Oracle PL/SQL Programming

THIRD EDITION

Oracle PL/SQL Programming

Steven Feuerstein
with Bill Pribyl

O'REILLY®

Beijing • Cambridge • Farnham • Köln • Paris • Sebastopol • Taipei • Tokyo

Oracle PL/SQL Programming, Third Edition
by Steven Feuerstein with Bill Pribyl

Published by O'Reilly & Associates, Inc., 1005 Gravenstein Highway North, Sebastopol, CA 95472.

O'Reilly & Associates books may be purchased for educational, business, or sales promotional use. Online editions are also available for most titles (*safari.oreilly.com*). For more information, contact our corporate/institutional sales department: (800) 998-9938 or *corporate@oreilly.com*.

Editor: Deborah Russell

Production Editor: Emily Quill

Cover Designer: Edie Freedman

Interior Designer: David Futato

Printing History:

September 1995: First Edition.

September 1997: Second Edition.

September 2002: Third Edition.

ISBN: 0-596-00381-1
[M]

To my wife, Veva, my parents, Sheldon and Joan Feuerstein, and to the children in my life: Ilana Belle Rosenthal, Markus Finnbar Walsh, Danielle and Benjamin DeUrso, Timnah and Masada Sela, Nikolas Silva, Ian and Michaela McCauseland, Ciera, Brian, Michael Daniels, and Marc Silva, and of course my very own boys, Eli and Chris.

—Steven Feuerstein

To my father, who told me "that's no hill for a stepper" enough times that it finally sank in.

—Bill Pribyl

Table of Contents

Part II. PL/SQL Program Structure

Part III. PL/SQL Program Data

Part VI. Advanced PL/SQL Topics

Preface

Millions of application developers and database administrators around the world use software provided by Oracle Corporation to build complex systems that manage vast quantities of data. At the heart of much of Oracle's software is PL/SQL—a programming language that provides procedural extensions to Oracle's version of SQL (Structured Query Language), and serves as the programming language within the Oracle Developer toolset (most notably Forms Developer and Reports Developer).

PL/SQL figures prominently as an enabling technology in almost every new product released by Oracle Corporation. Software professionals use PL/SQL to perform many kinds of programming functions, including:

- Implementing crucial business rules in the Oracle Server with PL/SQL-based stored procedures and database triggers
- Generating and managing XML documents entirely within the database
- Linking World Wide Web pages to an Oracle database
- Implementing and automating database administration tasks—from establishing row-level security to managing rollback segments within PL/SQL programs

PL/SQL was modeled after Ada,* a programming language designed for the United States Department of Defense. Ada is a high-level language that emphasizes data abstraction, information hiding, and other key elements of modern design strategies.

As a result of this very smart design decision by Oracle, PL/SQL is a powerful language that incorporates many of the most advanced elements of procedural languages, including:

- A full range of datatypes from number to string, and including complex data structures such as records (which are similar to rows in a relational table),

* The language was named "Ada" in honor of Ada Lovelace, a mathematician who is regarded by many to have been the world's first computer programmer. For more information about Ada, visit *http://www.adahome.com*.

collections (which are Oracle's version of arrays), and even XMLType for managing XML documents in Oracle and through PL/SQL

- An explicit and highly readable block structure that makes it easy to enhance and maintain PL/SQL applications
- Conditional, iterative, and sequential control statements, including a CASE statement and three different kinds of loops
- Exception handlers for use in event-based error handling
- Named, reusable code elements such as functions, procedures, triggers, object types (akin to object-oriented classes), and packages (collections of related programs and variables)

PL/SQL is integrated tightly into Oracle's SQL language: you can execute SQL statements directly from your procedural program without having to rely on any kind of intermediate API (Application Programming Interface) like JDBC (Java DataBase Connectivity) or ODBC (Open DataBase Connectivity). Conversely, you can also call your own PL/SQL functions from within a SQL statement.

Oracle developers who want to be successful in the 21st century must learn to use PL/SQL to full advantage. This is a two-step process. First, you must become familiar with and learn how to use the language's ever-expanding set of features; and second, after gaining competence in the individual features, you must learn how to put these constructs together to build complex applications.

For these reasons and more, Oracle developers need a solid, comprehensive resource for the base PL/SQL language. You need to know about the basic building blocks of PL/SQL, but you also need to learn by example so that you can avoid some of the trial-and-error. As with any programming language, PL/SQL has a right way and many wrong ways (or at least "not as right" ways) to handle just about any task. It is our hope that this book will help you learn how to use the PL/SQL language in the most effective and efficient way possible.

Objectives of This Book

What, specifically, will this book help you do?

Take full advantage of PL/SQL

Oracle's reference manuals may describe all the features of the PL/SQL language, but they don't tell you how to apply the technology. In fact, in some cases, you'll be lucky to even understand how to use a given feature after you've made your way through the railroad diagrams. Books and training courses tend to cover the same standard topics in the same limited way. In this book, we'll venture beyond the basics to the far reaches of the language, finding the nonstandard ways that a particular feature can be tweaked to achieve a desired result.

Use PL/SQL to solve your problems

You don't spend your days and nights writing PL/SQL modules so that you can rise to a higher plane of existence. You use PL/ SQL to solve problems for your company or your customers. In this book, we try hard to help you tackle real-world problems, the kinds of issues developers face on a daily basis (at least those problems that can be solved with mere software). To do this, we've packed the book with examples—not just small code fragments, but substantial application components that you can apply immediately to your own situations. There is a good deal of code in the book itself, and much more on the accompanying web site. In a number of cases, we use the code examples to guide you through the analytical process needed to come up with a solution. In this way you'll see, in the most concrete terms, how to apply PL/SQL features and undocumented applications of those features to a particular situation.

Write efficient, maintainable code

PL/SQL and the rest of the Oracle products offer the potential for incredible development productivity. If you aren't careful, however, this capability will simply let you dig yourself into a deeper, darker hole than you've ever found yourself in before. We would consider this book a failure if it only helped programmers write more code in less time; we want to help you develop the skills and techniques to build applications that readily adapt to change and that are easily understood and maintained. We want to teach you to use comprehensive strategies and code architectures that allow you to apply PL/SQL in powerful, general ways to the problems you face.

Structure of This Book

Both the authors and O'Reilly & Associates are committed to providing comprehensive, useful coverage of PL/SQL over the life of the language. The first edition of this book covered most of PL/SQL's features as they existed through PL/SQL Release 2.3. The second edition added coverage of Oracle8's new PL/SQL features, but separated that content from the rest of the book. The third edition, which you are now holding, takes a different approach. It includes all PL/SQL language features up to and including Oracle9*i* Release 2 (9.2). So regardless of the version you are using, from Oracle 7.3.4 (although we hope you won't be using that one much longer) to Oracle9*i*, this book will help you answer your questions. And this information is now completely integrated; there is no separate section for Oracle9*i*. Instead, you simply go to the section of the book with the feature you are interested in, and you will see what is available in the various versions.

When Steven first started writing about PL/SQL in 1994, it was actually possible to offer comprehensive coverage of the language in a single, albeit large, volume. By 1997, that was no longer the case, which is why there are many additional books from O'Reilly on such topics as the built-in or Oracle-supplied packages (e.g.,

DBMS_SQL); see "The O'Reilly PL/SQL Series" in Chapter 1 for information about these other books. Now, in 2002, the rapid developments in the PL/SQL language made us wonder: how can we provide a user guide and reference to the PL/SQL language without creating a tome so unwieldy that reading the book becomes as much a physical as a mental workout?

We took the following steps in shaping the book:

- First, and most importantly, we added crucial content that had been missing for years, most notably the treatment of database triggers.
- Next, we decided to leverage the Internet more fully. Rather than take up page after page with extended (and often hard to follow) code examples, we have shifted such topics to the book's Web Companion, available on the O'Reilly web site at *http://www.oreilly.com/catalog/oraclep3* (see "About the Code" for details). Don't worry—the book is still absolutely packed full of code; we're just more concise than in the past.
- With much reluctance, we moved entire chapters from the second edition to the book's web site. These include the second edition's Chapter 17, *Calling PL/SQL Functions in SQL*, and Chapter 22, *Code Design Tips*. (Code design tips are also covered extensively in *Oracle PL/SQL Best Practices*).
- We reorganized a number of chapters, both to improve the flow of the book and to reduce the overall page count. For example, rather than treating character data separately from character functions, we now have a single chapter that covers everything relating to strings. We combined several chapters, most notably the old Chapters 24 through 26 (covering debugging, tuning, and tracing) into a single chapter. Large swaths of text, mostly anecdotes, that didn't make it into the third edition can be found on the web site.
- A new and more compact O'Reilly interior book design saved us a good 10% in overall page count over the previous format. The new format was also crucial in squeezing more code onto lines and pages.

We are very happy with the results, and hope that you will be too. There is more information than ever before, but we managed to present it without losing that "trademark" sense of humor and conversational tone that readers have told us for years make the book readable, understandable, and highly useful.

One comment regarding the "voice" behind the text. You may notice that in some parts of this book we use the word "we," and in others "I." One characteristic of this book (and one for which readers have expressed appreciation) is the personal voice that's inseparable from the text. Consequently, even with the addition of coauthors to the book (and, in the third edition, significant contributions from several other people), we've decided to maintain the use of "I" when an author speaks in his own voice.

Rather than leave you guessing as to which author is represented by the "I" in a given chapter, we thought we'd offer this quick guide for the curious:

Chapter	Author	Chapter	Author
1	Steven	13	Steven
2	Bill	14	Steven
3	Bill and Steven	15	Steven
4	Jonathan and Steven	16	Steven
5	Steven	17	Steven
6	Steven	18	Darryl
7	Steven	19	Steven
8	Jonathan and Steven	20	Bill
9	Jonathan and Steven	21	Bill
10	Jonathan and Steven	22	Steven
11	Steven and Bill	23	Bill
12	Jonathan		

About the Contents

The third edition of *Oracle PL/SQL Programming* is divided into six parts:

Part I, Programming in PL/SQL
: We start from the very beginning in Chapter 1: where did PL/SQL come from? What is it good for? We offer a very quick review of some of the main features of the PL/SQL language. Chapter 2 is designed to get you and up and running PL/SQL programs as quickly as possible: it contains clear, straightforward instructions for executing PL/SQL code in SQL*Plus and a few other common environments. Chapter 3 reviews fundamentals of the PL/SQL language: what makes up a PL/SQL statement, an introduction to the block structure, how to write comments in PL/SQL, and so on.

Part II, PL/SQL Program Structure
: Chapters 4 through 6 explore conditional (IF and CASE) and sequential (e.g., GOTO and NULL) control statements, loops, and exception handling in the PL/SQL language. This section of the book will teach you to construct blocks of code that correlate to the complex requirements of your applications.

Part III, PL/SQL Program Data
: Just about every program you write will manipulate data, and much of that data will be local to (defined in) your PL/SQL procedure or function. Chapters 7 through 12 concentrate exhaustively on the various types of program data you can define in PL/SQL, such as numbers, strings, records, and collections. You will learn about the new datatypes introduced in Oracle9*i*, such as INTERVAL, TIMESTAMP, XMLType, and others. These chapters also cover the various

built-in functions provided by Oracle that allow you to manipulate and modify data.

Part IV, SQL in PL/SQL
: Chapters 13 through 15 address one of the most central elements of PL/SQL code construction: the connection to the underlying database, which takes place through SQL. These chapters show you how to define transactions that update, insert, and delete tables in the database; how to query information from the database for processing in a PL/SQL program; and how to execute SQL statements dynamically, using native dynamic SQL (NDS), which was introduced in Oracle8*i*.

Part V, PL/SQL Application Construction
: This is where it all comes together. You know about declaring and working with variables, and you're an expert in error handling and loop construction. Now, in Chapters 16 through 19, you'll learn about the building blocks of applications, which include procedures, functions, triggers, and packages. Chapter 19 discusses how to manage your PL/SQL code base, including suggestions for tuning and debugging that code.

Part VI, Advanced PL/SQL Topics
: A language as mature and rich as PL/SQL is full of features that you may not use on a day-to-day basis, but that may sometimes be the difference between success and failure. Chapter 20 contains an exploration into the PL/SQL runtime architecture, including PL/SQL's use of memory and the differences between server-side and client-side PL/SQL. Chapter 21 offers an in-depth guide to the object-oriented features of Oracle (object types and object views). Chapters 22 and 23 show you how to invoke Java and C code from your PL/SQL applications.

If you are an accomplished programmer who is just new to PL/SQL, reading this book from beginning to end should improve your skills and deepen your understanding. If you're already a proficient PL/SQL programmer, you'll probably want to dip into the appropriate sections to extract particular techniques for immediate application. Whether you use this book as a teaching guide or as a reference, we hope that it will help you to use PL/SQL effectively.

What This Book Does Not Cover

Long as this book is, it doesn't contain everything. The Oracle environment is huge and complex, and in this book we've focused our attention on the core PL/SQL language itself. The following topics are therefore outside the scope of this book and are not covered, except in an occasional and peripheral fashion:

The SQL language
: We assume that you already have a working knowledge of the SQL language, and that you know how to write SELECTs, UPDATEs, INSERTs, and DELETEs.

Administration of Oracle databases
: While DBAs can use this book to learn how to write the PL/SQL needed to build and maintain databases, this book does not explore all the nuances of the Data Definition Language (DDL) of Oracle's SQL.

Application and database tuning
: We don't cover detailed tuning issues in this book, although Chapter 19 does discuss the tracing, tuning, and debugging of PL/SQL programs. There are other books that delve deeply into Oracle application tuning.

Oracle tool-specific technologies independent of PL/SQL
: This book does not attempt to show you how to build applications in a tool like Oracle's Forms Developer, even though the implementation language is PL/SQL. We have chosen to focus on core language capabilities, centered on what you can do with PL/SQL from within the database. However, most everything covered in this book is applicable to PL/SQL inside Forms Developer and Reports Developer.

National Language Support in Oracle
: This book does not offer comprehensive coverage of Oracle's National Language Support (NLS) capabilities for developing applications for multiple languages.

Conventions Used in This Book

The following conventions are used in this book:

Italic
: Used for file and directory names, for URLs, and for emphasis when introducing a new term.

`Constant width`
: Used for code examples.

`Constant width bold`
: Indicates user input in examples showing an interaction. Also, in some code examples, highlights the statements being discussed.

`Constant width italic`
: In some code examples, indicates an element (e.g., a filename) that you supply.

UPPERCASE
: In code examples, generally indicates PL/SQL keywords.

lowercase
: In code examples, generally indicates user-defined items such as variables, parameters, etc.

punctuation
: In code examples, enter exactly as shown.

indentation
: In code examples, helps to show structure but is not required.

--
: In code examples, a double hyphen begins a single-line comment that extends to the end of a line.

/ and */*
: In code examples, these characters delimit a multiline comment that can extend from one line to another.

.
: In code examples and related discussions, a dot qualifies a reference by separating an object name from a component name. For example, dot notation is used to select fields in a record and to specify declarations within a package.

[ ]
: In syntax descriptions, square brackets enclose optional items.

{ }
: In syntax descriptions, curly brackets enclose a set of items from which you must choose only one.

|
: In syntax descriptions, a vertical bar separates the items enclosed in curly brackets, as in {TRUE | FALSE}.

...
: In syntax descriptions, ellipses indicate repeating elements. An ellipsis also shows that statements or clauses irrelevant to the discussion were left out.

Indicates a tip, suggestion, or general note. For example, we'll tell you if a certain setting is version-specific.

Indicates a warning or caution. For example, we'll tell you if a certain setting has some kind of negative impact on the system.

Which Platform or Version?

In general, all of the discussions and examples in this book apply regardless of the machine and/or operating system you are using. In those cases where a feature is in any way version-dependent—for example, if you can use it only in Oracle versions Oracle8*i* or Oracle9*i*—we note that in the text.

There are many versions of PL/SQL, and you may even find that you need to use multiple versions in your development work. Chapter 1 describes the versions of PL/SQL still in common use and what you should know about them; see the section called "Working with Multiple Versions of PL/SQL."

About the Code

We have provided all of the code included in this book on the book's web page on the O'Reilly web site. Go to:

http://www.oreilly.com/catalog/oraclep3

and click on the Examples link to go to the book's Web Companion.

As we mentioned earlier, you will also find the entire contents of some of the chapters included in the second edition of this book, but removed or condensed in the third edition. These may be especially helpful to readers who are running older versions of Oracle.

To find a particular example on the site, look for the filename cited in the text. For many examples, you will find filenames in the following form provided as a comment at the beginning of the example shown in the book:

```
/* File on web: fullname.pkg */
```

Comments and Questions

We have tested and verified the information in this book and in the source code to the best of our ability, but given the amount of text and the rapid evolution of technology, you may find that features have changed or that we have made mistakes. If so, please notify us by writing to:

O'Reilly & Associates
1005 Gravenstein Highway
Sebastopol, CA 95472
800-998-9938 (in the U.S. or Canada)
707-829-0515 (international or local)
707-829-0104 (FAX)

You can also send messages electronically. To be put on the mailing list or request a catalog, send email to:

info@oreilly.com

To ask technical questions or comment on the book, send email to:

bookquestions@oreilly.com

As mentioned in the previous section, we have a web site for this book where you can find code, updated links, chapters from previous editions of the book, and errata (previously reported errors and corrections are available for public view). You can access this web site at:

> *http://www.oreilly.com/catalog/oraclep3*

For more information about this book and others, see the O'Reilly web site:

> *http://www.oreilly.com*

Acknowledgments

Since *Oracle PL/SQL Programming* was first published in 1995, it has had a busy and productive history as the "go to" text on how to use the PL/SQL language. For that, we first of all express our appreciation to all of our readers.

Maintaining *Oracle PL/SQL Programming* as an accurate, readable, and up-to-date reference to PL/SQL has, from the start, been a big (all right, we admit it—sometimes overwhelming) job; it certainly would not have been possible without the help of many Oracle specialists, friends, and family, and of course the incredible staff at O'Reilly & Associates.

You will find below rather detailed thank yous for those who helped pull together the third edition of *Oracle PL/SQL Programming*. Following that, you will find an acknowledgment of the many people who were instrumental in the first and second editions. If you want to read the full text of the acknowledgments from these earlier editions, please visit the web site.

First and foremost, we thank Jonathan Gennick, Darryl Hurley, Bryn Llewellyn, and Steve Adams, four outstanding Oracle technologists, for their substantial contributions to this book. Jonathan wrote or substantially updated five chapters, and Darryl contributed the fine chapter on database triggers and contributed many insights on Oracle's internationalization features. Bryn Llewellyn, Oracle's PL/SQL Product Manager, provided crucial information on Oracle9*i*'s new features, answered endless questions about various PL/SQL features with bottomless patience, and reviewed a large number of chapters. Steve gave us excellent and detailed feedback on PL/SQL's runtime architecture.

With such a big book, we needed lots of reviewers, especially because we asked them to test each code snippet and program in the book to keep to an absolute minimum the number of errors that made it into the printed version. We are deeply grateful to the following men and women of the Oracle PL/SQL world, who took time away from the rest of their lives to help make *Oracle PL/SQL Programming* the best book it could be: Don Bales, Dick Bolz, Dan Clamage, Steve Cosner, Gerard Hartgers, Dwayne King, Larry Elkins, Chandrasekharan Iyer, Vadim Loevski, Giovanni Jaramillo, Rakesh Patel, James Padfield, Peter Linsley, Christopher Racicot, Alex Romankevich, Scott Sowers, JT Thomas, Edward Van Hatten, Simon St. Laurent, Tony Crawford, Geoff Chester, and Andre Vergison.

Once we felt good about the technical content, it was time for the remarkable crew at O'Reilly & Associates, led by our good friend, Deborah Russell, to transform our many chapters and code examples into a book worthy of the O'Reilly imprint. Many thanks to Emily Quill, production manager for the book; Rob Romano, who created the excellent figures; Julie Flanagan, able editorial assistant who helped throughout the project; and the rest of the crew.

And here are the many people we thanked (and continue to be grateful to) for their contributions to the first and second editions of this book:

Jennifer Blair, Eric Camplin, Joe Celko, Avery Cohen, Thomas Dunbar, R. James Forsythe, Mike Gangler, Gabriel Hoffman, Karen Peiser, Pete Schaffer, David Thompson, Cailein Barclay, Sunil Bhargava, Boris Burshteyn, Gray Clossman, Radhakrishna Hari, James Mallory, Nimesh Mehta, Jeff Muller, Dave Posner, Chris Racicot, Peter Vasterd, Zona Walcott, Sohaib Abassi, Per Brondum, Ivan Chong, Bill Dwight, Steve Ehrlich, Bushan Fotedar, Ken Jacobs, Nimish Mehta, Steve Muench, Sri Rajan, Mark Richter, Bill Hinman, Tony Ziemba, John Cordell, Beverly Gibson, Mike Sierra, Gigi Estabrook, Edie Freedman, Donna Woonteiler, Chris Reilley, Michelle Willey, Debby Cunha, Michael Deutsch, John Files, Juliette Muellner, Cory Willing, Seth Maislin, Kismet McDonough Chan, Clairemarie Fisher O'Leary, Eric Givler, Bert Scalzo, John Beresniewicz, Tom White, Steve Hilker, Thomas Kurian, Radhakrishna Hari, Shirish Puranik, Kannan Muthukkaruppan, Jane Ellin, Kimo Carter, Madeleine Newell, Rob Romano, Nancy Priest, Seth Maislin, Fred Polizo, Donald Herkimer, Ervan Darnell, Gary Cernosek, Patrick Pribyl, Bill Watkins, Debra Luik, and Leo Lok.

Finally, Steven thanks his wife, Veva Silva, and two sons, Chris Silva and Eli Feuerstein, for their support and tolerance of so much of his time and attention.

And Bill extends his most heartfelt gratitude to his immediate family, for putting up with writing into the wee hours ("Mommy, Daddy fell asleep at the computer again!") and remaining a constant source of love and good humor.

PART I

Programming in PL/SQL

This first part of the book introduces PL/SQL, explains how to create and run PL/SQL code, and presents language fundamentals. Chapter 1 asks the fundamental questions: Where did PL/SQL come from? What is it good for? What are the main features of the PL/SQL language? Chapter 2 is designed to get you and up and running PL/SQL programs as quickly as possible; it contains clear, straightforward instructions for executing PL/SQL code in SQL*Plus and a few other common environments. Chapter 3 answers basic questions about the language structure and keywords: What makes up a PL/SQL statement? What is the PL/SQL block structure all about? How do I write comments in PL/SQL?

In this chapter:

CHAPTER 1

Introduction to PL/SQL

This chapter introduces PL/SQL, its origins, and its various versions. It also offers a guide to additional resources for PL/SQL developers and some words of advice.

What Is PL/SQL?

PL/SQL stands for "Procedural Language extensions to the Structured Query Language." SQL is the now-ubiquitous language for both querying *and* updating—never mind the name—of relational databases. Oracle Corporation introduced PL/SQL to overcome some limitations in SQL and to provide a more complete programming solution for those who sought to build mission-critical applications to run against the Oracle database.

PL/SQL has several defining characteristics:

It is a highly structured, readable, and accessible language
: Modeled after the Ada language, PL/SQL incorporates some of the latest and greatest in language design. If you are new to programming, PL/SQL is a great place to start. If you are experienced in other programming languages, you will very easily adapt to the new syntax. The accessibility of PL/SQL also means that you can write code that is easily maintained and enhanced over time, a critical aspect of high-quality software development.

PL/SQL is a standard and portable language for Oracle development
: If you write a PL/SQL procedure or function to execute from within the Personal Oracle database sitting on your laptop, you can move that same procedure to a database on your corporate network and execute it there without any changes (assuming compatibility of Oracle versions, of course!). "Write once, run everywhere" was the mantra of PL/SQL long before Java appeared. For PL/SQL, though, "everywhere" means "everywhere there is an Oracle database."

PL/SQL is an embedded language

PL/SQL was not designed to be used as a "standalone" language, but instead to be invoked from within a "host" environment. So, for example, you can run PL/SQL programs from within the database (through, say, the SQL*Plus interface). Alternatively, you can define and execute PL/SQL programs from within an Oracle Developer form or report (this approach is called *client-side PL/SQL*). You cannot, however, create a PL/SQL "executable" that runs all by itself. Chapter 2 provides all the information you need to get up and running with this embedded language.

PL/SQL is a high-performance, highly integrated database language

These days, you have a number of choices when it comes to writing software to run against the Oracle database. You can use Java and JDBC (or SQLJ); you can use Visual Basic and ODBC; you can go with Delphi, C++, and so on. You will find, however, that it is easier to write highly efficient code to access the Oracle database in PL/SQL than it is in any other language. In particular, Oracle offers certain PL/SQL-specific enhancements such as the FORALL statement that can improve database performance by an order of magnitude or more.

The Origins of PL/SQL

Oracle has a history of leading the software industry in providing declarative, non-procedural approaches to designing both databases and applications. The Oracle Server technology is among the most advanced, powerful, and stable relational databases in the world. Its application development tools, such as Oracle Forms, can offer high levels of productivity by relying heavily on a "paint-your-screen" approach in which extensive default capabilities allow developers to avoid heavy customized programming efforts.

The Early Years of PL/SQL

In Oracle's early years, this declarative approach, combined with its groundbreaking relational technology, was enough to satisfy developers. But as the industry matured, expectations rose and requirements became more stringent. Developers needed to get "under the skin" of the products. They needed to build complicated formulas, exceptions, and rules into their forms and database procedures.

In 1991, Oracle Corporation released Oracle Version 6.0, a major advance in its relational database technology. A key component of Oracle Version 6.0 was the so-called "procedural option" or PL/SQL. At roughly the same time, Oracle released its long-awaited upgrade to SQL*Forms Version 2.3 (the original name for the product now known as Oracle Forms or Forms Developer). SQL*Forms V3.0 incorporated the PL/SQL engine for the first time on the tools side, allowing developers to code their procedural logic in a natural, straightforward manner.

This first release of PL/SQL was very limited in its capabilities. On the server side, you could use PL/SQL only to build "batch-processing" scripts of procedural and SQL statements. In other words, you could not store procedures or functions for execution at some later time. You could not construct a modular application or store complex business rules in the server. On the client side, SQL*Forms V3.0 did allow you to create procedures and functions, although support for functions was not documented, and was therefore not used by many developers for years. In addition, this release of PL/SQL did not implement array support and could not interact with the operating system (for input or output). It was a far cry from a full-fledged programming language.

But for all its limitations, PL/SQL was warmly, even enthusiastically, received in the developer community. The hunger for the ability to code a simple IF statement inside SQL*Forms was strong. The need to perform multi-SQL statement batch processing was overwhelming.

What few developers realized at the time was that the original motivation and driving vision behind PL/SQL extended beyond the desire for programmatic control within products like SQL*Forms. Very early in the life cycle of Oracle's database and tools, Oracle Corporation had recognized two key weaknesses in their architecture: lack of portability and problems with execution authority.

Improved Application Portability

The concern about portability might seem odd to those of us familiar with Oracle Corporation's marketing and technical strategies. One of the hallmarks of the Oracle solution from the early 1980s was its portability. At the time that PL/SQL came along, the C-based RDBMS ran on many different operating systems and hardware platforms. SQL*Plus and SQL*Forms adapted easily to a variety of terminal configurations. Yet for all that coverage, there were still many applications that needed the more sophisticated and granular control offered by host languages like COBOL, C, and FORTRAN. As soon as a developer stepped outside the port-neutral Oracle tools, the resulting application would no longer be portable.

The PL/SQL language was (and is) intended to widen the range of application requirements that can be handled entirely in operating-system-independent programming tools. Today, Java and other programming languages have also made great strides in portability. Yet PL/SQL stands out as an early pioneer in this field and, of course, it continues to allow developers to write highly portable application code.

Improved Execution Authority and Transaction Integrity

An even more fundamental issue than portability was execution authority. The RDBMS and the SQL language give you the capability to tightly control access to, and changes in, any particular database table. For example, with the GRANT command you can make sure that only certain roles and users have the ability to perform an UPDATE on a given table. On the other hand, this GRANT statement can't ensure that the full set of UPDATEs performed by a user or application is done correctly. In other words, the database can't guarantee the integrity of a transaction that spans more than one table, as is common with most business transactions.

The PL/SQL language was intended by Oracle to provide tight control and management over logical transactions. One way that PL/SQL does this is with implementation of execution authority. Instead of granting to a role or user the authority to update a table, you grant privileges only to execute a procedure, which controls and provides access to the underlying data structures. The procedure is owned by a separate Oracle RDBMS account, which, in turn, is granted the actual update privileges on those tables needed to perform the transaction. The procedure therefore becomes the "gatekeeper" for the transaction. The only way that a program (whether it's an Oracle Forms application or a Pro*C executable) can execute the transfer is through the procedure. In this way, transaction integrity is guaranteed.

Humble Beginnings, Steady Improvement

In the time that Oracle has been working to make Java available as an alternative to PL/SQL in the database, it has also made steady, fundamental improvements to the PL/SQL language itself. It has added a great variety of supplied (or *built-in*) packages that extend the PL/SQL language in numerous ways and directions. It has introduced object-oriented capabilities, implemented a variety of array-like data structures, and in general improved the breadth and depth of the language.

As powerful as SQL is, it simply does not offer the flexibility and power that developers need to create full-blown applications. Oracle's PL/SQL language ensures that we can stay entirely within the operating-system-independent Oracle environment and still write highly efficient applications that meet our users' requirements.

PL/SQL has come a long way from its humble beginnings. With Version 1.0, it was not uncommon for a developer to have to tell his or her manager, "You can't do that with PL/SQL." Today, that statement has moved from fact to excuse. If you are ever confronted with a requirement and find yourself saying, "There's no way to do that," don't repeat it to your manager. Instead, dig deeper into the language, or explore the range of built-in PL/SQL packages offered by Oracle. There is a very good chance that PL/SQL will today allow you to do pretty much whatever you need to do.

In the next section, we take a look at some examples of PL/SQL programs that will familiarize you with the basics of PL/SQL programming.

So This Is PL/SQL

If you are completely new to programming or to working with PL/SQL (or even SQL, for that matter), learning PL/SQL may seem an intimidating prospect. If this is the case, don't fret! We are confident that you will find it easier than you think. There are two reasons for our optimism:

- Computer languages in general are not that hard to learn, at least compared to a second or third "human language." The reason? It's simply that computers are not particularly smart (they "think"—perform operations—rapidly, but not at all creatively). We must rely on a very rigid syntax in order to tell a computer what we want it to do. So the resulting language is also rigid (no exceptions!) and therefore easier for us to pick up.
- PL/SQL truly is an easy language as compared to other programming languages. It relies on a highly structured "block" design with different sections, all identified with explicit, self-documenting keywords.

Let's take a look at a few examples that demonstrate some of the key elements of both PL/SQL structure and functionality.

Integration with SQL

One of the most important aspects of PL/SQL is its tight integration with SQL. You don't need to rely on any intermediate software "glue" like ODBC (Open DataBase Connectivity) or JDBC (Java DataBase Connectivity) to run SQL statements in your PL/SQL programs. Instead, you just insert the UPDATE or SELECT into your code, as shown here:

```
DECLARE
   l_book_count INTEGER;

BEGIN
   SELECT COUNT(*)
     INTO l_book_count
     FROM books
    WHERE author LIKE '%FEUERSTEIN, STEVEN%';

   DBMS_OUTPUT.PUT_LINE (
      'Steven has written (or co-written) ' ||
       l_book_count ||
       ' books.');

   -- Oh, and I changed my name, so...
   UPDATE books
      SET author = REPLACE (author, 'STEVEN', 'STEPHEN')
    WHERE author LIKE '%FEUERSTEIN, STEVEN%';
END;
```

Let's take a more detailed look at this code in the following table:

Line(s)	Description
1–3	This is the declaration section of this so-called "anonymous" PL/SQL block, in which I declare an integer variable to hold the number of books that I have authored or coauthored. (I'll say much more about the PL/SQL block structure in Chapter 3.)
4	The BEGIN keyword indicates the beginning of my execution section—the code that will be run when I pass this block to SQL*Plus.
5–8	I run a query to determine the total number of books I have authored or coauthored. Line 6 is of special interest: the INTO clause shown here is actually not part of the SQL statement, but instead serves as the "bridge" from the database to local PL/SQL variables.
10–13	I use the DBMS_OUTPUT.PUT_LINE built-in procedure (i.e., a procedure in the DBMS_OUTPUT package supplied by Oracle) to display the number of books.
15	This single-line comment explains the purpose of the UPDATE.
16–18	I have decided to change the spelling of my first name to "Stephen", so I issue an update against the books table. I take advantage of the built-in REPLACE function to locate all instances of "STEVEN" and replace them with "STEPHEN".

Control and Conditional Logic

PL/SQL offers a full range of statements that allow us to very tightly control which lines of our programs execute. These statements include:

IF and CASE statements
: These implement conditional logic; for example, "If the page count of a book is greater than 1000, then..."

A full complement of looping or iterative controls
: These include the FOR loop, the WHILE loop, and the simple loop.

The GOTO statement
: Yes, PL/SQL even offers a GOTO that allows you to branch unconditionally from one part of your program to another. That doesn't mean, however, that you should actually *use* it.

Here is a procedure (a reusable block of code that can be called by name) that demonstrates some of these features:

```
CREATE OR REPLACE PROCEDURE pay_out_balance (
   account_id_in IN accounts.id%TYPE)
IS
   l_balance_remaining NUMBER;
BEGIN
   LOOP
      l_balance_remaining := account_balance (account_id_in);

      IF l_balance_remaining < 1000
      THEN
         EXIT;
      ELSE
```

```
13           apply_balance (account_id_in, l_balance_remaining);
14        END IF;
15     END LOOP;
16  END pay_out_balance;
```

Let's take a more detailed look at this code in the following table:

Line(s)	Description
1–2	This is the header of a procedure that pays out the balance of an account to cover outstanding bills. Line 2 is the parameter list of the procedure, in this case consisting of a single incoming value (the identification number of the account).
3–4	This is the declaration section of the procedure. Notice that instead of using a DECLARE keyword, the keyword IS (or AS) is used to separate the header from the declarations.
6–15	Here is an example of a simple loop. This loop relies on an EXIT statement (see line 11) to terminate the loop; FOR and WHILE loops specify the termination condition differently.
7	Here I call the account_balance function to retrieve the balance for this account. This is an example of a call to a reusable program within another reusable program. Line 13 demonstrates the calling of another procedure within this procedure.
9–14	An IF statement that can be interpreted as follows: if the account balance has fallen below $1000, then stop allocating funds to cover bills. Otherwise, apply the balance to the next charge.

When Things Go Wrong

The PL/SQL language offers a powerful mechanism for both raising and handling errors. In the following procedure, I obtain the name and balance of an account from its ID. I then check to see if the balance is too low; if it is, I explicitly raise an exception, which stops my program from continuing:

```
CREATE OR REPLACE PROCEDURE check_account (
   account_id_in IN accounts.id%TYPE)
IS
   l_balance_remaining       NUMBER;
   l_balance_below_minimum   EXCEPTION;
   l_account_name            accounts.name%TYPE;
BEGIN
   SELECT name
     INTO l_account_name
     FROM accounts
    WHERE id = account_id_in;

   l_balance_remaining := account_balance (account_id_in);

   DBMS_OUTPUT.put_line (
      'Balance for ' || l_account_name ||
       ' = ' || l_balance_remaining);

   IF l_balance_remaining < 1000
   THEN
      RAISE l_balance_below_minimum;
   END IF;

```

```
24  EXCEPTION
25     WHEN NO_DATA_FOUND
26     THEN
27        -- No account found for this ID
28        log_error (...);
29
30     WHEN l_balance_below_minimum
31     THEN
32        log_error (...);
33        RAISE;
34  END;
```

Let's take a more detailed look at the error-handling aspects of this code in the following table:

Line(s)	Description
5	I declare my own exception, called l_balance_below_minimum. Oracle provides a set of predefined exceptions, such as DUP_VAL_ON_INDEX, but I need something specific to my application, so I must define it myself in this case.
8–11	This query retrieves the name for the account. If there is no account for this ID, then Oracle will raise the predefined NO_DATA_FOUND exception, causing the program to stop.
19–22	If the balance is too low, I will explicitly raise my own exception, as I have encountered a serious problem with this account.
24	The EXCEPTION keyword denotes the end of the executable section and the beginning of the exception section in which errors are handled.
25–28	This is the error-handling section for the situation where the account is not found. If NO_DATA_FOUND was the exception raised, it will be "trapped" here and the error will be logged.
30–33	This is the error-handling section for the situation where the account balance has gotten too low (my application-specific exception). If l_balance_below_minimum was raised, it will be "trapped" here and the error will be logged. Then, due to the seriousness of the error, I will re-raise the same exception, propagating that error out of the current procedure and into the PL/SQL block that called it.

Chapter 6 takes you on an extensive tour of the error-handling mechanisms of PL/SQL.

There is, of course, much more that can be said about PL/SQL—which is why you have about another 950 pages of material to study in this book! However, these initial examples should give you a good feel for the kind of code you will write with PL/SQL, some of its most important syntactical elements, and the ease with which one can write—and read—PL/SQL code.

About PL/SQL Versions

Each version of the Oracle database comes with its own corresponding version of PL/SQL. As you use more up-to-date versions of PL/SQL, an increasing array of functionality will be available to you. One of our biggest challenges as PL/SQL programmers is simply "keeping up." We need to constantly educate ourselves about the new features in each version—figuring out how to use them and how to apply them to our applications, and determining which new techniques are so useful that we should modify existing applications to take advantage of them.

Table 1-1 summarizes the major elements in each of the versions (past and present) of PL/SQL in the database. It offers a very high-level glimpse of the new features available in each version. Following the table, you will find more detailed descriptions of "what's new" in PL/SQL in the latest Oracle versions, Oracle8*i* and Oracle9*i*.

The Oracle Developer product suite also comes with its own version of PL/SQL, and it generally lags behind the version available in the Oracle RDBMS itself. This chapter (and the book as whole) concentrates on server-side PL/SQL programming.

Table 1-1. Oracle database and corresponding PL/SQL versions

Oracle version	PL/SQL version	Characteristics
Oracle6	1.0	Initial version of PL/SQL, used primarily as a scripting language in SQL*Plus (it was not yet possible to create named, reusable, and callable programs) and also as a programming language in SQL*Forms 3.
Oracle7	2.0	Major upgrade to Version 1. Adds support for stored procedures, functions, packages, programmer-defined records, PL/SQL tables, and many package extensions, including DBMS_OUTPUT and DBMS_PIPE.
Oracle 7.1	2.1	Supports programmer-defined subtypes, enables the use of stored functions inside SQL statements, and offers dynamic SQL with the DBMS_SQL package. With Version 2.1, you can now execute SQL DDL statements from within PL/SQL programs.
Oracle 7.3	2.3	Enhances functionality of PL/SQL tables, offers improved remote dependency management, adds file I/O capabilities to PL/SQL with the UTL_FILE package, and completes the implementation of cursor variables.
Oracle8	8.0	The new version number reflects Oracle's effort to synchronize version numbers across related products. PL/SQL8 is the version of PL/SQL that supports the many enhancements of Oracle8, including large objects (LOBs), object-oriented design and development, collections (VARRAYs and nested tables), and Oracle/AQ (the Oracle/Advanced Queuing facility).
Oracle8*i*	8.1	The first of Oracle's *i* series (the "Internet database"), the corresponding release of PL/SQL offers a truly impressive set of added functionality, including a new version of dynamic SQL (native dynamic SQL), support for Java in the database, the invoker rights model, execution authority option, autonomous transactions, and high-performance "bulk" DML and queries.
Oracle9*i* Release 1	9.0	Oracle9*i* came fairly quickly on the heels of Oracle8*i*. The first release of this version showcases the following features for PL/SQL developers: support for inheritance in object types, table functions and cursor expressions (allowing for parallelization of PL/SQL function execution), multi-level collections (collections within collections), and the CASE statement and expression.
Oracle9*i* Release 2	9.2	The most recent version of the Oracle product set, Oracle9*i* Release 2 puts a major emphasis on XML (Extensible Markup Language), but also has some treats for PL/SQL developers, including associative arrays (index-by tables that can be indexed by VARCHAR2 strings in addition to integers), record-based DML (allowing you to perform an insert using a record, for example), and a thorough rewrite of UTL_FILE (now allowing you to copy, remove, and rename files).

Oracle8i New Features

Oracle8*i* is for many developers still a relatively new release of Oracle, so we thought it would be useful to describe some of the most important Oracle8*i* PL/SQL features covered in this book. They are summarized in the following sections, and covered more thoroughly in the indicated chapters.

Autonomous transactions

One long-standing request from PL/SQL developers has been the ability to execute and then save or cancel certain Data Manipulation Language (DML) statements (INSERT, UPDATE, DELETE) without affecting the overall session's transaction. You can now do this with autonomous transactions.

Where would you find autonomous transactions useful in your applications? Here are some ideas:

Logging mechanism
: This is the classic example of the need for an autonomous transaction. You need to log error information in a database table, but don't want that log entry to be a part of the logical transaction.

Reusable application components
: You are building an Internet application. You want to combine components from many different vendors and layers, and they need to interact in certain well-defined ways. If when one component commits, it affects all other aspects of your application, it will not function well in this environment. Autonomous transactions solve this problem.

When you define a PL/SQL block (anonymous block, procedure, function, packaged procedure, packaged function, or database trigger) as an autonomous transaction, you isolate the DML in that block from the rest of your session. That block becomes an independent transaction that is started by another transaction, referred to as the *main transaction*. Within the autonomous transaction block, the main transaction is suspended. You perform your SQL operations, commit or roll back those operations, and then resume the main transaction.

There isn't much involved in defining a PL/SQL block as an autonomous transaction. You simply include the following statement in your declaration section:

```
PRAGMA AUTONOMOUS_TRANSACTION;
```

Here is a very simple logging mechanism that relies on the autonomous transaction feature to save changes to the log without affecting the rest of the session's transaction:

```
PROCEDURE write_log (
   code IN INTEGER, text IN VARCHAR2)
IS
   PRAGMA AUTONOMOUS_TRANSACTION;
```

```
BEGIN
   INSERT INTO log VALUES (
      code, text,
      USER, SYSDATE
      );
   COMMIT:
END;
```

Of course, there are all sorts of rules and some restrictions to be aware of. See Chapter 13 for all the details.

Invoker rights

Back in the old days of Oracle7 and Oracle 8.0, whenever you executed a stored program, it executed under the authority of the owner of that program. This "rights model" was known as *definer rights*. This was not a big deal if your entire application—code, data, and users—worked out of the same Oracle account; however, that scenario probably fit about 0.5% of all Oracle shops. Definer rights proved to be a real pain in the neck for the other 99.5%, because usually code was stored in one schema and then shared through GRANT EXECUTE statements with other users (directly or through roles).

That centralized, stored code would not automatically apply the privileges of a user (also known as an *invoker*) to the code's objects. The user might not have had DELETE privileges on a table, but the stored code did, so delete away! In some circumstances, that is just how you wanted it to work, but in others, particularly when you were executing programs relying on dynamic SQL (with either DBMS_SQL or native dynamic SQL), awesome complications ensued.

In Oracle 8.1, PL/SQL has been enhanced so that at the time of compilation, you can decide whether a program (or all programs in a package) should run under the authority of the definer (the only choice in Oracle 8.0 and below) or of the invoker of that program.

The syntax to support this *invoker rights* feature is simple enough. Here is a generic "run DDL" engine that relies on the new native dynamic SQL statement EXECUTE IMMEDIATE:

```
CREATE OR REPLACE PROCEDURE runddl (ddl_in in VARCHAR2)
   AUTHID CURRENT_USER
IS
BEGIN
   EXECUTE IMMEDIATE ddl_in;
END;
/
```

The AUTHID CURRENT_USER clause before the IS keyword indicates that when the runddl procedure executes, it should run under the authority of the invoker (or "current user"), not under the authority of the definer.

Chapter 20 explores both the definer and invoker rights execution models.

Native dynamic SQL (NDS)

Ever since Oracle 7.1, we PL/SQL developers have been able to use the built-in DBMS_SQL package to execute dynamic SQL and PL/SQL. This means that at runtime, you can construct the query, a DELETE TABLE, a CREATE TABLE, or even a PL/SQL block, as a string—and then execute it. *Dynamic SQL* is extremely handy when you are building ad hoc query systems, when you need to execute Data Definition Language (DDL) inside PL/SQL, and just generally when you don't know in advance exactly what you or the user will want to do. Dynamic SQL is a frequent requirement in web-based applications.

But there are some problems with DBMS_SQL; for example, it is a very complicated package; it only works with Oracle7 datatypes (no object types or INTERVALs need apply); and it is relatively slow.

So our dear friends at PL/SQL Central in Redwood Shores took pity on us all and re-implemented dynamic SQL directly in the PL/SQL language itself. This is called *native dynamic SQL* (NDS).

NDS introduces the EXECUTE IMMEDIATE statement to the PL/SQL language, and expands the OPEN FOR statement (for cursor variables) to support dynamic query strings to handle multi-row queries. The following function uses NDS to return the number of rows in whatever table you specify:

```
CREATE OR REPLACE FUNCTION tabCount (
   tab IN VARCHAR2, whr IN VARCHAR2 := NULL)
   RETURN INTEGER
IS
   retval INTEGER;
BEGIN
   EXECUTE IMMEDIATE
      'SELECT COUNT(*)
         FROM ' || tab ||
      ' WHERE ' || NVL (whr, '1=1')
      INTO retval;
   RETURN retval;
END;
```

Those of you familiar with DBMS_SQL will find this code a breath of fresh air. See Chapter 15 for extensive coverage of this wonderful new capability.

Bulk binds and collects

One of the major priorities of Oracle's PL/SQL development team is to speed up the performance of their language. This effort cannot come a moment too soon. We developers have been complaining about runtime performance for years, and finally the development team has responded (although, to be brutally honest, it seems to me that the intensive tuning steps taken in Oracle 8.0 were motivated at least partly by the need to make PL/SQL fast enough to support object types).

One area of improvement concerns the execution of *bulk DML* inside PL/SQL. Consider, for example, the following code that deletes each employee identified by the employee number found in the nested table list:

```
/* File on web: bulktiming.sql */
CREATE TYPE empnos_list_t IS VARRARY(100) OF NUMBER;
CREATE OR REPLACE del_emps (list_in IN empnos_list_t)
IS
BEGIN
   FOR listnum IN list_in.FIRST.. list_in.LAST
   LOOP
      DELETE FROM emp WHERE empno = list_in (listnum);
   END LOOP;
END;
```

Easy to write, easy to read—but what about performance? Whenever this program issues its DELETE, a context switch takes place from PL/SQL to SQL to execute that command. If there are 100 elements in the list, there are at least 100 switches, with corresponding performance degradation.

Acknowledging this common requirement and its overhead, Oracle now offers a bulk bind variation on the FOR loop—the FORALL statement. With this statement, you can recode the del_emps procedure as follows:

```
CREATE OR REPLACE del_emps (list_in IN empnos_list_t)
IS
BEGIN
   FORALL listnum IN list_in.FIRST.. list_in.LAST
   LOOP
      DELETE FROM emp WHERE empno = list_in (listnum);
END;
```

Now there will be many fewer context switches; all of the DELETE operations will be bundled into a single bulk operation and passed to the SQL layer together.

In addition to the FORALL bulk DML operator, Oracle 8.1 also offers the BULK COLLECT variation on the INTO clause of an implicit query. This operation allows you to retrieve multiple rows in a single context switch.

Chapter 13 gives you the inside scoop on FORALL, and BULK COLLECT is covered in Chapter 14.

New trigger capabilities

Oracle8*i* expands significantly the use of triggers to administer a database and "publish" information about events taking place within the database. By employing database triggers on the newly defined system events and by using Oracle Advanced Queuing (AQ) within those triggers, you can take advantage of the publish/subscribe capabilities of Oracle8*i*.

The database event publication feature allows applications to subscribe to database events just as they subscribe to messages from other applications. The trigger syntax is extended to support system and other data events on a database or a schema. Trigger syntax also supports a CALL to a procedure as the trigger body.

You can now define a programmatic trigger on the following actions:

- DML statements (DELETE, INSERT, and UPDATE)
- DDL events (e.g., CREATE, DROP, and ALTER)
- Database events (SERVERERROR, LOGON, LOGOFF, STARTUP, and SHUTDOWN)

These are the new trigger features available in Oracle8*i*:

Triggers on nested table columns
: The CAST...MULTISET operation allows you to trigger activity when only an attribute in a nested table column is modified.

Database-level event triggers
: You can now define triggers to respond to such system events as LOGON, DATABASE SHUTDOWN, and even SERVERERROR.

Schema-level event triggers
: You can now define triggers to respond to such user- or schema-level events as CREATE, DROP, and ALTER.

Chapter 18 covers these new trigger features, as well as the more traditional DML triggers with which you can define actions on INSERT, UPDATE, and DELETE statements.

Calling Java from PL/SQL

Java is a very powerful language, more robust in many ways than PL/SQL. Java also offers hundreds of classes that provide clean, easy-to-use application programming interfaces (APIs) to a wide range of functionality. In Oracle8*i* and above, you can now invoke *Java Stored Procedures* (which are, in reality, Java methods stored in the database) from within your PL/SQL applications. You do so by constructing a "wrapper" or PL/SQL layer that encapsulates a call to a Java method, thereby making it available to any environment that can invoke PL/SQL programs.

Here is an example of such a wrapper, allowing me to delete files from PL/SQL:

```
CREATE OR REPLACE PACKAGE xfile
IS
   FUNCTION delete (file IN VARCHAR2) RETURN INTEGER
   AS LANGUAGE JAVA
      NAME 'JFile1.delete (java.lang.String) return int';
END;
```

Java in the Oracle database is a big topic; Java programming all by itself is an even bigger topic. Complete treatment of either is outside the scope of this book, but Chapter 22 will give you all the information you need to leverage Java from within your PL/SQL programs.

Oracle9i New Features

Oracle9*i* Release 1 and Release 2 have added exciting new functionality to the PL/SQL language. These are summarized in the following sections and are covered more thoroughly in the indicated chapters.

Record-based DML

New to Oracle9*i* Release 2, you can now use records in INSERT and UPDATE statements. Here is an example:

```
CREATE OR REPLACE PROCEDURE set_book_info (
   book_in IN books%ROWTYPE)
IS
BEGIN
   INSERT INTO books VALUES (book_in);
EXCEPTION
   WHEN DUP_VAL_ON_INDEX
   THEN
      UPDATE books SET ROW = book_in
       WHERE isbn = book_in.isbn;
END;
```

This enhancement offers some very compelling advantages over working with individual variables or fields within a record:

Very concise code
: You can "stay above the fray" and work completely at the record level. There is no need to declare individual variables or to decompose a record into its fields when passing that data to the DML statement.

More robust code
: By working with %ROWTYPE records and not explicitly manipulating fields in those records, your code is less likely to break as changes are made to the tables and views upon which the records are based.

You can find additional information about record-based DML in Chapter 13.

Table functions

A *table function* is a function that returns a result set (in the form of a PL/SQL collection) and can be called in the FROM clause of a query. Table functions were available in a very limited fashion in Oracle8*i*, but Oracle9*i* has greatly expanded the scope and usefulness of these functions. In Oracle9*i* it is now possible for you to write functions that do the following:

Return rows from a result set in "pipelined fashion"
: This means that data is returned while the function is still executing.

Participate fully in parallel query execution
: In other words, the function can be run simultaneously within multiple "slave processes" against different, partitioned elements of data.

Here is an example of the header of a pipelined table function that can run in parallel, defined so that all the rows for a given department go to the same slave process, and all rows are delivered consecutively:

```
CREATE OR REPLACE FUNCTION my_transform_fn (
      p_input_rows in employee_info.recur_t )
  RETURN employee_info.transformed_t
  PIPELINED
  CLUSTER P_INPUT_ROWS BY (department)
  PARALLEL_ENABLE
    ( PARTITION P_INPUT_ROWS BY HASH (department))
```

You can find additional information about table functions, pipelining, and parallel execution in Chapter 16.

New and improved datatypes

Oracle now offers dramatically improved support for timestamps, time zone management, and interval calculations (the amount of time between two dates or timestamps). The following block showcases a number of aspects of these new datatypes and associated functions:

```
DECLARE
  boss_free TIMESTAMP(0) WITH TIME ZONE;
  steven_leaves TIMESTAMP(0) WITH TIME ZONE;
  window_for_conversation INTERVAL DAY(3) TO SECOND(3);
BEGIN
  boss_free := TO_TIMESTAMP_TZ (
    '29-JAN-2002   12:00:00.0   US/Pacific     PST',
    'DD-MON-YYYY HH24:MI:SSXFF   TZR            TZD' );

  steven_leaves := TO_TIMESTAMP_TZ (
    '29-JAN-2002   16:45:00.0   US/Central     CST',
    'DD-MON-YYYY HH24:MI:SSXFF   TZR            TZD' );

  window_for_conversation := steven_leaves - boss_free;

  DBMS_OUTPUT.PUT_LINE (
     TO_CHAR (window_for_conversation, 'HH:MI:SSXFF' ));

  -- Implicit conversion from TimeZone to Date...
  DBMS_OUTPUT.PUT_LINE ( ADD_MONTHS (boss_free, -5 ) );

END;
```

Chapter 10 explores these new datatypes in detail.

On a completely different front, Oracle has now incorporated XML functionality directly into the database with the addition of the XMLType datatype (implemented as an object type). Oracle has committed itself to supporting XML, and with its own XML native datatype hopes to blur the lines between SQL and XML. In Oracle9*i*, you can issue SQL queries against XML documents stored in table columns. You can also use XPath syntax to search the contents of those documents.

Here is an example of inserting an XML document into a table (notice the use of the CREATEXML method of the XMLType object type to convert a string to an XML document):

```
INSERT INTO env_analysis
     VALUES ('ACME SILVERPLATING',
             TO_DATE ('15-02-2001', 'DD-MM-YYYY'),
        XMLTYPE.CREATEXML (
        '<?xml version="1.0"?>
        <report>
           <site>1105 5th Street</site>
           <substance>PCP</substance>
           <level>1054</level>
        </report>'));
```

The following CREATE statement utilizes XPath syntax to create a function-based index on the first 26 characters of the customer's name on a purchase order:

```
CREATE UNIQUE INDEX i_purchase_order_reference
ON purchaseorder p (
   SUBSTR(XMLTYPE.GETSTRINGVAL(
          XMLTYPE.EXTRACT(
                 p.PODOCUMENT,
            '/PurchaseOrder/Customer/text( )')),1,26)
);
```

Chapter 12 provides a lot more detail on the XMLType datatype.

Inheritance for object types

Oracle first introduced the *object type* (the closest that Oracle comes to a "class" in the, ahem, classical sense of object orientation) in Oracle8, but it was plagued by a severe lack of standard object functionality, most notably *inheritance*.

In Oracle9*i*, you can now define a hierarchy of object types in which the attributes and methods of a supertype are inherited or overwritten by the subtype. The following three object type specification definitions offer a simple example of such a hierarchy (in which food is the root, desserts are types of food, and cakes are types of desserts).

```
CREATE TYPE food_t AS OBJECT (
   name VARCHAR2(100),
   food_group  VARCHAR2 (100),
   grown_in    VARCHAR2 (100),
   MEMBER FUNCTION price RETURN NUMBER
   )
   NOT FINAL;
/
CREATE TYPE dessert_t UNDER food_t (
   contains_chocolate    CHAR(1),
   year_created          NUMBER(4),
   OVERRIDING MEMBER FUNCTION price RETURN NUMBER
   )
   NOT FINAL;
```

```
/
CREATE TYPE cake_t UNDER dessert_t (
   diameter      NUMBER,
   inscription   VARCHAR2(200)
   -- The cake_t type has no distinct pricing calculator.
   );
/
```

Notice that the dessert_t type overrides the root's price function, but the cake_t type inherits the price function from dessert_t.

With inheritance, there is now a much more compelling reason to give object types a serious evaluation for use in your applications. You can find out more about object types and inheritance in Chapter 21.

Enhancements to PL/SQL collections

PL/SQL collections are array-like structures that allow you to maintain lists of information. These lists can be of simple data, such as strings, or more complex structures, such as records. In Oracle9*i*, Oracle extends the features of collections with two major enhancements:

- Support for multiple-level collections (i.e., collections within collections).
- The ability to index the contents of one type of collection (*associative arrays*, previously known as *index-by tables*) by strings as well as integers.

Here is an example of using strings for the index values or row numbers in a collection:

```
DECLARE
   TYPE population_t IS TABLE OF NUMBER INDEX BY VARCHAR2(64);
   country_population population_t;
   continent_population population_t;

   howmany NUMBER;
   row_id VARCHAR2(64);
BEGIN
   country_population('Colymphia') := 100000;
   country_population('Ribalizia') := 750000;

   howmany := country_population('Colymphia');
   row_id := continent_population.FIRST;

   DBMS_OUTPUT.PUT_LINE (continent_population(row_id));
END;
/
```

Multi-level collections allow us to emulate *N*-dimensional arrays and, more generally, model arbitrarily complex data. For more information about these new collection features, check out Chapter 11.

Native compilation of PL/SQL code

Prior to Oracle9*i*, compilation of PL/SQL source code always results in a representation (usually referred to as *bytecode*) that is stored in the database and is interpreted at runtime by a virtual machine implemented within Oracle that, in turn, runs natively on the given platform. Oracle9*i* introduces a new approach. PL/SQL source code may optionally be compiled into native object code that is linked into Oracle. Native compilation can result in significant improvement in overall application performance. (Its impact is felt in compute-intensive programs, but will not affect SQL performance.)

For instructions on how to take advantage of native compilation, see Chapter 19.

Working with Multiple Versions of PL/SQL

You need to be aware of the version of Oracle you are running in order to know which features are available for your use. You may sometimes even have to write PL/SQL programs that can run on different versions of Oracle. In this case, you have two options:

- Avoid relying on any "advanced" features of PL/SQL—that is, features that appear in a later version of the language, but not in a version that you must write for. This can be termed the "lowest common denominator" approach.
- Maintain multiple versions of your programs for each of the different versions of Oracle (assuming that there are features you want, or need to take advantage of, in later versions). It is hard to maintain code using this approach. If you are in this situation, you might want to take a look at the *oneversion.sql* script available on the O'Reilly site. This script shows how you can determine the Oracle version from the data dictionary and then use SQL*Plus substitution variables to turn portions of your program on or off, as appropriate for a particular version.

Resources for PL/SQL Developers

O'Reilly & Associates published the first edition of this book back in 1995. At that time, *Oracle PL/SQL Programming* made quite a splash. It was the first independent (i.e., not emanating from Oracle) book on PL/SQL, and it fulfilled a clear and intensely felt need of developers around the world. Since that time, resources—books, development environments, utilities, and web sites—for PL/SQL programmers have proliferated. (Of course, this book is still by far the most important and valuable of these resources!)

The following sections describe very briefly many of these resources. By taking full advantage of these resources, many of which are available either free or at a relatively low cost, you will greatly improve your development experience (and resulting code).

The O'Reilly PL/SQL Series

Over the years, the Oracle PL/SQL series from O'Reilly & Associates has grown to include quite a long list of books. We've summarized the whole set below. Please check out the Oracle area of the O'Reilly web site (*http://oracle.oreilly.com*) for much more complete information.

Oracle PL/SQL Programming, by Steven Feuerstein with Bill Pribyl
: The thousand-page tome you are reading now. The desk-side companion of a great many professional PL/SQL programmers, this book is designed to cover every feature in the core PL/SQL language. The second edition covered Oracle versions through Oracle8, but this third edition covers all PL/SQL versions through Oracle9*i*.

Learning Oracle PL/SQL, by Bill Pribyl with Steven Feuerstein
: A comparatively gentle introduction to the language, ideal for new programmers and those who know a language other than PL/SQL.

Oracle PL/SQL Best Practices, by Steven Feuerstein
: A relatively short book that describes more than 100 best practices that will help you produce high-quality PL/SQL code. Having this book is kind of like having a "lessons learned" document written by an in-house PL/SQL expert. Current through Oracle8*i*.

Oracle PL/SQL Developer's Workbook, by Steven Feuerstein with Andrew Odewahn
: Contains a series of questions and answers intended to help the PL/SQL programmer develop and test his or her understanding of the language. Current through Oracle8*i*.

Oracle PL/SQL Language Pocket Reference, by Steven Feuerstein, Bill Pribyl, and Chip Dawes (covers Oracle 8i)

Oracle PL/SQL Built-ins Pocket Reference, by Steven Feuerstein, John Beresniewicz, and Chip Dawes (covers Oracle 8)
: Two tiny "quick reference" books that might actually fit in your coat pocket.

Oracle Built-in Packages, by Steven Feuerstein, Charles Dye, and John Beresniewicz
: A reference guide to all of the prebuilt packages that Oracle supplies with the core database server. The use of these packages can sometimes simplify the difficult and tame the impossible. Current through Oracle8.

Oracle PL/SQL Programming: Guide to Oracle8i Features, by Steven Feuerstein
: A companion to the *Oracle PL/SQL Programming* book that presents an overview of the great new PL/SQL features that appeared in Oracle8*i*.

Advanced Oracle PL/SQL Programming with Packages, by Steven Feuerstein
: A book designed to communicate the rationale and means of improving your programs by writing your own PL/SQL packages. Covers Oracle7.

Oracle Web Applications: PL/SQL Developer's Introduction, by Andrew Odewahn
A good book to get Oracle developers started building database-driven web applications. Includes some introductory material on both PL/SQL and programming for the Web. Current through Oracle8*i*.

Oracle PL/SQL CD Bookshelf
Contains an electronic version of most of the above books, plus a hardcopy version of the *Guide to Oracle8i Features*. Current through Oracle8*i*.

Other Printed Resources

In addition to the O'Reilly books listed in the previous section, there are other printed resources you should be aware of:

Oracle documentation
Oracle has come a long, long way from its early days of scattered and inadequate product documentation. The HTML documents that come with the RDBMS are an excellent source of information on the incredible array of technologies now offered by Oracle.

Oracle Press and other publishers
Oracle Press offers its own PL/SQL series by Scott Urman. Other technical publishers offer introductory texts for PL/SQL or include coverage of PL/SQL within broader Oracle-related books.

Oracle Professional from Pinnacle Publishing
This monthly, printed newsletter (with accompanying online edition) offers in-depth articles on Oracle technology. Each issue features a PL/SQL article (usually written by Steven Feuerstein) that explores either new features or applications of PL/SQL technology.

http://www.oracleprofessionalnewsletter.com/

Oracle Magazine from Oracle Corporation
A monthly publication that covers a wide variety of Oracle technology, *Oracle Magazine* often introduces new PL/SQL functionality and gives you a solid foundation for understanding how all the Oracle pieces fit together.

http://www.oramag.com/

PL/SQL on the Internet

There are also some excellent web sites available to PL/SQL programmers:

Oracle Technology Network
Join the Oracle Technology Network (OTN), sometimes called TechNet, which "provides services and resources that developers need to build, test, and deploy applications" based on Oracle technology. Boasting membership in the millions,

OTN is a great place to download Oracle software, documentation, and lots of sample code. Check out:

http://technet.us.oracle.com/

or the PL/SQL page more specifically:

http://otn.oracle.com/tech/pl_sql/content.html

PL/SQL Pipeline

We also recommend that you join the PL/SQL Pipeline, described as "a free Internet portal community hosted by Quest Software. This site is designed to inform, educate, and inspire IT professionals around the world. The Pipeline is regularly monitored by a host of industry-recognized authors and experts." The PL/SQL Pipeline offers archives of training materials and useful code. The Pipetalk forum features many active discussions and, in essence, free consulting for developers and DBAs around the world.

http://www.quest-pipelines.com

PL/Net.org

PLNet.org is a repository of open source software, maintained by Bill Pribyl, that is written in PL/SQL or is otherwise for the benefit of PL/SQL developers. You can read more about the project's background or check out the FAQ (Frequently Asked Questions). You will also be directed to a number of utilities, such as utPLSQL, the unit-testing framework for PL/SQL developers.

http://plnet.org

Open Directory Project

Courtesy of the "dmoz" (Directory Mozilla) project, you can find a choice set of links to PL/SQL sites. There is also a subcategory called "Tools" with a fairly comprehensive set of links to both commercial and noncommercial developer tools. Links on these pages are maintained by a team of volunteer editors, currently including Bill Pribyl.

http://dmoz.org/Computers/Programming/Languages/PL-SQL/

Oracle FAQ

This site offers "independent and useful information on Oracle products to the Oracle community. On this site you will find FAQs, Scripts, Tips, News, Jobs, Directories, Message forums, Chat boards, and many more features to make your journey with Oracle more worthwhile."

http://www.orafaq.com/faq.htm

Development Tools and Utilities

If you currently write your software in Notepad and then run and test code exclusively in SQL*Plus, you are wasting dozens (if not hundreds) of hours of your time—prime development time—each year. If you continue to debug your programs by inserting endless numbers of calls to DBMS_OUTPUT.PUT_LINE, you are missing out on the ease of use and effectiveness of source code debuggers.

Today, there is a plethora of tools available to PL/SQL developers to help get our work done more effectively. These tools range from commercial, high-end integrated development environments (IDEs), to inexpensive replacements for SQL*Plus, to single-purpose utilities.

It is not within the scope of this book to provide a review of these tools, nor will we recommend any particular tools. However, the following list offers a smattering of products and URLs that will get you started in exploring the possibilities:

TOAD (Tool for Oracle Application Developers)
: The most popular of all the PL/SQL IDEs, TOAD is famous for its tabbed browser and "Swiss Army Knife" approach. Available in both commercial and freeware versions.

  http://www.quest.com/toad

SQL Navigator
: Also from Quest, this IDE has been around a long time—and it shows in the depth of its support for PL/SQL and Java programming in the database.

  http://www.quest.com/sql_navigator

PL/SQL Developer
: A fine and relatively inexpensive entry from the Netherlands, PL/SQL Developer offers a large number of features in a very nicely designed package. It also allows third-party developers to provide plug-ins to extend the base product's functionality.

  http://www.allroundautomations.nl/plsqldev.html

TOra (Toolkit for Oracle)
: This toolkit includes a browser, PL/SQL editor, and debugger for Linux or Microsoft Windows. TOra is available in open source and commercial forms.

  http://www.globecom.se/tora/

Some Words of Advice

Since 1995, when the first edition of this book was published, we have had the opportunity to train, assist, and work with tens of thousands of PL/SQL developers. In the process, we have learned an awful lot from our students and readers, and have also gained some insights into the way we all do our work in the world of PL/SQL. We hope that you will not find it too tiresome if we share some advice with you on how you can work more effectively with this powerful programming language.

Don't Be in Such a Hurry!

We are almost always working under tight deadlines, or playing catch-up from one setback or another. We have no time to waste, and lots of code to write. So let's get right to it—right?

Wrong. If we dive too quickly into the depths of code construction, slavishly converting requirements to hundreds, thousands, or even tens of thousands of lines of code, we will end up with a total mess that is almost impossible to debug and maintain. Don't respond to looming deadlines with panic; you are more likely to meet those deadlines if you do some careful planning.

We strongly encourage you to resist these time pressures and make sure to do the following before you start a new application, or even a specific program in an application:

Construct test cases and test scripts before you write your code
: You should determine how you want to verify a successful implementation *before* you write a single line of a program. By taking this approach (adopted from the Extreme Programming methodology), you are more likely to get the interface of your programs correct, and be able to thoroughly identify what it is your program needs to do.

Establish clear rules for how developers will write the SQL statements in the application
: In general, we recommend that individual developers not write a whole lot of SQL. Instead, those single-row queries and inserts and updates should be "hidden" behind prebuilt and thoroughly tested procedures and functions (this is called *data encapsulation*). These programs can be optimized, tested, and maintained much more effectively than SQL statements (many of them redundant) scattered throughout your code.

Establish clear rules for how developers will handle exceptions in the application
: Best of all, create a single error-handling package that hides all the details of how an error log is kept, determines how exceptions are raised and propagated up through nested blocks, avoids hardcoding of application-specific exceptions (those –20,*NNN* errors), and more. Make sure that all developers use this package and do *not* write their own complicated, time-consuming, and error-prone error-handling code.

Use "stepwise refinement" (a.k.a. top-down design) to limit the complexity of the requirements you must deal with at any given time
: If you use this approach, you will find that the executable sections of your modules are shorter and easier to understand. This will make your code easier to maintain and enhance over time. Local or nested modules play a key role in following this design principle.

These are just a few of the important things to keep in mind *before* you start writing all that code. Just remember: in the world of software development, haste not only makes waste, it virtually guarantees a generous offering of bugs and lost weekends.

Don't Be Afraid to Ask for Help

Chances are, if you are a software professional, you are a fairly smart individual. You studied hard, you honed your skills, and now you make a darn good living writing code. You can solve almost any problem you are handed, and that makes you proud.

Unfortunately, your success can also make you egotistical, arrogant, and reluctant to seek out help when you are stumped. This dynamic is one of the most dangerous and destructive aspects of software development.

Software is written by human beings; it is important, therefore, to recognize that human psychology plays a key role in software development. Here is one example:

Joe, the senior developer in a team of six, has a problem with his program. He studies it for hours, with increasing frustration, but cannot figure out the source of the bug. He wouldn't think of asking any of his peers to help, because they all have less experience then he does. Finally, though, he is at wits' end and "gives up." Sighing, he picks up his phone and touches an extension: "Sandra, could you come over here and take a look at my program? I've got a problem I can't figure out." Sandra stops by and, with the quickest glance at Joe's program, points out what should have been obvious to him long ago. Hurray! The program is fixed and Joe expresses gratitude, but in fact he is secretly embarrassed.

Thoughts like "Why didn't I see that?" and "If I'd only spent another five minutes doing my own debugging I would have found it" run though Joe's mind. This is understandable, but also very thick-headed. The bottom line is that we are often unable to identify our own problems because we are too close to our own code. Sometimes, all we need is a fresh perspective, the relatively objective view of someone with nothing at stake. It has nothing to do with seniority, expertise, or competence.

We strongly suggest that you establish the following guidelines in your organization:

Reward admissions of ignorance
: Hiding what you don't know about an application or its code is very dangerous. Develop a culture that welcomes questions and requests for help.

Ask for help
: If you cannot figure out the source of a bug in 30 minutes, immediately ask for help. You might even set up a "buddy system," so that everyone is assigned a person who is *expected* to be asked for assistance. Don't let yourself (or others in your group) go for hours banging your head against the wall in a fruitless search for answers.

Set up a formal peer code review process

Don't let any code go to QA or production without being read and critiqued (in a positive, constructive manner) by one or more other developers in your group.

Take a Creative, Even Radical Approach

We all tend to fall into ruts, in almost every aspect of our lives. People are creatures of habit: you learn to write code in one way; you assume certain limitations about a product; you turn aside possible solutions without serious examination because you just *know* it can't be done. Developers become downright prejudiced about their own programs, and often not in positive ways. They are often overheard saying things like:

> "It can't run any faster than that; it's a pig."
>
> "I can't make it work the way the user wants; that'll have to wait for the next version."
>
> "If I were using X or Y or Z product, it would be a breeze. But with this stuff, everything is a struggle."

But the reality is that your program could almost always run a little faster. And the screen could in fact function *just* the way the user wants it to. And although each product has its limitations, strengths, and weaknesses, you should never have to wait for the next version. Isn't it so much more satisfying to be able to tell your therapist that you tackled the problem head-on, accepted no excuses, and crafted a solution?

How do you do this? Break out of the confines of your hardened views and take a fresh look at the world (or maybe just your cubicle). Reassess the programming habits you've developed. Be creative—step away from the traditional methods, from the often limited and mechanical approaches constantly reinforced in our places of business.

Try something new: experiment with what may seem to be a radical departure from the norm. You will be surprised at how much you will learn and grow as a programmer and problem-solver. Over the years, I have surprised myself over and over with what is really achievable when I stopped saying "You can't do that!" and instead simply nodded quietly and murmured "Now, if I do it this way…"

In this chapter:

CHAPTER 2

Creating and Running PL/SQL Code

Before exploring the "meat and potatoes" of writing PL/SQL programs, you might benefit from some practical information about how to compile and run those programs. This chapter surveys a range of tools, in particular SQL*Plus, from which you can invoke your PL/SQL programs, and provides the specifics you'll need to get started.

If you already have some experience with database programming, you probably realize that there are lots of different ways and places to use SQL (Structured Query Language). Well, the same is true for PL/SQL; not only can you invoke it from a variety of other languages, it can execute in two different runtime environments:

- "Inside" the Oracle database server, as stored code. If you call PL/SQL from SQL*Plus, Java, or any other language, this is typically where it's going to run.
- In one of Oracle's application development environments such as Oracle Forms or Oracle Reports, as a program that executes on a client computer. (Alternately, these tools can run on a "middle tier," operated across the network from a browser-only or "thin" client.)

Let's begin by looking at the first option, running on the Oracle server. Here you have additional options for the front end from which you launch your code. Some of the most popular programming tools include:

- Oracle's command-line tool, SQL*Plus, which connects to an Oracle server where you can run PL/SQL statements.
- A host language such as C, C++, Java, Visual Basic, COBOL, Ada, or FORTRAN, for which Oracle provides a runtime library and/or precompiler that allows you to embed SQL and PL/SQL calls into your program.

Because the number of execution tools at your disposal will probably far exceed your time to assimilate them, it makes sense to concentrate on one or two, and learn them really well. So, while this chapter shows some examples of using PL/SQL with a variety of tools, the main concentration is on SQL*Plus.

SQL*Plus

The granddaddy of Oracle front ends, Oracle's SQL*Plus provides a *command-line interpreter* for both SQL and PL/SQL. That is, it accepts database statements from the user, then sends them off to the Oracle server, and finally displays the results.

Often maligned for its primitive user interface, SQL*Plus is one of my favorite Oracle tools. I actually *like* the lack of fancy gizmos or complicated menus. When I started using Oracle (circa 1986), this product's predecessor was boldly named UFI—*User Friendly Interface*. Almost two decades later, even Oracle9*i*'s version of SQL*Plus is still unlikely to win any user friendliness awards, but at least it doesn't crash very often.

Today there are several different styles of executing SQL*Plus:

*As a console program**
: This is a program that runs from a shell or command prompt (an environment that is sometimes called a *console*).

As a pseudo-GUI program
: This form of SQL*Plus is available only on Microsoft Windows. I call it a "pseudo-GUI" because it looks pretty much like the console program but with bitmapped fonts; few other features distinguish it from the console program. In fact, Oracle is already phasing out support for this product, with even "extended" support terminating in September 2005.

*Via iSQL*Plus (in Oracle9i or later)*
: This program executes from a web browser connected to a middle-tier machine running Oracle's HTTP server and *i*SQL*Plus server.

*Via SQL*Plus Worksheet*
: This is merely a Java GUI front end on the console version of SQL*Plus. Although it does maintain some statement history, there is little else to commend this version.

Figure 2-1 is a screen shot of a SQL*Plus console-style session.

Usually, I prefer the console program because:

- It tends to draw the screen faster, which can be significant for long queries
- It has more complete command-line history (on Microsoft Windows platforms, at least)
- It has a much easier way of changing visual characteristics such as font, color, and scroll buffer size
- I'm just an old command-line guy anyway

* Oracle calls this the "command-line interface" version of SQL*Plus, but I find that somewhat confusing, because two of the four styles provide a command-line interface.

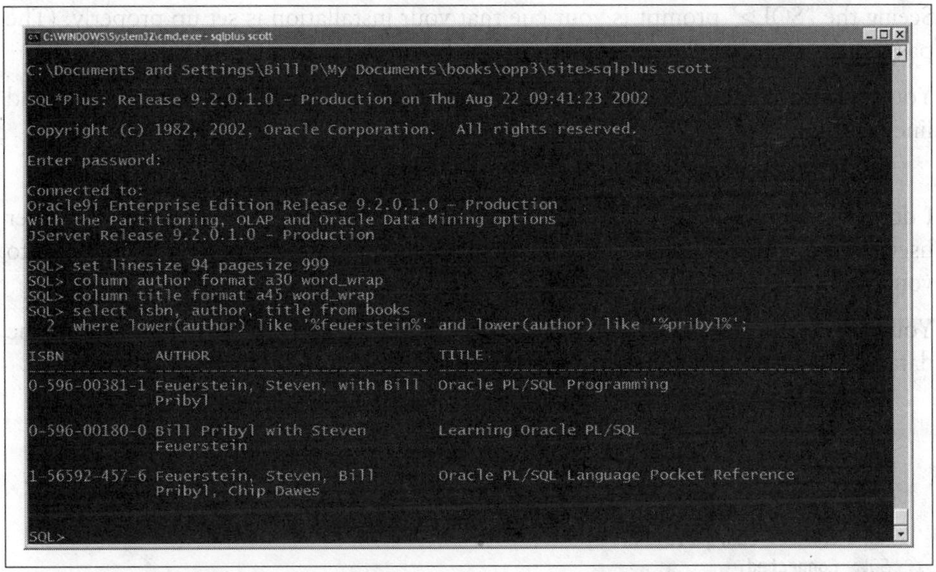

```
C:\Documents and Settings\Bill P\My Documents\books\opp3\site>sqlplus scott

SQL*Plus: Release 9.2.0.1.0 - Production on Thu Aug 22 09:41:23 2002

Copyright (c) 1982, 2002, Oracle Corporation.  All rights reserved.

Enter password:

Connected to:
Oracle9i Enterprise Edition Release 9.2.0.1.0 - Production
With the Partitioning, OLAP and Oracle Data Mining options
JServer Release 9.2.0.1.0 - Production

SQL> set linesize 94 pagesize 999
SQL> column author format a30 word_wrap
SQL> column title format a45 word_wrap
SQL> select isbn, author, title from books
  2  where lower(author) like '%feuerstein%' and lower(author) like '%pribyl%';

ISBN          AUTHOR                         TITLE
------------- ------------------------------ ---------------------------------------------
0-596-00381-1 Feuerstein, Steven, with Bill  Oracle PL/SQL Programming
              Pribyl

0-596-00180-0 Bill Pribyl with Steven        Learning Oracle PL/SQL
              Feuerstein

1-56592-457-6 Feuerstein, Steven, Bill       Oracle PL/SQL Language Pocket Reference
              Pribyl, Chip Dawes

SQL>
```

*Figure 2-1. SQL*Plus in a console session*

That said, I am also rather fond of the way *i*SQL*Plus automatically formats query output into HTML tables. It's really useful when you're trying to display a lot of columns from the database; you'll see an example in the later section, "Running a SQL Statement."

Starting Up SQL*Plus

To start the console version of SQL*Plus, you can simply type "sqlplus" at the operating system prompt (designated by "OS>").

```
OS> sqlplus
```

This works for both Unix-based and Microsoft operating systems. SQL*Plus should display a startup banner and then prompt you for a username and password.

```
SQL*Plus: Release 9.2.0.1.0 - Production on Thu Jun 20 10:41:17 2002

Copyright (c) 1982, 2002, Oracle Corporation.  All rights reserved.

Enter user-name: bob
Enter password: swordfish

Connected to:
Oracle9i Enterprise Edition Release 9.2.0.1.0 - Production
With the Partitioning, OLAP and Oracle Data Mining options
JServer Release 9.2.0.1.0 - Production

SQL>
```

Seeing the "SQL>" prompt is your cue that your installation is set up properly. (The password, "swordfish" in this case, won't echo on the screen.)

You can also launch SQL*Plus with the username and password on the command line:

```
OS> sqlplus bob/swordfish
```

I do *not* recommend this, because some operating systems provide a way for other users to see your command-line arguments, which would allow them to break into your account.

You can use the /NOLOG option to start up SQL*Plus without connecting to the database, and supply the username and password via the CONNECT command.

```
OS> sqlplus /nolog

SQL*Plus: Release 9.2.0.1.0 - Production on Thu Jun 20 10:42:22 2002

Copyright (c) 1982, 2002, Oracle Corporation.  All rights reserved.
SQL> CONNECT bob/swordfish
SQL> Connected.
```

If the computer where you're running SQL*Plus also has a properly configured Oracle Net* installation, *and* you have been authorized by the database administrator to connect to remote databases (that is, database servers running on other computers), you will be able to connect to these other databases from SQL*Plus. This requires knowing something called an Oracle Net *connect identifier* (also known as a *service name*) that you must supply along with your username and password. A connect identifier could look like this:

```
test01.ariel.datacraft.com
```

To use this identifier, you can append it to your username and password, separated by an at-sign (@) symbol:

```
SQL> CONNECT bob/swordfish@test01.ariel.datacraft.com
SQL> Connected.
```

When starting the pseudo-GUI version of SQL*Plus, supplying your credentials is straightforward, although it calls the connect identifier a "Host String" (see Figure 2-2). If you want to connect to a database server running on the local machine, just leave the "Host String" field blank.

To run *i*SQL*Plus, put the correct URL into your browser (probably *http://hostname/isqlplus*) and supply your connection information as in Figure 2-3.

* Oracle Net is the current name for the product previously known as Net8 or SQL*Net.

Log On

User Name: bob

Password: *********

Host String: test01.ariel.datacraft.com

OK Cancel

*Figure 2-2. The GUI login screen of SQL*Plus*

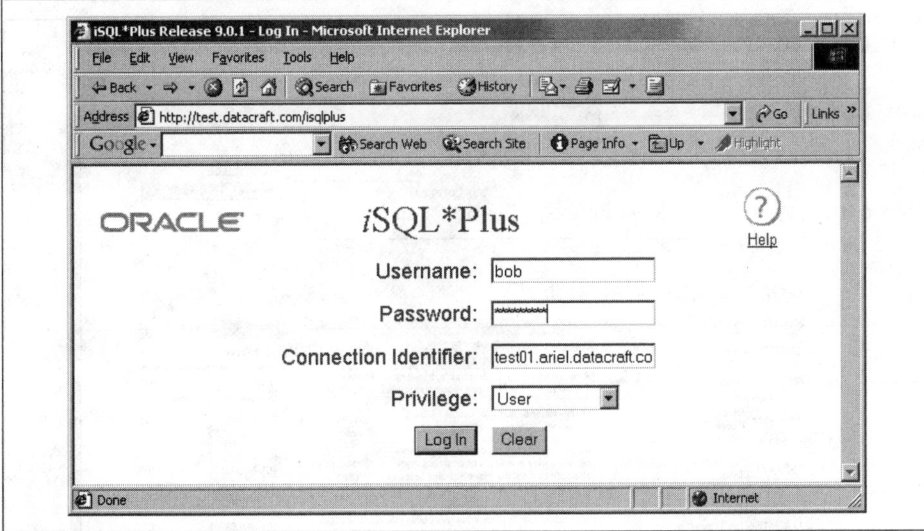

*Figure 2-3. The iSQL*Plus login page*

Once you have SQL*Plus running, you can do any of several things; the most common are:

- Run a SQL statement
- Compile and store a PL/SQL program in the database
- Run a PL/SQL program
- Issue a SQL*Plus-specific command
- Run a script that might contain a mix of the above

Let's take a look at each of these in turn.

Running a SQL Statement

In the console version of SQL*Plus, the query:

```
SELECT * FROM books;
```

produces output similar to that shown in Figure 2-1. (Well, I cheated a bit in that figure, because I used some column formatting commands. If this were a book about SQL*Plus or how to display database data, I would expound on the many ways SQL*Plus lets you control the appearance of the output by setting various formatting and display preferences. You can take my word for it, though; there are more options than you can shake a stick at.)

If you want "pretty" output, you may be better off with *i*SQL*Plus. Here, you enter the statement in the "Enter statements" field and press the "Execute" button. Output appears in a table in your browser, as in Figure 2-4.

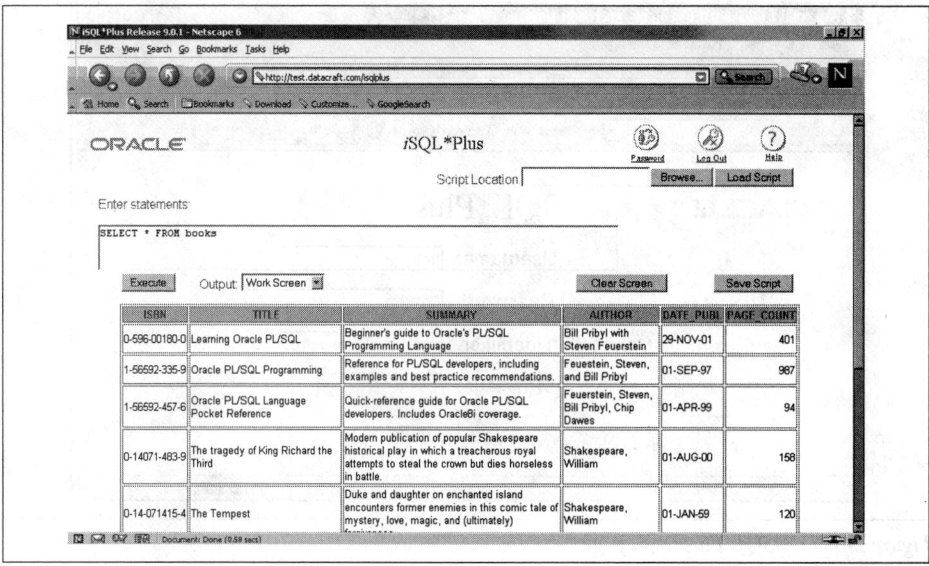

ISBN	TITLE	SUMMARY	AUTHOR	DATE_PUBL	PAGE_COUNT
0-596-00180-0	Learning Oracle PL/SQL	Beginner's guide to Oracle's PL/SQL Programming Language	Bill Pribyl with Steven Feuerstein	29-NOV-01	401
1-56592-335-9	Oracle PL/SQL Programming	Reference for PL/SQL developers, including examples and best practice recommendations.	Feuestein, Steven, and Bill Pribyl	01-SEP-97	987
1-56592-457-6	Oracle PL/SQL Language Pocket Reference	Quick-reference guide for Oracle PL/SQL developers. Includes Oracle8i coverage.	Feuerstein, Steven, Bill Pribyl, Chip Dawes	01-APR-99	94
0-14071-483-9	The tragedy of King Richard the Third	Modern publication of popular Shakespeare historical play in which a treacherous royal attempts to steal the crown but dies horseless in battle.	Shakespeare, William	01-AUG-00	158
0-14-071415-4	The Tempest	Duke and daughter on enchanted island encounters former enemies in this comic tale of mystery, love, magic, and (ultimately)	Shakespeare, William	01-JAN-59	120

*Figure 2-4. Query with result in iSQL*Plus*

You must terminate SQL statements in the console or pseudo-GUI with a semicolon, but the terminator is not required when entering a single statement in *i*SQL*Plus.

Running a PL/SQL Program

So, here we go (drum roll please). Let's type a short PL/SQL program into SQL*Plus:

```
SQL> BEGIN
  2     DBMS_OUTPUT.PUT_LINE('Hey look, ma!');
```

```
  3  END;
  4  /

PL/SQL procedure successfully completed.

SQL>
```

Oops. While "successful," this particular program is supposed to invoke PL/SQL's built-in program that echoes back some text. SQL*Plus's somewhat annoying default behavior is to suppress such output. To get it to display properly, you must use a SQL*Plus command to turn on SERVEROUTPUT.

```
SQL> SET SERVEROUTPUT ON
SQL> BEGIN
  2     DBMS_OUTPUT.PUT_LINE('Hey look, Ma!');
  3  END;
  4  /
Hey look, Ma!

PL/SQL procedure successfully completed.

SQL>
```

I generally put the SERVEROUTPUT command in my startup file (see the discussion of *login.sql* in the later section, "Loading your own custom environment automatically on startup"), causing it to be enabled until one of the following occurs:

1. You disconnect, log off, or otherwise end your session
2. You explicitly set SERVEROUTPUT to OFF
3. Oracle discards session state either at your request or due to a compilation error (see "Healing Invalids" in Chapter 20)

When you enter SQL or PL/SQL statements into the console or pseudo-GUI SQL*Plus, the program assigns a number to each line after the first. Why does it number the lines? Two main reasons: first, to help you designate which line to edit with the built-in line editor (which you might actually use one day); and second, if Oracle detects an error in your code, it will usually report the error accompanied by a line number. You'll have plenty of opportunities to see *that* behavior in action.

To tell SQL*Plus that you're done entering a PL/SQL statement, you must usually include a trailing slash (see line 4 above). Although mostly harmless, the slash has several important characteristics:

- The meaning of the slash is "execute the most recently entered statement," regardless of whether the statement was SQL or PL/SQL.
- The slash is a command unique to SQL*Plus; it is *not* part of the PL/SQL language, nor is it part of SQL.
- It must appear on a line by itself—no other commands can be included on the line.

- In most versions of SQL*Plus prior to Oracle9*i*, if you accidentally precede the slash with any spaces, it doesn't work! Beginning with Oracle9*i*, SQL*Plus correctly overlooks leading whitespace. Trailing space doesn't matter in any version.

As a convenience feature, SQL*Plus offers PL/SQL users an EXECUTE command, which saves typing the BEGIN, END, and trailing slash. So the following is equivalent to the short program I ran earlier:

```
SQL> EXECUTE DBMS_OUTPUT.PUT_LINE('Hey look, Ma!')
```

A trailing semicolon is optional, but I prefer to omit it. As with most SQL*Plus commands, EXECUTE can be abbreviated and is case-insensitive, so most interactive use gets reduced to:

```
SQL> exec dbms_output.put_line('Hey look, Ma!')
```

Running a Script

Assuming that you know the filename of a SQL or PL/SQL script, the easiest way to run it is to use the SQL*Plus "at-sign" (@) command.* For example, to create the prototype error-handling package discussed in Chapter 6, you can run it from SQL*Plus by entering:

```
SQL> @errpkg.pkg
```

Or, if you prefer words to at-signs, you can use the equivalent START command:

```
SQL> START errpkg.pkg
```

and you will get identical results. Either way, this command causes SQL*Plus to do the following:

1. Open the file named *errpkg.pkg*.
2. Attempt to execute all of the SQL, PL/SQL, and SQL*Plus statements in the file, one by one.
3. When complete, close the file and return you to the SQL*Plus prompt (unless the file invokes the EXIT statement, which will cause SQL*Plus to quit).

For example:

```
SQL> @errpkg.pkg

Package created.

Package body created.

SQL>
```

As you can see, the results of running the script appear on the screen.

* START, @, and @@ commands are available in the non-browser versions of SQL*Plus. In *i*SQL*Plus, you can use the "Browse" and "Load Script" buttons for a similar result.

In my example, I've used a filename extension of *pkg*. By default, though, SQL*Plus assumes a file extension of *sql*. So if I were using the defaults and left off the *.pkg*, as below, SQL*Plus would have searched for a file named *errpkg.sql* and given me an error:

```
SQL> @errpkg
SP2-0310: unable to open file "errpkg.sql"
```

SP2-0310 is the Oracle-supplied error number, and "SP2" means that it is unique to SQL*Plus. (For more details about SQL*Plus error messages, refer to Oracle's *SQL*Plus User's Guide and Reference*).

As you might expect, if your script file is in another directory, you can precede the filename with the path:*

```
SQL> @/files/src/release/1.0/errpkg.pkg
```

The idea of running scripts in other directories raises an interesting question. What if *errpkg.pkg* is located in this other directory and, in turn, calls other scripts? It might contain the lines:

```
REM  Filename: errpkg.pkg
@errpkg.pks
@errpkg.pkb
```

(Any line beginning with REM is a comment or "remark" that SQL*Plus ignores.) Executing the *errpkg.pkg* script is supposed to run *errpkg.pks* and *errpkg.pkb*. But because I have not included path information, where will SQL*Plus look for these other files? The answer: it looks only in the current directory (see the upcoming sidebar). And that's probably not where they are.

To address this problem, Oracle created a variation on the @ command: the @@ command. This double at-sign means "look for the file *relative* to the directory of the currently executing file." So, the preferred way of writing the calls in the *errpkg.pkg* script would be:

```
REM  Filename: errpkg.pkg
@@errpkg.pks
@@errpkg.pkb
```

Other SQL*Plus Tasks

There are dozens of commands specific to SQL*Plus, but I only have space to mention a few more that are particularly important or particularly confusing. For a thorough treatment of this venerable product, you might want to get a copy of Jonathan Gennick's book *Oracle SQL*Plus: The Definitive Guide* (O'Reilly) or, for quick reference, his *Oracle SQL*Plus Pocket Reference*.

* As a pleasant surprise, you can use forward slashes as directory delimiters on both Unix and Microsoft operating systems, at least as of Oracle8*i*. This allows your scripts to port more easily between operating systems.

Setting your preferences

As with many command-line environments, you can change the behavior of SQL*Plus by changing the value of some of its built-in variables and settings. We've already seen one example, the SET SERVEROUTPUT statement. There are many options on the SQL*Plus SET command, such as SET SUFFIX (changes the default file extension) and SET LINESIZE *n* (sets the maximum number of characters in each displayed line before wrapping). To see all the SET values applicable to your current session, use the command:

```
SQL> SHOW ALL
```

If you're using the GUI version of SQL*Plus, you can also view and set these preferences by choosing the Options → Environment menu option.

SQL*Plus also has the ability to create and manipulate its own in-memory variables, and it sets aside a few special variables that will affect its behavior. Actually, there are two separate types of variables in SQL*Plus: DEFINEs and bind variables. To assign a value to a DEFINE variable, you can use the DEFINE command:

```
SQL> DEFINE x = "the answer is 42"
```

To view the value of x, specify:

```
SQL> DEFINE x
DEFINE X               = "the answer is 42" (CHAR)
```

You would refer to such a variable using an ampersand (&). SQL*Plus does a simple substitution before sending the statement to Oracle, so you may need single-quote marks around it.

```
SELECT '&x' FROM DUAL;
```

For bind variables, you first declare the variable. Then you can use it in PL/SQL, and display it using the SQL*Plus PRINT command:

```
SQL> VARIABLE x VARCHAR2(10)
SQL> BEGIN
  2     :x := 'hullo';
  3  END;
  4  /

PL/SQL procedure successfully completed.

SQL> PRINT :x

X
--------------------------------
hullo
```

This can get a little bit confusing because there are now two different "x" variables, one that has been DEFINEd and one that has been declared.

```
SQL> SELECT :x, '&x' FROM DUAL;
old   1: SELECT :x, '&x' FROM DUAL
new   1: SELECT :x, 'the answer is 42' FROM DUAL
```

```
:X                                'THEANSWERIS42'
--------------------------------- ---------------
hullo                             the answer is 42
```

Just remember that DEFINEs are always character strings expanded by SQL*Plus, and declared variables are used as true bind variables in SQL and PL/SQL.

The "Current Directory" in SQL*Plus

Any time you launch SQL*Plus from an operating system command prompt, SQL*Plus treats the operating system's current directory as its own current directory. In other words, if you start up using:

```
C:\BILL\FILES> sqlplus
```

then any file operations inside SQL*Plus (like opening or running a script) will default to the directory *C:\BILL\FILES*.

The same is true if you start the GUI version from the operating system prompt with the command:

```
C:\BILL\FILES> sqlplusw
```

If you use a shortcut or menu option to launch SQL*Plus, the "current" directory is the one the operating system associates with the launch mechanism. So how would you change the current directory once you're inside SQL*Plus? Depends on the version. In the console program, you can't do it. You have to exit, change directories in the operating system, and restart SQL*Plus. In the GUI version, though, completing a File → Open or File → Save menu command will have the side effect of changing the current directory. If you're running *i*SQL*Plus, the concept of the current directory is relevant only in the browser's file save and retrieve dialogs, so the behavior will vary by browser.

Saving output to a file

Frequently, you will want to save output from a SQL*Plus session to a file—perhaps because you are generating a report, or because you want a record of your actions, or because you are dynamically generating commands to execute later. At any rate, an easy way to do this in SQL*Plus is to use its SPOOL command:

```
SQL> SPOOL report01.txt
SQL> @run_report

...output scrolls past and gets written to the file report01.txt...

SQL> SPOOL OFF
```

The first command, SPOOL report01.txt, tells SQL*Plus to save everything from that point forward into the file *report01.txt*. The last command, SPOOL OFF, tells SQL*Plus to stop saving the output and to close the file.

The SPOOL command works fine in the GUI version of SQL*Plus, but it does not work explicitly when using *i*SQL*Plus. Instead, save output to a file by setting the *i*SQL*Plus "Output:" drop-down menu to "File."

Exiting SQL*Plus

To exit SQL*Plus and return to the operating system, use the EXIT command:

```
SQL> EXIT
```

If you happen to be spooling a file when you exit, SQL*Plus will stop spooling and close it.

What happens if you exit with any pending (uncommitted) changes to the database? These changes are normally caused by running SQL or PL/SQL, which manipulates data in the database but is not followed by an explicit COMMIT or ROLLBACK. So what happens to the pending transactions depends on the AUTOCOMMIT setting. The default, AUTOCOMMIT ON, will attempt to commit any uncommitted changes. If you have changed the default by using:

```
SQL> SET AUTOMCOMMIT OFF
```

then Oracle will "roll back" any uncommitted changes.

To disconnect from the database but remain connected to SQL*Plus, use the command DISCONNECT, which will look something like this in action:

```
SQL> DISCONNECT
Disconnected from Oracle9i Enterprise Edition Release 9.2.0.1.0 - Production
With the Partitioning, OLAP and Oracle Data Mining options
JServer Release 9.2.0.1.0 - Production
SQL>
```

Why might you want to use DISCONNECT? If you're writing a script that changes connections in midstream, it's safer to disconnect before reconnecting. Otherwise, if you happen to be using operating system authentication, the script might reconnect itself automatically...maybe to the wrong account.

Editing a statement

SQL*Plus keeps the most recently issued statement in a buffer, and you can edit this statement using either the built-in line editor (which is sort of a pain unless you're an old gray-haired programmer like me) or an external editor of your choosing. To start with, I'll show how to set and use an external editor.

Use the EDIT command to have SQL*Plus save the buffer to a file, temporarily pause SQL*Plus, and invoke the editor:

```
SQL> EDIT
```

By default, the file will be saved with the name *afiedt.buf*, but you can change that with SET EDITFILE. Or, if you want to edit an existing file, just supply its name as an argument to EDIT:

```
SQL> EDIT errpkg.pkg
```

Once you've saved the file and exited the editor, the SQL*Plus session will read the contents of the newly edited file into its buffer, and then resume.

The default editors that Oracle assumes are:

For Unix, Linux, and relatives
: ed

For Microsoft Windows variants
: Notepad

Although these default values are actually hardcoded into the *sqlplus* executable, you can easily change them by assigning your own value to the SQL*Plus _EDITOR variable. Here's an example:

```
SQL> DEFINE _EDITOR = /bin/vi
```

where */bin/vi* is the full path to an editor that's popular among a handful of strange people (yes, me). I recommend using the editor's full pathname here, for security reasons.

If you really want to use the line editor (and it can be really handy), the essential commands you need to know are:

L
: List the most recent statement.

n
: Make the *n*th line of the statement the current line.

DEL
: Delete the current line.

C */old/new/*
: In the current line, change the first occurrence of *old* to *new*. The delimiter (here a forward slash) can be any arbitrary character.

n text
: Make *text* the current text of line *n*.

I
: Insert a line below the current line. To insert a new line prior to line 1, use a line zero command (e.g., 0 *text*).

By the way, EDIT works just fine in the GUI version of SQL*Plus, or you can copy and paste as well. If you are using *i*SQL*Plus, EDIT won't work, but you can either copy and paste from its editing window or use the "Save Script" and "Load Script" buttons.

Loading your own custom environment automatically on startup

To customize your SQL*Plus environment and have it assign your preferences from one session to the next, you will want to edit one or both of its auto-startup scripts. The way SQL*Plus behaves on startup is:

1. It searches for the file *sqlplus/admin/glogin.sql* in the Oracle home directory and, if found, executes any commands it contains. This "global" login script applies to everyone who executes SQL*Plus from that Oracle home, no matter which directory they start in.
2. Next, it searches for and runs the file *login.sql* in the current directory.

The startup script can contain the same kinds of statements as any other SQL*Plus script: SET commands, SQL statements, column formatting commands, and the like.

Neither file is required to be present. If both files are present, both get executed; in the case of conflicting preferences or variables, the later setting prevails.

Here are a few of my favorite *login.sql* settings:

```
REM Number of lines of SELECT statement output before re-printing headers
SET PAGESIZE 999

REM Width of displayed page, expressed in characters
SET LINESIZE 132

REM Enable display of DBMS_OUTPUT messages
SET SERVEROUTPUT ON SIZE 1000000 FORMAT WRAPPED

REM Change editor SQL*Plus invokes with "ed" command
DEFINE _EDITOR = vi

REM Format misc columns commonly retrieved from data dictionary
COLUMN segment_name FORMAT A30 WORD_WRAP
COLUMN object_name FORMAT A30 WORD_WRAP
```

In *i*SQL*Plus, there is no notion of the current directory, so there is no way to have a personal *login.sql* file. Only the *glogin.sql* on the server running *i*SQL*Plus has any effect.

Error Handling in SQL*Plus

The way SQL*Plus communicates success depends on the class of command you are running. With most SQL*Plus-specific commands, you can calibrate success by the absence of an error message. Successful SQL and PL/SQL commands, on the other hand, usually result in some kind of positive textual feedback.

If SQL*Plus encounters an error in a SQL or PL/SQL statement, it will, by default, report the error and continue processing. This behavior is desirable when you're working interactively. But, when you're executing a script, there are many cases in which you want an error to cause SQL*Plus to terminate. Use the following command to make that happen:

```
SQL> WHENEVER SQLERROR EXIT SQL.SQLCODE
```

Thereafter in this session, SQL*Plus will terminate if the database server returns any error messages in response to a SQL or PL/SQL statement. The SQL.SQLCODE part means that, when SQL*Plus terminates, it will set its "return code" to a nonzero value, which you can detect in the calling environment.* Otherwise SQL*Plus always ends with a 0 return code, which may falsely imply that the script succeeded.

A more common form of this command would be:

```
SQL> WHENEVER SQLERROR SQL.SQLCODE EXIT ROLLBACK
```

which means that you also want SQL*Plus to roll back any uncommitted changes prior to exiting.

Why You Will Love and Hate SQL*Plus

In addition to the features you just read about, here are some particular features of SQL*Plus that you will come to know and love:

- With SQL*Plus, you can run "batch" programs, supplying application-specific arguments on the *sqlplus* command line, and referring to them in the script using &1 (first argument), &2 (second argument), etc.
- SQL*Plus provides complete and up-to-date support for all SQL and PL/SQL statements. This can be important when you're using features unique to Oracle. Third-party environments may not provide 100% coverage; for example, some still don't understand Oracle's object types, which were introduced several years ago. (See Chapter 21 for a discussion of using object types in PL/SQL.)
- SQL*Plus runs on all of the same hardware and operating system platforms on which the Oracle server runs.

But as with any tool, there are going to be some irritations:

- In console versions of SQL*Plus, the statement buffer is limited to the most recently used statement; SQL*Plus offers no further command history.
- When you switch users by issuing a CONNECT command in the middle of a session or a script, SQL*Plus does not rerun the *login.sql* (or *glogin.sql*) startup script, causing SERVEROUTPUT to get disabled. This also causes no end of trouble for folks who create fancy prompts in their *login.sql* file—for example, a prompt such as "TEST9i>" will remain even after doing a CONNECT to the PROD9i database. You have to remember to run the startup after every reconnect.

* Using, for example, $? in the Unix shell, or %ERRORLEVEL% in Microsoft Windows.

- With SQL*Plus, there are no modern command-interpreter features such as automatic completion of keywords or hints about which database objects are available while typing in a statement.
- Online help consists of minimal documentation of the SQL*Plus command set. (Use HELP *command* to get help on a specific command.)
- There is no ability to change the current directory once you've started SQL*Plus. This can be annoying when opening or saving scripts if you don't like typing full pathnames. If you discover that you're in an inconvenient directory, you have to quit SQL*Plus, change directories, and restart SQL*Plus.
- SQL*Plus looks only in the startup directory for *login.sql*; it would be better if it always searched in my home directory, so I wouldn't need a copy of *login.sql* in every directory where I work.

The bottom line is that SQL*Plus is something of a "real programmer's" tool that is neither warm nor fuzzy. But it is ubiquitous, doesn't crash, and is likely to be supported as long as there is an Oracle Corporation.

Performing Essential PL/SQL Tasks

Let's turn to the highlights of creating, running, deleting, and otherwise managing PL/SQL programs, using SQL*Plus as the front end. Don't expect to be overwhelmed with detail here; treat this section as a glimpse of topics that will be covered in much greater detail in the chapters ahead.

Creating a Stored Program

To build your own stored PL/SQL program, you use one of SQL's CREATE statements. For example, if you want to create a stored function named wordcount that counts words in a string, you can do so using a CREATE FUNCTION statement:

```
CREATE FUNCTION wordcount (str IN VARCHAR2)
   RETURN PLS_INTEGER
AS
   declare local variables go here
BEGIN
   implement algorithm here
END;
/
```

As with the simple BEGIN-END blocks shown earlier, running this statement from SQL*Plus requires a trailing slash on a line by itself.

Assuming that the database administrator has granted you Oracle's CREATE PROCEDURE privilege, this statement will cause Oracle to compile and store this stored function in your schema; if your code compiles, you'll probably see a success message such as:

```
Function created.
```

If a table or stored program named wordcount already exists in your Oracle schema, CREATE FUNCTION will fail with the error message *ORA-00955: name is already used by an existing object.* That is one of the reasons that Oracle provides the OR REPLACE OPTION, which you will want to use probably 99% of the time.

```
CREATE OR REPLACE FUNCTION wordcount (str IN VARCHAR2)
   RETURN PLS_INTEGER
AS
   same as before
```

The OR REPLACE option avoids the side effects of dropping and re-creating the program; in other words, it preserves any object privileges you have granted to other users or roles. Fortunately, it only replaces objects of the same type, and it won't automatically drop a table named wordcount just because you decided to create a function by that name.

As with anonymous blocks used more than once, programmers generally store these statements in files in the operating system. I could create a file *wordcount.fun* for this function and use the SQL*Plus @ command to run it:

```
SQL> @wordcount.fun

Function created.
```

As this example shows, SQL*Plus does not, by default, echo the contents of scripts. You can, however, SET ECHO ON to see the source code scroll past the screen, including the line numbers that Oracle assigns; this setting can be helpful when troubleshooting. Let's introduce an error into the program by commenting out a variable declaration.

```
SQL> /* File on web: wordcount.fun */
SQL> SET ECHO ON
SQL> @wordcount.fun
SQL> CREATE OR REPLACE FUNCTION wordcount (str IN VARCHAR2)
  2     RETURN PLS_INTEGER
  3  AS
  4  /* words PLS_INTEGER := 0;  ***Commented out for intentional error*** */
  5     len PLS_INTEGER := NVL(LENGTH(str),0);
  6     inside_a_word BOOLEAN;
  7  BEGIN
  8     FOR i IN 1..len + 1
  9     LOOP
 10        IF ASCII(SUBSTR(str, i, 1)) < 33 OR i > len
 11        THEN
 12           IF inside_a_word
 13           THEN
 14              words := words + 1;
 15              inside_a_word := FALSE;
```

```
16           END IF;
17        ELSE
18           inside_a_word := TRUE;
19        END IF;
20     END LOOP;
21     RETURN words;
22  END;
23  /

Warning: Function created with compilation errors.

SQL>
```

We get a "warning" message that is completely inadequate for debugging the problem; you will want to look at the full text of the error message. The quickest way to do this is with the SHOW ERRORS command, abbreviated as SHOW ERR:

```
SQL> SHOW ERR
Errors for FUNCTION WORDCOUNT:

LINE/COL ERROR
-------- -------------------------------------------------
14/13    PLS-00201: identifier 'WORDS' must be declared
14/13    PL/SQL: Statement ignored
21/4     PL/SQL: Statement ignored
21/11    PLS-00201: identifier 'WORDS' must be declared
```

(Why SQL*Plus makes you show errors as a second step, I don't know.) The compiler has detected both occurrences of the variable, reporting the exact line and column numbers. Behind the scenes, SHOW ERRORS is really just querying Oracle's USER_ERRORS view in the data dictionary. To see more detail about any server-based error, you can look it up by its identifier—PLS-00201 in this case—in Oracle's *Database Error Messages* document.

It's common practice to append a SHOW ERRORS command after every scripted CREATE statement that builds a stored PL/SQL program. So, a "good practices" file template for building stored programs in SQL*Plus might begin with the following form:

```
CREATE OR REPLACE program-type
AS
   your code
/

SHOW ERRORS
```

(I don't usually include SET ECHO ON in scripts, but rather type it at the command line when needed.)

When your program contains an error that the compiler can detect, CREATE will still cause Oracle to store the program in the database, though in an invalid state. If, however, you mistype part of the CREATE syntax, Oracle won't be able to figure out what you are trying to do, and won't store the code.

Show Other Errors

Many Oracle programmers know only one form of the SQL*Plus command:

```
SQL> SHOW ERRORS
```

and they incorrectly believe that they must query the USER_ERRORS view directly to see anything but the error messages from the most recent compile. However, you can append to SHOW ERRORS an object category and a name, and it will display the latest errors for any object:

```
SQL> SHOW ERRORS category object
```

For example, to view the latest errors for the wordcount procedure, specify:

```
SQL> SHOW ERRORS PROCEDURE wordcount
```

Use caution when interpreting the output:

```
No errors.
```

This message actually means one of three things: (1) the object did compile successfully; (2) you gave it the wrong category (for example, function instead of procedure); or (3) no object by that name exists!

The complete list of categories this command recognizes varies by version, but in Oracle9*i* it includes the following:

```
DIMENSION
FUNCTION
JAVA SOURCE
JAVA CLASS
PACKAGE
PACKAGE BODY
PROCEDURE
TRIGGER
TYPE
TYPE BODY
VIEW
```

Executing a Stored Program

We've already looked at two different ways to invoke a stored program: one is to wrap it in a simple PL/SQL block, and another is to use the SQL*Plus EXECUTE command. You can also use stored programs inside other stored programs. For example, you can use a function like wordcount any place that you could use an integer expression. Here is a short illustration of how I might test the wordcount function with a strange input (CHR(9) is an ASCII "tab" character):

```
BEGIN
   DBMS_OUTPUT.PUT_LINE('There are ' || wordcount(CHR(9)) || ' words in a tab');
END;
/
```

I have embedded wordcount as part of an expression and supplied it as an argument to DBMS_OUTPUT.PUT_LINE. Here, PL/SQL automatically casts the integer to a string so it can concatenate it with two other literal expressions; the result is:

```
There are 0 words in a tab
```

You can also invoke many PL/SQL functions inside SQL statements. Here are several examples of how you can use the wordcount function.

- Apply the function in a select list to compute the number of words in a table column:

  ```
  SELECT isbn, wordcount(description) FROM books;
  ```

- Use the ANSI-compliant CALL statement, binding the function output to a SQL*Plus variable, and display the result:

  ```
  VARIABLE words NUMBER
  CALL wordcount('some text') INTO :words;
  PRINT :words
  ```

- Same as above, but execute the function from a remote database as defined in the database link *test.newyork.ora.com*:

  ```
  CALL wordcount@test.newyork.ora.com('some text') INTO :words;
  ```

- Execute the function, owned by schema bill, while logged in to any schema that has appropriate authorization:

  ```
  SELECT bill.wordcount(description) FROM books WHERE id = 10007;
  ```

Showing Stored Programs

Sooner or later you will want to get a list of the stored programs you own, and you may also need to view the most recent version of its source that Oracle has saved in its data dictionary. This is one task that you will find far easier if you use some kind of GUI-based navigation assistant (Chapter 1 mentions a few such tools), but if you lack such a tool, it's not too hard to write a few SQL statements that will pull the desired information out of the data dictionary.

For example, to see a complete list of your programs (and tables, indexes, etc.), query the USER_OBJECTS view, as in:

```
SELECT * FROM USER_OBJECTS;
```

This view shows name, type, creation time, latest compile times, status (valid or invalid), and other useful information.

If all you need is the summary of a PL/SQL program's callable interface in SQL*Plus, the easiest command to use is DESCRIBE.

```
SQL> DESCRIBE wordcount
FUNCTION wordcount RETURNS BINARY_INTEGER
 Argument Name                  Type                    In/Out Default?
 ------------------------------ ----------------------- ------ --------
 STR                            VARCHAR2                IN
```

For the complete source code of your stored programs, query USER_SOURCE or TRIGGER_SOURCE. (Querying from these data dictionary views is discussed in further detail in Chapter 19.)

Managing Grants and Synonyms for Stored Programs

When you first create a PL/SQL program, normally no one but you or the database administrator can execute it. To give another user the authority to execute your program, issue a GRANT statement:

```
GRANT EXECUTE ON wordcount TO scott;
```

To remove the privilege, use REVOKE:

```
REVOKE EXECUTE ON wordcount FROM scott;
```

You could also grant the EXECUTE privilege to a role:

```
GRANT EXECUTE ON wordcount TO all_mis;
```

Or, if appropriate, you could allow any Oracle user on the current database to run the program:

```
GRANT EXECUTE ON wordcount TO PUBLIC;
```

If you grant a privilege to an individual like Scott, and to a role of which the user is a member, and later grant it to PUBLIC, Oracle remembers all three grants. Any one of the grants is sufficient to permit the individual to run the program, so if you ever decide you don't want Scott to run it, you must revoke the privilege from Scott, and revoke it from PUBLIC, and finally revoke it from the role (or revoke the role from Scott).

To view a list of privileges you have granted to other users and roles, you can query the USER_TAB_PRIVS_MADE data dictionary view. Somewhat nonintuitively, PL/SQL program names appear in the table_name column:

```
SQL> SELECT table_name, grantee, privilege
  2    FROM USER_TAB_PRIVS_MADE
  3   WHERE table_name = 'WORDCOUNT';

TABLE_NAME                     GRANTEE                        PRIVILEGE
------------------------------ ------------------------------ -----------
WORDCOUNT                      PUBLIC                         EXECUTE
WORDCOUNT                      SCOTT                          EXECUTE
WORDCOUNT                      MIS_ALL                        EXECUTE
```

When Scott does have the EXECUTE privilege on wordcount, he will probably want to create a synonym for the program to avoid having to prefix it with the name of the schema that owns it:

```
SQL> CONNECT scott/tiger
Connected.
SQL> CREATE OR REPLACE SYNONYM wordcount FOR bill.wordcount;
```

Now he can execute the program in his programs by referring only to the synonym:

```
IF wordcount(localvariable) > 100 THEN...
```

This is a good thing, because if the owner changes, only the synonym (and not any stored program) needs modification.

It's possible to create a synonym for a procedure, function, package, or—in the most recent Oracle versions—user-defined type. Synonyms for procedures, functions, or packages can hide not only the schema but also the actual database; you can create a synonym for remote programs as easily as local programs. However, a synonym for a procedure or function *inside* a package or type will not work.

Removing a synonym is easy:

```
DROP SYNONYM wordcount;
```

Dropping a Stored Program

If you really, truly don't need a particular stored program any more, you can drop it using SQL's DROP statement:

```
DROP FUNCTION wordcount;
```

You can drop packages and types in their entirety:

```
DROP PACKAGE pkgname;
DROP TYPE typename;
```

Or you can drop only the body without invalidating the corresponding specification:

```
DROP PACKAGE BODY pkgname;
DROP TYPE BODY typename;
```

Any time you drop a program that other programs call, the callers will be marked invalid.

Hiding the Source Code of a Stored Program

When you create a PL/SQL program as described above, the source code will be available in clear text in the data dictionary, and any DBA will be able to view or even alter it. To protect trade secrets or to prevent tampering with your code, you might want some way to encrypt or otherwise obscure your PL/SQL source code before delivering it.

Oracle provides a command-line utility called *wrap* that converts many CREATE statements into a combination of plain text and hex. It's not true encryption, but it does go a long way toward hiding your code. Here are a few extracts from a wrapped file:

```
CREATE OR REPLACE FUNCTION wordcount wrapped
0
abcd
```

```
abcd
...snip...
1WORDS:
10:
1LEN:
1NVL:
1LENGTH:
1INSIDE_A_WORD:
1BOOLEAN:
...snip...
a5 b 81 b0 a3 a0 1c 81
b0 91 51 a0 7e 51 a0 b4
2e 63 37 :4 a0 51 a5 b a5
b 7e 51 b4 2e :2 a0 7e b4
2e 52 10 :3 a0 7e 51 b4 2e
d :2 a0 d b7 19 3c b7 :2 a0
d b7 :2 19 3c b7 a0 47 :2 a0
```

If you need true encryption—for example, to deliver information such as a password that really needs to be secure—you may not be able to rely on this facility.*

To learn more about the *wrap* utility, skip to Chapter 19.

Oracle's PL/SQL-Based Developer Tools

If you want to use PL/SQL for all of your programming needs, including the user interface, one way to accomplish that goal is to use two of Oracle's developer tools, commonly known as Forms and Reports. The programmer's tools are part of what Oracle currently calls the Oracle9*i* Developer Suite, which also includes a Java developer environment and a software configuration manager. Another tool, which was known as Oracle Graphics, is no longer sold as a separate product, but its functionality is available in Forms and Reports.

Included with the Forms Builder and Reports Developer products is a runtime engine that allows programmers to run their own applications; actually deploying your applications for end users, though, involves licensing a runtime environment such as Oracle9*i* Forms Services or Oracle9*i* Reports Services. These "services" are components of yet another product, Oracle9*i* Application Server, which would typically run on a mid-tier server machine, offering forms and reports to end users via Java-enabled browsers. However, older versions of Oracle Forms and Oracle Reports—still in use in many Oracle shops—run in a so-called "fat client" arrangement, in which the runtime software resides on every end user's desktop machine.

Throughout this book, you will notice references to Oracle's "client-side" developer tools, which refer to these tools. From the perspective of the database, everything is

* Oracle does provide a way to incorporate DES (Data Encryption Standard) security into your own applications using the built-in package DBMS_OBFUSCATION_TOOLKIT.

a client, even though you may be running multi-tier arrangements instead of just client and server.

Figure 2-5 shows what the Oracle9*i* Forms Builder user interface looks like. Look closely and you can see the built-in PL/SQL editor in the second subwindow from the right.

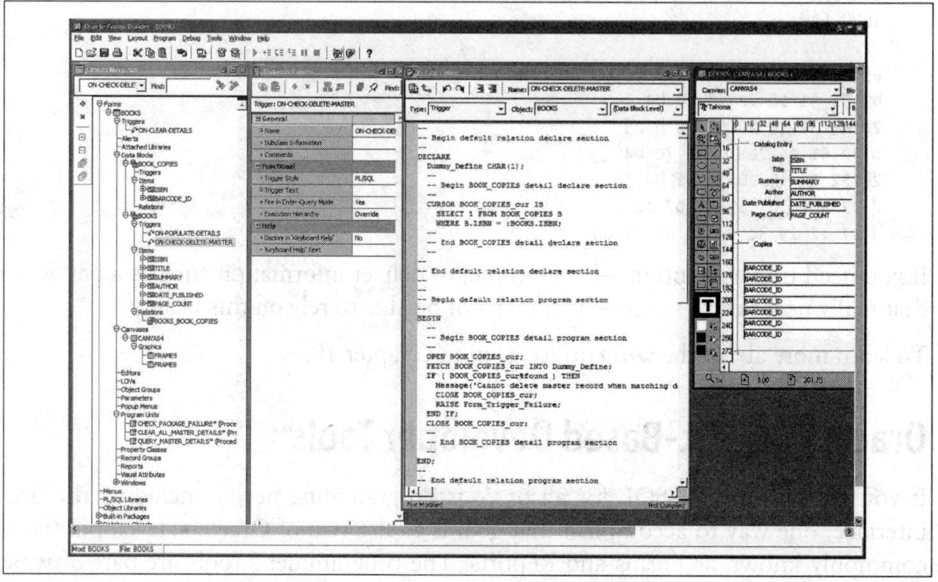

Figure 2-5. The programmer's user interface in Oracle Forms Builder

To help provide the kind of functionality that most users expect, Oracle provides an assortment of extensions to PL/SQL that are unique to the developer tools. For example, in Oracle Forms, PL/SQL programs can:

- Use on-screen item values as bind variables—for example, in a block named bk with a user-enterable field named isbn, the notation :bk.isbn would bind its value for the current record.
- Populate drop-down lists using data obtained from a database table.
- Automatically execute logic on end-user events such as clicking the mouse or navigating out of an input item.
- Control the appearance of the user interface, for example by displaying or hiding input items or windows.

Client-side PL/SQL can exist in one of three places in the application.

Triggers
: These PL/SQL blocks fire on specific application events such as startup, mouse click, or data validation.

Program units inside a particular application
These are available to call from any other PL/SQL program in the same application.

A PL/SQL library of your own reusable client-side programs
You can call these from any client-side application.

And, of course, you can call *server-side* PL/SQL programs from inside these applications as well. However, there are a number of limitations in the way that Oracle has implemented these calls. For example, you can't use server-side package variables or cursors directly in a client-side program (you have to put a wrapper function around them instead).

Moving PL/SQL Programs Between Client and Server

Moving PL/SQL code between the client and the server can be easy, but only if you haven't used any nonportable aspects of the language. For example, Figure 2-6 shows the result of doing a "drag and drop" of two stored packages from the database to a client-side PL/SQL library; the bodies didn't compile, as indicated by an asterisk. This reflects the fact that the packages use PL/SQL features that are not supported on the client side. One of the features is native dynamic SQL. To resolve this problem, I could eliminate the offending programs from the package body, or possibly convert the code to use the client-side EXEC_SQL built-in.

I had another problem with these packages: while the client-side PL/SQL engine can handle programmer-defined exceptions raised with the RAISE_APPLICATION_ERROR built-in on the server, client applications cannot themselves raise this exception. A workaround might involve centralizing your programmer-defined client exceptions in a client package specification.

Often, PL/SQL developed for the client is not a good candidate to move to the server, because it is likely to contain many things that limit its portability. For example, if the code contains references to client-specific bind variables like :bks.isbn, or uses Oracle Forms–specific built-ins like SHOW_ALERT or EXECUTE_QUERY, it will fail to compile on the server.

If you are doing a lot of work with Oracle's client tools, you may want to get a copy of *Oracle Developer Advanced Forms & Reports*, by Peter Koletzke and Paul Dorsey. As its title indicates, though, it is not a "starter" book.

Calling PL/SQL from Other Languages

Sooner or later, you will probably want to call PL/SQL from C, Java, Perl, Visual Basic, or any number of other places. This seems like a reasonable request, but if you've ever done cross-language work before, you may be all too familiar with some of the intricacies of mating up language-specific datatypes—especially composite datatypes like arrays, records, and objects—not to mention differing parameter

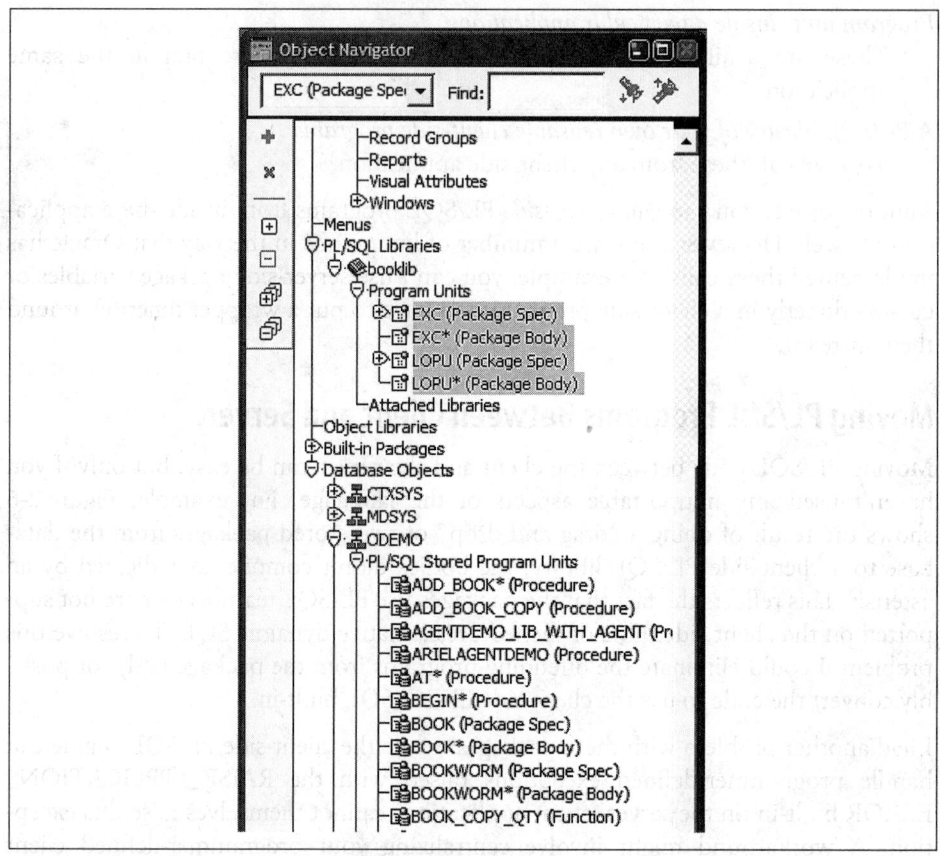

Figure 2-6. The Object Navigator in Oracle Forms shows the result of dragging and dropping two packages from the server to the client

semantics or vendor extensions to "standard" application programming interfaces (APIs) like Oracle DataBase Connectivity (ODBC).

I will show a few examples. Let's say that I've written a PL/SQL function that accepts an ISBN expressed as a string and returns the corresponding book title:

```
/* File on web: booktitle.fun */
CREATE OR REPLACE FUNCTION booktitle (isbn_in IN VARCHAR2)
   RETURN VARCHAR2
IS
   l_isbn books.title%TYPE;
   CURSOR icur IS SELECT title FROM books WHERE isbn = isbn_in;
BEGIN
   OPEN icur;
   FETCH icur INTO l_isbn;
   CLOSE icur;
   RETURN l_isbn;
END;
/
```

In SQL*Plus, I could call this in several different ways. The shortest way would be as follows:

```
SQL> EXEC DBMS_OUTPUT.PUT_LINE(booktitle('0-596-00180-0'))
Learning Oracle PL/SQL

PL/SQL procedure successfully completed.
```

Let's see how I might call this function from the following environments:

- C, using Oracle's precompiler (Pro*C)
- Java, using JDBC
- Perl, using Perl DBI and DBD::Oracle
- PL/SQL Server Pages

These examples are very contrived—for example, the username and password are hardcoded, and the programs simply display the output to stdout. Moreover, I'm not even going to pretend to describe every line of code. Still, these examples will give you an idea of some of the patterns you may encounter in different languages.

C: Using Oracle's Precompiler (Pro*C)

Oracle supplies at least two different C-language interfaces to Oracle: one called OCI (Oracle Call Interface), which is largely the domain of rocket scientists; and the other called Pro*C. OCI provides hundreds of functions from which you must code low-level operations such as open, parse, bind, define, execute, fetch...and that's just for a single query. Because the simplest OCI program that does anything interesting is about 200 lines long, I thought I'd show a Pro*C example instead.

Pro*C is a precompiler technology that allows you to construct source files containing a mix of C, SQL, and PL/SQL. You run this through Oracle's *proc* program, and out comes C code:

```
/* File on web: callbooktitle.pc */
#include <stdio.h>
#include <string.h>

EXEC SQL BEGIN DECLARE SECTION;
    VARCHAR uid[20];
    VARCHAR pwd[20];
    VARCHAR isbn[15];
    VARCHAR btitle[400];
EXEC SQL END DECLARE SECTION;

EXEC SQL INCLUDE SQLCA.H;

int sqlerror();

int main()
{
    /* VARCHARs actually become a struct of a char array and a length */
```

```
        strcpy((char *)uid.arr,"scott");
        uid.len = (short) strlen((char *)uid.arr);
        strcpy((char *)pwd.arr,"tiger");
        pwd.len = (short) strlen((char *)pwd.arr);

        /* this is a cross between an exception and a goto */
        EXEC SQL WHENEVER SQLERROR DO sqlerror( );

        /* connect and then execute the function */
        EXEC SQL CONNECT :uid IDENTIFIED BY :pwd;
        EXEC SQL EXECUTE
           BEGIN
              :btitle := booktitle('0-596-00180-0');
           END;
        END-EXEC;

        /* show me the money */
        printf("%s\n", btitle.arr);

        /* Disconnect from ORACLE. */
        EXEC SQL COMMIT WORK RELEASE;
        exit(0);
    }

    sqlerror( )
    {
        EXEC SQL WHENEVER SQLERROR CONTINUE;
        printf("\n% .70s \n", sqlca.sqlerrm.sqlerrmc);
        EXEC SQL ROLLBACK WORK RELEASE;
        exit(1);
    }
```

As you can see, Pro*C is not an approach for which language purists will be pining away. And trust me, you don't want to mess with the C code that this generates. Nevertheless, many companies find that Pro*C (or Pro*Cobol or any of several other languages Oracle supports) serves a reasonable middle ground between, say, Visual Basic (too slow and clunky) and OCI (too hard).

For more information about Pro*C, the best source is Oracle's own documentation.

Java: Using JDBC

As with C, Oracle provides a number of different Java approaches to connecting to the database. The embedded SQL approach, known as SQLJ, is similar to Oracle's other precompiler technology, although a bit more debugger-friendly. A more popular and Java-centric approach is known as JDBC, which doesn't really stand for anything, but the usual interpretation is "Java DataBase Connectivity."

```
/* File on web: callbooktitle.java */
import java.sql.*;

public class book
```

```
{
  public static void main(String[] args) throws SQLException
  {
    // initialize the driver and try to make a connection

    DriverManager.registerDriver (new oracle.jdbc.driver.OracleDriver ());
    Connection conn =
       DriverManager.getConnection("jdbc:oracle:thin:@localhost:1521:o92",
                                   "scott", "tiger");

   // prepareCall uses ANSI92 "call" syntax
   CallableStatement cstmt = conn.prepareCall("{? = call booktitle(?)}");

   // get those bind variables and parameters set up
   cstmt.registerOutParameter(1, Types.VARCHAR);
   cstmt.setString(2, "0-596-00180-0");

   // now we can do it, get it, close it, and print it
   cstmt.executeUpdate( );
   String bookTitle = cstmt.getString(1);
   conn.close( );
   System.out.println(bookTitle);
  }
}
```

This particular example uses the thin driver, which provides great compatibility and ease of installation (all the network protocol smarts exists in a Java library), at some expense of communications performance. An alternative approach would be to use what's known as the oci driver. Don't worry, there's no rocket scientist programming required to use it, despite the name!

To learn more about Java programming with Oracle, see *Java Programming with Oracle JDBC* by Don Bales and *Java Programming with Oracle SQLJ* by Jason Price, both from O'Reilly.

Perl: Using Perl DBI and DBD::Oracle

Much beloved by the system administration community, Perl is something of the mother of all open source languages. Now nearly in Version 6, it does just about everything and seems to run everywhere. And, with nifty auto-configuration tools such as CPAN (Comprehensive Perl Archive Network), it's a cinch to install community-supplied modules such as the DataBase Interface (DBI) and the corresponding Oracle driver, DBD::Oracle.

```
/* File on web: callbooktitle.pl */
#!/usr/bin/perl

use strict;
use DBI qw(:sql_types);

# either make the connection or DIE
my $dbh = DBI->connect(
```

```
        'dbi:Oracle:o92',
        'scott',
        'tiger',
        {
            RaiseError => 1,
            AutoCommit => 0
        }
    ) || die "Database connection not made: $DBI::errstr";

my $retval;

# make parse call to Oracle, get statement handle
eval {
    my $func = $dbh->prepare(q{
        BEGIN
            :retval := booktitle(isbn_in => :bind1);
        END;
    });

# bind the parameters and execute
    $func->bind_param(":bind1", "0-596-00180-0");
    $func->bind_param_inout(":retval", \$retval, SQL_VARCHAR);
    $func->execute;

};

if( $@ ) {
    warn "Execution of stored procedure failed: $DBI::errstr\n";
    $dbh->rollback;
} else {
   print "Stored procedure returned: $retval\n";
}

   # don't forget to disconnect
$dbh->disconnect;
```

Perl is one of those languages in which it is shamelessly easy to write code that is impossible to read. It's not a particularly fast or small language, either, but there are compiled versions that at least address the speed problem.

For more information about Perl and Oracle, see *Perl for Oracle DBAs* by Andy Duncan and Jared Still, and *Programming the Perl DBI* by Alligator Descartes, both from O'Reilly. There are also many excellent books on the Perl language.

PL/SQL Server Pages

Although the PL/SQL Server Pages (PSP) environment is proprietary to Oracle, I thought I would mention it because it's a quick way to get a web page up and running. PSP is another precompiler technology; it gives you the ability to embed PL/SQL into HTML pages.

```
/* File on web: favorite_plsql_book.psp */
<%@ page language="PL/SQL" %>
```

```
<%@ plsql procedure="favorite_plsql_book" %>
<HTML>
   <HEAD>
      <TITLE>My favorite book about PL/SQL</TITLE>
   </HEAD>
   <BODY>
      <%= booktitle( '0-596-00180-0') %>
   </BODY>
</HTML>
```

That `<%= %>` line means "process this as PL/SQL and return the result to the page." When properly installed on a web server connected to an Oracle database, this page will display as in Figure 2-7.

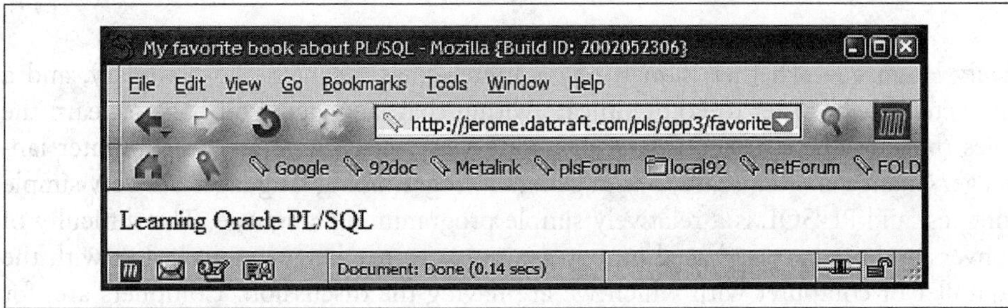

Figure 2-7. Output from a PL/SQL Server Page

I'm rather fond of PL/SQL Server Pages as a good way to put together data-driven web sites fairly quickly.

For more information about PL/SQL Server Pages, see *Learning Oracle PL/SQL* by the authors of the book you're reading now.

And What Else?

We've seen how to use PL/SQL in SQL*Plus and in a number of other common environments and programming languages. There are still more places you can use PL/SQL:

- Embedded in COBOL or FORTRAN and processed with Oracle's precompiler
- Called from Visual Basic, using some flavor of ODBC
- Called from the Ada programming language, via a technology called SQL*Module
- Executed automatically, as triggers on events in the Oracle database such as table updates
- Scheduled to execute on a recurring basis inside the Oracle database, via the DBMS_JOB built-in package

We'll take a look at some of these approaches in upcoming chapters.

CHAPTER 3

Language Fundamentals

In this chapter:

- PL/SQL Block Structure
- The PL/SQL Character Set
- Identifiers
- Literals
- The Semicolon Delimiter
- Comments
- The PRAGMA Keyword
- Labels

Every language—whether human or computer—has a syntax, a vocabulary, and a character set. In order to communicate within that language, you have to learn the rules that govern its usage. Many of us are wary of learning a new computer language. Change is often scary, but in general, programming languages are very simple tongues, and PL/SQL is a relatively simple programming language. The difficulty of conversing in languages based on bytes is not with the language itself, but with the compiler or computer with which we are having the discussion. Compilers are, for the most part, rather dull-witted. They are not creative, sentient beings. They are not capable of original thought. Their vocabulary is severely limited. Compilers just happen to think their dull thoughts very, very rapidly—and very inflexibly.

If I hear someone ask "gottabuck?", I can readily interpret that sentence and decide how to respond. On the other hand, if I instruct PL/SQL to "gimme the next half-dozen records," I will not get very far in my application. To use the PL/SQL language, you must dot your i's and cross your t's—syntactically speaking. So, this chapter covers the fundamental language rules that will help you converse with the PL/SQL compiler—the PL/SQL block structure, character set, lexical units, and PRAGMA keyword.

PL/SQL Block Structure

Virtually all programming languages give you a way to organize logically related elements into programming units. In PL/SQL, the fundamental unit of organization is the *block*, which is at the core of two key language concepts.

Modularization

The PL/SQL block is the basic unit of code from which you will build modules, such as procedures and functions, which in turn comprise applications. As the lowest organizational unit, well-designed blocks are fundamental to achieving code that other programmers can easily use and maintain.

Scope

The block provides a scope or context for logically related objects. In the block, you group together declarations and executable statements that belong together.

You can create anonymous blocks (blocks of code that have no name) and named blocks, which are procedures and functions. Furthermore, you can build packages in PL/SQL that group together multiple procedures and functions.

Sections of the PL/SQL Block

Each PL/SQL block has up to four different sections, only one of which is mandatory:

Header

Used only for named blocks. The header determines the way the named block or program must be called. Optional.

Declaration section

Identifies variables, cursors, and sub-blocks that are referenced in the execution and exception sections. Optional.

Execution section

Statements the PL/SQL runtime engine will execute at runtime. Mandatory.

Exception section

Handles exceptions to normal processing (warnings and error conditions). Optional.

Figure 3-1 shows the structure of the PL/SQL block for a procedure.

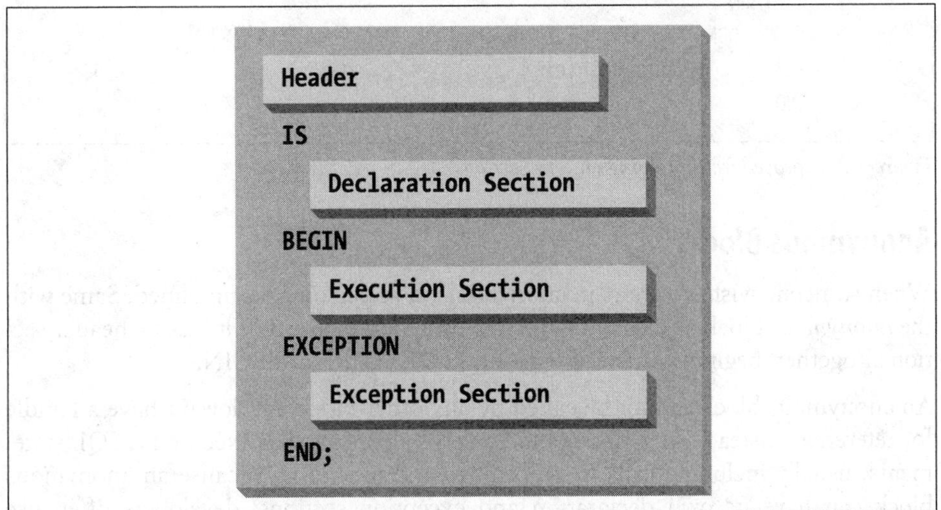

Figure 3-1. The PL/SQL block structure

The ordering of the sections in a block generally corresponds to the way you would write your programs and the way they are executed:

1. Define the type of block (procedure, function, anonymous) and the way it is called (header).
2. Declare any variables used in that block (declaration section).
3. Use those local variables and other PL/SQL objects to perform the required actions (execution section).
4. Handle any problems that arise during the execution of the block (exception section).

Figure 3-2 shows a procedure containing all four sections. In practice, there is often quite a bit of iteration among these steps when creating your own blocks; don't expect perfection on your first pass!

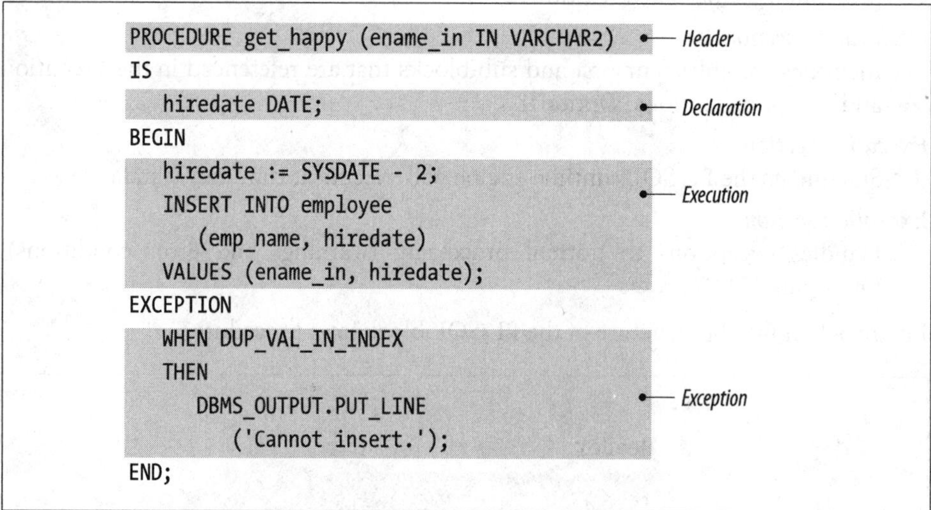

Figure 3-2. A procedure containing all four sections

Anonymous Blocks

When someone wishes to remain anonymous, that person goes unnamed. Same with the *anonymous* block in PL/SQL, which is shown in Figure 3-3: it lacks a header section altogether, beginning instead with either DECLARE or BEGIN.

An anonymous block cannot be called by any other block—it doesn't have a handle for reference. Instead, anonymous blocks serve as scripts that execute PL/SQL statements, usually including calls to procedures and functions. Because an anonymous block can have its own declaration and exception sections, developers often use anonymous blocks to provide a scope for identifiers and exception handling within a larger program. I'll explore these characteristics in the following sections.

```
BEGIN
   DBMS_OUTPUT.PUT_LINE ('Hello world');
END;
```

Execution Only

Figure 3-3. An anonymous block without declaration and exception sections

The structure of an anonymous block

The general format of an anonymous PL/SQL block is as follows:

```
[ DECLARE
   ... optional declaration statements ... ]

BEGIN
   ... executable statements ...

[ EXCEPTION
   ... optional exception handler statements ... ]

END;
```

The square brackets indicate an optional part of the syntax. You must have BEGIN and END statements, and you must have at least one executable statement.

Examples of anonymous blocks

The following examples show the different combinations of block sections, all of which comprise valid PL/SQL blocks:

- An anonymous block with BEGIN-END terminators, but no declaration or exception sections:

```
BEGIN
    -- Show current date in default format
    DBMS_OUTPUT.PUT_LINE (SYSDATE);
END;
```

- An anonymous block with a declaration section, but no exception section:

```
DECLARE
    l_right_now DATE := SYSDATE;
BEGIN
    DBMS_OUTPUT.PUT_LINE (l_right_now);
END;
```

- An anonymous block containing declaration, execution, and exception sections:

```
DECLARE
    -- Call a pre-defined function to obtain the hiredate
    -- of the employee named "FEUERSTEIN".
    l_hiredate DATE := employee_pkg.date_of_hire ('FEUERSTEIN');

    l_right_now DATE := SYSDATE;
    l_old_timer EXCEPTION;
```

```
BEGIN
   IF l_hiredate < ADD_MONTHS (l_right_now, 6)
   THEN
      RAISE l_old_timer;
   ELSE
      l_hiredate := right_now;
   END IF;
EXCEPTION
   WHEN l_old_timer
   THEN
      DBMS_OUTPUT.PUT_LINE
         ('You are not eligible for orientation.');
   WHEN OTHERS
   THEN
      DBMS_OUTPUT.PUT_LINE
         ('Error encountered: ' || SQLCODE);
END;
```

Anonymous blocks execute a series of statements and then terminate, thus acting like procedures. In fact, all anonymous blocks are "anonymous procedures."

Anonymous blocks in different environments

Anonymous blocks are used in various environments where PL/SQL code is either executed directly or enclosed in some program in that environment (see Table 3-1). The enclosing object provides the context and possibly a means of naming the program.

Table 3-1. Anonymous blocks in different environments

Enclosing object	Environment(s)	Description
Client-side trigger	Oracle development tools	"Bare" executable statements in the Forms Builder or Reports Builder trigger(s), packaged as an anonymous block by the tool and sent to the PL/SQL engine. (See Chapter 18 for a discussion of triggers.)
Database trigger	Table-level data manipulation or database event	Trigger "body." While the trigger has a name, the PL/SQL code itself is unnamed (anonymous).
Script	SQL*Plus or equivalent	Ad hoc programs and batch-processing scripts that call procedures and/or functions. Also, the SQL*Plus EXECUTE command translates its argument into an anonymous block by enclosing it between BEGIN and END statements.
Compiled program	Embedded languages (Pro*C, etc.); OCI (Oracle Call Interface)	Anonymous blocks embedded in execute statements inside the database server.

Whenever you attach PL/SQL code to a trigger or field in a tool like Forms Builder, that code establishes an anonymous PL/SQL block. When you write this code, you can enter a fully specified PL/SQL block (declaration, execution, and exception sections), or you can enter only the execution section.

Named Blocks

While anonymous PL/SQL blocks can be found throughout most Oracle applications, the majority of code you write will be in named blocks. You've seen a few short examples of stored procedures in this book already (as in Figure 3-1), and you probably know that the big difference is in the header. A procedure header looks like this:

```
PROCEDURE [schema.]name [ ( parameter [, parameter ... ] ) ]
   [AUTHID {DEFINER | CURRENT_USER}]
```

A function header is similar, but includes the RETURN keyword:

```
FUNCTION [schema.]name [ ( parameter [, parameter ... ] ) ]
   RETURN return_datatype
   [AUTHID {DEFINER | CURRENT_USER}]
   [DETERMINISTIC]
   [PARALLEL ENABLE ...]
   [PIPELINED]
```

Because Oracle allows you to invoke some functions from within SQL statements, the function header includes more optional components than the procedure header, corresponding to the greater control that Oracle gives you over a function's runtime behavior.

For a more complete discussion of procedures and functions, see Chapter 16.

Nested Blocks

A *nested block* lives inside another block. Here's an example showing a procedure containing an anonymous, nested block:

```
PROCEDURE calc_totals
IS
   year_total NUMBER;
BEGIN
   year_total := 0;

   /* Beginning of nested block */
   DECLARE
      month_total NUMBER;
   BEGIN
      month_total := year_total / 12;
   END set_month_total;
   /* End of nested block */

END;
```

The /* and */ delimiters indicate comments (see the "Comments" section later in this chapter). You can nest anonymous blocks within anonymous blocks to more than one level, as shown in Figure 3-4.

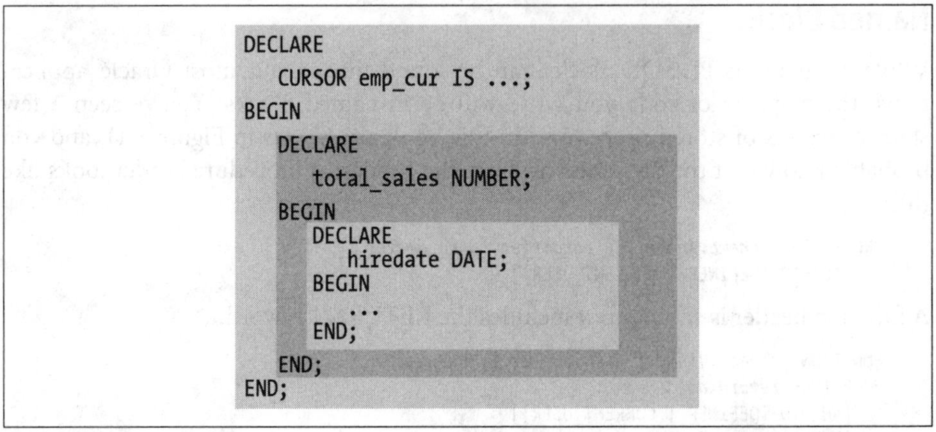

```
DECLARE
   CURSOR emp_cur IS ...;
BEGIN
   DECLARE
      total_sales NUMBER;
   BEGIN
      DECLARE
         hiredate DATE;
      BEGIN
         ...
      END;
   END;
END;
```

Figure 3-4. Anonymous blocks nested three levels deep

Other terms you may hear for nested block are *enclosed block*, *child block*, or *sub-block*; the outer PL/SQL block may be called the *enclosing block* or the *parent block*.

Scope

The general advantage of nesting a block is that you create a *scope* for all the declared objects and executable statements in that block. You can use this feature not only to improve your control over runtime behavior, but also to reduce the likelihood of a programmer's accidentally modifying the wrong variable.

Variables, exceptions, modules, and a few other structures are local to the block that declares them. When the block stops executing, you can no longer reference any of these structures. For example, in the calc_totals procedure above, I can reference elements from the outer block, like the year_total variable, anywhere in the program; however, elements declared within an inner block are not available to the outer block.

One of the most common reasons to create a nested block is to take advantage of the exception section that comes with that block. By trapping the exception inside the program, you can allow your program to continue processing rather than ending with an error. For example, if I'm unsure that a particular record exists in the database, I might want to do something like this:

```
BEGIN

  BEGIN  /* nested block */
      INSERT INTO book_copies (isbn, qty)
      VALUES (:newisbn, :copies);
  EXCEPTION
    WHEN DUP_VAL_ON_INDEX
    THEN
      UPDATE book_copies SET qty = :copies WHERE isbn = :newisbn;
```

```
      END; /* nested block */

      books.distribute_inventory_report;
   END;
```

Using the nested block provides a convenient way for me to ensure that the table has the desired record before running the books.distribute_inventory_report procedure. It also prevents the program from aborting due to a DUP_VAL_ON_INDEX exception. Of course, for other errors, such as *ORA-00942: Table or view does not exist*, you might actually *want* the program to terminate. The important point to keep in mind is that *you* are in control and get to choose what happens. See Chapter 6 for more information about error handling.

Visibility

Once a variable is in scope, another important property is its *visibility*—that is, whether you can refer to it using only its name, or whether you need to attach a prefix in front of it.

"Visible" identifiers

First, I'd like to make an observation about the simple case:

```
DECLARE
   first_day DATE;
   last_day DATE;
BEGIN
   first_day := SYSDATE;
   last_day := ADD_MONTHS (first_day, 6);
END;
```

Because both the first_day and last_day variables are declared in the same block where they are used, I can conveniently refer to them using only their identifiers, which are visible. A visible identifier might actually reference any of the following:

- A loop index variable (but it's visible and in-scope only inside the loop)
- An identifier declared in the current block
- An identifier declared in a block that encloses the current block
- A standalone database object (table, view, sequence, etc.) or PL/SQL object (procedure, function, type) that you own
- A standalone database object or PL/SQL object on which you have appropriate privilege and that is the target of an Oracle synonym that you can see

PL/SQL also allows the possibility of referring to in-scope items that are not directly visible, as the next section describes.

Qualified identifiers

A common example of an identifier that isn't visible is anything declared in a package specification, such as a variable, datatype, procedure, or function. To refer to one of these elements outside of that package, you merely need to prefix it with a dotted qualifier, similar to the way you would qualify a column name with the name of its table. For example:

price_util.compute_means
: A program named compute_means inside the price_util package

math.pi
: A constant named pi, declared and initialized in a math package

:GLOBAL.company_id
: A global variable in Oracle Forms

(Although the descriptions indicate what kinds of globals these are, you can't necessarily tell by looking—definitely an argument in favor of good naming conventions!)

You can use an additional qualifier to indicate the owner of the object. For example:

```
scott.price_util.compute_means
```

could refer to the compute_means procedure in the price_util package owned by the Oracle user account scott.

Qualifying identifier names with module names

When necessary, PL/SQL offers many ways to qualify an identifier so that a reference to the identifier can be resolved. Using packages, for example, you can create variables with "global" scope. Suppose that I create a package called company_pkg and declare a variable named last_company_id in that package's specification, as follows:

```
PACKAGE company_pkg
IS
   last_company_id NUMBER;
   ...
END company_pkg;
```

Then, when I reference that variable outside of the package, I must preface the identifier name with the package name:

```
IF new_company_id = company_pkg.last_company_id THEN
```

Because a variable declared in a package specification is global in your session, the last_company_id variable can be referenced in any program, but it is not visible unless it is qualified.

I can also qualify the name of an identifier with the module in which it is defined:

```
PROCEDURE calc_totals
IS
   salary NUMBER;
```

```
BEGIN
   ...
   DECLARE
      salary NUMBER;
   BEGIN
      salary := calc_totals.salary;
   END;
   ...
END;
```

The first declaration of salary creates an identifier whose scope is the entire procedure. In the nested block, however, I declare another identifier with the same name. So when I reference the variable "salary" inside the inner block, it will always be resolved first against the declaration in the inner block, where that variable is visible without any qualification. If I wish to make reference to the procedure-wide salary variable inside the inner block, I must qualify that variable name with the name of the procedure (cal_totals.salary).

PL/SQL goes to a lot of trouble and has established many rules for determining how to resolve such naming conflicts. While it is good to be aware of such issues, you would be much better off never having to rely on these guidelines. Use unique names for your identifiers in different nested blocks so that you can avoid naming conflicts altogether.

The PL/SQL Character Set

A PL/SQL program consists of a sequence of statements, each made up of one or more lines of text. The precise characters available to you will depend on what database character set you're using. For example, Table 3-2 illustrates the available characters in the US7ASCII character set.

Table 3-2. Characters available to PL/SQL in the US7ASCII character set

Type	Characters
Letters	A-Z, a-z
Digits	0–9
Symbols	~!@#$%&*()_-+=|[]{}:;"'<>,.?/^
Whitespace	Tab, space, newline, carriage return

Every keyword in PL/SQL is made from various combinations of characters in this character set. Now you just have to figure out how to put them all together!

By default, PL/SQL is a case-insensitive language. That is, uppercase letters are treated the same way as lowercase letters except when characters are surrounded by single quotes, which makes them a literal string.

A number of these characters—both singly and in combination with other characters—have a special significance in PL/SQL. Table 3-3 lists these special symbols.

Table 3-3. Simple and compound symbols in PL/SQL

Symbol	Description
;	Semicolon: terminates declarations and statements
%	Percent sign: attribute indicator (cursor attributes like %ISOPEN and indirect declaration attributes like %ROWTYPE); also used as multibyte wildcard symbol with the LIKE condition
_	Single underscore: single-character wildcard symbol in LIKE condition
@	At- sign: remote location indicator
:	Colon: host variable indicator, such as :block.item in Oracle Forms
**	Double asterisk: exponentiation operator
<> or != or ^= or ~=	Ways to denote the "not equal" relational operator
||	Double vertical bar: concatenation operator
<<and >>	Label delimiters
<= and >=	Less than or equal, greater than or equal relational operators
:=	Assignment operator
=>	Association operator for positional notation
..	Double dot: range operator
--	Double dash: single-line comment indicator
/* and */	Beginning and ending multiline comment block delimiters

Characters are grouped together into lexical units, also called *atomics* of the language because they are the smallest individual components. A lexical unit in PL/SQL is any of the following:

- Identifier
- Literal
- Delimiter
- Comment

These are described in the following sections.

Identifiers

An *identifier* is a name for a PL/SQL object, including any of the following:

- Constant
- Scalar variable
- Composite variable (record or collection)
- Exception

- Procedure
- Function
- Package
- Type
- Cursor
- Reserved word
- Label

Default properties of PL/SQL identifiers are summarized below:

- Up to 30 characters in length
- Must start with a letter
- Can include $ (dollar sign), _ (underscore), and # (pound sign)
- Cannot contain spaces

If the only difference between two identifiers is the case of one or more letters, PL/SQL normally treats those two identifiers as the same.* For example, the following identifiers are all considered by PL/SQL to be the same:

```
lots_of_$MONEY$
LOTS_of_$MONEY$
Lots_of_$Money$
```

The following strings are valid names of identifiers:

```
company_id#
primary_acct_responsibility
First_Name
FirstName
address_line1
S123456
```

The following identifiers are all illegal in PL/SQL:

```
1st_year                          -- Starts with numeral
procedure-name                    -- Contains invalid character "-"
minimum_%_due                     -- Contains invalid character "%"
maximum_value_exploded_for_detail -- Name is too long
company ID                        -- Cannot have embedded spaces in name
```

Identifiers are the handles for objects in your program. Be sure to name your objects carefully so the names describe the objects and their uses. Avoid identifier names like X1 and temp; they are too ambiguous to mean anything to you or to anyone else reading your code.

* The compiler accomplishes this by internally converting program text into uppercase during an early compiler phase.

Although rarely done in practice, you can actually break some of these rules by surrounding identifiers with double quotation marks. I don't recommend programming like this, but you may one day have to deal with some "clever" code such as:

```
SQL> DECLARE
  2     "pi" CONSTANT NUMBER := 3.141592654;
  3     "PI" CONSTANT NUMBER := 3.14159265358979323846;
  4     "2 pi" CONSTANT NUMBER := 2 * "pi";
  5  BEGIN
  6     DBMS_OUTPUT.PUT_LINE('pi: ' || "pi");
  7     DBMS_OUTPUT.PUT_LINE('PI: ' || pi);
  8     DBMS_OUTPUT.PUT_LINE('2 pi: ' || "2 pi");
  9* END;
 10 /

pi: 3.141592654
PI: 3.14159265358979323846
2 pi: 6.283185308
```

Notice that line 7 refers to pi without quotation marks. Because the compiler accomplishes its case-independence by defaulting identifiers and keywords to uppercase, the variable that line 7 refers to is the one declared on line 3 as `"PI"`.

On rare occasions, you may need to use the double-quote trick in SQL statements to refer to database objects that exist with mixed-case names. I've seen this happen when a programmer used Microsoft Access to create the Oracle tables.

Reserved Words

Of course, you don't get to name all the identifiers in your programs. The PL/SQL language recognizes certain identifiers (such as BEGIN, IF, and THEN) as having special meaning.

There are two kinds of built-in identifiers that PL/SQL provides:

- Language keywords
- Identifiers from the STANDARD package

In both cases you should not—and, in many cases, cannot—redefine the identifier for your program's own use.

Language keywords

The PL/SQL compiler recognizes certain words as having certain semantics no matter what. For example, one very important reserved word is END, which terminates programs, IF statements, and loops. If you try to declare a variable named "end", as I do below:

```
DECLARE
   end VARCHAR2(10) := 'blip';   /* Will not work! Can't use END as name. */
BEGIN
```

```
    DBMS_OUTPUT.PUT_LINE (end);
END;
/
```

then you will get the subsequent compile error:

```
PLS-00103: Encountered the symbol "END" when expecting one of the following:
```

The appearance of the word "end" in the declaration section signals to PL/SQL the premature termination of that anonymous block.

Identifiers from STANDARD package

In addition to avoiding identifiers that duplicate keywords, you should also avoid using identifiers that duplicate names Oracle has defined in a special package named STANDARD. Oracle defines quite a few identifiers in this package, including built-in exceptions like DUP_VAL_ON_INDEX, functions like UPPER, REPLACE, and TO_DATE, and subtypes such as STRING. You can view a list of functions and procedures defined in STANDARD with this command:

```
SQL> DESC SYS.STANDARD
```

You may occasionally find that you want to use the name of a built-in from STANDARD. You can still reference the built-in form by prefixing it with STANDARD, as follows:

```
DECLARE
   dup_val_on_index EXCEPTION;  -- local re-declaration
BEGIN
   ...
   INSERT INTO ...  /* may raise the built-in exception */
   ...
   RAISE dup_val_on_index;  -- resolves to the locally declared exception
EXCEPTION
   WHEN dup_val_on_index
   THEN
      /* handle the locally declared exception */
   ...
   WHEN STANDARD.DUP_VAL_ON_INDEX
   THEN
      /* handle the usual exception */
   ...
END;
```

Approaches to avoiding reserved words

Finding a valid name for your identifier should be the least of your problems, as there are thousands and thousands of permutations of the legal characters. The question is, how will you know if you inadvertently use a reserved word in your own program? By some counts, there are hundreds of words known to PL/SQL!

You could just ignore this issue and deal with the compiler errors as they come up. This is what a lot of people do, but it can be a real drain on a workday because sometimes the error messages are completely off the wall. Some people use a high-priced development environment with a snazzy syntax-directed editor that alerts you to possible problems as you type. Personally, my favorite solution is to use a cheap (as in free) editor that is aware of PL/SQL's keywords and just highlights them automatically.*

I have compiled a small list of the Oracle9*i* PL/SQL reserved words, shown in Table 3-4 (and available in the *reserved.txt* file on the O'Reilly site). Starting from the list of keywords Oracle publishes in the V$RESERVED_WORDS data dictionary view, I tried to declare a variable, and then a procedure, using the word as its identifier. If the compiler prevented me doing from one or both of those operations, I put the keyword on the list.

Table 3-4. Absolute minimal list of words to avoid using as PL/SQL identifiers

ACCESS	CURSOR	INDEXES	OPTION	START
ADD	DATE	INITIAL	OR	SUCCESSFUL
ALL	DECIMAL	INSERT	ORDER	SYNONYM
ALTER	DECLARE	INTEGER	OVERLAPS	SYSDATE
AND	DEFAULT	INTERSECT	PACKAGE	TABLE
ANY	DELETE	INTO	PCTFREE	THEN
AS	DESC	IS	PRIOR	TO
ASC	DISTINCT	LEVEL	PRIVILEGES	TRIGGER
AT	DROP	LIKE	PROCEDURE	TYPE
AUDIT	ELSE	LOCK	PUBLIC	UID
BEGIN	END	LONG	RAW	UNION
BETWEEN	EXCLUSIVE	MAXEXTENTS	RENAME	UNIQUE
BY	EXISTS	MINUS	RESOURCE	UPDATE
CASE	FILE	MLSLABEL	RETURN	USE
CHAR	FLOAT	MODE	REVOKE	USER
CHECK	FOR	MODIFY	ROLLBACK	VALIDATE
CLOSE	FROM	NOAUDIT	ROW	VALUES
CLUSTER	FUNCTION	NOCOMPRESS	ROWID	VARCHAR
COLUMN	GRANT	NOT	ROWNUM	VARCHAR2
COLUMNS	GROUP	NOWAIT	ROWS	VIEW
COMMENT	HAVING	NULL	SAVEPOINT	WHEN
COMMIT	IDENTIFIED	NUMBER	SELECT	WHENEVER
COMPRESS	IF	OF	SESSION	WHERE
CONNECT	IMMEDIATE	OFFLINE	SET	WITH
CREATE	IN	ON	SHARE	
CURRENT	INCREMENT	ONLINE	SIZE	
DEFAULT	INDEX	OPEN	SMALLINT	

If you are running Oracle 8.1.5 or later, you can ask your DBA to grant you privilege to execute this statement:

```
SQL> SELECT * FROM V$RESERVED_WORD;
```

* As a matter of fact, I helped create a syntax highlighting file and an automatic indentation file for an open source editor known as *vim* (derived from *vi*). Very cool. Visit the book's web site for details.

Although the list is overwhelmingly long, it does not even include all the identifiers in STANDARD; the PL/SQL compiler does not care if you carelessly reuse identifiers declared there. All the more reason to use an intelligent editor.

Whitespace and Keywords

Identifiers must be separated by at least one space or by a delimiter, but you can format your text by adding additional spaces, line breaks (newlines and/or carriage returns), and tabs wherever you can put a space, without changing the meaning of your entry.

The two statements shown below are therefore equivalent:

```
IF too_many_orders
THEN
   warn_user;
ELSIF no_orders_entered
THEN
   prompt_for_orders;
END IF;

IF too_many_orders THEN warn_user;
ELSIF no_orders_entered THEN prompt_for_orders;
END IF;
```

You may not, however, place a space or carriage return or tab within a lexical unit, such as a compound delimiter like the "not equals" symbol (!=). The following statement raises a compile error:

```
IF max_salary ! = min_salary THEN
```

because there is a space between the ! and the =.

Literals

A literal is a value that is not represented by an identifier; it is simply a value. A literal may be composed of one of the following types of data:

Number
  415, 21.6, or NULL

String
  'This is my sentence' or '01-FEB-2003' or NULL

Boolean
  TRUE, FALSE, or NULL

Notice that there is no direct way to code a true date literal. The value '01-FEB-2003' is a string literal (any sequence of characters enclosed by single quotes). You can convert such a string to a date in PL/SQL or SQL, but a date has only an internal binary representation in Oracle.

A string literal can be composed of zero or more characters from the PL/SQL character set. A literal of zero characters is represented as '' (two consecutive single quotes with no characters between them). At least through Oracle9*i*, this zero-length string literal has the value NULL,* and a datatype of CHAR (fixed-length string).

Unlike identifiers, string literals in PL/SQL are case-sensitive. The following two literals are different:

```
'Steven'
'steven'
```

The following condition, for example, evaluates to FALSE:

```
IF 'Steven' = 'steven'
```

Embedding Single Quotes Inside a String

The trickiest part of working with string literals comes when you need to include a single quote inside a string literal (as part of the literal itself). Generally, the rule is that you write two single quotes next to each other inside a string if you want the literal to contain a single quote in that position. The following table shows the literal in one column and the resulting "internal" string in the second column:

Literal	Actual value
`'There''s no business like show business.'`	`There's no business like show business.`
`'"Hound of the Baskervilles"'`	`"Hound of the Baskervilles"`
`'NLS_LANGUAGE=''ENGLISH'''`	`NLS_LANGUAGE='ENGLISH'`
`''''`	`'`
`'''hello'''`	`'hello'`
`''''''`	`''`

Here's a summary of how to embed single quotes in a literal:

- To place a single quote inside the literal, put two single quotes together.
- To place a single quote at the beginning or end of a literal, put three single quotes together.
- To create a string literal consisting of one single quote, put four single quotes together.
- To create a string literal consisting of two single quotes together, put six single quotes together.

* Don't be fooled by the inconsistent Oracle documentation, which states that a zero-length string is not the same as NULL, as in the ANSI standard.

Two single quotes together is not the same as a double quote character. A double quote character does not have any special significance inside a string literal. It is treated the same as a letter or number.

Numeric Literals

Numeric literals can be integers or real numbers (a number that contains a fractional component). Note that PL/SQL considers the number 154.00 to be a real number, even though the fractional component is zero and the number is actually an integer. Internally, integers and reals have a different representation, and there is some small overhead involved in converting between the two.

You can also use scientific notation to specify a numeric literal. Use the letter "E" (upper- or lowercase) to multiply a number by 10 to the *n*th power—for example, 3.05E19, 12e-5.

Boolean Literals

Oracle provides two literals to represent Boolean values: TRUE and FALSE. These values are not strings; you should not put quotes around them. Use Boolean literals to assign values to Boolean variables, as in:

```
DECLARE
   enough_money BOOLEAN; -- Declare a Boolean variable
BEGIN
   enough_money := FALSE; -- Assign it a value
END;
```

You do not, on the other hand, need to refer to the literal value when checking the value of a Boolean expression. Instead, just let that expression speak for itself, as shown in the conditional clause of the following IF statement:

```
DECLARE
   enough_money BOOLEAN;
BEGIN
   IF enough_money
   THEN
      ...
```

The Semicolon Delimiter

A PL/SQL program is made up of a series of declarations and statements. These are defined *logically*, as opposed to physically. In other words, they are not terminated with the physical end of a line of code; instead, they are terminated with a semicolon (;). In fact, a single statement is often spread over several lines to make it more readable. The following IF statement takes up four lines and is indented to reinforce the logic behind the statement:

```
IF salary < min_salary (2003)
THEN
   salary := salary + salary*.25;
END IF;
```

There are two semicolons in this IF statement. The first semicolon indicates the end of the single executable statement within the IF-END IF construct. The second semicolon terminates the IF statement itself. This same statement could also be placed on a single physical line and have exactly the same result:

```
IF salary < min_salary (2003) THEN salary := salary + salary*.25; END IF;
```

The semicolons are still needed to terminate each logical, executable statement, even if they are nested inside one another. Unless you're *trying* to create unreadable code, I suggest that you not combine the different components of the IF statement on a single line. I also recommend that you place no more than one statement or declaration on each line.

Comments

Inline documentation, otherwise known as *comments*, is an important element of a good program. While this book offers many suggestions on how to make your program self-documenting through good naming practices and modularization, such techniques are seldom enough by themselves to communicate a thorough understanding of a complex program.

PL/SQL offers two different styles for comments: single-line and multiline block comments.

Single-Line Comment Syntax

The single-line comment is initiated with two hyphens (--), which cannot be separated by a space or any other characters. All text after the double hyphen to the end of the physical line is considered commentary and is ignored by the compiler. If the double hyphen appears at the beginning of the line, the whole line is a comment.

Remember: the double hyphen comments out the remainder of a physical line, not a logical PL/SQL statement. In the following IF statement, I use a single-line comment to clarify the logic of the Boolean expression:

```
IF salary < min_salary (2003) -- Function returns min salary for year.
THEN
   salary := salary + salary*.25;
END IF;
```

Multiline Comment Syntax

While single-line comments are useful for documenting brief bits of code or ignoring a line that you do not want executed at the moment, the multiline comment is superior for including longer blocks of commentary.

Multiline comments start with a slash-asterisk (/*) and end with an asterisk-slash (*/). PL/SQL considers all characters found between these two sequences of symbols to be part of the comment, and they are ignored by the compiler.

The following example of multiline comments shows a header section for a procedure. I use the vertical bars in the left margin so that, as the eye moves down the left edge of the program, it can easily pick out the chunks of comments:

```
PROCEDURE calc_revenue (company_id IN NUMBER) IS
/*
| Program: calc_revenue
| Author: Steven Feuerstein
| Change history:
|    9/23/94 - Start program
|    06-JUN-1999 - Y2K okay
*/
BEGIN
   ...
END;
```

You can also use multiline comments to block out lines of code for testing purposes. In the following example, the additional clauses in the EXIT statement are ignored so that testing can concentrate on the a_delimiter function:

```
EXIT WHEN a_delimiter (next_char)
/*
             OR
          (was_a_delimiter AND NOT a_delimiter (next_char))
*/
;
```

The PRAGMA Keyword

The PRAGMA keyword is used to signify that the remainder of the PL/SQL statement is a *pragma*, or directive, to the compiler. Also called a *pseudoinstruction*, a pragma simply passes information to the compiler rather than getting transformed into a particular execution.

The syntax for using the PRAGMA keyword is as follows:

```
PRAGMA instruction;
```

where *instruction* is a statement providing instructions to the compiler. The PL/SQL compiler will accept such directives anywhere in the declaration section.

PL/SQL offers the following pragmas:

AUTONOMOUS_TRANSACTION
: Tells the PL/SQL runtime engine to commit or roll back any changes made to the database inside the current block without affecting the main or outer transaction. See Chapter 13 for more information. Introduced in Oracle8*i*.

EXCEPTION_INIT
: Tells the compiler to associate a particular error number with an identifier you have declared as an exception in your program. See Chapter 6 for more information.

RESTRICT_REFERENCES
: Tells the compiler the purity level (freedom from side effects) of a packaged program. See Chapter 16 for more information.

SERIALLY_REUSABLE
: Tells the PL/SQL runtime engine that package-level data should not persist between references to that data. See Chapter 17 for more information. Introduced in Oracle8.

The following block demonstrates the use of the EXCEPTION_INIT pragma to name a built-in exception that would otherwise have only a number.

```
DECLARE
   no_such_sequence EXCEPTION;
   PRAGMA EXCEPTION_INIT (no_such_sequence, -2289);
BEGIN
   ...
EXCEPTION
   WHEN no_such_sequence
   THEN
      ...
END;
```

Labels

A PL/SQL label is a way to name a particular part of your program. Syntactically, a label has the format:

```
<<identifier>>
```

where *identifier* is a valid PL/SQL identifier (up to 30 characters in length and starting with a letter, as discussed earlier in the "Identifiers" section). There is no terminator; labels appear directly in front of the thing they're labeling, which must be an executable statement—even if it is merely the NULL statement.

```
BEGIN
   ...
   <<the_spot>>
   NULL;
```

Because anonymous blocks are themselves executable statements, a label can "name" an anonymous block for the duration of its execution. For example:

```
<<insert_but_ignore_dups>>
BEGIN
   INSERT INTO catalog
   VALUES (...);
EXCEPTION
   WHEN DUP_VAL_ON_INDEX
   THEN
      NULL;
END insert_but_ignore_dups;
```

One reason you might label a block is to improve the readability of your code. When you give something a name, you self-document that code. You also clarify your own thinking about what that code is supposed to do, sometimes ferreting out errors in the process.

Another reason to use a block label is to allow you to qualify references to elements from an enclosing block that have duplicate names in the current, nested block. Here's a schematic example:

```
<<outerblock>>
DECLARE
   counter INTEGER := 0;
BEGIN
   ...
   DECLARE
      counter INTEGER := 1;
   BEGIN
      IF counter = outerblock.counter
      THEN
         ...
      END IF;
   END;
END;
```

Without the block label, there would be no way to distinguish between the two "counter" variables. Again, though, a better solution would probably have been to use distinct variable names.

A third function of labels is to serve as the target of a GOTO statement. However, these days, GOTO statements are virtually nonexistent, thanks to Edsger Dijkstra's now-legendary essay on the subject* (and the fact that exception handling is usually a better way to go). In all the PL/SQL code I've ever seen, I recall only one GOTO.

Although few programs I've seen or worked on require the use of labels, there is one final use of this feature that is more significant than the previous three combined: a

* "Go To Statement Considered Harmful," which originally appeared in the March 1968 *Communications of the ACM*, was influential enough to introduce the phrase *considered harmful* into the lexicon of computerese.

label can serve as a target for the EXIT statement in nested loops. Here's the example code:

```
BEGIN
   <<outer_loop>>
   LOOP
      LOOP
         EXIT outer_loop;
      END LOOP;
      some_statement;
   END LOOP;
END;
```

Without the <<outer_loop>> label, the EXIT statement would have exited only the inner loop and would have executed some_statement. But I didn't want it to do that. So, in this case, the label provides functionality that PL/SQL does not offer in any other straightforward way.

PART II

PL/SQL Program Structure

This part of the book presents the basic PL/SQL programming elements and statement constructs. Chapters 4 through 6 describe conditional (IF and CASE) and sequential control statements (e.g., GOTO and NULL), loops, and exception handling in the PL/SQL language. When you complete this section of the book you will know how to construct blocks of code that correlate to the complex requirements in your applications.

In this chapter:

- IF Statements
- CASE Statements
- The GOTO Statement
- The NULL Statement

CHAPTER 4

Conditional and Sequential Control

This chapter describes two types of PL/SQL control statements: conditional control statements and sequential control statements. Almost every piece of code you write will require conditional control, which is the ability to direct the flow of execution through your program based on a condition. You do this with IF-THEN-ELSE and CASE statements (CASE statements are new in Oracle9*i*). There are also CASE expressions; while not the same as CASE statements, they can sometimes be used to eliminate the need for an IF or CASE statement altogether. Far less often, you will need to tell PL/SQL to transfer control unconditionally via the GOTO statement, or explicitly to do nothing via the NULL statement.

IF Statements

In your programs, you need to be able to implement requirements such as:

> If the salary is between ten and twenty thousand, then apply a bonus of $1500.
> If the salary is between twenty and forty thousand, apply a bonus of $1000.
> If the salary is over forty thousand, give the employee a bonus of $500.

or:

> If the user preference includes the toolbar, display the toolbar when the window first opens.

The IF statement allows you to design conditional logic into your programs. The IF statement comes in three flavors, as shown in the following table:

IF type	Characteristics

`IF`
`THEN`
`END IF;`
	This is the simplest form of the IF statement. The condition between IF and THEN determines whether the set of statements between THEN and END IF should be executed. If the condition evaluates to FALSE, the code is not executed.

`IF`
`THEN`
`ELSE`
`END IF;`
	This combination implements an either/or logic: based on the condition between the IF and THEN keywords, execute the code either between THEN and ELSE or between ELSE and END IF. One of these two sections of executable statements is performed.

IF type	Characteristics

IF
THEN
ELSIF
ELSE
END IF;
	This last and most complex form of the IF statement selects an action from a series of mutually exclusive conditions and then executes the set of statements associated with that condition. If you're writing IF statements like this in Oracle9*i*, you should consider using *searched CASE* statements instead.

The IF-THEN Combination

The general format of the IF-THEN syntax is as follows:

```
IF condition
THEN
   ... sequence of executable statements ...
END IF;
```

The *condition* is a Boolean variable, constant, or expression that evaluates to TRUE, FALSE, or NULL. If *condition* evaluates to TRUE, then the executable statements found after the THEN keyword and before the matching END IF statement are executed. If *condition* evaluates to FALSE or NULL, those statements are not executed.

The following IF condition compares two different numeric values. Remember that if one of these two values is NULL, then the entire expression returns NULL; in the following example, the bonus is not given:

```
IF salary > 40000
THEN
   give_bonus (employee_id,500);
END IF;
```

It's not necessary to put the IF, THEN, and END IF keywords on their own lines. In fact, line breaks don't matter at all for any type of IF statement. We could just as easily write:

```
IF salary > 40000 THEN give_bonus (employee_id,500); END IF;
```

Putting everything on one line is perfectly fine for simple IF statements such as the one shown here. However, when writing IF statements of any complexity at all, you'll find that readability is much greater when you format the statement such that each keyword begins a new line. For example, the following code would be very difficult to follow if it were all crammed on a single line. Actually, it's difficult to follow as it appears on three lines:

```
IF salary > 40000 THEN INSERT INTO employee_bonus (eb_employee_id, eb_bonus_amt)
VALUES (employee_id, 500); UPDATE emp_employee SET emp_bonus_given=1 WHERE emp_
employee_id=employee_id; END IF;
```

Ugh! Who'd want to spend time figuring that out? It's much more readable when formatted nicely:

```
IF salary > 40000
THEN
   INSERT INTO employee_bonus
```

```
        (eb_employee_id, eb_bonus_amt)
        VALUES (employee_id, 500);

    UPDATE emp_employee
    SET emp_bonus_given=1
    WHERE emp_employee_id=employee_id;
END IF;
```

This readability issue becomes even more important when using the ELSE and ELSIF keywords, and when nesting one IF statement inside the other. Take full advantage of indents and formatting to make the logic of your IF statements easily decipherable. Future maintenance programmers will thank you.

The IF-THEN-ELSE Combination

Use the IF-THEN-ELSE format when you want to choose between two mutually exclusive actions. The format of this either/or version of the IF statement is as follows:

```
IF condition
THEN
   ... TRUE sequence of executable statements ...
ELSE
   ... FALSE/NULL sequence of executable statements ...
END IF;
```

The *condition* is a Boolean variable, constant, or expression. If *condition* evaluates to TRUE, then the executable statements found after the THEN keyword and before the ELSE keyword are executed (the "TRUE sequence of executable statements"). If *condition* evaluates to FALSE or NULL, then the executable statements that come after the ELSE keyword and before the matching END IF keywords are executed (the "FALSE/NULL sequence of executable statements").

Notice that the ELSE clause does not have a THEN associated with it.

The important thing to remember is that one of the two sequences of statements will *always* execute, because IF-THEN-ELSE is an either/or construct. Once the appropriate set of statements has been executed, control passes to the statement immediately following the END IF keyword.

Following is an example of the IF-THEN-ELSE construct that builds upon the IF-THEN example shown in the previous section:

```
IF salary <= 40000
THEN
   give_bonus (employee_id, 0);
ELSE
   give_bonus (employee_id, 500);
END IF;
```

In this example, employees with a salary greater than 40,000 will get a bonus of 500 while all other employees will get no bonus at all. Or will they? What happens if salary, for whatever reason, happens to be NULL for a given employee? In that case, the statements following the ELSE will be executed, and the employee in question will get the bonus that is supposed to go only to highly paid employees. That's not good! If we're not sure that salary will never be NULL, we can protect ourselves against this problem using the NVL function:

```
IF NVL(salary,0) <= 40000
THEN
   give_bonus (employee_id, 0);
ELSE
   give_bonus (employee_id, 500);
END IF;
```

The NVL function will return zero any time salary is NULL, ensuring that any employees with a NULL salary also get a zero bonus.

Using Boolean Flags

Often, it's convenient to use Boolean variables as flags so that we don't need to evaluate the same Boolean expression more than once. When doing so, remember that the result of a Boolean expression can be assigned directly to a Boolean variable. For example, rather than write:

```
IF :customer.order_total > max_allowable_order
THEN
   order_exceeds_balance := TRUE;
ELSE
   order_exceeds_balance := FALSE;
END IF;
```

we can instead write the following, much simpler, expression:

```
order_exceeds_balance := :customer.order_total > max_allowable_order;
```

Now, whenever we need to test in our code whether an order's total exceeded the maximum, we can write the following, easily understandable, IF statement:

```
IF order_exceeds_balance
THEN
...
```

If you have not had much experience with Boolean variables, it may take you a little while to learn how to integrate them smoothly into your code. It is worth the effort, though. The result is cleaner, more readable code.

The IF-THEN-ELSIF Combination

This last form of the IF statement comes in handy when you have to implement logic that has many alternatives; it is not an either/or situation. The IF-ELSIF formulation provides a way to handle multiple, mutually exclusive alternatives. The general format for this variation of the IF statement is:

```
IF condition-1
THEN
   statements-1
ELSIF condition-N
THEN
   statements-N
[ELSE
   else_statements]
END IF;
```

Be very careful to use ELSIF, not ELSEIF. The inadvertent use of ELSEIF is a fairly common syntax error. ELSE IF (two words) doesn't work either.

Logically speaking, the IF-THEN-ELSIF construct is one way of implementing CASE statement functionality in PL/SQL. Of course, if you are using Oracle9*i* or higher, you are probably better off actually using a CASE statement (discussed later in this chapter).

NULLs in IF Statements

Be very cognizant of the effect of NULL values in IF expressions. One NULL value in an expression will usually cause the entire expression to be NULL, and a NULL is neither TRUE nor FALSE. For example, while seemingly equivalent, the following two IF statements do not have the same effect:

```
IF x = 2 THEN
   DBMS_OUTPUT.PUT_LINE('x contains 2');
ELSE
   DBMS_OUTPUT.PUT_LINE('x doesn''t contain 2');
END IF;

IF x <> 2 THEN
   DBMS_OUTPUT.PUT_LINE('x doesn''t contain 2');
ELSE
   DBMS_OUTPUT.PUT_LINE('x contains 2');
END IF;
```

The difference between these two statements lies in what happens when the variable x is NULL. When x is NULL, the first IF-THEN-ELSE statement will display "x doesn't contain 2"; the second statement will display "x contains 2". Why? Because when x is NULL, the IF expression is not considered to be TRUE, and control passes to the ELSE clause.

Protect yourself from inadvertent NULL-related bugs by using functions such as NVL or by explicitly checking for the NULL case using the IS NULL predicate.

Each ELSIF clause must have a THEN after its *condition*. Only the ELSE keyword does not need the THEN keyword. The ELSE clause in the IF-ELSIF is the "otherwise" of the statement. If none of the conditions evaluate to TRUE, then the statements in the ELSE clause are executed. But the ELSE clause is optional. You can code an IF-ELSIF that has only IF and ELSIF clauses. In this case, if none of the conditions are TRUE, then no statements inside the IF block are executed.

Following is an implementation of the complete bonus logic described at the beginning of this chapter using the IF-THEN-ELSEIF combination:

```
IF salary BETWEEN 10000 AND 20000
THEN
   give_bonus(employee_id, 1500);
ELSIF salary BETWEEN 20000 AND 40000
THEN
   give_bonus(employee_id, 1000);
ELSIF salary > 40000
THEN
   give_bonus(employee_id, 500);
ELSE
   give_bonus(employee_id, 0);
END IF;
```

The conditions in the IF-ELSIF are always evaluated in the order of first condition to last condition. If two conditions evaluate to true, the statements for the first such condition are executed. With respect to the current example, a salary of 20,000 will result in a bonus of 1500 even though that 20,000 salary also satisfies the condition for a 1000 bonus (BETWEEN is inclusive). Once a condition evaluates to TRUE, the remaining conditions are not evaluated at all.

The CASE statement available beginning in Oracle9*i* represents a better solution to the bonus problem than the IF-THEN-ELSIF solution shown in this section. See the upcoming section "CASE Statements."

Even though overlapping conditions are allowed in an IF-THEN-ELSIF statement, it's best to avoid them when possible. In our case, the original spec is a bit ambiguous about how to handle boundary cases such as 20,000. Assuming that the intent is to give the highest bonuses to the lowest-paid employees (which seems like a reasonable approach to us), we would dispense with the BETWEEN operator and use the following less-than/greater-than logic. Note that we've also dispensed with the ELSE clause just to illustrate that it is optional:

```
IF salary >= 10000 AND salary <= 20000
THEN
   give_bonus(employee_id, 1500);
ELSIF salary > 20000 AND salary <= 40000
THEN
```

```
    give_bonus(employee_id, 1000);
ELSIF salary > 40000
THEN
    give_bonus(employee_id, 400);
END IF;
```

By taking steps to avoid overlapping conditions in an IF-THEN-ELSIF, we are eliminating a possible (probable?) source of confusion for programmers who come after us. We also eliminate the possibility of inadvertent bugs being introduced as a result of someone's reordering the ELSIF clauses.

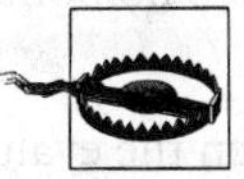

The language does not require that ELSIF conditions be mutually exclusive. Always be aware of the possibility that two or more conditions might apply to a given value, and that consequently the order of those ELSIF conditions might be important.

Nested IF Statements

You can nest any IF statement within any other IF statement. The following IF statement shows several layers of nesting:

```
IF condition1
THEN
   IF condition2
   THEN
      statements2
   ELSE
      IF condition3
      THEN
         statements3
      ELSIF condition4
      THEN
         statements4
      END IF;
   END IF;
END IF;
```

Nested IF statements are often necessary to implement complex logic rules, but you should use them carefully. Nested IF statements, like nested loops, can be very difficult to understand and debug. If you find that you need to nest more than three levels deep in your conditional logic, you should review that logic and see if there is a simpler way to code the same requirement. If not, then consider creating one or more local modules to hide the innermost IF statements.

A key advantage to the nested IF structure is that it defers evaluation of inner conditions. The conditions of an inner IF statement are evaluated only if the condition for the outer IF statement that encloses them evaluates to TRUE. Therefore, the obvious reason to nest IF statements is to evaluate one condition only when another condition is true. For example, in our code to award bonuses, we might write the following:

```
IF award_bonus(employee_id) THEN
   IF print_check (employee_id) THEN
      DBMS_OUTPUT.PUT_LINE('Check issued for ' || employee_id);
   END IF;
END IF;
```

This is reasonable, because we want to print a message for each bonus check issued, but we don't want to print a bonus check for a zero amount in cases where no bonus was given.

Another situation in which you'd want to use nested IF statements is when the evaluation of a condition is very expensive in terms of CPU or memory utilization. In such a case, you may want to defer that processing to an inner IF statement so that it is executed only when absolutely necessary. This is especially true of code that will be performed frequently or in areas of the application where quick response time is critical. The following IF statement illustrates this concept:

```
IF condition1 AND condition2
THEN
   ...
END IF;
```

The PL/SQL runtime engine evaluates both conditions in order to determine whether the Boolean expression evaluates to TRUE. Suppose that *condition2* is an expression that PL/SQL can process simply and efficiently, such as:

```
total_sales > 100000
```

but that *condition1* is a much more complex and CPU-intensive expression, perhaps calling a stored function that executes a query against the database. If *condition2* is evaluated in a tenth of a second to FALSE, and *condition1* is evaluated in three seconds to TRUE, then it has taken more than three seconds to determine that the code inside the IF statement should not be executed.

Now consider this next version of the same IF statement:

```
IF condition2
THEN
   IF condition1
   THEN
      ...
   END IF;
END IF;
```

Now *condition1* will be evaluated only if *condition2* evaluates to TRUE. In those situations where total_sales <= 100000, the user will never have to wait the extra three seconds to continue.

Avoiding Syntax Gotchas

Keep in mind these points about IF statement syntax:

Always match up an IF with an END IF
: In all three variations of the IF statement, you must close off the executable statements associated with the conditional structure with an END IF keyword.

You must have a space between the keywords END and IF
: If you type ENDIF instead of END IF, the compiler will get very confused and give you the following hard-to-understand error messages:

```
ORA-06550: line 14, column 4:
PLS-00103: Encountered the symbol ";" when expecting one of the following:
```

The ELSIF keyword should not have an embedded "E"
: If you type ELSEIF in place of ELSIF, the compiler will get very confused and not recognize the ELSEIF as part of the IF statement. It will interpret it as a variable or procedure name.

Place a semicolon (;) only after the END IF keywords
: The keywords THEN, ELSE, and ELSIF should not have a semicolon after them. They are not standalone executable statements and, unlike END IF, do not complete a statement. If you include a semicolon after these keywords, the compiler will issue messages indicating that it is looking for a statement of some kind before the semicolon.

CASE Statements

New to PL/SQL in Oracle9*i*, the CASE statement allows you to select one sequence of statements to execute out of many possible sequences. CASE statements themselves are not new; they have long been implemented in other programming languages. They've been part of the SQL standard since 1992, although Oracle SQL didn't support CASE until the release of Oracle8*i*, and PL/SQL didn't support CASE until Oracle9*i*.

Oracle9*i* (and higher) supports the following two types of CASE statements:

Simple CASE statement
: Associates each of one or more sequences of PL/SQL statements with a value. Chooses which sequence of statements to execute based on an expression that returns one of those values.

Searched CASE statement
: Chooses which of one or more sequences of PL/SQL statements to execute by evaluating a list of Boolean conditions. The sequence of statements associated with the first condition that evaluates to TRUE is executed.

In addition to CASE statements, PL/SQL also supports CASE expressions. A CASE expression is very similar in form to a CASE statement, and allows you to choose which of one or more expressions to evaluate. The result of a CASE expression is a single value, whereas the result of a CASE statement is the execution of a sequence of PL/SQL statements.

Simple CASE Statements

A simple CASE statement allows you to choose which of several sequences of PL/SQL statements to execute based on the results of a single expression. Simple CASE statements take the following form:

```
CASE expression
WHEN result1 THEN
   statements1
WHEN result2 THEN
   statements2
...
ELSE
   statements_else
END CASE;
```

The ELSE portion of the statement is optional. When evaluating such a CASE statement, PL/SQL first evaluates *expression*. It then compares the result of *expression* with *result1*. If the two results match, *statements1* is executed. Otherwise, *result2* is checked, and so forth.

Following is an example of a simple CASE statement that uses the employee type as a basis for selecting the proper bonus algorithm:

```
CASE employee_type
WHEN 'S' THEN
   award_salary_bonus(employee_id);
WHEN 'H' THEN
   award_hourly_bonus(employee_id);
WHEN 'C' THEN
   award_commissioned_bonus(employee_id);
ELSE
   RAISE invalid_employee_type;
END CASE;
```

This CASE statement has an explicit ELSE clause; however, the ELSE is optional. When you do not explicitly specify an ELSE clause of your own, PL/SQL implicitly uses the following:

```
ELSE
   RAISE CASE_NOT_FOUND;
```

In other words, if you do not specify an ELSE clause, and none of the results in the WHEN clauses match the result of the CASE expression, PL/SQL will raise a CASE_NOT_FOUND error. This behavior is different from what we're used to with IF statements. When an IF statement lacks an ELSE clause, nothing happens when the condition is not met. With CASE, the analogous situation leads to an error.

By now you're probably wondering how, or even whether, the bonus logic shown earlier in this chapter can be implemented using a simple CASE statement. At first glance, it doesn't appear possible. However, a bit of creative thought yields the following solution:

```
CASE TRUE
WHEN salary >= 10000 AND salary <=20000 THEN
   give_bonus(employee_id, 1500);
WHEN salary > 20000 AND salary <= 40000
   give_bonus(employee_id, 1000);
WHEN salary > 40000
   give_bonus(employee_id, 500);
ELSE
   give_bonus(employee_id, 0);
END CASE;
```

The point we are trying to make with this solution, aside from the fact that you sometimes need to code creatively, is that the *expression* and *result* elements shown in the earlier syntax diagram can be either scalar values or expressions that evaluate to scalar values.

If you look back to the earlier IF-THEN-ELSIF statement implementing this same bonus logic, you'll see that we specified an ELSE clause for the CASE implementation, whereas we didn't specify an ELSE for the IF-THEN-ELSIF solution. The reason for the addition of the ELSE is simple: if no bonus conditions are met, the IF statement does nothing, effectively resulting in a zero bonus. A CASE statement, however, will raise an error if no conditions are met—hence the need to code explicitly for the zero bonus case.

While our previous CASE TRUE statement may look like a clever hack, it's really an explicit implementation of the searched CASE statement, which we talk about in the next section.

Searched CASE Statements

A searched CASE statement evaluates a list of Boolean expressions and, when it finds an expression that evaluates to TRUE, executes a sequence of statements associated with that expression. Essentially, a searched CASE statement is the equivalent of the CASE TRUE statement shown in the previous section.

Searched CASE statements have the following form:

```
CASE
WHEN expression1 THEN
   statements1
WHEN expression2 THEN
   statements2
```

```
...
ELSE
   statements_else
END CASE;
```

A searched CASE statement is a perfect fit for the problem of implementing the bonus logic. For example:

```
CASE
WHEN salary >= 10000 AND salary <=20000 THEN
   give_bonus(employee_id, 1500);
WHEN salary > 20000 AND salary <= 40000 THEN
   give_bonus(employee_id, 1000);
WHEN salary > 40000 THEN
   give_bonus(employee_id, 500);
ELSE
   give_bonus(employee_id, 0);
END CASE;
```

As with simple CASE statements, the following rules apply:

- Execution ends once a sequence of statements has been executed. If more than one expression evaluates to TRUE, only the statements associated with the first such expression are executed.
- The ELSE clause is optional. If no ELSE is specified and no expressions evaluate to TRUE, then a CASE_NOT_FOUND exception is raised.
- WHEN clauses are evaluated in order, from top to bottom.

Following is an implementation of our bonus logic that takes advantage of the fact that WHEN clauses are evaluated in the order in which we write them. The individual expressions are simpler, but is the intent of the statement as easily grasped?

```
CASE
WHEN salary > 40000 THEN
   give_bonus(employee_id, 500);
WHEN salary > 20000 THEN
   give_bonus(employee_id, 1000);
WHEN salary >= 10000 THEN
   give_bonus(employee_id, 1500);
ELSE
   give_bonus(employee_id, 0);
END CASE;
```

If a given employee's salary is 20,000, then the first expression and second expression will evaluate to FALSE. The third expression will evaluate to TRUE, and that employee will be awarded a bonus of 1500. If an employee's salary is 21,000, then the second expression will evaluate to TRUE, and the employee will be awarded a bonus of 1000. Execution of the CASE statement will cease with the first WHEN condition that evaluates to TRUE, so a salary of 21,000 will never reach the third condition.

It's arguable whether you should take this approach to writing CASE statements. You should certainly be aware that it's possible to write such a statement, and you should watch for such order-dependent logic in programs that you are called upon to modify or debug.

Order-dependent logic can be a subtle source of bugs when you decide to reorder the WHEN clauses in a CASE statement. Consider the following searched CASE statement in which, assuming a salary of 20,000, both WHEN expressions evaluate to TRUE:

```
CASE
WHEN salary BETWEEN 10000 AND 20000 THEN
   give_bonus(employee_id, 1500);
WHEN salary BETWEEN 20000 AND 40000 THEN
   give_bonus(employee_id, 1000);
...
```

Imagine the results if a future programmer unthinkingly decides to make the code neater by reordering the WHEN clauses in descending order by salary. Don't scoff at this possibility! We programmers frequently fiddle with perfectly fine, working code to satisfy some inner sense of order. Following is the CASE statement rewritten with the WHEN clauses in descending order:

```
CASE
WHEN salary BETWEEN 20000 AND 40000 THEN
   give_bonus(employee_id, 1000);
WHEN salary BETWEEN 10000 AND 20000 THEN
   give_bonus(employee_id, 1500);
...
```

Looks good, doesn't it? Unfortunately, because of the slight overlap between the two WHEN clauses, we've introduced a subtle bug into the code. Now an employee with a salary of 20,000 gets a bonus of 1000 rather than the intended 1500. There may be cases where overlap between WHEN clauses is desirable, but avoid it when feasible. Always remember that order matters, and resist the urge to fiddle with working code.

Because WHEN clauses are evaluated in order, you may be able to squeeze some extra efficiency out of your code by listing the most likely WHEN clauses first. In addition, if you have WHEN clauses with "expensive" expressions (e.g., requiring lots of CPU and memory), you may want to list those last in order to minimize the chances that they will be evaluated. See the previous discussion under "Nested IF Statements" for an example of this issue.

Use searched CASE statements when you wish to use Boolean expressions as a basis for identifying a set of statements to execute. Use simple CASE statements when you can base that decision on the result of a single expression.

Nested CASE Statements

CASE statements can be nested just as IF statements can. For example, the following rather difficult-to-follow implementation of our bonus logic uses a nested CASE statement:

```
CASE
WHEN salary >= 10000 THEN
   CASE
   WHEN salary <= 20000 THEN
      give_bonus(employee_id, 1500);
   WHEN salary > 20000 THEN
      give_bonus(employee_id, 1000);
   END CASE;
WHEN salary > 40000 THEN
   give_bonus(employee_id, 500);
WHEN salary < 10000 THEN
   give_bonus(employee_id,0);
END CASE;
```

Any type of statement may be used within a CASE statement, so we could replace the inner CASE statement with an IF statement. Likewise, any type of statement, including CASE statements, may be nested within an IF statement.

CASE Expressions

CASE expressions do for expressions what CASE statements do for statements. Simple CASE expressions let you choose an expression to evaluate based on a scalar value that you provide as input. Searched CASE expressions evaluate a list of expressions to find the first one that evaluates to TRUE, and then return the results of an associated expression.

CASE expressions take the following two forms:

```
Simple_Case_Expression :=
   CASE expression
   WHEN result1 THEN
      result_expression1
   WHEN result2 THEN
      result_expression2
   ...
   ELSE
      result_expression_else
   END;

Searched_Case_Expression :=
   CASE
   WHEN expression1 THEN
      result_expression1
   WHEN expression2 THEN
      result_expression2
   ...
```

```
ELSE
   result_expression_else
END;
```

A CASE expression returns a single value, the result of whichever result expression is chosen. Each WHEN clause must be associated with exactly one expression (no statements). Do not use semicolons or END CASE to mark the end of the CASE expression. CASE expressions are terminated by a simple END.

Following is an example of a simple CASE expression being used with the DBMS_OUTPUT package to output the value of a Boolean variable. Recall that PUT_LINE is not overloaded to handle Boolean types. In this example, the CASE expression converts the Boolean value in a character string, which PUT_LINE can then handle:

```
DECLARE
   boolean_true BOOLEAN := TRUE;
   boolean_false BOOLEAN := FALSE;
   boolean_null BOOLEAN;

   FUNCTION boolean_to_varchar2 (flag IN BOOLEAN) RETURN VARCHAR2 IS
   BEGIN
      RETURN
      CASE flag
      WHEN TRUE THEN 'True'
      WHEN FALSE THEN 'False'
      ELSE 'NULL' END;
   END;

BEGIN
   DBMS_OUTPUT.PUT_LINE(boolean_to_varchar2(boolean_true));
   DBMS_OUTPUT.PUT_LINE(boolean_to_varchar2(boolean_false));
   DBMS_OUTPUT.PUT_LINE(boolean_to_varchar2(boolean_null));
END;
```

A searched CASE expression can be used to implement our bonus logic, returning the proper bonus value for any given salary:

```
DECLARE
  salary NUMBER := 20000;
  employee_id NUMBER := 36325;

  PROCEDURE give_bonus (emp_id IN NUMBER, bonus_amt IN NUMBER) IS
  BEGIN
    DBMS_OUTPUT.PUT_LINE(emp_id);
    DBMS_OUTPUT.PUT_LINE(bonus_amt);
  END;

BEGIN
   give_bonus(employee_id,
              CASE
              WHEN salary >= 10000 AND salary <=20000 THEN 1500
              WHEN salary > 20000 AND salary <= 40000 THEN 1000
              WHEN salary > 40000 THEN 500
```

```
                 ELSE 0
                 END);
END;
```

You can use a CASE expression anywhere you can use any other type of expression. The following example uses a CASE expression to compute a bonus amount, multiplies that amount by 10, and assigns the result to a variable that is displayed via DBMS_OUTPUT:

```
DECLARE
  salary NUMBER := 20000;
  employee_id NUMBER := 36325;
  bonus_amount NUMBER;
BEGIN
   bonus_amount :=
      CASE
      WHEN salary >= 10000 AND salary <=20000 THEN 1500
      WHEN salary > 20000 AND salary <= 40000 THEN 1000
      WHEN salary > 40000 THEN 500
      ELSE 0
      END * 10;

   DBMS_OUTPUT.PUT_LINE(bonus_amount);
END;
```

Unlike with the CASE statement, no error is raised in the event that no WHEN clause is selected in a CASE expression. Instead, when no WHEN conditions are met, a CASE expression will return NULL.

The GOTO Statement

Certain PL/SQL control structures offer structured methods for processing executable statements in your program. You use an IF statement or a CASE statement to test a condition to determine which parts of your code to execute; you use a LOOP variation (described in Chapter 5) to execute a section of code more than once. In addition to these well-structured approaches to program control, PL/SQL offers the GOTO. The GOTO statement performs unconditional branching to another executable statement in the same execution section of a PL/SQL block. As with other constructs in the language, if you use GOTO appropriately and with care, your programs will be stronger for it.

The general format for a GOTO statement is:

```
GOTO label_name;
```

where *label_name* is the name of a label identifying the target statement. This GOTO label is defined in the program as follows:

```
<<label_name>>
```

CASE in SQL Statements

Support for CASE in SQL statements preceded support for CASE in PL/SQL; Oracle8*i* introduced the searched CASE expression in SQL. Unfortunately, much to the frustration of PL/SQL programmers everywhere, SQL statements executed from within PL/SQL could not use CASE expressions. For example, from SQL*Plus you could execute:

```
SELECT
   CASE
      WHEN DUMMY='X' THEN 'Dual is OK'
      ELSE 'Dual is messed up'
   END
FROM DUAL;
```

However, the following PL/SQL code would not work:

```
DECLARE
   dual_message VARCHAR2(20);
BEGIN
   SELECT CASE
            WHEN DUMMY='X' THEN 'Dual is OK'
            ELSE 'Dual is messed up'
            END INTO dual_message
   FROM DUAL;
   DBMS_OUTPUT.PUT_LINE (dual_message);
END;
```

This frustration goes away in Oracle9*i*. In Oracle9*i*, you can have both searched and simple CASE statements, and they can be used equally from SQL, from PL/SQL, and from SQL within PL/SQL.

You must surround the label name with double enclosing angle brackets (<< >>). When PL/SQL encounters a GOTO statement, it immediately shifts control to the first executable statement following the label. Following is a complete code block containing both a GOTO and a label:

```
BEGIN
   GOTO second_output;

   DBMS_OUTPUT.PUT_LINE('This line will never execute.');

   <<second_output>>
   DBMS_OUTPUT.PUT_LINE('We are here!');
END;
```

Contrary to popular opinion (including mine), the GOTO statement can come in handy. There are cases where a GOTO statement can simplify the logic in your program. On the other hand, because PL/SQL provides so many different control constructs and modularization techniques, you can almost always find a better way to do something than with a GOTO.

Restrictions on the GOTO Statement

There are several restrictions on the GOTO statement:

- At least one executable statement must follow a label.
- The target label must be in the same scope as the GOTO statement.
- The target label must be in the same part of the PL/SQL block as the GOTO.

These restrictions are described in detail in the following sections.

At least one executable statement must follow a label

A label itself is not an executable statement (notice that it does not have a semicolon after the label brackets), so it cannot take the place of one. All of the uses of the <<all_done>> label in the following code are illegal because the labels are not followed by an executable statement:

```
IF status_inout = 'COMPLETED'
THEN
   <<all_done>> /* Illegal! */
ELSE
   schedule_activity;
END IF;

DECLARE
   CURSOR company_cur IS ...;
BEGIN
   FOR company_rec IN company_cur
   LOOP
      apply_bonuses (company_rec.company_id);
      <<all_done>> /* Illegal! */
   END LOOP;
END;

FUNCTION new_formula (molecule_in IN NUMBER) RETURN VARCHAR2
IS
BEGIN
   ... construct formula for molecule ...
   RETURN formula_string;

   <<all_done>> /* Illegal! */

END;
```

Keywords such as END, THEN, ELSE, ELSIF, and END LOOP do not represent executable statements, and thus such keywords cannot be immediately preceded by a label.

The target label must be in the same scope as the GOTO statement

A GOTO statement's target label must be in the same scope as the GOTO statement. In the context of the GOTO statement, each of the following constructs maintains its own scope:

- Functions
- Procedures
- Anonymous blocks
- IF statements
- LOOP statements
- Exception handlers
- CASE statements

The following code examples show common programming errors. Each illustrates an attempt to branch to a label that is out of scope, and each generates the following PL/SQL error:

```
PLS-00375: illegal GOTO statement; this GOTO cannot branch to label
```

IF conditions

The only way to enter an IF statement is through an evaluation of an IF condition to TRUE. Therefore, this code produces an error:

```
GOTO label_inside_IF;
IF status = 'NEW'
THEN
   <<label_inside_IF>> /* Out of scope! */
   show_new_one;
END IF;
```

Likewise, you can't jump into the middle of a CASE statement.

BEGIN statements

The only way to enter a block-within-a-block is through the sub-block's BEGIN statement. PL/SQL insists on orderly entrances and exits. This code produces an error because it doesn't comply with this structure:

```
GOTO label_inside_subblock;
BEGIN
   <<label_inside_subblock>> /* Crosses block boundary! */
   NULL;
END;
```

Scope of IF statements

Each IF clause of the IF statement is its own scope. A GOTO may not transfer from one clause to another. This code produces an error:

```
IF status = 'NEW'
THEN
   <<new_status>>
   GOTO old_status; /* Crosses IF clause boundary! */
ELSIF status = 'OLD'
```

```
      THEN
         <<old_status>>
         GOTO new_status; /* Crosses IF clause boundary! */
      END IF;
```

Likewise, you can't jump from one clause to another within a CASE statement.

Don't jump into the middle of a loop

You cannot jump into the middle of a loop with a GOTO. This code produces an error:

```
FOR month_num IN 1 .. 12
LOOP
   <<do_a_month>>
   schedule_activity (month_num);
END LOOP;
GOTO do_a_month; /* Can't go back into loop. */
```

Don't GOTO a local module

You cannot issue a GOTO from the main body of a block to a label in a function, procedure, or other module defined within that block. This code produces an error:

```
DECLARE
   FUNCTION local_null IS
   BEGIN
      <<descrip_case_statement>>
      NULL;
   END;
BEGIN
   GOTO descrip_case_statement; /* Label not visible here. */
END;
```

The target label must be in the same part of the PL/SQL block as the GOTO

The target label must be in the same part of the PL/SQL block as the GOTO statement. A GOTO in the execution section may not go to a label in the exception section; a GOTO in the exception section may not go to a label in the execution section. A GOTO in an exception handler may reference a label in the same handler. The following code example generates the same PL/SQL error shown in the previous section (PLS-00375):

```
BEGIN
   /*
   || The label and GOTO must be in the same section!
   */
   GOTO out_of_here;
EXCEPTION
   WHEN OTHERS
   THEN
      <<out_of_here>> /* Out of scope! */
      NULL;
END;
```

The NULL Statement

Usually when you write a statement in a program, you want it to do something. There are cases, however, when you want to tell PL/SQL to do absolutely nothing, and that is where the NULL statement comes in handy. The NULL statement has the following format:

```
NULL;
```

Well, you wouldn't want a do-nothing statement to be complicated, would you? The NULL statement is simply the reserved word NULL followed by a semicolon (;) to indicate that this is a statement and not a NULL value. The NULL statement does nothing except pass control to the next executable statement.

Why would you want to use the NULL statement? There are several reasons, described in the following sections.

Improving Program Readability

There are many situations in your program where you logically do not want to take any action. In most of these cases, PL/SQL will let you write nothing and the program will execute as you wish. The only drawback is the ambiguity surrounding this solution: it is not clear to a person examining the program that you purposely took no action.

For example, when you write an IF statement, you do not have to include an ELSE clause. To produce a report based on a selection, you can code:

```
IF :report.selection = 'DETAIL'
THEN
   exec_detail_report;
END IF;
```

What should the program be doing if the report selection is not 'DETAIL'? One would assume that the program is supposed to do nothing. But because this is not explicitly stated in the code, one is left to wonder if perhaps there was an oversight. If, on the other hand, you include an explicit ELSE clause that does nothing, you state very clearly, "Don't worry, I thought about this possibility and I really want nothing to happen."

```
IF :report.selection = 'DETAIL'
THEN
   exec_detail_report;
ELSE
   NULL; -- Do nothing
END IF;
```

Nullifying a Raised Exception

The optional exception section of a program contains one or more exception handlers. These handlers trap and handle errors that have been raised in your program. The structure and flow of the exception section is similar in structure and flow to a conditional CASE statement, as follows:

```
EXCEPTION
   WHEN exception_name1
   THEN
      executable_statements;

   WHEN exception_nameN
   THEN
      executable_statements;
   WHEN OTHERS
   THEN
      executable_statements;
END;
```

If *exception_name1* is raised, then execute its statements; if *exception_nameN* is raised, then execute its statements; and so on. The WHEN OTHERS clause handles any exceptions not handled in the previous WHEN clauses (it is just like the ELSE clause of the IF statement). When you don't want to write any special code to handle an exception, you can use the NULL statement to make sure that a raised exception halts execution of the current PL/SQL block, but does not propagate any exceptions to enclosing blocks:

```
PROCEDURE calc_avg_sales
BEGIN
   :sales.avg := :sales.month1 / :sales.total;
EXCEPTION
   WHEN ZERO_DIVIDE
   THEN
      :sales.avg := 0;
      RAISE FORM_TRIGGER_FAILURE;
   WHEN OTHERS
   THEN
      NULL;
END;
```

If total sales are zero, then an exception is raised, the average is set to zero, and the trigger processing in Oracle Forms is halted. If any other exceptions occur (such as VALUE_ERROR, which would be raised if the number generated by the calculation is larger than the sales.avg item allows), the WHEN OTHERS clause gets control, handles the exception by doing nothing (i.e., executes the NULL statement), and processing continues. Because the exception is handled, it is not raised to the enclosing block.

See Chapter 6 for more detailed information about exceptions.

Using NULL After a Label

In some cases, you can pair NULL with GOTO to avoid having to execute additional statements. Most of you will never have to use the GOTO statement; there are very few occasions where it is truly needed. If you ever do use GOTO, however, you should remember that when you GOTO a label, at least one executable statement must follow that label. In the following example, I use a GOTO statement to quickly move to the end of my program if the state of my data indicates that no further processing is required:

```
PROCEDURE process_data (data_in IN orders%ROWTYPE,
                        data_action IN VARCHAR2) IS
BEGIN
   -- First in series of validations.
   IF data_in.ship_date IS NOT NULL
   THEN
      status := validate_shipdate (data_in.ship_date);
      IF status != 0 THEN GOTO end_of_procedure;
   END IF;

   -- Second in series of validations.
   IF data_in.order_date IS NOT NULL
   THEN
      status := validate_orderdate (data_in.order_date);
      IF status != 0 THEN GOTO end_of_procedure;
   END IF;

   ... more validations ...

   << end_of_procedure >>
   NULL;
END;
```

With this approach, if I encounter an error in any single section, I use the GOTO to bypass all remaining validation checks. Because I do not have to do anything at the termination of the procedure, I place a NULL statement after the label because at least one executable statement is required there. Even though NULL does nothing, it is still an executable statement.

CHAPTER 5

Iterative Processing with Loops

In this chapter:

This chapter explores the iterative control structures of PL/SQL, otherwise known as *loops*, which let you execute the same code repeatedly. PL/SQL provides three different kinds of loop constructs:

- The simple or infinite loop
- The FOR loop (numeric and cursor)
- The WHILE loop

Each type of loop is designed for a specific purpose with its own nuances, rules for use, and guidelines for high-quality construction. As we explain each loop, we'll provide a table describing the following properties of the loop:

Property	Description
How the loop is terminated	A loop executes code repetitively. How do you make the loop stop executing its body?
When the test for termination takes place	Does the test for termination take place at the beginning or end of the loop? What are the consequences?
Reason to use this loop	What are the special factors you should consider to determine if this loop is right for your situation?

Loop Basics

Why are there three different kinds of loops? To provide you with the flexibility you need to write the most straightforward code to handle any particular situation. Most situations that require a loop could be written with any of the three loop constructs. If you do not pick the construct best-suited for that particular requirement, however, you could end up having to write many additional lines of code. The resulting module would also be harder to understand and maintain.

Examples of Different Loops

To give you a feeling for the way the different loops solve their problems in different ways, consider the following three procedures. In each case, the procedure executes the same body of code inside a loop:

```
set_rank (ranking_level);
```

where set_rank performs a ranking for the specified level.

The simple loop

My procedure accepts a maximum ranking as an argument and then sets the rank until the level exceeds the maximum. Notice the IF statement used to guard against executing the loop when the maximum rank is negative. Notice also the EXIT WHEN statement used to terminate the loop:

```
PROCEDURE set_all_ranks (max_rank_in IN INTEGER)
IS
   ranking_level  NUMBER  (3) := 1;
BEGIN
   LOOP
      EXIT WHEN ranking_level > max_rank_in;
      set_rank (ranking_level);
      ranking_level :=   ranking_level + 1;
   END LOOP;
END set_all_ranks;
```

The FOR loop

In this case, I rank for the fixed range of values, from 1 to the maximum number:

```
PROCEDURE set_all_ranks (max_rank_in IN INTEGER)
IS
BEGIN
   FOR ranking_level IN 1 .. max_rank_in
   LOOP
      set_rank (ranking_level);
   END LOOP;
END set_all_ranks;
```

The WHILE loop

My procedure accepts a maximum ranking as an argument and then sets the rank until the level exceeds the maximum. Notice that the condition that terminates the loop comes on the same line as the WHILE keyword:

```
PROCEDURE set_all_ranks (max_rank_in IN INTEGER)
IS
   ranking_level NUMBER(3) := 1;
BEGIN
   WHILE ranking_level <= max_rank_in
   LOO
      set_rank (ranking_level);
      ranking_level := ranking_level + 1;
   END LOOP;
END set_all_ranks;
```

In the above example, the FOR loop clearly requires the smallest amount of code. Yet I could use it in this case only because I knew that I would run the body of the loop a specific number of times (max_rank_in). In many other situations, the number of times a loop must execute varies, so the FOR loop cannot be used.

Structure of PL/SQL Loops

While there are differences among the three loop constructs, every loop has two parts: the loop boundary and the loop body.

Loop boundary
: This is composed of the reserved words that initiate the loop, the condition that causes the loop to terminate, and the END LOOP statement that ends the loop.

Loop body
: This is the sequence of executable statements inside the loop boundary that execute on each iteration of the loop.

Figure 5-1 shows the boundary and body of a WHILE loop.

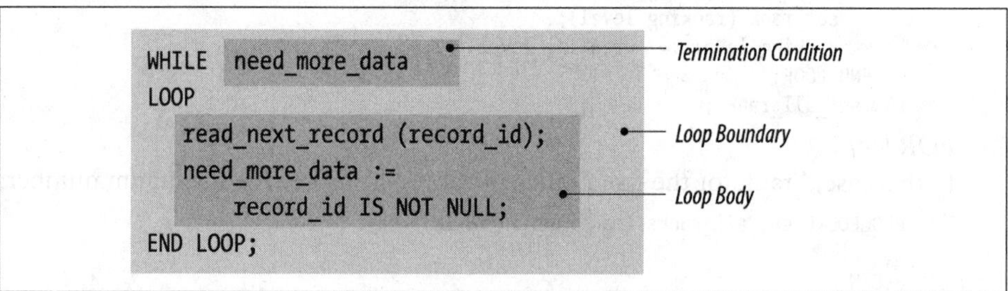

Figure 5-1. The boundary and body of the WHILE loop

In general, think of a loop much as you would a procedure or a function. The body of the loop is a black box, and the condition that causes loop termination is the interface to that black box. Code outside the loop should not have to know about the inner workings of the loop. Keep this in mind as you go through the different kinds of loops and examples in the rest of the chapter.

In addition to the examples you will find in this chapter, I have included several lengthy code samples utilizing PL/SQL loops in the Oracle Forms environment in the following files, available on the O'Reilly site:

highrec.doc and highrec.fp
: Demonstrate highlighting items in an Oracle Forms record.

ofquery.doc, postqry.fp, and preqry.fp
: Demonstrate automatic post- and pre-query processing in Oracle Forms.

The Simple Loop

The structure of the simple loop is the most basic of all the loop constructs. It consists of the LOOP keyword, the body of executable code, and the END LOOP keywords, as shown here:

```
LOOP
   executable statement(s)
END LOOP;
```

The loop boundary consists solely of the LOOP and END LOOP reserved words. The body must consist of at least one executable statement. The following table summarizes the properties of the simple loop:

Property	Description
How the loop is terminated	The simple loop is terminated when an EXIT statement is executed in the body of the loop. If this statement is not executed, the simple loop becomes a true infinite loop.
When the test for termination takes place	The test takes place inside the body of the loop—and then only if an EXIT or EXIT WHEN statement is executed. Therefore, the body—or part of the body—of the simple loop will always execute at least once.
Reason to use this loop	Use the simple loop when: • You are not sure how many times you will want the loop to execute, and • You want the loop to run at least once.

This loop is useful when you want to guarantee that the body (or at least part of the body) will execute at least one time. Because there is no condition associated with the loop boundary that determines whether or not it should execute, the body of the loop will always execute the first time.

The simple loop will terminate only when an EXIT (or its close cousin, EXIT WHEN) statement is executed in its body, or when an exception is raised (and goes unhandled) within the body of the loop.

Terminating a Simple Loop: EXIT and EXIT WHEN

Be very careful when you use simple loops. Make sure they always have a way to stop. To force a simple loop to stop processing, execute an EXIT or EXIT WHEN statement within the body of the loop. The syntax for these statements is as follows:

```
EXIT;
EXIT WHEN condition;
```

where *condition* is a Boolean expression.

The following example demonstrates how the EXIT forces the loop to immediately halt execution and pass control to the next statement after the END LOOP statement. The account_balance procedure returns the amount of money remaining in the account specified by the account ID. If there is less than $1000 left, the EXIT statement is executed and the loop is terminated. Otherwise, the program applies the balance to the outstanding orders for that account.

```
LOOP
   balance_remaining := account_balance (account_id);
   IF balance_remaining < 1000
   THEN
      EXIT;
   ELSE
      apply_balance (account_id, balance_remaining);
   END IF;
END LOOP;
```

You can use an EXIT statement only within a LOOP.

PL/SQL also offers the EXIT WHEN statement, which supports conditional termination of the loop. Essentially, the EXIT WHEN combines an IF-THEN statement with the EXIT statement. Using the same example, the EXIT WHEN changes the loop to:

```
LOOP
   /* Calculate the balance */
   balance_remaining := account_balance (account_id);

   /* Embed the IF logic into the EXIT statement */
   EXIT WHEN balance_remaining < 1000;

   /* Apply balance if still executing the loop */
   apply_balance (account_id, balance_remaining);
END LOOP;
```

Notice that the loop no longer requires an IF statement to determine when it should exit. Instead, that conditional logic is embedded inside the EXIT WHEN statement.

So when should you use EXIT WHEN, and when is the stripped-down EXIT more appropriate?

- EXIT WHEN is best used when there is a single conditional expression that determines whether or not a loop should terminate. The previous example demonstrates this scenario clearly.
- In situations with multiple conditions for exiting or when you need to set a "return value" coming out of the loop based on different conditions, you are probably better off using an IF or CASE statement, with EXIT statements in one or more of the clauses.

The following example demonstrates a preferred use of EXIT. It is taken from a function that determines if two files are equal (i.e., contain the same content):

```
   ...
   IF (end_of_file1 AND end_of_file2)
   THEN
      retval := TRUE;
```

```
         EXIT;
      ELSIF (checkline != againstline)
      THEN
         retval := FALSE;
         EXIT;
      ELSIF (end_of_file1 OR end_of_file2)
      THEN
         retval := FALSE;
         EXIT;
      END IF;
   END LOOP;
```

Emulating a REPEAT UNTIL Loop

PL/SQL does not provide a REPEAT UNTIL loop in which the condition is tested after the body of the loop is executed and thus guarantees that the loop always executes at least once. You can, however, emulate a REPEAT UNTIL with a simple loop, as follows:

```
LOOP
   ... body of loop ...
   EXIT WHEN boolean_condition;
END LOOP;
```

where *boolean_condition* is a Boolean variable or an expression that evaluates to a Boolean value of TRUE or FALSE.

The WHILE Loop

The WHILE loop is a conditional loop that continues to execute as long as the Boolean condition defined in the loop boundary evaluates to TRUE. Because the WHILE loop execution depends on a condition and is not fixed, you should use a WHILE loop if you don't know in advance the number of times a loop must execute.

Here is the general syntax for the WHILE loop:

```
WHILE condition
LOOP
   executable statement(s)
END LOOP;
```

where *condition* is a Boolean variable or an expression that evaluates to a Boolean value of TRUE, FALSE, or NULL. Each time an iteration of the loop's body is to be executed, the condition is checked. If it evaluates to TRUE, then the body is executed. If it evaluates to FALSE or NULL, then the loop terminates and control passes to the next executable statement following the END LOOP statement.

The following table summarizes the properties of the WHILE loop:

Property	Description
How the loop is terminated	The WHILE loop terminates when the Boolean expression in its boundary evaluates to FALSE or NULL.
When the test for termination takes place	The test for termination of a WHILE loop takes place in the loop boundary. This evaluation occurs prior to the first and each subsequent execution of the body. The WHILE loop, therefore, is not guaranteed to execute its loop even a single time.
Reason to use this loop	Use the WHILE loop when: • You are not sure how many times you must execute the loop body, and • You will want to conditionally terminate the loop, and • You don't have to execute the body at least one time.

The WHILE loop's condition is tested at the beginning of the loop's iteration, before the body of the loop is executed. There are two consequences to this pre-execution test:

- All the information needed to evaluate the condition must be set before the loop is executed for the first time.
- It is possible that the WHILE loop will not execute even a single time.

Here is an example of a WHILE loop from the *datemgr.pkg* file available on the O'Reilly site. It shows a boundary condition consisting of a complex Boolean expression. There are two reasons for the WHILE loop to stop: either I have run out of date masks to attempt a conversion, or I have successfully performed a conversion (and date_converted is now TRUE):

```
WHILE mask_index <= mask_count AND NOT date_converted
LOOP
   BEGIN
      /* Try to convert string using mask in table row */
      retval := TO_DATE (value_in, fmts (mask_index));
     date_converted := TRUE;
   EXCEPTION
      WHEN OTHERS
      THEN
         retval := NULL;
         mask_index:= mask_index+ 1;
   END;
END LOOP;
```

The Numeric FOR Loop

There are two kinds of PL/SQL FOR loops: the numeric FOR loop and the cursor FOR loop. The numeric FOR loop is the traditional and familiar "counted" loop. The number of iterations of the FOR loop is known when the loop starts; it is specified in the range scheme found between the FOR and LOOP keywords in the boundary.

The range scheme implicitly declares the loop index (if it has not already been declared), specifies the start and end points of the range, and optionally dictates the order in which the loop index proceeds (from lowest to highest or highest to lowest).

Here is the general syntax of the numeric FOR loop:

```
FOR loop index IN [REVERSE] lowest number .. highest number
LOOP
   executable statement(s)
END LOOP;
```

You must have at least one executable statement between the LOOP and END LOOP keywords.

The following table summarizes the properties of the numeric FOR loop:

Property	Description
How the loop is terminated	The numeric FOR loop terminates unconditionally when the number of times specified in its range scheme has been satisfied. You can also terminate the loop with an EXIT statement, but this is not recommended.
When the test for termination takes place	After each execution of the loop body, PL/SQL checks the value of the loop index. When it exceeds the upper bound of the range scheme, the loop terminates. If the lower bound is greater than the upper bound of the range scheme, the loop never executes its body.
Reason to use this loop	Use the numeric FOR loop when you want to execute a body of code a fixed number of times and do not want to halt that looping prematurely.

Rules for Numeric FOR Loops

Follow these rules when you use numeric FOR loops:

- Do not declare the loop index. PL/SQL automatically and implicitly declares it as a local variable with datatype INTEGER. The scope of this index is the loop itself; you cannot reference the loop index outside the loop.
- Expressions used in the range scheme (both for lowest and highest bounds) are evaluated once, when the loop starts. The range is not re-evaluated during the execution of the loop. If you make changes within the loop to the variables that you used to determine the FOR loop range, those changes will have no effect.
- Never change the values of either the loop index or the range boundary from within the loop. This is an extremely bad programming practice. PL/SQL will either produce a compile error or ignore your instructions; in either case, you'll have problems.
- Use the REVERSE keyword to force the loop to decrement from the upper bound to the lower bound. You must still make sure that the first value in the range specification (the *lowest number* in *lowest number .. highest number*) is less than the second value. Do not reverse the order in which you specify these values when you use the REVERSE keyword.

Examples of Numeric FOR Loops

The following examples demonstrate some variations of the numeric FOR loop syntax:

- The loop executes ten times; loop_counter starts at 1 and ends at 10:

```
FOR loop_counter IN 1 .. 10
LOOP
   ... executable statements ...
END LOOP;
```

- The loop executes ten times; loop_counter starts at 10 and ends at 1:

```
FOR loop_counter IN REVERSE 1 .. 10
LOOP
   ... executable statements ...
END LOOP;
```

- Here is a loop that doesn't execute even once. I specified REVERSE, so the loop index, loop_counter, will start at the highest value and end with the lowest. I then mistakenly concluded that I should switch the order in which I list the highest and lowest bounds:

```
FOR loop_counter IN REVERSE 10 .. 1
LOOP
   /* This loop body will never execute even once! */
END LOOP;
```

  Even when you specify a REVERSE direction, you must still list the lowest bound before the highest bound. If the first number is greater than the second number, the body of the loop will not execute at all. If the lowest and highest bounds have the same value, the loop will execute just once.

- The loop executes for a range determined by the values in the variable and expression:

```
FOR calc_index IN start_period_number ..
            LEAST (end_period_number, current_period)
LOOP
   ... executable statements ...
END LOOP;
```

  In this example, the number of times the loop will execute is determined at runtime. The boundary values are evaluated once, before the loop executes, and then applied for the duration of loop execution.

Handling Nontrivial Increments

PL/SQL does not provide a "step" syntax whereby you can specify a particular loop index increment. In all variations of the PL/SQL numeric FOR loop, the loop index is always incremented or decremented by one.

If you have a loop body that you want executed for a nontrivial increment (something other than one), you will have to write some cute code. For example, what if you want your loop to execute only for even numbers between 1 and 100? You can make use of the numeric MOD function, as follows:

```
FOR loop_index IN 1 .. 100
LOOP
   IF MOD (loop_index, 2) = 0
   THEN
      /* We have an even number, so perform calculation */
      calc_values (loop_index);
   END IF;
END LOOP;
```

Or you can use simple multiplication inside a loop with half the iterations:

```
FOR even_number IN 1 .. 50
LOOP
   calc_values (even_number*2);
END LOOP;
```

In both cases, the calc_values procedure executes only for even numbers. In the first example, the FOR loop executes 100 times; in the second example, it executes only 50 times.

Whichever approach you decide to take, be sure to document this kind of technique clearly. You are, in essence, manipulating the numeric FOR loop to do something for which it is not designed. Comments would be very helpful for the maintenance programmer who has to understand why you would code something like that.

The Cursor FOR Loop

A cursor FOR loop is a loop that is associated with (and actually defined by) an explicit cursor or a SELECT statement incorporated directly within the loop boundary. Use the cursor FOR loop only if you need to fetch and process each and every record from a cursor, which is often the case with cursors.

The cursor FOR loop is one of my favorite PL/SQL features. It leverages fully the tight and effective integration of the procedural constructs with the power of the SQL database language. It reduces the volume of code you need to write to fetch data from a cursor. It greatly lessens the chance of introducing loop errors in your programming—and loops are one of the more error-prone parts of a program. Does this loop sound too good to be true? Well, it isn't—it's all true!

Here is the basic syntax of a cursor FOR loop:

```
FOR record_index IN [cursor_name, (explicit SELECT statement)]
LOOP
   executable statement(s)
END LOOP;
```

where *record_index* is a record declared implicitly by PL/SQL with the %ROWTYPE attribute against the cursor specified by *cursor_name*.

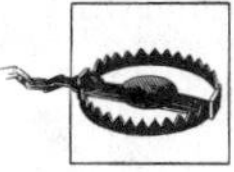

Do not declare a record explicitly with the same name as the loop index record. It is not needed (PL/SQL declares one for its use within the loop implicitly) and can lead to logic errors. For tips on accessing information about a cursor FOR loop's record outside or after loop execution, see the later section titled "Obtaining Information About FOR Loop Execution."

You can also embed a SELECT statement directly in the cursor FOR loop, as shown in this example:

```
FOR book_cur IN (SELECT * FROM book)
LOOP
   show_usage;
END LOOP;
```

You should, however, avoid this formulation, as it results in the embedding of SELECT statements in "unexpected" places in your code, making it more difficult to maintain and enhance your logic.

The following table summarizes the properties of the cursor FOR loop where *record_index* is a record declared implicitly by PL/SQL with the %ROWTYPE attribute against the cursor specified by *cursor_name*:

Property	Description
How the loop is terminated	The cursor FOR loop terminates unconditionally when all of the records in the associated cursor have been fetched. You can also terminate the loop with an EXIT statement, but this is not recommended.
When the test for termination takes place	After each execution of the loop body, PL/SQL performs another fetch. If the %NOTFOUND attribute of the cursor evaluates to TRUE, then the loop terminates. If the cursor returns no rows, then the loop never executes its body.
Reason to use this loop	Use the cursor FOR loop when you want to fetch and process every record in a cursor.

You should use a cursor FOR loop whenever you need to unconditionally fetch all rows from a cursor (i.e., there are no EXITs or EXIT WHENs inside the loop that cause early termination). Let's take a look at how you can use the cursor FOR loop to streamline your code and reduce opportunities for error.

Example of Cursor FOR Loops

Suppose I need to update the bills for all pets staying in my pet hotel, the Share-a-Din-Din Inn. The following example contains an anonymous block that uses a cursor, occupancy_cur, to select the room number and pet ID number for all occupants of the Inn. The procedure update_bill adds any new changes to that pet's room charges:

```
DECLARE
   CURSOR occupancy_cur IS
      SELECT pet_id, room_number
```

```
 4          FROM occupancy WHERE occupied_dt = TRUNC (SYSDATE;)
 5      occupancy_rec occupancy_cur%ROWTYPE;
 6   BEGIN
 7      OPEN occupancy_cur;
 8      LOOP
 9         FETCH occupancy_cur INTO occupancy_rec;
10         EXIT WHEN occupancy_cur%NOTFOUND;
11         update_bill
12            (occupancy_rec.pet_id, occupancy_rec.room_number);
13      END LOOP;
14      CLOSE occupancy_cur;
15   END;
```

This code leaves nothing to the imagination. In addition to defining the cursor (line 2), you must explicitly declare the record for the cursor (line 5), open the cursor (line 7), start up an infinite loop (line 8), fetch a row from the cursor set into the record (line 9), check for an end-of-data condition with the cursor attribute (line 10), and finally perform the update (line 11). When you are all done, you have to remember to close the cursor (line 14).

If I convert this PL/SQL block to use a cursor FOR loop, then I have:

```
DECLARE
   CURSOR occupancy_cur IS
      SELECT pet_id, room_number
        FROM occupancy WHERE occupied_dt = TRUNC (SYSDATE;)
BEGIN
   FOR occupancy_rec IN occupancy_cur
   LOOP
      update_bill (occupancy_rec.pet_id, occupancy_rec.room_number);
   END LOOP;
END;
```

Here you see the beautiful simplicity of the cursor FOR loop! Gone is the declaration of the record. Gone are the OPEN, FETCH, and CLOSE statements. Gone is the need to check the %FOUND attribute. Gone are the worries of getting everything right. Instead, you say to PL/SQL, in effect:

> You and I both know that I want each row and I want to dump that row into a record that matches the cursor. Take care of that for me, will you?

And PL/SQL does take care of it, just the way any modern programming language should.

As with all other cursors, you can pass parameters to the cursor in a cursor FOR loop. If any of the columns in the select list of the cursor is an expression, remember that you must specify an alias for that expression in the select list. Within the loop, the only way to access a particular value in the cursor record is with the dot notation (*cursor_name.column_name*, as in occupancy_rec.room_number), so you need a column name associated with the expression.

Loop Labels

You can give a name to a loop by using a label. (We introduced labels in Chapter 3.) A *loop label* in PL/SQL has the following format:

```
<<label_name>>
```

where *label_name* is the name of the label, and that loop label appears immediately before the LOOP statement:

```
<<all_emps>>
FOR emp_rec IN emp_cur
LOOP
   ...
END LOOP;
```

The label can also appear optionally after the END LOOP reserved words, as the following example demonstrates:

```
<<year_loop>>
WHILE year_number <= 1995
LOOP

   <<month_loop>>
   FOR month_number IN 1 .. 12
   LOOP
      ...
   END LOOP month_loop;

END LOOP year_loop;
```

The loop label is potentially useful in several ways:

- When you have written a loop with a large body (say one that starts at line 50, ends on line 725, and has 16 nested loops inside it), use a loop label to tie the end of the loop back explicitly to its start. This visual tag will make it easier for a developer to maintain and debug the program. Without the loop label, it can be very difficult to keep track of which LOOP goes with which END LOOP.
- You can use the loop label to qualify the name of the loop indexing variable (either a record or a number). Again, this can be helpful for readability. Here is an example:

```
<<year_loop>>
FOR year_number IN 1800..1995
LOOP
   <<month_loop>>
   FOR month_number IN 1 .. 12
   LOOP
      IF year_loop.year_number = 1900 THEN ... END IF;
   END LOOP month_loop;
END LOOP year_loop;
```

- When you have nested loops, you can use the label both to improve readability and to increase control over the execution of your loops. You can, in fact, stop the execution of a specific named outer loop by adding a loop label after the EXIT keyword in the EXIT statement of a loop, as follows:

  ```
  EXIT loop_label;
  EXIT loop_label WHEN condition;
  ```

  While it is possible to use loop labels in this fashion, I recommend that you avoid it. It leads to very unstructured logic (quite similar to GOTOs) that is hard to debug. If you feel that you need to insert code like this, you should consider restructuring your loop, and possibly switching from a FOR loop to a simple or WHILE loop.

Tips for Iterative Processing

Loops are very powerful and useful constructs, but they are structures that you should use with care. Performance issues within a program often are traced back to loops, and any problem within a loop is magnified by its repeated execution. The logic determining when to stop a loop can be very complex. This section offers some tips on how to write loops that are clean, easy to understand, and easy to maintain.

Use Understandable Names for Loop Indexes

Software programmers should not have to make Sherlock Holmes–like deductions about the meaning of the start and end range values of the innermost FOR loops in order to understand their purpose. Use names that self-document the purposes of variables and loops. That way, other people will understand your code, and you will remember what your own code does when you review it three months later.

How would you like to try to understand—much less maintain—code that looks like this?

```
FOR i IN start_id .. end_id
LOOP
   FOR j IN 1 .. 7
   LOOP
      FOR k IN 1 .. 24
      LOOP
         build_schedule (i, j, k);
      END LOOP;
   END LOOP;
END LOOP;
```

It is hard to imagine that someone would write code based on such generic integer variable names (right out of Algebra 101), yet it happens all the time. The habits we pick up in our earliest days of programming have an incredible half-life. Unless you are constantly vigilant, you will find yourself writing the most abominable code. In the case above, the solution is simple—use variable names for the loop indexes that are meaningful and therefore self-documenting:

```
FOR focus_account IN start_id .. end_id
LOOP
   FOR day_in_week IN 1 .. 7
   LOOP
      FOR month_in_biyear IN 1 .. 24
      LOOP
         build_schedule (focus_account, day_in_week, month_in_biyear);
      END LOOP;
   END LOOP;
END LOOP;
```

Now that I have provided descriptive names for those index variables, we discover that the innermost loop actually spanned two sets of twelve months ($12 \times 2 = 24$).

The Proper Way to Say Goodbye

One important and fundamental principle in structured programming is "one way in, one way out." "One way in" is not an issue with PL/SQL: no matter what kind of loop you are using, there is always only one entry point into the loop—the first executable statement following the LOOP keyword. It is quite possible, however, to construct loops that have multiple exit paths. Avoid this practice. Having multiple ways of terminating a loop results in code that is much harder to debug and maintain.

In particular, you should follow these guidelines for loop termination:

- Do not use EXIT or EXIT WHEN statements within FOR and WHILE loops. You should use a FOR loop only when you want to iterate through *all* the values (integer or record) specified in the range. An EXIT inside a FOR loop disrupts this process and subverts the intent of that structure. A WHILE loop, on the other hand, specifies its termination condition in the WHILE statement itself.
- Do not use the RETURN or GOTO statements within a loop—again, these cause the premature, unstructured termination of the loop. It can be tempting to use these constructs because in the short run they appear to reduce the amount of time spent writing code. In the long run, however, you (or the person left to clean up your mess) will spend more time trying to understand, enhance, and fix your code over time.

Let's look at an example of loop termination issues with the cursor FOR loop. As you have seen, the cursor FOR loop offers many advantages when you want to loop through all of the records returned by a cursor. This type of loop is not appropriate, however, when you need to apply conditions to each fetched record to determine if you should halt execution of the loop. Suppose that you need to scan through each record from a cursor and stop when a total accumulation of a column (like the number of pets) exceeds a maximum, as shown in the following code. Although you can do this with a cursor FOR loop by issuing an EXIT statement inside the loop, that is an inappropriate use of this construct:

```
 1 DECLARE
 2    CURSOR occupancy_cur IS
 3       SELECT pet_id, room_number
 4         FROM occupancy WHERE occupied_dt = TRUNC (SYSDATE;)
 5    pet_count INTEGER := 0;
 6 BEGIN
 7    FOR occupancy_rec IN occupancy_cur
 8    LOOP
 9       update_bill
10          (occupancy_rec.pet_id, occupancy_rec.room_number);
11       pet_count := pet_count + 1;
12       EXIT WHEN pet_count >= :GLOBAL.max_pets;
13    END LOOP;
14 END;
```

The FOR loop explicitly states: "I am going to execute the body of this loop *n* times" (where *n* is a number in a numeric FOR loop, or the number of records in a cursor FOR loop). An EXIT inside the FOR loop (line 12) short-circuits this logic. The result is code that's difficult to follow and debug.

If you need to terminate a loop based on information fetched by the cursor FOR loop, you should use a WHILE loop or a simple loop in its place. Then the structure of the code will more clearly state your intentions.

Obtaining Information About FOR Loop Execution

FOR loops are handy and concise constructs. They handle lots of the "administrative work" in a program; this is especially true of cursor FOR loops. There is, however, a trade-off: by letting Oracle do so much of the work for us, we have limited access to information about the end results of that loop after the loop has been terminated.

Suppose that I want to know how many records I processed in a cursor FOR loop and then execute some logic based on that value. It would be awfully convenient to write code like this:

```
BEGIN
   FOR book_rec IN books_cur (author_in => 'FEUERSTEIN,STEVEN')
   LOOP
      ... process data ...
   END LOOP;
   IF books_cur%ROWCOUNT > 10 THEN ...
```

but if I try it, I get the runtime error *ORA-01001: invalid cursor*. This makes sense, because the cursor is implicitly opened and closed by Oracle. So how can you get this information from a loop that is closed? You will need to declare a variable in the block housing that FOR loop, and then set its value inside the FOR loop so that you can obtain the necessary information about the FOR loop after it has closed. This technique is shown below:

```
DECLARE
   book_count PLS_INTEGER;
BEGIN
   FOR book_rec IN books_cur (author_in => 'FEUERSTEIN,STEVEN')
   LOOP
      ... process data ...
      book_count := books_cur%ROWCOUNT;
   END LOOP;
   IF book_count > 10 THEN ...
```

SQL Statement as Loop

You actually can think of a SQL statement such as SELECT as a loop. After all, such a statement specifies an action to be taken on a set of data; the SQL engine then "loops through" the data set and applies the action. In some cases, you will have a choice between using a PL/SQL loop and a SQL statement to do the same or similar work. Let's look at an example and then draw some conclusions about how you can decide which approach to take.

I need to write a program to move the information for pets who have checked out of the pet hotel from the occupancy table to the occupancy_history table. As a seasoned PL/SQL developer, I immediately settle on a cursor FOR loop. For each record fetched (implicitly) from the cursor (representing a pet who has checked out), the body of the loop first inserts a record into the occupancy_history table and then deletes the record from the occupancy table:

```
DECLARE
   CURSOR checked_out_cur IS
      SELECT pet_id, name, checkout_date
        FROM occupancy WHERE  checkout_date IS NOT NULL;
BEGIN
   FOR checked_out_rec IN checked_out_cur
   LOOP
      INSERT INTO occupancy_history (pet_id, name, checkout_date)
         VALUES (checked_out_rec.pet_id, checked_out_rec.name,
                 checked_out_rec.checkout_date);
      DELETE FROM occupancy WHERE pet_id = checked_out_rec.pet_id;
   END LOOP;
END;
```

This code does the trick. But was it necessary to do it this way? I can express precisely the same logic and get the same result with nothing more than an INSERT-SELECT FROM followed by a DELETE, as shown here:

```
BEGIN
   INSERT INTO occupancy_history (pet_id, NAME, checkout_date)
      SELECT pet_id, NAME, checkout_date
        FROM occupancy WHERE checkout_date IS NOT NULL;
```

```
    DELETE FROM occupancy WHERE checkout_date IS NOT NULL;
END;
```

What are the advantages to this approach? I have written less code, and my code will run more efficiently because I have reduced the number of "context switches" (moving back and forth between the PL/SQL and SQL execution engines). I execute just a single INSERT and a single DELETE.

There are, however, disadvantages to the 100% SQL approach. SQL statements are generally all-or-nothing propositions. In other words, if any one of those individual rows from occupancy_history fails, then the entire INSERT fails; no records are inserted or deleted. Also, the WHERE clause had to be coded twice. Though not a significant factor in this example, it may well be when substantially more complex queries are involved. The initial cursor FOR loop thus obviated the need to potentially maintain complex logic in multiple places.

PL/SQL offers more flexibility as well. Suppose, for example, that I want to transfer as many of the rows as possible, and simply write a message to the error log for any transfers of individual rows that fail. In this case, I really do need to rely on the cursor FOR loop, but with the added functionality of an EXCEPTION section:

```
BEGIN
   FOR checked_out_rec IN checked_out_cur
   LOOP
      BEGIN
         INSERT INTO occupancy_history ...
         DELETE FROM occupancy ...
      EXCEPTION
         WHEN OTHERS THEN
            log_checkout_error (checked_out_rec);
      END;
   END LOOP;
END;
;
```

PL/SQL offers the ability to access and process a single row at a time, and to take action (and, perhaps, complex procedural logic based on the contents of that specific record). When that's what you need, use a blend of PL/SQL and SQL. If, on the other hand, your requirements allow you to use native SQL, you will find that you can use less code and that it will run more efficiently.

CHAPTER 6

Exception Handlers

In this chapter:

- How PL/SQL Deals with Errors
- Defining Exceptions
- Raising Exceptions
- Handling Exceptions

It is a sad fact of life that most programmers never take the time to properly bulletproof their programs. Instead, wishful thinking often reigns. Most of us find it hard enough—and more than enough work—to simply write the code that implements the positive aspects of an application: maintaining customers, generating invoices, and so on. It is devilishly difficult, from both a psychological standpoint and a resources perspective, to focus on the negative: for example, what happens when the user presses the wrong key? If the database is unavailable, what should I do?

As a result, we write applications that assume the best of all possible worlds, hoping that our programs are bug-free, that users will enter only the correct data in only the correct fashion, and that all systems (hardware and software) will always be a "go."

Of course, harsh reality dictates that no matter how hard you try, there will always be one more bug in your application. And your users will somehow always find just the right sequence of keystrokes to make a form implode. The challenge is clear: either you spend the time up-front to properly debug and bulletproof your programs, or you fight an unending series of rear-guard battles, taking frantic calls from your users and putting out the fires.

You know what you should do. Fortunately, PL/SQL offers a powerful and flexible way to trap and handle errors. It is entirely feasible within the PL/SQL language to build an application that fully protects the user and the database from errors.

How PL/SQL Deals with Errors

In the PL/SQL language, errors of any kind are treated as *exceptions*—situations that should not occur—in your program. An exception can be one of the following:

- An error generated by the system (such as "out of memory" or "duplicate value in index")
- An error caused by a user action
- A warning issued by the application to the user

PL/SQL traps and responds to errors using an architecture of *exception handlers*. The exception handler mechanism allows you to cleanly separate your error processing code from your executable statements. It also provides an *event-driven* model, as opposed to a linear code model, for processing errors. In other words, no matter how a particular exception is raised, it is handled by the same exception handler in the exception section.

When an error occurs in PL/SQL, whether it's a system error or an application error, an exception is raised. The processing in the current PL/SQL block's execution section halts, and control is transferred to the separate exception section of the current block, if one exists, to handle the exception. You cannot return to that block after you finish handling the exception. Instead, control is passed to the enclosing block, if any.

Figure 6-1 illustrates how control is transferred to the exception section when an exception is raised.

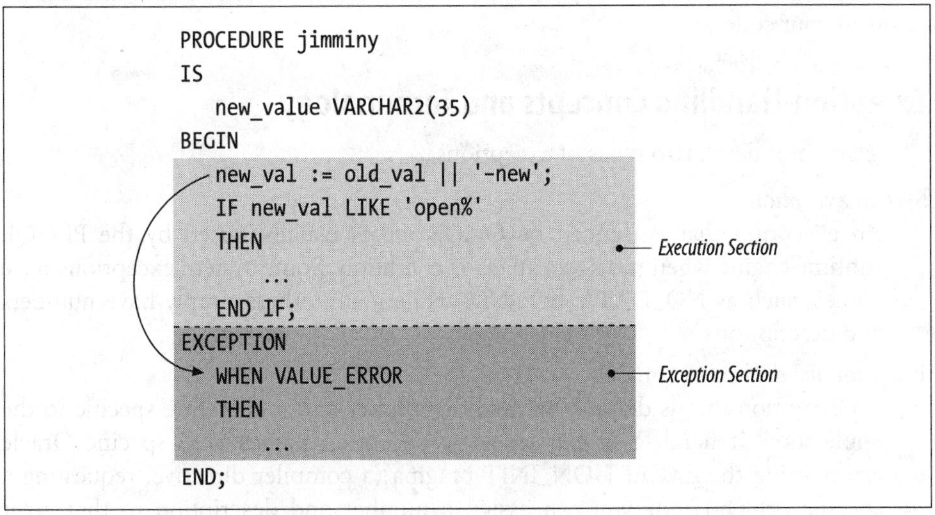

```
PROCEDURE jimminy
IS
   new_value VARCHAR2(35)
BEGIN
   new_val := old_val || '-new';
   IF new_val LIKE 'open%'
   THEN
      ...
   END IF;
EXCEPTION
   WHEN VALUE_ERROR
   THEN
      ...
END;
```


Figure 6-1. Exception-handling architecture

Adopting an Exception-Handling Strategy

PL/SQL exception handling is very powerful and flexible, but it can also be confusing and tricky. It is extremely important to establish a consistent strategy and architecture for error handling in your application *before* you write any code. To do that, you must answer questions like these:

- How and when do I log errors so that they can be reviewed and corrected?
- How and when do I report the occurrence of errors back to the user?

Linked tightly to these very high-level questions are more concrete issues, such as:

- Should I include an exception-handling section in every one of my PL/SQL blocks?
- Should I have an exception-handling section only in the top-level or outermost blocks?
- How should I manage my transactions when errors occur?

Part of the complexity of exception handling is that there is no single right answer to any of these questions. It depends at least in part on the application architecture and the way it is used (batch process versus user-driven transactions, for example). However you answer these questions for your application, I strongly suggest that you "codify" the strategy and rules for error handling within a standardized package. I address this topic at the end of the chapter.

The rest of this chapter introduces the concepts behind PL/SQL exception handling, explains the different types of exceptions, and shows how to both raise and handle errors in your code.

Exception-Handling Concepts and Terminology

There are, in general, two types of exceptions:

System exception
: An exception that is defined by Oracle and is usually raised by the PL/SQL runtime engine when it detects an error condition. Some system exceptions have names, such as NO_DATA_FOUND, while many others simply have numbers and descriptions.

Programmer-defined exception
: An exception that is defined by the programmer and is therefore specific to the application at hand. You can associate exception names with specific Oracle errors using the EXCEPTION_INIT pragma (a compiler directive, requesting a specific behavior), or you can assign a number and description to that error using RAISE_APPLICATION_ERROR.

The following terms will be used throughout this chapter:

Exception section
: The optional section in a PL/SQL block (anonymous block, procedure, function, trigger, or initialization section of a package) that contains one or more "handlers" for exceptions. The structure of an exception section is very similar to a CASE statement, which we discussed in Chapter 4.

Raise
: Stops execution of the current PL/SQL block by notifying the runtime engine of an error. Oracle itself can raise exceptions, or your own code can raise an exception with either the RAISE or RAISE_APPLICATION_ERROR command.

Handle (used as a verb), handler (used as a noun)
: "Traps" an error within an exception section. You can then write code in the *handler* to process that error, which might involve recording the error occurrence in a log, displaying a message to the user, or propagating an exception out of the current block.

Scope
: The portion of code (whether in a particular block or for an entire session) in which an exception can be raised. Also, that portion of code for which an exception section can trap and handle exceptions that are raised.

Propagation
: The process by which exceptions are passed from one block to its enclosing block if the exception goes unhandled in that block.

Unhandled exception
: An exception is said to go "unhandled" when it propagates without being handled out of the outermost PL/SQL block. Control then passes back to the host execution environment, at which point that environment/program determines how to respond to the exception (roll back the transaction, display an error, ignore it, etc.).

Un-named or anonymous exception
: An exception that has an error code and a description associated with it, but does not have a name that can be used in a RAISE statement or in an exception handler WHEN clause.

Named exception
: An exception that has been given a name, either by Oracle in one of its built-in packages or by a developer. You can also associate a name with this exception through the use of the EXCEPTION_INIT pragma, or leave it defined only by its name (which can be used to both raise and handle the exception).

Defining Exceptions

Before an exception can be raised or handled, it must be defined. Oracle predefines thousands of exceptions, mostly by assigning numbers and messages to those exceptions. Oracle also assigns names to a few of the most commonly encountered exceptions.

You can define or declare your own exceptions for use in your applications in two different ways, described in the following sections.

Declaring Named Exceptions

The exceptions that PL/SQL has declared in the STANDARD package (and other built-in packages) cover internal or system-generated errors. Many of the problems a user will encounter (or cause) in an application, however, are specific to that application. Your program might need to trap and handle errors such as "negative balance in account" or "call date cannot be in the past." While different in nature from "division by zero," these errors are still exceptions to normal processing and should be handled gracefully by your program.

One of the most useful aspects of the PL/SQL exception-handling model is that it does not make any structural distinction between internal errors and application-specific errors. Once an exception is raised, it can and should be handled in the exception section, regardless of the type or source of error.

Of course, to handle an exception, you must have a name for that exception. Because PL/SQL cannot name these exceptions for you (they are specific to your application), you must do so yourself by declaring an exception in the declaration section of your PL/SQL block. You declare an exception by listing the name of the exception you want to raise in your program followed by the keyword EXCEPTION:

```
exception_name EXCEPTION;
```

The following declaration section of the calc_annual_sales procedure contains two programmer-defined exception declarations:

```
PROCEDURE calc_annual_sales
   (company_id_in IN company.company_id%TYPE)
IS
   invalid_company_id   EXCEPTION;
   negative_balance     EXCEPTION;

   duplicate_company    BOOLEAN;
BEGIN
   ... body of executable statements ...
EXCEPTION
         ...
   WHEN NO_DATA_FOUND   -- system exception
   THEN
      ...
   WHEN invalid_company_id
   THEN

   WHEN negative_balance
   THEN
      ...
END;
```

The names for exceptions are similar in format to (and "read" just like) Boolean variable names, but can be referenced in only two ways:

- In a RAISE statement in the execution section of the program (to raise the exception), as in:

```
RAISE invalid_company_id;
```

- In the WHEN clauses of the exception section (to handle the raised exception), as in:

```
WHEN invalid_company_id THEN
```

Associating Exception Names with Error Codes

Oracle has given names to just a handful of exceptions. Thousands of other error conditions within the RDBMS are defined by nothing more than an error number and a message. In addition, a developer can raise exceptions using RAISE_APPLICATION_ERROR (covered later under "Raising Exceptions") that consist of nothing more than an error number (between –20000 and –20999) and an error message.

Exceptions without names are perfectly legitimate, but they can lead to code that is hard to read and maintain. Suppose, for example, that I write a program in which I know Oracle might raise a date-related error, such as *ORA-01843: not a valid month*. I could write an exception handler to trap that error with code that looks like this:

```
EXCEPTION
   WHEN OTHERS THEN
      IF SQLCODE = -1843 THEN
```

but that is very obscure code, begging for a comment—or some sort of clarity.

SQLCODE is a built-in function that returns the number of the last error raised; it is discussed later in this chapter under "Handling Exceptions."

Using EXCEPTION_INIT

With the EXCEPTION_INIT pragma, I can replace the WHEN clause shown in the previous example with something like this:

```
EXCEPTION
   WHEN invalid_month THEN
```

No more hardcoded literal error numbers that are difficult to remember. Now I have a self-documenting name. Let's see how we can accomplish this.

EXCEPTION_INIT is a compile-time command or *pragma* used to associate a name with an internal error code. EXCEPTION_INIT instructs the compiler to associate an identifier, declared as an EXCEPTION, with a specific error number. Once you have made that association, you can then raise that exception by name and write an explicit WHEN handler that traps the error.

The pragma EXCEPTION_INIT must appear in the declaration section of a block; the exception named must have already been defined in that same block, an enclosing block, or a package specification. Here is the syntax in an anonymous block:

```
DECLARE
   exception_name EXCEPTION;
   PRAGMA EXCEPTION_INIT (exception_name, integer);
```

where *exception_name* is the name of an exception and *integer* is a literal integer value, the number of the Oracle error with which you want to associate the named exception. The error number can be any integer value with these constraints:

- It cannot be –1403 (the error code for NO_DATA_FOUND). If for some reason you want to associate your own named exception with this error, you need to pass 100 to the EXCEPTION_INIT pragma. (NO_DATA_FOUND is the only error I know of in Oracle that has two different error numbers, a consequence of ANSI standards compliance requiring the use of the error 100 for this condition.)
- It cannot be 0 or any positive number besides 1.
- It cannot be a negative number less than –10000000.

Let's look at an example. In the following program code, I declare and associate an exception for this error:

```
ORA-2292 violated integrity constraining (OWNER.CONSTRAINT) -
         child record found.
```

This error occurs if I try to delete a parent record while there are child records still in that table. (A *child record* is a record with a foreign key reference to the parent table.)

```
PROCEDURE delete_company (company_id_in IN NUMBER)
IS
   /* Declare the exception. */
   still_have_employees EXCEPTION;

   /* Associate the exception name with an error number. */
   PRAGMA EXCEPTION_INIT (still_have_employees, -2292);
BEGIN
   /* Try to delete the company. */
   DELETE FROM company
    WHERE company_id = company_id_in;
EXCEPTION
   /* If child records were found, this exception is raised! */
   WHEN still_have_employees
   THEN
      DBMS_OUTPUT.PUT_LINE
         (' Please delete employees for company first.');
END;
```

Recommended uses of EXCEPTION_INIT

You will find this pragma most useful in two circumstances:

- Giving names to otherwise anonymous system exceptions that you commonly reference in your code. In other words, Oracle did not predefine a name for the error; you have only the number with which to work.
- Assigning names to the application-specific errors you raise using RAISE_APPLICATION_ERROR (see "Raising Exceptions"). This allows you to handle such errors by name, rather than simply by number.

In both cases, I recommend that you centralize your usage of EXCEPTION_INIT into packages so that the definitions of exceptions are not scattered throughout your code. Suppose, for example, that I am doing lots of work with dynamic SQL (described in Chapter 15). I might then encounter "invalid column name" errors as I construct my dynamic queries. I don't want to have to remember what the code is for this error, and it's silly to define my pragmas in 20 different programs. So instead I predefine my own "system exceptions" in my own dynamic SQL package:

```
CREATE OR REPLACE PACKAGE dynsql
IS
   invalid_table_name EXCEPTION;
      PRAGMA EXCEPTION_INIT (invalid_table_name, -903);
   invalid_column_name EXCEPTION;
      PRAGMA EXCEPTION_INIT (invalid_column_name, -904);
```

and now I can trap for these errors in any program as follows:

```
WHEN dynsql.invalid_column_name THEN ...
```

I also suggest that you take this same approach when working with the –20,*NNN* error codes passed to RAISE_APPLICATION_ERROR. Avoid hardcoding these literals directly into your application; instead, build (or generate) a package that assigns names to those error numbers. Here is an example of such a package:

```
PACKAGE errnums
IS
   en_too_young CONSTANT NUMBER := -20001;
   exc_too_young EXCEPTION;
   PRAGMA EXCEPTION_INIT
     (exc_too_young, -20001);

   en_sal_too_low CONSTANT NUMBER := -20002;
   exc_sal_too_low EXCEPTION;
   PRAGMA EXCEPTION_INIT
     (exc_sal_too_low , -20002);
END errnums;
```

By relying on such a package, I can write code like the following, without embedding the actual error number in the logic:

```
PROCEDURE validate_emp (birthdate_in IN DATE)
IS
   min_years CONSTANT PLS_INTEGER := 18
BEGIN
   IF ADD_MONTHS (SYSDATE, min_years * 12 * -1) < birthdate_in
   THEN
      RAISE_APPLICATION_ERROR
         (errnums.en_too_young,
          'Employee must be at least ' || min_years || ' old.');
   END IF;
END;
```

About Named System Exceptions

Oracle gives names to a relatively small number of system exceptions by including EXCEPTION_INIT pragma statements in built-in package specifications.

The most important and commonly used set of named exceptions may be found in the STANDARD package in PL/SQL. This package is one of the two default packages of PL/SQL (the other is DBMS_STANDARD). This means that you can reference these exceptions without including the package name as a prefix. So, for instance, if I want to raise the NO_DATA_FOUND exception in my code, I can do so with either of these statements:

```
WHEN NO_DATA_FOUND THEN
WHEN STANDARD.NO_DATA_FOUND THEN
```

You can find predefined exceptions in other built-in packages such as DBMS_LOB, the package used to manipulate large objects. Here is an example of one such definition in that package's specification:

```
invalid_argval EXCEPTION;
    PRAGMA EXCEPTION_INIT(invalid_argval, -21560);
```

Because DBMS_LOB is not a default package, when I reference this exception, I need to include the package name:

```
WHEN DBMS_LOB.invalid_argval THEN...
```

Many of the STANDARD-based predefined exceptions are listed in Table 6-1, each with its Oracle error number, the value returned by a call to SQLCODE, and a brief description. SQLCODE is a PL/SQL built-in function that returns the status code of the last-executed SQL or DML statement. SQLCODE returns zero if the last statement executed without errors. In all but one case (100, the ANSI standard error number for NO_DATA_FOUND), the SQLCODE value is the same as the Oracle error code.

Table 6-1. Predefined exceptions in PL/SQL

Name of exception Oracle error/SQLCODE	Description
CURSOR_ALREADY_OPEN ORA-6511 SQLCODE=-6511	You tried to OPEN a cursor that was already OPEN. You must CLOSE a cursor before you try to OPEN or re-OPEN it.
DUP_VAL_ON_INDEX ORA-00001 SQLCODE=-1	Your INSERT or UPDATE statement attempted to store duplicate values in a column or columns in a row that is restricted by a unique index.
INVALID_CURSOR ORA-01001 SQLCODE=-1001	You made reference to a cursor that did not exist. This usually happens when you try to FETCH from a cursor or CLOSE a cursor before that cursor is OPENed.
INVALID_NUMBER ORA-01722 SQLCODE = -1722	PL/SQL executes a SQL statement that cannot convert a character string successfully to a number. This exception is different from the VALUE_ERROR exception, as it is raised only from within a SQL statement.

Table 6-1. Predefined exceptions in PL/SQL (continued)

Name of exception Oracle error/SQLCODE	Description
LOGIN_DENIED ORA–01017 SQLCODE= –1017	Your program tried to log into the Oracle RDBMS with an invalid username-password combination. This exception is usually encountered when you embed PL/SQL in a 3GL language.
NO_DATA_FOUND ORA–01403 SQLCODE= +100	This exception is raised in three different scenarios: (1) You executed a SELECT INTO statement (implicit cursor) that returned no rows. (2) You referenced an uninitialized row in a local PL/SQL table. (3) You read past end-of-file with the UTL_FILE package.
NOT_LOGGED_ON ORA–01012 SQLCODE= –1012	Your program tried to execute a call to the database (usually with a DML statement) before it had logged into the Oracle RDBMS.
PROGRAM_ERROR ORA–06501 SQLCODE= –6501	PL/SQL encounters an internal problem. The message text usually also tells you to "Contact Oracle Support."
STORAGE_ERROR ORA–06500 SQLCODE= –6500	Your program ran out of memory, or memory was in some way corrupted.
TIMEOUT_ON_RESOURCE ORA–00051 SQLCODE= –51	A timeout occurred in the RDBMS while waiting for a resource.
TOO_MANY_ROWS ORA–01422 SQLCODE= –1422	A SELECT INTO statement returned more than one row. A SELECT INTO can return only one row; if your SQL statement returns more than one row, you should place the SELECT statement in an explicit CURSOR declaration and FETCH from that cursor one row at a time.
TRANSACTION_BACKED_OUT ORA–00061 SQLCODE= –61	The remote part of a transaction is rolled back, either with an explicit ROLLBACK command or as the result of some other action (such as a failed SQL/DML on the remote database).
VALUE_ERROR ORA–06502 SQLCODE= –6502	PL/SQL encountered an error having to do with the conversion, truncation, or invalid constraining of numeric and character data. This is a very general and common exception. If this type of error is encountered in a SQL DML statement within a PL/SQL block, then the INVALID_NUMBER exception is raised.
ZERO_DIVIDE ORA–01476 SQLCODE= –1476	Your program tried to divide by zero.

Here is an example of how you might use the exceptions table. Suppose that your program generates an unhandled exception for error ORA–6511. Looking up this error, you find that it is associated with the CURSOR_ALREADY_OPEN exception. Locate the PL/SQL block in which the error occurs and add an exception handler for CURSOR_ALREADY_OPEN, as shown here:

```
EXCEPTION
   WHEN CURSOR_ALREADY_OPEN
   THEN
      CLOSE my_cursor;
END;
```

Of course, you would be even better off analyzing your code to determine proactively which of the predefined exceptions might occur. Then you could decide which of those exceptions you want to handle specifically, which should be covered by the WHEN OTHERS clause, and which would best be left unhandled.

Scope of an Exception

The *scope* of an exception is that portion of the code that is "covered" by that exception. An exception covers a block of code if it can be raised in that block. The following table shows the scope for each of the different kinds of exceptions:

Exception type	Description of scope
Named system exceptions	These exceptions are globally available because they are not declared in or confined to any particular block of code. You can raise and handle a named system exception in any block.
Named programmer-defined exceptions	These exceptions can be raised and handled only in the execution and exception sections of the block in which they are declared (and all nested blocks). If the exception is defined in a package specification, its scope is every program whose owner has EXECUTE authority on that package.
Anonymous system exceptions	These exceptions can be handled in any PL/SQL exception section via the WHEN OTHERS section. If they are assigned a name, then the scope of that name is the same as that of the named programmer-defined exception.
Anonymous programmer-defined exceptions	These exceptions are defined only in the call to RAISE_APPLICATION_ERROR, and then are passed back to the calling program.

Consider the following example of the exception overdue_balance declared in the procedure check_account. The scope of that exception is the check_account procedure, and nothing else:

```
PROCEDURE check_account (company_id_in IN NUMBER)
IS
   overdue_balance EXCEPTION;
BEGIN
   ... executable statements ...
   LOOP
      ...
      IF ... THEN
         RAISE overdue_balance;
      END IF;
   END LOOP;
EXCEPTION
   WHEN overdue_balance THEN ...
END;
```

I can RAISE the overdue_balance inside the check_account procedure, but I cannot raise that exception from a program that calls check_account. The following anonymous block will generate a compile error, as shown below:

```
DECLARE
   company_id NUMBER := 100;
BEGIN
   check_account (100);
EXCEPTION
   WHEN overdue_balance /* PL/SQL cannot resolve this reference. */
   THEN ...
END;

PLS-00201: identifier "OVERDUE_BALANCE" must be declared
```

The check_account procedure is a "black box" as far as the anonymous block is concerned. Any identifiers—including exceptions—declared inside check_account are invisible outside of that program.

Raising Exceptions

There are three ways that an exception may be raised in your application:

- Oracle might raise the exception when it detects an error.
- You might raise an exception with the RAISE statement.
- You might raise an exception with the RAISE_APPLICATION_ERROR built-in procedure.

We've already looked at how Oracle raises exceptions. Now let's examine the different mechanisms you can use to raise exceptions.

The RAISE Statement

Oracle offers the RAISE statement so that you can, at your discretion, raise a named exception. You can raise an exception of your own or a system exception. The RAISE statement can take one of three forms:

```
RAISE exception_name;
RAISE package_name.exception_name;
RAISE;
```

The first form (without a package name qualifier) can be used to raise an exception you have defined in the current block (or an outer block containing that block) or to raise a system exception defined in the STANDARD package. Here are two examples, first raising a programmer-defined exception:

```
DECLARE
   invalid_id EXCEPTION; -- All IDs must start with the letter 'X'.
   id_value VARCHAR2;
BEGIN
   id_value := id_for ('SMITH');
   IF SUBSTR (id_value, 1, 1) != 'X'
   THEN
      RAISE invalid_id;
   END IF;
   ...
END;
```

And then you can always raise a system exception as needed:

```
BEGIN
   IF total_sales = 0
   THEN
      RAISE ZERO_DIVIDE; -- Defined in STANDARD package
   ELSE
```

```
      RETURN (sales_percentage_calculation  (my_sales, total_sales));
   END IF;
END;
```

The second form does require a package name qualifier. If an exception has been declared inside a package (other than STANDARD) and you are raising that exception outside that package, you must qualify your reference to that exception in your RAISE statement, as in:

```
IF days_overdue (isbn_in, borrower_in) > 365
THEN
   RAISE overdue_pkg.book_is_lost;
END IF;
```

The third form of the RAISE statement does not require an exception name, but can be used only within a WHEN clause of the exception section. Its syntax is simply:

```
RAISE;
```

Use this form when you want to re-raise (or propagate out) the same exception from within an exception handler, as you see here:

```
EXCEPTION
   WHEN NO_DATA_FOUND
   THEN
      -- Use common package to record all the "context" information,
      -- such as error code, program name, etc.
      errlog.putline (company_id_in);
      -- And now pass NO_DATA_FOUND unhandled to the enclosing block.
      RAISE;
```

This feature is useful when you want to log the fact that an error occurred, but then pass that same error out to the enclosing block. That way, you record where the error occurred in your application, but still stop the enclosing block(s) without losing the error information.

Raising exceptions in nested blocks

When you declare an exception in a block, it is local to that block, but global to all the blocks enclosed by that block (nested blocks). In the version of check_account shown in the following example, the procedure contains an anonymous sub-block that also raises the overdue_balance. Because the sub-block is enclosed by the procedure block, PL/SQL can resolve the reference to that exception:

```
PROCEDURE check_account (company_id_in IN NUMBER)
IS
   overdue_balance EXCEPTION;
BEGIN
   ... executable statements ...

   -- Start of sub-block inside check_account
   BEGIN
      ... statements within sub-block ...
```

```
      RAISE overdue_balance;  -- Exception raised in sub-block.
   END;
   -- End of sub-block inside check_account

   LOOP
      ...
      IF ... THEN
         RAISE overdue_balance; -- Exception raised in main block.
      END IF;
   END LOOP;

EXCEPTION
   WHEN overdue_balance THEN ... -- Exception handled in main block.
END;
```

When the overdue_balance exception is raised in either the sub-block or the main block, control is transferred immediately to the main block—the only exception section in the entire procedure. Because overdue_balance was declared for the whole procedure, the name is known throughout all sub-blocks.

Using RAISE_APPLICATION_ERROR

Oracle provides the RAISE_APPLICATION_ERROR procedure (defined in the default DBMS_STANDARD package) to raise application-specific errors in your application. The advantage to using RAISE_APPLICATION_ERROR instead of RAISE (which can also raise an application-specific, explicitly declared exception) is that you can associate an error message with the exception.

When this procedure is run, execution of the current PL/SQL block halts immediately, and any changes made to OUT or IN OUT arguments (if present) will be reversed. Changes made to global data structures, such as packaged variables, and to database objects (by executing an INSERT, UPDATE, or DELETE) will *not* be rolled back. You must execute an explicit ROLLBACK in your exception section to reverse the effect of DML operations.

The header for this procedure (defined in package DBMS_STANDARD) is shown here:

```
PROCEDURE RAISE_APPLICATION_ERROR (
   num binary_integer,
   msg varchar2,
   keeperrorstack boolean default FALSE);
```

where *num* is the error number and must be a value between –20,999 and –20,000 (just think: Oracle needs all the rest of those negative integers for its *own* exceptions!); *msg* is the error message and must be no more than 2K characters in length (any text beyond that limit will be ignored); and *keeperrorstack* indicates whether you want to add the error to any already on the stack (TRUE) or replace the existing errors (the default, FALSE).

Oracle is supposed to have set aside the range of –20,999 and –20,000 for use by its customers, but be warned: several built-in packages, including DBMS_OUTPUT and DBMS_DESCRIBE, use error numbers –20,000 through –20,005. This is very rude, but they do it. See the package documentation for descriptions of usage.

Let's take a look at one useful application of this built-in. Suppose that I need to support error messages in different languages for my user community. I create a separate error_table to store all these messages, segregated by the string_language value. I then create a procedure to raise the specified error, grabbing the appropriate error message from the table based on the NLS_LANGUAGE parameter value:

```
/* File on web: raise_by_language.sp */
CREATE OR REPLACE PROCEDURE raise_by_language (code_in IN PLS_INTEGER)
IS
   l_message error_table.error_string;
BEGIN
   SELECT error_string
     INTO l_message
     FROM error_table, v$nls_parameters v
    WHERE error_number = code_in
      AND string_language  = v.VALUE
      AND v.parameter = 'NLS_LANGUAGE';

   RAISE_APPLICATION_ERROR (code_in, l_message);
END;
```

When you make use of RAISE_APPLICATION_ERROR, it is entirely up to you to manage the error numbers and messages. This can get tricky and messy ("Gee, which number should I use? Well, I doubt that anyone would be using –20774!"). To help manage your error codes and provide a consistent interface with which developers can handle server errors, consider building a table to store all the –20,*NNN* error numbers you use, along with their associated exception names and error messages. Developers can then view these already-defined errors via a screen and choose the one that fits their situation. See the *msginfo.pkg* file available on the O'Reilly site for one such example of a table, along with code that will generate a package containing declarations of each of the "registered" exceptions.

Handling Exceptions

Once an exception is raised, the current PL/SQL block stops its regular execution and transfers control to the exception section. The exception is then either handled by an exception handler in the current PL/SQL block or passed to the enclosing block.

To handle or trap an exception once it is raised, you must write an exception handler for that exception. In your code, your exception handlers must appear after all the executable statements in your program but before the END statement of the block. The EXCEPTION keyword indicates the start of the exception section and the individual exception handlers:

```
DECLARE
   ... declarations ...
BEGIN
   ... executable statements ...
[ EXCEPTION
   ... exception handlers ... ]
END;
```

The syntax for an exception handler is as follows:

```
WHEN exception_name [ OR exception_name ... ]
THEN
      executable statements
```

or:

```
WHEN OTHERS
THEN
   executable statements
```

You can have multiple exception handlers in a single exception section. The exception handlers are structured much like a conditional CASE statement, as shown in the following table:

Exception section	English-like translation

EXCEPTION
   WHEN NO_DATA_FOUND
   THEN
      executable_statements1;
	If the NO_DATA_FOUND exception is raised, then execute the first set of statements.

WHEN payment_overdue THEN executable_statements2;	If the payment is overdue, then execute the second set of statements.
WHEN OTHERS THEN executable_statements3; END;	If any other exception is encountered, then execute the third set of statements.

An exception is handled if an exception that is named in a WHEN clause matches the exception that was raised. Notice that the WHEN clause traps errors only by exception name, not by error codes. If a match is found, then the executable statements associated with that exception are run. If the exception that has been raised is not handled or does not match any of the named exceptions, the executable statements associated with the WHEN OTHERS clause (if present) will be run. Only one exception handler can catch a particular error. After the statements for that handler are executed, control passes immediately out of the block.

The WHEN OTHERS clause is optional; if it is not present, then any unhandled exception is immediately propagated back to the enclosing block, if any. The WHEN OTHERS clause must be the last exception handler in the exception section. If you place any other WHEN clauses after WHEN OTHERS, you will receive the following compilation error:

```
PLS-00370: OTHERS handler must be last among the exception handlers of a block
```

Combining Multiple Exceptions in a Single Handler

You can, within a single WHEN clause, combine multiple exceptions together with an OR operator, just as you would combine multiple Boolean expressions:

```
WHEN invalid_company_id OR negative_balance
THEN
```

You can also combine application and system exception names in a single handler:

```
WHEN balance_too_low OR ZERO_DIVIDE OR DBMS_LDAP.INVALID_SESSION
THEN
```

You cannot, however, use the AND operator, because only one exception can be raised at a time.

Unhandled Exceptions

If an exception is raised in your program and it is not handled by an exception section in either the current or enclosing PL/SQL blocks, that exception is *unhandled*. PL/SQL returns the error that raised the unhandled exception all the way back to the application environment from which PL/SQL was run. That environment (a tool like SQL*Plus, Oracle Forms, or a Java program) then takes an action appropriate to the situation; in the case of SQL*Plus, a ROLLBACK of any DML changes from within that top-level block's logic is automatically performed.

One key decision to make about your application architecture is whether you want to allow unhandled exceptions to occur at all. They are handled differently by different front ends, and in some cases none too gracefully. If your PL/SQL programs are being called from a non-PL/SQL environment, you may want to design your outermost blocks or programs to do the following:

- Trap any exception that might have propagated out to that point.
- Log the error so that a developer can analyze what might be the cause of the problem.
- Pass back a status code, description, and any other information needed by the host environment to make a determination about an appropriate action to take.

Using SQLCODE and SQLERRM in Handler Clauses

You can use the WHEN OTHERS clause in the exception section to trap any otherwise unhandled exceptions. Once inside the exception handler, however, you will often want to know which error occurred. You can use the SQLCODE function to obtain this information. SQLCODE returns the current error number (0 indicates that there is no error on the error stack); SQLERRM returns the error message for the current error or whatever error number you pass to it.

Combined with WHEN OTHERS, SQLCODE provides a way for you to handle different, specific exceptions without having to use the EXCEPTION_INIT pragma. In the next example, I trap two parent-child exceptions, –2292 and –2291, and then take an action appropriate to each situation:

```
PROCEDURE delete_company (company_id_in IN NUMBER)
IS
BEGIN
   DELETE FROM company  WHERE company_id = company_id_in;
EXCEPTION
   WHEN OTHERS
   THEN
      /*
      || Anonymous block inside the exception handler lets me declare
      || local variables to hold the error code information.
      */
      DECLARE
         error_code NUMBER := SQLCODE;
         error_msg  VARCHAR2 (512) := SQLERRM; -- Maximum length of SQLERRM string.
      BEGIN
         IF error_code = -2292
         THEN
            /* Child records found. Delete those too! */
            DELETE FROM employee WHERE company_id = company_id_in;

            /* Now delete parent again. */
            DELETE FROM company   WHERE company_id = company_id_in;

         ELSIF error_code = -2291
         THEN
            /* Parent key not found. */
            DBMS_OUTPUT.PUTLINE  (' Invalid company ID: '||TO_CHAR (company_id_in));
         ELSE
            /* This is like a WHEN OTHERS inside a WHEN OTHERS! */
            DBMS_OUTPUT.PUTLINE  (' Error deleting company, error: '||error_msg);
         END IF;
      END; -- End of anonymous block.

END delete_company;
```

Continuing Past Exceptions

When an exception is raised in a PL/SQL block, normal execution is halted and control is transferred to the exception section. You can never return to the execution section once an exception is raised in that block. In some cases, however, the ability to continue past exceptions is exactly the desired behavior.

Consider the following scenario: I need to write a procedure that performs a series of DML statements against a variety of tables (delete from one table, update another, insert into a final table). My first pass at writing this procedure might produce code like the following:

```
PROCEDURE change_data IS
BEGIN
   DELETE FROM employee WHERE ... ;
   UPDATE company SET ... ;
   INSERT INTO company_history SELECT * FROM company WHERE ... ;
END;
```

This procedure certainly contains all the appropriate DML statements. But one of the requirements for this program is that, although these statements are executed in sequence, they are logically independent of each other. In other words, even if the DELETE fails, I want to go on and perform the UPDATE and INSERT.

With the current version of change_data, I cannot make sure that all three DML statements will at least be attempted. If an exception is raised from the DELETE, for example, then the entire program's execution will halt and control will be passed to the exception section, if there is one. The remaining SQL statements will not be executed.

How can I get the exception to be raised and handled without terminating the program as a whole? The solution is to place the DELETE within its own PL/SQL block. Consider this next version of the change_data program:

```
PROCEDURE change_data IS
BEGIN
   BEGIN
      DELETE FROM employee WHERE ... ;
   EXCEPTION
      WHEN OTHERS THEN NULL;
   END;

   BEGIN
      UPDATE company SET ... ;
   EXCEPTION
      WHEN OTHERS THEN NULL;
   END;

   BEGIN
      INSERT INTO company_history SELECT * FROM company WHERE ... ;
   EXCEPTION
      WHEN OTHERS THEN NULL;
   END;
END;
```

With this new format, if the DELETE raises an exception, control is immediately passed to the exception section. But what a difference! Because the DELETE statement is now in its own block, it can have its own exception section. The WHEN OTHERS clause in that section smoothly handles the error by doing nothing. Control is then passed out of the DELETE's block and back to the enclosing change_data procedure.

Execution in this enclosing block then continues to the next statement in the procedure. A new anonymous block is then entered for the UPDATE statement. If the UPDATE statement fails, the WHEN OTHERS in the UPDATE's own exception section traps the problem and returns control to change_data, which blithely moves on to the INSERT statement (contained in its very own block).

Figure 6-2 shows this process for two sequential DELETE statements.

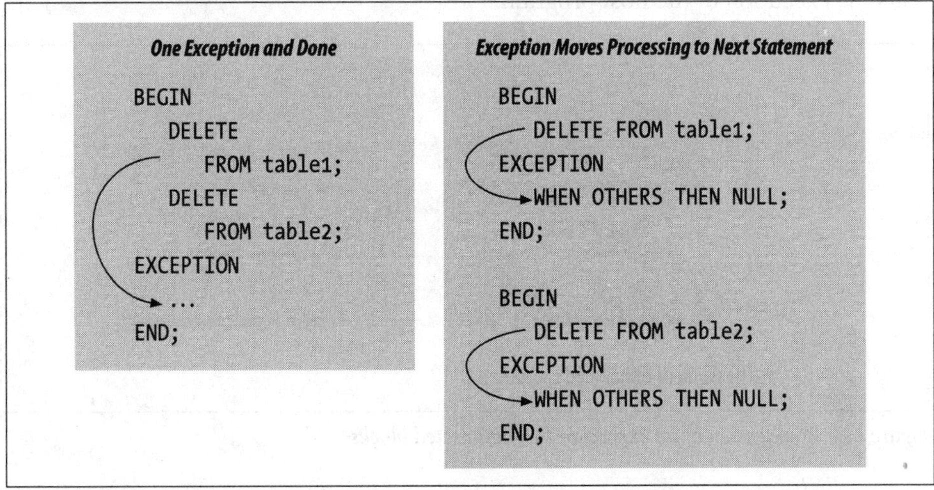

Figure 6-2. Sequential DELETEs, using two different approaches to scope

To summarize: a raised exception will always be handled in the current block—if there is a matching handler present. You can create a "virtual block" around any statement(s) by prefacing it with a BEGIN and following it with an EXCEPTION section and an END statement. In this way you can control the scope of failure caused by an exception by establishing "buffers" of anonymous blocks in your code.

You can also take this strategy a step further and move the code you want to isolate into separate procedures or functions. Of course, these named PL/SQL blocks may also have their own exception sections and will offer the same protection from total failure. One key advantage of using procedures and functions is that you hide all the BEGIN-EXCEPTION-END statements from the mainline program. The program is then easier to read, understand, maintain, and reuse in multiple contexts.

Propagation of an Unhandled Exception

The scope rules for exceptions determine the block in which an exception can be raised. The rules for exception propagation address the way in which an exception is handled after it is raised.

When an exception is raised, PL/SQL looks for an exception handler in the current block (anonymous block, procedure, or function) of the exception. If it does not find a match, then PL/SQL *propagates* the exception to the enclosing block of that current block. PL/SQL then attempts to handle the exception by raising it once more in the enclosing block. It continues to do this in each successive enclosing block until there are no more blocks in which to raise the exception (see Figure 6-3). When all blocks are exhausted, PL/SQL returns an unhandled exception to the application environment that executed the outermost PL/SQL block. An unhandled exception halts the execution of the host program.

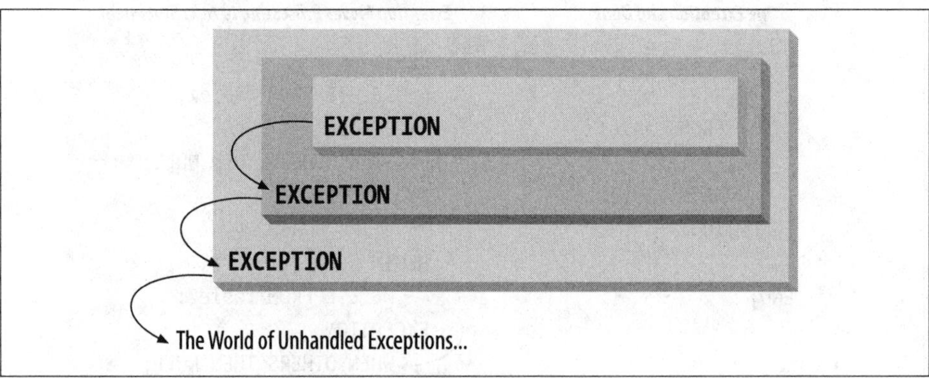

Figure 6-3. Propagation of an exception through nested blocks

Losing exception information

The architecture of PL/SQL exception handling leads to an odd situation regarding local, programmer-defined exceptions: you can lose crucial information (what error occurred?) unless you are careful.

Consider the following situation. I declare an exception as follows:

```
BEGIN
    <<local_block>>
    DECLARE
        case_is_not_made EXCEPTION;
    BEGIN
        ...
    END local_block;
```

but neglect to include an exception section. The scope of the case_is_not_made exception is inside local_block's execution and exception sections. If the exception is not handled there and instead propagates to the enclosing block, then there is no way to know that the case_is_not_made exception was raised. You really don't know what error was raised, only that some error was raised.

How can this be so? Because all user-defined exceptions have the same error number and error message: 1 and "User-defined error", respectively. Not very informative. Only the exception's name is unique. But outside of local_block, that name, that exception, no longer exists.

As a consequence, when you are working with locally defined (and raised) exceptions, you must always include an exception handler specifically for that error by name.

```
PROCEDURE list_my_faults IS
BEGIN
  ...
   DECLARE                                                    Nested Block 1
      too_many_faults EXCEPTION;
   BEGIN
      ... executable statements before new block ...
      BEGIN                                                   Nested Block 2
         SELECT SUM (faults) INTO num_faults FROM profile ... ;
         IF num_faults > 100
         THEN
            RAISE too_many_faults;
         END IF;
      EXCEPTION
         WHEN NO_DATA_FOUND THEN ... ;
      END;
      ... executable statements after Nested Block 2 ...
   EXCEPTION
      WHEN too_many_faults THEN ... ;
   END;
END list_my_faults;
```

Figure 6-4. Propagation of exception handling to first nested block

Examples of propagation

Let's look at a few examples of how exceptions propagate through enclosing blocks. Figure 6-4 shows how the exception raised in the inner block, too_many_faults, is handled by the next enclosing block. The innermost block has an exception section, so PL/SQL first checks to see if too_many_faults is handled in this section. Because it was not handled, PL/SQL closes that block and raises the too_many_faults exception in the enclosing block, Nested Block 1. Control immediately passes to the exception section of Nested Block 1. (The executable statements after Nested Block 2 are not executed.) PL/SQL scans the exception handlers and finds that too_many_faults is handled in this block, so the code for that handler is executed, and control passes back to the main list_my_faults procedure.

Notice that if the NO_DATA_FOUND exception had been raised in the innermost block (Nested Block 2), then the exception section for Nested Block 2 would have handled the exception. Then control would pass back to Nested Block 1, and the executable statements that come after Nested Block 2 would be executed.

In Figure 6-5, the exception raised in the inner block is handled by the outermost block. The outermost block is the only one with an exception section, so when Nested Block 2 raises the too_many_faults exception, PL/SQL terminates execution of that block and raises that exception in the enclosing block, Nested Block 1. Again, this block has no exception section, so PL/SQL immediately terminates Nested Block 1 and passes control to the outermost block, the list_my_faults procedure. This procedure does have an exception section, so PL/SQL scans the exception handlers, finds a match for too_many_faults, executes the code for that handler, and then returns control to whatever program called list_my_faults.

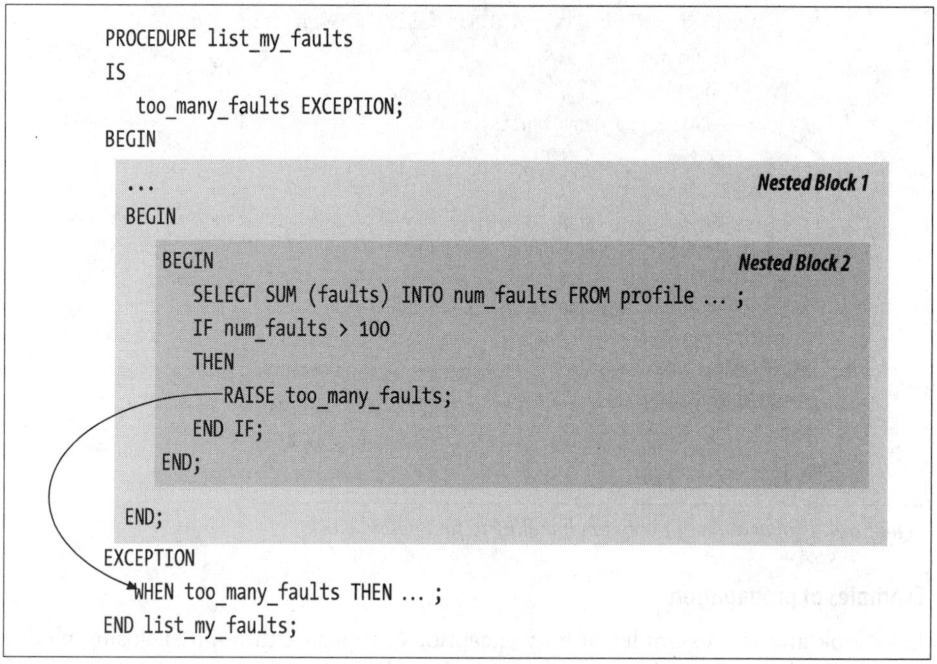

```
PROCEDURE list_my_faults
IS
   too_many_faults EXCEPTION;
BEGIN
  ...                                                  Nested Block 1
  BEGIN
     BEGIN                                             Nested Block 2
        SELECT SUM (faults) INTO num_faults FROM profile ... ;
        IF num_faults > 100
        THEN
           RAISE too_many_faults;
        END IF;
     END;
  END;
EXCEPTION
   WHEN too_many_faults THEN ... ;
END list_my_faults;
```

Figure 6-5. Exception raised in nested block handled by outermost block

Using Standardized Error Handler Programs

Robust and consistent error handling is an absolutely crucial element of a properly constructed application. This consistency is important for two very different audiences: the user and the developer. If the user is presented with easy-to-understand, well-formatted information when an error occurs, she will be able to report that error more effectively to the support team and will feel more comfortable using the application. If the application handles and logs errors in the same way throughout the entire application, the support and maintenance programmers will be able to fix and enhance the code much more easily.

Sounds like a sensible approach, doesn't it? Unfortunately, and especially in development teams of more than a handful of people, the end result of exception handling is usually very different from what I just described. A more common practice is that each developer strikes out on his or her own path, following different principles, writing to different kinds of logs, and so on. Without standardization, debugging and maintenance becomes a nightmare. Here's an example of the kind of code that typically results:

```
EXCEPTION
   WHEN NO_DATA_FOUND
   THEN
      v_msg :='No company for id '||TO_CHAR (v_id);
      v_err :=SQLCODE;
      v_prog :='fixdebt';
      INSERT INTO errlog VALUES
         (v_err,v_msg,v_prog,SYSDATE,USER);

   WHEN OTHERS
   THEN
      v_err :=SQLCODE;
      v_msg :=SQLERRM;
      v_prog :='fixdebt';
      INSERT INTO errlog VALUES
         (v_err,v_msg,v_prog,SYSDATE,USER);
      RAISE;
```

At first glance, this code might seem quite sensible, and can in fact be explained as follows:

> If I don't find a company for this ID, grab the SQLCODE value, set the program name and message, and write a row to the log table. Then allow the enclosing block to continue (it's not a very severe error in this case). If any other error occurs, grab the error code and message, set the program name, write a row to the log table, and then propagate out the same exception, causing the enclosing block to stop (I don't know how severe the error is).

So what's wrong with all that? The mere fact that I can actually explain everything that is going on is an indication of the problem. I have *exposed* and hardcoded all the steps I take to get the job done. The result is that (a) I write a lot of code, and (b) if anything changes, I have to change a lot of code. Just to give you one example, notice that I am writing to a database table for my log. This means that the log entry has become a part of my logical transaction. If I need to roll back that transaction, I lose my error log.

There are several ways to correct this problem (e.g., write to a file, or use autonomous transactions to save my error log without affecting my main transaction). The problem is that, with the way I have written my code above, I have to apply my correction in potentially hundreds of different programs.

Now consider a rewrite of this same exception section using a standardized package:

```
EXCEPTION
   WHEN NO_DATA_FOUND
   THEN
      errpkg.record_and_continue (
         SQLCODE, 'No company for id ' || TO_CHAR (v_id));
   WHEN OTHERS
   THEN
      errpkg.record_and_stop;
END;
```

My error-handling package hides all the implementation details; I simply decide which of the handler procedures I want to use by viewing the specification of the package. If I want to record the error and then continue, I call the record_and_continue program. If I want to record and then stop, clearly I want to use the record_and_stop program. How does it record the error? How does it stop the enclosing block (i.e., how does it propagate the exception)? I don't know and I don't care. Whatever it does, it does it according to the standards defined for my application.

All I know is that I can now spend more time building the interesting elements of my application, rather than worrying over the tedious, low-level administrivia.

The *errpkg.pkg* file available on the O'Reilly site contains a prototype of such a standardized error-handling package. You will need to complete its implementation before putting it to use in your application, but it will give you a very clear sense of how to construct such a utility. You might also check out the plvexc package of the PL/Vision library, a collection of 60+ packages that are a part of Quest Software's PL/SQL Knowledge Expert. The plvexc package provides a complete, working implementation of a generic, reusable error-handling infrastructure component.

PART III

PL/SQL Program Data

Just about every program you write will manipulate data—and much of that data is "local" (i.e., defined in) your PL/SQL procedure or function. This part of the book concentrates exhaustively on the various types of program data you can define in PL/SQL, such as numbers, strings, records, and collections. You will learn about the new datatypes introduced in Oracle9*i*, such as INTERVAL, TIMESTAMP, XMLType, and others. Chapters 7 through 12 also cover the various built-in functions provided by Oracle that allow you to manipulate and modify data.

In this chapter:

CHAPTER 7

Working with Program Data

Almost every PL/SQL block you write will define and manipulate *program data*. Program data consists of data structures that exist only within your PL/SQL session (physically, within the Program Global Area, or PGA, for your session); they are not stored in the database. Program data can be:

Variables or constants
: The values of variables can change during a program's execution. The values of constants are static once they are set at the time of declaration.

Scalar or composite
: Scalars are made up of a single value, such as a number or a string. Composite data consists of multiple values, such as a record, a collection, or an object type instance.

Containers
: Containers may contain information obtained from the database, or data that was never in the database and might not ever end up there.

Before you can work with program data inside your PL/SQL code, you must declare those data structures, giving them names and datatypes.

This chapter describes how you declare program data. It covers the rules governing the format of the names you give them. It offers a quick reference to all the different types of data supported in PL/SQL and explores the concept of datatype conversion. The chapter finishes with some recommendations for working with program data. The remaining chapters in this part of the book describe specific types of program data.

Naming Your Program Data

To work with a variable or a constant you must first declare it, and when you declare it you give it a name. Here are the rules that PL/SQL insists you follow when naming your data structures (these are the same rules applied to names of database objects, such as tables and columns):

- Can be up to 30 characters in length
- Must start with a letter
- Can then be composed of any of the following: letters, numerals, $, #, and _
- All names are case-insensitive (unless those names are placed within double quotes).

Given these rules, the following names are valid:

```
l_total_count
first_12_years
total_#_of_trees
salary_in_$
```

These next three names are not only valid, but considered identical by PL/SQL because it is *not* a case-sensitive language:

```
diapers_changed_week1
DIAPERS_CHANGED_WEEK1
Diapers_Changed_Week1
```

The next three names are invalid, for the reasons indicated:

```
1st_account -- Starts with a number instead of a letter
favorite_ice_cream_flavors_that_dont_contain_nuts -- Too long
email_address@business_loc -- Contains invalid character (@)
```

There are some exceptions to these rules (why are we not surprised?). If you embed a name within double quotes when you declare it, you can bypass all the above rules *except* the maximum length of 30 characters. For example, all of the following declarations are valid:

```
DECLARE
   "truly_lower_case" INTEGER;
   "     " DATE; -- Yes, a name consisting of five spaces!
   "123_go!" VARCHAR2(10);
BEGIN
   "123_go!"  := 'Steven';
END;
```

Note that when you reference these strange names in your execution section, you will need to do so within double quotes, as shown. Otherwise, your code will not compile.

Why would you use double quotes? There is little reason to do so in PL/SQL programs. It is a technique sometimes employed when creating database objects because it preserves case-sensitivity (in other words, if I CREATE TABLE "docs", then the name of the table is docs and not DOCS), but in general, you should avoid using double quotes in PL/SQL.

Another exception to these naming conventions has to do with the names of Java objects, which can be up to 4K in length. See Chapter 22 for more details about this variation and what it means for PL/SQL developers.

Here are two key recommendations for naming your variables, constants, and types:

Make sure the name accurately reflects its usage and is understandable "at a glance"
: You might even take a moment to write down—in noncomputer terms—what the variable represents. You can then easily extract an appropriate name from this statement. For example, if a variable represents the "total number of calls made about lukewarm coffee," a good name for that variable might be total_calls_on_cold_coffee, or tot_cold_calls, if you are allergic to five-word variable names. A bad name for that variable would be totcoffee, or t_#_calls_lwcoff, both too cryptic to get the point across.

Establish consistent, sensible naming conventions
: Such conventions usually involve the use of prefixes and/or suffixes to indicate type and usage. For example, all local variables should be prefixed with "l_" while global variables defined in packages have a "g_" prefix. All record types should have a suffix of "_rt", and so on. You can download a comprehensive set of naming conventions from O'Reilly's Oracle page at *http://oracle.oreilly.com*. Click on "Oracle PL/SQL Best Practices," then "Examples." The download contains a standards document for your use. (The direct URL is *http://examples.oreilly.com/orbestprac/*.)

Overview of PL/SQL Datatypes

Whenever you declare a variable or a constant, you must assign it a datatype. (PL/SQL is, with very few exceptions, a "strongly typed" language; see the sidebar for a definition.) PL/SQL offers a comprehensive set of predefined scalar and composite datatypes, and starting with Oracle8 you can create your own user-defined types (also known as *abstract datatypes*).

Virtually all of these predefined datatypes are defined in the PL/SQL STANDARD package. Here, for example, are the statements that define the Boolean datatype and two of the numeric datatypes:

```
create or replace package STANDARD is

  type BOOLEAN is (FALSE, TRUE);

  type NUMBER is NUMBER_BASE;
  subtype INTEGER is NUMBER(38,);
```

When it comes to datatypes, PL/SQL supports the "usual suspects" and a whole lot more. This section provides a quick overview of the various predefined datatypes. They are covered in detail in Chapters 8 through 12, 14, and 21; you will find detailed references to specific chapters in the following sections.

> ### What Does "Strongly Typed" Mean?
>
> "A strongly typed programming language is one in which each type of *data* (such as integer, character, hexadecimal, packed decimal, and so forth) is predefined as part of the programming language, and all constants or variables defined for a given program must be described with one of the data types. Certain operations may be allowable only with certain data types. The language *compiler* enforces the data typing and use compliance. An advantage of strong data typing is that it imposes a rigorous set of rules on a programmer and thus guarantees a certain consistency of results. A disadvantage is that it prevents the programmer from inventing a data type not anticipated by the developers of the programming language and it limits how "creative" one can be in using a given data type." (Definition courtesy of *www.whatis.com*)

Character Data

PL/SQL supports both fixed- and variable-length strings as both traditional character and Unicode character data. CHAR and NCHAR are fixed-length datatypes; VARCHAR2 and NVARCHAR2 are variable-length datatypes. Here is a declaration of a variable-length string that can hold up to 2000 characters:

```
DECLARE
   l_accident_description VARCHAR2(2000);
```

Chapter 8 explores the rules for character data, provides many examples, and explains the built-in functions provided to manipulate strings in PL/SQL.

Oracle also supports very large character strings, known as LONGs (pre-Oracle8) and LOBs (large objects) in Oracle8 and above. These datatypes allow you to store and manipulate very large amounts of data—a LOB can hold up to 4 GB of information. The character LOB datatypes are CLOB and NCLOB (multibyte format). CLOB stands for character large object, and NCLOB for National Language Support character large object.

There are, by the way, many rules restricting the use of LONGs. We recommend that you avoid using LONGs in all releases of the RDBMS from Oracle8 onwards.

Chapter 12 explores the rules for large objects, provides many examples, and explains the built-in functions and DBMS_LOB package provided to manipulate large objects in PL/SQL.

Numbers

PL/SQL supports both real and integer datatypes. The base datatype for all variations is NUMBER. INTEGER supports only whole numbers, while POSITIVE and

NATURAL are variations of INTEGER. Here is an example of declaring a numeric datatype that can have only one of three values (1, –1, and NULL):

```
DECLARE
   l_direction SIGNTYPE;
```

Chapter 9 explores the rules for numeric data, provides many examples, and explains the built-in functions provided to manipulate numbers in PL/ SQL.

Dates, Timestamps, and Intervals

Prior to Oracle9*i*, the Oracle world of dates was limited to the DATE datatype, which stored both dates and times (down to the nearest second). Oracle9*i* introduces two sets of new, related datatypes: INTERVALs and TIMESTAMPs. These datatypes greatly expand the capability of PL/SQL developers to write programs that manipulate and store dates and times with very high granularity, and also compute and store intervals of time.

Here is an example of a function that computes the age of a person:

```
CREATE OR REPLACE FUNCTION age (dob_in IN DATE)
   RETURN INTERVAL YEAR TO MONTH
IS
   retval INTERVAL YEAR TO MONTH;
BEGIN
   RETURN (SYSDATE - dob_in) YEAR TO MONTH;
END;
```

Chapter 10 explores the rules for date-related data, provides many examples, and explains the built-in functions provided to manipulate dates, timestamps, and intervals in PL/SQL.

Booleans

PL/SQL supports a true Boolean datatype. A variable of this type can have one of only three values: TRUE, FALSE, and NULL.

Booleans help us write very readable code, especially involving complex logical expressions. Here's an example of a Boolean declaration, along with an assignment of a default value to that variable:

```
DECLARE
   l_eligible_for_discount BOOLEAN :=
      customer_in.balance > min_balance AND
      customer_in.pref_type = 'MOST FAVORED' AND
      customer_in.disc_eligibility;
```

Chapter 12 explores the rules for Boolean data and provides examples of usage.

Binary Data

Oracle supports several forms of *binary data* (unstructured data that is not interpreted or processed by Oracle), including RAW, LONG RAW, BFILE, and BLOB. The BFILE datatype stores unstructured binary data in operating system files outside the database. RAW is a variable-length datatype like the VARCHAR2 character datatype, except that Oracle utilities do not perform character conversion when transmitting RAW data.

Chapter 12 explores the rules for binary data, provides many examples, and explains the built-in functions and DBMS_LOB package provided to manipulate BFILEs and other binary data in PL/SQL.

ROWIDs

Oracle provides two proprietary datatypes, ROWID and UROWID, used to represent the address of a row in a table. ROWID represents the unique address of a row in its table; UROWID represents the logical position of a row in an index-organized table (IOT). ROWID is also a SQL pseudonym that can be included in SQL statements.

Chapter 12 explores the rules for working with the ROWID and UROWID datatypes.

REF Cursors

The REF CURSOR datatype allows developers to declare cursor variables, which can be used with static and dynamic SQL statements to implement very flexible requirements. This datatype supports two forms: the strong REF CURSOR and the weak REF CURSOR. The latter is one of the very few weakly typed datatypes you can declare.

Here is an example of a strong REF CURSOR declaration (I associate the cursor variable with a specific record structure with %ROWTYPE):

```
DECLARE
   TYPE book_data_t IS REF CURSOR RETURN book%ROWTYPE;
   book_curs_var book_data_t;
```

And here are two weak REF CURSOR declarations in which I do not associate any particular structure with the resulting variable. The second line showcases SYS_REFCURSOR, a predefined weak REF CURSOR type.

```
DECLARE
   TYPE book_data_t IS REF CURSOR;
   book_curs_var book_data_t;
```

Chapter 14 explores REF CURSORs and cursor variables in much more detail.

Internet Datatypes

Oracle9*i* offers native support for several Internet-related technologies and types of data, specifically XML (Extensible Markup Language) and URIs (Universal Resource Identifiers). Oracle provides datatypes used to handle XML and URI data, as well as a class of URIs called DBUri-REFs used to access data stored within the database itself. Oracle also provides a new set of types to store and access both external and internal URIs from within the database.

The XMLType allows you to query and store XML data in the database using functions like SYS_XMLGEN and the DBMS_XMLGEN package. It also allows you to use native operators in the SQL language to perform searching with the XPath language.

The URI-related types, including URIType and HttpURIType, are all part of an object type inheritance hierarchy and can be used to store URLs to external web pages and files, as well as to refer to data within the database.

Chapter 12 explores the rules for working with XMLType and URI types, provides many examples, and explains the built-in functions and packages provided to manipulate these datatypes.

"Any" Datatypes

Most of the time, our programming tasks are fairly straightforward and very specific to the requirement at hand. At other times, however, we write more generic kinds of code. For those situations, the "Any" datatypes might come in very handy.

The "Any" types are new to Oracle9*i* and are very different from any other kind of datatype available in Oracle. They let you dynamically encapsulate and access type descriptions, data instances, and sets of data instances of any other SQL type. I can use these types (and the methods defined for them, as they are object types) to do things like determine the type of data stored in a particular nested table—without having access to the actual declaration of that table type!

The "Any" datatypes include AnyType, AnyData, and AnyDataSet.

Chapter 12 explores the rules for working with the "Any" datatypes and provides some working examples of this new and exciting technology.

User-Defined Datatypes

With the introduction of object types in Oracle8, you can now use Oracle built-in datatypes and other user-defined datatypes to create arbitrarily complex types of your own that model closely the structure and behavior of data in systems.

Chapter 21 explores this powerful feature in more detail and explores how to take advantage of Oracle9*i*'s addition of support for object type inheritance.

Declaring Program Data

Before you can make a reference to a variable constant, you must declare it. (The only exception to this rule is for the index variables of FOR loops.) All declarations must be made in the declaration section of your anonymous block, procedure, function, trigger, object type body, or package body. (See Chapter 3 for more details on the structure of the PL/SQL block and its declaration section.)

You can declare many types of data and data structures in PL/SQL, including variables, constants, TYPES (such as a type of collection or a type of record), and exceptions. This chapter focuses on the declarations of variables and constants. (See Chapter 11 for an explanation of TYPE statements. See Chapter 6 to learn how to declare exceptions.)

Declaring a Variable

When you declare a variable, PL/SQL allocates memory for the variable's value and names the storage location so that the value can be retrieved and changed. The declaration also specifies the datatype of the variable; this datatype is then used to validate values assigned to the variable.

The basic syntax for a declaration is:

```
name datatype [NOT NULL] [default assignment];
```

where *name* is the name of the variable or constant to be declared, and *datatype* is the datatype or subtype that determines the type of data that can be assigned to the variable. You can include a NOT NULL clause, which means that if your code assigns a NULL to this variable, Oracle will raise an exception. The [*default assignment*] clause allows you to initialize the variable with a value; this is optional for all declarations except those of constants.

The following examples illustrate declarations of variables of different datatypes:

```
DECLARE
    -- Simple declaration of numeric variable
    l_total_count NUMBER;

    -- Declaration of number that rounds to nearest hundredth (cent):
    l_dollar_amount NUMBER (10,2);

    -- A single date value, assigned a default value of "right now"
    -- and it can never be NULL
    l_right_now DATE NOT NULL  DEFAULT SYSDATE;

    -- Using the assignment operator for the default value specification
    l_favorite_flavor VARCHAR2(100) := `Anything with chocolate, actually';

    -- Two-step declaration process for associative array.
    -- First, the type of table:
```

```
TYPE list_of_books_t IS TABLE OF book%ROWTYPE INDEX BY BINARY_INTEGER;

-- And now the specific list to be manipulated in this block:
oreilly_oracle_books list_of_books_t;
```

The DEFAULT and assignment operator syntax for assigning a default value are equivalent and can be interchanged. So which should you use? I like to use the assignment operator (:=) to set default values for constants, and the DEFAULT syntax for variables. In the case of the constant, the assigned value is not really a default but an initial (and unchanging) value, so the DEFAULT syntax feels misleading to me.

Declaring Constants

There are just two differences between declaring a variable and declaring a constant: for a constant, you include the CONSTANT keyword, and you must supply a default value. So the syntax for the declaration of a constant is:

```
name CONSTANT datatype [NOT NULL] := | DEFAULT default_value;
```

The value of a constant is set upon declaration and may not change thereafter.

Here are some examples of declarations of constants:

```
DECLARE
   -- The current year number; it's not going to change during my session.
   l_curr_year CONSTANT PLS_INTEGER :=
      TO_NUMBER (TO_CHAR (SYSDATE, 'YYYY'));

   -- Using the DEFAULT keyword
   l_author CONSTANT VARCHAR2(100) DEFAULT 'Bill Pribyl';

   -- Declare a complex datatype as a constant
   -- this isn't just for scalars!
   l_stevenCONSTANT  person_ot :=
     person_ot ('HUMAN', 'Steven Feuerstein', 175, '09-23-1958');
```

Unless otherwise stated, the information provided in the rest of this chapter for variables also applies to constants.

An unnamed constant is a literal value, such as 2 or Bobby McGee. A literal does not have a name, although it does have an implied (undeclared) datatype.

Constrained Declarations

A declaration is *constrained* when you specify a number constraining or restricting the magnitude of the value that can be assigned to that variable. A datatype is *unconstrained* when there are no such restrictions.

Consider the datatype NUMBER. It supports up to 38 digits of precision—and uses up the memory needed for all those digits. If your variable does not require this much memory, you could declare a number with a constraint, such as the following:

```
itty_bitty_# NUMBER(1);

large_but_constrained_# NUMBER(20,5);
```

Constrained variables require less memory than unconstrained number declarations like this:

```
no_limits_here NUMBER;
```

The NOT NULL Clause

If you do assign a default value, you can also specify that the variable must be NOT NULL. For example, the following declaration initializes the company_name variable to PCS R US and makes sure that the name can never be set to NULL:

```
company_name VARCHAR2(60) NOT NULL DEFAULT 'PCS R US';
```

If your code includes a line like this:

```
company_name := NULL;
```

then PL/SQL will raise the VALUE_ERROR exception. In addition, you will receive a compilation error with this next declaration, because the declaration does not include an initial or default value:

```
company_name VARCHAR2(60) NOT NULL; -- must assign a value if declared NOT NULL!
```

Anchored Declarations

You can and often will declare variables using "hardcoded" or explicit datatypes, as follows:

```
l_company_name VARCHAR2(100);
```

Oracle offers an alternative method, called *anchoring*, that offers some significant advantages, particularly when the variable you are declaring is related to or will be populated from another source, such as a row in a table.

When you "anchor" a datatype, you tell PL/SQL to set the datatype of your variable based on the datatype of an already defined data structure—another PL/SQL variable, a predefined TYPE or SUBTYPE, a database table, or a specific column in a table. PL/SQL offers two kinds of anchoring:

Scalar anchoring
: Use the %TYPE attribute to define your variable based on a table's column or some other PL/SQL scalar variable.

Record anchoring
: Use the %ROWTYPE attribute to define your record structure based on a table or a predefined PL/SQL explicit cursor.

The syntax for an anchored datatype is:

```
variable name type attribute%TYPE [optional default value assignment];
variable name table_name | cursor_name%ROWTYPE [optional default value assignment];
```

where *variable name* is the name of the variable you are declaring, and *type attribute* is either a previously declared PL/SQL variable name or a table column specification in the format *table.column*.

This anchoring reference is resolved at the time the code is compiled; there is no runtime overhead to anchoring. The anchor also establishes a dependency between the code and the anchored element (the table, cursor, or package containing the variable referenced). This means that if those elements are changed, the code in which the anchoring takes place is marked INVALID. When it is recompiled, the anchor will again be resolved, thereby keeping the code current with the anchored element.

Figure 7-1 shows how the datatype is drawn from both a database table and a PL/ SQL variable.

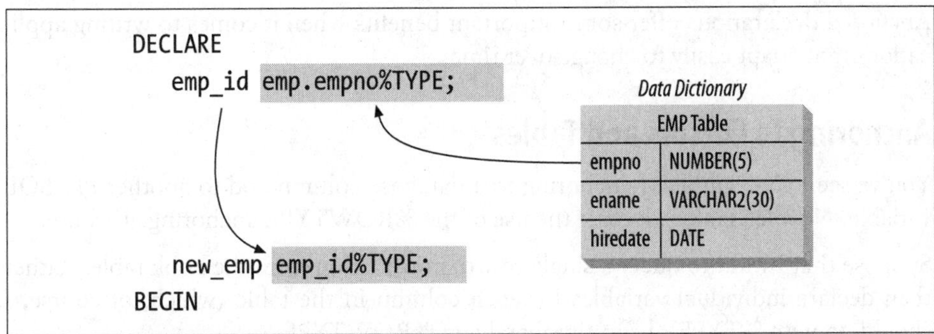

Figure 7-1. Anchored declarations with %TYPE

Here is an example of anchoring a variable to a database column:

```
l_company_id company.company_id%TYPE;
```

You can also anchor against PL/SQL variables; this is usually done to avoid redundant declarations of the same hardcoded datatype. In this case, the best practice is to create a "reference" variable in a package and then reference that package variable in %TYPE statements. (You could also create SUBTYPEs in your package; this topic is covered later in the chapter.) The following example shows just a portion of a package intended to make it easier to work with Oracle Advanced Queuing (AQ):

```
/* File on web: aq.pkg */
CREATE OR REPLACE PACKAGE aq
IS
```

```
/* Standard datatypes for use with Oracle AQ. */
   SUBTYPE msgid_type IS RAW(16);
   SUBTYPE name_type IS VARCHAR2(49);
   ...
END aq;
```

AQ message IDs are of type RAW(16). Rather than have to remember that (and hardcode it into my application again and again), I can simply declare an AQ message ID as follows:

```
DECLARE
   my_ msg_id aq.msgid_type;
BEGIN
```

Then, if Oracle ever changes its datatype for a message ID, I can change my SUBTYPE definition in the aq package and all declarations will be updated with the next recompilation.

Anchored declarations provide an excellent illustration of the fact that PL/SQL is not just a procedural-style programming language, but was designed specifically as an extension to the Oracle SQL language. A very thorough effort was made by Oracle Corporation to tightly integrate the programming constructs of PL/SQL to the underlying SQL database.

Anchored declarations offer some important benefits when it comes to writing applications that adapt easily to change over time.

Anchoring to Cursors and Tables

You've seen an example of anchoring to a database column and to another PL/ SQL variable. Now let's take a look at the use of the %ROWTYPE anchoring attribute.

Suppose that I want to query a single row of information from the book table. Rather than declare individual variables for each column in the table (which, of course, I should do with %TYPE), I can simply rely on %ROWTYPE:

```
DECLARE
   l_book book%ROWTYPE;
BEGIN
   SELECT * INTO l_book
      FROM book
    WHERE isbn = '1-56592-335-9'
   process_book (l_book);
END;
```

Suppose, now, that I only want to retrieve the author and title from the book table. In this case, I will build an explicit cursor and then %ROWTYPE against that cursor:

```
DECLARE
   CURSOR book_cur IS
      SELECT author, title FROM book
       WHERE  isbn = '1-56592-335-9'
```

```
   l_book book_cur%ROWTYPE;
BEGIN
   OPEN book_cur;
   FETCH book_cur INTO l_book;
   process_book (l_book);
END;
```

Finally, here is an example of an *implicit* use of the %ROWTYPE declaration: the cursor FOR loop.

```
BEGIN
   FOR book_rec IN (SELECT * FROM book)
   LOOP
      process_book (book_rec);
   END LOOP;
END;
```

Now let's explore some of the benefits of anchored declarations.

Benefits of Anchored Declarations

All the declarations you have seen so far—character, numeric, date, Boolean— specify explicitly the type of data for that variable. In each of these cases, the declaration contains a direct reference to a datatype and, in most cases, a constraint on that datatype. You can think of this as a kind of hardcoding in your program. While this approach to declarations is certainly valid, it can cause problems in the following situations:

Synchronization with database columns
: The PL/SQL variable "represents" database information in the program. If I declare explicitly and then change the structure of the underlying table, my program may not work properly.

Normalization of local variables
: The PL/SQL variable stores calculated values used throughout the application. What are the consequences of repeating (hardcoding) the same datatype and constraint for each declaration in all of my programs?

Let's take a look at each of these scenarios in detail.

Synchronization with database columns

Databases hold information that needs to be stored and manipulated. Both SQL and PL/SQL perform these manipulations. Your PL/SQL programs often read data from a database into local program variables, and then write information from those variables back into the database.

Suppose that I have a company table with a column called NAME and a datatype of VARCHAR2(60). I can therefore create a local variable to hold this data as follows:

```
DECLARE
   cname VARCHAR2(60);
```

and then use this variable to represent this database information in my program. Now consider an application that uses the company entity. There may be a dozen different screens, procedures, and reports that contain this same PL/SQL declaration, VARCHAR2(60), over and over again. And everything works just fine...until the business requirements change or the DBA has a change of heart. With a very small effort, the definition of the name column in the company table changes to VARCHAR2(100) in order to accommodate longer company names. Suddenly the database can store names that will raise VALUE_ERROR exceptions when FETCHed into the company_name variable.

My programs have now become incompatible with the underlying data structures. All declarations of cname (and all the variations programmers employed for this data throughout the system) must be modified—otherwise, my application is simply a ticking time bomb, just waiting to fail. My variable, which is a local representation of database information, is no longer synchronized with that database column.

Normalization of local variables

Another drawback to explicit declarations arises when working with PL/SQL variables that store and manipulate calculated values not found in the database. Suppose that my programmers built an application to manage my company's finances. I am very bottom-line-oriented, so many different programs make use of a total_revenue variable, declared as follows:

```
total_revenue NUMBER (10,2);
```

Yes, I like to track my total revenue down to the last penny. In 1992, when specifications for the application were first written, the maximum total revenue I ever thought I could possibly obtain from any single customer was $99 million, so we used the NUMBER(10,2) declaration. Then, in 1995, my proposal to convert B-2 bombers into emergency transport systems to deliver Midwestern wheat to famine regions was accepted: a $2 billion contract! I was just about ready to pop the corks on the champagne when my lead programmer told me the bad news: I wouldn't be able to generate reports on this newest project and customer, because those darn total_revenue variables were too small!

What a bummer...I had to fire the guy.

Just kidding. Instead, we quickly searched out any and all instances of the revenue variables so that we could change the declarations. This was a time-consuming job because we had spread equivalent declarations throughout the entire application. I had, in effect, denormalized my local data structures, with the usual consequences on maintenance. If only I had a way to define each of the local total_revenue variables in relation to a single datatype.

If only they had used %TYPE!

Anchoring to NOT NULL Datatypes

When you declare a variable, you can also specify the need for the variable to be NOT NULL. This NOT NULL declaration constraint is transferred to variables declared with the %TYPE attribute. If I include a NOT NULL in my declaration of a source variable (one that is referenced afterwards in a %TYPE declaration), I must also make sure to specify a default value for the variables that make use of that source variable. Suppose that I declare max_available_date NOT NULL in the following example:

```
DECLARE
   max_available_date DATE NOT NULL :=
         LAST_DAY (ADD_MONTHS (SYSDATE, 3));
   last_ship_date max_available_date%TYPE;
```

The declaration of last_ship_date will then fail to compile, with the following message:

```
a variable declared NOT NULL must have an initialization assignment.
```

If you use a NOT NULL variable in a %TYPE declaration, the new variable must have a default value provided. The same is not true, however, for variables declared with %TYPE where the source is a database column defined as NOT NULL. This NOT NULL constraint is *not* automatically transferred to the variable.

Programmer-Defined Subtypes

With the SUBTYPE statement, PL/SQL allows you to define your own subtypes or aliases of predefined datatypes, sometimes referred to as *abstract datatypes*. In PL/SQL, a subtype of a datatype is a variation that specifies the same set of rules as the original datatype, but that might allow only a subset of the datatype's values.

There are two kinds of subtypes, constrained and unconstrained:

Constrained subtype
: A subtype that restricts or constrains the values normally allowed by the datatype itself. POSITIVE is an example of a constrained subtype of BINARY_INTEGER. The package STANDARD, which predefines the datatypes and the functions that are part of the standard PL/SQL language, declares the subtype POSITIVE as follows:

```
SUBTYPE POSITIVE IS BINARY_INTEGER RANGE 1 .. 2147483647;
```

A variable that is declared POSITIVE can store only integer values greater than zero.

Unconstrained subtype
: A subtype that does not restrict the values of the original datatype in variables declared with the subtype. FLOAT is an example of an unconstrained subtype of NUMBER. Its definition in the STANDARD package is:

```
SUBTYPE FLOAT IS NUMBER;
```

In other words, an unconstrained subtype provides an alias or alternate name for the original datatype. Prior to Oracle8*i*, PL/SQL developers could define only unconstrained subtypes; now, constrained subtypes are allowed as well, as shown below:

```
CREATE OR REPLACE PACKAGE utility
AS
   SUBTYPE big_string IS VARCHAR2(32767);
   SUBTYPE big_db_string IS VARCHAR2(4000);
END utility;
```

In order to make a subtype available, you first have to declare it in the declaration section of an anonymous PL/SQL block, procedure, function, or package. You've already seen the syntax for declaring a subtype used by PL/SQL in the STANDARD package. The general format of a subtype declaration is:

```
SUBTYPE subtype_name IS base_type;
```

where *subtype_name* is the name of the new subtype and *base_type* is the datatype on which the subtype is based.

Be aware that an anchored subtype does not carry over the NOT NULL constraint to the variables it defines. Nor does it transfer a default value that was included in the original declaration of a variable or column specification.

Conversion Between Datatypes

There are many different situations in which you need to convert data from one datatype to another. You can perform this conversion in two ways:

Implicitly
: By allowing the PL/SQL runtime engine to take its "best guess" at performing the conversion

Explicitly
: By calling a PL/SQL function or operator to do the conversion

In this section I will first review how and when PL/SQL performs implicit conversions, and will then focus attention on the programs available for explicit conversions.

Implicit Data Conversion

Whenever PL/SQL detects that a conversion is necessary, it attempts to change the values as required to perform the operation. You would probably be surprised to learn how often PL/SQL is performing conversions on your behalf. Figure 7-2 shows what kinds of implicit conversions PL/SQL can perform.

With implicit conversions you can specify literal values in place of data with the correct internal format, and PL/SQL will convert that literal as necessary. In the

From \ To	BINARY_INTEGER	BLOB	CHAR	CLOB	DATE	LONG	NUMBER	PLS_INTEGER	RAW	UROWID	VARCHAR2
BINARY_INTEGER	NA		●			●	●	●			●
BLOB		NA							●		
CHAR	●		NA	●	●	●	●	●	●	●	●
CLOB			●	NA							●
DATE			●		NA	●					●
LONG			●			NA			●		●
NUMBER	●		●			●	NA	●			●
PLS_INTEGER	●		●			●	●	NA			●
RAW		●	●			●			NA		●
UROWID			●							NA	●
VARCHAR2	●		●	●	●	●	●	●	●	●	NA

Figure 7-2. Implicit conversions performed by PL/SQL

following example, PL/SQL converts the literal string "125" to the numeric value 125 in the process of assigning a value to the numeric variable:

```
DECLARE
   a_number NUMBER;
BEGIN
   a_number := '125';
END;
```

You can also pass parameters of one datatype into a module and then have PL/SQL convert that data into another format for use inside the program. In the following procedure, the second parameter is a date. When I call that procedure, I pass a string value in the form DD-MON-YY, and PL/SQL converts that string automatically to a date:

```
PROCEDURE change_hiredate
   (emp_id_in IN INTEGER, hiredate_in IN DATE)

change_hiredate (1004, '12-DEC-94');
```

Limitations of implicit conversion

As shown in Figure 7-2, conversions are limited; PL/SQL cannot convert any arbitrary datatype to any other datatype. Furthermore, some implicit conversions raise exceptions. Consider the following assignment:

```
DECLARE
   a_number NUMBER;
```

```
BEGIN
   a_number := 'abc';
END;
```

PL/SQL cannot convert "abc" to a number and so will raise the VALUE_ERROR exception when it executes this code. It is up to you to make sure that if PL/SQL is going to perform implicit conversions, it is given values it can convert without error.

Drawbacks of implicit conversion

There are several drawbacks to implicit conversion:

- Each implicit conversion PL/SQL performs represents a loss, however small, in the control you have over your program. You do not expressly perform or direct the performance of the conversion; you simply make an assumption that it will take place and that it will have the intended effect. There is always a danger in making this assumption. If Oracle changes the way and circumstances under which it performs conversions, your code could then be affected.
- The implicit conversion that PL/SQL performs depends on the context in which the code occurs. As a result, a conversion might occur in one program and not in another, even though they appear to be the same. The conversion that PL/SQL performs is not necessarily the one you might expect.
- Your code is easier to read and understand if you explicitly convert data where needed. Such conversions provide documentation of variances in datatypes between tables or between code and tables. By removing an assumption and a hidden action from your code, you remove a potential misunderstanding as well.

As a consequence, I recommend that you avoid allowing either the SQL or PL/SQL languages to perform implicit conversions on your behalf. Instead, use a conversion function to guarantee that the right kind of conversion takes place.

Explicit Datatype Conversion

Oracle provides a comprehensive set of conversion functions and operators to be used in SQL and PL/SQL; a complete list is shown in Table 7-1. Most of these functions are described in other chapters (for those, the table indicates the chapter number). For functions not described elsewhere, brief descriptions are provided later in this chapter.

Table 7-1. The built-in conversion functions

Name	Description	Chapter
ASCIISTR	Converts a string in any character set to an ASCII string in the database character set.	8
CAST	Converts one built-in datatype or collection-typed value into another built-in datatype or collection-typed value; this very powerful conversion mechanism can be used as a substitute for traditional functions like TO_DATE.	7, 9, 10

Table 7-1. The built-in conversion functions (continued)

Name	Description	Chapter
CHARTOROWID	Converts a string to a ROWID.	7
CONVERT	Converts a string from one character set to another.	7
FROM_TZ	Adds time zone information to a TIMESTAMP value, thus converting it into a TIMESTAMP WITH TIME ZONE value.	10
HEXTORAW	Converts from hexadecimal to raw format.	7
MULTISET	Maps a database table to a collection.	11
NUMTODSINTERVAL	Converts a number (or numeric expression) to an INTERVAL DAY TO SECOND literal.	10
NUMTOYMINTERVAL	Converts a number (or numeric expression) to an INTERVAL YEAR TO MONTH literal.	10
RAWTOHEX, RAWTONHEX	Converts from raw value to hexadecimal.	7
REFTOHEX	Converts a REF value into a character string containing the hexadecimal representation of the REF value.	21
ROWIDTOCHAR, ROWIDTONCHAR	Converts a binary ROWID value to a character string.	7
TABLE	Maps a collection to a database table; this is the inverse of MULTISET.	11
THE	Maps a single column value in a single row into a virtual database table.	11
TO_CHAR, TO_NCHAR (number version)	Converts a number to a string (VARCHAR2 or NVARCHAR2, respectively).	9
TO_CHAR, TO_NCHAR (date version)	Converts a date to a string.	10
TO_CHAR, TO_NCHAR (character version)	Converts character data between the database character set and the national character set.	8
TO_BLOB	Converts from a RAW value to a BLOB.	12
TO_CLOB, TO_NCLOB	Converts from a VARCHAR2, NVARCHAR2, or NCLOB value to a CLOB (or NCLOB).	12
TO_DATE	Converts a string to a date.	10
TO_DSINTERVAL	Converts a character string of a CHAR, VARCHAR2, NCHAR, or NVARCHAR2 datatype to an INTERVAL DAY TO SECOND type.	10
TO_LOB	Converts from a LONG to a LOB.	12
TO_MULTI_BYTE	Where possible, converts single-byte characters in the input string to their multi-byte equivalents.	8
TO_NUMBER	Converts a string to a number.	9
TO_RAW	Converts from a BLOB to a RAW.	12
TO_SINGLE_BYTE	Converts multibyte characters in the input string to their corresponding single-byte characters.	8
TO_TIMESTAMP	Converts a character string to a value of type TIMESTAMP.	10
TO_TIMESTAMP_TZ	Converts a character string to a value of type TO_TIMESTAMP_TZ.	10
TO_TIMESTAMP_LTZ	Converts a character string to a value of type TO_TIMESTAMP_LTZ.	10
TO_YMINTERVAL	Converts a character string of a CHAR, VARCHAR2, NCHAR, or NVARCHAR2 datatype to an INTERVAL YEAR TO MONTH type.	10

Table 7-1. The built-in conversion functions (continued)

Name	Description	Chapter
TRANSLATE ... USING	Converts supplied text into the character set specified for conversions between the database character set and the national character set.	8
UNISTR	Takes as its argument a string in any character set and returns it in Unicode in the database Unicode character set.	8

The CHARTOROWID function

The CHARTOROWID function converts a string of either type CHAR or VARCHAR2 to a value of type ROWID. The specification of the CHARTOROWID function is:

```
FUNCTION CHARTOROWID (string_in IN CHAR) RETURN ROWID
FUNCTION CHARTOROWID (string_in IN VARCHAR2) RETURN ROWID
```

In order for CHARTOROWID to successfully convert the string, it must be of the format:

```
BBBBBBBB.RRRR.FFFF
```

where *BBBBBBBB* is the number of the block in the database file, *RRRR* is the number of the row in the block, and *FFFF* is the number of the database file. All three numbers must be in hexadecimal format. If the input string does not conform to the above format, PL/SQL raises the VALUE_ERROR exception.

The CAST function

The CAST function, added to the PL/SQL toolbox in Oracle8, is a very handy and flexible conversion mechanism. It converts from one (and almost any) built-in datatype or collection-typed value into another built-in datatype or collection-typed value. CAST will be a familiar operator to anyone working with object-oriented languages in which it is often necessary to "cast" an object of one class into that of another.

With Oracle's CAST function, you can convert an unnamed expression (a number, a date, or even the result set of a subquery) or a named collection (a nested table, for instance) into a datatype or named collection of a compatible type.

Figure 7-3 shows the supported conversion between built-in datatypes. Note the following:

- You cannot cast LONG, LONG RAW, any of the LOB datatypes, or the Oracle-supplied types.
- "DATE" in the figure includes DATE, TIMESTAMP, TIMESTAMP WITH TIMEZONE, INTERVAL DAY TO SECOND, and INTERVAL YEAR TO MONTH.
- To cast a named collection type into another named collection type, the elements of both collections must be of the same type.
- You cannot cast a UROWID to a ROWID if the UROWID contains the value of a ROWID of an index-organized table.

From \ To	CHAR, VARCHAR2	NUMBER	DATE	RAW	ROWID, UROWID	NCHAR, NVARCHAR2
CHAR, VARCHAR2	●	●	●	●	●	
NUMBER	●	●				
DATE	●		●			
RAW	●			●		
ROWID, UROWID	●				●	
NCHAR, NVARCHAR2		●	●	●	●	●

Figure 7-3. Casting built-in datatypes

First let's take a look at using CAST as a replacement for scalar datatype conversion. I can use it in a SQL statement:

```
SELECT employee_id, cast (hire_date AS  VARCHAR2 (30))
  FROM employee;
```

and I can use it in native PL/SQL syntax:

```
DECLARE
   hd_display VARCHAR2 (30);
BEGIN
   hd_display := CAST (SYSDATE AS  VARCHAR2);
END;
```

A much more interesting application of CAST comes into play when you are working with PL/SQL collections (nested tables and VARRAYs). For these datatypes, you use CAST to convert from one type of collection to another. You can also use CAST to manipulate (from within a SQL statement) a collection that has been defined as a PL/SQL variable.

Chapter 11 covers these topics in more detail, but the following example should give you a sense of the syntax and possibilities. First I create two nested table types and a relational table:

```
CREATE TYPE names_t AS TABLE OF VARCHAR2 (100);

CREATE TYPE authors_t AS TABLE OF VARCHAR2 (100);

CREATE TABLE favorite_authors (name VARCHAR2(200))
```

I would then like to write a program that blends together data from the favorite_authors table with the contents of a nested table declared and populated in my program. Consider the following block:

```
/* File on web: cast.sql */
DECLARE
   scifi_favorites   authors_t
```

```
 3         := authors_t ('Sheri S. Tepper', 'Orson Scott Card', 'Gene Wolfe');
 4  BEGIN
 5     DBMS_OUTPUT.put_line ('I recommend that you read books by:');
 6
 7     FOR rec IN  (SELECT column_value favs
 8                    FROM TABLE (CAST (scifi_favorites AS  names_t))
 9                  UNION
10                   SELECT NAME
11                     FROM favorite_authors)
12     LOOP
13        DBMS_OUTPUT.put_line (rec.favs);
14     END LOOP;
15  END;
```

On lines 2 and 3, I declare a local nested table and populate it with a few of my favorite science fiction/fantasy authors. In lines 7 through 11, I use the UNION operator to merge together the rows from favorite_authors with those of scifi_ favorites. To do this, I *cast* the PL/SQL nested table (local and not visible to the SQL engine) as a type of nested table known in the database. Notice that I am able to cast a collection of type authors_t to a collection of type names_t; this is possible because they are of compatible types. Once the cast step is completed, I call the TABLE operator to ask the SQL engine to treat the nested table as a relational table. Here is the output I see on my screen:

```
I recommend that you read books by:
Gene Wolfe
Orson Scott Card
Robert Harris
Sheri S. Tepper
Tom Segev
Toni Morrison
```

The CONVERT function

The CONVERT function converts strings from one character set to another character set. The specification of the CONVERT function is:

```
FUNCTION CONVERT
   (string_in IN VARCHAR2,
    new_char_set VARCHAR2
    [, old_char_set VARCHAR2])
RETURN VARCHAR2
```

The third argument, *old_char_set,* is optional. If this argument is not specified, then the default character set for the database instance is used.

The CONVERT function does *not* translate words or phrases from one language to another. CONVERT simply substitutes the letter or symbol in one character set with the corresponding letter or symbol in another character set. (Note that a character set is not the same thing as a human language.)

Two commonly used character sets are US7ASCII (U.S. 7-bit ASCII character set) and F7DEC (DEC French 7-bit character set).

The HEXTORAW function

The HEXTORAW function converts a hexadecimal string from type CHAR or VARCHAR2 to type RAW. The specification of the HEXTORAW function is:

```
FUNCTION HEXTORAW (string_in IN CHAR) RETURN RAW
FUNCTION HEXTORAW (string_in IN VARCHAR2) RETURN RAW
```

The RAWTOHEX function

The RAWTOHEX function converts a value from type RAW to a hexadecimal string of type VARCHAR2. The specification of the RAWTOHEX function is:

```
FUNCTION RAWTOHEX (binary_value_in IN RAW) RETURN VARCHAR2
```

RAWTOHEX always returns a variable-length string value, even if its mirror conversion function is overloaded to support both types of input.

The ROWIDTOCHAR function

The ROWIDTOCHAR function converts a binary value of type ROWID to a string of type VARCHAR2. The specification of the ROWIDTOCHAR function is:

```
FUNCTION ROWIDTOCHAR (row_in IN ROWID ) RETURN VARCHAR2
```

The string returned by this function has the format:

```
BBBBBBBB.RRRR.FFFF
```

where *BBBBBBBB* is the number of the block in the database file, *RRRR* is the number of the row in the block, and *FFFF* is the number of the database file. All three numbers are in hexadecimal format; for example:

```
11/14/1994      1988      2018
```

CHAPTER 8
Strings

In this chapter:

- The Impact of Character Sets
- String Datatypes
- String Issues
- String Functions
- NLS Functions

Variables with character datatypes store text and are manipulated by character functions. Because character strings are "free-form," there are few rules concerning their content. For example, you can store numbers and letters, as well as any combination of special characters, in a character-type variable. There are, however, several different kinds of character datatypes, each of which serves a particular purpose.

CLOB (character large object) and LONG, while arguably character types, cannot be used in the same manner as the character types discussed in this chapter, and are more usefully thought of as *large object types*. We discuss large object types in Chapter 12.

The Impact of Character Sets

Working with strings used to be a short and simple topic. However, as applications have grown more international in nature, Oracle's support for different character sets, especially Unicode, has expanded, and a good understanding of character set issues is now almost a necessity when working with strings.

What Is a Character Set?

A *character set* is a mapping between a set of characters meaningful to humans and a set of bit sequences used to represent those characters in a computer or on a disk. 7-bit ASCII is a commonly used character set in the United States. Each 7-bit ASCII character is represented as a sequence of seven bits within an eight-bit byte. The letter G, then, is represented as 0100 0111. Look at that same string of bits as a number, and you end up with 0x47 (hexadecimal) or 71 (decimal). With seven bits, you can represent only 128 characters, enough to handle American English and little else. The characters that a character set's designers choose to represent, together with their underlying numeric values, form the definition of a character set.

7-bit ASCII was one of the first character sets to be defined, and it's very U.S.-centric. By that we mean that the people who defined 7-bit ASCII did not choose to represent any letters needed by languages other than English. As a result, many, many other character sets have been defined by various standards organizations and companies in order to handle characters used by other languages. Many of these character sets are supersets of ASCII that make use of the eighth bit to represent an additional 128 characters. For example, the Microsoft Windows Code Page 1251 8-bit Latin/Cyrillic character set is compatible with ASCII, but also represents Cyrillic characters.

256 characters is enough for most western character sets, such as those based on the Latin or Cyrillic alphabets. However, 256 characters is nowhere near enough to represent Asian languages such as Japanese, Korean, and Chinese—such languages have far more than 256 characters. Consequently, character sets for those languages typically use two or even more bytes per character. Such character sets are referred to as *multibyte character sets*.

Unicode is a relative newcomer on the character set scene. Unicode refers to a class of character sets that have been developed to incorporate all known characters into one character set. Different Unicode character sets are available, but each encompasses the same, or almost the same, universal set of characters.

For authoritative information on Unicode, visit *http://unicode.org*.

Types of Character Sets

Character sets can be categorized in many different ways, but the distinctions that matter most to PL/SQL programmers are the following:

- Single-byte versus multibyte
- Fixed-width versus variable-width

Let's return for a moment to the 7-bit ASCII character set. The seven bits used to represent each character fit into a single byte, and each character is represented using a separate byte. Consequently, 7-bit ASCII is considered a *single-byte* character set. It's also considered a *fixed-width* character set, in that each character is represented using the same number of bytes (one in this case) as every other character.

Character sets capable of representing more than 256 characters—for example, the Unicode UTF-8 character set—often use single bytes to represent the traditional ASCII characters and perhaps some other commonly used characters, and multiple bytes to represent everything else. In UTF-8 characters are represented by as many as three bytes; for example, the letter G is represented numerically as 71 (or 0x41 in hexadecimal), whereas the Euro symbol (€) is represented as three bytes: 0xE282AC. In addition, some UTF-8 characters may be represented using surrogate pairs, which are special sequences of two characters that always use a total of four bytes. Character sets such as UTF-8 are *multibyte* because they use more than one byte for some characters, and they are *variable-width* because the number of bytes used per character is not always the same.

A third class of character sets is *multibyte* and *fixed-width*. The Unicode UTF-16 character set is a good example of this class, as each UTF-16 character is represented using exactly two bytes. The letter A, for example, is represented as two bytes with values of 0 and 65 respectively.

There is no such thing as a variable-width, single-byte character set. Single-byte character sets, by definition, always use one byte per character, and are thus always fixed-width.

Database Character Set Versus National Language Character Set

Every Oracle database has not one, but two character sets associated with it:

A database character set
: Used for CHAR and VARCHAR2 columns; for table names, column names, PL/SQL variable names, and other such identifiers; and for SQL statements and most string literals.

A national language character set
: Used for NCHAR and NVARCHAR2 columns, and for string literals prefixed with an N (see "Specifying String Constants" later in this chapter).

Why two character sets? Historically, this came about largely for performance reasons. With two character sets, it became possible to use the database character set for single-byte ASCII characters, and to use the national character set for fixed-width multibyte characters. With this scenario, your database character set still supports ASCII, you can still support multibyte characters, and you don't take a performance hit from having to deal with multibyte characters all of the time.

If you're not certain which two character sets your database supports, you can query the NLS_DATABASE_PARAMETERS view in the Oracle data dictionary to find out:

```
SQL> SELECT *
  2  FROM nls_database_parameters
  3  WHERE parameter IN ('NLS_CHARACTERSET','NLS_NCHAR_CHARACTERSET');

PARAMETER                      VALUE
------------------------------ ----------------------------------------
NLS_CHARACTERSET               WE8MSWIN1252
NLS_NCHAR_CHARACTERSET         AL16UTF16
```

The NLS_CHARACTERSET parameter returns Oracle's name for the database character set. The NLS_NCHAR_CHARACTERSET parameter returns Oracle's name for the national character set used for NCHAR and NVARCHAR2 types.

The character set "names" that Oracle uses are really convenient abbreviations recognized by the Oracle software. These abbreviations are not necessarily recognized by standards bodies, and they are not usually official character set names. For example, AL16UTF16 is Oracle's abbreviation for Unicode UTF-16. With some exceptions, you can often learn useful information about a character set just from the name Oracle uses for it. Figure 8-1 illustrates Oracle's character set naming convention.

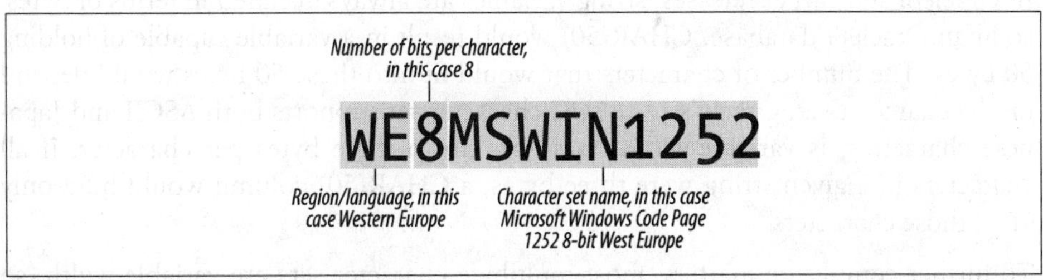

Figure 8-1. Oracle's character set naming convention

The key item in the naming convention is the second element, indicating the number of bits per character. If it's 7 or 8, you can be confident that you are dealing with a single-byte, fixed-width character set. If it is 16, 32, or any other value higher than 8, you are dealing with a multibyte character set. Most multibyte character sets are variable-length, but the name alone won't tell you that.

Sometimes you will see an S or a C on the end of a character set name. Such a suffix indicates a character set that can be used only on the server (S) or only on the client (C).

The naming convention shown in Figure 8-1 isn't universally applied to all Oracle character sets. For example, UTF8, Oracle's name for the UTF-8 character set, does not conform to the naming convention just described.

Character Set Issues

One byte or two? Fixed or variable? Does all this really matter? Yes, it does. When you are declaring string variables, the character set matters in different ways:

- It affects the maximum number of characters you can fit into a string.
- It impacts the interpretation of results returned by certain string functions.
- It can affect sort order (i.e., whether one string is greater or less than another).

Bytes versus characters

One of the first issues you need to wrap your mind around is that of bytes versus characters. Consider the following declaration for a string variable:

```
feature_name CHAR(50);
```

Does this declaration allow for 50 characters or for 50 bytes? If your database character set is of the single-byte variety, then the distinction hardly matters: 50 characters is the same as 50 bytes. But if your database uses a multibyte character set, then you really do need to know whether you are getting a 50-byte variable, or a variable capable of holding 50 multibyte characters.

In Oracle8*i* and earlier releases, string variables are always declared in terms of bytes, so in an Oracle8*i* database, CHAR(50) would result in a variable capable of holding 50 bytes. The number of characters that would fit into these 50 bytes would depend on the character set. Oracle's JA16EUC character set supports both ASCII and Japanese characters, is variable-width, and uses up to three bytes per character. If all characters in a given string were three bytes, a CHAR(50) column would hold only 16 of those characters.

To further complicate matters, most multibyte character sets are variable-width, so the number of characters that will fit into 50 bytes will vary. For example, the Unicode UTF-8 character set is a variable-width character set where characters are represented by up to three bytes. To prepare for the case in which the UTF-8 characters all have three bytes (surrogate pairs aren't considered here), you'd need to declare that variable as a CHAR(150) to be absolutely certain a variable could hold any 50 UTF-8 characters.

Oracle9i string declarations

Beginning with Oracle9*i*, you have the option when declaring string variables of specifying whether your length is in terms of bytes or in terms of characters. For example, to declare a CHAR variable capable of holding 50 bytes, you can do the following:

```
feature_name CHAR(50 BYTE)
```

However, if you want to be certain that your variable can hold 50 characters from the underlying character set, you would declare as follows:

```
feature_name CHAR(50 CHAR)
```

And what of the following simple declaration?

```
feature_name CHAR(50)
```

This is ambiguous unless you know a critical piece of information about how the database has been configured. You need to know the setting of the NLS_LENGTH_SEMANTICS parameter, which you can find using the following query:

```
SQL> SELECT *
  2  FROM nls_session_parameters
```

```
  3  WHERE parameter = 'NLS_LENGTH_SEMANTICS';

PARAMETER                      VALUE
------------------------------ ------------------
NLS_LENGTH_SEMANTICS           BYTE
```

A value of BYTE is the default NLS_LENGTH_SEMANTICS setting, indicating that byte semantics are the default and that CHAR(50) is the same as CHAR(50 BYTE). A value of CHAR indicates character semantics, in which case CHAR(50) would be interpreted as CHAR(50 CHAR). Be aware that your DBA can change the NLS_LENGTH_SEMANTICS setting from its default using an ALTER SYSTEM command; you yourself can change it at the session level via the ALTER SESSION command. If you have any doubts about NLS_LENGTH_SEMANTICS, query the NLS_SESSION_PARAMETERS view for the current setting.

Your use of the BYTE and CHAR qualifiers has an effect that outlasts a variable's declaration. The qualifiers also affect the way in which certain string functions treat the variables and whether CHAR variables are padded (or not padded) with spaces to their maximum length. Consider the following two tables, created on a system using UTF-8 as the database character set:

```
SQL> DESCRIBE utest
 Name        Null?    Type
 ----------- -------- -------------
 UCHAR                CHAR(1 CHAR)

SQL> DESCRIBE utest2
 Name        Null?    Type
 ----------- -------- -------------
 UCHAR2               CHAR(3)
```

One column has been declared using character semantics, while the other has been declared using byte semantics. Yet both columns consume three bytes, as the following data dictionary query demonstrates:

```
SQL> SELECT table_name, column_name, data_length, char_length, char_used
  2  FROM user_tab_columns
  3  WHERE column_name IN ('UCHAR','UCHAR2');

TABLE_NAME COLUMN_NAM DATA_LENGTH CHAR_LENGTH CHAR_USED
---------- ---------- ----------- ----------- ---------
UTEST      UCHAR                3           1 C
UTEST2     UCHAR2               3           3 B
```

You can see that both columns use three bytes (DATA_LENGTH), and that Oracle has kept track of whether character or byte semantics were used to declare the columns (CHAR_USED).

The following PL/SQL code snippet shows the effect of the differing semantics on the operation of the LENGTH function:

```
DECLARE
   uchar utest.uchar%TYPE;
   uchar2 utest2.uchar2%TYPE;
BEGIN
   uchar := 'ã';
   uchar2 := 'ã';
   DBMS_OUTPUT.PUT_LINE(LENGTH(uchar));
   DBMS_OUTPUT.PUT_LINE(LENGTH(uchar2));
   DBMS_OUTPUT.PUT_LINE(LENGTHB(uchar));
   DBMS_OUTPUT.PUT_LINE(LENGTHB(uchar2));
END;
```

The output is:

```
1
2
2
3
```

The key to understanding this output lies in knowing that the LENGTH function (which you'll learn more about later in this chapter) always returns the length of a string in terms of characters. Likewise, LENGTHB counts the number of bytes occupied by the characters in a string, not the number of bytes used to declare the string. Here are some things to note about this code example:

- The uchar and uchar2 variable declarations are based on the underlying database columns. Therefore, each variable occupies three bytes.
- Both variables are set to the single character ã, which is represented in Unicode UTF-8 using two bytes.
- Because uchar was declared using character semantics, its length is reported in terms of characters. ã is one character. The length of uchar will always be one character.
- Because uchar2 was declared using byte semantics, there is one byte left over after the two-byte character ã. This extra byte is filled with a space character (as is always the case with extra bytes in CHAR strings). The resulting length, however, is still reported in terms of characters.
- The fact that both variables consume three bytes is not reflected in the values returned by LENGTH because that function is counting characters, not bytes.
- LENGTHB returns the length of each variable in terms of bytes, but the semantics used to declare each variable still affect the results. LENGTHB counts not the number of physical bytes occupied by the variable, but rather the number of bytes occupied by each variable's *value*. The value ã in uchar is two bytes long. The value in uchar2, however, is ã followed by a space character, for a total of three bytes.

Because of the confusion that can arise when character and byte semantics are mixed, Oracle recommends that you not use the CHAR and BYTE qualifiers and instead rely on the database default, which you can set using NLS_LENGTH_SEMANTICS. There isn't yet a large enough body of knowledge on this issue to enable us to agree or disagree with Oracle's recommendation. However, we strongly believe that if you are using multibyte character sets, you must familiarize yourself with the issues we've described in this section, and understand how the CHAR and BYTE qualifiers affect the operation of string variables.

Character function semantics

Character functions such as SUBSTR and INSTR deal with positions inside a string. SUBSTR, for example, allows you to specify starting and ending positions for a substring you want to extract from a containing string. You can choose to express such positions in terms of bytes or characters. Functions such as SUBSTR and INSTR always deal in characters; functions such as SUBSTRB and INSTRB (note the trailing B) always deal in bytes. If you're working with multibyte character sets, it matters which function you use in any given situation. When using Unicode, you have even more character function variations to learn about.

Code points and code units

When working with Unicode, there is more than just bytes and characters to deal with. You must also understand something about code points and code units. In Unicode, a *code point* is a numeric value corresponding to an entry in an encoding table. For example, 0x0061 is the code point for the letter "a". Code points are sometimes combined in order to form one character. The code point for the letter "a" can be combined with 0x0303, the code point corresponding to the tilde to form the character ã. The 0x0303 code point happens to represent a *combining diacritical mark*, meaning that it is always used to modify a character, never used standalone.

In Unicode, it's not only possible for multiple code points to represent one character, but one code point can represent many characters. If you find that confusing, don't feel bad—we do too.

While a code point represents a specific mapping of a character to a numeric value in an encoding table, a *code unit* refers to the actual representation of the code point. Take, for example, the Unicode code point 0x0061 representing the letter "a". The UTF-8 representation of that code point uses just one byte: 0x61. That one byte is a code unit. The UTF-16 representation, on the other hand, uses two bytes to represent the code point: 0x0061. Those two bytes together form one code unit. As you can see, the code unit size (i.e., the number of bytes in the code unit) varies depending on which form of Unicode is being used. Sometimes, a code point value is too large for the underlying code unit. In such cases, the code point is represented using two or more code units. For example, the code point 0x1D11E, which represents the musical symbol G clef (𝄞), is represented in UTF-16 using two code units: 0xD834 and 0xDD1E. Neither value represents a code point by itself—only together do the two code units represent a code point, and in this case the code point in turn represents a single character.

The distinction between bytes, characters, code points, and code units becomes important when you work with string functions such as LENGTH and INSTR. When you want the length of a string, do you want it in terms of bytes, characters, code points, or code units? Oracle9*i* supports variations of these functions that allow you to choose the semantics that you wish to use for a given invocation; for example, you can use LENGTHC to look at the length of a string in terms of the number of Unicode characters it holds. Certain Unicode characters can be represented in multiple ways. In UTF-16, the character ã can be represented as the single code point 0x00E3 or as the two code points 0x0061 and 0x0303. The standard LENGTH function will see the two code points as two characters. The LENGTHC function will recognize that 0x0061 followed by 0x0303 represents only a single character.

Unicode has many subtle facets. We've been told there may be unusual cases where a single Unicode character could be interpreted as multiple characters by a person who speaks the language in question. Because of subtle issues like this one, we strongly recommend that you become familiar with the resources at *http://unicode.org* if you work with Unicode.

In addition to LENGTH and LENGTHC, you should also consider LENGTH2 and LENGTH4. LENGTH2 counts the number of code units in a string, and LENGTH4 counts the number of code points in a string. This is why it's important to understand the distinction between code units and code points. Other character string functions, such as SUBSTR and INSTR, also have the same variations as LENGTH.

In Oracle's documentation you'll see references to UCS-2 and UCS-4. These acronyms are where the 2 and 4 in LENGTH2 and LENGTH4 come from. Originally defined by an ISO standard that mirrored the Unicode specification, the UCS-2 and UCS-4 acronyms are now obsolete. Whenever you see UCS-2, think code unit. Whenever you see UCS-4, think code point.

Equality of Unicode strings

When testing two character strings for equality, PL/SQL doesn't take into account the fact that a single Unicode character may have more than one representation. A string containing the single code point 0x00E3 to represent the character ã is not considered the equivalent of a string containing the two code points 0x0061 and 0x0303. For example:

```
DECLARE
   x NVARCHAR2(30);
```

```
    y NVARCHAR2(30);
BEGIN
    x := UNISTR('\00E3');
    y := UNISTR('\0061\0303');
    IF x = y THEN
       DBMS_OUTPUT.PUT_LINE('x = y');
    ELSIF x <> y THEN
       DBMS_OUTPUT.PUT_LINE('x <> y');
    END IF;
END;
```

The output is:

```
x <> y
```

You can use the COMPOSE function, described later in this chapter, to deal with this particular situation. In this specific instance, you would write:

```
IF COMPOSE(x) = COMPOSE(y)
```

There is one situation where COMPOSE won't help, though, and that is when a character can be represented both by a surrogate pair and by its code point value.

In Oracle9*i* Release 1, you must call COMPOSE from within a SQL statement. In Release 2, you can also invoke COMPOSE in a PL/SQL statement.

Sort order

Sort order is perhaps the only character set issue that is not an extension of the basic bytes-versus-characters issue. Different character sets use different numeric values for the various characters represented. This affects comparison statements in which one string or character is compared to another. Is the uppercase letter "A" greater than or less than the lowercase letter "a"? It depends. If you're using an ASCII-based character set, you'll find that uppercase letters are "less than" lowercase letters. If you're using EBCDIC, however, you'll find the opposite to be true.

String Datatypes

Oracle supports four string datatypes, which are summarized in Table 8-1. Which type you should use depends on your answers to the following two questions:

- Are you working with variable-length or fixed-length strings?
- Do you wish to use the database character set or the national character set?

Table 8-1. PL/SQL's string datatypes

	Fixed-length	Variable-length
Database character set	CHAR	VARCHAR2
National character set	NCHAR	NVARCHAR2

You will rarely need or want to use the fixed-length CHAR and NCHAR datatypes in Oracle-based applications; in fact, we recommend that you never use these types unless there is a specific requirement for fixed-length strings. See the upcoming "String Issues" section for a description of problems you may encounter when mixing fixed- and variable-length string variables.

The VARCHAR2 Datatype

VARCHAR2 variables store variable-length character strings. When you declare a variable-length string, you must also specify a maximum length for the string, which can range from 1 to 32767 bytes. You may specify the maximum length in terms of characters or bytes, but either way the length is ultimately defined in bytes. The general format for a VARCHAR2 declaration is:

```
variable_name VARCHAR2 (max_length [CHAR | BYTE]);
```

where:

variable_name
: Is the name of the variable you wish to declare.

max_length
: Is the maximum length of the variable.

CHAR
: Indicates that *max_length* is expressed in terms of characters.

BYTE
: Indicates that *max_length* represents a number of bytes.

When you specify the maximum length of a VARCHAR2 string in terms of characters (using the CHAR qualifier), the actual length in bytes is determined using the largest number of bytes that the database character set uses to represent a character. For example, the Unicode UTF-8 character set uses up to three bytes for some characters; thus, if UTF-8 is your underlying character set, declaring a VARCHAR2 variable with a maximum length of 100 characters is equivalent to declaring the same variable with a maximum length of 300 bytes.

If you omit the CHAR or BYTE qualifier when declaring a VARCHAR2 variable, then whether the size is in characters or bytes depends on the NLS_LENGTH_SEMANTICS parameter. NLS_LENGTH_SEMANTICS defaults to BYTE, so you'll find in practice that omitting the qualifier usually results in byte-sized variables.

Following are some examples of VARCHAR2 declarations:

```
DECLARE
   small_string VARCHAR2(4);
   line_of_text VARCHAR2(2000);
   feature_name VARCHAR2(100 BYTE); -- 100 byte string
   emp_name VARCHAR2(30 CHAR); -- 30 character string
```

The maximum length allowed for PL/SQL VARCHAR2 variables is 32,767 bytes, a much higher maximum than that for the VARCHAR2 datatype in the Oracle RDBMS (2000 bytes prior to Oracle8*i*, and 4000 bytes in Oracle8*i* and above). This size limit applies regardless of whether you declare the variable's size in terms of characters or bytes. As a result of PL/SQL's much higher size limit, if you plan to store a PL/SQL VARCHAR2 value into a VARCHAR2 database column, you must remember that only the first 2000 or 4000 bytes can be inserted, depending on which release of Oracle you are using. Neither PL/SQL nor SQL automatically resolves this inconsistency.

If you need to work with strings greater than 4000 bytes in length (or 2000 prior to Oracle8*i*), consider storing those strings in CLOB (character large object) columns. See Chapter 12 for information on CLOBs.

The CHAR Datatype

The CHAR datatype specifies a fixed-length character string. When you declare a fixed-length string, you also specify a maximum length for the string, which can range from 1 to 32767 bytes. (Again, this is much higher than that for the CHAR datatype in the Oracle RDBMS, which is only 2000, or 255 prior to Oracle8*i*. You can specify the length in terms of bytes or in terms of characters. For example, the following two declarations create strings of 100 bytes and 100 characters respectively:

```
feature_name CHAR(100 BYTE);
feature_name CHAR(100 CHAR);
```

The actual number of bytes in a 100-character string depends on the underlying database character set. If you are using a variable-width character set, PL/SQL will allocate enough bytes to the string to accommodate the specified number of worst-case characters. For example, UTF-8 uses between one and three bytes per character, so PL/SQL will assume the worst and allocate three bytes × 100 characters, for a total of 300 bytes.

If you leave off the BYTE or CHAR qualifier, the results will depend on the setting of the NLS_LENGTH_SEMANTICS parameter. Assuming the default setting, the following declaration results in a 100-byte string:

```
feature_name CHAR(100);
```

If you do not specify a length for the string, PL/SQL declares a string of one byte. Suppose you declare a variable as follows:

```
feature_name CHAR;
```

As soon as you assign a string of more than one character to feature_name, PL/ SQL will raise the generic VALUE_ERROR exception. It will not tell you where it encountered this problem. So if you do get this error, check your variable declarations for a

Is Fixed-Length Really Fixed?

You can get very unusual results when you declare CHAR variables using byte semantics and use those variables to store characters in a multibyte character set. The following example was generated on a system using UTF-8 as the database character set:

```
DECLARE
   x CHAR(3);
BEGIN
   --Assign a single-byte character
   x := 'a';
   DBMS_OUTPUT.PUT_LINE(LENGTH(x));

   --and now a two-byte character
   x := 'ã';
   DBMS_OUTPUT.PUT_LINE(LENGTH(x));

   --and now two characters for a total
   --of three bytes
   x := 'ãa';
   DBMS_OUTPUT.PUT_LINE(LENGTH(x));
END;
```

The output is:

```
3
2
2
```

Isn't it interesting that the length of a supposedly fixed-length string changes? Isn't it even more interesting that the length of ã is exactly the same as the length of ãa? What's happening here is that the LENGTH function is counting characters. In the first case, the string has the letter "a" followed by two spaces, for a total of three characters. In the next case, it's the two-byte character ã followed by only one space, for a total of two characters in three bytes. In the last case, it's the two-byte character ã followed by the single-byte letter "a", also for a total of two characters.

Run this same piece of code with x declared as CHAR(3 CHAR), and the length will consistently be three characters. Thus, when working with multibyte characters, it might be best to always use character semantics in your declarations.

lazy use of CHAR. To avoid mistakes and to prevent future programmers from wondering about your intent, you should *always* specify a length when you use the CHAR datatype. Several examples follow:

```
yes_or_no CHAR (1) DEFAULT 'Y';
line_of_text    CHAR (80 CHAR); --Always a full 80 characters!
whole_paragraph CHAR (10000 BYTE); --Think of all the spaces...
```

Because CHAR is fixed-length, PL/SQL will right-pad any value assigned to a CHAR variable with spaces to the maximum length specified in the declaration.

Prior to Oracle7, the CHAR datatype was variable-length; Oracle did not support a fixed-length character string datatype and prided itself on that fact. To improve compatibility with IBM relational databases and to comply with ANSI standards, Oracle7 reintroduced CHAR as a fixed-length datatype and offered VARCHAR2 as the variable-length datatype.

The NVARCHAR2 and NCHAR Datatypes

The NVARCHAR2 and NCHAR datatypes represent character data using the national character set rather than the database character set. In addition, they are always declared using character semantics (no CHAR qualifier applies). Other than those two differences, NVARCHAR2 and NCHAR are just like their counterparts, VARCHAR2 and CHAR. Use NVARCHAR2 for variable-length strings in the national character set, and use NCHAR for fixed-length strings in the national character set.

Following are some example declarations:

```
line_of_text NVARCHAR2(2000); -- 2000 characters, variable-length
feature_name NCHAR(100); -- 100 characters, fixed-length
```

Prior to Oracle9*i*, the national character set could be any one of a large number of single- and multibyte character sets. Beginning with Oracle9*i*, the national character set used by NCHAR and NVARCHAR2 variables must be either UTF-8 (multibyte, variable-width) or UTF-16 (multibyte, fixed-width).

See the "Database Character Set Versus the National Language Character Set" section earlier in this chapter for a more detailed explanation of database and national character sets.

The NVARCHAR2 and NCHAR types have been improved in Oracle9*i*, and you may now freely mix them in expressions involving VARCHAR2 and CHAR. Prior to Oracle9*i*, for example, if you attempted to compare a VARCHAR2 value with an NVARCHAR2 value, PL/SQL would return a *PLS-00561: character set mismatch* error. In Oracle9*i*, such expressions are possible. Of course, you pay a penalty in terms of efficiency, because PL/SQL must implicitly convert the values to a common character set.

String Subtypes

PL/SQL supports several subtypes, listed in Table 8-2, that you can use when declaring character string variables. Many of these subtypes exist for the ostensible purpose of providing compatibility with the ANSI SQL standard. It's unlikely that you'll ever need to use these—we never do—but you should be aware that they exist.

Table 8-2. PL/SQL subtypes and their equivalents

Subtype	Equivalent PL/SQL type
CHAR VARYING	VARCHAR2
CHARACTER	CHAR
CHARACTER VARYING	VARCHAR2
NATIONAL CHAR	NCHAR
NATIONAL CHAR VARYING	NVARCHAR2
NATIONAL CHARACTER	NCHAR
NATIONAL CHARACTER VARYING	NVARCHAR2
NCHAR VARYING	NVARCHAR2
STRING	VARCHAR2
VARCHAR	VARCHAR2

Each subtype listed in the table is equivalent to the base PL/SQL type shown in the right-hand column. For example, the following declarations all have the same effect:

```
feature_name VARCHAR2(100);
feature_name CHARACTER VARYING(100);
feature_name CHAR VARYING(100);
feature_name STRING(100);
```

The VARCHAR subtype deserves special mention. For years now Oracle has been threatening to change the meaning of VARCHAR (to something not equivalent to VARCHAR2) and warning against its use. We agree with Oracle's recommendation. If there's a possibility of VARCHAR's being changed, it's senseless to depend on its current behavior. Don't use VARCHAR; use VARCHAR2.

String Issues

Most of the time, working with strings is very straightforward. However, there are some subtle issues you should be aware of, as described in the next few sections.

Empty Strings Are NULL Strings

One issue that often causes great consternation, especially to people who come to Oracle after working with other databases, is that Oracle treats empty strings as NULLs. This is contrary to the ANSI SQL standard, which recognizes the difference between an empty string and a string variable that is NULL.

The following code demonstrates Oracle's behavior:

```
/* File on web: empty_is_null.tst */
DECLARE
   empty_varchar2 VARCHAR2(10) := '';
   empty_char CHAR(10) := '';
BEGIN
```

```
    IF empty_varchar2 IS NULL THEN
       DBMS_OUTPUT.PUT_LINE('empty_varchar2 is NULL');
    END IF;

    IF '' IS NULL THEN
       DBMS_OUTPUT.PUT_LINE(''''' is NULL');
    END IF;

    IF empty_char IS NULL THEN
       DBMS_OUTPUT.PUT_LINE('empty_char is NULL');
    END IF;
END;
```

The output is:

```
empty_varchar2 is NULL
'' is NULL
```

You'll notice in this example that the CHAR variable is not considered NULL. That's because CHAR variables, as fixed-length character strings, are never truly empty. The CHAR variable in this example is padded with blanks until it is exactly 10 characters in length. The VARCHAR2 variable, however, is NULL, as is the zero-length string literal.

You have to really watch for this behavior in IF statements that compare two VARCHAR2 values. Consider a program that queries the user for a name, and then compares that name to a value read in from the database:

```
DECLARE
   user_entered_name VARCHAR2(30);
   name_from_database VARCHAR2(30);
   ...
BEGIN
...
IF user_entered_name <> name_from_database THEN
...
```

If the user entered an empty string instead of a name, the IF condition shown in this example would never be TRUE. That's because a NULL is never not-equal, nor equal, to any other value. One alternative approach to this IF statement is the following:

```
IF (user_entered_name <> name_from_database)
   OR (user_entered_name IS NULL) THEN
```

This is just one way of dealing with the "empty string is NULL" issue; it's impossible to provide a solution that works in all cases. You must think through what you are trying to accomplish, recognize that any empty strings will be treated as NULLs, and code appropriately.

Mixing CHAR and VARCHAR2 Values

If you make use of both fixed-length (CHAR) and variable-length (VARCHAR2) strings in your PL/SQL code, you should be aware of how Oracle handles the interactions between these two datatypes, as described in the following sections.

Database-to-variable conversion

When you SELECT or FETCH data from a CHAR database column into a VARCHAR2 variable, the trailing spaces are retained. If you SELECT or FETCH from a VARCHAR2 database column into a CHAR variable, PL/SQL automatically pads the value with spaces out to the maximum length. In other words, the type of the variable, not the column, determines the variable's resulting value.

Variable-to-database conversion

When you INSERT or UPDATE a CHAR variable into a VARCHAR2 database column, the SQL kernel does not trim the trailing blanks before performing the change. When the following PL/SQL is executed, the company_name in the new database record is set to "ACME SHOWERS••••••••" (where • indicates a space). It is, in other words, padded out to 20 characters, even though the default value was a string of only 12 characters.

```
DECLARE
   comp_id#   NUMBER;
   comp_name  CHAR(20) := 'ACME SHOWERS';
BEGIN
   SELECT company_id_seq.NEXTVAL
      INTO comp_id#
      FROM dual;
   INSERT INTO company (company_id, company_name)
      VALUES (comp_id#, comp_name);
END;
```

On the other hand, when you INSERT or UPDATE a VARCHAR2 variable into a CHAR database column, the SQL kernel automatically pads the variable-length string with spaces out to the maximum (fixed) length specified when the table was created, and places that expanded value into the database.

String comparisons

Suppose your code contains a string comparison such as the following:

```
IF company_name = parent_company_name ...
```

PL/SQL must compare company_name to parent_company_name. It performs the comparison in one of two ways, depending on the types of the two variables:

- If a comparison is made between two CHAR variables, then PL/SQL uses a blank-padding comparison.
- If at least one of the strings involved in the comparison is variable-length, then PL/SQL performs a non-blank-padding comparison.

The following code snippet illustrates the difference between these two comparison methods:

```
DECLARE
   company_name CHAR(30)
```

```
      := 'Feuerstein and Friends';
   char_parent_company_name CHAR(35)
      := 'Feuerstein and Friends';
   varchar2_parent_company_name VARCHAR2(35)
      := 'Feuerstein and Friends';
BEGIN
   --Compare two CHARs, so blank-padding is used
   IF company_name = char_parent_company_name THEN
      DBMS_OUTPUT.PUT_LINE ('first comparison is TRUE');
   ELSE
      DBMS_OUTPUT.PUT_LINE ('first comparison is FALSE');
   END IF;

   --Compare a CHAR and a VARCHAR2, so nonblank-padding is used
   IF company_name = varchar2_parent_company_name THEN
      DBMS_OUTPUT.PUT_LINE ('second comparison is TRUE');
   ELSE
      DBMS_OUTPUT.PUT_LINE ('second comparison is FALSE');
   END IF;
END;
```

The output is:

```
first comparison is TRUE
second comparison is FALSE
```

The first comparison is between two CHAR values, so blank-padding is used: PL/SQL blank-pads the shorter of the two values out to the length of the longer value. It then performs the comparison. In this example, PL/SQL adds five spaces to the end of the value in company_name and then performs the comparison between company_name and char_parent_company_name. The result is that both strings are considered equal. Note that PL/SQL does not actually change the company_name variable's value. It copies the value to another memory structure and then modifies this temporary data for the comparison.

The second comparison involves a VARCHAR2 value, so PL/SQL performs a non-blank-padding comparison. It makes no changes to any of the values, uses the existing lengths, and performs the comparison. In this case, the first 22 characters of both strings are the same, "Feuerstein and Friends", but the fixed-length company_name is padded with eight space characters, whereas the variable-length varchar2_company_name is not. Because one string has trailing blanks and the other does not, the two strings are not considered equal.

The fact that one VARCHAR2 value causes non-blank-padding comparisons is also true of expressions involving more than two variables, as well as of expressions involving the IN operator. For example:

```
IF menu_selection NOT IN
      (save_and_close, cancel_and_exit, 'OPEN_SCREEN')
   THEN ...
```

If any of the four strings in this example (menu_selection, the two named constants, and the single literal) is declared VARCHAR2, then exact comparisons without modification are performed to determine if the user has made a valid selection. Note that a literal like OPEN_SCREEN is always considered a fixed-length CHAR datatype.

Character functions and CHAR arguments

A character function is a function that takes one or more character values as parameters and returns either a character value or a number value. When a character function returns a character value, that value is always of type VARCHAR2 (variable length), with the exceptions of UPPER and LOWER. These functions convert to upper- and lowercase, respectively, and return CHAR values (fixed length) if the strings they are called on to convert are fixed-length CHAR arguments.

Specifying String Constants

By now you've seen a number of string constants in this chapter's examples, so you know that you specify a string constant by enclosing it within single quotes:

```
'Brighten the corner where you are'
```

If you wish to embed a single quote within a string constant, you can do so by typing the single quote twice:

```
'Aren''t you glad you''re learning PL/SQL?'
```

Normally, string constants are represented using the database character set. If such a string constant is assigned to an NCHAR or NVARCHAR2 variable, it will be implicitly converted to the national character set. Oracle performs such conversions when necessary, and you rarely need to worry about them. Occasionally, however, you may find yourself faced with the need to explicitly specify a string constant to be represented in the national character set. You can do so using the N prefix:

```
N'This string will be represented using the national character set.'
```

While not strictly a PL/SQL issue, you'll often find that ampersand (&) characters cause problems if you're executing PL/SQL code via SQL*Plus. SQL*Plus uses ampersands to prefix SQL*Plus variables, and when an ampersand is encountered, SQL*Plus will prompt you for a value. For example:

```
SQL> BEGIN
  2     DBMS_OUTPUT.PUT_LINE ('Generating & saving test data.');
  3  END;
  4  /
Enter value for saving:
```

There are several solutions to this problem. One that works well is to issue the SQL*Plus command SET DEFINE OFF to disable SQL*Plus's variable substitution feature. Other solutions can be found in Jonathan Gennick's book *Oracle SQL*Plus: The Definitive Guide* (O'Reilly).

String Functions

PL/SQL provides a rich set of string functions that allow you to get information about strings and modify the contents of those strings in very high-level, powerful ways. Table 8-3 shows the string functions covered in detail in this section. The remaining functions are specific to Oracle's National Language Support (NLS) and Trusted Oracle features. National Language Support functions are covered later in this chapter in the "NLS Functions" section.

Table 8-3. String functions

Name	Description
ASCII	Returns the ASCII code of a character.
ASCIISTR	Converts a string to a string of ASCII characters.
CHR	Returns the character associated with the specified collating code.
COMPOSE	Takes a Unicode string and returns it in a fully normalized form.
CONCAT	Concatenates two strings into one.
DECOMPOSE	Takes a Unicode string and returns it in with any precomposed characters decomposed into separate elements.
GREATEST	Returns the string that would come last (if sorted alphabetically).
INITCAP	Sets the first letter of each word to uppercase. All other letters are set to lowercase.
INSTR, INSTRB, INSTRC, INSTR2, INSTR4	Returns the location in a string of the specified substring.
LEAST	Returns the string that would come first (if sorted alphabetically).
LENGTH, LENGTHB, LENGTHC, LENGTH2, LENGTH4	Returns the length of a string.
LOWER	Converts all letters to lowercase.
LPAD	Pads a string on the left with the specified characters.
LTRIM	Trims the left side of a string of all specified characters.
REPLACE	Replaces a character sequence in a string with a different set of characters.
RPAD	Pads a string on the right with the specified characters.
RTRIM	Trims the right side of a string of all specified characters.
SOUNDEX	Returns the "soundex" of a string.
SUBSTR, SUBSTRB, SUBSTRC, SUBSTR2, SUBSTR4	Returns the specified portion of a string.
TO_CHAR	Converts national character set data into its database character set equivalent.
TO_MULTI_BYTE	Takes a string as input and, where possible, converts any single-byte characters to their multibyte equivalents. In UTF-8, for example, many characters can be represented using one byte or using multiple bytes.
TO_SINGLE_BYTE	Does the reverse of TO_MULTI_BYTE, converting multibyte characters to their single-byte equivalents.
TRANSLATE	Translates single characters in a string to different characters.

Table 8-3. String functions (continued)

Name	Description
TRANSLATE...USING	Translates character data between character sets.
TRIM	Combines functionality of RTRIM and LTRIM.
UNISTR	Does the reverse of ASCIISTR, converting a string into Unicode.
UPPER	Converts all letters in the string to uppercase.

The following sections briefly describe each of the PL/SQL string functions.

ASCII

The ASCII function returns the NUMBER code that represents the specified character in the database character set. The specification of the ASCII function is:

```
FUNCTION ASCII (single_character IN VARCHAR2) RETURN NUMBER
```

where *single_character* is the character to be located in the collating sequence. Even though the function is named ASCII, it will return the code location in whatever the database character set is set to, such as EBCDIC Code Page 500 or 7-bit ASCII. Remember that the collating code for uppercase letters is different from that for lowercase letters. For example, in the 7-bit ASCII character set, ASCII ("a") returns 97. ASCII ("A") returns 65 because the uppercase letters come before the lowercase letters in the sequence.

If you pass more than one character in the parameter to ASCII, it returns the collating code for the first character and ignores the other characters. As a result, the following calls to ASCII all return the same value of 100:

```
ASCII ('defg')
ASCII ('d')
ASCII ('d_e_f_g')
```

ASCIISTR

The ASCIISTR function takes a string in any character set and converts it into a string of ASCII characters. Any non-ASCII characters are represented using the form \XXXX, where XXXX represents the Unicode value for the character. The specification for ASCIISTR is:

```
FUNCTION ASCIISTR (string1 IN VARCHAR2) RETURN VARCHAR2;
```

Following is an example of ASCIISTR in use:

```
BEGIN
   DBMS_OUTPUT.PUT_LINE(
      ASCIISTR('The letter ã is not an ASCII character.')
   );
END;
```

The output is:

```
The letter \00E3 is not an ASCII character.
```

The UNISTR function, described later in this chapter, is the inverse of ASCIISTR.

For information on Unicode, including the underlying bytecodes used to represent characters in the Unicode character set, visit *http://unicode.org*.

CHR

The CHR function is the inverse of ASCII. It returns a VARCHAR2 character (length 1) that corresponds to the location in the collating sequence provided as a parameter. The specification of the CHR function is:

```
FUNCTION CHR (code_location IN NUMBER) RETURN VARCHAR2
```

where *code_location* is the number specifying the location in the collating sequence.

The CHR function is especially valuable when you need to make reference to a nonprintable character in your code. For example, the location in the standard ASCII collating sequence for the newline character is 10 (the ASCII linefeed). The CHR function gives you a way to search for the newline character in a string, and perform operations on a string based on the presence of that control character.

You can also insert a linefeed into a character string using the CHR function. For example, suppose you have to build a report that displays the address of a company. A company can have up to four address strings (in addition to city, state, and zip code). You need to put each address string on a new line, but you don't want any blank lines embedded in the address. The following SELECT will not do the trick:

```
SELECT name, address1, address2, address3, address4,
       city || ', ' || state || ' ' || zipcode location
  FROM company;
```

Assuming that each column (report field) goes on a new line, you will end up using six lines per address, no matter how many of these address strings are NULL. For example:

```
HAROLD HENDERSON
22 BUNKER COURT
SUITE 100


WYANDANCH, MN 66557
```

You can use the CHR function to suppress these internal blank lines as follows:

```
SELECT name ||
       DECODE (address1, NULL, NULL, CHR (10) || address1) ||
       DECODE (address2, NULL, NULL, CHR (10) || address2) ||
       DECODE (address3, NULL, NULL, CHR (10) || address3) ||
       DECODE (address4, NULL, NULL, CHR (10) || address4) ||
       CHR (10) ||
       city || ', ' || state || ' ' || zipcode
  FROM company;
```

Now the query returns a single formatted column per company. The DECODE statement offers IF-THEN logic within SQL and executes as follows: "If the address string is NULL then concatenate NULL; otherwise insert a linefeed character concatenated with the address string." In this way, blank address lines are ignored, and the address will be scrunched down to:

```
HAROLD HENDERSON
22 BUNKER COURT
SUITE 100
WYANDANCH, MN 66557
```

By default, the CHR function translates the character code you specify into a character from the database character set. If you wish to use a character from the national character set instead, you can use the USING NCHAR_CS clause:

```
DECLARE
   x NVARCHAR2(30);
BEGIN
   x := CHR(65 USING NCHAR_CS);
   ...
```

The NCHR function also provides this same functionality.

COMPOSE

COMPOSE takes a Unicode string as input and returns that string in its fully normalized form. The specification for COMPOSE is:

```
FUNCTION COMPOSE (string1 IN VARCHAR2) RETURN VARCHAR2
```

Unicode allows certain characters to be represented in multiple ways. For example, the ã character that you've seen throughout this chapter can be represented in the following two ways:

```
ã = \00E3
ã = a\0303
```

In the first case, \00E3 is the Unicode code point (in hexadecimal) for the character ã. In the second case, \0303 is a nonspacing Unicode character representing the addition of a ˜ to the preceding character. Thus, ã is built up starting with a simple "a" and then adding the ˜ on top. The complete character \00E3 is known as a *precomposed character*. The COMPOSE function takes decomposed strings such as "a\0303" and converts them into their composed counterparts. For example:

```
DECLARE
   x VARCHAR2(30);
   y VARCHAR2(30);
BEGIN
   SELECT COMPOSE(UNISTR('a\0303 is a composed character')),
          ASCIISTR(COMPOSE(UNISTR('a\0303 is a composed character')))
   INTO x, y
   FROM dual;

   DBMS_OUTPUT.PUT_LINE(x);
   DBMS_OUTPUT.PUT_LINE(y);
END;
```

The output is:

```
ã is a composed character
\00E3 is a composed character
```

In Oracle9*i* Release 1, COMPOSE must be called from a SQL statement; it cannot be used in a PL/SQL expression. In Oracle9*i* Release 2, however, you can invoke COMPOSE from a PL/SQL expression.

CONCAT

The CONCAT function concatenates by taking two VARCHAR2 strings and returning them appended together in the order specified. The specification of the CONCAT function is:

```
FUNCTION CONCAT (string1 IN VARCHAR2, string2 IN VARCHAR2)
                RETURN VARCHAR2
```

CONCAT always appends *string2* to the end of *string1*. If either string is NULL, CONCAT returns the non-NULL argument all by its lonesome. If both strings are NULL, CONCAT returns NULL. Here are some examples of uses of CONCAT (where → means that the function returns the value shown):

```
CONCAT ('abc', 'defg') → 'abcdefg'
CONCAT (NULL, 'def') → 'def'
CONCAT ('ab', NULL) → 'ab'
CONCAT (NULL, NULL) → NULL
```

I have a confession to make about CONCAT: I have never used it in all my years of PL/SQL coding. In fact, I never even noticed it was available until I did the research for this book. How can this be? I certainly have performed many acts of concatenation in my time. However, PL/SQL (and the Oracle RDBMS) offers a second concatenation operator—the double vertical bars (||). For example:

```
DECLARE
   x VARCHAR2(100);
BEGIN
   x := 'abc' || 'def' || 'ghi';
   DBMS_OUTPUT.PUT_LINE(x);
END;
```

The output is:

```
abcdefghi
```

To perform the identical concatenation using CONCAT, we'd need to nest one call to CONCAT inside another:

```
x := CONCAT(CONCAT('abc','def'),'efg');
```

You can see that the || operator is not only much easier to use than CONCAT, but results in much more readable code.

DECOMPOSE

DECOMPOSE is the opposite of the COMPOSE function. It takes a Unicode string as input, and returns that string with any precomposed characters decomposed into their separate elements. Its specification is:

```
FUNCTION DECOMPOSE(string1 IN VARCHAR2) RETURN VARCHAR2
```

The following example undoes the effect of the COMPOSE example shown earlier:

```
DECLARE
   x VARCHAR2(30);
BEGIN
   x := 'ã is a composed character';
   SELECT ASCIISTR(DECOMPOSE(x))
   INTO x
   FROM dual;

   DBMS_OUTPUT.PUT_LINE(x);
END;
```

The output is:

```
a\0303 is a composed character
```

In this case, the character ã in the input string has been decomposed into the letter "a" followed by the nonspacing character \0303 (indicating the tilde).

Like COMPOSE, DECOMPOSE cannot be invoked directly from a PL/SQL expression in Oracle *9i* Release 1; you must invoke it from a SQL statement. This restriction is removed in Oracle*9i* Release 2.

GREATEST

GREATEST takes one or more strings as input, and returns the string that would come last (i.e., that is the greatest) if the inputs were to be sorted in ascending order. The ordering of the strings is based on character code in the database character set. GREATEST has the following specification:

```
FUNCTION GREATEST (string1 IN VARCHAR2, string2 IN VARCHAR2,...)
   RETURN VARCHAR2
```

Following is an example:

```
BEGIN
   DBMS_OUTPUT.PUT_LINE(GREATEST('Jonathan','Steven','Bill'));
END;

Steven
```

Also see the LEAST function, which is the opposite of GREATEST.

INITCAP

The INITCAP function reformats the case of the string argument, setting the first letter of each word to uppercase and the remainder of the letters to lowercase. A word is a set of characters separated by a space or nonalphanumeric character (such as # or _). The specification of INITCAP is:

```
FUNCTION INITCAP (string_in IN VARCHAR2) RETURN VARCHAR2
```

Here are some examples of the impact of INITCAP on your strings:

- Shift all lowercase to mixed case:

  ```
  INITCAP ('this is lower') → 'This Is Lower'
  ```

- Shift all uppercase to mixed case:

```
INITCAP ('BIG>AND^TALL') → 'Big>And^Tall'
```

- Shift a confusing blend of cases to consistent initcap format:

```
INITCAP ('wHatISthis_MESS?') → 'Whatisthis_Mess?'
```

- Create Visual Basic–style variable names (I use REPLACE, explained later, to strip out the embedded spaces):

```
REPLACE (INITCAP ('ALMOST_UNREADABLE_VAR_NAME'), '_', NULL)
   → 'AlmostUnreadableVarName'
```

When and why would you use INITCAP? Many Oracle shops like to store all character string data, such as names and addresses, in uppercase for consistency. This practice makes it easier to search for records that match certain criteria.

The problem with storing all the data in uppercase is that, while it is a convenient "machine format," it is not particularly readable or presentable. How easy is it to scan a page of information that looks like the following?

```
CUSTOMER TRACKING LIST - GENERATED ON 12-MAR-1994
LAST PAYMENT WEDNESDAY: PAUL JOHNSON, 123 MADISON AVE - $1200
LAST PAYMENT MONDAY: HARRY SIMMERSON, 555 AXELROD RD - $1500
```

It is hard for the eye to pick out the individual words and different types of information; all that text just blends together. Furthermore, solid uppercase has a "machine" or even "mainframe" feel to it; you'd never actually type it that way. A mixture of upper- and lowercase can make your output much more readable and friendly in appearance:

```
Customer Tracking List - Generated On 12-Mar-1994
Last Payment Wednesday: Paul Johnson, 123 Madison Ave - $1200
Last Payment Monday: Harry Simmerson, 555 Axelrod Rd - $1500
```

Can you see any problems with using INITCAP to format output? There are a couple of drawbacks to the way it works. First, as with the string "BIG AND TALL", INITCAP is not very useful for generating titles because it doesn't know that little words like "and" and "the" should not be capitalized. That is a relatively minor problem compared with the second one: INITCAP is completely ignorant of real-world surname conventions. Names with internal capital letters, in particular, cannot be generated with INITCAP. Consider the following example in which the "D" in "McDonald's" ends up in lowercase.

```
INITCAP ('HAMBURGERS BY THE BILLIONS AT MCDONALDS')
 → 'Hamburgers By The Billions At Mcdonalds'
```

For these reasons, use INITCAP with caution when printing reports or displaying data. The information it produces may not always be formatted correctly.

INSTR, INSTRB, INSTRC, INSTR2, and INSTR4

The INSTR family of functions allow you to search a string to find a match for a substring. If the substring is found, the functions return the position, in the source string, of the first character of the substring. If there is no match, then the functions return 0.

The five INSTR functions differ only in terms of how they look at the string and substring:

INSTR
: Strings consist of characters. The return value indicates the character position at which the substring is found.

INSTRB
: Strings consist of bytes. The return value indicates the byte position at which the substring is found.

INSTRC
: Strings consist of Unicode characters. Decomposed Unicode characters are recognized (e.g., a\0303 is recognized as being the same as \00E3 or ã).

INSTR2
: Looks at strings in terms of Unicode code units.

INSTR4
: Looks at strings in terms of Unicode code points.

All of the INSTR functions share the same specification:

```
FUNCTION INSTR
   (string1 IN VARCHAR2,
    string2 IN VARCHAR2
   [,start_position IN NUMBER := 1
   [, nth_appearance IN NUMBER := 1]])
RETURN NUMBER
```

where *string1* is the string searched by INSTR for the position in which the *nth_appearance* of *string2* is found. The *start_position* parameter is the character (not byte) position in the string where the search will start. It is optional and defaults to 1 (the beginning of *string1*). The *nth_appearance* parameter is also optional and defaults to 1.

Both the *start_position* and the *nth_appearance* parameters can be literals (like 5 or 157), variables, or complex expressions, as follows:

```
INSTR (company_name, 'INC', (last_location + 5) * 10)
```

If *start_position* is negative, then INSTR counts back *start_position* number of characters from the end of the string, and then searches from that point toward the beginning of the string for the *n*th match. Figure 8-2 illustrates the two directions in which INSTR searches, depending on whether the *start_position* parameter is positive or negative.

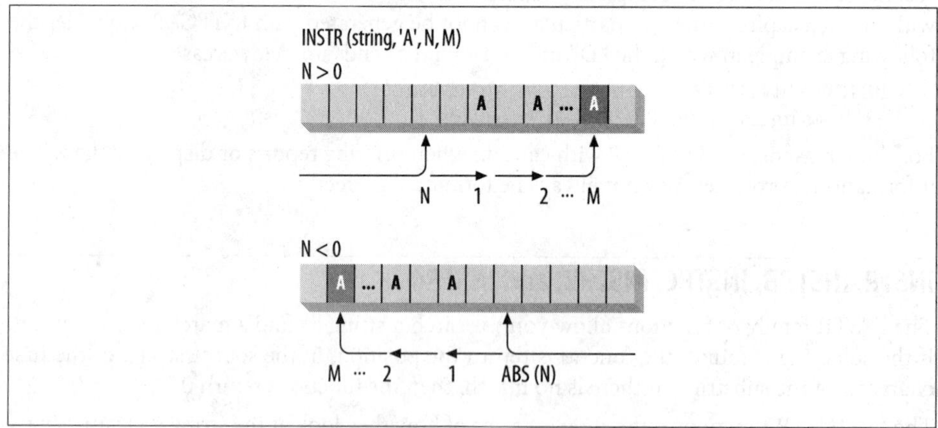

Figure 8-2. Forward and reverse searches with INSTR

We have found INSTR to be a very handy function, especially when used to the fullest extent possible. Most programmers make use of (and may only be aware of) only the first two parameters. Use INSTR to search from the end of the string? Search for the *n*th appearance as opposed to just the first appearance? "Wow!" many programmers would say, "I didn't know it could do that." Take the time to get familiar with INSTR and use *all* of its power.

In Oracle7, if *nth_appearance* is not positive (i.e., if it is 0 or negative), then INSTR always returns 1. In Oracle8, a value of 0 or a negative number for *nth_appearance* causes INSTR to raise the VALUE_ERROR exception.

Let's look at some examples of INSTR. In these examples, you will see all four parameters used in all their permutations. As you write your own programs, keep in mind the different ways in which INSTR can be used to extract information from a string; it can greatly simplify the code you write to parse and analyze character data.

- Find the first occurrence of "archie" in "bug-or-tv-character?archie":

  ```
  INSTR ('bug-or-tv-character?archie', 'archie') → 21
  ```

  The starting position and the *n*th appearance both defaulted to 1.

- Find the last occurrence of "ar" in "bug-or-tv-character?archie".

  ```
  INSTR ('bug-or-tv-character?archie', 'ar', -1) → 21
  ```

  Were you thinking that the answer might be 6? Remember that the character position returned by INSTR is always calculated from the leftmost character of the string as position 1. The easiest way to find the last of anything in a string is to specify a negative number for the starting position. I did not have to specify the *n*th appearance (leaving me with a default value of 1), because the last occurrence is also the first when searching backwards.

- Find the second-to-last occurrence of "a" in "bug-or-tv-character?archie":

  ```
  INSTR ('bug-or-tv-character?archie', 'a', -1, 2) → 15
  ```

  No surprises here. Counting from the back of the string, INSTR passes over the "a" in archie because that is the last occurrence, and searches for the next occurrence. Again, the character position is counted from the leftmost character, not the rightmost character, in the string.

- Find the position of the letter "t" closest to (but not past) the question mark in the string "bug-or-tv-character?archie tophat":

  ```
  search_string := 'bug-or-tv-character?archie tophat';
  tee_loc :=
     INSTR (search_string, 't',
            -1 * (LENGTH (search_string) - INSTR (search_string, '?') +1));
  ```

  I dynamically calculate the location of the question mark (actually, the first question mark in the string; I assume that there is only one). Then I subtract that from the full length of the string and multiply by –1 because I need to count the number of characters from the end of the string. I then use that value to kick off the search for the closest prior "t".

This example is a good reminder that any of the parameters to INSTR can be complex expressions that call other functions or perform their own calculations. This fact is also highlighted in the next INSTR example.

- Use INSTR to confirm that a user entry is valid. In the following code, I check to see if the command selected by the user is found in the list of valid commands. If so, I execute that command:

```
IF INSTR ('|ADD|DELETE|CHANGE|VIEW|CALC|', '|' || cmd || '|') > 0
THEN
   execute_command (cmd);
ELSE
   DBMS_OUTPUT.PUT_LINE
      (' You entered an invalid command. Please try again...');
END IF;
```

  In this case, I use the concatenation operator to construct the string that I will search for in the command list. I have to append a vertical bar (|) to the selected command because it is used as a delimiter in the command list. I also use the call to INSTR in a Boolean expression. If INSTR finds a match in the string, it returns a nonzero value; the Boolean expression therefore evaluates to TRUE, and I can go on with my processing. Otherwise, I display an error message.

The following code example, generated using Unicode UTF-8 as the database character set, illustrates the difference in semantics between INSTR and INSTRB, the two variations of INSTR that you are most likely to use:

```
DECLARE
   --The underlying database datatype for this example is Unicode UTF-8
   x CHAR(30 CHAR) := 'The character ã is two-bytes.';
BEGIN
   --Find the location of "is" in terms of characters
   DBMS_OUTPUT.PUT_LINE(INSTR(x,'is'));

   --Find the location of "is" in terms of bytes
   DBMS_OUTPUT.PUT_LINE(INSTRB(x,'is'));
END;
```

The output is:

```
17
18
```

The difference in the location of the word "is" comes about because the character ã is represented in Unicode UTF-8 using two bytes. Thus, while "is" is 17 characters into the string, it is at the same time 18 bytes into the string.

The INSTRC function is capable of recognizing decomposed characters. As described in the section on COMPOSE, an alternate representation of ã is a\0303. The following example demonstrates that INSTRC recognizes this alternate representation, whereas INSTR does not:

```
DECLARE
   --The underlying database datatype for this example is Unicode UTF-8
   x CHAR(40 CHAR) := UNISTR('The character a\0303 could be composed.');
BEGIN
   --INSTR won't see that a\0303 is the same as ã
   DBMS_OUTPUT.PUT_LINE(INSTR(x,'ã'));
```

```
   --INSTRC, however, will recognize that a\0303 = ã
   DBMS_OUTPUT.PUT_LINE(INSTRC(x,'ã'));
END;
```

The output is:

```
0
15
```

According to INSTR, the string x does not contain ã at all. INSTRC, on the other hand, recognizes that a\0303 is an alternate representation for the same character. The UNISTR function is used in the declaration of x to convert the ASCII string that we can read into a Unicode string for the example.

The INSTR2 and INSTR4 functions allow you to search for code units and code points respectively, which may not correspond to complete characters. For the following example, AL16UTF16 is used as the national language character set. The character ã is represented in the string x as two code points: one for "a", and the other (\0303) for the tilde that goes above the "a". INSTRC and INSTR4 are then used to search for the location of the \0303 code point:

```
DECLARE
   --The underlying database datatype for this example is Unicode UTF-16
   x NCHAR(40) := UNISTR('The character a\0303 could be composed.');
BEGIN
   --Find the location of "\0303" using INSTRC
   DBMS_OUTPUT.PUT_LINE(INSTRC(x,UNISTR('\0303')));

   --Find the location of "\0303" using INSTR4
   DBMS_OUTPUT.PUT_LINE(INSTR4(x,UNISTR('\0303')));
END;
```

The output is:

```
0
16
```

The INSTRC function works with full characters, and is of no use when you need to search for a code point that does not represent a complete character. INSTR4, on the other hand, is able to locate the \0303 code point. The return value of 16 indicates that \0303 is the 16th code point in the string.

INSTR2 works like INSTR4, but allows you to search for UCS-4 code units. Look at the following example:

```
DECLARE
  x NCHAR(40) := UNISTR('This is a \D834\DD1E test');
BEGIN
  DBMS_OUTPUT.PUT_LINE (INSTR2(x, UNISTR('\D834')));
  DBMS_OUTPUT.PUT_LINE (INSTR4(x, UNISTR('\D834')));
END;

11
0
```

\D834\DD1E (the musical G clef) is a surrogate pair; each value in a surrogate pair is a code unit. Together, the two code units represent a single code point. This example shows how INSTR2 matches on just the high surrogate, whereas INSTR4 does not. That's because INSTR2 matches in terms of code *units*, whereas INSTR4 matches in terms of code *points*. Matching on just one code unit of a surrogate is sort of equivalent to searching and matching on the first byte of a multibyte character. Normally, you don't want to do this.

LEAST

LEAST takes one or more strings as input and returns the string that would come first (i.e., that is the least) if the inputs were to be sorted in ascending order. The ordering of the strings is based on character code in the database character set. LEAST has the following specification:

```
FUNCTION LEAST (string1 IN VARCHAR2, string2 IN VARCHAR2,...)
   RETURN VARCHAR2
```

Following is an example:

```
BEGIN
   DBMS_OUTPUT.PUT_LINE(LEAST('Gennick','Pribyl','Feuerstein'));
END;

Feuerstein
```

Also see the GREATEST function, which is the opposite of LEAST.

LENGTH, LENGTHB, LENGTHC, LENGTH2, and LENGTH4

The LENGTH family of functions returns the length of a string. The length can be returned in any of the following units:

LENGTH
: Characters

LENGTHB
: Bytes

LENGTHC
: Unicode characters, normalizing where possible

LENGTH2
: Code units

LENGTH4
: Code points

The same pattern is used for the specification of all LENGTH functions:

```
FUNCTION LENGTH (string1 VARCHAR2) RETURN NUMBER
```

If *string1* is NULL, then LENGTH returns NULL—not zero! Remember that a NULL string is a "nonvalue." Therefore, it cannot have a length, even a zero length.

The LENGTH function, in fact, will never return zero; it will always return either NULL or a positive number.

An exception is when LENGTH is used against a CLOB. It is possible for a CLOB to hold zero bytes and yet not be NULL. In that one case, LENGTH will return zero.

Here are some examples of LENGTH:

```
LENGTH (NULL) → NULL
LENGTH ('') → NULL -- Same as a NULL string.
LENGTH ('abcd') → 4
LENGTH ('abcd ') → 5
```

If *string1* is a fixed-length CHAR datatype, then LENGTH counts the trailing blanks in its calculation. So the LENGTH of a fixed-length string is always the declared length of the string. If you want to compute the length of the nonblank characters in *string1*, you will need to use the RTRIM function to remove the trailing blanks (RTRIM is discussed later in this chapter). In the following example, *length1* is set to 60 and *length2* is set to 14.

```
DECLARE
   company_name CHAR(60) := 'ACME PLUMBING';
   length1 NUMBER;
   length2 NUMBER;
BEGIN
   length1 := LENGTH (company_name);
   length2 := LENGTH (RTRIM (company_name));
END;
```

The following example uses an NVARCHAR2 variable and the AL16UTF16 character set to highlight the differences between LENGTH, LENGTHB, and LENGTHC. Remember that AL16UTF16 is Oracle's name for UTF-16, a character set in which each character is represented using two bytes.

```
DECLARE
   --NVARCHAR2 = UTF-16 in this example.
   x NVARCHAR2(50) :=
      UNISTR('The character ã and its decomposed equivalent: a\0303');
BEGIN
   DBMS_OUTPUT.PUT_LINE(LENGTH(x));
   DBMS_OUTPUT.PUT_LINE(LENGTHB(x));
   DBMS_OUTPUT.PUT_LINE(LENGTHC(x));
END;
```

The output is:

```
49
98
48
```

LENGTH counts characters, but sees a\0303 as two separate, two-byte characters. LENGTHB counts bytes, returning a value that is twice the number of two-byte characters reported by LENGTH. LENGTHC counts Unicode characters, and recognizes that a\0303 really represents the single character ã.

LOWER

The LOWER function converts all letters in the specified string to lowercase. The specifications for the LOWER function are:

```
FUNCTION LOWER (string1 IN CHAR) RETURN CHAR
FUNCTION LOWER (string1 IN VARCHAR2) RETURN VARCHAR2
```

As noted earlier, LOWER and UPPER return a fixed-length string if the incoming string is fixed-length. LOWER will not change any characters in the string that are not letters, as case is irrelevant for numbers and special characters.

Here are some examples of the effect of LOWER:

```
LOWER ('BIG FAT LETTERS') → 'big fat letters'
LOWER ('123ABC') → '123abc'
```

LOWER and UPPER are useful for guaranteeing a consistent case when comparing strings. PL/SQL is not a case-sensitive language with regard to its own syntax and names of identifiers, but it *is* sensitive to case in character strings, whether they are found in named constants, literals, or variables. The string "ABC" is not the same as "abc", and this can cause problems in your programs if you are not careful and consistent in your handling of such values.

LPAD

By default, PL/SQL strips all trailing blanks from a character string unless it is declared with a fixed-length CHAR datatype. There are occasions, however, when you really want some spaces (or even some other characters) added to the front or back of your string. LPAD (and its right-leaning cousin, RPAD) give you this capability. The LPAD function returns a string padded to the left (hence the "L") to a specified length and with a specified pad string. The specification of the LPAD function is:

```
FUNCTION LPAD
   (string1 IN VARCHAR2,
    padded_length IN NUMBER
    [, pad_string IN VARCHAR2])
RETURN VARCHAR2
```

LPAD returns *string1* padded on the left to length *padded_length* with the optional character string *pad_string*. If you do not specify *pad_string*, then *string1* is padded on the left with spaces. You must specify the *padded_length*. If *string1* already has a length equal to *padded_length*, then LPAD returns *string1* without any additional characters. If *padded_length* is smaller than the length of *string1*, LPAD effectively truncates *string1*—it returns only the first *padded_length* characters of the incoming *string1*.

As you can see, LPAD can do a lot more than just add spaces to the left of a string. Let's look at some examples of how useful LPAD can be.

- Display the number padded left with zeros to a length of 10:

  ```
  LPAD ('55', 10, '0') → '0000000055'
  ```

- Display the number padded left with zeros to a length of 5:

  ```
  LPAD ('12345678', 5, '0') → '12345'
  ```

  LPAD interprets its *padded_length* as the maximum length of the string that it may return. As a result, it counts *padded_length* number of characters from the left (start of the string) and then simply returns that substring of the incoming value.

- Place the phrase "sell!" in front of the names of selected stocks, up to a string length of 43.

  ```
  LPAD ('HITOP TIES', 43, 'sell!')
  →
    'sell!sell!sell!sell!sell!sell!selHITOP TIES'
  ```

Because the length of "HITOP TIES" is 10 and the length of "sell!" is 5, there is no room for seven full repetitions of the pad string. As a result, the seventh repetition (counting from the left) of "sell!" lost its last two characters. So you can see that LPAD does not pad by adding to the left of the original string until it runs out of room. Instead, it figures out how many characters it must pad by to reach the total, constructs that full padded fragment, and finally appends the original string to this fragment.

LTRIM

The LTRIM function is the opposite of LPAD. Whereas LPAD adds characters to the left of a string, LTRIM removes, or trims, characters from the left of the string. And just like LPAD, LTRIM offers much more flexibility than simply removing leading blanks. The specification of the LTRIM function is:

```
FUNCTION LTRIM (string1 IN VARCHAR2 [, trim_string IN VARCHAR2])
RETURN VARCHAR2
```

LTRIM returns *string1* with all leading characters removed up to the first character not found in the *trim_string*. The second parameter is optional and defaults to a single space.

There is one important difference between LTRIM and LPAD. LPAD pads to the left with the specified string, and repeats that string (or pattern of characters) until there is no more room. LTRIM, on the other hand, removes all leading characters that appear in the trim string, not as a pattern, but as individual candidates for trimming.

Here are some examples:

- Trim all leading blanks from "   Way Out in Right Field":

  ```
  LTRIM ('    Way Out in Right Field') → 'Way Out in Right Field'
  ```

  Because we did not specify a trim string, it defaults to a single space, so all leading spaces are removed.

- Remove all numbers from the front of the string:

  ```
  my_string := '70756234LotsaLuck';

  LTRIM (my_string, '0987612345') → 'LotsaLuck'
  ```

  By specifying every possible digit in the trim string, we ensure that any and all numbers will be trimmed, regardless of the order in which they occur (and the order in which we place them in the trim string).

What if we wanted to remove only a specific pattern, say the letters "abc", from the front of the string? We couldn't use LTRIM because it trims off any matching individual characters. To remove a leading pattern from a string—or to replace one pattern with another—you will want to make use of the REPLACE function, which is discussed next.

The TRIM function implements ANSI-standard trim functionality.

REPLACE

The REPLACE function returns a string in which all occurrences of a specified match string are replaced with a replacement string. REPLACE is useful for searching a pattern of characters, and then changing all instances of that pattern in a single function call. The specification of the REPLACE function is:

```
FUNCTION REPLACE (string1 IN VARCHAR2, match_string IN VARCHAR2
                  [, replace_string IN VARCHAR2])
RETURN VARCHAR2
```

If you do not specify the replacement string, then REPLACE simply removes all occurrences of the *match_string* in *string1*. If you specify neither a match string nor a replacement string, REPLACE returns NULL.

Here are several examples using REPLACE:

- Remove all instances of the letter "C" in the string "CAT CALL":

  ```
  REPLACE ('CAT CALL', 'C') → 'AT ALL'
  ```

  Because we did not specify a replacement string, REPLACE changed all occurrences of "C" to NULL.

- Replace all occurrences of "99" with "100" in the following string:

  ```
  REPLACE ('Zero defects in period 99 reached 99%!', '99', '100')
  →
          'Zero defects in period 100 reached 100%!'
  ```

- Handle occurrences of a single quote within a query criteria string. The single quote is a string terminator symbol, indicating the start and/or end of the literal string. I once ran into this requirement when building query-by-example strings in Oracle Forms. If the user enters a string with a single quote in it, such as:

  ```
  Customer didn't have change.
  ```

  and then the program concatenates that string into a larger string, the resulting SQL statement (created dynamically by Oracle Forms in Query Mode) fails because there are unbalanced single quotes in the string. You can resolve this problem by converting that single quote into two single quotes in a row, thereby telling SQL that you really intend for one quote to be part of the string. Use the following REPLACE to do this:

  ```
  criteria_string := REPLACE (criteria_string, '''', '''''');
  ```

  The four quotes in the second parameter resolve to a string containing one single quote. The six quotes in the third parameter resolve to a string containing two single quotes. In each case, the outer pair of quotes delimits the string, and each pair of single quotes inside that outer pair are interpreted as just one single quote within the string.

- Remove all leading instances of "abc" from the string:

  ```
  "abcabcccccI LOVE CHILIabc"
  ```

  This is the behavior we were looking at in the previous section on LTRIM. We want to remove all instances of the pattern "abc" from the beginning of the string, but we do not want to remove that pattern throughout the rest of the string. In addition, we want to remove "abc" only as a pattern; if we encounter three contiguous c's ("ccc"), on the other hand, they should not be removed from the string. This task is less straightforward than it might at first seem. If we simply apply REPLACE to the string, it will remove all occurrences of "abc", instead of just the leading instances. For example:

```
REPLACE ('abcabccccI LOVE CHILIabc', 'abc') → 'cccI LOVE CHILI'
```

That is not what we want in this case. If we use LTRIM, on the other hand, we will be left with none of the leading c's, as demonstrated in a previous example:

```
LTRIM ('abcabccccI LOVE CHILIabc', 'abc') → 'I LOVE CHILIabc'
```

And this is not quite right either. We want to be left with "cccI LOVE CHILIabc" (please do not ask why), and it turns out that the way to get it is to use a combination of LTRIM and REPLACE. Suppose that we create a local variable as follows:

```
my_string   := 'abcabccccI LOVE CHILIabc';
```

Then the following statement will achieve the desired effect by nesting calls to REPLACE and LTRIM within one another:

```
REPLACE
   (LTRIM
      (REPLACE (my_string, 'abc', '@'), '@'), '@', 'abc')
→
      'cccI LOVE CHILIabc'
```

Here is how we would describe in English what the above statement does:

> First replace all occurrences of "abc" with the special character "@" (which we are assuming does not otherwise appear in the string). Then trim off all leading instances of "@". Finally, replace all remaining occurrences of "@" with "abc".

Voilà, as they say in many of the finer restaurants in Paris. Now let's pull apart this single, rather complex statement into separate PL/SQL steps corresponding to the "natural language" description:

Replace all occurrences of "abc" with the special character "@" (which we are assuming does not otherwise appear in the string). Notice that this only affects the "abc" pattern, and not any individual appearances of "a", "b", or "c".

```
REPLACE ('abcabccccI LOVE CHILIabc', 'abc', '@')
      → '@@cccI LOVE CHILI@'
```

Trim off all leading instances of "@".

```
LTRIM ('@@cccI LOVE CHILI@', '@') → 'cccI LOVE CHILI@'
```

Notice that LTRIM now leaves the c's in place, because we didn't ask it to remove "a" or "b" or "c"—just "@". In addition, it left the trailing "@" in the string because LTRIM deals only with characters on the leading end of the string.

Replace all remaining occurrences of "@" with "abc".

```
REPLACE ('cccI LOVE CHILI@', '@', 'abc') → 'cccI LOVE CHILIabc'
```

And we are done. We used the first REPLACE to temporarily change the occurrences of "abc" so that LTRIM could distinguish between the pattern we wanted to get rid of and the extra characters that needed to be preserved. Then a final call to REPLACE restored the pattern in the string.

RPAD

The RPAD function adds characters to the end of a character string. It returns a string padded to the right (hence the "R") to a specified length and with an optional pad string. The specification of the RPAD function is:

```
FUNCTION RPAD
   (string1 IN VARCHAR2,
    padded_length IN NUMBER
    [, pad_string IN VARCHAR2])
RETURN VARCHAR2
```

RPAD returns *string1* padded on the right to length *padded_length* with the optional character string *pad_string*. If you do not specify *pad_string*, then *string1* is padded on the right with spaces. You must specify the *padded_length*. If *string1* already has a length equal to *padded_length*, then RPAD returns *string1* without any additional characters. If *padded_length* is smaller than the length of *string1*, RPAD effectively truncates *string1*, returning only the first *padded_length* characters of the incoming *string1*.

Let's look at some examples of RPAD:

- Display the number padded right with zeros to a length of 10:

  ```
  RPAD ('55', 10, '0') → '5500000000'
  ```

  I could also use TO_CHAR to convert from a number to a character (I don't know offhand why you would do this, but it's good to remember that there are usually at least two or three ways to solve any problem):

  ```
  TO_CHAR (55 * 10000000) → '5500000000'
  ```

- Display the number padded right with zeros to a length of 5:

  ```
  RPAD ('12345678', 5) → '12345'
  ```

  RPAD interprets its *padded_length* as the maximum length of the string that it may return. As a result, it counts *padded_length* number of characters from the left (start of the string) and then simply returns that substring of the incoming value. This is the same behavior as that found with LPAD, described earlier in this chapter. Remember that RPAD does not return the rightmost five characters (in the above case "45678").

- Place the phrase "sell!" after the names of selected stocks, up to a string length of 43:

  ```
  RPAD ('HITOP TIES', 43, 'sell!')
  →
     'HITOP TIESsell!sell!sell!sell!sell!sell!sel'
  ```

  Because the length of "HITOP TIES" is 10 and the length of "sell!" is 5, there is no room for seven full repetitions of the pad string. As a result, the seventh repetition of "sell!" loses its last two characters.

You can use RPAD (and LPAD) to generate repetitive sequences of characters. For example, you can create a string of 60 dashes to use as a border in a report:

```
RPAD ('-', 60, '-')
→
'------------------------------------------------------------'
```

I have used this technique in SQL*Reportwriter V1.1 where graphical objects like boxes are not really available. I can include the RPAD in a SELECT statement in the report, and then use the corresponding field in text elements to provide lines to break up the data in a report.

RTRIM

The RTRIM function is the opposite of RPAD and the companion to LTRIM. While RPAD adds characters to the right of a string, RTRIM removes, or trims, characters from the end portion of the string. Just as with RPAD, RTRIM offers much more flexibility than simply removing trailing blanks. The specification of the RTRIM function is:

```
FUNCTION RTRIM (string1 IN VARCHAR2 [, trim_string IN VARCHAR2])
RETURN VARCHAR2
```

RTRIM returns *string1* with all trailing characters removed up to the first character not found in the *trim_string*. The second parameter is optional and defaults to a single space.

Here are some examples of RTRIM:

- Trim all trailing blanks from a string:

  ```
  RTRIM ('Way Out in Right Field                    ')
   → 'Way Out in Right Field'
  ```

  Because I did not specify a trim string, it defaults to a single space, so all trailing spaces are removed.

- Trim all the characters in "BAM! ARGH!" from the end of a string:

  ```
  my_string := 'Sound effects: BAM!ARGH!BAM!HAM';
  RTRIM (my_string, 'BAM! ARGH!') → 'Sound effects:'
  ```

  This use of RTRIM strips off all the letters at the end of the string that are found in "BAM!ARGH!". This includes "BAM" and "HAM", so those words too are removed from the string even though "HAM" is not listed explicitly as a "word" in the trim string. Also, the inclusion of two exclamation marks in the trim string is unnecessary, because RTRIM is not looking for the word "ARGH!", but for each of the letters in "ARGH!".

The TRIM function implements ANSI-standard trim functionality.

SOUNDEX

The SOUNDEX function allows you to perform string comparisons based on phonetics (the way a word sounds) as opposed to semantics (the way a word is spelled).* SOUNDEX returns a character string that is the "phonetic representation" of the argument. The specification of the SOUNDEX function is as follows:

```
FUNCTION SOUNDEX (string1 IN VARCHAR2) RETURN VARCHAR2
```

Here are some of the values SOUNDEX generated, and their variations according to the input string:

```
SOUNDEX ('smith') → 'S530'
SOUNDEX ('SMYTHE') → ''S530'
```

* Oracle Corporation uses the algorithm in Donald Knuth's *The Art of Computer Programming*, Volume 3, to generate the phonetic representation.

```
SOUNDEX ('smith smith') → 'S532'
SOUNDEX ('smith z') → 'S532'
SOUNDEX ('feuerstein') → 'F623'
SOUNDEX ('feuerst') → 'F623'
```

Keep the following SOUNDEX rules in mind when using this function:

- The SOUNDEX value always begins with the first letter in the input string.
- SOUNDEX uses only the first five consonants in the string to generate the return value.
- Only consonants are used to compute the numeric portion of the SOUNDEX value. Except for leading vowels, all vowels are ignored.
- SOUNDEX is not case-sensitive. Upper- and lowercase letters return the same SOUNDEX value.

The SOUNDEX function is useful for ad hoc queries, and any other kinds of searches where the exact spelling of a database value is not known or easily determined.

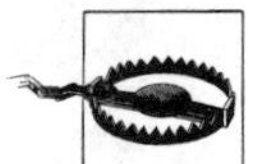

The SOUNDEX algorithm is English-centric and may not work well (or at all) for other languages.

SUBSTR, SUBSTRB, SUBSTRC, SUBSTR2, and SUBSTR4

The SUBSTR family of functions is one of the most common and useful set of character functions. The SUBSTR functions allow you to extract a subset of contiguous characters from a string. The substring is specified by starting position and length, and the functions differ in the units they use:

SUBSTR
: Starting position and length are in terms of characters.

SUBSTRB
: Starting position and length are in terms of bytes. When you use a single-byte character set, SUBSTRB and SUBSTR will return the same results.

SUBSTRC
: Starting position and length are in terms of Unicode characters, after any decomposed characters have been composed.

SUBSTR2
: Starting position and length are in terms of code units.

SUBSTR4
: Starting position and length are in terms of code points.

All of the function specifications follow the same pattern:

```
FUNCTION SUBSTR
   (string_in IN VARCHAR2,
    start_position_in IN NUMBER
    [, substr_length_in IN NUMBER])
RETURN VARCHAR2
```

where the arguments are as follows:

string_in
: The source string

start_position_in
: The starting position of the substring in *string_in*

substr_length_in
: The length of the substring desired (the number of characters to be returned in the substring)

The last parameter, *substr_length_in*, is optional. If you do not specify a substring length, then SUBSTR returns all the characters to the end of *string_in* (from the starting position specified). The *substr_length_in* argument, if present, must be greater than zero.

The starting position cannot be zero. If it is less than zero, then the substring is retrieved from the back of the string. SUBSTR counts backwards *substr_length_in* number of characters from the end of *string_in*. In this case, however, the characters that are extracted are still to the right of the starting position. See Figure 8-3 for an illustration of how the different arguments are used by SUBSTR.

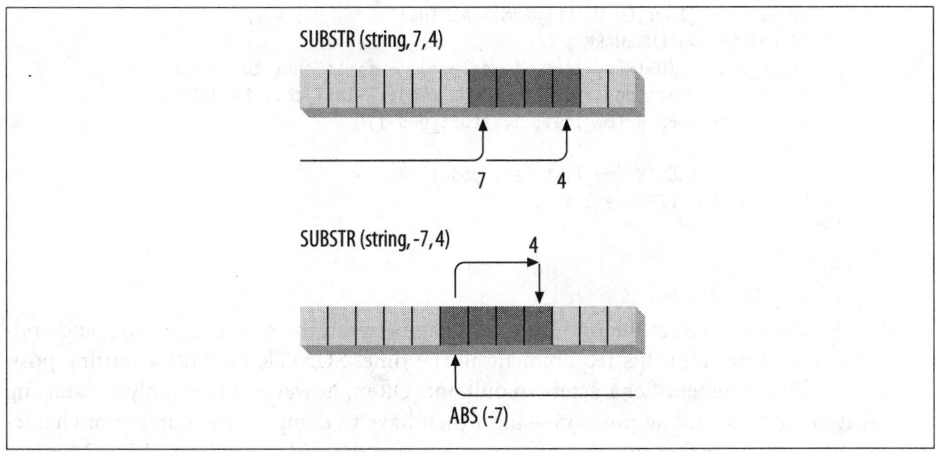

Figure 8-3. How arguments are used by SUBSTR

You will find that in practice SUBSTR is very forgiving. Even if you violate the rules for the values of the starting position and the number of characters to be substringed, SUBSTR will not generate errors. Instead, for the most part, it will return NULL—or the entire string—as its answer.

Here are some examples of SUBSTR:

- Return the last character in a string:

  ```
  SUBSTR ('Another sample string', -1) → 'g'
  ```

  This is the cleanest way to get the single last character. A more direct, but also more cumbersome approach is this:

  ```
  SUBSTR
     ('Sample string', LENGTH ('Sample string'), 1) → 'g'
  ```

In other words, calculate the LENGTH of the string and the one character from the string that starts at that last position. Yuck.

- Remove an element from a string list. This is, in a way, the opposite of SUBSTR: I want to extract a portion or substring of a string and leave the rest of it intact. Oddly enough, I will use SUBSTR to perform this task. Suppose that my screen maintains a list of selected temperatures as follows:

  ```
  |HOT|COLD|LUKEWARM|SCALDING|
  ```

  The vertical bar delimits the different items on the list. When the user deselects "LUKEWARM", I have to remove it from the list. The best way to accomplish this task is to determine the starting and ending positions of the item to be removed, and then use SUBSTR to take apart the list and put it back together—without the specified item. Let's walk through this process a step at a time. For example:

  ```
  DECLARE
     my_list VARCHAR2(50);
     to_delete VARCHAR2(20);
     start_pos NUMBER;
     end_pos NUMBER;
  BEGIN
     my_list := '|HOT|COLD|LUKEWARM|SCALDING|';
     to_delete := 'LUKEWARM';
     start_pos := INSTR(my_list, to_delete); --first char to delete
     end_pos := start_pos + LENGTH(to_delete); --last char to delete
     my_list := SUBSTR (my_list, 1, start_pos-1)
                ||
                SUBSTR (my_list, end_pos+1);
  DBMS_OUTPUT.PUT_LINE(my_list);
  END;
  ```

  The output is:

  ```
  |HOT|COLD|SCALDING|
  ```

- Use SUBSTR to extract the portion of a string between the specified starting and ending points. I run into this requirement all the time. SUBSTR requires a starting position and the number of characters to pull out. Often, however, I have only the starting position and the ending position—and I then have to compute the number of characters in between. Is that just the difference between the end and start positions? Or is it one more or one less than that? Invariably, I get it wrong the first time and have to scribble a little example on scrap paper to prove the formula to myself.

  So to save you the trouble, I offer a tiny function called betwnstr (for "BETWeeN STRing"). This function encapsulates the calculation you must perform to come up with the number of characters between the start and end positions, which is *end_position* – *start_position* + 1.

  ```
  /* File on web: betwnstr.sf */
  FUNCTION betwnstr
     (string_in IN VARCHAR2, start_in IN INTEGER, end_in IN INTEGER)
     RETURN VARCHAR2
  IS
  BEGIN
     RETURN SUBSTR (string_in, start_in, end_in - start_in + 1);
  END;
  ```

While this function does not provide the full flexibility offered by SUBSTR (for example, with negative starting positions), it offers a starting point for the kind of encapsulation you should be performing in these situations.

Like the INSTR and LENGTH families of functions, SUBSTR offers permutations useful in dealing with multibyte character sets and Unicode. The following PL/SQL block illustrates the difference between character and byte semantics:

```
DECLARE
   --NVARCHAR2 = UTF-16 in this example.
   x NVARCHAR2(50 CHAR) :=
      UNISTR('The character a\0303 is the same as ã');
BEGIN
   DBMS_OUTPUT.PUT_LINE(SUBSTR(x,25,4));
   DBMS_OUTPUT.PUT_LINE(SUBSTRB(x,49,8));
END;
```

The output is:

```
same
same
```

The word "same" occupies four characters beginning at character position 25. In terms of bytes, though, it occupies eight bytes beginning at byte position 49. Because we're using the UTF-16 character set, each character occupies two bytes. The first 24 characters occupy the first 48 bytes; thus the 25th character begins at the 49th byte, and occupies bytes 49 and 50.

TO_CHAR

The TO_CHAR function converts national character set data into its database character set equivalent. The specification of TO_CHAR, at least for this usage, is as follows:

```
FUNCTION TO_CHAR(char_data IN NVARCHAR2) RETURN VARCHAR2
```

The TO_CHAR function is defined to accept any of the following types as input: NCHAR, NVARCHAR2, CLOB, and NCLOB. The return type is always VARCHAR2.

Following is an example of TO_CHAR's being used to translate a string from the national character set into the database character set:

```
DECLARE
   a VARCHAR2(30);
   b NVARCHAR2(30) := 'Corner? What corner?';
BEGIN
   a := TO_CHAR(b);
END;
```

See the discussion of TO_NCHAR under "NLS Functions" later in this chapter for information on converting in the other direction. Also see the TRANSLATE...USING function.

TO_CHAR may also be used to convert date and time values, as well as numbers, into human-readable form. These uses of TO_CHAR are described in Chapter 10 (dates and times) and Chapter 9 (numbers).

TO_MULTI_BYTE

TO_MULTI_BYTE translates single-byte characters to their multibyte equivalents. Some multibyte character sets, notably UTF-8, provide for more than one representation of a given character. In UTF-8, for example, letters such as "G" can be represented using one byte or using three bytes. TO_MULTI_BYTE lets you convert between the two representations. The function specification is as follows:

```
FUNCTION TO_MULTI_BYTE (string IN VARCHAR2) RETURN VARCHAR2
```

The datatype of the input value that you pass to TO_MULTI_BYTE determines the output datatype. The output datatype will always match the input datatype.

Following is an example of TO_MULTI_BYTE being used to convert the letter G into its multibyte representation. This example was generated on a system using UTF-8 as the national character set.

```
DECLARE
   g_one_byte NVARCHAR2 (1 CHAR) := 'G';
   g_three_bytes NVARCHAR2 (1 CHAR);
   g_one_again NVARCHAR2(1 CHAR);
   dump_output VARCHAR2(30);
BEGIN
   --Convert single-byte "G" to its multibyte representation
   g_three_bytes := TO_MULTI_BYTE(g_one_byte);
   DBMS_OUTPUT.PUT_LINE(LENGTHB(g_one_byte));
   DBMS_OUTPUT.PUT_LINE(LENGTHB(g_three_bytes));
   SELECT DUMP(g_three_bytes) INTO dump_output FROM dual;
   DBMS_OUTPUT.PUT_LINE(dump_output);

   --Convert that multibyte representation back to a single byte
   g_one_again := TO_SINGLE_BYTE(g_three_bytes);
   DBMS_OUTPUT.PUT_LINE(g_one_again || ' is ' ||
                        TO_CHAR(LENGTHB(g_one_again))
                        || ' byte again.');
END;
```

The output is:

```
1
3
Typ=1 Len=3: 239,188,167
G is 1 byte again.
```

As you can see, the call to TO_MULTI_BYTE in line 8 returned a three-byte UTF-8 representation of the letter G. We then invoked TO_SINGLE_BYTE to convert that three-byte representation back into one byte.

TO_SINGLE_BYTE

TO_SINGLE_BYTE translates multibyte characters to their single-byte equivalents—exactly the reverse of what TO_MULTI_BYTE does. The specification is as follows:

```
FUNCTION TO_SINGLE_BYTE (string IN VARCHAR2) RETURN VARCHAR2
```

The datatype returned by TO_SINGLE_BYTE will always correspond to the input datatype. See the discussion of TO_MULTI_BYTE for an example of TO_SINGLE_BYTE in use.

TRANSLATE

The TRANSLATE function is a variation on REPLACE. REPLACE replaces every instance of a set of characters with another set of characters; that is, REPLACE works with entire words or patterns. TRANSLATE replaces single characters at a time, translating the *n*th character in the search set to the *n*th character in the replacement set. The specification of the TRANSLATE function is as follows:

```
FUNCTION TRANSLATE
   (string_in IN VARCHAR2,
    search_set IN VARCHAR2,
    replace_set VARCHAR2)
RETURN VARCHAR2
```

where *string_in* is the string in which characters are to be translated, *search_set* is the set of characters to be translated (if found), and *replace_set* is the set of characters that will be placed in the string. Unlike REPLACE, where the last argument can be left off, you must include all three arguments when you use TRANSLATE. Any of the three arguments may, however, be NULL, in which case TRANSLATE always returns NULL.

Here are some examples of TRANSLATE:

```
TRANSLATE ('abcd', 'ab', '12') → '12cd'

TRANSLATE ('12345', '15', 'xx') → 'x234x'

TRANSLATE ('grumpy old possum', 'uot', '%$*') →  'gr%mpy $ld p$ss%m'

TRANSLATE ('my language needs the letter e', 'egms', 'X')
 →
   'y lanuaX nXXd thX lXttXr X';

TRANSLATE ('please go away', 'a', NULL) → NULL
```

You can deduce a number of the usage rules for TRANSLATE from the above examples, but we'll spell them out here:

- If the search set contains a character not found in the string, then no translation is performed for that character.
- If the string contains a character not found in the search set, then that character is not translated.
- If the search set contains more characters than the replace set, then the "trailing" search characters that have no match in the replace set are removed from the string. In the following example, "a", "b", and "c" are changed to "z", "y", and "x", respectively. But the letter "d" is removed from the return string entirely because it had no corresponding character in the replace set.

  ```
  TRANSLATE ('abcdefg', 'abcd', 'zyx') → 'zyxefg'
  ```

In these cases, NULL is the matching "character" for all extra characters in the search set. When you replace a character with NULL, it is the same as removing that character from the string.

- If any of the three arguments is NULL, then the result of the translation is NULL. This is consistent with a basic tenet of NULLs: apply an operation to an unknown value, and you always get an unknown value.

The TRANSLATE function comes in handy when you need to change a whole set of characters in a string, regardless of the order in which they appear.

TRANSLATE...USING

This function exists to provide ANSI compatibility, and translates character data between character sets. Because TRANSLATE...USING is so unusual, we provide the syntax for using it, rather than its specification:

```
TRANSLATE(text USING {CHAR_CS | NCHAR_CS}
```

where:

text
: Is the text you wish to translate. This may be a character variable, an expression, or a literal text string.

CHAR_CS
: Specifies that the input text should be converted into the database character set.

NCHAR_CS
: Specifies that the input text should be converted into the national character set.

The output datatype will be either VARCHAR2 or NVARCHAR2, depending on whether you are converting to the database or the national character set, respectively.

Following is a simple example showing the use of this function:

```
DECLARE
   a VARCHAR2(30) := 'Corner? What corner?';
   b NVARCHAR2(30);
BEGIN
   b := TRANSLATE(a USING NCHAR_CS);
END;
```

In this example, the characters in the string are represented using the database character set. TRANSLATE...USING converts those characters into their national character set equivalents.

In Oracle9*i* you can simply assign a VARCHAR2 to an NVARCHAR2, (and vice versa), and Oracle will handle the conversion implicitly. If you wish to make such a conversion explicit, you can use TO_CHAR and TO_NCHAR to convert text to database and national character sets, respectively. Oracle recommends the use of TO_CHAR and TO_NCHAR over TRANSLATE...USING, because those functions support a greater range of input datatypes.

TRIM

Oracle added the TRIM function in the Oracle8*i* release to increase compliance with the ANSI SQL standard. TRIM combines the functionality of RTRIM and LTRIM into one function. TRIM is a bit different from other SQL functions in that it allows the use of keywords where you would normally expect arguments. Well, what do you expect from a function designed by a committee?

TRIM is unusual in the same manner as TRANSLATE...USING, so again we provide syntax rather than a specification:

```
TRIM ([LEADING | TRAILING | BOTH] [trim_character] FROM trim_source)
```

where:

trim_source
: Is the string you wish to trim.

trim_character
: Specifies the character you wish to remove from one or both ends of the string. The default is to trim spaces.

LEADING | TRAILING | BOTH
: Indicates whether you wish to trim from the beginning of the string (LEADING), from the end of the string (TRAILING), or both (BOTH). The default is to trim from both ends.

Following are some examples of TRIM:

- Remove leading and trailing spaces from a string:

```
TRIM( '    Brighten the corner where you are.    ');
   → 'Brighten the corner where you are'
```

- Remove only leading spaces:

```
x := '    Brighten the corner where you are.    ';
TRIM (LEADING FROM x)
     → 'Brighten the corner where you are.    '
```

- Remove trailing periods:

```
x := 'Brighten the corner where you are.';
y := '.';
TRIM (TRAILING y FROM x)
     → 'Brighten the corner where you are'
```

Given that TRIM is ANSI-standard, is there any reason to ever again use RTRIM or LTRIM? It turns out that there is. When using TRIM, you can specify only one character to trim. Using LTRIM and RTRIM, you can specify a string of characters to trim. For example:

```
RTRIM('Brighten the corner where you are.,:!..;:', '.,;:!')
  → 'Brighten the corner where you are'
```

With one function call, RTRIM has removed all trailing punctuation from the input string. Such a feat is simply not possible using TRIM. Well, it's possible if you wish to write a recursive PL/SQL function of your own that in turn invoked TRIM once for each possible punctuation character...but why bother?

UNISTR

UNISTR is the opposite of ASCIISTR, and converts a string into Unicode. You can represent non-printable characters in the input string using the *\XXXX* notation, where *XXXX* represents the Unicode code point value for a character. The specification for UNISTR is:

```
FUNCTION UNISTR (string1 IN VARCHAR2) RETURN VARCHAR2;
```

Following is an example of UNISTR in use:

```
BEGIN
   DBMS_OUTPUT.PUT_LINE(
      UNISTR('The letter \00E3 is not an ASCII character.')
   );
END;

The letter ã is not an ASCII character.
```

To find Unicode code point values, visit *http://www.unicode.org/charts/*.

UNISTR gives you convenient access to the entire universe of Unicode characters, even those you cannot type directly from your keyboard.

UPPER

The UPPER function converts all letters in the specified string to uppercase. UPPER (and LOWER) is an overloaded function, and will return a fixed-length string if the incoming string is fixed-length. The specifications for the UPPER function are:

```
FUNCTION UPPER (string1 IN CHAR) RETURN CHAR
FUNCTION UPPER (string1 IN VARCHAR2) RETURN VARCHAR2
```

UPPER will not change any characters in the string that are not letters, as case is irrelevant for numbers and special characters such as the dollar sign.

Here are some examples of the effect of UPPER:

```
UPPER ('Munising MI 49862') → 'MUNISING MI 49862'
UPPER ('Jenny') → 'JENNY'
```

The UPPER and LOWER functions are useful for guaranteeing a consistent case when comparing strings.

NLS Functions

Oracle provides a subset of string functions oriented toward work with the national language character set. These functions (summarized in Table 8-4) handle cases where the underlying character set matters to the results. For example, if you were using an ASCII character set as your database character set and an EBCDIC character set as your national language character set, you would find that the two character sets had different letters associated with the code 65. You can use CHR to translate 65 to the associated character in the database character set, and the NLS function NCHR to translate 65 to a character in the national language character set.

Table 8-4. National language support functions

Name	Description
NCHR	Returns a value from the national language character set.
NLS_INITCAP	Uppercases the first letter of each word (like INITCAP) and allows you to specify a linguistic sorting sequence.
NLS_LOWER	Lowercases a string in accordance with language-specific rules.
NLS_UPPER	Uppercases a string in accordance with language-specific rules.
NLSSORT	Returns a string of bytes that can be used to sort a string in accordance with language-specific rules.
TO_NCHAR	Converts database character set data into its national character set equivalent.

NCHR

NCHR functions similarly to CHR, but returns a value from the national language character set. The specification is:

```
FUNCTION NCHR(code_location NUMBER) RETURN NVARCHAR2;
```

Values returned by NCHR should generally be assigned to NVARCHAR2 or NCHAR2 variables. To do otherwise is to force a character set conversion that you probably don't need. Following is an example of using NCHR:

```
DECLARE
   x NVARCHAR2(30);
BEGIN
   x := NCHR(65);
   ...
```

The CHR function's USING NCHAR_CS clause provides the same functionality as NCHR.

NLS_INITCAP

The NLS_INITCAP function uppercases the first letter of each word in a string, just as the INITCAP function does. NLS_INITCAP also allows you to specify a linguistic sorting sequence that affects the definition of "first letter." The syntax for using NLS_INITCAP is:

```
NLS_INITCAP(string1, [, 'NLS_SORT=sort_sequence_name'])
```

The following example illustrates the difference between INITCAP and NLS_INITCAP:

```
BEGIN
   DBMS_OUTPUT.PUT_LINE(INITCAP('ijzen'));
   DBMS_OUTPUT.PUT_LINE(NLS_INITCAP('ijzen','NLS_SORT=XDUTCH'));
END;
```

The output is:

```
Ijzen
IJzen
```

In the Dutch language, the character sequence "ij" is treated as a single character. NLS_INITCAP correctly recognizes this as a result of the NLS_SORT specification, and uppercases the word "ijzen" (Dutch for "iron") appropriately.

NLS_INITCAP returns a VARCHAR2 value. The inputs can be from any character set.

NLS_LOWER

The NLS_LOWER function lowercases a string in accordance with language-specific rules. The syntax for calling NLS_LOWER is:

```
NLS_LOWER(string1, [, 'NLS_SORT=sort_sequence_name'])
```

See NLS_INITCAP for a description of how the NLS_SORT specification can affect the results.

NLS_UPPER

The NLS_UPPER function uppercases a string in accordance with language-specific rules. The syntax and usage are the same as for NLS_LOWER.

NLSSORT

The NLSSORT function returns a string of bytes that can be used to sort a string value in accordance with language-specific rules. The string returned is of the RAW datatype. The syntax for invoking NLSSORT is as follows:

```
NLSSORT(string1, [, 'NLS_SORT=sort_sequence_name'])
```

Following is an example of how NLSSORT can be used to ensure that two string values are compared according to language rules:

```
IF NLSSORT(x, 'NLS_SORT=XFRENCH') > NLSSORT(y, 'NLS_SORT=XFRENCH') THEN...
```

In this case, the IF statement is testing to see whether the string x is "greater" than the string y. If a simple x > y comparison were used, the results would depend simply on whether the binary representation of x was greater than y. For some languages, the underlying binary representation does not correlate to the sort sequence. The RAW strings returned by NLSSORT allow you to compare two values in the appropriate way for the ordering of characters in the language being used.

TO_NCHAR

TO_NCHAR is an overloaded function that can be used to convert either numbers, dates, or character strings to character strings in the national character set. The two TO_NCHAR functions (one for numbers, one for dates) work just like the TO_CHAR function described in Chapter 9. The one difference is that the return value is an NVARCHAR2 rather than a VARCHAR2.

This version of TO_NCHAR converts database character set data into its national character set equivalent. TO_NCHAR is the opposite of TO_CHAR, which is described in the previous section, "Character Functions." The specification of TO_NCHAR is as follows:

```
FUNCTION TO_NCHAR(char_data IN VARCHAR2) RETURN NVARCHAR2
```

TO_NCHAR can accept any of the following types as input: CHAR, VARCHAR2, CLOB, and NCLOB. The return type is always NVARCHAR2.

Following is an example of TO_NCHAR's translating a string from the database character set into the national character set:

```
DECLARE
   a VARCHAR2(30) := 'Corner? What corner?';
   b NVARCHAR2(30);
BEGIN
   b := TO_NCHAR(a);
END;
```

If you're planning to use TO_NCHAR, you should also review the use of TRANSLATE...USING, described earlier. Also be aware that TO_NCHAR may be used in the same manner as TO_CHAR to convert dates, times, and numbers into human-readable form. Such uses are described in Chapters 9 and 10.

CHAPTER 9
Numbers

In this chapter:

- Numeric Datatypes
- Number Conversions
- Numeric Functions

Where would we be without numbers? While those of us who are math-challenged might prefer a text-only view of the world, the reality is that much of the data in any database is numeric. How much inventory do we have? How much money do we owe? At what rate is our business growing? These are just some of the questions that we expect to answer using numbers from databases.

When working with numbers in PL/SQL, you need to have at least a passing familiarity with the following:

- The numeric datatypes at your disposal. It also helps to know in what situations they are best used.
- Conversion between numbers and their textual representations. How else do you expect to get those numbers into and out of your database?
- PL/SQL's rich library of built-in numeric functions. After all, you don't want to reinvent the wheel.

Each of these topics is discussed in this chapter. We'll begin by looking at the datatypes themselves.

Numeric Datatypes

PL/SQL, just like the Oracle RDBMS, offers a variety of numeric datatypes to suit different purposes. There are basically three numeric datatypes you need to know about:

- NUMBER
- PLS_INTEGER
- BINARY_INTEGER

In practice, you may encounter other numeric types, such as FLOAT and DECIMAL. These are really nothing more than alternate names for the three core numeric types just listed. We'll talk about these alternate names later, in the section "Numeric Subtypes."

Oracle's numeric types are designed to perform identically across all platforms that Oracle supports, enhancing portability. For example, a NUMBER division performed on Intel hardware will be rounded in the same manner and yield the same results as a NUMBER division performed on Sun hardware. Oracle achieves this portability by implementing its own math routines rather than using the underlying hardware-based math functions. An exception is the PLS_INTEGER type, which trades hardware-independence for execution speed.

The NUMBER Type

The NUMBER datatype is by far the most common numeric datatype you'll encounter in the world of Oracle and PL/SQL programming. NUMBER is the only numeric datatype supported directly by the Oracle database engine. In fact, the importance of NUMBER relative to the other numeric types is so great that you could probably go through your entire career using only NUMBER in your PL/SQL programs.

Use the NUMBER datatype to store integer, fixed, or floating-point numbers of just about any size, up to a maximum of 38 significant digits. However, you can set an assumed decimal point anywhere from 127 positions to the left (scale of 127) through 84 positions to the right (scale of –84) of those 38 significant digits. Effectively, then, the NUMBER type supports the following range of absolute values:

$1x10^{-127}$ through $9.99999999999999999999999999999999999999x10^{+121}$ (38 nines)

This range is what we came up with in our testing using Oracle9*i* Release 1. However, in the *Oracle9i SQL Reference*, Oracle specifies the range as 1.0×10^{-130} through $9.9...9 \times 10^{125}$ (38 nines).

The simplest way to declare a NUMBER variable is simply to specify the keyword NUMBER:

```
DECLARE
   x NUMBER;
```

Such a declaration results in a floating-point NUMBER. Oracle will allocate space for up to the maximum of 38 digits, and the decimal point will float to best accommodate whatever values you assign to the variable.

Generally, when you declare a variable of type NUMBER, you also specify the variable's precision and scale, as follows:

```
NUMBER (precision, scale)
```

Such a declaration results in a fixed-point number. The *precision* is the total number of significant digits that the number contains. The amount of memory that Oracle sets aside for a NUMBER directly relates to the *precision* you specify. The *scale* dictates the number of digits to the right or left of the decimal point, and also affects the point at which rounding occurs. Both the *precision* and the *scale* values must be literal, integer values; you cannot use variables or constants in the declaration. Legal values for *precision* range from 1 to 38, and legal values for *scale* range from –84 to 127.

When declaring fixed-point numbers, the value for *scale* is usually less than the value for *precision*. For example, you might declare a variable holding a monetary amount as NUMBER(9,2). Figure 9-1 shows how to interpret such a declaration.

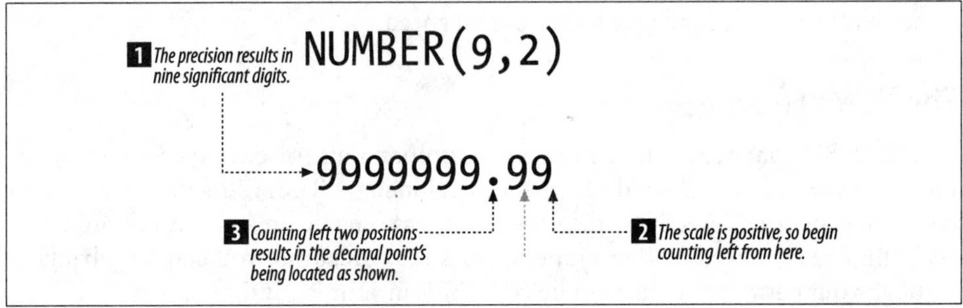

Figure 9-1. A typical fixed-point NUMBER declaration

As Figure 9-1 illustrates, a declaration of NUMBER(9,2) results in a fixed-point number consisting of seven digits to the left of the decimal point and two digits to the right of the decimal point. Such a variable can hold values into the millions. Values stored in the variable will be rounded to a maximum of two decimal places, as shown in Table 9-1.

Table 9-1. Rounding of NUMBER(9,2) values

Original value	Rounded value that is actually stored
1,234.56	1,234.56
1,234,567.984623	1,234,567.98
1,234,567.985623	1,234,567.99
1,234,567.995623	1,234,568.00
10,000,000.00	Too large a number for the variable; results in an overflow error
-10,000,000.00	Too small a number for the variable; results in an underflow error

The last two values in Table 9-1 result in overflow and underflow because they require more significant digits to represent than the variable can handle. Values in the tens of millions require at least eight significant digits to the left of the decimal point. You can't round such values to fit into only seven digits, so you get overflow and underflow errors.

Things get more interesting when you declare a variable with a *scale* that exceeds the variable's *precision*, or when you use a negative value for *scale*. Figure 9-2 illustrates the effect of a *scale* exceeding a variable's *precision*. Figure 9-3 illustrates the effect of using a negative *scale*.

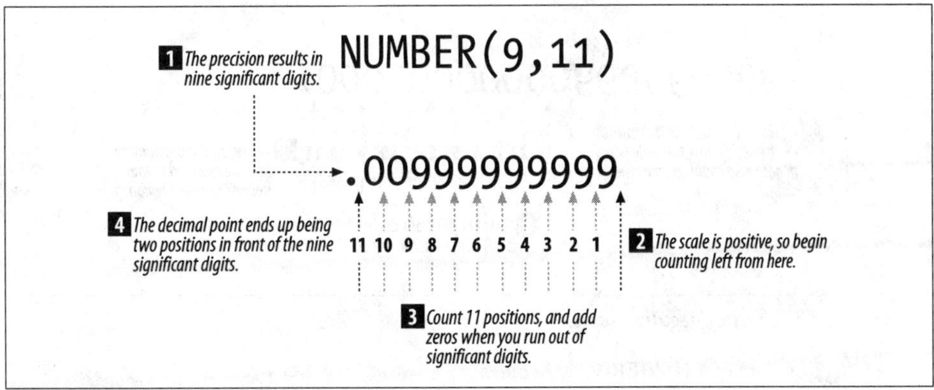

Figure 9-2. The effect of scale exceeding precision

The variable illustrated in Figure 9-2 has the same number of significant digits as the variable in Figure 9-1, but those significant digits are used differently. Because the *scale* is 11, those nine significant digits can represent only absolute values less than 0.01. Values are rounded to the nearest hundred-billionth. Table 9-2 shows the results of storing some carefully chosen example values into a NUMBER(9,11) variable.

Table 9-2. Rounding of NUMBER(9,11) values

Original value	Rounded value that is actually stored
0.00123456789	0.00123456789
0.000000000005	0.00000000001
0.000000000004	0.00000000000
0.01	Too large a number for the variable; requires a significant digit in the hundredth's position; results in an overflow error
-0.01	Too small a number for the variable; requires a significant digit in the hundredth's position; results in an underflow error

Negative *scale* values extend the decimal point out to the right, in the opposite direction of the positive scale. Figure 9-3 illustrates a variable declared NUMBER(9,–11).

Again we've used nine significant digits, but look where the decimal point is now! Rather than representing small values down to the hundred-billionth, the smallest value we can now represent precisely is 100 billion. Values less than 100 billion are rounded up or down to the nearest 100 billion, as illustrated in Table 9-3.

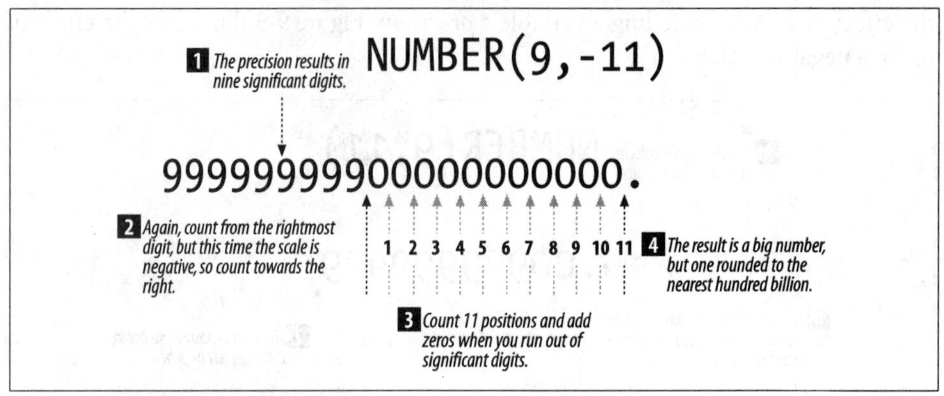

Figure 9-3. The effect of negative scale

Table 9-3. Rounding of NUMBER(9,-11) values

Original value	Rounded value that is actually stored
50,000,000,000.123	100,000,000,000.
49,999,999,999.999	0.
150,000,975,230,001	150,000,000,000,000
100,000,000,000,000,000,000 or 1 x 1020.	Too large a number for the variable; requires a significant digit in the hundred-quintillion's position; results in an overflow error
-100,000,000,000,000,000,000 or -1 x 1020.	Too small a number for the variable; requires a significant digit in the hundred-quintillion's position; results in an underflow error

As Figure 9-3 and Table 9-3 illustrate, negative scales allow us to represent some very large numbers, but only at the sacrifice of precision in the less-significant digits. Any absolute value less than 50 trillion is rounded to zero when stored in a NUMBER(9,-11) variable.

When declaring NUMBER variables using *precision* and *scale*, bear in mind that *scale* is optional and defaults to zero. For example, the following declarations are equivalent:

```
x NUMBER(9,0);
x NUMBER(9);
```

Both of these declarations result in integer variables (i.e., zero digits past the decimal point) containing nine significant digits. The range of integer values that can be represented using nine significant digits is –999,999,999 through 999,999,999.

Given the wide range and versatility of the NUMBER datatype, it's no wonder that it's so widely used. Using simply NUMBER in your declarations, you can represent floating-point values. By including *precision* and *scale*, you can represent fixed-point decimal numbers. By setting *scale* to zero or omitting it entirely, you can represent integer values. One datatype covers all the bases.

The PLS_INTEGER Type

The PLS_INTEGER datatype is available in PL/SQL Release 2.3 and above, and stores signed integers in the range –2,147,483,647 through 2,147,483,647. Values are stored using your hardware platform's native integer format.

Following is an example of some PLS_INTEGER declarations:

```
DECLARE
    loop_counter PLS_INTEGER;
    days_in_standard_year CONSTANT PLS_INTEGER := 365;
    emp_vacation_days PLS_INTEGER DEFAULT 14;
```

The PLS_INTEGER datatype was designed for speed. When you perform arithmetic using PLS_INTEGER values, the Oracle software uses native machine arithmetic, whereas arithmetic with other numeric types requires Oracle's platform-independent arithmetic library. As a result, it's faster to manipulate PLS_INTEGER values than it is to manipulate NUMBER values. Because PLS_INTEGER values are integers, you generally won't run into any compatibility issues as you move from one hardware platform to the next.

For efficiency reasons, Oracle recommends that you use PLS_INTEGER for all integer calculations that do not fall outside its range. Bear in mind, however, that if your use of PLS_INTEGER results in frequent conversions to and from the NUMBER type, you may be better off using NUMBER to begin with. You'll gain the greatest efficiency when you use PLS_INTEGER for integer arithmetic (and for loop counters) in cases where you can avoid conversions back and forth to the NUMBER type.

The BINARY_INTEGER Type

The BINARY_INTEGER datatype also allows you to store signed integers in a binary format. Unlike with PLS_INTEGER, native machine arithmetic is not used; BINARY_INTEGER arithmetic uses Oracle's platform-independent library code. BINARY_INTEGER was the first of PL/SQL's binary, integer datatypes. However, Oracle now recommends that you use PLS_INTEGER instead. Use BINARY_INTEGER only if you need to maintain compatibility with code written prior to PL/SQL Release 2.3.

The range of magnitude of a BINARY_INTEGER is –2,147,483,647 through 2,147,483,647. If you will be performing intensive calculations with integer values, you might see a performance improvement by declaring your variables as BINARY_INTEGER rather than NUMBER. But to be honest, in most situations this slight savings will not be noticeable.

Numeric Subtypes

Oracle also provides a number of *numeric subtypes*. Most of the time, these subtypes are simply alternate names for the three basic types we've just discussed. These alternate names offer compatibility with ANSI SQL, SQL/DS, and DB2 datatypes, and usually have the same range of legal values as their base type. Sometimes, subtypes offer additional functionality by restricting values to a subset of those supported by their base type. These subtypes are described in Table 9-4.

Table 9-4. Predefined numeric subtypes

Subtype	Compatibility	Corresponding Oracle datatype/notes
DEC (*precision, scale*)	ANSI	NUMBER (*precision, scale*)
DECIMAL (*precision, scale*)	IBM	NUMBER (*precision, scale*)
DOUBLE PRECISION	ANSI	NUMBER
FLOAT	ANSI, IBM	NUMBER
FLOAT (*binary_precision*)	ANSI, IBM	NUMBER, but NUMBERs can't be declared using binary precision
INT	ANSI	NUMBER
INTEGER	ANSI, IBM	NUMBER
NATURAL	N/A	BINARY_INTEGER, but allows only non-negative values (0 and higher)
NATURALN	N/A	Same as NATURAL, but with the additional restriction of never being NULL
NUMERIC (*precision, scale*)	ANSI	NUMBER (*precision, scale*)
POSITIVE	N/A	BINARY_INTEGER, but allows only positive values (1 and higher)
POSITIVEN	N/A	Same as POSITIVE, but with the additional restriction of never being NULL
REAL	ANSI	NUMBER
SIGNTYPE	N/A	BINARY_INTEGER, limited to the values –1, 0, and 1
SMALLINT	ANSI, IBM	NUMBER (38)

The NUMERIC, DECIMAL, and DEC datatypes can declare only fixed-point numbers. DOUBLE PRECISION and REAL are equivalent to NUMBER. FLOAT allows floating decimal points with binary precisions that range from 63 to 126 bits. We don't find it all that useful to define a number's precision in terms of bits rather than digits. We also don't find much use for the ANSI/IBM compatible subtypes, and we don't believe you will either.

The subtypes that we do sometimes find useful are the BINARY_INTEGER subtypes. NATURAL and POSITIVE are both subtypes of BINARY_INTEGER. These subtypes constrain the values you can store in a variable, and their use can make a program more self-documenting. For example, if you have a variable whose values must always be non-negative, you could declare that variable to be NATURAL (0 and higher) or POSITIVE (1 and higher), improving the self-documenting aspect of your code. Bear in mind, though, that you may get better performance out of PLS_INTEGER than out of BINARY_INTEGER and its subtypes.

Number Conversions

Computers work with numbers best when those numbers are in some sort of binary format. We humans, on the other hand, prefer to see our numbers in the form of character strings containing digits, commas, and other punctuation. PL/SQL allows you to convert numbers back and forth between human- and machine-readable form. Most commonly, you'll perform such conversions using the TO_CHAR and TO_NUMBER functions. In order to use these functions to their fullest extent, you need to understand number format models.

Number Format Models

Number formats are used with both the TO_CHAR and TO_NUMBER functions. You use number formats in calls to TO_CHAR to specify exactly how a numeric value should be translated into a VARCHAR2 string. You can specify the punctuation to use, the location of the positive or negative sign, and other useful items. Conversely, you use number formats in calls to TO_NUMBER to specify how a string representing a numeric value should be interpreted.

A number format mask can comprise one or more elements from Table 9-5. The resulting character string (or the converted numeric value) will reflect the combination of the format model elements that you use. You will find examples of different applications of the format models in the descriptions of both the TO_CHAR and TO_NUMBER functions.

Format elements with a description starting with "Prefix:" can be used only at the beginning of a format mask; when a description starts with "Suffix:", it can be used only at the end of a format mask. Most format elements are described in terms of their effect on a conversion of a number to its character string representation. Bear in mind that the majority of such elements may also be used in the converse manner, to specify the format of a character string to be converted into a number.

Table 9-5. Number format model elements

Format element	Description
9	Each 9 represents a significant digit to be returned. Leading zeros in a number are displayed as blanks.
0	Each zero represents a significant digit to be returned. Leading zeros in a number are displayed as zeros.
$	Prefix: puts a dollar sign in front of a number.
B	Prefix: returns a zero value as blanks, even if the 0 format element is used to show leading zeros.
MI	Suffix: places a minus sign (-) after the number if it is negative. If the number is positive, a trailing space is placed after the number.
S	Prefix: places a plus sign (+) in front of a positive number and a minus sign (-) in front of a negative number.
PR	Suffix: places angle brackets (< and >) around a negative value. Positive values will be given a leading and a trailing space.

Table 9-5. Number format model elements (continued)

Format element	Description
D	Specifies the location of the decimal point in the returned value. All format elements to the left of the D will format the integer component of the value. All format elements to the right of the D will format the fractional part of the value. The character used for the decimal point is determined by the database parameter NLS_NUMERIC_CHARACTERS.
G	Specifies the location of the group separator (for example, a comma to separate thousands as in 6,754) in the returned value. The character used for the group separator is determined by the database parameter NLS_NUMERIC_CHARACTERS.
C	Specifies the location of the ISO currency symbol in the returned value. The NLS_ISO_CURRENCY parameter specifies the ISO currency symbol.
L	Specifies the location of the local currency symbol (such as $) in the return value. The NLS_CURRENCY parameter specifies the local currency symbol.
, (comma)	Specifies that a comma be returned in that location in the return value. This comma is used as a group separator (see the G format element).
. (period)	Specifies that a period be returned in that location in the return value. This period is used as a decimal point (see the D format element).
V	Multiplies the number to the left of the V in the format model by 10 raised to the *n*th power, where *n* is the number of 9s found after the V in the format model.
EEEE	Suffix: specifies that the value be returned in scientific notation.
RN or rn	Specifies that the return value be converted to upper- or lowercase Roman numerals. The range of valid numbers for conversion to Roman numerals is between 1 and 3999. The value must be an integer. RN returns uppercase Roman numerals, while rn returns lowercase Roman numerals.
FM	Prefix: removes any leading or trailing blanks from the return value.
TM	Prefix: returns a number using the minimum number of characters. TM stands for "text minimum." Follow TM with one 9 if you want a regular, decimal notation (the default). Follow TM with one E if you want scientific notation.
U	Places a Euro symbol at the specified location. The NLS_DUAL_CURRENCY parameter controls the character returned by this format element.
X	Returns a number in hexadecimal value. You can precede this element with 0s to return leading zeros, or with FM to trim leading and trailing blanks. X cannot be used in combination with any other format elements.

Notice that sometimes two elements can be used to specify the same thing, or seemingly the same thing. For example, you can use the dollar sign ($), comma (,), and period (.), or you can use the L, G, and D elements, respectively. The letter elements respect your current NLS settings, and return the proper characters for whatever language you are using. For example, some European languages use a comma rather than a period to represent the decimal point. The dollar-sign, comma, and period format elements are U.S.-centric, and always return those three characters. We recommend that you use the NLS-sensitive format model elements such as L, G, and D unless you have a specific reason to do otherwise.

> **Denoting Monetary Units**
>
> Table 9-5 shows four format elements you can use to denote currency symbols. These elements are $, L, and C, and U, and you may be wondering about the differences among them.
>
> - The $ format element is U.S.-centric and always returns a dollar sign ($).
> - The L format element respects your current NLS_CURRENCY setting, which specifies your local currency indicator. If, for example, you set your NLS_TERRITORY to indicate that you're in the United Kingdom, NLS_CURRENCY will default to £, and the L format element will result in the £ being used as the currency indicator.
> - The C format element is similar to the L element, but it results in the ISO currency indicator, as specified by your current NLS_ISO_CURRENCY setting. For the United Kingdom you'll get GBP (for Great Britain Pounds), while for the United States you'll get USD (for U.S. Dollars), and so forth.
> - The U format element was added to support the Euro, and uses the currency indicator specified by NLS_DUAL_CURRENCY. For countries that support the Euro, the NLS_DUAL_CURRENCY setting will default to the Euro symbol (€).
>
> To view your current NLS_CURRENCY and NLS_ISO_CURRENCY settings, you can query the NLS_SESSION_PARAMETERS system view.

The TO_NUMBER Function

The TO_NUMBER function converts both fixed- and variable-length strings to numbers using an optional format mask. Use TO_NUMBER whenever you need to convert the character string representation of a number into its corresponding numeric value. Invoke TO_NUMBER as follows:

```
TO_NUMBER(string [,format [,nls_params]])
```

where:

string
: Is a string containing the character representation of a number.

format
: Is an optional format mask that specifies how TO_NUMBER should interpret the character representation of the number contained in the first parameter.

nls_params
: Is an optional string specifying various NLS parameter values. You can use this to override your current, session-level NLS parameter settings.

Using TO_NUMBER with no format

In many straightforward cases, you can use TO_NUMBER to convert strings to numbers without specifying any format string at all. For example, all of the following conversions work just fine:

```
DECLARE
   a NUMBER;
   b NUMBER;
   c NUMBER;
   d NUMBER;

   n1 VARCHAR2(20) := '-123456.78';
   n2 VARCHAR2(20) := '+123456.78';
BEGIN
   a := TO_NUMBER('123.45');
   b := TO_NUMBER(n1);
   c := TO_NUMBER(n2);
   d := TO_NUMBER('1.25E2');
END;
```

Generally, you should be able to use TO_NUMBER without specifying a format when the following conditions apply:

- Your number is represented using only digits and a single decimal point.
- Any sign is leading, and must be either minus (–) or plus (+). If no sign is present, the number is assumed to be positive.
- Scientific notation is used—for example, 1.25E2.

If your character strings don't meet these criteria or if you need to round values to a specific number of decimal digits, then you need to invoke TO_NUMBER with a format model.

Using TO_NUMBER with a format model

Using TO_NUMBER with a format model enables you to deal with a much wider range of numeric representations than TO_NUMBER would otherwise recognize. For example, you can specify the location of group separators and the currency symbol:

```
a := TO_NUMBER('$123,456.78','L999G999D99');
```

You don't necessarily need to specify the exact number of digits in your format model. TO_NUMBER is forgiving in this respect so long as your model contains more digits than are in your actual value. For example, the following will work:

```
a := TO_NUMBER('$123,456.78','L999G999G999D99');
```

However, if you have more digits to the left or to the right of the decimal point than your format allows, the conversion will fail with an *ORA-06502: PL/SQL: numeric or value error*. The first of the following conversions will fail because the string contains ten digits to the left of the decimal, while the format calls for only nine. The second conversion will fail because there are too many digits to the right of the decimal point:

```
a := TO_NUMBER('$1234,567,890.78','L999G999G999D99');
a := TO_NUMBER('$234,567,890.789','L999G999G999D99');
```

You can force leading zeros using the 0 format element:

```
a := TO_NUMBER('001,234','000G000');
```

You can recognize angle-bracketed numbers as negative numbers using the PR element:

```
a := TO_NUMBER('<123.45>','999D99PR');
```

However, not all format elements can be used to convert strings into numbers. Some elements, such as RN for Roman numerals, are output-only. The following attempt to convert the Roman numeral representation of a value into a number will fail:

```
a := TO_NUMBER('cxxiii','rn');
```

EEEE is another output-only format, but that's OK because you don't need it to convert values that are correctly represented in scientific notation. You can simply do:

```
a := TO_NUMBER('1.23456E-24');
```

Passing NLS settings to TO_NUMBER

Many of the number format model elements listed in Table 9-5 ultimately derive their meaning from one of the NLS parameters. For example, the G element represents the numeric group separator, which is the second character in the NLS_NUMERIC_CHARACTERS setting in effect when the conversion takes place. You can view current NLS parameter settings by querying the NLS_SESSION_PARAMETER view:

```
SQL> SELECT * FROM nls_session_parameters

PARAMETER                  VALUE
-------------------------  ---------------
NLS_LANGUAGE               AMERICAN
NLS_TERRITORY              AMERICA
NLS_CURRENCY               $
NLS_ISO_CURRENCY           AMERICA
NLS_NUMERIC_CHARACTERS     .,
NLS_CALENDAR               GREGORIAN
NLS_DATE_FORMAT            DD-MON-RR
```

Some NLS parameter settings are by default dependent on others. For example, set NLS_TERRITORY to AMERICA, and Oracle defaults NLS_NUMERIC_CHARACTERS TO ".,". If you need to, you can then override the NLS_NUMERIC_CHARACTERS setting (using an ALTER SESSION command, for example).

On rare occasions, you may want to override specific NLS parameter settings for a single call to TO_NUMBER. In the following example, we invoke TO_NUMBER and specify NLS settings corresponding to NLS_TERRITORY=FRANCE:

```
a := TO_NUMBER('F123.456,78','L999G999D99',
               'NLS_NUMERIC_CHARACTERS='',.'''
               || ' NLS_CURRENCY=''F'''
               || ' NLS_ISO_CURRENCY=FRANCE');
```

Because our NLS parameter string is so long, we've broken it up into three separate strings concatenated together so that our example fits nicely on the page. Note our doubling of quote characters. The setting we want for NLS_NUMERIC_CHARACTERS is:

```
NLS_NUMERIC_CHARACTERS=',.'
```

We need to embed this setting into our NLS parameter string, and to embed quotes within a string we must double them, so we end up with:

```
'NLS_NUMERIC_CHARACTERS='',.'''
```

The three NLS parameters we've set in this example are the only three you can set via TO_NUMBER. We don't know why that is. It certainly would be much more convenient if we could simply do the following:

```
a := TO_NUMBER('F123.456,78','L999G999D99','NLS_TERRITORY=FRANCE');
```

But unfortunately, NLS_TERRITORY is not something you can set via a call to TO_NUMBER. You are limited to specifying NLS_NUMERIC_CHARACTERS, NLS_CURRENCY, and NLS_ISO_CURRENCY.

For detailed information on setting the various NLS parameters, please see *Oracle's Globalization Support Guide*, which is part of the Oracle9*i* Database documentation set.

Avoid using the third argument to TO_NUMBER—we believe it's better to rely on session settings to drive the way in which PL/SQL interprets format model elements such as L, G, and D. Instead of your having to hardcode such information throughout your programs, session settings can be controlled by the user outside the bounds of your code.

The TO_CHAR Function

The TO_CHAR function is the converse of TO_NUMBER, and converts numbers to their character representations. Using an optional format mask, you can be quite specific about the form those character representations take. Invoke TO_CHAR as follows:

```
TO_CHAR(number [,format [,nls_params]])
```

where:

number
: Is a number that you wish to represent in character form. This number may be of any of PL/SQL's numeric types: NUMBER, PLS_INTEGER, and BINARY_INTEGER.

format
: Is an optional format mask that specifies how TO_CHAR should present the number in character form.

nls_params
: Is an optional string specifying various NLS parameter values. You can use this to override your current session-level NLS parameter settings.

If you wish your results to be in the national character set, you can use TO_NCHAR in place of TO_CHAR. In that case, be certain you provide your number format string in the national character set as well. Otherwise, you may receive output consisting of all number signs.

Using TO_CHAR with no format

As with TO_NUMBER, you can invoke TO_CHAR without specifying a format mask:

```
DECLARE
   b VARCHAR2(30);
BEGIN
   b := TO_CHAR(123456789.01);
   DBMS_OUTPUT.PUT_LINE(b);
END;
```

The output is:

```
123456789.01
```

Unlike the case with TO_NUMBER, you aren't likely to find this use of TO_CHAR very useful. At the very least, you may want to format your numeric output with group separators to make it more readable.

Using TO_CHAR with a format model

When converting numbers into their character string equivalents, you'll most often invoke TO_CHAR with a format model. For example, you can output a monetary amount as follows:

```
DECLARE
   b VARCHAR2(30);
BEGIN
   b := TO_CHAR(123456789.01,'L999G999G999D99');
   DBMS_OUTPUT.PUT_LINE(b);
END;
```

The output (in the U.S.) is:

```
$123,456,789.01
```

The format model elements in Table 9-5 give you a lot of flexibility, and you should experiment with them to learn the finer points of how they work. The following example specifies that leading zeros be maintained, but the B format element is used to force any zero values to blanks. Notice that the B element precedes the number elements (the 0s) but follows the currency indicator (the L):

```
DECLARE
   b VARCHAR2(30);
   c VARCHAR2(30);
BEGIN
   b := TO_CHAR(123.01,'LB000G000G009D99');
   DBMS_OUTPUT.PUT_LINE(b);

   b := TO_CHAR(0,'LB000G000G009D99');
   DBMS_OUTPUT.PUT_LINE(b);
END;
```

The output is:

```
$000,000,123.01
```

You see only one line of output from this example, and that's from the first conversion. The second conversion involves a zero value, and the B format element causes TO_CHAR to return that value as a blank string, even though the format otherwise specifies that leading zeros be returned. As an experiment, try this same example on your system, but leave off the B.

Not all combinations of format elements are possible. For example, you can't use LRN to place a currency symbol in front of a value expressed in Roman numerals. Oracle doesn't document every such nuance. It takes some experience and some experimenting to get a feel for what's possible and what's not.

The V format element

The V format element is unusual enough to warrant a special explanation. The V element allows you to scale a value, and its operation is best explained through a good illustration, which you'll find in Figure 9-4.

Why would you ever need such functionality? Look no further than the stock market for an example. The standard trading unit for stocks is 100 shares, and stock sales are sometimes reported in terms of the number of 100-share units sold. Thus, a sales figure of 123 actually represents 123 units of 100 shares, or 12,300 shares. The

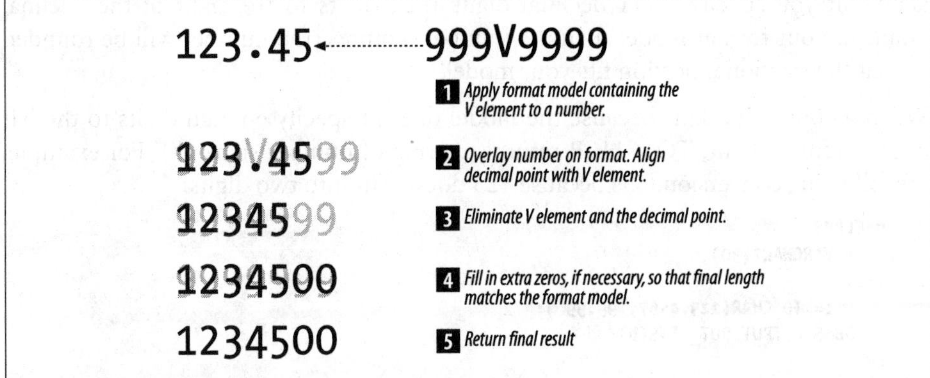
123.45
999V9999
1 Apply format model containing the V element to a number.
123V4599
2 Overlay number on format. Align decimal point with V element.
1234599
3 Eliminate V element and the decimal point.
1234500
4 Fill in extra zeros, if necessary, so that final length matches the format model.
1234500
5 Return final result

Figure 9-4. The V number format element

following example shows how V can be used to scale a value such as 123 in recognition of the fact that it really represents 100s:

```
DECLARE
   shares_sold NUMBER := 123;
BEGIN
   DBMS_OUTPUT.PUT_LINE(
      TO_CHAR(shares_sold,'999G9V99')
   );
END;
```

The output is:

```
12,300
```

Notice that the format model in this example includes the G element to specify the location of the group separator (the comma) in the displayed number. You can specify group separators only to the left of the V element, not to the right. This is unfortunate. Consider the following, perfectly reasonable format model:

```
TO_CHAR(123.45,'9G99V9G999');
```

You would hope to get the result formatted as 1,234,500. However, the G to the right of the V is invalid. You can use 9G99V9999 to get a result of 1,234500, or you can use 999V9999 to get a result of 1234500. Neither result is as readable as we would like it to be.

You probably won't use the V element very often, but it's worth knowing about this bit of interesting functionality.

Rounding when converting numbers to character strings

When converting character strings to numbers, you'll get an error any time you have more digits to the left or right of the decimal point than the format model allows. When converting numbers to characters, however, you'll get an error only if the number requires more digits to the left of the decimal point than the format model allows. If you specify fewer decimal digits (i.e., digits to the right of the decimal point) in your format model than the number requires, the number will be rounded so that the fractional portion fits your model.

When a conversion fails because the model doesn't specify enough digits to the left of the decimal point, TO_CHAR returns a string of number signs (#). For example, the following conversion fails because 123 doesn't fit into two digits:

```
DECLARE
   b VARCHAR2(30);
BEGIN
   b := TO_CHAR(123.4567,'99.99');
   DBMS_OUTPUT.PUT_LINE(b);
END;

######
```

It's perfectly OK, however, for your model not to include enough digits to cover the fractional portion of a value. In such cases, rounding occurs. For example:

```
BEGIN
   DBMS_OUTPUT.PUT_LINE(TO_CHAR(123.4567,'999.99'));
   DBMS_OUTPUT.PUT_LINE(TO_CHAR(123.4567,'999'));
END;

123.46
123
```

Digits 5 and higher are rounded up, which is why 123.4567 is rounded up to 123.46. Digits less than 5 are rounded down, so 123.4xxx will always be rounded down to 123.

Dealing with spaces when converting numbers to character strings

A reasonably common problem encountered when converting numbers to character strings is that TO_CHAR always leaves room for the minus sign even when numbers are positive. By default, TO_CHAR will leave one space in front of a number for use by a potential minus sign (–):

```
DECLARE
   b VARCHAR2(30);
   c VARCHAR2(30);
BEGIN
   b := TO_CHAR(-123.4,'999.99');
   c := TO_CHAR(123.4,'999.99');
   DBMS_OUTPUT.PUT_LINE(':' || b || ' ' || TO_CHAR(LENGTH(b)));
   DBMS_OUTPUT.PUT_LINE(':' || c || ' ' || TO_CHAR(LENGTH(c)));
END;
```

The output is:

```
:-123.40 7
: 123.40 7
```

Notice that both converted values have the same length, seven characters, even though the positive number requires only six characters when displayed in character form. That leading space can be a big help if you are trying to get columns of numbers to line up. However, it can be a bit of a pain if for some reason you need a compact number with no spaces whatsoever.

Use the PR element, and your positive numbers will have one leading space and one trailing space to accommodate the potential enclosing angle-brackets. Spaces will be left to accommodate whatever sign-indicator you choose in your format model.

There are a couple of approaches you can take if you really need your numbers converted to characters without leading or trailing spaces. One approach is to use the TM format model element to get the "text minimum" representation of a number:

```
DECLARE
   b VARCHAR2(30);
   c VARCHAR2(30);
BEGIN
   b := TO_CHAR(-123.4,'TM9');
   c := TO_CHAR(123.4,'TM9');
   DBMS_OUTPUT.PUT_LINE(':' || b || ' ' || TO_CHAR(LENGTH(b)));
   DBMS_OUTPUT.PUT_LINE(':' || c || ' ' || TO_CHAR(LENGTH(c)));
END;
```

The output is:

```
:-123.4 6
:123.4 5
```

The TM approach works, but it's a relatively new format element that is not available in older releases of PL/SQL (before Oracle8*i*). TM also doesn't allow you to specify any other formatting information. You can't, for example, specify TM999.99 in order to get a fixed two decimal digits. If you need to specify other formatting information or if TM is not available in your release of PL/SQL, you'll need to trim the results of the conversion:

```
DECLARE
   b VARCHAR2(30);
   c VARCHAR2(30);
BEGIN
   b := LTRIM(TO_CHAR(-123.4,'999.99'));
   c := LTRIM(TO_CHAR(123.4,'999.99'));
   DBMS_OUTPUT.PUT_LINE(':' || b || ' ' || TO_CHAR(LENGTH(b)));
   DBMS_OUTPUT.PUT_LINE(':' || c || ' ' || TO_CHAR(LENGTH(c)));
END;
```

The output is:

```
:-123.40 7
:123.40 6
```

Here we've used LTRIM to remove any potential leading spaces, and we've successfully preserved our fixed two digits to the right of the decimal-point. Use RTRIM if you are placing the sign to the right of the number (e.g., via the MI element) or TRIM if you are using something like PR that affects both sides of the number.

Passing NLS settings to TO_CHAR

As with TO_NUMBER, you have the option of passing a string of NLS parameter settings to TO_CHAR. For example:

```
BEGIN
   DBMS_OUTPUT.PUT_LINE(
      TO_CHAR(123456.78,'999G999D99','NLS_NUMERIC_CHARACTERS='',.''')
   );
END;
```

The output is:

```
123.456,78
```

The three NLS parameters you can set this way are NLS_NUMERIC_CHARACTERS, NLS_CURRENCY, and NLS_ISO_CURRENCY. See "Passing NLS settings to TO_NUMBER" earlier in this chapter for an example of all three being set at once.

Using CAST

The CAST function is newly supported in Oracle9*i*, and can be used to convert numbers to strings and vice versa. The general format of the CAST function is as follows:

```
CAST (expression AS datatype)
```

The following example shows CAST being used first to convert a NUMBER to a VARCHAR2 string, and then to convert the characters in a VARCHAR2 string into their corresponding numeric value:

```
DECLARE
   a NUMBER := 123.45;
   a1 VARCHAR2(30);
   b VARCHAR2(30) := '-123.45';
   b1 NUMBER;
BEGIN
   a1 := CAST (a AS VARCHAR2);
   b1 := CAST (b AS NUMBER);
   DBMS_OUTPUT.PUT_LINE(a1);
   DBMS_OUTPUT.PUT_LINE(b1);
END;
```

The output is:

```
123.45
-123.45
```

CAST has the disadvantage of not supporting the use of number format models. An advantage to CAST, however, is that it is part of the ANSI SQL standard, whereas the TO_CHAR and TO_NUMBER functions are not. If writing 100% ANSI-compliant code is important to you, you should investigate the use of CAST. Otherwise, we recommend using the traditional TO_NUMBER and TO_CHAR functions.

Because PL/SQL is not part of the ANSI standard, it's by definition not possible to write 100% ANSI-compliant PL/SQL code, so CAST seems to bring no real benefit to PL/SQL number conversions. CAST can, however, be used in the effort to write 100% ANSI-compliant SQL statements (such as SELECT, INSERT, etc.).

Implicit Conversions

A final method of handling conversions between numbers and strings is to just leave it all to PL/SQL. Such conversions are referred to as *implicit conversions*, because you don't explicitly specify them in your code. Following are some straightforward implicit conversions that will work just fine:

```
DECLARE
   a NUMBER;
   b VARCHAR2(30);
BEGIN
   a := '-123.45';
   b := -123.45;
...
```

We have several problems with implicit conversions. We are strong believers in maintaining control over our code, and when you use an implicit conversion you are giving up some of that control. You should always know when conversions are taking place, and the best way to do that is to code them explicitly. Don't just let them happen. If you rely on implicit conversions, you lose track of when conversions are occurring, and your code is less efficient as a result. Explicit conversions also make your intent clear to other programmers, making your code more self-documenting and easier to understand.

Another problem with implicit conversions is that while they may work just fine (or seem to) in simple cases, sometimes they can be ambiguous. Consider the following:

```
DECLARE
   a NUMBER;
BEGIN
   a := '123.400' || 999;
```

What value will the variable "a" hold when this code executes? It all depends on how PL/SQL evaluates the expression on the right side of the assignment operator. If PL/SQL begins by converting the string to a number, you'll get the following result:

```
a := '123.400' || 999;
a := 123.4 || 999;
a := '123.4' || '999';
a := '123.4999';
a := 123.4999;
```

On the other hand, if PL/SQL begins by converting the number to a string, you'll get the following result:

```
a := '123.400' || 999;
a := '123.400' || '999';
a := '123.400999';
a := 123.400999;
```

Which is it? Do you know? Even if you *do* know, do you really want to leave future programmers guessing and scratching their heads when they look at your code? It would be much clearer, and therefore better, to write the conversion explicitly:

```
a := TO_NUMBER('123.400' || TO_CHAR(999));
```

This expression, by the way, represents how Oracle will evaluate the original example. Isn't it much easier to understand at a glance now that we've expressed the conversions explicitly?

Conversion Between Numeric Types

PL/SQL supports three numeric types, NUMBER, PLS_INTEGER, and BINARY_INTEGER, and you may be wondering about conversions among these three types. There's no ambiguity when converting between numeric types, so PL/SQL handles such conversions implicitly. There are no functions that allow you to go between these types, and any such functions would be superfluous.

Be aware, however, that conversions between the three numeric types can and do occur, and that they do exact a cost (albeit a small one) in terms of execution time. Try to minimize such conversions.

Most, if not all, of the numeric functions discussed in the next section of this chapter expect NUMBER inputs. Invoke those functions with PLS_INTEGER or BINARY_INTEGER arguments, and you are forcing a conversion to take place.

Isolate your use of PLS_INTEGER or BINARY_INTEGER from any NUMBER variables or numeric functions that your program may be using.

Numeric Functions

PL/SQL implements a number of functions that are useful when working with numbers. We list those functions in Table 9-6, and describe each of them in detail in the sections that follow.

Table 9-6. PL/SQL's built-in numeric functions

Name	Description
ABS	Returns the absolute value of a number.
ACOS	Returns the inverse cosine.

Table 9-6. PL/SQL's built-in numeric functions (continued)

Name	Description
ASIN	Returns the inverse sine.
ATAN	Returns the inverse tangent.
ATAN2	Returns the inverse tangent of a value, but allows you to pass that value differently than when using ATAN.
BITAND	Performs an AND operation on the bits from two positive integer numbers.
CEIL	Returns the smallest integer greater than or equal to the specified number.
COS	Returns the cosine.
COSH	Returns the hyperbolic cosine.
EXP (*n*)	Returns the number *e* raised to the *n*th power, where *e* = 2.71828183...
FLOOR	Returns the largest integer equal to or less than the specified number.
LN (*a*)	Returns the natural logarithm of *a*.
LOG (*a*, *b*)	Returns the logarithm, base *a*, of *b*.
MOD (*a*, *b*)	Returns the remainder of *a* divided by *b*.
POWER (*a*, *b*)	Returns *a* raised to the *b*th power.
ROUND (*a*, [*b*])	Returns *a* rounded to *b* decimal places.
SIGN (*a*)	Returns 1 if *a* is positive, 0 if *a* is 0, and –1 if *a* is less than 0 (i.e., negative).
SIN	Returns the sine.
SINH	Returns the hyperbolic sine.
SQRT	Returns the square root of a number.
TAN	Returns the tangent.
TANH	Returns the hyperbolic tangent.
TRUNC (*a*, [*b*])	Returns *a* truncated to *b* decimal places.

Note that the trigonometric and logarithmic functions are available only in PL/SQL Version 2.0 and subsequent releases. The inverse trigonometric functions are available only in PL/SQL Release 2.3 and higher.

When using the trigonometric functions, be aware that all angles are expressed in radians, not in degrees. You can convert between radians and degrees as follows:

```
radians = π * degrees / 180 – From degrees to radians

degrees = radians * 180 / π – From radians to degrees
```

Oracle Corporation did not implement a function for π (pi) itself. However, you can obtain the value for π through the following call:

```
ACOS (-1)
```

The inverse cosine (ACOS) of –1 happens to be defined as exactly π. Of course, because π is a never-ending decimal number, you always have to work with an approximation. Use the ROUND function if you wish to round the results of ACOS(–1) to a specific number of decimal places.

We'll look quickly at the rounding and truncation functions, and then provide summaries of each of PL/SQL's built-in numeric functions. For each, we'll include the specification, some examples, and a brief description.

Rounding and Truncation Functions

There are four different numeric functions that perform rounding and truncation actions: CEIL, FLOOR, ROUND, and TRUNC. It is easy to get confused about which to use in a particular situation. Table 9-7 compares these functions.

Table 9-7. Comparison of functions that perform rounding and truncation actions

Function	Summary
CEIL	Returns the smallest integer that is greater than the specified value. This integer is the "ceiling" over your value.
FLOOR	Returns the largest integer that is less than the specified value. This integer is the "floor" under your value.
ROUND	Performs rounding on a number. You can round with a positive number of decimal places (the number of digits to the right of the decimal point) and also with a negative number of decimal places (the number of digits to the right of the decimal point).
TRUNC	Truncates a number to the specified number of decimal places. TRUNC simply discards all values beyond the decimal places provided in the call.

Figure 9-5 illustrates the use of the functions for different values and decimal place rounding. See "The ROUND and TRUNC Functions" in Chapter 10 for a discussion of rounding and truncating dates.

	1.75	1.3	55.56	55.56	Input
Function	**0**	**0**	**1**	**-1**	Number of decimal places
ROUND	2	1	55.6	60	
TRUNC	1	1	55.5	50	
FLOOR	1	1	55	55	
CEIL	2	2	56	56	

Figure 9-5. Impact of rounding and truncating functions

The following sections describe each of the PL/SQL numeric functions.

ABS

The ABS function returns the absolute value of the input. The specification for the ABS function is:

```
FUNCTION ABS (n NUMBER) RETURN NUMBER;
```

The ABS function can help simplify your code logic. For example, in one program we reviewed, line items and amounts for a profit and loss statement were footed or balanced. If the variance on the line amount was greater than $100, either positive or negative, that line item was flagged as "in error." The first version of the code that implemented this requirement looked like this (variance_table is a PL/SQL table holding the variance for each line item):

```
IF variance_table (line_item_nu) BETWEEN 1 AND 100 OR
   variance_table (line_item_nu) BETWEEN -100 AND -1
THEN
   apply_variance (statement_id);
ELSE
   flag_error (statement_id, line_item_nu);
END IF;
```

There are two ways to express this logic. First, instead of hardcoding the maximum allowable variance, we put the value in a named constant. Second, we use ABS so that we perform the range check only once. With these changes, the above code can be rewritten as follows:

```
IF ABS (variance_table (line_item_nu))
   BETWEEN min_variance AND max_variance
THEN
   apply_variance (statement_id);
ELSE
   flag_error (statement_id, line_item_nu);
END IF;
```

ACOS

The ACOS function returns the inverse cosine. The specification for the ACOS function is:

```
FUNCTION ACOS (n NUMBER) RETURN NUMBER;
```

where the number *n* must be between –1 and 1, and the value returned by ACOS is between 0 and π.

ASIN

The ASIN function returns the inverse sine. The specification for the ASIN function is:

```
FUNCTION ASIN (n NUMBER) RETURN NUMBER;
```

where the number *n* must be between –1 and 1, and the value returned by ASIN is between $-\pi/2$ and $\pi/2$.

ATAN

The ATAN function returns the inverse tangent. The specification for the ATAN function is:

```
FUNCTION ATAN (n NUMBER) RETURN NUMBER;
```

where the number *n* must be between –infinity and infinity, and the value returned by ATAN is between $-\pi/2$ and $\pi/2$.

ATAN2

The ATAN2 function returns the inverse tangent of *n/m*. The specification for the ATAN2 function is:

```
FUNCTION ATAN (n NUMBER, m NUMBER) RETURN NUMBER;
```

where the numbers *n* and *m* must be between –infinity and infinity, and the value returned by ATAN is between $-\pi$ and π. The result of ATAN2(*n*,*m*) is defined to be identical to ATAN(n/m).

BITAND

The BITAND function performs a logical AND between two positive, integer arguments. The specification for BITAND is:

```
FUNCTION BITAND (n NUMBER, m NUMBER) RETURN NUMBER;
```

The following example illustrates how BITAND might be used to read the bits in an integer used to contain on/off-type flags.

```
DECLARE
   --Declare a flag variable, the bits of which are interpreted
   --as follows:
   ---    0000
   ---       |--0=male, 1=female
   ---      |---0=part-time, 1=full-time
   ---     |----0=hourly, 1=salaried
   ---    |-----0=office, 1=factory
   bit_flags PLS_INTEGER;
BEGIN
   --Initialize the flag variable to indicate a female,
   --full-time employee. Note that 3 is represented in
   --binary as 11.
   bit_flags := 3;
...
   --Do some things if the employee is full-time
   IF BITAND(bit_flags, 2) <> 0 THEN
      DBMS_OUTPUT.PUT_LINE('Employee is full-time.');
         ...
```

To set an individual bit in an integer value, you can use an incantation such as the following. The first resets the full-time bit in the flag variable used in the previous example, while the second sets the same bit:

```
bit_flags := BITAND(bit_flags,13);
bit_flags := BITAND(bit_flags,13) + 2;
```

These incantations work by using BITAND with a mask that returns the current state of all bits *except* the one that we want to set (or reset, as the case may be). The value 13 is represented in binary as 1101. Consequently, the value returned by BITAND in this case is guaranteed to have the full-time bit set to zero. If we want to leave it that way, we can. Otherwise, to set the bit, we add the value 2. The binary representation of 2 is 10, causing the second bit to be set. These incantations work regardless of the bit's original value.

If you limit yourself to positive numbers, the largest power of 2 that you can store in a PLS_INTEGER variable is 2^{30}. This effectively gives you 30 bits to play with.

CEIL

The CEIL ("ceiling") function returns the smallest integer greater than or equal to the specified number. The specification for the CEIL function is:

```
FUNCTION CEIL (n NUMBER) RETURN NUMBER;
```

Here are some examples of the effect of CEIL:

```
CEIL (6) → 6
CEIL (119.1) → 120
CEIL (-17.2) → -17
```

For a comparison of CEIL with several other numeric functions, see Table 9-7 and Figure 9-5 earlier in the "Rounding and Truncation Functions" section.

COS

The COS trigonometric function returns the cosine of the specified angle. The specification for the COS function is:

```
FUNCTION COS (angle NUMBER) RETURN NUMBER;
```

where *angle* must be expressed in radians. If your angle is specified in degrees, then you should call COS as follows:

```
my_cosine := COS (ACOS(-1)*angle_in_degrees/180);
```

COSH

The COSH trigonometric function returns the hyperbolic cosine of the specified number. The specification for the COSH function is:

```
FUNCTION COSH (n NUMBER) RETURN NUMBER;
```

If n is a real number and i is the imaginary square root of -1, then the relationship between COS and COSH can be expressed as follows:

```
COS (i * n) = COSH (n)
```

EXP

The EXP function returns the value e raised to the nth power, where n is the input argument. The specification for the EXP function is:

```
FUNCTION EXP (n NUMBER) RETURN NUMBER;
```

The number e (approximately equal to 2.71828) is the base of the system of natural logarithms.

FLOOR

The FLOOR function, the opposite of the CEIL function, returns the largest integer that is less than or equal to the input number. The specification for the FLOOR function is:

```
FUNCTION FLOOR (n NUMBER) RETURN NUMBER;
```

Here are some examples of the values returned by FLOOR:

```
FLOOR (6.2) → 6
FLOOR (-89.4) → -90
```

For a comparison of FLOOR with several other numeric functions, see Table 9-7 and Figure 9-5 earlier in the "Rounding and Truncation Functions" section.

LN

The LN function returns the natural logarithm of the input. The specification for the LN function is:

```
FUNCTION LN (n NUMBER) RETURN NUMBER;
```

The argument *n* must be greater than or equal to 0. If you pass LN a negative argument, you will receive the following error:

```
ORA-01428: argument '-1' is out of range
```

LOG

The LOG function returns the base *b* logarithm of the input value. The specification for the LOG function is:

```
FUNCTION LOG (b NUMBER, n NUMBER) RETURN NUMBER;
```

The argument *n* must be greater than or equal to 0. The base *b* must be greater than 1. If you pass LOG an argument that violates either of these rules, you will receive the following error:

```
ORA-01428: argument '-1' is out of range
```

MOD

The MOD function returns the remainder of one number when divided by a second number. The specification for the MOD function is:

```
FUNCTION MOD (dividend NUMBER, divisor NUMBER) RETURN NUMBER;
```

If the *divisor* is zero, then the *dividend* is returned unchanged. Here are some examples of MOD:

```
MOD (10, 5) → 0
MOD (2, 1) → 0
MOD (3,2) → 1
```

You can use MOD to determine quickly if a number is odd or even:

```
FUNCTION is_odd (num_in IN NUMBER) RETURN BOOLEAN
IS
```

```
BEGIN
   RETURN MOD (num_in, 2) = 1;
END;

FUNCTION is_even (num_in IN NUMBER) RETURN BOOLEAN
IS
BEGIN
   RETURN MOD (num_in, 2) = 0;
END;
```

POWER

The POWER function raises the first argument to the power indicated by the second argument. The specification for the POWER function is:

```
FUNCTION POWER (base NUMBER, power NUMBER) RETURN NUMBER;
```

If base is negative, then *power* must be an integer. The following expression calculates the range of valid values for a BINARY_INTEGER variable ($-2^{31}-1$ through $2^{31}-1$):

```
POWER (-2, 31) - 1 .. POWER (2, 31) - 1
```

or:

```
-2147483649 .. 2147483647
```

ROUND

The ROUND function returns the first argument rounded to the number of decimal places specified in the second argument. The specification for the ROUND function is:

```
FUNCTION ROUND (n NUMBER, [decimal_places NUMBER]) RETURN NUMBER;
```

The *decimal_places* argument is optional and defaults to 0, which means that *n* will be rounded to zero decimal places, a whole number. The value of *decimal_ places* can be less than zero. A negative value for this argument directs ROUND to round digits to the left of the decimal point rather than to the right. Here are some examples:

```
ROUND (153.46) → 153
ROUND (153.46, 1) → 153.5
ROUND (153, -1) → 150
```

For a comparison of ROUND with several other numeric functions, see Table 9-7 and Figure 9-5 earlier in the "Rounding and Truncation Functions" section.

SIGN

The SIGN function returns the sign of the input number. The specification for the SIGN function is:

```
FUNCTION SIGN (n NUMBER) RETURN NUMBER;
```

This function returns one of these three values:

–1	*n* is less than zero
0	*n* is equal to zero
+1	*n* is greater than zero

SIN

The SIN trigonometric function returns the sine of the specified angle. The specification for the SIN function is:

```
FUNCTION SIN (angle NUMBER) RETURN NUMBER;
```

where *angle* must be expressed in radians. If your angle is specified in degrees, then you should call SIN as follows:

```
my_sine := SIN (ACOS(-1)*angle_in_degrees/180);
```

SINH

The SINH trigonometric function returns the hyperbolic sine of the specified number. The specification for the SINH function is:

```
FUNCTION SINH (n NUMBER) RETURN NUMBER;
```

If *n* is a real number and *i* is the imaginary square root of –1, then the relationship between SIN and SINH can be expressed as follows:

```
SIN (i * n) = i * SINH (n)
```

SQRT

The SQRT function returns the square root of the input number. The specification for the SQRT function is:

```
FUNCTION SQRT (n NUMBER) RETURN NUMBER;
```

where *n* must be greater than or equal to 0. If *n* is negative, you will receive the following error:

```
ORA-01428: argument '-1' is out of range
```

TAN

The TAN trigonometric function returns the tangent of the specified angle. The specification for the TAN function is:

```
FUNCTION TAN (angle NUMBER) RETURN NUMBER;
```

where *angle* must be expressed in radians. If your angle is specified in degrees, then you should call TAN as follows:

```
my_tane := TAN (ACOS(-1)*angle_in_degrees/180);
```

TANH

The TANH trigonometric function returns the hyperbolic tangent of the specified number. The specification for the TANH function is:

```
FUNCTION TANH (n NUMBER) RETURN NUMBER;
```

If *n* is a real number and *i* is the imaginary square root of –1, then the relationship between TAN and TANH can be expressed as follows:

```
TAN (i * n) = i * TANH (n)
```

TRUNC

The TRUNC function truncates the first argument to the number of decimal places specified by the second argument. The specification for the TRUNC function is:

```
FUNCTION TRUNC (n NUMBER, [decimal_places NUMBER]) RETURN NUMBER;
```

The *decimal_places* argument is optional and defaults to 0, which means that *n* will be truncated to zero decimal places, a whole number. The value of *decimal_ places* can be less than zero. A negative value for this argument directs TRUNC to truncate or zero-out digits to the left of the decimal point rather than to the right. Here are some examples:

```
TRUNC (153.46) → 153
TRUNC (153.46, 1) → 153.4
TRUNC (-2003.16, -1) → -2000
```

For a comparison of ROUND with several other numeric functions, see Table 9-7 and Figure 9-5 earlier in the "Rounding and Truncation Functions" section.

CHAPTER 10
Dates and Timestamps

In this chapter:

- Date and Time Datatypes
- Date and Timestamp Conversions
- Date/Time Arithmetic
- Date/Time Functions

Most of our applications require the storage and manipulation of dates and times. Dates are quite complicated: not only are they highly formatted data, but there are myriad rules for determining valid values and valid calculations (leap days and years, national and company holidays, date ranges, etc.). Fortunately, the Oracle RDBMS and PL/SQL offer us lots of help in handling date information.

First of all, both the RDBMS and PL/SQL provide you with a set of true datetime datatypes that store both date and time information using a standard, internal format. No matter how you choose to represent datetime values when you enter them or display them, such values are represented in a consistent manner within PL/SQL and the RDBMS.

For any datetime value, Oracle stores some or all of the following information:

Year
Month
Day
Hour
Minute
Second
Fractional second
Time zone hour displacement
Time zone minute displacement
Time zone region name
Time zone abbreviation

Support for true datetime datatypes is only half the battle. You also need a language that can manipulate those values in a natural and intelligent manner—as actual dates and times. Oracle provides us with a comprehensive suite of functions with which to manipulate date and time information. Need to convert a character string to a date? No problem. Oracle has you covered with the TO_DATE function, which can interpret and validate a variety of different date formats. Need to convert times between time zones? Again, Oracle has you covered—use the NEW_TIME function.

Not only do you have a rich set of built-in datetime functions to work with, you can perform certain types of datetime arithmetic directly on any datetime value. For example, computing the number of days between two dates is as simple as subtracting one from another.

With all this datetime power at your disposal, it's important to understand your choices. To that end, the next section discusses the various datetime datatypes available from PL/SQL. Next we talk about conversions, and show you how to get datetime values into and out of your datetime variables. In the remaining sections of the chapter, we describe the datetime functions that are available and show you how to work with and manipulate the various datetime datatypes that Oracle supports.

Date and Time Datatypes

It used to be that you didn't have any choices. Life then was simple. In the days of Oracle8*i*, Oracle8, and prior releases, if you needed to work with datetime values, you used the DATE datatype, end of story. With Oracle9*i*, however, Oracle introduced a slew of new datetime datatypes and related functionality.

Much of the new datetime functionality in Oracle9*i* focuses on the new TIMESTAMP and INTERVAL families of datatypes. Related to these are the new timestamp and interval expressions. Not only is this new functionality useful, it also brings Oracle into greater conformance with current ANSI/ISO SQL standards.

The DATE Datatype

DATE is the original datetime datatype supported by Oracle, and is the only one available through Oracle8*i*. An Oracle DATE stores the following information as a fixed-length, seven-byte value:

Year
Month
Day
Hour
Minute
Second

You cannot actually specify these internal values in an assignment statement. Instead you rely on implicit conversion of character and numeric values to an actual date, or explicit conversion with the TO_DATE function. See "Date and Timestamp Conversions" later in this chapter.

Declaring DATE variables

The syntax for declaring DATE variables is as follows:

```
var_name [CONSTANT] DATE [:= | DEFAULT initial_value]
```

In this syntax, *var_name* is the name of the variable you are declaring. Once you declare a DATE variable, you can use it to store just date values, or combined date and time values.

Datetime values always have a time component. The question is whether you ignore it or use it.

Following are some examples of DATE declarations:

```
DECLARE
   todays_date CONSTANT DATE := SYSDATE;
   hire_date DATE DEFAULT SYSDATE;
   end_of_year DATE := TO_DATE('12/31/2002', 'MM/DD/YYYY');
```

When to use DATE

Use DATE if you're developing programs for existing systems that use DATE columns within the database. Use DATE if you expect to deploy an application against a pre-Oracle9*i* database. And, of course, you'll have to use DATE if you are currently working with Oracle8*i*, Oracle8, or some prior release. But for new development that will be deployed only against Oracle9*i* or higher, consider using one of the new TIMESTAMP datatypes.

Limitations of DATE

DATE has two limitations you should be aware of:

- The DATE datatype does not resolve time to anything less than increments of a single second. Thus, DATE is not very useful for tracking real-time activities that occur at subsecond intervals.
- DATE values do not include time zone information. This can be a problem if users of your system span multiple time zones. When you retrieve a DATE value from the database, you have to "just know" what time zone it represents.

The newer TIMESTAMP datatypes overcome these limitations, allowing you to resolve time down to the billionth of a second and to store time zone information with your datetime values.

If you are using a release prior to Oracle9*i* and you need to track time at subsecond intervals, you can store the information as a number. You can obtain subsecond timings using the DBMS_UTILITY package's GET_TIME function.

The TIMESTAMP Datatypes

Oracle9*i* introduced three TIMESTAMP datatypes. All three allow for time to be resolved to the billionth of a second; two accommodate time zones, but in different ways. The three types are:

TIMESTAMP
: Stores date and time without respect to time zone. Except for being able to resolve time to the billionth of a second, TIMESTAMP is the equivalent of DATE.

TIMESTAMP WITH TIME ZONE
: Stores the time zone along with each date and time value.

TIMESTAMP WITH LOCAL TIME ZONE
: Stores a date and time that is assumed to be in the local time zone. For database columns of this type, the "local" time zone is the database time zone. For PL/SQL variables of this type, the "local" time zone is the session time zone. Values that move between database columns and PL/SQL variables are converted from one time zone into the other.

The nuances of these three types, especially the TIMESTAMP WITH LOCAL TIME ZONE type, can be a bit difficult to understand at first. Figure 10-1 shows the effects of the different datetime datatypes on a datetime value as it moves from a user in one time zone through the database to another user in a different time zone.

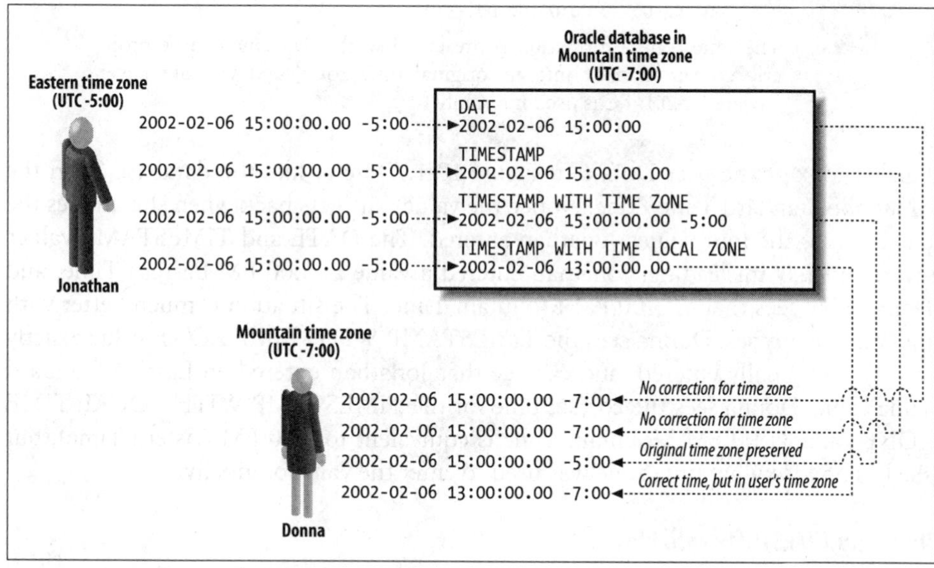

Figure 10-1. Effect of different datetime datatypes

The figure shows the user Jonathan in the Eastern Time Zone, which is five hours behind Coordinated Universal Time (UTC). (See the sidebar for a description of

UTC.) Jonathan stores the same datetime value in four database fields. The datetime value (in the figure) is represented using ANSI/ISO standard notation, and in this case represents 3:00 PM (15:00:00.00) Eastern Standard Time (-5:00) on Feb 6, 2002 (2002-02-06).

The database in the figure is in the Mountain Standard Time Zone. Notice how the database representation varies with each of the different datetime datatypes. DATE and TIMESTAMP totally ignore the time zone difference between the user and the database. They also don't preserve the original time zone, so that information is lost along with any knowledge of the time the user really was referring to.

The TIMESTAMP WITH TIME ZONE column preserves the time zone information and represents the exact time, from his point of view, that Jonathan entered the values. Compare this with the behavior of the TIMESTAMP WITH LOCAL TIME ZONE column. Here, you see that the time has been converted from Eastern Time into Mountain Time, the database's local time zone. The correct time has been preserved, but the point of view has been lost; we no longer know the time zone in which the time was entered.

Figure 10-1 is conceptual with respect to TIMESTAMP WITH TIME ZONE. Internally, Oracle represents all TIMESTAMP WITH TIME ZONE values in UTC time. This is no doubt to make date comparisons and arithmetic efficient. With respect to the figure, the internal representation would be:

```
2002-02-06 20:00:00:00.00 -5:00
```

The time zone information is preserved so the datetime can be properly converted back into its original time zone, and you are never "aware" that UTC is used internally.

Finally, look at the user Donna in Figure 10-1. Donna, like the database, is in the Mountain Standard Time Zone. Notice the values she gets back when she queries the database for the four values Jonathan entered. The DATE and TIMESTAMP values are completely misleading. Jonathan entered a value at 3:00 PM Eastern Time, and Donna now sees that as 3:00 PM Mountain Time. The situation is much better with the other datatypes. Donna sees the TIMESTAMP WITH TIME ZONE value exactly as it was originally entered, and can see that Jonathan entered an Eastern Standard Time value. Donna sees the correct time for the TIMESTAMP WITH LOCAL TIME ZONE value (1:00 PM Mountain Time is equivalent to 3:00 PM Eastern Time), but she has no idea what time zone was used to enter the value originally.

Declaring TIMESTAMP variables

The syntax for declaring TIMESTAMP variables is a bit more complex than that for declaring DATEs. Most of the TIMESTAMP types are composed of multiple words,

> **Coordinated Universal Time**
>
> Coordinated Universal Time, abbreviated UTC, is measured using highly accurate and precise atomic clocks, and forms the basis of our worldwide system of civil time. Time zones, for example, are all defined with respect to how far they are in terms of hours and minutes from UTC. UTC is atomic time, and is periodically adjusted through the mechanism of leap seconds to keep it in sync with time as determined by the rotation of the earth.
>
> You may be familiar with Greenwich Mean Time (GMT). GMT is an obsolete term in scientific circles, but is often used colloquially. For most practical purposes, GMT is equivalent to UTC, but the two are not really the same.
>
> Why the acronym UTC and not CUT? The standards body couldn't agree on whether to use the English acronym CUT or the French acronym TUC, so they compromised on UTC, which matches neither language. See *http://www.boulder.nist.gov/timefreq/general/misc.htm#Anchor-14550*.
>
> For more information on UTC, see the U.S. Naval Observatory document "What is Universal Time?" at *http://aa.usno.navy.mil/faq/docs/UT.html*. Also see the National Institute of Standards and Technology document on UTC at *http://physics.nist.gov/GenInt/Time/world.html*.

which takes a bit of getting used to. The TIMESTAMP types also allow you to specify the number of decimal digits used for fractional seconds. The syntax is as follows:

```
TIMESTAMP [(precision)]
TIMESTAMP [(precision)] WITH TIME ZONE
TIMESTAMP [(precision)] WITH LOCAL TIME ZONE
```

The *precision* in these declarations refers to the number of decimal digits allocated for recording values to the fraction of a second. The default *precision* is 6, which means that you can track time down to 0.000001 seconds. The allowable range for *precision* is 0 through 9.

A TIMESTAMP(0) variable behaves identically to a DATE variable.

When to use TIMESTAMPs

There are two key reasons to use TIMESTAMP variables:

- You need to track time down to the fraction of a second
- You need to deal with time from different time zones

All TIMESTAMP types support fractional seconds, so if that's all you're interested in, you can use TIMESTAMP. However, if time zones are important to you, consider using TIMESTAMP WITH TIME ZONE or TIMESTAMP WITH LOCAL TIME ZONE.

The TIMESTAMP WITH TIME ZONE datatype incorporates time zone information with its datetime value. There is never any ambiguity as to what time such a value represents because the time zone is part of the value. Use TIMESTAMP WITH TIME ZONE when dealing with data from multiple time zones, especially when it is important to preserve knowledge of the originating time zone.

Actually, under very specific circumstances, daylight savings time allows for potential ambiguity in TIMESTAMP WITH TIME ZONE values. This can be controlled. See the later "Date and Timestamp Conversions" section for details.

If knowing the correct time is important but knowing the originating time zone is not, you can use TIMESTAMP WITH LOCAL TIME ZONE. With this datatype, datetime values are automatically converted into your local time zone. Be careful with this type, though, because in three-tier environments the "local" time zone can easily end up being your web application server's time zone, and not the time zone of the user actually seeing the data displayed in a web browser.

The TIMESTAMP WITH LOCAL TIME ZONE datatype is also helpful when you need to migrate existing database DATE columns to TIMESTAMPs. You can't change a DATE column directly into a TIMESTAMP WITH TIME ZONE because DATEs have no time zone information. On the other hand, if you wish to treat all DATE values as being in the database's local time zone, you can convert a DATE column into a TIMESTAMP WITH LOCAL TIME ZONE. Datetime values in the resulting column will then be automatically converted between the database time zone and the user's session time zone. Such a conversion is perhaps more of a database administration issue than a programming issue, but the possibility is worth understanding.

The INTERVAL Datatypes

INTERVAL datatypes are new in Oracle9*i*. To better understand what they represent, step back a bit and think about the different kinds of datetime data we deal with on a daily basis:

Instants

An *instant* is a point in time with respect to a given granularity. When we plan to wake up at a given hour in the morning, that hour represents an instant. The granularity, then, would be to the hour, or possibly to the minute. DATE and all the TIMESTAMP datatypes allow you to represent instants of time.

Intervals
: An *interval* refers not to a specific point in time, but to a specific *amount* of time. We use intervals all the time in our daily lives. We work for eight hours a day (we hope), we take an hour for lunch (in our dreams!), and so forth. Oracle9*i*'s two new INTERVAL types allow us to represent time intervals.

Periods
: A *period* refers to an interval of time that begins or ends at a specific instant. For example: "I woke up at 8:00 AM today and worked for eight hours." Here, the 8-hour interval beginning at 8:00 AM today would be considered a period. Oracle has no datatype to directly support periods, nor does ANSI/ISO define one.

The two INTERVAL datatypes introduced in Oracle9*i* conform to the ANSI/ISO standard, and are as follows:

INTERVAL YEAR TO MONTH
: Allows you to define an interval of time in terms of years and months.

INTERVAL DAY TO SECOND
: Allows you to define an interval of time in terms of days, hours, minutes, and seconds (including fractional seconds).

Declaring INTERVAL variables

Compared to other PL/SQL variable declarations, the syntax for declaring INTERVAL variables is a bit unusual. You not only have multiple-word type names, but in one case you specify not one, but two precisions:

```
var_name INTERVAL YEAR [(year_precision)] TO MONTH
```

or:

```
var_name INTERVAL DAY [(day_precision)] TO SECOND [(frac sec_prec)]
```

where:

var_name
: Is the name of the INTERVAL variable that you wish to declare.

year_precision
: Is the number of digits (from 0 to 4) that you wish to allow for a year value. The default is 2.

day_precision
: Is the number of digits (from 0 to 9) that you wish to allow for a day value. The default is 2.

frac_sec_prec
: Is the number of digits (from 0 to 9) that you wish to allow for fractional seconds (i.e., the fractional seconds precision). The default is 6.

It is the nature of intervals that you need only worry about precision at the extremes. INTERVAL YEAR TO MONTH values are always normalized such that the number of months is between 0 and 11. In fact, Oracle will not allow you to specify a month greater than 11; an interval of 1 year, 13 months must be expressed as 2 years, 1 month. The *year_precision* fixes the maximum size of the interval. Likewise, the *day_precision* in INTERVAL DAY TO SECOND fixes the maximum size of that interval.

You don't need to specify a precision for the hour, minute, and second values for an INTERVAL DAY TO SECOND variable for the same reason you don't specify a precision for month in an INTERVAL YEAR TO MONTH. The intervals are always normalized so that any values for hour, minute, and second are within the normal ranges of 0–23 for hours, 0–59 for minutes, and 0–59 for seconds (excluding fractional seconds).

The fractional second precision (*frac_sec_prec*) is necessary because INTERVAL DAY TO SECOND values can resolve intervals down to the fraction of a second. INTERVAL YEAR TO MONTH values don't handle fractional months, so no fractional month precision is necessary.

When to use INTERVALs

INTERVAL types are new to Oracle, so let's look at a few examples of how they might be used. We hope to spark your natural creativity here so you can begin to think about how you might use INTERVAL types in systems you develop.

Imagine for a moment that you work for a food cannery. Canned goods must be stamped with an expiration date, and it's your job to write the software to compute this date for whatever item is being canned at the moment. This is a problem that calls for the use of intervals. The food in a can is good for a certain interval of time, and the expiration date marks the end of that interval. Because canned goods last for long periods of time, we're talking intervals in terms of years and months.

To further complicate matters, each different type of canned food may have a different expiration date. Canned vegetables tend to last longer than canned meats, and the expiration dates for pet food can be pushed out further than for human food. You decide to create a table to store the "good for" interval for each product that your company cans. One possibility for that table is:

```
CREATE TABLE good_for (
    product_id NUMBER,
    good_for_period INTERVAL YEAR(2) TO MONTH NOT NULL
);
```

You then realize (when you've been programming for enough years, experience speaks to you in powerful and mysterious ways) that you will need a PL/SQL function to return the expiration date for a product, given its "good for" period of time. The function can be very concisely expressed as follows:

```
CREATE OR REPLACE FUNCTION expiration_date (
    good_for_period_in IN shelf_life.good_for_period%TYPE
)
```

```
    RETURN DATE
IS
BEGIN
-- Truncate the current date so that we are left
-- with only the date, and not the time of day.
    RETURN TRUNC (SYSDATE) + good_for_period_in;
END;
```

Had we used the first solution (two number columns for years and months, rather than an INTERVAL column), our computation would have been more complicated:

```
expiration_date :=
    ADD_MONTHS(TRUNC(SYSDATE),
               (good_for_years_in * 12) + good_for_months_in
    );
```

The interval solution has several advantages over the other:

- It's easier to code, which means fewer coding errors and less debugging.
- It's easier to read and understand after you code it.
- The use of INTERVAL YEAR TO MONTH in the good_for table ensures that only valid year/month intervals will be stored. You never have to worry about interpreting a value such as 1 year and 24 months.

Another use for INTERVAL types is when you need to look at the difference between two dates. Consider the following example, which computes an employee's length of service:

```
DECLARE
   start_date DATE;
   end_date DATE;
   service_interval INTERVAL YEAR TO MONTH;
   years_of_service NUMBER;
   months_of_service NUMBER;
BEGIN
   --Normally, we would retrieve start and end dates from a database.
   start_date := TO_DATE('29-DEC-1988','dd-mon-yyyy');
   end_date := TO_DATE ('26-DEC-1995','dd-mon-yyyy');

   --Determine and display years and months of service:
   service_interval := (end_date - start_date) YEAR TO MONTH;
   DBMS_OUTPUT.PUT_LINE(service_interval);

   --Use the new EXTRACT function to grab individual
   --year and month components.
   years_of_service := EXTRACT(YEAR FROM service_interval);
   months_of_service := EXTRACT(MONTH FROM service_interval);
   DBMS_OUTPUT.PUT_LINE(years_of_service || ' years and '
                        || months_of_service || ' months');
END;
```

The line that performs the actual calculation to get years and months of service is:

```
service_interval := (end_date - start_date) YEAR TO MONTH;
```

The YEAR TO MONTH is part of the interval expression syntax, about which you'll read more in the later section "Date/Time Arithmetic." You can see, however, that computing the interval is as simple as subtracting one date from another. Had we not used an INTERVAL type, we would have had to code something like the following:

```
months_of_service := ROUND(months_between(end_date, start_date));
years_of_service := TRUNC(months_of_service/12);
months_of_service := MOD(months_of_service,12);
```

Again, the non-INTERVAL solution is much more complex to code and to understand afterwards.

The INTERVAL YEAR TO MONTH type displays rounding behavior, and it's important you understand the ramifications of that. See the section "Date/Time Arithmetic" for details about this issue.

Why Two INTERVAL Datatypes?

We were initially puzzled about the need for two INTERVAL datatypes. We noticed that between the two types, all portions of a TIMESTAMP value were accounted for, but the decision to treat year and month separately from days, hours, minutes, and seconds seemed at first rather arbitrary. Why not simply have one INTERVAL type that covers all possibilities? It turns out that we can blame this state of affairs on the long-dead Roman Emperor Julius Caesar, who designed our calendar and determined most of our month lengths.

The reason for having two INTERVAL types with a dividing line at the month level is that months are the only datetime component for which the length of time in question varies. Think about having an interval of 1 month and 30 days. How long is that, really? Is it less than two months? The same as two months? More than two months? If the one month is January, then 30 days gets you past February and into March, resulting in a 61-day interval that is a bit more than "two months" long. If the one month is February, then the interval is exactly two months (but only 59 or 60 days). If the one month is April, then the interval is slightly less than two months, for a total of 60 days.

Rather than sort out and deal with all the complications differing month lengths pose for interval comparison, date arithmetic, and normalization of datetime values, the ANSI standard "breaks" the datetime model into two parts, year and month, and everything else. (For more, see C. J. Date's *A Guide to the SQL Standard*, 3rd Edition, Addison-Wesley, 1993).

Date and Timestamp Conversions

Now that you understand Oracle's array of datetime datatypes, it's time to look at how you get dates into and out of datetime variables. Human-readable datetime values are character strings such as "March 5, 2002" and "10:30 AM", so this discussion centers around the conversion of datetime values from character strings to Oracle's internal representation, and vice versa.

PL/SQL validates and stores dates that fall from January 1, 4712 B.C. through December 31, 9999 A.D. (Oracle documentation indicates a maximum date of December 31, 4712; run the *showdate.sql* script, available on the O'Reilly site, to verify the range on your version.) If you enter a date without a time (many applications do not require the tracking of time, so PL/SQL lets you leave it off), the time portion of the value defaults to midnight (12:00:00 AM).

Oracle can interpret just about any date or time format you throw at it. Key to that flexibility is the concept of a *date format model*, which is a string of special characters that define a date's format to Oracle. Because they form the basis of date conversion, we talk about date format models first, and then show you how to use them to get dates into and out of PL/SQL datetime variables.

Date Format Models

In Versions 6 and earlier of the Oracle RDBMS, the default format for dates as character values was DD-MON-YY, a cause of consternation for many developers and users. While this format is common in many parts of the world, very few people use it in the United States.

Beginning with Oracle7, your database administrator can specify your own default date format (which takes effect on the initialization or startup of the RDBMS instance) with the NLS_DATE_FORMAT parameter as follows:

```
NLS_DATE_FORMAT = 'MM/DD/YYYY'
```

The default date format is also set implicitly with another initialization parameter, NLS_ TERRITORY. When you specify an NLS_TERRITORY value, you set conventions for date format, date language, numeric formats, currency symbols, and week start day.

You also have the option of specifying a date format at the session level, a capability that can come in handy if your particular needs differ from those of the majority of database users. Use the ALTER SESSION command to specify a session-level default date format. The following example works in Oracle8*i* or higher, and sets the default date format to MM/DD/YYYY:

```
BEGIN
   EXECUTE IMMEDIATE 'ALTER SESSION SET NLS_DATE_FORMAT=''MM/DD/YYYY''';
END;
```

To check the default date format in effect for your session at any given time, issue the following query against the NLS_SESSION_PARAMETERS data dictionary view:

```
SELECT value
FROM nls_session_parameters
WHERE parameter='NLS_DATE_FORMAT';
```

Regardless of how the default date format is set, both developers and users must be aware of this format when working with dates. In the upcoming sections "String-to-Date Conversions" and "Date-to-String Conversions," you'll learn how to specify date format models for individual conversions rather than relying on the database or session default model.

As you can see, format models (such as MMDDYY and Month DD, YYYY) play an important role in the conversion of date and character data. Date format models are made up of elements. For example, the elements in the MM/DD/YYYY model are:

MM
DD
YYYY
The two forward-slash (/) characters.

Table 10-1 shows the full set of date format elements and explains how to use them in all their variations. Following the table are examples showing some of these variations. You can use the format elements in any combination, in any order. However, when specifying NLS_DATE_FORMAT, you cannot specify the same date element twice; for example, you can specify only one of MONTH, MON, and MM because all three refer to the month.

Older releases of Oracle would allow you to specify the same date element twice. For example, the model "Mon (MM) DD, YYYY" specifies the month twice. Beginning in Oracle9*i*, you may specify an element only once in a format model.

Some elements in Table 10-1 apply only when translating datetime values from Oracle's internal format into character strings, and not vice versa. Such elements can't be used in a default date model (i.e., with NLS_DATE_FORMAT) because the default date model applies to conversions in both directions. These elements are noted as "Output-only" in the table.

Table 10-1. Date format model elements

Element	Description
SCC or CC	The century. If the SCC format is used, any B.C. dates are prefaced with a minus sign (–). Output-only.
SYYYY or YYYY	The four-digit year. If the SYYYY format is used, any B.C. dates are prefaced with a minus sign (–).
IYYY	The four-digit ISO standard year. Output-only.
YYY or YY or Y	The last three, two, or one digits of the year. The current century is the default when using these elements to convert a character string value into a date.
IYY or IY or I	The last three, two, or one digits of the ISO standard year. Output-only.
Y,YYY	The four-digit year with a comma.
SYEAR, YEAR SYear, Year, syear, or year	The year spelled out in words (e.g., "two thousand two"). The S prefix places a negative sign in front of B.C. dates. The format may be upper-, mixed-, or lowercase. Output-only.

Table 10-1. Date format model elements (continued)

Element	Description
RR	The last two digits of the year. This format is used to display years in centuries other than our own. See the section called "The RR element."
RRRR	Same as RR when used for output; accepts four-digit years when used for input.
BC or AD	The B.C. or A.D. indicator, without periods.
B.C. or A.D.	The B.C. or A.D. indicator, with periods.
E	The abbreviated era name. Valid only for the following calendars: Japanese Imperial, ROC Official, and Thai Buddha. Input-only.
EE	The full era name.
Q	The quarter of the year, from 1 through 4. January through March are in the first quarter, April through June in the second quarter, etc. Output-only.
MM	The number of the month in the year, from 01 through 12. January is month number 01, September is 09, etc.
RM	The Roman numeral representation of the month number, from I through XII. January is I, September is IX, etc.
MONTH, Month, or month	The name of the month, in upper-, mixed-, or lowercase format.
MON, Mon, or mon	The abbreviated name of the month, as in JAN for January. This also may be in upper-, mixed-, or lowercase format.
WW	The week of the year, from 1 through 53. Output-only.
IW	The week of the year, from 1 through 52 or 1 through 53, based on the ISO standard. Output-only.
W	The week of the month, from 1 through 5. Week 1 starts on the first day of the month and ends on the seventh. Output-only.
DDD	The day of the year, from 1 through 366.
DD	The day of the month, from 1 through 31.
D	The day of the week, from 1 through 7. The day of the week that is decreed the first day is specified implicitly by the NLS_TERRITORY initialization parameter for the database instance.
DAY, Day, or day	The name of the day in upper-, mixed, or lowercase format.
DY, Dy, or dy	The abbreviated name of the day, as in TUE for Tuesday.
J	The Julian day format of the date (counted as the number of days since January 1, 4712 B.C., the earliest date supported by the Oracle RDBMS).
AM or PM	The meridian indicator (morning or evening) without periods.
A.M. or P.M.	The meridian indicator (morning or evening) with periods.
TZD	The abbreviated time zone name; for example, EST, PST, etc. This is an input-only format, which may seem odd at first.
TZH	The time zone hour displacement. For example, -5 indicates a time zone five hours earlier than UTC.
TZM	The time zone minute displacement. For example, -5:30 indicates a time zone that is five hours, thirty minutes earlier than UTC. A few such time zones do exist.
TZR	The time zone region. For example, "US/Eastern" is the region in which EST (Eastern Standard Time) and EDT (Eastern Daylight Time) are valid.
HH or HH12	The hour of the day, from 1 through 12. HH12 is output-only.

Table 10-1. Date format model elements (continued)

Element	Description
HH24	The hour of the day, from 0 through 23.
MI	The minutes component of the datetime value, from 0 through 59.
SS	The seconds component of the datetime value, from 0 through 59.
SSSSS	The number of seconds since midnight of the time component. Values range from 0 through 86399, with each hour comprising 3600 seconds.
FF	The fractional seconds. Only valid when used with TIMESTAMP values. Always use FF (two Fs) regardless of the number of decimal digits you wish to see or use. Any other number of Fs is invalid.
X	The local radix character. In American English, this is a period (.). This element can be placed in front of FF so that fractional seconds are properly interpreted and represented.
TH	Suffix that converts a number to its ordinal format; for example, 4 becomes 4th and 1 becomes 1st. This element can appear at the end of any element that results in a number. For example, "DDth-Mon-YYYY' results in output such as "15th-Nov-1961". The return value is always in English, regardless of the date language.
SP	Suffix that converts a number to its spelled format. This element can appear at the end of any element that results in a number. For example, a mask such as "DDth-Mon-Yyyysp" results in output such as "15th-Nov-One Thousand Nine Hundred Sixty-One". The return value is always in English, regardless of the date language. (Note that Yyyy resulted in mixed-case words).
SPTH	Suffix that converts a number to its spelled and ordinal format; for example, 4 becomes FOURTH and 1 becomes FIRST. This element can appear at the end of any element that results in a number. For example, a mask such as "Ddspth Mon, Yyyysp" results in output such as "Fifteenth Nov, One Thousand Nine Hundred Sixty-One". The return value is always in English, regardless of the date language.
FX	Element that requires exact pattern matching between data and format model. (FX stands for Format eXact.) See "The FX element" later in this chapter.
FM	Element that toggles suppression of blanks in output from conversion. (FM stands for Fill Mode.) See "The FM element" later in this chapter.
Other text	Any punctuation, such as a comma (,) or slash (/) or hyphen (-), will be reproduced in the formatted output of the conversion. You can also include text within double quotes (" ") and the text will be represented as entered in the converted value. See the examples in the section "TO_CHAR" for an illustration of this element.

Note that whenever a date format returns a spelled value (words rather than numbers, as with MONTH, MON, DAY, DY, AM, and PM), the language used to spell these words is determined by the National Language Support parameters, NLS_DATE_LANGUAGE and NLS_LANGUAGE, or by the optional date language argument you can pass to both TO_ CHAR and TO_DATE.

Here are some examples of date format masks composed of the above format elements:

```
'Month DD, YYYY'
'MM/DD/YY Day A.M.'
'Year Month Day HH24:MI:SS'
'J'
'SSSSS-YYYY-MM-DD'
'"A beautiful summer morning on the" DDth" day of "Month'
```

See the description of the TO_CHAR and TO_DATE functions for more examples of the use and resulting values of these masks.

ISO Dates

The IYY and IW elements represent the ISO (International Standards Organization) year and week. The ISO calendar is a good example of "design by committee." The first day of the ISO year is always a Monday and is determined by the following rules:

- When January 1 falls on a Monday, the ISO year begins on the same day.
- When January 1 falls on a Tuesday through Thursday, the ISO year begins on the preceding Monday.
- When January 1 falls on a Friday through Sunday, the ISO year begins on the following Monday.

These rules lead to some strange situations. For example, 31-Dec-2001 is considered to be the first day of ISO year 2002, and if you display that date using the IYYY format, 31-Dec-2002 is exactly what you'll get.

ISO weeks always begin on Mondays and are numbered from the first Monday of the ISO year.

String-to-Date Conversions

The first issue you'll face when working with dates is that of getting date (and time) values into your PL/SQL datetime variables. You do that by converting datetime values from character strings to Oracle's internal format. Such conversions can be done implicitly via assignment of a character string directly to a datetime variable, or they can be done explicitly via one of Oracle's built-in conversion functions.

Implicit conversion is risky, and we don't recommend it. Following is an example of implicit conversion from a character string to a DATE variable:

```
DECLARE
   birthdate DATE;
BEGIN
   birthdate := '15-Nov-1961';
END;
```

Such a conversion relies on the NLS_DATE_FORMAT setting, and will work fine until the day your DBA decides to change that setting. On that day, all your date-related code will break. Changing NLS_DATE_FORMAT at the session level can also break such code.

Rather than rely on implicit conversions and the NLS_DATE_FORMAT setting, it's far safer to convert dates explicitly via one of the built-in conversion functions. The functions not only make it clear in your code that a type conversion is occurring, they allow you to specify the exact datetime format being used.

The next few sections describe the built-in conversion functions in greater detail. You'll also find a section on a new feature in Oracle9*i*, the timestamp literal. A *timestamp literal* is an ANSI/ISO-standard text format used for datetime values; it represents one more option available to you for converting text to a datetime value.

TO_DATE

The TO_DATE function converts a character string to a true DATE datatype. The specification of the TO_DATE function is overloaded for string and number input:

```
FUNCTION TO_DATE (string_in IN VARCHAR2
   [, format_mask IN VARCHAR2
   [, nls_language IN VARCHAR2 ]]
   )
RETURN DATE;

FUNCTION TO_DATE
  (number_in IN NUMBER
   [, format_mask IN VARCHAR2   [, nls_language IN VARCHAR2 ]])
RETURN DATE;
```

The second version of TO_DATE can be used only with the format mask of J for Julian date. The Julian date is the number of days that have passed since January 1, 4712 B.C. Only in this use of TO_DATE can a number be passed as the first parameter of TO_ DATE.

For all other cases the parameters are as follows:

string_in
: Is the string variable, literal, named constant, or expression to be converted.

format_mask
: Is the format mask TO_DATE will use to convert the string. The format mask defaults to the NLS_DATE_FORMAT setting.

nls_language
: Optionally specifies the language to be used to interpret the names and abbreviations of both months and days in the string. The format of *nls_language* is as follows:

```
'NLS_DATE_LANGUAGE=language'
```

where *language* is a language recognized by your instance of the database. You can usually determine the acceptable languages by checking your installation guide.

The following example converts the string "123188" to a date:

```
TO_DATE ('123188', 'MMDDYY')
```

In the next example, the *nls_language* parameter is used to specify that the Spanish language is used for the name of the month:

```
TO_DATE ('Abril 12 1991', 'Month DD YYYY', 'NLS_DATE_LANGUAGE=Spanish')
```

Any Oracle errors between ORA-01800 and ORA-01899 are related to the internal Oracle date function and can arise when you encounter date conversion errors. You can learn additional nuances of date conversion rules by perusing the different errors and reading about the documented causes of these errors. Some of these rules are:

- A date literal passed to TO_CHAR for conversion to a date cannot be longer than 220 characters.
- You cannot include both a Julian date element (J) and the day of year element (DDD) in a single format mask.
- You cannot include multiple elements for the same component of the date/time in the mask. For example, the format mask YYYY-YYY-DD-MM is illegal because it includes two year elements, YYYY and YYY.
- You cannot use the 24-hour time format (HH24) and a meridian element (e.g., AM) in the same mask.

The TO_TIMESTAMP family

There are three TIMESTAMP datatypes, and each one has an associated conversion function. When converting a character string to a TIMESTAMP value, use the particular function designed for your target datatype:

TO_TIMESTAMP
: Converts a character string to a value of type TIMESTAMP

TO_TIMESTAMP_TZ
: Converts a character string to a value of type TO_TIMESTAMP_TZ

TO_TIMESTAMP_LTZ
: Converts a character string to a value of type TO_TIMESTAMP_LTZ

The specifications for these three functions all follow the same pattern. Unlike the case with TO_DATE, none of the TO_TIMESTAMP functions is overloaded to accept a NUMBER for the datetime value. Let's look at the specification of TO_TIMESTAMP as a representative case:

```
FUNCTION TO_TIMESTAMP (
      string_in IN VARCHAR2
   [, format_mask IN VARCHAR2
   [, nls_language IN VARCHAR2 ]]
   )
RETURN DATE;
```

The parameters are very similar to those of TO_DATE:

string_in
: Is a character string representing a datetime value.

format_mask
: Is a string of elements from Table 10-1 describing the format of the input string. The format mask defaults to one of the following NLS parameters:

NLS_TIMESTAMP_FORMAT
For TO_TIMESTAMP and TO_TIMESTAMP_LTZ

NLS_TIMESTAMP_TZ_FORMAT
For TO_TIMESTAMP_TZ

nls_language
Optionally specifies the language to be used to interpret the names and abbreviations of both months and days in the string.

The format elements described in Table 10-1 apply when using the TO_TIMESTAMP family of functions. For example, the following calls to TO_TIMESTAMP convert character strings to TIMESTAMP values:

```
DECLARE
   a TIMESTAMP;
   b TIMESTAMP;
BEGIN
   a := TO_TIMESTAMP('24-Feb-2002 09.00.00.50 PM');
   b := TO_TIMESTAMP('02/24/2002 09:00:00.50 PM',
                     'mm/dd/yyyy hh:mi:ssxff AM');
   DBMS_OUTPUT.PUT_LINE(a);
   DBMS_OUTPUT.PUT_LINE(b);
END;
```

The output is:

```
24-FEB-02 09.00.00.500000 PM
24-FEB-02 09.00.00.500000 PM
```

Note the decimal seconds (.50) and the use of XFF in the format mask. The X format element specifies the location of the radix character, in this case a period (.), separating the whole seconds from the fractional seconds. We could just as easily have specified a period, as in ".FF", but we chose to use X instead. The difference is that when X is specified, Oracle determines the correct radix character based on the current NLS_TERRITORY setting.

The TO_TIMESTAMP_TZ and TO_TIMESTAMP_LTZ functions can convert character strings that include time zone information. And while time zones seem simple on the surface, they are anything but, as we'll see in the next section.

Dealing with time zones

The possible presence of time zone information makes the use of TO_TIMESTAMP_TZ and TO_TIMESTAMP_LTZ more complex than the TO_DATE and TO_TIMESTAMP functions. You may specify time zone information in any of the following ways:

- As a positive or negative displacement of some number of hours and minutes from UTC time (sometimes referred to inappropriately as GMT or Greenwich Mean Time); for example, -5:00 is equivalent to U.S. Eastern Standard Time. Displacements must fall into the range -12:59 and +13:59.

- Using a time zone region name such as US/Eastern, US/Pacific, and so forth.
- Using a combination of time zone region name and abbreviation, as in US/Eastern EDT.

Let's look at some examples. We'll begin with a simple example that leaves off time zone information entirely:

```
TO_TIMESTAMP_TZ ('123188 083015.50', 'MMDDYY HHMISS.FF')
```

The date and time in this example work out to be 31-Dec-1998 at 15 1/2 seconds past 8:30 AM. Because no time zone is specified, Oracle will assume that your current session time zone applies. Every Oracle session is associated with a time zone, which you can check using the following query:

```
SQL> SELECT SESSIONTIMEZONE FROM DUAL;

SESSIONTIMEZONE
---------------------------------------
-05:00
```

The notation -05:00 indicates that your session time zone is five hours and zero minutes behind UTC. Such a difference equates to Eastern Standard Time in the United States. A displacement of +10:00, on the other hand, equates to Australian Eastern Standard Time.

Next, let's represent the time zone using a displacement of hours and minutes from UTC. Note the use of the TZH and TZM to denote the location of the hour and minute displacements in the input string:

```
TO_TIMESTAMP_TZ ('123188 083015.50 -5:00', 'MMDDYY HHMISS.FF TZH:TZM')
```

In this example, the datetime value is interpreted as being an Eastern Standard Time value (regardless of your session time zone).

The next example shows the time zone being specified using a time zone region name. The following example specifies America/Detroit, which is equivalent to Eastern Time in the United States. Note the use of TZR in the format mask to designate where the time zone region name appears in the input string.

```
TO_TIMESTAMP_TZ ('27-Oct-2002 01:30:00.00 America/Detroit',
                 'dd-Mon-yyyy hh:mi:ssxff TZR')
```

This example is interesting in that it represents Eastern Time, not Eastern Standard Time. The difference is that "Eastern Time" can refer to either Eastern Standard Time or Eastern Daylight Time, depending on whether daylight savings time is in effect. And it might be in effect! We've carefully crafted this example to make it ambiguous. 27-Oct-2002 is the date on which Eastern Daylight Time ends, and at 2:00 AM time rolls back to 1:00 AM. So on that date, 1:30 AM actually comes around twice! The first time it's 1:30 AM Eastern Daylight Time, and the second time it's 1:30 AM Eastern Standard Time. So what time is it, really, when we say it's 1:30 AM on 27-Oct-2002?

The time zone region name alone doesn't distinguish between standard time and daylight savings time. To remove the ambiguity, you also must specify a time zone abbreviation, which we've done in the next example. Note the addition of TZD in the format mask to mark the location of the abbreviation:

```
TO_TIMESTAMP_TZ ('27-Oct-2002 01:30:00.00 America/Detroit EDT',
                 'dd-Mon-yyyy hh:mi:ssxff TZR TZD')
```

To avoid ambiguity, we recommend that you either specify a time zone offset using hours and minutes (as in -5:00) or use a combination of region name and time zone abbreviation. If you use region name alone and there's ambiguity with respect to daylight savings time, Oracle will resolve the ambiguity by assuming that standard time applies.

If you set the session parameter ERROR_ON_OVERLAP_TIME to TRUE, Oracle will give you an error whenever you specify an ambiguous time.

You can get a complete list of the time zone region names and time zone abbreviations that Oracle supports by querying the V$TIMEZONE_NAMES view. Any database user can access that view. When you query it, notice that time zone abbreviations are not unique (see the sidebar).

A Time Zone Standard?

As important as time zones are, you would think there would be some sort of international standard specifying their names and abbreviations. Well, there isn't one. Not only are time zone abbreviations not standardized, but there is also some duplication. For example, EST is used in the U.S. for Eastern Standard Time, and also in Australia for Eastern Standard Time, and we assure you that the two Eastern Standard Times are not at all the same! This is why the TO_TIMESTAMP functions do not allow you to specify time zone using the abbreviation alone.

Because there is no time zone standard, you might as well ask the source of all those time zone region names in V$TIMEZONE_NAMES. Oracle's source for that information can be found at *ftp://elsie.nci.nih.gov/pub*. Look especially at the file named *tzdata_2002c.tar.gz*.

Date and timestamp literals

Date and timestamp literals are part of the ANSI SQL standard, and are newly supported in Oracle9*i*. They represent yet another option for you to use in getting values into datetime variables. A *date literal* consists of the keyword DATE followed by a date (and only a date) value in the following format:

```
DATE 'YYYY-MM-DD'
```

A *timestamp literal* consists of the keyword TIMESTAMP followed by a datetime value in a very specific format:

```
TIMESTAMP 'YYYY-MM-DD HH:MI:SS[.FFFFFFFFF] [{+|-}HH:MI]'
```

The FFFFFFFFF represents fractional seconds and is optional. If you specify fractional seconds, you may use anywhere from one to nine digits. The time zone displacement (+HH:MI) is optional and may use either a plus or a minus sign as necessary. The hours are always with respect to a 24-hour clock.

If you omit the time zone displacement in a timestamp literal, the time zone will default to the session time zone.

The following PL/SQL block shows several valid date and timestamp literals:

```
DECLARE
   a TIMESTAMP WITH TIME ZONE;
   b TIMESTAMP WITH TIME ZONE;
   c TIMESTAMP WITH TIME ZONE;
   d TIMESTAMP WITH TIME ZONE;
   e DATE;
BEGIN
   --Two digits for fractional seconds
   a := TIMESTAMP '2002-02-19 11:52:00.00 -05:00';

   --Nine digits for fractional seconds, 24-hour clock, 14:00 = 2:00 PM
   b := TIMESTAMP '2002-02-19 14:00:00.000000000 -5:00';

   --No fractional seconds at all
   c := TIMESTAMP '2002-02-19 13:52:00 -5:00';

   --No time zone, defaults to session time zone
   d := TIMESTAMP '2002-02-19 13:52:00';

   --A date literal
   e := DATE '2002-02-19';
END;
```

The format for timestamp literals is prescribed by the ANSI/ISO standards, and cannot be changed by you or by the DBA. Thus, it's safe to use timestamp literals whenever you need to embed a specific datetime value in your code.

When using a timestamp literal, you may also specify the time zone using a time zone region name. For example, the following block shows that 10:52 -8:00 (Pacific Standard Time in the U.S.) is equivalent to 13:52 U.S. Eastern Standard Time:

```
DECLARE
   a TIMESTAMP WITH TIME ZONE;
   b TIMESTAMP WITH TIME ZONE;
BEGIN
   a := TIMESTAMP '2002-02-19 10:52:00 -8:00';
```

```
      b := TIMESTAMP '2002-02-19 13:52:00 EST';

      IF a = b THEN
         dbms_output.put_line('a = b');
      END IF;
   END;
```

The output is:

```
   a = b
```

Our use of EST in this example may be confusing, but it serves to illustrate an important point: EST is listed in V$TIMEZONE_NAMES as both a region name (the TZNAME column) and an abbreviation (the TZABBREV column). As a region name, EST may be used to specify time zone information in a timestamp literal. In this example, it's clear that EST is being interpreted as U.S. Eastern Standard Time.

The FX element

PL/SQL offers the FX (format exact) element as a modifier to a format mask. FX specifies that an exact match must be performed for a character argument and date format mask in a call to the TO_DATE function.

If FX is not specified, the TO_DATE function does not require that the character string match the format precisely. It makes the following allowances:

- Extra blanks in the character string are ignored. Blanks are not significant data in any part of a date value, except to delimit separate parts of the date and time:

  ```
  TO_DATE ('Jan        15        1994', 'MON DD YYYY')
  ```

- Numeric values, such as the day number or the year, do not have to include leading zeros to fill out the mask. As long as the numbers are in the right place in the string (as determined, usually, by the delimiter characters in the string), TO_DATE can convert the numeric values properly:

  ```
  TO_DATE ('1-1-4', 'DD-MM-YYYY')
  TO_DATE ('7/16/94', 'MM/DD/YY')
  ```

- Punctuation in the string to be converted can simply match the length and position of punctuation in the format. In the following example, my format mask specifies hyphen (-) delimiters, and the string that I pass it uses caret (^) delimiters. Even so, TO_DATE has no problem making the match. For example:

  ```
  TO_DATE ('JANUARY^1^94', 'Month-dd-yy')
  ```

This kind of flexibility is great—until you want to actually restrict a user or even a batch process from entering data in a nonstandard format. In some cases, it simply is not OK when a date string has a pound sign (#) instead of a hyphen (-) between the day and month numbers. For these situations, you can use the FX modifier to enforce an exact match between string and format model.

With FX, there is no flexibility in the interpretation of the string. It cannot have extra blanks if none are found in the model. Its numeric values must include leading zeros if the format model specifies additional digits. And the punctuation and literals must exactly match the punctuation and quoted text of the format mask (except for case, which is always ignored). In all but the first of the following examples:

```
TO_DATE ('Jan 15 1994', 'fxMON DD YYYY')
TO_DATE ('1-1-4', 'fxDD-MM-YYYY')
TO_DATE ('7/16/94', 'FXMM/DD/YY')
TO_DATE ('JANUARY^1^ the year of 94', 'FXMonth-dd-"WhatIsaynotdo"yy')
```

PL/SQL raises one of the following errors:

```
ORA-01861: literal does not match format string
ORA-01862: the numeric value does not match the length of the format item
```

The FX modifier can be specified in upper-, lower-, or mixed-case; the effect is the same.

The FX modifier is a toggle, and can appear more than once in a format model. Each time it appears in the format, it changes the effect of the modifier. By default (that is, if FX is not specified anywhere in a format mask), an exact match is not required in any part of the string. So the first time FX appears in the format, it turns on exact matching for any following elements. The second time it appears, it indicates that an exact match is not required for any following elements, and so on.

The following example specifies FX three times. As a result, an exact match is required for the day number and the year number, but not the month number:

```
TO_DATE ('07-1-1994', 'FXDD-FXMM-FXYYYY')
```

This next attempt at date conversion will raise ORA-01862 because the year number is not fully specified:

```
TO_DATE ('07-1-94', 'FXDD-FXMM-FXYYYY') -- Invalid string for format!
```

You can use FM (fill mode) in the format model of a call to the TO_DATE function to fill a string with blanks or zeros. This action matches the format model (the opposite of the suppression action). You can, in other words, use FM to guarantee that a format exact match required by FX will succeed. Later in this chapter, in the section "The FM element," you'll see how the FM modifier can strip leading blanks and zeros from the output of a call to TO_CHAR.

The following call to TO_DATE will return a date because the "fm" at the beginning of the format mask turns on fill mode for the entire string, thus changing the 1 to 01 and 94 to 1994:

```
TO_DATE ('07-1-94', 'FXfmDD-FXMM-FXYYYY')
```

You can also include multiple references to both FM and FX in the same format string, to toggle both or either of these modifiers.

The RR element

The recent millennium change caused an explosion of interest in using four-digit years as people suddenly realized the ambiguity inherent in the commonly used two-digit year. For example, does 1-Jan-45 refer to 1945 or 2045? In spite of this realization, habits are tough to break and existing systems can be difficult to change, so you may find yourself still needing to allow your users to enter dates using two-digit years rather than four-digit years.

Using two-digit years is especially problematic when the century and millennium are close to changing. The YY format element always defaults to the current century, so when it is November 1999 and your user enters 1/1/1 or 1-JAN-1, they will enter into the database the date of January 1, 1901, not January 1, 2001.

What's an information systems manager to do? One solution is to go into all your screens and change or add trigger logic so that if the user enters a year number less than ten (or whatever you decide the cutoff to be), then the next century will be assumed. That would work, but it's a very undesirable prospect.

Fortunately, Oracle provides a format element to take care of this problem: the RR format model. With RR you can enter dates from the 21st century before the year 2000, and dates from the 20th century (like the birthdays of employees and customers) after the year 2000. Here is how RR works.

In the following discussion, we use the term "century" colloquially. RR's 20th century is composed of the years 1900–1999, and its 21st century is composed of the years 2000–2099. We realize this is not the proper definition of century, but it's a definition that makes it easier to explain RR's behavior.

If the current year is in the first half of the century (years 0 through 49), then:

- If you enter a date in the first half of the century (i.e., from 0 through 49), RR returns the current century.
- If you enter a date in the latter half of the century (i.e., from 50 through 99), RR returns the previous century.

On the other hand, if the current year is in the latter half of the century (years 50 through 99), then:

- If you enter a date in the first half of the century, RR returns the next century.
- If you enter a date in the latter half of the century, RR returns the current century.

Confusing? We had to think about it for awhile too. The RR rules are an attempt to make the best guess as to which century is intended when a user leaves off that information. Here are some examples of the impact of RR. Notice that for year 88 and year 18, SYSDATE returns a current date in the 20th and 21st centuries, respectively:

```
SELECT TO_CHAR (SYSDATE, 'MM/DD/YYYY') "Current Date",
       TO_CHAR (TO_DATE ('14-OCT-88', 'DD-MON-RR'), 'YYYY') "Year 88",
       TO_CHAR (TO_DATE ('14-OCT-18', 'DD-MON-RR'), 'YYYY') "Year 18"
  FROM dual;

Current Date Year 88 Year 18
------------ ------- -------
  02/25/2002    1988    2018
```

When we reach the year 2050, RR will interpret the same dates differently:

```
SELECT TO_CHAR (SYSDATE, 'MM/DD/YYYY') "Current Date",
       TO_CHAR (TO_DATE ('10/14/88', 'MM/DD/RR'), 'YYYY') "Year 88",
       TO_CHAR (TO_DATE ('10/14/18', 'MM/DD/RR'), 'YYYY') "Year 18"
  FROM dual;

Current Date Year 88 Year 18
------------ ------- -------
  02/25/2050    2088    2118
```

Of course, if you use the RR format now and want to enter a date that falls in the latter half of the 21st century (e.g., entering 75 for 2075), you will need to add special logic to your code. Masks with the RR format model will convert such two-digit years into the previous century until we reach the year 2050. Likewise, you'll need special logic if you wish to enter dates that fall in the early 20th century, as RR currently recognizes years 00-49 as part of the 21st century.

There are a number of ways you can activate the RR logic in your current applications. The cleanest and simplest way is to change the default format mask for dates in your database instance(s). You can do this by changing the NLS_DATE_FORMAT initialization parameter as follows:

```
NLS_DATE_FORMAT = 'MM/DD/RR'
```

or:

```
NLS_DATE_FORMAT = 'DD-MON-RR'
```

depending on what the previous format was. Then, if you have not hardcoded the date format mask anywhere else in your screens or reports, you are done. Bring down and restart the database, and then your application will allow users to enter dates in the 21st century. If you do have date format masks in the format property for an Oracle Forms item or in an Oracle Reports query or field, you will need to change those modules to reflect the new approach embodied by RR.

Date-to-String Conversions

Getting values into datetime variables is half the battle. The other half is getting them out again in some sort of human-readable format. Oracle provides the TO_CHAR function for that purpose.

TO_CHAR

The TO_CHAR function can be used to convert a datetime value to a variable-length string. This single function works for DATE types as well as for all the types in the TIMESTAMP family. TO_CHAR is also used to convert numbers to character strings, as covered in Chapter 9. The following specification describes TO_CHAR for datetime values:

```
FUNCTION TO_CHAR
   (date_in IN DATE
    [, format_mask IN VARCHAR2
    [, nls_language IN VARCHAR2]])
RETURN VARCHAR2
```

where:

date_in
: Is the date to be converted to character format.

format_mask
: Is the mask made up of one or more of the date format elements. See Table 10-1 for a list of date format elements.

nls_language
: Is a string specifying a date language.

Both the *format_mask* and *nls_language* parameters are optional.

If you wish your results to be in the national character set, you can use TO_NCHAR in place of TO_CHAR. In this case, be certain you provide your date format string in the national character set as well. Otherwise, you may receive *ORA-01821: date format not recognized* errors.

If *format_mask* is not specified, the default date format for the database instance is used. This format is DD-MON-RR, unless your DBA has used the NLS_DATE_FORMAT initialization parameter to specify some other format. You can also change the default format for a given session using the ALTER SESSION command:

```
ALTER SESSION SET NLS_DATE_FORMAT = 'MM/DD/YYYY';
```

If the NLS language parameter is not specified, then the default date language for the instance is used. This is either the language for the instance specified by the NLS_LANGUAGE parameter, or the date language specified by the initialization parameter NLS_DATE_LANGUAGE.

Here are some examples of TO_CHAR's being used for date conversion:

- Notice that there are two blanks between month and day and a leading zero for the fifth day:

  ```
  TO_CHAR (SYSDATE, 'Month DD, YYYY') → 'February  05, 1994'
  ```

- Use the FM fill mode element to suppress blanks and zeros:

```
TO_CHAR (SYSDATE, 'FMMonth DD, YYYY') → 'February 5, 1994'
```

- Note the case difference on the month abbreviations of the next two examples. You get exactly what you ask for with Oracle date formats!

```
TO_CHAR (SYSDATE, 'MON DDth, YYYY') → 'FEB 05TH, 1994'
TO_CHAR (SYSDATE, 'fmMon DDth, YYYY') → 'Feb 5TH, 1994'
```

  The TH format is an exception to the capitalization rules. Even if you specify lowercase "th" in a format string, Oracle will use uppercase TH in the output.

- Show the day of year, the month, and the week for the date:

```
TO_CHAR (SYSDATE, 'DDD DD D ') → '036 05 7'
TO_CHAR (SYSDATE, 'fmDDD DD D ') → '36 5 7'
```

- Here's some fancy formatting for reporting purposes:

```
TO_CHAR (SYSDATE, '"In month "RM" of year "YEAR')
   → 'In month II   of year NINETEEN NINETY FOUR'
```

- For TIMESTAMP variables, you can specify the time down to the millisecond:

```
TO_CHAR (A_TIMESTAMP, 'YYYY-MM-DD HH:MI:SS.FF AM TZH:TZM')
   → a value like: 2002-02-19 01:52:00.123457000 PM -05:00
```

Be careful when dealing with fractional seconds. The FF format element represents fractional seconds in the output format model, and you'll be tempted to use the number of Fs to control the number of decimal digits in the output. Don't do that! It doesn't work. The following example attempts to use FFFFF to specify five decimal digits:

```
DECLARE
   A TIMESTAMP WITH TIME ZONE;
BEGIN
   A := TIMESTAMP '2002-02-19 13:52:00.123456789 -5:00';
   DBMS_OUTPUT.PUT_LINE(TO_CHAR(a,'YYYY-MM-DD HH:MI:SS.FFFFF AM TZH:TZM'));
END;
```

The output is:

```
DECLARE
*
ERROR at line 1:
ORA-01821: date format not recognized
ORA-06512: at line 5
```

If you want only five decimal digits, then you must declare your timestamp variable as TIMESTAMP(5). For example:

```
DECLARE
   A TIMESTAMP(5) WITH TIME ZONE;
BEGIN
   A := TIMESTAMP '2002-02-19 13:52:00.123456789 -5:00';
   DBMS_OUTPUT.PUT_LINE(TO_CHAR(a,'YYYY-MM-DD HH:MI:SS.FF AM TZH:TZM'));
END;
```

The output is:

```
2002-02-19 01:52:00.123460000 PM -05:00

PL/SQL procedure successfully completed.
```

Note the rounding that occurred. The number of seconds input was 00.123456789. That value was rounded (not truncated) to five decimal digits: 00.12346.

It's unfortunate that Oracle ties the number of decimal digits displayed directly to the precision of the timestamp variable in question. We believe you should be able to control the display precision independently of the stored precision. NUMBERs work that way; TIMESTAMPs should too.

It's easy to slip up and specify an incorrect date format, and the introduction of TIMESTAMP types has made this even easier. Format elements that are valid with TIMESTAMP types are not valid for the DATE type. Note the results in the following example when FF, TZH, and TZM are used to convert a DATE value to a character string:

```
DECLARE
   A DATE;
BEGIN
   A := SYSDATE;
   DBMS_OUTPUT.PUT_LINE(TO_CHAR(A,'YYYY-MM-DD HH:MI:SS.FF AM TZH:TZM'));
END;
```

The output is:

```
   A := SYSDATE;
*
ERROR at line 4:
ORA-01821: date format not recognized
ORA-06512: at line 5
```

The error message you get in this case, *ORA-01821: date format not recognized*, is confusing and misleading. The date format is just fine. The problem is that it's being applied to the wrong datatype. Watch for this when you write code. If you get this error, check not only the date format, but also the datatype that you are trying to convert.

Converting time zones to character strings

Time zones add complexity to the problem of converting datetime values to character strings. Time zone information consists of the following elements:

- A displacement from UTC in terms of hours and minutes
- A time zone region name
- A time zone abbreviation

All these elements are stored separately in a TIMESTAMP WITH TIME ZONE variable. The displacement from UTC is always present, but whether you can display the region name or abbreviation depends on whether you've specified that information to begin with. Look closely at this example:

```
DECLARE
   A TIMESTAMP WITH TIME ZONE;
   B TIMESTAMP WITH TIME ZONE;
   C TIMESTAMP WITH TIME ZONE;
BEGIN
     A := TO_TIMESTAMP_TZ('2002-06-18 13:52:00.123456789 -5:00',
                          'YYYY-MM-DD HH24:MI:SS.FF TZH:TZM');
     B := TO_TIMESTAMP_TZ('2002-06-18 13:52:00.123456789 US/Eastern',
                          'YYYY-MM-DD HH24:MI:SS.FF TZR');
     C := TO_TIMESTAMP_TZ('2002-06-18 13:52:00.123456789 US/Eastern EDT',
                          'YYYY-MM-DD HH24:MI:SS.FF TZR TZD');

     DBMS_OUTPUT.PUT_LINE(TO_CHAR(A,
        'YYYY-MM-DD HH:MI:SS.FF AM TZH:TZM TZR TZD'));
     DBMS_OUTPUT.PUT_LINE(TO_CHAR(B,
        'YYYY-MM-DD HH:MI:SS.FF AM TZH:TZM TZR TZD'));
     DBMS_OUTPUT.PUT_LINE(TO_CHAR(C,
        'YYYY-MM-DD HH:MI:SS.FF AM TZH:TZM TZR TZD'));
  END;
```

The output is:

```
2002-06-18 01:52:00.123457000 PM -05:00 -05:00
2002-06-18 01:52:00.123457000 PM -04:00 US/EASTERN EDT
2002-06-18 01:52:00.123457000 PM -04:00 US/EASTERN EDT
```

Note the following with respect to the display of time zone information:

- For A, we specified time zone in terms of a displacement from UTC. Thus, when A was displayed, only the displacement could be displayed.
- In the absence of a region name for A, Oracle provided the time zone displacement. This is preferable to providing no information at all.
- For B, we specified a time zone region. That region was translated internally into an offset from UTC, but the region name was preserved. Thus, both the UTC offset and the region name could be displayed.
- For B, Oracle correctly recognized that daylight savings time is in effect during the month of June. As a result, the value of B was implicitly associated with the EDT abbreviation.
- For C, we specified a time zone region and an abbreviation, and both those values could be displayed. No surprises here.

There's a one-to-many relationship between UTC offsets and time zone regions; the offset alone is not enough to get you to a region name. That's why you can't display a region name unless you specify one to begin with.

The FM element

PL/SQL offers the FM element as a modifier to a format mask. FM (fill mode) controls the suppression of padded blanks and leading zeros in values returned by the TO_CHAR function.

By default, the following format mask results in both padded blanks and leading zeros (there are five spaces between the month name and the day number):

```
TO_CHAR (SYSDATE, 'Month DD, YYYY') → 'April     05, 1994'
```

With the FM modifier at the beginning of the format mask, however, both the extra blank and the leading zeros disappear:

```
TO_CHAR (SYSDATE, 'FMMonth DD, YYYY') → April 5, 1994'
```

The modifier can be specified in upper-, lower-, or mixed-case; the effect is the same.

The FM modifier is a toggle, and can appear more than once in a format model. Each time it appears in the format, it changes the effect of the modifier. By default (that is, if FM is not specified anywhere in a format mask), blanks are not suppressed and leading zeros are included in the result value. So the first time FM appears in the format, it indicates that blanks and leading zeros are suppressed for any following elements. The second time it appears, it indicates that blanks and leading zeros are not suppressed for any following elements, and so on.

The following example suppresses the padded blank at the end of the month name, but preserves the leading zero on the day number with a second specification of FM:

```
TO_CHAR (SYSDATE, 'fmMonth FMDD, YYYY') → April 05, 1994'
```

If you do not use FM in your mask, a converted date value is always right-padded with blanks to a fixed length (that length is dependent on the different format elements you use). If you do use FM, the length of your return value may vary depending on the actual values returned by the different format elements.

The FM modifier can also be used in the format model of a call to the TO_DATE function to fill a string with blanks or zeros to match the format model. This variation of FM was explored earlier in the discussion of the FX modifier.

Interval Conversions

Unlike datetime values, which represent specific points in time, intervals represent *lengths* of time. The text representation of those lengths is reasonably complex, and Oracle provides a number of ways for you to convert the character representation of an interval into its internal representation.

An interval is composed of one or more datetime elements. For example, you might choose to express an interval in terms of years and months. Table 10-2 lists the standard names for each of these elements. These are the names you must use in conjunction with the conversion functions and expressions described in the following sections.

Table 10-2. Interval element names

Name	Description
YEAR	Some number of years, ranging from 1 through 999,999,999.
MONTH	Some number of months, ranging from 0 through 11.
DAY	Some number of days, ranging from 0 to 999,999,999.
HOUR	Some number of hours, ranging from 0 through 23.
MINUTE	Some number of minutes, ranging from 0 through 59.
SECOND	Some number of seconds, ranging from 0 through 59.999999999.

The names shown in Table 10-2 are not case-sensitive when used with the interval conversion functions. For example, YEAR, Year, and year are all equivalent.

The NUMTO family of functions

The NUMTOYMINTERVAL and NUMTODSINTERVAL functions allow you to convert single numeric values into one of the interval datatypes. You do this by associating your numeric value with one of the interval elements listed in Table 10-2.

The function NUMTOYMINTERVAL (pronounced "num to Y M interval") converts a numeric value to an interval of type INTERVAL YEAR TO MONTH. The function NUMTODSINTERVAL (pronounced "num to D S interval") likewise converts a numeric value to an interval of type INTERVAL DAY TO SECOND.

Following is an example of NUMTOYMINTERVAL's being used to convert 10.5 to an INTERVAL YEAR TO MONTH value. The second argument, Year, indicates that the number represents some number of years.

```
DECLARE
   A INTERVAL YEAR TO MONTH;
BEGIN
   A := NUMTOYMINTERVAL (10.5,'Year');
   DBMS_OUTPUT.PUT_LINE(A);
END;
```

The output is:

```
+10-06
```

As you can see, 10.5 years was converted to an interval of 10 years, 6 months. Any fractional number of years (in this case 0.5) will be converted to an equivalent number of months, with the result being rounded to an integer. Thus, 10.9 years will convert to an interval of 10 years, 10 months.

The next example converts a numeric value to an interval of type INTERVAL DAY TO SECOND:

```
DECLARE
   A INTERVAL DAY TO SECOND;
BEGIN
```

```
    A := NUMTODSINTERVAL (1440,'Minute');
    DBMS_OUTPUT.PUT_LINE(A);
END;
```

The output is:

```
+01 00:00:00.000000

PL/SQL procedure successfully completed.
```

As you can see, Oracle has automatically taken care of normalizing the input value of 1440 minutes to an interval value of 1 day. This is great, because now you don't need to do that work yourself. You can easily display any number of minutes (or seconds or days or hours) in a normalized format that makes sense to the reader. Prior to the introduction of the interval datatypes, you would have needed to write your own code to translate a minute value into the correct number of days, hours, minutes, and seconds.

The TO_xxINTERVAL functions

The NUMTO functions are fine if you are converting numeric values to intervals, but what about character string conversions? For those, you can use TO_YMINTERVAL and TO_DSINTERVAL, depending on whether you are converting to an INTERVAL YEAR TO MONTH or an INTERVAL DAY TO SECOND.

TO_YMINTERVAL converts a character string value into an INTERVAL YEAR TO MONTH value, and is invoked as follows:

```
TO_YMINTERVAL('Y-M')
```

where *Y* represents some number of years and *M* represents some number of months. You must supply both values and separate them using a dash.

Likewise, TO_DSINTERVAL converts a character string into an INTERVAL DAY TO SECOND value. Invoke TO_DSINTERVAL using the following format:

```
TO_DSINTERVAL('D HH:MI:SS')
```

where *D* is some number of days, and *HH:MI:SS* represents hours, minutes, and seconds.

The following example shows an invocation of each of these functions:

```
DECLARE
   A INTERVAL YEAR TO MONTH;
   B INTERVAL DAY TO SECOND;
   C INTERVAL DAY TO SECOND;
BEGIN
   A := TO_YMINTERVAL('40-3'); --my age
   B := TO_DSINTERVAL('10 1:02:10');
   C := TO_DSINTERVAL('10 1:02:10.123'); --fractional seconds
END;
```

When invoking either function, you must supply all relevant values. You cannot, for example, invoke TO_YMINTERVAL specifying only a year, or invoke TO_DS_INTERVAL leaving off the seconds. You can, however, omit the fractional seconds.

Interval value expressions

Interval value expressions are similar to timestamp expressions, and represent one more option for converting character strings to interval values. They are also more flexible than the TO_xxINTERVAL family of functions.

Interval value expressions take on the following form:

```
INTERVAL 'character_representation' start_element TO end_element
```

where:

character_representation
: Is the character string representation of the interval. See "The TO_xxINTERVAL functions" for a description of how the two interval data types are represented in character form.

start_element
: Specifies the leading element in the interval.

end_element
: Specifies the trailing element in the interval.

Unlike the TO_xxINTERVAL functions, interval expressions allow you to specify an interval using any sequence of datetime elements from Table 10-2. There are only two restrictions:

- You must use a consecutive sequence of elements
- You cannot transition from a month to a day within the same interval

Following are several valid examples:

```
DECLARE
   A INTERVAL YEAR TO MONTH;
   B INTERVAL YEAR TO MONTH;
   C INTERVAL DAY TO SECOND;
   D INTERVAL DAY TO SECOND;
BEGIN
   /* Some YEAR TO MONTH examples */
   A := INTERVAL '40-3' YEAR TO MONTH;
   B := INTERVAL '40' YEAR;

   /* Some DAY TO SECOND examples */
   C := INTERVAL '10 1:02:10.123' DAY TO SECOND;

   /* Fails in Oracle9i, Release 1 because of a bug */
   --D := INTERVAL '1:02' HOUR TO MINUTE;

   /* Following are two workarounds for defining intervals,
```

```
      such as HOUR TO MINUTE, that represent only a portion of the
      DAY TO SECOND range. */
   SELECT INTERVAL '1:02' HOUR TO MINUTE
   INTO D
   FROM dual;

   D := INTERVAL '1' HOUR + INTERVAL '02' MINUTE;
END;
```

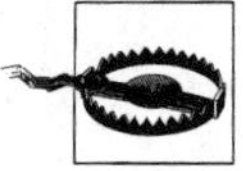

In Oracle9*i* Releases 1 and 2, the expression INTERVAL '1:02' HOUR TO MINUTE will work from a SQL statement, but not from a PL/SQL statement. Furthermore, you'll get an error about using the keyword BULK in the wrong context. This is now a known bug that we expect to see fixed in a future release.

Because there is no one interval type that includes both month and day, any interval that attempts to include both is invalid. For example, the following interval expression will generate an error:

```
INTERVAL '1-15' MONTH TO DAY
```

Likewise, there is no mechanism for skipping over an element. You can't, for example, specify values for days and minutes without also specifying some number of hours.

One very convenient thing that Oracle *will* do for you is to normalize interval values. In the following example, 72 hours and 15 minutes is normalized to 3 days, 0 hours, and 15 minutes:

```
DECLARE
   A INTERVAL DAY TO SECOND;
BEGIN
   SELECT INTERVAL '72:15' HOUR TO MINUTE INTO A FROM DUAL;
   DBMS_OUTPUT.PUT_LINE(A);
END;
```

The output is:

```
+03 00:15:00.000000
```

Oddly, Oracle will normalize only the high-end value (hours in this example). An attempt to specify an interval of 72:75 (72 hours and 75 minutes) results in an error.

Formatting intervals for display

So far in this section on interval conversion, we've relied on Oracle's implicit conversion mechanism to format interval values for display. You may be thinking that you could use TO_CHAR in conjunction with a format mask to gain more control over how an interval is displayed. Amazingly enough, you'd be wrong! TO_CHAR is completely useless when it comes to formatting interval values. For example:

```
DECLARE
   A INTERVAL YEAR TO MONTH;
```

```
BEGIN
   A := INTERVAL '40-3' YEAR TO MONTH;

   DBMS_OUTPUT.PUT_LINE(TO_CHAR(A,'YY "Years" and MM "Months"'));
END;
```

The output is:

```
+000040-03
```

Frankly, we don't understand what the people at Oracle were thinking when they decided against adding interval support to the TO_CHAR function.

If you're not satisfied with the default conversion of intervals to character strings, you can use the EXTRACT function (new in Oracle9*i*):

```
DECLARE
   A INTERVAL YEAR TO MONTH;
BEGIN
   A := INTERVAL '40-3' YEAR TO MONTH;

   DBMS_OUTPUT.PUT_LINE(
      EXTRACT(YEAR FROM A) || ' Years and '
      || EXTRACT(MONTH FROM A) || ' Months'
   );
END;
```

The output is:

```
40 Years and 3 Months
```

Using EXTRACT is certainly not as convenient as using TO_CHAR, but the EXTRACT approach, described in the next section, has the advantage of actually working.

The CAST and EXTRACT Functions

The CAST and EXTRACT functions are ANSI-standard functions (from SQL/92 forward) that are newly supported in Oracle. CAST made its appearance in Oracle8 as a mechanism for explicitly identifying collection types, and it was enhanced in Oracle8*i* to enable conversion between built-in datatypes. With respect to date and time, you can use CAST to convert datetime values to and from character strings. The EXTRACT function is new in Oracle9*i*, and allows you to pluck an individual datetime element from a datetime or interval value.

The CAST function

With respect to date and time, you can use the CAST function as follows:

- To convert a character string into a datetime value
- To convert a datetime value into a character string
- To convert one datetime type (e.g., DATE) into another (e.g., TIMESTAMP)

When used to convert datetimes to and from character strings, CAST respects the following NLS parameter settings:

NLS_DATE_FORMAT
: When casting to or from a DATE

NLS_TIMESTAMP_FORMAT
: When casting to or from a TIMESTAMP or a TIMESTAMP WITH LOCAL TIME ZONE

NLS_TIMESTAMP_TZ_FORMAT
: When casting to or from a TIMESTAMP WITH TIME ZONE

The following example shows a representative of each type of CAST that is relevant when working with datetimes:

```
DECLARE
   a TIMESTAMP WITH TIME ZONE;
   b VARCHAR2(40);
   c TIMESTAMP WITH LOCAL TIME ZONE;
BEGIN
   a := CAST ('24-Feb-2002 09.00.00.00 PM US/Eastern'
              AS TIMESTAMP WITH TIME ZONE);
   b := CAST (a AS VARCHAR2);
   c := CAST (a AS TIMESTAMP WITH LOCAL TIME ZONE);

   DBMS_OUTPUT.PUT_LINE(a);
   DBMS_OUTPUT.PUT_LINE(b);
   DBMS_OUTPUT.PUT_LINE(c);
END;
```

The output is:

```
24-FEB-02 09.00.00.000000 PM US/EASTERN
24-FEB-02 09.00.00.000000 PM US/EASTERN
24-FEB-02 09.00.00.000000 PM
```

This example generates a TIMESTAMP WITH TIME ZONE from a character string, converts that value to a VARCHAR2, and finally converts it to a TIMESTAMP WITH LOCAL TIME ZONE. Note that no time zone conversion is done when the value is CAST from TIMESTAMP WITH TIME ZONE to TIMESTAMP WITH LOCAL TIME ZONE. In that case, the time zone information is lost.

In a SQL statement, you can specify the size of a datatype in a CAST, as in CAST (x AS VARCHAR2(40)). However, PL/SQL does not allow you to specify the size of the target datatype.

The EXTRACT function

The EXTRACT function is an ANSI-standard function used to extract date components from a datetime value. Use the following format when invoking EXTRACT:

```
EXTRACT (component_name, FROM {datetime | interval})
```

In this syntax, *component_name* is the name of a datetime element listed in Table 10-3. Component names are not case-sensitive. Replace *datetime* or *interval* with a valid datetime or interval value. The function's return type depends on the component you are extracting.

Table 10-3. Datetime component names for use with EXTRACT

Component name	Return datatype
YEAR	NUMBER
MONTH	NUMBER
DAY	NUMBER
HOUR	NUMBER
MINUTE	NUMBER
SECOND	NUMBER
TIMEZONE_HOUR	NUMBER
TIMEZONE_MINUTE	NUMBER
TIMEZONE_REGION	VARCHAR2
TIMEZONE_ABBR	VARCHAR2

The following example shows EXTRACT being used to check whether the current month is November:

```
BEGIN
   IF EXTRACT (MONTH FROM SYSDATE) = 11 THEN
      DBMS_OUTPUT.PUT_LINE('It is November');
   ELSE
      DBMS_OUTPUT.PUT_LINE('It is not November');
   END IF;
END;
```

Use EXTRACT when you need to use a datetime element to control program flow, as in this example, or when you need a datetime element as a numeric value. Don't be tempted to use EXTRACT as a means of converting a datetime value to a character string, as in the following example:

```
BEGIN
   DBMS_OUTPUT.PUT_LINE('Today''s date is: ' ||
      EXTRACT(MONTH FROM SYSDATE) || '/' ||
      EXTRACT(DAY FROM SYSDATE) || '/' ||
      EXTRACT(YEAR FROM SYSDATE));
END;
```

The output is:

```
Today's date is: 2/24/2002
```

Look at how clumsy this is! EXTRACT is not designed to convert a datetime to a character string, as it returns mainly numeric values, not character string values. In this example, all those numbers are implicitly converted to character strings. Not only that, EXTRACT returns only numbers, not day names or month names or any of the other good things TO_CHAR provides. Use TO_CHAR to convert datetimes to character strings. Use EXTRACT when you just need to programmatically look at a value.

Date/Time Arithmetic

PL/SQL supports arithmetic involving datetime values, numeric values, and interval values. For example, you can add a given number of days to a date, or you can subtract two dates in order to determine the interval of time between them. Date arithmetic prior to the release of Oracle9*i* is a very simple topic. Oracle9*i*'s addition of INTERVAL types makes it much more complex.

Traditional Date Arithmetic

Prior to Oracle9*i*, date arithmetic meant doing one of two things:

- Adding or subtracting numeric values, representing some number of days, from DATE values.
- Subtracting one DATE from another in order to determine the number of days between them.

In Oracle9*i* this functionality is still available, but only with the DATE datatype.

You also could (and still can) make use of date functions such as ADD_MONTHS and MONTHS_BETWEEN. We discuss these later in the section "Date/Time Functions."

Adding and subtracting numeric values

Integer values represent days when doing date arithmetic. To move a date one day into the future, simply add 1 to the date as shown:

```
hire_date + 1
```

You can even add a fractional value to a date. A fractional value represents less than one day. You'll find fractional values most useful when you work in multiples of the values shown in Table 10-4.

Table 10-4. Fractional values in date arithmetic

Value	Represents
1/24	One hour
1/1440	One minute
1/86400	One second

In the following example, 8/24 is added to hire_date to change the time component from midnight to the more reasonable 8:00 AM:

```
DECLARE
   start_time DATE := DATE '2000-09-01';
BEGIN
   DBMS_OUTPUT.PUT_LINE(TO_CHAR(start_time,'YYYY-MM-DD HH:MI AM'));
   DBMS_OUTPUT.PUT_LINE(TO_CHAR(start_time+8/24,'YYYY-MM-DD HH:MI AM'));
END;
```

The output is:

```
2000-09-01 12:00 AM
2000-09-01 08:00 AM
```

Note that we specified 8/24 for 8 hours, and not 1/3 or the decimal equivalent of 0.33333333. By using 8/24, we make it reasonably clear to other programmers that we are adding 8 hours to the date. Always use one of the denominators shown in Table 10-4 when adding or subtracting numbers to a DATE. Once you memorize those denominators, the implications of any date arithmetic that uses them becomes very easy to understand. Following are some examples:

- To add 12 hours to a date, use 12/24 rather than 1/2.
- To add 1 day and 12 hours to a date value, use either 1+12/24 or 36/24, but never 1.5.
- You can specify one minute as 60 seconds (60/86400) or 1 minute (1/1440), depending on whether your application drives you to think in terms of minutes or seconds.

Avoid using denominators other than those shown in Table 10-4. Quick! How much time does 1/48 represent? Hmmm...had to think about that, didn't you? If we'd asked about 30/1440, you would have known immediately that we were talking about 30 minutes. For the record, 30/1440 reduces to 1/48 and represents 30 minutes. Use 1/48 for your math homework, but use 30/1440 for clarity in your code.

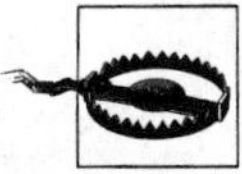

Adding or subtracting numbers to or from any of the TIMESTAMP types causes an implicit conversion to DATE.

Add or subtract numeric values as shown in this section only when using DATE variables. The following example demonstrates that a TIMESTAMP WITH TIME ZONE is implicitly converted to type DATE when a numeric value is added to it:

```
DECLARE
   start_time TIMESTAMP WITH TIME ZONE
      := TIMESTAMP '2000-09-01 00:00:00.00 -7:00';
BEGIN
   DBMS_OUTPUT.PUT_LINE(start_time);
   DBMS_OUTPUT.PUT_LINE(start_time+8/24);
   DBMS_OUTPUT.PUT_LINE(TO_CHAR(start_time+8/24,'DD-MON-YY HH.MI.SS'));
END;
```

The output is:

```
01-SEP-00 12.00.00.000000 AM -07:00
01-SEP-00
01-SEP-00 08.00.00
```

Ignore the time zone for a moment, and you can see that in each case 8 hours have been added to the time of day. Note that the second line of output is formatted as a DATE value, not a timestamp—that's evidence right there of the implicit conversion. The third line of output shows that the time of day was preserved during the implicit cast, but rest assured that the time zone and any fractional seconds have not been preserved.

Computing the difference between two dates

You can't add two DATE values. If you think about that logically, it makes sense. What does it mean, for example, to add 15-Nov-1961 to 18-Jun-1961? On the other hand, you can subtract one DATE value from another, resulting in the difference in days between the two dates. For example:

```
BEGIN
   DBMS_OUTPUT.PUT_LINE (
      TO_DATE('15-Nov-1961','dd-Mon-yyyy')
      - TO_DATE('18-Jun-1961','dd-Mon-yyyy')
   );
END;
```

The output is:

```
150
```

From this, you can see that 18-Jun-1961 falls 150 days prior to 15-Nov-1961. Be careful with the results of subtracting two DATE values, because if any time-of-day components are involved, you'll get a fractional result. Look at the same subtraction again; this time we've added some carefully chosen times:

```
BEGIN
   DBMS_OUTPUT.PUT_LINE (
      TO_DATE('15-Nov-1961 12:01 am','dd-Mon-yyyy hh:mi am')
      - TO_DATE('18-Jun-1961 11:59 pm','dd-Mon-yyyy hh:mi am')
   );
END;
```

The output is:

```
149.00138888888888888888888888888888889
```

If you're interested in the number of calendar days between the two dates shown in this example, the result is clearly not correct. It *is* correct from the standpoint of measuring the number of 24-hour periods between the two DATE values, but most humans want to know that the two dates are 150 days apart, not that one DATE value is 149.00139 24-hour periods distant from the other. You can get correct results by applying the TRUNC function to each of the date values:

```
BEGIN
   DBMS_OUTPUT.PUT_LINE (
      TRUNC(TO_DATE('15-Nov-1961 12:01 am','dd-Mon-yyyy hh:mi am'))
      - TRUNC(TO_DATE('18-Jun-1961 11:59 pm','dd-Mon-yyyy hh:mi am'))
   );
END;
```

The output is:

```
150
```

TRUNC eliminates any time-of-day component from the two DATE values, making the resulting subtraction equivalent to the first example in this section, and the result is the number of calendar days between the two dates. TRUNC is a very useful function when working with DATEs, and is discussed in detail later in the "Date/Time Functions" section.

The result of subtracting one DATE from another is a NUMBER. The result of subtracting one TIMESTAMP type from another is an INTERVAL DAY TO SECOND.

Interval Arithmetic

Oracle9*i* introduces the concept of an INTERVAL datatype, leading to a whole new level of complexity when it comes to date arithmetic. But the concept of an interval isn't really new. If you've been doing date arithmetic in older releases of Oracle, then you've already been working with intervals. Date arithmetic involving numbers, as described in the previous section, is nothing more than date arithmetic using intervals expressed in terms of days and fractions of a day. Think back to the problem of adding one day to a date. In Oracle9*i*, you can do either of the following:

```
hire_date + 1;

hire_date + INTERVAL '1' DAY;
```

See, we've been working with intervals all along. Oracle has just now formalized the concept, and in the process has given us two more interval types to work with. Beginning in Oracle9*i*, you can express intervals in any of the following terms:

INTERVAL YEAR TO MONTH type
: Allows us to express intervals in terms of years and months

INTERVAL DAY TO SECOND type
: Allows us to express intervals in terms of days, hours, minutes, and seconds

Numeric values
: Allow us to express intervals in terms of days and fractions of a day

With this in mind, date arithmetic in Oracle9*i* can be reduced to the following three types of operations:

- Adding or subtracting an interval to or from a datetime value
- Subtracting one datetime value from another in order to determine the interval between the two values
- Adding or subtracting one interval to or from another interval

The only thing that's really new here is the terminology and the INTERVAL datatypes. Don't let these intimidate you. The first two bullets correspond to the first two bullets in the previous section; only the terminology has changed. Even the third bullet represents nothing new—we've always been able to add and subtract date intervals. It's just that pre-Oracle9*i*, that meant adding and subtracting numbers, whereas now, when working with the new TIMESTAMP family of types, you can add or subtract INTERVAL datatypes.

Adding and subtracting intervals to/from datetimes

The fundamental concept of adding an interval of time to a datetime value is the same in Oracle9*i* as in prior releases. In Oracle8*i* you can do:

```
hire_date + 1;
```

In Oracle9*i* you can do the same thing, as well as:

```
hire_date + INTERVAL '1' DAY;
```

Nothing is new here but the INTERVAL DAY TO SECOND datatype. The expression INTERVAL '1' DAY yields a value of the INTERVAL DAY TO SECOND datatype. We specified only a number of days, so hours, minutes, and seconds will default to zero. See "Interval value expressions" earlier in this chapter for more details on writing the kinds of interval expressions we've used here.

The following code snippet contains some more examples of interval arithmetic in Oracle9*i*:

```
DECLARE
   hire_date TIMESTAMP WITH TIME ZONE;

   a INTERVAL YEAR TO MONTH;
   b INTERVAL DAY TO SECOND;
BEGIN
   hire_date := TIMESTAMP '2000-09-01 00:00:00 -5:00';
   DBMS_OUTPUT.PUT_LINE(hire_date);

   a := INTERVAL '1-2' YEAR TO MONTH;
   b := INTERVAL '3 4:5:6.7' DAY TO SECOND;

   --Add some years and months
   hire_date := hire_date + a;
   DBMS_OUTPUT.PUT_LINE(hire_date);
```

```
    --Add some days, hours, minutes, and seconds
    hire_date := hire_date + b;
    DBMS_OUTPUT.PUT_LINE(hire_date);
END;
```

The output is:

```
01-SEP-00 12.00.00.000000 AM -05:00
01-NOV-01 12.00.00.000000 AM -05:00
04-NOV-01 04.05.06.700000 AM -05:00
```

Computing the interval between two datetimes

If you compute the interval between two DATE values, the result is the number of 24-hour periods (not the same as days) between the two values. If the number was an integer, then the difference was an exact number of days. If the number was a fractional number, then the difference included some number of hours, minutes, and seconds as well.

A significant drawback to the old mechanism for computing intervals is that you get fractional numbers as a result. Look at the following example, which you may remember from the previous section:

```
BEGIN
    DBMS_OUTPUT.PUT_LINE (
        TO_DATE('15-Nov-1961 12:01 am','dd-Mon-yyyy hh:mi am')
        - TO_DATE('18-Jun-1961 11:59 pm','dd-Mon-yyyy hh:mi am')
    );
END;
```

The output is:

```
149.00138888888888888888888888888888889
```

The 149 days you can understand, but you probably wonder what exactly is represented by .00138888888888888888888888888888889. How many hours is that? You might be able to work out the corresponding number of hours, minutes, and seconds, but you might not get an accurate result, especially with that repeating decimal in the value. Oracle9*i* to the rescue! The new INTERVAL types make it easy to compute an interval in terms that make sense to us humans. For example:

```
DECLARE
    a INTERVAL DAY(3) TO SECOND(0);
BEGIN
    --Compute interval and assign to an INTERVAL DAY TO SECOND variable
    a := TO_TIMESTAMP('15-Nov-1961 12:01 am','dd-Mon-yyyy hh:mi am')
         - TO_TIMESTAMP('18-Jun-1961 11:59 pm','dd-Mon-yyyy hh:mi am');

    DBMS_OUTPUT.PUT_LINE(a);
END;
```

The output is:

```
+149 00:02:00
```

In this example, we subtract one date from the other and assign the resulting difference to a variable of the INTERVAL DAY TO SECOND type. Instead of a number with a repeating fraction that we can't easily understand, the result is an interval that can be expressed exactly as 149 days, zero hours, two minutes, and zero seconds.

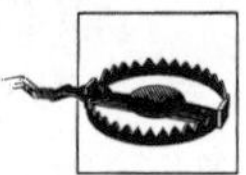

Values of the INTERVAL types can be returned only from subtractions involving the new TIMESTAMP types.

Oddly, or seemingly so, PL/SQL doesn't seem to support the return of an INTERVAL YEAR TO MONTH value as the difference between two timestamps. Thus, neither of the calculations for "c" in the following block will be successful:

```
DECLARE
   a TIMESTAMP;
   b TIMESTAMP;
   c INTERVAL YEAR TO MONTH;
BEGIN
   a := TO_TIMESTAMP('15-Nov-1961 12:01 am','dd-Mon-yyyy hh:mi am');
   b := TO_TIMESTAMP('18-Jun-1961 11:59 pm','dd-Mon-yyyy hh:mi am');

   c := a - b;
   c := CAST(a - b AS INTERVAL YEAR TO MONTH);
END;
```

Regardless of whether we use the CAST operator, we can't compute the difference between two timestamps as an INTERVAL YEAR TO MONTH. Oracle provides no official explanation for this—in fact, the documentation doesn't even mention that you cannot perform such a calculation. After some thought we've come up with the following explanation:

1. Any given expression yields a result in a defined datatype. In the case of subtracting two timestamps, the resulting datatype is always INTERVAL DAY TO SECOND.
2. The result type of an expression can't depend on the type of the variable to which it is assigned. PL/SQL can't look at the left side of the assignment operator and change the semantics of the expression on the right side.
3. When the result of an expression is of a type not matching the type of the target variable on the left side of the assignment operator, PL/SQL performs an implicit conversion.
4. An implicit conversion from INTERVAL DAY TO SECOND to INTERVAL YEAR TO MONTH is not possible, because the number of days in a month varies from month to month. Fundamentally, this is the same reason for not allowing an INTERVAL datatype to span MONTH and DAY to begin with (see "The INTERVAL Datatypes" earlier in this chapter).

Intervals can be negative or positive. So far, all the intervals we've shown have been positive. In the context of subtraction, a positive interval indicates that you've subtracted a date in the past from a more recent date. For example:

```
15-Nov-1961 - 18-Jun-1961 = +150
```

A negative interval indicates that you've subtracted a more recent date from a date further in the past, as in:

```
18-Jun-1961 - 15-Nov-1961 = -150
```

Fundamentally, the sign of the result indicates the directionality of the interval; we'll talk more about that in the upcoming section "Adding and subtracting intervals." It's somewhat unfortunate that there's no absolute value function that applies to intervals in the same way that the ABS function applies to numeric values.

CASTing DATEs to TIMESTAMPs

Recall from the previous section that each expression yields a result of a defined datatype. The result of a subtraction involving two TIMESTAMPs is a value of type INTERVAL DAY TO SECOND. To maintain compatibility with prior releases, the result of a subtraction involving two DATEs is still a numeric value. Consequently, if you wish to subtract one DATE from another and return an INTERVAL DAY TO SECOND value, you will need to CAST your DATEs into TIMESTAMPs. For example:

```
DECLARE
   a DATE;
   b DATE;
   c INTERVAL DAY(3) TO SECOND(0);
BEGIN
   a := TO_DATE('15-Nov-1961 12:01 am','dd-Mon-yyyy hh:mi am');
   b := TO_DATE('18-Jun-1961 11:59 pm','dd-Mon-yyyy hh:mi am');

   c := CAST(a AS TIMESTAMP) - CAST(b AS TIMESTAMP);

   DBMS_OUTPUT.PUT_LINE(c);
END;
```

The output is:

```
+149 00:02:00
```

If you mix DATEs and TIMESTAMPs in the same subtraction expression, PL/SQL will implicitly cast the DATEs into TIMESTAMPs. For example:

```
DECLARE
   a DATE;
   b TIMESTAMP;
   c INTERVAL DAY(3) TO SECOND(0);
   d INTERVAL DAY(3) TO SECOND(0);
BEGIN
   a := TO_DATE('15-Nov-1961 12:01 am','dd-Mon-yyyy hh:mi am');
```

```
   b := TO_TIMESTAMP('18-Jun-1961 11:59 pm','dd-Mon-yyyy hh:mi am');

   c := a - b;
   d := b - a;

   DBMS_OUTPUT.PUT_LINE(c);
   DBMS_OUTPUT.PUT_LINE(d);
END;
```

The output is:

```
+149 00:02:00
-149 00:02:00
```

When mixing datatypes in a single expression, it's probably best to use explicit casting (or some other mechanism) to remove all doubt about which way implicit conversions are occurring.

Adding and subtracting intervals

Unlike the case with datetime values, it makes perfect sense to add one interval to another. It also makes sense to subtract one interval from another. The one rule you need to keep in mind is that whenever you add or subtract two intervals, they must be of the same type. For example:

```
DECLARE
   a1 INTERVAL DAY TO SECOND := '2 3:4:5.6';
   b1 INTERVAL DAY TO SECOND := '1 1:1:1.1';

   a2 INTERVAL YEAR TO MONTH := '2-10';
   b2 INTERVAL YEAR TO MONTH := '1-1';

   a3 NUMBER := 3;
   b3 NUMBER := 1;
BEGIN
   DBMS_OUTPUT.PUT_LINE(a1 - b1);
   DBMS_OUTPUT.PUT_LINE(a2 - b2);
   DBMS_OUTPUT.PUT_LINE(a3 - b3);
END;
```

The output is:

```
+000000001 02:03:04.500000000
+000000001-09
2
```

This example shows the results of three interval subtractions. The first two involve INTERVAL DAY TO SECOND and INTERVAL YEAR TO MONTH. The third shows the subtraction of two numbers. Remember: when working with DATE types, the interval between two DATE values is expressed as a NUMBER.

Multiplying and dividing intervals

Multiplication and division have no application to dates, but you can multiply an interval by a number and divide an interval by a number. Following are some examples:

```
DECLARE
   a1 INTERVAL DAY TO SECOND := '2 3:4:5.6';
   a2 INTERVAL YEAR TO MONTH := '2-10';
   a3 NUMBER := 3;
BEGIN
   --Show some interval multiplication
   DBMS_OUTPUT.PUT_LINE(a1 * 2);
   DBMS_OUTPUT.PUT_LINE(a2 * 2);
   DBMS_OUTPUT.PUT_LINE(a3 * 2);

   --Show some interval division
   DBMS_OUTPUT.PUT_LINE(a1 / 2);
   DBMS_OUTPUT.PUT_LINE(a2 / 2);
   DBMS_OUTPUT.PUT_LINE(a3 / 2);
END;
```

The output is:

```
+000000004 06:08:11.200000000
+000000005-08
6
+000000001 01:32:02.800000000
+000000001-05
1.5
```

Unconstrained INTERVAL types

Intervals can be declared with varying levels of precision, and values of different precisions are not entirely compatible with each other. Look at the following example, which shows how fractional-seconds digits can be lost as a result of careless assignment between two variables declared slightly differently:

```
DECLARE
   A INTERVAL DAY TO SECOND;
   C INTERVAL DAY(9) TO SECOND(2);
BEGIN
   A := '10 0:0:0.123456';
   C := A;
   DBMS_OUTPUT.PUT_LINE (A);
   DBMS_OUTPUT.PUT_LINE (C);
END;
```

The output is:

```
+10 00:00:00.123456
+000000010 00:00:00.12
```

The value assigned to A specifies 0.123456 seconds, which works because the default precision for INTERVAL DAY TO SECOND variables is six digits past the decimal point. When the value of A is assigned to C, however, four of those digits were lost because of the way C was declared.

At first, this issue seems to be just a matter of keeping your datatypes straight, but it becomes a problem when writing procedures and functions that accept INTERVAL values as parameters. Notice the loss of precision when the value of B is doubled via a call to the function double_my_interval:

```
DECLARE
   B INTERVAL DAY(9) TO SECOND(9);

   FUNCTION double_my_interval (
      A IN INTERVAL DAY TO SECOND) RETURN INTERVAL DAY TO SECOND
   IS
   BEGIN
      RETURN A * 2;
   END;
BEGIN
   B := '1 0:0:0.123456789';
   DBMS_OUTPUT.PUT_LINE(B);
   DBMS_OUTPUT.PUT_LINE(double_my_interval(B));
END;
```

The output is:

```
+000000001 00:00:00.123456789
+02 00:00:00.246914
```

Not only have we lost digits in our fractional seconds, but we've also lost digits where the number of days is concerned. Had B been assigned a value of 100 days or more, the call to double_my_interval would have failed with an *ORA-01873: the leading precision of the interval is too small* error.

The issue here is that the default precision for INTERVAL types is not the same as the maximum precision. This problem is compounded by the fact that PL/SQL doesn't allow us to specify precision when declaring a function's or procedure's formal parameters. We can't, for example, do the following:

```
FUNCTION double_my_interval (
      A IN INTERVAL DAY(9) TO SECOND(9)) RETURN INTERVAL DAY TO SECOND
   IS
```

Fortunately, the good people who design PL/SQL had the foresight to provide us with two unconstrained datatypes just to solve this particular problem. These datatypes are:

YMINTERVAL_UNCONSTRAINED
: Accepts any INTERVAL YEAR TO MONTH value with no loss of precision

DSINTERVAL_UNCONSTRAINED
: Accepts any INTERVAL DAY TO SECOND value with no loss of precision

Using the DSINTERVAL_UNCONSTRAINED type, we can recode our earlier example as follows:

```
DECLARE
   B INTERVAL DAY(9) TO SECOND(9);

   FUNCTION double_my_interval (
      A IN DSINTERVAL_UNCONSTRAINED) RETURN DSINTERVAL_UNCONSTRAINED
   IS
   BEGIN
      RETURN A * 2;
   END;
BEGIN
   B := '100 0:0:0.123456789';
   DBMS_OUTPUT.PUT_LINE(B);
   DBMS_OUTPUT.PUT_LINE(double_my_interval(B));
END;
```

The output is:

```
+000000100 00:00:00.123456789
+000000200 00:00:00.246913578
```

Notice that we used DSINTERVAL_UNCONSTRAINED twice: once to specify the type of the formal parameter to double_my_interval, and once to specify the function's return type. As a result, we can now invoke the function on *any* INTERVAL DAY TO SECOND value with no loss of precision.

Date/Time Functions

Date arithmetic, described in the previous section, does not provide all the functionality you need when working with datetime values, so PL/SQL also implements a number of helpful, built-in datetime functions. You've already read about built-in conversion functions such as TO_DATE and NUMTOYMINTERVAL in previous sections. Table 10-5 briefly describes the other date-related functions at your disposal.

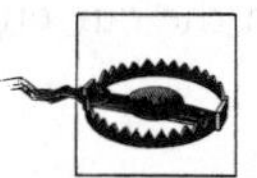

Avoid using Oracle's traditional DATE functions with the new timestamp types. Instead, use the new interval functionality whenever possible. Use DATE functions only with DATE values.

Many of the functions in the table accept DATE values as inputs. ADD_MONTHS is an example of one such function. You must be careful when you consider using such functions to operate on any of the new TIMESTAMP datatypes. While you can pass a TIMESTAMP type to one of these functions, Oracle implicitly converts that type to a DATE. Only then does the function perform its operation. As a result of this implicit conversion, fractional seconds and any time zone information will be lost. The result type from such functions will be of type DATE. For example, if you pass a

TIMESTAMP WITH TIME ZONE to ADD_MONTHS, you will get back a DATE without any time zone information and without any fractional seconds. Be careful!

Table 10-5. Built-in date functions

Name	Description
ADD_MONTHS	Adds a specified number of months to a date.
CURRENT_DATE	Returns the current date and time as a DATE value in the session time zone.
CURRENT_TIMESTAMP	Returns the current date and time as a TIMESTAMP WITH TIME ZONE value in the session time zone.
DBTIMEZONE	Returns the time zone offset (from UTC) of the database time zone in the form of a character string (e.g.,'-05:00').
FROM_TZ	Adds time zone information to a TIMESTAMP value, converting it to a TIMESTAMP WITH TIME ZONE.
LAST_DAY(*date*)	Returns the last day in the month containing the specified input date.
LOCALTIMESTAMP	Returns the current date and time as a TIMESTAMP value in the local time zone.
MONTHS_ BETWEEN	Calculates the number of months between two dates.
NEW_TIME	Shifts a DATE value from one time zone to another.
NEXT_DAY	Returns the date of the first weekday specified that is later than the date.
ROUND	Returns the date rounded to the specified format unit.
SESSIONTIMEZONE	Returns the time zone offset (from UTC) of the session time zone in the form of a character string (e.g.,'-05:00').
SYSDATE	Returns the current date and time from the Oracle server as a DATE value.
SYSTIMESTAMP	Returns the current date and time from the Oracle server as a TIMESTAMP WITH TIME ZONE value.
TRUNC	Truncates a DATE value to a specified format unit.
TZ_OFFSET	Returns the time zone offset from UTC (e.g., '-05:00') for a given time zone name, abbreviation, or offset.

Functions to Get the Date and Time

Getting the date and time in PL/SQL used to be easy: you used the SYSDATE function and that was it. In Oracle9*i*, you have a number of other options at your disposal, and you need to understand how they work and what your choices are. Following are the specifications for all the Oracle9*i* functions that return the current date and time:

```
CURRENT_DATE RETURN DATE
CURRENT_TIMESTAMP RETURN TIMESTAMP_TZ_UNCONSTRAINED
LOCALTIMESTAMP RETURN TIMESTAMP_UNCONSTRAINED
SYSDATE RETURN DATE
SYSTIMESTAMP RETURN TIMESTAMP_TZ_UNCONSTRAINED
```

The SQL reference manual shows an optional precision parameter for CURRENT_TIMESTAMP and LOCALTIMESTAMP. In Oracle9*i* Release 1, SQL supports that parameter; PL/SQL does not. PL/SQL does support the parameter in Oracle9*i* Release 2.

So which function should you use in a given situation? The answer depends on several factors, which you should probably consider in the following order:

1. You are using a release prior to Oracle8*i* or need to maintain compatibility with such a release. In this case, your choice is simple: use SYSDATE.
2. Time zone is an issue. The database is associated with a time zone, and so is each session; your session may be in a different time zone from the database. Do you want the time with respect to your time zone or with respect to the server's time zone?
3. Datatype is an issue. Some functions return DATE, one returns TIMESTAMP, and yet others return TIMESTAMP WITH TIME ZONE values. After deciding on session time versus server time, narrow your choice based on the function's return type.

Use Table 10-6 in conjunction with these three factors to help you decide which function to use. Note that, unfortunately, Oracle didn't maintain parallelism in its nomenclature. LOCALTIMESTAMP and SYSTIMESTAMP have parallel names but return different datatypes.

Table 10-6. Comparison of functions that return current date and time

Function	Time zone	Datatype
CURRENT_DATE	Session	DATE
CURRENT_TIMESTAMP	Session	TIMESTAMP WITH TIME ZONE
LOCALTIMESTAMP	Session	TIMESTAMP
SYSDATE	Server	DATE
SYSTIMESTAMP	Server	TIMESTAMP WITH TIME ZONE

For example, if you want the current date and time with respect to the session, and you want to put that value into a DATE variable, you should use the CURRENT_DATE function. On the other hand, if you are working with dates from different time zones using TIMESTAMP WITH TIME ZONE variables, choose the CURRENT_TIMESTAMP function.

If you decide to use a function that returns the time in the session time zone, be certain that your DBA has correctly configured the server and that you've correctly specified your session time zone. The following example illustrates the difference between CURRENT_TIMESTAMP, which is used to get the time in the server's time zone, and SYSTIMESTAMP, which is used to get the time in the session's time zone.

```
BEGIN
   DBMS_OUTPUT.PUT_LINE(CURRENT_TIMESTAMP);
   DBMS_OUTPUT.PUT_LINE(SYSTIMESTAMP);
END;
```

The output is:

```
24-FEB-02 04.55.54.803009000 PM -08:00
24-FEB-02 07.55.54.804221000 PM -05:00
```

In this example, the session is on U.S. Pacific Standard Time (-8:00) while the server is on U.S. Eastern Standard Time (-5:00). Note the time difference of three hours between the two values. Also note the respective time zone displacements.

What if there's no function to return a value in the datatype that you need? For example, what if you need the server time in a TIMESTAMP variable? The good news is that you can allow Oracle to convert the types for you. Even better might be to use an explicit CAST. For example:

```
DECLARE
   a TIMESTAMP;
   b TIMESTAMP;
BEGIN
   a := CAST(SYSTIMESTAMP AS TIMESTAMP);
   b := SYSDATE;
   DBMS_OUTPUT.PUT_LINE(TO_CHAR(a,'DD-MON-YYYY HH:MI:SS AM'));
   DBMS_OUTPUT.PUT_LINE(TO_CHAR(a,'DD-MON-YYYY HH:MI:SS AM'));
END;
```

The output is:

```
24-FEB-2002 06:46:39 PM
24-FEB-2002 06:46:39 PM
```

The call to SYSTIMESTAMP uses CAST to make the conversion from TIMESTAMP WITH TIME ZONE to TIMESTAMP explicit. The call to SYSDATE allows the conversion from DATE to TIMESTAMP to happen implicitly.

Be cognizant of hardware and operating-system limitations if you are using these functions for subsecond timing purposes. The CURRENT_TIMESTAMP, LOCALTIMESTAMP, and SYSTIMESTAMP functions return values in either the TIMESTAMP WITH TIME ZONE or TIMESTAMP datatypes. These datatypes allow you to resolve time down to the billionth of a second. That's all well and good, but think about where that time comes from. Oracle (probably) gets the time from the operating system, and the operating system depends at some level on the hardware. If your operating system or underlying hardware tracks time only to the hundredth of a second, Oracle won't be able to return results any finer than that. For example, when using Suse Linux 7.2 on an Intel x86 processor we can resolve time only to the millionth of a second (six digits), whereas we do seem to get values resolved to the billionth of a second when running Windows XP on the same hardware.

The Time Zone Functions

Sometimes you need to know what time zone your session or your database is in. You might also want to determine the offset from UTC for a given time zone. Use the following three functions to do these things:

```
DBTIMEZONE RETURN VARCHAR2
SESSIONTIMEZONE RETURN VARCHAR2
TZ_OFFSET (time_zone) RETURN VARCHAR2
```

DBTIMEZONE and SESSIONTIMEZONE return the database and session time zones, respectively. The time zones are identified by their offsets from UTC. For example:

```
BEGIN
   DBMS_OUTPUT.PUT_LINE(DBTIMEZONE);
   DBMS_OUTPUT.PUT_LINE(SESSIONTIMEZONE);
END;
```

The output is:

```
-07:00
-08:00
```

But what time zones do these offsets really represent? Recall that the V$TIMEZONE_NAMES view returns a list of time zone names and abbreviations. You can use the TZ_OFFSET function to get the current time zone offset for a given time zone region. The following query returns a list of all the time zone regions that currently correspond to an offset of -07:00. The query was executed when daylight savings time was not in effect; if it were in effect, you'd get different results. For example, America/Denver is UTC -07:00 during most of the year, but UTC -06:00 when daylight savings time is in effect.

```
SELECT TZNAME, TZABBREV
FROM V$TIMEZONE_NAMES
WHERE SUBSTR(TZ_OFFSET(TZNAME),1,6) = '-07:00';

TZNAME                                   TZABBREV
---------------------------------------- ----------
America/Denver                           LMT
America/Denver                           MST
America/Denver                           MWT
America/Denver                           MDT
America/Edmonton                         LMT
America/Edmonton                         MST
America/Edmonton                         MDT
```

Why the use of the SUBSTR function in this example? In Oracle9*i* Release 1, there appears to be a bug with the TZ_OFFSET function in that it returns an extra zero byte at the end of the string. For example:

```
SELECT TZ_OFFSET('US/EASTERN') offset,
       LENGTH(TZ_OFFSET('US/EASTERN')) length,
       DUMP(TZ_OFFSET('US/EASTERN')) dump
FROM dual;
```

```
OFFSET     LENGTH DUMP
------- ---------- ----------------------------------
-05:00           7 Typ=1 Len=7: 45,48,53,58,48,48,0
```

Note the zero byte at the end of the DUMP, and consider what happens when the following SELECT is issued:

```
SELECT TZNAME
FROM V$TIMEZONE_NAMES
WHERE TZ_OFFSET(TZNAME) = '-07:00';

      *
ERROR at line 3:
ORA-01875: time zone minute must be between -59 and 59
```

At worst, this SELECT should return no rows, and in our testing on Windows XP this is indeed the result we got. Under Linux, however, we received the rather strange error you see here. Use SUBSTR to remove the extraneous zero, and you should be OK.

The ADD_MONTHS Function

The ADD_MONTHS function returns a new date with the specified number of months added to the input date. The specification for ADD_MONTHS is as follows:

```
FUNCTION ADD_MONTHS (date_in IN DATE, month_shift NUMBER) RETURN DATE
FUNCTION ADD_MONTHS (month_shift NUMBER, date_in IN DATE) RETURN DATE
```

ADD_MONTHS is an overloaded function. You can specify the date first and then the number of months by which you want to shift that date, or you can list the *month_shift* parameter first and then the date. Either order is acceptable, and both arguments are required.

If the *month_shift* parameter is positive, ADD_MONTHS returns a date for that number of months into the future. If the number is negative, ADD_MONTHS returns a date for that number of months in the past. Here are some examples that use ADD_MONTHS:

- Move ahead by 3 months:

  ```
  ADD_MONTHS ('12-JAN-1995', 3) → 12-APR-1995
  ```

- Move back by 12 months:

  ```
  ADD_MONTHS (-12, '12-MAR-1990') → 12-MAR-1989
  ```

ADD_MONTHS always shifts the date by whole months. You can provide a fractional value for the *month_shift* parameter, but ADD_MONTHS will round down to the next whole number nearest zero, as shown in the following example. Pay special attention to the direction in which a negative value of months is rounded.

```
BEGIN
   --Adding 1.9999 is the same as adding 1
   DBMS_OUTPUT.PUT_LINE(ADD_MONTHS ('28-FEB-1989', 1.9999));
   DBMS_OUTPUT.PUT_LINE(ADD_MONTHS ('28-FEB-1989', 1));
```

```
    DBMS_OUTPUT.PUT_LINE(ADD_MONTHS ('28-FEB-1989', -1.9999));
    DBMS_OUTPUT.PUT_LINE(ADD_MONTHS ('28-FEB-1989', -1));
END;
```

The output is:

```
31-MAR-1989
31-MAR-1989
31-JAN-1989
31-JAN-1989
```

If you want to shift a date by a fraction of a month, simply add or subtract the required number of days. PL/SQL supports direct arithmetic operations between date values. For more information, see "Date/Time Arithmetic" earlier in this chapter.

If the input date to ADD_MONTHS does not fall on the last day of the month, the date returned by ADD_MONTHS falls on the same day in the new month as in the original month. If the day number of the input date is greater than the last day of the month returned by ADD_MONTHS, the function sets the day number to the last day in the new month. The following example illustrates both of these rules. The first call to ADD_MONTHS advances 15-Jan one month to 15-Feb. Because there is no 31st day in February, the second call returns the last day in February:

```
BEGIN
    DBMS_OUTPUT.PUT_LINE(ADD_MONTHS ('15-JAN-1995', 1));
    DBMS_OUTPUT.PUT_LINE(ADD_MONTHS ('31-JAN-1995', 1));
END;
```

The output is:

```
15-FEB-1995
28-FEB-1995
```

This behavior is perfectly reasonable. However, what if the input date falls on the last day of the month, and the new month has more days than the original month? If you shift two months forward from 28-FEB-1994, do you get back 30-APR-1994 (the last day of April) or 28-APR-1994 (the same day in the new month as in the old month)? The answer is that if the input date represents the last day of the month, so will the output date:

```
BEGIN
    DBMS_OUTPUT.PUT_LINE(ADD_MONTHS ('28-FEB-1994', 2));
END;

30-APR-1994
```

If you pass to ADD_MONTHS a day representing the last day of the month, PL/SQL always returns the last day of the resulting month, regardless of the number of actual days in each of the months. This behavior makes sense in some situations, but not in others. Be aware of it! (See the upcoming sidebar for a function that can help you get around this quirk.)

Getting Around ADD_MONTH's Month-End Quirk

The fact that ADD_MONTHS always returns a month-end date whenever the input date represents a month-end date is sometimes inconvenient. The following PL/SQL function, my_add_months, will preserve the original day of the month whenever possible:

```
FUNCTION my_add_months (
   date_in IN DATE, months_shift IN NUMBER)
RETURN DATE IS
   date_out DATE;
   day_in NUMBER;
   day_out NUMBER;
BEGIN
   date_out := ADD_MONTHS(date_in, months_shift);
   day_in := TO_NUMBER(TO_CHAR(date_in,'DD'));
   day_out := TO_NUMBER(TO_CHAR(date_out,'DD'));
   IF day_out > day_in
   THEN
      date_out := date_out - (day_out - day_in);
   END IF;
   RETURN date_out;
END;
```

The only time this function adjusts the day of the month is when the day happens to be beyond the end of the target month. Add 1 month to 31-Jan-2002, and because February has only 28 days you'll get 28-Feb-2002 as the result. However, add 1 to 28-Feb-2002, and you'll get 28-Mar-2002—the day is preserved whenever possible. This function also preserves any time-of-day components such as hours, minutes, and seconds.

The FROM_TZ Function

The FROM_TZ function adds time zone information to a TIMESTAMP value, thus converting the TIMESTAMP value into a TIMESTAMP WITH TIME ZONE value. The specification is:

```
FUNCTION FROM_TZ (timestamp_value IN TIMESTAMP,
                  time_zone IN VARCHAR2)
```

You can specify the time zone using either an offset from UTC or a time zone region name. The result returned by the function is the same date and time passed as input, but with the addition of the time zone information that you specify.

Following are two examples of using FROM_TZ:

```
DECLARE
   w TIMESTAMP := CAST('24-Jun-2002 3.41.00.00 PM' AS TIMESTAMP);
   x TIMESTAMP WITH TIME ZONE;
   y TIMESTAMP WITH TIME ZONE;
BEGIN
   x := FROM_TZ(w,'-5:00');
   y := FROM_TZ(w,'US/Eastern');
```

```
    DBMS_OUTPUT.PUT_LINE(x);
    DBMS_OUTPUT.PUT_LINE(y);
END;
```

The output is:

```
24-JUN-02 03.41.00.000000 PM -05:00
24-JUN-02 03.41.00.000000 PM US/EASTERN
```

You can see that the date and time fields remain unchanged from those passed as input to FROM_TZ. The only difference is that the time zone information has been tacked onto the original TIMESTAMP values, making them into TIMESTAMP WITH TIME ZONE values.

The LAST_DAY Function

The LAST_DAY function returns the date of the last day of the month for a given date. The specification is:

```
FUNCTION LAST_DAY (date_in IN DATE) RETURN DATE
```

This function is useful because the number of days in a month varies throughout the year. With LAST_DAY, for example, you do not have to try to figure out if February of this or that year has 28 or 29 days. Just let LAST_DAY figure it out for you.

Here are some examples of LAST_DAY in action:

```
BEGIN
    --Go to the last day in the month:
    DBMS_OUTPUT.PUT_LINE(LAST_DAY ('12-JAN-99'));

    --If already on the last day, just stay on that day:
    DBMS_OUTPUT.PUT_LINE(LAST_DAY ('31-JAN-99'));

    --Get the last day of the month three months ago:
    DBMS_OUTPUT.PUT_LINE(LAST_DAY (ADD_MONTHS (SYSDATE, 3)));

    --Tell me the number of days until the end of the current month:
    DBMS_OUTPUT.PUT_LINE(LAST_DAY (SYSDATE) - SYSDATE);
END;
```

The output is:

```
31-JAN-0099
31-JAN-0099
31-MAY-2002
4
```

The MONTHS_BETWEEN Function

The MONTHS_BETWEEN function calculates the number of months between two dates and returns that difference as a number. The specification is:

```
FUNCTION MONTHS_BETWEEN (date1 IN DATE, date2 IN DATE)
    RETURN NUMBER
```

Getting the First Day of the Month

Oracle has a LAST_DAY function, so why not a FIRST_DAY? Believe it or not, such a function would have its use. We've written quite a few queries where we've had to determine both the first and last day of the month for any arbitrary date a user enters. A convenient incantation to return the first day of the month for any date is:

```
ADD_MONTHS(LAST_DAY(x),-1)+1
```

This discussion depends on the behavior of ADD_MONTHS with respect to month-end dates. First, we use LAST_DAY to compute the last day of the current month. Then we add –1 months (using ADD_MONTHS), which is guaranteed to get us the last day of the previous month. Finally, we add 1 to advance the day to the first of the current month.

While this approach may seem a tad convoluted, it avoids the need for string manipulation and preserves any time-of-day component that is part of the input value.

The following rules apply to MONTHS_BETWEEN:

- If *date1* comes after *date2*, then MONTHS_BETWEEN returns a positive number.
- If *date1* comes before *date2*, then MONTHS_BETWEEN returns a negative number.
- If *date1* and *date2* are in the same month, then MONTHS_BETWEEN returns a fraction (a value between –1 and +1).
- If *date1* and *date2* both fall on the last day of their respective months, then MONTHS_BETWEEN returns a whole number (no fractional component).
- If *date1* and *date2* are in different months and at least one of the dates is not the last day of the month, MONTHS_BETWEEN returns a fractional number. The fractional component is calculated on a 31-day month basis, and also takes into account any differences in the time component of *date1* and *date2*.

Here are some examples of the uses of MONTHS_BETWEEN:

```
BEGIN
   --Calculate two ends of month, the first earlier than the second:
   DBMS_OUTPUT.PUT_LINE(
      MONTHS_BETWEEN ('31-JAN-1994', '28-FEB-1994'));

   --Calculate two ends of month, the first later than the second:
   DBMS_OUTPUT.PUT_LINE(
      MONTHS_BETWEEN ('31-MAR-1995', '28-FEB-1994'));

   --Calculate when both dates fall in the same month:
   DBMS_OUTPUT.PUT_LINE(
      MONTHS_BETWEEN ('28-FEB-1994', '15-FEB-1994'));
```

```
   --Perform months_between calculations with a fractional component:
   DBMS_OUTPUT.PUT_LINE(
      MONTHS_BETWEEN ('31-JAN-1994', '1-MAR-1994'));
   DBMS_OUTPUT.PUT_LINE(
      MONTHS_BETWEEN ('31-JAN-1994', '2-MAR-1994'));
   DBMS_OUTPUT.PUT_LINE(
      MONTHS_BETWEEN ('31-JAN-1994', '10-MAR-1994'));
END;
```

The output is:

```
-1
13
.4193548387096774193548387096774193548387
-1.03225806451612903225806451612903225806
-1.06451612903225806451612903225806451613
-1.32258064516129032258064516129032258065
```

If you detect a pattern here, you are right. As noted, MONTHS_BETWEEN calculates the fractional component of the number of months by assuming that each month has 31 days. Therefore, each additional day over a complete month counts for 1/31 of a month, and:

```
1 divided by 31 = .032258065—more or less!
```

According to this rule, the number of months between January 31, 1994 and February 28, 1994 is 1—a nice, clean integer. But the number of months between January 31, 1994 and March 1, 1994, has an additional .032258065 added to it.

The ROUND and TRUNC Functions

The ROUND function rounds a date value to the nearest date as specified by a format mask. The TRUNC function truncates a date as specified by a format mask. ROUND and TRUNC for datetimes are analogous to ROUND and TRUNC for numbers. (See the "Rounding and Truncation Functions" section in Chapter 9.) Their specifications are as follows:

```
FUNCTION ROUND (date_in IN DATE [, format_mask VARCHAR2]) RETURN DATE

FUNCTION TRUNC (date_in IN DATE [, format_mask VARCHAR2]) RETURN DATE
```

A common use for both functions is to set the time-of-day component of a DATE value to midnight (12:00:00 AM). By convention, midnight is the value you use when you care only about the date itself, not the time. The difference between the two functions lies in whether they disregard the time component entirely or use it to round the resulting DATE value up or down. Let's look at the different results from the two functions in the following example:

```
DECLARE
   date_in DATE := TO_DATE('24-Feb-2002 05:16:00 PM'
                   ,'DD-MON-YYYY HH:MI:SS AM');
   date_rounded DATE;
```

```
      date_truncated DATE;
   BEGIN
      date_rounded := ROUND(date_in);
      date_truncated := TRUNC(date_in);

      DBMS_OUTPUT.PUT_LINE(
         TO_CHAR(date_rounded, 'DD-MON-YYYY HH:MI:SS AM'));
      DBMS_OUTPUT.PUT_LINE(
         TO_CHAR(date_truncated,'DD-MON-YYYY HH:MI:SS AM'));
   END;
```

The result is:

```
25-FEB-2002 12:00:00 AM
24-FEB-2002 12:00:00 AM
```

Look at the value for *date_rounded*. Do you see that the day has been advanced from 24-Feb to 25-Feb? That's because the time, 5:16 PM, was closer to midnight of the following day (the 25th) than it was to the 24th. In contrast, the value for *date_truncated* is still the 24th. The TRUNC function simply eliminated the time-of-day information. The ROUND function respected the time of day, eliminated it, but also advanced the date by one day. Had the time of day been 5:16 AM, the rounding would have been downward, and both functions would have returned the same result.

By default, the functions round or truncate to the date, as those operations tend to be by far the most common. However, using one of the format mask elements shown in Table 10-7, you can round to any other datetime element that you wish.

Table 10-7. Format mask elements for ROUND and TRUNC

Format mask	Rounds or truncates to
CC or SSC	Century
SYYY, YYYY, YEAR, SYEAR, YYY, YY, or Y	Year (rounds up to next year starting on July 1)
IYYY, IYY, IY, or I	Standard ISO year
Q	Quarter (rounds up on the sixteenth day of the second month of the quarter)
MONTH, MON, MM, or RM	Month (rounds up on the sixteenth day, which is not necessarily the same as the middle of the month)
WW	Same day of the week as the first day of the year
IW	Same day of the week as the first day of the ISO year
W	Same day of the week as the first day of the month
DDD, DD, or J	Day
DAY, DY, or D	Starting day of the week
HH, HH12, HH24	Hour
MI	Minute

The following example shows TRUNC being used to truncate a datetime value to the beginning of the year and the beginning of the month, respectively:

```
DECLARE
   date_in DATE := TO_DATE('24-Feb-2002 05:36:00 PM'
                    ,'DD-MON-YYYY HH:MI:SS AM');
   trunc_to_year DATE;
   trunc_to_month DATE;

BEGIN
   trunc_to_year := TRUNC(date_in,'YYYY');
   trunc_to_month := TRUNC(date_in,'MM');

   DBMS_OUTPUT.PUT_LINE(
      TO_CHAR(trunc_to_year, 'DD-MON-YYYY HH:MI:SS AM'));
   DBMS_OUTPUT.PUT_LINE(
      TO_CHAR(trunc_to_month,'DD-MON-YYYY HH:MI:SS AM'));
END;
```

The output is:

```
01-JAN-2002 12:00:00 AM
01-FEB-2002 12:00:00 AM
```

As you can see, TRUNC has enabled us to instantly jump back to the first of the year and the first of the month.

If you read the earlier sidebar, "Getting the First Day of the Month," you might wonder why you shouldn't use TRUNC to get the first day of the month. You can, as long as you don't care about the time of day. If you need to preserve the time of day, use the method shown in the sidebar. Otherwise, use TRUNC.

The following example shows ROUND being used in a few different ways. First, it is used to determine the century closest to 24-Feb-2002 and also to 24-Feb-1902. Then, it is used to round a datetime value to the nearest hour.

```
DECLARE
   date_in_1 DATE := TO_DATE('24-Feb-2002','DD-MON-YYYY');
   date_in_2 DATE := TO_DATE('24-Feb-1902','DD-MON-YYYY');
   date_in_3 DATE := TO_DATE('24-Feb-2002 05:36:00 PM'
                      ,'DD-MON-YYYY HH:MI:SS AM');

   round_1 DATE;
   round_2 DATE;
   round_3 DATE;

BEGIN
   round_1 := ROUND(date_in_1,'CC');
   round_2 := ROUND(date_in_2,'CC');
   round_3 := ROUND(date_in_3,'HH');

   DBMS_OUTPUT.PUT_LINE(TO_CHAR(round_1,'DD-MON-YYYY HH:MI:SS AM'));
```

```
   DBMS_OUTPUT.PUT_LINE(TO_CHAR(round_2,'DD-MON-YYYY HH:MI:SS AM'));
   DBMS_OUTPUT.PUT_LINE(TO_CHAR(round_3,'DD-MON-YYYY HH:MI:SS AM'));
END;
```

The output is:

```
01-JAN-2001 12:00:00 AM
01-JAN-1901 12:00:00 AM
24-FEB-2002 06:00:00 PM
```

Actually, rounding to the century doesn't return the century; it returns the date and time at which the century begins. And Oracle respects the scientific definition of century, not the popular definition, so, for example, the 21st century began in 2001, not 2000. The explanation of the third line of output in this example is straightforward: 5:36 PM was rounded to the nearest hour, which was 6:00 PM on the same date.

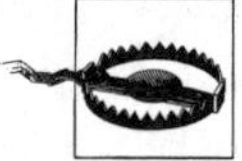

When you're using TRUNC or ROUND, be aware that unwanted datetime components do not "go away." All DATE variables specify values for year, month, day, hour, minute, and second. When 5:36 PM is rounded to 6:00 PM, the minutes component is still there; it's just been set to zero.

The TRUNC function is very useful in leveling the playing field with regard to the time component when comparing two DATE variables. Consider the following comparison:

```
IF request_date BETWEEN start_date AND end_date
THEN
...
```

The date component of request_date and start_date might be the same, but if your application does not specify a time component for each of its dates, the comparison might fail. If, for example, the user enters a request_date and the screen does not include a time component, the time for request_date will be midnight (12:00 AM) of that day. If start_date was set from SYSDATE, however, its time component will reflect the time at which the assignment was made. Because 12:00 AM comes before any other time of the day, a comparison that looks to the naked eye like a match might well fail.

If you are not sure about the time components of your date fields and variables and want to make sure that your operations on dates disregard the time component, TRUNCate them:

```
IF TRUNC (request_date) BETWEEN TRUNC (start_date) AND TRUNC (end_date)
THEN
...
```

TRUNC resets the time of day to midnight (12:00:00 AM). In this example, all datetime values are truncated to midnight, so the time will never cause this comparison to fail.

The NEW_TIME Function

I don't know about you, but I am simply unable to remember the time in Anchorage when it is 3:00 PM in Chicago. Fortunately for me, PL/SQL provides the NEW_TIME function. This function converts dates (along with their time components) from one time zone to another. The specification for NEW_ TIME is:

```
FUNCTION NEW_TIME (date_in DATE, zone1 VARCHAR2, zone2 VARCHAR2)
   RETURN DATE
```

where *date_in* is the original date, *zone1* is the starting point for the zone switch (usually, but not restricted to, your own local time zone), and *zone2* is the time zone in which the date returned by NEW_TIME should be placed.

If you're writing software that must work across time zones, we recommend using the newer TIMESTAMP WITH TIME ZONE functionality rather than using NEW_TIME with DATE values.

The valid time zones are shown in Table 10-8.

Table 10-8. Time zone abbreviations and descriptions

Time zone abbreviation	Description
AST	Atlantic Standard Time
ADT	Atlantic Daylight Time
BST	Bering Standard Time
BDT	Bering Daylight Time
CST	Central Standard Time
CDT	Central Daylight Time
EST	Eastern Standard Time
EDT	Eastern Daylight Time
GMT	Greenwich Mean Time
HST	Alaska-Hawaii Standard Time
HDT	Alaska-Hawaii Daylight Time
MST	Mountain Standard Time
MDT	Mountain Daylight Time
NST	Newfoundland Standard Time
PST	Pacific Standard Time
PDT	Pacific Daylight Time
YST	Yukon Standard Time
YDT	Yukon Daylight Time

Be aware that NEW_TIME does not accept all of the time zone abbreviations returned by V$TIMEZONE_NAMES. Use only those abbreviations listed in Table 10-8.

The specification of time zones to NEW_TIME is not case-sensitive, as the following example shows:

```
BEGIN
   DBMS_OUTPUT.PUT_LINE(
      TO_CHAR (NEW_TIME (TO_DATE ('09151994 12:30 AM',
                                  'MMDDYYYY HH:MI AM'),
                         'CST', 'hdt'),
               'Month DD, YYYY HH:MI AM'));
END;
```

The output is:

```
September 14, 1994 09:30 PM
```

So, when it was 12:30 in the morning of September 15, 1994 in Chicago, it was 9:30 in the evening of September 14, 1994 in Anchorage.

By the way, I used TO_DATE with a format mask to make sure that a time other than the default of midnight would be used in the calculation of the new date and time. I then used TO_CHAR with another format mask (this one intended to make the output more readable) to display the date and time, because by default PL/SQL will not include the time component unless specifically requested to do so.

Even though NEW_TIME converts between time zones, it does not respect the time zones in the TIMESTAMP WITH TIME ZONE datatype. The following example demonstrates this:

```
DECLARE
   a TIMESTAMP WITH TIME ZONE
      := TO_TIMESTAMP_TZ ('09151994 12:30 AM -5:00',
                          'MMDDYYYY HH:MI AM TZH:TZM');
BEGIN
   DBMS_OUTPUT.PUT_LINE(a);

   DBMS_OUTPUT.PUT_LINE(
      TO_CHAR (NEW_TIME (a,'CST', 'hdt'),
               'Month DD, YYYY HH:MI AM'));
END;
```

The output is:

```
15-SEP-94 12.30.00.000000 AM -05:00
September 14, 1994 09:30 PM
```

Notice that the shifted time in this example is 9:30 PM, just as in the previous example. The NEW_TIME function takes a DATE as input. When the TIMESTAMP

WITH TIME ZONE value is converted to a DATE, the time zone information is lost. The end result is that 12:30 AM gets shifted +9:00 hours from CST to HDT.

The NEXT_DAY Function

The NEXT_DAY function returns the date of the first day after the specified date that falls on the specified day of the week. Here is the specification for NEXT_ DAY:

```
FUNCTION NEXT_DAY (date_in IN DATE, day_name IN VARCHAR2) RETURN DATE
```

The *day_name* must be a day of the week in your session's date language (specified by the NLS_DATE_LANGUAGE database initialization parameter). The time component of the returned date is the same as that of the input date, *date_in*. If the day of the week of the input date matches the specified *day_name*, then NEXT_DAY will return the date seven days (one full week) after *date_in*. NEXT_ DAY does not return the input date if the day names match.

Here are some examples of the use of NEXT_DAY. Let's figure out the date of the first Monday and Wednesday in 1997 in all of these examples:

```
BEGIN
   --You can use both full and abbreviated day names:
   DBMS_OUTPUT.PUT_LINE(NEXT_DAY ('01-JAN-1997', 'MONDAY'));
   DBMS_OUTPUT.PUT_LINE(NEXT_DAY ('01-JAN-1997', 'MON'));

   --The case of the day name doesn't matter a whit:
   DBMS_OUTPUT.PUT_LINE(NEXT_DAY ('01-JAN-1997', 'monday'));

   --NEXT_DAY of Wednesday moves the date up a full week:
   DBMS_OUTPUT.PUT_LINE(NEXT_DAY ('01-JAN-1997', 'WEDNESDAY'));

   --If the date language were Spanish:
   EXECUTE IMMEDIATE 'ALTER SESSION SET NLS_DATE_LANGUAGE="SPANISH"';
   DBMS_OUTPUT.PUT_LINE(NEXT_DAY ('01-ENE-1997', 'LUNES'));
END;
```

The output is:

```
06-JAN-97
06-JAN-97
06-JAN-97
08-JAN-97
06-ENE-97
```

CHAPTER 11
Records and Collections

In this chapter:

Records and collections are examples of *composite data structures*, which means that they are composed of more than one element or component, each with its own value. *Records* in PL/SQL programs are very similar in concept and structure to the rows of a database table. The record as a whole does not have a value of its own; instead, each individual component or field has a value, and the record gives you a way to store and access these values as a group. Records can greatly simplify your life as a programmer, allowing you to write and manage your code more efficiently by shifting from field-level declarations and manipulation to record-level operations.

A *collection* is a data structure that acts like a list or single-dimensional array. Collections are, in fact, the closest you can get to traditional arrays in the PL/SQL language. You can use collections to manage lists of information in your programs. This chapter will help you decide which of the three different types of collections (associative array, nested table, or VARRAY) best fit your program requirements, and will show you how to define and manipulate those structures.

First, let's get to know records. They are simpler, and are often used within collections.

Records in PL/SQL

A record is similar in structure to a row in a database table. Each row in a table has one or more columns of various datatypes. A record is composed of one or more fields. There are three different ways to define a record, but once defined, the same rules apply for referencing and changing fields in a record. Let's take a look at some of the benefits of using records. Then we'll examine the different ways to define a record, and finish up with examples of using records in your programs.

Benefits of Using Records

The record data structure provides a high-level way of addressing and manipulating data defined inside PL/SQL programs (as opposed to stored in database tables). This approach offers several benefits, described in the following sections.

Data abstraction

When you abstract something, you generalize it, distancing yourself from the nitty-gritty details and concentrating on the big picture. When you create modules, you abstract the individual actions of the module into a name. The name (and program specification) represents those actions.

When you create a record, you abstract all the different attributes or fields of the subject of that record. You establish a relationship between those different attributes, and give that relationship a name by defining a record.

Aggregate operations

Once you have stored information in records, you can perform operations on whole blocks of data at a time, rather than on each individual attribute. This kind of aggregate operation reinforces the abstraction of the record. Very often, you are not really interested in making changes to individual components of a record, but instead to the object that represents all of those different components.

Suppose that in my job I need to work with companies. I don't really care about whether a company has two lines of address information or three; instead, I want to work at the level of the company itself, making changes to, deleting, or analyzing the status of a company. In all of these cases I am talking about a whole row in the database, not any specific column. The company record hides all that information from me, yet makes it accessible if and when I need it. This orientation brings you closer to viewing your data as a collection of objects, with rules applied to those objects.

Leaner, cleaner code

Using records also helps you to write cleaner code and less of it. When I use records, I invariably produce programs that have fewer lines of code, are less vulnerable to change, and need fewer comments. Records also cut down on variable sprawl; instead of declaring many individual variables, I declare a single record. This lack of clutter creates aesthetically attractive code that requires fewer resources to maintain.

Use of PL/SQL records can have a dramatic, positive impact on your programs, both in initial development and in ongoing maintenance. To ensure that I get the most out of record structures, I have set the following guidelines for my code development:

Create corresponding cursors and records

Whenever I create a cursor in my programs, I also create a corresponding record (except in the case of cursor FOR loops). I always FETCH into a record, rather than into individual variables. In those few instances when this involves a little extra work, I marvel at the elegance of the approach and compliment myself on my commitment to principle. And in Oracle9*i* Release 2, I can even use records with DML statements!

Create table-based records
: Whenever I need to store table-based data within my programs, I create a new (or use a predefined) table-based record to store that data. I keep my variable use to a minimum and dynamically link my program data structures to my RDBMS data structures with the %ROWTYPE attribute.

Pass records as parameters
: Whenever appropriate, I pass records rather than individual variables as parameters in my procedural interfaces. This way, my procedure calls are less likely to change over time, making my code more stable. There is a downside to this technique, however: if a record is passed as an OUT or IN OUT parameter, its field values are saved by the PL/SQL program in case of a rollback. This can use up memory and consume unnecessary CPU cycles. (Oracle has introduced a NOCOPY parameter hint that may help in some cases. See Chapter 16 for details.)

Declaring Records

You can declare a record in one of three ways:

Table-based record
: Use the %ROWTYPE attribute with a table name to declare a record in which each field corresponds to—and has the same name as—a column in a table. Here is an example declaring a record named one_book with the same structure as the books table:

```
DECLARE
   one_book books%ROWTYPE;
```

Cursor-based record
: Use the %ROWTYPE with an explicit cursor or cursor variable in which each field corresponds to a column or aliased expression in the cursor SELECT statement. Here is an example declaring a record with the same structure as an explicit cursor:

```
DECLARE
   CURSOR my_books_cur IS
      SELECT * FROM books
       WHERE author LIKE '%FEUERSTEIN%';

   one_SF_book my_books_cur%ROWTYPE;
```

Programmer-defined record

Use the TYPE RECORD statement to define a record in which each field is defined explicitly (with its name and datatype) in the TYPE statement for that record; a field in a programmer-defined record can even be another record. In the following example, I declare a record TYPE containing some information about my book writing career and an "instance" of that type, a record:

```
DECLARE
   TYPE book_info_rt IS RECORD (
      author books.author%TYPE,
      category VARCHAR2(100),
      total_page_count POSITIVE);

   steven_as_author book_info_rt;
```

Notice that when I declare a record based on a record TYPE, I do not use the %ROWTYPE attribute. The book_info_rt element already is a TYPE.

The general format of the %ROWTYPE declaration is:

```
record_name [schema_name.]object_name%ROWTYPE;
```

The *schema_name* is optional (if not specified, then the schema under which the code is compiled is used to resolve the reference). The *object_name* can be an explicit cursor, cursor variable, table, view, or synonym.

Here is an example of the creation of a record based on a cursor variable:

```
DECLARE
   TYPE book_rc IS REF CURSOR RETURN books%ROWTYPE;
   book_cv book_rc;

   one_book book_cv%ROWTYPE;
BEGIN
   ...
```

The other way to declare and use a record is to do so implicitly, with a cursor FOR loop. In the following block, the book_rec record is not defined in the declaration section; PL/SQL automatically declares it for me with the %ROWTYPE attribute against the loop's query:

```
BEGIN
   FOR book_rec IN (SELECT * FROM books)
   LOOP
      calculate_total_sales (book_rec);
   END LOOP;
END;
```

By far the most interesting and complicated way to declare a record is with the TYPE statement, so let's explore that feature in a bit more detail.

Programmer-Defined Records

Table- and cursor-based records are great when you need to create program data matching those structures. Yet do these kinds of records cover all of our needs for composite data structures? What if I want to create a record that has nothing to do with either a table or a cursor? What if I want to create a record whose structure is derived from several different tables and views? Should I really have to create a "dummy" cursor just so I can end up with a record of the desired structure? For just these kinds of situations, PL/SQL offers programmer-defined records, declared with the TYPE...RECORD statement.

With the programmer-defined record, you have complete control over the number, names, and datatypes of fields in the record. To declare a programmer-defined record, you must perform two distinct steps:

1. Declare or define a record TYPE containing the structure you want in your record.
2. Use this record TYPE as the basis for declarations of your own actual records having that structure.

Declaring programmer-defined record TYPEs

You declare a record type with the TYPE statement. The TYPE statement specifies the name of the new record structure, and the components or fields that make up that record. The general syntax of the record TYPE definition is:

```
TYPE type_name IS RECORD
   (field_name1 datatype1,
    field_name2 datatype2,
    ...
    field_nameN datatypeN
   );
```

where *field_nameN* is the name of the *N*th field in the record, and *datatypeN* is the datatype of that *N*th field. The datatype of a record's field can be any of the following:

- Hardcoded, scalar datatype (VARCHAR2, NUMBER, etc.).
- Programmer-defined SUBTYPE.
- Anchored declarations using %TYPE or %ROWTYPE attributes. In the latter case, we have created a *nested record*—one record inside another.
- PL/SQL collection type; a field in a record can be a list or even a collection.
- REF CURSOR, in which case the field contains a cursor variable.

Here is an example of a record TYPE statement:

```
TYPE company_rectype IS RECORD
   (comp# company.company_id%TYPE,
    name  company.name%TYPE);
```

You can declare a record TYPE in a local declaration section or in a package specification; the latter approach allows you to globally reference that record type in any PL/SQL block compiled in the schema that owns the package, or in the PL/SQL blocks of any schema that has EXECUTE privileges on the package.

Declaring the record

Once you have created your own customized record types, you can use those types in declarations of specific records. The actual record declarations have the following format:

```
record_name record_type;
```

where *record_name* is the name of the record, and *record_type* is the name of a record type that you have defined with the TYPE...RECORD statement.

To build a customer sales record, for example, I would first establish a record type called customer_sales_rectype, as follows:

```
TYPE customer_sales_rectype IS RECORD
   (customer_id   NUMBER (5),
    customer_name customer.name%TYPE,
    total_sales   NUMBER (15,2)
   );
```

This is a three-field record structure that contains the primary key and name information for a customer, as well as a calculated, total amount of sales for the customer. I can then use this new record type to declare records with the same structure as this type:

```
prev_customer_sales_rec customer_sales_rectype;
top_customer_rec customer_sales_rectype;
```

Notice that I do not need the %ROWTYPE attribute, or any other kind of keyword, to denote this as a record declaration. The %ROWTYPE attribute is only needed for table and cursor records.

In addition to specifying the datatype, you can supply default values for individual fields in a record with the DEFAULT or := syntax. You can also apply constraints to the declaration of a record's fields. You can specify that a field in a record be NOT NULL (in which case you must also assign a default value). Finally, each field name within a record must be unique.

Examples of programmer-defined record declarations

Suppose that I declare the following subtype, a cursor, and an associative array data structure:*

* *Associative array* is the Oracle9*i* name for an index-by table, as explained later in the discussion of collections.

```
DECLARE SUBTYPE long_line_type IS VARCHAR2(2000);

CURSOR company_sales_cur IS
   SELECT name, SUM (order_amount) total_sales
     FROM company c, order o
    WHERE c.company_id = o.company_id;

TYPE employee_ids_tabletype IS
   TABLE OF employee.employee_id%TYPE
   INDEX BY BINARY_INTEGER;
```

I can then define the following programmer-defined record in that same declaration section:

- A programmer-defined record that is a subset of the company table, plus a PL/SQL table of employees. I use the %TYPE attribute to link the fields in the record directly to the table. I then add a third field, which is actually an associative array of employee ID numbers.

  ```
  TYPE company_rectype IS RECORD
     (company_id    company.company_id%TYPE,
      company_name  company.name%TYPE,
      new_hires_tab employee_ids_tabletype);
  ```

- A mish-mash of a record that demonstrates the different kinds of field declarations in a record, including the NOT NULL constraint, the use of a subtype, the %TYPE attribute, a default value specification, an associative array, and a nested record. These varieties are shown here.

  ```
  TYPE mishmash_rectype IS RECORD
     (emp_number NUMBER(10) NOT NULL,
      paragraph_text long_line_type,
      company_nm company.name%TYPE,
      total_sales company_sales.total_sales%TYPE := 0,
      new_hires_tab employee_ids_tabletype,
      prefers_nonsmoking_fl BOOLEAN := FALSE,
      new_company_rec company_rectype
     );
  ```

As you can see, PL/SQL offers tremendous flexibility in designing your own record structures. Your records can represent tables, views, and SELECT statements in a PL/SQL program. They can also be arbitrarily complex, with fields that are actually records within records or associative arrays.

Working with Records

Regardless of how you define a record (based on a table, cursor, or explicit record TYPE statement), you work with the resulting record in the same ways. You can work with the data in a record at the "record level," or you can work with individual fields of the record.

Record-level operations

When you work at the record level, you avoid any references to individual fields in the record. Here are the record-level operations currently supported by PL/SQL:

- You can copy the contents of one record to another (as long as they are compatible in structure, i.e., have the same number of fields and the same or convertible datatypes).
- You can assign a value of NULL to a record with a simple assignment.
- You can define and pass the record as an argument in a parameter list.
- You can RETURN a record back through the interface of a function.

Several record-level operations are not yet supported:

- You cannot use the IS NULL syntax to see if all fields in the record have NULL values. Instead, you must apply the IS NULL operator to each field individually.
- You cannot compare two records—for example, you cannot ask if the records (the values of their fields) are the same or different, or if one record is greater than or less than another. Unfortunately, to answer these kinds of questions, you must compare each field individually. We cover this topic and provide a utility that generates such comparison code in the later section "Comparing Records."
- Prior to Oracle9*i* Release 2, you cannot insert into a database table with a record. Instead, you must pass each individual field of the record for the appropriate column. For more information on record-based DML, see Chapter 13.

You can perform record-level operations on any records with compatible structures. In other words, the records must have the same number of fields and the same or convertible datatypes, but they don't have to be the same type. Suppose that I have created the following table:

```
CREATE TABLE cust_sales_roundup (
   customer_id NUMBER (5),
   customer_name VARCHAR2 (100),
   total_sales NUMBER (15,2)
   );
```

Then the three records defined as follows all have compatible structures, and I can "mix-and-match" the data in these records as shown:

```
DECLARE
   cust_sales_roundup_rec cust_sales_roundup%ROWTYPE;

   CURSOR cust_sales_cur IS SELECT * FROM cust_sales_roundup;
   cust_sales_rec cust_sales_cur%ROWTYPE;

   TYPE customer_sales_rectype IS RECORD
      (customer_id NUMBER(5),
       customer_name customer.name%TYPE,
       total_sales NUMBER(15,2)
      );
```

```
    prefererred_cust_rec customer_sales_rectype;
BEGIN
    -- Assign one record to another.
    cust_sales_roundup_rec := cust_sales_rec;
    prefererred_cust_rec := cust_sales_rec;
END;
```

Let's look at some other examples of record-level operations.

- In this example, I'll assign a default value to a record. You can initialize a record at the time of declaration by assigning it another, compatible record. In the following program, I assign an IN argument record to a local variable. I might do this so that I can modify the values of fields in the record:

  ```
  PROCEDURE compare_companies
     (prev_company_rec IN company%ROWTYPE)
  IS
     curr_company_rec company%ROWTYPE := prev_company_rec;
  BEGIN
     ...
  END;
  ```

- In this next initialization example, I create a new record type and record. I then create a second record type using the first record type as its single column. Finally, I initialize this new record with the previously defined record:

  ```
  DECLARE
     TYPE first_rectype IS RECORD (
        var1 VARCHAR2(100) := 'WHY NOT');

     first_rec first_rectype;

     TYPE second_rectype IS RECORD
        (nested_rec first_rectype := first_rec);
  BEGIN
     ...
  END;
  ```

- I can also perform assignments within the execution section, as you might expect. In the following example I declare two different rain_forest_history records and then set the current history information to the previous history record:

  ```
  DECLARE
     prev_rain_forest_rec rain_forest_history%ROWTYPE;
     curr_rain_forest_rec rain_forest_history%ROWTYPE;
  BEGIN
     ... initialize previous year rain forest data ...

     -- Transfer data from previous to current records.
     curr_rain_forest_rec := prev_rain_forest_rec;
  ```

  The result of this aggregate assignment is that the value of each field in the current record is set to the value of the corresponding field in the previous record. I could also have accomplished this with individual direct assignments from the previous to current records. This would have required four separate assignments and lots of typing; whenever possible, use record-level operations to save time and make your code less vulnerable to change.

- I can move data directly from a row in a table to a record in a program by fetching directly into a record. Here are several examples:

```
DECLARE
   /*
   || Declare a cursor and then define a record based on that cursor
   || with the %ROWTYPE attribute.
   */
   CURSOR cust_sales_cur IS
      SELECT customer_id, name, SUM (total_sales) tot_sales
        FROM cust_sales_roundup
       WHERE sold_on < ADD_MONTHS (SYSDATE, -3)
      GROUP BY customer_id, name;

   cust_sales_rec cust_sales_cur%ROWTYPE;
BEGIN
   /* Move values directly into record by fetching from cursor */

   OPEN cust_sales_cur;
   FETCH cust_sales_cur INTO cust_sales_rec;
```

  In this next block, I declare a programmer-defined TYPE that matches the data retrieved by the implicit cursor. Then I SELECT directly into a record based on that type.

```
DECLARE
   TYPE customer_sales_rectype IS RECORD
      (customer_id   NUMBER (5),
       customer_name customer.name%TYPE,
       total_sales   NUMBER (15,2)
      );
   top_customer_rec  customer_sales_rectype;
BEGIN
   /* Move values directly into the record: */
   SELECT customer_id, name, SUM (total_sales)
     INTO top_customer_rec
     FROM cust_sales_roundup
    WHERE sold_on < ADD_MONTHS (SYSDATE, -3)
     GROUP BY customer_id, name;
```

- I can declare a function that returns a record, and also demonstrate the ability to "null out" a record with a direct assignment.

```
CREATE OR REPLACE FUNCTION best_seller (
   week_in IN PLS_INTEGER,
   year_in IN PLS_INTEGER)
   RETURN books%ROWTYPE
IS
   return_value books%ROWTYPE;
BEGIN
```

```
      SELECT *
        INTO return_value
        FROM books B
       WHERE week_number = week_in
         AND year = year_in
         AND sales = (SELECT MAX (sales) FROM book_sales BS
                       WHERE BS.isbn = B.isbn
                         AND week_number = week_in
                         AND year = year_in);
      RETURN return_value;
   EXCEPTION
      WHEN NO_DATA_FOUND OR TOO_MANY_ROWS
      THEN
         -- Make sure to return NULL.
         return_value := NULL;
         RETURN return_value;
   END best_seller;
```

Whenever possible, try to work with records at the aggregate level: the record as a whole, and not individual fields. The resulting code is much easier to write and maintain. There are, of course, many situations in which you need to manipulate individual fields of a record. Let's take a look at how you would do that.

Field-level operations

When you need to access a field within a record (to either read or change its value), you must use dot notation, just as you would when identifying a column from a specific database table. The syntax for such a reference is:

```
[schema_name.][package_name.]record_name.field_name
```

You need to provide a package name only if the record is defined in the specification of a package that is different from the one you are working on at that moment. You need to provide a schema name only if the package is owned by a schema different from that in which you are compiling your code.

Once you have used dot notation to identify a particular field, all the normal rules in PL/SQL apply as to how you can reference and change the value of that field. Let's take a look at some examples.

The assignment operator (:=) changes the value of a particular field. In the first assignment, total_sales is zeroed out. In the second assignment, a function is called to return a value for the Boolean flag output_generated (it is set to either TRUE or FALSE):

```
BEGIN
   top_customer_rec.total_sales := 0;

   report_rec.output_generated :=
      check_report_status (report_rec.report_id);
END;
```

In the next example I create a record based on the rain_forest_history table, populate it with values, and then insert a record into that same table:

```
DECLARE
   rain_forest_rec rain_forest_history%ROWTYPE;
BEGIN
   /* Set values for the record */
   rain_forest_rec.country_code  := 1005;
   rain_forest_rec.analysis_date :=
      ADD_MONTHS (TRUNC (SYSDATE), -3);
   rain_forest_rec.size_in_acres := 32;
   rain_forest_rec.species_lost  := 425;

   /* Insert a row in the table using the record values */
   INSERT INTO rain_forest_history
          (country_code, analysis_date, size_in_acres, species_lost)
   VALUES
      (rain_forest_rec.country_code,
       rain_forest_rec.analysis_date,
       rain_forest_rec.size_in_acres,
       rain_forest_rec.species_lost);
   ...
END;
```

Notice that because the analysis_date field is of type DATE, I can assign any valid DATE expression to that field. The same goes for the other fields, and this is even true for more complex structures.

Suppose that I have created a nested record structure; that is, one of the fields in my "outer" record is actually another record. In the following example I declare a record type for all the elements of a phone number (phone_rectype), and then declare a record type that collects all the phone numbers for a person together in a single structure (contact_set_rectype).

```
DECLARE
   TYPE phone_rectype IS RECORD
      (intl_prefix   VARCHAR2(2),
       area_code     VARCHAR2(3),
       exchange      VARCHAR2(3),
       phn_number    VARCHAR2(4),
       extension     VARCHAR2(4)
      );
   TYPE contact_set_rectype IS RECORD
      (day_phone#    phone_rectype, /* Nested record */
       eve_phone#    phone_rectype, /* Nested record */
       fax_phone#    phone_rectype, /* Nested record */
   home_phone#   phone_rectype, /* Nested record */
       cell_phone#   phone_rectype  /* Nested record */
      );
   auth_rep_info_rec contact_set_rectype;
BEGIN
```

Although I still use the dot notation to refer to a field with nested records, now I might have to refer to a field that is nested several layers deep inside the structure. To do this I must include an extra dot for each nested record structure, as shown in the following assignment, which sets the fax phone number's area code to the home phone number's area code:

```
auth_rep_info_rec.fax_phone#.area_code :=
   auth_rep_info_rec.home_phone#.area_code;
```

Finally, here is an example demonstrating references to packaged records (and package-based record TYPEs). Suppose I want to plan out my summer reading (for all those days I will be lounging about in the sand outside my Caribbean hideaway). I create a package specification as follows:

```
CREATE OR REPLACE PACKAGE summer
IS
   TYPE reading_list_rt IS RECORD (
      favorite_author  VARCHAR2 (100),
      title            VARCHAR2 (100),
      finish_by        DATE);

   must_read reading_list_rt;
   wifes_favorite reading_list_rt;
END summer;

CREATE OR REPLACE PACKAGE BODY summer
IS
BEGIN -- Initialization section
   must_read.favorite_author := 'Tepper, Sheri S.';
   must_read.title := 'Gate to Women''s Country';
END summer;
```

With this package compiled in the database, I can then construct my reading list as follows:

```
DECLARE
   first_book summer.reading_list_rt;
   second_book summer.reading_list_rt;
BEGIN
   summer.must_read.finish_by := TO_DATE ('01-AUG-2002', 'DD-MON-YYYY');
   first_book := summer.must_read;

   second_book.favorite_author := 'Morris, Benny';
   second_book.title := 'Righteous Victims';
   second_book.finish_by := TO_DATE ('01-SEP-2002', 'DD-MON-YYYY');
END;
```

I declare two local book records. I then assign a "finish by" date to the packaged must-read book (notice the *package.record.field* syntax) and assign that packaged record to my first book of the summer record. I then assign values to individual fields for the second book of the summer.

By the way, when you work with the UTL_FILE built-in package for file I/O in PL/SQL, you follow these same rules. The UTL_FILE.FILE_TYPE datatype is actually a record TYPE definition. So when you declare a file handle, you are really declaring a record from a package-based TYPE:

```
DECLARE
   my_file_id UTL_FILE.FILE_TYPE;
```

Comparing Records

How can you check to see if two records are equal (i.e., that each corresponding field contains the same value)? It would be wonderful if PL/SQL would allow you to perform a direct comparison, as in:

```
DECLARE
   first_book summer.reading_list_rt := summer.must_read;
   second_book summer.reading_list_rt := summer.wifes_favorite;
BEGIN
   IF first_book = second_book
   THEN
      lots_to_talk_about;
   END IF;
END;
```

Unfortunately, you cannot do that. Instead, to test for record equality, you must write code that compares each field individually. If a record doesn't have many fields, this isn't too cumbersome. For the reading list record, you would write something like this:

```
DECLARE
   first_book summer.reading_list_rt := summer.must_read;
   second_book summer.reading_list_rt := summer.wifes_favorite;
BEGIN
   IF first_book.favorite_author = second_book.favorite_author
      AND
      first_book.title = second_book.title
      AND
      first_book.finish_by = second_book.finish_by
   THEN
      lots_to_talk_about;
   END IF;
END;
```

There is one complication to keep in mind. If your requirements indicate that two NULL records are equal (equally NULL), you will have to modify each comparison to something like this:

```
(first_book.favorite_author  = second_book.favorite_author
   OR( first_book.favorite_author IS NULL AND
       second_book.favorite_author IS NULL)
```

Any way you look at it, this is pretty tedious coding. Wouldn't it be great if we could generate code to do this for us? In fact, it's not all that difficult to do precisely that—

at least if the records you want to compare are defined with %ROWTYPE against a table or view. In this case, you can obtain the names of all fields from the ALL_TAB_COLUMNS data dictionary view and then format the appropriate code out to the screen or to a file.

Better yet, you don't have to figure all that out yourself. Instead, you can download and run the "records equal" generator designed by Dan Spencer; you will find his package on the O'Reilly web site in the *gen_record_comparison.pkg* file.

Collections in PL/SQL

A *collection* is a datatype that offers a way to store singly dimensioned arrays in PL/SQL. Great. So what does that mean? You will use collections to create lists of related information, either in your PL/SQL program or in the column of a database table. Here are some of the ways we've found collections handy:

- Emulate bidirectional or random-access cursors. PL/SQL only allows you to fetch forward through a cursor's result set. But if I load the result set of a cursor into a collection, I can move back and forth through that set, and can instantly (and repetitively) access any particular row in the set.
- Improve performance of lookups by storing lists of subordinate information directly in the column of a table (as a nested table or VARRAY), rather than normalizing that data into a separate relational table. (Nested tables, VARRAYs, and associative arrays are collection types described in the upcoming section "Types of Collections.")
- Keep track of data elements selected in a program for special processing.
- Cache database information that is static and frequently queried to speed up performance of those queries.

In the following sections we'll show how to create and use collection types both in the database and in PL/SQL programs, and show the syntax for creating collection types. We'll present the three different initialization techniques with additional examples, and review the built-in "methods," such as NEXT, DELETE, and TRIM, for managing collection content. Although we can't cover every aspect of SQL's use of collections (for example, as columns in tables), the examples will give you a sense of how important—and useful—these new devices can be, despite their complexity.

A Simple Collection Example

Collections are much more complex in structure and syntax than scalar variables such as dates and numbers. Let's take a look at a very simple example, and then use that to explore some of the concepts and terminology associated with collections. Take a look at the following code.

```
1   DECLARE
2      TYPE list_of_dates_t IS TABLE OF DATE;
3
4      TYPE list_of_names_t IS TABLE OF VARCHAR2 (100)
5         INDEX BY BINARY_INTEGER;
6
7      birthdays      list_of_dates_t
8                           := list_of_dates_t ();
9      happyfamily    list_of_names_t;
10  BEGIN
11     birthdays.EXTEND;
12     birthdays (1) := '23-SEP-1958';
13     birthdays.EXTEND;
14     birthdays (2) := '01-OCT-1986';
15
16     happyfamily (-15070) := 'Steven';
17     happyfamily (88) := 'Veva';
18     happyfamily (909) := 'Chris';
19     happyfamily (2020202020) :='Eli';
20
21     DBMS_OUTPUT.put_line (birthdays.COUNT);
22     DBMS_OUTPUT.put_line (happyfamily.FIRST);
23  END;
```

Here is the output from running this script:

```
   2
-15070
```

The following table steps through the code and draws out some concepts and definitions:

Line(s)	Description
2–5	Declarations of types of collections. To work with a collection (list), you must first define its type and then declare specific collections from those types. You see here two different collection types: a nested table type on line 2 and an associative array type on lines 4–5.
7–8	Actual declaration of a nested table. Notice that you must also initialize the nested table by calling a constructor, a function with the same name as the TYPE that is automatically provided by PL/SQL.
9	Declaration of an associative array. No constructor is needed for these types of collections.
11–14	I define two rows in the nested table with a standard assignment operator. Notice, however, that I must explicitly extend or make room for those rows. If I do not extend first, an assignment like this will raise an error. Notice also that I populate the rows in the birthdays nested table sequentially.
16–19	I populate the happyfamily collection with four names. I do not have to extend with associative arrays; simply by assigning a value to a row number, I conjure that row into existence. Notice that I did not add rows sequentially. In fact, I chose my row numbers randomly, using both positive and negative numbers. This is an example of a sparse collection.
21	I take advantage of the collection method called COUNT to obtain the number of rows defined in my birthdays nested table.
22	Finally, I use the collection method FIRST to obtain the first or lowest row number in use in my happyfamily collection.

Types of Collections

Oracle supports three different types of collections:

Associative arrays
: These are singly dimensioned, unbounded, sparse collections of homogeneous elements that are available only in PL/SQL. They were called *PL/SQL tables* in PL/SQL 2 and *index-by tables* in Oracle8 and Oracle8*i* (because when you declare such a collection, you explicitly state that they are "indexed by" the row number). And now, in Oracle9*i*, the name has changed to *associative arrays*. The motivation for the name change is that in Oracle9*i*, the INDEX BY syntax can be used to "associate" or index contents by VARCHAR2 or PLS_INTEGER.

Nested tables
: These are also singly dimensioned, unbounded collections of homogeneous elements. They are initially dense but can become sparse through deletions. Nested tables can be defined in both PL/SQL and the database (for example, as a column in a table).

VARRAYs
: Like the other two collection types, VARRAYs (variable-sized arrays) are also singly dimensioned collections of homogeneous elements. However, they are always bounded and never sparse. Like nested tables, they can be used in PL/SQL and in the database. Unlike nested tables, when you store and retrieve a VARRAY, its element order is preserved.

Glossary of Collection Terms

The following glossary should help you understand and absorb collections more smoothly.

Collection
: A term that can have several different meanings:

  - A nested table, associative array, or VARRAY datatype
  - A PL/SQL variable of type nested table, associative array, or VARRAY
  - A table column of type nested table or VARRAY

  Regardless of the particular type or usage, however, a collection is a list of items.

One-dimensional or single-dimensional
: Essentially, a collection has just a single column of information in each row, and is in this way similar to a one-dimensional array. You cannot define a collection so that it can be referenced as follows:

  ```
  my_table (10, 44)
  ```

  This is a two-dimensional structure and not currently supported.

Homogeneous elements

A collection can have only a single column, and that column must have a datatype declared when the collection TYPE is defined. Thus, all rows in a collection contain values of the same datatype and the collection is, therefore, homogeneous. This datatype can, however, be a composite or complex datatype itself; you can declare a table of records, for example. And with Oracle9*i*, you can define multilevel collections. This kind of collection has, as its column datatype, another collection or a record that contains a collection.

Unbounded versus bounded

A collection is said to be *bounded* if there are predetermined limits to the possible values for row numbers in that collection. It is *unbounded* if there are no upper or lower limits on those row numbers. VARRAYs or variable-sized arrays are always bounded; when you define them, you specify the maximum number of rows allowed in that collection (the first row number is always 1). Nested tables and associative arrays are only theoretically bounded. We describe them as unbounded, because from a theoretical standpoint there is no limit to the number of rows you can define in them.

The theoretical limits of an associative array are:

Lowest value: $-2^{31} + 1$
Highest value: $2^{31} - 1$

The theoretical limits of a nested table are:

Lowest value: 1
Highest value: $2^{31} - 1$

This means that you can define up to approximately 4.3 billion rows in an associative array, and about 2.14 billion rows in a nested table. This is only a theoretical bound, because you will run out of real memory in your computer before you use that many rows. We therefore say that associative arrays and nested tables are unbounded.

Sparse versus dense

A collection (or array or list) is called *dense* if all rows between the first and last row are defined and given a value (including NULL). A collection is considered *sparse* if rows do not have to be defined and populated sequentially; there can be gaps between defined rows, as demonstrated in the previous example. VARRAYs are always dense. Nested tables always start as dense collections, but can be made sparse. Associative arrays can be sparse or dense, depending on how you fill the collection.

Sparseness, it turns out, is a very valuable feature, as it gives you the flexibility to populate rows in a collection using a primary key or other intelligent key data as the row number. By doing so, you can define an order on the data in a collection or greatly enhance the performance of lookups.

Indexed by integers
: All collections support the ability to reference a row via the row number, an integer value. The associative array TYPE declaration makes that explicit, but the same rule holds true for the other collection types.

Indexed by strings
: In Oracle9*i* Release 2, Oracle makes it possible to index an associative array by string values instead of by numeric row numbers. This feature is not available for nested tables or VARRAYs.

Outer table
: This refers to the "enclosing" table in which you have used a nested table or VARRAY as a column's datatype.

Inner table
: This is the "enclosed" collection that is implemented as a column in a table; also known as a "nested table column."

Store table
: This is the physical table that Oracle creates to hold values of the inner table (a nested table column).

Making Sense of Collections

We have noticed over the years that relatively few developers know about and use collections. This always comes as a surprise, because we have found them to be so handy. One challenge is that collections are relatively complicated. Three different types of collections, multiple steps involved in defining and using them, usage in both PL/SQL programs and database objects, more complex syntax than simply working with individual variables: all of these factors conspire to limit usage of collections.

We have organized this chapter so that we can be comprehensive in our treatment of collections, avoid redundancy in treatment of similar topics across different collection types, and offer guidance in your usage of collections. The resulting chapter is rather long. Here is a quick guide to the remainder of its contents:

Declaring collection types and collections
: First, we start by showing you how to declare different types (or templates) of collections, along with the syntax to instantiate specific collections from those types.

Collection built-ins
: Next, we explore the many built-in functions or methods that Oracle provides to help you examine and manipulate the contents of a collection.

Working with collections
: Now it is time to build on all those "preliminaries" to explore some of the nuances of working with collections, including the initialization process

necessary for nested tables and VARRAYs, different ways to populate and access collection data, and so on.

We then finish up the chapter with (a) a look at collection "pseudo-functions" designed to let us manipulate collections as relational tables, and vice versa; and (b) some details on how to maintain collections in the database and choose the most appropriate collection type.

Declaring Collection Types and Collections

Before you can work with a collection, you must declare it. When you declare a collection, it must be based on a collection type. So the first thing you must learn to do is define a collection type.

There are two different ways of creating user-defined collection types:

- You can define a nested table type or VARRAY type "in the database" using the CREATE TYPE command. This makes the datatype available to use for a variety of purposes: columns in database tables, variables in PL/SQL programs, and attributes of object types.
- You can declare the collection type within a PL/SQL program using TYPE...IS... syntax. This collection type will then be available only for use within the block in which the TYPE is defined.

Declaring an Associative Array

As with a record, an associative array is declared in two stages:

1. Define a particular associative array structure (made up of strings, dates, etc.) using the TYPE statement. The result of this statement is a datatype you can use in declaration statements.
2. Declare the actual collection based on that table type. The declaration of an associative array is a specific instance of a generic datatype.

Defining the table TYPE

The TYPE statement for an associative array has the following format:

```
TYPE table_type_name IS TABLE OF datatype [ NOT NULL ]
   INDEX BY [ BINARY_INTEGER | VARCHAR2 (size_limit)];
```

where *table_type_name* is the name of the table structure you are creating, and *datatype* is the datatype of the single column in the table. You can optionally specify that the table be NOT NULL, meaning that every row in the table must have a value.

Prior to Oracle9*i* Release 2, the only way you could specify an index for an associative array (a.k.a., index-by table) was:

```
INDEX BY BINARY_INTEGER
```

With Oracle9*i* Release 2, you can now also specify:

```
INDEX BY VARCHAR2 (size_limit)
```

The rules for the table type name are the same as for any identifier in PL/SQL: the name can be up to 30 characters in length, it must start with a letter, and it can include some special characters such as underscore (_) and dollar sign ($). (This feature is explored later in the section "Using VARCHAR2 Associative Arrays".)

The datatype of the table type's column can be any of the following:

Scalar datatype
: Any PL/SQL-supported scalar datatype, such as VARCHAR2, CLOB, POSITIVE, DATE, or BOOLEAN.

Anchored datatype
: A datatype inferred from a column, previously defined variable, or cursor expression using the %TYPE attribute.

Here are some examples of associative array type declarations:

```
TYPE company_keys_tabtype IS TABLE OF company.company_id%TYPE NOT NULL
   INDEX BY BINARY_INTEGER;

TYPE booklist_tabtype IS TABLE OF books%ROWTYPE
   INDEX BY BINARY_INTEGER;

TYPE books_by_author_tabtype IS TABLE OF books%ROWTYPE
   INDEX BY VARCHAR2(100);
```

Declaring the collection

Once you have created your table type, you can reference that table type to declare the actual collection. The general format for a collection declaration is:

```
collection_name table_type;
```

where *collection_name* is the name of the collection and *table_type* is the name of a previously declared table type. In the following example I create a general table type for primary keys from the company and employee tables, and then use that table type to create two collections of primary keys:

```
CREATE OR REPLACE PACKAGE company_pkg
IS
   /* Create a generic table type for primary keys */
   TYPE primary_keys_tabtype IS TABLE OF NUMBER NOT NULL
      INDEX BY BINARY_INTEGER;

   /* Declare two tables based on this table type */
   company_keys_tab primary_keys_tabtype;
   emp_keys_tab primary_keys_tabtype;

END company_pkg;
```

Declaring a Nested Table or VARRAY

As with associative arrays, you must define a type before you can declare an actual nested table or VARRAY. You can define these types either in the database or in a PL/SQL block.

To create a nested table datatype that lives in the database (and not just your PL/SQL code), specify:

```
CREATE [ OR REPLACE ] TYPE type_name AS | IS
   TABLE OF element_datatype [ NOT NULL ];
```

To create a VARRAY datatype that lives in the database (and not just your PL/SQL code), specify:

```
CREATE [ OR REPLACE ] TYPE type_name AS | IS
   VARRAY (max_elements) OF element_datatype [ NOT NULL ];
```

To drop a type, specify:

```
DROP TYPE type_name [ FORCE ];
```

To declare a nested table datatype in PL/SQL, use the declaration:

```
TYPE type_name IS TABLE OF element_datatype [ NOT NULL ];
```

To declare a VARRAY datatype in PL/SQL, use the declaration:

```
TYPE type_name IS VARRAY (max_elements)
   OF element_datatype [ NOT NULL ];
```

where:

OR REPLACE
: Allows you to rebuild an existing type as long as there are no other database objects that depend on it. This is useful primarily because it preserves grants.

type_name
: Is a legal SQL or PL/SQL identifier. This will be the identifier to which you refer later when you use it to declare variables or columns.

element_datatype
: Is the type of the collection's elements. All elements are of a single type, which can be most scalar datatypes, an object type, or a REF object type. If the elements are objects, the object type itself cannot have an attribute that is a collection. In PL/SQL, if you are creating a collection with RECORD elements, its fields can be only scalars or objects. Explicitly disallowed collection datatypes are BOOLEAN, NCHAR, NCLOB, NVARCHAR2, REF CURSOR, TABLE, and VARRAY (non-SQL datatype).

NOT NULL
: Indicates that a variable of this type cannot have any null elements. However, the collection can be atomically null (uninitialized).

max_elements
: Is the maximum number of elements allowed in the VARRAY. Once declared, this cannot be altered.

FORCE
: Tells Oracle to drop the type even if there is a reference to it in another type. For example, if an object type definition uses a particular collection type, you can still drop the collection type using the FORCE keyword.

Note that the only syntactic difference between declaring nested table types and declaring associative array types in a PL/SQL program is the absence of the INDEX BY clause for nested table types.

The syntactic differences between nested table and VARRAY type declarations are:

- The use of the keyword VARRAY
- The limit on VARRAY's number of elements

Examples of declaring nested tables and VARRAYs

Here are some examples of declaring nested tables in PL/SQL. First, I create a nested table type in the database:

```
CREATE OR REPLACE TYPE Color_tab_t AS TABLE OF VARCHAR2(30);
```

Next, I declare some PL/SQL variables. There is no reason you must use only types that you have created in the database. You can also declare them locally, or mix and match from both sources:

```
DECLARE
   -- A variable that will hold a list of available font colors
   font_colors Color_tab_t;

   /* The next variable will later hold a temporary copy of
   || font_colors. Note that we can use %TYPE to refer to the
   || datatype of font_colors. This illustrates two different
   || ways of declaring variables of the Color_tab_t type.
   */
   font_colors_save font_colors%TYPE;

   -- Variable to hold a list of paint colors
   paint_mixture Color_array_t;

   /* As with Oracle7 index-by tables, you can define
   || a table datatype here within a declaration section...
   */
   TYPE Number_t IS TABLE OF NUMBER;

   /* ...and then you can use your new type in the declaration
   || of a local variable. The next line declares and initializes
   || in a single statement. Notice the use of the constructor,
   || Number_t(value, value, ...), to the right of the ":="
   */
```

```
    my_favorite_numbers Number_t := Number_t(42, 65536);

    /* Or you can just refer to the Color_tab_t datatype in the
    || data dictionary. This next line declares a local variable
    || my_favorite_colors to be a "nested" table and initializes it
    || with two initial elements using the default constructor.
    */
    my_favorite_colors Color_tab_t := Color_tab_t('PURPLE', 'GREEN');

END;
```

This code also illustrates default constructors (special functions Oracle provides whenever you create a type) that serve to initialize and/or populate their respective types. A constructor has the same name as the type, and accepts as arguments a comma-separated list of elements. See the section "Initializing Collection Variables" for more information.

Where Collections Can Be Used

The following sections describe the different places in your code where a collection can be declared and used. Because a collection type can be defined in the database itself (nested tables and VARRAYs only), you can find collections not only in PL/SQL programs, but also inside tables and object types.

Collections as Components of a Record

Using a collection type in a record is similar to using any other type. You can use VARRAYs, nested tables, associative arrays, or any combination thereof in RECORD datatypes. For example:

```
DECLARE
   TYPE toy_rec_t IS RECORD (
      manufacturer INTEGER,
      shipping_weight_kg NUMBER,
      domestic_colors Color_array_t,
      international_colors Color_tab_t
   );
```

RECORD types cannot live in the database; they are available only within PL/SQL programs. Logically, however, you can achieve a similar result by using *object types* in place of RECORD types. Briefly, object types can have a variety of attributes; you can include the two new collection types as attributes within objects; you can also define a collection whose elements are themselves objects. For a complete discussion of object types, see Chapter 21.

Collections as Program Parameters

Collections can also serve as module parameters. In this case, you cannot return a user-defined type that is declared in the module itself. You will instead use types that you have built outside the scope of the module, either via CREATE TYPE or via public declaration in a package. The following function provides a pseudo "UNION ALL" operation on two input parameters of type Color_tab_t. That is, it creates an OUT parameter that is the superset of the colors of the two input parameters. The full implementation of this function may be found in the *make_colors_superset.sp* file on the O'Reilly site.

```
CREATE PROCEDURE make_colors_superset (first_colors IN Color_tab_t,
   second_colors IN Color_tab_t, superset OUT Color_tab_t)
```

And here is an example of how you would call such a program:

```
DECLARE
   my_colors    Color_tab_t;
   your_colors  Color_tab_t;
   our_colors   Color_tab_t;
BEGIN
   make_colors_superset (
      my_colors,
      your_colors,
      our_colors
     );
END;
```

Check out the later section "Passing Associative Arrays as Parameters" for details.

Collections as Datatypes of a Function's Return Value

In the next example, we have defined Color_tab_t as the type of a function return value, and also used it as the datatype of a local variable. The same restriction about scope applies to this usage—types must be declared outside the module's scope.

```
CREATE FUNCTION true_colors (whose_id IN NUMBER) RETURN Color_tab_t
AS
   l_colors Color_tab_t;
BEGIN
   SELECT favorite_colors INTO l_colors
     FROM personality_inventory
    WHERE person_id = whose_id;
   RETURN l_colors;
EXCEPTION
   WHEN NO_DATA_FOUND
   THEN
      RETURN NULL;
END;
```

This example also illustrates a long-awaited feature: the retrieval of a complex data item in a single fetch. This is so cool that it bears repeating, so we'll talk more about it later in this chapter.

How would you use this function in a PL/SQL program? Because it acts in the place of a variable of type Color_tab_t, you can do one of two things with the returned data:

1. Assign the entire result to a collection variable
2. Assign a single element of the result to a variable (as long as the variable is of a type compatible with the collection's elements)

Option one is easy. Notice, by the way, that this is another circumstance where you don't have to initialize the collection variable explicitly:

```
DECLARE
   color_array Color_tab_t;
BEGIN
   color_array := true_colors (8041);
END;
```

With option two, we actually give the function call a subscript. The general form is:

```
variable_of_element_type := function ( ) (subscript);
```

Or, in the case of the true_colors function:

```
DECLARE
   one_of_my_favorite_colors VARCHAR2(30);
BEGIN
   one_of_my_favorite_colors := true_colors (whose_id=>8041) (1);
END;
```

Note that this code has a small problem: if there is no record in the database table where person_id is 8041, the attempt to read its first element will raise a COLLECTION_IS_NULL exception. We should trap and deal with this exception in a way that makes sense to the application.

In the previous example, I've used named parameter notation (whose_id=>) for readability, although it is not strictly required. (See Chapter 16 for more details.)

Collection as "Columns" in a Database Table

Using a nested table or VARRAY, you can store and retrieve nonatomic data in a single column of a table. For example, the employee table used by the HR department could store the date of birth for each employee's dependents in a single column, as shown in Table 11-1.

Table 11-1. Storing a column of dependents as a collection in a table of employees

Id (NUMBER)	Name (VARCHAR2)	Dependents_ages (Dependent_birthdate_t)
10010	Zaphod Beeblebrox	12-JAN-1763 4-JUL-1977 22-MAR-2021
10020	Molly Squiggly	15-NOV-1968 15-NOV-1968

Table 11-1. Storing a column of dependents as a collection in a table of employees (continued)

Id (NUMBER)	Name (VARCHAR2)	Dependents_ages (Dependent_birthdate_t)
10030	Joseph Josephs	
10040	Cepheus Usrbin	27-JUN-1995 9-AUG-1996 19-JUN-1997
10050	Deirdre Quattlebaum	21-SEP-1997

It's not terribly difficult to create such a table. First we define the collection type:

```
CREATE TYPE Dependent_birthdate_t AS VARRAY(10) OF DATE;
```

Now we can use it in the table definition:

```
CREATE TABLE employees (
   id NUMBER,
   name VARCHAR2(50),
   ...other columns...,
   Dependents_ages Dependent_birthdate_t
);
```

We can populate this table using the following INSERT syntax, which relies on the type's default constructor to transform a list of dates into values of the proper datatype:

```
INSERT INTO employees VALUES (42, 'Zaphod Beeblebrox', ...,
   Dependent_birthdate_t( '12-JAN-1765', '4-JUL-1977', '22-MAR-2021'));
```

Now let's look at an example of a nested table datatype as a column. When we create the outer table personality_inventory, we must tell Oracle what we want to call the "store table:"

```
CREATE TABLE personality_inventory (
   person_id NUMBER,
   favorite_colors Color_tab_t,
   date_tested DATE,
   test_results BLOB)
NESTED TABLE favorite_colors STORE AS favorite_colors_st;
```

The NESTED TABLE...STORE AS clause tells Oracle that we want the store table for the favorite_colors column to be called favorite_colors_st. There is no preset limit on how large this store table, which is located "out of line" (or separate from the rest of that row's data to accommodate growth) can grow.

You cannot directly manipulate data in the store table, and any attempt to retrieve or store data directly into favorite_colors_st will generate an error. The only path by which you can read or write the store table's attributes is via the outer table. (See the later section called "Collection Pseudo-Functions" for a few examples of doing so.) You cannot even specify storage parameters for the store table; it inherits the physical attributes of its outermost table.

One chief difference between nested tables and VARRAYs surfaces when we use them as column datatypes. Although using a VARRAY as a column's datatype can achieve much the same result as a nested table, VARRAY data must be predeclared to be of a maximum size, and is actually stored "inline" with the rest of the table's data. For this reason, Oracle Corporation says that VARRAY columns are intended for "small" arrays, and that nested tables are appropriate for "large" arrays.

Collections as Attributes of an Object Type

In this example, we are modeling automobile specifications. Each Auto_spec_t object will include a list of manufacturer's colors in which you can purchase the vehicle.

```
CREATE TYPE Auto_spec_t AS OBJECT (
   make VARCHAR2(30),
   model VARCHAR2(30),
   available_colors Color_tab_t
);
```

Because there is no data storage required for the object type, it is not necessary to designate a name for the companion table at the time we issue the CREATE TYPE... AS OBJECT statement.

When the time comes to implement the type as, say, an object table, you could do this:

```
CREATE TABLE auto_specs OF Auto_spec_t
   NESTED TABLE available_colors STORE AS available_colors_st;
```

This statement requires a bit of explanation. When you create a "table of objects," Oracle looks at the object type definition to determine what columns you want. When it discovers that one of the object type's attributes, available_colors, is in fact a nested table, Oracle treats this table as it did in earlier examples; in other words, it wants to know what to name the store table. So the phrase:

```
...NESTED TABLE available_colors STORE AS available_colors_st
```

says that you want the available_colors column to have a store table named available_colors_st.

See Chapter 21 for more information about Oracle object types.

Collection Built-Ins (Methods)

PL/SQL offers a number of built-in functions and procedures, known as *collection methods*, that let you obtain information about and modify the contents of collections. Here is the complete list of these programs:

Method (function or procedure)	Description
COUNT function	Returns the current number of elements in a collection.
DELETE procedure	Removes one or more elements from the "middle" of a nested table. Reduces COUNT if the element is not already DELETEd. Can be used for VARRAYS, but only to delete the entire contents of the collection.
EXISTS function	Returns TRUE or FALSE to indicate whether the specified element exists.
EXTEND procedure	Increases the number of elements in a collection. Increases COUNT. Does not apply to associative arrays.
FIRST, LAST functions	Return the smallest (FIRST) and largest (LAST) subscripts in use.
LIMIT function	Returns the maximum number of allowed elements in a VARRAY.
PRIOR, NEXT functions	Return the subscript immediately before (PRIOR) or after (NEXT) a specified subscript. You should always use PRIOR and NEXT to traverse a collection, especially if you are working with sparse (or potentially sparse) collections.
TRIM procedure	Removes collection elements at the "end" of the collection. Reduces COUNT if elements are not DELETEd.

These programs are referred to as "methods" because the syntax for using the collection built-ins is different from the normal syntax used to call procedures and functions. Collection methods employ a "member method" syntax that's common in object-oriented languages such as C++.

To give you a feel for member-method syntax, consider the LAST function. It returns the greatest index value in use in the associative array. Using standard function syntax, you might expect to call LAST as follows:

```
IF LAST (company_table) > 10 THEN ... /* Invalid syntax */
```

In other words, you would pass the associative array as an argument. In contrast, by using the member-method syntax, the LAST function is a method that "belongs to" the object—in this case, the associative array. So the correct syntax for using LAST is:

```
IF company_table.LAST > 10 THEN ... /* Correct syntax */
```

The general syntax for calling these associative array built-ins is either of the following:

- An operation that takes no arguments:

  ```
  table_name.operation
  ```

- An operation that takes a row index for an argument:

  ```
  table_name.operation(index_number [, index_number])
  ```

The following statement, for example, returns TRUE if the 15th row of the company_tab associative array is defined:

```
company_tab.EXISTS(15)
```

The collection methods are not available from within SQL; they can be used only in PL/SQL programs.

The COUNT Method

Use COUNT to compute the number of elements defined in an associative array, nested table, or VARRAY. If elements have been DELETEd or TRIMmed from the collection, they are not included in COUNT.

The specification for COUNT is:

```
FUNCTION COUNT RETURN PLS_INTEGER;
```

Let's look at an example. Before I do anything with my collection, I verify that it contains some information:

```
DECLARE
  volunteer_list volunteer_list_ar := volunteer_list_ar('Steven');
BEGIN
   IF volunteer_list.COUNT > 0
   THEN
      assign_tasks (volunteer_list);
   END IF;
END;
```

Boundary considerations

If COUNT is applied to an initialized collection with no elements, it returns zero. It also returns zero if it's applied to an empty associative array.

Exceptions possible

If COUNT is applied to an uninitialized nested table or a VARRAY, it raises the COLLECTION_IS_NULL predefined exception. Note that this exception is not possible for associative arrays, which do not require initialization.

The DELETE Method

Use DELETE to remove one, some, or all elements of an associative array, nested table, or VARRAY. DELETE without arguments removes all of the elements of a collection. DELETE(*i*) removes the *i*th element from the nested table or associative array. DELETE(*i,j*) removes all elements in an inclusive range beginning with *i* and ending with *j*. When you use parameters, DELETE actually keeps a placeholder for the "removed" element, and you can later reassign a value to that element.

In physical terms, PL/SQL actually releases the memory only when your program deletes a sufficient number of elements to free an entire page of memory (unless you DELETE all the elements, which frees all the memory immediately). This de-allocation happens automatically and requires no accommodations or devices in your code.

When DELETE is applied to VARRAYs, you can issue DELETE only without arguments (i.e., remove all rows). In other words, you cannot delete individual rows of a VARRAY, possibly making it sparse. The only way to remove a row from a VARRAY is to TRIM from the end of the collection.

The overloaded specification for this method is as follows:

```
PROCEDURE DELETE;
PROCEDURE DELETE (i PLS_INTEGER);
PROCEDURE DELETE (i PLS_INTEGER, j PLS_INTEGER);
```

The following procedure removes everything but the last element in the collection. It actually makes use of four collection methods: FIRST, to obtain the first defined row; LAST, to obtain the last defined row; PRIOR, to determine the next-to-last row; and DELETE to remove all but the last.

```
CREATE PROCEDURE keep_last (the_list IN OUT List_t)
AS
   first_elt PLS_INTEGER := the_list.FIRST;
   next_to_last_elt PLS_INTEGER := the_list.PRIOR(the_list.LAST);
BEGIN
   the_list.DELETE(first_elt, next_to_last_elt);
END;
```

Here are some additional examples:

- Delete all the rows from the names table:

  ```
  names.DELETE;
  ```

- Delete the 77th row from the globals table:

  ```
  globals.DELETE (77);
  ```

- Delete all the rows in the temperature readings table between the 0th row and the –15,000th row, inclusively:

  ```
  temp_readings.DELETE (-15000, 0);
  ```

Boundary considerations

If *i* and/or *j* refer to nonexistent elements, DELETE attempts to "do the right thing" and will not raise an exception. For example, if you have three elements in a TABLE item and DELETE(-5,1), the first element will be deleted. However, DELETE(-5) will do nothing.

Exceptions possible

If DELETE is applied to an uninitialized nested table or a VARRAY, it raises the COLLECTION_ IS_NULL predefined exception.

The EXISTS Method

Use the EXISTS method with nested tables, associative arrays, and VARRAYs to determine if the specified row exists within the collection. It returns TRUE if the element exists, FALSE otherwise. It never returns NULL. If you have used TRIM or DELETE to remove a row that existed previously, EXISTS for that row number returns FALSE.

The specification of this method is:

```
FUNCTION EXISTS (i IN PLS_INTEGER) RETURN BOOLEAN;
```

In the following block, I check to see if my row exists, and if so I set it to NULL.

```
DECLARE
   my_list Color_tab_t := Color_tab_t();
   element INTEGER := 1;
BEGIN
   ...
   IF my_list.EXISTS(element)
   THEN
     my_list(element) := NULL;
   END IF;
END;
```

Boundary considerations

If EXISTS is applied to an uninitialized (atomically null) nested table or a VARRAY, or an initialized collection with no elements, it simply returns FALSE. You can use EXISTS beyond the COUNT without raising an exception.

Exceptions possible

If *i* is not an integer and cannot be converted to an integer, EXISTS will raise the VALUE_ERROR exception. This exception is possible for any collection method that accepts an argument.

The EXTEND Method

Adding an element to a nested table or VARRAY requires a separate allocation step. Making a "slot" in memory for a collection element is independent from assigning a value to it. If you haven't initialized the collection with a sufficient number of elements (null or otherwise), you must first use the EXTEND procedure on the variable. Do not use EXTEND with associative arrays.

EXTEND appends element(s) to a collection. EXTEND with no arguments appends a single null element. EXTEND(*n*) appends *n* null elements. EXTEND(*n*,*i*) appends *n* elements and sets each to the same value as the *i*th element; this form of EXTEND is required for collections with NOT NULL elements.

Here is the overloaded specification of EXTEND:

```
PROCEDURE EXTEND (n PLS_INTEGER:=1);
PROCEDURE EXTEND (n PLS_INTEGER, i PLS_INTEGER);
```

In the following example, the push procedure extends my list by a single row and populates it:

```
CREATE PROCEDURE push (the_list IN OUT List_t, new_value IN VARCHAR2)
AS
BEGIN
   the_list.EXTEND;
   the_list(the_list.LAST) := new_value;
END;
```

I can also use EXTEND to add 10 new rows to my list, all with the same value. First I extend a single row and populate explicitly. Then I extend again, this time by 9 rows, and specify the row number with new_value as the initial value for all my new rows.

```
CREATE PROCEDURE push_ten (the_list IN OUT List_t, new_value IN VARCHAR2)
AS
   l_copyfrom PLS_INTEGER;
BEGIN
   the_list.EXTEND;
   l_copyfrom := the_list.LAST;
   the_list(l_copyfrom) := new_value;
   the_list.EXTEND (9, l_copyfrom);
END;
```

Boundary considerations

If you have DELETEd or TRIMmed from the end of a collection, EXTEND will "jump over" (skip) the deleted elements when it assigns a new index. If *n* is null, EXTEND will do nothing.

Exceptions possible

If EXTEND is applied to an uninitialized nested table or a VARRAY, it raises the COLLECTION_IS_NULL predefined exception. An attempt to EXTEND a VARRAY beyond its declared limit raises the SUBSCRIPT_BEYOND_LIMIT exception.

The FIRST and LAST Methods

Use the FIRST and LAST methods with nested tables, associative arrays, and VARRAYs to return, respectively, the lowest and highest index in use in the collection. The specifications for these functions are:

```
FUNCTION FIRST RETURN PLS_INTEGER;
FUNCTION LAST RETURN PLS_INTEGER;
```

For example, the following code scans from the start to the end of my collection:

```
FOR indx IN holidays.FIRST .. holidays.LAST
LOOP
   send_everyone_home (indx);
END LOOP;
```

Please remember that this kind of loop will only work (i.e., not raise a NO_DATA_FOUND exception) if the collection is densely populated.

In the next example, I use LAST to concisely specify that I want to add a row onto the end of an associative array. I use a cursor FOR loop to transfer data from the database to an associative array of records. When the first record is fetched, the companies collection is empty, so the LAST operator will return NULL. I then use NVL to produce a starting row of 1.

```
FOR company_rec IN company_cur
LOOP
   companies (NVL (companies.LAST, 0) + 1).company_id :=
      company_rec.company_id;
END LOOP;
```

Boundary considerations

FIRST and LAST return NULL when they are applied to initialized collections that have no elements. For VARRAYs, which have at least one element, FIRST is always 1, and LAST is always equal to COUNT.

Exceptions possible

If FIRST and LAST are applied to an uninitialized nested table or a VARRAY, they raise the COLLECTION_ IS_NULL predefined exception.

The LIMIT Method

Use the LIMIT method to determine the maximum number of elements that can be defined in a VARRAY. This function will return NULL if it is applied to nested tables or to associative arrays. The specification for LIMIT is:

```
FUNCTION LIMIT RETURN PLS_INTEGER;
```

The following conditional expression makes sure that there is still room in my VARRAY before extending:

```
IF my_list.LAST < my_list.LIMIT
THEN
   my_list.EXTEND;
END IF;
```

Boundary considerations

There are no boundary considerations for LIMIT.

Exceptions possible

If LIMIT is applied to an uninitialized nested table or a VARRAY, it raises the COLLECTION_ IS_NULL predefined exception.

The PRIOR and NEXT Methods

Use the PRIOR and NEXT methods with nested tables, associative arrays, and VARRAYs to navigate through the contents of a collection. The specifications for these functions are:

```
FUNCTION PRIOR (i PLS_INTEGER) RETURN PLS_INTEGER;
FUNCTION NEXT (i PLS_INTEGER) RETURN PLS_INTEGER;
```

PRIOR returns the next-lower index in use relative to *i*; NEXT returns the next higher. In the following example, this function returns the sum of elements in a List_t collection of numbers:

```
CREATE FUNCTION compute_sum (the_list IN List_t) RETURN NUMBER
AS
   row_index PLS_INTEGER := the_list.FIRST;
   total NUMBER := 0;
BEGIN
   LOOP
      EXIT WHEN row_index IS NULL;
      total := total + the_list(row_index);
      row_index := the_list.NEXT(row_index);
   END LOOP;
   RETURN total;
END;
```

Here is that same program working from the last to the very first defined row in the collection:

```
CREATE FUNCTION compute_sum (the_list IN List_t) RETURN NUMBER
AS
   row_index PLS_INTEGER := the_list.LAST;
   total NUMBER := 0;
BEGIN
   LOOP
      EXIT WHEN row_index IS NULL;
      total := total + the_list(row_index);
      row_index := the_list.PRIOR(row_index);
   END LOOP;
   RETURN total;
END;
```

In this case, it doesn't matter which direction you move through the collection. In other programs, though, it can make a big difference.

Boundary considerations

If PRIOR and NEXT are applied to initialized collections that have no elements, they return NULL. If *i* is greater than or equal to COUNT, NEXT returns NULL; if *i* is less than or equal to FIRST, PRIOR returns NULL.

Currently, if the collection has elements, and *i* is greater than COUNT, PRIOR returns LAST; if *i* is less than FIRST, NEXT returns FIRST. However, do not rely on this behavior in future Oracle versions.

Exceptions possible

If PRIOR and NEXT are applied to an uninitialized nested table or a VARRAY, they raise the COLLECTION_IS_NULL predefined exception.

The TRIM Method

Use TRIM to remove *n* elements from the end of a nested table or VARRAY. Without arguments, TRIM removes exactly one element. As we've already mentioned, confusing behavior occurs if you combine DELETE and TRIM actions on a collection; for example, if an element that you are trimming has previously been DELETEd, TRIM "repeats" the deletion but counts this as part of *n*, meaning that you may be TRIMming fewer actual elements than you think.

Attempting to TRIM an associative array will produce a compile-time error.

The specification for TRIM is:

```
PROCEDURE TRIM (n PLS_INTEGER:=1);
```

The following function pops the last value off of a list and returns it to the invoking block. The "pop" action is implemented by trimming the collection by a single row after extracting the value.

```
CREATE FUNCTION pop (the_list IN OUT List_t) RETURN VARCHAR2
AS
   l_value VARCHAR2(30);
BEGIN
   IF the_list.COUNT >= 1
   THEN
      /* Save the value of the last element in the collection
      || so it can be returned
      */
      l_value := the_list(the_list.LAST);
      the_list.TRIM;
   END IF;
```

```
    RETURN l_value;
END;
```

Boundary considerations

If *n* is null, TRIM will do nothing.

Exceptions possible

The TRIM method will raise the SUBSCRIPT_BEYOND_COUNT predefined exception if you attempt to TRIM more elements than actually exist. If TRIM is applied to an uninitialized nested table or a VARRAY, it raises the COLLECTION_IS_NULL predefined exception.

If you use TRIM and DELETE on the same collection, you can get some very surprising results. Consider this scenario: if you DELETE an element at the end of a nested table variable and then do a TRIM on the same variable, how many elements have you removed? You might think that you have removed two elements, but, in fact, you have removed only one. The placeholder that is left by DELETE is what TRIM acts upon. To avoid confusion, Oracle Corporation recommends using either DELETE or TRIM, but not both, on a given collection.

Working with Collections

By now, you have learned how to define a TYPE of collection, whether in the database or in your code base. You also know how to declare collections based on those types. Now let's examine the kind of code you need to write to actually work with those collections. There are three main programming tasks you need to understand:

- How to properly initialize the collection variable
- How to assign values to elements without raising exceptions
- How to add and remove "slots" for elements

In addition, to fully exploit the programming utility of collections, you need to learn how to retrieve and store sets of data with them. This leads into our section on pseudo-functions, which allow you to perform magic tricks with collections. (OK, maybe it's not real magic, but you're almost guaranteed to say "How did they do that?" the first time you try to program this stuff.)

Initializing Collection Variables

With an associative array datatype, initialization is a nonissue. Simply declaring an associative array variable initializes it in an "empty" state. Then you can just assign values to subscripted table elements as you desire. Index values (subscripts) can be almost any positive or negative integer. A program can even assign subscripts to associative arrays arbitrarily, skipping huge ranges of subscripts without paying a memory or performance penalty.* So if you are working with associative arrays, you can skip to the next section on assigning elements to a collection.

The allocation scheme for nested tables and VARRAYs is different from that of associative arrays. First of all, if you don't initialize a collection of those types, it will be atomically null, and any attempt to read or write an element of an atomically null collection will generate a runtime error. For example:

```
DECLARE
   /* The variable cool_colors is not initialized in its
   || declaration; it is "atomically null."
   */
   cool_colors Color_tab_t;
BEGIN
   IF cool_colors IS NULL THEN          -- valid; will be TRUE
      ...
   IF cool_colors(1) IS NULL THEN       -- exception raised
      ...
   cool_colors(1) := 'BLUE';            -- exception raised
```

You must initialize the collection before using it. There are three ways you can initialize a collection:

- Explicitly, using a constructor
- Implicitly, via a direct assignment of another collection variable
- Implicitly, via a fetch from the database

There is no requirement that you initialize any particular number of elements in a collection. Zero, one, or more are fine, and you can always add more values later. In particular, don't be confused by VARRAYs. Just because you specify a limit on the number of elements it can hold does not imply that you have to put that many elements in when you initialize it.

Initializing explicitly with a constructor

Earlier, we saw declarations that looked like this:

```
my_favorite_colors Color_tab_t := Color_tab_t('PURPLE', 'GREEN');
my_favorite_numbers Number_t := Number_t(42, 65536);
```

Color_tab_t() is the constructor function supplied by Oracle when we created the Color_tab_t collection type. This function accepts an arbitrary number of arguments, as long as each argument is of the "proper" datatype—which in this case is VARCHAR2(30), because our original type definition statement was the following:

```
CREATE TYPE Color_tab_t AS TABLE OF VARCHAR2(30);
```

* This sparseness makes it possible to use an associative array as an in-memory representation of almost any database table that uses an integer primary key.

At initialization, Oracle allocates to the variable an amount of memory necessary to hold the values you supply as arguments. Initialization both creates and populates the "slots" for the elements.

So, if I want to fix the earlier invalid example, I can simply initialize the variable:

```
DECLARE
   cool_colors Color_tab_t := Color_tab_t('VIOLET');  -- initialize
BEGIN
   IF cool_colors(1) IS NULL THEN    -- This is OK now!
```

What do you suppose Oracle does with the following initialization?

```
working_colors Color_tab_t := Color_tab_t();
```

This is a way of creating an empty collection. "Empty" is a kind of enigmatic state in which the collection is not atomically null but still has no data. Whenever you create such an empty collection, you'll need to "extend" the collection variable later when you want to put elements into it. (See the discussion of the EXTEND method earlier in this chapter.)

Initializing implicitly during direct assignment

You can copy the entire contents of one collection to another as long as both are built from the exact same datatype. When you do so, initialization comes along "for free."

Here's an example illustrating the implicit initialization that occurs when we assign wedding_colors to be the value of earth_colors.

```
DECLARE
   earth_colors Color_tab_t := Color_tab_t('BRICK', 'RUST', 'DIRT');
   wedding_colors Color_tab_t;
BEGIN
   wedding_colors := earth_colors;
   wedding_colors(3) := 'CANVAS';
END;
```

This code initializes wedding_colors and creates three elements that match those in earth_colors. These are independent variables rather than pointers to identical values; changing the third element of wedding_colors to CANVAS does not have any effect on the third element of earth_colors.

Note that assignment is not possible when datatypes are merely "type-compatible." Even if you have created two different types with the exact same definition, the fact that they have different names makes them different types.

Initializing implicitly via fetch

If you use a collection as a type in a database table, Oracle provides some very elegant ways of moving the collection between PL/SQL and the table. As with direct assignment, when you use FETCH or SELECT INTO to retrieve a collection and drop it into a collection variable, you get automatic initialization of the variable. Collections can turn out to be incredibly useful!

Although we mentioned this briefly in an earlier example, let's take a closer look at how you can read an entire collection in a single fetch. First, we want to create a table containing a collection and populate it with a couple of values:

```
CREATE TABLE color_models (
   model_type VARCHAR2(12),
   colors Color_tab_t)
NESTED TABLE colors STORE AS color_model_colors_tab;

INSERT INTO color_models
   VALUES ('RGB', Color_tab_t('RED','GREEN','BLUE'));
```

Now we can show off the neat integration features. With one trip to the database we can retrieve all the values of the colors column for a given row, and deposit them into a local variable:

```
DECLARE
   l_colors Color_tab_t;
BEGIN
   /* Retrieve all the nested values in a single fetch.
   || This is the cool part.
   */
   SELECT colors INTO l_colors FROM color_models
      WHERE model_type = 'RGB';
   ...
END;
```

Pretty neat, huh? Here are a few important things to notice:

- Oracle, not the programmer, assigns the subscripts of l_colors when fetched from the database.
- Oracle's assigned subscripts begin with 1 (as opposed to 0, as in some other languages) and increment by 1.
- Fetching satisfies the requirement to initialize the local collection variable before assigning values to elements. We didn't initialize l_colors with a constructor, but PL/SQL knew how to deal with it.

You can also make changes to the contents of the nested table and just as easily move the data back into a database table. Just to be mischievous, let's create a Fuschia-Green-Blue color model:

```
DECLARE
   color_tab Color_tab_t;
BEGIN
   SELECT colors INTO color_tab FROM color_models
      WHERE model_type = 'RGB';
   FOR element IN 1..color_tab.COUNT
   LOOP
      IF color_tab(element) = 'RED'
```

```
      THEN
         color_tab(element) := 'FUSCHIA';
      END IF;
   END LOOP;
   /* Here is the cool part of this example. Only one insert
   || statement is needed -- it sends the entire nested table
   || back into the color_models table in the database.
   */
   INSERT INTO color_models VALUES ('FGB', color_tab);
END;
```

VARRAY integration

Does this database-to-PL/SQL integration work for VARRAYs too? You bet, although there are a couple of differences.

First of all, realize that when you store and retrieve the contents of a nested table in the database, Oracle makes no promises about preserving the order of the elements. This makes sense, because the server is just putting the nested data into a store table behind the scenes, and we all know that relational databases don't give two hoots about row order. By contrast, storing and retrieving the contents of a VARRAY *do* preserve the order of the elements.

Preserving the order of VARRAY elements is a fairly useful capability. It makes it possible to embed meaning in the order of the data, which is something you cannot do in a pure relational database. For example, if you want to store someone's favorite colors in rank order, you can do it with a single VARRAY column. Every time you retrieve the column collection, its elements will be in the same order as when you last stored it. In contrast, abiding by a pure relational model, you would need two columns, one for an integer corresponding to the rank, and one for the color.

This order-preservation of VARRAYs suggests some possibilities for interesting utility functions. For example, you could fairly easily code a tool that would allow the insertion of a new "favorite" at the low end of the list by "shifting up" all the other elements.

A second difference between integration of nested tables and integration of VARRAYs with the database is that some SELECT statements you could use to fetch the contents of a nested table will have to be modified if you want to fetch a VARRAY. (See the "Collection Pseudo-Functions" section later for some examples.)

Assigning Values to Elements

You can assign values to rows in a collection with the standard assignment operator of PL/SQL, as shown here:

```
countdown_test_list (43) := 'Internal pressure';
company_names_table (last_name_row+10) := 'Johnstone Clingers';
```

You can also perform an "aggregate assignment" of the contents of an entire collection to another collection of similar type. Here is an example of such a transfer:

```
DECLARE
   TYPE name_table IS TABLE OF VARCHAR2(100) INDEX BY BINARY_INTEGER;
   old_names name_table;
   new_names name_table;
BEGIN
   /* Assign values to old_names table */
   old_names(1) := 'Smith';
   old_names(2) := 'Harrison';

   /* Assign values to new_names table */
   new_names(111) := 'Hanrahan';
   new_names(342) := 'Blimey';

   /* Transfer values from new to old */
   old_names := new_names;

   /* This assignment will raise NO_DATA_FOUND */
   DBMS_OUTPUT.PUT_LINE (old_names (1));
END;
```

A collection-level assignment completely replaces the previously defined rows in the collection. In the preceding example, rows 1 and 2 in old_names are defined before the last, aggregate assignment.

After the assignment, only rows 111 and 342 in the old_names collection have values. As a result (and as explained in the following discussion), if I try to then reference the contents of row 1 in old_names, PL/SQL will raise a NO_DATA_FOUND exception.

If you are working with associative arrays, you can assign a value (of the appropriate type) to any valid row number in the collection (a row number must be between $-2^{31} + 1$ and $2^{31} - 1$). The simple act of assigning the value creates the row and deposits the value in that row.

In contrast to associative arrays, you can't assign values to arbitrarily numbered subscripts of nested tables and VARRAYs; instead, the indexes (at least initially) are monotonically increasing integers, assigned by the PL/SQL engine. That is, if you initialize *n* elements, they will have subscripts 1 through *n*—and those are the only rows to which you can assign a value.

Before you try to assign a value to a row in a nested table or VARRAY, you must make sure that it has been extended to include or initialize that row. Use the EXTEND operator, discussed later in this chapter, to make new rows available in nested tables and VARRAYs.

Referencing an Undefined Row

Rows in collections exist only if:

- You assign a value to a row in an associative array. The mere act of assignment creates that row.
- You explicitly extend a VARRAY or nested table, creating the row. Once created, you can assign a value to that row.

If you attempt to reference a row (either to set or read its value), PL/SQL will raise one of three exceptions, as illustrated by the following code:

```
CREATE TYPE strings_nt IS TABLE OF VARCHAR2 (100);
```

```
DECLARE
   TYPE strings_ibt IS TABLE OF VARCHAR2 (100)
      INDEX BY BINARY_INTEGER;

   strings   strings_nt := strings_nt ();
   ibt_strings strings_ibt;
BEGIN
     BEGIN
        IF ibt_strings(2) = 'a' THEN NULL; END IF;
    EXCEPTION
    WHEN OTHERS
       THEN DBMS_OUTPUT.put_line (   'a. ' || SQLERRM);
    END;
    BEGIN
       strings.EXTEND; strings (2) := 'b';
    EXCEPTION
       WHEN OTHERS
          THEN DBMS_OUTPUT.put_line (   'b. ' || SQLERRM);
    END;

   BEGIN
       strings (0) := 'c';
    EXCEPTION
    WHEN OTHERS
       THEN DBMS_OUTPUT.put_line (   'c. ' || SQLERRM);
    END;
 END;
```

Here is the output when this script is run:

```
a. ORA-01403: no data found
b. ORA-06533: Subscript beyond count
c. ORA-06532: Subscript outside of limit
```

The following table provides an explanation of the code.

Line	Description
9	I try to read the second row in an associative array that has no rows defined in it (it was just declared three lines previously). So PL/SQL raises the NO_DATA_FOUND exception.
15	I extend a single row, but then try to assign a value to the second row of a nested table. I have not, however, extended twice, so that subscript is invalid and "beyond count."
22	I try to assign a value to row 0 of the nested table, and that is a definite no-no. It is not a valid row number, either for nested tables or for VARRAYs (though it is fine for associative arrays).

Working with Collections of Composites

When Oracle first made collections available in PL/SQL 2 (corresponding to Oracle7), you were able to create associative arrays of scalar values: dates, numbers, strings, and so on. But that was about it, making collections (back then called "PL/SQL tables") awkward and of limited use.

But that was long ago. Now, depending on the version of Oracle you are using, collections support much more complex data structures:

Collections of records (Oracle 7.3.4 and above)
: You can define and manipulate collections of records (as long as those records do not contain as fields other records or collections).

Collections of object type instances, etc. (Oracle8 and above)
: You can define collections of object type instances (a.k.a. "objects"), records, LOBs, XML datatypes, and all other noncollection datatypes.

Collections of collections (Oracle9i and above)
: You can define multilevel collections, including collections of collections and collections of datatypes that contain, as an attribute or a field, another collection.

Let's take a look at examples of each of these variations.

Collections of records

You define a collection of records by specifying a record type (through either %ROWTYPE or a programmer-defined record type) in the TABLE OF clause of the collection definition. This technique applies only to collection TYPEs that are declared inside a PL/SQL program. Nested table and VARRAY TYPEs defined in the database cannot reference %ROWTYPE record structures.

Here is an example of a collection of records based on a custom record TYPE:

```
CREATE OR REPLACE PACKAGE compensation_pkg
IS
   TYPE reward_rt IS RECORD (
      nm VARCHAR2(2000),
      sal NUMBER,
      comm NUMBER
   );
```

```
   TYPE reward_tt IS TABLE OF reward_rt
      INDEX BY BINARY_INTEGER
   END compensation_pkg;
```

With these types defined in my package specification, I can now declare collections in other programs like this:

```
DECLARE
   holiday_bonuses compensation_pkg.reward_tt ;
```

Collections of records come in especially handy when you want to create in-memory (PGA) collections that have the same structure (and, at least in part, data) as database tables. Why would I want to do this? Suppose that I am running a batch process on Sunday at 3 AM against tables that are only modified during the week. I need to do some intensive analysis that involves multiple passes against the tables' data. I could simply query the data repetitively from the database, but that is a relatively slow, intensive process.

Alternately, I can copy the data from the table or tables into a collection and then move much more rapidly (and randomly) through my result set. I am, in essence, emulating bidirectional cursors in my PL/SQL code. Let's first look at a very simple example of moving data from a table to a collection. I will then provide a comprehensive prototype of emulation of a bidirectional cursor.

It actually takes very little code to transfer data from a table—or any query, in fact—to a collection.

```
DECLARE
   CURSOR hairstyles_cur IS
      SELECT * FROM hairstyles;
   TYPE local_hairstyles_tab IS TABLE OF hairstyles_cur%ROWTYPE
      INDEX BY BINARY_INTEGER;
   local_hairstyles local_hairstyles_tab;
BEGIN
   FOR hairstyles_rec IN hairstyles_cur
   LOOP
      local_hairstyles (hairstyles_rec.code) := hairstyles_rec;
   END LOOP;
END;
```

In this case, I am using the hairstyles code, which is an integer value, as the row number for the hairstyle information. This is an example of filling an associative array nonsequentially. Why would I do this? Because now if I have the hairstyle code (which could come from another program or be entered by the user through a screen interface), I can immediately retrieve the hairstyles description without doing another lookup from the database.

So that's the basic idea. Now let's take a look at emulating a bidirectional cursor. In this case, I want to read my data just once from the database and then be able to move back and forth through my dataset without any more roundtrips to the SGA. There are two basic approaches I can take:

- Embed all of the collection code in my main program
- Create a separate package to encapsulate access to the data in the collection

I generally choose the second approach for most situations. In other words, I find it useful to create separate, well-defined, and highly reusable APIs to complex data structures and logic. Here is the package specification for my bidirectional cursor emulator:

```
/* File on web: bidir.pkg */
CREATE OR REPLACE PACKAGE bidir
IS
   FUNCTION rowforid (id_in IN employee.employee_id%TYPE)
      RETURN employee%ROWTYPE;

   FUNCTION firstrow RETURN PLS_INTEGER;
   FUNCTION lastrow RETURN PLS_INTEGER;

   FUNCTION rowCount RETURN PLS_INTEGER;

   FUNCTION end_of_data RETURN BOOLEAN;

   PROCEDURE setrow (nth IN PLS_INTEGER);

   FUNCTION currrow RETURN employee%ROWTYPE;

   PROCEDURE nextrow;
   PROCEDURE prevrow;
END;
```

So how do you use this API? Here is an example of a program using this API to read through the result set for the employee table, first forward and then backward:

```
DECLARE
   l_employee   employee%ROWTYPE;
BEGIN
   LOOP
      EXIT WHEN bidir.end_of_data;
      l_employee := bidir.currrow;
      DBMS_OUTPUT.put_line (l_employee.last_name);
      bidir.nextrow;
   END LOOP;

   bidir.setrow (bidir.lastrow);

   LOOP
      EXIT WHEN bidir.end_of_data;
      l_employee := bidir.currrow;
      DBMS_OUTPUT.put_line (l_employee.last_name);
      bidir.prevrow;
   END LOOP;
END;
```

An astute reader will now be asking: when is the collection loaded up with the data? Or even better: where is the collection? There is no evidence of a collection anywhere in the code I have presented.

Let's take the second question first. The reason you don't see the collection is that I have hidden it behind my package specification. A user of the package never touches the collection and doesn't have to know anything about it. That is the whole point of the API. You just call one or another of the programs that will do all the work of traversing the collection (data set) for you.

Now, when and how is the collection loaded? This may seem a bit magical until you read about packages in Chapter 17. If you look in the package body, you will find that it has an initialization section as follows:

```
BEGIN -- Package initialization
   FOR rec IN  (SELECT * FROM employee)
   LOOP
      employees (rec.employee_id) := rec;
   END LOOP;

   g_currrow := firstrow;
END;
```

Note that g_currrow is defined in the package body and therefore was not listed in the specification above.

This means that the very first time I reference any element in the package specification, this code is run automatically, transferring the contents of the employee table to my employees collection. When does that happen in my sample program shown earlier? Inside my loop, when I call the bidir.end_of_data function to see if I am done looking through my data set!

I encourage you to examine the package implementation. The code is very basic and easy to understand; the benefits of this approach can be dramatic.

Collections of other complex datatypes

There is nothing special about defining and using collections of any of the newer datatypes, but it can be a little off-putting if you don't have much experience with these datatypes. Here is an example of a collection of objects:

```
/* File on web: object_collection.sql */
CREATE TYPE pet_t IS OBJECT (
   tag_no   INTEGER,
   name     VARCHAR2 (60),
   MEMBER FUNCTION set_tag_no (new_tag_no IN INTEGER)
      RETURN pet_t));

DECLARE
```

```
   TYPE pets_t IS TABLE OF pet_t;

   pets   pets_t :=
     pets_t (pet_t (1050, 'Sammy'), pet_t (1075, 'Mercury'));
BEGIN
   FOR indx IN pets.FIRST .. pets.LAST
   LOOP
      DBMS_OUTPUT.put_line (pets (indx).name);
      pets(indx).set_tag_no (indx);
   END LOOP;
END;
```

Once I have my object type defined, I can declare a collection based on that type and then populate it with instances of those object types. You can just as easily declare collections of LOBs, XMLTypes, and so on. All the normal rules that apply to variables of those datatypes also apply to individual rows of a collection of that datatype.

Multilevel collections

In Oracle9*i* you can now nest collections within collections—also referred to as support for *multilevel collections*. Let's take a look at an example and then discuss how you can use this feature in your applications.

Suppose that I want to build a system to maintain information about my pets. Besides their standard information, such as breed, name, and so on, I would like to keep track of their visits to the veterinarian. So I create a vet visit object type:

```
CREATE TYPE vet_visit_t IS OBJECT (
   visit_date  DATE,
   reason      VARCHAR2 (100)
   );
```

Notice that objects instantiated from this type are not associated with a pet (i.e., a foreign key to a pet table or object). You will soon see why I don't need to do that. Now I create a nested table of vet visits (we are supposed to go at least once a year):

```
CREATE TYPE vet_visits_t IS TABLE OF vet_visit_t
```

With these data structures defined, I now declare my object type to maintain information about my pets:

```
CREATE TYPE pet_t IS OBJECT (
   tag_no   INTEGER,
   name     VARCHAR2 (60),
   petcare vet_visits_t,
   MEMBER FUNCTION set_tag_no (new_tag_no IN INTEGER) RETURN pet_t)
   NOT FINAL;
```

This object type has three attributes and one member method. Any object instantiated from this type will have associated with it a tag number, name, and a list of visits to the vet. You can also modify the tag number for that pet by calling the set_tag_no program. Finally, I have declared this object type to be NOT FINAL so that I can extend this generic pet object type, taking advantage of Oracle9*i*'s support for object type inheritance. (I might, for example, define a dog subtype of the generic pet supertype. See Chapter 21 for more details.)

So I have now declared an object type that contains as an attribute a nested table. I don't need a separate database table to keep track of these veterinarian visits; they are a part of my object.

Now let's take advantage of the new multilevel collections features of Oracle9*i*. In the following example, lines 1–10 define a multilevel collection; once the collection is populated, lines 11–14 access the collection.

```
   /* File on web: multilevel_collections.sql */
 1 DECLARE
 2    TYPE bunch_of_pets_t IS TABLE OF pet_t INDEX BY BINARY_INTEGER;
 3    my_pets   bunch_of_pets_t;
 4 BEGIN
 5    my_pets (1) :=
 6          pet_t (100, 'Mercury',
 7             vet_visits_t (
 8                vet_visit_t ('01-Jan-2001', 'Clip wings'),
 9                vet_visit_t ('01-Apr-2002', 'Check cholesterol'))
10          );
11    DBMS_OUTPUT.PUT_LINE (my_pets (1).name);
12    DBMS_OUTPUT.PUT_LINE (my_pets (1).petcare (2).reason);
13    DBMS_OUTPUT.put_line (my_pets.COUNT);
14    DBMS_OUTPUT.put_line (my_pets(1).petcare.LAST);
15 END;
```

The output from running this script is:

```
Mercury
Check cholesterol
1
2
```

The following table explains what's going on in the code:

Line(s)	Description
2–3	I declare a local associative array TYPE, in which each row contains a single pet object. I then declare a collection to keep track of my "bunch of pets."
5–10	I assign an object of type pet_t to the first row in this associative array. As you can see, the syntax required when working with nested, complex objects of this sort can be quite intimidating. So let's parse the various steps required. To instantiate an object of type pet_t, I must provide a tag number, a name, and a list of vet visits, which is a nested table. To provide a nested table of type vet_visits_t, I must call the associated constructor (of the same name). I can either provide a null or empty list, or initialize the nested table with some values. I do this in lines 8 and 9. Each row in the vet_visits_t collection is an object of type vet_visit_t, so again I must use the object constructor and pass in a value for each attribute (date and reason for visit).
11	I display the value of the name attribute of the pet object in row 1 of the my_pets associative array.
12	I display the value of the reason attribute of the vet visit object in row 2 of the nested table, which in turn resides in the first row of the my_pets associative array. That's a mouthful, and it is a "line-full" of code.
13–14	I demonstrate how you can use the collection methods (in this case, COUNT and LAST) on both outer and nested collections.

In this example we have the good fortune to be working with collections that, at each level, actually have names: the my_pets associative array and the petcare nested table. This is not always the case, as is illustrated in the next example.

Unnamed nested collections

Suppose I need to build an application to maintain nicknames for people across different languages. In fact, for starters, I need to support four languages and three different sources for nicknames, as I capture in my package with named constants:

```
/* File on web: multilevel_collections2.sql */
CREATE OR REPLACE PACKAGE nicknames
IS
   french           CONSTANT PLS_INTEGER := 1005;
   american_english CONSTANT PLS_INTEGER := 1013;
   german           CONSTANT PLS_INTEGER := 2005;
   arabic           CONSTANT PLS_INTEGER := 3107;

   from_family       CONSTANT PLS_INTEGER := 88;
   from_friends      CONSTANT PLS_INTEGER := 99;
   from_colleagues   CONSTANT PLS_INTEGER := 111;
```

To support all of these nicknames elegantly, I create two types of multilevel collections, as shown in the next section of my package:

```
CREATE OR REPLACE PACKAGE nicknames
IS
   ...
   TYPE strings_t IS TABLE OF VARCHAR2 (30)
      INDEX BY BINARY_INTEGER;

   TYPE nickname_set_t IS TABLE OF strings_t
      INDEX BY BINARY_INTEGER;

   TYPE multiple_sets_t IS TABLE OF nickname_set_t
      INDEX BY BINARY_INTEGER;
```

A collection based on nickname_set_t has for each of its rows a collection of strings, which will be nicknames. One row will contain family nicknames, another will contain nicknames bestowed upon the person by her colleagues, and so on. A collection based on multiple_sets_t has for each of its rows a set of nicknames. One row will contain English nicknames, another French nicknames, and so on. Notice that the single column of each of the nickname_set_t and multiple_sets_t types is nameless, defined only by its datatype.

This package also contains a series of translation functions (to_French, to_German, to_Arabic). Each function accepts a set of nicknames in English and returns a translated set of nicknames in a collection of the same type. Here is one of the headers:

```
FUNCTION to_french (nicknames_in IN nickname_set_t)
   RETURN nickname_set_t;
```

Great! With the nicknames package compiled, I can then utilize all of that functionality. The following program demonstrates the use of multilevel collections with anonymous columns:

```
CREATE OR REPLACE PROCEDURE set_steven_nicknames
IS
   steven_nicknames       nicknames.nickname_set_t;
   universal_nicknames    nicknames.multiple_sets_t;
BEGIN
   steven_nicknames (99) (1000) := 'Steve';
   steven_nicknames
      (nicknames.from_colleagues) (2000) := 'Troublemaker';
   steven_nicknames
      (nicknames.from_colleagues) (3000) := 'All-around Great Guy';
   steven_nicknames
      (nicknames.from_family) (789) := 'Whiner';


   universal_nicknames (nicknames.american_english)
      := steven_nicknames;
   universal_nicknames (nicknames.french) :=
      nicknames.to_french (steven_nicknames);
   universal_nicknames (nicknames.german) :=
      nicknames.to_german (steven_nicknames);
   universal_nicknames (nicknames.arabic) :=
      nicknames.to_arabic (steven_nicknames);

   DBMS_OUTPUT.PUT_LINE (
      universal_nicknames
         (nicknames.american_english)
         (nicknames.from_colleagues)
         (2000));

   DBMS_OUTPUT.PUT_LINE (
      universal_nicknames(1005)(111)(2000));
END;
```

Here is the output from this script (assuming that the translation programs were actually implemented—which they are not!):

```
Troublemaker
Provocateur
```

In the following table, let's step through the code and get comfortable with this sometimes-contorted syntax.

Line(s)	Description
3–4	I define two collections, one to hold all of my nicknames, and another to hold my nicknames in various languages.
6–12	I populate my steven_nicknames collection with three colleague-based nicknames and one family nickname. Line 6 uses all hardcoded literals. Lines 7–12 rely on predefined constants. The actual row numbers holding the strings can be any values. You can see on line 6 the syntax you must use to specify a row within a multilevel, anonymous collection: `steven_nicknames (99) (1000)` With this assignment, I place the string "Steve" into the 1000th row of the collection, which is in turn the 99th row of the nickname set. Because the collections that make up each row in the nickname set collection are anonymous, I simply "string together" subscript indicators.
15–22	Now I move up another level within my collection hierarchy. I have set my nicknames in English, so it is time to translate them to French, German, and Arabic. Once translated, I deposit those collections into the appropriate row in the universal_nicknames collection. I rely again on the predefined constants to make sure I get them right—and to make my code more readable.
24–31	In the final lines of the procedure, I display information from the collection, showing a triple subscripting, first relying on named constants and then showing the syntax explicitly with literal values. `universal_nicknames(1005)(111)(2000))`

Yes, the syntax can get very complicated, especially if you are working with anonymous columns in your collections. You can get around that easily by working with collections of object types or records, in which case each column will have a name (either of the object type attribute or the record's field).

I don't know about you, but when I worked with this kind of complex structure, I found myself wondering how deeply I could nest these multilevel collections. So I decided to find out. I built a small code generator that allows me to pass in the number of levels of nesting. It then constructs a procedure that declares *N* collection TYPEs, each one being a TABLE OF the previous table TYPE. Finally, it assigns a value to the string that is all the way at the heart of the nested collections.

I found that I was able to create a collection of at least 250 nested collections before my computer ran into a memory error! I find it hard to believe that any PL/SQL developer will even come close to that level of complexity. So for all intents and purposes, there is no limit to the nesting of collections supported by Oracle. If you would like to run this same experiment in your own system, check out the *gen_multcoll.sp* file available on the O'Reilly site.

Multilevel collections can be complicated to understand and maintain, but they offer tremendous flexibility and elegance of implementation.

Sequential and Nonsequential Associative Arrays

Associative arrays can be sparse; there is no requirement that you fill and use row 1, then row 2, and so on. This means that you generally have a choice when populating and using an associative array:

Fill it sequentially

Starting from row 0 or 1 (or whatever is appropriate for your code), you add new values to the collection by appending them to the end of the collection. This technique is valuable when the order in which items are added to the list is important.

Fill it non-sequentially

In this case, you use the row number as some kind of "intelligent key," usually the primary key values from a database table. The ability to randomly (i.e., non-sequentially) place values in a table can come in very handy when the primary key value for the table's row is not sequentially derived, but is instead based on data in your application.

Let's look at an example of each of these approaches.

Sequential usage

I want to replace Oracle's TO_DATE function with my own better function. What would make it better? I would like to be able to convert virtually any date represented as a string into a real date, regardless of the format of that string—and without having to make the user provide or hardcode the format.

Here's my idea: I will populate a collection with a variety of date format masks. Then my_to_date will try to convert the string using each of the masks in turn until one of them works. You can see the straightforward code for this function in the following example. In this case, the order in which I place the format masks in my collection affects how the strings are converted. In other words, a string like 04-02-01 can be interpreted as MM-DD-RR or DD-MM-RR. The order of masks in the array decides the matter.

```
/* File on web: mytodate.sf */
CREATE OR REPLACE FUNCTION my_to_date (value_in IN VARCHAR2)
   RETURN DATE
IS
   TYPE mask_t IS TABLE OF VARCHAR2 (30) INDEX BY BINARY_INTEGER;
   fmts            mask_t;

   retval          DATE    := NULL;
   mask_index      INTEGER := 1;
   date_converted  BOOLEAN := FALSE;

   PROCEDURE init_fmts
   IS
   BEGIN
      fmts (1) := 'DD-MON-RR';
      fmts (2) := 'DD-MON-YYYY';
      fmts (3) := 'DD-MON';
      fmts (4) := 'MM/DD';
      ...
   END;
```

```
BEGIN
   init_fmts;

   WHILE  mask_index IS NOT NULL AND NOT date_converted
   LOOP
      BEGIN
         retval := TO_DATE (value_in, fmts (mask_index));
         date_converted := TRUE;
      EXCEPTION
         WHEN OTHERS THEN
            mask_index := fmts.NEXT (mask_index);
            IF mask_index IS NULL THEN RAISE; END IF;
      END;
   END LOOP;

   RETURN retval;
END my_to_date;
```

Nonsequential usage

In many applications, we find ourselves writing and executing the same queries over and over again. In some cases, the queries are retrieving static data, such as codes and descriptions that rarely (if ever) change. Well, if the data isn't changing—especially during a user session—then why would I need to keep querying the information from the database? Even if the data is cached in the System Global Area (SGA), I still need a network roundtrip to find that information in the data buffers and return it to the session program area (the Program Global Area, or PGA).

Here's an idea: set as a rule that for a given static lookup table, a user will never query a row from the table more than once in a session. After the first time, it will be stored in the session's PGA and be instantly available for future requests. This is very easy to do with collections. Essentially, you use the collection's index as an intelligent key.

Let's take a look at an example. I have a hairstyles table that contains a numeric code (primary key) and a description of the hairstyle (e.g., "Pageboy", "Shag"). These styles are timeless and rarely change.

Here is the body of a package that utilizes a collection to cache code-hairstyle pairs and minimizes trips to the database.

```
/* File on web: justonce.sql */
CREATE OR REPLACE PACKAGE BODY justonce
IS
   TYPE desc_t IS TABLE OF hairstyles.description%TYPE
      INDEX BY BINARY_INTEGER;
   descriptions   desc_t;

   FUNCTION description (code_in IN hairstyles.code%TYPE)
      RETURN hairstyles.description%TYPE
   IS
```

```
10        return_value   hairstyles.description%TYPE;
11
12        FUNCTION desc_from_database RETURN hairstyles.description%TYPE
13        IS
14           CURSOR desc_cur IS
15              SELECT description FROM hairstyles WHERE code = code_in;
16           desc_rec   desc_cur%ROWTYPE;
17        BEGIN
18           OPEN desc_cur;
19           FETCH desc_cur INTO desc_rec;
20           RETURN desc_rec.description;
21        END;
22     BEGIN
23        RETURN descriptions (code_in);
24     EXCEPTION
25        WHEN NO_DATA_FOUND THEN
26           descriptions (code_in) := desc_from_database;
27           RETURN descriptions (code_in);
28     END;
29  END justonce;
```

The table provides a description of the interesting aspects of this program:

Line(s)	Description
3–5	Declare a collection type and the collection to hold my cached descriptions.
7–8	Header of my retrieval function. The interesting thing about the header is that it is not interesting at all. There is no indication that this function is doing anything but the typical query against the database to retrieve the description for the code. The implementation is hidden, which is just the way you want it.
12–21	That very traditional query from the database. But in this case it is just a private function within my main function, which is fitting becasue it is not the main attraction.
23	The entire execution section! Simply return the description that is stored in the row indicated by the code number. The first time I run this function for a given code, the row will not be defined. So PL/SQL raises NO_DATA_FOUND (see lines 25–27). For all subsequent requests for this code, however, the row is defined and the function returns the value immediately.
25–27	So the data hasn't yet been queried in this session. Fine. Trap the error, look up the description from the database, and deposit it in the collection. Then return that value. Now we are set to divert all subsequent lookup attempts.

So how much of a difference does this caching make? Using the local Oracle9*i* database on my laptop, I ran some tests and found that it took just under 2 seconds to execute 10,000 queries against the hairstyles table. That's pretty darned fast. Yet it took only .1 second to retrieve that same information 10,000 times using the above function. That's more than an order of magnitude improvement—and that's with a local database. The superiority of the collection caching technique would be even greater in a real-world situation.

Here are some final notes on the collection caching technique:

- This technique is a classic tradeoff between CPU and memory. Each session has its own copy of the collection (this is program data and is stored in the PGA). If you have 10,000 users, the total memory required for these 10,000 small caches could be considerable. You should use this approach only with small, static tables.

- Your static table should have an integer primary key to be used as the row in the collection. If the primary key is concatenated or a string, you could use the DBMS_UTILITY.GET_HASH_VALUE function to produce a hashed value usable as a collection index value. The resulting complexity and overhead would, however, make the technique less attractive.

You can learn more about data caching and its applicability to your requirements in Chapters 17 and 20.

Passing Associative Arrays as Parameters

We've already seen an example of how you can use collections as module parameters. Let's take a look at the one subtlety involved if that collection happens to be an associative array.

A collection TYPE is just another type of data to the PL/SQL engine, so it should come as no surprise that you can pass a collection as a parameter in a procedure or a function. With this approach you can, in a single call, pass all the values in a table into the module. In the following package specification I define two modules that pass PL/SQL tables as parameters. The send_promos procedure sends a promotional mailing to all the companies in my table. The companies_overdue function returns a table filled with the names of companies that have overdue bills.

```
CREATE OR REPLACE PACKAGE company_pkg
IS
   /* Nested table that matches the company table in structure */
   TYPE companies_tabtype IS TABLE OF company%ROWTYPE;

   /* Parameter is a table of company primary keys */
   PROCEDURE send_promos (companies_in IN companies_tabtype);

   /* Function returns a table of company names */
   FUNCTION companies_overdue (overdue_date_in IN DATE)
      RETURN companies_tabtype;
END company_pkg;
```

Now that I have a package containing both the table type and the programs referencing those types, I can call these programs. The only tricky part is remembering that you must declare a collection based on the matching type before you can use any of the programs. This step is shown in the following procedure:

```
CREATE OR REPLACE PROCEDURE send_invoices
IS
   indx PLS_INTEGER;

   /* Declare a nested table based on the packaged type. */
```

```
   companies company_pkg. companies_tabtype;
BEGIN
   companies := company_pkg.companies_overdue (SYSDATE-30);

   indx := companies.FIRST;
   LOOP
      EXIT WHEN indx IS NULL;
      send_invoice (companies(indx).company_id);
      indx := companies.NEXT (indx);
   END LOOP;
END;
```

PL/SQL-to-Server Integration

To provide another demonstration of how collections can ease the burden of transferring data between the server and the PL/SQL application program, let's look at a new example. The main entity in this example is the apartment complex. We use a nested table of objects to hold the list of apartments for each apartment complex.

Each apartment is described by the following attributes:

```
CREATE TYPE Apartment_t AS OBJECT (
   unit_no NUMBER,
   square_feet NUMBER,
   bedrooms NUMBER,
   bathrooms NUMBER,
   rent_in_dollars NUMBER
);
```

We can now define the nested table type that will hold a list of these apartment objects:

```
CREATE TYPE Apartment_tab_t AS TABLE OF Apartment_t;
```

Using this type as the type of a column, here is the definition of our database table:

```
CREATE TABLE apartment_complexes
  (name VARCHAR2(75),
   landlord_name VARCHAR2(45),
   apartments Apartment_tab_t)
NESTED TABLE apartments STORE AS apartments_store_tab;
```

If you're curious, the INSERT statements to populate such a table look like the following (note the use of nested constructors to create the collection of objects):

```
INSERT INTO apartment_complexes VALUES
   ('RIVER OAKS FOUR', 'MR. JOHNSON',
     Apartment_tab_t(
        Apartment_t(1, 780, 2, 1, 975),
        Apartment_t(2, 1200, 3, 2, 1590),
        Apartment_t(3, 690, 1, 1.5, 800),
        Apartment_t(4, 690, 1, 2, 450),
        Apartment_t(5, 870, 2, 2, 990)
     )
   );
```

```
INSERT INTO apartment_complexes VALUES
   ('GALLERIA PLACE', 'MS. DODENHOFF',
     Apartment_tab_t(
        Apartment_t(101, 1000, 3, 2, 1295),
        Apartment_t(102, 800, 2, 1, 995),
        Apartment_t(103, 800, 2, 1, 995),
        Apartment_t(201, 920, 3, 1.5, 1195),
        Apartment_t(202, 920, 3, 1.5, 1195),
        Apartment_t(205, 1000, 3, 2, 1295)
     )
  );
```

Now, at last, we can show off some wonderful features of storing collections in the database.

Imagine that we are the new managers of the River Oaks Four apartments and not nearly as committed to affordable housing as the previous manager. We want to demolish any unit that rents for less than $500 and raise the rent on everything else by 15%.

```
DECLARE
   /* Declare the cursor that will retrieve the collection of
   || apartment objects. Since we know we're going to update the
   || record, we can lock it using FOR UPDATE.
   */
   CURSOR aptcur IS
      SELECT apartments  FROM apartment_complexes
       WHERE name = 'RIVER OAKS FOUR'
         FOR UPDATE OF apartments;

   /* Need a local variable to hold the collection of fetched
   || apartment objects.
   */
   l_apartments apartment_tab_t;
   which INTEGER;
BEGIN
   /* A single fetch is all we need! */
   OPEN aptcur;
   FETCH aptcur INTO l_apartments;
   CLOSE aptcur;

   /* Iterate over the apartment objects in the collection and
   || delete any elements of the nested table that meet the
   || criteria.
   */
   which := l_apartments.FIRST;
   LOOP
      EXIT WHEN which IS NULL;
      IF l_apartments(which).rent_in_dollars < 500
      THEN
         l_apartments.DELETE(which);
      END IF;
      which := l_apartments.NEXT(which);
   END LOOP;
```

```
   /* Now iterate over the remaining apartments and raise the
   || rent. Notice that this code will skip any deleted
   || elements.
   */
   which := l_apartments.FIRST;
   LOOP
      EXIT WHEN which IS NULL;
      l_apartments(which).rent_in_dollars :=
         l_apartments(which).rent_in_dollars * 1.15;
      which := l_apartments.NEXT(which);

   END LOOP;

   /* Finally, ship the entire apartment collection back to the
   || server -- in a single statement!
   */
   UPDATE apartment_complexes
      SET apartments = l_apartments
    WHERE name = 'RIVER OAKS FOUR';

END;
```

To me, one of the most significant aspects of this example is the single-statement fetch (and store). This PL/SQL fragment emulates the creating of a *client-side cache* of data, which is an essential concept in many object-oriented and client/server architectures. Using this kind of approach with collections can reduce network traffic and improve the quality of your code.

Using VARCHAR2 Associative Arrays

In Oracle9*i* Release 2, Oracle has finally "loosened up" on the way we can define and manipulate PL/SQL-specific collections, now called *associative arrays*. Specifically, we can "index by" strings in addition to integer values (i.e., row numbers). This gives us significant additional flexibility. Let's look at some examples and explore applications of this new feature.

Here is a block of code that demonstrates the basics:

```
/* File on web: assoc_array.sql */
DECLARE
   TYPE population_type IS
      TABLE OF NUMBER INDEX BY VARCHAR2(64);
   country_population population_type;
   continent_population population_type;
   howmany NUMBER;
   limit VARCHAR2(64);
BEGIN
   country_population('Greenland') := 100000;
   country_population('Iceland') := 750000;

   howmany := country_population('Greenland');
```

```
    continent_population('Australia') := 30000000;

    continent_population('Antarctica') :=
       1000; -- Creates new entry
    continent_population('Antarctica') := 1001;
       -- Replaces previous value

    limit := continent_population.FIRST;
    DBMS_OUTPUT.PUT_LINE (limit);
    DBMS_OUTPUT.PUT_LINE (continent_population(limit));

    limit := continent_population.LAST;
    DBMS_OUTPUT.PUT_LINE (limit);
    DBMS_OUTPUT.PUT_LINE (continent_population(limit));
END;
```

Here is the output from the script:

```
Antarctica
1001
Australia
30000000
```

Recall that with this type of associative array, the values returned by calls to the FIRST, LAST, PRIOR, and NEXT methods are strings and not numbers. Also note that you cannot use %TYPE to declare the associative array type. You must use a literal, hardcoded declaration.

So why would you want to index by string instead of number? Suppose that you need to do some heavy processing of employee information in your program. You need to go back and forth over the set of selected employees, searching by the employee ID number, last name, and Social Security number (or appropriate national identification number for non-U.S. countries).

```
DECLARE
   TYPE name_t IS TABLE OF employee%ROWTYPE INDEX BY VARCHAR2(100);

   TYPE id_t IS TABLE OF employee%ROWTYPE INDEX BY BINARY_INTEGER;

   by_name   name_t;
   by_ssn    name_t;
   by_id     id_t;

      ceo_name employee.last_name%TYPE := 'ELLISON';

   PROCEDURE load_arrays IS
   BEGIN
      FOR rec IN  (SELECT * FROM employee)
      LOOP
         -- Load up all three arrays in single pass to database table.
         by_name (rec.last_name) := rec;
         by_ssn (rec.ssn) := rec;
         by_id (rec.employee_id) := rec;
      END LOOP;
```

```
   END;
BEGIN
   load_arrays;

   -- Now I can retrieve information by name or ID:

   IF by_name (ceo_name).salary > by_id (7645).salary
   THEN
      make_adjustment (by_name);
   END IF;
END;
```

As you can see in the preceding example, it doesn't take a whole lot of code to build multiple, highly efficient entry points into cached data transferred from a relational table. Still, to make it even easier for you to implement these techniques in your application, I have built a utility, which you will find in the *genaa.sp* file on the O'Reilly site, that will actually generate a package to implement caching for the specified relational table. It populates a collection based on the integer primary key and another collection for each unique index defined on the table (indexed by BINARY_INTEGER or VARCHAR2, depending on the type(s) of the column(s) in the index).

Finally, the file, *summer_reading.pkg*, offers another example of the use of VARCHAR2-indexed associative arrays to manipulate lists of information within a PL/SQL program.

Emulating Alternative Indexes in Collections

Prior to Oracle9*i* Release 2, you could index associative arrays only by BINARY_INTEGER. This means that if I populate a collection with many rows of data about books and I need to find the row that contains a certain title, I must scan the entire collection. This is slow and cumbersome. Is there a better way? One thing you can consider is building your own alternate index into the contents of your collection. The most effective and efficient way to do this is with the Oracle built-in hashing function, DBMS_UTILITY.GET_HASH_VALUE. This function accepts a string and returns an integer value. Ideally, this value is unique for every different string, but in reality there is no way to guarantee this uniqueness. As a result, you must write "conflict resolution" logic in your code.

Sounds intimidating, doesn't it? It is actually fairly straightforward. However, let me note two things:

- A full exploration of such algorithms is a bit outside the scope of this book.
- You don't have to write such an algorithm—I've done it for you already! The *altind.pkg* file on the O'Reilly site shows you exactly how to write this code. It is designed for the manipulation of employee information, but you can easily adapt it to your own needs.

Here is the basic idea. As you populate your main collection with the information you need to manipulate (several times over, in different directions, etc.), you also hash the alternative index value (such as the name of the employee) and use that hash value as the row number in your index collection. So when you are done with your data load, you have filled two collections. Then, when you need to find a row based on a string (employee name), you hash the name to a number, go to that row, get the row number for the main collection, and then grab the desired data. Figure 11-1 provides a graphical representation of these steps.

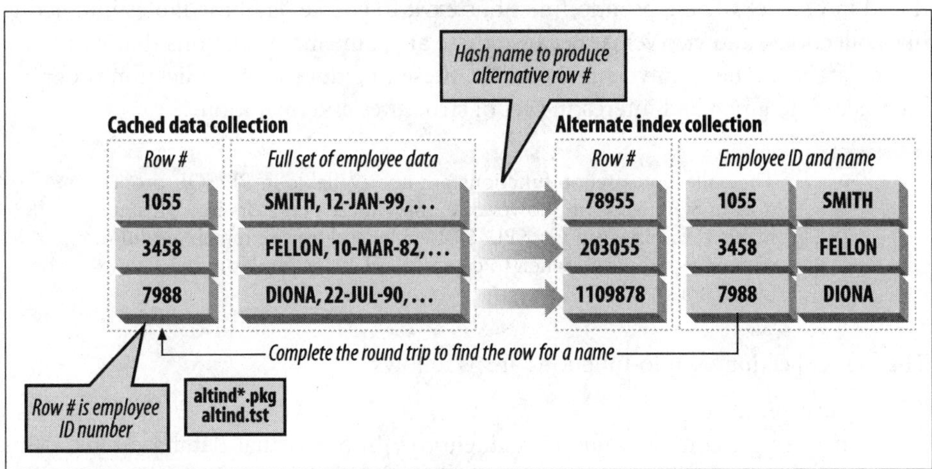

Figure 11-1. Populating and accessing a hash index

It is probably best to set up this data in the initialization section of your package, as I show for altind here:

```
CREATE OR REPLACE PACKAGE BODY altind
IS
   ... body of package ...

   PROCEDURE loadcache IS
   BEGIN
      loadtab.DELETE;
      hashtab.DELETE;

      FOR rec IN ( SELECT * FROM employee)
      LOOP
         loadtab (rec.employee_id) := rec;
         add_to_altind (rec.last_name, rec.employee_id);
      END LOOP;
   END;

BEGIN
   loadcache;
END;
```

For more details about how to apply this technique in your environment, check out the *altind.pkg* file.

Collection Pseudo-Functions

I've been working with Oracle's SQL for more than thirteen years and PL/SQL for more than eight, but my brain has rarely turned as many cartwheels over SQL's semantics as it did when I first contemplated the *collection pseudo-functions* introduced in Oracle8. These pseudo-functions exist to coerce database tables into acting like collections, and vice versa. Because there are some manipulations that work best when data is in one form versus the other, these functions give application programmers access to a rich and interesting set of structures and operations.

The collection pseudo-functions are not available in PL/SQL proper, only in SQL. You can, however, employ these operators in SQL statements that appear in your PL/ SQL code, and it is extremely useful to understand how and when to do so. We'll see examples in the following sections.

The four collection pseudo-functions are as follows:

THE (now deprecated)
: Maps a single column value in a single row into a virtual database table. This pseudo-function allows you to manipulate the elements of a persistent collection.

CAST
: Maps a collection of one type to a collection of another type. This can encompass mapping a VARRAY into a nested table.

MULTISET
: Maps a database table to a collection. With MULTISET and CAST, you can actually retrieve rows from a database table as a collection-typed column.

TABLE
: Maps a collection to a database table. This is the inverse of MULTISET.

Oracle introduced these pseudo-functions in order to manipulate collections that live in the database. They are important to our PL/SQL programs for several reasons, not least of which is that they provide an incredibly efficient way to move data between the database and the application.

Yes, these pseudo-functions can be puzzling. But if you're the kind of person who gets truly excited by arcane code, these SQL extensions introduced in Oracle8 will make you jumping-up-and-down silly.

The THE Pseudo-Function

If you have a column that's a nested table and you want to insert, update, or delete from the contents of this column, you cannot do so with any SQL statement you know from "traditional" SQL. Instead, you will need to use the strangely named keyword THE, which helps tell Oracle which row from the outer table you want to deal with.

The THE function has been replaced in Oracle8*i* and above by the TABLE operator, which is discussed in the next section.

Earlier, we created the color_models table:

```
CREATE TABLE color_models (
   model_type VARCHAR2(12),
   colors Color_tab_t)
NESTED TABLE colors STORE AS color_model_colors_tab;
```

We had inserted a row with model_type='RGB', and a colors column containing ('RED', 'GREEN', 'BLUE'). Imagine now that we've populated color_models with a half dozen or so records. One question that might have come into your mind is: how can we retrieve all of the colors for a single model using a SELECT statement?

```
SELECT VALUE(c) FROM
   THE(SELECT colors FROM color_models
        WHERE model_type = 'RGB') c;
```

OK, you can exhale now. The meaning of this statement is "retrieve the individual elements of the RGB color model." Or, more literally, "retrieve the value of each element of the colors nested table within the color_models outer table." Sure enough, it displays the following:

```
VALUE(C)
------------------------------
RED
GREEN
BLUE
```

I guess it's really not that weird; we're just substituting a subquery for a table in the FROM clause.

Another way you could have expressed the previous query is using the predefined alias COLUMN_VALUE, as shown in the following example. COLUMN_VALUE is a way of referring to elements of a nested table of scalars. It is a syntactic shortcut to achieve the same result as the previous example.

```
SELECT COLUMN_VALUE FROM
   THE(SELECT colors FROM color_models
        WHERE model_type = 'RGB');
```

You can also use a THE subquery as the target of an INSERT, UPDATE, or DELETE statement. Here are some examples:

```
BEGIN
   -- change BLUE to BURGUNDY inside the collection
   UPDATE THE(SELECT colors FROM color_models WHERE model_type = 'RGB')
      SET COLUMN_VALUE = 'BURGUNDY'
    WHERE COLUMN_VALUE = 'BLUE';
   -- add a silly extra color
   INSERT INTO THE (
      SELECT colors FROM color_models WHERE model_type = 'RGB')
      VALUES ('EXTRA-COLOR');
   -- show the current colors
   SELECT COLUMN_VALUE
     FROM THE(SELECT colors FROM color_models WHERE model_type = 'RGB');
   -- delete the extra color
   DELETE THE(SELECT colors FROM color_models WHERE model_type = 'RGB')
    WHERE COLUMN_VALUE = 'EXTRA-COLOR';
END;
```

The TABLE Pseudo-Function

The TABLE operator casts or converts a collection-valued column into something you can SELECT from. It sounds complicated, but this section presents an example that's not too hard to follow.

Looking at it another way, let's say that you have a database table with a column of a collection type. How can you figure out which rows in the table contain a collection that meets certain criteria? That is, how can you select from the database table, putting a WHERE clause on the collection's contents? Wouldn't it be nice if you could just say:

```
SELECT *
  FROM table_name
 WHERE collection_column
       HAS CONTENTS 'whatever';    -- invalid; imaginary syntax!
```

Logically, that's exactly what you can do with the TABLE function. Going back to our color_models database table, how could we get a listing of all color models that contain the color RED? Here's the real way to do it:

```
SELECT *
  FROM color_models c
 WHERE 'RED' IN
       (SELECT * FROM TABLE(c.colors));
```

which, in SQL*Plus, returns:

```
MODEL_TYPE   COLORS
------------ ------------------------------------------------------
RGB          COLOR_TAB_T('RED', 'GREEN', 'BLUE')
```

The query means "go through the color_models table and return all rows whose list of colors contains at least one RED element." Had there been more rows with a RED element in their colors column, these rows too would have appeared in our SQL*Plus result set.

As illustrated above, TABLE accepts an alias-qualified collection column as its argument:

```
TABLE(alias_name.collection_name)
```

TABLE returns the contents of this collection coerced into a virtual database table. Hence, you can SELECT from it. In our example, it's used in a subquery.

Does the TABLE pseudo-function remind you vaguely of the THE pseudo-function? Recall our THE example:

```
SELECT VALUE(c) FROM
   THE(SELECT colors FROM color_models
         WHERE model_type = 'RGB') c;
```

which returns:

```
VALUE(C)
------------------------------
RED
GREEN
BLUE
```

What is the difference between THE and TABLE? Both return something that, for purposes of the rest of the SQL statement, serves as a "virtual database table." So the difference between the functions must lie in that on which they operate—their "inputs." The TABLE function operates on a (column-typed) nested table. In contrast, the pseudo-function THE operates on a SELECT statement's result set that contains exactly one row with one column, which is a (column-typed) nested table.

As it turns out, the TABLE function gets called "under the covers" whenever you use THE as the target of an INSERT, UPDATE, or DELETE statement. This under-the-covers call coerces the results of the subquery into a virtual database table upon which the DML makes sense to operate.

To repeat an earlier admonition, none of the collection pseudo-functions is available from within PL/SQL, but PL/SQL programmers will certainly want to know how to use these gizmos in their SQL statements!

You will also find the pseudo-functions, particularly TABLE, very handy when you are taking advantage of Oracle9*i*'s new table function capability. A table function is a function that returns a collection, and it can be used in the FROM clause of a query. This functionality is explored in Chapter 16.

Personally, I find these new features fascinating, and I enjoy the mental calisthenics required to understand and use them. Maybe mine isn't a universal sentiment, but at least you must admit that Oracle hasn't let its language technology get tired!

The CAST Pseudo-Function

The new THE pseudo-function does not work directly on VARRAYs. It is, however, possible to use the CAST function on a VARRAY so that we can emulate the SELECT statement shown in the previous section.

Casting a named collection

Here is an example of casting a named collection. Suppose that we have created the color_ models table based on a VARRAY type as follows:

```
CREATE TYPE Color_array_t AS VARRAY(16) OF VARCHAR2(30);

CREATE TABLE color_models_a (
   model_type VARCHAR2(12),
   colors Color_array_t);
```

We can CAST the VARRAY colors column as a nested table and apply the pseudo-function THE to the result:

```
SELECT COLUMN_VALUE FROM
   THE(SELECT CAST(colors AS Color_tab_t)
         FROM color_models_a
        WHERE model_type = 'FGB');
```

CAST performs an on-the-fly conversion of the Color_array_t collection type to the Color_tab_t collection type.

A subtle difference exists between what you can accomplish with CAST and what you can accomplish with THE. As we saw in the previous section, THE can serve on either the left-hand side or the right-hand side of an INSERT, UPDATE, or DELETE statement. THE subqueries can be part of either the source or the target of these DML statements. By contrast, CAST works only in SELECTs or on the right-hand side of DML statements.

Casting an unnamed collection

It is also possible to cast a "bunch of records"—such as the result of a subquery—as a particular collection type. Doing so requires the MULTISET function, covered in the next section.

The MULTISET Pseudo-Function

The MULTISET function exists only for use within CASTs. MULTISET allows you to retrieve a set of data and convert it on the fly to a collection type. The simplest form is this:

```
SELECT CAST (MULTISET (SELECT field FROM table) AS collection-type)
   FROM DUAL;
```

So if we happened to have a relational table of colors:

```
CREATE TABLE some_colors (
   color_name VARCHAR2(30),
   color_classification VARCHAR2(30));
```

and we wanted to CAST to a collection so we could fetch a set of them at once, we could do this:

```
DECLARE
   some_hot_colors Color_tab_t;
BEGIN
   SELECT CAST(MULTISET(SELECT color_name
                          FROM some_colors
                         WHERE color_classification = 'HOT')
            AS Color_tab_t)
     INTO some_hot_colors
     FROM DUAL;
END;
```

Another way to use MULTISET involves a correlated subquery in the SELECT list:

```
SELECT outerfield,
  CAST(MULTISET(SELECT field FROM whateverTable
                 WHERE correlationCriteria)
    AS collectionTypeName)
  FROM outerTable;
```

This technique is useful for making joins look as if they include a collection. For example, suppose that we had a detail table that listed, for each bird in our table, the countries where that species lives:

```
CREATE TABLE birds (
   genus VARCHAR2(128),
   species VARCHAR2(128),
   colors Color_array_t,
   PRIMARY KEY (genus, species)
);

CREATE TABLE bird_habitats (
   genus VARCHAR2(128),
   species VARCHAR2(128),
   country VARCHAR2(60),
   FOREIGN KEY (genus, species) REFERENCES birds (genus, species)
);

CREATE TYPE Country_tab_t AS TABLE OF VARCHAR2(60);
```

We should then be able to smush the master and detail tables together in a single SELECT that converts the detail records into a collection type. This feature has enormous significance for client/server programs because the number of roundtrips can be cut down without the overhead of duplicating the master records with each and every detail record:

```
DECLARE
   CURSOR bird_curs IS
```

```
        SELECT b.genus, b.species,
           CAST(MULTISET(SELECT bh.country FROM bird_habitats bh
                          WHERE bh.genus = b.genus
                            AND bh.species = b.species)
             AS country_tab_t)
          FROM birds b;
   bird_row bird_curs%ROWTYPE;
BEGIN
   OPEN bird_curs;
   FETCH bird_curs into bird_row;
   CLOSE bird_curs;
END;
```

As with the CAST pseudo-function, MULTISET cannot serve as the target of an INSERT, UPDATE, or DELETE statement.

Sorting Contents of Collections

One of the wonderful aspects of pseudo-functions is that you can apply SQL operations against the contents of PL/SQL data structures (nested tables and VARRAYs, at least). You can, for example, use ORDER BY to select information from the nested table in the order you desire. Here, I populate a database table with some of my favorite authors:

```
CREATE TYPE names_t AS TABLE OF VARCHAR2 (100);

CREATE TYPE authors_t AS TABLE OF VARCHAR2 (100);

CREATE TABLE favorite_authors (name varchar2(200))

BEGIN
   INSERT INTO favorite_authors VALUES ('Robert Harris');
   INSERT INTO favorite_authors VALUES ('Tom Segev');
   INSERT INTO favorite_authors VALUES ('Toni Morrison');
END;
```

Now I would like to blend this information with data from my PL/SQL program:

```
DECLARE
   scifi_favorites   authors_t
      := authors_t ('Sheri S. Tepper', 'Orson Scott Card', 'Gene Wolfe');
BEGIN
   DBMS_OUTPUT.put_line ('I recommend that you read books by:');

   FOR rec IN  (SELECT column_value favs
                  FROM TABLE (cast (scifi_favorites AS  names_t))
                UNION
                SELECT NAME
                  FROM favorite_authors)
   LOOP
      DBMS_OUTPUT.put_line (rec.favs);
   END LOOP;
END;
```

Notice that I can use UNION to combine data from my database table and collection. I can also apply this technique only to PL/SQL data to sort the contents being retrieved:

```
DECLARE
   scifi_favorites   authors_t
      := authors_t ('Sheri S. Tepper', 'Orson Scott Card', 'Gene Wolfe');
BEGIN
   DBMS_OUTPUT.put_line ('I recommend that you read books by:');

   FOR rec IN  (SELECT column_value favs
                  FROM TABLE (cast (scifi_favorites AS  names_t))
                 ORDER BY column_value)
   LOOP
      DBMS_OUTPUT.put_line (rec.favs);
   END LOOP;
END;
```

Maintaining Collections

Here are some not-so-obvious bits of information that will assist you in using nested tables and VARRAYS. This sort of housekeeping is not necessary or relevant when working with associative arrays.

Privileges

When they live in the database, collection datatypes can be shared by more than one Oracle user (schema). As you can imagine, privileges are involved. Fortunately, it's not complicated; only one Oracle privilege—EXECUTE—applies to collection types.

If you are Scott and you want to grant Joe permission to use Color_tab_t in his programs, all you need to do is grant the EXECUTE privilege to him:

```
GRANT EXECUTE on Color_tab_t TO JOE;
```

Joe can then refer to the type using *schema.type* notation. For example:

```
CREATE TABLE my_stuff_to_paint (
   which_stuff VARCHAR2(512),
   paint_mixture SCOTT.Color_tab_t
)
NESTED TABLE paint_mixture STORE AS paint_mixture_st;
```

EXECUTE privileges are also required by users who need to run PL/SQL anonymous blocks that use the object type. That's one of several reasons that named PL/SQL modules—packages, procedures, functions—are generally preferred. Granting EXECUTE on the module confers the grantor's privileges to the grantee while executing the module.

For tables that include collection columns, the traditional SELECT, INSERT, UDPATE, and DELETE privileges still have meaning, as long as there is no requirement to build a collection for any columns. However, if a user is going to INSERT or

UPDATE the contents of a collection column, that user must have the EXECUTE privilege on the type because that is the only way to use the default constructor.

Collections and the Data Dictionary

There are a few new entries in the data dictionary that will be very helpful in managing your nested table and VARRAY collection types (see Table 11-2). The shorthand dictionary term for user-defined types is simply TYPE. Collection type definitions are found in the USER_SOURCE view (or DBA_SOURCE, or ALL_SOURCE).

Table 11-2. Data dictionary entries for collection types

To answer the question...	Use this view	As in
What collection types have I created?	USER_TYPES	`SELECT type_name FROM user_types WHERE typecode = 'COLLECTION';`
What was the original type definition of collection Foo_t?	USER_SOURCE	`SELECT text FROM user_source WHERE name = 'FOO_T' AND type = 'TYPE' ORDER BY line;`
What columns implement Foo_t?	USER_TAB_COLUMNS	`SELECT table_name, column_name FROM user_tab_columns WHERE data_type = 'FOO_T';`
What database objects are dependent on Foo_t?	USER_DEPENDENCIES	`SELECT name, type FROM user_dependencies WHERE referenced_name = 'FOO_T';`

Choosing a Collection Type

Which collection type makes sense for your application? In some cases, the choice is obvious. In others, there may be several acceptable choices. This section provides some guidance. Table 11-3 illustrates many of the differences between associative arrays, nested tables, and VARRAYs.

As a PL/SQL developer, I find myself leaning toward using associative arrays as a first instinct. Why is this? They involve the least amount of coding. You don't have to initialize or extend them. They have historically been the most efficient collection type (although this distinction will probably fade over time). However, if you want to store your collection within a database table, you cannot use an associative array. The question then becomes: nested table or VARRAY?

Beyond these very high-level determinants, review the following guidelines for additional assistance in making your choice:

- If you intend to store large amounts of persistent data in a column collection, your only option is a nested table. Oracle will then use a separate table behind the scenes to hold the collection data, so you can allow for almost limitless growth.

- If you want to preserve the order of elements stored in the collection column and if your dataset will be small, use a VARRAY. What is "small"? I tend to think in terms of how much data you can fit into a single database block; if you span blocks, you get row chaining, which decreases performance. The database block size is established at database creation time and is typically 2K, 4K, or 8K.
- Here are some other indications that a VARRAY would be appropriate: you don't want to worry about deletions occurring in the middle of the data set; your data has an intrinsic upper bound; or you expect, in general, to retrieve the entire collection simultaneously.
- If you need sparse associative arrays (for example, for "data-smart" storage), your only practical option is an associative array. True, you could allocate and then delete elements of a nested table variable (as illustrated in the later section on NEXT and PRIOR methods), but it is inefficient to do so for anything but the smallest collections.
- If your PL/SQL program needs to run under both Oracle7 and Oracle8, associative arrays are again your only option. And if your PL/SQL application requires negative subscripts, you also have to use associative arrays.

Table 11-3. Comparing Oracle collection types

Characteristic	Associative array	Nested table	VARRAY
Dimensionality	Single	Single	Single
Usable in SQL?	No	Yes	Yes
Usable as column datatype in a table?	No	Yes; data stored "out of line" (in separate table)	Yes; data stored "in line" (in same table)
Uninitialized state	Empty (cannot be null); elements undefined	Atomically null; illegal to reference elements	Atomically null; illegal to reference elements
Initialization	Automatic, when declared	Via constructor, fetch, assignment	Via constructor, fetch, assignment
In PL/SQL, elements referenced via	BINARY_INTEGER (-2,147,483,647 .. 2,147,483,647) VARCHAR2 (Oracle9*i* Release 2 and above)	Positive integer between 1 and 2,147,483,647	Positive integer between 1 and 2,147,483,647
Sparse?	Yes	Initially, no; after deletions, yes	No
Bounded?	No	Can be extended	Yes
Can assign value to any element at any time?	Yes	No; may need to EXTEND first	No; may need to EXTEND first, and cannot EXTEND past upper bound
Means of extending	Assign value to element with a new subscript	Use built-in EXTEND procedure (or TRIM to condense), with no predefined maximum	EXTEND (or TRIM), but only up to declared maximum size

Table 11-3. Comparing Oracle collection types (continued)

Characteristic	Associative array	Nested table	VARRAY
Can be compared for equality?	No	No	No
Retains ordering and subscripts when stored in and retrieved from database?	N/A	No	Yes

In this chapter:

- The BOOLEAN Datatype
- The RAW Datatype
- The UROWID and ROWID Datatypes
- The LOB Datatypes
- Working with LOBs
- Predefined Object Types

CHAPTER 12

Miscellaneous Datatypes

In this chapter, we'll explore all the native PL/SQL datatypes that we haven't yet covered. These include the BOOLEAN and UROWID/ROWID types, as well as the LOB (large object) family of types. We'll also discuss some useful, predefined object types, including XMLType, which enables you to store XML data in a database column, and ANYDATA type, which allows you to store, well, just about anything.

The BOOLEAN Datatype

The Oracle RDBMS/SQL language offers features not found in PL/SQL, such as the Oracle SQL DECODE construct. PL/SQL, on the other hand, has a few tricks up its sleeve that are unavailable in native SQL. One particularly pleasant example of this is the BOOLEAN datatype.* Boolean data may only be TRUE, FALSE, or NULL. A Boolean is a "logical" datatype.

The Oracle RDBMS does not support a Boolean datatype. You can create a table with a column of datatype CHAR(1) and store either "Y" or "N" in that column to indicate TRUE or FALSE. That is a poor substitute, however, for a datatype that stores actual Boolean values (or NULL). Because there is no counterpart for the PL/SQL Boolean in the Oracle RDBMS, you can neither SELECT into a Boolean variable nor insert a TRUE or FALSE value directly into a database column.

Boolean values and variables are very useful in PL/SQL. Because a Boolean variable can only be TRUE, FALSE, or NULL, you can use that variable to explain what is happening in your code. With Booleans you can write code that is easily readable because it is more English-like. You can replace a complicated Boolean expression involving many different variables and tests with a single Boolean variable that directly expresses the intention and meaning of the text.

* The Boolean is named after George Boole, who lived in the first half of the 19th century and is considered the father of symbolic logic. One therefore capitalizes "Boolean," whereas the other datatypes get no respect.

Here is an example of an IF statement with a single Boolean variable (or function—you really can't tell the difference just by looking at this line of code):

```
IF report_requested
THEN
   print_report (report_id);
END IF;
```

The beauty of this technique is that it not only makes your code a bit more self-documenting, it also has the potential to insulate your code from future change. For example, consider the human interface that needs to precede the previous code fragment. How do we know that a report was requested? Perhaps we ask the user to answer a question with a Y or an N, or perhaps the user must place a check in a checkbox or select an option from a drop-down list. The point is that it doesn't matter. We can freely change the human interface of our code, and, as long as that interface properly sets the report_requested Boolean variable, the actual reporting functionality will continue to work correctly.

In the previous example, we used a single Boolean variable in our condition. If the variable report_requested evaluates to TRUE, then the report prints. Otherwise, the print step is skipped. We *could* code that same IF statement as follows:

```
IF report_requested = TRUE
THEN
   print_report (report_id);
END IF;
```

While the code in this example is logically equivalent to the "IF report_requested" formulation, it is superfluous and works against the nature of a Boolean variable. A Boolean variable itself evaluates to TRUE, FALSE, or NULL; you don't have to test the variable against those values. If you name your Boolean variables properly, you will be able to easily read the logic and intent of your IF-THEN logic by leaving out the unnecessary parts of the statement.

The fact that Boolean variables can be NULL has implications for IF...THEN...ELSE statements. For example, look at the difference in behavior between the following two statements:

```
IF report_requested
THEN
   --Executes if report_requested = TRUE
ELSE
   --Executes if report_requested = FALSE or IS NULL
END IF;

IF NOT report_requested
THEN
   --Executes if report_requested = FALSE
ELSE
   --Executes if report_requeste = TRUE or IS NULL
END IF;
```

If you need separate logic for each of the three possible cases, you can write a three-pronged IF statement as follows:

```
IF report_requested
THEN
   --Executes if report_requested = TRUE
ELSIF NOT report_requested
   --Executes if report_requested = FALSE
ELSE
   --Executes if report_requested IS NULL
END IF;
```

For more details on the effects of NULLs in IF statements, refer back to Chapter 4.

The RAW Datatype

The RAW datatype allows you to store and manipulate relatively small amounts of binary data. Unlike the case with VARCHAR2 and other character types, RAW data never undergoes any kind of character set conversion when traveling back and forth between your PL/SQL programs and the database. RAW variables are declared as follows:

```
variable_name RAW(maximum_size)
```

The value for *maximum_size* may range from 1 through 32767. Be aware that while a RAW PL/SQL variable can hold up to 32,767 bytes of data, a RAW database column can hold only 2000 bytes.

RAW is not a type that we use or encounter very often. It's useful mainly when you need to deal with small amounts of binary data. When dealing with the large amounts of binary data found in images, sound files, and the like, you should look into using the BLOB (binary large object) type. BLOB is described later in this chapter (see "The BLOB Datatype").

The UROWID and ROWID Datatypes

The UROWID and ROWID types allow you to work with database rowids in your PL/SQL programs. A rowid is a *row identifier*—a binary value that identifies a row of data in an Oracle table. Referencing rowids in UPDATE and DELETE statements can sometimes lead to desirable improvements in processing speed, as access by rowid is typically the fastest way to locate or retrieve a particular row in the database—faster even than a search by primary key. Figure 12-1 contrasts the use of a rowid in an UPDATE statement with the use of column values such as those for a primary key.

In the history of Oracle, the ROWID type came first. As Oracle added functionality such as index-organized tables (IOTs) and gateways to other types of databases, Oracle developed new types of rowids and hence had to develop a new datatype capable of holding them. Enter the UROWID datatype. The U in UROWID stands for Universal, and a UROWID variable can contain any type of ROWID from any type of table.

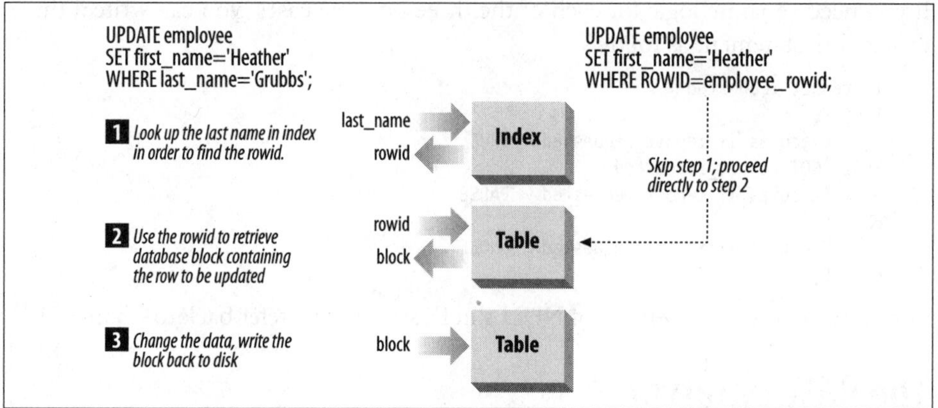
UPDATE employee
SET first_name='Heather'
WHERE last_name='Grubbs';
1 Look up the last name in index in order to find the rowid.
2 Use the rowid to retrieve database block containing the row to be updated
3 Change the data, write the block back to disk
last_name
rowid
Index
rowid
block
Table
block
Table
UPDATE employee
SET first_name='Heather'
WHERE ROWID=employee_rowid;
Skip step 1; proceed directly to step 2

Figure 12-1. ROWIDs take you directly to rows in a table

We recommend the use of UROWID for all new development involving rowids. The ROWID type provides backward compatibility, but can't accommodate all types of rowids now encountered in an Oracle database. UROWID is safer because it accommodates any type of rowid.

Getting at Rowids

In the Oracle RDBMS, ROWID is a *pseudocolumn* that is a part of every table you create. The rowid is an internally generated and maintained binary value that identifies a row of data in your table. ROWID is called a pseudocolumn because a SQL statement may include it in places where you would normally use a column, but it is not an actual column that you create for the table. Instead, the RDBMS generates the rowid for each row as it is inserted into the database, and returns that value to you via the ROWID pseudocolumn. You cannot change the value of a rowid.

You can use the UROWID datatype to store rowids from the database in your PL/SQL program. You can SELECT or FETCH the rowid for a row into a ROWID variable; for example:

```
DECLARE
    employee_rowid UROWID;
    employee_salary NUMBER;
BEGIN
    --Retrieve employee information that we might want to modify
    SELECT rowid, salary INTO employee_rowid, employee_salary
    FROM employee
    WHERE last_name='Grubbs' AND first_name='John';
END;
```

You may find yourself wondering just what a rowid looks like, or what kind of data a UROWID value really contains. Unless you're a DBA, there's probably no reason to care. In fact, we're fairly certain that unless you are writing some kind of database administration utility, you shouldn't write programs that are concerned with the contents of rowids. However, if you are curious, you can SELECT rowids from SQL*Plus. Following are some rowids from an index-organized table:

```
SQL> SELECT rowid FROM employee;

ROWID
----------------------------------
*BAIACiICwQL+
*BAIACiICwQP+
```

and following are some from a regular table:

```
SQL> SELECT rowid FROM rtest;

ROWID
------------------
AAAH2pAAIAAAAoSAAA
AAAH2pAAIAAAAoSAAB
```

If you're using Oracle7, you'll see different results.

If you need to work with rowids at a detailed level, extracting the individual component values that make up a rowid, you will want to use the built-in package, DBMS_ROWID. You can read about DBMS_ROWID in *Oracle Built-in Packages* (O'Reilly) or in the Oracle manual *Supplied PL/SQL Packages and Types Reference*. In general, and certainly for uses such as we describe in this chapter, you should treat rowids as opaque values, meaning that you shouldn't worry about looking at and understanding the actual data they contain.

Using Rowids

So you can get a rowid value into your PL/SQL program, but what use can you then make of it? One potentially very useful application of rowids is in repeating access to a given database row. Recall the example from the previous section in which we retrieved the salary for a specific employee. What if we later want to modify that salary? One solution would be to issue an UPDATE statement with the same WHERE clause as the one we used in our original SELECT:

```
DECLARE
   employee_rowid UROWID;
   employee_salary NUMBER;
BEGIN
   --Retrieve employee information that we might want to modify
   SELECT rowid, salary INTO employee_rowid, employee_salary
   FROM employee
   WHERE last_name='Grubbs' AND first_name='John';

   /* Do a bunch of processing to compute a new salary */

   UPDATE employee
```

```
        SET salary = employee_salary
      WHERE last_name='Grubbs' AND first_name='John';
END;
```

While this code will certainly work, it has the disadvantage of having to repeat the same access path for the UPDATE as was used for the SELECT. Most likely, one or more indexes will be consulted in order to determine the rowid for the employee row in question. But those indexes were just consulted for the SELECT statement, so why go through all the trouble of looking up the same rowid twice? Why indeed! Because we retrieved the rowid in our SELECT statement, we can simply supply that rowid to the UPDATE, thus bypassing the need to do any kind of index lookup:

```
DECLARE
   employee_rowid UROWID;
   employee_salary NUMBER;
BEGIN
   --Retrieve employee information that we might want to modify
   SELECT rowid, salary INTO employee_rowid, employee_salary
   FROM employee
   WHERE last_name='Grubbs' AND first_name='John';

   /* Do a bunch of processing to compute a new salary */

   UPDATE employee
      SET salary = employee_salary
    WHERE rowid = employee_rowid;
END;
```

If employee is a regular, heap-organized table, the rowid in the UPDATE statement's WHERE clause points directly to the location of the row on disk. If employee is an index-organized table, that may or may not be the case depending on how volatile the table is; nevertheless, the rowid still represents the fastest way of accessing a given row.

An often better way to achieve the same effect as using ROWID in an UPDATE or DELETE statement is to use an explicit cursor to retrieve data, and then use the WHERE CURRENT OF CURSOR clause to modify or delete it. See Chapter 14 for detailed information on this technique.

Do rowids ever change?

Do rowids ever change? That's a good question. If you're going to retrieve a rowid and use it later on, you need to know whether rowids ever expire. Physical rowids, used for standard, heap-organized tables, never change. Only if you delete a row and reinsert it—as you might when doing an export followed by an import—will you get a new rowid for a row. But we just said that physical rowids never change! Are we contradicting ourselves? By no means. When you delete a row and reinsert it, you are really inserting a new row with the same values, and the new row will get a new rowid.

Logical rowids, used in index-organized tables, are not as long-lived as physical rowids. Additionally, logical rowids can change when you change a row's primary key. We're not in the habit of writing applications that change primary keys, so in actual practice this doesn't seem like much of a limitation. It is, however, something to keep in mind when you are writing applications that make use of rowids, especially if any of your application tables are index-organized.

Everything is a tradeoff. The use of rowids can make your applications more efficient, but the tradeoff is that you now have a few more things to think and worry about.

Using rowids in Oracle Forms

You can make use of the rowid in an Oracle Forms application to access the row in the database corresponding to the record on the screen. When you create a base-table block in Oracle Forms, it automatically includes the rowid in the block as an "invisible pseudoitem." You do not see it on your item list, but you can reference it in your triggers and PL/SQL program units. For example, to update the name of an employee displayed on the screen, you could issue the following statement:

```
UPDATE employee
   SET last_name = :employee.last_name
 WHERE rowid = :employee.rowid;
```

Using rowids in a cursor FOR loop

You can also use the rowid inside a cursor FOR loop (or any other loop that FETCHes records from a cursor) to make changes to the row just FETCHed, as follows:

```
PROCEDURE remove_internal_competitors IS
BEGIN
   FOR emp_rec IN
      (SELECT connections, rowid
         FROM employee
        WHERE sal > 500000)
   LOOP
      IF emp_rec.connections IN ('President', 'CEO')
      THEN
         send_holiday_greetings;
      ELSE
         DELETE FROM employee
          WHERE rowid = emp_rec.rowid;
      END IF;
   END LOOP;
END;
```

The DELETE uses the rowid stored in the emp_rec record to immediately get rid of anyone making more than $500,000 who does not have known connections to the President or CEO. Note that the DBA controls who may have EXECUTE privilege to this stored procedure. So one must now wonder: does the DBA have connections to the President or CEO? Well, in any case, use of the rowid guarantees the fastest possible DELETE of that employee.

Of course, the above procedure could also simply have fetched the employee_id (the primary key of the employee table) and executed a DELETE based on that real column, as in the following:

```
DELETE FROM employee WHERE employee_id = emp_id;
```

Is the use of rowids worth the effort?

We aren't convinced that the theoretical performance gains of searching by rowid justify its use. The resulting code is harder to understand than the application-specific use of the primary key. You also must understand how rowids might change. We've heard of people storing rowids in tables, only to have everything break when the DBA does an export/import to reorganize storage. It's best, in our opinion, not to store rowids in database columns.

A further issue with respect to rowids concerns portability. The rowid is not a part of the ANSI SQL standard; instead, it reflects directly the internal storage structure of the Oracle RDBMS. References to rowids could cause portability problems in the future, as non-Oracle databases do not recognize or support rowids. If you are building applications that may need to work against non-Oracle data sources, you should avoid any references to the rowid pseudocolumn and to the UROWID and ROWID datatypes.

The LOB Datatypes

Oracle and PL/SQL support several variations of LOB (large object) datatypes. LOBs can store large amounts—up to four gigabytes—of binary data (such as images) or character text data.

Within PL/SQL you can declare LOB variables of the following datatypes:

BFILE
: Binary file. Declares a variable that holds a file locator pointing to an operating-system file outside the database. Oracle treats the data in the file as binary data.

BLOB
: Binary large object. Declares a variable that holds a LOB locator pointing to a large binary object stored inside the database.

CLOB
: Character large object. Declares a variable that holds a LOB locator pointing to a large block of single-byte, fixed-width character data stored inside the database.

NCLOB
: National Language Support (NLS) character large object. Declares a variable that holds a LOB locator pointing to a large block of single-byte, fixed-width multibyte, or variable-width multibyte character data stored inside the database.

There are two types of LOBs: internal and external. Internal LOBs (BLOBs, CLOBs, and NCLOBs) are stored in the database and can participate in a transaction in the database server. External LOBs (BFILEs) represent binary data stored in operating-system files outside the database tablespaces. External LOBs cannot participate in transactions; in other words, you cannot commit or roll back changes to a BFILE. Instead, you must rely on the underlying filesystem for data integrity.

The BFILE Datatype

Use the BFILE datatype to access large binary objects (up to four gigabytes in size) in files outside the database. This variable gives you read-only, bytestream I/O access to these files, which can reside on a hard disk, CD-ROM, or other such device.

When you declare a BFILE variable, you allocate memory to store the *file locator* of the BFILE, not the BFILE contents itself. This file locator contains a directory alias as well as a filename. See the later section "BFILEs Are Different" for more information about the file locator.

Here is an example of a declaration of a BFILE variable:

```
DECLARE
   web_page BFILE;
```

The BLOB Datatype

Use the BLOB datatype to store large binary objects inside the database. Data for all but very small BLOB values is stored "out of line," which means that when a table has a BLOB column, a row of data for that table contains a pointer, or *locator*, to the actual location of the BLOB data (thus it is not "in line" with the other column values of the row). Extremely small BLOB values may be stored inline.

The BLOB variable's locator then points to a large binary object. BLOBs can be up to four gigabytes in size, and they participate fully in transactions. In other words, any changes you make to a BLOB (via the DBMS_LOB built-in package, for example) can be rolled back or committed along with other outstanding changes in your transaction. BLOB locators cannot, however, span transactions or sessions.

Here is an example of a declaration of a BLOB variable:

```
DECLARE
   photo BLOB;
```

The CLOB Datatype

Use the CLOB datatype to store large blocks of single-byte character data inside the database. Variable-width character sets are not supported in CLOBs. As with BLOBs, large CLOBs are stored "out of line."

A CLOB variable contains a locator, which then points to the large block of single-byte character data. CLOBs can be up to four gigabytes in size, and they participate fully in transactions. In other words, any changes you make to a CLOB can be rolled back or committed along with other outstanding changes in your transaction. Like BLOB locators, CLOB locators cannot span transactions or sessions.

Here is an example of a declaration of a CLOB variable:

```
DECLARE
   directions CLOB;
```

LONG and LONG RAW

If you've been around Oracle for a few years, you've probably noticed that so far we've omitted any discussion of two datatypes: LONG and LONG RAW. This is intentional. In the database, LONG and LONG RAW allow you to store large amounts (up to two gigabytes) of character and binary data, respectively. The maximum lengths of the PL/SQL types, however, are much shorter: only 32,760 bytes, which is less than the 32,767 bytes supported by VARCHAR2 and RAW. Given this rather odd length limitation, we recommend using VARCHAR2 and RAW, instead of LONG and LONG RAW, in your PL/SQL programs.

If you're retrieving LONG and LONG RAW columns that may contain more than 32,767 bytes of data, you won't be able to store the returned values in VARCHAR2 or RAW variables. This is an unfortunate restriction, and a good reason to avoid LONG and LONG RAW to begin with.

LONG and LONG RAW are obsolete types, maintained only for backward compatibility. Oracle doesn't recommend their use, and neither do we. For new applications where you have a choice, use CLOB and BLOB instead. For existing applications, Oracle's *Oracle9i Application Developer's Guide—Large Objects (LOBs)* provides guidance for migrating existing data from LONG to LOB columns.

The NCLOB Datatype

Use the NCLOB datatype to store large blocks of text represented using single-byte, fixed-width multibyte, or variable-width multibyte character sets inside the database. NCLOB is to CLOB what NVARCHAR2 is to VARCHAR2. Refer back to Chapter 8 for an introduction to character sets.

In Oracle8, variable-width character sets were not supported by NCLOB columns. Beginning with Oracle8*i*, NCLOBs do support variable-width characters.

An NCLOB variable contains a locator, which then points to the large block of character data. NCLOBs can be up to four gigabytes in size, and they participate fully in transactions. In other words, any changes you make to an NCLOB can be rolled back or committed along with other outstanding changes in your transaction. Like BLOB and CLOB locators, NCLOB locators cannot span transactions or sessions.

Here is an example of a declaration of an NCLOB variable:

```
DECLARE
   directions NCLOB;
```

Working with LOBs

The topic of working with large objects is, well, large, and we can't begin to cover every aspect of LOB programming in this chapter. What we can and will do, however, is provide you with a good introduction to the topic of LOB programming aimed especially at PL/SQL developers. We'll discuss some of the issues to be aware of and show examples of fundamental LOB operations. All of this, we hope, will provide you with a good foundation for your future LOB programming endeavors.

We will first introduce the different types of LOBs available to PL/SQL developers. Then it's time to learn about LOB locators and how to create LOBs. We will show you how to use DBMS_LOB to manipulate LOB contents and also introduce new, native syntax in Oracle9*i* that lets you work with LOBs using built-in functions like SUBSTR directly (albeit with an impact on performance, as is noted in that section).

Before getting into the meat of this section, please note that all LOB examples are based on the following table definition:

```
CREATE TABLE waterfalls (
   falls_name VARCHAR2(80),
   falls_photo BLOB,
   falls_directions CLOB,
   falls_description NCLOB,
   falls_web_page BFILE);
```

This table contains rows about waterfalls located in Michigan's Upper Peninsula. Figure 12-2 shows the Dryer Hose, a falls frequented by ice-climbers, in its frozen state.

The table implements one column for each of the four LOB types. Photos consist of large amounts of binary data, so the falls_photo column is defined as a BLOB. Directions and descriptions are text, so those columns are CLOB and NCLOB, respectively. Normally, you'd use either CLOB or NCLOB for both, but we wanted to provide an example that made use of each LOB type. Finally, the master copy of the web page for each waterfall is stored in an HTML file outside the database. We use a BFILE column to point to that HTML file. We'll use these columns in our examples to demonstrate various facets of working with LOB data in PL/SQL programs.

Figure 12-2. The Dryer Hose in Munising, Michigan

In our discussion of large objects, we'll frequently use the acronym LOB to refer to CLOBs, BLOBs, NCLOBs, and BFILEs in general. We'll use specific type names only when discussing something specific to a type.

Understanding LOB Locators

Fundamental to working with LOBs is the concept of a *LOB locator*. A LOB locator is a pointer to large object data in a database. By way of explanation, let's look at what happens when you select a BLOB column into a BLOB PL/SQL variable:

```
DECLARE
   photo BLOB;
BEGIN
   SELECT falls_photo
```

```
  INTO photo
  FROM waterfalls
 WHERE falls_name='Tannery Falls';
```

What, exactly, is in the photo variable after the SELECT statement executes? Is the photo itself retrieved? No. Only a pointer to the photo is retrieved. You end up with the situation shown in Figure 12-3.

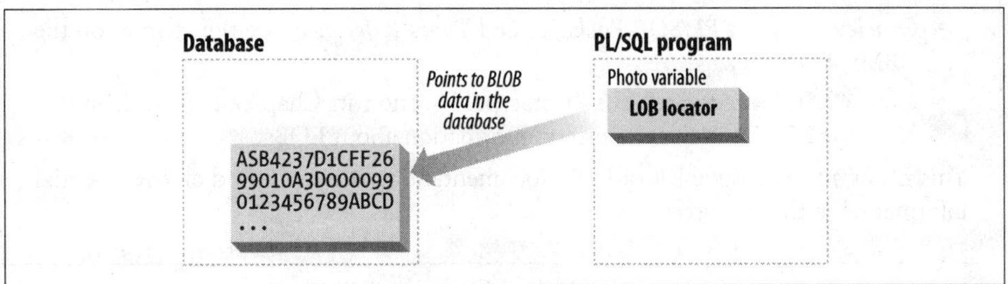

Figure 12-3. A LOB locator points to its associated large object data within the database

This is different from the way in which other database column types work. Database LOB columns store LOB locators, and those locators point to the real data stored elsewhere in the database. Likewise, PL/SQL LOB variables hold those same LOB locators, which point to LOB data within the database. To work with LOB data, you first retrieve a LOB locator, and you then use a built-in package named DBMS_LOB to retrieve and/or modify the actual LOB data. For example, to retrieve the binary photo data from the falls_photo BLOB column used in the previous example, you would go through the following steps:

1. Issue a SELECT statement to retrieve the LOB locator for the photo you wish to display.
2. Open the LOB via a call to DBMS_LOB.OPEN.
3. Make a call to DBMS_LOB.GETCHUNKSIZE to get the optimal chunk size to use when reading (and writing) the LOB's value.
4. Make a call to DBMS_LOB.GETLENGTH to get the number of bytes or characters in the LOB value.
5. Make multiple calls to DBMS_LOB.READ in order to retrieve the LOB data.
6. Close the LOB, if you previously opened it.

Not all of these steps are necessary, and don't worry if you don't understand them fully right now. We'll explain all the steps and operations shortly.

LOB locators and the need to use the DBMS_LOB package add a certain amount of complexity to working with LOBs as opposed to working with other datatypes. However, there are good reasons for the approach Oracle chose. Remember that LOB columns can hold up to four gigabytes of data. Imagine for a moment what might happen without LOB locators if you selected several 4 GB LOB columns in one SELECT statement. First off, your PL/SQL program would need to retrieve *all*

Oracle's LOB Documentation

If you are working with LOBs, we strongly recommend that you familiarize yourself with the following portions of Oracle's documentation set:

- *Oracle9i Application Developer's Guide—Large Objects (LOBs)*. Contains complete information on LOB programming.
- *Oracle9i Supplied PL/SQL Packages and Types Reference*. See the chapter on the DBMS_LOB package.
- *Oracle9i SQL Reference*. The "Datatypes" section in Chapter 2, *Basic Elements of Oracle SQL*, contains important information about LOBs.

This is not an exhaustive list of LOB documentation, but you'll find all the essential information in these sources.

that LOB data as part of executing the SELECT statement. Worse yet, you'd need enough memory to hold all that data. And what if you didn't really need to see all the LOB data in a particular column, but only part of it? LOB locators enable SQL statements involving LOB columns to execute more quickly because only the locators are moved back and forth. Once you have the locator, you can retrieve all of a LOB's data or only a small portion of the data. If you need to see only 100 bytes out of a 4 GB LOB, you're much better off retrieving just the 100 bytes you need instead of retrieving the entire four gigabytes.

The bottom line is that LOB columns hold pointers, not data, and those pointers are what you get when you SELECT a LOB column into a PL/SQL LOB variable. This leads to the rather interesting issue of empty LOBs versus NULL LOBs.

Empty Versus NULL LOBs

Now that you understand the distinction between a LOB locator and the value to which it points, you need to wrap your mind around another key concept: the *empty LOB*. An empty LOB is what you have when a LOB locator doesn't point to any LOB data. This is not the same as a NULL LOB, which is a LOB column (or variable) that doesn't hold a LOB locator. Clear as mud, right? Let's look at some example code:

```
SQL> DECLARE
   directions CLOB;
BEGIN
   IF directions IS NULL THEN
      DBMS_OUTPUT.PUT_LINE('directions is NULL');
   ELSE
      DBMS_OUTPUT.PUT_LINE('directions is not NULL');
   END IF;
END;
/

directions is NULL
```

Here we've declared a CLOB variable, which is NULL because we haven't yet assigned it a value. You're used to this behavior, right? It's the same with any other datatype: declare a variable without assigning a value and the result is NULL. Let's press ahead and create a LOB locator for the variable. The following code uses a call to EMPTY_CLOB in conjunction with an INSERT statement to create a LOB locator. Subsequently, a SELECT statement retrieves that same LOB locator from the database and places it into the directions variable. We'll talk more about the reasons for this somewhat cumbersome approach in the next section. For now, focus on the output from this code snippet.

First the code:

```
DECLARE
   directions CLOB;
BEGIN
   --Delete any existing rows for 'Munising Falls' so that this
   --example can be executed multiple times
   DELETE
     FROM waterfalls
    WHERE falls_name='Munising Falls';

   --Insert a new row using EMPTY_CLOB( ) to create a LOB locator
   INSERT INTO waterfalls
             (falls_name,falls_directions)
      VALUES ('Munising Falls',EMPTY_CLOB( ));

   --Retrieve the LOB locater created by the previous INSERT statement
   SELECT falls_directions
     INTO directions
     FROM waterfalls
    WHERE falls_name='Munising Falls';

   IF directions IS NULL THEN
      DBMS_OUTPUT.PUT_LINE('directions is NULL');
   ELSE
      DBMS_OUTPUT.PUT_LINE('directions is not NULL');
   END IF;

   DBMS_OUTPUT.PUT_LINE('Length = '
                        || DBMS_LOB.GETLENGTH(directions));
END;
```

and now the output:

```
directions is not NULL
Length = 0
```

EMPTY_CLOB is a built-in function that returns a CLOB locator, which we've stored in the database and then retrieved. Our CLOB variable is now no longer NULL because it contains a value: the locator. However, the results from the call to DBMS_LOB.GETLENGTH indicate that there is no data being pointed to; thus, the directions CLOB is an empty LOB. This is important to understand because the way in which you test for the presence or absence of data is more complicated with a LOB than it is for other datatypes.

A simple IS NULL test suffices for traditional scalar datatypes:

```
IF some_number IS NULL THEN
   --You know there is no data
```

If an IS NULL test on a NUMBER or a VARCHAR2 (or any other scalar type) returns TRUE, you know that the variable holds no data. With LOBs, however, you not only need to check for nullity (no locator), but you also need to check the length:

```
IF some_clob IS NULL THEN
   --There is no data
ELSEIF DBMS_LOB.GETLENGTH(some_clob) = 0 THEN
   --There is no data
ELSE
   --Only now is there data
END IF;
```

As illustrated in this example, you can't check the length of a LOB without first having a locator. Thus, to determine whether a LOB holds data, you must first check for the presence of a locator using an IS NULL test, and then check for a non-zero length.

Creating a LOB

In the previous section, we used the following code to create a LOB locator:

```
--Insert a new row using EMPTY_CLOB( ) to create a LOB locator
INSERT INTO waterfalls
         (falls_name,falls_directions)
   VALUES ('Munising Falls',EMPTY_CLOB( ));
```

We then issued a SELECT statement to retrieve the new locator from a table. That sure seems like a cumbersome approach, doesn't it? You're probably wondering why we didn't just do the following:

```
directions := EMPTY_CLOB( );
```

It turns out that there is a very good reason why we took the approach we did. Remember that a CLOB variable (such as directions) really holds a LOB locator that points to the actual LOB data in the database. The key words to focus on here are *in the database*. LOBs do not exist in memory. They exist on disk in one or more of the database files. Furthermore, the physical details of how and where a given LOB is stored are specified as part of the table definition of the table containing the LOB. When we invoke the EMPTY_CLOB() function, we get an empty LOB (perhaps "empty LOB locator" would be a better term) that does not point to any specific location on disk. It's not until we store that empty LOB into a column in a database table that Oracle finishes filling in the blanks to produce a locator that we can use. When we insert our empty LOB into the waterfalls table, Oracle sees that the LOB locator is incomplete, decides on a location for the LOB based on storage information that the DBA provided as part of the waterfall table's definition, updates the LOB locator to point to that location, and finally stores the new locator as part of the table row that we are inserting. Only after all that can we actually work with the LOB. Of course, to get the newly completed LOB locator, we need to select it back again from the row that we just inserted.

It's worth noting that you don't necessarily need to embed the call to EMPTY_CLOB() within the INSERT statement. We can assign the results of EMPTY_CLOB to a CLOB variable, and then insert that variable into our table:

```
--Insert a new row using EMPTY_CLOB( ) to create a LOB locator
directions := EMPTY_CLOB( );
INSERT INTO waterfalls
         (falls_name,falls_directions)
  VALUES ('Munising Falls',directions);
```

Note that even after this code executes, directions is still an empty LOB. A subsequent SELECT statement is necessary to retrieve the updated, nonempty LOB from the database.

When working with BLOBs, use EMPTY_BLOB( ) to create an empty BLOB. Use EMPTY_CLOB( ) for CLOBs and NCLOBs.

Beginning with Oracle8*i*, it is possible to work with LOBs without having to insert rows into your database. You do this using temporary LOBs, which are discussed in the later section, "Temporary LOBs."

Writing into a LOB

Once you have a valid LOB locator, you can write data into that LOB using one of two procedures from the built-in DBMS_LOB package:

DBMS_LOB.WRITE
: Allows you to write data randomly into a LOB

DBMS_LOB.WRITEAPPEND
: Allows you to append data to the end of a LOB

Following is an extension of the previous examples in this chapter. It begins by creating a LOB locator for the directions column in the waterfalls table. After creating the locator, we use DBMS_LOB.WRITE to begin writing directions to Munising Falls into the CLOB column. We then use DBMS_LOB.WRITEAPPEND to finish the job:

```
DECLARE
   directions CLOB;
   amount BINARY_INTEGER;
   offset INTEGER;
```

```
   first_direction VARCHAR2(100);
   more_directions VARCHAR2(500);
BEGIN
   --Delete any existing rows for 'Munising Falls' so that this
   --example can be executed multiple times
   DELETE
     FROM waterfalls
    WHERE falls_name='Munising Falls';

   --Insert a new row using EMPTY_CLOB( ) to create a LOB locator
   INSERT INTO waterfalls
             (falls_name,falls_directions)
      VALUES ('Munising Falls',EMPTY_CLOB( ));

   --Retrieve the LOB locator created by the previous INSERT statement
   SELECT falls_directions
     INTO directions
     FROM waterfalls
    WHERE falls_name='Munising Falls';

   --Open the LOB; not strictly necessary, but best to open/close LOBs.
   DBMS_LOB.OPEN(directions, DBMS_LOB.LOB_READWRITE);

   --Use DBMS_LOB.WRITE to begin
   first_direction := 'Follow I-75 across the Mackinac Bridge.';
   amount := LENGTH(first_direction);  --number of characters to write
   offset := 1; --begin writing to the first character of the CLOB
   DBMS_LOB.WRITE(directions, amount, offset, first_direction);

   --Add some more directions using DBMS_LOB.WRITEAPPEND
   more_directions := ' Take US-2 west from St. Ignace to Blaney Park.'
                   || ' Turn north on M-77 and drive to Seney.'
                   || ' From Seney, take M-28 west to Munising.';
   DBMS_LOB.WRITEAPPEND(directions,
                        LENGTH(more_directions), more_directions);

   --Add yet more directions
   more_directions := ' In front of the paper mill, turn right on H-58.'
                   || ' Follow H-58 to Washington Street. Veer left onto'
                   || ' Washington Street. You''ll find the Munising'
                   || ' Falls visitor center across from the hospital at'
                   || ' the point where Washington Street becomes'
                   || ' Sand Point Road.';
   DBMS_LOB.WRITEAPPEND(directions,
                        LENGTH(more_directions), more_directions);

   --Close the LOB, and we are done.
   DBMS_LOB.CLOSE(directions);
END;
```

In this example, we used both WRITE and WRITEAPPEND solely to demonstrate the use of both procedures. Because our LOB had no data to begin with, we could have done all the work using only WRITEAPPEND. Notice that we opened and closed the LOB; while this is not strictly necessary, it is a good idea, especially if you are using Oracle Text. Otherwise, any Oracle Text domain- and function-based indexes will be updated with each WRITE or WRITEAPPEND call, rather than being updated once when you call CLOSE.

In the section on BFILEs, we show how to read LOB data directly from an external operating-system file.

When writing to a LOB, as we have done here, there is no need to update the LOB column in the table. That's because the LOB locator does not change. We did not change the contents of falls_directions (the LOB locator). Rather, we added data to the LOB to which the locator pointed.

LOB updates take place within the context of a transaction. We did not COMMIT in our example code. You should issue a COMMIT after executing the PL/SQL block if you want the Munising Falls directions to remain permanently in your database. If you issue a ROLLBACK after executing the PL/SQL block, all the work done by this block will be undone.

Our example writes to a CLOB column. You write BLOB data in the same manner, except that your inputs to WRITE and WRITEAPPEND should be of the RAW type instead of the VARCHAR2 type.

The following SQL*Plus example shows one way you can see the data just inserted by our example. The next section will show you how to retrieve the data using the various DBMS_LOB procedures.

```
SQL> SET LONG 2000
SQL> COLUMN falls_directions WORD_WRAPPED FORMAT A70
SQL> SELECT falls_directions
  2  FROM waterfalls
  3  WHERE falls_name='Munising Falls';

FALLS_DIRECTIONS
----------------------------------------------------------------------
Follow I-75 across the Mackinac Bridge. Take US-2 west from St. Ignace
to Blaney Park. Turn north on M-77 and drive to Seney. From Seney,
take M-28 west to Munising. In front of the paper mill, turn right on
H-58. Follow H-58 to Washington Street. Veer left onto Washington
Street. You'll find the Munising Falls visitor center across from the
hospital at the point where Washington Street becomes Sand Point Road.
```

Reading from a LOB

To retrieve data from a LOB, you use the DBMS_LOB.READ procedure. First, of course, you must retrieve the LOB locator. When reading from a CLOB, you specify an offset in terms of characters. Reading begins at the offset that you specify, and the first character of a CLOB is always number 1. When you are working with BLOBs, offsets are in terms of bytes. Note that when you are calling DBMS_LOB.READ, you must specify the number of characters (or bytes) that you wish to read. Given that LOBs are large, it's reasonable to plan on doing more than one read to get at all the data.

The following example retrieves and displays the directions to Munising Falls. We've carefully chosen the number of characters to read both to accommodate DBMS_OUTPUT's line-length restriction and to ensure a nice-looking line break in the final output.

```
DECLARE
   directions CLOB;
   directions_1 VARCHAR2(300);
   directions_2 VARCHAR2(300);
   chars_read_1 BINARY_INTEGER;
   chars_read_2 BINARY_INTEGER;
   offset INTEGER;
BEGIN
   --Retrieve the LOB locator inserted previously
   SELECT falls_directions
     INTO directions
     FROM waterfalls
    WHERE falls_name='Munising Falls';

   --Begin reading with the first character
   offset := 1;

   --Attempt to read 229 characters of directions, chars_read_1 will
   --be updated with the actual number of characters read
   chars_read_1 := 229;
   DBMS_LOB.READ(directions, chars_read_1, offset, directions_1);

   --If we read 229 characters, update the offset and try to
   --read 255 more.
   IF chars_read_1 = 229 THEN
      offset := offset + chars_read_1;
      chars_read_2 := 255;
      DBMS_LOB.READ(directions, chars_read_2, offset, directions_2);
   ELSE
      chars_read_2 := 0;
      directions_2 := '';
   END IF;

   --Display the total number of characters read
   DBMS_OUTPUT.PUT_LINE('Characters read = ' ||
                        TO_CHAR(chars_read_1+chars_read_2));

   --Display the directions
   DBMS_OUTPUT.PUT_LINE(directions_1);
   DBMS_OUTPUT.PUT_LINE(directions_2);
END;
```

The output from this code is as follows:

```
Characters read = 414
Follow I-75 across the Mackinac Bridge. Take US-2 west from St. Ignace to Blaney
Park. Turn north on M-77 and drive to Seney. From Seney, take M-28 west to
Munising. In front of the paper mill, turn right on H-58. Follow H-58 to
Washington Street. Veer left onto Washington Street. You'll find the Munising
Falls visitor center across from the hospital at the point where Washington
Street becomes Sand Point Road.
```

The chars_read_1 (amount to read) parameter, which is the second parameter you pass to DBMS_LOB.READ, is an IN OUT parameter, and DBMS_LOB.READ will update it to reflect the number of characters (or bytes) actually read. You'll know you've reached the end of a LOB when the number of characters or bytes read is less than the number you requested. It seems to us a bit inconvenient that the offset is not updated in the same manner. When reading several sequential portions of a LOB, you must update the offset each time based on the number of characters or bytes just read.

You can use DBMS_LOB.GET_LENGTH(*lob_locator*) to retrieve the length of a LOB. The length is returned as a number of bytes for BLOBs and BFILEs, and as a number of characters for CLOBs.

BFILEs Are Different

As mentioned earlier, the BLOB, CLOB, and NCLOB types represent *internal LOBs*, meaning that they are stored within the database. A BFILE, on the other hand, is an *external LOB* type. BFILEs are very different from internal LOBs in three important ways:

- The value of a BFILE is stored in an operating-system file, not within the database.
- BFILEs do not participate in transactions (i.e., changes to a BFILE cannot be rolled back or committed). However, changes to a BFILE locator can be rolled back and committed.
- From within PL/SQL and Oracle in general, you can only read BFILEs. Oracle does not allow you to write BFILE data. You must generate the external files—to which BFILE locators point—completely outside of the Oracle database system.

When you work with BFILEs in PL/SQL, you still do work with a LOB locator. In the case of a BFILE, however, the locator simply points to a file stored on the server. For this reason, two different rows in a database table can have a BFILE column that points to the same file.

A BFILE locator is composed of a directory alias and a filename. You use the BFILENAME function, which we'll describe shortly, to return a locator based on those two pieces of information. A *directory alias* is simply an Oracle-specific name for an operating-system directory. Directory aliases allow your PL/SQL programs to work with directories in an operating-system-independent manner. If you have the CREATE ANY DIRECTORY privilege, you can create a directory alias and grant access to it as follows:

```
CREATE DIRECTORY bfile_data AS 'c:\PLSQL Book\Ch12_Misc_Datatypes';

GRANT READ ON DIRECTORY bfile_data TO gennick;
```

Creating directory aliases and dealing with access to those aliases are more database administration functions than PL/SQL issues, so we won't go too deeply into those topics. The examples here should be enough to get you started. To learn more about directory aliases, talk to your DBA or read the section in Oracle's *SQL Reference Manual* on the CREATE DIRECTORY command.

Creating a BFILE locator

BFILE locators are trivial to create; you simply invoke the BFILENAME function and pass it a directory alias and a filename. Unlike locators for other LOB types, you don't need to store a BFILE locator in the database prior to using it. In the following example we create a BFILE locator for the HTML file containing the Tannery Falls web page. We then store that locator into the waterfalls table.

```
DECLARE
   web_page BFILE;
BEGIN
   --Delete row for Tannery Falls so this example can
   --be executed multiple times
   DELETE FROM waterfalls WHERE falls_name='Tannery Falls';

   --Invoke BFILENAME to create a BFILE locator
   web_page := BFILENAME('BFILE_DATA','Tannery Falls.htm');

   --Save our new locator in the waterfalls table
   INSERT INTO waterfalls (falls_name, falls_web_page)
      VALUES ('Tannery Falls',web_page);
END;
```

A BFILE locator is simply a combination of directory alias and filename. The actual file and directory don't even need to exist. That is, Oracle allows you to create directory aliases for directories that do not yet exist, and BFILENAME allows you to create BFILE locators for files that do not yet exist. There are times when it's convenient to do these things.

The directory name you specify in calls to BFILENAME is case-sensitive, and its case must match that shown by the ALL_DIRECTORIES data dictionary view. We first used lowercase bfile_data in our example, only to be greatly frustrated by errors when we tried to access our external BFILE data (as in the next section). In most cases, you'll want to use all-uppercase for the directory name in a call to BFILENAME.

Accessing BFILEs

Once you have a BFILE locator, you can access the data from an external file in much the same manner as you would access a BLOB. One difference is that you must use DBMS_LOB.FILEOPEN to open the external file before reading, and you must later use DBMS_LOB.FILECLOSE to close the file after you are done. The following example retrieves the first 60 bytes of HTML from the Tannery Falls web page. The results, which are of the RAW type, are cast to a character string using the built-in UTL_RAW.CAST_TO_VARCHAR2 function.

```
DECLARE
   web_page BFILE;
   html RAW(60);
   amount BINARY_INTEGER := 60;
   offset INTEGER := 1;
BEGIN
   --Retrieve the LOB locator for the web page
   SELECT falls_web_page
     INTO web_page
     FROM waterfalls
    WHERE falls_name='Tannery Falls';

   --Open the locator, read 60 bytes, and close the locator
   DBMS_LOB.OPEN(web_page);
   DBMS_LOB.READ(web_page, amount, offset, html);
   DBMS_LOB.CLOSE(web_page);

   --Uncomment following line to display results in hex
   --DBMS_OUTPUT.PUT_LINE(RAWTOHEX(html));

   --Cast RAW results to a character string we can read
   DBMS_OUTPUT.PUT_LINE(UTL_RAW.CAST_TO_VARCHAR2(html));
END;
```

The output from this code will appear as follows:

```
<!DOCTYPE HTML PUBLIC "-//W3C//DTD HTML 4.0 Transitional//EN
```

The maximum number of BFILEs that can be opened within a session is established by the database initialization parameter, SESSION_MAX_OPEN_FILES. This parameter defines an upper limit on the number of files opened simultaneously in a session (not just BFILEs, but all kinds of files, including those opened using the UTL_FILE package).

Remember that from within the Oracle database, you can only read BFILEs. The BFILE type is ideal when you want to access binary data, such as a collection of images, that is generated outside the database environment. For example, you might upload a collection of images from a digital camera to your server and create a BFILE locator to point to each of those images. You could then access the images from your PL/SQL programs.

Using BFILEs to load LOB columns

In addition to allowing you to access binary file data created outside the Oracle database environment, BFILEs provide a convenient means to load data from external files into internal LOB columns. Up through Oracle9*i* Release 1, you can use the DBMS_LOB.LOADFROMFILE function to read binary data from a BFILE and store it into a BLOB column. Oracle9*i* Release 2 introduced the following, much improved, functions:

DBMS_LOB.LOADCLOBFROMFILE
: Loads CLOBs from BFILEs. Takes care of any needed character set translation.

DBMS_LOB.LOADBLOBFROMFILE
: Loads BLOBs from BFILEs. Does the same thing as DBMS_LOB.LOADFROMFILE, but with an interface that is consistent with that of LOADCLOBFROMFILE.

Imagine that we had directions to Tannery Falls in an external text file named *TanneryFalls.directions* in a directory pointed to by the BFILE_DATA directory alias. The following example shows how we could use DBMS_LOB.LOADCLOBFROMFILE to load the directions into the falls_directions CLOB column in the waterfalls table:

```
DECLARE
   Tannery_Falls_Directions BFILE
      := BFILENAME('BFILE_DATA','TanneryFalls.directions');
   directions CLOB;
   destination_offset INTEGER := 1;
   source_offset INTEGER := 1;
   language_context INTEGER := DBMS_LOB.default_lang_ctx;
   warning_message INTEGER;
BEGIN
   --Delete row for Tannery Falls, so this example
   --can run multiple times.
   DELETE FROM waterfalls WHERE falls_name='Tannery Falls';

   --Insert a new row using EMPTY_CLOB() to create a LOB locator
   INSERT INTO waterfalls
             (falls_name,falls_directions)
      VALUES ('Tannery Falls',EMPTY_CLOB());

   --Retrieve the LOB locator created by the previous INSERT statement
   SELECT falls_directions
     INTO directions
     FROM waterfalls
    WHERE falls_name='Tannery Falls';

   --Open the target CLOB and the source BFILE
   DBMS_LOB.OPEN(directions, DBMS_LOB.LOB_READWRITE);
   DBMS_LOB.OPEN(Tannery_Falls_Directions);

   --Load the contents of the BFILE into the CLOB column
```

```
    DBMS_LOB.LOADCLOBFROMFILE(directions, Tannery_Falls_Directions,
                              DBMS_LOB.LOBMAXSIZE,
                              destination_offset, source_offset,
                              NLS_CHARSET_ID('US7ASCII'),
                              language_context, warning_message);

    --Check for the only possible warning message.
    IF warning_message = DBMS_LOB.WARN_INCONVERTIBLE_CHAR THEN
         dbms_output.put_line(
            'Warning! Some characters couldn''t be converted.');
    END IF;

    --Close both LOBs
    DBMS_LOB.CLOSE(directions);
    DBMS_LOB.CLOSE(Tannery_Falls_Directions);
END;
```

The real work in this snippet of code is done by the call to DBMS_LOB.LOADCLOBFROMFILE. That procedure reads data from the external file, performs any character set translation that's necessary, and writes the data to the CLOB column. We use the new DBMS_LOB.LOBMAXSIZE constant to specify the amount of data to load. We really want *all* the data from the external file, and DBMS_LOB.LOBMAXSIZE is as much as a CLOB will hold.

The destination and source offsets both begin at 1. We want to begin reading with the first character in the BFILE, and we want to begin writing to the first character of the CLOB. To facilitate multiple, sequential calls to LOADCLOBFROMFILE, the procedure will update both of these offsets to point one character past the most recently read character. Because they are IN OUT parameters, we must use variables and not constants in our procedure call.

The call to NLS_CHARSET_ID returns the character set ID number for the character set used by the external file. The LOADCLOBFROMFILE procedure will then convert the data being loaded from that character set to the database character set. The only possible warning message that LOADCLOBFROMFILE can return is that some characters were not convertible from the source to the target character set. We check for this warning in the IF statement following the load.

A warning is not the same as a PL/SQL error; the load will still have occurred, just as we requested.

The following SQL*Plus example shows the data loaded from our external file using LOADCLOBFROMFILE:

```
SQL> SET LONG 2000
SQL> COLUMN falls_directions WORD_WRAPPED FORMAT A70
SQL> SELECT falls_directions
     FROM waterfalls
     WHERE falls_name='Tannery Falls';
```

```
FALLS_DIRECTIONS
----------------------------------------------------------------------
From downtown Munising, take Munising Avenue east. It will
shortly turn into H-58. Watch for Washington Street veering
off to your left. At that intersection you'll see a wooden
stairway going into the woods on your right. Go up that
stairway and follow the trail to the falls. Do not park
on H-58! You'll get a ticket. You can park on Nestor Street,
which is just uphill from the stairway.
```

Temporary LOBs

So far, we've been talking about permanently storing large amounts of unstructured data by means of the various LOB datatypes. Such LOBs are known as *persistent LOBs*. Many applications have a need for *temporary LOBs* that act like local variables but do not exist permanently in the database. This section discusses temporary LOBs and the use of the DBMS_LOB built-in package to manipulate them.

Oracle8*i* and subsequent releases of Oracle's database software support the creation, freeing, access, and update of temporary LOBs through the Oracle Call Interface (OCI) and DBMS_LOB calls. The default lifetime of a temporary LOB is the lifetime of the session that created it, but such LOBs may be explicitly freed sooner by the application. Temporary LOBs are ideal as transient workspaces for data manipulation, and because no logging is done and no redo records are generated, they offer better performance than persistent LOBs do. In addition, whenever you rewrite or update a LOB, Oracle copies the entire LOB to a new segment. By avoiding all the associated redo and logging, applications that perform lots of piecewise operations on LOBs should see significant performance improvements with temporary LOBs.

A temporary LOB is empty when it is created—you don't need to (and, in fact, you will not be able to) use the EMPTY_CLOB and EMPTY_BLOB functions to initialize LOB locators for a temporary LOB. By default, all temporary LOBs are deleted at the end of the session in which they were created. If a process dies unexpectedly or if the database crashes, then temporary LOBs are deleted and the space for temporary LOBs is freed.

Temporary LOBs are just like persistent LOBs in that they exist on disk inside your database. Don't let the word "temporary" fool you into thinking that they are memory structures. Temporary LOBs are written to disk, but instead of being associated with a specific LOB column in a specific table, they are written to disk in your session's temporary tablespace. Thus, if you use temporary LOBs, you need to make sure that your temporary tablespace is large enough to accommodate them.

Let's examine the processes for creating and freeing temporary LOBs. Then we'll look at how you can test to see whether a LOB locator points to a temporary or a permanent LOB. We'll finish up by covering some of the administrative details to consider when you're working with temporary LOBs.

Creating a temporary LOB

Before you can work with a temporary LOB, you need to create it. One way to do this is with a call to the DBMS_LOB.CREATETEMPORARY procedure. This procedure creates a temporary BLOB or CLOB and its corresponding index in your default temporary tablespace. The header is:

```
DBMS_LOB.CREATETEMPORARY (
   lob_loc IN OUT NOCOPY [ BLOB | CLOB CHARACTER SET ANY_CS ],
   cache   IN BOOLEAN,
   dur     IN PLS_INTEGER := DBMS_LOB.SESSION);
```

The parameters to DBMS_LOB.CREATETEMPORARY are listed in Table 12-1.

Table 12-1. CREATETEMPORARY parameters

Parameter	Description
lob_loc	Receives the locator to the LOB.
cache	Specifies whether the LOB should be read into the buffer cache.
dur	Controls the duration of the LOB. The *dur* argument can be one of the following two named constants: *DBMS_LOB.SESSION* Specifies that the temporary LOB created should be cleaned up (memory freed) at the end of the session. This is the default. *DBMS_LOB.CALL* Specifies that the temporary LOB created should be cleaned up (memory freed) at the end of the current program call in which the LOB was created.

Another way to create a temporary LOB is to declare a LOB variable in your PL/SQL code and assign a value to it. For example, the following code creates both a temporary BLOB and a temporary CLOB:

```
DECLARE
   temp_clob CLOB;
   temp_blob BLOB;
BEGIN
   --Assigning a value to a null CLOB or BLOB variable causes
   --PL/SQL to implicitly create a session-duration temporary
   --LOB for you.
   temp_clob :=' http://www.nps.gov/piro/';
   temp_blob := HEXTORAW('7A');
END;
```

We don't really have a strong preference as to which method you should use to create a temporary LOB, but we do believe the use of DBMS_LOB.CREATETEMPORARY makes the intent of your code a bit more explicit.

Freeing a temporary LOB

The DBMS_LOB.FREETEMPORARY procedure frees a temporary BLOB or CLOB in your default temporary tablespace. The header for this procedure is:

```
PROCEDURE DBMS_LOB.FREETEMPORARY (
   lob_loc IN OUT NOCOPY
      [ BLOB | CLOB CHARACTER SET ANY_CS ]);
```

In the following example, we again create two temporary LOBs. Then we explicitly free them:

```
DECLARE
   temp_clob CLOB;
   temp_blob BLOB;
BEGIN
   --Assigning a value to a null CLOB or BLOB variable causes
   --PL/SQL to implicitly create a session-duration temporary
   --LOB for you.
   temp_clob :=' http://www.exploringthenorth.com/alger/alger.html';
   temp_blob := HEXTORAW('7A');

   DBMS_LOB.FREETEMPORARY(temp_clob);
   DBMS_LOB.FREETEMPORARY(temp_blob);
END;
```

After a call to FREETEMPORARY, the LOB locator that was freed (*lob_loc* in the previous specification) is marked as invalid. If an invalid LOB locator is assigned to another LOB locator through an assignment operation in PL/SQL, then the target of the assignment is also freed and marked as invalid.

PL/SQL will implicitly free temporary LOBs when they go out of scope at the end of a block.

Checking to see whether a LOB is temporary

The ISTEMPORARY function tells you if the LOB locator (*lob_loc* in the following specification) points to a temporary or a persistent LOB. The function returns an integer value: 1 means that it is a temporary LOB, and 0 means that it is not (it's a persistent LOB instead).

```
DBMS_LOB.ISTEMPORARY (
   lob_loc IN [ BLOB | CLOB CHARACTER SET ANY_CS ])
  RETURN INTEGER;
```

This function is designed to be called from within SQL; that, presumably, is the reason Oracle did not define ISTEMPORARY to be a Boolean function.

Managing temporary LOBs

Temporary LOBs are handled quite differently from normal, persistent, internal LOBs. With temporary LOBs, there is no support for transaction management, consistent read operations, rollbacks, and so forth. There are various consequences of this lack of support:

- If you encounter an error when processing with a temporary LOB, you must free that LOB and start your processing over again.

- You should not assign multiple LOB locators to the same temporary LOB. Lack of support for consistent read and undo operations can cause performance degradation with multiple locators.
- If a user modifies a temporary LOB while another locator is pointing to it, a copy (referred to by Oracle as a *deep copy*) of that LOB is made. The different locators will then no longer see the same data. To minimize these deep copies, use the NOCOPY compiler hint whenever you're passing LOB locators as arguments.
- To make a temporary LOB permanent, you must call the DBMS_LOB.COPY program and copy the temporary LOB into a permanent LOB.
- Temporary LOB locators are unique to a session. You cannot pass a locator from one session to another (through a database pipe, for example) and make the associated temporary LOB visible in that other session.

Oracle offers a new V$ view called V$TEMPORARY_LOBS that shows how many cached and uncached LOBs exist per session. Your DBA can combine information from V$TEMPORARY_LOBS and the DBA_SEGMENTS data dictionary view to see how much space a session is using for temporary LOBs.

Native LOB Operations in Oracle9i

Almost since the day Oracle unleashed LOB functionality to the vast hordes of Oracle database users, programmers and query-writers have wanted to treat LOBs as very large versions of regular, scalar variables. Particularly, users wanted to treat CLOBs as very large character strings, passing them to SQL functions, using them in SQL statement WHERE clauses, and so forth. To the dismay of many, CLOBs could not be used interchangeably with VARCHAR2s. For example, in Oracle8 and Oracle8*i*, you could not apply a character function to a CLOB column:

```
SELECT SUBSTR(falls_directions,1,60)
FROM waterfalls;
```

Beginning in Oracle9*i* Release 1, however, you can now use CLOBs interchangeably with VARCHAR2s in a wide variety of situations:

- You can pass CLOBs to most SQL and PL/SQL VARCHAR2 functions.
- In PL/SQL, but not in SQL, you can use various relational operators such as less-than (<), greater-than (>), and equals (=) with LOB variables.
- You can assign CLOB values to VARCHAR2 variables and vice versa. You can also select CLOB values into VARCHAR2 variables and vice versa. This is because PL/SQL now implicitly converts between the CLOB and VARCHAR2 types.

Oracle refers to these new capabilities as offering "SQL semantics" for LOBs. From a PL/SQL developer's standpoint, it means that you can manipulate LOBs using native operators rather than a supplied package.

Following is an example showing some of the new things you can do with LOBs in Oracle9*i*:

```
DECLARE
   name CLOB;
   name_upper CLOB;
   directions CLOB;
   blank_space VARCHAR2(1) := ' ';
BEGIN
   --Retrieve a VARCHAR2 into a CLOB, apply a function to a CLOB
   SELECT falls_name, SUBSTR(falls_directions,1,500)
   INTO name, directions
   FROM waterfalls
   WHERE falls_name = 'Munising Falls';

   --Uppercase a CLOB
   name_upper := UPPER(name);

   -- Compare two CLOBs
   IF name = name_upper THEN
      DBMS_OUTPUT.PUT_LINE('We did not need to uppercase the name.');
   END IF;

   --Concatenate a CLOB with some VARCHAR2 strings
   IF INSTR(directions,'Mackinac Bridge') <> 0 THEN
      DBMS_OUTPUT.PUT_LINE('To get to ' || name_upper || blank_space
                           || 'you must cross the Mackinac Bridge.');
   END IF;
END;
```

This example will output the following message:

```
To get to MUNISING FALLS you must cross the Mackinac Bridge.
```

The small piece of code in this example does several interesting things:

- The falls_name column is a VARCHAR2 column, yet it is retrieved into a CLOB variable. This is a demonstration of implicit conversion between the VARCHAR2 and CLOB types.
- The SUBSTR function is used to limit retrieval to only the first 500 characters of the directions to Munising Falls. Further, the UPPER function is used to uppercase the falls name. This demonstrates the application of SQL and PL/SQL functions to LOBs.
- The IF statement that compares name to name_upper is a bit forced, but it demonstrates that relational operators may now be applied to LOBs.
- The uppercased falls name, a CLOB, is concatenated with some string constants and one VARCHAR2 string (blank_space). This shows that CLOBs may now be concatenated.

There are many restrictions and caveats that you need to be aware of when using this functionality. For example, not every function that takes a VARCHAR2 input will accept a CLOB in its place; there are some exceptions. Likewise, not all relational operators are supported for use with LOBs. All of these restrictions and caveats are described in detail in the section called "SQL Semantics Support for LOBs" in Chapter 7 of Oracle's *Modeling and Design Application Developer's Guide—Large Objects*. If you're using this new functionality, we strongly suggest that you take a look at that section of the manual.

SQL semantics for LOBs apply only to internal LOBs: CLOBs, BLOBs, and NCLOBs. SQL semantics support does not apply to BFILEs.

SQL semantics may yield temporary LOBs

One issue you will need to understand when applying SQL semantics to LOBs is that the result is often the creation of a temporary LOB. Think about applying the UPPER function to a CLOB:

```
DECLARE
   directions CLOB;
BEGIN
   SELECT UPPER(falls_directions)
   INTO directions
   FROM waterfalls
   WHERE falls_name = 'Munising Falls';
END;
```

Because they are potentially very large objects, CLOBs are stored on disk. Oracle can't uppercase the CLOB being retrieved because that would mean changing its value on disk, in effect changing a value that we simply want to retrieve. Nor can Oracle make the change to an in-memory copy of the CLOB because the value may not fit in memory, and also because what is being retrieved is only a locator that points to a value that must be on disk. The only option is for the database software to create a temporary CLOB in your temporary tablespace. The UPPER function then copies data from the original CLOB to the temporary CLOB, uppercasing the characters during the copy operation. The SELECT statement then returns a LOB locator pointing to the temporary CLOB, not to the original CLOB. There are two extremely important ramifications to all this:

- You cannot use the locator returned by a function or expression to update the original LOB. The directions variable in our example cannot be used to update the persistent LOB stored in the database because it really points to a temporary LOB returned by the UPPER function.
- Disk space and CPU resources are expended to create a temporary LOB, which can be of considerable size. We'll discuss this issue more in the next section, "Performance impact of using SQL semantics."

If we wish to retrieve an uppercase version of the directions to Munising Falls while still maintaining the ability to update the directions, we'll need to retrieve two LOB locators:

```
DECLARE
   directions_upper CLOB;
   directions_persistent CLOB;
BEGIN
   SELECT UPPER(falls_directions), falls_directions
   INTO directions_upper, directions_persistent
   FROM waterfalls
   WHERE falls_name = 'Munising Falls';
END;
```

Now we can access the uppercase version of the directions via the locator in directions_upper, and we can modify the original directions via the locator in directions_persistent. There's no performance penalty in this case from retrieving the extra locator. The performance hit comes from uppercasing the directions and placing them into a temporary CLOB. The locator in directions_persistent is simply plucked as-is from the database table.

In general, any character-string function to which you normally pass a VARCHAR2, and that normally returns a VARCHAR2 value, will return a temporary CLOB when you pass in a CLOB as input. Similarly, expressions that return CLOBs will most certainly return temporary CLOBs. Temporary CLOBs and BLOBs cannot be used to update the LOBs that you originally used in an expression or function.

Performance impact of using SQL semantics

You'll need to give some thought to performance when you are using the new SQL semantics for LOBs functionality. Remember that the "L" in LOB stands for "large," and that "large" can be as much as four gigabytes. Consequently, you may encounter some serious performance issues if you indiscriminately treat LOBs the same as any other type of variable or column. Have a look at the following query, which attempts to identify all waterfalls for which a visit might require a trip across the Mackinac Bridge:

```
SELECT falls_name
FROM waterfalls
WHERE INSTR(UPPER(falls_directions),'MACKINAC BRIDGE') <> 0;
```

Think about what Oracle must do to resolve this query. For every row in the waterfalls table, it must take the falls_directions column, uppercase it, and place those results into a temporary CLOB (residing in your temporary tablespace). Then it must apply the INSTR function to that temporary LOB to search for the string 'MACKINAC BRIDGE'. In our examples, the directions have been fairly short. Imagine, however, that falls_directions were truly a large LOB, and that the average column size were one gigabyte. Think of the drain on your temporary tablespace as Oracle allocated the necessary room for the temporary LOBs created when uppercasing the directions. Then think of all the time required to make a copy of each CLOB in order to uppercase it, the time required to allocate and deallocate space for temporary CLOBs in your temporary tablespace, and the time required for the INSTR function to search character-by-character through an average of 1 GB per CLOB. Such a query would surely bring the wrath of your DBA down upon you.

Oracle Text and SQL Semantics

If you need to execute queries that look at uppercase versions of CLOB values and you need to do so efficiently, Oracle Text may hold the solution. For example, you might reasonably expect to write a query such as the following some day:

```
SELECT falls_name
FROM waterfalls
WHERE INSTR(UPPER(falls_directions),
            'MACKINAC BRIDGE') <> 0;
```

If falls_directions is a CLOB column, this query may not be all that efficient. However, if you are using Oracle Text, you can define a case-insensitive Oracle Text index on that CLOB column, and then use the CONTAINS predicate to efficiently evaluate the query:

```
SELECT falls_name
FROM waterfalls
WHERE
   CONTAINS(falls_directions,'mackinac bridge') > 0;
```

For more information on CONTAINS and case-insensitive indexes using Oracle Text, see the *Oracle Text Application Developer's Guide*.

Because of all the performance ramifications of applying SQL semantics to LOBs, Oracle's documentation suggests that you limit such applications to LOBs that are 100 KB or less in size. We ourselves don't have a specific size recommendation to pass on to you; you should consider each case in terms of your particular circumstances and how badly you need to accomplish a given task. We encourage you, however, to always give thought to the performance implications of using SQL semantics for LOBs, and possibly to run some tests to experience these implications, so that you can make a reasonable decision based on your circumstances.

LOB Conversion Functions

Oracle provides several conversion functions that are sometimes useful when working with large object data, described in Table 12-2.

Table 12-2. LOB conversion functions

Function	Description
TO_CLOB (*character_data*)	Converts character data into a CLOB. The input to TO_CLOB can be any of the following character types: VARCHAR2, NVARCHAR2, CHAR, NCHAR, CLOB, and NCLOB. If necessary (for example, if the input is NVARCHAR2), input data is converted from the national character set into the database character set.
TO_BLOB(*raw_data*)	Similar to TO_CLOB, but converts RAW or LONG RAW data into a BLOB.
TO_NCLOB (*character_data*)	Does the same as TO_CLOB, except that the result is an NCLOB using the national character set.
TO_LOB (*long_data*)	Accepts either LONG or LONG RAW data as input, and converts that data into a CLOB or a BLOB, respectively. TO_LOB may be invoked only from the SELECT list of a subquery in an INSERT...SELECT...FROM statement.
TO_RAW	Takes a BLOB as input and returns the BLOB's data as a RAW value.

The TO_LOB function is designed specifically to enable one-time conversion of LONG and LONG RAW columns into CLOB and BLOB columns, because LONG and LONG RAW are now considered obsolete. The TO_CLOB and TO_NCLOB functions provide a convenient mechanism for converting character large object data between the database and national language character sets.

Predefined Object Types

Oracle9*i* implements a collection of useful, predefined object types. These include:

XMLType
: Use this to store and manipulate XML data.

Various URI types
: Use these to store uniform resource identifiers (such as HTML addresses).

Various "Any" types
: Use these to define a PL/SQL variable that can hold any type of data.

In the following sections, we provide brief introductions to these predefined object types and then point you to sources of more information.

The XMLType Type

XML (Extensible Markup Language) is fast becoming a very important technology to understand. Did we say "fast becoming"? Strike that—XML is important *right now*, and the predefined object type XMLType enables you to store XML data in an Oracle database and manipulate that XML data from within SQL and PL/SQL.

XML is a huge subject that we can't hope to cover in detail. Instead, we will settle for familiarizing you with XMLType so that you understand how important it is and what you can do with it. To learn more about using XML with Oracle, we recommend Steve Muench's book, *Building Oracle XML Applications* (O'Reilly). To learn more about XML in general, you might try *Learning XML* by Erik T. Ray (O'Reilly).

In Oracle9*i* Release 1, you need to use the "SYS." prefix when referencing the XMLType object type. Release 2 allows synonyms to point to object types, and the database creation script (*$ORACLE_HOME/rdbms/admin/dbmsxmlt.sql*) that creates XMLType now also creates the public synonym XMLTYPE, which points to the SYS.XMLType predefined object type.

Using XMLType, you can easily create a table to hold XML data:

```
CREATE TABLE falls (
   fall_id NUMBER,
   fall SYS.XMLType
);
```

The fall column in this table is of XMLType and can hold XML data. To store XML data into this column, you must invoke the static CreateXML method, passing it your XML data. CreateXML accepts XML data as input and instantiates a new XMLType object to hold that data.

The new object is then returned as the method's result, and it is that object that you must store in the column. CreateXML is overloaded to accept both VARCHAR2 strings and CLOBs as input.

Use the following INSERT statements to create three XML documents in the falls table:

```
INSERT INTO falls VALUES (1, XMLType.CreateXML(
   '<?xml version="1.0"?>
    <fall>
       <name>Munising Falls</name>
       <county>Alger</county>
       <state>MI</state>
       <url>
          http://michiganwaterfalls.com/munising_falls/munising_falls.html
       </url>
    </fall>'));

INSERT INTO falls VALUES (2, XMLType.CreateXML(
   '<?xml version="1.0"?>
    <fall>
       <name>Au Train Falls</name>
       <county>Alger</county>
       <state>MI</state>
       <url>
          http://michiganwaterfalls.com/autrain_falls/autrain_falls.html
       </url>
    </fall>'));
```

```
INSERT INTO falls VALUES (3, XMLType.CreateXML(
   '<?xml version="1.0"?>
   <fall>
      <name>Laughing Whitefish Falls</name>
      <county>Alger</county>
      <state>MI</state>
   </fall>'));
```

You can query XML data in the table using various XMLType methods. The existsNode method used in the following example allows you to test for the existence of a specific XML node in an XML document. The built-in SQL EXISTSNODE function, also in the example, performs the same test. Whether you use the method or the built-in function, you identify the node of interest using an XPath expression.* Both of the following statements produce the same output:

```
SQL> SELECT fall_id
  2  FROM falls f
  3  WHERE f.fall.existsNode('/fall/url') > 0;

SQL> SELECT fall_id
  2  FROM falls
  3  WHERE EXISTSNODE(fall,'/fall/url') > 0;

   FALL_ID
----------
         1
         2
```

You can, of course, also work with XML data from within PL/SQL. In the following example we retrieve the fall column for Munising Falls into a PL/SQL variable that is also of XMLType. Thus, we retrieve the entire XML document into our PL/SQL program, where we can work further with it. After retrieving the document, we extract and print the text from the /fall/url node.

```
<<demo_block>>
DECLARE
   fall XMLType;
   url VARCHAR2(80);
BEGIN
   --Retrieve XML for Munising Falls
   SELECT fall INTO demo_block.fall
   FROM falls f
   WHERE f.fall_id = 1;

   --Extract and display the URL for Munising Falls
   url := fall.extract('/fall/url/text( )').getStringVal;
   DBMS_OUTPUT.PUT_LINE(url);
END;
```

* XPath is a syntax used to describe parts of an XML document. Among other things, you can use XPath to specify a particular node, or attribute value, in an XML document.

We'd like to call your attention to the following two lines:

`SELECT fall INTO demo_block.fall`
: Our variable name, fall, matches the name of the column in the database table. In our SQL query, therefore, we qualify our variable name with the name of our PL/SQL block.

`url := fall.extract('/fall/url/text( )').getStringVal;`
: To get the text of the URL, we invoke two of XMLType's methods:

  `extract`
  : Returns an XML document, of XMLType, containing only the specified fragment of the original XML document. Use XPath notation to specify the fragment that you want returned.

  `getStringVal`
  : Returns the text of an XML document.

In our example, we apply the getStringVal method to the XML document returned by the extract method, thus retrieving the text for the Munising Fall's URL. The extract method returns the contents of the <url> node as a XMLType object, and getStringVal then returns that content as a text string that we can display.

You can even index XMLType columns to allow for efficient retrieval of XML documents based on their content. You do this by creating a function-based index, for which you need the QUERY REWRITE privilege. The following example creates a function-based index on the first 80 characters of each falls name:

```
CREATE INDEX falls_by_name
   ON falls f (
      SUBSTR(
         XMLType.getStringVal(
            XMLType.extract(f.fall,'/fall/name/text()')
         ),1,80
      )
   );
```

We had to use the SUBSTR function in the creation of this index. The getStringVal method returns a string that is too long to index, resulting in an *ORA-01450: maximum key length (3166) exceeded* error. Thus, when creating an index like this, you need to use SUBSTR to restrict the results to some reasonable length.

If you decide to use XMLType in any of your applications, be sure to consult Oracle's documentation for more complete and current information. XMLType was introduced in Oracle9*i* Release 1. Oracle added a great deal of XML functionality in Oracle9*i* Release 2, and if you are using Release 2 you should take the time to become familiar with the latest XML capabilities. Oracle's *Application Developer's Guide—XML* is an important, if not critical, reference for developers working with XML. The *SQL Reference* also has some useful information on XMLType and on the built-in SQL functions that support XML.

The URI Types

The URI types consist of a supertype and a collection of subtypes that provide support for storing URIs in PL/SQL variables and in database columns. UriType is the supertype, and a UriType variable can hold any instance of one of the subtypes:

HttpUriType
: A subtype of UriType that is specific to HTTP URLs, which usually point to web pages.

DBUriType
: A subtype of UriType that supports URLs that are XPath expressions.

XDBUriType
: A subtype of UriType that supports URLs that reference Oracle XML DB objects. XML DB is Oracle's name for a set of XML technologies built into the database.

To facilitate your work with URIs, Oracle9*i* also implements a UriFactory package that automatically generates the appropriate URI type for whatever URI you pass to it.

The URI types are created by the script named *dbmsuri.sql $ORACLE_HOME/rdbms/admin directory*. All the types and subtypes are owned by the user SYS, and as with XMLType in Oracle9*i* Release 1 you must use a "SYS." prefix to reference them (no longer necessary in Release 2).

The following code example demonstrates the use of HttpUriType.

```
DECLARE
   WebPageURL HttpUriType;
   WebPage CLOB;
BEGIN
   --Create an instance of the type pointing
   --to a message from Jonathan Gennick
   WebPageURL := HttpUriType.createUri(
                  'http://gennick.com/message.plsql');

   --Retrieve the message via HTTP
   WebPage := WebPageURL.getclob( );

   --Display the message
   DBMS_OUTPUT.PUT_LINE((SUBSTR(WebPage,1,60)));
END;
```

The output from this code example will be:

```
Brighten the corner where you are.
```

For more information on the use of the UriType family, see the *Oracle9i XML API Reference—XDK and Oracle XML DB*.

The "Any" Types

A new family of types known as the "Any" types enables you to write programs to manipulate data when you don't know the type of that data until runtime. Member functions support introspection, allowing you to determine the type of a value at runtime and to access that value.* The following predefined types belong to this family:

AnyData
: Can hold a single value of any type, whether it's a built-in scalar datatype, a user-defined object type, a nested table, a large object, a varying array (VARRAY), or any other type not listed here.

AnyDataSet
: Can hold a set of values of any type, as long as all values are of the same type.

AnyType
: Can hold a description of a type. Think of this as an AnyData without the data.

The "Any" types are created by a script named *dbmsany.sql* found in *$ORACLE_HOME/rdbms/admin*, and are owned by the user SYS, and as with XMLType in Oracle9*i* Release 1, you must use a "SYS." prefix to reference them (no longer necessary in Release 2).

In addition to creating the "Any" types, the *dbmsany.sql* script also creates a package named DBMS_TYPES that defines the constants in the following list. You can use these constants in conjunction with introspection functions such as GETTYPE in order to determine the type of data held by a given AnyData or AnyDataSet variable. The specific numeric values assigned to the constants are not important; rely on the constants, not on their underlying values.

TYPECODE_DATE
TYPECODE_NUMBER
TYPECODE_RAW
TYPECODE_CHAR
TYPECODE_VARCHAR2
TYPECODE_VARCHAR
TYPECODE_MLSLABEL
TYPECODE_BLOB
TYPECODE_BFILE
TYPECODE_CLOB
TYPECODE_CFILE
TYPECODE_TIMESTAMP
TYPECODE_TIMESTAMP_TZ

* An introspection function is one that you can use in a program to examine and learn about variables declared by your program. In essence, your program learns about itself—hence the term *introspection*.

TYPECODE_TIMESTAMP_LTZ
TYPECODE_INTERVAL_YM
TYPECODE_INTERVAL_DS
TYPECODE_REF
TYPECODE_OBJECT
TYPECODE_VARRAY
TYPECODE_TABLE
TYPECODE_NAMEDCOLLECTION
TYPECODE_OPAQUE

The following example creates two user-defined types representing two kinds of geographic features. The subsequent PL/SQL block then uses SYS.AnyType to define a heterogeneous array of features (i.e., each array element can be of a different datatype).

First, you'll need to create the following two types:

```
CREATE OR  REPLACE TYPE waterfall AS OBJECT (
   name VARCHAR2(30),
   height NUMBER
);

CREATE OR REPLACE TYPE river AS OBJECT (
   name VARCHAR2(30),
   length NUMBER
);
```

Next, execute the following PL/SQL code block:

```
DECLARE
   TYPE feature_array IS VARRAY(2) OF SYS.AnyData;
   features feature_array;
   wf waterfall;
   rv river;
   ret_val NUMBER;
BEGIN
   --Create an array where each element is of
   --a different object type
   features := feature_array(
                  AnyData.ConvertObject(
                     waterfall('Grand Sable Falls',30)),
                  AnyData.ConvertObject(
                     river('Manistique River', 85.40))
               );

   --Display the feature data
   FOR x IN 1..features.COUNT LOOP
      --Execute code pertaining to whatever object type
      --we are currently looking at. NOTE! Replace GENNICK
      --with whatever schema you are using.
       CASE features(x).GetTypeName
       WHEN 'GENNICK.WATERFALL' THEN
```

```
            ret_val := features(x).GetObject(wf);
            DBMS_OUTPUT.PUT_LINE('Waterfall: '
               || wf.name || ', Height = ' || wf.height || ' feet.');
         WHEN 'GENNICK.RIVER' THEN
            ret_val := features(x).GetObject(rv);
            DBMS_OUTPUT.PUT_LINE('River: '
               || rv.name || ', Length = ' || rv.length || ' miles.');
         END CASE;
   END LOOP;
END;
```

Finally, your output should appear as follows:

```
Waterfall: Grand Sable Falls, Height = 30 feet.
River: Manistique River, Length = 85.4 miles.
```

Let's look at this code one piece at a time. The features are stored in a VARRAY, which is initialized as follows:

```
features := feature_array(
               AnyData.ConvertObject(
                  waterfall('Grand Sable Falls',30)),
               AnyData.ConvertObject(
                  river('Manistique River, 85.40))
            );
```

Working from the inside out and focusing on Grand Sable Falls, you can interpret this code as follows:

`waterfall('Grand Sable Falls',30)`
: Invokes the constructor for the waterfall type to create an object of that type.

`AnyData.ConvertObject(`
: Converts the waterfall object into an instance of SYS.AnyData, allowing it to be stored in our array of SYS.AnyData objects.

`feature_array(`
: Invokes the constructor for the array. Each argument to feature_array is of type AnyData. The array is built from the two arguments we pass.

VARRAYs were discussed in Chapter 11, and you can read about object types in more detail in Chapter 21.

The next significant part of the code is the FOR loop in which each object in the features array is examined. A call to:

```
features(x).GetTypeName
```

returns the fully qualified type name of the current features object. For user-defined objects, the type name is prefixed with the schema name of the user who created the object. We had to include this schema name in our WHEN clauses; for example:

```
WHEN 'GENNICK.WATERFALL' THEN
```

If you're running this example on your own system, be sure to replace the schema we used (GENNICK) with the one that is valid for you.

For built-in types such as NUMBER, DATE, and VARCHAR2, GetTypeName will return just the type name. Schema names apply only to user-defined types (i.e., those created using CREATE TYPE).

Once we determined which datatype we were dealing with, we retrieved the specific object using the following call:

```
ret_val := features(x).GetObject(wf);
```

In our example, we ignored the return code. There are two possible return code values:

DBMS_TYPES.SUCCESS
: The value (or object, in our case) was successfully returned.

DBMS_TYPES.NO_DATA
: No data was ever stored in the AnyData variable in question, so no data can be returned.

Once we had the object in a variable, it was an easy enough task to write a DBMS_OUTPUT statement specific to that object type. For example, to print information about waterfalls, we used:

```
DBMS_OUTPUT.PUT_LINE('Waterfall: '
   || wf.name || ', Height = ' || wf.height || ' feet.');
```

For more information on the "Any" family of types:

- Visit Chapter 21, which examines the "Any" datatypes from an object-oriented perspective.
- Check out the *Oracle9i Supplied PL/SQL Packages and Types Reference* and the *Oracle9i SQL Reference*.
- Try out the *anynums.pkg* and *anynums.tst* scripts on the O'Reilly web site.

From an object-oriented design standpoint, there are better ways of dealing with multiple feature types than the method we used in this section's example. In the real world, however, not everything is ideal, and our example does serve the purpose of demonstrating the utility of the SYS.AnyData predefined object type.

PART IV
SQL in PL/SQL

This part of the book addresses a central element of PL/SQL code construction: the connection to the underlying Oracle database (which takes places through SQL (Structured Query Language). Chapters 13 through 15 show you how to define transactions that update, insert, and delete tables in the database; query information from the database for processing in a PL/SQL program; and execute SQL statements dynamically, using native dynamic SQL (NDS), which was introduced in Oracle8*i*.

In this chapter:

- DML in PL/SQL
- Bulk DML with the FORALL Statement
- Transaction Management
- Autonomous Transactions

CHAPTER 13
DML and Transaction Management

PL/SQL is tightly integrated with the Oracle database via the SQL language. From within PL/SQL, you can execute any Data Manipulation Language (DML) statements—specifically INSERTs, UPDATEs, DELETEs, and, of course, queries.

You cannot, however, execute Data Definition Language (DDL) statements in PL/SQL unless you run them as dynamic SQL. This topic is covered in Chapter 15.

You can also join multiple SQL statements together logically as a transaction, so that they are either saved ("committed" in SQL parlance) together, or rejected in their entirety ("rolled back"). This chapter examines the SQL statements available inside PL/SQL to establish and manage transactions.

To appreciate the importance of transactions in Oracle, it helps to consider the "ACID" principle: a transaction has Atomicity, Consistency, Isolation, and Durability. These concepts are defined as follows:

Atomicity
: A transaction's changes to a state are atomic: either they all happen or none happens.

Consistency
: A transaction is a correct transformation of state. The actions taken as a group do not violate any integrity constraints associated with that state.

Isolation
: Many transactions may be executing concurrently, but from any given transaction's point of view, other transactions appear to have executed before or after its own execution.

Durability
: Once a transaction completes successfully, the changes to the state are made permanent and survive any subsequent failures.

A transaction can either be saved by performing a COMMIT or be erased by requesting a ROLLBACK. In either case, the affected locks on resources are released (a ROLLBACK TO might release only some of the locks). The session can then start a new transaction. The default behavior in a PL/SQL program is that there is one transaction per session, and all changes that you make are a part of that transaction. By using a feature called *autonomous transactions*, however, you can create nested transactions within the main, session-level transaction. This feature was added to PL/SQL in Oracle8*i* and is covered near the end of this chapter in the section "Autonomous Transactions."

DML in PL/SQL

From within any PL/SQL block of code you can execute DML statements (INSERTs, UPDATEs, and DELETEs) against any and all data structures to which you have access.

Access to these data structures is determined at the time of compilation when you're using the *definer rights model*. If you instead use the *invoker rights model* with the AUTHID CURRENT_USER compile option, access privileges are determined at runtime. See Chapter 20 for more details.

A Quick Introduction to DML

It is outside the scope of this book to provide complete reference information about the features of DML statements in the Oracle SQL language. Instead, we provide a quick overview of the basic syntax, and then explore special features relating to DML inside PL/SQL, including:

- Examples of each DML statement
- Cursor attributes for DML statements
- Special PL/SQL features for DML statements, such as the RETURNING clause

For detailed information, I encourage you to peruse Oracle documentation or a SQL-specific text.

There are three DML statements available in the SQL language:

INSERT
: Inserts one or more new rows into a table

UPDATE
: Updates the values of one or more columns in an existing row in a table

DELETE
: Removes one or more rows from a table

The INSERT statement

Here is the syntax of the two basic types of INSERT statements:

- Insert a single row with an explicit list of values.

```
INSERT INTO table [(col1, col2, ..., coln)]
   VALUES (val1, val2, ..., valn);
```

- Insert one or more rows into a table as defined by a SELECT statement against one or more other tables.

```
INSERT INTO table [(col1, col2, ..., coln)]
AS
   SELECT ...;
```

Let's look at some examples of INSERT statements executed within a PL/SQL block. First, I insert a new row into the book table. Notice that I do not need to specify the names of the columns if I provide a value for each column.

```
BEGIN
   INSERT INTO book
        VALUES ('1-56592-335-9',
           'Oracle PL/SQL Programming',
           'Reference for PL/SQL developers,' ||
           'including examples and best practice ' ||
           'recommendations.',
           'Feuerstein,Steven, with Bill Pribyl',
           TO_DATE ('01-SEP-1997','DD-MON-YYYY'),
           987);
END;
```

I can also list the names of the columns and provide the values as variables, instead of literal values:

```
DECLARE
   l_isbn book.isbn%TYPE := '1-56592-335-9';
   ... other declarations of local variables
BEGIN
   INSERT INTO books (
        isbn, title, summary, author,
        date_published, page_count)
      VALUES (
         l_isbn, l_title, l_summary, l_author,
         l_date_published, l_page_count);
```

Here is an example of an INSERT SELECT FROM statement that creates "sequels" for each of my existing books. Notice that as I retrieve data from the existing book rows, I change the values of the columns. For example, I create a "dummy" ISBN and add one year to the publication date. Ah, if only it were that easy to update my oeuvre!:

```
BEGIN
   INSERT INTO books (
        isbn, title, summary, author,
        date_published, page_count)
```

```
    SELECT SUBSTR (isbn, 1, LENGTH(isbn)-1) || 'X'
           title || ' - Part Deux',
           summary || ' plus newer stuff',
           author,
           ADD_MONTHS (date_published, 12),
           page_count
      FROM books
     WHERE UPPER (author) LIKE '%FEUERSTEIN, STEVEN%';
END;
```

The UPDATE statement

Now let's take a look at the UPDATE statement. You can update one or more columns in one or more rows using UPDATE. Here is the basic syntax:

```
UPDATE table
   SET col1 = val1
       [, col2 = val2, ... colN = valN]
[WHERE where clause];
```

The WHERE clause is optional; if you do not supply one, all rows in the table are updated. Here are some examples of UPDATEs:

- Uppercase all the titles of books in the book table.

  ```
  UPDATE books SET title = UPPER (title);
  ```

- Run a utility procedure that removes the time component from the publication date of books written by specified authors (the argument in the procedure) and uppercases the titles of those books. As you can see, you can run an UPDATE statement "standalone" or within a PL/SQL block:

  ```
  CREATE OR REPLACE PROCEDURE remove_time (
     author_in IN VARCHAR2)
  IS
  BEGIN
     UPDATE books
        SET title = UPPER (title),
            date_published =
               TRUNC (date_published)
      WHERE author LIKE author_in;
  END;
  ```

The DELETE statement

Finally, let's look at the DELETE statement. You can use DELETE to remove one, some, or all the rows in a table. Here is the basic syntax:

```
DELETE FROM table
 [WHERE where clause];
```

The WHERE clause is optional in a DELETE statement. If you do not supply one, all rows in the table are deleted. Here are some examples of DELETEs:

- Delete all the books from the books table:

  ```
  DELETE FROM books;
  ```

- Delete all the books from the books table that were published prior to a certain date and return the number of rows deleted:

```
CREATE OR REPLACE PROCEDURE remove_books (
   date_in            IN      DATE,
   removal_count_out  OUT     PLS_INTEGER)
IS
BEGIN
   DELETE FROM books
         WHERE date_published < date_in;

   removal_count_out := SQL%ROWCOUNT;
END;
```

Of course, all of these DML statements can become qualitatively more complex as you deal with real-world entities. You can, for example, update multiple columns with the contents of a subquery. As of Oracle9*i*, you can replace a table name with a *table function* that returns a result set upon which the DML statement acts.

As I mentioned, this chapter is limited to exploring the intersection point of DML and PL/SQL. It will answer such questions as: How can you take full advantage of DML from within the PL/SQL language? And how do you manage transactions that are created implicitly when you execute DML statements?

First, let's take a look at the cursor attributes that Oracle provides for the implicit cursors "behind" your DML statements.

Cursor Attributes for DML Operations

Oracle allows you to access information about the most recently executed implicit cursor by referencing one of the following special implicit cursor attributes:

SQL%FOUND
SQL%NOTFOUND
SQL%ROWCOUNT
SQL%ISOPEN

Implicit cursor attributes return information about the execution of an INSERT, UPDATE, DELETE, or SELECT INTO statement. Cursor attributes for SELECT INTOs are covered in Chapter 14. In this section, we'll discuss how to take advantage of the SQL% attributes for DML statements.

First of all, remember that the values of implicit cursor attributes always refer to the most recently executed SQL statement, regardless of the block in which the implicit cursor is executed. And before Oracle opens the first SQL cursor in the session, all the implicit cursor attributes yield NULL. (The exception is %ISOPEN, which returns FALSE.)

Table 13-1 summarizes the significance of the values returned by these attributes for implicit cursors.

Table 13-1. Implicit SQL cursor attributes for DML statements

Name	Description
SQL%FOUND	Returns TRUE if one or more rows were modified (created, changed, removed) successfully.
SQL%NOTFOUND	Returns TRUE if no rows were modified by the DML statement.
SQL%ROWCOUNT	Returns number of rows modified by the DML statement.
SQL%ISOPEN	Always returns FALSE for implicit cursors, because Oracle opens and closes implicit cursors automatically.

Now let's see how we can use cursor attributes with implicit cursors.

- Use SQL%FOUND to determine if your DML statement affected any rows. For example, from time to time an author will change his name and want the new name used for all of his books. So I create a small procedure to update the name and then report back via a Boolean variable the number of book entries affected:

```
CREATE OR REPLACE PROCEDURE change_author_name (
   old_name_in        IN      books.author%TYPE,
   new_name_in        IN      books.author%TYPE,
   changes_made_out   OUT     BOOLEAN)
IS
BEGIN
   UPDATE books
      SET author = new_name_in
    WHERE author = old_name_in;

   changes_made_out := SQL%FOUND;
END;
```

- Use SQL%NOTFOUND to confirm that your DML statement did not affect any rows. This is the inverse of SQL%FOUND.
- Use SQL%ROWCOUNT when you need to know exactly how many rows were affected by your DML statement. Here is a reworking of the above name-change procedure that returns a bit more information:

```
CREATE OR REPLACE PROCEDURE change_author_name (
   old_name_in        IN      books.author%TYPE,
   new_name_in        IN      books.author%TYPE,
   rename_count_out   OUT     PLS_INTEGER)
IS
BEGIN
   UPDATE books
      SET author = new_name_in
    WHERE author = old_name_in;

   rename_count_out := SQL%ROWCOUNT;
END;
```

RETURNING Information from DML Statements

Suppose that I perform an UPDATE or DELETE, and then need to get information about the results of that statement for future processing. Rather than perform a distinct query following the DML statement, I can add a RETURNING clause to an INSERT, UPDATE, or DELETE and retrieve that information directly into variables in my program. With the RETURNING clause, you can reduce network round trips, consume less server CPU time, and minimize the number of cursors opened and managed in the application.

Here are some examples that demonstrate the capabilities of this feature.

- The following very simple block shows how I use the RETURNING clause to retrieve a value (the new salary) that was computed within the UPDATE statement:

```
DECLARE
   myname  employee.last_name%TYPE;
   mysal   employee.salary%TYPE;
BEGIN
   FOR rec IN (SELECT *
                 FROM employee)
   LOOP
      UPDATE    employee
            SET salary = new_compensation (rec)
          WHERE employee_id = rec.employee_id
      RETURNING salary, last_name
           INTO mysal, myname;
      DBMS_OUTPUT.PUT_LINE ('New salary for ' ||
         myname || ' = ' || mysal;
   END LOOP;
END;
```

- In the following block, I take advantage of RETURNING to obtain a LOB locator so that I can move the contents of a BFILE image into a BLOB in the database:

```
DECLARE
   pic_file BFILE := BFILENAME('WEB_PIX', 'memories.jpg');
   pic_blob_loc BLOB := EMPTY_BLOB( );
BEGIN
   INSERT INTO web_graphic_blobs
      VALUES (1, pic_blob_loc)
      RETURNING image INTO pic_blob_loc;
   DBMS_LOB.FILEOPEN(pic_file, DBMS_LOB.FILE_READONLY);
   DBMS_LOB.LOADFROMFILE(dest_lob => pic_blob_loc,
      src_lob => pic_file,
      amount => DBMS_LOB.GETLENGTH(pic_file));
   DBMS_LOB.FILECLOSE(pic_file);
END;
/
```

- Suppose that I perform an UPDATE that modifies more than one row. In this case, I can return information not just into a single variable, but into a collection using the BULK COLLECT syntax. This technique is shown below in a FORALL statement:

```
DECLARE
   names name_varray;
```

```
      new_salaries number_varray;
   BEGIN
      populate_names_array (names);

      FORALL indx IN names.FIRST .. names.LAST
         UPDATE compensation
            SET salary = new_compensation (names(indx))
          WHERE name = names (indx)
          RETURNING salary BULK COLLECT INTO new_salaries;
      ...
   END;
```

DML and Exception Handling

When an exception occurs in a PL/SQL block, Oracle does not roll back any of the changes made by DML statements in that block. It is up to you, the manager of the application's logical transaction, to decide what sort of behavior should occur.

Consider the following procedure:

```
CREATE OR REPLACE PROCEDURE empty_library (
   pre_empty_count OUT PLS_INTEGER)
IS
BEGIN
   -- The tabCount function returns the number
   -- of rows in the specified table, using
   -- Native Dynamic SQL. See Chapter 15 for details.
   pre_empty_count := tabcount ('books');

   DELETE FROM books;
   RAISE NO_DATA_FOUND;
END;
```

Notice that I set the value of the OUT parameter before I raise the exception. Now let's run an anonymous block that calls this procedure, and examine the after-effects:

```
DECLARE
   table_count   NUMBER := -1;
BEGIN
   INSERT INTO books
        VALUES (...);

   empty_library (table_count);
EXCEPTION
   WHEN OTHERS
   THEN
      DBMS_OUTPUT.put_line (tabcount ('books'));
      DBMS_OUTPUT.put_line (table_count);
END;
```

The output is:

```
0
-1
```

Notice that my rows remain deleted from the books table even though an exception was raised; Oracle did not perform an automatic rollback. My table_count variable, however, retains its original value. Oracle does perform a kind of rollback on the program variables involved when an exception occurs.

So it is up to you to perform rollbacks—or rather, to decide if you want to perform a rollback—in programs that perform DML. Here are some things to keep in mind in this regard:

- If your block is an autonomous transaction (described later in this chapter), then you must perform a rollback or commit (usually a rollback) when an exception is raised.
- You can use *savepoints* to control the scope of a rollback. In other words, you can roll back to a particular savepoint and thereby preserve a portion of the changes made in your session. Savepoints are also explored later in this chapter.
- If an exception propagates past the outermost block (i.e., it goes "unhandled"), then in most host execution environments for PL/SQL like SQL*Plus, an unqualified rollback is automatically executed, reversing any outstanding changes.

DML and Records

New to Oracle9*i* Release 2, you can now use records in INSERT and UPDATE statements. Here is an example:

```
CREATE OR REPLACE PROCEDURE set_book_info (
   book_in IN books%ROWTYPE)
IS
BEGIN
   INSERT INTO books VALUES book_in;
EXCEPTION
   WHEN DUP_VAL_ON_INDEX
   THEN
      UPDATE books SET ROW = book_in
       WHERE isbn = book_in.isbn;
END;
```

This enhancement offers some compelling advantages over working with individual variables or fields within a record:

Very concise code
: You can "stay above the fray" and work completely at the record level. There is no need to declare individual variables or decompose a record into its fields when passing that data to the DML statement.

More robust code
: By working with %ROWTYPE records and not explicitly manipulating fields in those records, your code is less likely to break as changes are made to the tables and views upon which the records are based.

In the section "Restrictions on record-based inserts and updates," you will find a list of restrictions on using records in DML statements. First, let's take a look at how you can take advantage of record-based DML for the two supported statements, INSERT and UPDATE.

Record-based inserts

You can INSERT using a record both with single-row inserts and bulk inserts (via the FORALL statement). You can also use records that are based on %ROWTYPE declarations against the table to which the insert is made, or on an explicit record TYPE that is compatible with the structure of the table.

Here are some examples.

- Insert a row into the books table with a %ROWTYPE record:

  ```
  DECLARE
     my_book books%ROWTYPE;
  BEGIN
     my_book.isbn := '1-56592-335-9';
     my_book.title := 'ORACLE PL/SQL PROGRAMMING';
     my_book.summary := 'General user guide and reference';
     my_book.author := 'FEUERSTEIN, STEVEN AND BILL PRIBYL';
     my_book.page_count := 1000;

     INSERT INTO books VALUES my_book;
  END;
  ```

  Notice that you do not include parentheses around the record specifier. If you use this format:

  ```
  INSERT INTO books VALUES (my_book);
  ```

  then you will get an *ORA-00947: not enough values* exception.

  You can also use a record based on a programmer-defined record TYPE to perform the INSERT, but that record type must be 100% compatible with the table %ROWTYPE definition. You may not, in other words, INSERT using a record that covers only a subset of the table's columns.

- Perform record-based inserts with the FORALL statement. You can also work with collections of records and insert all those records directly into a table within the FORALL statement, as in:

  ```
  DECLARE
     TYPE book_list_t IS TABLE OF books%ROWTYPE;
     my_books book_list_t := book_list_t();
  BEGIN
     my_books.EXTEND (2);

     my_books(1).isbn := '1-56592-335-9';
     my_books(1).title := 'ORACLE PL/SQL PROGRAMMING';

     my_books(2).isbn := '0-596-00121-5';
     my_books(2).title := 'ORACLE PL/SQL BEST PRACTICES';
  ```

```
    FORALL indx IN my_books.FIRST .. my_books.LAST
        INSERT INTO books VALUES my_books(indx);
END;
```

Record-based updates

With Oracle9*i* Release 2, you can also perform updates of an entire row with a record. The following example inserts a row into the books table with a %ROWTYPE record. Notice that I use a new keyword, ROW, to indicate that I am updating the entire row with a record:

```
DECLARE
   my_book books%ROWTYPE;
BEGIN
   my_book.isbn := '1-56592-335-9';
   my_book.title := 'ORACLE PL/SQL PROGRAMMING';
   my_book.summary := 'General user guide and reference';
   my_book.author := 'FEUERSTEIN, STEVEN AND BILL PRIBYL';
   my_book.page_count := 980; -- new page count for 3rd edition

   UPDATE books
      SET ROW = my_book
    WHERE isbn = my_book.isbn;
END;
```

There are some restrictions on record-based updates:

- You must update an entire row with the ROW syntax. You cannot update a subset of columns (although this may be supported in future releases).
- You cannot perform an update using a subquery.

Using records with the RETURNING clause

DML statements can include a RETURNING clause that returns column values (and expressions based on those values) from the affected row(s). You can return into a record, or even a collection of records:

```
DECLARE
   my_book_new_info books%ROWTYPE;
   my_book_return_info books%ROWTYPE;
BEGIN
   my_book.isbn := '1-56592-335-9';
   my_book.title := 'ORACLE PL/SQL PROGRAMMING';
   my_book.summary := 'General user guide and reference';
   my_book.author := 'FEUERSTEIN, STEVEN AND BILL PRIBYL';
   my_book.page_count := 980; -- new page count for 3rd edition

   UPDATE books
      SET ROW = my_book_new_info
    WHERE isbn = my_book.isbn
    RETURNING isbn, title, summary, author, page_count INTO
              my_book_return_info;
END;
```

Notice that I must list each of my individual columns in the RETURNING clause. Oracle does not yet support use of the * syntax.

If I am updating more than one row, I can use the BULK COLLECT feature (see Chapter 14 for more information) to retrieve my RETURNING information for each row updated into a collection.

```
DECLARE
   my_book_new_info books%ROWTYPE;

   TYPE book_list_t IS TABLE OF books INDEX BY BINARY_INTEGER;
   my_books book_lis_t;
BEGIN
   -- The publisher switches to a new format for their Oracle books,
   -- which means that all page counts will go down by 10%.

   UPDATE books
      SET page_count = page_count * .9
    WHERE UPPER (title) LIKE '%ORACLE%'
    RETURNING isbn, title, summary, author, page_count
      BULK COLLECT INTO my_books;
END;
```

Restrictions on record-based inserts and updates

As you begin to explore these new capabilities and put them to use, keep in mind the following:

- You can use a record variable only (a) on the right side of the SET clause in UPDATEs; (b) in the VALUES clause of an INSERT; or (c) in the INTO subclause of a RETURNING clause.
- You must (and can only) use the ROW keyword on the left side of a SET clause. In this case, you may not have any other SET clauses (i.e., you cannot SET a row and then SET an individual column).
- If you INSERT with a record, you cannot pass individual values for columns.
- You cannot INSERT or UPDATE with a record that contains a nested record or with a function that returns a nested record.
- You cannot use records in DML statements that are executed dynamically (EXECUTE IMMEDIATE). This would require Oracle to support the binding of a PL/SQL record type into a SQL statement, and only SQL types can be bound in this way.

Bulk DML with the FORALL Statement

Oracle introduced a significant enhancement to PL/SQL's DML capabilities for Oracle8*i* and above with the FORALL statement. FORALL tells the PL/SQL runtime engine to bulk bind into the SQL statement all of the elements of one or more collections before sending anything to the SQL engine. Why would this be useful? We all know that PL/SQL is tightly integrated with the underlying SQL engine in the Oracle database. PL/SQL is the database programming language of choice for Oracle—even though you can now (at least theoretically) use Java inside the database as well.

But this tight integration does not necessarily mean that no overhead is associated with running SQL from a PL/SQL program. When the PL/SQL runtime engine processes a block of code, it executes the procedural statements within its own engine but passes the SQL statements on to the SQL engine. The SQL layer executes the SQL statements and then returns information to the PL/SQL engine, if necessary.

This transfer of control (shown in Figure 13-1) between the PL/SQL and SQL engines is called a *context switch*. Each time a switch occurs, there is additional overhead. There are a number of scenarios in which many switches occur and performance degrades. In Oracle8*i* and above, Oracle now offers two enhancements to PL/SQL that allow you to bulk together multiple context switches into a single switch, thereby improving the performance of your applications. These enhancements are FORALL, which is explored in this chapter, and BULK COLLECT, which is explained in Chapter 14.

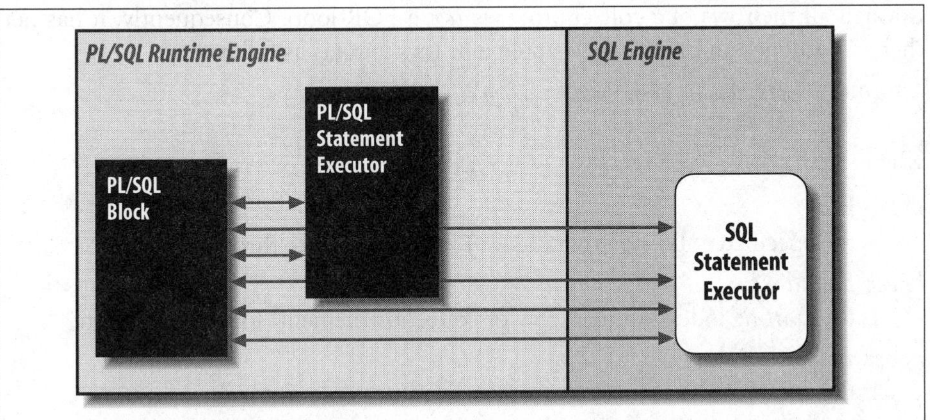

Figure 13-1. Context switching between PL/SQL and SQL

When the statement is bulk bound and passed to SQL, the SQL engine executes the statement once for each index number in the range. In other words, the same SQL statements are executed, but they are all run in the same round trip to the SQL layer, minimizing the context switches. This is shown in Figure 13-2.

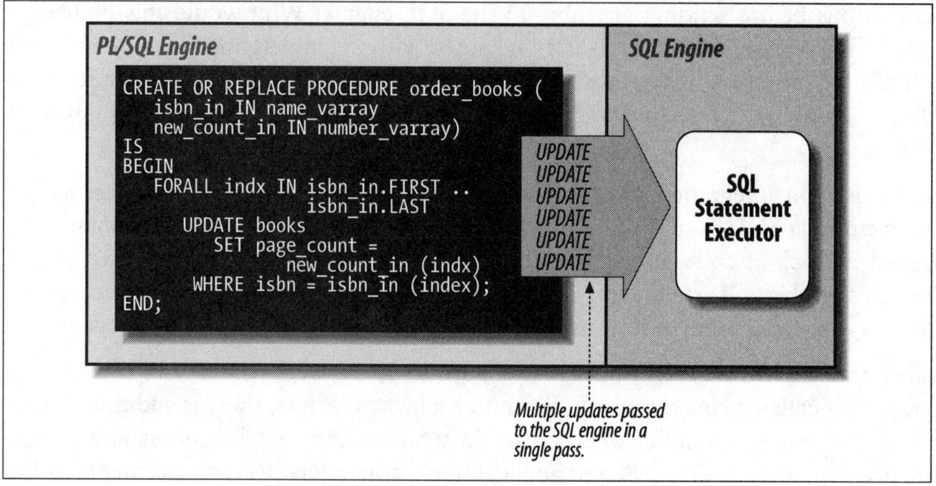
PL/SQL Engine
SQL Engine
CREATE OR REPLACE PROCEDURE order_books (
isbn_in IN name_varray
new_count_in IN number_varray)
IS
BEGIN
FORALL indx IN isbn_in.FIRST ..
isbn_in.LAST
UPDATE books
SET page_count =
new_count_in (indx)
WHERE isbn = isbn_in (index);
END;
UPDATE
UPDATE
UPDATE
UPDATE
UPDATE
UPDATE
SQL
Statement
Executor
Multiple updates passed
to the SQL engine in a
single pass.

Figure 13-2. One context switch with FORALL

The FORALL Statement

Although the FORALL statement contains an iteration scheme (i.e., it iterates through all the rows of a collection), it is not a FOR loop. Consequently, it has neither a LOOP nor an END LOOP statement. Its syntax is as follows:

```
FORALL index_row IN lower_bound ... upper_bound
   sql_statement;
```

where:

index_row
: Is the specified collection that the FORALL will iterate through

lower_bound
: Is the starting index number (row or collection element) for the operation

upper_bound
: Is the ending index number (row or collection element) for the operation

sql_statement
: Is the SQL statement to be performed on each collection element

You must follow these rules when using FORALL:

- The body of the FORALL statement must be a single DML statement—an INSERT, UPDATE, or DELETE.
- The DML statement must reference collection elements, indexed by the *index_row* variable in the FORALL statement. The scope of the *index_row* variable is the FORALL statement only; you may not reference it outside of that statement. Note, though, that the upper and lower bounds of these collections do not have to span the entire contents of the collection(s).

- Do not declare a variable for *index_row*. It is declared implicitly as PLS_INTEGER by the PL/SQL engine.
- The lower and upper bounds must specify a valid range of consecutive index numbers for the collection(s) referenced in the SQL statement. Sparsely filled collections will raise the following error:

  ```
  ORA-22160: element at index [3] does not exist
  ```

  See the *diffcount.sql* file on O'Reilly site for an example of this scenario.
- The collection subscript referenced in the DML statement cannot be an expression. For example, the following script:

  ```
  DECLARE
     names name_varray := name_varray( );
  BEGIN
     FORALL indx IN names.FIRST .. names.LAST
        DELETE FROM emp WHERE ename = names(indx+10);
  END;
  ```

  will cause the following error:

  ```
  PLS-00430: FORALL iteration variable INDX is not allowed in this context
  ```

Context-Switching Problem Scenarios

Before we look at the details of FORALL, let's examine the scenarios in which excessive context switches are likely to cause problems. These scenarios may occur when you are processing multiple rows of information stored (or to be deposited) in a collection (a VARRAY, nested table, or associative array).

Suppose, for example, that I need to write a procedure to update the page count of specified books in my books table. Inputs to my program are two collections, one that contains the ISBN numbers of the books to be updated and another that holds the page counts for those books. Here's the solution I would have written prior to Oracle 8.1 (taking advantage of two previously defined variable array types, name_varray and number_varray):

```
CREATE OR REPLACE PROCEDURE order_books (
   isbn_in IN name_varray,
   new_count_in IN number_varray)
IS
BEGIN
   FOR indx IN isbn_in.FIRST .. isbn_in.LAST
   LOOP
      UPDATE books
         SET page_count = new_count_in (indx)
       WHERE isbn = isbn_in (indx);
   END LOOP;
END;
```

If I needed to insert 100 rows, then I would be performing at least 100 context switches, because each update is processed in a separate trip to the SQL engine. Figure 13-3 illustrates this excessive (but previously unavoidable) switching.

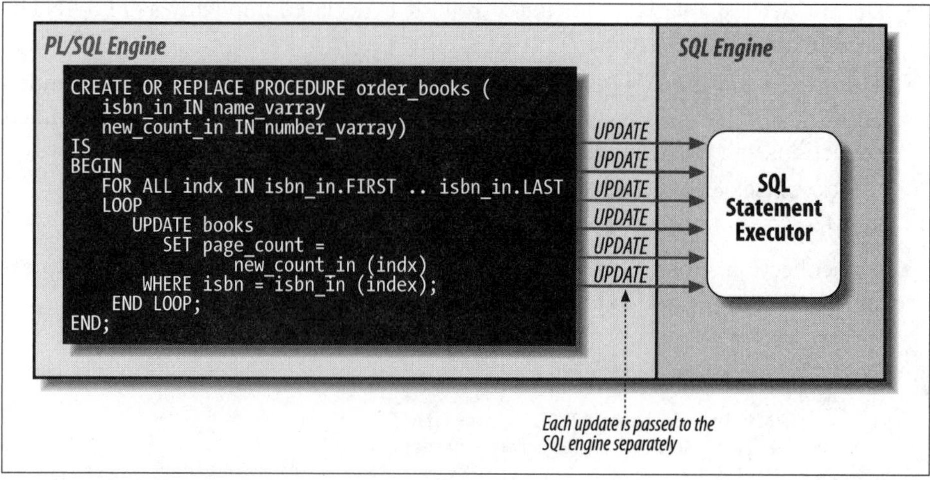
PL/SQL Engine
SQL Engine
CREATE OR REPLACE PROCEDURE order_books (
isbn_in IN name_varray
new_count_in IN number_varray)
IS
BEGIN
FOR ALL indx IN isbn_in.FIRST .. isbn_in.LAST
LOOP
UPDATE books
SET page_count =
new_count_in (indx)
WHERE isbn = isbn_in (index);
END LOOP;
END;
UPDATE
UPDATE
UPDATE
UPDATE
UPDATE
UPDATE
SQL
Statement
Executor
Each update is passed to the
SQL engine separately

Figure 13-3. Excessive context switching for multiple UPDATEs

You can also run into lots of switching when you fetch multiple rows of information from a cursor into a collection. Here is an example of the kind of code that cries out for the bulk collection feature:

```
DECLARE
   CURSOR major_polluters IS
      SELECT name, mileage
        FROM cars_and_trucks
       WHERE vehicle_type IN ('SUV', 'PICKUP');
   names name_varray := name_varray( );
   mileages number_varray := number_varray( );
BEGIN
   FOR bad_car IN major_polluters
   LOOP
      names.EXTEND;
      names (major_polluters%ROWCOUNT) := bad_car.name;
      mileages.EXTEND;
      mileages (major_polluters%ROWCOUNT) := bad_car.mileage;
   END LOOP;

   ... now work with data in the arrays ...
END;
```

If you find yourself writing code like either of these examples, you will be much better off switching to one of the bulk operations explored in the following sections. In particular, you should keep an eye out for these cues in your code:

- A recurring SQL statement inside a PL/SQL loop. (It doesn't have to be a FOR loop, but that is the most likely candidate.)
- Some parameter that can be made a bind variable. You need to be able to load those values into a collection to have it processed by FORALL.

FORALL Examples

Here are some examples of the use of the FORALL statement:

- Let's rewrite the order_books procedure to use FORALL:

  ```
  CREATE OR REPLACE PROCEDURE order_books (
     isbn_in IN name_varray,
     new_count_in IN number_varray)
  IS
  BEGIN
     FORALL indx IN isbn_in.FIRST .. isbn_in.LAST
        UPDATE books
           SET page_count = new_count_in (indx)
         WHERE isbn = isbn_in (indx);
  END;
  ```

  Notice that the only changes in this example are to change FOR to FORALL, and to remove the LOOP and END LOOP keywords. This use of FORALL accesses and passes to SQL each of the rows defined in the two collections. Figure 13-2 shows the change in behavior that results.

- The next example shows how the DML statement can reference more than one collection. In this case, I have three collections: denial, patient_name, and illnesses. Only the first two are subscripted, and so individual elements of the collection are passed to each INSERT. The third column in health_coverage is a collection listing preconditions. Because the PL/SQL engine bulk binds only subscripted collections, the illnesses collection is placed in that column for each row inserted:

  ```
  FORALL indx IN denial.FIRST .. denial.LAST
     INSERT INTO health_coverage
        VALUES (denial(indx), patient_name(indx), illnesses);
  ```

- Use the RETURNING clause in a FORALL statement to retrieve information about each separate DELETE statement. Notice that the RETURNING clause in FORALL must use BULK COLLECT INTO (the corresponding "bulk" operation for queries):

  ```
  CREATE OR REPLACE FUNCTION remove_emps_by_dept (deptlist dlist_t)
     RETURN enolist_t
  IS
     enolist enolist_t;
  BEGIN
     FORALL aDept IN deptlist.FIRST..deptlist.LAST
        DELETE FROM emp WHERE deptno IN deptlist(aDept)
           RETURNING empno BULK COLLECT INTO enolist;
     RETURN enolist;
  END;
  ```

Cursor Attributes for FORALL

You can use cursor attributes after you execute a FORALL statement to get information about the DML operation run within FORALL. Oracle also offers an additional attribute, %BULK_ROWCOUNT, to give you more granular information about the results of the bulk DML statement.

Table 13-2 describes the significance of the values returned by these attributes for FORALL.

Table 13-2. Implicit SQL cursor attributes for DML statements

Name	Description
SQL%FOUND	Returns TRUE if the last execution of the SQL statement modified one or more rows.
SQL%NOTFOUND	Returns TRUE if the last execution of the SQL statement modified one or more rows.
SQL%ROWCOUNT	Returns the total number of rows processed by all executions of the SQL statement, not just the last statement.
SQL%ISOPEN	Always returns FALSE and should not be used.
SQL%BULK_ROWCOUNT	Returns a collection that tells you the number of rows processed by each corresponding SQL statement executed via FORALL. Note: when %BULK_ROWCOUNT(i) is zero, %FOUND and %NOTFOUND are FALSE and TRUE, respectively.

Let's now explore the %BULK_ROWCOUNT composite attribute. This attribute, designed specifically for use with FORALL, has the semantics of (acts like) an associative array or collection. Oracle deposits in the *N*th element in this collection the number of rows processed by the *N*th execution of the FORALL's INSERT, UPDATE, or DELETE. If no rows were affected, the *N*th row will contain a zero value.

Here is an example of using %BULK_ROWCOUNT (and the overall %ROWCOUNT attribute as well):

```
DECLARE
   TYPE isbn_list IS TABLE OF VARCHAR2(13);

   my_books  isbn_list
   := isbn_list (
         '1-56592-375-8',
         '0-596-00121-5',
         '1-56592-849-0',
         '1-56592-335-9',
         '1-56592-674-9',
         '1-56592-675-7',
         '0-596-00180-0',
         '1-56592-457-6'
      );
BEGIN
   FORALL book_index IN
         my_books.FIRST..my_books.LAST
```

```
        UPDATE books
           SET page_count
         WHERE isbn = my_books (book_index);

    -- Did I update the total number of books I expected?
    IF SQL%ROWCOUNT != 8
    THEN
        DBMS_OUTPUT.PUT_LINE (
           'We are missing a book!');
    END IF;

    -- Did the 4th UPDATE statement affect any rows?
    IF SQL%BULK_ROWCOUNT(4) = 0
    THEN
        DBMS_OUTPUT.PUT_LINE (
           'What happened to Oracle PL/SQL Programming?');;
    END IF;
END;
```

Here are some tips on how this attribute works:

- The FORALL statement and %BULK_ROWCOUNT use the same subscripts or row numbers in the collections. For example, if the collection passed to FORALL has data in rows 10 through 200, then the %BULK_ROWCOUNT pseudo-collection will also have rows 10 through 200 defined and populated. Any other rows will be undefined.
- When the INSERT affects only a single row (when you specify a VALUES list, for example), a row's value in %BULK_ROWCOUNT will be equal to 1. For INSERT...SELECT statements, however, %BULK_ROWCOUNT can be greater than 1.
- The value in a row of the %BULK_ROWCOUNT pseudo-array for deletes and inserts may be any natural number (0 or positive); these statements can modify more than one row, depending on their WHERE clauses.

ROLLBACK Behavior with FORALL

The FORALL statement allows you to pass multiple SQL statements all together (in bulk) to the SQL engine. This means that as far as context switching is concerned, you have one SQL "block," but these blocks are still treated as individual DML operations.

What happens when one of those DML statements fails? Here is the default behavior:

- The FORALL statement stops executing. It isn't possible to request that the FORALL skip over the offending statement and continue on to the next row in the collection.
- The DML statement being executed is rolled back to an implicit savepoint marked by the PL/SQL engine before execution of the statement.
- Any previous DML operations in that FORALL statement that already executed without error are not rolled back.

Continuing Past Exceptions with FORALL

Oracle9*i* offers a new clause, SAVE EXCEPTIONS, which can be used inside a FORALL statement. By including this clause, you instruct Oracle to continue processing even when an error has occurred. Oracle will then "save the exception" (or multiple exceptions, if more than one error occurs). When the DML statement completes, it will then raise the ORA-24381 exception. In the exception section, you can then access a pseudo-collection called SQL%BULK_EXCEPTIONS to obtain error information.

Here is an example, followed by an explanation of what is going on:

```
/* File on web: bulkexc.sql */
CREATE OR REPLACE PROCEDURE bulk_exceptions (
   whr_in IN VARCHAR2 := NULL)
IS
   TYPE namelist_t IS TABLE OF VARCHAR2 (100);
   enames_with_errors namelist_t := -- Max of 10 characters in emp.
      namelist_t ('LITTLE', 'BIGBIGGERBIGGEST', 'SMITHIE', '');
   bulk_errors EXCEPTION;
   PRAGMA EXCEPTION_INIT ( bulk_errors, -24381 );
BEGIN
   FORALL indx IN
         enames_with_errors.FIRST ..
         enames_with_errors.LAST
      SAVE EXCEPTIONS
      EXECUTE IMMEDIATE
         'UPDATE emp SET ename = :newname'
         USING enames_with_errors(indx);
EXCEPTION
   WHEN bulk_errors
   THEN
      FOR indx IN 1 .. SQL%BULK_EXCEPTIONS.COUNT
      LOOP
         DBMS_OUTPUT.PUT_LINE (
            'Error ' || indx || ' occurred during ' ||
            'iteration ' || SQL%BULK_EXCEPTIONS(indx).ERROR_INDEX ||
            ' updating name to ' ||
               enames_with_errors (
                  SQL%BULK_EXCEPTIONS(indx).ERROR_INDEX));
         DBMS_OUTPUT.PUT_LINE (
            'Oracle error is ' ||
            SQLERRM (-1 * SQL%BULK_EXCEPTIONS(indx).ERROR_CODE));
      END LOOP;
END;
```

When I run this code (with SERVEROUTPUT turned on), I see these results:

```
SQL> exec bulk_exceptions

Error 1 occurred during iteration 2 updating name to BIGBIGGERBIGGEST
Oracle error is ORA-01401: inserted value too large for column

Error 2 occurred during iteration 4 updating name to
Oracle error is ORA-01407: cannot update () to NULL
```

In other words, Oracle encountered two exceptions as it processed the DML for the names collection. It did not stop with the first exception, but continued on, cataloguing a third.

The following table describes the error-handling functionality in this code:

Line(s)	Description
4–6	Declare and populate a collection that will drive the FORALL statement. I have intentionally placed data in the collection that will raise two errors.
8–9	Declare a named exception to make the exception section more readable.
11–17	Execute a dynamic UPDATE statement with FORALL using the enames_with_errors collection.

19	Trap the "bulk exceptions error" by name. I could also have written code like:
	`WHEN OTHERS THEN`
	`   IF SQLCODE = -24381`

20	Use a numeric FOR loop to scan through the contents of the SQL%BULKEXCEPTIONS pseudo-collection. Note that I can call the COUNT method to determine the number of defined rows (errors raised), but I cannot call other methods, such as FIRST and LAST.
22–30	Extract the information from the collection and display (or log) error information.
24	The ERROR_INDEX field of each pseudo-collection's row returns the row number in the driving collection of the FORALL statement for which an exception was raised.
30	The ERROR_CODE field of each pseudo-collection's row returns the error number of the exception that was raised. Note that this value is stored as a positive integer; you will need to multiple it by –1 before passing it to SQLERRM or displaying the information.

Transaction Management

The Oracle RDBMS provides a very robust transaction model, as you might expect from a relational database. Your application code determines what constitutes a *transaction*, which is the logical unit of work that must be either saved with a COMMIT statement or rolled back with a ROLLBACK statement. A transaction begins implicitly with the first SQL statement issued since the last COMMIT or ROLLBACK (or with the start of a session), or continues after a ROLLBACK TO SAVEPOINT.

PL/SQL provides the following statements for transaction management:

COMMIT
: Saves all outstanding changes since the last COMMIT or ROLLBACK and releases all locks.

ROLLBACK
: Erases all outstanding changes since the last COMMIT or ROLLBACK and releases all locks.

ROLLBACK TO SAVEPOINT
: Erases all changes made since the specified savepoint was established, and releases locks that were established within that range of the code.

SAVEPOINT
: Establishes a savepoint, which then allows you to perform partial ROLLBACKs.

SET TRANSACTION
: Allows you to begin a read-only or read-write session, establish an isolation level, or assign the current transaction to a specified rollback segment.

LOCK TABLE
: Allows you to lock an entire database table in the specified mode. This overrides the default row-level locking usually applied to a table.

These statements are explained in more detail in the following sections.

The COMMIT Statement

When you COMMIT, you make permanent any changes made by your session to the database in the current transaction. Once you COMMIT, your changes will be visible to other Oracle sessions or users. The syntax for the COMMIT statement is:

```
COMMIT [WORK] [COMMENT text];
```

The WORK keyword is optional and can be used to improve readability.

The COMMENT keyword specifies a comment that is then associated with the current transaction. The text must be a quoted literal and can be no more than 50 characters in length. The COMMENT text is usually employed with distributed transactions, and can be handy for examining and resolving in-doubt transactions within a two-phase commit framework. It is stored in the data dictionary along with the transaction ID.

Note that COMMIT releases any row and table locks issued in your session, such as with a SELECT FOR UPDATE statement. It also erases any savepoints issued since the last COMMIT or ROLLBACK.

Once you COMMIT your changes, you cannot roll them back with a ROLLBACK statement.

The following statements are all valid uses of COMMIT:

```
COMMIT;
COMMIT WORK;
COMMIT COMMENT 'maintaining account balance'.
```

The ROLLBACK Statement

When you perform a ROLLBACK, you undo some or all changes made by your session to the database in the current transaction. Why would you want to erase changes? From an ad hoc SQL standpoint, the ROLLBACK gives you a way to erase mistakes you might have made, as in:

```
DELETE FROM orders;
```

"No, no! I meant to delete only the orders before May 1995!" No problem—just issue ROLLBACK. From an application coding standpoint, ROLLBACK is important because it allows you to clean up or restart from a clean state when a problem occurs.

The syntax for the ROLLBACK statement is:

```
ROLLBACK [WORK] [TO [SAVEPOINT] savepoint_name];
```

There are two basic ways to use ROLLBACK: without parameters or with the TO clause to indicate a savepoint at which the ROLLBACK should stop. The parameterless ROLLBACK undoes all outstanding changes in your transaction.

The ROLLBACK TO version allows you to undo all changes and release all acquired locks that were issued since the savepoint identified by *savepoint_name* was marked. (See the next section on the SAVEPOINT statement for more information on how to mark a savepoint in your application.)

The *savepoint_name* is an undeclared Oracle identifier. It cannot be a literal (enclosed in quotes) or variable name.

All of the following uses of ROLLBACK are valid:

```
ROLLBACK;
ROLLBACK WORK;
ROLLBACK TO begin_cleanup;
```

When you roll back to a specific savepoint, all savepoints issued after the specified *savepoint_name* are erased, but the savepoint to which you roll back is not. This means that you can restart your transaction from that point and, if necessary, roll back to that same savepoint if another error occurs.

Immediately before you execute an INSERT, UPDATE, or DELETE, PL/SQL implicitly generates a savepoint. If your DML statement then fails, a rollback is automatically performed to that implicit savepoint. In this way, only the last DML statement is undone.

The SAVEPOINT Statement

SAVEPOINT gives a name to, and marks a point in, the processing of your transaction. This marker allows you to ROLLBACK TO that point, erasing any changes and releasing any locks issued after that savepoint, but preserving any changes and locks that occurred before you marked the savepoint.

The syntax for the SAVEPOINT statement is:

```
SAVEPOINT savepoint_name;
```

where *savepoint_name* is an undeclared identifier. This means that it must conform to the rules for an Oracle identifier (up to 30 characters in length, starting with a letter, containing letters, numbers, and #, $, or _), but that you do not need to (and are not able to) declare that identifier.

Savepoints are not scoped to PL/SQL blocks. If you reuse a savepoint name within the current transaction, that savepoint is "moved" from its original position to the current point in the transaction, regardless of the procedure, function, or anonymous block in which the SAVEPOINT statements are executed. As a corollary, if you issue a savepoint inside a recursive program, a new savepoint is executed at each level of recursion, but you can only roll back to the most recently marked savepoint.

The SET TRANSACTION Statement

The SET TRANSACTION statement allows you to begin a read-only or read-write session, establish an isolation level, or assign the current transaction to a specified rollback segment. This statement must be the first SQL statement processed in a transaction, and it can appear only once. This statement comes in the following four flavors.

SET TRANSACTION READ ONLY;
: This version defines the current transaction as read-only. In a read-only transaction, all subsequent queries see only those changes that were committed before the transaction began (providing a read-consistent view across tables and queries). This statement is useful when you are executing long-running, multiple query reports and you want to make sure that the data used in the report is consistent.

SET TRANSACTION READ WRITE;
: This version defines the current transaction as read-write.

SET TRANSACTION ISOLATION LEVEL SERIALIZABLE | READ COMMITTED;
: This version defines how transactions that modify the database should be handled. You can specify a serializable or read-committed isolation level. When you specify SERIALIZABLE, a data manipulation statement (UPDATE, INSERT, DELETE) that attempts to modify a table already modified in an uncommitted transaction will fail. To execute this command, you must set the database initialization parameter COMPATIBLE to 7.3.0 or higher.

  If you specify READ COMMITTED, a DML statement that requires row-level locks held by another transaction will wait until those row locks are released.

SET TRANSACTION USE ROLLBACK SEGMENT `rollback_segname`;
: This version assigns the current transaction to the specified rollback segment and establishes the transaction as read-write. This statement cannot be used in conjunction with SET TRANSACTION READ ONLY.

The LOCK TABLE Statement

This statement allows you to lock an entire database table with the specified lock mode. By doing this, you can share or deny access to that table while you perform operations against it. The syntax for this statement is:

```
LOCK TABLE table_reference_list IN lock_mode MODE [NOWAIT];
```

where *table_reference_list* is a list of one or more table references (identifying either a local table/view or a remote entity through a database link), and *lock_ mode* is the mode of the lock, which can be one of the following:

ROW SHARE
ROW EXCLUSIVE
SHARE UPDATE
SHARE
SHARE ROW EXCLUSIVE
EXCLUSIVE

If you specify the NOWAIT keyword, Oracle will not wait for the lock if the table has already been locked by another user. If you leave out the NOWAIT keyword, Oracle waits until the table is available (and there is no set limit on how long Oracle will wait). Locking a table never stops other users from querying or reading the table.

The following LOCK TABLE statements show valid variations:

```
LOCK TABLE emp IN ROW EXCLUSIVE MODE;
LOCK TABLE emp, dept IN SHARE MODE NOWAIT;
LOCK TABLE scott.emp@new_york IN SHARE UPDATE MODE;
```

Autonomous Transactions

Before the release of PL/SQL 8.1, each Oracle session could have at most one active transaction at a given time. In other words, any and all changes made in your session had to be either saved or erased in their entirety. This restriction has long been considered a drawback in the PL/SQL world. Developers have requested the ability to execute and save or cancel certain DML statements (INSERT, UPDATE, DELETE) without affecting the overall session's transaction.

You can now accomplish this goal with the autonomous transaction feature of PL/SQL 8.1 and above. When you define a PL/SQL block (anonymous block, procedure, function, packaged procedure, packaged function, database trigger) as an *autonomous transaction*, you isolate the DML in that block from the caller's transaction context. That block becomes an independent transaction that is started by another transaction, referred to as the *main transaction*.

Within the autonomous transaction block, the main transaction is suspended. You perform your SQL operations, commit or roll back those operations, and resume the main transaction. This flow of transaction control is illustrated in Figure 13-4.

Defining Autonomous Transactions

There isn't much involved in defining a PL/SQL block as an autonomous transaction. You simply include the following statement in your declaration section:

```
PRAGMA AUTONOMOUS_TRANSACTION;
```

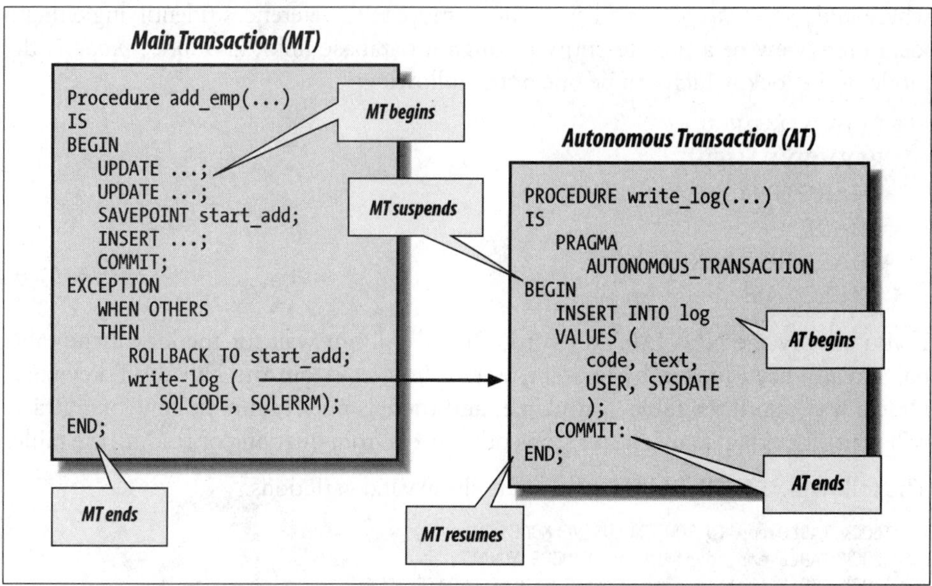

Figure 13-4. Flow of transaction control between main, nested, and autonomous transactions

The pragma instructs the PL/SQL compiler to establish a PL/SQL block as autonomous or independent. For the purposes of the autonomous transaction, a PL/SQL block can be any of the following:

- Top-level (but not nested) anonymous PL/SQL blocks
- Functions and procedures, defined either in a package or as standalone programs
- Methods (functions and procedures) of an object type
- Database triggers

You can put the autonomous transaction pragma anywhere in the declaration section of your PL/SQL block. You would probably be best off, however, placing it before any data structure declarations. That way, anyone reading your code will immediately identify the program as an autonomous transaction.

This pragma is the only syntax change made to PL/SQL to support autonomous transactions. COMMIT, ROLLBACK, the DML statements—all the rest is as it was before. However, these statements have a different scope of impact and visibility when executed within an autonomous transaction, and you will need to include a COMMIT or ROLLBACK in your program.

When to Use Autonomous Transactions

Where would you find autonomous transactions useful in your applications? First, let's reinforce the general principle: you will want to define your program module as an autonomous transaction whenever you want to isolate the changes made in that module from the caller's transaction context.

Here are some specific ideas:

Logging mechanism
: On the one hand, you need to log an error to your database log table. On the other hand, you need to roll back your core transaction because of the error. And you don't want to roll back over other log entries. What's a person to do? Go autonomous!

Commits and rollbacks in your database triggers
: If you define a trigger as an autonomous transaction, then you can commit and/or roll back in that code. Developers have been asking for this capability for a long time.

Retry counter
: Suppose that you want to let a user try to get access to a resource *N* times before an outright rejection; you also want to keep track of attempts between connections to the database. This persistence requires a COMMIT, but one that should remain independent of the transaction. For an example of such a utility, see *retry.pkg* and *retry.tst* on the O'Reilly site.

Software usage meter
: You want to keep track of how often a program is called during an application session. This information is not dependent on, and cannot affect, the transaction being processed in the application.

Reusable application components
: This usage goes to the heart of the value of autonomous transactions. As we move more and more into the dispersed, multi-layered world of the Internet, it becomes ever more important to be able to offer standalone units of work (also known as *cartridges*) that get their job done without any side effects on the calling environment. Autonomous transactions will play a crucial role in this area.

Before we look at how you might use autonomous transactions for these scenarios, let's get a clearer picture about what you can and cannot do with autonomous transactions.

Rules and Restrictions on Autonomous Transactions

While it is certainly very easy to add the autonomous transaction pragma to your code, there are some rules and restrictions on the use of this feature.

- You can make only a top-level anonymous block an autonomous transaction. This will work:

```
DECLARE
   PRAGMA AUTONOMOUS_TRANSACTION;
   myempno NUMBER;
```

```
BEGIN
   INSERT INTO emp VALUES (myempno, ...);
   COMMIT;
END;
```

whereas this construction:

```
DECLARE
   myempno NUMBER;
BEGIN
   DECLARE
      PRAGMA AUTONOMOUS_TRANSACTION;
   BEGIN
      INSERT INTO emp VALUES (myempno, ...);
      COMMIT;
   END;
END;
```

results in this error:

```
PLS-00710: PRAGMA AUTONOMOUS_TRANSACTION cannot be declared here
```

- If an autonomous transaction attempts to access a resource held by the main transaction (which has been suspended until the autonomous routine exits), a deadlock can occur in your program. Here is a simple example to demonstrate the problem. I create a procedure to perform an update, and then call it after having already updated all rows:

```
/* File on web: autondlock.sql */
CREATE OR REPLACE PROCEDURE
   update_salary (dept_in IN NUMBER)
IS
   PRAGMA AUTONOMOUS_TRANSACTION;

   CURSOR myemps IS
      SELECT empno FROM emp
       WHERE deptno = dept_in
         FOR UPDATE NOWAIT;
BEGIN
   FOR rec IN myemps
   LOOP
      UPDATE emp SET sal = sal * 2
       WHERE empno = rec.empno;
   END LOOP;
   COMMIT;
END;

BEGIN
   UPDATE emp SET sal = sal * 2;
   update_salary (10);
END;
```

The results are not pretty:

```
ERROR at line 1:
ORA-00054: resource busy and acquire with NOWAIT specified
```

- You cannot mark all subprograms in a package (or all methods in an object type) as autonomous with a single PRAGMA declaration. You must indicate autonomous transactions explicitly in each program. One consequence of this rule is that you cannot tell by looking at the package specification which (if any) programs will run as autonomous transactions.
- To exit without errors from an autonomous transaction program, you must perform an explicit commit or rollback. If the program (or any program called by it) has transactions pending, the runtime engine will raise the exception shown below—and then will roll back those uncommitted transactions.

  ```
  ORA-06519: active autonomous transaction detected and rolled back
  ```
- The COMMIT and ROLLBACK statements end the active autonomous transaction, but they do not force the termination of the autonomous routine. You can, in fact, have multiple COMMIT and/or ROLLBACK statements inside your autonomous block.
- You can roll back only to savepoints marked in the current transaction. When you are in an autonomous transaction, therefore, you cannot roll back to a savepoint set in the main transaction. If you try to do so, the runtime engine will raise this exception:

  ```
  ORA-01086: savepoint 'your savepoint' never established
  ```
- The TRANSACTIONS parameter in the Oracle initialization file specifies the maximum number of transactions allowed concurrently in a session. If you use lots of autonomous transaction programs in your application, you might exceed this limit, in which case you will see the following exception:

  ```
  ORA-01574: maximum number of concurrent transactions exceeded
  ```

  In this case, increase the value for TRANSACTIONS. The default value is 75.

Using autonomous transactions from within SQL

Ever since Oracle 7.3, you have been able to call your own functions from within SQL—provided that you follow the rules. The main one is this: you are not allowed to update the database. And you certainly can't save or cancel changes from within the function.

With the autonomous transaction feature, however, the picture changes a good deal. An autonomous transaction program never violates the two database-related purity levels, RNDS (reads no database state) and WNDS (writes no database state), even if the program actually does read from or write to the database. This is possible because those purity levels or constraints apply to the SQL statement (which, in this case, is the main transaction), but an autonomous transaction's DML actions never affect the main transaction.

So as long as you define a program to be an autonomous transaction, you can also call it directly or indirectly in a SQL statement. Of course, if your program cannot assert another purity level, such as WNPS (writes no package state), you may be restricted from calling that program in certain parts of the SQL statement, such as the WHERE clause.

As an example, suppose that I want to keep a trace of all the rows that have been touched by a query. I create this table:

```
/* File on web: trcfunc.sql */
CREATE TABLE query_trace (
   table_name VARCHAR2(30),
   rowid_info ROWID,
   queried_by VARCHAR2(30),
   queried_at DATE
   );
```

I then create this simple function to perform the audit:

```
CREATE OR REPLACE FUNCTION traceit (
   tab IN VARCHAR2,
   rowid_in IN ROWID)
   RETURN INTEGER
IS
BEGIN
   INSERT INTO query_trace VALUES (tab, rowid_in, USER, SYSDATE);
   RETURN 0;
END;
```

When I try to use this function inside a query, I get the expected error:

```
SQL> select ename, traceit ('emp', rowid) from emp;
                   *
ERROR at line 1:
ORA-14551: cannot perform a DML operation inside a query
```

However, if I now transform traceit into an autonomous transaction by adding the pragma (and committing my results before the RETURN statement!), the results are very different. My query works, and the query_trace table is filled:

```
SQL> SELECT ename, traceit ('emp', ROWID) FROM emp;

ENAME      TRACEIT('EMP',ROWID)
---------- --------------------
KING                          0
...
MILLER                        0
14 rows selected.

SQL> SELECT table_name, rowid_info, queried_by,
  2         TO_CHAR (queried_at, 'HH:MI:SS') queried_at
  3     FROM query_trace;

TABLE_NAME ROWID_INFO         QUERIED_BY QUERIED_AT
---------- ------------------ ---------- ----------
emp        AAADEPAACAAAAgOAAA SCOTT      05:32:54
...
emp        AAADEPAACAAAAgOAAN SCOTT      05:36:50
```

You have other options when it comes to tracing queries: you can write to the screen with the DBMS_OUTPUT built-in package or send information to a pipe with DBMS_PIPE. Now that autonomous transactions are available, if you do want to send information to a database table (or delete rows, update data, etc.), you can take that route instead, but be sure to carefully analyze the overhead of this approach.

Transaction visibility

The default behavior of autonomous transactions is that once a COMMIT or a ROLLBACK occurs in the autonomous transaction, those changes are visible immediately in the main transaction. But what if you want to hide those changes from the main transaction? You want them saved or erased—no question about that—but the information should not be available to the main transaction.

Oracle offers a SET TRANSACTION statement option to achieve this effect.

```
SET TRANSACTION ISOLATION LEVEL SERIALIZABLE;
```

The default isolation level is READ COMMITTED, which means that as soon as changes are committed, they are visible to the main transaction.

As is usually the case with the SET TRANSACTION statement, you must call it before you initiate your transactions (i.e., issue any SQL statements); in addition, the setting affects your entire session, not just the current program. The following script demonstrates the SERIALIZABLE isolation level at work (the *autonserial.sql* file available from the O'Reilly site will let you run these steps yourself).

First, I create my autonomous transaction procedure:

```
/* File on web: autonserial.sql */
CREATE OR REPLACE PROCEDURE empty_todo_list
IS
   PRAGMA AUTONOMOUS_TRANSACTION;
BEGIN
   DELETE FROM tasks WHERE task_type = 'TODO';
   COMMIT;
END;
```

Then I run a script that sets the isolation level to SERIALIZABLE, and display the number of rows that appear in the tasks table at the following times:

- Before I call empty_todo_list
- After I call empty_todo_list but before the main transaction is committed or rolled back

After I commit in the main transaction, here is the script I run:

```
DECLARE
   PROCEDURE showcount (str VARCHAR2) IS
      num INTEGER;
   BEGIN
      SELECT COUNT(*) INTO num FROM emp2;
```

```
        DBMS_OUTPUT.PUT_LINE (str || ' ' || num);
    END;
BEGIN
    SET TRANSACTION ISOLATION LEVEL SERIALIZABLE;
    showcount ('Before isolated AT delete');
    empty_todo_list;
    showcount ('After isolated AT delete');
    COMMIT;
    showcount ('After MT commit');
END;
```

Here is the output from running the script:

```
Before isolated AT delete 14
After isolated AT delete 14
After MT commit 0
```

Autonomous Transactions Examples

This section provides some complete examples of using autonomous transactions in your applications.

Building an autonomous logging mechanism

A very common requirement in applications is keeping a log of errors that occur during transaction processing. The most convenient repository for this log is a database table; with a table, all the information is retained in the database, and you can use SQL to retrieve and analyze the log.

One problem with a database table log, however, is that entries in the log become a part of your transaction. If you perform a ROLLBACK (or if one is performed to you), you can easily erase your log. How frustrating! You can get fancy and use savepoints to preserve your log entries while cleaning up your transaction, but that approach is not only fancy, it is complicated. With autonomous transactions, however, logging becomes simpler, more manageable, and less error prone.

Suppose that I have a log table defined as follows:

```
/* File on web: log.pkg */
CREATE TABLE logtab (
    code INTEGER,
    text VARCHAR2(4000),
    created_on DATE,
    created_by VARCHAR2(100),
    changed_on DATE,
    changed_by VARCHAR2(100),
    machine VARCHAR2(100),
    program VARCHAR2(100)
    );
```

I can use it to store errors (SQLCODE and SQLERRM) that have occurred, or even for non-error-related logging. The machine and program columns record information available from the virtual V$SESSION table, as you will see.

So I have my table. Now, how should I write to my log? Here's what you should not do:

```
EXCEPTION
   WHEN OTHERS
   THEN
      v_code := SQLCODE;
      v_msg := SQLERRM;
      INSERT INTO logtab VALUES (
         v_code, v_msg, SYSDATE, USER, SYSDATE, USER, NULL, NULL);
END;
```

In other words, never expose your underlying logging mechanism by explicitly inserting into it your exception sections and other locations. Instead, you should build a layer of code around the table (this is known as *encapsulation*). There are two reasons to do this:

- If you ever change your table's structure, all those uses of the log table will not be disrupted.
- People will be able to use the log table in a much easier, more consistent manner.

So here is my very simple logging package. It consists of two procedures:

```
CREATE OR REPLACE PACKAGE log
IS
   PROCEDURE putline (
      code_in IN INTEGER, text_in IN VARCHAR2);

   PROCEDURE saveline (
      code_in IN INTEGER, text_in IN VARCHAR2);
END;
```

What is the difference between putline and saveline? The log.saveline procedure (as you will see in the package body) is an autonomous transaction routine, whereas log.putline simply performs the insert. Here is the package body:

```
/* File on web: log.pkg */
CREATE OR REPLACE PACKAGE BODY log
IS
   PROCEDURE putline (
      code_in IN INTEGER, text_in IN VARCHAR2)
   IS
   BEGIN
      INSERT INTO logtab
           VALUES (
              code_in,
              text_in,
              SYSDATE,
              USER,
```

```
                SYSDATE,
                USER
             );
   END;

   PROCEDURE saveline (
      code_in IN INTEGER, text_in IN VARCHAR2)
   IS
      PRAGMA AUTONOMOUS_TRANSACTION;
   BEGIN
      putline (code_in, text_in);
      COMMIT;
   EXCEPTION WHEN OTHERS THEN ROLLBACK;
   END;
BEGIN
   OPEN sess; FETCH sess INTO rec; CLOSE sess;
END;
```

Here are some comments on this implementation that you might find helpful:

- I obtain some useful information from V$SESSION when the package is initialized (the values will not change during my session, so I should query it only once) and incorporate that into the log.
- The putline procedure performs the straight insert. You would probably want to add some exception handling to this program if you applied this idea in your production application.
- The saveline procedure calls the putline procedure (I don't want any redundant code), but does so from within the context of an autonomous transaction.

With this package in place, my error handler shown earlier can be as simple as this:

```
EXCEPTION
   WHEN OTHERS
   THEN
      log.saveline (SQLCODE, SQLERRM);
END;
```

No muss, no fuss. Developers don't have to concern themselves with the structure of the log table; they don't even have to know they are writing to a database table. And because I have used an autonomous transaction, they can rest assured that no matter what happens in their application, the log entry has been saved.

Using autonomous transactions in a database trigger

The grand new benefit of autonomous transactions for database triggers (described in Chapter 18) is that inside those triggers you can now issue COMMITs and ROLLBACKs, statements that are otherwise not allowed in database triggers. The changes you commit and roll back will not, however, affect the main transaction that caused the database trigger to fire; they will apply only to DML activity taking place inside the trigger itself (or through stored program units called within the trigger).

Why is this valuable? You may want to take an action in the database trigger that is not affected by the ultimate disposition of the transaction that caused the trigger to fire. For example, suppose that you want to keep track of each action against a table, whether or not the action completed. You might even want to be able to detect which actions failed. Let's see how you can use autonomous transactions to do this.

Creating a database trigger. First, let's construct a simple autonomous transaction trigger on the bonus_compensation table that writes a simple message to the bonus_comp_history table. Here are the two table definitions:

```
/* File on web: autontrigger.sql */
CREATE TABLE bonus_compensation (
   company VARCHAR2(100),
   name VARCHAR2(100),
   compensation NUMBER,
   reason VARCHAR2(200));

CREATE TABLE bonus_comp_history (
   name VARCHAR2(100),
   description VARCHAR2(500),
   occurred_on DATE);
```

Here is the BEFORE INSERT trigger to run all the elements in the script:

```
CREATE OR REPLACE TRIGGER bef_ins_bonus_comp
BEFORE INSERT ON bonus_compensation FOR EACH ROW
DECLARE
   PRAGMA AUTONOMOUS_TRANSACTION;
BEGIN
   INSERT INTO bonus_comp_history VALUES (
      :new.name, 'BEFORE INSERT', SYSDATE);
   COMMIT;
END;
```

With this trigger in place, I am now certain to track every insert attempt, as shown in the steps below:

```
BEGIN
   -- What happens when programmers write the
   -- compensation calculation programs:

   INSERT INTO bonus_compensation VALUES (
      'Quest', 'Steven', 100, 'Monthly e-seminar series');

   INSERT INTO bonus_compensation VALUES (
      'Quest', 'Steven', 250, 'Big smile at conferences');

   ROLLBACK;
END;

SQL> SELECT name,
  2         description,
  3         TO_CHAR (occurred_on,
```

```
             'MM/DD/YYYY HH:MI:SS') occurred_on
  FROM bonus_comp_history;

NAME                 DESCRIPTION                 OCCURRED_ON
-------------------- --------------------------- -------------------
Steven               BEFORE INSERT               03/17/1999 04:00:56
Steven               BEFORE INSERT               03/17/1999 04:00:56
```

You will find in the *autontrigger.sql* script available on the O'Reilly site all of the statements needed to create these objects and run your own test. You can even add your CEO's name to the series of INSERTs if he or she fits the bill.

Fine-tuning the database trigger. Unfortunately, there is something of a problem with the trigger I just defined. I defined the trigger as an autonomous transaction because I performed the alert in the body of the trigger. But what if I want to perform some additional DML for the main transaction here in the trigger? It won't be rolled back with the rest of the transaction if a rollback occurs. This is unacceptable from the perspective of data integrity.

Generally, I would recommend that you not make a database trigger itself the autonomous transaction. Instead, push all of the independent DML activity (such as writing to the audit or history table) into its own procedure, make that procedure the autonomous transaction, and have the trigger call the procedure.

The *autontrigger2.sql* script available on the O'Reilly site contains the following reworking of the database trigger. First, I create the audit procedure:

```
/* File on web: autontrigger2.sql */
CREATE OR REPLACE PROCEDURE audit_bonus_comp (
   name IN VARCHAR2,
   description IN VARCHAR2,
   occurred_on IN DATE
   )
IS
   PRAGMA AUTONOMOUS_TRANSACTION;
BEGIN
   INSERT INTO bonus_comp_history VALUES (
      audit_bonus_comp.name,
      audit_bonus_comp.description,
      audit_bonus_comp.occurred_on
      );
   COMMIT;
END;
```

Then I change the trigger to the following.

```
CREATE OR REPLACE TRIGGER aft_ins_bonus_comp
AFTER INSERT ON bonus_compensation FOR EACH ROW
DECLARE
   ok BOOLEAN := is_valid_comp_info (:NEW.name);
BEGIN
   IF ok
```

```
      THEN
         audit_bonus_comp (
            :new.name, 'AFTER INSERT', SYSDATE);
      ELSE
         RAISE VALUE_ERROR;
      END IF;
   END;
```

Note the following differences:

- The trigger is now an AFTER INSERT trigger rather than a BEFORE INSERT trigger. I want to wait until after the INSERT to the compensation table takes place. Then I will perform my audit.
- When the is_valid_comp_info function returns FALSE, I will not even perform an audit. Instead, I will stop the transaction by raising an error. This demonstrates the other reason that the trigger itself should not be autonomous. In some situations, I always want to perform my audit, but under other circumstances, I may want to stop my main transaction by raising an exception. I can't have both of those events happen if the exception is raised in the same block and transaction as the audit DML.

As you take advantage of the new autonomous transaction pragma, plan how you will be using these new code elements. You will almost always be better off hiding the details of your new, independent transactions behind a procedural interface.

CHAPTER 14
Data Retrieval

In this chapter:

- Cursor Basics
- Working with Implicit Cursors
- Working with Explicit Cursors
- BULK COLLECT
- SELECT...FOR UPDATE
- Cursor Variables
- Cursor Expressions (Oracle9i)

One of the hallmarks of the PL/SQL language is its tight integration with the Oracle database, both for changing data in database tables and for extracting information from those tables. This chapter explores the many features available in PL/SQL to query data from the database and make that data available within PL/SQL programs.

When you execute a SQL statement from PL/SQL, the Oracle RDBMS assigns a private work area for that statement and also manages the data specified by the SQL statement in the System Global Area (SGA). The private work area contains information about the SQL statement and the set of data returned or affected by that statement.

PL/SQL provides a number of different ways to name this work area and manipulate the information within it; all of these ways involve defining and working with cursors. They include:

Implicit cursors
: A simple and direct SELECT...INTO retrieves a single row of data into local program variables. It's the easiest (and often the most efficient) path to your data, but can often lead to coding the same or similar SELECTs in multiple places in your code.

Explicit cursors
: You can declare the query explicitly in your declaration section (local block or package). In this way, you can open and fetch from the cursor in one or more programs, with a granularity of control not available with implicit cursors.

Cursor variables
: Offering an additional level of flexibility, cursor variables (declared from a REF CURSOR type) allow you to pass a *pointer* to a query's underlying result set from one program to another. Any program with access to that variable can open, fetch from, or close the cursor.

Cursor expressions
: New to Oracle9*i*, the CURSOR expression transforms a SELECT statement into a REF CURSOR result set and can be used in conjunction with table functions to improve the performance of applications.

Dynamic SQL queries
: Oracle allows you to construct and execute queries dynamically at runtime using either native dynamic SQL (NDS) (new to Oracle8*i* and covered in Chapter 15) or DBMS_SQL Details on this built-in package are available in *Oracle Built-in Packages* (O'Reilly).

This chapter explores implicit cursors, explicit cursors, cursor variables, and cursor expressions in detail.

Cursor Basics

In its simplest form, you can think of a *cursor* as a pointer into a table in the database. For example, the following cursor declaration associates the entire employee table with the cursor named employee_cur:

```
CURSOR employee_cur IS SELECT * FROM employee;
```

Once I have declared the cursor, I can open it:

```
OPEN employee_cur;
```

Then I can fetch rows from it:

```
FETCH employee_cur INTO employee_rec;
```

Finally, I can close the cursor:

```
CLOSE employee_cur;
```

In this case, each record fetched from this cursor represents an entire record in the employee table. You can, however, associate any valid SELECT statement with a cursor. In the next example I have a join of three tables in my cursor declaration:

```
DECLARE
   CURSOR joke_feedback_cur
   IS
      SELECT J.name, R.laugh_volume, C.name
        FROM joke J, response R, comedian C
       WHERE J.joke_id = R.joke_id
         AND J.joker_id = C.joker_id;
BEGIN
   ...
END;
```

Here, the cursor does not act as a pointer into any actual table in the database. Instead, the cursor is a pointer into the virtual table or implicit view represented by the SELECT statement (SELECT is called a virtual table because the data it produces has the same structure as a table—rows and columns—but it exists only for the duration of the execution of the SQL statement). If the triple join returns 20 rows, each containing three columns, then the cursor functions as a pointer into those 20 rows.

Some Data Retrieval Terms

You have lots of options in PL/SQL for executing SQL, and all of them occur as some type of cursor inside your PL/SQL program. Before diving into the details of the various approaches, this section will familiarize you with the types and terminology of data retrieval.

Static SQL
: A SQL statement is *static* if its content is determined at compile time.

Dynamic SQL
: A SQL statement is *dynamic* if it is constructed at runtime and then executed, so you don't completely specify the SQL statement in the code you write. You can execute dynamic SQL either through the use of the built-in DBMS_SQL package (available in all versions of Oracle) or with native dynamic SQL (introduced in Oracle8*i* and described in Chapter 15).

Result set
: This is the set of rows identified by Oracle as fulfilling the request for data specified by the SQL statement. The result set is cached in the System Global Area to improve the performance of accessing and modifying the data in that set. Oracle maintains a pointer into the result set, which we will refer to as the *current row*.

Implicit cursor
: PL/SQL declares and manages an implicit cursor every time you execute a SQL DML statement (INSERT, UPDATE, or DELETE) or a SELECT INTO that returns a single row from the database directly into a PL/SQL data structure. This kind of cursor is called "implicit" because Oracle automatically handles many of the cursor-related operations for you, such as allocating a cursor, opening the cursor, fetching records, and even closing the cursor (although this is not an excuse to write code that relies on this behavior).

Explicit cursor
: This is a SELECT statement that you declare as a cursor explicitly in your application code. You then also explicitly perform each operation against that cursor (open, fetch, close, etc.). You will generally use explicit cursors when you need to retrieve multiple rows from data sources using static SQL.

Cursor variable
: This is a variable you declare that references or points to a cursor object in the database. As a true variable, a cursor variable can change its value (i.e., the cursor or result set it points to) as your program executes. The variable can refer to different cursor objects (queries) at different times. You can also pass a cursor

variable as a parameter to a procedure or function. Cursor variables are very useful when passing result set information from a PL/SQL program to another environment, such as Java or Visual Basic.

Cursor attribute
A cursor attribute takes the form *%attribute_name* and is appended to the name of a cursor or cursor variable. The attribute returns information about the state of the cursor, such as "is the cursor open?" and "how many rows have been retrieved for this cursor?" Cursor attributes work in slightly different ways for implicit and explicit cursors and for dynamic SQL. These variations are explored throughout this chapter.

SELECT FOR UPDATE
This statement is a special variation of the normal SELECT that proactively issues row locks on each row of data retrieved by the query. Use SELECT FOR UPDATE only when you need to "reserve" data you are querying to ensure that no one changes the data while you are processing it.

Bulk processing
In Oracle8*i* and above, PL/SQL offers the BULK COLLECTION syntax for queries that allows you to fetch multiple rows from the database in a single or "bulk" step.

Typical Query Operations

Regardless of the type of cursor, PL/SQL performs the same operations to execute a SQL statement from within your program. In some cases, PL/SQL takes these steps for you. In others, such as with explicit cursors, you will code and execute these steps yourself.

Parse
The first step in processing a SQL statement is to parse it to make sure it is valid and to determine the execution plan (using either the rule-based or cost-based optimizer, depending on how your DBA has set the OPTIMIZER_MODE parameter for your database).

Bind
When you bind, you associate values from your program (host variables) with placeholders inside your SQL statement. With static SQL, the PL/SQL engine itself performs these binds. With dynamic SQL, you must explicitly request a binding of variable values if you wish to use bind variables.

Open
When you open a cursor, the bind variables are used to determine the result set for the SQL statement. The pointer to the active or current row is set to the first row. Sometimes you will not explicitly open a cursor; instead, the PL/SQL engine will perform this operation for you (as with implicit cursors or native dynamic SQL).

Execute
In the execute phase, the statement is run within the SQL engine.

Fetch
If you are performing a query, the FETCH command retrieves the next row from the cursor's result set. Each time you fetch, PL/SQL moves the pointer forward in the result set. When you are working with explicit cursors, remember that FETCH does nothing (does not raise an error) if there are no more rows to retrieve.

Close
This step closes the cursor and releases all memory used by the cursor. Once closed, the cursor no longer has a result set. Sometimes you will not explicitly close a cursor; instead, the PL/SQL engine will perform this operation for you (as with implicit cursors or native dynamic SQL).

Figure 14-1 shows how some of these different operations are used to fetch information from the database into your PL/SQL program.

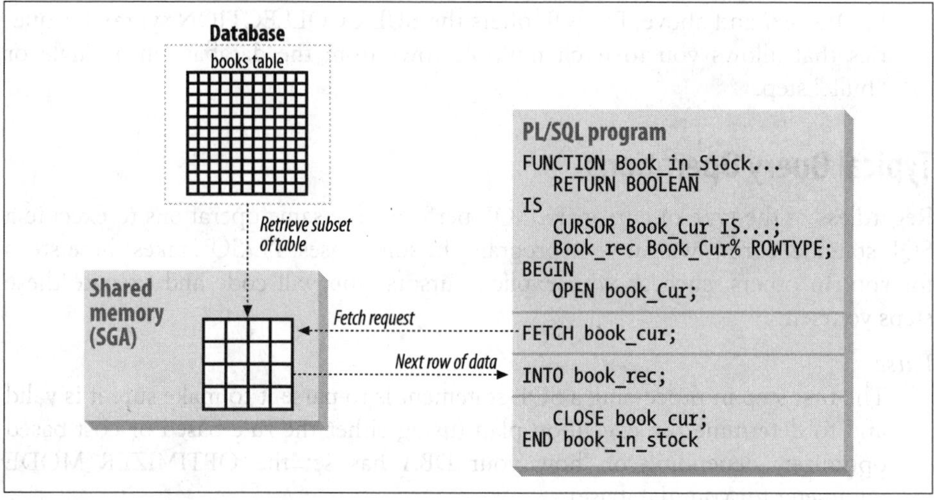

Figure 14-1. Simplified view of cursor fetch operation

Introduction to Cursor Attributes

This section describes each of the different cursor attributes at a high level. They are explored in more detail for each of the kinds of cursors throughout this chapter, as well as in Chapters 13 and 15.

PL/SQL offers a total of six cursor attributes, as shown in Table 14-1.

Table 14-1. Cursor attributes

Name	Description
%FOUND	Returns TRUE if record was fetched successfully, FALSE otherwise.
%NOTFOUND	Returns TRUE if record was not fetched successfully, FALSE otherwise.
%ROWCOUNT	Returns number of records fetched from cursor at that point in time.
%ISOPEN	Returns TRUE if cursor is open, FALSE otherwise.
%BULK_ROWCOUNT	Returns the number of records modified by the FORALL statement for each collection element.
%BULK_EXCEPTIONS	Returns exception information for rows modified by the FORALL statement for each collection element.

To reference a cursor attribute, attach it to the name of the cursor or cursor variable about which you want information. Here are some examples:

- Is the explicit cursor still open?

```
DECLARE
   CURSOR happiness_cur IS SELECT simple_delights FROM ...;
BEGIN
   OPEN happiness_cur;
   ...
   IF happiness_cur%ISOPEN THEN ...
```

- How many rows did I retrieve from the implicit cursor? (Notice that the "name" of my cursor in this case is "SQL".)

```
DECLARE
   TYPE num_tab IS TABLE OF NUMBER;
   deptnums   num_tab;
BEGIN
   SELECT deptno
     BULK COLLECT INTO deptnums
     FROM dept;

   DBMS_OUTPUT.PUT_LINE (SQL%ROWCOUNT);
END;
```

The following sections offer brief descriptions of each of the cursor attributes.

The %FOUND attribute

The %FOUND attribute reports on the status of your most recent FETCH against the cursor. This attribute evaluates to TRUE if the most recent FETCH against the explicit cursor returned a row, or FALSE if no row was returned.

If the cursor has not yet been opened, a reference to the %FOUND attribute raises the INVALID_CURSOR exception. You can evaluate the %FOUND attribute of any open cursor because you reference the cursor by name.

In the following example, I loop through all the callers in the caller_cur cursor, assign all calls entered before today to that particular caller, and then fetch the next record. If I have reached the last record, then the explicit cursor's %FOUND attribute is set to FALSE and I exit the simple loop. After my UPDATE statement, I check the implicit cursor's %FOUND attribute as well.

```
OPEN caller_cur;
LOOP
   FETCH caller_cur INTO caller_rec;
   EXIT WHEN NOT caller_cur%FOUND;

   UPDATE call
      SET caller_id = caller_rec.caller_id
    WHERE call_timestamp < SYSDATE;
   IF SQL%FOUND THEN
      DBMS_OUTPUT.PUT_LINE (
         'Calls updated for ' || caller_rec.caller_id);
   END IF;
END LOOP;
CLOSE caller_cur;
```

The %NOTFOUND attribute

The %NOTFOUND attribute is the opposite of %FOUND. It returns TRUE if the explicit cursor is unable to fetch another row because the last row was fetched. If the cursor is unable to return a row because of an error, the appropriate exception is raised.

If the cursor has not yet been opened, a reference to the %NOTFOUND attribute raises the INVALID_CURSOR exception. You can evaluate the %NOTFOUND attribute of any open cursor because you reference the cursor by name.

When should you use %FOUND and when should you use %NOTFOUND? Use whichever formulation fits most naturally in your code. In the previous example, I issued the following statement to exit my loop:

```
EXIT WHEN NOT caller_cur%FOUND;
```

An alternate and perhaps more readable formulation might use %NOTFOUND instead, as follows:

```
EXIT WHEN caller_cur%NOTFOUND;
```

The %ROWCOUNT attribute

The %ROWCOUNT attribute returns the number of records fetched from a cursor at the time the attribute is queried. When you first open a cursor, its %ROWCOUNT is set to zero. If you reference the %ROWCOUNT attribute of a cursor that is not open, you will raise the INVALID_CURSOR exception. After each record is fetched, %ROWCOUNT is increased by one.

Use %ROWCOUNT to verify that the expected number of rows have been fetched (or updated, in the case of DML) or to stop your program from executing after a certain number of iterations.

The %ISOPEN attribute

The %ISOPEN attribute returns TRUE if the cursor is open; otherwise, it returns FALSE.

The %BULK_ROWCOUNT attribute

The %BULK_ROWCOUNT attribute, designed for use with the FORALL statement, returns the number of rows processed by each DML execution. This attribute has the semantics of an associative array. It is covered in more detail in Chapter 13.

The %BULK_EXCEPTIONS attribute

The %BULK_EXCEPTIONS attribute, designed for use with the FORALL statement, returns exception information that may have been raised by each DML execution. This attribute has the semantics of an associative array of records. It is covered in more detail in Chapter 13.

You can reference cursor attributes in your PL/SQL code, as shown in the preceding example, but you cannot use those attributes inside a SQL statement. For example, if you try to use the %ROWCOUNT attribute in the WHERE clause of a SELECT:

```
SELECT caller_id, company_id
   FROM caller
 WHERE company_id = company_cur%ROWCOUNT;
```

you will get a compile error:

```
PLS-00229: Attribute expression within SQL expression
```

Referencing PL/SQL Variables in a Cursor

Because a cursor must be associated with a SELECT statement, every cursor must reference at least one table from the database and determine from that (and from the WHERE clause) which rows will be returned in the active set. This does not mean, however, that a PL/SQL cursor's SELECT may return only database information.

The list of expressions that appears after the SELECT keyword and before the FROM keyword is called the *select list*. In native SQL, this select list may contain both columns and expressions (SQL functions on those columns, constants, etc.). In PL/SQL, the select list of a SELECT may contain PL/SQL variables and complex expressions.

In the following cursor, the SELECT statement retrieves rows based on the employee table, but the information returned in the select list contains a combination of table columns, a PL/SQL variable, and a bind variable from the host environment (such as an Oracle Forms item):

```
DECLARE
   /* A local PL/SQL variable */
```

```
   projected_bonus NUMBER := 1000;
   /*
   || Cursor adds $1000 to the salary of each employee
   || hired more than three years ago.
   */
   CURSOR employee_cur
   IS
      SELECT employee_id,
             salary + projected_bonus new_salary, /* Column alias */
             :review.evaluation                   /* Bind variable */
        FROM employee
       WHERE hiredate < ADD_MONTHS (SYSDATE, -36);

BEGIN
   ...
END;
```

You can reference local PL/SQL program data (PL/SQL variables and constants), as well as host language bind variables in the WHERE, GROUP BY, and HAVING clauses of the cursor's SELECT statement.

Identifier precedence in a cursor

Be careful about naming identifiers when you mix PL/SQL variables in with database columns. It is, for instance, common practice to give a variable the same name as the column whose data it represents. This makes perfect sense until you want to reference both the local variables and the column in a SQL statement.

In the following example, I want to fetch each employee who was hired more than three years ago and, using a local variable, add $1000 to his or her salary. The employee table has a column named "salary", and unfortunately this procedure relies on a local variable of the same name to achieve its ends. Although this code will compile without error, it will not produce the desired result:

```
PROCEDURE improve_QOL
IS
   /* Local variable with same name as column: */
   salary NUMBER := 1000;

   CURSOR double_sal_cur
   IS
      SELECT salary + salary
        FROM employee
       WHERE hiredate < ADD_MONTHS (SYSDATE, -36);
BEGIN
   ...
END;
```

Instead of adding $1000 to each person's salary, this code will instead double the salary. Inside the SQL statement, any unqualified reference to "salary" is resolved using the column named "salary".

I can achieve the desired effect by qualifying the PL/SQL variable with the name of the procedure, as follows:

```
CURSOR double_sal_cur
IS
   SELECT salary + improve_QOL.salary
     FROM employee
    WHERE hiredate < ADD_MONTHS (SYSDATE, -36);
```

In this situation, I am informing the compiler that the second reference to "salary" is that variable "owned" by the improve_QOL procedure. It will then add the current value of that variable to the salary column value.

Using standard naming conventions

Another common practice for avoiding naming conflicts between SQL and PL/SQL is to use standard naming conventions for PL/SQL variables, thus minimizing the possibility of a conflict. Suppose, for example, that the standard in my company is that all locally declared variables have a prefix of "l_" in their names. The declaration of my salary variable would then be:

```
PROCEDURE improve_QOL
IS
   /* Local variable with same name as column: */
   l_salary NUMBER := 1000;
```

and my cursor would look like this:

```
CURSOR double_sal_cur
IS
   SELECT salary + l_salary
     FROM employee
    WHERE hiredate < ADD_MONTHS (SYSDATE, -36);
```

This will generally work just fine, except for one "nightmare" scenario: what if the DBA comes along six months from now and adds a column to the employee table named "l_salary"? Then the SQL query will definitely not work as planned. Sure, that isn't a likely move by the DBA, but it is definitely in the realm of possibility.

For this reason, qualification of PL/SQL variables with their scope names inside SQL statements offers the highest guarantee that you will avoid conflicts.

Choosing Between Explicit and Implicit Cursors

In years past, it was common for "Oracle gurus" (including yours truly) to solemnly declare that you should never use implicit cursors for single-row fetches, and then explain that implicit cursors follow the ANSI standard and always perform two fetches, making them less efficient than explicit cursors (for which you can just fetch a single time).

The first two editions of this book repeated that "wisdom," but it is time to break from tradition. The bottom line is that from Oracle8 onwards, as a result of Oracle optimization, it is very likely that your implicit cursor will run more—not less—efficiently than the equivalent explicit cursor.

So does that mean that you should now always use implicit cursors? Not at all. There are still good reasons to use explicit cursors, including the following:

- In some cases, explicit cursors will be more efficient. You should test your critical, often-executed queries in both formats to see which will be better in that particular situation.
- Explicit cursors offer much tighter programmatic control. If a row is not found, for example, Oracle will not raise an exception, instead forcing the execution block to shut down.

I suggest that the question to answer is not "implicit or explicit?," but rather, "encapsulate or expose?" And the answer is (new wisdom revealed):

> You should always encapsulate your single-row query, hiding the query behind a function interface, and passing back the data through the RETURN clause.

Don't worry about explicit versus implicit. Worry about how you can tune and maintain your code if single-row queries are duplicated throughout your code. Take the time to encapsulate them behind functions, preferably package-based functions.

Working with Implicit Cursors

PL/SQL declares and manages an implicit cursor every time you execute a SQL DML statement (INSERT, UPDATE, or DELETE) or a SELECT INTO that returns a single row from the database directly into a PL/SQL data structure. This kind of cursor is called *implicit* because Oracle implicitly or automatically handles many of the cursor-related operations for you, such as allocation of a cursor, opening the cursor, fetching, and so on.

The implicit DML statements are covered in Chapter 13. This chapter is concerned only with the implicit SQL query.

An implicit cursor is a SELECT statement that has the following special characteristics:

- The SELECT statement appears in the executable section of your block; it is not defined in the declaration section, as explicit cursors are.
- The query contains an INTO clause (or BULK COLLECT INTO for bulk processing). The INTO clause is a part of the PL/SQL (not the SQL) language and is the mechanism used to transfer data from the database into local PL/SQL data structures.

- You do not open, fetch, or close the SELECT statement; all of these operations are done for you.

The general structure of an implicit query is as follows:

```
SELECT column_list
  [BULK COLLECT] INTO PL/SQL variable list
  ...rest of SELECT statement...
```

If you use an implicit cursor, Oracle performs the open, fetches, and close for you automatically; these actions are outside your programmatic control. You can, however, obtain information about the most recently executed SQL statement by examining the values in the implicit SQL cursor attributes, as explained later in this chapter.

In the following sections, the term *implicit cursor* means a SELECT INTO statement that retrieves (or attempts to retrieve) a single row of data. Later we'll discuss the SELECT BULK COLLECT INTO variation that allows you to retrieve multiple rows of data with a single implicit query.

Implicit Cursor Examples

A common use of implicit cursors is to perform a lookup based on a primary key. In the following example, I look up the title of a book based on its ISBN number:

```
DECLARE
   l_title book.title%TYPE;
BEGIN
   SELECT title
     INTO l_title
     FROM book
    WHERE isbn = '0-596-00121-5';
```

Once I have fetched the title into my local variable, l_title, I can manipulate that information—for example, by changing the variable's value, displaying the title, or passing the title on to another PL/SQL program for processing.

Here is an example of an implicit query that retrieves an entire row of information into a record:

```
DECLARE
   l_book book%ROWTYPE;
BEGIN
   SELECT *
     INTO l_book
     FROM book
    WHERE isbn = '0-596-00121-5';
```

You can also retrieve group-level information from a query. The following single-row query calculates and returns the total salary for a department. Once again, PL/SQL creates an implicit cursor for this statement:

```
SELECT SUM (salary)
  INTO department_total
  FROM employee
 WHERE department_number = 10;
```

Because PL/SQL is so tightly integrated with the Oracle database, you can also easily retrieve complex datatypes, such as objects and collections, within your implicit cursor.

All of these illustrate the use of implicit queries to retrieve a single row's worth of information. If you want to retrieve more than one row, you must use either an explicit cursor for that query or the BULK COLLECT INTO clause (available only in Oracle8*i* and above) in your query. Both of these approaches are discussed later in this chapter.

As mentioned earlier, I recommend that you always "hide" single-row queries like those shown above behind a function interface. This concept was explored in detail in the section "Choosing Between Explicit and Implicit Cursors."

Error Handling with Implicit Cursors

The implicit cursor version of the SELECT statement is kind of a black box. You pass the SQL statement to the SQL layer in the database, and it returns a single row of information. You can't get inside the separate operations of the cursor, such as the open, fetch, and close stages. You are also stuck with the fact that Oracle will automatically raise exceptions from within the implicit SELECT for two common outcomes:

- The query does not find any rows matching your criteria. In this case, Oracle raises the NO_DATA_FOUND exception.
- The SELECT statement returns more than one row. In this case, Oracle raises the TOO_ MANY_ROWS exception.

When either of these scenarios occurs (as well as any other exceptions raised when executing a SQL statement), execution of the current block terminates and control is passed to the exception section. You have no control over this process flow; you cannot tell Oracle that with this implicit cursor, you actually expect to not find any rows and it is not an error. Instead, whenever you code an implicit cursor, you should include an exception section that traps and handles these two exceptions (and perhaps others, depending on your application logic).

In the following block of code, I query the title of a book based on its ISBN number, but I also anticipate the possible problems that arise:

```
DECLARE
   l_isbn book.isbn%TYPE := '0-596-00121-5';
   l_title book.title%TYPE;
```

```
BEGIN
   SELECT title
     INTO l_title
     FROM book
    WHERE isbn = l_isbn;
EXCEPTION
   WHEN NO_DATA_FOUND
   THEN
      display.line ('Unknown book: ' || l_isbn);
   WHEN TOO_MANY_ROWS
   THEN
      errpkg.record_and_stop ('Data integrity error for: ' || l_isbn);
      RAISE;
END;
```

One of the problems with using implicit queries is that there is an awesome temptation to make assumptions about the data being retrieved, such as:

- "There can never possibly be more than one row in the book table for a given ISBN; we have constraints in place to guarantee that."
- "There will always be an entry in the book table for Steven and Bill's *Oracle PL/SQL Programming*. I don't have to worry about NO_DATA_FOUND."

The consequence of such assumptions is often that we neglect to include exception handlers for our implicit queries.

Now, it may well be true that today, with the current set of data, a query will return only a single row. If the nature of the data ever changes, however, you may find that the SELECT statement that formerly identified a single row now returns several. Your program will raise an exception, the exception will not be properly handled, and this could cause problems in your code.

You should, as a rule, always include handlers for NO_DATA_FOUND and TOO_MANY_ROWS whenever you write an implicit query. More generally, you should include error handlers for any errors that you can reasonably anticipate will occur in your program. The action you take when an error does arise will vary. Consider the code that retrieves a book title for an ISBN. Implemented below as a function, notice that my two error handlers act very differently: NO_DATA_FOUND returns a value, while TOO_MANY_ROWS logs the error and re-raises the exception, causing the function to actually fail. (See Chapter 6 for more information about the errpkg package.)

```
CREATE OR REPLACE FUNCTION book_title (
   isbn_in   IN   book.isbn%TYPE
)
   RETURN book.title%TYPE
IS
   return_value   book.title%TYPE;
BEGIN
  SELECT title
    INTO return_value
```

```
      FROM book
      WHERE isbn = l_isbn;

      RETURN return_value;
   EXCEPTION
      WHEN NO_DATA_FOUND
      THEN
        RETURN NULL;
      WHEN TOO_MANY_ROWS
      THEN
        errpkg.record_and_stop (   'Data integrity error for: '
                  || l_isbn);
        RAISE;
   END;
```

Here is the reasoning behind these varied treatments: the point of my function is to return the name of a book, which can never be NULL. The function can also be used to validate an ISBN (i.e., "does a book exist for this ISBN?"). For this reason, I really don't want my function to raise an exception when no book is found for an ISBN; that may actually constitute a successful condition, depending on how the function is being used. The logic may be, "If a book does not exist with this ISBN, then it can be used for a new book," which might be coded as:

```
IF book_title ('0-596-00121-7') IS NULL
THEN ...
```

In other words, the fact that no book exists for that ISBN is not an error and should not be treated as one within my general lookup function.

On the other hand, if the query raises the TOO_MANY_ROWS exception, I have a real problem: there should never be two different books with the same ISBN number. So in this case, I need to log the error and then stop the application from continuing.

Implicit SQL Cursor Attributes

Oracle allows you to access information about the most recently executed implicit cursor by referencing the special implicit cursor attributes shown in Table 14-2. The table describes the significance of the values returned by these attributes for implicit SQL cursors. Because the cursors are implicit, they have no name and therefore the keyword "SQL" is used to denote the implicit cursor.

Table 14-2. Implicit SQL cursor attributes for queries

Name	Description
SQL%FOUND	Returns TRUE if one row (or more in the case of BULK COLLECT INTO) was fetched successfully.
SQL%NOTFOUND	Returns TRUE if a row was not fetched successfully (in which case Oracle will also raise the NO_DATA_FOUND exception).
SQL%ROWCOUNT	Returns the number of rows fetched from the specified cursor.
SQL%ISOPEN	Always returns FALSE for implicit cursors, because Oracle opens and closes implicit cursors atomically.

These cursor attributes return information about the execution of an INSERT, UPDATE, DELETE, or SELECT INTO statement. All the implicit cursor attributes return NULL if no implicit cursors have yet been executed in the session. Otherwise, the values of the attributes always refer to the most recently executed SQL statement, regardless of the block or program from which the SQL statement was executed.

Let's make sure we understand the implications of this last point. Consider the following two programs:

```
CREATE OR REPLACE PROCEDURE remove_from_circulation
   (isbn_in in book.isbn%TYPE)
IS
BEGIN
   DELETE FROM book
         WHERE   isbn = isbn_in;
END;

CREATE OR REPLACE PROCEDURE show_book_count
IS
   l_count   INTEGER;
BEGIN
   SELECT COUNT (*)
     INTO l_count
     FROM book;

   -- No such book!
   remove_from_circulation ('0-000-00000-0');

   DBMS_OUTPUT.put_line (SQL%FOUND);
END;
```

No matter how many rows of data are in the book table, we will always see "0" displayed in the output window. Because I call remove_from_circulation after my SELECT INTO statement, the SQL%FOUND reflects the outcome of my silly, impossible DELETE statement, and not the query.

If you want to make certain that you are checking the values for the right SQL statement, you should save attribute values to local variables immediately after execution of the SQL statement. I demonstrate this technique in the following example:

```
CREATE OR REPLACE PROCEDURE show_book_count
IS
   l_count   INTEGER;
   l_foundsome BOOLEAN;
BEGIN
   SELECT COUNT (*)
     INTO l_count
     FROM book;

   -- Take snapshot of attribute value:
   l_foundsome := SQL%FOUND;
```

```
   -- No such book!
   remove_from_circulation ('0-000-00000-0');

   -- Now I can go back to the previous attribute value.
   DBMS_OUTPUT.put_line (l_foundsome);
END;
```

Now let's see how the cursor attributes work with implicit cursors.

SQL%FOUND
: Use SQL%FOUND to determine if any rows were retrieved. SQL%FOUND will return TRUE if your SELECT INTO statement returned one or more rows; otherwise, it returns FALSE.

SQL%NOT FOUND
: The SQL%NOT FOUND attribute acts in just the opposite fashion, returning TRUE if no rows were found (which, by the way, means that PL/SQL will have raised a NO_DATA_FOUND exception), and FALSE otherwise.

SQL%ISOPEN
: The SQL%ISOPEN attribute is of no interest for SELECT INTOs (or any other implicit cursor). It always returns FALSE, because implicit cursors are opened and closed implicitly before you can reference SQL%ISOPEN to check their status.

SQL%ROWCOUNT
: Use SQL%ROWCOUNT to determine the number of rows fetched by your SELECT INTO statement. This will generally return a value of 1 unless you are using BULK COLLECT INTO. If the value is 0, that means that no rows were found and once again PL/SQL will have raised a NO_DATA_FOUND exception.

SQL%ROWCOUNT returns 1 even when you select an aggregation of several rows into a variable. In fact:

```
SELECT COUNT (*) INTO l_count FROM dual WHERE 1=2;
```

will also set SQL%ROWCOUNT to 1 because 0 was successfully fetched into l_count.

Working with Explicit Cursors

An explicit cursor is a SELECT statement that is explicitly defined in the declaration section of your code and, in the process, assigned a name. There is no such thing as an explicit cursor for UPDATE, DELETE, and INSERT statements.

With explicit cursors, you have complete control over the different PL/SQL steps involved in retrieving information from the database. You decide when to OPEN the cursor, when to FETCH records from the cursor (and therefore from the table or tables in the SELECT statement of the cursor), how many records to fetch, and when to CLOSE the cursor. Information about the current state of your cursor is available through examination of cursor attributes. This granularity of control makes the explicit cursor an invaluable tool for your development effort.

Let's look at an example. The following function determines (and returns) the level of jealousy I should feel for my friends, based on their location.

```
1  CREATE OR REPLACE FUNCTION jealousy_level (
2     NAME_IN   IN   friends.NAME%TYPE) RETURN NUMBER
3  AS
4     CURSOR jealousy_cur
5     IS
6        SELECT location FROM friends
7         WHERE NAME = UPPER (NAME_IN);
8
9     jealousy_rec   jealousy_cur%ROWTYPE;
10    retval         NUMBER;
11 BEGIN
12    OPEN jealousy_cur;
13
14    FETCH jealousy_cur INTO jealousy_rec;
15
16    IF jealousy_cur%FOUND
17    THEN
18       IF jealousy_rec.location = 'PUERTO RICO'
19          THEN retval := 10;
20       ELSIF jealousy_rec.location = 'CHICAGO'
21          THEN retval := 1;
22       END IF;
23    END IF;
24
25    CLOSE emptyp_cur;
26
27    RETURN level_out;
28 END;
```

This PL/SQL block performs the following cursor actions:

Line(s)	Action
4–7	Declare the cursor
9	Declare a record based on that cursor
12	Open the cursor
14	Fetch a single row from the cursor
16	Check a cursor attribute to determine if a row was found
18–22	Examine the contents of the fetched row to calculate my level of jealousy
25	Close the cursor

The next few sections examine each of these steps in detail. In these sections, the word "cursor" refers to an explicit cursor unless otherwise noted.

Declaring Explicit Cursors

To use an explicit cursor, you must first declare it in the declaration section of your PL/SQL block or in a package, as shown here:

```
CURSOR cursor_name [ ( [ parameter [, parameter ...] ) ]
   [ RETURN return_specification ]
   IS SELECT_statement
      [FOR UPDATE [OF [column list]];
```

where *cursor_name* is the name of the cursor, *return_specification* is an optional RETURN clause for the cursor, and *SELECT_statement* is any valid SQL SELECT statement. You can also pass arguments into a cursor through the optional parameter list described later in the section "Cursor Parameters." Once you have declared a cursor, you can OPEN it and FETCH from it.

Here are some examples of explicit cursor declarations:

A cursor without parameters

The result set of this cursor is the set of company ID numbers for each record in the table:

```
CURSOR company_cur IS
   SELECT company_id FROM company;
```

A cursor with parameters

The result set of this cursor is the name of the company that matches the company ID passed to the cursor via the parameter:

```
CURSOR name_cur (company_id_in IN NUMBER)
IS
   SELECT name FROM company
    WHERE company_id = company_id_in;
```

A cursor with a RETURN clause

The result set of this cursor is all columns (in the same structure as the underlying table) from all employee records in department 10:

```
CURSOR emp_cur RETURN employee%ROWTYPE
IS
   SELECT * FROM employee
    WHERE department_id = 10;
```

Naming your cursor

The name of an explicit cursor can be up to 30 characters in length and follows the rules for any other identifier in PL/SQL. A cursor name is not a PL/SQL variable. Instead, it is an undeclared identifier used to point to or refer to the query. You cannot assign values to a cursor, nor can you use it in an expression. You can only reference that explicit cursor by name within OPEN, FETCH, and CLOSE statements, and use it to qualify the reference to a cursor attribute.

Declaring cursors in packages

You can declare explicit cursors in any declaration section of a PL/SQL block. This means that you can declare such cursors within packages and at the package level; not within a particular procedure or function in the package. We'll explore packages in general in Chapter 17. You may want to look ahead at that chapter to acquaint yourself with the basics of packages before plunging into the topic of declaring cursors in packages.

Here are two examples:

```
CREATE OR REPLACE PACKAGE book_info
IS
   CURSOR titles_cur
   IS
      SELECT title
        FROM book;

   CURSOR books_cur (title_filter_in IN book.title%TYPE)
      RETURN book%ROWTYPE
   IS
      SELECT *
        FROM book
       WHERE title LIKE title_filter_in;
END;
```

The first cursor, titles_cur, returns just the titles of books. The second cursor, books_cur, returns a record for each row in the book table whose title passes the filter provided as a parameter (such as "All books that contain 'PL/SQL'"). Notice that the second cursor also utilizes the RETURN clause of a cursor, in essence declaring publicly the structure of the data that each FETCH against that cursor will return.

The RETURN clause of a cursor may be made up of any of the following datatype structures:

- A record defined from a database table, using the %ROWTYPE attribute
- A record defined from another, previously defined cursor, also using the %ROWTYPE attribute
- A record defined from a programmer-defined record

The number of expressions in the cursor's select list must match the number of columns in the record identified by *table_name*%ROWTYPE, *cursor*%ROWTYPE, or *record_type*. The datatypes of the elements must also be compatible. For example, if the second element in the select list is type NUMBER, then the second column in the RETURN record cannot be type VARCHAR2 or BOOLEAN.

Before exploring the RETURN clause and its advantages, let's first address a different question: why should you bother putting cursors into packages? Why not simply declare your explicit cursors wherever you need them directly in the declaration sections of particular procedures, functions, or anonymous blocks?

The answer is simple and persuasive. By defining cursors in packages, you can more easily reuse those queries and avoid writing the same logical retrieval statement over and over again throughout your application. By implementing that query in just one place and referencing it in many locations, you make it easier to enhance and maintain that query. You will also realize some performance gains by minimizing the number of times your queries will need to be parsed.

If you declare cursors in packages for reuse, you do need to be aware of one important factor. Data structures, including cursors, that are declared at the "package level" (not inside any particular function or procedure) maintain their values or persist for your entire session. This means that a packaged cursor will stay until you explicitly close it or until your session ends. Cursors declared in local blocks of code close automatically when that block terminates execution.

Now let's explore this RETURN clause and why you might want to take advantage of it. One of the interesting variations on a cursor declaration within packages involves the ability to separate the cursor's header from its body. The header of a cursor, much like the header of a function, is just that information a developer needs in order to write code to work with the cursor: the cursor's name, any parameters, and the type of data being returned. The body of a cursor is its SELECT statement.

Here is a rewrite of the books_cur in the book_info package that illustrates this technique:

```
CREATE OR REPLACE PACKAGE book_info
IS
   CURSOR books_cur (title_filter_in IN book.title%TYPE)
      RETURN book%ROWTYPE
END;

CREATE OR REPLACE PACKAGE BODY book_info
IS
   CURSOR books_cur (title_filter_in IN book.title%TYPE)
      RETURN book%ROWTYPE
   IS
      SELECT *
        FROM book
       WHERE title LIKE title_filter_in;
END;
```

Notice that everything up to but not including the IS keyword is the specification, while everything following the IS keyword is the body.

There are two reasons that you might want to divide your cursor as shown above:

Hide information
: Packaged cursors are essentially black boxes. This is advantageous to developers because they never have to code or even see the SELECT statement. They only need to know what records the cursor returns, in what order it returns them, and

which columns are in the column list. Among other things, this means they do not "second guess" the author of the cursor, believing they can improve upon the query. They simply use it as another predefined element in their application.

Minimize recompilation
: If I hide the query definition inside the package body, I can make changes to the SELECT statement without making any changes to the cursor header in the package specification. This allows me to enhance, fix, and recompile my code without recompiling my specification, which means that all the programs dependent on that package will not be marked invalid and will not need to be recompiled.

Opening Explicit Cursors

The first step in using a cursor is to define it in the declaration section. The next step is to open that cursor. The syntax for the OPEN statement is simplicity itself:

```
OPEN cursor_name [ ( argument [, argument ...] ) ];
```

where *cursor_name* is the name of the cursor you declared and the *arguments* are the values to be passed if the cursor was declared with a parameter list.

Oracle also offers the OPEN *cursor* FOR syntax, which is utilized in both cursor variables (see the "Cursor Variables" section) and native dynamic SQL (see Chapter 15).

When you open a cursor, PL/SQL executes the query for that cursor. It also identifies the active set of data—that is, the rows from all involved tables that meet the criteria in the WHERE clause and join conditions. The OPEN does not actually retrieve any of these rows—that action is performed by the FETCH statement.

Regardless of when you perform the first fetch, however, the read consistency model in the Oracle RDBMS guarantees that all fetches will reflect the data as it existed when the cursor was opened. In other words, from the moment you open your cursor until the moment that cursor is closed, all data fetched through the cursor will ignore any inserts, updates, and deletes performed after the cursor was opened.

Furthermore, if the SELECT statement in your cursor uses a FOR UPDATE clause, all the rows identified by the query are locked when the cursor is opened. (This feature is covered in the section "SELECT...FOR UPDATE" later in this chapter.)

If you try to open a cursor that is already open you will get the following error:

```
ORA-06511: PL/SQL: cursor already open
```

You can be sure of a cursor's status by checking the %ISOPEN cursor attribute before you try to open the cursor:

```
IF NOT company_cur%ISOPEN
THEN
   OPEN company_cur;
END IF;
```

The later section "Explicit Cursor Attributes" explains the different cursor attributes and how to best make use of them in your programs.

If you are using a cursor FOR loop, you do not need to open the cursor explicitly. Instead, the PL/SQL engine does that for you.

Fetching from Explicit Cursors

A SELECT statement establishes a virtual table—its return set is a series of rows determined by the WHERE clause (or lack thereof), with columns determined by the column list of the SELECT. So a cursor represents that virtual table within your PL/SQL program. In almost every situation, the point of declaring and opening a cursor is to return, or fetch, the rows of data from the cursor and then manipulate the information retrieved. PL/SQL provides a FETCH statement for this action.

The general syntax for a FETCH is:

```
FETCH cursor_name INTO record_or_variable_list;
```

where *cursor_name* is the name of the cursor from which the record is fetched, and *record_or_variable_list* is the PL/SQL data structure(s) into which the next row of the active set of records is copied. You can fetch into a record structure (declared with the %ROWTYPE attribute or TYPE declaration statement) or you can fetch into a list of one or more variables (PL/SQL variables or application-specific bind variables such as Oracle Forms items).

Examples of explicit cursors

The following examples illustrate the variety of possible fetches:

- Fetch into a PL/SQL record:

```
DECLARE
   CURSOR company_cur is SELECT ...;
   company_rec company_cur%ROWTYPE;
BEGIN
   OPEN company_cur;
   FETCH company_cur INTO company_rec;
```

- Fetch into a variable:

```
FETCH new_balance_cur INTO new_balance_dollars;
```

- Fetch into the row of a PL/SQL table row, a variable, and an Oracle Forms bind variable:

```
FETCH emp_name_cur INTO emp_name (1), hiredate, :dept.min_salary;
```

You should always fetch into a record that was defined with %ROWTYPE against the cursor; avoid fetching into lists of variables. Fetching into a record usually means that you write less code and have more flexibility to change the select list without having to change the FETCH statement.

Fetching past the last row

Once you open an explicit cursor, you can FETCH from it until there are no more records left in the active set. Oddly enough, though, you can also continue to FETCH past the last record.

In this case, PL/SQL will not raise any exceptions. It just won't actually be doing anything. Because there is nothing left to fetch, it will not alter the values of the variables in the INTO list of the FETCH. More specifically, the FETCH operation will not set those values to NULL.

You should therefore never test the values of INTO variables to determine if the FETCH against the cursor succeeded. Instead, you should check the value of the %FOUND or %NOTFOUND attributes, as explained in the upcoming "Explicit Cursor Attributes" section.

Column Aliases in Explicit Cursors

The SELECT statement of the cursor includes the list of columns that are returned by that cursor. As with any SELECT statement, this column list may contain either actual column names or column expressions, which are also referred to as *calculated* or *virtual columns*.

A *column alias* is an alternative name you provide to a column or column expression in a query. You may have used column aliases in SQL*Plus in order to improve the readability of ad hoc report output. In that situation, such aliases are completely optional. In an explicit cursor, on the other hand, column aliases are required for calculated columns when:

- You FETCH into a record declared with a %ROWTYPE declaration against that cursor.
- You want to reference the calculated column in your program.

Consider the following query. For all companies with sales activity during 2001, the SELECT statement retrieves the company name and the total amount invoiced to that company (assume that the default date format mask for this instance is DD-MON-YYYY):

```
SELECT company_name, SUM (inv_amt)
  FROM company C, invoice I
 WHERE C.company_id = I.company_id
   AND I.invoice_date BETWEEN '01-JAN-2001' AND '31-DEC-2001';
```

If you run this SQL statement in SQL*Plus, the output will look something like this:

```
COMPANY_NAME                          SUM (INV_AMT)
------------
ACME TURBO INC.                       1000
WASHINGTON HAIR CO.                   25.20
```

SUM (INV_AMT) does not make a particularly attractive column header for a report, but it works well enough for a quick dip into the data as an ad hoc query. Let's now use this same query in an explicit cursor and add a column alias:

```
DECLARE
   CURSOR comp_cur IS
      SELECT company_name, SUM (inv_amt) total_sales
        FROM company C, invoice I
       WHERE C.company_id = I.company_id
         AND I.invoice_date BETWEEN '01-JAN-2001' AND '31-DEC-2001';
   comp_rec comp_cur%ROWTYPE;
BEGIN
   OPEN comp_cur;
   FETCH comp_cur INTO comp_rec;
   ...
END;
```

With the alias in place, I can get at that information just as I would any other column or expression in the query:

```
IF comp_rec.total_sales > 5000
THEN
   DBMS_OUTPUT.PUT_LINE
      (' You have exceeded your credit limit of $5000 by ' ||
       TO_CHAR (5000-comp_rec.total_sales, '$9999'));
END IF;
```

If you fetch a row into a record declared with %ROWTYPE, the only way to access the column or column expression value is by the column name—after all, the record obtains its structure from the cursor itself.

Closing Explicit Cursors

Early on I was taught to clean up after myself, and I tend to be a bit obsessive (albeit selectively) about this later in life. Cleaning up after oneself is an important rule to follow in programming and can be crucial when it comes to cursor management. So be sure to close a cursor when you are done with it!

Here is the syntax for a CLOSE cursor statement:

```
CLOSE cursor_name;
```

where *cursor_name* is the name of the cursor you are closing.

Here are some special considerations regarding the closing of explicit cursors:

- If you declare and open a cursor in a procedure, be sure to close it again. Otherwise, you've just programmed a memory leak—and that's not good! Strictly speaking, a cursor (like any other data structure) should be automatically closed and destroyed when it goes out of scope. In fact, in many cases PL/SQL does check for and implicitly close any open cursors at the end of a procedure call, function call, or anonymous block. However, the overhead involved in doing that is significant, so for the sake of efficiency there are cases where PL/SQL does *not* immediately check for and close any open cursors. In addition, REF CURSORs are, by design, never closed implicitly. The one thing you can count on is that whenever the outermost PL/SQL block ends and control is returned to SQL or some other calling program, PL/SQL will at that point implicitly close any cursors (but not REF CURSORS) left open by that block or nested blocks.

Nested anonymous blocks provide an example of one case (at least in Oracle9*i* Release 1) where PL/SQL does not implicitly close cursors. For an interesting discussion of this issue see Jonathan Gennick's article, "Does PL/SQL Implicitly Close Cursors?," at *http://gennick.com/open_cursors.html*.

- If you declare a cursor in a package at the package level and then open it in a particular block or program, that cursor will stay open until you explicitly close it or until your session closes. Therefore, it is extremely important that you include your CLOSE statement for any packaged cursors as soon as you are done with them (and in the exception section as well), as in the following:

```
BEGIN
   OPEN my_package.my_cursor;

   ... Do stuff with the cursor

   CLOSE my_package.my_cursor;
EXCEPTION
   WHEN OTHERS
   THEN
      CLOSE my_package.my_cursor;
END;
```

- If you have opened a SELECT FOR UPDATE query, it is especially important to close the cursor as soon as you are done, as this query causes row-level locks to be applied.
- You should close a cursor only if it is currently open. You can check a cursor's status with the %ISOPEN cursor attribute before you try to close the cursor:

```
IF company_cur%ISOPEN
THEN
   CLOSE company_cur;
END IF;
```

- If you leave too many cursors open, you may exceed the value set by the database initialization parameter, OPEN_CURSORS. If this happens, you will encounter the dreaded error message:

  ```
  ORA-01000: maximum open cursors exceeded
  ```

  If you get this message, check your usage of package-based cursors to make sure they are closed when no longer needed.

Explicit Cursor Attributes

Oracle offers four attributes (%FOUND, %NOTFOUND, %ISOPEN, %ROWCOUNT) that allow you to retrieve information about the state of your cursor. Reference these attributes using this syntax:

```
cursor%attribute
```

where *cursor* is the name of the cursor you have declared.

Table 14-3 describes the significance of the values returned by these attributes for explicit cursors.

Table 14-3. Values returned by cursor attributes

Name	Description
cursor%FOUND	Returns TRUE if a record was fetched successfully.
cursor%NOTFOUND	Returns TRUE if a record was not fetched successfully.
cursor%ROWCOUNT	Returns the number of records fetched from the specified cursor at that point in time.
cursor%ISOPEN	Returns TRUE if the specified cursor is open.

Table 14-4 shows you the attribute values you can expect to see both before and after the specified cursor operations.

Table 14-4. Cursor attribute values

	%FOUND	%NOTFOUND	%ISOPEN	%ROWCOUNT
Before OPEN	ORA-01001 raised	ORA-01001 raised	FALSE	ORA-01001 raised
After OPEN	NULL	NULL	TRUE	0
Before first FETCH	NULL	NULL	TRUE	0
After first FETCH	TRUE	FALSE	TRUE	1
Before subsequent FETCH(es)	TRUE	FALSE	TRUE	1
Before subsequent FETCH(es)	TRUE	FALSE	TRUE	Data dependent
Before last FETCH	TRUE	FALSE	TRUE	Data dependent
After last FETCH	FALSE	TRUE	TRUE	Data dependent
Before CLOSE	FALSE	TRUE	TRUE	Data dependent
After CLOSE	Exception	Exception	FALSE	Exception

Here are some things to keep in mind as you work with cursor attributes for explicit cursors:

- If you try to use %FOUND, %NOTFOUND, or %ROWCOUNT before the cursor is opened or after it is closed, Oracle will raise an INVALID_CURSOR error (ORA-01001).
- If the result set was empty after the very first FETCH, then attributes will return values as follows: %FOUND = FALSE, %NOTFOUND = TRUE, and %ROWCOUNT = 0.
- If you are using BULK COLLECT, it is possible for %ROWCOUNT to return a value other than 0 or 1; it will, in fact, return the number of rows fetched into the associated collections. For more details, see the section "BULK COLLECT."

The following code showcases many of these attributes:

```
CREATE OR REPLACE PACKAGE bookinfo_pkg
IS
   CURSOR bard_cur
       IS SELECT title, date_published
     FROM books
    WHERE UPPER(author) LIKE 'SHAKESPEARE%';
END bookinfo_pkg;

DECLARE
   bard_rec   bard_cur%ROWTYPE;
BEGIN
   -- Check to see if the cursor is already opened.
   -- This is possible, since it is a packaged cursor.
   -- If so, first close it and then re-open it to
   -- ensure a "fresh" result set.
   IF bookinfo_pkg.bard_cur%ISOPEN
   THEN
      CLOSE bookinfo_pkg.bard_cur;
   END IF;

   OPEN bookinfo_pkg.bard_cur;

   -- Fetch each row, but stop when I've displayed the
   -- first five works by Shakespeare or when I have
   -- run out of rows.
   LOOP
      FETCH bookinfo_pkg.bard_cur INTO bard_rec;
      EXIT WHEN bookinfo_pkg.bard_cur%NOTFOUND
             OR bookinfo_pkg.bard_cur%ROWCOUNT = 6;
      DBMS_OUTPUT.put_line (
           bcur%ROWCOUNT
         || ') '
         || rec.title
         || ', published in '
         || TO_CHAR (rec.date_published, 'YYYY')
      );
```

```
    END LOOP;

    CLOSE bcur;
END;
```

Cursor Parameters

You are probably familiar with the use of parameters with procedures and functions. Parameters provide a way to pass information into and out of a module. Used properly, parameters improve the usefulness and flexibility of modules.

PL/SQL allows you to pass parameters into cursors. The same rationale for using parameters in modules applies to parameters for cursors:

Makes the cursor more reusable
: Instead of hardcoding a value into the WHERE clause of a query to select particular information, you can use a parameter and then pass different values to the WHERE clause each time a cursor is opened.

Avoids scoping problems
: When you pass parameters instead of hardcoding values, the result set for that cursor is not tied to a specific variable in a program or block. If your program has nested blocks, you can define the cursor at a higher-level (enclosing) block and use it in any of the sub-blocks with variables defined in those local blocks.

You can specify as many cursor parameters as you need. When you OPEN the cursor, you need to include an argument in the parameter list for each parameter, except for trailing parameters that have default values.

When should you parameterize your cursor? I apply the same rule of thumb to cursors as to procedures and functions; if I am going to use the cursor in more than one place with different values for the same WHERE clause, I should create a parameter for the cursor.

Let's take a look at the difference between parameterized and unparameterized cursors. First, here is a cursor without any parameters:

```
CURSOR joke_cur IS
   SELECT name, category, last_used_date
     FROM joke;
```

The result set of this cursor is all the rows in the joke table. If I just wanted to retrieve all jokes in the HUSBAND category, I would need to add a WHERE clause:

```
CURSOR joke_cur IS
   SELECT name, category, last_used_date
     FROM joke
    WHERE category = 'HUSBAND';
```

I didn't use a cursor parameter to accomplish this task, nor did I need to. The joke_cur cursor now retrieves only those jokes about husbands. That's all well and good, but what if I also wanted to see lightbulb jokes and then chicken-and-egg jokes and finally, as my ten-year-old niece would certainly demand, all my knock-knock jokes?

Generalizing cursors with parameters

I really don't want to write a separate cursor for each category—that is definitely not a data-driven approach to programming. Instead, I would much rather be able to change the joke cursor so that it can accept different categories and return the appropriate rows. The best (though not the only) way to do this is with a cursor parameter:

```
DECLARE
   /*
   || Cursor with parameter list consisting of a single
   || string parameter.
   */
   CURSOR joke_cur (category_in VARCHAR2)
   IS
      SELECT name, category, last_used_date
        FROM joke
       WHERE category = UPPER (category_in);

   joke_rec joke_cur%ROWTYPE;

BEGIN
   /* Now when I open the cursor, I also pass the argument */
   OPEN joke_cur (:joke.category);
   FETCH joke_cur INTO joke_rec;
```

I added a parameter list after the cursor name and before the IS keyword. I took out the hardcoded "HUSBAND" and replaced it with "UPPER (category_in)" so that I could enter "HUSBAND", "husband", or "HuSbAnD" and the cursor would still work. Now when I open the cursor, I specify the value I wish to pass as the category by including that value (which can be a literal, a constant, or an expression) inside parentheses. At the moment the cursor is opened, the SELECT statement is parsed and bound using the specified value for category_in. The result set is identified and the cursor is ready for fetching.

Opening cursors with parameters

I can OPEN that same cursor with any category I like. Now I don't have to write a separate cursor to accommodate this requirement:

```
OPEN joke_cur (:jokes_pkg.category);
OPEN joke_cur ('husband');
OPEN joke_cur ('politician');
OPEN joke_cur (:jokes_pkg.relation || ' IN-LAW');
```

The most common place to use a parameter in a cursor is in the WHERE clause, but you can make reference to it anywhere in the SELECT statement, as shown here:

```
DECLARE
   CURSOR joke_cur (category_in VARCHAR2)
   IS
      SELECT name, category_in, last_used_date
        FROM joke
       WHERE category = UPPER (category_in);
```

Instead of returning the category from the table, I simply pass back the category_in parameter in the select list. The result will be the same either way because my WHERE clause restricts categories to the parameter value.

Scope of cursor parameters

The scope of the cursor parameter is confined to that cursor. You cannot refer to the cursor parameter outside of the SELECT statement associated with the cursor. The following PL/SQL fragment will not compile because the program_name identifier is not a local variable in the block. Instead, it is a formal parameter for the cursor and is defined only inside the cursor:

```
DECLARE
   CURSOR scariness_cur (program_name VARCHAR2)
   IS
      SELECT SUM (scary_level) total_scary_level
        FROM tales_from_the_crypt
       WHERE prog_name = program_name;
BEGIN
   program_name := 'THE BREATHING MUMMY'; /* Illegal reference */
   OPEN scariness_cur (program_name);
END;
```

Cursor parameter modes

The syntax for cursor parameters is very similar to that of procedures and functions, with the restriction that a cursor parameter can be an IN parameter only. You cannot specify OUT or IN OUT modes for cursor parameters. The OUT and IN OUT modes are used to pass values out of a procedure through that parameter. This doesn't make sense for a cursor. Values cannot be passed back out of a cursor through the parameter list. Information is retrieved from a cursor only by fetching a record and copying values from the column list with an INTO clause. (See Chapter 16 for more information on parameter mode).

Default values for parameters

Cursor parameters can be assigned default values. Here is an example of a parameterized cursor with a default value:

```
CURSOR emp_cur (emp_id_in NUMBER := 0)
IS
```

```
SELECT employee_id, emp_name
  FROM employee
 WHERE employee_id = emp_id_in;
```

So if Joe Smith's employee ID is 1001, the following statements would set my_ emp_ id to 1001 and my_emp_name to JOE SMITH:

```
OPEN emp_cur (1001);
FETCH emp_cur INTO my_emp_id, my_emp_name;
```

Because the emp_id_in parameter has a default value, I can also open and fetch from the cursor without specifying a value for the parameter. If I do not specify a value for the parameter, the cursor uses the default value.

BULK COLLECT

Oracle8*i* introduced a very powerful new feature that improves the efficiency of queries in PL/SQL: the BULK COLLECT clause. With BULK COLLECT you can retrieve multiple rows of data through either an implicit or an explicit query with a single roundtrip to and from the database. BULK COLLECT reduces the number of context switches between the PL/SQL and SQL statement executors and thereby reduces the overhead of retrieving data.

Take a look at the following code snippet. I need to retrieve hundreds of rows of data on automobiles that have a poor environmental record. I place that data into a set of collections so that I can easily and quickly manipulate the data for both analysis and reporting.

```
DECLARE
   CURSOR major_polluters_cur
   IS
      SELECT name, mileage
        FROM transportation
       WHERE TYPE = 'AUTOMOBILE'
         AND mileage < 20;
   names name_varray;
   mileages number_varray;
BEGIN
   FOR bad_car IN major_polluters
   LOOP
      names.EXTEND;
      names (major_polluters%ROWCOUNT) := bad_car.NAME;
      mileages.EXTEND;
      mileages (major_polluters%ROWCOUNT) := bad_car.mileage;
   END LOOP;
   -- Now work with data in the collections
END;
```

This certainly gets the job done, but the job might take a long time to complete. Consider this: if the transportation table contains 2,000 vehicles, then the PL/SQL engine issues 2,000 individual fetches against the cursor in the System Global Area (SGA).

To help out in this scenario, use the BULK COLLECT clause for the INTO element of your query. By using this clause in your cursor (explicit or implicit) you tell the SQL engine to bulk bind the output from the multiple rows fetched by the query into the specified collections before returning control to the PL/SQL engine. The syntax for this clause is:

```
... BULK COLLECT INTO collection_name[, collection_name] ...
```

where *collection_name* identifies a collection.

Here are some rules and restrictions to keep in mind when using BULK COLLECT:

- Prior to Oracle9*i*, you could use BULK COLLECT only with static SQL. With Oracle9*i*, you can use BULK COLLECT with both dynamic and static SQL. See Chapter 15 for more details and an example.
- You can use BULK COLLECT keywords in any of the following clauses: SELECT INTO, FETCH INTO, and RETURNING INTO.
- The collections you reference can store only scalar values (strings, numbers, dates). In other words, you cannot fetch a row of data into a record structure that is a row in a collection.
- The SQL engine automatically initializes and extends the collections you reference in the BULK COLLECT clause. It starts filling the collections at index 1, inserts elements consecutively (densely), and overwrites the values of any elements that were previously defined.
- You cannot use the SELECT...BULK COLLECT statement in a FORALL statement.

Let's explore these rules and the usefulness of BULK COLLECT through a series of examples.

First, here is a recoding of the "major polluters" example using BULK COLLECT:

```
DECLARE
   names name_varray;
   mileages number_varray;
BEGIN
   SELECT name, mileage
     FROM transportation
     BULK COLLECT INTO names, mileages
       WHERE TYPE = 'AUTOMOBILE'
         AND mileage < 20;
   -- Now work with data in the collections
END;
```

I am now able to remove the initialization and extension code from the row-by-row fetch implementation.

I don't have to rely on implicit cursors to get this job done. Here is another reworking of the major polluters example, retaining the explicit cursor:

```
DECLARE
   CURSOR major_polluters IS
```

```
        SELECT name, mileage
          FROM transportation
         WHERE TYPE = 'AUTOMOBILE'
           AND mileage < 20;
   names name_varray;
   mileages number_varray;
BEGIN
   OPEN major_polluters;
   FETCH major_polluters BULK COLLECT INTO names, mileages;
   -- Now work with data in the collections
END;
```

Limiting Rows Retrieved with BULK COLLECT

Oracle provides a LIMIT clause for BULK COLLECT that allows you to limit the number of rows fetched from the database. The syntax is:

```
FETCH ... BULK COLLECT INTO ... [LIMIT rows];
```

where *rows* can be any literal, variable, or expression that evaluates to a NUMBER (otherwise, Oracle will raise a VALUE_ERROR exception).

Let's take a look at an example. Suppose that my transportation table has a very large number of rows of vehicles that qualify as major polluters. I don't want to retrieve more than 5,000 rows. I can then add the LIMIT clause:

```
DECLARE
   CURSOR major_polluters IS
      SELECT name
        FROM transportation
       WHERE TYPE = 'AUTOMOBILE' AND mileage < 20;
   names name_varray;
BEGIN
   OPEN major_polluters;
   FETCH major_polluters
      BULK COLLECT INTO names
      LIMIT 5000;
   ...
END;
```

Bulk Fetching of Multiple Columns

As you have seen in previous examples, you certainly can bulk fetch the contents of more than one column. It would be most elegant if we could fetch those multiple columns into a single collection of records. This feature became available in Oracle9*i* Release 2.

Suppose that I would like to retrieve all the information in my transportation table for each vehicle whose mileage is less than 20 miles per gallon. In Oracle9*i* Release 2 and above, I can do so with a minimum of coding fuss:

```
DECLARE
   -- Declare the type of collection
```

```
    TYPE VehTab IS TABLE OF transportation%ROWTYPE;

    -- Instantiate a particular collection from the TYPE.
    gas_guzzlers VehTab;
BEGIN
    SELECT *
      BULK COLLECT INTO gas_guzzlers
      FROM transportation
     WHERE mileage < 20;
    ...
```

Prior to Oracle9*i* Release 2, the above code would raise this exception:

```
PLS-00597: expression 'GAS_GUZZLERS' in the INTO list is of wrong type
```

If you are running Oracle8*i* or Oracle9*i* Release 1, you will need to declare multiple collections and then fetch individually into those collections:

```
DECLARE
    guzzler_type name_varray;
    guzzler_name name_varray;
    guzzler_mileage number_varray;

    CURSOR low_mileage_cur IS
        SELECT vehicle_type, name, mileage
          FROM transportation WHERE mileage < 10;
BEGIN
    OPEN low_mileage_cur;
    FETCH low_mileage_cur BULK COLLECT
     INTO guzzler_type, guzzler_name, guzzler_mileage;
END;
```

Note that you can use the LIMIT clause with a BULK COLLECT into a collection of records, just as you would with any other BULK COLLECT statement.

Using the RETURNING Clause with Bulk Operations

You've now seen BULK COLLECT put to use for both implicit and explicit query cursors. You can also use BULK COLLECT inside a FORALL statement, in order to take advantage of the RETURNING clause.

The RETURNING clause, introduced in Oracle8, allows you to obtain information (such as a newly updated value for a salary) from a DML statement. RETURNING can help you avoid additional queries to the database to determine the results of DML operations that just completed.

Suppose that Congress has passed a law requiring that a company pay its highest-compensated employee no more than 50 times the salary of its lowest-paid employee. I work in the IT department of the newly merged company Northrop-Ford-Mattel-Yahoo-ATT, which employs a total of 250,000 workers. The word has come down from on high: the CEO is not taking a pay cut, so we need to increase the salaries of everyone who makes less than 50 times his 2004 total compensation package of $145 million—and decrease the salaries of all upper management except for the CEO. After all, somebody's got to make up for this loss in profit.

Wow! I have lots of updating to do, and I want to use FORALL to get the job done as quickly as possible. However, I also need to perform various kinds of processing on the employee data and then print a report showing the change in salary for each affected employee. That RETURNING clause would come in awfully handy here, so let's give it a try.

See the *onlyfair.sql* file on the O'Reilly site for all of the steps shown here, plus table creation and INSERT statements.

First, I'll create a reusable function to return the compensation for an executive:

```
/* File on web: onlyfair.sql */
FUNCTION salforexec (title_in IN VARCHAR2) RETURN NUMBER
IS
   CURSOR ceo_compensation IS
      SELECT salary + bonus + stock_options +
             mercedes_benz_allowance + yacht_allowance
        FROM compensation
       WHERE title = title_in;
   big_bucks NUMBER;
BEGIN
   OPEN ceo_compensation;
   FETCH ceo_compensation INTO big_bucks;
   RETURN big_bucks;
END;
```

In the main block of the update program, I declare a number of local variables and the following query to identify underpaid employees and overpaid employees who are not lucky enough to be the CEO:

```
DECLARE
   big_bucks NUMBER := salforexec ('CEO');
   min_sal NUMBER := big_bucks / 50;
   names name_varray;
   old_salaries number_varray;
   new_salaries number_varray;

   CURSOR affected_employees (ceosal IN NUMBER)
   IS
      SELECT name, salary + bonus old_salary
        FROM compensation
       WHERE title != 'CEO'
         AND ((salary + bonus < ceosal / 50)
              OR (salary + bonus > ceosal / 10)) ;
```

At the start of my executable section, I load all of this data into my collections with a BULK COLLECT query:

```
OPEN affected_employees (big_bucks);
FETCH affected_employees
   BULK COLLECT INTO names, old_salaries;
```

Then I can use the names collection in my FORALL update:

```
FORALL indx IN names.FIRST .. names.LAST
   UPDATE compensation
      SET salary =
         GREATEST(
            DECODE (
               GREATEST (min_sal, salary),
                  min_sal, min_sal,
               salary / 5),
            min_sal )
    WHERE name = names (indx)
    RETURNING salary BULK COLLECT INTO new_salaries;
```

I use DECODE to give an employee either a major boost in yearly income or an 80% cut in pay to keep the CEO comfy. I end it with a RETURNING clause that relies on BULK COLLECT to populate a third collection: the new salaries.

Finally, because I used RETURNING and don't have to write another query against the compensation table to obtain the new salaries, I can immediately move to report generation:

```
FOR indx IN names.FIRST .. names.LAST
LOOP
   DBMS_OUTPUT.PUT_LINE (
      RPAD (names(indx), 20) ||
      RPAD (' Old: ' || old_salaries(indx), 15) ||
      ' New: ' || new_salaries(indx)
      );
END LOOP;
```

Here, then, is the report generated from the *onlyfair.sql* script:

```
John DayAndNight       Old: 10500     New: 2900000
Holly Cubicle          Old: 52000     New: 2900000
Sandra Watchthebucks Old: 22000000  New: 4000000
```

Now everyone can afford quality housing and health care. And tax revenue at all levels will increase, so public schools can get the funding they need.

The RETURNING column values or expressions returned by each execution in FORALL are added to the collection after the values returned previously. If you use RETURNING inside a non-bulk FOR loop, previous values are overwritten by the latest DML execution.

SELECT...FOR UPDATE

When you issue a SELECT statement against the database to query some records, no locks are placed on the selected rows. In general, this is a wonderful feature because the number of records locked at any given time is kept to the absolute minimum: only those records that have been changed but not yet committed are locked. Even then, others will be able to read those records as they appeared before the change (the "before image" of the data).

There are times, however, when you will want to lock a set of records even before you change them in your program. Oracle offers the FOR UPDATE clause of the SELECT statement to perform this locking.

When you issue a SELECT...FOR UPDATE statement, the RDBMS automatically obtains exclusive row-level locks on all the rows identified by the SELECT statement, holding the records "for your changes only" as you move through the rows retrieved by the cursor. No one else will be able to change any of these records until you perform a ROLLBACK or a COMMIT—but other sessions can still read the data.

Here are two examples of the FOR UPDATE clause used in a cursor:

```
CURSOR toys_cur IS
   SELECT name, manufacturer, preference_level, sell_at_yardsale_flag
     FROM my_sons_collection
    WHERE hours_used = 0
      FOR UPDATE;

CURSOR fall_jobs_cur IS
   SELECT task, expected_hours, tools_required, do_it_yourself_flag
     FROM winterize
    WHERE year = TO_CHAR (SYSDATE, 'YYYY')
      FOR UPDATE OF task;
```

The first cursor uses the unqualified FOR UPDATE clause, while the second cursor qualifies the FOR UPDATE with a column name from the query.

You can use the FOR UPDATE clause in a SELECT against multiple tables. In this case, rows in a table are locked only if the FOR UPDATE clause references a column in that table. In the following example, the FOR UPDATE clause does not result in any locked rows in the winterize table:

```
CURSOR fall_jobs_cur
IS
  SELECT w.task, w.expected_hours,
         w.tools_required,
         w.do_it_yourself_flag
    FROM winterize w, husband_config hc
   WHERE YEAR = TO_CHAR (SYSDATE, 'YYYY')
     AND w.task_id = hc.task_id
  FOR UPDATE OF husband_config.max_procrastination_allowed;
```

The FOR UPDATE OF clause mentions only the max_procrastination_allowed column; no columns in the winterize table are listed.

The OF list of the FOR UPDATE clause does not restrict you to changing only those columns listed. Locks are still placed on all rows; the OF list just gives you a way to document more clearly what you intend to change. If you simply state FOR

UPDATE in the query and do not include one or more columns after the OF keyword, the database will then lock all identified rows across all tables listed in the FROM clause.

Furthermore, you do not have to actually UPDATE or DELETE any records just because you issue a SELECT...FOR UPDATE statement—that act simply states your intention to be able to do so.

Finally, you can append the optional keyword NOWAIT to the FOR UPDATE clause to tell Oracle not to wait if the table has been locked by another user. In this case, control will be returned immediately to your program so that you can perform other work or simply wait for a period of time before trying again. Without the NOWAIT clause, your process will block until the table is available. There is no limit to the wait time unless the table is remote. For remote objects, the Oracle initialization parameter, DISTRIBUTED_LOCK_TIMEOUT, is used to set the limit.

Releasing Locks with COMMIT

As soon as a cursor with a FOR UPDATE clause is OPENed, all rows identified in the result set of the cursor are locked and remain locked until your session issues either a COMMIT statement to save any changes or a ROLLBACK statement to cancel those changes. When either of these actions occurs, the locks on the rows are released. As a result, you cannot execute another FETCH against a FOR UPDATE cursor after you COMMIT or ROLLBACK. You will have lost your position in the cursor.

Consider the following program, which assigns winterization chores:*

```
DECLARE
   /* All the jobs in the Fall to prepare for the Winter */
   CURSOR fall_jobs_cur
   IS
      SELECT task, expected_hours, tools_required, do_it_yourself_flag
        FROM winterize
       WHERE year = TO_NUMBER (TO_CHAR (SYSDATE, 'YYYY'))
         AND completed_flag = 'NOTYET'
       FOR UPDATE OF task;
BEGIN
   /* For each job fetched by the cursor... */
   FOR job_rec IN fall_jobs_cur
   LOOP
      IF job_rec.do_it_yourself_flag = 'YOUCANDOIT'
      THEN
         /*
```

* Caveat: I don't want to set false expectations, especially with my wife. The code in this block is purely an example. In reality, I set the max_procrastination_allowed to five years and let my house decay until I can afford to pay someone else to do something, or my wife does it, or she gives me an ultimatum. Now you know why I decided to write a book...

```
         || I have found my next job. Assign it to myself (like someone
         || else is going to do it!) and then commit the changes.
         */
         UPDATE winterize SET responsible = 'STEVEN'
          WHERE task = job_rec.task
            AND year = TO_CHAR (SYSDATE, 'YYYY');
         COMMIT;
      END IF;
   END LOOP;
END;
```

Suppose this loop finds its first YOUCANDOIT job. It then commits an assignment of a job to STEVEN. When it tries to FETCH the next record, the program raises the following exception:

```
ORA-01002: fetch out of sequence
```

If you ever need to execute a COMMIT or ROLLBACK as you FETCH records from a SELECT FOR UPDATE cursor, you should include code (such as a loop EXIT or other conditional logic) to halt any further fetches from the cursor.

The WHERE CURRENT OF Clause

PL/SQL provides the WHERE CURRENT OF clause for both UPDATE and DELETE statements inside a cursor. This clause allows you to easily make changes to the most recently fetched row of data.

To update columns in the most recently fetched row, specify:

```
UPDATE table_name
   SET set_clause
 WHERE CURRENT OF cursor_name;
```

To delete the row from the database for the most recently fetched record, specify:

```
DELETE
  FROM table_name
 WHERE CURRENT OF cursor_name;
```

Notice that the WHERE CURRENT OF clause references the cursor, not the record into which the next fetched row is deposited.

The most important advantage to using WHERE CURRENT OF to change the last row fetched is that you do not have to code in two (or more) places the criteria used to uniquely identify a row in a table. Without WHERE CURRENT OF, you would need to repeat the WHERE clause of your cursor in the WHERE clause of the associated UPDATEs and DELETEs. As a result, if the table structure changed in a way that affected the construction of the primary key, you would have to update each SQL statement to support this change. If you use WHERE CURRENT OF, on the other hand, you modify only the WHERE clause of the SELECT statement.

This might seem like a relatively minor issue, but it is one of many areas in your code where you can leverage subtle features in PL/SQL to minimize code redundancies. Utilization of WHERE CURRENT OF, %TYPE and %ROWTYPE declaration attributes, cursor FOR loops, local modularization, and other PL/SQL language constructs can significantly reduce the pain of maintaining your Oracle-based applications.

Let's see how this clause would improve the example in the previous section. In the jobs cursor FOR loop, I want to UPDATE the record that was currently FETCHed by the cursor. I do this in the UPDATE statement by repeating the same WHERE used in the cursor because "(task, year)" makes up the primary key of this table:

```
WHERE task = job_rec.task
  AND year = TO_CHAR (SYSDATE, 'YYYY');
```

This is a less than ideal situation, as explained above: I have coded the same logic in two places, and this code must be kept synchronized. It would be so much more convenient and natural to be able to code the equivalent of the following statements:

- "Delete the row I just fetched."
- "Update these columns in that row I just fetched."

A perfect fit for WHERE CURRENT OF! The next version of my winterization program uses this clause. I have also switched from a FOR loop to a simple loop because I want to exit conditionally from the loop:

```
DECLARE
   CURSOR fall_jobs_cur IS SELECT ... same as before ... ;
   job_rec fall_jobs_cur%ROWTYPE;
BEGIN
   OPEN fall_jobs_cur;
   LOOP
      FETCH fall_jobs_cur INTO job_rec;

      IF fall_jobs_cur%NOTFOUND
      THEN
         EXIT;

      ELSIF job_rec.do_it_yourself_flag = 'YOUCANDOIT'
      THEN
         UPDATE winterize SET responsible = 'STEVEN'
          WHERE CURRENT OF fall_jobs_cur;
         COMMIT;
         EXIT;
      END IF;
   END LOOP;
   CLOSE fall_jobs_cur;
END;
```

Cursor Variables

A cursor variable is a variable that points to or references an underlying cursor. Unlike an explicit cursor, which names the PL/SQL work area for the result set, a cursor variable is a reference to that work area. Explicit and implicit cursors are static in that they are tied to specific queries. The cursor variable can be opened for any query, even for different queries within a single program execution.

The most important benefit of the cursor variable is that it provides a mechanism for passing results of queries (the rows returned by fetches against a cursor) between different PL/SQL programs—even between client and server PL/SQL programs. Prior to PL/SQL Release 2.3, you would have had to fetch all data from the cursor, store it in PL/SQL variables (perhaps a PL/SQL table), and then pass those variables as arguments. With cursor variables, you simply pass the reference to that cursor. This improves performance and streamlines your code.

It also means that the cursor is, in effect, shared among the programs that have access to the cursor variable. In a client-server environment, for example, a program on the client side could open and start fetching from the cursor variable, and then pass that variable as an argument to a stored procedure on the server. This stored program could then continue fetching and pass control back to the client program to close the cursor. You can also perform the same steps between different stored programs on the same or different database instances.

This process, shown in Figure 14-2, offers dramatic new possibilities for data sharing and cursor management in PL/SQL programs.

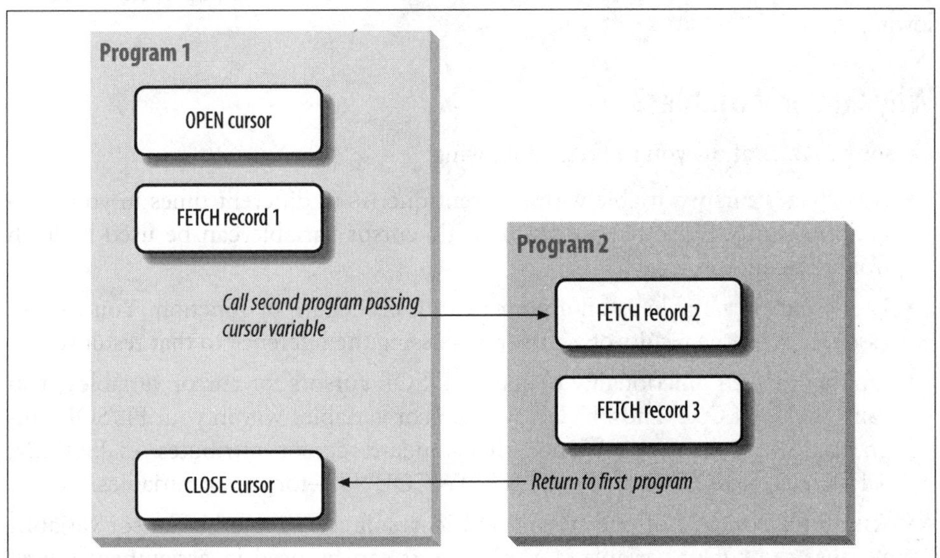

Figure 14-2. Referencing a cursor variable across two programs

The code you write to take advantage of cursor variables is very similar to that for explicit cursors. The following example declares a cursor type (called a REF CURSOR type) for the company table, then opens, fetches from, and closes the cursor:

```
DECLARE
   /* Create the cursor type. */
   TYPE company_curtype IS REF CURSOR RETURN company%ROWTYPE;

   /* Declare a cursor variable of that type. */
   company_curvar company_curtype;

   /* Declare a record with same structure as cursor variable. */
   company_rec company%ROWTYPE;
BEGIN
   /* Open the cursor variable, associating with it a SQL statement. */
   OPEN company_curvar FOR SELECT * FROM company;

   /* Fetch from the cursor variable. */
   FETCH company_curvar INTO company_rec;

   /* Close the cursor object associated with variable. */
   CLOSE company_curvar;
END;
```

That looks an awful lot like explicit cursor operations, except for the following:

- The REF CURSOR type declaration
- The OPEN FOR syntax that specified the query at the time of the open

Although the syntax is similar, the very fact that the cursor variable is a variable opens up many new opportunities in your programs. These are explored in the following sections.

Why Cursor Variables?

Cursor variables allow you to do the following:

- Associate a cursor variable with different queries at different times in your program execution. In other words, a single cursor variable can be used to fetch from different result sets.
- Pass a cursor variable as an argument to a procedure or function. You can, in essence, share the results of a cursor by passing the reference to that result set.
- Employ the full functionality of static PL/SQL cursors for cursor variables. You can OPEN, CLOSE, and FETCH with cursor variables within your PL/SQL programs. You can also reference the standard cursor attributes—%ISOPEN, %FOUND, %NOTFOUND, and %ROWCOUNT—for cursor variables.
- Assign the contents of one cursor (and its result set) to another cursor variable. Because the cursor variable is a variable, it can be used in assignment operations. There are restrictions on referencing this kind of variable, however, as we'll discuss later in this chapter.

Similarities to Static Cursors

One of the key design requirements for cursor variables was that, when possible, the semantics used to manage cursor objects would be the same as that of static cursors. While the declaration of a cursor variable and the syntax for opening it are enhanced, the following cursor operations for cursor variables are the same as for static cursors:

The CLOSE statement

In the following example, I declare a REF CURSOR type and a cursor variable based on that type. Then I close the cursor variable using the same syntax as for a static cursor:

```
DECLARE
   TYPE var_cur_type IS REF CURSOR;
   var_cur var_cur_type;
BEGIN
   CLOSE var_cur;
END;
```

Cursor attributes

You can use any of the four cursor attributes with exactly the same syntax as for a static cursor. The rules governing the use and values returned by those attributes match that of explicit cursors. If I have declared a variable cursor as in the previous example, I could use all the cursor attributes as follows:

```
var_cur%ISOPEN
var_cur%FOUND
var_cur%NOTFOUND
var_cur%ROWCOUNT
```

Fetching from the cursor variable

You use the same FETCH syntax when fetching from a cursor variable into local PL/SQL data structures. There are, however, additional rules applied by PL/SQL to make sure that the data structures of the cursor variable's row (the set of values returned by the cursor object) match that of the data structures to the right of the INTO keyword. These rules are discussed in the later section "Rules for Cursor Variables."

Because the syntax for these aspects of cursor variables is the same as for the already familiar explicit cursors, the following sections will focus on features that are unique to cursor variables.

Declaring REF CURSOR Types

Just as with a PL/SQL table or a programmer-defined record, you must perform two distinct declaration steps in order to create a cursor variable:

1. Create a referenced cursor TYPE (as of Oracle9*i*, you can use the predefined, weakly typed SYS_REFCURSOR REF CURSOR type).
2. Declare the actual cursor variable based on that type.

The syntax for creating a referenced cursor type is as follows:

```
TYPE cursor_type_name IS REF CURSOR [ RETURN return_type ];
```

where *cursor_type_name* is the name of the type of cursor and *return_type* is the RETURN data specification for the cursor type. The *return_type* can be any of the data structures valid for a normal cursor RETURN clause, and is defined using the %ROWTYPE attribute or by referencing a previously defined record TYPE.

Notice that the RETURN clause is optional with the REF CURSOR type statement. Both of the following declarations are valid:

```
TYPE company_curtype IS REF CURSOR RETURN company%ROWTYPE;
TYPE generic_curtype IS REF CURSOR;
```

The first form of the REF CURSOR statement is called a *strong type* because it attaches a record type (or row type) to the cursor variable type at the moment of declaration. Any cursor variable declared using that type can be used only with SQL statement and FETCH INTO data structures that match the specified record type. The advantage of a strong REF TYPE is that the compiler can determine whether or not the developer has properly matched up the cursor variable's FETCH statements with its cursor object's query list.

The second form of the REF CURSOR statement, in which the RETURN clause is missing, is called a *weak type*. This cursor variable type is not associated with any record data structures. Cursor variables declared without the RETURN clause can be used in more flexible ways than the strong type. They can be used with any query, with any rowtype structure, and can vary even within the course of a single program.

Declaring Cursor Variables

The syntax for declaring a cursor variable is:

```
cursor_name cursor_type_name;
```

where *cursor_name* is the name of the cursor and *cursor_type_name* is the name of the type of cursor previously defined with a TYPE statement.

Here is an example of the creation of a cursor variable:

```
DECLARE
   /* Create a cursor type for sports cars. */
   TYPE sports_car_cur_type IS REF CURSOR RETURN car%ROWTYPE;

   /* Create a cursor variable for sports cars. */
   sports_car_cur sports_car_cur_type;
BEGIN
   ...
END;
```

It is important to distinguish between declaring a cursor variable and creating an actual cursor object—the result set identified by the cursor SQL statement. A constant is nothing more than a value, whereas a variable points to its value. Similarly, a static cursor acts as a constant, whereas a cursor variable references or points to a cursor object. These distinctions are shown in Figure 14-3. Notice that two different cursor variables in different programs are both referring to the same cursor object.

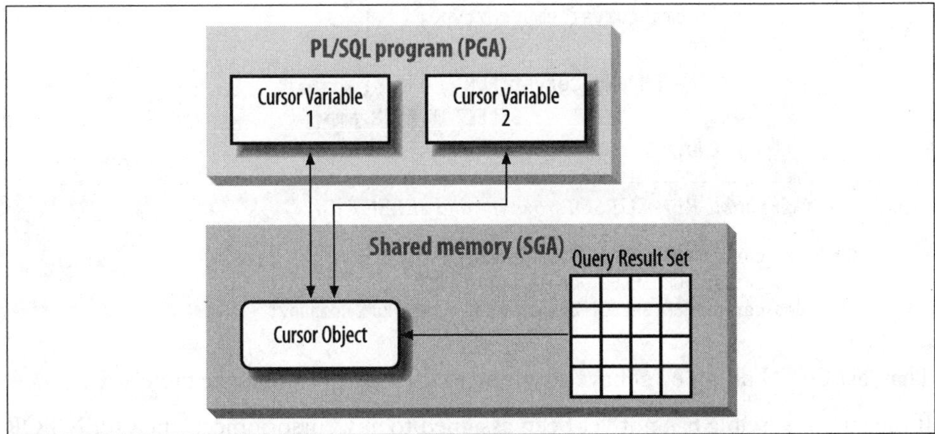

Figure 14-3. The referencing character of cursor variables

Declaration of a cursor variable does not create a cursor object. To do that, you must use the OPEN FOR syntax to create a new cursor object and assign it to the variable.

Opening Cursor Variables

You assign a value (the cursor object) to a cursor when you OPEN the cursor. So the syntax for the traditional OPEN statement allows for cursor variables to accept a SELECT statement after the FOR clause, as shown below:

```
OPEN cursor_name FOR select_statement;
```

where *cursor_name* is the name of a cursor or cursor variable and *select_statement* is a SQL SELECT statement.

For strong REF CURSOR type cursor variables, the structure of the SELECT statement (the number and datatypes of the columns) must match or be compatible with the structure specified in the RETURN clause of the TYPE statement. Figure 14-4 shows an example of the kind of compatibility required. "Rules for Cursor Variables" contains the full set of compatibility rules.

If *cursor_name* is a cursor variable defined with a weak REF CURSOR type, you can OPEN it for any query, with any structure. In the following example, I open (assign a value to) the cursor variable three times, with three different queries:

```
DECLARE
   TYPE emp_curtype IS REF CURSOR;
   emp_curvar emp_curtype;
BEGIN
```

```
DECLARE
   TYPE emp_curtype IS
      REF CURSOR RETURN emp%ROWTYPE;
   emp_curvar emp_curtype;
BEGIN
   OPEN emp_curvar FOR
              SELECT * FROM emp;
END;
```

Figure 14-4. Compatible REF CURSOR rowtype and SELECT list

```
   OPEN emp_curvar FOR SELECT * FROM emp;
   OPEN emp_curvar FOR SELECT employee_id FROM emp;
   OPEN emp_curvar FOR SELECT company_id, name FROM company;
END;
```

That last OPEN didn't even have anything to do with the employee table!

If the cursor variable has not yet been assigned to any cursor object, the OPEN FOR statement implicitly creates an object for the variable. If at the time of the OPEN the cursor variable is already pointing to a cursor object, OPEN FOR does not create a new object. Instead, it reuses the existing object and attaches a new query to that object. The cursor object is maintained separately from the cursor or query itself.

Fetching from Cursor Variables

As mentioned earlier, the syntax for a FETCH statement using a cursor variable is the same as that for static cursors:

```
FETCH cursor_variable_name INTO record_name;
FETCH cursor_variable_name INTO variable_name, variable_name ...;
```

When the cursor variable is declared with a strong REF CURSOR type, the PL/SQL compiler makes sure that the data structures listed after the INTO keyword are compatible with the structure of the query associated with the cursor variable.

If the cursor variable is of the weak REF CURSOR type, the PL/SQL compiler cannot perform the same kind of check it performs for a strong REF CURSOR type. Such a cursor variable can FETCH into any data structures because the REF CURSOR type is not identified with a rowtype at the time of declaration. At compile time, there is no way to know which cursor object (and associated SQL statement) will be assigned to that variable.

Consequently, the check for compatibility must happen at runtime, when the FETCH is about to be executed. At this point, if the query and the INTO clause do not structurally match, then the PL/SQL runtime engine will raise the predefined ROWTYPE_MISMATCH exception. Note that PL/SQL will use implicit conversions if necessary and possible.

Handling the ROWTYPE_MISMATCH exception

You can trap the ROWTYPE_MISMATCH exception and then attempt to FETCH from the cursor variable using a different INTO clause. But even though you are executing the second FETCH statement in your program, you will still retrieve the first row in the result set of the cursor object's query. This functionality comes in handy for weak REF CURSOR types.

In the following example, a centralized real estate database stores information about properties in a variety of tables: one for homes, another for commercial properties, and so on. There is also a single, central table that stores addresses and building types (home, commercial, etc.). I use a single procedure to open a weak REF CURSOR variable for the appropriate table based on the street address. Each individual real estate office can then call that procedure to scan through the matching properties. Here are the steps:

1. Define my weak REF CURSOR type:

   ```
   TYPE building_curtype IS REF CURSOR;
   ```

2. Create the procedure. Notice that the mode of the cursor variable parameter is IN OUT:

   ```
   PROCEDURE open_site_list
      (address_in IN VARCHAR2,
       site_cur_inout IN OUT building_curtype)
   IS
      home_type CONSTANT INTEGER := 1;
      commercial_type CONSTANT INTEGER := 2;

      /* A static cursor to get building type. */
      CURSOR site_type_cur IS
         SELECT site_type FROM property_master
          WHERE address = address_in;
      site_type_rec site_type_cur%ROWTYPE;

   BEGIN
      /* Get the building type for this address. */
      OPEN site_type_cur;
      FETCH site_type_cur INTO site_type_rec;
      CLOSE site_type_cur;

      /* Now use the site type to select from the right table.*/
      IF site_type_rec.site_type =  home_type
      THEN
         /* Use the home properties table. */
         OPEN site_cur_inout FOR
             SELECT * FROM home_properties
              WHERE address LIKE '%' || address_in || '%';

      ELSIF site_type_rec.site_type =  commercial_type
      THEN
         /* Use the commercial properties table. */
   ```

```
            OPEN site_cur_inout FOR
               SELECT * FROM commercial_properties
                WHERE address LIKE '%' || address_in || '%';
         END IF;
      END open_site_list;
```

3. Now that I have my open procedure, I can use it to scan properties.

In the following example, I pass in the address and then try to fetch from the cursor, assuming a home property. If the address actually identifies a commercial property, PL/SQL will raise the ROWTYPE_MISMATCH exception on account of the incompatible record structures. The exception section then fetches again, this time into a commercial building record, and the scan is complete.

```
DECLARE
   /* Declare a cursor variable. */
   building_curvar building_curtype;

   /* Define record structures for two different tables. */
   home_rec home_properties%ROWTYPE;
   commercial_rec commercial_properties%ROWTYPE;
BEGIN
   /* Get the address from the user. */
   prompt_for_address (address_string);

   /* Assign a query to the cursor variable based on the address. */
   open_site_list (address_string, building_curvar);

   /* Give it a try! Fetch a row into the home record. */
   FETCH building_curvar INTO home_rec;

   /* If I got here, the site was a home, so display it. */
   show_home_site (home_rec);
EXCEPTION
   /* If the first record was not a home... */
   WHEN ROWTYPE_MISMATCH
   THEN
      /* Fetch that same 1st row into the commercial record. */
      FETCH building_curvar INTO commercial_rec;

      /* Show the commercial site info. */
      show_commercial_site (commercial_rec);
END;
```

Rules for Cursor Variables

This section examines in more detail the rules and issues regarding the use of cursor variables in your programs. These include rowtype matching rules, cursor variable aliases, and scoping issues.

Remember that the cursor variable is a reference to a cursor object or query in the database. It is not the object itself. A cursor variable is said to refer to a given query if either of the following is true:

- An OPEN statement FOR that query was executed with the cursor variable.
- A cursor variable was assigned a value from another cursor variable that refers to that query.

You can perform assignment operations with cursor variables and also pass these variables as arguments to procedures and functions. In order to perform such actions between cursor variables (and to bind a cursor variable to a parameter), the different cursor variables must follow a set of compile-time and runtime rowtype matching rules.

Compile-time rowtype matching rules

These are the rules that PL/SQL follows at compile time:

- Two cursor variables (including procedure parameters) are compatible for assignments and argument passing if any of the following is true:
  - — Both variables (or parameters) are of a strong REF CURSOR type with the same *rowtype_name*.
  - — Both variables (or parameters) are of a weak REF CURSOR type, regardless of the *rowtype_name*.
  - — One variable (or parameter) is of any strong REF CURSOR type, and the other is of any weak REF CURSOR type.
- A cursor variable (or parameter) of a strong REF CURSOR type may be OPEN FOR a query that returns a rowtype that is structurally equal to the *rowtype_name* in the original type declaration.
- A cursor variable (or parameter) of a weak REF CURSOR type may be OPEN FOR any query. The FETCH from such a variable is allowed INTO any list of variables or record structure.

If either of the cursor variables is of the weak REF CURSOR type, then the PL/SQL compiler cannot really validate whether the two different cursor variables will be compatible. That will happen at runtime; the rules are covered in the next section.

Runtime rowtype matching rules

These are the rules that PL/SQL follows at runtime:

- A cursor variable (or parameter) of a weak REF CURSOR type may be made to refer to a query of any rowtype regardless of the query or cursor object to which it may have referred earlier.

- A cursor variable (or parameter) of a strong REF CURSOR type may be made to refer only to a query that matches structurally the *rowtype_name* of the RETURN clause of the REF CURSOR type declaration.
- Two records (or lists of variables) are considered structurally matching with implicit conversions if both of the following are true:
  - The number of fields is the same in both records (or lists).
  - For each field in one record (or variable in one list), a corresponding field in the second list (or a variable in the second list) has the same PL/SQL datatype, or one that can be converted implicitly by PL/SQL to match the first.
- For a cursor variable (or parameter) used in a FETCH statement, the query associated with the cursor variable must structurally match (with implicit conversions) the record or list of variables of the INTO clause of the FETCH statement. This same rule is used for static cursors.

Cursor variable aliases

If you assign one cursor variable to another cursor variable, they become *aliases* for the same cursor object; they share the reference to the cursor object (result set of the cursor's query). Any action taken against the cursor object through one variable is also available to and reflected in the other variable.

This anonymous block illustrates the way cursor aliases work:

```
1  DECLARE
2     TYPE curvar_type IS REF CURSOR;
3     curvar1 curvar_type;
4     curvar2 curvar_type;
5     story fairy_tales%ROWTYPE;
6  BEGIN
7     OPEN curvar1 FOR SELECT * FROM fairy_tales;
8     curvar2 := curvar1;
9     FETCH curvar1 INTO story;
10    FETCH curvar2 INTO story;
11    CLOSE curvar2;
12    FETCH curvar1 INTO story;
13 END;
```

The following table provides an explanation of the cursor variable actions.

Line(s)	Description
2–5	Declares my weak REF CURSOR type and cursor variables.
7	Creates a cursor object and assigns it to curvar1 by opening a cursor for that cursor variable.
8	Assigns that same cursor object to the second cursor variable, curvar2. (Now we have two cursor variables that can be used to manipulate the same result set!)
9	Fetches the first record using the curvar1 variable.

Line(s)	Description
10	Fetches the second record using the curvar2 variable. (Notice that it doesn't matter which of the two variables you use. The pointer to the current record resides with the cursor object, not with any particular variable.)
11	Closes the cursor object referencing curvar2.
12	Will raise the INVALID_CURSOR exception when I try to fetch again from the cursor object. (When I closed the cursor through curvar2, it also closed it as far as curvar1 was concerned.)

Any change of state in a cursor object will be seen through any cursor variable that is an alias for that cursor object.

Scope of cursor object

The scope of a cursor variable is the same as that of a static cursor: the PL/SQL block in which the variable is declared (unless declared in a package, which makes the variable globally accessible). The scope of the cursor object to which a cursor variable is assigned, however, is a different matter.

Once an OPEN FOR creates a cursor object, that cursor object remains accessible as long as at least one active cursor variable refers to that cursor object. This means that you can create a cursor object in one scope (PL/SQL block) and assign it to a cursor variable. Then, by assigning that cursor variable to another cursor variable with a different scope, the cursor object remains accessible even if the original cursor variable has gone out of scope.

In the following example, I use nested blocks to demonstrate how the cursor object can persist outside of the scope in which it was originally created:

```
DECLARE
   /* Define weak REF CURSOR type, cursor variable
      and local variable */
   TYPE curvar_type IS REF CURSOR;
   curvar1 curvar_type;
   do_you_get_it VARCHAR2(100);
BEGIN
   /*
   || Nested block which creates the cursor object and
   || assigns it to the curvar1 cursor variable.
   */
   DECLARE
      curvar2 curvar_type;
   BEGIN
      OPEN curvar2 FOR SELECT punch_line FROM jokes;
      curvar1 := curvar2;
   END;
   /*
   || The curvar2 cursor variable is no longer active,
   || but "the baton" has been passed to curvar1, which
   || does exist in the enclosing block. I can therefore
   || fetch from the cursor object, through this other
   || cursor variable.
```

```
    */
    FETCH curvar1 INTO do_you_get_it;
    CLOSE curvar1;
END;
```

Passing Cursor Variables as Arguments

You can pass a cursor variable as an argument in a call to a procedure or a function. When you use a cursor variable in the parameter list of a program, you need to specify the mode of the parameter and the datatype (the REF CURSOR type).

Identifying the REF CURSOR type

In your program header, you must identify the REF CURSOR type of your cursor variable parameter. To do this, that cursor type must already be defined.

If you are creating a local module within another program (see Chapter 16 for information about local modules), you can define the cursor type in the same program. It will then be available for the parameter. This approach is shown here:

```
DECLARE
   /* Define the REF CURSOR type. */
   TYPE curvar_type IS REF CURSOR RETURN company%ROWTYPE;

   /* Reference it in the parameter list. */
   PROCEDURE open_query (curvar_out OUT curvar_type)
   IS
      local_cur curvar_type;
   BEGIN
      OPEN local_cur FOR SELECT * FROM company;
      curvar_out := local_cur;
   END;
BEGIN
   ...
END;
```

If you are creating a standalone procedure or function, then the only way you can reference a pre-existing REF CURSOR type is by placing that TYPE statement in a package. All variables declared in the specification of a package act as globals within your session, so you can then reference this cursor type using the dot notation shown in the second example:

- Create the package with a REF CURSOR type declaration:

```
PACKAGE company
IS
   /* Define the REF CURSOR type. */
   TYPE curvar_type IS REF CURSOR RETURN company%ROWTYPE;
END package;
```

- In a standalone procedure, reference the REF CURSOR type by prefacing the name of the cursor type with the name of the package:

```
PROCEDURE open_company (curvar_out OUT company.curvar_type) IS
BEGIN
   ...
END;
```

Setting the parameter mode

Just like other parameters, a cursor variable argument can have one of the following three modes:

IN
: Can only be read by the program

OUT
: Can only be written to by the program

IN OUT
: Can be read or written to by the program

Remember that the value of a cursor variable is the reference to the cursor object, not the state of the cursor object. In other words, the value of a cursor variable does not change after you fetch from or close a cursor.

Only two operations, in fact, may change the value of a cursor variable (that is, the cursor object to which the variable points):

- An assignment to the cursor variable
- An OPEN FOR statement

If the cursor variable is already pointing to a cursor object, the OPEN FOR doesn't actually change the reference. It simply changes the query associated with the object.

The FETCH and CLOSE operations affect the state of the cursor object, but not the reference to the cursor object itself, which is the value of the cursor variable.

Here is an example of a program that has cursor variables as parameters:

```
PROCEDURE assign_curvar
   (old_curvar_in IN company.curvar_type,
    new_curvar_out OUT company.curvar_type)
IS
BEGIN
   new_curvar_out := old_curvar_in;
END;
```

This procedure copies the old company cursor variable to the new variable. The first parameter is an IN parameter because it appears only on the right-hand side of the assignment. The second parameter must be an OUT (or IN OUT) parameter because its value is changed inside the procedure. Notice that the curvar_type is defined within the company package.

Cursor Variable Restrictions

Cursor variables are subject to the following restrictions; note that Oracle may remove some of these in future releases.

- Cursor variables cannot be declared in a package because they do not have a persistent state.
- You cannot use RPCs (remote procedure calls) to pass cursor variables from one server to another.
- If you pass a cursor variable as a bind variable or host variable to PL/SQL, you will not be able to fetch from it from within the server unless you also open it in that same server call.
- The query you associate with a cursor variable in an OPEN FOR statement cannot use the FOR UPDATE clause. (This is allowed in Oracle9*i* and above.)
- You cannot test for cursor variable equality, inequality, or nullity using comparison operators.
- You cannot assign NULLs to a cursor variable. Attempts to do so will result in a *PLS-00382 Expression is of wrong type* error message.
- Database columns cannot store cursor variable values. You will not be able to use REF CURSOR types to specify column types in statements to CREATE TABLEs.
- The elements in a nested table, associative array, or VARRAY cannot store the values of cursor variables. You will not be able to use REF CURSOR types to specify the element type of a collection.

Cursor Expressions (Oracle9i)

Oracle has introduced a powerful new feature in the SQL language: the cursor expression. A *cursor expression*, denoted by the CURSOR operator, returns a nested cursor from within a query. Each row in the result set of this nested cursor can contain the usual range of values allowed in a SQL query; it can also contain other cursors as produced by subqueries.

The CURSOR syntax, though first introduced in Oracle8*i* SQL, was not available from within PL/SQL programs. This deficiency is corrected in Oracle9*i*: SQL statements within a PL/SQL procedure or function can take advantage of the CURSOR expression.

You can therefore use cursor expressions to return a large and complex set of related values retrieved from one or more tables. You can then process the cursor expression result set using nested loops that fetch from the rows of the result set, and then additional rows from any nested cursors within those rows.

Cursor expressions can get complicated, given how complex the queries and result sets can be. Nevertheless, it's good to know all the possible ways to retrieve data from the Oracle RDBMS.

You can use cursor expressions in any of the following:

- Explicit cursor declarations
- Dynamic SQL queries
- REF CURSOR declarations and variables

You cannot use a cursor expression in an implicit query.

The syntax for a cursor expression is very simple:

```
CURSOR (subquery)
```

Oracle opens the nested cursor defined by a cursor expression implicitly as soon as it fetches the row containing the cursor expression from the parent or outer cursor. This nested cursor is closed when:

- You explicitly close the cursor.
- The outer, parent cursor is executed again, closed, or canceled.
- An exception is raised while fetching from a parent cursor. The nested cursor is closed along with the parent cursor.

Using Cursor Expressions

The following procedure demonstrates the use of nested CURSOR expressions. The top-level query fetches just two pieces of data: the city location and a nested cursor containing departments in that city. This nested cursor, in turn, fetches a nested cursor with a CURSOR expression—in this case, one containing the names of all the employees in each department.

I could have performed this same retrieval with separate explicit cursors, opened and processed in a nested fashion. The CURSOR expression gives us the option of a different approach, and one that can be much more concise and efficient, given that all the processing takes place in the SQL statement executor and thus reduces context switching.

```
CREATE OR REPLACE PROCEDURE emp_report (p_locid NUMBER)
IS
   TYPE refcursor IS REF CURSOR;

-- The query returns only 2 columns, but the second column is
-- a cursor that lets us traverse a set of related information.
   CURSOR all_in_one_cur is
      SELECT l.city,
             CURSOR (SELECT d.department_name,
                            CURSOR(SELECT e.last_name
                                     FROM employees e
```

```
                                        WHERE e.department_id =
                                                 d.department_id)
                                            AS ename
                           FROM departments d
                          WHERE l.location_id = d.location_id) AS dname
        FROM locations l
       WHERE l.location_id = p_locid;

   departments_cur    refcursor;
   employees_cur   refcursor;

   v_city     locations.city%TYPE;
   v_dname    departments.department_name%TYPE;
   v_ename    employees.last_name%TYPE;
BEGIN
   OPEN all_in_one_cur;

   LOOP
      FETCH all_in_one_cur INTO v_city, departments_cur;
      EXIT WHEN all_in_one_cur%NOTFOUND;

      -- Now I can loop through departments and I do NOT need to
      -- explicitly open that cursor. Oracle did it for me.
      LOOP
         FETCH departments_cur INTO v_dname, employees_cur;
         EXIT WHEN departments_cur%NOTFOUND;

         -- Now I can loop through employees for that department.
         -- Again, I do not need to open the cursor explicitly.
         LOOP
            FETCH employees_cur INTO v_ename;
            EXIT WHEN employees_cur%NOTFOUND;
            DBMS_OUTPUT.put_line (
                  v_city
               || ' '
               || v_dname
               || ' '
               || v_ename
            );
         END LOOP;
      END LOOP;
   END LOOP;

   CLOSE all_in_one_cur;
END;
```

Restrictions on Cursor Expressions

There are a number of restrictions on the use of cursor expressions:

- You cannot use a cursor expression with an implicit cursor because no mechanism is available to fetch the nested cursor INTO a PL/SQL data structure.

- Cursor expressions can appear only in the outermost SELECT list of the query specification.
- You can place cursor expressions only in a SELECT statement that is not nested in any other query expression, except when it is defined as a subquery of the cursor expression itself.
- A cursor expression can be used as an argument to table functions, called within the FROM clause of a SELECT statement.
- Cursor expressions cannot be used when declaring a view.
- You cannot perform BIND and EXECUTE operations on cursor expressions when using the CURSOR expression in dynamic SQL.

CHAPTER 15

Dynamic SQL and Dynamic PL/SQL

Dynamic SQL refers to SQL statements that are constructed and executed at runtime. Dynamic is the opposite of static. *Static SQL* refers to SQL statements that are fixed at the time a program is compiled. *Dynamic PL/SQL* refers to entire PL/SQL blocks of code that are constructed dynamically, then compiled and executed.

Time for a confession: I have had more fun writing dynamic SQL and dynamic PL/SQL programs than just about anything else I have ever done with the PL/SQL language. By constructing and executing dynamically, you gain a tremendous amount of flexibility. You can also build extremely generic and widely useful reusable code.

So what can you do with dynamic SQL and dynamic PL/SQL?* Here are just a few ideas:

Execute DDL statements
: You can only execute queries and DML statements with static SQL inside PL/SQL. What if you want to create a table or drop an index? Time for dynamic SQL!

Build back-ends for web-based applications
: These might allow users to specify which columns they want to see and vary the order in which they see the data. In other words, you can support full ad hoc querying and updating applications.

Write a generic string parsing engine
: Such a parsing engine might accept a delimited list and deposit the elements of that list into your collection.

Ever since Oracle Version 7.1, we PL/SQL developers have been able to use the built-in DBMS_SQL package to execute dynamic SQL. In Oracle8*i*, we were given a second option for executing dynamically constructed SQL statements: *native dynamic*

* For the remainder of this chapter, any reference to "dynamic SQL" also includes dynamic PL/SQL blocks, unless otherwise stated.

SQL (NDS). The DBMS_SQL package is examined in depth in the book *Oracle Built-in Packages* (described in Chapter 1). In this chapter, we'll concentrate on NDS, which is easier to write and faster to execute. Also, unlike DBMS_SQL, NDS is a *native* part of the PL/SQL language, so it makes sense to cover it here. There are times, however, when you will want to use DBMS_SQL. You will find at the end of this chapter a comparison of the two approaches and recommendations for selecting the implementation path for your dynamic SQL needs.

NDS Statements

One of the nicest things about NDS is its simplicity. Unlike DBMS_SQL, which has dozens of programs and lots of rules to follow, NDS has been integrated into the PL/SQL language by adding one new statement, EXECUTE IMMEDIATE, which executes a specified SQL statement immediately, and by enhancing the existing OPEN FOR statement, which allows you to perform multiple-row dynamic queries.

The EXECUTE IMMEDIATE and OPEN FOR statements will not be directly accessible from Oracle Forms Builder and Oracle Reports Builder until the PL/SQL version in those tools are upgraded to Oracle8*i* or Oracle9*i*. Prior to that, you will need to create stored programs that hide calls to these constructs; you will then be able to execute those stored programs from within your client-side PL/SQL code.

The EXECUTE IMMEDIATE Statement

Use EXECUTE IMMEDIATE to execute (immediately!) the specified SQL statement. Here is the syntax of this statement:

```
EXECUTE IMMEDIATE SQL_string
   [INTO {define_variable[, define_variable]... | record}]
   [USING [IN | OUT | IN OUT] bind_argument
       [, [IN | OUT | IN OUT] bind_argument]...];
```

where:

SQL_string
: Is a string expression containing the SQL statement or PL/SQL block.

define_variable
: Is a variable that receives a column value returned by a query.

record
: Is a record based on a user-defined TYPE or %ROWTYPE that receives an entire row returned by a query.

bind_argument
: Is an expression whose value is passed to the SQL statement or PL/SQL block, or an identifier that serves as an input and/or output variable to the function or procedure that is called in the PL/SQL block.

INTO clause

Is used for single-row queries; for each column value returned by the query, you must supply an individual variable or field in a record of a compatible type.

USING clause

Allows you to supply bind arguments for the SQL string. This clause is used for both dynamic SQL and PL/SQL, which is why you can specify a parameter mode. This usage is relevant only for PL/SQL, however; the default is IN, which is the only kind of bind argument you would have for SQL statements.

You can use EXECUTE IMMEDIATE for any SQL statement or PL/SQL block except for multiple-row queries. If *SQL_string* ends with a semicolon, it will be treated as a PL/SQL block; otherwise, it will be treated as either DML (Data Manipulation Language—SELECT, INSERT, UPDATE, or DELETE) or DDL (Data Definition Language—e.g., CREATE TABLE). The string may contain placeholders for bind arguments, but you cannot use bind values to pass in the names of schema objects, such as table names or column names.

When the statement is executed, the runtime engine replaces each placeholder (an identifier with a colon in front of it, such as :salary_value) in the SQL string with its corresponding bind argument (by position). You can pass numeric, date, and string expressions. You cannot, however, pass a Boolean, because it is a PL/SQL datatype. Nor can you pass a NULL literal value. Instead, you must pass a variable of the correct type that has a value of NULL.

NDS supports all SQL datatypes. So, for example, define variables and bind arguments can be collections, large objects (LOBs), instances of an object type, and REFs. On the other hand, NDS does not support datatypes that are specific to PL/SQL, such as Booleans, associative arrays, and user-defined record types. The INTO clause may, however, contain a PL/SQL record.

Let's take a look at a few examples:

- Create an index:

  ```
  EXECUTE IMMEDIATE 'CREATE INDEX emp_u_1 ON employee (last_name)';
  ```

  It can't get much easier than that, can it?

- Create a stored procedure that will execute any DDL statement:

  ```
  CREATE OR REPLACE PROCEDURE execDDL (ddl_string IN VARCHAR2)
  IS
  BEGIN
     EXECUTE IMMEDIATE ddl_string;
  END;
  ```

  With execDDL in place, I can create that same index as follows:

  ```
  execDDL ('CREATE INDEX emp_u_1 ON employee (last_name)');
  ```

- Obtain the count of rows in any table, in any schema, for the specified WHERE clause:

```
/* File on web: tabcount.sf */
CREATE OR REPLACE FUNCTION tabCount (
   tab IN VARCHAR2,
   whr IN VARCHAR2 := NULL,
   sch IN VARCHAR2 := NULL)
   RETURN INTEGER
IS
   retval INTEGER;
BEGIN
   EXECUTE IMMEDIATE
      'SELECT COUNT(*)
         FROM ' || NVL (sch, USER) || '.' || tab ||
      ' WHERE ' || NVL (whr, '1=1')
      INTO retval;
   RETURN retval;
END;
```

So now I never again have to write SELECT COUNT(*), whether in SQL*Plus or within a PL/SQL program. Instead I can do the following:

```
BEGIN
   IF tabCount ('emp', 'deptno = ' || v_dept) > 100
   THEN
      DBMS_OUTPUT.PUT_LINE ('Growing fast!');
   END IF;
```

- Here's a function that lets you update the value of any numeric column in any table. It's a function because it returns the number of rows that have been updated.

```
/* File on web: updnval.sf */
CREATE OR REPLACE FUNCTION updNVal (
   tab IN VARCHAR2,
   col IN VARCHAR2,
   val IN NUMBER,
   whr IN VARCHAR2 := NULL,
   sch IN VARCHAR2 := NULL)
   RETURN INTEGER
IS
BEGIN
   EXECUTE IMMEDIATE
      'UPDATE ' || NVL (sch, USER) || '.' || tab ||
      '   SET ' || col || ' = :the_value
        WHERE ' || NVL (whr, '1=1')
     USING val;
   RETURN SQL%ROWCOUNT;
END;
```

That is a very small amount of code to achieve all that flexibility! This example introduces the bind argument—after the UPDATE statement is parsed, the PL/SQL engine replaces the :the_value placeholder with the value in the val variable. Notice also that I am able to rely on the SQL%ROWCOUNT cursor attribute that I have already been using for static DML statements.

- Suppose that I need to run a different stored procedure at 9 AM each day of the week. Each program's name has the structure DAYNAME_set_schedule. Each procedure has the same four arguments: you pass in employee_id and hour for the first meeting of the day; it returns the name of the employee and the number of appointments for the day. I can use dynamic PL/SQL to handle this situation:

```
/* File on web: run9am.sp */
CREATE OR REPLACE PROCEDURE run_9am_procedure (
   id_in IN employee.employee_id%TYPE,
   hour_in IN INTEGER)
IS
   v_apptCount INTEGER;
   v_name VARCHAR2(100);
BEGIN
   EXECUTE IMMEDIATE
      'BEGIN ' || TO_CHAR (SYSDATE, 'DAY') ||
         '_set_schedule (:id, :hour, :name, :appts); END;'
     USING IN
       id_in, IN hour_in, OUT v_name, OUT v_apptCount;

   DBMS_OUTPUT.PUT_LINE (
      'Employee ' || v_name || ' has ' || v_apptCount ||
      ' appointments on ' || TO_CHAR (SYSDATE));
END;
```

As you can see, EXECUTE IMMEDIATE provides a very easy and accessible syntax!

The OPEN FOR Statement

The OPEN FOR statement is not brand-new to PL/SQL in Oracle8*i*; it was first offered in Oracle7 to support cursor variables. Now it is deployed in an especially elegant fashion to implement multiple-row dynamic queries. With DBMS_SQL, you go through a painful series of steps to implement multirow queries: parse, bind, define each column individually, execute, fetch, extract each column value individually. That's a lot of code to write!

For native dynamic SQL, Oracle took an existing feature and syntax—that of cursor variables—and extended it in a very natural way to support dynamic SQL. The next section explores multirow queries in detail. Let's now look at the syntax of the OPEN FOR statement:

```
OPEN {cursor_variable | :host_cursor_variable} FOR SQL_string
   [USING bind_argument[, bind_argument]...];
```

where:

cursor_variable
: Is a weakly typed cursor variable

:host_cursor_variable
: Is a cursor variable declared in a PL/SQL host environment such as an Oracle Call Interface (OCI) program

SQL_string
: Contains the SELECT statement to be executed dynamically

USING clause
: Follows the same rules as in the EXECUTE IMMEDIATE statement

If you are not familiar with cursor variables, you might want to review Chapter 14. Here you will learn how to use cursor variables with NDS.

Following is an example that demonstrates the declaration of a weak REF CURSOR type, a cursor variable based on that type, and the opening of a dynamic query using the OPEN FOR statement:

```
CREATE OR REPLACE PROCEDURE show_parts_inventory (
   parts_table IN VARCHAR2,
   where_in IN VARCHAR2 := NULL)
IS
   TYPE query_curtype IS REF CURSOR;
   dyncur query_curtype;
BEGIN
   OPEN dyncur FOR
      'SELECT * FROM ' || parts_table
      ' WHERE ' || NVL (where_in, '1 = 1');
   ...
```

Once you have opened the query with the OPEN FOR statement, the syntax used to fetch rows, close the cursor variable, and check the attributes of the cursor are all the same as for static cursor variables and hardcoded explicit cursors. The next section demonstrates all of this syntax through examples.

Multirow Queries with Cursor Variables

Now that you have seen the syntax of OPEN FOR and are familiar with cursor variables, let's explore the nuances involved in multirow queries with NDS.

When you execute an OPEN FOR statement, the PL/SQL runtime engine does the following:

1. Associates a cursor variable with the query found in the query string
2. Evaluates any bind arguments and substitutes those values for the placeholders found in the query string
3. Executes the query
4. Identifies the result set
5. Positions the cursor on the first row in the result set
6. Zeros out the rows-processed count returned by %ROWCOUNT

Note that any bind arguments (provided in the USING clause) in the query are evaluated only when the cursor variable is opened. This means that if you want to use a different set of bind arguments for the same dynamic query, you must issue a new OPEN FOR statement with those arguments.

To perform a multirow query, you follow these steps:

1. Declare a REF CURSOR type (if one is not already available, as it could be if defined in a package specification)
2. Declare a cursor variable based on the REF CURSOR
3. OPEN the cursor variable FOR your query string
4. Use the FETCH statement to fetch one row at a time from the query
5. Check cursor attributes (%FOUND, %NOTFOUND, %ROWCOUNT, %ISOPEN) as necessary
6. Close the cursor variable using the normal CLOSE statement

Here is a simple program to display the specified column of any table for the rows indicated by the WHERE clause (it will work for number, date, and string columns):

```
/* File on web: showcol.sp */
CREATE OR REPLACE PROCEDURE showcol (
   tab IN VARCHAR2,
   col IN VARCHAR2,
   whr IN VARCHAR2 := NULL)
IS
   TYPE cv_type IS REF CURSOR;
   cv cv_type;
   val VARCHAR2(32767);
BEGIN
   /* Construct the very dynamic query and open the cursor. */
   OPEN cv FOR
      'SELECT ' || col ||
      '  FROM ' || tab ||
      ' WHERE ' || NVL (whr, '1 = 1');

   LOOP
      /* Fetch the next row, and stop if no more rows. */
      FETCH cv INTO val;
      EXIT WHEN cv%NOTFOUND;

      /* Display the data, with a header before the first row. */
      IF cv%ROWCOUNT = 1
      THEN
         DBMS_OUTPUT.PUT_LINE (RPAD ('-', 60, '-'));
         DBMS_OUTPUT.PUT_LINE (
            'Contents of ' ||
            UPPER (tab) || '.' || UPPER (col));
         DBMS_OUTPUT.PUT_LINE (RPAD ('-', 60, '-'));
      END IF;
      DBMS_OUTPUT.PUT_LINE (val);
   END LOOP;

   CLOSE cv; --All done, so clean up!
END;
```

Here are some examples of output from this procedure:

```
SQL> exec showcol ('emp', 'ename', 'deptno=10')
--------------------------------------------------
Contents of EMP.ENAME
--------------------------------------------------
CLARK
KING
MILLER
```

I can even combine columns:

```
BEGIN
   showcol (
      'emp',
      'ename || ''-$'' || sal',
      'comm IS NOT NULL');
END;
/
--------------------------------------------------
Contents of EMP.ENAME || '-$' || SAL
--------------------------------------------------
ALLEN-$1600
WARD-$1250
MARTIN-$1250
TURNER-$1500
```

FETCH into Variables or Records

The FETCH statement in the showcol procedure shown in the previous section fetches into an individual variable. You could also FETCH into a sequence of variables, as shown here:

```
DECLARE
   TYPE cv_type IS REF CURSOR;
   cv cv_type;
   mega_bucks company.ceo_compensation%TYPE;
   achieved_by company.cost_cutting%TYPE;
BEGIN
   OPEN cv FOR
      'SELECT ceo_compensation, cost_cutting
         FROM company
        WHERE ' || NVL (whr, '1 = 1');

   LOOP
      FETCH cv INTO mega_bucks, achieved_by;
```

Working with a long list of variables in the FETCH list can be cumbersome and inflexible—you have to declare the variables, keep that set of values synchronized with the FETCH statement, and so on. To ease our troubles, NDS allows us to fetch into a record, as shown here:

```
DECLARE
   TYPE cv_type IS REF CURSOR;
   cv cv_type;
   ceo_info company%ROWTYPE;
```

```
BEGIN
   OPEN cv FOR
      'SELECT *
        FROM company
       WHERE ' || NVL (whr, '1 = 1');

   LOOP
      FETCH cv INTO ceo_info;
```

Of course, in many situations you will not want to do a SELECT *; this statement can be very inefficient if your table has hundreds of columns and you need to work with only three. A better approach is to create record TYPEs that correspond to different requirements. The best place to put these structures is in a package specification so that they can be used throughout your application. Here's one such package:

```
CREATE OR REPLACE PACKAGE company_struc
IS
   TYPE dynsql_curtype IS REF CURSOR;

   TYPE ceo_info_rt IS RECORD (
      mega_bucks company.ceo_compensation%TYPE,
      achieved_by company.cost_cutting%TYPE);

END company_struc;
```

With this package in place, I can rewrite my CEO-related code as follows:

```
DECLARE
   cur company_struc.dynsql_curtype;
   rec company_struc.ceo_info_rt;
BEGIN
   OPEN cv FOR
      'SELECT ceo_compensation, cost_cutting
        FROM company
       WHERE ' || NVL (whr, '1 = 1');

   LOOP
      FETCH cv INTO rec;
```

The USING Clause in OPEN FOR

As with the EXECUTE IMMEDIATE statement, you can pass in bind arguments when you open a cursor. You can only provide IN arguments for a query. By using bind arguments, you can also improve the performance of your SQL and make it easier to write and maintain that code. In addition, you can potentially dramatically reduce the number of distinct parsed statements that are cached in the SGA, and thereby increasing the likelihood that your preparsed statement is still in the SGA the next time you need it. (See the "Binding Variables" section later in this chapter for information about this technique.)

Let's revisit the showcol procedure. That procedure accepted a completely generic WHERE clause. Suppose that I have a more specialized requirement: I want to display (or in some way process) all column information for rows that contain a date column with a value within a certain range. In other words, I want to be able to satisfy this query:

```
SELECT ename
  FROM emp
 WHERE hiredate BETWEEN x AND y;
```

as well as this query:

```
SELECT flavor
  FROM favorites
 WHERE preference_period BETWEEN x AND y;
```

I also want to make sure that the time component of the date column does not play a role in the WHERE condition.

Here is the header for the procedure:

```
/* File on web: showdtcol.sp */
PROCEDURE showcol (
   tab IN VARCHAR2,
   col IN VARCHAR2,
   dtcol IN VARCHAR2,
   dt1 IN DATE,
   dt2 IN DATE := NULL)
```

The OPEN FOR statement now contains two placeholders and a USING clause to match:

```
OPEN cv FOR
      'SELECT ' || col ||
      '   FROM ' || tab ||
      ' WHERE ' || dtcol ||
         ' BETWEEN TRUNC (:startdt)
               AND TRUNC (:enddt)'
   USING dt1, NVL (dt2, dt1+1);
```

I have crafted this statement so that if the user does not supply an end date, the WHERE clause returns rows whose date column is the same day as the dt1 provided. The rest of the showcol procedure remains the same, except for some cosmetic changes in the display of the header.

The following call to this new version of showcol asks to see the names of all employees hired in 1982:

```
BEGIN
   showcol ('emp',
      'ename', 'hiredate',
      '01-jan-82', '31-dec-82');
END;

----------------------------------------------------------------------
Contents of EMP.ENAME for HIREDATE between 01-JAN-82 and 31-DEC-82
----------------------------------------------------------------------
MILLER
```

Generic GROUP BY Procedure

How many times have you written a query along these lines:

```
SELECT some-columns, COUNT(*)
  FROM your-table
 GROUP BY some-columns;
```

And then there is the variation involving the HAVING clause (you don't want to see *all* the counts; you just want to see those groupings where there is more than one identical value, and so on). These are very common requirements, but with NDS, you can easily build a program that does all the work for you, for any table, and for any single column (and this is extensible to multiple columns as well).

Here is the header of such a procedure:

```
/* File on web: countby.sp */
PROCEDURE countBy (
   tab IN VARCHAR2,
   col IN VARCHAR2,
   atleast IN INTEGER := NULL,
   sch IN VARCHAR2 := NULL,
   maxlen IN INTEGER := 30)
```

where:

tab
: Is the name of the table.

col
: Is the name of the column.

sch
: Is the name of the schema (default of NULL = USER).

atleast
: If you supply a non-NULL value for *atleast*, then the SELECT statement includes a HAVING COUNT(*) greater than that value.

maxlen
: Is used for formatting of the output.

You can look at the *countby.sp* file available on the O'Reilly site to see the full implementation; here is all the code except that for the formatting (header string and so on):

```
IS
   TYPE cv_type IS REF CURSOR;
   cv cv_type;
   SQL_string VARCHAR2(2000) :=
      'SELECT ' || col || ', COUNT(*)
         FROM ' || NVL (sch, USER) || '.' || tab ||
      ' GROUP BY ' || col;
```

```
   v_val VARCHAR2(32767);
   v_count INTEGER;
BEGIN
   IF atleast IS NOT NULL
   THEN
      SQL_string := SQL_string || ' HAVING COUNT(*) >= ' || atleast;
   END IF;

   OPEN cv FOR SQL_String;

   LOOP
      FETCH cv INTO v_val, v_count;
      EXIT WHEN cv%NOTFOUND;
      DBMS_OUTPUT.PUT_LINE (RPAD (v_val, maxlen) || ' ' || v_count);
   END LOOP;

   CLOSE cv;
END;
```

As you start to build more and more of these generic utilities, you will find that it doesn't take very much code or effort—you just have to think through the steps of the SQL string construction carefully.

Generic GROUP BY Package

Simply displaying information is useful for test purposes, but in many cases you want to work with the queried information further. Let's build on the countby procedure shown in the previous section to provide an implementation in which the results of the dynamic query are stored in an associative array for subsequent analysis.

Here is the specification of the package:

```
/* File on web: countby.pkg */
CREATE OR REPLACE PACKAGE grp
IS
   TYPE results_rt IS RECORD (
      val VARCHAR2(4000),
      countby INTEGER);

   TYPE results_tt IS TABLE OF results_rt
      INDEX BY BINARY_INTEGER;

   FUNCTION countBy (
      tab IN VARCHAR2,
      col IN VARCHAR2,
      atleast IN INTEGER := NULL,
      sch IN VARCHAR2 := NULL,
      maxlen IN INTEGER := 30)
      RETURN results_tt;
END grp;
```

The implementation of the countby function is virtually the same as the procedure. The main difference is that I now have a record structure to fetch into and an associative array to fill. You can see both of these changes in the loop that fetches the rows:

```
LOOP
   FETCH cv INTO rec;
   EXIT WHEN cv%NOTFOUND;
   retval(cv%ROWCOUNT) := rec;
END LOOP;
```

With this package in place, I can very easily build programs that access this analytical information. Here is one example:

```
/* File on web: countby.tst */
DECLARE
   results grp.results_tt;
   indx PLS_INTEGER;
   minrow PLS_INTEGER;
   maxrow PLS_INTEGER;
BEGIN
   results := grp.countby ('employee', 'department_id');

   /* Find min and max counts. */
   indx := results.FIRST;
   LOOP
      EXIT WHEN indx IS NULL;

      IF minrow IS NULL OR
         minrow > results(indx).countby
      THEN
         minrow := indx;
      END IF;

      IF maxrow IS NULL OR
         maxrow < results(indx).countby
      THEN
         maxrow := indx;
      END IF;

      /* Perform other processing as well... */

      /* Move to next group count. */
      indx := results.NEXT(indx);
   END LOOP;
END;
```

Binding Variables

You have seen several examples of the use of bind variables or arguments with NDS. Let's now go over the various rules and special situations you may encounter when binding.

Binding Versus Concatenation

In most situations, you can take two different paths to insert program values into your SQL string: binding and concatenation. The following table contrasts these approaches for a dynamic UPDATE statement.

Binding	Concatenation

`EXECUTE IMMEDIATE`
`'UPDATE ' || tab`
`'SET sal = :new_sal'`
`USING v_sal;`
	`EXECUTE IMMEDIATE`
	`'UPDATE ' || tab`
	`'SET sal = ' || v_sal;`

Binding involves the use of placeholders and the USING clause; concatenation shortcuts that process by adding the values directly to the SQL string. When should you use each approach? I recommend that you bind arguments whenever possible (see the next section for limitations on binding) rather than rely on concatenation. There are two reasons for taking this approach:

Binding is faster
: When you bind in a value, the SQL string does not contain the value, just the placeholder name. Therefore, you can bind different values to the same SQL statement without changing that statement. Because it is the same SQL statement, your application can more likely take advantage of the preparsed cursors that are cached in the System Global Area (SGA) of the database.

Binding is easier to write and maintain
: When you bind, you don't have to worry about datatype conversion; it is all handled for you by the NDS engine. In fact, binding minimizes datatype conversion because it works with the native datatypes. If you use concatenation, you will often need to write very complex, error-prone string expressions involving multiple single quotes, TO_DATE and TO_CHAR function calls, and so on. For example, consider the following comparison of concatenation and binding for a more complex statement:

```
/* Binding */
EXECUTE IMMEDIATE
   'UPDATE employee SET salary = :val
     WHERE hire_date BETWEEN :lodate AND :hidate'
   USING v_start, v_end;

/* Concatenation */
EXECUTE IMMEDIATE
 'UPDATE employee SET salary = ' || val_in ||
 ' WHERE hire_date BETWEEN ' ||
    ' TO_DATE (''' || TO_CHAR (v_start)  || ''')' ||
    ' AND ' ||
    ' TO_DATE (''' || TO_CHAR (v_end)  || ''')';
```

So bind whenever possible. But when is binding not an option?

Limitations on Binding

You can bind into your SQL statement only those expressions (literals, variables, complex expressions) that replace placeholders for data values inside the dynamic string. You cannot bind in the names of schema elements (tables, columns, etc.) or entire chunks of the SQL statement (such as the WHERE clause). For those parts of your string, you must use concatenation.

For example, suppose you want to create a procedure that will truncate the specified view or table. Your first attempt might look something like this:

```
CREATE OR REPLACE PROCEDURE truncobj (
   nm IN VARCHAR2,
   tp IN VARCHAR2 := 'TABLE',
   sch IN VARCHAR2 := NULL)
IS
BEGIN
   EXECUTE IMMEDIATE
      'TRUNCATE :trunc_type :obj_name'
      USING tp, NVL (sch, USER) || '.' || nm;
END;
```

This code seems perfectly reasonable. But when you try to run the procedure you'll get this error:

```
ORA-03290: Invalid truncate command - missing CLUSTER or TABLE keyword
```

And if you rewrite the procedure to simply truncate tables, as follows:

```
EXECUTE IMMEDIATE 'TRUNCATE TABLE :obj_name' USING nm;
```

Then the error becomes:

```
ORA-00903: invalid table name
```

Why does NDS (and DBMS_SQL) have this restriction? When you pass a string to EXECUTE IMMEDIATE, the runtime engine must first parse the statement. The parse phase guarantees that the SQL statement is properly defined. PL/SQL can tell that the following statement is valid:

```
'UPDATE emp SET sal = :xyz'
```

without having to know the value of :xyz. But how can PL/SQL know if the following statement is well formed?

```
'UPDATE emp SET :col_name = :xyz'
```

Even if you don't pass in nonsense for col_name, it won't work. For that reason, you must use concatenation:

```
CREATE OR REPLACE PROCEDURE truncobj (
   nm IN VARCHAR2,
   tp IN VARCHAR2 := 'TABLE',
   sch IN VARCHAR2 := NULL)
IS
BEGIN
```

```
    EXECUTE IMMEDIATE
        'TRUNCATE ' || tp || ' ' || NVL (sch, USER) || '.' || nm;
END;
```

Argument Modes

Bind arguments can have one of three modes:

IN
: Read-only value (the default mode)

OUT
: Write-only variable

IN OUT
: Can read the value coming in and write the value going out

When you are executing a dynamic query, all bind arguments must be of mode IN, except when you are taking advantage of the RETURNING clause, as shown here:

```
CREATE OR REPLACE PROCEDURE wrong_incentive (
    company_in IN INTEGER,
    new_layoffs IN NUMBER
    )
IS
    sql_string VARCHAR2(2000);
    sal_after_layoffs NUMBER;
BEGIN
    sql_string :=
       'UPDATE ceo_compensation
           SET salary = salary + 10 * :layoffs
         WHERE company_id = :company
        RETURNING salary INTO :newsal';

    EXECUTE IMMEDIATE sql_string
      USING new_layoffs, company_in, OUT sal_after_layoffs;

    DBMS_OUTPUT.PUT_LINE (
       CEO compensation after latest round of layoffs $' || sal_after_layoffs);
END;
```

Besides being used with the RETURNING clause, OUT and IN OUT bind arguments come into play mostly when you are executing dynamic PL/SQL. In this case, the modes of the bind arguments must match the modes of any PL/SQL program parameters, as well as the usage of variables in the dynamic PL/SQL block.

Here are some guidelines for the use of the USING clause with dynamic PL/SQL execution:

- A bind variable of mode IN can be provided as any kind of expression of the correct type: a literal value, named constant, variable, or complex expression. The expression is evaluated and then passed into the dynamic PL/SQL block.

- You must provide a variable to receive the outgoing value for a bind variable of mode OUT or IN OUT.
- You can bind values only to variables in the dynamic PL/SQL block that have a SQL type. If a procedure has a Boolean parameter, for example, that Boolean cannot be set (or retrieved) with the USING clause.

Let's take a look at how this works with a few examples. Here is a procedure with IN, OUT, and IN OUT parameters:

```
PROCEDURE analyze_new_technology (
   tech_name IN VARCHAR2,
   analysis_year IN INTEGER,
   number_of_adherents IN OUT NUMBER,
   projected_revenue OUT NUMBER,
   ) ... ;
```

Because I have four parameters, any dynamic invocation of this procedure must include a USING clause with four elements. Because I have two IN parameters, the first two of those elements can be literal values or expressions. The second two elements must be the names of variables, as the parameter modes are OUT or IN OUT. Here is an example of a dynamic invocation of this procedure:

```
DECLARE
   devoted_followers NUMBER;
   est_revenue NUMBER;
BEGIN
   EXECUTE IMMEDIATE
      'BEGIN
          analyze_new_technology (:p1, :p2, :p3, :p4);        END;'
   USING 'Java', 2002, devoted_followers, est_revenue;
END;
```

Duplicate Placeholders

In a dynamically constructed and executed SQL string, NDS associates placeholders with USING clause bind arguments by *position* rather than by name. The treatment of multiple placeholders with the same name varies, however, according to whether you are using dynamic SQL or dynamic PL/SQL. You need to follow these rules:

- When you are executing a dynamic SQL string (DML or DDL—in other words, the string does *not* end in a semicolon), you must supply an argument for each placeholder, even if there are duplicates.
- When you are executing a dynamic PL/SQL block (the string ends in a semicolon), you must supply an argument for each unique placeholder.

Here is an example of a dynamic SQL statement with duplicate placeholders; notice the repetition of the val_in argument:

```
CREATE OR REPLACE PROCEDURE updnumval (
   col_in     IN   VARCHAR2,
```

```
   start_in   IN   DATE, end_in  IN   DATE,
   val_in     IN   NUMBER)
IS
   dml_str VARCHAR2(32767) :=
      'UPDATE emp SET ' || col_in || ' = :val
        WHERE hiredate BETWEEN :lodate AND :hidate
        AND :val IS NOT NULL';
BEGIN
   EXECUTE IMMEDIATE dml_str
  USING val_in, start_in, end_in, val_in;
END;
```

And here is a dynamic PL/SQL block with a duplicate placeholder; notice that val_in is supplied only once:

```
CREATE OR REPLACE PROCEDURE updnumval (
   col_in     IN   VARCHAR2,
   start_in   IN   DATE, end_in IN  DATE,
   val_in     IN   NUMBER)
IS
   dml_str VARCHAR2(32767) :=
      'BEGIN
          UPDATE emp SET ' || col_in || ' = :val
           WHERE hiredate BETWEEN :lodate AND :hidate
           AND :val IS NOT NULL;
       END;';
BEGIN
   EXECUTE IMMEDIATE dml_str
  USING val_in, start_in, end_in;
END;
```

Passing NULL Values

You will encounter special moments when you want to pass a NULL value as a bind argument, as follows:

```
EXECUTE IMMEDIATE
   'UPDATE employee SET salary = :newsal
     WHERE hire_date IS NULL'
   USING NULL;
```

You will, however, get this error:

```
PLS-00457: in USING clause, expressions have to be of SQL types
```

Basically, this is saying that NULL has no datatype, and "no datatype" is not a valid SQL datatype.

So what should you do if you need to pass in a NULL value? You can do one of two things:

- Hide the NULL value behind a variable façade, most easily done with an uninitialized variable, as shown here:

  ```
  DECLARE
     /* Default initial value is NULL */
  ```

```
    no_salary_when_fired NUMBER;
BEGIN
    EXECUTE IMMEDIATE
      'UPDATE employee SET salary = :newsal
        WHERE hire_date IS NULL'
      USING no_salary_when_fired;
END;
```

- Use a conversion function to convert the NULL value to a typed value explicitly:

```
BEGIN
    EXECUTE IMMEDIATE
      'UPDATE employee SET salary = :newsal
        WHERE hire_date IS NULL'
      USING TO_NUMBER (NULL);
END;
```

Working with Objects and Collections

One of the most important advantages of NDS over DBMS_SQL is its support for post-Oracle7 datatypes, such as objects and collections. You don't need to change the structure of the code you write in NDS to use it with these datatypes.

Suppose that I am building an internal administrative system for the national health management corporation Health$.Com. To reduce costs, the system will work in a distributed manner, creating and maintaining separate tables of customer information for each for-profit hospital owned by Health$.Com.

I'll start by defining an object type (person) and VARRAY type (preexisting_conditions), as follows:

```
CREATE TYPE person AS OBJECT (
   name VARCHAR2(50), dob DATE, income NUMBER);

CREATE TYPE preexisting_conditions IS TABLE OF VARCHAR2(25);
```

Once these types are defined, I can build a package to manage my most critical health-related information—data needed to maximize profits at Health$.Com. Here is the specification:

```
/* File on web: health$.pkg */
CREATE OR REPLACE PACKAGE health$
AS
   PROCEDURE setup_new_hospital (hosp_name IN VARCHAR2);

   PROCEDURE add_profit_source (
      hosp_name IN VARCHAR2,
      pers IN Person,
      cond IN preexisting_conditions);

   PROCEDURE minimize_risk  (
      hosp_name VARCHAR2,
      min_income IN NUMBER := 100000,
```

```
      max_preexist_cond IN INTEGER := 0);

   PROCEDURE show_profit_centers (hosp_name VARCHAR2);
END health$;
```

With this package, I can do the following:

- Set up a new hospital, which means create a new table to hold information about that hospital. Here's the implementation from the body:

  ```
  FUNCTION tabname (hosp_name IN VARCHAR2) IS
  BEGIN
     RETURN hosp_name || '_profit_center';
  END;

  PROCEDURE setup_new_hospital (hosp_name IN VARCHAR2) IS
  BEGIN
     EXECUTE IMMEDIATE
        'CREATE TABLE ' || tabname (hosp_name) || ' (
           pers Person,
           cond preexisting_conditions)
           NESTED TABLE cond STORE AS cond_st';
  END;
  ```

- Add a "profit source" (formerly known as a "patient") to the hospital, including his or her pre-existing conditions. Here's the implementation from the body:

  ```
  PROCEDURE add_profit_source (
     hosp_name IN VARCHAR2,
     pers IN Person,
     cond IN preexisting_conditions)
  IS
  BEGIN
     EXECUTE IMMEDIATE
        'INSERT INTO ' || tabname (hosp_name) ||
            ' VALUES (:revenue_generator, :revenue_inhibitors)'
        USING pers, cond;
  END;
  ```

  The use of objects and collections is transparent. I could be inserting scalars like numbers and dates, and the syntax and code would be the same.

- Minimize the risk to the health maintenance organization's bottom line by removing any patients who have too many pre-existing conditions or too little income. This is the most complex of the programs; here is the implementation:

  ```
  PROCEDURE minimize_risk (
     hosp_name VARCHAR2,
     min_income IN NUMBER := 100000,
     max_preexist_cond IN INTEGER := 1)
  IS
     cv RefCurTyp;
     human Person;
     known_bugs preexisting_conditions;

     v_table VARCHAR2(30) := tabname (hosp_name);
  ```

```
   v_rowid ROWID;
BEGIN
   /* Find all rows with more than the specified number
      of preconditions and deny them coverage. */
   OPEN cv FOR
      'SELECT ROWID, pers, cond
         FROM ' || v_table || ' alias
        WHERE (SELECT COUNT(*) FROM TABLE (alias.cond))
               > ' ||
               max_preexist_cond ||
         ' OR
               alias.pers.income < ' || min_income;
   LOOP
      FETCH cv INTO v_rowid, human, known_bugs;
      EXIT WHEN cv%NOTFOUND;
      EXECUTE IMMEDIATE
         'DELETE FROM ' || v_table ||
         ' WHERE ROWID = :rid'
         USING v_rowid;
   END LOOP;
   CLOSE cv;
END;
```

I decided to retrieve the ROWID of each profit source so that when I do the DELETE it would be easy to identify the row. It would be awfully convenient to make the query FOR UPDATE, and then use "WHERE CURRENT OF cv" in the DELETE statement, but that is not possible for two reasons: (1) The cursor variable would have to be globally accessible to be referenced inside a dynamic SQL statement, and (2) You cannot declare cursor variables in packages because they don't have persistent state. See the later section "Dynamic PL/SQL" for more details.

Building Applications with NDS

By now, you should have a solid understanding of how native dynamic SQL works in PL/SQL. This section covers some topics you should be aware of as you start to build production applications with this new PL/SQL feature.

Sharing NDS Programs with Invoker Rights

I have created a number of useful generic programs in my presentation on NDS, including functions and procedures that do the following:

- Execute any DDL statement
- Return the count of rows in any table
- Return the count for each grouping by specified column

These are pretty darn useful utilities, and I want to let everyone on my development team use them. So I compile them into the COMMON schema and grant EXECUTE authority on the programs to PUBLIC.

However, there is a problem with this strategy. When Sandra connects to her SANDRA schema and executes this command:

```
SQL> exec COMMON.execDDL ('create table temp (x date)');
```

she will inadvertently create a table in the COMMON schema—unless I take advantage of the invoker rights model, which is described in Chapter 20. The invoker rights model means that you define your stored programs so that they execute under the authority of and the privileges of the invoking schema rather than the defining schema (which is the default in Oracle 8.1 and the only option prior to Oracle 8.1).

Fortunately, it's easy to take advantage of this new feature. Here is a version of my execDDL procedure that executes any DDL statement—but always has an impact on the calling or invoking schema:

```
CREATE OR REPLACE PROCEDURE execDDL (ddl_string IN VARCHAR2)
   AUTHID CURRENT_USER
IS
BEGIN
   EXECUTE IMMEDIATE ddl_string;
END;
```

I recommend that you use the AUTHID CURRENT_USER clause in all of your dynamic SQL programs, particularly in those you plan to share among a group of developers.

Error Handling

Any robust application needs to anticipate and handle errors. Error detection and correction with dynamic SQL can be especially challenging.

Sometimes the most challenging aspect of building and executing dynamic SQL programs is getting the string of dynamic SQL correct. You might be combining a list of columns in a query with a list of tables and then a WHERE clause that changes with each execution. You have to concatenate all that stuff, getting the commas right, the ANDs and ORs right, and so on. What happens if you get it wrong?

Well, Oracle raises an error. This error usually tells you exactly what is wrong with the SQL string, but that information can still leave much to be desired. Consider the following nightmare scenario: I am building the most complicated PL/SQL application ever. It uses dynamic SQL left and right, but that's OK. I am a pro at the new NDS. I can, in a flash, type EXECUTE IMMEDIATE, OPEN FOR, and all the other statements I need. I blast through the development phase, and rely on some standard exception-handling programs I have built to display an error message when an exception is encountered.

Then the time comes to test my application. I build a test script that runs through a lot of my code; I place it in a file named *testall.sql* (you'll find it on the O'Reilly site). With trembling fingers, I start my test:

```
SQL> @testall
```

And, to my severe disappointment, here is what shows up on my screen:

```
ORA-00942: table or view does not exist
ORA-00904: invalid column name
ORA-00921: unexpected end of SQL command
ORA-00936: missing expression
```

Now, what am I supposed to make of all these error messages? Which error message goes with which SQL statement? Bottom line: when you do lots of dynamic SQL, it is very easy to get very confused and waste lots of time debugging your code—unless you take precautions as you write your dynamic SQL.

Here are my recommendations:

- Always include an error-handling section in code that calls EXECUTE IMMEDIATE and OPEN FOR.
- In each handler, record and/or display the error message and the SQL statement when an error occurs.
- You might also want to consider adding a "trace" in front of these statements so that you can easily watch the dynamic SQL as it constructed and executed.

How do these recommendations translate into changes in your code? First, let's apply these changes to the execDDL routine, and then generalize from there. Here is the starting point:

```
CREATE OR REPLACE PROCEDURE execDDL (ddl_string IN VARCHAR2)
   AUTHID CURRENT_USER IS
BEGIN
   EXECUTE IMMEDIATE ddl_string;
END;
```

Now let's add an error-handling section to show us problems when they occur:

```
/* File on web: execddl.sp */
CREATE OR REPLACE PROCEDURE execDDL (ddl_string IN VARCHAR2)
   AUTHID CURRENT_USER IS
BEGIN
   EXECUTE IMMEDIATE ddl_string;
EXCEPTION
   WHEN OTHERS
   THEN
      DBMS_OUTPUT.PUT_LINE (
         'Dynamic SQL Failure: ' || SQLERRM);
      DBMS_OUTPUT.PUT_LINE (
         '   on statement: "' || ddl_string || '"');
      RAISE;
END;
```

When I use this version to attempt to create a table using really bad syntax, this is what I see:

```
SQL> exec execddl ('create table x')
Dynamic SQL Failure: ORA-00906: missing left parenthesis
   on statement: "create table x"
```

Of course, in your production version, you might want to consider something a bit more sophisticated than the DBMS_OUTPUT built-in package.

With DBMS_SQL, if your parse request fails and you do not explicitly close your cursor in the error section, that cursor remains open (and uncloseable), leading to possible *ORA-01000: maximum open cursors exceeded* errors. This will not happen with NDS; cursor variables declared in a local scope are automatically closed—and the memory released—when the block terminates.

Now let's broaden our view a bit: when you think about it, the execDDL procedure is not really specific to DDL statements. It can be used to execute any SQL string that does not require either USING or INTO clauses. From that perspective, we now have a single program that can and should be used in place of a direct call to EXECUTE IMMEDIATE—it has all that error handling built in. I supply such a procedure in the ndsutil package (see the later "NDS Utility Package" section).

We could even create a similar program for OPEN FOR—again, only for situations that do not require a USING clause. Because OPEN FOR sets a cursor value, we would probably want to implement it as a function, which would return a type of weak REF CURSOR. This leads right to a packaged implementation along these lines:

```
PACKAGE ndsutil
IS
   TYPE cv_type IS REF CURSOR;
   FUNCTION openFor (sql_string IN VARCHAR2) RETURN cv_type;
END;
```

The NDS utility package (available from the O'Reilly site in *ndsutil.pkg*) contains the complete implementation of this function; the body is quite similar to the execDDL procedure shown earlier.

Dynamic PL/SQL

Dynamic PL/SQL offers some of the most interesting and challenging coding opportunities. Think of it: while a user is running your application, you can take advantage of NDS to do any of the following:

- Create a program, including a package that contains globally accessible data structures
- Obtain (and modify) by name the value of global variables
- Call functions and procedures whose names are not known at compile time

I have used this technique to build very flexible code generators, softcoded calculation engines for users, and much more. Dynamic PL/SQL allows you to work at a higher level of generality, which can be both challenging and exhilarating.

There are some rules and tips you need to keep in mind when working with dynamic PL/SQL blocks and NDS:

- The dynamic string must be a valid PL/SQL block. It must start with the DECLARE or BEGIN keyword, and end with an END statement and semicolon. The string will not be considered PL/SQL code unless it ends with a semicolon.
- In your dynamic block, you can access only PL/SQL code elements that have global scope (standalone functions and procedures, and elements defined in the specification of a package). Dynamic PL/SQL blocks execute outside the scope of the local enclosing block.
- Errors raised within a dynamic PL/SQL block can be trapped and handled by the local block in which the string was run with the EXECUTE IMMEDIATE statement.

Let's explore these rules. First, I will build a little utility to execute dynamic PL/SQL:

```
/* File on web: dynplsql.sp */
CREATE OR REPLACE PROCEDURE dynPLSQL (blk IN VARCHAR2)
IS
BEGIN
   EXECUTE IMMEDIATE
      'BEGIN ' || RTRIM (blk, ';') || '; END;';
END;
```

This one program encapsulates many of the rules mentioned previously for PL/SQL execution. By enclosing the string within a BEGIN-END pairing, I guarantee that whatever I pass in is executed as a valid PL/SQL block. For instance, I can execute the calc_totals procedure dynamically as simply as this:

```
SQL> exec dynPLSQL ('calc_totals');
```

Now let's use this program to examine what kind of data structures you can reference within a dynamic PL/SQL block. In the following anonymous block, I want to use dynamic SQL to assign a value of 5 to the local variable num:

```
<<dynamic>>
DECLARE
   num NUMBER;
BEGIN
   dynPLSQL ('num := 5');
END;
```

This string is executed within its own BEGIN-END block, which appears to be a nested block within the anonymous block named "dynamic". Yet when I execute this script I receive the following error:

```
PLS-00201: identifier 'NUM' must be declared
ORA-06512: at "SCOTT.DYNPLSQL", line 4
```

The PL/SQL engine is unable to resolve the reference to the variable named num. I get the same error even if I qualify the variable name with its block name:

```
<<dynamic>>
DECLARE
   num NUMBER;
BEGIN
   /* Also causes a PLS-00302 error! */
   dynPLSQL ('dynamic.num := 5');
END;
```

Now suppose that I define the num variable inside a package called dynamic:

```
CREATE OR REPLACE PACKAGE dynamic
IS
   num NUMBER;
END;
```

I am now able to execute the dynamic assignment to this newly defined variable successfully:

```
BEGIN
   dynPLSQL ('dynamic.num := 5');
END;
```

What's the difference between these two pieces of data? In my first attempt, the variable num is defined locally in the anonymous PL/SQL block. In my second attempt, num is a public global variable defined in the dynamic package. This distinction makes all the difference with dynamic PL/SQL.

It turns out that a dynamically constructed and executed PL/SQL block is not treated as a nested block; instead, it is handled as if it were a procedure or function called from within the current block. So any variables local to the current or enclosing blocks are not recognized in the dynamic PL/SQL block; you can make references only to globally defined programs and data structures. These PL/SQL elements include standalone functions and procedures and any elements defined in the specification of a package.

Fortunately, the dynamic block is executed within the context of the calling block. If you have an exception section within the calling block, it will trap exceptions raised in the dynamic block. So if I execute this anonymous block in SQL*Plus:

```
BEGIN
   dynPLSQL ('undefined.packagevar := ''abc''');
EXCEPTION
   WHEN OTHERS THEN DBMS_OUTPUT.PUT_LINE (SQLCODE);
END;
```

I will not get an unhandled exception.

The assignment performed in this anonymous block is an example of indirect referencing. I don't reference the variable directly, but instead do so by specifying the name of the variable. Oracle Forms Builder product (formerly known as SQL*Forms and Oracle Forms) offers an implementation of indirect referencing with the NAME_IN and COPY programs. This feature allows developers to build logic that can be shared across all forms in the application. PL/SQL does not support indirect referencing, but you can implement it with dynamic PL/SQL. See the *dynvar.pkg* file on the O'Reilly site for an example of such an implementation.

The following sections offer a few examples of dynamic PL/SQL to spark your interest and, perhaps, inspire your creativity.

Dramatic code reduction

This is a true story, I kid you not. During a consulting stint at an insurance company here in Chicago, I was asked to see what I could do about a particularly vexing program. It was very large and continually increased in size—soon it would be too large to even compile. Much to my amazement, this is what the program looked like:

```
CREATE OR REPLACE PROCEDURE process_line (line IN INTEGER)
IS
BEGIN
   IF    line = 1 THEN process_line1;
   ELSIF line = 2 THEN process_line2;
   ...
   ELSIF line = 514 THEN process_line514;
   ...
   ELSIF line = 2057 THEN process_line2057;
   END IF;
END;
```

Each one of those line numbers represented fine print in an insurance policy that helped the company achieve its primary objective (minimizing the payment of claims). For each line number, there was a "process_line" program that handled those details. And as the insurance company added more and more exceptions to the policy, the program got bigger and bigger. Not a very scalable approach to programming!

To avoid this kind of mess, a programmer should be on the lookout for repetition of code. If you can detect a pattern, you can either create a reusable program to encapsulate that pattern, or you can explore the possibility of expressing that pattern as a dynamic SQL construction.

At the time, I fixed the problem using DBMS_SQL, but dynamic SQL would have been a perfect match. Here's the NDS implementation:

```
CREATE OR REPLACE PROCEDURE process_line (line IN INTEGER)
IS
```

```
BEGIN
   EXECUTE IMMEDIATE
      'BEGIN process_line' || line || '; END;';
END;
```

From thousands of lines of code down to one executable statement! Of course, in most cases, identification of the pattern and conversion of that pattern into dynamic SQL will not be so straightforward. Still, the potential gains are enormous.

Generic calculator function

Suppose I have to build a GUI application that allows users to select their calculation of choice, enter the arguments, and then display the results. There are a dozen different calculations, accepting from one to five arguments, all returning a single value.

I could write a separate screen for each calculation. However, that approach is not only labor-intensive, but also high-maintenance. Every time a new calculation is added to the mix, I have to go in and write another screen. Yuck! Wouldn't it be nice if I could softcode my application so that when users need access to another calculation, they can essentially add it themselves?

So I build a set of database tables to store header-level information about the calculation, including a description, the name of the calculation function, the number of arguments, descriptions of each argument, and so forth. But now I need a utility that will run any of the calculations I send to it. This is where dynamic PL/SQL comes into play.

Here is the header of a function that accepts up to five arguments and runs whatever function is requested:

```
/* File on web: dyncalc.sf */
CREATE OR REPLACE FUNCTION dyncalc (
   oper_in IN VARCHAR2,
   nargs_in IN INTEGER := 0,
   arg1_in IN VARCHAR2 := NULL,
   arg2_in IN VARCHAR2 := NULL,
   arg3_in IN VARCHAR2 := NULL,
   arg4_in IN VARCHAR2 := NULL,
   arg5_in IN VARCHAR2 := NULL
   )
   RETURN VARCHAR2
```

The implementation uses the EXECUTE IMMEDIATE statement in a cascading IF statement. Here is a portion of the function body:

```
ELSIF nargs_in = 2
THEN
   EXECUTE IMMEDIATE v_code || '(:1, :2); END;'
      USING OUT retval, arg1_in, arg2_in;
ELSIF nargs_in = 3
THEN
```

```
EXECUTE IMMEDIATE v_code || '(:1, :2, :3); END;'
   USING OUT retval, arg1_in, arg2_in, arg3_in;
```

No rocket science here. But it gets the job done, as shown in this SQL*Plus session:

```
SQL> BEGIN
       DBMS_OUTPUT.PUT_LINE (dyncalc('sysdate'));
       DBMS_OUTPUT.PUT_LINE (dyncalc('power', 2, 2, 44));
       DBMS_OUTPUT.PUT_LINE (
          dyncalc ('greatest', 5, 66, 5, 88, 1020, -4));
    END;
    /
05-MAY-99
17592186044416
1020
```

The dyncalc function has some design limitations, but these can be addressed by shifting from a series of hardcoded parameters (arg1_in through arg5_in) to a single array to pass in all argument values. This technique is demonstrated in the *dyncalc.pkg* file available from the O'Reilly site.

You will find an even more interesting example of dynamic PL/SQL in the *str2list.pkg*. This package offers a very generic string-parsing engine that parses any delimited string and deposits the individual items into the collection of your choice.

NDS Utility Package

To make it easier for you to take advantage of the various generic utilities discussed in this chapter, I have created a single package called ndsutil. This package, available from the O'Reilly site in *ndsutil.pkg*, contains the programs listed in Table 15-1.

Table 15-1. Contents of the NDS utility package on the O'Reilly site

Name	Description
execImmed	A substitute for EXECUTE IMMEDIATE that does not need a USING or INTO clause; includes error handling.
openFor	A substitute for OPEN FOR that does not need a USING clause; includes error handling.
showCol	Shows the contents of a single column in the specified table.
tabCount	Returns the number of rows in the specified table, with an optional WHERE clause.
countBy	Returns the number of rows in the specified table for a particular GROUP BY expression, with an optional HAVING clause.
dynPLSQL	Executes a dynamic PL/SQL string, automatically making sure that it is a valid block and that it ends in a semicolon. The USING clause is not allowed.

The package is defined using the invoker rights mode (AUTHID CURRENT_USER). This means that no matter who owns the package, any external references in the dynamic SQL you execute via ndsutil are resolved according to the authority of the invoking schema, not the owner.

All programs contain exception sections that display the error and the offending SQL. Procedures then re-raise the error, whereas functions generally return NULL or a NULL/empty structure.

Comparing NDS and DBMS_SQL

Native dynamic SQL is covered in this book because it is a part of the native PL/SQL language. DBMS_SQL, on the other hand, is a built-in package, so we describe it in detail in the *Oracle Built-in Packages* book (O'Reilly). But is there any reason to use DBMS_SQL now that NDS is available?

Eyeballing Equivalent Implementations

First, let's compare the DBMS_SQL and NDS implementations of a program that displays all the employees for the specified and very dynamic WHERE clause.

The DBMS_SQL implementation:

```
CREATE OR REPLACE PROCEDURE showemps (where_in IN VARCHAR2 := NULL)
IS
   cur INTEGER := DBMS_SQL.OPEN_CURSOR;
   rec employee%ROWTYPE;
   fdbk INTEGER;
BEGIN
   DBMS_SQL.PARSE
     (cur,
      'SELECT employee_id, last_name
         FROM employee
        WHERE ' || NVL (where_in, '1=1'),
       DBMS_SQL.NATIVE);

   DBMS_SQL.DEFINE_COLUMN (cur, 1, 1);
   DBMS_SQL.DEFINE_COLUMN (cur, 2, user, 30);

   fdbk := DBMS_SQL.EXECUTE (cur);
   LOOP
      /* Fetch next row. Exit when done. */
      EXIT WHEN DBMS_SQL.FETCH_ROWS (cur) = 0;
      DBMS_SQL.COLUMN_VALUE (cur, 1, rec.employee_id);
      DBMS_SQL.COLUMN_VALUE (cur, 2, rec.last_name);
      DBMS_OUTPUT.PUT_LINE (
         TO_CHAR (rec.employee_id) || '=' ||  rec.last_name);
   END LOOP;

   DBMS_SQL.CLOSE_CURSOR (cur);
END;
```

The NDS implementation:

```
CREATE OR REPLACE PROCEDURE showemps (where_in IN VARCHAR2 := NULL)
IS
```

```
   TYPE cv_typ IS REF CURSOR;
   cv cv_typ;
   v_id employee.employee_id%TYPE;
   v_nm employee.last_name%TYPE;
BEGIN
   OPEN cv FOR
      'SELECT employee_id, last_name
         FROM employee
        WHERE ' || NVL (where_in, '1=1');
   LOOP
      FETCH cv INTO v_id, v_nm;
      EXIT WHEN cv%NOTFOUND;
      DBMS_OUTPUT.PUT_LINE ( TO_CHAR (v_id) || '=' || v_nm);
   END LOOP;
   CLOSE cv;
END;
```

As you can see (and this is true in general), you'll write dramatically less code using NDS. And because the code you write will rely less on built-in packaged programs and more on native, standard elements of PL/SQL, that code is easier to build, read, and maintain.

What Are NDS and DBMS_SQL Good For?

Here are the reasons you should use NDS whenever possible:

- NDS is always at least a little bit more efficient than DBMS_SQL, and sometimes significantly more efficient.
- NDS is much easier to write; you need less code, and the code you write is more intuitive, leading to many fewer bugs. This reality is demonstrated in the next section, "Eyeballing Equivalent Implementations."
- NDS works with all SQL datatypes, including user-defined objects and collection types (variable arrays, nested tables, and associative arrays). DBMS_SQL works only with Oracle7-compatible datatypes.
- NDS allows you to fetch multiple columns of information directly into a PL/SQL record. With DBMS_SQL, you must fetch into individual variables.

Given this situation, why would anyone use DBMS_SQL ever again? Because NDS cannot do everything. The following list shows what can be handled only (or most easily) with DBMS_SQL:

- DBMS_SQL supports "Method 4" dynamic SQL, which means that at compile time you don't know how many columns you will be querying and/or how many bind variables will need to be set. Method 4 is the most complex form of dynamic SQL, and NDS doesn't support it directly. With NDS, you have to hardcode the number of elements in the USING and INTO clauses. If you don't know how many values you are binding until you execute the SQL statement, you can't very easily write the USING clause of your EXECUTE IMMEDIATE statement.

Now, to be completely honest, you can get around this restriction by constructing not just the dynamic query string, but also a dynamic PL/SQL block containing the dynamic query string with the variable number of INTO and USING elements. However, that is a very complicated workaround, in which you would be running an EXECUTE IMMEDIATE statement inside a dynamic string.

- DBMS_SQL allows you to describe the columns of your dynamic cursor, returning information about each column in an associative array of records. This capability offers the possibility of writing very generic cursor-processing code. See *desccols.pkg* for a demonstration of how to use this feature.
- With DBMS_SQL, you can parse arbitrarily long SQL and PL/SQL statements by relying on a collection to pass the dynamic statement. In NDS, you are restricted to a string of no more than 32 KB in length.
- You can call DBMS_SQL programs from within client-side PL/SQL code, such as an Oracle Forms library. You cannot yet do the same for NDS statements because they are not supported in the version of PL/SQL available in the developer tools.

The bottom line is that the NDS implementation will be able to handle 80 to 90% of the dynamic SQL requirements you are likely to face. It is good to know, however, that there is still a place for DBMS_SQL. (Especially since I wrote a 100-page chapter on that package in *Oracle Built-in Packages!*)

PART V

PL/SQL Application Construction

This part of the book is where it all comes together. By now, you've learned the basics. You know about declaring and working with variables. You're an expert on error handling and loop construction. Now it's time to build an application—and you do that by constructing the building blocks, made up of procedures, functions, packages, and triggers, as described in Chapters 16 through 18. The final chapter in this part, Chapter 19, discusses managing your PL/SQL code base, including suggestions for tuning and debugging that code.

In this chapter:

CHAPTER 16

Procedures, Functions, and Parameters

Earlier parts of this book have explored in detail all of the components of the PL/SQL language: cursors, exceptions, loops, variables, and so on. While you certainly need to know about these components when you write applications using PL/SQL, putting the pieces together to create well-structured, easily understood, and smoothly maintainable programs is even more important.

Few of our tasks are straightforward. Few solutions can be glimpsed in an instant and immediately put to paper or keyboard. The systems we build are usually large and complex, with many interacting and sometimes conflicting components. Furthermore, as users deserve, demand, and receive applications that are easier to use and vastly more powerful than their predecessors, the inner world of those applications becomes correspondingly more complicated.

One of the biggest challenges in our profession today is finding ways to reduce the complexity of our environment. When faced with a massive problem to solve, the mind is likely to recoil in horror. Where do I start? How can I possibly find a way through that jungle of requirements and features?

A human being is not a massively parallel computer. Even the brightest of our bunch have trouble keeping track of more than seven tasks (plus or minus two) at one time. We need to break down huge, intimidating projects into smaller, more manageable components, and then further decompose those components into individual programs with an understandable scope. We can then figure out how to build and test those programs, after which we can construct a complete application from these building blocks.

Whether you use "top-down design" (a.k.a. step-wise refinement, which is explored in detail in the "Local Modules" section of this chapter) or some other methodology, there is absolutely no doubt that you will find your way to a high-quality and easily maintainable application by modularizing your code into procedures, functions, and object types.

Modular Code

Modularization is the process by which you break up large blocks of code into smaller pieces (modules) that can be called by other modules. Modularization of code is analogous to normalization of data, with many of the same benefits and a few additional advantages. With modularization, your code becomes:

More reusable
: By breaking up a large program or entire application into individual components that "plug-and-play" together, you will usually find that many modules are used by more than one other program in your current application. Designed properly, these utility programs could even be of use in other applications!

More manageable
: Which would you rather debug: a 10,000-line program or five individual 2,000-line programs that call each other as needed? Our minds work better when we can focus on smaller tasks. You can also test and debug on a smaller scale (called *unit testing*) before individual modules are combined for a more complicated system test.

More readable
: Modules have names, and names describe behavior. The more you move or hide your code behind a programmatic interface, the easier it is to read and understand what that program is doing. Modularization helps you focus on the big picture rather than on the individual executable statements.

More reliable
: The code you produce will have fewer errors. The errors you do find will be easier to fix because they will be isolated within a module. In addition, your code will be easier to maintain because there is less of it and it is more readable.

Once you become proficient with the different iterative, conditional, and cursor constructs of the PL/SQL language (the IF statement, loops, etc.), you are ready to write programs. You will not really be ready to build an application, however, until you understand how to create and combine PL/SQL modules.

PL/SQL offers the following structures that modularize your code in different ways:

Procedure
: A program that performs one or more actions and is called as an executable PL/SQL statement. You can pass information into and out of a procedure through its parameter list.

Function
: A program that returns a single value and is used just like a PL/ SQL expression. You can pass information into a function through its parameter list.

Database trigger
: A set of commands that are triggered to execute (e.g., log in, modify a row in a table, execute a DDL statement) when an event occurs in the database.

Package

A named collection of procedures, functions, types, and variables. A package is not really a module (it's more of a meta-module), but it is so closely related that I mention it here.

Object type or instance of an object type.

Oracle's version of (or attempt to emulate) an object-oriented class. Object types encapsulate state and behavior, combining data (like a relational table) with rules (procedures and functions that operate on that data).

Packages are discussed in Chapter 17; database triggers are explored in Chapter 18. You can read more about object types in Chapter 21. This chapter focuses on how to build procedures and functions, and how to design the parameter lists that are an integral part of well-designed modules.

I use the term *module* to mean either a function or a procedure. As is the case with many other programming languages, modules can call other named modules. You can pass information into and out of modules with parameters. Finally, the modular structure of PL/SQL also integrates tightly with exception handlers to provide all-encompassing error-checking techniques (see Chapter 6).

This chapter explores how to define procedures and functions, and then dives into the details of setting up parameter lists for these programs. We also examine some of the more "exotic" aspects of program construction, including local modules, overloading, forward referencing, deterministic functions, and table functions.

Procedures

A *procedure* is a module that performs one or more actions. Because a procedure call is a standalone executable statement in PL/SQL, a PL/SQL block could consist of nothing more than a single call to a procedure. Procedures are key building blocks of modular code, allowing you to both consolidate and reuse your program logic.

The general format of a PL/SQL procedure is as follows:

```
PROCEDURE [schema.]name [( parameter [, parameter ...] ) ]
   [AUTHID DEFINER | CURRENT_USER]
IS
   [declarations]

BEGIN
   executable statements

[ EXCEPTION
     exception handlers]

END [name];
```

where each element is used in the following ways:

schema
: Optional name of the schema that will own this procedure. The default is the current user. If different from the current user, that user will need privileges to create a procedure in another schema.

name
: The name of the procedure, which comes directly after the keyword PROCEDURE.

parameters
: An optional list of parameters that you define to both pass information into the procedure, and send information out of the procedure back to the calling program.

AUTHID clause
: Determines whether the procedure will execute under the authority of the definer (owner) of the procedure or under the authority of the current user. The former is known as the *definer rights model*, the latter as the *invoker rights model.*

declarations
: The declarations of local identifiers for that procedure. If you do not have any declarations, there will be no statements between the IS and BEGIN statements.

executable statements
: The statements that the procedure executes when it is called. You must have at least one executable statement after the BEGIN and before the END or EXCEPTION keywords.

exception handlers
: The optional exception handlers for the procedure. If you do not explicitly handle any exceptions, then you can leave out the EXCEPTION keyword and simply terminate the execution section with the END keyword.

Figure 16-1 shows the apply_discount procedure, which contains all four sections of the named PL/SQL block as well as a parameter list.

Calling a Procedure

A procedure is called as an executable PL/SQL statement. In other words, a call to a procedure must end with a semicolon (;) and be executed before and after other SQL or PL/SQL statements (if they exist) in the execution section of a PL/SQL block.

The following executable statement runs the apply_discount procedure:

```
BEGIN
   apply_discount( new_company_id, 0.15 );  -- 15% discount
END;
```

```
PROCEDURE apply_discount                                              Header
 (company_id_in IN company.company_id%TYPE, discount_in IN NUMBER)
IS
 min_discount CONSTANT NUMBER:=.05;
 max_discount CONSTANT NUMBER:=.25;                                   Declaration
 invalid_discount EXCEPTION;
BEGIN
 IF discount_in BETWEEN min_discount AND max_discount
  THEN
   UPDATE item
    SET item_amount:=item_amount*(1-discout_in);
   WHERE EXISTS (SELECT 'x' FROM order
     WHERE order.order_id=item.order_id                               Execution
      AND order.company_id=company_id_in);
  IF SQL%ROWCOUNT = 0 THEN RAISE NO_DATA_FOUND; END IF;
 ELSE
  RAISE invalid_discount;
 END IF;
EXCEPTION
 WHEN invalid_discount
 THEN
  DBMS_OUTPUT.PUT_LINE('The specified discount is invalid.');
                                                                      Exception
 WHEN NO_DATA_FOUND
 THEN
  DBMS_OUTPUT.PUT_LINE('No orders in the system for company:'||
     TO_CHAR(company_id_in));
END apply_discount;
```

Figure 16-1. The apply_discount procedure

If the procedure does not have any parameters, then you call the procedure without any parentheses:

```
display_store_summary;
```

In Oracle8*i* and later, you can also include empty open and close parentheses as well, as in:

```
display_store_summary( );
```

The Procedure Header

The portion of the procedure definition that comes before the IS keyword is called the *procedure header*. The header provides all the information a programmer needs to call that procedure, namely:

- The procedure name
- The AUTHID clause, if any
- The parameter list, if any

A programmer does not need to know about the inside of the procedure to be able to call it properly from another program.

The header for the apply_discount procedure mentioned in the previous section is:

```
PROCEDURE apply_discount
   (company_id_in IN company.company_id%TYPE,
    discount_in IN NUMBER)
```

It consists of the module type, the name, and a list of two parameters.

The Procedure Body

The body of the procedure is the code required to implement that procedure, and consists of the declaration, execution, and exception sections of the function. Everything after the IS keyword in the procedure makes up that procedure's body. The exception and declaration sections are optional. If you have no exception handlers, leave off the EXCEPTION keyword and simply enter the END statement to terminate the procedure. If you have no declarations, the BEGIN statement simply follows immediately after the IS keyword.

You must supply at least one executable statement in a procedure. That is generally not a problem; instead, watch out for execution sections that become extremely long and hard to manage. You should work hard to keep the execution section compact and readable. See later sections in this chapter for more specific guidance on this topic, expecially the "Improving readability" section.

The END Descriptor

You can append the name of the procedure directly after the END keyword when you complete your procedure, as shown here:

```
PROCEDURE display_stores (region_in IN VARCHAR2) IS
BEGIN
   ...
END display_stores;
```

This name serves as a label that explicitly links the end of the program with its beginning. You should, as a matter of habit, use an END descriptor. It is especially important to do so when you have a procedure that spans more than a single page, or is one in a series of procedures and functions in a package body.

The RETURN Statement

The RETURN statement is generally associated with a function, as it is required to RETURN a value from a function (or else raise an exception). Interestingly, PL/SQL also allows you to use a RETURN statement in a procedure. The procedure version of the RETURN does not take an expression; it therefore cannot pass a value back to the calling program unit. The RETURN simply halts execution of the procedure and returns control to the calling code.

You do not see this usage of RETURN very often, and for good reason. Use of the RETURN in a procedure usually leads to very unstructured code, because there would then be at least two paths out of the procedure, making execution flow hard to understand and maintain. Avoid using both RETURN and GOTO to bypass proper control structures and process flow in your program units.

Functions

A *function* is a module that returns a value. Unlike a procedure call, which is a standalone executable statement, a call to a function can exist only as part of an executable statement, such as an element in an expression or the value assigned as the default in a declaration of a variable.

Because a function returns a value, it is said to have a datatype. A function can be used in place of an expression in a PL/SQL statement having the same datatype as the function.

Functions are particularly important constructs for building modular code. For example, every single business rule or formula in your application should be placed inside a function. Every single-row query should also be defined within a function, so that it can be easily and reliably reused.

Some programmers prefer to rely less on functions, and more on procedures that return status information through the parameter list. If you are one of these programmers, make sure that your business rules, formulas, and single-row queries are tucked away into your procedures!

An application short on function definition and usage is likely to be difficult to maintain and enhance over time.

Structure of a Function

The structure of a function is the same as that of a procedure, except that the function also has a RETURN clause. The general format of a function is as follows:

```
FUNCTION [schema.]name [( parameter [, parameter ...] ) ]
   RETURN return_datatype
   [AUTHID DEFINER | CURRENT_USER]
   [DETERMINISTIC]
   [PARALLEL ENABLE ...]
   [PIPELINED]
IS
   [declaration statements]
```

```
BEGIN
   executable statements

[EXCEPTION
   exception handler statements]

END [ name ];
```

where each element is used in the following ways:

schema
: Optional name of the schema that will own this function. The default is the current user. If different from the current user, that user will need privileges to create a function in another schema.

name
: The name of the procedure comes directly after the keyword FUNCTION.

parameters
: An optional list of parameters that you define to both pass information into the procedure and send information out of the procedure back to the calling program.

return_datatype
: The datatype of the value returned by the function. This is required in the function header and is explained in more detail in the next section.

AUTHID clause
: Determines whether the procedure will execute under the authority of the definer (owner) of the procedure or under the authority of the current user. The former is known as the *definer rights model*, the latter as the *invoker rights model.*

DETERMINISTIC clause
: An optimization hint that lets the system use a saved copy of the function's return result, if available. The query optimizer can choose whether to use the saved copy or re-call the function.

PARALLEL_ENABLE clause
: An optimization hint that enables the function to be executed in parallel when called from within a SELECT statement.

PIPELINED clause
: Specifies that the results of this table function should be returned iteratively via the PIPE ROW command.

declaration statements
: The declarations of local identifiers for that function. If you do not have any declarations, there will be no statements between the IS and BEGIN statements.

executable statements
: The statements the function executes when it is called. You must have at least one executable statement after the BEGIN and before the END or EXCEPTION keywords.

exception handler statements

The optional exception handlers for the function. If you do not explicitly handle any exceptions, then you can leave out the EXCEPTION keyword and simply terminate the execution section with the END keyword.

Figure 16-2 illustrates the PL/SQL function and its different sections. Notice that the tot_sales function does not have an exception section.

```
FUNCTION tot_sales
 (company_id_in IN company.company_id%TYPE,
  status_in IN order.status_code%TYPE:=NULL)
RETURN NUMBER
IS
 /*Internal upper-cased version of status code */
 status_int order.status_code%TYPE:=UPPER(status_in);

 /*Parameterized cursor returns total discounted sales. */
 CURSOR sales_cur (status_in IN status_code%TYPE) IS
  SELECT SUM (amount*discount)
   FROM item
  WHERE EXISTS (SELECT 'X' FROM order
     WHERE order.order_id=item.order_id
     AND company_id=company_id_in
     AND status_code LIKE status_in);

 /*Return value for function*/
 return_value NUMBER;
BEGIN
 OPEN sales_cur (status_int);
 FETCH sales_cur INTO return_value;
 IF sales_cur%NOTFOUND
 THEN
    CLOSE sales_cur;
    RETURN NULL;
 ELSE
    CLOSE sales_cur;
    RETURN return_value;
 END IF;
END tot_sales;
```


Figure 16-2. The tot_sales function

The RETURN Datatype

A PL/SQL function can return virtually any kind of data known to PL/SQL, from scalars (single, primitive values like dates and strings) to complex structures like collections, object types, cursor variables, and LOBs (large objects). You may not, however, return an exception through a function, because in PL/SQL exceptions do not have a type.

Here are some examples of RETURN clauses in functions:

- Return a string from a standalone function:

```
CREATE OR REPLACE FUNCTION favorite_nickname (
   name_in IN VARCHAR2) RETURN VARCHAR2
IS ...
END;
```

- Return a DATE from an object type member function:

```
CREATE TYPE pet_t IS OBJECT (
   tag_no                        INTEGER,
   NAME                          VARCHAR2 (60),
   breed VARCHAR2(100),
   dob DATE,
   MEMBER FUNCTION age (new_tag_no IN INTEGER)
      RETURN DATE
)
```

- Return a record with the same structure as the books table:

```
CREATE OR REPLACE PACKAGE book_info
IS
   FUNCTION onerow (isbn_in IN books.isbn%TYPE)
     RETURN books%ROWTYPE;
...
```

- Return a cursor variable with the specified REF CURSOR type (based on a record type):

```
CREATE OR REPLACE PACKAGE book_info
IS
   TYPE overdue_rt IS RECORD (
      isbn books.isbn%TYPE,
      days_overdue PLS_INTEGER);

   TYPE overdue_rct IS REF CURSOR RETURN overdue_rt;

   FUNCTION overdue_info (username_in IN lib_users.username%TYPE)
     RETURN overdue_rct;
...
```

The END Descriptor

You can append the name of the function directly after the END keyword when you complete your function, as shown here:

```
FUNCTION tot_sales (company_in IN INTEGER) RETURN NUMBER
IS
BEGIN
   ...
END tot_sales;
```

This name serves as a label that explicitly links the end of the program with its beginning. You should, as a matter of habit, use an END descriptor. It is especially important to do so when you have a function that spans more than a single page or that is one in a series of functions and procedures in a package body.

Calling a Function

A function is called as part of an executable PL/SQL statement wherever an expression can be used. The following examples illustrate how the various functions defined in the section "The RETURN Datatype" can be invoked.

- Assign the default value of a variable with a function call:

```
DECLARE
   v_nickname VARCHAR2(100) :=
      favorite_nickname ('Steven');
```

- Use a member function for the pet object type in a conditional expression:

```
DECLARE
   my_parrot pet_t :=
      pet_t (1001, 'Mercury', 'African Grey',
             TO_DATE ('09/23/1996', 'MM/DD/YYYY'));
BEGIN
   IF my_parrot.age < INTERVAL '50' YEAR -- 9i INTERVAL type
   THEN
      DBMS_OUTPUT.PUT_LINE ('Still a youngster!');
   END IF;
```

- Retrieve a single row of book information directly into a record:

```
DECLARE
   my_first_book books%ROWTYPE;
BEGIN
   my_first_book := book_info.onerow ('1-56592-335-9');
   ...
```

- Obtain a cursor variable to overdue book information for a specific user:

```
DECLARE
   my_overdue_info overdue_rct;
BEGIN
   my_overdue_info :=
      book_info.overdue_info ('STEVEN_FEUERSTEIN');
   ...
```

- Call a function of one's own making from within a CREATE VIEW statement, utilizing a CURSOR expression to pass a result set as an argument to that function:

```
CREATE OR REPLACE VIEW young_managers AS
  SELECT managers.employee_id manager_employee_id
    FROM employees managers
    WHERE Most_Reports_Before_Manager
      (
        CURSOR ( SELECT reports.hire_date FROM employees reports
```

```
                WHERE reports.manager_id = managers.employee_id
             ),
        managers.hire_date
      ) = 1;
```

Functions Without Parameters

If a function has no parameters, the function call is written without parentheses. The following code illustrates this with a call to a method named "age" of the pet_t object type:

```
IF my_parrot.age < INTERVAL '50' YEAR -- 9i INTERVAL type
```

In Oracle8*i* and later, you can also include empty open and close parentheses, as in:

```
IF my_parrot.age( ) < INTERVAL '50' YEAR
```

The Function Header

The portion of the function definition that comes before the IS keyword is called the *function header*. The header provides all the information a programmer needs to call that function, namely:

- The function name
- Modifiers to the definition and behavior of the function (e.g., is it deterministic? Does it run in parallel execution? Is it pipelined?)
- The parameter list, if any
- The RETURN datatype

A programmer should not need to look at the inside of the function (its body) in order to be able to call it properly from another program.

The header for the tot_sales function discussed earlier is:

```
FUNCTION tot_sales
   (company_id_in IN company.company_id%TYPE,
    status_in IN order.status_code%TYPE := NULL)
RETURN NUMBER
```

It consists of the module type, the name, a list of two parameters, and a RETURN datatype of NUMBER. This means that any PL/SQL statement or expression that references a numeric value can make a call to tot_sales to obtain that value. Here is one such statement:

```
DECLARE
   v_sales NUMBER;
BEGIN
   v_sales := tot_sales (1505, 'ACTIVE');
   ...
```

The Function Body

The body of the function is the code required to implement the function. It consists of the declaration, execution, and exception sections of the function. Everything after the IS keyword in the function makes up that function's body.

Once again, the declaration and exception sections are optional. If you have no exception handlers, simply leave off the EXCEPTION keyword and enter the END statement to terminate the function. If you have no declarations, the BEGIN statement simply follows immediately after the IS keyword.

A function's execution section should have a RETURN statement in it, although it is not necessary for the function to compile. If, however, your function finishes executing without processing a RETURN statement, Oracle will raise the following error (a sure sign of a very poorly designed function):

```
ORA-06503: PL/SQL: Function returned without value
```

The RETURN Statement

A function must have at least one RETURN statement in its execution section of statements. It can have more than one RETURN, but only one is executed each time the function is called. The RETURN statement that is executed by the function determines the value that is returned by that function. When a RETURN statement is processed, the function terminates immediately and returns control to the calling PL/SQL block.

The RETURN clause in the header of the function is different from the RETURN statement in the execution section of the body. While the RETURN clause indicates the datatype of the return or result value of the function, the RETURN statement specifies the actual value that is returned. You have to specify the RETURN datatype in the header, but then also include at least one RETURN statement in the function. The datatype indicated in the RETURN clause in the header must be compatible with the datatype of the returned expression in the RETURN statement.

RETURN any valid expression

The RETURN statement can return any expression compatible with the datatype indicated in the RETURN clause. This expression can be composed of calls to other functions, complex calculations, and even data conversions. All of the following usages of RETURN are valid:

```
RETURN 'buy me lunch';
RETURN POWER (max_salary, 5);
RETURN (100 - pct_of_total_salary (employee_id));
RETURN TO_DATE ('01' || earliest_month || initial_year, 'DDMMYY');
```

You can also return complex data structures such as object type instances, collections, and records.

An expression in the RETURN statement is evaluated when the RETURN is executed. When control is passed back to the calling block, the result of the evaluated expression is passed along, too.

Multiple RETURNs

In the tot_sales function shown in Figure 16-2, I used two different RETURN statements to handle different situations in the function, which can be described as follows:

> If I cannot obtain sales information from the cursor, I return NULL (which is different from zero). If I do get a value from the cursor, I return it to the calling program. In both of these cases, the RETURN statement passes back a value: in one case the NULL value, and in the other the return_value variable.

While it is certainly possible to have more than one RETURN statement in the execution section of a function, you are generally better off having just one: the last line in your execution section. The next section explains this.

RETURN as last executable statement

Generally, the best way to make sure that your function always returns a value is to make the last executable statement your RETURN statement. Declare a variable named return_value (which clearly indicates that it will contain the return value for the function), write all the code to come up with that value, and then, at the very end of the function, RETURN the return_value, as shown here:

```
FUNCTION do_it_all (parameter_list) RETURN NUMBER IS
   return_value NUMBER;
BEGIN
   ... lots of executable statements ...
   RETURN return_value;
END;
```

Here is a rewrite of the logic in Figure 16-2 to fix the problem of multiple RETURN statements.

```
IF sales_cur%NOTFOUND
THEN
   return_value:= NULL;
END IF;
CLOSE sales_cur;
RETURN return_value;
```

Parameters

Procedures and functions can both use *parameters* to pass information back and forth between the module and the calling PL/SQL block.

The parameters of a module are at least as important as the code that implements the module (the module's body). Sure, you have to make certain that your module fulfills its promise. But the whole point of creating a module is that it can be called, ideally by more than one other module. If the parameter list is confusing or badly designed, it will be very difficult for other programmers to make use of the module, and the result is that few will bother. And it doesn't matter how well you implemented a program if no one uses it.

Many developers do not give enough attention to a module's set of parameters. Considerations regarding parameters include:

The number of parameters
: Too few parameters can limit the reusability of your program; with too many parameters, no one will want to reuse your program. Certainly, the number of parameters is largely determined by program requirements, but there are different ways to define parameters (such as bundling multiple parameters in a single record).

The types of parameters
: Should you use read-only, write-only, or read-write parameters?

The names of parameters
: How should you name your parameters so that their purpose in the module is properly and easily understood?

Default values for parameters
: How do you set defaults? When should a parameter be given defaults, and when should the programmer be forced to enter a value?

PL/SQL offers many different features to help you design parameters effectively. This section covers all elements of parameter definition.

Defining Parameters

Formal parameters are defined in the parameter list of the program. A parameter definition parallels closely the syntax for declaring variables in the declaration section of a PL/SQL block. There are two important distinctions: first, a parameter has a passing mode while a variable declaration does not; and second, a parameter declaration must be unconstrained.

A *constrained declaration* is one that constrains or limits the kind of value that can be assigned to a variable declared with that datatype. An *unconstrained declaration* is one that does not limit values in this way. The following declaration of the variable company_name constrains the variable to 60 characters:

```
DECLARE
   company_name VARCHAR2(60);
```

When you declare a parameter, however, you must leave out the constraining part of the declaration:

```
PROCEDURE display_company (company_name IN VARCHAR2) IS ...
```

Actual and Formal Parameters

We need to distinguish between two different kinds of parameters: actual and formal parameters. The *formal parameters* are the names that are declared in the parameter list of the header of a module. The *actual parameters* are the values or expressions placed in the parameter list of the actual call to the module.

Let's examine the differences between actual and formal parameters using the example of tot_sales. Here, again, is the tot_sales header:

```
FUNCTION tot_sales
   (company_id_in IN company.company_id%TYPE,
    status_in IN order.status_code%TYPE := NULL)
RETURN std_types.dollar_amount;
```

The formal parameters of tot_sales are:

company_id_in
: The primary key of the company

status_in
: The status of the orders to be included in the sales calculation

These formal parameters do not exist outside of the function. You can think of them as placeholders for real or actual parameter values that are passed into the function when it is used in a program.

When you use tot_sales in your code, the formal parameters disappear. In their place you list the actual parameters or variables whose values will be passed to tot_sales. In the following example, the company_id variable contains the primary key pointing to a company record. In the first three calls to tot_sales, a different, hardcoded status is passed to the function. The last call to tot_sales does not specify a status; in this case, the function assigns the default value (provided in the function header) to the status_in parameter:

```
new_sales     := tot_sales (company_id, 'N');
paid_sales    := tot_sales (company_id, 'P');
shipped_sales := tot_sales (company_id, 'S');
all_sales     := tot_sales (company_id);
```

When tot_sales is called, all the actual parameters are evaluated. The results of the evaluations are then assigned to the formal parameters inside the function to which they correspond (note that this is true only for IN and IN OUT parameters; parameters of OUT mode are not copied in).

The formal parameter and the actual parameter that corresponds to it (when called) must be of the same or compatible datatypes. PL/SQL will perform datatype conversions for you in many situations. Generally, however, you are better off avoiding all implicit datatype conversions. Use a formal conversion function like TO_CHAR or TO_DATE (see Chapter 10), so that you know exactly what kind of data you are passing into your modules.

Matching Actual and Formal Parameters in PL/SQL

How does PL/SQL know which actual parameter goes with which formal parameter when a program is executed? PL/SQL offers two ways to make the association:

Positional notation
: Associate the actual parameter implicitly (by position) with the formal parameter.

Named notation
: Associate the actual parameter explicitly (by name) with the formal parameter.

Positional notation

In every example so far, I have employed positional notation to guide PL/SQL through the parameters. With positional notation, PL/SQL relies on the relative positions of the parameters to make the correspondence: it associates the *N*th actual parameter in the call to a program with the *N*th formal parameter in the program's header.

With the following tot_sales example, PL/SQL associates the first actual parameter, :order.company_id, with the first formal parameter, company_id_in. It then associates the second actual parameter, *N*, with the second formal parameter, status_in:

```
new_sales := tot_sales (:order.company_id, 'N');

FUNCTION tot_sales
   (company_id_in IN company.company_id%TYPE,
    status_in IN order.status_code%TYPE := NULL)
RETURN std_types.dollar_amount;
```

Now you know the name for the way compilers pass values through parameters to modules. Positional notation, shown graphically in Figure 16-3, is certainly the most obvious method.

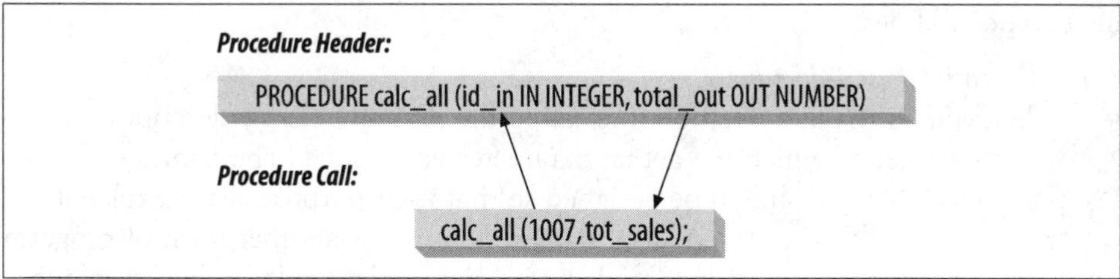

Figure 16-3. Matching actual with formal parameters (positional notation)

Named notation

With named notation, you explicitly associate the formal parameter (the name of the parameter) with the actual parameter (the value of the parameter) right in the call to the program, using the combination symbol =>.

The general syntax for named notation is:

```
formal_parameter_name => argument_value
```

Because you provide the name of the formal parameter explicitly, PL/SQL no longer needs to rely on the order of the parameters to make the association from actual to formal. So, if you use named notation, you do not need to list the parameters in your call to the program in the same order as the formal parameters in the header. You can call tot_sales for new orders in either of these two ways:

```
new_sales :=
   tot_sales (company_id_in => :order.company_id, status_in =>'N');

new_sales :=
   tot_sales (status_in =>'N', company_id_in => :order.company_id);
```

You can also mix named and positional notation in the same program call:

```
:order.new_sales := tot_sales (:order.company_id, status_in =>'N');
```

If you do mix notation, however, you must list all of your positional parameters before any named notation parameters, as shown in the preceding example. Positional notation has to have a starting point from which to keep track of positions, and the only starting point is the first parameter. If you place named notation parameters in front of positional notation, PL/SQL loses its place. Both of the following calls to tot_sales will fail. The first statement fails because the named notation comes first. The second fails because positional notation is used, but the parameters are in the wrong order. PL/SQL will try to convert 'N' to a NUMBER (for company_id):

```
:order.new_sales := tot_sales (company_id_in => :order.company_id, 'N');
:order.new_sales := tot_sales ('N', company_id_in => :order.company_id);
```

Benefits of named notation

Now that you are aware of the different ways to notate the order and association of parameters, you might be wondering why you would ever use named notation. Here are two possibilities:

Named notation is self-documenting
: When you use named notation, the call to the program clearly describes the formal parameter to which the actual parameter is assigned. The names of formal parameters can and should be designed so that their purpose is self-explanatory. In a way, the descriptive aspect of named notation is another form of program documentation. If you are not familiar with all of the modules called by an application, the listing of the formal parameters helps reinforce your understanding of a particular program call. In some development environments, the standard for parameter notation is named notation for just this reason. This is especially true when the formal parameters are named following the convention of appending the passing mode as the last token. Then, the direction of data can be clearly seen simply by investigating the procedure or function call.

Named notation gives you complete flexibility over parameter specification

You can list the parameters in any order you want. (This does not mean, however, that you should randomly order your arguments when you call a program!) You can also include only the parameters you want or need in the parameter list. Complex applications may at times require procedures with literally dozens of parameters. Any parameter with a default value can be left out of the call to the procedure. By using named notation, the developer can use the procedure by passing only the values needed for that usage.

Remember that whether you use named or positional notation, the actual module (both header and body) remains unchanged. The only difference is in the way the module is called.

Parameter Modes

When you define the parameter, you also specify the way in which it can be used. There are three different modes of parameters:

Mode	Description	Parameter usage
IN	Read-only	The value of the actual parameter can be referenced inside the module, but the parameter cannot be changed.
OUT	Write-only	The module can assign a value to the parameter, but the parameter's value cannot be referenced. Note that in some cases, Oracle will allow you to reference OUT parameters in ways that seem inconsistent with its definition. You should avoid such usages.
IN OUT	Read-write	The module can both reference (read) and modify (write) the parameter.

The mode determines how the program can use and manipulate the value assigned to the formal parameter. You specify the mode of the parameter immediately after the parameter name and before the parameter's datatype and optional default value. The following procedure header uses all three parameter modes:

```
PROCEDURE predict_activity
   (last_date_in IN DATE,
    task_desc_inout IN OUT VARCHAR2,
    next_date_out OUT DATE)
```

The predict_activity procedure takes in two pieces of information: the date of the last activity and a description of the activity. It then returns or sends out two pieces of information: a possibly modified task description and the date of the next activity. Because the task_desc_inout parameter is IN OUT, the program can both read the value of the argument and change the value of that argument.

Let's look at each of these parameter modes in detail.

IN mode

An IN parameter allows you to pass values into the module, but will not pass anything out of the module and back to the calling PL/SQL block. In other words, for the purposes of the program, IN parameters function like constants. Just like constants, the value of the formal IN parameter cannot be changed within the program. You cannot assign values to the IN parameter or in any other way modify its value.

IN is the default mode; if you do not specify a parameter mode, the parameter is automatically considered IN. I recommend, however, that you always specify a parameter mode so that your intended use of the parameter is documented explicitly in the code itself.

IN parameters can be given default values in the program header (see the later section "Default Values").

The actual value for an IN parameter can be a variable, a named constant, a literal, or a complex expression. All of the following calls to display_title are valid:

```
DECLARE
   happy_title CONSTANT VARCHAR2(30)    := 'HAPPY BIRTHDAY';
   changing_title VARCHAR2(30) := 'Happy Anniversary';
   spc VARCHAR2(1) := CHR(32) -- ASCII code for a single space;
BEGIN
   display_title ('Happy Birthday');              -- a literal
   display_title (happy_title);                   -- a constant

   changing_title := happy_title;
   display_title (changing_title);                -- a variable
   display_title ('Happy' || spc || 'Birthday'); -- an expression
   display_title (INITCAP (happy_title));         -- another expression
END;
```

What if you want to transfer data out of your program? For that, you will need an OUT or an IN OUT parameter.

OUT mode

An OUT parameter is the opposite of the IN parameter, but perhaps you already had that figured out. Use the OUT parameter to pass a value back from the program to the calling PL/SQL block. An OUT parameter is like the return value for a function, but it appears in the parameter list and you can have as many as you like.

Inside the program, an OUT parameter acts like a variable that has not been initialized. In fact, the OUT parameter has no value at all until the program terminates successfully (unless you have requested use of the NOCOPY hint, which is described in a moment). During the execution of the program, any assignments to an OUT parameter are actually made to an internal copy of the OUT parameter. When the program terminates successfully and returns control to the calling block, the value in that local copy is then transferred to the actual OUT parameter. That value is then available in the calling PL/SQL block.

There are several consequences of these rules concerning OUT parameters:

- You cannot assign an OUT parameter's value to another variable or even use it in a reassignment to itself. Note that in some cases, Oracle will allow you to reference OUT parameters in ways that seem inconsistent with its definition. You should avoid such usages.
- You also cannot provide a default value to an OUT parameter. You can only assign a value to an OUT parameter inside the body of the module.
- Any assignments made to OUT parameters are rolled back when an exception is raised in the program. Because the value for an OUT parameter is not actually assigned until a program completes successfully, any intermediate assignments are therefore ignored. Unless an exception handler traps the exception and then assigns a value to the OUT parameter, no assignment is made to that parameter. The variable will retain the same value it had before the program was called.
- An actual parameter corresponding to an OUT formal parameter must be a variable. It cannot be a constant, literal, or expression because these formats do not provide a receptacle in which PL/SQL can place the OUTgoing value.

IN OUT mode

With an IN OUT parameter, you can pass values into the program and return a value back to the calling program (either the original, unchanged value or a new value set within the program). The IN OUT parameter shares two restrictions with the OUT parameter:

- An IN OUT parameter cannot have a default value.
- An IN OUT actual parameter or argument must be a variable. It cannot be a constant, literal, or expression because these formats do not provide a receptacle in which PL/SQL can place the outgoing value.

Beyond these restrictions, none of the other restrictions apply.

You can use the IN OUT parameter in both sides of an assignment because it functions like an initialized, rather than uninitialized, variable. PL/SQL does not lose the value of an IN OUT parameter when it begins execution of the program. Instead, it uses that value as necessary within the program.

The combine_and_format_names procedure shown here combines the first and last names into a full name in the format specified ("LAST, FIRST" or "FIRST LAST"). I need the incoming names for the combine action, and I will uppercase the first and last names for future use in the program (thereby enforcing the application standard of all-uppercase for names of people and things). This program uses all three parameter modes: IN, IN OUT, and OUT.

```
PROCEDURE combine_and_format_names
   (first_name_inout IN OUT VARCHAR2,
    last_name_inout IN OUT VARCHAR2,
    full_name_out OUT VARCHAR2,
    name_format_in IN VARCHAR2 := 'LAST, FIRST')
IS
BEGIN
   /* Upper-case the first and last names. */
   first_name_inout := UPPER (first_name_inout);
   last_name_inout := UPPER (last_name_inout);

   /* Combine the names as directed by the name format string. */
   IF name_format_in = 'LAST, FIRST'
   THEN
      full_name_out := last_name_inout || ', ' || first_name_inout;

   ELSIF name_format_in = 'FIRST LAST'
   THEN
      full_name_out := first_name_inout || ' ' || last_name_inout;
   END IF;
END;
```

The first name and last name parameters must be IN OUT. The full_name_out is just an OUT parameter because I create the full name from its parts. If the actual parameter used to receive the full name has a value going into the procedure, I certainly don't want to use it! Finally, the name_format_in parameter is a mere IN parameter because it is used to determine how to format the full name, but is not changed or changeable in any way.

Each parameter mode has its own characteristics and purpose. You should choose carefully which mode to apply to your parameters so that they are used properly within the module.

The NOCOPY Parameter Mode Hint

Starting with Version 8.1, PL/SQL offers an option for definitions of parameters: the NOCOPY clause. NOCOPY is a hint to the compiler about how you would like the PL/SQL engine to work with the data structure being passed in as an OUT or IN OUT parameter. To understand NOCOPY and its potential impact, it will help to review how PL/SQL handles parameters. There are two ways of passing parameter values: by reference and by value.

By reference
: When an actual parameter is passed by reference, it means that a pointer to the actual parameter is passed to the corresponding formal parameter. Both the actual and formal parameters then reference, or point to, the same location in memory that holds the value of the parameter.

By value
: When an actual parameter is passed by value, the value of the actual parameter is copied into the corresponding formal parameter. If the program then

terminates without an exception, the formal parameter value is copied back to the actual parameter. If an error occurs, the changed values are not copied back to the actual parameter.

Parameter passing in PL/SQL without the use of NOCOPY follows these rules:

Parameter mode	Passed by value or reference? (default behavior)
IN	By reference
OUT	By value
IN OUT	By value

We can infer from these definitions and rules that when a large data structure (such as a collection, a record, or an instance of an object type) is passed as an OUT or IN OUT parameter, that structure will be passed by value, and your application could experience performance and memory degradation as a result of all this copying. The NOCOPY hint is a way for you to attempt to avoid this. The syntax of this feature is as follows:

```
parameter_name [ IN | IN OUT | OUT | IN OUT NOCOPY | OUT NOCOPY ] parameter_datatype
```

You can specify NOCOPY only in conjunction with the OUT or IN OUT mode. Here is a parameter list that uses the NOCOPY hint for both of its IN OUT arguments:

```
PROCEDURE analyze_results (
   date_in IN DATE,
   values IN OUT NOCOPY numbers_varray,
   validity_flags IN OUT NOCOPY validity_rectype
   );
```

There are two things you should keep in mind about NOCOPY:

- The corresponding actual parameter for an OUT parameter under the NOCOPY hint is set to NULL whenever the subprogram containing the OUT parameter is called.
- NOCOPY is a hint, not a command. This means that the compiler might silently decide that it cannot fulfill your request for a NOCOPY parameter treatment. The next section lists the restrictions on NOCOPY that might cause this to happen.

Restrictions on NOCOPY

A number of situations will cause the PL/SQL compiler to ignore the NOCOPY hint and instead use the default by-value method to pass the OUT or IN OUT parameter. These situations are the following:

The actual parameter is an element of an associative array

You can request NOCOPY for an entire associative array (which could be an entire record structure), but not for an individual element in the table. A suggested workaround is to copy the structure to a standalone variable, either scalar or record, and then pass that as the NOCOPY parameter. That way, at least you aren't copying the entire structure.

Certain constraints are applied to actual parameters
Some constraints will result in the NOCOPY hint's being ignored; these include a scale specification for a numeric variable and the NOT NULL constraint. You can, however, pass a string variable that has been constrained by size.

The actual and formal parameters are record structures
One or both records were declared using %ROWTYPE or %TYPE, and the constraints on corresponding fields in these two records are different.

In passing the actual parameter, the PL/SQL engine must perform an implicit datatype conversion
A suggested workaround is this: because you are always better off performing explicit conversions anyway, do that and then pass the converted value as the NOCOPY parameter.

The subprogram requesting the NOCOPY hint is used in an external or remote procedure call
In these cases, PL/SQL will always pass the actual parameter by value.

Impact of NOCOPY

Depending on your application, NOCOPY can improve the performance of programs with IN OUT or OUT parameters. As you might expect, these potential gains come with a tradeoff: if a program terminates with an unhandled exception, you cannot trust the values in a NOCOPY actual parameter.

What do I mean by "trust"? Let's review how PL/SQL behaves concerning its parameters when an unhandled exception terminates a program. Suppose that I pass an IN OUT record to my calculate_totals procedure. The PL/SQL runtime engine first makes a copy of that record and then, during program execution, makes any changes to that copy. The actual parameter itself is not modified until calculate_totals ends successfully (without propagating back an exception). At that point, the local copy is copied back to the actual parameter, and the program that called calculate_totals can access that changed data. If calculate_totals terminates with an unhandled exception, however, the calling program can be certain that the actual parameter's value has not been changed.

That certainty disappears with the NOCOPY hint. When a parameter is passed by reference (the effect of NOCOPY), any changes made to the formal parameter are also made immediately to the actual parameter. Suppose that my calculate_totals program reads through a 10,000-row collection and makes changes to each row. If an error is raised at row 5000 and propagated out of calculate_totals unhandled, my actual parameter collection will be only half-changed.

As a result, you should be very judicious in your use of the NOCOPY hint. Use it only when you know that you have a performance problem relating to your parameter passing, and be prepared for the potential consequences when exceptions are raised.

Default Values

As you have seen from previous examples, you can provide default values for IN parameters. If an IN parameter has a default value, you do not need to include that parameter in the call to the program. Likewise, a parameter's default value is used by the program only if the call to that program does not include that parameter in the list. You must, of course, include an actual parameter for any IN OUT parameters.

The parameter default value works the same way as a specification of a default value for a declared variable. There are two ways to specify a default value: either with the keyword DEFAULT or with the assignment operator (:=), as the following example illustrates:

```
PROCEDURE astrology_reading
   (sign_in IN VARCHAR2 := 'LIBRA',
    born_at_in IN DATE DEFAULT SYSDATE) IS
```

By using default values, you can call programs with different numbers of actual parameters. The program uses the default value of any unspecified parameters, and overrides the default values of any parameters in the list that have specified values. Here are all the different ways you can ask for your astrology reading using positional notation:

```
BEGIN
   astrology_reading ('SCORPIO',
      TO_DATE ('12-24-2001 17:56:10', 'MM-DD-YYYY HH24:MI:SS');
   astrology_reading ('SCORPIO');
   astrology_reading;
END;
```

The first call specifies both parameters explicitly. In the second call, only the first actual parameter is included, so born_at_in is set to the current date and time. In the third call, no parameters are specified, so we cannot include the parentheses. Both of the default values are used in the body of the procedure.

What if you want to specify a birth time, but not a sign? To "skip over" leading parameters that have default values, you will need to use named notation. By including the name of the formal parameter, you can list only those parameters to which you need to pass values. In this (thankfully) last request for a star-based reading of my fate, I have successfully passed in a default of Libra as my sign and an overridden birth time of 5:56 PM.

```
BEGIN
   astrology_reading (
      born_at_in =>
         TO_DATE ('12-24-2001 17:56:10', 'MM-DD-YYYY HH24:MI:SS');
END;
```

Local Modules

A *local module* is a procedure or function that is defined in the declaration section of a PL/SQL block (anonymous or named). This module is considered local because it is defined only within the parent PL/SQL block. It cannot be called by any other PL/SQL blocks defined outside that enclosing block.

Figure 16-4 shows how blocks that are external to a procedure definition cannot "cross the line" into the procedure to directly invoke any local procedures or functions.

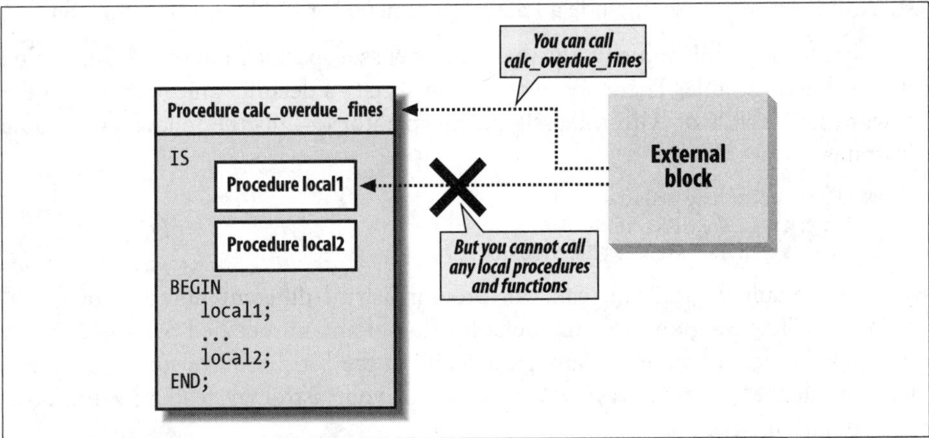

Figure 16-4. Local modules are hidden and inaccessible outside the program

The syntax for defining the procedure or function is exactly the same as that used for creating standalone modules.

The following anonymous block, for example, declares a local procedure:

```
DECLARE
   PROCEDURE show_date (date_in IN DATE) IS
   BEGIN
      DBMS_OUTPUT.PUT_LINE (TO_CHAR (date_in, 'Month DD, YYYY');
   END;
BEGIN
   ...
END;
```

Local modules must be located after all of the other declaration statements in the declaration section. You must declare your variables, cursors, exceptions, types, records, tables, and so on before you type in the first PROCEDURE or FUNCTION keyword.

The following sections explore the benefits of local modules and offer a number of examples.

Benefits of Local Modularization

There are two central reasons to create local modules:

To reduce the size of the module by stripping it of repetitive code
: This is the most common motivation to create a local module; you can see its impact in the next example. The code reduction leads to higher code quality because you have fewer lines to test and fewer potential bugs. It takes less effort to maintain the code because there is less to maintain. And when you do have to make a change, you make it in one place in the local module and the effects are felt immediately throughout the parent module.

To improve the readability of your code
: Even if you do not repeat sections of code within a module, you still may want to pull out a set of related statements and package them into a local module. This can make it easier to follow the logic of the main body of the parent module.

The following sections examine these benefits.

Reducing code volume

Let's look at an example of reducing code volume. The calc_percentages procedure takes numeric values from the sales package (sales_pkg), calculates the percentage of each sales amount against the total sales provided as a parameter, and then formats the number for display in a report or form. The example you see here has only three calculations, but I extracted it from a production application that actually performed 23 of these computations!

```
PROCEDURE calc_percentages (tot_sales_in IN NUMBER)
IS
BEGIN
   :profile.food_sales_stg :=
      TO_CHAR ((sales_pkg.food_sales / tot_sales_in ) * 100,
               '$999,999');
   :profile.service_sales_stg :=
      TO_CHAR ((sales_pkg.service_sales / tot_sales_in ) * 100,
               '$999,999');
   :profile.toy_sales_stg :=
      TO_CHAR ((sales_pkg.toy_sales / tot_sales_in ) * 100,
               '$999,999');
END;
```

This code took a long time (relatively speaking) to write, is larger than necessary, and is maintenance-intensive. What if I need to change the format to which I convert the numbers? What if the calculation of the percentage changes? I will have to change each of the individual calculations.

With local modules, I can concentrate all the common, repeated code into a single function, which is then called repeatedly in calc_percentages. The local module version of this procedure is shown here:

```
PROCEDURE calc_percentages (tot_sales_in IN NUMBER)
IS
   /* Define a function right inside the procedure! */
   FUNCTION pct_stg (val_in IN NUMBER) RETURN VARCHAR2
   IS
   BEGIN
      RETURN TO_CHAR ((val_in/tot_sales_in ) * 100, '$999,999');
   END;
BEGIN
   :profile.food_sales_stg := pct_stg (sales_pkg.food_sales);
   :profile.service_sales_stg := pct_stg (sales_pkg.service_sales);
   :profile.toy_sales_stg := pct_stg (sales_pkg.toy_sales);
END;
```

All of the complexities of the calculation, from the division by tot_sales_in to the multiplication by 100 to the formatting with TO_CHAR, have been transferred to the function pct_stg. This function is defined in the declaration section of the procedure. By calling this function from within the body of calc_percentages, the executable statements of the procedure are much more readable and maintainable. Now, if the formula for the calculation changes in any way, I make the change just once in the function and it takes effect in all the assignments.

Improving readability

You can use local modules to dramatically improve the readability and maintainability of your code. In essence, local modules allow you to follow "top-down design" or "stepwise refinement" methodologies very closely. You can also use the same technique to "decompose" or "refactor" an existing program so that it is more readable.

The bottom-line result of using local modules in this way is that you can dramatically reduce the size of your execution sections (you are transferring many lines of logic from an "inline" location in the execution section to a local module callable in that section). By keeping your execution sections small, you will find that it is much easier to read and understand the logic.

I suggest that you adopt as a guideline in your coding standards that execution sections of PL/SQL blocks be no longer than 60 lines (the amount of text that can fit on a screen or page). This may sound crazy, but if you follow the techniques in this section, you will find it not only possible but highly advantageous.

Suppose that I have a series of WHILE loops (some of them nested) whose bodies contain a series of complex calculations and deep nestings of conditional logic. Even with extensive commenting, it can be difficult to follow the program flow over several pages, particularly when the END IF or END LOOP of a given construct is not even on the same page as the IF or LOOP statement that began it.

In contrast, if you pull out sequences of related statements, place them in one or more local modules, and then call those modules in the body of the program, the result is a program that can literally document itself. The assign_workload procedure offers a simplified version of this scenario that still makes clear the gains offered by local modules:

```
PROCEDURE assign_workload (department_in IN emp.deptno%TYPE)
IS
   CURSOR emps_in_dept_cur (department_in IN emp.deptno%TYPE)
   IS
      SELECT * FROM emp WHERE deptno = department_in;

   PROCEDURE assign_next_open_case
      (emp_id_in IN NUMBER, case_out OUT NUMBER)
   IS
   BEGIN ...  full implementation ... END;

   FUNCTION next_appointment (case_id_in IN NUMBER)
      RETURN DATE
   IS
   BEGIN ...  full implementation ... END;

   PROCEDURE schedule_case
       (case_in IN NUMBER, date_in IN DATE)
   IS
   BEGIN ...  full implementation ... END;

BEGIN /* main */
   FOR emp_rec IN emps_in_dept_cur (department_in)
   LOOP
      IF analysis.caseload (emp_rec.emp_id) <
         analysis.avg_cases (department_in);
      THEN
         assign_next_open_case (emp_rec.emp_id, case#);
         schedule_case
            (case#, next_appointment (case#));
      END IF;
   END LOOP
END assign_workload;
```

The assign_workload procedure has three local modules:

```
assign_next_open_case
next_appointment
schedule_case
```

It also relies on two packaged programs that already exist and can be easily plugged into this program: analysis.caseload and analysis.avg_cases. For the purposes of understanding the logic behind assign_workload, it doesn't really matter what code is executed in each of them. I can rely simply on the names of those modules to read through the main body of this program. Even without any comments, a reader can still gain a clear understanding of what each module is doing. Of course, if you want to rely on named objects to self-document your code, you'd better come up with very good names for the functions and procedures.

Scope of Local Modules

The modularized declaration section looks a lot like the body of a package, as you will see in Chapter 17. A package body also contains definitions of modules. The big difference between local modules and package modules is their scope. Local modules can be called only from within the block in which they are defined; package modules can—at a minimum—be called from anywhere in the package. If the package modules are also listed in the package specification, they can be called by any other program in your application.

You should therefore use local modules only to encapsulate code that does not need to be called outside of the current program. Otherwise, go ahead and create a package!

Sprucing Up Your Code with Local Modules

These days it seems that whenever I write a program with more than 20 lines and any complexity whatsoever, I end up creating several local modules. Doing so helps me see my way through to a solution much more easily; I can conceptualize my code at a higher level of abstraction by assigning a name to a whole sequence of statements; and I can perform top-down design and stepwise refinement of my requirements. Finally, by modularizing my code even within a single program, I make it very easy to later extract a local module and make it a truly independent, reusable procedure or function.

I hope that as you read this, a program you have written comes to mind. Perhaps you can go back and consolidate some repetitive code, clean up the logic, and make the program actually understandable to another human being. Don't fight the urge. Go ahead and modularize your code.

Module Overloading

When more than one program in the same scope share the same name, the programs are said to be *overloaded*. PL/SQL supports the overloading of procedures and functions in the declaration section of a block (named or anonymous), package specifications and bodies, and object type definitions. Overloading is a very powerful concept, and you should exploit it fully to improve the usability of your software.

Here is a very simple example of three overloaded modules defined in the declaration section of an anonymous block (therefore, all are local modules):

```
DECLARE
   /* First version takes a DATE parameter. */
   FUNCTION value_ok (date_in IN DATE) RETURN BOOLEAN IS
```

```
   BEGIN
      RETURN date_in <= SYSDATE;
   END;

   /* Second version takes a NUMBER parameter. */
   FUNCTION value_ok (number_in IN NUMBER) RETURN BOOLEAN  IS
   BEGIN
      RETURN number_in > 0;
   END;

   /* Third version is a procedure! */
   PROCEDURE value_ok (number_in IN NUMBER) RETURN BOOLEAN  IS
   BEGIN
      IF number_in > 0 THEN
         DBMS_OUTPUT.PUT_LINE (number_in || 'is OK!');
      ELSE
         DBMS_OUTPUT.PUT_LINE (number_in || 'is not OK!');
      END IF;
   END;

BEGIN
```

When the PL/SQL runtime engine encounters the following statement:

```
IF value_ok (SYSDATE) THEN ...
```

the actual parameter list is compared with the formal parameter lists of the various overloaded modules, searching for a match. If one is found, PL/SQL executes the code in the body of the program with the matching header.

Another name for overloading is *static polymorphism*. The term *polymorphism* refers to the ability of a language to define and selectively use more than one form of a program with the same name. When the decision on which form to use is made at compilation time, it is called *static polymorphism*. When the decision is made at runtime, it is called *dynamic polymorphism*; this type of polymorphism is available through inherited object types.

Overloading can greatly simplify your life and the lives of other developers. This technique consolidates the call interfaces for many similar programs into a single module name, transferring the burden of knowledge from the developer to the software. You do not have to try to remember, for instance, the six different names for programs adding values (dates, strings, Booleans, numbers, etc.) to various PL/SQL tables. Instead, you simply tell the compiler that you want to add a value, and pass it that value. PL/SQL and your overloaded programs figure out what you want to do and then do it for you.

When you build overloaded modules, you spend more time in design and implementation than you might with separate, standalone modules. This additional time up-front will be repaid handsomely down the line, as you and others will find it much easier and more efficient to use your programs.

Benefits of Overloading

There are three different scenarios that benefit from overloading:

Supporting many data combinations
: When applying the same action to different kinds or combinations of data, overloading does not provide a single name for different activities, so much as it provides different ways of requesting the same activity. This is the most common motivation for overloading.

Fitting the program to the user
: To make your code as useful as possible, you may construct different versions of the same program that correspond to different patterns of use. This often involves overloading functions and procedures. A good indicator of the need for this form of overloading is when you find yourself writing unnecessary code. For example, when working with DBMS_SQL, you will call the DBMS_SQL.EXECUTE function, but for DDL statements, the value returned by this function is ignored. Oracle should have overloaded this function as a procedure, so that I could simply execute a DDL statement like this:

```
BEGIN
   DBMS_SQL.EXECUTE ('CREATE TABLE xyz ...');
```

as opposed to:

```
DECLARE
   feedback PLS_INTEGER;
BEGIN
   feedback := DBMS_SQL.EXECUTE ('CREATE TABLE xyz ...');
```

and then ignoring the feedback.

Overloading by type, not value
: This is the least common application of overloading. In this scenario, you use the type of data, not its value, to determine which of the overloaded programs should be executed. This really comes in handy only when you are writing very generic software. The DBMS_SQL.DEFINE_COLUMN is a good example of this approach to overloading. I need to tell DBMS_SQL the type of each of my columns being selected from the dynamic query. To indicate a numeric column, I can make a call as follows:

```
DBMS_SQL.DEFINE_COLUMN (cur, 1, 1);
```

or I could do this:

```
DBMS_SQL.DEFINE_COLUMN (cur, 1, DBMS_UTILITY.GET_TIME);
```

It doesn't matter which I do; I just need to say "this is a number," but not any particular number. Overloading is an elegant way to handle this requirement.

Let's look at an example of the most common type of overloading, and then review restrictions and guidelines on overloading.

Supporting many data combinations

Use overloading to apply the same action to different kinds or combinations of data. As noted previously, this kind of overloading does not provide a single name for different activities so much as different ways of requesting the same activity. We illustrate this kind of overloading with the DBMS_OUTPUT.PUT_LINE procedure, which doesn't even overload for the Boolean datatype.

Here is the relevant part of the DBMS_OUTPUT package specification:

```
CREATE OR REPLACE PACKAGE DBMS_OUTPUT
AS
   PROCEDURE put_line (a VARCHAR2);
   PROCEDURE put_line (a NUMBER);
END DBMS_OUTPUT;
```

And that's it for overloadings of PUT_LINE! As mentioned above, this overloading is very inadequate. You cannot even ask DBMS_OUTPUT to display a Boolean variable's value, for example. To see such a value, you must write an IF statement, as in:

```
IF l_student_is_registered
THEN
   DBMS_OUTPUT.PUT_LINE ('TRUE');
ELSE
   DBMS_OUTPUT.PUT_LINE ('FALSE');
END IF;
```

Now, isn't that silly? And a big waste of your time? Fortunately, it is very easy to fix this problem. Just build your own package, with lots of overloadings, on top of DBMS_OUTPUT.PUT_LINE. Here is a very abbreviated example of such a package. You can extend it easily, as I do with the do.pl procedure (why type all those characters just to say "show me", right?). A portion of the package specification is shown here:

```
/* File on web: do.pkg */
CREATE OR REPLACE PACKAGE DO
IS
   PROCEDURE pl (boolean_in IN BOOLEAN);

   /* Display a string. */
   PROCEDURE pl (char_in IN VARCHAR2);

   /* Display a string and then a Boolean value. */
   PROCEDURE pl (
      char_in       IN   VARCHAR2,
      boolean_in    IN   BOOLEAN
   );

   PROCEDURE pl (xml_in IN SYS.XMLType);

END DO;
```

This package simply sits on top of DBMS_OUTPUT.PUT_LINE and enhances it. With do.pl, I can now display a Boolean value without writing my own IF statement, as in:

```
DECLARE
   v_is_valid BOOLEAN :=
      book_info.is_valid_isbn ('5-88888-66');
BEGIN
   do.pl (v_is_valid);
```

Better yet, I can get really fancy and even apply do.pl to complex datatypes like the new XMLType:

```
/* File on web: xmltype.sql */
DECLARE
   one_report XMLTYPE;
BEGIN
   SELECT ea.report INTO one_report
     FROM env_analysis ea
    WHERE company = 'SMOKESTAX INC';

   do.pl (one_report);
END;
```

Restrictions on Overloading

There are several restrictions on how you can overload programs. When the PL/SQL engine compiles and runs your program, it has to be able to distinguish between the different overloaded versions of a program; after all, it can't run two different modules at the same time. So when you compile your code, PL/SQL will reject any improperly overloaded modules. It cannot distinguish between the modules by their names, because by definition they are the same in all overloaded programs. Instead, PL/SQL uses the parameter lists of these sibling programs to determine which one to execute and/or the types of the programs (procedure versus function). As a result, the following restrictions apply to overloaded programs.

The datatype family of at least one of the parameters of overloaded programs must differ
: INTEGER, REAL, DECIMAL, FLOAT, etc., are NUMBER subtypes. CHAR, VARCHAR2, and LONG are character subtypes. If the parameters differ only by datatype within the supertype or family of datatypes, PL/SQL does not have enough information to determine the appropriate program to execute.

Overloaded programs with parameter lists that differ only by name must be called using named notation
: If you don't use the name of the argument, how can the compiler distinguish between calls to two overloaded programs? Please note, however, that it is always risky to use named notation as an enforcement paradigm. One should avoid situations where named notation yields different semantic meaning from positional notation.

The parameter list of overloaded programs must differ by more than parameter mode
: Even if a parameter in one version is IN and that same parameter in another version is IN OUT, PL/SQL cannot tell the difference at the point in which the program is called.

Overloaded functions must differ by more than their return type (the datatype specified in the RETURN clause of the function)
: At the time that the overloaded function is called, the compiler doesn't know what type of data that function will return. The compiler therefore cannot determine which version of the function to use if all the parameters are the same.

All of the overloaded programs must be defined within the same PL/SQL scope or block (anonymous block, standalone procedure or function, or package)
: You cannot define one version in one block (scope level) and define another version in a different block. You cannot overload two standalone programs; one simply replaces the other.

Forward Declarations

PL/SQL is rather fussy about its requirement that you declare elements before using them in your code. Otherwise, how can PL/SQL be sure that the way you are using the construct is appropriate? Because modules can call other modules, however, you may encounter situations where it is completely impossible to define all modules before any references to those modules are made. What if program A calls program B and program B calls program A? PL/SQL supports *recursion*, including mutual recursion, in which two or more programs directly or indirectly call each other.

If you find yourself committed to mutual recursion, you will be very glad to hear that PL/SQL supports the *forward declaration* of local modules, which means that modules are declared in advance of the actual definition of that program. This declaration makes that program available to be called by other programs even before the program definition.

Remember that both procedures and functions have a header and a body. A forward declaration consists simply of the program header followed by a semicolon (;). This construction is called the *module header*. This header, which must include the parameter list (and a RETURN clause if it's a function), is all the information PL/SQL needs about a module in order to declare it and resolve any references to it.

The following example illustrates the technique of forward declaration. I define two mutually recursive functions within a procedure. Consequently, I have to declare just the header of my second function, total_cost, before the full declaration of net_profit:

```
PROCEDURE perform_calcs (year_in IN INTEGER)
IS
   /* Header only for total_cost function. */
```

```
   FUNCTION total_cost (...)  RETURN NUMBER;

   /* The net_profit function uses total_cost. */
   FUNCTION net_profit (...) RETURN NUMBER    IS
   BEGIN
      RETURN tot_sales (...) - total_cost (. . .);
   END;

   /* The total_cost function uses net_profit. */
   FUNCTION total_cost (...)  RETURN NUMBER    IS
   BEGIN
      IF <condition based on parameters>
      THEN
         RETURN net_profit (...) * .10;
      ELSE
         RETURN <parameter value>;
      END IF;
   END;
BEGIN
   . . .
END;
```

Here are some rules to remember concerning forward declarations:

- You cannot make forward declarations of a variable or cursor. This technique works only with modules (procedures and functions).
- The definition for a forwardly declared program must be contained in the declaration section of the same PL/SQL block (anonymous block, procedure, function, or package body) in which you code the forward declaration.

In some situations, forward declarations are absolutely required; in most situations, they just help make your code more readable and presentable. As with every other advanced or unusual feature of the PL/SQL language, use forward declarations only when you really need the functionality. Otherwise, the declarations simply add to the clutter of your program, which is the last thing you want.

Advanced Topics

The following sections are most appropriate for experienced PL/SQL programmers. Here, I'll touch on a number of advanced modularization topics, including calling functions in SQL, using table functions, and using deterministic functions.

Calling Your Function Inside SQL

Oracle allows you to call your own custom-built functions from within SQL. In essence, this flexibility allows you to customize the SQL language to adapt to application-specific requirements.

Requirements for calling functions in SQL

There are several requirements that a programmer-defined PL/SQL function must meet in order to be callable from within a SQL statement:

- The function must be stored in the database. A function defined in a client-side PL/SQL environment cannot be called from within SQL; there would be no way for SQL to resolve the reference to the function.
- All of the function's parameters must use the IN mode. Neither IN OUT nor OUT parameters are allowed in SQL-embedded stored functions—you should never have IN OUT and OUT parameters in functions, period. Whether or not you are going to use that function inside a SQL statement, such parameters constitute side effects of the main purpose of the function, which is to return a single value.
- The datatypes of the function's parameters, as well as the datatype of the RETURN clause of the function, must be recognized within the Oracle Server. While all of the Oracle Server datatypes are valid within PL/SQL, PL/SQL has added new datatypes that are not (yet) supported in the database. These datatypes include BOOLEAN, BINARY_INTEGER, associative arrays, PL/SQL records, and programmer-defined subtypes.
- Prior to Oracle8*i*, functions defined in packages must have an associated RESTRICT_REFEFRENCES pragma defined for them. If you want to call from SQL a function defined in a package, you will need to add a pragma to the package specification asserting explicitly that this function is valid for SQL execution. See the later section "The PRAGMA RESTRICT_REFERENCES (Oracle8 and earlier)" for more details on this step.

By default, user-defined functions that execute in SQL operate on a single row of data, not on an entire column of data that crosses rows, as the group functions SUM, MIN, and AVG do. It is possible to write aggregate functions to be called inside SQL, but this requires taking advantage of the ODCIAggregate interface, which is part of Oracle's Extensibility Framework. See the Oracle documentation for more details on this functionality.

Restrictions on user-defined functions in SQL

In order to guard against nasty side effects and unpredictable behavior, the Oracle RDBMS makes it impossible for your stored function in SQL to take any of the following actions:

- The stored function may not modify database tables. It cannot execute an INSERT, DELETE, or UPDATE statement. Note that this restriction is relaxed if your function is defined as an autonomous transaction (described in Chapter 13); in this case, any changes made in your function occur independently of the outer transaction in which the query was executed.

- A stored function that is called remotely or through a parallelized action may not read or write the values of package variables. The Oracle Server does not support side effects that cross user sessions.
- A stored function can update the values of package variables only if that function is called in a select list, or a VALUES or SET clause. If the stored function is called in a WHERE or GROUP BY clause, it cannot write package variables.
- Prior to Oracle8, you cannot call RAISE_APPLICATION_ERROR from within the stored function.
- The stored function may not call another module (stored procedure or function) that breaks any of the preceding rules. A function is only as pure as the most impure module that it calls.
- The stored function may not reference a view that breaks any of the preceding rules. A view is a stored SELECT statement; that view's SELECT may use stored functions.

Replacing DECODEs with IF statements

The DECODE function offers IF-like capabilities in the nonprocedural SQL environment provided by the Oracle Server. You can use the DECODE syntax to create matrix reports with a fixed number of columns or to perform complex IF-THEN-ELSE logic within a query. The downside to DECODE is that it can be difficult to write and very difficult to maintain. Consider the following example of using DECODE to determine whether a date is within the prescribed range and, if so, to add to the count of rows that fulfill this requirement:

```
SELECT FC.year_number,
       SUM (DECODE (GREATEST (ship_date, FC.q1_sdate),
                    ship_date,
                    DECODE (LEAST (ship_date, FC.q1_edate),
                            ship_date, 1,
                            0),
                    0)) Q1_results,
       SUM (DECODE (GREATEST (ship_date, FC.q2_sdate),
                    ship_date,
                    DECODE (LEAST (ship_date, FC.q2_edate),
                            ship_date, 1,
                            0),
                    0)) Q2_results,
       SUM (DECODE (GREATEST (ship_date, FC.q3_sdate),
                    ship_date,
                    DECODE (LEAST (ship_date, FC.q3_edate),
                            ship_date, 1,
                            0),
                    0)) Q3_results,
       SUM (DECODE (GREATEST (ship_date, FC.q4_sdate),
                    ship_date,
                    DECODE (LEAST (ship_date, FC.q4_edate),
                            ship_date, 1,
```

```
                              0),
                         0)) Q4_results
  FROM orders O,
       fiscal_calendar FC
 GROUP BY year_number;
```

The result set for this query might look like this:

```
YEAR NUMBER    Q1 RESULTS    Q2 RESULTS    Q3 RESULTS    Q4 RESULTS
------------   ----------    ----------    ----------    ----------
1993           12000         14005         22000         40000
1994           10000         15000         21000         55004
```

While it is very handy to use DECODE to produce such a report, the SQL required to accomplish the task is more than a little frightening. Here is how you might try to interpret the Q1 RESULTS nested DECODE:

> If the ship date is greater than or equal to the first quarter start date and less than or equal to the first quarter end date, then add one to the sum of the total number of orders shipped in that quarter. Otherwise, add zero.

Unfortunately, unless you are experienced in interpreting DECODE statements, you may find it difficult to glean this understanding from that convoluted SQL statement. The repetition in that single SELECT also cries out for modularization, which we can supply with the following stored function (incr_in_range means "increment if in the range"):

```
FUNCTION incr_in_range
   (ship_date_in IN DATE, sdate_in IN DATE, edate_in IN DATE)
   RETURN INTEGER
IS
BEGIN
   IF ship_date_in BETWEEN sdate_in AND edate_in
   THEN
      RETURN 1;
   ELSE
      RETURN 0;
   END IF;
END;
```

Yep, that's all there is to it! With the incr_in_range function, that long and winding SELECT statement simply becomes:

```
SELECT FC.year_number,
       SUM (incr_in_range (ship_date, q1_sdate, q1_edate)) Q1_results,
       SUM (incr_in_range (ship_date, q2_sdate, q2_edate)) Q2_results,
       SUM (incr_in_range (ship_date, q3_sdate, q3_edate)) Q3_results,
       SUM (incr_in_range (ship_date, q4_sdate, q4_edate)) Q4_results
  FROM orders O,
       fiscal_calendar FC
 GROUP BY year_number;
```

This stored function gets rid of the code redundancy and makes the SELECT statement much more readable. In addition, this function could be used in other SQL statements to perform the same logic.

The PRAGMA RESTRICT_REFERENCES (Oracle8 and earlier)

Prior to Oracle8*i*, if you wanted to invoke within SQL a function that was defined inside a package specification, you would have had to provide a RESTRICT_REFERENCES pragma (a compiler directive or instruction) for that function. This pragma asserts the "purity level" of the function, in essence promising Oracle that the function has the specified side effects (or, more to the point, lack thereof).

Working with the RESTRICT_REFERENCES pragma can be very frustrating, so it was a great relief to many a PL/SQL developer when in Oracle8*i* this pragma was made unnecessary. However, this section talks briefly about some of the rules associated with this pragma for those still using Oracle8 and earlier.

You need a separate PRAGMA statement for each packaged function you wish to use in a SQL statement, and it must come after the function declaration in the package specification. To assert a purity level with the pragma, use the following syntax:

```
PRAGMA RESTRICT_REFERENCES
   (function_name, WNDS [, WNPS] [, RNDS] [, RNPS])
```

where *function_name* is the name of the function whose purity level you wish to assert, and the four codes have the following meanings:

WNDS
: Writes No Database State. Asserts that the function does not modify any database tables.

WNPS
: Writes No Package State. Asserts that the function does not modify any package variables.

RNDS
: Reads No Database State. Asserts that the function does not read any database tables.

RNPS
: Reads No Package State. Asserts that the function does not read any package variables.

Here is an example of two different purity-level assertions for functions in the company_financials package:

```
PACKAGE company_financials
IS
   FUNCTION company_type (type_code_in IN VARCHAR2)
      RETURN VARCHAR2;

   FUNCTION company_name (
      company_id_in IN company.company_id%TYPE)
      RETURN VARCHAR2;

   PRAGMA RESTRICT_REFERENCES (
      company_type, WNDS, RNDS, WNPS, RNPS);
```

```
   PRAGMA RESTRICT_REFERENCES (company_name, WNDS, WNPS, RNPS);
END company_financials;
```

In this package, the company_name function reads from the database to obtain the name for the specified company. Notice that I placed both pragmas together at the bottom of the package specification; the pragma does not need to immediately follow the function specification. I also went to the trouble of specifying the WNPS and RNPS arguments for both functions. Oracle recommends that you assert the highest possible purity levels so that the compiler will never reject the function unnecessarily.

If a function you want to call in SQL calls a procedure or function in a package, you must also provide a RESTRICT_REFERENCES pragma for that program. You cannot call a procedure directly in SQL, but if it is going to be executed indirectly from within SQL, it still must follow the rules.

If your function violates its pragma, you will receive the PLS-00452 error: *subprogram* 'program' *violates its associated pragma*. Suppose, for example, that the body of the company_financials package looks like this:

```
CREATE OR REPLACE PACKAGE BODY company_financials
IS
   FUNCTION company_type (type_code_in IN VARCHAR2)
      RETURN VARCHAR2
   IS
      v_sal NUMBER;
   BEGIN
      SELECT sal INTO v_sal FROM emp WHERE empno = 1;
      RETURN 'bigone';
   END;

   FUNCTION company_name (company_id_in IN company.company_id%TYPE)
      RETURN VARCHAR2
   IS
   BEGIN
      UPDATE emp SET sal = 0;
      RETURN 'bigone';
   END;
END company_financials;
```

When I attempt to compile this package body I will get the following error:

```
3/4     PLS-00452: Subprogram 'COMPANY_TYPE' violates its associated pragma
```

because the company_type function reads from the database and I have asserted the RNDS purity level. If I remove that silly SELECT statement, I will then receive this error:

```
11/4    PLS-00452: Subprogram 'COMPANY_NAME' violates its associated pragma
```

because the company_name function updates the database and I have asserted the WNDS level. You will sometimes look at your function and say, "Hey, I absolutely do not violate my purity level. There is no UPDATE, DELETE, or UPDATE around." Maybe not. But there is a good chance that you are calling a built-in package or in some other way breaking the rules. Again, if you are running Oracle8*i* and above, you no longer need to deal with RESTRICT_REFERENCES. The runtime engine will automatically check your code for any violations.

Table Functions

Oracle8*i* and Oracle9*i* now make it possible for you to write table functions. These functions return a result set (collection) that can be treated like a relational table in the FROM clause of a query (Oracle8*i* and Oracle9*i*). That's why they are called table functions! We'll look at table functions in the following sections, focusing on the special varieties of table functions available in Oracle9*i*:

Pipelined functions
: These functions return a result set in "pipelined fashion," meaning that data is returned while the function is still executing (Oracle9*i*-specific). These pipelined table functions can then be used to "daisy-chain" data transformations without having to rely on local PL/SQL data structures to hold intermediate forms of the data.

Transformative functions
: These functions participate fully in parallel query execution. In other words, table functions of this kind can be run simultaneously within multiple slave processes against different, partitioned elements of data (Oracle9*i*-specific).

Let's explore how to define table functions and put them to use in your application.

Calling a function in a FROM clause

To call a function from within a FROM clause, you must do the following:

- Define the RETURN datatype of the function to be a collection (either a nested table or a VARRAY).
- Make sure that all of the other parameters to the function are of mode IN and have SQL datatypes. (You cannot call a function with a Boolean argument inside a query.)
- Embed the call to the function inside the TABLE and CAST operators.

Here is an example that works for both Oracle8*i* and Oracle9*i*. First, I will create a nested table type based on an object type of pets:

```
CREATE TYPE pet_t IS OBJECT (
   NAME                          VARCHAR2 (60),
   breed                         VARCHAR2 (100),
   dob                           DATE);

CREATE TYPE pet_nt IS TABLE OF pet_t;
```

Now I will create a function named pet_family. It accepts two pet objects as arguments: the mother and the father. Then, based on the breed, it returns a nested table with the entire family defined in the collection:

```
CREATE OR REPLACE FUNCTION pet_family (dad_in IN pet_t, mom_in IN pet_t)
   RETURN pet_nt
IS
   l_count PLS_INTEGER;
   retval   pet_nt := pet_nt ();

   PROCEDURE extend_assign (pet_in IN pet_t) IS
   BEGIN
      retval.EXTEND;
      retval (retval.LAST) := pet_in;
   END;
BEGIN
   extend_assign (dad_in);
   extend_assign (mom_in);

   IF    mom_in.breed = 'RABBIT'   THEN l_count := 12;
   ELSIF mom_in.breed = 'DOG'      THEN l_count := 4;
   ELSIF mom_in.breed = 'KANGAROO' THEN l_count := 1;
   END IF;

   FOR indx IN 1 .. l_count
   LOOP
      extend_assign (pet_t ('BABY' || indx, mom_in.breed, SYSDATE));
   END LOOP;

   RETURN retval;
END;
```

Now I can call this function in the FROM clause of a query, as follows:

```
SQL> SELECT *
  2    FROM TABLE (CAST (
  3                   pet_family (
  4                      pet_t ('Hoppy', 'RABBIT', SYSDATE),
  5                      pet_t ('Hippy', 'RABBIT', SYSDATE)
  6                   ) AS  pet_nt
  7                ));

NAME       BREED      DOB
---------- ---------- ---------
Hoppy      RABBIT     27-FEB-02
Hippy      RABBIT     27-FEB-02
BABY1      RABBIT     27-FEB-02
BABY2      RABBIT     27-FEB-02
...
BABY11     RABBIT     27-FEB-02
BABY12     RABBIT     27-FEB-02
```

This functionality is available in both Oracle8*i* and Oracle9*i;* we'll now explore the additional features new in Oracle9*i*.

Creating a pipelined function

A *pipelined function* is one that returns a result set as a collection, but does so iteratively. In other words, Oracle no longer waits for the function to run to completion, storing all the rows it computes in the PL/SQL collection, before it delivers the first rows. Instead, as each row is ready to be assigned into the collection, it is "piped out" of the function.

Here is a rewrite of the pet_family function as a pipelined function:

```
 1  CREATE FUNCTION pet_family (dad_in IN pet_t, mom_in IN pet_t)
 2     RETURN pet_nt PIPELINED
 3  IS
 4     l_count PLS_INTEGER;
 5     retval   pet_nt := pet_nt ();
 6
 7  BEGIN
 8     PIPE ROW (dad_in);
 9     PIPE ROW (mom_in);
10
11     IF    mom_in.breed = 'RABBIT'   THEN l_count := 12;
12     ELSIF mom_in.breed = 'DOG'      THEN l_count := 4;
13     ELSIF mom_in.breed = 'KANGAROO' THEN l_count := 1;
14     END IF;
15
16     FOR indx IN 1 .. l_count
17     LOOP
18        PIPE ROW (pet_t ('BABY' || indx, mom_in.breed, SYSDATE));
19     END LOOP;
20
21     RETURN;
22  END;
```

The following table notes several changes to our original functionality:

Line(s)	Description
2	The PIPELINED keyword is necessary to tell Oracle that rows are to be returned iteratively.
8, 9, 18	Rather than assign rows of data to the collection, you simply prepare the row of information (it must have the same structure as a row in the collection type specified in the RETURN clause of the function) and then use PIPE ROW to pipe it back out of the function.
21	An unqualified RETURN (formerly allowed only in procedures) is used in pipelined functions. Nothing is actually returned at this point, except control to the calling block.

I can invoke a pipelined function within a SQL statement (as you already saw) or I can use a simpler syntax:

```
SELECT *
  FROM TABLE (pet_family (
                 pet_t ('Bob', 'KANGAROO', SYSDATE),
                 pet_t ('Sally', 'KANGAROO', SYSDATE)));
```

In other words, I no longer need to employ the CAST AS syntax to explicitly cast into a recognized database collection type.

So what is the advantage of a pipelined function? If your application can take advantage of or needs to start working with rows of data before the entire set has been identified, then a pipelined function can make an enormous difference. At the end of the next section, we'll present a script that performs a comparison of performance.

Building a transformative function

A *transformative function* is a pipelined function that accepts as a parameter a result set (via a CURSOR expression) and returns a result set. This functionality is also new to Oracle9*i* and can have a very positive effect on application performance.

You can define a table function with an IN argument of type REF CURSOR and call it with a CURSOR expression as the actual parameter—all inside a SQL statement. This technique allows you to "pipe" data from one function to the next, or from one SQL operation to the next, without needing to rely on any intermediate storage of data. Here is an example of how you can use this functionality:

All the code shown here may be found in the *tabfunc.sql* script on the O'Reilly site.

Consider the following scenario. I have a table of stock ticker information that contains a single row for the openand close prices of stock:

```
CREATE TABLE StockTable (
  ticker VARCHAR2(10),
  open_price NUMBER,
  close_price NUMBER);
```

I need to transform (or *pivot*) that information into another table:

```
CREATE TABLE TickerTable (
  ticker VARCHAR2(10),
  PriceType VARCHAR2(1),
  price NUMBER);
```

In other words, a single row in StockTable becomes two rows in TickerTable.

There are many ways to achieve this goal. For example, when using traditional methods in pre-Oracle9*i* versions of the database, I could write code like this:

```
FOR rec IN  (SELECT * FROM stocktable)
LOOP
   INSERT INTO tickertable
               (ticker, pricetype, price)
        VALUES (rec.ticker, 'O', rec.open_price);

   INSERT INTO tickertable
               (ticker, pricetype, price)
        VALUES (rec.ticker, 'C', rec.close_price);
END LOOP;
```

It works, but for very large volumes of data, perhaps it is not as efficient as it could be. Let's see if I can use a transformative function to do the job more quickly.

I create a collection type to use in my function:

```
CREATE TYPE TickerType AS OBJECT (
  ticker VARCHAR2(10),
  PriceType VARCHAR2(1),
  price NUMBER);

CREATE TYPE TickerTypeSet AS TABLE OF TickerType;
```

I then create a package defining a REF CURSOR type based on this collection type. I do this in a package specification so that it can be referenced by my function:

```
CREATE OR REPLACE PACKAGE refcur_pkg
IS
   TYPE refcur_t IS REF CURSOR
      RETURN StockTable%ROWTYPE;
END refcur_pkg;
```

And here is my stock pivot function:

```
CREATE OR REPLACE FUNCTION StockPivot (
   p refcur_pkg.refcur_t) RETURN TickerTypeSet
   PIPELINED
IS
  out_rec TickerType := TickerType(NULL,NULL,NULL);
  in_rec p%ROWTYPE;
BEGIN
  LOOP
    FETCH p INTO in_rec;
    EXIT WHEN p%NOTFOUND;

    -- first row
    out_rec.ticker := in_rec.Ticker;
    out_rec.PriceType := 'O';
    out_rec.price := in_rec.Open_Price;
    PIPE ROW(out_rec);

    -- second row
    out_rec.PriceType := 'C';
    out_rec.Price := in_rec.Close_Price;
    PIPE ROW(out_rec);
  END LOOP;
  CLOSE p;
  RETURN ;
END;
```

And here is that same function defined in a nonpipelined way:

```
CREATE OR REPLACE FUNCTION StockPivot_nopl (
   p refcur_pkg.refcur_t)
   RETURN TickerTypeSet
IS
  out_rec TickerType := TickerType(NULL,NULL,NULL);
```

```
    in_rec p%ROWTYPE;
    retval TickerTypeSet := TickerTypeSet( );
  BEGIN
    retval.DELETE;
    LOOP
      FETCH p INTO in_rec;
      EXIT WHEN p%NOTFOUND;
      out_rec.ticker := in_rec.Ticker;

      out_rec.PriceType := 'O';
      out_rec.price := in_rec.Open_Price;
      retval.EXTEND;
      retval(retval.LAST) := out_rec;

      out_rec.PriceType := 'C';
      out_rec.Price := in_rec.Close_Price;
      retval.EXTEND;
      retval(retval.LAST) := out_rec;

    END LOOP;
    CLOSE p;
    RETURN retval;
  END;
```

So many different approaches to solving the same problem! How does one choose among them? Well, if you have lots of data to process, you will certainly want to choose the most efficient implementation. You will find in the *tabfunc.sql* file* an anonymous block that compares the performance of the following four approaches:

- A direct insert from SELECT using the pipelined function:

```
INSERT INTO tickertable
   SELECT *
     FROM TABLE (StockPivot (CURSOR(SELECT * FROM StockTable)));
```

- A direct insert from SELECT using the nonpipelined function:

```
INSERT INTO tickertable
   SELECT *
    FROM TABLE (StockPivot_nopl (CURSOR(SELECT * FROM StockTable)));
```

- A deposit of pivoted data into a local collection. You can then use a simple loop to transfer the collection's contents to the table:

```
OPEN curvar FOR
   SELECT * FROM stocktable;
mystock := stockpivot_nopl (curvar);
indx := mystock.FIRST;

LOOP
   EXIT WHEN indx IS NULL;
```

* The *tabfunc.sql* file relies on the PL/Vision timer mechanism, PLVtmr, to calculate elapsed time. You can install this package by running the *:plvtmr.pkg* script.

```
      INSERT INTO tickertable
                (ticker, pricetype, price)
         VALUES (mystock (indx).ticker, mystock (indx).pricetype,
                 mystock (indx).price);

   END LOOP;
```

- The "old-fashioned" method. Use a cursor FOR loop to expand each single row from stocktable into the two rows of the tickertable:

```
      FOR rec IN  (SELECT * FROM stocktable)
      LOOP
         INSERT INTO tickertable
                  (ticker, pricetype, price)
              VALUES (rec.ticker, 'O', rec.open_price);

         INSERT INTO tickertable
                  (ticker, pricetype, price)
              VALUES (rec.ticker, 'C', rec.close_price);
      END LOOP;
```

When I execute the block comparing these four aproaches in my SQL*Plus session, I see these results:

```
All SQL with Pipelining function Elapsed: 2.47 seconds.
All SQL with non-pipelining function Elapsed: 1.78 seconds.
Intermediate collection Elapsed: 6.71 seconds.
Cursor FOR Loop and two inserts Elapsed: 6.9 seconds.
```

I draw two conclusions from this output:

- The ability of the table function (whether pipelined or regular) to transform data "in-line" (i.e., within a single SQL statement) noticeably improves performance.
- Pipelining doesn't help us in this scenario; it actually seems to slow things down a bit. In fact, I am not really taking advantage of pipelining in this code. In all cases, I am waiting until the logic has executed to completion before I do anything with my data (or compute elapsed time).

I would expect (or hope, at least) to see some improvement in elapsed time when executing this logic in parallel or, more generally, when we get the first *N* number of rows and start processing them before all of the data has been retrieved. The file *tabfunc.sql* offers a simulation of such a scenario.

I compare the time it takes to execute each of these statements:

```
-- With pipelining
INSERT INTO tickertable
   SELECT *
     FROM TABLE (StockPivot (CURSOR(SELECT * FROM StockTable)))
WHERE ROWNUM < 10;

-- Without pipelining
INSERT INTO tickertable
   SELECT *
```

```
    FROM TABLE (StockPivot_nopl (CURSOR(SELECT * FROM StockTable)))
WHERE ROWNUM < 10;
```

And the contrasting timings are very interesting:

```
Pipelining first 10 rows Elapsed: .08 seconds.
No pipelining first 10 rows Elapsed: 1.77 seconds.
```

Clearly, piping rows back does work and does make a difference!

Enabling a function for parallel execution

One enormous step forward for PL/SQL in Oracle9*i* is the ability to execute functions within a parallel query context. Prior to Oracle9*i*, a call to a PL/SQL function inside SQL caused serialization of that query—a major problem for data warehousing applications. With Oracle9*i*, you can now add information to the function header to instruct the runtime engine how that function can and should be used.

In general, if you would like your function to execute in parallel, it must have a single, strongly typed REF CURSOR input parameter.* Here are some examples:

- Specify that the function can run in parallel and that the data passed to that function can be partitioned arbitrarily:

  ```
  CREATE OR REPLACE FUNCTION my_transform_fn (
       p_input_rows in employee_info.recur_t )
    RETURN employee_info.transformed_t
    PIPELINED
    PARALLEL_ENABLE ( PARTITION p_input_rows BY ANY )
  ```

  In this example, the keyword ANY expresses the programmer's assertion that the results are independent of the order in which the function gets the input rows. When this keyword is used, the runtime system randomly partitions the data among the query slaves. This keyword is appropriate for use with functions that take in one row, manipulate its columns, and generate output rows based on the columns of this row only. If your program has other dependencies, the outcome will be unpredictable.

- Specify that the function can run in parallel, that all the rows for a given department go to the same slave, and that all of these rows are delivered consecutively:

  ```
  CREATE OR REPLACE FUNCTION my_transform_fn (
       p_input_rows in employee_info.recur_t )
    RETURN employee_info.transformed_t
    PIPELINED
    CLUSTER P_INPUT_ROWS BY (department)
    PARALLEL_ENABLE
      ( PARTITION P_INPUT_ROWS BY HASH (department) )
  ```

  Oracle uses the term *clustered* to signify this type of delivery, and *cluster key* for the column (in this case, "department") on which the aggregation is done. But

* The input REF CURSOR need *not* be strongly typed to be partitioned by ANY.

significantly, the algorithm does *not* care in what order of cluster key it receives each successive cluster, and Oracle doesn't guarantee any particular order here. This allows for a quicker algorithm than if rows were required to be clustered and delivered in the order of the cluster key. It scales as *order N* rather than *order N.log(N)*, where *N* is the number of rows.

In this example, we can choose between HASH (department) and RANGE (department), depending on what we know about the distribution of the values. HASH is quicker than RANGE and is the natural choice to be used with CLUSTER...BY.

- Specify that the function can run in parallel and that the rows that are delivered to a particular slave process, as directed by PARTITION... BY (for that specified partition), will be locally sorted by that slave. The effect will be to parallelize the sort:

```
CREATE OR REPLACE FUNCTION my_transform_fn (
   p_input_rows in employee_info.recur_t )
RETURN employee_info.transformed_t
PIPELINED
ORDER P_INPUT_ROWS BY (C1)
PARALLEL_ENABLE
  ( PARTITION P_INPUT_ROWS BY RANGE (C1) )
```

Because the sort is parallelized, there should be no ORDER...BY in the SELECT used to invoke the table function. (In fact, an ORDER...BY clause in the SELECT statement would subvert the attempt to parallelize the sort.) Thus it's natural to use the RANGE option together with the ORDER...BY option. This will be slower than CLUSTER...BY, and so should be used only when the algorithm depends on it.

The CLUSTER...BY construct can't be used together with the ORDER...BY in the declaration of a table function. This means that an algorithm that depends on clustering on one key, c1, and then on ordering within the set row for a given value of c1 by, say, c2, would have to be parallelized by using the ORDER ... BY in the declaration in the table function.

Deterministic Functions

A function is called *deterministic* if it returns the same result value whenever it is called with the same values for its arguments. The following function (a simple encapsulation on top of SUBSTR) is such a function:

```
CREATE OR REPLACE FUNCTION betwnStr (
   string_in IN VARCHAR2,start_in IN INTEGER, end_in IN INTEGER
   )
   RETURN VARCHAR2 IS
BEGIN
   RETURN (
```

```
      SUBSTR (
         string_in, start_in, end_in - start_in + 1));
END;
```

As long as I pass in, for example, "abcdef" for the string, 3 for the start, and 5 for the end, betwnStr will always return "cde". Now, if that is the case, why not have Oracle save the results associated with a set of arguments? Then when I next call the function with those arguments, it can return the result without executing the function!

You can achieve this effect by adding the DETERMINISTIC clause to the function's header, as in the following:

```
CREATE OR REPLACE FUNCTION betwnStr (
   string_in IN VARCHAR2,start_in IN INTEGER, end_in IN INTEGER
   )
   RETURN VARCHAR2 DETERMINISTIC IS
BEGIN
   RETURN (
      SUBSTR (
         string_in, start_in, end_in - start_in + 1));
END;
```

The decision to use a saved copy of the function's return result (if such a copy is available) is made by the Oracle query optimizer. Saved copies can come from a materialized view, a function-based index, or a repetitive call to the same function in the same SQL statement.

You must declare a function DETERMINISTIC in order for it to be called in the expression of a function-based index, or from the query of a materialized view if that view is marked REFRESH FAST or ENABLE QUERY REWRITE.

Oracle has no way of reliably checking to make sure that the function you declare to be deterministic actually is free of any side effects. It is up to you to use this feature responsibly. Your deterministic function should not rely on package variables, nor should it access the database in a way that might affect the result set.

Go Forth and Modularize!

As the PL/SQL language and Oracle tools mature, you will find that you are being asked to implement increasingly complex applications with this technology. To be quite frank, you don't have much chance of success with such large-scale projects without an intimate familiarity with the modularization techniques available in PL/SQL.

While this book cannot possibly provide a full treatment of modularization in PL/SQL, it should give you some solid pointers and a foundation on which to build. There is still much more for you to learn: the full capabilities of packages, the awesome range of package extensions that Oracle now provides with the tools and database, the various options for code reusability, and more.

Behind all that technology, however, you must develop an instinct, a sixth sense, for modularization. Develop a deep and abiding allergy to code redundancy and to the hardcoding of values and formulas. Apply a fanatic's devotion to the modular construction of true black boxes that easily plug-and-play in and across applications.

You will find yourself spending more time in the design phase and less time in debug mode. Your programs will be more readable and more maintainable. They will stand as elegant testimonies to your intellectual integrity. You will be the most popular kid in the class. But enough already! I am sure you are properly motivated.

Go forth and modularize!

In this chapter:

CHAPTER 17
Packages

A *package* is a grouping or packaging of PL/SQL code elements. Packages provide a structure (both logically and physically) in which you can organize your programs and other PL/SQL elements such as cursors, TYPEs, and variables. They also offer significant, unique functionality, including the ability to "hide" logic and data from view, and to define and manipulate "global" or session-persistent data.

In the first two editions of this book, I wrote that "Packages are among the least understood and most underutilized features of PL/ SQL. That is a shame, because the package structure is also one of the most useful constructs for building well-designed PL/SQL-based applications." Fortunately, only the second of these statements is still true. Over the years, many developers have come to recognize and take advantage of the power of packages.

Why Packages?

The package is a powerful and important element of the PL/SQL language. It should be the cornerstone of any complex application development project. What makes the package so powerful and important? Consider the following advantages of the use of packages:

Easier enhancement and maintenance of applications

As more and more of the production PL/SQL code base moves into maintenance mode, the quality of PL/SQL applications will be measured as much by the ease of maintenance as it is by overall performance. Packages can make a *big* difference in this regard. From data encapsulation (hiding all calls to SQL statements behind a procedural interface to avoid repetition), to enumerating constants for literal or "magic" values, to grouping together logically related functionality, package-driven design and implementation lead to far fewer points of failure in an application.

Improved overall application performance

By using packages, you can improve the performance of your code in a number of ways. Persistent package data can dramatically improve the response time of queries by caching (and not requerying) static data. Oracle's memory management with packages optimizes access to compiled code (see Chapter 20 for more details).

Ability to shore up application or built-in weaknesses

It is quite straightforward to construct a package on top of existing functionality where there are drawbacks. (Consider, for example, the UTL_FILE and DBMS_OUTPUT built-in packages in which crucial functionality is badly or partially implemented.) You don't have to accept these weaknesses; instead, you can build your own package on top of Oracle's to correct as many of the problems as possible. For example, the *do.pkg* script we'll look at later in this chapter offers a substitute for the DBMS_OUTPUT.PUT_LINE built-in that adds an overloading for the XMLType datatype. Sure, you can get some of the same effect with standalone procedures or functions, but overloading and other package features make this approach vastly preferable

Packages are conceptually very simple. The challenge, I have found, is to figure out how to fully exploit them in an application. As a first step, we'll take a look at a simple package and see how, even in that basic code, we can reap many of the benefits of packages. Then we'll look at the special syntax used to define packages.

Before diving in, however, I would like to make an overall recommendation:

Always construct your application around packages; avoid standalone procedures and functions. Even if today you think that only one procedure is needed for a certain area of functionality, in the future you will almost certainly have two, then three, and then a dozen. At which point you will find yourself saying, "Gee, I should really collect those together in a package!" Which is fine, except that now you have to go back to all the invocations of those unpackaged procedures and functions and add in the "PACKAGE." prefix. So start with a package and save yourself the trouble!

Demonstrating the Power of the Package

A package consists of up to two chunks of code: the *specification* (required) and the *body* (optional, but almost always present). The specification defines how a developer can use the package: which programs can be called, what cursors can be opened, and so on. The body contains the implementation of the programs (and, perhaps, cursors) listed in the specification, plus other code elements as needed.

Suppose that I need to write code to retrieve the "full name" of an employee whose name is in the form "last, first." That seems easy enough to write out:

```
CREATE OR REPLACE PROCEDURE process_employee (
   employee_id_in IN employee.employee_id%TYPE)
IS
   l_fullname VARCHAR2(100);
BEGIN
   SELECT last_name || ',' || first_name
     INTO l_fullname
     FROM employee
    WHERE employee_id = employee_id_in;
    ...
END;
```

Yet there are many problems lurking in this seemingly transparent code:

- I have hardcoded the length of the fullname variable. I did this because it is a *derived* value, the concatenation of two column values. I did not, therefore, have a column against which I could %TYPE the declaration. This could cause difficulties over time if the last_name or first_name columns are expanded.
- I have also hardcoded or explicitly placed in this block the *formula* (an application rule, really) for creating a full name. What's wrong with that, you wonder? What if next week I get a call from the users: "We want to see the names in first-space-last format." Yikes! Time to hunt through all my code for the last-comma-first constructions.
- Finally, this very common query will likely appear in a variety of formats in multiple places in my application. This SQL redundancy can make it very hard to maintain my logic—and optimize its performance.

What's a developer to do? I would like to be able to change the way I write my code to avoid the above hardcodings. To do that, I need to write these things once (one definition of a "full name" datatype, one representation of the formula, one version of the query) and then call them wherever needed. Packages to the rescue!

Take a look at the following package specification:

```
   /* File on web: fullname.pkg */
 1 CREATE OR REPLACE PACKAGE employee_pkg
 2 AS
 3     SUBTYPE fullname_t IS VARCHAR2 (200);
 4
 5     FUNCTION fullname (
 6        last_in  employee.last_name%TYPE,
 7        first_in  employee.first_name%TYPE)
 8        RETURN fullname_t;
 9
10     FUNCTION fullname (
11        employee_id_in IN employee.employee_id%TYPE)
12        RETURN fullname_t;
13 END employee_pkg;
```

What I have done here is essentially *list* the different elements I want to use. On line 3, I declare a "new" datatype using SUBTYPE called fullname_t. It is currently defined to have a maximum of 200 characters, but that can be easily changed if needed.

I then declare a function called fullname (lines 5 through 8). It accepts a last name and a first name and returns the full name. Notice that the way the full name is constructed is not visible in the package specification. That's a good thing, as you will soon see.

Finally, on lines 10–12, I have a second function, also called fullname; this version accepts a primary key for an employee and returns the full name for that employee. This repetition is an example of *overloading*, which we explored in Chapter 16.

Now, before I even show you the implementation of this package, let's rewrite the original block of code using my packaged elements (notice the use of dot notation, which is very similar to its use in the form *table.column)*:

```
DECLARE
   l_name employee_pkg.fullname_t;
   employee_id_in   employee.employee_id%type := 1;
BEGIN
   l_name := employee_pkg.fullname (employee_id_in);
   ...
END;
```

I declare my variable using the new datatype, and then simply call the appropriate function to do all the work for me. The name formula and the SQL query have been moved from my application code to a separate "container" holding employee-specific functionality. The code is cleaner and simpler. If I need to change the formula for last name or expand the total size of the full name datatype, I can go to the package specification or body, make the changes, and recompile any affected code, and the code will automatically take on the updates.

Speaking of the package body, here is the implementation of employee_pkg:

```
CREATE OR REPLACE PACKAGE BODY employee_pkg
AS
   FUNCTION fullname (
      last_in employee.last_name%TYPE,
      first_in employee.first_name%TYPE
   )
      RETURN fullname_t
   IS
   BEGIN
      RETURN   last_in || ',' || first_in;
   END;

   FUNCTION fullname (employee_id_in IN employee.employee_id%TYPE)
      RETURN fullname_t
   IS
      retval   fullname_t;
   BEGIN
      SELECT fullname (last_name, first_name) INTO retval
```

```
19          FROM employee
20         WHERE employee_id = employee_id_in;
21
22        RETURN retval;
23     EXCEPTION
24        WHEN NO_DATA_FOUND THEN RETURN NULL;
25
26        WHEN TOO_MANY_ROWS THEN errpkg.record_and_stop;
27     END;
28  END employee_pkg;
```

Lines 3–11 are nothing but a function wrapper around the last-comma-first formula. Lines 13–27 showcase a typical single-row query lookup built around an implicit query. Notice, though, that on line 18, the query calls that self-same fullname function to return the combination of the two name components.

So now if my users call and say "first-space-last, please!", I will not groan and work late into the night, hunting down occurrences of || ', ' ||. Instead, I will change the implementation of my employee_pkg.fullname in about five seconds flat and astound my users by announcing that they are good to go.

And that, dear friends, gives you some sense of the beauty and power of packages.

Some Package-Related Concepts

Before diving into the details of package syntax and structure, you should be familiar with a few concepts:

Information hiding
: Information hiding is the practice of removing from view information about one's system or application. Why would a developer ever want to hide information? Couldn't it get lost? Information hiding is actually quite a valuable principle and coding technique. First of all, humans can deal with only so much complexity at a time. A number of researchers have demonstrated that remembering more than seven (plus or minus two) items in a group for example, is challenging for the average human brain (this is known as the "human hrair limit," a term that comes from the book *Watership Down*). By hiding unnecessary detail, you can focus on the important stuff. Second, not everyone needs to know—or should be allowed to know—all the details. I might need to call a function that calculates CEO compensation, but the formula itself could very well be confidential. In addition, if the formula changes, the code is insulated from that change.

Public and private
: Closely related to information hiding is the fact that packages are built around the concepts of public and private elements. *Public* code is defined in the package specification and is available to any schema that has EXECUTE authority on the package. *Private* code, on the other hand, is defined in and visible only from

within the package. External programs using the package cannot see or use private code.

When you build a package, you decide which of the package elements are public and which are private. You also can hide all the details of the package body from the view of other schemas/developers. In this way, you use the package to hide the implementation details of your programs. This is most important when you want to isolate the most volatile aspects of your application, such as platform dependencies, frequently changing data structures, and temporary workarounds.

Package specification
: The package specification contains the definition or specification of all the publicly available elements in the package that may be referenced outside of the package. The specification is like one big declaration section; it does not contain any PL/SQL blocks or executable code. If a specification is well designed, a developer can learn from it everything necessary to use the package. There should never be any need to go "behind" the interface of the specification and look at the implementation, which is in the body.

Package body
: The body of the package contains all the code required to implement elements defined in the package specification. The body may also contain private elements, which do not appear in the specification and therefore cannot be referenced outside of the package. The body of the package resembles a standalone module's declaration section. It contains both declarations of variables and the definitions of all package modules. The package body may also contain an execution section, which is called the *initialization section* because it is run only once, to initialize the package.

Initialization
: Initialization should not be a new concept for a programmer. In the context of packages, however, it takes on a specific meaning. Rather than initializing the value of a single variable, you can initialize the entire package with arbitrarily complex code. Oracle takes responsibility for making sure that the package is initialized only once per session.

Session persistence
: As a database programmer, the concept of persistence should also be familiar. After all, a database is all about persistence: I insert a row into the database on Monday, fly to the Bahamas for the rest of the week, and when I return to work on the following Monday, my row is still in the database. It persisted!

Another kind of persistence is *session persistence*. This means that if I connect to Oracle (establish a session) and execute a program that assigns a value to a package-level variable (i.e., a variable declared in a package, outside of any program in the package), that variable is set to persist for the length of my session, and it retains its value even if the program that performed the assignment has ended.

It turns out that the package is the construct that offers support in the Oracle PL/SQL language for session-persistent data structures.

Diagramming Privacy

Let's go back to the public-private dichotomy for a moment. The distinction drawn between public and private elements in a package gives PL/SQL developers unprecedented control over their data structures and programs. A fellow named Grady Booch came up with a visual way to describe this aspect of a package (now called, naturally, the *Booch diagram*).

Take a look at Figure 17-1. Notice the two labels "inside" and "outside." "Outside" consists of all the programs you write that are *not* a part of the package at hand (the *external programs*). "Inside" consists of the package body (the internals or implementation of the package).

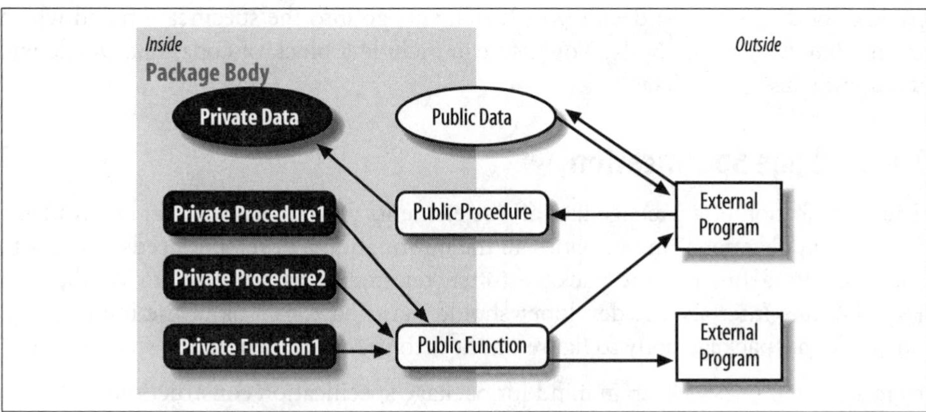

Figure 17-1. Booch diagram showing public and private package elements

Here are the conclusions we can draw from the Booch diagram:

- External programs cannot cross the boundary from outside to inside. That is, an external program may not reference or call any elements defined inside the package. They are private and invisible outside of the package.
- Those elements defined in the package specification (labeled "public" in the figure) straddle the boundary between inside and outside. These programs can be called by an external program (from the outside), can be called or referenced by a private program, and can, in turn, call or reference any other element in the package.

- Public elements of the package therefore offer the only path to the inside of the package. In this way, the package specification acts as a control mechanism for the package as a whole.
- If you find that a formerly private object (such as a module or a cursor) should instead be made public, simply add that object to the package specification and recompile. It will then be visible outside of the package.

Rules for Building Packages

The package is a deceptively simple construct. In a small amount of time, you can learn all the basic elements of package syntax and rules, but you can spend weeks (or more) uncovering all the nuances and implications of the package structure. In this section, we review the rules you need to know in order to build packages. Later in the chapter, we'll take a look at the circumstances under which you will want to build packages.

To construct a package, you must build a specification and, in almost every case, a package body. You must decide which elements go into the specification and which are hidden away in the body. You also can include a block of code that Oracle will use to initialize the package.

The Package Specification

The specification of a package lists all the elements in that package that are available for use in applications, and provides all the information a developer needs in order to use elements defined in the package (often referred to as an "API" or Application Programming Interface). A developer should never have to look at the implementation code in a package body to figure out how to use an element in the specification.

Here are some rules to keep in mind for package specification construction:

- You can declare variables and constants of almost any datatype, such as numbers, strings, and collections, at the package level (i.e., not within a particular procedure or function in the package). This is referred to as *package-level data*; generally, you should avoid declaring variables in the package specification, although constants are always "safe."

  You cannot declare cursor variables (variables defined from a REF CURSOR type) in a package specification (or body). Cursor variables are not allowed to *persist* at the session level (see "Working with Package Data" for more information about package data persistence).
- You can declare almost any type of data structure, such as a collection type, a record type, or a REF CURSOR type.

- You can declare procedures and functions in a package specification, but you can include only the header of the program (everything up to but not including the IS or AS keyword).
- You can include explicit cursors in the package specification. An explicit cursor can take one of two forms: it can include the SQL query as a part of the cursor declaration, or you can "hide" the query inside the package body and provide only a RETURN clause in the cursor declaration. This topic is covered in more detail in the section "Working with packaged cursors."
- If you declare any procedures or functions in the package specification or if you declare a CURSOR without its query, then you *must* provide a package body in order to implement those code elements.
- You can include an AUTHID clause in a package specification, which determines whether any references to data objects will be resolved according to the privileges of the owner of the package (AUTHID DEFINER) or of the invoker of the package (AUTHID CURRENT_USER). See Chapter 20 for more information on this feature.
- You can include an optional package name label after the END statement of the package, as in:

  ```
  END my_package;
  ```

Here is a very simple package specification illustrating these rules:

```
CREATE OR REPLACE PACKAGE favorites_pkg
   AUTHID CURRENT_USER
IS
   -- Two constants; notice that I give understandable
   -- names to otherwise obscure values.

   c_chocolate CONSTANT PLS_INTEGER := 16;
   c_strawberry CONSTANT PLS_INTEGER := 29;

   -- A nested table TYPE declaration
   TYPE codes_nt IS TABLE OF INTEGER;

   -- A nested table declared from the generic type.
   my_favorites codes_nt;

   -- A REF CURSOR returning favorites information.
   TYPE fav_info_rct IS REF CURSOR RETURN favorites%ROWTYPE;

   -- A procedure that accepts a list of favorites
   -- (using a type defined above) and displays the
   -- favorite information from that list.
   PROCEDURE show_favorites (list_in IN codes_nt);

   -- A function that returns all the information in
   -- the favorites table about the most popular item.
```

```
    FUNCTION most_popular RETURN fav_info_rct;

END favorites_pkg; -- End label for package
```

As you can see, a package specification is, in structure, essentially the same as a declaration section of a PL/SQL block. One difference, however, is that a package specification may *not* contain any implementation code.

The Package Body

The package body contains all the code required to implement the package specification. A package body is not always needed; see "When to Use Packages" for examples of package specifications without bodies. A package body is required when any of the following conditions is true:

The package specification contains a cursor declaration with a RETURN clause
: You will then need to specify the SELECT statement in the package body.

The package specification contains a procedure or function declaration
: You will then need to complete the implementation of that module in the package body.

You wish to execute code in the initialization section of the package body
: The package specification does not support an execution section (executable statements within a BEGIN...END); you can do this only in the body.

Structurally, a package body is very similar to a procedure definition. Here are some rules particular to package bodies:

- A package body can have declaration, execution, and exception sections. The declaration section contains the complete implementation of any cursors and programs defined in the specification, and also the definition of any private elements (not listed in the specification). The declaration section can be empty as long as there is an initialization section.
- The execution section of a package is known as the *initialization section*; this optional code is executed when the package is instantiated for a session. We discuss this topic in the following section.
- The exception section handles any exceptions raised in the initialization section. You can have an exception section at the bottom of a package body only if you have defined an initialization section.
- A package body may consist of the following combinations: just a declaration section; just an execution section; execution and exception sections; or declaration, execution, and exception sections.
- You may not include an AUTHID clause in the package body; it must go in the package specification. Anything declared in the specification may be referenced (used) within the package body.

- The same rules and restrictions for declaring package-level data structures apply to the body as well as to the specification—for example, you cannot declare a cursor variable.
- You can include an optional package name label after the END statement of the package, as in:

```
END my_package;
```

Here is an implementation of the favorites_pkg body:

```
CREATE OR REPLACE PACKAGE BODY favorites_pkg
IS
   -- A private variable
   g_most_popular   PLS_INTEGER := c_strawberry;

   -- Implementation of procedure
   PROCEDURE show_favorites (list_in IN codes_nt) IS
   BEGIN
      FOR indx IN list_in.FIRST .. list_in.LAST
      LOOP
         DBMS_OUTPUT.put_line (list_in (indx));
      END LOOP;
   END show_favorites;

   -- Implement the function
   FUNCTION most_popular RETURN fav_info_rct
   IS
      retval fav_info_rct;
      null_cv fav_info_rct;
   BEGIN
      OPEN retval FOR
      SELECT *
        FROM favorites
       WHERE code = g_most_popular;
      RETURN retval;
   EXCEPTION
      WHEN NO_DATA_FOUND THEN RETURN null_cv;
   END most_popular;

END favorites_pkg; -- End label for package
```

See the section "When to Use Packages" for other examples of package bodies.

Initializing Packages

Packages can contain data structures that persist for your entire session (this topic is covered in more detail in the later section "Working with Package Data"). The first time your session makes use of a package (whether by calling a program defined in the package, reading or writing a variable, or using a locally declared variable TYPE), Oracle initializes that package. This involves one or all of the following steps:

1. Instantiate any package-level data (such as a number variable or a string constant).
2. Assign default values to variables and constants as specified in their declarations.
3. Execute a block of code, called the *initialization section*, that is specifically designed to "initialize" the package, complementing the preceding steps.

Oracle executes these steps just once per session, and not until you need that information (i.e., on the "first touch" of that package).

A package may be reinitialized in a session if that package was recompiled since last use or if the package state for your entire session was reset, as is indicated by the following error:

```
ORA-04068: existing state of packages has been discarded
```

The initialization section of a package consists of all the statements following the BEGIN statement at the end of the package (and outside any procedure or function's definitions) and through to the END statement for the entire package body. Here is what an initialization section in favorites_pkg might look like:

```
CREATE OR REPLACE PACKAGE BODY favorites_pkg
IS
   g_most_popular   PLS_INTEGER;

   PROCEDURE show_favorites (list_in IN codes_nt) ... END;

   FUNCTION most_popular RETURN fav_info_rct ... END;

   PROCEDURE analyze_favorites (year_in IN INTEGER) ... END;

-- Initialization section
BEGIN
   g_most_popular := c_chocolate;

   -- Use new Oracle9i EXTRACT to get year number from SYSDATE!
   analyze_favorites (EXTRACT (YEAR FROM SYSDATE));
END favorites_pkg;
```

The initialization section is a powerful mechanism: PL/SQL automatically detects when this code should be run. You do not have to explicitly execute the statements, and you can be sure that they are run only once. Why would you use an initialization section? The following sections explore some specific reasons.

Execute complex initialization logic

You can, of course, assign default values to package data directly in the declaration statement. This approach has several possible problems:

- The logic required to set the default value may be quite complex and not easily invoked as a default value assignment.

- If the assignment of the default value raises an exception, that exception cannot be trapped within the package: it will instead propagate out unhandled. This issue is covered in more detail in the section "When initialization fails."

Using the initialization section to initialize data offers several advantages over default value assignments. First, you have the full flexibility of an execution section in which to define, structure, and document your steps; and, if an exception is raised, you can handle it within the initialization section's exception section.

Cache static session information

Another great motivation for including an initialization section in your package is to cache information that is static (unchanging) throughout the duration of your session. If the data values don't change, why endure the overhead of querying or recalculating those values again and again?

In addition, if you want to make sure that the information is retrieved just once in your session, then the initialization section is an ideal, automatically managed way to get this to happen.

There is an important and typical tradeoff when working with cached package data: memory versus CPU. By caching data in package variables, you can improve the elapsed time performance of data retrieval. This is accomplished by moving the data closer to the user, into the Program Global Area of *each* user. If there are 1000 distinct sessions, then there are 1000 copies of the cached data. This agreement decreases the CPU usage, but takes up more memory.

See the section "Caching Static Session Data" near the end of this chapter for more details on this technique.

Avoid side effects when initializing

Avoid setting the values of global data in other packages within the initialization section (or anywhere else in those other packages, for that matter). This precaution can prevent havoc in code execution and potential confusion for maintenance programmers. Keep the initialization section code focused on the current package. Remember that this code is executed whenever your application first tries to use a package element. You don't want your users sitting idle while the package performs some snazzy, expensive setup computations that could be parceled out to different packages or triggers in the application.

```
CREATE OR REPLACE PACKAGE BODY company IS
BEGIN
   /*
   || Initialization section of company_pkg updates the global
   || package data of a different package. This is a no-no!
   */
   SELECT SUM (salary)
     INTO employee_pkg.max_salary
```

```
        FROM employee;
END company;
```

If your initialization requirements seem different from those we've illustrated, you should consider alternatives to the initialization section, such as grouping your startup statements together into a procedure in the package. Give the procedure a name like init_environment; then, at the appropriate initialization point in your application, call the init_environment procedure to set up your session.

When initialization fails

There are several steps to initialize a package: declare data, assign default values, run the initialization section. What happens when an error occurs, causing the failure of this initialization process? It turns out that even if a package fails to complete its initialization steps, Oracle marks the package as having been initialized and does *not* attempt to run the startup code again during that session. To verify this behavior, consider the following package:

```
/* File on web: valerr.pkg */
CREATE OR REPLACE PACKAGE valerr
IS
   FUNCTION get RETURN VARCHAR2;
END valerr;
/
CREATE OR REPLACE PACKAGE BODY valerr
IS
   -- Note: this is a package-level, but private global variable
   v VARCHAR2(1) := 'ABC';

   FUNCTION get RETURN VARCHAR2
   IS
   BEGIN
      RETURN v;
   END;
BEGIN
   DBMS_OUTPUT.PUT_LINE ('Before I show you v...');

EXCEPTION
  WHEN OTHERS
  THEN
    DBMS_OUTPUT.PUT_LINE ('Trapped the error!');

END valerr;
```

Suppose that I connect to SQL*Plus and try to run the valerr.get function (for the first time in that session). This is what I see:

```
SQL> exec DBMS_OUTPUT.PUT_LINE (valerr.get)
*
ERROR at line 1:
ORA-06502: PL/SQL: numeric or value error: character string buffer too small
```

In other words, my attempt in the declaration of the v variable to assign a value of "ABC" caused a VALUE_ERROR exception. The exception section at the bottom of the package did *not* trap the error; it can only trap errors raised in the initialization section itself. And so the exception goes unhandled. Notice, however, that when I call that function a second time in my session, I do not get an error:

```
SQL> BEGIN
       DBMS_OUTPUT.PUT_LINE ('V is set to ' || NVL (valerr.get, 'NULL'));
     END;
     /
V is set to NULL
```

How curious! The statement "Before I show you v..." is never displayed; in fact, it is never executed. This packaged function fails the first time, but not the second or any subsequent times. Here we have one of those classic "unreproducible errors," and within the PL/SQL world, this is the classic cause of such a problem: a failure in package initialization.

These errors are very hard to track down. The best way to avoid such errors and also aid in detection is to move the assignments of default values to the initialization section, where the exception section can gracefully handle errors and report on their probable case, as shown here:

```
CREATE OR REPLACE PACKAGE BODY valerr
IS
   v VARCHAR2(1);

   FUNCTION get RETURN VARCHAR2 IS BEGIN ... END;
BEGIN
   v := 'ABC';

EXCEPTION
  WHEN OTHERS
  THEN
    DBMS_OUTPUT.PUT_LINE ('Error initializing valerr:');
    DBMS_OUTPUT.PUT_LINE (SQLERRM);

END valerr;
```

Rules for Calling Packaged Elements

It doesn't really make any sense to talk about running or executing a package (after all, it is just a container for code elements). However, you will certainly want to run or reference those elements defined in a package.

A package owns its objects, just as a table owns its columns. To reference an element defined in the package specification *outside of* the package itself, you must use the same dot notation to fully specify the name of that element. Let's look at some examples.

The following package specification declares a constant, an exception, a cursor, and several modules:

```
CREATE OR REPLACE PACKAGE pets_inc
IS
   max_pets_in_facility CONSTANT INTEGER := 120;
   pet_is_sick EXCEPTION;

   CURSOR pet_cur (pet_id_in IN pet.id%TYPE) RETURN pet%ROWTYPE;

   FUNCTION next_pet_shots (pet_id_in IN pet.id%TYPE) RETURN DATE;
   PROCEDURE set_schedule (pet_id_in IN pet.id%TYPE);

END pets_inc;
```

To reference any of these objects, I preface the object name with the package name, as follows:

```
DECLARE
   -- Base this constant on the id column of the pet table.
   c_pet CONSTANT pet.id%TYPE:= 1099;
   v_next_apppointment DATE;
BEGIN
   IF pets_inc.max_pets_in_facility > 100
   THEN
      OPEN pets_inc.pet_cur (c_pet);
   ELSE
      v_next_appointment:= pets_inc.next_pet_shots (c_pet);
   END IF;
EXCEPTION
   WHEN pets_inc.pet_is_sick
   THEN
      pets_inc.set_schedule (c_pet);
END;
```

To summarize, there are two rules to follow in order to reference and use elements in a package:

- When you reference elements defined in a package specification from outside of that package (an external program), you must use dot notation in the form *package_name.element_name*.
- When you reference package elements from within the package (specification or body), you do not need to include the name of the package. PL/SQL will automatically resolve your reference within the scope of the package.

Working with Package Data

Package data consists of variables and constants that are defined at the *package level*—that is, not within a particular function or procedure in the package. The scope of the package data is therefore not a single program, but rather the package as a whole. In the PL/SQL runtime architecture, package data structures *persist* (hold their values) for the duration of a session (rather than the duration of execution for a particular program).

If package data is declared inside the package body, then that data persists for the session but can be accessed only by elements defined in the package itself (private data).

If package data is declared inside the package specification, then that data persists for the session and is directly accessible (to both read and modify the value) by any program that has EXECUTE authority on that package (public data). Public package data is very similar to and potentially as dangerous as GLOBAL variables in Oracle Forms.

If a packaged procedure opens a cursor, that cursor remains open and is available throughout the session. It is not necessary to define the cursor in each program. One module can open a cursor while another performs the fetch. Additionally, package variables can carry data across the boundaries of transactions because they are tied to the session rather than to a single transaction.

Global Within a Single Oracle Session

As a result of the SGA architecture, package data structures act like globals within the PL/SQL environment. Remember, however, that they are accessible only within a single Oracle session or connection; package data is not shared across sessions. If you need to share data between different Oracle sessions, you must use the DBMS_PIPE package. (See *Oracle Built-In Packages* for more information about this package.)

You need to be careful about assuming that different parts of your application maintain a single Oracle connection. There are times when a tool may establish a new connection to the database to perform an action. If this occurs, the data you have stored in a package in the first connection will not be available.

For example, suppose that an Oracle Forms application has saved values to data structures in a package. When the form calls a stored procedure, this stored procedure can access these same package-based variables and values as the form can because they share a single Oracle connection. But now suppose that the form kicks off a report using Oracle Reports. By default, Oracle Reports uses a second connection to the database (with the same username and password) to run the report. Even if this report accesses the same package and data structures, the values in those data structures will not match those used by the form. The report is using a different Oracle connection and a new instantiation of the package data structures.

Just as there are two types of data structures in a package (public and private), there are also two types of global package data to consider: global public data and global private data. The next two sections explore the differences between these kinds of package data.

Global Public Data

Any data structure declared in the specification of a package is a global public data structure, meaning that any program outside of the package can access it. You can, for example, define a PL/SQL table in a package specification and use it to keep a running list of all employees selected for a raise. You can also create a package of constants that are used throughout all your programs. Other developers will then reference the packaged constants instead of hardcoding the values in their programs. You are also allowed to change global public data structures unless they are declared as CONSTANTs in the declaration statement.

Global data is the proverbial "loose cannon" of programming. It is very convenient to declare and is a great way to have all sorts of information available at any point in time. However, reliance on global data structures leads to unstructured code that is full of side effects.

Recall that the specification of a module should give you all the information you need to understand how to call and use that module. However, it is not possible to determine if a package reads and/or writes to global data structures from the package's specification. Because of this, you cannot be sure of what is happening in your application and which program changes what data.

It is always preferable to pass data as parameters in and out of modules. That way, reliance on those data structures is documented in the specification and can be accounted for by developers. On the other hand, you should create named global data structures for information that truly is global to an application, such as constants and configuration information.

Packaged Cursors

One particularly interesting type of package data is the explicit cursor, which was introduced in Chapter 14. I can declare a cursor in a package, in either the body or the specification. The state of this cursor (i.e., whether it is opened or closed, the pointer to the location in the result set) persists for the session, just like any other packaged data. This means that it is possible to open a packaged cursor in one program, fetch from it in a second, and close it in a third. This flexibility can be an advantage and also a potential problem.

Let's first look at some of the nuances of declaring packaged cursors, and then move on to how you can open, fetch, and close such cursors.

Declaring packaged cursors

If you are declaring an explicit cursor in a package specification, you have two options:

- Declare the entire cursor, including the query, in the specification. This is exactly the same as if you were declaring a cursor in a local PL/SQL block.
- Declare only the header of the cursor and do not include the query itself. In this case, the query is defined in the package body only. You have, in effect, hidden the implementation of the cursor.

If you declare only the header, then you must add a RETURN clause to a cursor definition that indicates the data elements returned by a fetch from the cursor. Of course, these data elements are actually determined by the SELECT statement for that cursor, but the SELECT statement appears only in the body, not in the specification.

The RETURN clause may be made up of either of the following datatype structures:

- A record defined from a database table using the %ROWTYPE attribute
- A record defined from a programmer-defined record

If you declare a cursor in a package body, the syntax is the same as if you were declaring it in a local PL/SQL block.

Here is a simple package specification that shows both of these approaches:

```
   /* File on web: pkgcur.sql */
 1 CREATE OR REPLACE PACKAGE book_info
 2 IS
 3    CURSOR byauthor_cur (
 4       author_in   IN   books.author%TYPE
 5    )
 6    IS
 7       SELECT *
 8         FROM books
 9        WHERE author = author_in;
10
11    CURSOR bytitle_cur (
12       title_filter_in  IN   books.title%TYPE
13    ) RETURN books%ROWTYPE;
14
15    TYPE author_summary_rt IS RECORD (
16       author                        books.author%TYPE,
17       total_page_count              PLS_INTEGER,
18       total_book_count              PLS_INTEGER);
19
20    CURSOR summary_cur (
21       author_in   IN   books.author%TYPE
22    ) RETURN author_summary_rt;
23 END book_info;
```

On lines 3–9 you can see a very typical explicit cursor definition, fully defined in the package specification. On lines 11–13, I define a cursor without a query. In this case, I am telling whoever is looking at the specification that if they open and fetch from this cursor they will receive a single row from the books table for the specified "title filter," the implication being that wild cards are accepted in the description of the title. On lines 15–18, I define a new record type to hold summary information for a particular author, and on lines 20–22, I declare a cursor that returns summary information (just three values) for a given author.

Let's take a look at the package body and then see what kind of code needs to be written to work with these cursors.

```
CREATE OR REPLACE PACKAGE BODY book_info
IS
   CURSOR bytitle_cur (
      title_filter_in   IN   books.title%TYPE
   ) RETURN books%ROWTYPE
   IS
      SELECT *
        FROM books
       WHERE title LIKE UPPER (title_filter_in);

   CURSOR summary_cur (
      author_in   IN   books.author%TYPE
   ) RETURN author_summary_rt
   IS
      SELECT author, SUM (page_count), COUNT (*)
        FROM books
       WHERE author = author_in;
END book_info;
```

Because I had two cursors with a RETURN clause in my book information package specification, I must finish defining those cursors in the body. The select list of the query that I now add to the header must match, in number of items and datatype, the RETURN clause in the package specification; in this case, they do. If they do not match or the RETURN clause is not specified in the body, then the package body will fail to compile with one of the following errors:

```
20/11     PLS-00323: subprogram or cursor '<cursor>' is declared in a
          package specification and must be defined in the package body

5/13      PLS-00400: different number of columns between cursor SELECT
          statement and return value
```

Working with packaged cursors

Now let's see how we can take advantage of packaged cursors. First of all, you do not need to learn any new syntax to open, fetch from, and close packaged cursors; you just have to remember to prepend the package name to the name of the cursor. So if I want to get information about all the books having to do with PL/SQL, I can write a block like this:

```
DECLARE
   onebook    book_info.bytitle_cur%ROWTYPE;
BEGIN
   OPEN book_info.bytitle_cur ('%PL/SQL%');
```

```
    LOOP
       EXIT WHEN book_info.bytitle_cur%NOTFOUND;
       FETCH book_info.bytitle_cur INTO onebook;
       book_info.display (onebook);
    END LOOP;

    CLOSE book_info.bytitle_cur;
END;
```

As you can see, I can %ROWTYPE a packaged cursor and check its attributes just as I would with a locally defined explicit cursor. Nothing new there!

There are some hidden issues lurking in this code, however. Because my cursor is declared in a package specification, its scope is not bound to any given PL/SQL block. Suppose that I run this code:

```
BEGIN -- Only open...
   OPEN book_info.bytitle_cur ('%PEACE%');
END;
```

and then, in the same session, I run the anonymous block with the LOOP shown above. I will then get this error:

```
ORA-06511: PL/SQL: cursor already open
```

This happened because in my "only open" block, I neglected to close the cursor. Even though the block terminated, my packaged cursor did not close.

Given the persistence of packaged cursors, you should always keep the following rules in mind:

- Never assume that a packaged cursor is closed (and ready to be opened).
- Never assume that a packaged cursor is opened (and ready to be closed).
- Always be sure to explicitly close your packaged cursor when you are done with it.

These three rules also apply to working with other kinds of cursors—such as locally defined explicit cursors and DBMS_SQL cursors—but they are absolutely crucial for packaged cursors.

If you neglect these rules, you might well execute an application that makes certain assumptions, and then pays the price in unexpected and unhandled exceptions. So the question then becomes: how best can you remember and follow these rules? My suggestion is to build procedures that perform the open and close operations for you—and take all these nuances and possibilities into account.

The following package offers an example of this technique.

```
/* File on web: openclose.sql */
CREATE OR REPLACE PACKAGE personnel
IS
   CURSOR emps_for_dept (
```

```
      deptno_in IN employee.department_id%TYPE)
   IS
      SELECT * FROM employee
       WHERE department_id = deptno_in;

   PROCEDURE open_emps_for_dept(
      deptno_in IN employee.department_id%TYPE,
      close_if_open IN BOOLEAN := TRUE
      );

   PROCEDURE close_emps_for_dept;

END personnel;
```

I have a packaged cursor along with procedures to open and close the cursor. So if I want to loop through all the rows in the cursor, I would write code like this:

```
DECLARE
   one_emp personnel.emps_for_dept%ROWTYPE;
BEGIN
   personnel.open_emps_for_dept (1055);

   LOOP
      EXIT WHEN personnel.emps_for_dept%NOTFOUND;
      FETCH personnel.emps_for_dept INTO one_emp;
      ...
   END LOOP;

   personnel.close_emps_for_dept;
END;
```

I don't use explicit OPEN and CLOSE statements; instead, I call the corresponding procedures, which handle complexities related to packaged cursor persistence. I urge you to examine the *openclose.sql* file available from the O'Reilly site to study the implementation of these procedures.

You have a lot to gain by creating cursors in packages and making those cursors available to the developers on a project. Crafting precisely the data structures you need for your application is hard and careful work. These same structures—and the data in them—are used in your PL/SQL programs, almost always through the use of a cursor. If you do not package up your cursors and provide them "free of charge and effort" to all developers, each of them will write his or her own variations of these cursors, leading to all sorts of performance and maintenance issues. Packaging cursors is just one example of using packages to encapsulate access to data structures, which is explored further in "When to Use Packages."

One of the technical reviewers of this book, JT Thomas, offers the following alternative perspective:

"Rather than working with packaged cursors, you can get exactly the same effect by encapsulating logic and data presentation into views and publishing these to the developers. This allows the developers to then be responsible for properly maintaining their own cursors; the idea is that it is not possible to enforce proper maintenance given the toolset available with publicly accessible package cursors. Specifically, as far as I know, there is no way to enforce the usage of the open/close procedures, but the cursors will always remain visible to the developer directly opening/closing it; thus, this construct is still vulnerable. To make matters worse, however, the acceptance of publicly accessible packaged cursors and the open/close procedures might lull a team into a false sense of security and reliability."

Serializable Packages

As we have seen, package data by default persists for your entire session (or until the package is recompiled). This is an incredibly handy feature, but it has some drawbacks:

- Globally accessible (public *and* private) data structures persist, and that can cause undesired side effects. In particular, I can inadvertently leave packaged cursors open, causing "already open" errors in other programs.
- My programs can suck up lots of real memory (package data is managed in the user's memory area or User Global Area [UGA]) and then not release it if that data is stored in a package-level structure.

To help you manage the use of memory in packages, PL/SQL offers the SERIALLY_REUSABLE pragma. This pragma, which must appear in both the package specification and the body (if one exists), marks that package as *serially reusable*. For such packages, the duration of package state (the values of variables, the open status of a packaged cursor, etc.) can be reduced from a whole session to a single call of a program in the package.

To see the effects of this pragma, consider the following book_info package. I have created two separate programs: one to fill a list of books and another to show that list.

```
/* File on web: serialpkg.sql */
CREATE OR REPLACE PACKAGE book_info
IS
   PRAGMA SERIALLY_REUSABLE;
   PROCEDURE fill_list;

   PROCEDURE show_list;
END;
```

As you can see in the following package body, that list is declared as a private, but global, associative array:

```
/* File on web: serialpkg.sql */
CREATE OR REPLACE PACKAGE BODY book_info
IS
   PRAGMA SERIALLY_REUSABLE;

   TYPE book_list_t IS TABLE OF books%ROWTYPE INDEX BY BINARY_INTEGER;

   my_books   book_list_t;

   PROCEDURE fill_list IS
   BEGIN
      FOR rec IN (SELECT * FROM books WHERE AUTHOR LIKE '%FEUERSTEIN%')
      LOOP
         my_books (NVL (my_books.LAST, 0) + 1) := rec;
      END LOOP;
   END fill_list;

   PROCEDURE show_list IS
   BEGIN
      IF my_books.COUNT = 0
      THEN
         DBMS_OUTPUT.put_line ('** No books to show you...');
      ELSE
         FOR indx IN my_books.FIRST .. my_books.LAST
         LOOP
            DBMS_OUTPUT.put_line (my_books (indx).title);
         END LOOP;
      END IF;
   END show_list;
END;
```

To see the effect of this pragma, I fill and then show the list. In my first approach, these two steps are done in the same block, so the collection is still loaded and can be displayed:

```
SQL> BEGIN
      DBMS_OUTPUT.put_line (
         'Fill and show in same block:'
      );
      book_info.fill_list;
      book_info.show_list;
   END;
   /
Fill and show in same block:
Oracle PL/SQL Programming
Oracle PL/SQL Best Practices
Oracle PL/SQL Built-in Packages
```

In my second attempt, I fill and show the list in two separate blocks. As a result, my collection is now empty:

```
SQL> BEGIN
       DBMS_OUTPUT.put_line ('Fill in first block');
       book_info.fill_list;
     END;
     /
Fill in first block

SQL> BEGIN
       DBMS_OUTPUT.put_line ('Show in second block:');
       book_info.show_list;
     END;
     /
Show in second block:
** No books to show you...
```

Here are some things to keep in mind for serialized packages:

- The global memory for serialized packages is allocated in the System Global Area (SGA), not in the user's User Global Area (UGA). This approach allows the package work area to be reused. Each time the package is reused, its public variables are initialized to their default values or to NULL, and its initialization section is re-executed.
- The maximum number of work areas needed for a serialized package is the number of concurrent users of that package. The increased use of SGA memory is offset by the decreased use of UGA or program memory. Finally, Oracle ages out work areas not in use if it needs to reclaim memory from the SGA for other requests.

When to Use Packages

By now, we've covered the rules, syntax, and nuances of constructing packages. Let's now return to the list of reasons you might want to use PL/SQL packages and explore them in more detail. These scenarios include:

Encapsulating (hiding) data manipulation
: Rather than have developers write SQL statements (leading to inefficient variations and maintenance nightmares), provide an interface to those SQL statements.

Avoiding the hardcoding of literals
: Use a package with constants to give a name to the literal ("magic") value and avoid hardcoding it into individual (and multiple) programs. You can, of course, declare constants within procedures and functions as well. The advantage of a constant defined in a package specification is that it can be referenced outside of the package.

Improving the usability of built-in features
: Some of Oracle's own utilities, such as UTL_FILE and DBMS_OUTPUT, leave lots to be desired. Build your own package on top of Oracle's to correct as many of the problems as possible.

Grouping together logically related functionality
: If you have a dozen procedures and functions that all revolve around a particular aspect of your application, put them all into a package so that you can manage (and find) that code more easily.

Caching session-static data to improve application performance
: Take advantage of persistent package data to improve the response time of your application by caching (and not requerying) static data.

The following sections describe each of these scenarios.

Encapsulating Data Manipulation

Rather than have developers write their own SQL statements, you should provide an interface to those SQL statements. This is one of the most important motivations for building packages, yet is only rarely employed by developers.

With this approach, PL/SQL developers as a rule will not write SQL in their applications. Instead, they will call predefined, tested, and optimized code that does all the work for them; for example, an "add" procedure (overloaded to support records) that issues the INSERT statement and follows standard error-handling rules; a function to retrieve a single row for a primary key; and a variety of cursors that handle the common requests against the data structure (which could be a single table or a "business entity" consisting of multiple tables).

If you take this approach, developers will not necessarily need to understand how to join three or six different highly normalized tables to get the right set of data. They can just pick a cursor and leave the data analysis to someone else. They will not have to figure out what to do when they try to insert and the row already exists. The procedure has this logic inside it (and can be easily upgraded to use the Oracle*9i* MERGE statement).

Perhaps the biggest advantage of this approach is that as your data structures change, the maintenance headaches of updating application code are both minimized and centralized. The person who is expert at working with that table or object type makes the necessary changes within that single package, and the changes are then "rolled out" more or less automatically to all programs relying on that package.

Data encapsulation is a big topic and can be very challenging to implement in a comprehensive way. You will find an example of a table encapsulation package (built around the employee table) in the *te_employee.pks* and *te_employee.pkb* files on the O'Reilly web site. Let's take a look at what sort of impact this kind of package can have on your code. The *givebonus1.sp* file on the web site contains a procedure that gives the same bonus to each employee in the specified department, but only if he or she has been with the company for at least six months. Here are the parts of the give_bonus program that contains the SQL (see *givebonus1.sp* for the complete implementation):

```
CREATE OR REPLACE PROCEDURE give_bonus (
    dept_in IN employee.department_id%TYPE,
    bonus_in IN NUMBER)
IS
    v_name VARCHAR2(50);

    CURSOR by_dept_cur
    IS
       SELECT *
         FROM employee
        WHERE department_id = dept_in;
BEGIN
    /* Retrieve all information for the specified department. */
    SELECT name
      INTO v_name
      FROM department
     WHERE department_id = dept_in;

    /* For each employee in the specified department... */
    FOR rec IN by_dept_cur
    LOOP
       IF ADD_MONTHS (SYSDATE, -6) > rec.hire_date
       THEN
          UPDATE employee
             SET salary = rec.salary + bonus_in
           WHERE employee_id = rec.employee_id;
       END IF;
    END LOOP;
END;
```

Now let's compare that to the encapsulation alternative, which you will find in its entirety in *givebonus2.sp*:

```
CREATE OR REPLACE PROCEDURE give_bonus (
    dept_in IN employee.department_id%TYPE,
    bonus_in IN NUMBER)
IS
    dept_rec department%ROWTYPE;
    fdbk INTEGER;
BEGIN
    dept_rec := te_department.onerow (dept_in);

    /* Make sure packaged cursor is closed. */
    te_employee.close_emp_dept_lookup_all_cur;

    FOR rec IN te_employee.emp_dept_lookup_all_cur (
       dept_in)
    LOOP
       IF ADD_MONTHS (SYSDATE, -6) > rec.hire_date
```

```
         THEN
            te_employee.upd$salary (
               rec.employee_id,
               rec.salary + bonus_in,
               fdbk);
         END IF;
      END LOOP;
END;
/
```

All the SQL has been removed from the program, replaced with calls to reusable procedures and functions. This optimizes the SQL in my application and allows me to write more robust code in a more productive manner.

It is by no means a trivial matter to build (or generate) such packages and I recognize that most of you will not be willing or able to adopt a 100% encapsulated approach. You can, however, gain many of the advantages of data encapsulation without having to completely revamp your coding techniques. At a minimum, I suggest that you:

- Hide all your single-row queries behind a function interface. That way, you can make sure that error handling is performed and you can choose the best implementation (implicit or explicit cursors, for example).
- Identify the tables that are most frequently and directly manipulated by developers and build layers of code around them.
- Create packaged programs to handle complex transactions. If "add a new order" involves inserting two rows, updating six others, and so on, make sure to embed this logic inside a procedure that handles the complexity. Don't rely on individual developers to figure it out (and write it more than once!).

Avoiding Hardcoding of Literals

Virtually any application has a variety of "magic values"—literal values that have special significance in a system. These values might be type codes or validation limits. Your users will tell you that these magic values never change. "I will *always* have only 25 line items in my profit-and-loss," one will say. "The name of the parent company," swears another, "will *always* be ATLAS HQ." Don't take these promises at face value, and never code them into your programs. Consider the following IF statements:

```
IF footing_difference BETWEEN 1 and 100
THEN
   adjust_line_item;
END IF;

IF cust_status = 'C'
THEN
   reopen_customer;
END IF;
```

You are begging for trouble if you write code like this. You will be a much happier developer if you instead build a package of named constants as follows:

```
CREATE OR REPLACE PACKAGE config_pkg
IS
   closed_status     CONSTANT VARCHAR2(1) := 'C';
   open_status       CONSTANT VARCHAR2(1) := 'O';
   active_status     CONSTANT VARCHAR2(1) := 'A';
   inactive_status   CONSTANT VARCHAR2(1) := 'I';

   min_difference    CONSTANT NUMBER := 1;
   max_difference    CONSTANT NUMBER := 100;

   earliest_date     CONSTANT DATE := SYSDATE;
   latest_date       CONSTANT DATE := ADD_MONTHS (SYSDATE, 120);

END config_pkg;
```

Using this package, my two IF statements above now become:

```
IF footing_difference
   BETWEEN config_pkg.min_difference and config_pkg.max_difference
THEN
   adjust_line_item;
END IF;

IF cust_status = config_pkg.closed_status
THEN
   reopen_customer;
END IF;
```

If any of my magic values ever change, I simply modify the assignment to the appropriate constant in the configuration package. I do not need to change a single program module. Just about every application I have reviewed (and many that I have written) mistakenly includes hardcoded magic values in the program. In every single case (especially those that I myself wrote!), the developer had to make repeated changes to the programs, during both development and maintenance phases. It was often a headache, and sometimes a nightmare; I cannot emphasize strongly enough the importance of consolidating all magic values into a single package, with or without a body.

Improving Usability of Built-in Features

Some of Oracle's own utilities, such as UTL_FILE and DBMS_OUTPUT, leave lots to be desired. We all have our pet peeves, and not just about how Oracle builds utilities for us. What about that "ace" consultant who blew into town last year? Are you still trying to deal with the code mess he left behind? Maybe you can't *replace* any of this stuff, but you can certainly consider building your own package on top of theirs (their packages, their poorly designed data structures, etc.) to correct as many of the problems as possible.

Rather than fill up the pages of this book with examples, I've listed the filenames of a number of packages available on the O'Reilly site as companion code to this text. These demonstrate this use of packages and also offer some useful utilities. I suggest that you look through all the **.pkg* files on the site for other code you might find handy in your application.

filepath.pkg
: Adds support for a path to UTL_FILE. This allows you to search through multiple, specified directories to find the desired file.

dbparm.pkg
: Makes it easier to use the DBMS_UTILITY.GET_PARAMETER_VALUE utility to retrieve values from the initialization file (*INIT.ORA*).

do.pkg
: Improves the "print line" functionality of DBMS_OUTPUT to avoid the nuisances of its design drawbacks (it cannot display Booleans or strings longer than 255 bytes, for instance).

Grouping Together Logically Related Functionality

If you have a dozen procedures and functions that all revolve around a particular feature or aspect of your application, put them all into a package so that you can manage (and find) that code more easily. This is most important when coding the business rules for your application. When implementing business rules, follow these important guidelines:

- Do not hardcode them (usually repeatedly) into individual application components.
- Do not scatter them across many different standalone, hard-to-manage programs.

Before you start building an application, construct a series of packages that encapsulate all of its rules. Sometimes these rules are part of a larger package, such as a table encapsulation package. In other cases, you might establish a package that contains nothing *but* the key rules. Here is one example:

```
/* File on web: custrules.pkg */
CREATE OR REPLACE PACKAGE customer_rules
IS
    FUNCTION min_balance RETURN PLS_INTEGER;  /* Toronto */

    FUNCTION eligible_for_discount
        (customer_in IN customer%ROWTYPE)
        RETURN BOOLEAN;

    FUNCTION eligible_for_discount
        (customer_id_in IN customer.customer_id%TYPE)
        RETURN BOOLEAN;

END customer_rules;
```

The "eligible for discount" function is hidden away in the package so that it can be easily managed. I also use overloading to offer two different interfaces to the formula: one that accepts a primary key and establishes eligibility for that customer in the database, and a second that applies its logic to customer information already loaded into a %ROWTYPE record. Why did I do this? Because if a person has already queried the customer information from the database, he can use the %ROWTYPE overloading and avoid a second query.

Of course, not all "logically related functionality" has to do with business rules. I might need to add to the built-in string manipulation functions of PL/SQL. Rather than create twelve different standalone functions, I will create a "string enhancements" package and put all of the functions there. Then I and others know where to go to access that functionality.

Caching Static Session Data

Take advantage of persistent package data to improve the response time of your application by caching (and not requerying) static data. You can do this at a number of different levels; for each of the following items, I've listed a few helpful code examples available on the O'Reilly site:

- Cache a single value, such as the name of the session (returned by the USER function). Examples: *thisuser.pkg* and *thisuser.tst*.
- Cache a single row or set of information, such as the configuration information for a given user. Examples: *init.pkg* and *init.tst*.
- Cache a whole list of values, such as the contents of a static, reference code lookup table. Examples: *emplu.pkg* (employee lookup) and *emplu.tst*.

Use the test files to compare cached and noncached performance.

If you decide to take advantage of this technique, remember that this data is cached separately for each session that references the package. This means that if your cache of a row in a table consumes 20K and you have 1000 users, you have just used up 2 MB of real memory in your system—in addition to all the other memory consumed by Oracle.

Packages and Object Types

Packages are containers that allow you to group together data and code elements. Object types are containers that allow you to group together data and code elements. Do we need both? Do object types supersede packages, especially now that Oracle has added support for inheritance? When should you use a package and when should you use an object type? All very interesting and pertinent questions.

It is true that packages and object types share some features:

- Each can contain one or more programs and data structures.
- Each can (and usually does) consist of both a specification and a body.

There are, however, key differences between the two, including the following:

- An object type is a *template* for data; you can instantiate multiple object type instances (a.k.a. "objects") from that template. Each one of those instances has associated with it all of the attributes (data) and methods (procedures and functions) from the template. These instances can be stored in the database. A package, on the other hand, is a "one-off" structure and, in a sense, a static object type: you cannot declare instances of it.
- In Oracle9*i* and beyond, object types offer inheritance. That means that I can declare an object type to be "under" another type, and it *inherits* all the attributes and methods of that supertype. There is no concept of hierarchy or inheritance in packages. See Chapter 21 for lots more information about this.
- With packages, you can create private, hidden data and programs. This is not supported in object types, in which everything is publicly declared and accessible (although you can still hide the implementation of methods in the object type body).

So when should you use object types and when should you use packages? First of all, very few people use object types and even fewer attempt to take advantage of Oracle's "object-relational" model. For them, packages will remain the core building blocks of their PL/SQL-based applications.

If you do plan to exploit object types (definitely worth a serious look with the Oracle9*i* release), then I recommend that you consider putting much of your complex code into packages that are then called by methods in the object type. You then have more flexibility in designing the code that implements your object types, and you can share that code with other elements of your application.

In this chapter:

- DML Triggers
- DDL Triggers
- Database Event Triggers
- INSTEAD OF Triggers
- AFTER SUSPEND Triggers
- Maintaining Triggers

CHAPTER 18
Triggers

Database triggers are named program units that are executed in response to events that occur in the database. Triggers are critical elements of a well-designed application built on the Oracle database, and are used to do the following:

Perform validation on changes being made to tables
: Because the validation logic is attached directly to the database object, database triggers offer a strong guarantee that the required logic will always be executed and enforced.

Automate maintenance of the database
: Starting with Oracle8*i*, you can use database startup and shutdown triggers to automatically perform necessary initialization and cleanup steps. This is a distinct advantage over creating and running such steps as scripts external to the database.

Apply rules about acceptable database administration activity in a granular fashion
: You can use triggers to tightly control what kinds of actions are allowed on database objects, such as dropping or altering tables. Again, by putting this logic in triggers, you make it very difficult, if not impossible, for anyone to bypass the rules you have established.

Five different types of events can have trigger code attached to them:

Data Manipulation Language (DML) statements
: DML triggers are available to fire whenever a record is inserted into, updated in, or deleted from a table. These triggers can be used to perform validation, set default values, audit changes, and even disallow certain DML operations.

Data Definition Language (DDL) statements
: DDL triggers fire whenever DDL is executed—for example, whenever a table is created. These triggers can perform auditing and prevent certain DDL statements from occurring.

Database events

Database event triggers fire whenever the database starts up or is shut down, whenever a user logs on or off, and whenever an Oracle error occurs. For Oracle8*i* and above, these triggers provide a means of tracking activity in the database.

INSTEAD OF

INSTEAD OF triggers are essentially alternatives to DML triggers. They fire when inserts, updates, and deletes are about to occur; your code specifies what to do in place of these DML operations. INSTEAD OF triggers control operations on views, not tables. They can be used to make non-updateable views updateable and to override the behavior of views that are updateable.

Suspended statements

Oracle9*i* introduces the concept of suspended statements. Statements experiencing space problems (lack of tablespace or quota) can enter a suspended mode until the space problem is fixed. Triggers can be added to the mix to automatically alert someone of the problem or even fix it.

This chapter describes these types of triggers; for each, I'll provide syntax details, example code, and suggested uses. I'll also touch on trigger maintenance at the end of the chapter.

DML Triggers

Data Manipulation Language (DML) triggers fire when records are inserted into, updated within, or deleted from a particular table, as shown in Figure 18-1. These are the most common type of triggers, especially for developers; the other trigger types are used primarily by DBAs.

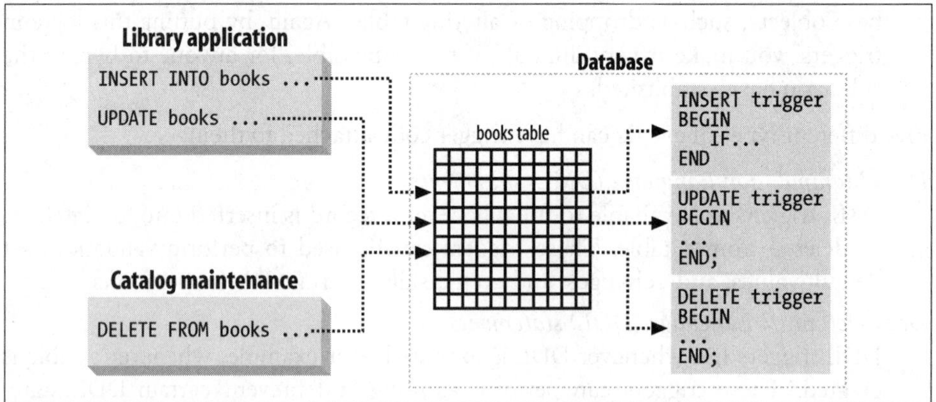

Figure 18-1. DML triggers fire in response to changes to a database table

There are many options regarding DML triggers. They can fire after or before a DML statement or they can fire after or before each row is processed within a statement. They can fire for INSERT, UPDATE, or DELETE statements, or combinations of the three.

There are also many ways to actually configure DML triggers. To determine what works for your environment, you will generally want to answer each of the following questions:

- Should the triggers fire once for the whole DML statement or once per row involved in the statement?
- Should the triggers fire before or after the whole statement completes or before or after each row is processed?
- Should the triggers fire for inserts, updates, deletes, or a combination thereof?

DML Trigger Concepts

Before diving into the syntax and examples, you may find it useful to review these DML trigger concepts and associated terminology.

BEFORE trigger
: A trigger that executes before a certain operation occurs, such as BEFORE INSERT.

AFTER trigger
: A trigger that executes after a certain operation occurs, such as AFTER UPDATE.

Statement-level trigger
: A trigger that executes for a SQL statement as a whole (which may, in turn, affect one or more individual rows in a database table).

Row-level trigger
: A trigger that executes for a single row that has been affected by the execution of a SQL statement. Suppose that the books table contains 1000 rows. Then the following UPDATE statement will modify 1000 rows:

```
UPDATE books SET title = UPPER (title);
```

And if I define a row-level update trigger on the books table, that trigger will fire 1000 times.

NEW pseudo-record
: A data structure named NEW that looks like and (mostly) acts like a PL/SQL record. This "pseudo-record" is available only within update and insert DML triggers; it contains the values for the affected row after any changes were made.

OLD pseudo-record
: A data structure named OLD that looks like and (mostly) acts like a PL/SQL record. This "pseudo-record" is available only within update and delete DML

triggers; it contains the values for the affected row before any changes were made.

WHEN clause
: The portion of the DML trigger that is run to determine whether or not the trigger code should be executed (allowing you to avoid unnecessary execution).

DML trigger scripts

To explore some of the concepts presented in the previous section, we have made the following scripts available on the O'Reilly site:

Concept	Files	Description

Statement-level and row-level triggers	*copy_tables.sql*
	statement_vs_row.sql
		Creates two identical tables, one with data and one empty.
		Creates two simple triggers, one statement-level and one row-level.
		After running these scripts, execute this statement and view the results (with SERVEROUTPUT turned on to watch the activity):
		`INSERT INTO to_table`
		`SELECT * FROM from_table;`

BEFORE and AFTER triggers	*before_vs_after.sql*	Creates BEFORE and AFTER triggers. After running the script, execute this statement and view the results:
		`INSERT INTO to_table`
		`SELECT * FROM from_table;`

Triggers for various DML operations	*one_trigger_per_type.sql*	Creates AFTER INSERT, UPDATE, and DELETE triggers on to_table. After running the script, execute these commands and view the results:
		`INSERT INTO to_table`
		`VALUES (1);`
		`UPDATE to_table`
		`SET col1 = 10;`
		`DELETE to_table;`

Transaction participation

By default, DML triggers participate in the transaction from which they were fired. This means that:

- If a trigger raises an exception, that part of the transaction will be rolled back.
- If the trigger performs any DML itself (such as inserting a row into a log table), then that DML becomes a part of the main transaction.
- You cannot issue a COMMIT or ROLLBACK from within a DML trigger.

If you define your DML trigger to be an autonomous transaction (discussed in Chapter 13), however, then any DML performed inside the trigger will be saved or rolled back without affecting the main transaction.

The following sections present the syntax for creating a DML trigger, provide reference information on various elements of the trigger definition, and explore an example that uses the many components and options for these triggers.

Creating a DML Trigger

To create (or replace) a DML trigger, use the syntax shown here:

```
1  CREATE [OR REPLACE] TRIGGER trigger name
2  {BEFORE | AFTER|
3  {INSERT | DELETE | UPDATE | UPDATE OF column list} ON table name
4  [FOR EACH ROW]
5  [WHEN (...)]
6  [DECLARE ... ]
7  BEGIN
8    ... executable statements ...
9  [EXCEPTION ... ]
10 END [trigger name];
```

The following table provides an explanation of these different elements:

Line(s)	Description
1	States that a trigger is to be created with the name supplied. Specifying OR REPLACE is optional. If the trigger exists and REPLACE is not specified, then your attempt to create the trigger anew will result in an ORA-4081 error.
2	Specifies if the trigger is to fire BEFORE or AFTER the statement or row is processed.
3	Specifies the type of DML to which the trigger applies: insert, update, or delete. Note that UPDATE can be specified for the whole record or just for a column list separated by commas. The columns can be combined (separated with an OR) and may be specified in any order. Line 3 also specifies the table to which the trigger is to apply. Remember that each DML trigger can apply to only one table.
4	If FOR EACH ROW is specified, then the trigger will activate for each row processed by a statement. If this clause is missing, the default behavior is to fire only once for the statement (a statement-level trigger).
5	An optional WHEN clause that allows you to specify logic to avoid unnecessary execution of the trigger.
6	Optional declaration section for the anonymous block that constitutes the trigger code. If you do not need to declare local variables, you do not need this keyword. Note that you should never try to declare the NEW and OLD pseudo-records. This is done automatically.
7–8	The execution section of the trigger. This is required and must contain at least one statement.
9	Optional exception section. This section will trap and handle (or attempt to handle) any exceptions raised in the execution section only.
10	Required END statement for the trigger. You can include the name of the trigger after the END keyword to explicitly document which trigger you are ending.

Here are a few examples of DML trigger usage:

- I want to make sure that whenever an employee is added or changed, all necessary validation is run. Notice that I pass the necessary fields of the NEW pseudo-record to individual check routines in this row-level trigger:

```
CREATE OR REPLACE TRIGGER validate_employee_changes
   AFTER INSERT OR UPDATE
   ON employee
```

```
    FOR EACH ROW
BEGIN
    check_age (:NEW.date_of_birth);
    check_resume (:NEW.resume);
END;
```

- The following BEFORE INSERT trigger captures audit information for the CEO compensation table. It also relies on the Oracle8*i* autonomous transaction feature to commit this new row without affecting the "outer" or main transaction:

```
CREATE OR REPLACE TRIGGER bef_ins_ceo_comp
    AFTER INSERT
    ON ceo_compensation
    FOR EACH ROW
DECLARE
    PRAGMA AUTONOMOUS_TRANSACTION;
BEGIN
    INSERT INTO ceo_comp_history
          VALUES (:NEW.name,
                  :OLD.compensation, :NEW.compensation,
                  'AFTER INSERT', SYSDATE);
    COMMIT;
END;
```

The WHEN clause

Use the WHEN clause to fine-tune the situations under which the body of the trigger code will actually execute. In the following example, I use the WHEN clause to make sure that the trigger code does not execute unless the new salary or new commission is changing to a *different* value:

```
CREATE OR REPLACE TRIGGER check_raise
   AFTER UPDATE OF salary, commission
   ON employee
   FOR EACH ROW
WHEN ((OLD.salary != NEW.salary OR
      (OLD.salary IS NULL AND NEW.salary IS NULL))
  OR
     (OLD.commission != NEW.commission OR
      (OLD.commission IS NULL AND NEW.commission IS NULL)))
BEGIN
   ...
```

In other words, if a user issues an UPDATE to a row and for some reason sets the salary to its current value, the trigger will and must fire, but the reality is that you really don't need any of the PL/SQL code in the body of the trigger to execute. By checking this condition in the WHEN clause, you avoid some of the overhead of starting up the PL/SQL block associated with the trigger.

The *genwhen.sp* file offers a procedure that will generate a WHEN clause to ensure that the new value is actually different from the old.

The WHEN clause can be used only with row-level triggers. You will get a compilation error (ORA-04077) if you try to use it with statement-level triggers.

In most cases, you will reference fields in the OLD and NEW pseudo-records in the WHEN clause, as in the example shown above. You may also, however, write code that invokes built-in functions, as in the following WHEN clause that uses SYSDATE to restrict inserts to between 9 AM and 5 PM:

```
CREATE OR REPLACE TRIGGER valid_when_clause
BEFORE INSERT ON frame
FOR EACH ROW
WHEN ( TO_CHAR(SYSDATE,'HH24') BETWEEN 9 AND 17 )
   ...
```

Here are some things to keep in mind when using the WHEN clause:

- Enclose the entire logical expression inside parentheses. These parentheses are optional in an IF statement, but required in the trigger WHEN clause.
- Do *not* include the ":" in front of the OLD and NEW names. This colon (indicating a host variable) is required in the body of the trigger PL/SQL code, but cannot be used in the WHEN clause.
- You can only invoke SQL built-in functions from within the WHEN clause; you will not be able to call user-defined functions or functions defined in built-packages (such as DBMS_UTILITY). Attempts to do so will generate an *ORA-04076: invalid NEW or OLD specification* error. If you need to invoke such functions, move that logic into the beginning of the trigger execution section.

Working with NEW and OLD pseudo-records

Whenever a row-level trigger fires, the PL/SQL runtime engine creates and populates two data structures that function much like records. They are the NEW and OLD pseudo-records ("pseudo" because they don't share all the properties of real PL/SQL records). OLD stores the original values of the record being processed by the trigger; NEW contains the new values. These records have the same structure as a record declared using %ROWTYPE on the table to which the trigger is attached.

Here are some rules to keep in mind when working with NEW and OLD:

- With triggers on INSERT operations, the OLD structure does not contain any data; there *is* no "old" set of values.
- With triggers on UPDATE operations, both the OLD and NEW structures are populated. OLD contains the values prior to the update; NEW contains the values the row will contain after the update is performed.
- With triggers on DELETE operations, the NEW structure does not contain any data; the record is about to be erased.

FOR EACH ROW Before WHEN

In some versions of PL/SQL, the compiler requires that FOR EACH ROW be specified before the WHEN clause because it assumes that a statement trigger is being created unless told otherwise.

```
SQL> CREATE OR REPLACE TRIGGER row_must_be_before_when
  2  BEFORE INSERT ON frame
  3  WHEN ( new.strike = 'Y' )
  4  FOR EACH ROW
  5  BEGIN NULL; END;
  8  /

ERROR at line 3:
ORA-04077: WHEN clause cannot be used with table level triggers

SQL> CREATE OR REPLACE TRIGGER row_must_be_before_when
  2  BEFORE INSERT ON frame
  3  FOR EACH ROW
  4  WHEN ( new.strike = 'Y' )
  5  BEGIN NULL; END;
  8  /

Trigger created.
```

- The NEW and OLD pseudo-records also contain the ROWID pseudo-column; this value is populated in both OLD and NEW with the same value, in all circumstances. Go figure!
- You cannot change the field values of the OLD structure; attempting to do so will raise the ORA-04085 error. You *can* modify the field values of the NEW structure.
- You cannot pass a NEW or OLD structure as a "record parameter" to a procedure or function called within the trigger. You can pass only individual fields of the pseudo-record. See the *gentrigrec.sp* script for a program that will generate code transferring NEW and OLD values to records that *can* be passed as parameters.
- When referencing the NEW and OLD structures within the anonymous block for the trigger, you must preface those keywords with a colon, as in:

```
IF :NEW.salary > 10000 THEN...
```

- You cannot perform record-level operations with the NEW and OLD structures. For example, the following statement will cause the trigger compilation to fail:

```
BEGIN :new := NULL; END;
```

You can also use the REFERENCING clause to change the names of the pseudo-records within the database trigger; this allows you to write code that is more self-documenting and application-specific. Here is one example:

```
CREATE OR REPLACE TRIGGER audit_update
   AFTER UPDATE
   ON frame
   REFERENCING OLD AS prior_to_cheat NEW AS after_cheat
   FOR EACH ROW
BEGIN
   INSERT INTO frame_audit
               (bowler_id,
                game_id,
                frame_number,
                old_strike,
                new_strike,
                old_spare,
                new_spare,
                old_score,
                new_score,
                change_date,
                operation)

        VALUES (:after_cheat.bowler_id,
                :after_cheat.game_id,
                :after_cheat.frame_number,
                :prior_to_cheat.strike,
                :after_cheat.strike,
                :prior_to_cheat.spare,
                :after_cheat.spare,
                :prior_to_cheat.score,
                :after_cheat.score,
                SYSDATE,
                'UPDATE');
END;
```

Run the *full_old_and_new.sql* script to take a look at the behavior of the OLD and NEW pseudo-records.

Determining the DML action within a trigger

Oracle offers a set of functions (also known as *operational directives*) that allow you to determine which DML action caused the firing of the current trigger. Each of these functions returns TRUE or FALSE, as described below.

INSERTING
: Returns TRUE if the trigger was fired by an insert into the table to which the trigger is attached, and FALSE if not.

UPDATING
: Returns TRUE if the trigger was fired by an update of the table to which the trigger is attached, and FALSE if not.

DELETING

Returns TRUE if the trigger was fired by a delete from the table to which the trigger is attached, and FALSE if not.

Using these directives, it is possible to create a single trigger that consolidates the actions required for each of the different types of operations. Here is one such trigger:

```
/* File on web: one_trigger_does_it_all.sql */
CREATE OR REPLACE TRIGGER three_for_the_price_of_one
BEFORE DELETE OR INSERT OR UPDATE ON account_transaction
FOR EACH ROW
BEGIN
  -- track who created the new row
  IF INSERTING
  THEN
    :NEW.created_by := USER;
    :NEW.created_date := SYSDATE;

  -- track deletion with special audit program
  ELSIF DELETING
  THEN
     audit_deletion(USER,SYSDATE);

  -- track who last updated the row
  ELSIF UPDATING
  THEN
    :NEW.LAST_UPDATED_BY := USER;
    :NEW.LAST_UPDATED_DATE := SYSDATE;
  END IF;
END;
```

The UPDATING function is overloaded with a version that takes a specific column name as an argument. This is handy for isolating specific column updates.

```
/* File on web: overloaded_update.sql */
CREATE OR REPLACE TRIGGER validate_update
BEFORE UPDATE ON account_transaction
FOR EACH ROW
BEGIN
  IF UPDATING ('ACCOUNT_NO')
  THEN
    errpkg.raise('Account number cannot be updated');
  END IF;
END;
```

Specification of the column name is not case-sensitive. The name is not evaluated until the trigger executes, and if the column does not exist in the table to which the trigger is attached, it will evaluate to FALSE.

Operational directives can be called from within any PL/SQL block, not just triggers. They will, however, only evaluate to TRUE within a DML trigger or code called from within a DML trigger.

DML Trigger Example: No Cheating Allowed!

One application function for which triggers are perfect is change auditing. Consider the example of Paranoid Pam (or Ms Trustful as we call her), who runs a bowling alley and has been receiving complaints about people cheating on their scores. She recently implemented a complete Oracle application known as Pam's Bowl-A-Rama Scoring System, and now wants to augment it to catch the cheaters.

The focal point of Pam's application is the frame table that records the score of a particular frame of a particular game for a particular player:

```
/* File on web: bowlerama_tables.sql */
CREATE TABLE frame
(bowler_id    NUMBER,
 game_id      NUMBER,
 frame_number NUMBER,
 strike       VARCHAR2(1) DEFAULT 'N',
 spare        VARCHAR2(1) DEFAULT 'N',
 score        NUMBER,
 CONSTRAINT frame_pk
 PRIMARY KEY (bowler_id, game_id, frame_number));
```

Pam augments the frame table with an audit version to catch all before and after values, so that she can compare them and identify fraudulent activity:

```
CREATE TABLE frame_audit
(bowler_id    NUMBER,
 game_id      NUMBER,
 frame_number NUMBER,
 old_strike   VARCHAR2(1),
 new_strike   VARCHAR2(1),
 old_spare    VARCHAR2(1),
 new_spare    VARCHAR2(1),
 old_score    NUMBER,
 new_score    NUMBER,
 change_date  DATE,
 operation    VARCHAR2(6));
```

For every change to the frame table, Pam would like to keep track of before and after images of the affected rows. So she creates the following single audit trigger:

```
/* File on web: bowlerama_full_audit.sql */
CREATE OR REPLACE TRIGGER audit_frames
AFTER INSERT OR UPDATE OR DELETE ON frame
FOR EACH ROW
BEGIN
  IF INSERTING THEN
    INSERT INTO frame_audit(bowler_id,game_id,frame_number,
                            new_strike,new_spare,new_score,
                            change_date,operation)
    VALUES(:NEW.bowler_id,:NEW.game_id,:NEW.frame_number,
           :NEW.strike,:NEW.spare,:NEW.score,
           SYSDATE,'INSERT');

```

```
13    ELSIF UPDATING THEN
14      INSERT INTO frame_audit(bowler_id,game_id,frame_number,
15                              old_strike,new_strike,
16                              old_spare,new_spare,
17                              old_score,new_score,
18                              change_date,operation)
19      VALUES(:NEW.bowler_id,:NEW.game_id,:NEW.frame_number,
20             :OLD.strike,:NEW.strike,
21             :OLD.spare,:NEW.spare,
22             :OLD.score,:NEW.score,
23             SYSDATE,'UPDATE');
24
25    ELSIF DELETING THEN
26      INSERT INTO frame_audit(bowler_id,game_id,frame_number,
27                              old_strike,old_spare,old_score,
28                              change_date,operation)
29      VALUES(:OLD.bowler_id,:OLD.game_id,:OLD.frame_number,
30             :OLD.strike,:OLD.spare,:OLD.score,
31             SYSDATE,'DELETE');
32    END IF;
33  END audit_frames;
```

Notice that for the INSERTING clause (lines 6–11), she relies on the NEW pseudo-record to populate the audit row. For UPDATING (lines 14–23), a combination of NEW and OLD information is used. For DELETING (lines 26–31), Pam only has OLD information with which to work. With this trigger in place, Pam can sit back and wait for action.

Of course, Pam doesn't announce her new auditing system. In particular, Sally Johnson (a very ambitious but not terribly skilled bowler) has no idea she is being watched. Sally has decided that she really wants to be the champion this year, and will stop at nothing to make it happen. Her father owns the bowling alley, she has access to SQL*Plus, and she knows that her bowler ID is 1. All that constitutes enough privilege and information to allow her to bypass the application GUI altogether, connect directly into SQL*Plus, and work some very unprincipled "magic."

Sally starts out by giving herself a strike in the first frame:

```
SQL> INSERT INTO frame
  2  (BOWLER_ID,GAME_ID,FRAME_NUMBER,STRIKE)
  3  VALUES(1,1,1,'Y');
1 row created.
```

But then she decides to be clever. She immediately downgrades her first frame to a spare to be less conspicuous:

```
SQL> UPDATE frame
  2  SET strike = 'N',
  3      spare = 'Y'
  4  WHERE bowler_id = 1
  5    AND game_id = 1
  6    AND frame_number = 1;
1 row updated.
```

Uh oh! Sally hears a noise in the corridor. She loses her nerve and tries to cover her tracks:

```
SQL> DELETE frame
  2  WHERE bowler_id = 1
  3    AND game_id = 1
  4    AND frame_number = 1;
1 row deleted.

SQL> COMMIT;
Commit complete.
```

She even verifies that her entries were deleted:

```
SQL> SELECT * FROM frame;
no rows selected
```

Wiping the sweat from her brow, Sally signs out, but vows to come back later and follow through on her plans.

Ever suspecting, Pam signs in and quickly discovers what Sally was up to by querying the audit table (Pam might also consider setting up an hourly job via DBMS_JOB to automate this part of the auditing procedure):

```
SELECT bowler_id,
       game_id,
       frame_number,
       old_strike,
       new_strike,
       old_spare,
       new_spare,
       change_date,
       operation
  FROM frame_audit;
```

Here is the output:

```
BOWLER_ID GAME_ID FRAME_NUMBER O N O N CHANGE_DA OPERAT
--------- ------- ------------ - - - - --------- ------
        1       1            1   Y   N 12-SEP-00 INSERT
        1       1            1 Y N N Y 12-SEP-00 UPDATE
        1       1            1 N   N   12-SEP-00 DELETE
```

Sally is so busted! The audit entries show what Sally was up to even though no changes remain behind in the frame table. All three statements were audited by Pam's DML trigger: the initial insert of a strike entry, the downgrade to a spare, and the subsequent removal of the record.

Applying the WHEN clause

After using her auditing system for many successful months, Pam undertakes an effort to further isolate potential problems. She reviews her application front end and determines that the strike, spare, and score fields are the only ones that can be changed. Thus her trigger can be more specific:

```
CREATE OR REPLACE TRIGGER audit_update
   AFTER UPDATE OF strike, spare, score
   ON frame
   REFERENCING OLD AS prior_to_cheat NEW AS after_cheat
   FOR EACH ROW
BEGIN
   INSERT INTO frame_audit (...)
     VALUES (...);
END;
```

After a few weeks of this implementation, Pam is still not happy with the auditing situation because audit entries are being created even when values are set equal to themselves. Updates like this one are producing useless audit records that show nothing changing:

```
SQL> UPDATE FRAME
  2  SET strike = strike;
   1 row updated.

SQL> SELECT old_strike,
  2         new_strike,
  3         old_spare,
  4         new_spare,
  5         old_score,
  6         new_score
  7    FROM frame_audit;

O N O N  OLD_SCORE  NEW_SCORE
- - - - ---------- ----------
Y Y N N
```

Pam needs to further isolate the trigger so that it fires only when values actually change. She does this using the WHEN clause shown here:

```
/* File on web: final_audit.sql */
CREATE OR REPLACE TRIGGER audit_update
AFTER UPDATE OF STRIKE, SPARE, SCORE ON FRAME
REFERENCING OLD AS prior_to_cheat NEW AS after_cheat
FOR EACH ROW
WHEN ( prior_to_cheat.strike != after_cheat.strike OR
       prior_to_cheat.spare != after_cheat.spare OR
       prior_to_cheat.score != after_cheat.score )
BEGIN
  INSERT INTO FRAME_AUDIT ( ... )
     VALUES ( ... );
END;
```

Now entries will appear in the audit table only if something did indeed change, allowing Pam to quickly identify possible cheaters. Pam performs a quick final test of her trigger.

```
SQL> UPDATE frame
  2  SET strike = strike;
1 row updated.
```

```
SQL> SELECT old_strike,
  2         new_strike,
  3         old_spare,
  4         new_spare,
  5         old_score,
  6         new_score
  7    FROM frame_audit;
no rows selected
```

Using pseudo-records to fine-tune trigger execution

Pam has implemented an acceptable level of auditing in her system; now she'd like to make it a little more user-friendly. Her most obvious idea is to have her system add 10 to the score for frames recording a strike or spare. This allows the scoreperson to track only the score for subsequent bowls while the system adds the strike score.

```
CREATE OR REPLACE TRIGGER set_score
BEFORE INSERT ON frame
FOR EACH ROW
WHEN ( NEW.score IS NULL )
BEGIN
  IF :NEW.strike = 'Y' OR :NEW.spare = 'Y'
  THEN
    :NEW.score := :NEW.score + 10;
  END IF;
END;
```

Remember that field values in the NEW records can be changed only in BEFORE row triggers.

Being a stickler for rules, Pam decides to add score validation to her set of triggers:

```
/* File on web: validate_score.sql */
CREATE OR REPLACE TRIGGER validate_score
   AFTER INSERT OR UPDATE
   ON frame
   FOR EACH ROW
BEGIN
   IF      :NEW.strike = 'Y' AND :NEW.score < 10
   THEN
      RAISE_APPLICATION_ERROR (
         -20001,
         'ERROR: Score For Strike Must Be >= 10'
      );
   ELSIF :NEW.spare = 'Y' AND :NEW.score < 10
   THEN
      RAISE_APPLICATION_ERROR (
         -20001,
         'ERROR: Score For Spare Must Be >= 10'
      );
   ELSIF :NEW.strike = 'Y' AND :NEW.spare = 'Y'
```

```
   THEN
      RAISE_APPLICATION_ERROR (
         -20001,
         'ERROR: Cannot Enter Spare And Strike'
      );
   END IF;
END;
```

Now when there is any attempt to insert a row that violates this condition, it will be rejected:

```
SQL> INSERT INTO frame VALUES (1,1,1,NULL,NULL,5);
INSERT INTO frame
            *
ERROR at line 1:
ORA-20000: ERROR: Score For Strike Must Be Less >= 10

SQL> INSERT INTO frame VALUES(1,1,1,'Y',NULL,5);
INSERT INTO frame
            *
ERROR at line 1:
ORA-20001: ERROR: Score For Strike Must >= 10
```

Multiple Triggers of the Same Type

Above and beyond all of the options presented for DML triggers, it is also possible to have multiple triggers of the same type attached to a single table. Switching from bowling to golf, consider the following example that provides a simple commentary of a golf score by determining its relationship to a par score of 72.

A single row-level BEFORE INSERT trigger would suffice:

```
/* File on web: golf_commentary.sql */
CREATE OR REPLACE TRIGGER golf_commentary
BEFORE INSERT ON golf_scores
FOR EACH ROW
BEGIN
  IF :NEW.score < 72 THEN
    :NEW.commentary := 'Under Par';
  ELSIF :NEW.score = 72 THEN
       :NEW.commentary := 'Par';
  ELSE
    :NEW.commentary := 'Over Par';
  END IF;
END;
```

However, the requirement could also be satisfied with three separate row-level BEFORE INSERT triggers with mutually exclusive WHEN clauses:

```
CREATE OR REPLACE TRIGGER golf_commentary_under_par
BEFORE INSERT ON golf_scores
FOR EACH ROW
WHEN (NEW.score < 72)
BEGIN
```

```
    :NEW.commentary := 'Under Par';
  END;

  CREATE OR REPLACE TRIGGER golf_commentary_par
  BEFORE INSERT ON golf_scores
  FOR EACH ROW
  WHEN (NEW.score = 72)
  BEGIN
    :NEW.commentary := 'Par';
  END;

  CREATE OR REPLACE TRIGGER golf_commentary_over_par
  BEFORE INSERT ON golf_scores
  FOR EACH ROW
  WHEN (NEW.score > 72)
  BEGIN
    :NEW.commentary := 'Over Par';
  END;
```

Both implementations are perfectly acceptable and have advantages and disadvantages. A single trigger is easier to maintain because all of the code is in one place, while separate triggers reduce parse and execution time when more complex processing is required.

One pitfall of multiple triggers is that there is no guarantee of the order in which they will fire. While this is not a concern in the above example, it could be a problem in others, as shown next.

What values will be shown by the final query?

```
/* File on web: multiple_trigger_seq.sql */
DROP TABLE incremented_values;

CREATE TABLE incremented_values
(value_inserted    NUMBER,
 value_incremented NUMBER);

CREATE OR REPLACE TRIGGER increment_by_one
BEFORE INSERT ON incremented_values
FOR EACH ROW
BEGIN
  :NEW.value_incremented := :NEW.value_incremented + 1;
END;
/

CREATE OR REPLACE TRIGGER increment_by_two
BEFORE INSERT ON incremented_values
FOR EACH ROW
BEGIN
  IF :NEW.value_incremented > 1 THEN
    :NEW.value_incremented := :NEW.value_incremented + 2;
  END IF;
END;
/
```

```
INSERT INTO incremented_values
VALUES(1,1);

SELECT *
  FROM incremented_values;
```

Any guesses? On my database I got this result:

```
SQL> SELECT *
  2    FROM incremented_values;

VALUE_INSERTED VALUE_INCREMENTED
-------------- -----------------
             1                 2
```

So the increment_by_two trigger fired first and did nothing because the value_incremented column was not greater than 1; then the increment_by_one trigger fired to increase the value_incremented column by 1. Is this the result you will receive? There is no guarantee. Will this result always be received? Again, there is no guarantee. Oracle explicitly states that there is no way to control or assure the order in which multiple triggers of the same type on a single table will fire. There are many theories, the most prevalent being that triggers fire in reverse order of creation or by order of object ID—but even those theories should not be relied upon.

Mutating Table Errors: Problem and Solution

When something mutates, it is changing. Something that is changing is hard to analyze and to quantify. A mutating table error (ORA-4091) occurs when a row-level trigger tries to examine or change a table that is already undergoing change (via an INSERT, UPDATE, or DELETE statement).

In particular, this error occurs when a row-level trigger attempts to read or write the table from which the trigger was fired. Suppose, for example, that I want to put a special check on my employee table to make sure that when a person is given a raise, that person's new salary is not more than 20% above the next-highest salary in their department.

I would therefore like to write a trigger like this:

```
CREATE OR REPLACE TRIGGER brake_on_raises
   BEFORE UPDATE OF salary ON employee
   FOR EACH ROW
DECLARE
   l_curr_max NUMBER;
BEGIN
   SELECT MAX (salary) INTO l_curr_max
     FROM employee;
   IF l_curr_max * 1.20 < :NEW.salary
   THEN
      errpkg.RAISE (
         employee_rules.en_salary_increase_too_large,
```

```
            :NEW.employee_id,
            :NEW.salary
         );
      END IF;
   END;
```

But when I try to perform an update that, say, doubles the salary of the PL/SQL programmer (yours truly), I get this error:

```
ORA-04091: table SCOTT.EMPLOYEE is mutating, trigger/function may not see it
```

Here are some guidelines to keep in mind regarding mutating table errors:

- In general, a row-level trigger may not read or write the table from which it has been fired. The restriction only applies to row-level triggers, however. Statement-level triggers are free to both read and modify the triggering table; this fact gives us a way to avoid the mutating table error, as discussed in the section "Getting around the mutating table error."
- If you make your trigger an autonomous transaction (by adding the PRAGMA AUTONOMOUS TRANSACTION statement and committing inside the body of the trigger), then you will be able to *query* the contents of the firing table. However, you will still not be allowed to modify the contents of the table.

Mutating tables and foreign keys

The mutating table error often arises in the context of foreign keys. Let's take a look at an example.

The staff at Humongous Bank have implemented their transaction system using Version 7.3.4 of Oracle, and they are feeling very magnanimous: they have decided to give away $100 to any customer who opens up a new account. As usual, they neglected to inform the applications team until the weekend before the promotion begins; thus poor Kay Fourohone is asked to work through the weekend to implement the new system.

Kay applies her stellar logic to the situation—every time an account is opened, a deposit of $100 must be made into my...I mean, the *new* account. This is a perfect application of DML triggers: every time an INSERT is performed on the account table, a trigger will put the deposit entry into the account transaction table. Kay is extremely happy because such a simple trigger will only take half a day to code, debug, test, and implement, leaving her the rest of the weekend to practice bowling before the league finals on Monday.

Knowing that the tables involved are account and account_transaction and that there is a foreign key between them on the account_id field, Kay creates the following trigger:

```
CREATE TRIGGER give_away_free_money
AFTER INSERT ON account
FOR EACH ROW
```

```
BEGIN
  INSERT INTO account_transaction
   (transaction_id,
    account_id,
    transaction_type,
    transaction_amount,
    comments)
  VALUES(account_transaction_seq.nextval,
      :NEW.account_id,
      'DEP',
      100,
      'Free Money!');
END;
```

Kay is so confident that this will work that she almost doesn't bother to test it. What could go wrong with such a simple chunk of code? She quickly gets her answer.

```
SQL> INSERT INTO account
  2  (account_id,account_owner)
  3  VALUES(1,'Test');

INSERT INTO account
            *
ERROR at line 1:
ORA-04091: table SCOTT.ACCOUNT is mutating, trigger/function may not see it
ORA-06512: at "SCOTT.GIVE_AWAY_FREE_MONEY", line 2
ORA-04088: error during execution of trigger 'SCOTT.GIVE_AWAY_FREE_MONEY'
```

The account table is indeed mutating during this transaction as a result of the initial INSERT statement. The trigger then attempts to insert a record into the account_transaction table, which in turn requires Oracle to validate the account_id against the account table. But because foreign key validation occurs before the trigger even fires, Oracle cannot be assured that the entry is valid.

Now you may be saying that this error makes no sense because all of the required information is easily available; the primary key is available from the original INSERT statement. While this is a valid argument, the fact remains that we've exposed a limitation of row-level triggers here.

As of Oracle 8.1.5, this error will no longer occur. The foreign key check now takes place after row-level triggers fire.

This limitation applies only to row-level triggers; statement-level triggers are immune because they do not process single rows. This immunity is what Kay will exploit to get around her mutation problem.

Getting around the mutating table error

So what should you do when confronted with this error? Some developers throw up their hands, abandon triggers, and seek another way of getting the same logic enforced. This is not necessary. Instead, you can rely on the fact that statement-level triggers are not restricted from accessing the firing table, and that package-level data structures persist for the duration of your session.

Here's the best way to look at it: within a row-level trigger, you need to take a certain action. But Oracle won't let you take that action. Instead, you must defer your action until it can be performed in a statement-level trigger. Fine. But if you are going to wait until later, you have to *remember* what it is you needed to do. PL/SQL collections (array-like structures, which we cover in Chapter 11) serve very well as your to-do list.

So in the row-level trigger, instead of taking the necessary action, you write all the information you need to remember in order to take that action at the statement level. Then when all the row-level triggers have fired, control passes to the statement-level trigger. And inside that trigger, you can scan through the contents of the collection and execute the code you originally wanted to perform at the row level. These steps are shown in Figure 18-2. Let's take a look at how Kay can apply this technique to her situation.

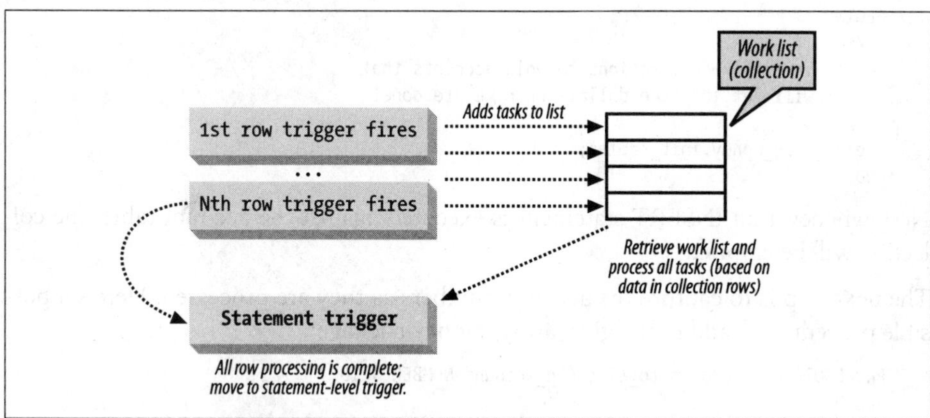

Figure 18-2. Using a collection as a work list to bypass mutating trigger errors

Kay can implement the following algorithm to subvert any chances of mutating:

1. Initialize collections in a PL/SQL package when the statement begins.
2. Store record identifiers in these collections as each row is processed.
3. Process each entry in the collections after the statement ends.

First a PL/SQL package is required. Here is the start of one that will help Kay out:

```
/* File on web: mutation_zone.sql */
CREATE OR REPLACE PACKAGE give_away_money AS

  PROCEDURE init_tables;

END give_away_money;
```

```
CREATE OR REPLACE PACKAGE BODY give_away_money
AS
  -- structure to hold account numbers
  TYPE v_account_table_type IS TABLE OF NUMBER
    INDEX BY BINARY_INTEGER;
  v_account_table v_account_table_type;

  /*----------------------------------------*/
  PROCEDURE init_tables IS
  /*----------------------------------------*/
  BEGIN -- Initialize the account list to empty
    v_account_table.DELETE;
  END init_tables;

END give_away_money;
```

This simple beginning takes care of cleaning out the collection to store account numbers as they are inserted. Next we have to hook up the init_tables procedure with a BEFORE statement trigger:

```
CREATE OR REPLACE TRIGGER before_insert_statement
BEFORE INSERT ON account
BEGIN
  /*
    || Initialize collections to hold accounts that
    || will get 100 free dollars when we are done!
  */
  give_away_money.init_tables;
END;
```

Now whenever an INSERT statement is executed against the account table, the collection will be emptied.

The next step is to capture the account numbers as they are processed. Here's a possible procedure to add to the give_away_money package:

```
PROCEDURE add_account_to_list ( p_account NUMBER ) IS
BEGIN
  v_account_table(NVL(v_account_table.LAST,0) + 1) := p_account;
END add_account_to_list;
```

It attaches to an AFTER INSERT row trigger like this:

```
CREATE OR REPLACE TRIGGER after_insert_row
AFTER INSERT ON account
FOR EACH ROW
BEGIN
  /*
    || Add the new account to the list of those in line for
    || 100 dollars.
  */
  give_away_money.add_account_to_list(:NEW.account_id);
END;
```

Last but not least, a procedure in the package finally gives the money away:

```
PROCEDURE give_it_away_now
IS
-- Create $100 deposits for accounts that have been created
  v_element PLS_INTEGER;
BEGIN
  v_element := v_account_table.FIRST;
  LOOP
    EXIT WHEN v_element IS NULL;
    INSERT INTO account_transaction
       (transaction_id,
        account_id,
        transaction_type,
        transaction_amount,
        comments)
    VALUES(account_transaction_seq.nextval,
        v_account_table(v_element),
        'DEP',
        100,
        'Free Money!');
    v_element := v_account_table.NEXT(v_element);
  END LOOP;
END give_it_away_now;
```

This procedure attaches to an AFTER INSERT statement trigger as such:

```
CREATE OR REPLACE TRIGGER after_insert_statement
AFTER INSERT ON account
BEGIN
  -- At long last we can give away the money!
  give_away_money.give_it_away_now;
END;
```

Now after dropping Kay's original trigger and replacing it with the new package and triggers, testing reveals the following behavior:

```
SQL> INSERT INTO account (account_id,account_owner)
  2     VALUES (1,'Test');

SQL> SELECT * FROM account_transaction
  2   WHERE account_id = 1;

TRANSACTION_ID ACCOUNT_ID TRA TRANSACTION_AMOUNT COMMENTS
-------------- ---------- --- ------------------ ------------------------------
             1          1 DEP                100 Free Money!
SQL> BEGIN
  2    FOR counter IN 20..25 LOOP
  3      INSERT INTO account
  4      (account_id,account_owner)
  5      VALUES(counter,'Test');
  6    END LOOP;
  7  END;
```

```
SQL> SELECT *
  2    FROM account_transaction
  3   WHERE account_id BETWEEN 20 AND 25

TRANSACTION_ID ACCOUNT_ID TRA TRANSACTION_AMOUNT COMMENTS
-------------- ---------- --- ------------------ ------------------------------
             2         20 DEP                100 Free Money!
             3         21 DEP                100 Free Money!
             4         22 DEP                100 Free Money!
             5         23 DEP                100 Free Money!
             6         24 DEP                100 Free Money!
             7         25 DEP                100 Free Money!

6 rows selected.
```

Thanks to the powerful interaction of statement-level triggers, row-level triggers and PL/SQL packages, Kay is free to enjoy the rest of her weekend without worrying about any mutation problems.

The dwindling mutation zone

As Oracle matures, it is getting better at handling the mutating table situation. As a matter of fact, starting with Oracle 8.1.5, Kay's original code would work fine. This is because the foreign key check is now done after the row-level triggers fire. One situation that remains vulnerable to painful mutation is when a foreign key specifies the ON DELETE CASCADE clause.

Consider this rudimentary example of a simple master table and detail table, with a foreign key constraint between them that includes the ON DELETE CASCADE clause:

```
CREATE TABLE master_table
(master_id NUMBER NOT NULL PRIMARY KEY);

CREATE TABLE detail_table
(detail_id NUMBER NOT NULL,
 master_id NUMBER NOT NULL,
   CONSTRAINT detail_to_emp
   FOREIGN KEY (master_id)
   REFERENCES master_table (master_id)
   ON DELETE CASCADE);

CREATE OR REPLACE TRIGGER after_delete_master
AFTER DELETE ON master_table
FOR EACH ROW
DECLARE
  CURSOR curs_count_detail IS
  SELECT COUNT(*)
    FROM detail_table;
  v_detail_count NUMBER;
BEGIN
  OPEN curs_count_detail;
```

```
    FETCH curs_count_detail INTO v_detail_count;
    CLOSE curs_count_detail;
  END;
```

Delete operations on the master_table cause associated detail_table records to disappear; then the trigger attempts to count the rows in detail_table. Oracle cannot guarantee an accurate result because it is unsure of how many rows remain. Thus, it is left with no choice but to loudly announce the potential mutation:

```
SQL> DELETE master_table;
*
ERROR at line 1:
ORA-04091: table SCOTT.DETAIL_TABLE is mutating, trigger/function may not see it
ORA-06512: at "SCOTT.AFTER_DELETE_MASTER", line 3
ORA-06512: at "SCOTT.AFTER_DELETE_MASTER", line 7
ORA-04088: error during execution of trigger 'SCOTT.AFTER_DELETE_MASTER'
```

Even this situation can be avoided using autonomous transactions as introduced in Oracle 8.1. This means that the trigger will fire as its own transaction in order to avoid the possibility of mutation.

```
CREATE OR REPLACE TRIGGER after_delete_master
AFTER DELETE ON master_table
FOR EACH ROW
DECLARE
  -- declare as autonomous
  PRAGMA AUTONOMOUS_TRANSACTION;
  CURSOR curs_count_detail IS
  SELECT COUNT(*)
    FROM detail_table;
  v_detail_count NUMBER;
BEGIN
  OPEN curs_count_detail;
  FETCH curs_count_detail INTO v_detail_count;
  DBMS_OUTPUT.PUT_LINE('detail count = ' || v_detail_count);
  CLOSE curs_count_detail;
END;
```

Now the trigger can execute because it is not a part of the actual delete transaction.

```
SQL> DELETE master_table;
detail count = 1

1 row deleted.
```

As you can see, the mutation zone is becoming less and less of a problem.

DDL Triggers

Oracle8 introduced a long-awaited feature: the firing of triggers when Data Definition Language (DDL) statements are executed. Simply put, DDL is any SQL statement used to create or modify a database object such as a table or an index. Here are some examples of DDL statements:

- CREATE TABLE / ALTER TABLE
- CREATE INDEX
- CREATE TRIGGER / DROP TRIGGER

Each of these statements results in the creation, alteration, or removal of a database object.

The syntax for creating these triggers is remarkably similar to that of DML triggers, except that the firing events differ and they are not applied to tables.

Creating a DDL Trigger

To create (or replace) a DDL trigger, use the syntax shown here:

```
1 CREATE [OR REPLACE] TRIGGER trigger name
2 {BEFORE | AFTER| {DDL event} ON {DATABASE | SCHEMA}
3 DECLARE
4 Variable declarations
5 BEGIN
6 ... some code...
7 END;
```

The following table summarizes what is happening in this code:

Line(s)	Description
1	Specifies that a trigger is to be created with the name supplied. Specifying OR REPLACE is optional. If the trigger exists and REPLACE is not specified, then good old Oracle error 4081 will appear stating just that.
2	This line has a lot to say. It defines whether the trigger will fire before or after the particular DDL event as well as whether it will fire for all operations within the database or just within the current schema.
3–7	These lines simply demonstrate the PL/SQL contents of the trigger.

Here's an example of a somewhat uninformed town crier trigger that announces the creation of all objects:

```
/* File on web: uninformed_town_crier.sql*/
SQL> CREATE OR REPLACE TRIGGER town_crier
  2  AFTER CREATE ON SCHEMA
  3  BEGIN
  4     DBMS_OUTPUT.PUT_LINE('I believe you have created something!');
  5  END;
  6  /
Trigger created.

SQL> SET SERVEROUTPUT ON
SQL> CREATE TABLE a_table
  2  (col1 NUMBER);
Table created.

SQL> CREATE INDEX an_index ON a_table(col1);
Index created.
```

```
SQL> CREATE FUNCTION a_function RETURN BOOLEAN AS
  2  BEGIN
  3    RETURN(TRUE);
  4  END;
  5  /
Function created.

SQL> /*-- flush the DBMS_OUTPUT buffer */
SQL> BEGIN NULL; END;
  2  /
I believe you have created something!
I believe you have created something!
I believe you have created something!

PL/SQL procedure successfully completed.
```

Text displayed using the DBMS_OUTPUT built-in package within DDL triggers will not display until you successfully execute a PL/SQL block, even if that block does nothing.

Over time, this town crier would be ignored due to a lack of information, always proudly announcing that something had been created but never providing any details. Thankfully, there is a lot more information available to DDL triggers, allowing for a much more nuanced treatment, as shown in this version:

```
/* File on web: informed_town_crier.sql */
SQL> CREATE OR REPLACE TRIGGER town_crier
  2  AFTER CREATE ON SCHEMA
  3  BEGIN
  4    -- use event attributes to provide more info
  5    DBMS_OUTPUT.PUT_LINE('I believe you have created a ' ||
  6                         ORA_DICT_OBJ_TYPE || ' called ' ||
  7                         ORA_DICT_OBJ_NAME);
  8  END;
  9  /
Trigger created.

SQL> SET SERVEROUTPUT ON
SQL> CREATE TABLE a_table
  2  (col1 NUMBER);
Table created.

SQL> CREATE INDEX an_index ON a_table(col1);
Index created.

SQL> CREATE FUNCTION a_function RETURN BOOLEAN AS
  2  BEGIN
  3    RETURN(TRUE);
  4  END;
  5  /
Function created.
```

```
SQL> /*-- flush the DBMS_OUTPUT buffer */
SQL> BEGIN NULL; END;
/
I believe you have created a TABLE called A_TABLE
I believe you have created a INDEX called AN_INDEX
I believe you have created a FUNCTION called A_FUNCTION

PL/SQL procedure successfully completed.
```

Much more attention will be paid now that the town crier is more forthcoming. The above examples touch upon two important aspects of DDL triggers: the specific events to which they can be applied and the event attributes available within the triggers.

Available Events

Table 18-1 lists the DDL events for which triggers can be coded. Each event can have a BEFORE and an AFTER trigger.

Table 18-1. Available DDL events

DDL event	Fires when...
CREATE	Any database object is created using the SQL CREATE command.
ALTER	Any database object is altered using the SQL ALTER command.
DROP	Any database object is dropped using the SQL DROP command.
ANALYZE	Any database object is analyzed using the SQL ANALYZE command.
ASSOCIATE STATISTICS	Statistics are associated with a database object.
AUDIT	Auditing is turned on using the SQL AUDIT command.
NOAUDIT	Auditing is turned off using the SQL NOAUDIT command.
COMMENT	Comments are applied to a database object.
DDL	Any of the events listed here occur.
DISASSOCIATE STATISTICS	Statistics are disassociated from a database object.
GRANT	Privileges are granted using the SQL GRANT command.
RENAME	A database object is renamed using the SQL RENAME command.
REVOKE	Privileges are revoked using the SQL REVOKE command.
TRUNCATE	A table is truncated using the SQL TRUNCATE command.

As with DML triggers, these DDL triggers fire when the event to which they are attached occurs within the specified database or schema. There is no limit to the number of trigger types that can exist in the database or schema.

Available Attributes

Oracle provides a set of functions (defined in the DBMS_STANDARD package) that provide information about what fired the DDL trigger and other information about the trigger state (e.g., the name of the table being dropped). Table 18-2 displays these trigger attribute functions. The following sections offer some examples of usage.

Table 18-2. DDL trigger event and attribute functions

Name	Description
ORA_SYSEVENT	Returns the type of event that caused the DDL trigger to fire (e.g., CREATE, DROP, or ALTER).
ORA_LOGIN_USER	Returns the name of the Oracle user for which the trigger fired.
ORA_INSTANCE_NUM	Returns the number of the database instance.
ORA_DATABASE_NAME	Returns the name of the database.
ORA_CLIENT_IP_ADDRESS	Returns the IP address of the client.
ORA_DICT_OBJ_TYPE	Returns the type of database object affected by the firing DDL (e.g., TABLE or INDEX).
ORA_DICT_OBJ_NAME	Returns the name of the database object affected by the firing DDL.
ORA_DICT_OBJ_OWNER	Returns the owner of the database object affected by the firing DDL.
ORA_IS_CREATING_NESTED_TABLE	Returns TRUE if a nested table is being created, or FALSE if not.
ORA_DES_ENCRYPTED_PASSWORD	Returns the DES-encrypted password of the current user.
ORA_IS_ALTER_COLUMN	Returns TRUE if the specified COLUMN_NAME argument is being altered, or FALSE if not.
ORA_IS_DROP_COLUMN	Returns TRUE if the specified COLUMN_NAME argument is indeed being dropped, or FALSE if not.
ORA_DICT_OBJ_NAME_LIST	Returns the count of objects affected. It also returns a complete list of objects affected in the NAME_LIST parameter, which is a collection of type DBMS_STANDARD.ORA_NAME_LIST_T.
ORA_DICT_OBJ_OWNER_LIST	Returns the count of objects affected. It also returns a complete list of object owners affected in the NAME_LIST parameter, which is a collection of type DBMS_STANDARD.ORA_NAME_LIST_T.
ORA_GRANTEE	Returns the count of grantees. The USER_LIST argument contains the full list of grantees, which is a collection of type DBMS_STANDARD.ORA_NAME_LIST_T.
ORA_WITH_GRANT_OPTION	Returns TRUE if privileges were granted with the GRANT option, or FALSE if not.
ORA_PRIVILEGE_LIST	Returns the number of privileges being granted or revoked. The PRIVILEGE_LIST argument contains the full list of privileges affected, which is a collection of type DBMS_STANDARD.ORA_NAME_LIST_T.
ORA_REVOKEE	Returns the count of revokees. The USER_LIST argument contains the full list of revokees, which is a collection of type DBMS_STANDARD.ORA_NAME_LIST_T.

Note the following about the event and attribute functions:

- The datatype ORA_NAME_LIST_T is defined in the DBMS_STANDARD package as:

  ```
  TYPE ora_name_list_t IS TABLE OF VARCHAR2(64);
  ```

  In other words, this is a nested table of strings, each of which can contain up to 64 characters.

- The DDL trigger event and attribute functions are also defined in the DBMS_STANDARD package. Oracle creates a standalone function (which adds the "ORA_" prefix to the function name) for each of the packaged functions by executing the *$ORACLE_HOME/rdbms/dbmstrig.sql* script during database creation. In some releases of Oracle, there are errors in this script that cause the standalone functions to not be visible or executable. Here is an example from the 8.1.7 script (notice the error in privileg_list):

  ```
  create public synonym ora_privilege_list for privileg_list
  ```

  While this particular problem was fixed in Oracle9*i*, you may encounter others. In this case, you should ask your DBA to check the script for problems and make the necessary corrections.
- The USER_SOURCE data dictionary view does not get updated until after both BEFORE and AFTER DDL triggers are fired. In other words, you cannot use these functions to provide a "before and after" version control system built entirely within the database and based on database triggers.

Working with Events and Attributes

The best way to demonstrate the possibilities offered by DDL trigger events and attributes is with a series of examples.

Here is a trigger that prevents any and all database objects from being created:

```
CREATE OR REPLACE TRIGGER no_create
   AFTER CREATE ON SCHEMA
BEGIN
   RAISE_APPLICATION_ERROR (
      -20000,
      'ERROR : Objects cannot be created in the production database.'
   );
END;
```

After installing this trigger, attempts at creating anything meet with failure:

```
SQL> CREATE TABLE demo (col1 NUMBER);
*
ERROR at line 1:
ORA-20000: Objects cannot be created in the production database.
```

That is a rather terse and uninformative error message. There was a failure, but what failed? Wouldn't it be nice to have a little more information in the error message, such as what I was attempting to create?

```
/* File on web: no_create.sql */
CREATE OR REPLACE TRIGGER no_create
AFTER CREATE ON SCHEMA
BEGIN
  RAISE_APPLICATION_ERROR (-20000,
       'Cannot create the ' || ORA_DICT_OBJ_TYPE ||
       ' named '            || ORA_DICT_OBJ_NAME ||
```

```
         ' as requested by '  || ORA_DICT_OBJ_OWNER ||
         ' in production.');
END;
```

With this trigger installed, an attempt to create my table now offers much more diagnostic information:

```
SQL> CREATE TABLE demo (col1 NUMBER);
*
ERROR at line 1:
ORA-20000: Cannot create the TABLE named DEMO as requested by SCOTT in production
```

I could even place this logic within a BEFORE DDL trigger, and take advantage of the ORA_SYSEVENT attribute to respond to specific events:

```
CREATE OR REPLACE TRIGGER no_create
BEFORE DDL ON SCHEMA
BEGIN
  IF ORA_SYSEVENT = 'CREATE'
  THEN
    RAISE_APPLICATION_ERROR (-20000,
       'Cannot create the ' || ORA_DICT_OBJ_TYPE ||
       ' named '            || ORA_DICT_OBJ_NAME ||
       ' as requested by '  || ORA_DICT_OBJ_OWNER);
  ELSIF ORA_SYSEVENT = 'DROP'
  THEN
     -- Logic for DROP operations
     ...
  END IF;
END;
```

What column did I touch?

I can use the ORA_IS_ALTER_COLUMN function to decipher which column was altered by an ALTER TABLE statement. Here is one example:

```
/* File on web: preserve_app_cols.sql  */
CREATE OR REPLACE TRIGGER preserve_app_cols
   AFTER ALTER ON SCHEMA
DECLARE
   -- Cursor to get columns in a table
   CURSOR curs_get_columns (cp_owner VARCHAR2, cp_table VARCHAR2)
   IS
      SELECT column_name
        FROM all_tab_columns
       WHERE owner = cp_owner AND table_name = cp_table;
BEGIN
   -- if it was a table that was altered...
   IF ora_dict_obj_type = 'TABLE'
   THEN
      -- for every column in the table...
      FOR v_column_rec IN curs_get_columns (
                             ora_dict_obj_owner,
                             ora_dict_obj_name
                          )
```

```
      LOOP
         -- Is the current column one that was altered?
         IF ORA_IS_ALTER_COLUMN (v_column_rec.column_name)
         THEN
            -- Reject change to "core application" column
            IF mycheck.is_application_column (
                  ora_dict_obj_owner,
                  ora_dict_obj_name,
                  v_column_rec.column_name
               )
            THEN
               RAISE_APPLICATION_ERROR (
                  'FAIL',
                  'Cannot alter core application attributes'
               );
            END IF; -- table/column is core
         END IF; -- current column was altered
      END LOOP; -- every column in the table
   END IF; -- table was altered
END;
```

Attempts to change core application attributes will now be stopped.

Remember that this logic will not work when the trigger is fired for the addition of new columns. That column information is not yet visible in the data dictionary when the DDL trigger fires.

I can check for attempts to drop specific columns as follows:

```
IF ORA_IS_DROP_COLUMN ('COL2')
THEN
  do something!
ELSE
  do something else!
END IF;
```

The ORA_IS_DROP_COLUMN and ORA_IS_ALTER_COLUMN functions are blissfully unaware of the table to which the column is attached; they work on column name alone.

Lists returned by attribute functions

Some of the attribute functions return two pieces of data: a list of items and a count of items. For example, the ORA_GRANTEE function returns a list and a count of users that were granted a privilege, and the ORA_PRIVILEGE_LIST function returns a list and a count of privileges granted. These two functions are perfect for use in AFTER GRANT triggers. The *what_privs.sql* file available on the O'Reilly site offers an extended example of how to use both of these functions. Below is just a portion of the total code:

```
/* File on web: what_privs.sql */
CREATE OR REPLACE TRIGGER what_privs
```

```
   AFTER GRANT ON SCHEMA
DECLARE
   v_grant_type      VARCHAR2 (30);
   v_num_grantees    BINARY_INTEGER;
   v_grantee_list    ora_name_list_t;
   v_num_privs       BINARY_INTEGER;
   v_priv_list       ora_name_list_t;
BEGIN
   -- Retrieve information about grant type and then the lists.
   v_grant_type := ORA_DICT_OBJ_TYPE;
   v_num_grantees := ORA_GRANTEE (v_grantee_list);
   v_num_privs := ORA_PRIVILEGE_LIST (v_priv_list);

   IF v_grant_type = 'ROLE PRIVILEGE'
   THEN
      DBMS_OUTPUT.put_line ('The following roles/privileges were granted'
      );

      -- For each element in the list, display the privilege.
      FOR counter IN 1 .. v_num_privs
      LOOP
         DBMS_OUTPUT.put_line ('Privilege ' || v_priv_list (counter)
         );
      END LOOP;
```

This trigger is great for detailing what privileges and objects are affected by grant operations, as shown below. In a more sophisticated implementation, you might consider storing this information in database tables so that you have a detailed history of changes that have occurred.

```
SQL> GRANT DBA TO book WITH ADMIN OPTION;
Grant succeeded.

SQL> EXEC DBMS_OUTPUT.PUT_LINE('Flush buffer');
        The following roles/privileges were granted
                Privilege UNLIMITED TABLESPACE
                Privilege DBA
        Grant Recipient BOOK
Flush buffer

SQL> GRANT SELECT ON x TO system WITH GRANT OPTION;
Grant succeeded.

SQL> EXEC DBMS_OUTPUT.PUT_LINE('Flush buffer');
        The following object privileges were granted
                Privilege SELECT
        On X with grant option
        Grant Recipient SYSTEM
Flush buffer
```

Dropping the Undroppable

We have shown that one use for DDL triggers is preventing a particular type of DDL on a particular object or type of object. But what if we create a trigger that prevents DROP DDL, and then attempt to drop the trigger itself? Will we be left with a trigger that is essentially undroppable? Fortunately, Oracle has thought of this scenario, as you can see here:

```
SQL> CREATE OR REPLACE TRIGGER undroppable
  2  BEFORE DROP ON SCHEMA
  3  BEGIN
  4    RAISE_APPLICATION_ERROR(-20000,'You cannot drop me! I am invincible!');
  5  END;

SQL> DROP TABLE employee;
*
ERROR at line 1:
ORA-20000: You cannot drop me! I am invincible!

SQL> DROP TRIGGER undroppable;
Trigger dropped.
```

Database Event Triggers

Database event triggers fire whenever database-wide events occur. There are five database event triggers:

STARTUP
: Fires when the database is opened.

SHUTDOWN
: Fires when the database is shut down normally.

SERVERERROR
: Fires when an Oracle error is raised.

LOGON
: Fires when an Oracle session begins.

LOGOFF
: Fires when an Oracle session terminates normally.

As any DBA will immediately see, these triggers offer stunning possibilities for automated administration and very granular control.

Creating a Database Event Trigger

The syntax used to create these triggers is quite similar to that used for DDL triggers:

```
CREATE [OR REPLACE] TRIGGER trigger name
{BEFORE | AFTER} {database event} ON {DATABASE | SCHEMA}
DECLARE
```

```
Variable declarations
BEGIN
... some code...
END;
```

There are restrictions regarding what events can be combined with what BEFORE and AFTER attributes. Some situations just don't make sense:

No BEFORE STARTUP triggers

Even if such triggers could be created, when would they fire? Attempts to create triggers of this type will be met by this straightforward error message:

```
ORA-30500: database open triggers and server error triggers cannot have BEFORE
type
```

No AFTER SHUTDOWN triggers

Again, when would they fire? Attempts to create such triggers are deflected with this message:

```
ORA-30501: instance shutdown triggers cannot have AFTER type
```

No BEFORE LOGON triggers

It would require some amazingly perceptive code to implement these triggers: "Wait, I think someone is going to log on—do something!" Being strictly reality-based, Oracles stops these triggers with this message:

```
ORA-30508: client logon triggers cannot have BEFORE type
```

No AFTER LOGOFF triggers

"No wait, please come back! Don't sign off!" Attempts to create such triggers are stopped with this message:

```
ORA-30509: client logoff triggers cannot have AFTER type
```

No BEFORE SERVERERROR

These triggers would be every programmer's dream! Think of the possibilities…

```
CREATE OR REPLACE TRIGGER BEFORE_SERVERERROR
BEFORE SERVERERROR ON DATABASE
BEGIN
  diagnose_impending_error;
  fix_error_condition;
  continue_as_if_nothing_happened;
END;
```

Unfortunately, our dreams are shattered by this error message:

```
ORA-30500: database open triggers and server error triggers cannot have BEFORE
type
```

The STARTUP Trigger

Startup triggers execute during database startup processing. This is a perfect place to perform housekeeping steps, such as pinning objects in the shared pool so that they do not "age out" with the least-recently-used algorithm.

In order to create startup event triggers, users must have been granted the ADMINISTER DATABASE TRIGGER privilege.

Here is an example of creating a STARTUP event trigger:

```
CREATE OR REPLACE TRIGGER startup_pinner
AFTER STARTUP ON DATABASE
BEGIN
  pin_plsql_packages;
  pin_application_packages;
END;
```

The SHUTDOWN Trigger

BEFORE SHUTDOWN triggers execute before database shutdown processing is performed. This is a great place to gather system statistics. Here is an example of creating a SHUTDOWN event trigger:

```
CREATE OR REPLACE TRIGGER after_shutdown
AFTER SHUTDOWN ON DATABASE
BEGIN
  gather_system_stats;
END;
```

SHUTDOWN triggers execute only when the database is shut down using NORMAL or IMMEDIATE mode. They do not execute when the database is shut down using ABORT mode or when the database crashes.

The LOGON Trigger

AFTER LOGON triggers fire when an Oracle session is begun. They are the perfect place to establish session context and perform other session setup tasks. Here is an example of creating a LOGON event trigger:

```
CREATE OR REPLACE TRIGGER after_logon
AFTER LOGON ON SCHEMA
DECLARE
  v_sql VARCHAR2(100) := 'ALTER SESSION ENABLE RESUMABLE ' ||
                         'TIMEOUT 10 NAME ' || '''' ||
                         'OLAP Session'     || '''';
BEGIN
  EXECUTE IMMEDIATE v_sql;
  DBMS_SESSION.SET_CONTEXT('OLAP Namespace',
                           'Customer ID',
                           load_user_customer_id);
END;
```

The LOGOFF Trigger

BEFORE LOGOFF triggers execute when sessions disconnect normally from the database. This is a good place to gather statistics regarding session activity. Here is an example of creating a LOGOFF event trigger:

```
CREATE OR REPLACE TRIGGER before_logoff
BEFORE LOGOFF ON DATABASE
BEGIN
  gather_session_stats;
END;
```

The SERVERERROR Trigger

AFTER SERVERERROR triggers fire after an Oracle error is raised, unless the error is one of the following:

ORA-00600
: Oracle internal error

ORA-01034
: Oracle not available

ORA-01403
: No data found

ORA-01422
: Exact fetch returns more than requested number of rows

ORA-01423
: Error encountered while checking for extra rows in an exact fetch

ORA-04030
: Out-of-process memory when trying to allocate *N* bytes

In addition, the AFTER SERVERERROR trigger will *not* fire when an exception is raised *inside* this trigger (to avoid an infinite recursive execution of the trigger).

AFTER SERVERERROR triggers do not provide facilities to fix the error, only to log information about the error. It is therefore possible to build some powerful logging mechanisms around these triggers.

Oracle also provides two built-in functions (again, defined in DBMS_STANDARD) that retrieve information about the error stack generated when an exception is raised:

ORA_SERVER_ERROR
: Returns the Oracle error number at the specified position in the error stack. It returns 0 if no error is found at that position.

ORA_IS_SERVERERROR
: Returns TRUE if the specified error number appears in the current exception stack.

SERVERERROR examples

Let's look at some examples of using the SERVERERROR functions. We'll start with a very simple example of a SERVERERROR trigger that echoes the fact that an error occurred.

```
CREATE OR REPLACE TRIGGER error_echo
AFTER SERVERERROR
ON SCHEMA
BEGIN
  DBMS_OUTPUT.PUT_LINE ('You experienced an error');
END;
```

Whenever an Oracle error occurs (assuming that SERVEROUTPUT is ON), the coded message above will display:

```
SQL> SET SERVEROUTPUT ON
SQL> EXEC DBMS_OUTPUT.PUT_LINE(TO_NUMBER('A'));
You experienced an error
BEGIN DBMS_OUTPUT.PUT_LINE(TO_NUMBER('A')); END;

*
ERROR at line 1:
ORA-06502: PL/SQL: numeric or value error: character to number conversion error
ORA-06512: at line 1
```

Note that the Oracle error message was delivered after the trigger message. This allows the Oracle error to be accessed and logged prior to the actual failure, as shown in the next example.

SERVERERROR triggers are automatically isolated in their own autonomous transaction (autonomous transactions were covered in Chapter 13). This means that you can, for example, write error information out to a log table and save those changes with a COMMIT, while not affecting the session transaction in which the error occurred.

The error_echo trigger guarantees that information about all but a handful of errors listed earlier will be automatically logged regardless of the application, user, or program in which the error was raised.

```
/* File on web: error_log.sql */
CREATE OR REPLACE TRIGGER error_echo
AFTER SERVERERROR
ON SCHEMA
DECLARE

  v_errnum  NUMBER;             -- the Oracle error #
  v_now     DATE := SYSDATE; -- current time
  v_counter NUMBER := 1;        -- stack counter
BEGIN

  -- for every error in the error stack...
```

```
    LOOP

      -- get the error number off the stack at this position
      v_errnum := ORA_SERVER_ERROR (v_counter);

      -- if the error # is zero then we are done
      EXIT WHEN v_errnum = 0;

      -- Write the error out to the log table.
      INSERT INTO error_log(username,
                            error_number,
                            sequence,
                            timestamp)
      VALUES(USER,
             v_errnum,
             v_counter,
             v_now);

      -- increment the counter and try again
      v_counter := v_counter + 1;

    END LOOP;  -- every error on the stack
  END;
```

Remember that all these new rows in the error_log have been committed by the time the END statement is reached, because the trigger is executed within an autonomous transaction. The following lines demonstrate this trigger in action:

```
SQL> EXEC DBMS_OUTPUT.PUT_LINE(TO_NUMBER('A'));
*
ERROR at line 1:
ORA-06502: PL/SQL: numeric or value error: character to number conversion error

SQL> SELECT * FROM error_log;

USERNAME                       ERROR_NUMBER   SEQUENCE TIMESTAMP
------------------------------ ------------ ---------- ---------
BOOK                                   6502          1 04-JAN-02
BOOK                                   6512          2 04-JAN-02
```

Why do two errors appear in the table when only one error was raised? The actual error stack generated by Oracle contains both ORA-06502 and ORA-06512, so they are both logged and denoted by their sequence of occurrence.

If you want to quickly determine if a certain error number is located in the stack without parsing it manually, use the companion function, ORA_IS_SERVERERROR. This function is very useful for monitoring specific errors that may require extra handling, such as user-defined exceptions. This is the kind of code you might write:

```
-- Special handling of user defined errors
-- 20000 through 20010 raised by calls to
-- RAISE_APPLICATION_ERROR
```

```
FOR errnum IN 20000 .. 20010
LOOP
  IF ORA_IS_SERVERERROR (errnum)
  THEN
     log_user_defined_error (errnum);
  END IF;
END LOOP;
```

All Oracle error numbers are negative, except for 1 (user-defined exception) and 100 (synonymous with –1403, NO_DATA_FOUND). When you specify an error number in the call to ORA_IS_SERVERERROR, however, you must supply a positive number, as shown in the above example.

Central error handler

While it is possible to implement separate SERVERERROR triggers in every schema in a database, I recommend creating a single central trigger with an accompanying PL/SQL package to provide the following features.

Centralized error logging
: There is only one trigger and package to maintain and keep in Oracle's memory.

Session-long searchable error log
: The error log can be accumulated over the course of a session rather than error by error. It can be searched to return details like the number of occurrences, the timestamp of the first and last occurrence, etc. The log can also be purged on demand.

Option to save error log
: The error log can be saved to a permanent table in the database if desired.

Viewable current log
: The current log of errors is viewable by specific error number and/or date range.

You can find the implementation of one such centralized error-handling package in the *error_log.sql* file on the O'Reilly site. Once this package is in place, we can create the SERVERERROR trigger as follows:

```
CREATE OR REPLACE TRIGGER error_log
AFTER SERVERERROR
ON DATABASE
BEGIN
  central_error_log.log_error;
END;
```

Here are some example usages. First, I will generate an error:

```
SQL> EXEC DBMS_OUTPUT.PUT_LINE(TO_NUMBER('A'));
*
ERROR at line 1:
ORA-06502: PL/SQL: numeric or value error: character to number conversion error
```

Now I can search for a specific error number and retrieve that information in a record:

```
DECLARE
  v_find_record central_error_log.v_find_record;
BEGIN
  central_error_log.find_error(6502,v_find_record);
  DBMS_OUTPUT.PUT_LINE('Total Found    = ' || v_find_record.total_found);
  DBMS_OUTPUT.PUT_LINE('Min Timestamp = ' || v_find_record.min_timestamp);
  DBMS_OUTPUT.PUT_LINE('Max Timestamp = ' || v_find_record.max_timestamp);
END;
```

The output is:

```
Total Found   = 1
Min Timestamp = 04-JAN-02
Max Timestamp = 04-JAN-02
```

Impact of Invalid Triggers

If database event triggers are in an invalid state, they can cause other actions to fail, as shown here:

Event	If invalid...
AFTER SERVERERROR	All transactions that encounter an Oracle error will be rolled back, and a message detailing the invalid trigger will display.
AFTER LOGON	Only users with the ADMINISTER DATABASE TRIGGER privilege will be able to log on.
BEFORE LOGOFF	Users will see an invalid trigger message when they disconnect from the database.
BEFORE SHUTDOWN	Message stating invalid trigger will display in the database alert log, but shutdown will proceed normally.
AFTER STARTUP	Message stating invalid trigger will display in the database alert log, but startup will proceed normally.

INSTEAD OF Triggers

INSTEAD OF triggers control insert, update, and delete operations on *views*, not tables. They can be used to make non-updateable views updateable and to override the default behavior of views that are updateable.

Creating an INSTEAD OF Trigger

To create (or replace) an INSTEAD OF trigger, use the syntax shown here:

```
CREATE [OR REPLACE TRIGGER] trigger_name
INTEAD OF operation
ON view name
FOR EACH ROW
BEGIN
  ... code goes here ...
END;
```

The table contains an explanation of this code:

Line(s)	Description
1	States that a trigger is to be created with the unique name supplied. Specifying OR REPLACE is optional. If the trigger exists and REPLACE is not specified, then your attempt to create the trigger anew will result in an ORA-4081 error.
2	This is where we see differences between INSTEAD OF triggers and other types of triggers. Because INSTEAD OF triggers aren't really triggered by an event, we don't need to specify AFTER or BEFORE or provide an event name. What we do specify is the operation that the trigger is to fire in place of (or instead of). Stating INSTEAD OF followed by one of INSERT, UPDATE, or DELETE accomplishes this.
3	This line is somewhat like the corresponding line for DDL and database event triggers in that the keyword ON is specified. The similarities end there: instead of specifying DATABASE or SCHEMA, we provide the name of the view to which the trigger is to apply.
4–7	Contains standard PL/SQL code.

INSTEAD OF triggers are best explained with an example. Let's use one of my favorite topics: pizza delivery! Before we can start pounding the dough, we have to put a system in place to monitor our deliveries. We will need three tables: one to track actual deliveries, one to track delivery areas, and one to track our massive fleet of drivers (remember the first rule of business— always think big!).

```
/* File on web: pizza_tables.sql */
CREATE TABLE delivery
(delivery_id NUMBER,
 delivery_start DATE,
 delivery_end DATE,
 area_id NUMBER,
 driver_id NUMBER);

CREATE TABLE area
   (area_id NUMBER, area_desc   VARCHAR2(30));

CREATE TABLE driver
   (driver_id NUMBER, driver_name   VARCHAR2(30));
```

For the sake of brevity I will not create any primary or foreign keys.

We will also need three sequences to provide unique identifiers for our tables.

```
CREATE SEQUENCE delivery_id_seq;
CREATE SEQUENCE area_id_seq;
CREATE SEQUENCE driver_id_seq;
```

To avoid having to explain relational database design and normalization to our employees, we will simplify deliveries into a single view displaying delivery, area, and driver information.

```
CREATE OR REPLACE VIEW delivery_info AS
SELECT d.delivery_id,
       d.delivery_start,
       d.delivery_end,
       a.area_desc,
```

```
        dr.driver_name
   FROM delivery      d,
        area          a,
        driver        dr
  WHERE a.area_id = d.area_id
    AND dr.driver_id = d.driver_id;
```

Because our system relies heavily on this view for query functionality, why not make it available for insert, update, and delete as well? This is where INSTEAD OF triggers come into play. We need to tell the database what to do when an insert, update or delete operation occurs against the delivery_info view; in other words, we need to tell it what to do instead of trying to insert, update, or delete. Let's start with the INSERT trigger.

The INSTEAD OF INSERT Trigger

Our INSERT trigger will perform four basic operations:

1. Ensure that the delivery_end value is NULL. All delivery completions must be done via an update.
2. Try to find the driver ID based on the name provided. If the name cannot be found, then assign a new ID and create a driver entry using the name and the new ID.
3. Try to find the area ID based on the name provided. If the name cannot be found, then assign a new ID and create an area entry using the name and the new ID.
4. Create an entry in the delivery table.

Bear in mind that this example is intended to demonstrate triggers—not how to effectively build a business system! After a while we will probably wind up with a multitude of duplicate driver and area entries. However, using this view speeds things up by not requiring drivers and areas to be predefined, and in the fast-paced world of pizza delivery, time is money!

```
/* File on web: pizza_triggers.sql */
CREATE OR REPLACE TRIGGER delivery_info_insert
INSTEAD OF INSERT ON delivery_info
DECLARE

  -- cursor to get the driver ID by name
  CURSOR curs_get_driver_id ( cp_driver_name VARCHAR2 ) IS
  SELECT driver_id
    FROM driver
   WHERE driver_name = cp_driver_name;
  v_driver_id NUMBER;

  -- cursor to get the area ID by name
  CURSOR curs_get_area_id ( cp_area_desc VARCHAR2 ) IS
  SELECT area_id
```

```
    FROM area
   WHERE area_desc = cp_area_desc;
  v_area_id NUMBER;

BEGIN

  /*
   || Make sure the delivery_end value is NULL
  */
  IF :NEW.delivery_end IS NOT NULL
  THEN
    RAISE_APPLICATION_ERROR (
      -20000,'Delivery end date value must be NULL when delivery created');
  END IF;

  /*
    || Try to get the driver ID using the name. If not found
    || then create a brand new driver ID from the sequence
  */
  OPEN curs_get_driver_id(UPPER(:NEW.driver_name));
  FETCH curs_get_driver_id INTO v_driver_id;
  IF curs_get_driver_id%NOTFOUND THEN
    SELECT driver_id_seq.nextval
      INTO v_driver_id
      FROM DUAL;
    INSERT INTO driver(driver_id,driver_name)
    VALUES(v_driver_id,UPPER(:NEW.driver_name));
  END IF;
  CLOSE curs_get_driver_id;

  /*
    || Try to get the area ID using the name. If not found
    || then create a brand new area ID from the sequence
  */
  OPEN curs_get_area_id(UPPER(:NEW.area_desc));
  FETCH curs_get_area_id INTO v_area_id;
  IF curs_get_area_id%NOTFOUND THEN
    SELECT area_id_seq.nextval
      INTO v_area_id
      FROM DUAL;
    INSERT INTO area(area_id,area_desc)
    VALUES(v_area_id,UPPER(:NEW.area_desc));
  END IF;
  CLOSE curs_get_area_id;

  /*
    || Create the delivery entry
  */
  INSERT INTO delivery(delivery_id,
                       delivery_start,
                       delivery_end,
                       area_id,
                       driver_id)
  VALUES(delivery_id_seq.nextval,
```

```
        NVL(:NEW.delivery_start,SYSDATE),
        NULL,
        v_area_id,
        v_driver_id);

END;
```

The INSTEAD OF UPDATE Trigger

Now let's move on to the UPDATE trigger. For the sake of simplicity, we will only allow updating of the delivery_end field, and only if it were NULL to start with. We can't have drivers resetting delivery times.

```
CREATE OR REPLACE TRIGGER delivery_info_update
   INSTEAD OF UPDATE
   ON delivery_info
DECLARE
   -- cursor to get the delivery entry
   CURSOR curs_get_delivery (cp_delivery_id NUMBER)
   IS
      SELECT delivery_end
        FROM delivery
       WHERE delivery_id = cp_delivery_id
      FOR UPDATE OF delivery_end;

   v_delivery_end   DATE;
BEGIN
   OPEN curs_get_delivery (:NEW.delivery_id);
   FETCH curs_get_delivery INTO v_delivery_end;

   IF v_delivery_end IS NOT NULL
   THEN
      RAISE_APPLICATION_ERROR (
         -20000, 'The delivery end date has already been set');
   ELSE
      UPDATE delivery
         SET delivery_end = :NEW.delivery_end
       WHERE CURRENT OF curs_get_delivery;
   END IF;

   CLOSE curs_get_delivery;
END;
```

The INSTEAD OF DELETE Trigger

The DELETE trigger is the simplest of all. It merely ensures that we are not deleting a completed entry, and then removes the delivery record. The driver and area records remain intact.

```
CREATE OR REPLACE TRIGGER delivery_info_delete
   INSTEAD OF DELETE
ON delivery_info
```

```
BEGIN
  IF :NEW.delivery_end IS NOT NULL
  THEN
     RAISE_APPLICATION_ERROR (
        -20000,'Completed deliveries cannot be deleted');
  END IF;

  DELETE delivery
   WHERE delivery_id = :NEW.delivery_id;
END;
```

Populating the Tables

Now, with a single INSERT focused on the delivery information we know (the driver and the area), all of the required tables are populated:

```
SQL> INSERT INTO delivery_info(delivery_id,
  2                            delivery_start,
  3                            delivery_end,
  4                            area_desc,
  5                            driver_name)
  6  VALUES
  7    (NULL, NULL, NULL, 'LOCAL COLLEGE', 'BIG TED');

1 row created.

SQL> SELECT * FROM delivery;

DELIVERY_ID DELIVERY_ DELIVERY_    AREA_ID  DRIVER_ID
----------- --------- --------- ---------- ----------
          1 13-JAN-02                    1          1

SQL> SELECT * FROM area;

   AREA_ID AREA_DESC
---------- ------------------------------
         1 LOCAL COLLEGE

SQL> SELECT * FROM driver;

 DRIVER_ID DRIVER_NAME
---------- ------------------------------
         1 BIG TED
```

AFTER SUSPEND Triggers

Oracle9*i* introduced a new type of trigger that fires whenever a statement is suspended. This might occur as the result of a space issue like exceeding an allocated tablespace quota. This functionality can be used in order to repair the conditions and allow the stalled operation to continue. AFTER SUSPEND triggers are a boon to busy developers tired of being held up by space errors, and to even busier DBAs who constantly have to resolve these errors.

For example, consider the situation faced by Batch Only, the star Oracle developer at Totally Controlled Systems. He is responsible for maintaining hundreds of programs that run overnight, performing lengthy transactions to summarize information and move it between disparate applications. At least twice a week, his pager goes off during the wee hours of the morning because one of his programs has encountered this Oracle error.

```
ERROR at line 1:
ORA-01536: space quota exceeded for tablespace 'USERS'
```

Batch then has the unenviable task of phoning Totally's Senior DBA, Don T. Planahead, and begging for a space quota increase. Don's usual question is, "How much do you need?" to which Batch can only feebly reply, "I don't know because the data load fluctuates so much." This leaves them both very frustrated, because Don wants control over the space allocation for planning reasons, and Batch doesn't want his night's sleep interrupted so often.

Setting Up for the AFTER SUSPEND Trigger

Thankfully, an AFTER SUSPEND trigger can eliminate the dark circles under both Don's and Batch's eyes. Here is how they work through the situation.

Batch discovers a particular point in his code that encounters the error most frequently. It is an otherwise innocuous INSERT statement at the end of a program that takes hours to run:

```
INSERT INTO monthly_summary (
   acct_no, trx_count, total_in, total_out)
VALUES (
   v_acct, v_trx_count, v_total_in, v_total_out);
```

What makes this most maddening is that the values take hours to calculate, only to be immediately lost when the final INSERT statement fails. At the very least, Batch wants the program to suspend itself while he contacts Don to get more space allocated. He discovers that this can be done with a simple ALTER SESSION statement.

```
ALTER SESSION ENABLE RESUMABLE TIMEOUT 3600 NAME 'Monthly Summary';
```

This means that whenever this Oracle session encounters an out-of-space error, it will go into a suspended (and potentially resumable) state for 3600 seconds (1 hour). This provides enough time for Totally's monitoring system to page Batch, for Batch to phone Don, and Don to allocate more space. It's not a perfect system, but at least the hours spent calculating the data are no longer wasted.

Another problem faced by Batch and Don is that when they try to diagnose the situation in the middle of the night, they are both so tired and grumpy that time is wasted on misunderstandings. Thankfully, the need for explanations can be alleviated by another feature of suspended/resumable statements: the DBA_RESUMABLE view. This shows all sessions that have registered for resumable statements with the ALTER SESSION command shown above.

The RESUMABLE system privilege must be granted to users before they can enable the resumable option.

Now, whenever Batch's programs go into the suspended state he only has to phone Don and mumble "Check the resumable view." Don then queries it from his DBA account to see what is going on.

```
SQL> run
  1  SELECT session_id,
  2         name,
  3         status,
  4         error_number
  5*   FROM dba_resumable

SESSION_ID NAME                 STATUS    ERROR_NUMBER
---------- -------------------- --------- ------------
         8 Monthly Summary      SUSPENDED         1536

1 row selected.
```

This shows that session 8 is suspended because of *ORA-01536: space quota exceeded for tablespace* 'tablespace_name'. From past experience, Don knows which schema and tablespace are involved, so he corrects the problem and mumbles into the phone "It's fixed." The suspended statement in Batch's code immediately resumes, and both Don and Batch can go back to sleep in their own beds.

Looking at the Actual Trigger

After a few weeks, both Don and Batch are tired of their repetitive, albeit abbreviated late-night conversations, so Don sets out to automate things with an AFTER SUSPEND trigger. Here is what he cooks up and installs in the DBA account:

```
/* File on web: smart_space_quota.sql */
CREATE OR REPLACE TRIGGER after_suspend
AFTER SUSPEND
ON DATABASE
DECLARE

  -- cursor to get the username for the current session
  CURSOR curs_get_username IS
  SELECT username
    FROM v$session
   WHERE audsid = SYS_CONTEXT('USERENV','SESSIONID');
  v_username VARCHAR2(30);
```

```
  -- cursor to get the quota for the user/tablespace
  CURSOR curs_get_ts_quota ( cp_tbspc VARCHAR2,
                             cp_user  VARCHAR2 ) IS
  SELECT max_bytes
    FROM dba_ts_quotas
   WHERE tablespace_name = cp_tbspc
     AND username = cp_user;
  v_old_quota NUMBER;
  v_new_quota NUMBER;

  -- hold information from SPACE_ERROR_INFO
  v_error_type        VARCHAR2(30);
  v_object_type       VARCHAR2(30);
  v_object_owner      VARCHAR2(30);
  v_tbspc_name        VARCHAR2(30);
  v_object_name       VARCHAR2(30);
  v_subobject_name VARCHAR2(30);

  -- SQL to fix things
  v_sql               VARCHAR2(1000);

BEGIN

  -- if this is a space related error...
  IF ORA_SPACE_ERROR_INFO ( error_type => v_error_type,
                            object_type => v_object_type,
                            object_owner => v_object_owner,
                            table_space_name => v_tbspc_name,
                            object_name => v_object_name,
                            sub_object_name => v_subobject_name ) THEN

    -- if the error is a tablespace quota being exceeded...
    IF v_error_type = 'SPACE QUOTA EXCEEDED' AND
       v_object_type = 'TABLE SPACE' THEN
      -- get the username
      OPEN curs_get_username;
      FETCH curs_get_username INTO v_username;
      CLOSE curs_get_username;

      -- get the current quota for the username and tablespace
      OPEN curs_get_ts_quota(v_object_name,v_username);
      FETCH curs_get_ts_quota INTO v_old_quota;
      CLOSE curs_get_ts_quota;

      -- create an ALTER USER statement and send it off to
      -- the fixer job because if we try it here we will raise
      -- ORA-30511: invalid DDL operation in system triggers
      v_new_quota := v_old_quota + 40960;
      v_sql := 'ALTER USER ' || v_username  || ' ' ||
               'QUOTA '      || v_new_quota || ' ' ||
               'ON '         || v_object_name;
      fixer.fix_this(v_sql);

    END IF;  -- tablespace quota exceeded
```

```
    END IF;  -- space related error

  END;
```

This creates a trigger that fires whenever a statement enters a suspended state and attempts to fix the problem. (Note that this particular example only handles tablespace quotas being exceeded.)

> **Invalid DDL Operation in System Triggers**
>
> AFTER SUSPEND triggers are not allowed to actually perform certain DDL (ALTER USER and ALTER TABLESPACE) to fix the problems they diagnose. They will simply raise the error *ORA-30511: Invalid DDL operation in system triggers*. One way to work around this situation is as follows:
>
> 1. Have the AFTER SUSPEND trigger write the SQL statement necessary to fix a problem in a table.
> 2. Create a PL/SQL package that reads SQL statements from the table and executes them.
> 3. Submit the PL/SQL package to DBMS_JOB to run every minute or so.

Now when Batch's programs encounter the tablespace quota problem, the database-wide AFTER SUSPEND trigger fires and puts a SQL entry in the "stuff to fix" table via the fixer package. In the background, a fixer job is running; it picks the SQL statement out of the table and executes it, thus alleviating the quota problem without requiring anyone to pick up the phone.

A complete AFTER_SUSPEND trigger and fixer package are available in the *fixer.sql* file on the O'Reilly site.

Creating the AFTER SUSPEND Trigger

The syntax used to create an AFTER SUSPEND trigger follows the same format as DDL and database event triggers. It declares the firing event (SUSPEND), the timing (AFTER), and the scope (DATABASE or SCHEMA):

```
CREATE [OR REPLACE] TRIGGER trigger_name
AFTER SUSPEND
ON {DATABASE | SCHEMA}
BEGIN
... code ...
END;
```

The ORA_SPACE_ERROR_INFO Function

Information on the cause of the statement suspension may be garnered using the ORA_SPACE_ERROR_INFO function shown in earlier examples. Now let's look at the syntax for specifying this function; the parameters are defined as shown in Table 18-3.

Table 18-3. ORA_SPACE_ERROR_INFO parameters

Parameter	Description
ERROR_TYPE	The type of space error; will be one of the following:
	SPACE QUOTA EXCEEDED: if a user has exceeded his or her quota for a tablespace.
	MAX EXTENTS REACHED: if an object attempts to go beyond its maximum extents specification.
	NO MORE SPACE: if there is not enough space in a tablespace to store the new information.
OBJECT_TYPE	The type of object encountering the space error.
OBJECT_OWNER	The owner of the object encountering the space error.
TABLE_SPACE_NAME	The tablespace encountering the space error.
OBJECT_NAME	The name of the object encountering the space error.
SUB_OBJECT_NAME	The name of the sub-object encountering the space error.

The function returns a Boolean value of TRUE if the suspension occurs because of one of the errors shown in the table, and FALSE if not.

The ORA_SPACE_ERROR_INFO function does not actually fix whatever space problems occur in your system; its role is simply to provide the information you need in order to take further action. In the earlier example, we saw how the quota error was addressed. Here are two additional examples of SQL you might supply to fix space problems diagnosed by the ORA_SPACE_ERROR_INFO function:

- Specify the following when your table or index has achieved its maximum extents and no more extents are available:

  ```
  ALTER <object_type> <object_owner>.<object_name> STORAGE (MAXEXTENTS UNLIMITED);
  ```

- Specify the following when your tablespace is completely out of space:

  ```
  /* Assume Oracle Managed Files (9i) being used so explicit
     datafile declaration not required */
  ALTER TABLESPACE <table_space_name> ADD DATAFILE;
  ```

The DBMS_RESUMABLE Package

If the ORA_SPACE_ERROR_INFO function returns FALSE, then the situation causing the suspended statement cannot be fixed. Thus, there is no rational reason for remaining suspended. Unfixable statements can be aborted from within the AFTER_SUSPEND trigger using the ABORT procedure in the DBMS_RESUMABLE package. The following provides an example of issuing this procedure:

```
/* File on web: local_abort.sql */
CREATE OR REPLACE TRIGGER after_suspend
AFTER SUSPEND
ON SCHEMA
DECLARE

  CURSOR curs_get_sid IS
  SELECT sid
    FROM v$session
   WHERE audsid = SYS_CONTEXT('USERENV','SESSIONID');
  v_sid        NUMBER;
  v_error_type VARCHAR2(30);
  ...

BEGIN

  IF ORA_SPACE_ERROR_INFO(...
    ...try to fix things...
  ELSE  -- cant fix the situation
    OPEN curs_get_sid;
    FETCH curs_get_sid INTO v_sid;
    CLOSE curs_get_sid;
    DBMS_RESUMABLE.ABORT(v_sid);
  END IF;

END;
```

The ABORT procedure takes a single argument, the ID of the session to abort. This allows ABORT to be called from a DATABASE- or SCHEMA-level AFTER SUSPEND trigger. The aborted session receives this error:

```
ORA-01013: user requested cancel of current operation
```

After all, the cancellation was requested by a user, but exactly which user is unclear.

In addition to the ABORT procedure, the DBMS_RESUMABLE package contains functions and procedures to get and set timeout values. In the following example, the GET_SESSION_TIMEOUT function returns the timeout value of the suspended session by session ID:

```
FUNCTION DBMS_REUSABLE.GET_SESSION_TIMEOUT (sessionid IN NUMBER)
     RETURN NUMBER;
```

The SET_SESSION_TIMEOUT function sets the timeout value of the suspended session by session ID:

```
PROCEDURE DBMS_REUSABLE.SET_SESSION_TIMEOUT (
  sessionid IN NUMBER, TIMEOUT IN NUMBER);
```

The GET_TIMEOUT function returns the timeout value of the current session:

```
FUNCTION DBMS_REUSABLE.GET_TIMEOUT RETURN NUMBER;
```

The SET_SESSION_TIMEOUT function sets the timeout value of the current session:

```
PROCEDURE DBMS_REUSABLE.SET_TIMEOUT (TIMEOUT IN NUMBER);
```

New timeout values take effect immediately but do not reset the counter to zero.

Trapped Multiple Times

AFTER SUSPEND triggers fire whenever a statement is suspended. Therefore, they can fire many times during the same statement. For example, suppose that the following hardcoded trigger is implemented:

```
/* File on web: increment_extents.sql */
CREATE OR REPLACE TRIGGER after_suspend
AFTER SUSPEND ON SCHEMA
DECLARE
  -- get the new max (current plus one)
  CURSOR curs_get_extents IS
  SELECT max_extents + 1
    FROM user_tables
   WHERE table_name = 'MONTHLY_SUMMARY';
  v_new_max NUMBER;

BEGIN
  - fetch the new maximum extent value
  OPEN curs_get_extents;
  FETCH curs_get_extents INTO v_new_max;
  CLOSE curs_get_extents;

  -- alter the table to take on the new value for maxextents
  EXECUTE IMMEDIATE 'ALTER TABLE MONTHLY_SUMMARY ' ||
                    'STORAGE ( MAXEXTENTS '        ||
                    v_new_max                      || ')';

  DBMS_OUTPUT.PUT_LINE('Incremented MAXEXTENTS to ' || v_new_max);
END;
```

If you start with an empty table with MAXEXTENTS (maximum number of extents) specified as 1, inserting four extents' worth of data produces this output:

```
SQL> @test

Incremented MAXEXTENTS to 2
Incremented MAXEXTENTS to 3
Incremented MAXEXTENTS to 4

PL/SQL procedure successfully completed.
```

To Fix or Not To Fix?

That is the question! The previous examples have shown how "lack of space" errors can be handled on the fly by suspending statements until intervention (human or automated) allows them to continue. Taken to an extreme, this approach allows applications to be installed with minimal tablespace, quota, and extent settings, and then to grow as required. While overdiligent DBAs may see this situation as nirvana, it does have its downsides:

Intermittent pauses
: Suspended statement pauses may wreak havoc with high-volume online transaction processing (OLTP) applications that require high throughput levels. This will be even more troublesome if the fix takes a long time.

Resource contention
: Suspended statements maintain their table locks, which may cause other statements to wait long periods of time or fail needlessly.

Management overhead
: The resources required to continuously add extents or datafiles, or increment quotas may wind up overwhelming those required to actually run the application

For these reasons I recommend that AFTER SUSPEND triggers be used judiciously. They are perfect for long-running processes that must be restarted after failure, as well as for incremental processes that require DML to undo their changes before they can be restarted. However, they are not well suited to OLTP applications.

Maintaining Triggers

Oracle offers a number of DDL statements that can help you manage your triggers. You can enable, disable, and drop triggers, view information about triggers, and check the status of triggers, as explained in the following sections.

Disabling, Enabling, and Dropping Triggers

Disabling a trigger causes it not to fire when its triggering event occurs. Dropping a trigger causes it to be removed from the database altogether. The SQL syntax for disabling triggers is relatively simple compared to that for creating them:

```
ALTER TRIGGER trigger_name DISABLE;
```

For example:

```
ALTER TRIGGER emp_after_insert DISABLE;
```

A disabled trigger can also be re-enabled as shown in the following example:

```
ALTER TRIGGER emp_after_insert ENABLE;
```

The ALTER TRIGGER command is concerned only with the trigger name; it does not require identifying the trigger type or anything else. You can also easily create stored procedures to handle these steps for you. The following procedure, for example, uses dynamic SQL to disable or enable all triggers on a table:

```
/* File on web: settrig.sp */
CREATE OR REPLACE PROCEDURE settrig (tab IN VARCHAR2, action IN VARCHAR2)
IS
   v_action         VARCHAR2 (10) := UPPER (action);
```

```
   v_other_action   VARCHAR2 (10) := 'DISABLED';
BEGIN
   IF v_action = 'DISABLE'
   THEN
      v_other_action := 'ENABLED';
   END IF;

   FOR rec IN (SELECT trigger_name
                 FROM user_triggers
                WHERE table_owner = USER
                  AND table_name = UPPER (tab)
                  AND status = v_other_action)
   LOOP
      EXECUTE IMMEDIATE 'ALTER TRIGGER ' || rec.trigger_name || ' ' || v_action;
      DBMS_OUTPUT.put_line (
         'Set status of '|| rec.trigger_name || ' to ' || v_action
      );
   END LOOP;
END;
```

The DROP TRIGGER command is just as easy; simply specify the trigger name, as shown in this example:

```
DROP TRIGGER emp_after_insert;
```

Viewing Triggers

You can ascertain lots of information about triggers by issuing queries against the following data dictionary views:

DBA_TRIGGERS
: All triggers in the database

ALL_TRIGGERS
: All triggers accessible to the current user

USER_TRIGGERS
: All triggers owned by the current user

Table 18-4 summarizes the most useful (and common) columns in these views.

Table 18-4. Useful columns in trigger views

Name	Description
TRIGGER_NAME	The name of the trigger
TRIGGER_TYPE	The type of the trigger; you can specify: For DML triggers: BEFORE_STATEMENT, BEFORE EACH ROW, AFTER EACH ROW, or AFTER STATEMENT. For DDL triggers: BEFORE EVENT or AFTER EVENT. For INSTEAD OF triggers: INSTEAD OF. For AFTER_SUSPEND triggers: AFTER EVENT.

Table 18-4. Useful columns in trigger views (continued)

Name	Description
TRIGGERING EVENT	The event that causes the trigger to fire: For DML triggers: UPDATE, INSERT, or DELETE For DDL triggers: The DDL operation (see full list in the DDL trigger section of this chapter) For database event triggers: ERROR, LOGON, LOGOFF, STARTUP, or SHUTDOWN For INSTEAD OF triggers: INSERT, UPDATE, or DELETE For AFTER SUSPEND triggers: SUSPEND
TABLE_OWNER	This column contains different information depending on the type of trigger. For DML triggers: The name of the owner of the table to which the trigger is attached. For DDL triggers: If database-wide then SYS; otherwise, the owner of the trigger For database event triggers: If database-wide then SYS; otherwise, the owner of the trigger For INSTEAD OF triggers: The owner of the view to which the trigger is attached For AFTER SUSPEND triggers: If database-wide then SYS; otherwise, the owner of the trigger
BASE_OBJECT_TYPE	The type of object to which the trigger is attached. For DML triggers: TABLE For DDL triggers: SCHEMA or DATABASE For database event triggers: SCHEMA or DATABASE For INSTEAD OF triggers: VIEW For AFTER SUSPEND triggers: SCHEMA or DATABASE
TABLE_NAME	For DML triggers: The name of the table the trigger is attached to. Other types of triggers: NULL
REFERENCING_NAMES	For DML (row-level) triggers: The clause used to define the aliases for the OLD and NEW records For other types of triggers: The text "REFERENCING NEW AS NEW OLD AS OLD"
WHEN_CLAUSE	For DML triggers: The trigger's conditional firing clause
STATUS	Trigger's status (ENABLED or DISABLED)
ACTION_TYPE	Indicates whether the trigger executes a call (CALL) or contains PL/SQL (PL/SQL).
TRIGGER_BODY	Text of the trigger body (LONG column)

Checking the Validity of Triggers

Oddly enough, the trigger views in the data dictionary do not display whether or not a trigger is in a valid state. If a trigger is created with invalid PL/SQL, it is saved in the database but marked as INVALID. You can query the USER_OBJECTS or ALL_OBJECTS views to determine this status, as shown here:

```
SQL> CREATE OR REPLACE TRIGGER invalid_trigger
AFTER DDL ON SCHEMA
BEGIN
  NULL
END;
/
```

```
Warning: Trigger created with compilation errors.

SQL> SELECT object_name,
  2         object_type,
  3         status
  4    FROM user_objects
  5   WHERE object_name = 'INVALID_TRIGGER';

OBJECT_NAME   OBJECT TYPE STATUS
------------- ----------- -------
INVALID_STATE TRIGGER     INVALID
```

CHAPTER 19

Managing PL/SQL Applications

In this chapter:

Writing the code for an application is just one step toward putting that production into application and then maintaining the code base. It is not possible within the scope of this book to fully address the entire lifecycle of application design, development, and deployment. We do have room, however, to offer some ideas and advice about the following topics:

Managing and analyzing code in the database
: When you compile PL/SQL programs, the source code is loaded into the data dictionary in a variety of forms (the text of the code, dependency relationships, parameter information, etc.). You can therefore use SQL to query these dictionaries to help you manage your code base.

Protecting stored code
: Oracle offers a way to "wrap" source code so that confidential and proprietary information can be hidden from prying eyes. This utility is most useful to vendors who sell applications based on PL/SQL stored code.

Using native compilation
: Beginning with Oracle9*i*, PL/SQL source code may optionally be compiled into native object code that is linked into Oracle. Native compilation can result in significant improvement in overall application performance (its impact is felt in compute-intensive programs, but does not affect SQL performance).

Testing PL/SQL programs
: This chapter offers suggestions for PL/SQL program testing based on the open source unit testing framework, utPLSQL.

Debugging PL/SQL programs
: Many development tools now offer graphical debuggers based on Oracle's DBMS_DEBUG API. These provide the most powerful way to debug programs, but they are still just a small part of the overall debugging process. This chapter will also explore some of the techniques and (dare I say) philosophical approaches you should utilize to debug effectively.

Tuning PL/SQL programs
: It is not within the scope of this book to offer comprehensive tuning recommendations for PL/SQL code. However, I will offer a roundup of some of the more useful and generally applicable tuning tips, along with instructions for how you can analyze your program's execution with built-in profiling and tracing utilities.

Managing and Analyzing Code in the Database

When you CREATE OR REPLACE a PL/SQL program, the source code for that program, along with other representations of that software, is stored in the database itself. This is a tremendous advantage for two key reasons:

Information about that code is available to you via the SQL language
: I can run a query against a data dictionary view that shows me all the programs that have been modified by a certain date, or tells me which programs are invalid and need to be recompiled.

The database manages dependencies between your stored objects
: For example, if a stored function relies on a certain table, and that table's structure is changed, the status of that function is automatically set to INVALID. Recompilation then takes place automatically when someone tries to execute that function.

This SQL interface to your code base allows you to manage your code repository—running analyses on your code, documenting what has been written and changed, and so on. The following sections introduce you to some of the most commonly accessed sources of information in the data dictionary.

Data Dictionary Views for PL/SQL Programmers

The Oracle data dictionary is a jungle! There are hundreds of views built on hundreds of tables, many complex interrelationships, special codes, and, all too often, non-optimized view definitions. In general, there are three types or levels of data dictionary views:

*USER_**
: Views that show information about the database objects owned by the currently connected schema.

*ALL_**
: Views that show information about all of the database objects to which the currently connected schema has access (either because it owns them or because it has been granted access to them).

*DBA_**
: Views that show information about all the objects in the database.

Because the stored objects are contained in tables in the data dictionary, you can use SQL itself to get information about the currently available programs. The following views are the most useful to understand:

USER_DEPENDENCIES
: The dependencies to and from objects you own.

USER_ERRORS
: The current set of errors for all stored objects you own. This view is accessed by the SHOW ERRORS SQL*Plus command, described in Chapter 2.

USER_OBJECTS
: The objects you own.

USER_OBJECT_SIZE
: The size of the objects you own.

USER_SOURCE
: The text source code for all objects you own.

USER_TRIGGERS
: The database triggers you own.

USER_ARGUMENTS
: The arguments (parameters) in all the procedures and functions in your schema.

You can view the structures of each of these views either with a DESC (describe) command in SQL*Plus or by referring to the appropriate Oracle documentation. The following sections provide some examples of the ways you can use these views.

Displaying Information About Stored Objects

The USER_OBJECTS view contains the following key information about an object:

OBJECT_NAME
: Name of the object

OBJECT_TYPE
: Type of the object

STATUS
: Status of the object: VALID or INVALID

Here are *some* of the types of objects (those most pertinent to PL/SQL developers) that are accessible through this view:

```
SQL> SELECT distinct object_type FROM user_objects;

OBJECT_TYPE
-------------
FUNCTION
INDEX
JAVA CLASS
JAVA SOURCE
```

```
LOB
PACKAGE
PACKAGE BODY
PROCEDURE
SEQUENCE
SYNONYM
TABLE
TRIGGER
TYPE
TYPE BODY
VIEW
```

You can see that USER_OBJECTS does more than keep track of PL/SQL code; you can use it to obtain a list of all PL/SQL objects currently in the database. I created and ran the following SQL*Plus script in a file called *psobj.sql*, which you'll find on the O'Reilly site:

```
/* File on web: psobj.sql */
SET PAGESIZE 66
COLUMN object_type FORMAT A20
COLUMN object_name FORMAT A30
COLUMN status FORMAT A10
BREAK ON object_type SKIP 1
SPOOL psobj.lis
SELECT object_type, object_name, status
  FROM user_objects
 WHERE object_type IN (
    'PACKAGE', 'PACKAGE BODY', 'FUNCTION', 'PROCEDURE',
    'TYPE', 'TYPE BODY')
 ORDER BY object_type, status, object_name
/
SPOOL OFF
```

The output from this script file contained the following list:

```
OBJECT_TYPE          OBJECT_NAME                    STATUS
-------------------- ------------------------------ ----------
FUNCTION             DEVELOP_ANALYSIS               INVALID
                     NUMBER_OF_ATOMICS              INVALID
                     FREQ_INSTR                     VALID

PACKAGE              CONFIG_PKG                     VALID
                     EXCHDLR_PKG                    VALID

PACKAGE BODY         EXCHDLR_PKG                    VALID

PROCEDURE            ASSESS_POPULARITY              INVALID
                     ASSERT_CONDITION               VALID

TYPE                 DESSERT_T                      VALID

TYPE BODY            DESSERT_T                      VALID
```

Notice that a number of my modules are marked as INVALID. This may be due to changes to the tables referenced in the modules, or changes to other programs called by these modules. The RDBMS automatically recompiles these objects when a program tries to call them. In other words, this recompilation takes place at runtime, when the user has caused these programs to be run and is waiting while the compilation occurs. You can avoid this automatic recompilation (and its impact on users) by manually compiling the INVALID modules yourself. The best way to do this is to use the excellent recompile utility, built by Solomon Yakobson and found in *recompile.sql* on the O'Reilly site.

Displaying and Searching Source Code

You should always maintain the source code of your programs in text files (or via a development tool specifically designed to store and manage PL/SQL code outside of the database). When you store these programs in the database, however, you can take advantage of SQL to analyze your source code across all modules, which may not be a straightforward task with your text editor.

The USER_SOURCE view contains all of the source code for objects owned by the current user. The structure of USER_SOURCE is as follows:

```
Name                             Null?    Type
-------------------------------- -------- ----
NAME                             NOT NULL VARCHAR2(30)
TYPE                                      VARCHAR2(12)
LINE                             NOT NULL NUMBER
TEXT                                      VARCHAR2(2000)
```

where NAME is the name of the object, TYPE is the type of the object (such as PROCEDURE, FUNCTION, PACKAGE, or PACKAGE BODY), LINE is the line number, and TEXT is the text of the source code.

USER_SOURCE is a very valuable resource for developers. With the right kind of queries, you can do things like:

- Display source code for a given line number
- Validate coding standards
- Identify possible bugs or weaknesses in your source code

Suppose, for example, that we have set as a rule that individual developers should never hardcode one of those application-specific error numbers between –20,999 and –20,000 (such hardcodings can lead to conflicting usages and lots of confusion). I can't stop a developer from writing code like this:

```
RAISE_APPLICATION_ERROR (-20306, 'Balance too low');
```

but I can create a package that allows me to identify all the programs that have such a line in them. I call it my "validate standards" package; it is very simple, and its main procedure looks like this:

```
/* File on web: valstd.pkg */
CREATE OR REPLACE PACKAGE BODY valstd
IS
   CURSOR objwith_cur (str IN VARCHAR2)
   IS
      SELECT name, text
        FROM USER_SOURCE
       WHERE UPPER (text) LIKE '%' || UPPER (str) || '%'
         AND name != 'VALSTD';

   PROCEDURE progwith (str IN VARCHAR2)
   IS
   BEGIN
      FOR prog_rec IN objwith_cur (str)
      LOOP
         do.pl (prog_rec.name, prog_rec.text);
      END LOOP;
   END;
END valstd;
```

Once this package is compiled into my schema, I can check for usages of –20,*NNN* numbers with this command:

```
SQL> EXEC valstd.progwith ('-20')
CHECK_BALANCE - RAISE_APPLICATION_ERROR (-20306, 'Balance too low');
MY_SESSION -    PRAGMA EXCEPTION_INIT(dblink_not_open,-2081);
VSESSTAT - CREATE DATE    : 1999-07-20
```

Notice that the third line in my output is not really a problem; it shows up only because I couldn't define my filter narrowly enough.

Another fine use of this package might be to find all declarations using the fixed-length CHAR datatype:

```
SQL> EXEC valstd.progwith ('-20')
```

This is a fairly crude analytical tool, but you could certainly make it more sophisticated. You could also have it generate HTML that is then posted on your intranet. You could then run the valstd scripts every Sunday night through a DBMS_JOB-submitted job, and each Monday morning developers could check the intranet for feedback on any fixes needed in their code.

Finally, here is a procedure you can run to identify any standalone procedures and functions (sorry, it doesn't work for packaged programs) that do not have an exception section. It isn't foolproof (for example, it will not identify itself), but it's better than nothing!

```
/* File on web: shownoexc.sp */
CREATE OR REPLACE PROCEDURE show_no_exc_sections
IS
   CURSOR check_for_exc (nm IN VARCHAR2)
   IS
      SELECT line
        FROM user_source
```

```
         WHERE NAME = nm AND INSTR (UPPER (text), 'EXCEPTION') > 0;

   check_rec    check_for_exc%ROWTYPE;
BEGIN
   FOR obj_rec IN (SELECT object_name, object_type
                     FROM user_objects
                    WHERE object_type IN ('PROCEDURE', 'FUNCTION'))
   LOOP
      OPEN check_for_exc (obj_rec.object_name);
      FETCH check_for_exc INTO check_rec;

      IF check_for_exc%FOUND
      THEN
         NULL;
      ELSE
         DBMS_OUTPUT.put_line (
               obj_rec.object_type
            || ' '
            || obj_rec.object_name
            || ' does not contain the EXCEPTION keyword.'
         );
      END IF;

      CLOSE check_for_exc;
   END LOOP;
END;
```

Protecting Stored Code

Virtually any application we write contains propriety information. If I write my application in PL/SQL and sell it commercially, I really don't want to let customers (or worse, competitors) see my secrets. Oracle offers a program known as *wrap* that hides most, if not all, of these secrets.

Some people refer to "wrapping" code as "encrypting" code, but wrapping is not true encryption. If you need to deliver information, such as a password, that *really* needs to be secure, you should not rely upon this facility. Note, however, that Oracle does provide a way to incorporate DES (Data Encryption Standard) security into your own applications using the built-in package DBMS_OBFUSCATION_TOOLKIT. See the Oracle documentation for details.

When you wrap PL/SQL source, you convert your readable ASCII text source code into unreadable ASCII text source code. This unreadable code can then be distributed to customers, regional offices, etc., for creation in new database instances. It is as portable as your original PL/SQL code, and is included in imports and exports. The Oracle database maintains dependencies for this wrapped code as it would for programs compiled from readable text. In short, a wrapped program is treated within the database just as normal PL/SQL programs are treated; the only difference is that prying eyes can't query the USER_SOURCE data dictionary to extract trade secrets.

How to Wrap Code

To wrap PL/SQL source code, you run the *wrap* executable. This program, named *wrap.exe*, is located in the *bin* directory of the Oracle instance. The format of the *wrap* command is:

```
wrap iname=infile [oname=outfile]
```

where *infile* points to the original, readable version of your program, and *outfile* is the name of the file that will contain the wrapped version of code. If *infile* does not contain a file extension, then the default of *sql* is assumed.

Versions of Oracle prior to Oracle8*i* offered *wrapNN.exec* executables where *NN* was the version number (e.g., *wrap72.exe* and *wrap73.exe*).

If you do not provide an oname argument, then *wrap* creates a file with the same name as *infile* but with a default extension of *plb*, which stands for "PL/SQL binary" (a misnomer, but it gets the idea across: binaries are, in fact, unreadable).

Here are some examples of using the *wrap* executable:

- Wrap a program, relying on all the defaults:

  ```
  c:\oracle\ora81\bin\wrap iname=secretprog
  ```

- Wrap a package body, specifying overrides of all the defaults. Notice that the wrapped file does not have to have the same filename or extension as the original:

  ```
  c:\oracle\ora81\bin\wrap iname=secretbody.spb oname=shhhhhh.bin
  ```

Working with Wrapped Code

I have found the following guidelines useful in working with wrapped code:

- Create batch files so that you can easily, quickly, and uniformly wrap one or more files. In Windows NT, I create *bat* files that contain lines like this in my source code directories:

  ```
  c:\orant\bin\wrap iname=plvrep.sps oname=plvrep.pls
  ```

  Of course, you can also create parameterized scripts and pass in the names of the files you want to wrap.

- To wrap your source code, you must place that code in an operating system file. If you are working within a PL/SQL development environment that allows you to build and maintain source directly in the database, you will have to "dump" this code to a file, wrap it, and then compile it back into the database—thereby wiping out your original, readable, and maintainable source code. This is not an issue as you deploy software to customers, but it could cause some uncomfortable situations as you develop and maintain applications.

- You can only wrap package specifications, package bodies, and standalone functions and procedures. You can run the wrapped binary against any other kind of SQL or PL/SQL statement, but those files will not be changed.
- You can tell that a program is wrapped by examining the program header. It will contain the keyword WRAPPED, as in:

  ```
  PACKAGE BODY package_name WRAPPED
  ```

  Even if you don't notice the keyword WRAPPED on the first line, you will immediately know that you are looking at wrapped code because the text in USER_SOURCE will look like this:

  ```
       LINE TEXT
  ------- ----------------------
         45 abcd
         46 95a425ff
         47 a2
         48 7 PACKAGE:
  ```

  and no matter how bad your coding style is, it surely isn't that bad!
- Wrapped code is much larger than the original source. I have found in my experience that a 57 KB readable package body turns into a 153 KB wrapped package body, while a 86 KB readable package body turns into a 357 KB wrapped package body. These increases in file size do result in increased requirements for storing source code in the database. The size of compiled code stays the same, although the time it takes to compile may increase.

Using Native Compilation

In pre-Oracle9*i* versions, compilation of PL/SQL source code always results in a representation (usually referred to as *bytecode*) that is stored in the database and is interpreted at runtime by a virtual machine implemented within Oracle that, in turn, runs natively on the given platform. Oracle9*i* introduces a new approach. PL/SQL source code may optionally be compiled into native object code that is linked into Oracle. (Note, however, that an anonymous PL/SQL block is *never* compiled natively.)

When would this feature come in handy? How do you turn on native compilation? This section addresses these questions.

PL/SQL is often used as a thin wrapper for executing SQL statements, setting bind variables, and handling result sets. For these kinds of programs, the execution speed of the PL/SQL code is rarely an issue; it is the execution speed of the SQL that determines the performance. (The efficiency of the context switch between the PL/SQL and the SQL operating environments might be an issue, but this is addressed very effectively by the FORALL and BULK COLLECT features introduced in Oracle8*i* and described in Chapter 13).

There are many other applications and programs, however, that rely on PL/SQL to perform computationally intensive tasks that are independent of the database. PL/SQL is, after all, a fully functional procedural language. Suppose, for example, that I wrote a program to find all right-angled triangles with all side lengths integer (a.k.a. perfect triangles). We must count only unique triangles—that is, those whose sides are not each the same integral multiple of the sides of a perfect triangle already found. (You will find the code to perform this function in the *perfect_triangles.sp* file on the O'Reilly site.)

This program implements an exhaustive search among candidate triangles with all possible combinations of lengths of the two shorter sides, each in the range 1 to a specified maximum. Testing whether the square root of the sum of the squares of the two short sides is within 0.01 of an integer coarsely filters each candidate. Triangles that pass this test are tested again by exactly applying Pythagoras's theorem using integer arithmetic. Candidate perfect triangles are then tested against the list of multiples of perfect triangles found so far. Each new unique perfect triangle is stored in a PL/SQL table, and its multiples (up to the maximum length) are stored in a separate PL/SQL table to facilitate uniqueness testing.

The implementation thus involves a doubly nested loop with the following steps at its heart: several arithmetic operations, casts, and comparisons; calls to procedures implementing comparisons driven by iteration through a PL/SQL table (with yet more arithmetic operations); and extension of PL/SQL tables where appropriate.

So what is the impact of native compilation on such code? We measured the elapsed time for p_max =5000 (i.e., 12.5 million repetitions of the heart of the loop) using interpreted and natively compiled versions of the procedure. The times were 548 seconds and 366 seconds respectively (on a Sun Ultra60 with no load apart from the test). Thus the natively compiled version was about 33% faster.

That's not bad for a semitransparent enhancement (i.e., no code changes were required in my application). And while native compilation may give only a marginal performance improvement for data-intensive programs, I have never seen it degrade performance. So how do you turn on native compilation? Read on…

One-Time DBA Setup

Native PL/SQL compilation is achieved by translating the PL/SQL source code into C source code that is then compiled on the given platform. The compiling and linking of the generated C source code is done using third-party utilities whose location has been specified by the DBA, typically in the *INIT.ORA* initialization parameter file.

The object code for each natively compiled PL/SQL library unit is stored in directories on the platform's filesystem, similarly under the DBA's control. Thus, native compilation takes longer than interpreted mode compilation; our tests have shown an increase of a factor of about two. That's because native compilation involves several extra steps: generating C code from the initial output of the PL/SQL compilation; writing this to the filesystem; invoking and running the C compiler; and linking the resulting object code into Oracle.

Oracle Corporation recommends that the C compiler be configured to do no optimization. Our tests have concurred that optimizing the generated C produces negligible improvement in runtime performance and substantially increases the compilation time.

Interpreted Versus Native Compilation Modes

The compilation mode is determined by the session parameter PLSQL_COMPILER_FLAGS. The user sets it as follows:

```
ALTER SESSION
   SET plsql_compiler_flags =
   'NATIVE' /* or 'INTERPRETED' */;
```

The compilation mode is then set for subsequently compiled PL/SQL library units during that session. The mode is stored with the library unit's metadata so that if the program is implicitly recompiled as a consequence of dependency checking, the mode the user intended will still be used.

You can determine the compilation mode by querying the data dictionary using the SELECT statement shown here:

```
SELECT o.object_name NAME,
       s.param_value comp_mode
  FROM USER_STORED_SETTINGS s,
       USER_OBJECTS o
 WHERE o.object_id = s.object_id
   AND param_name = 'plsql_compiler_flags'
   AND o.object_type IN ('PACKAGE', 'PROCEDURE', 'FUNCTION');
```

Here's one thing you need to be aware of: if you use the DBMS_UTILITY.COMPILE_SCHEMA built-in to attempt to recompile all invalid program units in your schema, it will use the current value of PLSQL_COMPILER_FLAGS rather than the compilation mode stored with each program unit.

Oracle recommends that all of the PL/SQL library units called from a given top-level unit be compiled in the same mode (see the sidebar). That's because there is a cost for the context switch when a library unit compiled in one mode invokes one compiled in the other mode. Significantly, this recommendation includes the Oracle-supplied library units. These are always shipped compiled in interpreted mode.

Upgrading an Entire Database to Native

The simplest way to follow Oracle's recommendation that all PL/SQL library units called from a given top-level unit be compiled in the same mode is to upgrade the whole database so that all PL/SQL library units are compiled NATIVE. A future release of the database (post-Oracle9*i* Release 2) will include a script to accomplish this, as well as a script to downgrade a whole database so that all PL/SQL library units are compiled INTERPRETED. For now, however, the best way to achieve this goal is to follow the instructions posted on the Oracle Technology Network at: *http://otn.oracle.com//tech/pl_sql/htdocs/README_2188517.htm*.

Our conclusion? If your application contains a significant amount of compute-intensive logic, you should seriously consider switching to native compilation.

Testing PL/SQL Programs

I get great satisfaction out of creating new things, and that is one of the reasons I so enjoy writing software. I love to take an interesting idea or challenge, and then come up with a way of using the PL/SQL language to meet that challenge.

I have to admit, though, that I don't really like having to take the time to test my software (nor do I like to write documentation for it). I do it, but I don't really do enough of it. And I have this funny feeling that I am not alone. The overwhelming reality is that developers generally perform an inadequate number of inadequate tests and figure that if the users don't find a bug, there is no bug. Why does this happen? Let me count the ways...

The psychology of success and failure
: We are so focused on getting our code to work correctly that we generally shy away from bad news—or from taking the chance of getting bad news. Better to do some cursory testing, confirm that everything seems to be working OK, and then wait for others to find bugs, if there are any (as if there were any doubt).

Deadline pressures
: Hey, it's Internet time! Time to market determines all. We need everything yesterday, so let's be just like Microsoft and Netscape—release pre-beta software as production and let our users test/suffer through our applications.

Management's lack of understanding
: IT management is notorious for not really understanding the software development process. If we are not given the time and authority to write (and I mean "write" in the broadest sense, including testing, documentation, refinement, etc.) code properly, we will always end up with buggy junk that no one wants to admit ownership of.

Overhead of setting up and running tests
: If it's a big deal to write and run tests, they won't get done. We'll decide that we don't have time; after all, there is always something else to work on. One consequence of this is that more and more of the testing is handed over to the QA department, if there is one. That transfer of responsibility is, on the one hand, positive. Professional quality assurance professionals can have a tremendous impact on application quality. Yet developers must take and exercise responsibility for unit testing their own code; otherwise, the testing/QA process is much more frustrating and extended.

The bottom line is that our code almost universally needs more testing. I recently spent a fair amount of time thinking about how to improve my testing procedures. I have studied test "frameworks" developed by other programmers who work primarily with object-oriented languages. An obsessive coder, I then proceeded to construct my own framework for unit testing PL/SQL programs, which I named utPLSQL. utPLSQL is now an open source project that is being used by developers around the world.

In the following sections, I take a look at the way we often test (or think we are testing) our code. I then introduce utPLSQL, give you a sense of how it works, and tell you where you can get the software.

Typical, Tawdry Testing Techniques

Say that I am writing a big application with lots of string manipulation. I've got a "hangnail" called SUBSTR—this function bothers me and I need to take care of it. What's the problem? SUBSTR is great when you know the starting location of a string and the number of characters you want. In many situations, though, I have only the start and end locations, and I need to figure out the number of characters. Is it:

```
mystring := SUBSTR (full_string, 5, 17); -- start and end? Nah...
mystring := SUBSTR (full_string, 5, 12); -- end - start?
mystring := SUBSTR (full_string, 5, 13); -- end - start + 1?
mystring := SUBSTR (full_string, 5, 11); -- end - start - 1?
```

Why should I have to remember stuff like this? I never do remember, in fact, and so I find myself time and again doing the "SUBSTR tango": take out a scrap of paper, write down "abcdefgh", put a mark over the "c" and another over the "g", count on my fingers, and then remember that the formula is "end – start + 1". Of course.

All right, so I do that a dozen times, I'm pretty sick of it, and now I'm determined to stop wasting my time. I decide to write a function of my own called "betwnstr" (return the STRing BETWeeN the start and end) that does the work and the remembering for me.

After just a few moments, I create the following function:

```
CREATE OR REPLACE FUNCTION betwnStr (
   string_in IN VARCHAR2,
```

```
    start_in IN INTEGER,
    end_in IN INTEGER
    )
    RETURN VARCHAR2
IS
BEGIN
    RETURN (
       SUBSTR (
          string_in,
          start_in,
          end_in - start_in + 1
          )
       );
END;
```

That was easy—and I can tell with just a glance that it will work—right? It seems so obvious. Yet…OK, I really should run some tests and to do that, I put together a test script:

```
BEGIN
   DBMS_OUTPUT.PUT_LINE (betwnstr ('abcdefgh', 3, 5));
END;
```

And when I run this script (saved in the *betwnstr.tst* file), everything looks hunky-dory:

```
SQL> @betwnstr.tst
cde
```

Am I done testing? Not really. There are lots of different conditions I ought to test before I say that betwnstr is ready for prime time. I can pass a starting location of 0 to SUBSTR, for example, and it acts just as though I passed it a value of 1. Will betwnstr work the same way? Best to check. So I go back into my test script, make the change, and run it:

```
BEGIN
   DBMS_OUTPUT.PUT_LINE (betwnstr ('abcdefgh', 5, 10));
END;
```

And when I run this script again, once more everything looks fine:

```
SQL>  @betwnstr.tst
efgh
```

After pondering for another thirty seconds or so, I come up with lots of other conditions/combinations:

Start	End
NULL	NOT NULL
NOT NULL	NULL
NULL	NULL
3 (positive number)	1 (smaller positive number)
3 (positive number)	100 (larger than length of string)

And so on. And the most likely path of testing these various conditions is to go back to *betwnstr.tst*, plug in the values, and run the test. After a while, I will be very satisfied that my code works correctly.

We could conclude that I have just performed a very thorough unit test of my program. There are, however, several drawbacks to this approach:

- It was necessary for me to visually ("manually") verify that the result of the betwnstr execution was correct. Is the correct answer really "def"? Perhaps it is "efg". I need to look at the original test and do the work in my head. This is both time-consuming and error-prone.
- Each time I set up a new test, I "lost" my previous test; I typed in new values over old values.
- There is a good chance that I will lose track of—or even immediately discard—my ad hoc test script when I am satisfied that the code works.

The consequences of this approach to testing are rather far-reaching. Suppose that I want to add functionality to this program, or I discover a problem after using it for a little while. There's one problem with betwnstr you might have already noticed: what if I pass it a negative starting position? If I do that with SUBSTR, it simply starts at the *N*th position from the end of string and then scans forward to extract the substring, as in:

```
BEGIN
   DBMS_OUTPUT.PUT_LINE (SUBSTR ('abcdefgh', -3, 5));
END;
```

This returns "fgh". If I pass those same arguments to betwnstr, I get some eerily similar but questionable results:

```
SQL> BEGIN
  2      DBMS_OUTPUT.PUT_LINE (SUBSTR ('abcdefgh', -3, 5));
  3      DBMS_OUTPUT.PUT_LINE (betwnstr ('abcdefgh', -3, 5));
  4  END;
  5  /
fgh
fgh
```

This doesn't really make sense, does it? What is the string between positions –3 and 5? Seems to me that betwnstr should accept –3 as start and –5 as end and return the substring "def"—or is it "fed"? I will leave the revised implementation of the betwnstr function as an exercise for the reader, because it is not relevant to unit testing. For now, just assume that I have modified betwnstr in some fairly substantial ways to support negative start and end positions.

Consider the situation I now face from a testing perspective. To be certain that my code works, I should run all the previous tests, plus an additional set of tests based on the variations of negative and positive values. But I didn't keep all those test cases! I ran the tests, the code worked, I was done.

Ah, but it isn't that simple, is it? I can tell you with total confidence that I have never written a piece of code that required just one round of testing. Software, if it is used by human beings, will change over time. That is the nature of the reality software seeks to emulate.

Now I face the task of re-creating the same tests I ran earlier. This makes me feel harried, short of time (because I am clearly wasting my time doing something I did before), and pressured. I know now that I should have kept all those tests intact, but I feel that to do so now would take extra time. I need to test, test quickly no matter how ugly the process, and get this code into production.

Does that sense of desperation sound familiar? It is a sure sign that you should slow down, even STOP, and reevaluate your path. So I will do that with betwnstr.

Certainly, it would make more sense to construct a series of tests in my test script, something like this:

```
SET SERVEROUTPUT ON FORMAT WRAPPED
BEGIN
   DBMS_OUTPUT.PUT_LINE (betwnstr ('abcdefgh', 3, 5));
   DBMS_OUTPUT.PUT_LINE (betwnstr ('abcdefgh', 0, 2));
   DBMS_OUTPUT.PUT_LINE (betwnstr ('abcdefgh', NULL, 5));
   DBMS_OUTPUT.PUT_LINE (betwnstr ('abcdefgh', 3, NULL));
   DBMS_OUTPUT.PUT_LINE (betwnstr ('abcdefgh', 3, 100));
   DBMS_OUTPUT.PUT_LINE (betwnstr ('abcdefgh', -3, -5));
   DBMS_OUTPUT.PUT_LINE (betwnstr ('abcdefgh', -3, 0));
END;
```

When I run this script (which I can do repeatedly with little incremental effort), I get the following output:

```
SQL> @betwnstr.tst
cde
abc

cdefgh
def
abcdef
```

This output is, unfortunately, very hard to analyze for correctness.

Doesn't it seem that there should be a better way to obtain a high level of confidence in one's code—to test comprehensively without taking lots of time to get the job done? I believe there is, and I spent a good part of June 2000 constructing a PL/SQL utility called utPLSQL to do just that.

If I were going to use utPLSQL to test betwnstr, I would open a SQL*Plus session and issue this statement:

```
SQL> exec utplsql.test ('betwnstr')
```

If there were a problem, it would be revealed with this kind of message sent to the screen:

```
> FFFFFFF   AA     III  L      U     U RRRRR   EEEEEEE
> F        A  A     I   L      U     U R    R  E
> F       A    A    I   L      U     U R     R E
> F      A      A   I   L      U     U R     R E
> FFFF   A      A   I   L      U     U RRRRRR  EEEE
> F      AAAAAAAA   I   L      U     U R   R   E
> F      A      A   I   L      U     U R    R  E
> F      A      A   I   L       U   U  R     R E
> F      A      A  III  LLLLLLL  UUU   R     R EEEEEEE
.
 FAILURE: "betwnstr"

FAILURE - EQ "normal" Expected "cde" and got "c"
FAILURE - EQ "zero start" Expected "abc" and got "a"
SUCCESS - ISNULL "null start" Expected "" and got ""
SUCCESS - ISNULL "big start small end" Expected "" and got ""
```

Assuming that I fixed the problem and the test turned out to be successful, I would simply see this:

```
SQL> exec utplsql.test ('betwnstr')
.
>    SSSS   U     U   CCC     CCC   EEEEEEE   SSSS     SSSS
>   S    S  U     U  C   C   C   C  E        S    S   S    S
>  S        U     U C     C C     C E       S        S
>   S       U     U C       C       E        S        S
>    SSSS   U     U C       C       EEEE      SSSS     SSSS
>        S  U     U C       C       E             S        S
>         S U     U C     C C     C E              S        S
>   S    S   U   U   C   C   C   C  E        S    S   S    S
>    SSSS     UUU     CCC     CCC   EEEEEEE   SSSS     SSSS
.
 SUCCESS: "betwnstr"

SUCCESS - EQ "normal" Expected "cde" and got "cde"
SUCCESS - EQ "zero start" Expected "abc" and got "abc"
SUCCESS - ISNULL "null start" Expected "" and got ""
SUCCESS - ISNULL "big start small end" Expected "" and got ""
```

Well, that's kind of nice, isn't it? utPLSQL tells me whether or not my test succeeded—and even reports on individual test cases. Now how is this possible?

Unfortunately, it is not all automatic. You need to build a test package that conforms to certain rules (mainly, how you name procedures in the specification). For example, the test package specification for betwnstr looks like this:

```
CREATE OR REPLACE PACKAGE ut_betwnstr
IS
   PROCEDURE ut_setup;
   PROCEDURE ut_teardown;

   -- For each program to test...
   PROCEDURE ut_betwnstr;
END ut_betwnstr;
```

In other words, I specify a test setup program that is run before my unit tests, and a teardown program that runs after the unit tests in order to perform cleanup operations. The ut_betwnstr procedure is the unit test program for betwnstr. Here is a portion of the implementation of this program:

```
PROCEDURE ut_BETWNSTR IS
BEGIN
   utAssert.eq (
      'normal',
      BETWNSTR('abcdefg', 3, 5),
      'def'
      );
   utAssert.isnull (
      'null start',
      BETWNSTR('abcdefg', NULL, 5),
      );
END ut_BETWNSTR;
```

Here I am making calls to utPLSQL assertion routines to check whether the outcome of a call to betwnstr matches what I would have expected. The result of this test is stored in a database table. After all unit tests are run, utPLSQL queries the contents of this table to display the results.

Figure 19-1 shows the "round trip" involved in utPLSQL's running the test programs, which in turn call assertion programs to populate the results table, which is then analyzed for test outcomes.

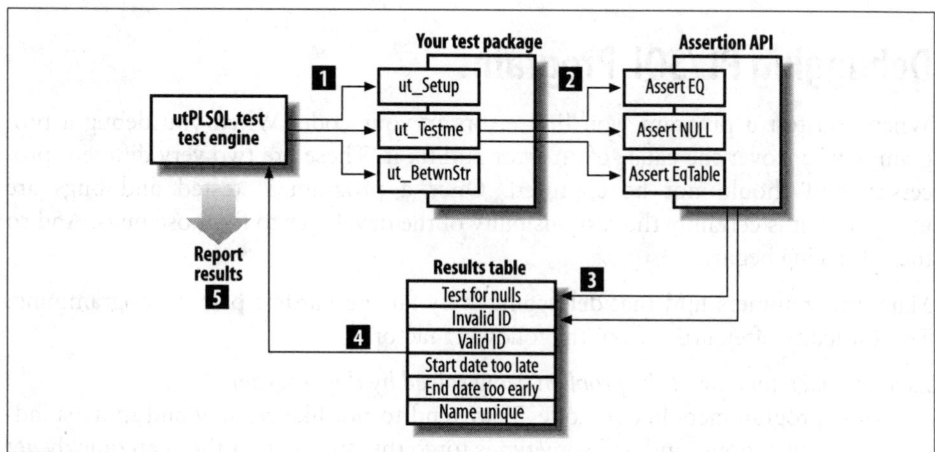

Figure 19-1. The utPLSQL architecture

Even without understanding all the details of the code and architecture, I hope that the following advantages are clear:

- I use a predefined testing engine (*utPLSQL.test*) to run my tests. This engine gives me a "red light, green light" response: did it work or fail? If it failed, utPLSQL gives me a message indicating which test case failed. The bottom line is that I have shifted to automated testing—I do not need to examine the results and think about whether or not they are correct.

- To use utPLSQL, I build a test routine (such as ut_betwnstr), which means that I automatically "cache" all of my tests to be run over and over again. After every change I make to the code, in fact, I can instantly and confidently test to make sure I didn't screw something up.

I believe that this sort of unit testing framework can be of tremendous help to just about any developer (including myself!).

For More Information...

While there is lots more to be said and demonstrated about utPLSQL, you should now have enough of an understanding of it to decide whether it might be of interest to you. To learn more about utPLSQL, the utAssert assertion routines, and the rest of this unit testing framework, visit the project home for utPLSQL at:

https://sourceforge.net/projects/utplsql/

You can download the software, join the distributed development team, and submit your requests for enhancements (and, sigh, bug reports). Even if you decide not to use utPLSQL, I hope that it will give you some ideas about how to improve your own testing procedures.

Debugging PL/SQL Programs

When you test a program, you find errors in your code. When you debug a program, you uncover the cause of an error and fix it. These are two very different processes, and should not be confused. Once a program is tested and bugs are uncovered, it is certainly the responsibility of the developer to fix those bugs. And so the debugging begins!

Many programmers find that debugging is by far the hardest part of programming. This difficulty often arises from the following factors:

Lack of understanding of the problem being solved by the program
: Most programmers like to code. They tend to not like reading and understanding specifications, and will sometimes forgo this step so that they can quickly get down to writing code. The chance of a program meeting its requirements under these conditions is slim at best.

Poor programming practice
: Programs that are hard to read (lack of documentation, too much documentation, inconsistent use of whitespace, bad choices for identifier names, etc.), programs that are not properly modularized, and programs that try to be too clever

present a much greater challenge to debug than programs that are well designed and structured.

The program simply contains too many errors
: Without the proper analysis and coding skills, you can end up with many more errors than are necessary. When you compile a program and get back five screens of compile errors, do you just want to scream and hide? It is easy to be so overwhelmed by your errors that you don't take the organized, step-by-step approach needed to fix those errors.

Limited debugging skills
: There are many different approaches to uncovering the causes of your problems. Some approaches only make life more difficult for you. If you have not been trained in the best way to debug your code, you can waste many hours, raise your blood pressure, and upset your manager.

The following sections review the debugging methods that you will want to avoid at all costs, and then offer recommendations for more effective debugging strategies.

The Wrong Way to Debug

As I present the various ways you shouldn't debug your programs, I expect that just about all of you will say to yourselves, "Well, that sure is obvious. Of course you shouldn't do that. I never do that."

And yet the very next time you sit down to do your work, you may very well follow some of these obviously horrible debugging practices.

If you happen to see little bits of yourself in the paragraphs that follow, I hope you will be inspired to mend your ways.

Disorganized debugging

When faced with a bug, you become a whirlwind of frenzied activity. Even though the presence of an error indicates that you did not fully analyze the problem and figure out how the program should solve it, you do not now take the time to understand the program. Instead you place MESSAGE statements (in Oracle Forms) or SRW.MESSAGE statements (in Oracle Reports) or DBMS_OUTPUT.PUT_LINE statements (in stored modules) all over your program in the hopes of extracting more clues.

You do not save a copy of the program before you start making changes because that would take too much time; you are under a lot of pressure right now, and you are certain that the answer will pop right out at you. You will just remove your debug statements later.

You spend lots of time looking at information that is mostly irrelevant. You question everything about your program, even though most of it uses constructs you've employed successfully for years.

You skip lunch but make time for coffee, lots of coffee, because it is free and you want to make sure your concentration is at the most intense level possible. Even though you have no idea what is causing the problem, you think that maybe if you try this one change it might help. You make the change and take several minutes to compile, generate, and run through the test case, only to find that the change didn't help—in fact, it seemed to have caused another problem because you hadn't thought through the impact of the change on your application.

So you back out of that change and try something else in hopes that it might work. But several minutes later you again find that it doesn't. A friend, noticing that your fingers are trembling, offers to help. But you don't know where to start explaining the problem because you don't really know what is wrong. Furthermore, you are kind of embarrassed about what you've done so far (turned the program into a minefield of tracing statements) and realize you don't have a clean version to show your friend. So you snap at the best programmer in your group and call your family to let them know you aren't going to be home for dinner that night.

Why? Because you are determined to fix that bug!

Irrational debugging

You execute your report and it comes up empty. You spent the last hour making changes both in the underlying data structures and in the code that queries and formats the data. You are certain, however, that your modifications could not have made the report disappear.

You call your internal support hotline to find out if there is a network problem, even though File Manager clearly shows access to network drives. You further probe as to whether the database has gone down, even though you just connected successfully. You spend another ten minutes of the support analyst's time running through a variety of scenarios before you hang up in frustration.

"They don't know anything over there," you fume. You realize that you will have to figure this one out all by yourself. So you dive into the code you just modified. You are determined to check every single line until you find the cause of your difficulty. Over the course of the next two hours, you talk aloud to yourself—a lot.

"Look at that! I called the stored procedure inside an IF statement. I never did that before. Maybe you can't call stored programs that way." So you remove the IF statement and instead use a GOTO statement to perform the branching to the stored procedure. But that doesn't fix the problem.

"My code seems fine. But it calls this other routine that Joe wrote ages ago." Joe has since moved on, making him a ripe candidate for the scapegoat. "It probably doesn't work anymore; after all, we did upgrade to a new voicemail system." So you decide to perform a standalone test of Joe's routine, which hasn't changed for two years and has no interface to voicemail. But his program seems to work fine—when it's not run from your program.

Now you are starting to get desperate. "Maybe this report should only run on weekends. Hey, can I put a local module in an anonymous block? Maybe I can use only local modules in procedures and functions! I think maybe I heard about a bug in this tool. Time for a workaround…"

You get angry and begin to understand why your eight-year-old hits the computer monitor when he can't beat the last level of Ultra Mystic Conqueror VII. And just as you are ready to go home and take it out on your dog, you realize that you are connected to the development database, which has almost no data at all. You switch to the test instance, run your report, and everything looks just fine.

Except, of course, for that GOTO and all the other workarounds you stuck in the report…

Debugging Tips and Strategies

In this chapter, I do not pretend to offer a comprehensive primer on debugging. The following tips and techniques, however, should improve upon your current set of error-fixing skills.

Use a source code debugger

The single most effective thing you can do to minimize the time spent debugging your code is to use a source code debugger. One is now available in just about every PL/SQL Integrated Development Environment (IDE). If you are using Quest's TOAD or SQL Navigator, Allround Automations' PL/SQL Developer, or Computer Associates' SQL Station (or any other such GUI tool), you will be able to set visual breakpoints in your code with the click of a mouse, step through your code line-by-line, watch variables as they change their values, and so on.

The other tips in this section apply whether or not you are using a GUI-based debugger, but there is no doubt that if you are still debugging the old-fashioned way (inserting calls to DBMS_OUTPUT.PUT_LINE in dozens of places in your code), you are wasting a lot of your time.

Gather data

Gather as much data as possible about when, where, and how the error occurred. It is very unlikely that the first occurrence of an error will give you all the information you will want or need to figure out the source of that error. Upon noticing an error, the temptation is to show off one's knowledge of the program by declaring, "Got it! I know what's going on and exactly how to fix it." This can be very gratifying when it turns out that you do have a handle on the problem, and that may be the case for simple bugs. Some problems can appear simple, however, and turn out to require extensive testing and analysis. Save yourself the embarrassment of pretending (or believing) that you know more than you actually do. Before rushing to change your code, take these steps:

Run the program again to see if the error is reproducible
: This will be the first indication of the complexity of the problem. It is almost impossible to determine the cause of a problem if you are unable to get it to occur predictably. Once you work out the steps needed to get the error to occur, you will have gained much valuable information about its cause.

Narrow the test case needed to generate the error
: I recently had to debug a problem in one of my Oracle Forms modules. A pop-up window would lose its data under certain circumstances. At first glance, the rule seemed to be: "For a new call, if you enter only one request, that request will be lost." If I had stopped testing at that point, I would have had to analyze all code that initialized the call record and handled the INSERT logic. Instead, I tried additional variations of data entry and soon found that the data was lost only when I navigated to the pop-up window directly from a certain item. Now I had a very narrow test case to analyze, and it became very easy to uncover the error in logic.

Examine the circumstances under which the problem does not occur
: "Failure to fail" can offer many insights into the reason an error does occur. It also helps you narrow down the sections of code and the conditions you have to analyze when you go back to the program.

The more information you gather about the problem at hand, the easier it will be to solve that problem. It is worth the extra time to assemble the evidence. So even when you are absolutely sure you are on to that bug, hold off and investigate a little further.

Remain logical at all times

Symbolic logic is the lifeblood of programmers. No matter which programming language you use, the underlying logical framework is a constant. PL/SQL has one particular syntax. The C language uses different keywords and the IF statement looks a little different. The elegance of LISP demands a very different way of building programs. But underneath it all, symbolic logic provides the backbone on which you hang the statements that solve your problems.

The reliance on logical and rational thought in programming is one reason that it is so easy for a developer to learn a new programming language. As long as you can take the statement of a problem and develop a logical solution step by step, the particulars of a language are secondary.

With logic at the core of our being, it amazes me to see how often we programmers abandon this logic and pursue the most irrational path to solving a problem. We engage in wishful thinking and highly superstitious, irrational, or dubious thought processes. Even though we know better—much better—we find ourselves questioning code that conforms to documented functionality, that has worked in the past, and that surely works at that moment. This irrationality almost always involves shifting the blame from oneself to the "other"—the computer, the compiler, Joe, the word processor, whatever. Anything and anybody but our own pristine selves!

When you attempt to shift blame, you only put off solving your problem. Computers and compilers may not be intelligent, but they are very fast and very consistent. All they can do is follow rules, and you write the rules in your program. So when you uncover a bug in your code, take responsibility for that error. Assume that *you* did something wrong—don't blame the PL/SQL compiler or Oracle Forms or the text editor.

If you do find yourself questioning a basic element or rule in the compiler that has always worked for you in the past, it is time to take a break. Better yet, it is time to get someone else to look at your code. It is amazing how another pair of eyes can focus your own analytical powers on the real causes of a problem.

Strive to be the Spock of Programming. Accept only what is logical. Reject that which has no explanation.

Analyze instead of trying

So you have a pile of data and all the clues you could ask for in profiling the symptoms of your problem. Now it is time to analyze that data. For many people, analysis takes the following form: "Hmm, this looks like it could be the answer. I'll make this change, recompile, and try it to see if it works."

What's wrong with this approach? When you try a solution to see what will happen, what you are really saying is:

- You are not sure that the change really is a solution. If you were sure, you wouldn't "try" it to see what would happen. You would make the change and then test that change.
- You have not fully analyzed the error to understand its causes. If you know why an error occurs, then you know if a particular change will fix that problem. If you are unsure about the source of the error, you will be tempted to simply try a change and examine the impact. This is, unfortunately, very faulty logic.
- Even if the change stops the error from occurring, you cannot be sure that your "solution" really solved anything. Because you are not sure why the problem occurred, the simple fact that the problem does not reappear in your particular

tests does not mean that you fixed the bug. The most you can say is that your change stopped the bug from occurring under certain, perhaps even most, circumstances.

To truly solve a problem, you must completely analyze the cause of the problem. Once you understand why the problem occurs, you have found the root cause and can take the steps necessary to make the problem go away in all circumstances.

When you identify a potential solution, perform a walk-through of your code based on that change. Don't execute your form. Examine your program and mentally try out different scenarios to test your hypothesis. Once you are certain that your change actually does address the problem, you can then perform a test of that solution. You won't be *trying* anything; you will be *verifying* a fix.

Analyze your bug fully before you test solutions. If you say to yourself, "Why don't I try this?" in the hope that it will solve the problem, then you are wasting your time and debugging inefficiently.

Take breaks and ask for help

We are often our own biggest obstacles when it comes to sorting out our problems, whether a program bug or a personal crisis. When you are stuck on the inside of a problem, it is hard to maintain an objective distance and take a fresh look.

When you are making absolutely no progress and feel that you have tried everything, try these two radical techniques:

- Take a break
- Ask for help

When I have struggled with a bug for any length of time without success, I not only become ineffective, I also tend to lose perspective. I pursue irrational and superstitious leads. I lose track of what I have already tested and what I have assumed to be right. I get too close to the problem to debug it effectively.

My frustration level usually correlates closely to the amount of time I have sat in my ergonomic chair and perched over my wrist-padded keyboard and stared at my low-radiation screen. Often the very simple act of stepping away from the workstation will clear my head and leave room for a solution to pop into place. Did you ever wake up the morning after a very difficult day at work to find the elusive answer sitting there at the end of your dream?

Make it a rule to get up and walk around at least once an hour when you are working on a problem—heck, even when you are writing your programs. Give your brain a chance to let its neural networks make the connections and develop new options for your programming. There is a whole big world out there. Even when your eyes are glued to the monitor and your source code, the world keeps turning. It never hurts to remind yourself of the bigger picture, even if that only amounts to taking note of the weather outside your air-conditioned cocoon.

Even more effective than taking a break is asking another person to look at your problem. There is something entirely magical about the dynamic of adding another pair of eyes to the situation. You might struggle with a problem for an hour or two, and finally, at the exact moment that you break down and explain the problem to a co-worker, the solution will jump out at you. It could be a mismatch on names, a false assumption, or a misunderstanding of the IF statement logic. Whatever the case, chances are that you yourself will find it (even though you couldn't for the last two hours) as soon as you ask someone else to find it for you.

And even if the error does not yield itself quite so easily, you still have lots to gain from the perspective of another person who (a) did not write the code and has no subconscious assumptions or biases about it, and (b) isn't mad at the program.

Other benefits accrue from asking for help. You improve the self-esteem and self-confidence of other programmers by showing that you respect their opinions. If you are one of the best developers in the group, then your request for help demonstrates that you, too, sometimes make mistakes and need help from the team. This builds the sense (and the reality) of teamwork, which will improve the overall development and testing efforts on the project.

Change and test one area of code at a time

One of my biggest problems when I debug my code is that I am overconfident about my development and debugging skills, so I try to address too many problems at once. I make five or ten changes, rerun my test, and get very unreliable and minimally useful results. I find that my changes cause other problems (a common phenomenon until a program stabilizes, and a sure sign that lots more debugging and testing is needed), that some, but not all, of the original errors are gone, and that I have no idea which changes fixed which errors and which changes caused new errors.

In short, my debugging effort is a mess, and I have to back out of changes until I have a clearer picture of what is happening in my program.

Unless you are making very simple changes, you should fix one problem at a time and then test that fix. The amount of time it takes to compile, generate, and test may increase, but in the long run you will be much more productive.

Another aspect of incremental testing and debugging is performing unit tests on individual modules before you test a program that calls these various modules. If you test the programs separately and determine that they work, when you debug your application as a whole (in a system test), you do not have to worry about whether those modules return correct values or perform the correct actions. Instead, you can concentrate on the code that calls the modules. (See the earlier section "Testing PL/SQL Programs" for more on unit testing.)

Tuning PL/SQL Programs

Tuning an Oracle application is a complex process—you need to tune the SQL in your code base, make sure the System Global Area (SGA) is properly configured, optimize algorithms, and so on. Tuning individual PL/SQL programs is a bit less daunting, but still more than enough of a challenge. Before spending lots of time improving the performance of your PL/SQL code, you should first:

Tune access to code and data in the SGA
: Before your code can be executed (and perhaps run too slowly), it must be loaded into the SGA of the Oracle instance. This process can benefit from a focused tuning effort, usually performed by a DBA. You will find more information about the SGA and the PL/SQL runtime architecture in Chapter 20.

Optimize your SQL
: In virtually any application you write against the Oracle RDBMS, the vast majority of tuning will take place by optimizing the SQL statements executed against your data. The potential inefficiencies of a 16-way join dwarf the usual issues found in a procedural block of code. To put it another way, if you have a program that runs in 20 hours and you need to reduce elapsed time to 30 minutes, virtually your only hope will be to concentrate on the SQL within your code. There are many third-party tools available to both DBAs and developers that perform very sophisticated analyses of SQL within applications and recommend more efficient alternatives.

Once you are confident that the "context" in which your PL/SQL code is run is not obviously inefficient, you should turn your attention to the code base. I suggest the following steps:

Write your application with best practices and standards in mind
: While you should not take clearly inefficient approaches to meeting requirements, you also should not obsess about the performance implications of every line in your code. Remember that most of the code you write will never be a bottleneck in your application's performance, so you don't have to optimize it. Instead, get the application done and then...

Analyze your application's execution profile
: Does it run quickly enough? If it does, great—you don't need to do any tuning (at the moment). If it's too slow, identify which specific elements of the application are causing the problem and then focus directly on those programs (or parts of programs). Once identified, you can then...

Tune your algorithms
: As a procedural language, PL/SQL is often used to implement complex formulas and algorithms. You can make use of conditional statements, loops, perhaps even GOTOs and (I hope) reusable modules to get the job done. These algorithms can be written in many different ways, some of which perform very badly.

How do you tune poorly written algorithms? This is a tough question with no easy answers. Tuning algorithms is much more complex than tuning SQL (which is "structured" and therefore lends itself more easily to automated analysis).

Take advantage of any PL/SQL-specific performance features
: Over the years, Oracle has added statements and optimizations that can make a substantial difference to the execution of your code. From the RETURNING clause to FORALL, make sure you aren't "living in the past" and paying the price in application inefficiencies.

It is outside the scope of this book to offer substantial advice on SQL tuning and database/SGA configuration. Even a comprehensive discourse on PL/SQL tuning alone would require multiple chapters. Furthermore, developers often find that many tuning tips have limited or no impact on their particular environments. In the remainder of this chapter, I will present some ideas on how to analyze performance of your code, and then offer a limited amount of tuning advice that will apply to the broadest range of applications.

Analyzing Performance of PL/SQL Code

Before you can tune your application, you need to figure out what is running slowly and where you should focus your efforts. Oracle and third-party vendors offer a variety of products to help you do this; generally they focus on analyzing the SQL statements in your code, offering alternative implementations, and so on. These tools are very powerful, yet they can also be very frustrating to PL/SQL developers. They tend to offer an overwhelming amount of performance data without telling you what you really want to know: how fast did a particular program run, and how much did the performance improve after making this change?

To answer these questions, Oracle offers a number of built-in utilities. The most useful are:

DBMS_PROFILER
: This built-in package allows you to turn on execution profiling in a session. Then, when you run your code, Oracle uses tables to keep track of detailed information about how long each line in your code took to execute. You can then run queries on these tables or—much preferred—use screens in products like TOAD or SQL Navigator to present the data in a clear, graphical fashion.

DBMS_UTILITY.GET_TIME
: Use this built-in function to calculate the elapsed time of your code down to the hundredth of a second. The scripts *tmr81.ot* and *plvtmr.pkg* (available on the O'Reilly site) offer an interface to this function that allows you to use "timers" (based on DBMS_UTILITY.GET_TIME) in your code. These make it possible to time exactly how long a certain operation took to run, and even to compare various implementations of the same requirement.

In case you do not have access to a tool that offers an interface to DBMS_PROFILER, here are some instructions and examples.

First of all, Oracle does not yet install DBMS_PROFILER for you automatically. To see if DBMS_PROFILER is installed and available, connect to your schema in SQL*Plus and issue this command:

```
SQL> DESC DBMS_PROFILER
```

If you then see the message:

```
ERROR:
ORA-04043: object dbms_profiler does not exist
```

you will have to install the program.

For Oracle 7.x and 8.0, you need to ask your DBA to run the following scripts under a SYSDBA account (the first creates the package specification, the second the package body):

$ORACLE_HOME/rdbms/admin/dbmspbp.sql
$ORACLE_HOME/rdbms/admin/prvtpbp.plb

For Oracle8*i* and Oracle9*i*, you need to run the *$ORACLE_HOME/rdbms/admin/profload.sql* file instead, also under a SYSDBA account.

You then need to run the *$ORACLE_HOME/rdbms/admin/proftab.sql* file in your own schema to create three tables populated by DBMS_PROFILER:

PLSQL_PROFILER_RUNS
: Parent table of runs

PLSQL_PROFILER_UNITS
: Program units executed in run

PLSQL_PROFILER_DATA
: Profiling data for each line in a program unit

Finally, you will probably find it helpful to take advantage of some sample queries and reporting packages offered by Oracle in the following files:

```
$ORACLE_HOME/plsql/demo/profrep.sql
$ORACLE_HOME/plsql/demo/profsum.sql
```

Once all these objects are defined, you gather profiling information for your application by writing code like this:

```
BEGIN
   DBMS_OUTPUT.PUT_LINE (
      DBMS_PROFILER.START_PROFILER (
         'showemps ' ||
         TO_CHAR (SYSDATE, 'YYYYMMDD HH24:MI:SS')
         )
      );
   showemps;
```

```
    DBMS_OUTPUT.PUT_LINE (
       DBMS_PROFILER.STOP_PROFILER);
END;
```

Once you have finished running your application code, you can run queries against the data in the PLSQL_PROFILER_ tables. Here is an example of such a query that displays those lines of code that consumed at least 1% of the total time of the run:

```
/* File on web: slowest.sql */
SELECT      TO_CHAR (
               p1.total_time / 10000000,
               '99999999')
         || '-'
         || TO_CHAR (p1.total_occur) AS time_count,
            p2.unit_owner || '.' || p2.unit_name unit,
            TO_CHAR (p1.line#)
         || '-'
         || p3.text text
    FROM plsql_profiler_data p1,
         plsql_profiler_units p2,
         all_source p3,
         plsql_profiler_grand_total p4
   WHERE p2.unit_owner NOT IN ('SYS', 'SYSTEM')
     AND p1.runid = &&firstparm
     AND (p1.total_time >= p4.grand_total / 100)
     AND p1.runid = p2.runid
     AND p2.unit_number = p1.unit_number
     AND p3.TYPE = 'PACKAGE BODY'
     AND p3.owner = p2.unit_owner
     AND p3.line = p1.line#
     AND p3.NAME = p2.unit_name
ORDER BY p1.total_time DESC;
```

As you can see, these queries are fairly complex (I modified one of the canned queries from Oracle to produce the above four-way join). That's why it is far better to rely on a graphical interface in a PL/SQL development tool.

After you have analyzed your code and identified bottlenecks, the following sections can help you determine what kinds of changes to make to your code to improve performance.

Tracing Execution of Your Code

Earlier versions of Oracle offered some PL/SQL trace capabilities, but Oracle8*i* provides an API that allows you to easily specify and control the tracing of the execution of PL/SQL procedures, functions, and exceptions. The DBMS_TRACE built-in package provides programs to start and stop PL/SQL tracing in a session. When tracing is turned on, the engine collects data as the program executes. The data is then written out to the Oracle Server trace file.

The PL/SQL trace facility provides a trace file that shows you the specific steps executed by your code. The DBMS_PROFILER package (described earlier in this chapter) offers a much more comprehensive analysis of your application, including timing information and counts of the number of times a specific line was executed.

Installing DBMS_TRACE

This package may not have been installed automatically with the rest of the built-in packages. To determine whether DBMS_TRACE is present, connect to SYS (or another account with SYSDBA privileges) and execute this command:

```
BEGIN DBMS_TRACE.CLEAR_PLSQL_TRACE; END;
```

If you see this error:

```
PLS-00201: identifier 'DBMS_TRACE.CLEAR_PLSQL_TRACE'
           must be declared
```

then you must install the package. To do this, remain connected as SYS (or another account with SYSDBA privileges) and run the following files in the order specified:

$ORACLE_HOME/rdbms/admin/dbmspbt.sql
$ORACLE_HOME/rdbms/admin/prvtpbt.plb

DBMS_TRACE programs

The following programs are available in the DBMS_TRACE package:

SET_PLSQL_TRACE
: Starts PL/SQL tracing in the current session

CLEAR_PLSQL_TRACE
: Stops the dumping of trace data for that session

PLSQL_TRACE_VERSION
: Gets the major and minor version numbers of the DBMS_TRACE package

To trace execution of your PL/SQL code, you must first start the trace with a call to:

```
DBMS_TRACE.SET_PLSQL_TRACE (trace_level INTEGER);
```

in your current session, where *trace_level* is one of the following values:

- Constants that determine which elements of your PL/SQL program will be traced:

```
DBMS_TRACE.trace_all_calls          constant INTEGER := 1;
DBMS_TRACE.trace_enabled_calls      constant INTEGER := 2;
DBMS_TRACE.trace_all_exceptions     constant INTEGER := 4;
DBMS_TRACE.trace_enabled_exceptions constant INTEGER := 8;
DBMS_TRACE.trace_all_sql            constant INTEGER := 32;
DBMS_TRACE.trace_enabled_sql        constant INTEGER := 64;
DBMS_TRACE.trace_all_lines          constant INTEGER := 128;
DBMS_TRACE.trace_enabled_lines      constant INTEGER := 256;
```

- Constants that control the tracing process:

```
DBMS_TRACE.trace_stop                constant INTEGER := 16384;
DBMS_TRACE.trace_pause               constant INTEGER := 4096;
DBMS_TRACE.trace_resume              constant INTEGER := 8192;
DBMS_TRACE.trace_limit               constant INTEGER := 16;
```

By combining the DBMS_TRACE constants, you can enable tracing of multiple PL/SQL language features simultaneously. Note that the constants that control the tracing behavior (such as DBMS_TRACE.trace_pause) should not be used in combination with the other constants (such as DBMS_TRACE.trace_enabled_calls).

To turn on tracing from all programs executed in your session, issue this call:

```
DBMS_TRACE.SET_PLSQL_TRACE (DBMS_TRACE.trace_all_calls);
```

To turn on tracing for all exceptions raised during the session, issue this call:

```
DBMS_TRACE.SET_PLSQL_TRACE (DBMS_TRACE.trace_all_exceptions);
```

You then run your code. When you are done, you stop the trace session by calling:

```
DBMS_TRACE.CLEAR_PLSQL_TRACE;
```

You can then examine the contents of the trace file. The names of these files are generated by Oracle; you will usually look at the modification dates to figure out which file to examine. The location of the trace files is discussed in the later section "Format of collected data."

Note that you cannot use PL/SQL tracing with the multithreaded server (MTS).

Controlling trace file contents

The trace files produced by DBMS_TRACE can get *really* big. You can focus the output by enabling only specific programs for trace data collection.

You cannot use this approach with remote procedure calls.

To enable a specific program for tracing, you can alter the session to enable any programs that are created or replaced in the session. To take this approach, issue this command:

```
ALTER SESSION SET PLSQL_DEBUG=TRUE;
```

If you don't want to alter your entire session, you can recompile a specific program unit in debug mode as follows (not applicable to anonymous blocks):

```
ALTER [PROCEDURE | FUNCTION | PACKAGE BODY] program_name COMPILE DEBUG;
```

After you have enabled the programs in which you're interested, the following call will initiate tracing just for those program units:

```
DBMS_TRACE.SET_PLSQL_TRACE (DBMS_TRACE.trace_enabled_calls);
```

You can also restrict the trace information to only those exceptions raised within enabled programs with this call:

```
DBMS_TRACE.SET_PLSQL_TRACE (DBMS_TRACE.trace_enabled_exceptions);
```

If you request tracing for all programs or exceptions and also request tracing only for enabled programs or exceptions, the request for "all" takes precedence.

Pausing and resuming the trace process

The SET_PLSQL_TRACE procedure can do more than just determine which information will be traced. You can also request that the tracing process be paused and resumed. The following statement, for example, requests that no information be gathered until tracing is resumed:

```
DBMS_TRACE.SET_PLSQL_TRACE (DBMS_TRACE.trace_pause);
```

DBMS_TRACE will write a record to the trace file to show when tracing was paused and/or resumed.

Use the DBMS_TRACE.trace_limit constant to request that only the last 8,192 trace events of a run be preserved. This approach helps ensure that you can turn tracing on without overwhelming the database with trace activity. When the trace session ends, only the last 8,192 records are saved.

Format of collected data

If you request tracing only for enabled program units and the current program unit is not enabled, no trace data is written. If the current program unit is enabled, call tracing writes out the program unit type, name, and stack depth. If the current program unit is enabled, call tracing writes out the program unit type, line number, and stack depth.

Exception tracing writes out the line number. Raising an exception records trace information on whether the exception is user-defined or predefined, and records the exception number in the case of predefined exceptions. If you raise a user-defined exception, you will always see an error code of 1.

Here is an example of the output from a trace of the showemps procedure:

```
*** 1999.06.14.09.59.25.394
*** SESSION ID:(9.7) 1999.06.14.09.59.25.344
------------ PL/SQL TRACE INFORMATION -----------
Levels set :  1
Trace:  ANONYMOUS BLOCK: Stack depth = 1
Trace:   PROCEDURE SCOTT.SHOWEMPS: Call to entry at line 5 Stack depth = 2
Trace:    PACKAGE BODY SYS.DBMS_SQL: Call to entry at line 1 Stack depth = 3
```

```
Trace:      PACKAGE BODY SYS.DBMS_SYS_SQL: Call to entry at line 1 Stack depth = 4
Trace:      PACKAGE BODY SYS.DBMS_SYS_SQL: ICD vector index = 21 Stack depth = 4
Trace:     PACKAGE PLVPRO.P: Call to entry at line 26 Stack depth = 3
Trace:     PACKAGE PLVPRO.P: ICD vector index = 6 Stack depth = 3
Trace:     PACKAGE BODY PLVPRO.P: Call to entry at line 1 Stack depth = 3
Trace:     PACKAGE BODY PLVPRO.P: Call to entry at line 1 Stack depth = 3
Trace:      PACKAGE BODY PLVPRO.P: Call to entry at line 1 Stack depth = 4
```

Improving Application Performance

Now that we have reviewed some of the ways you can analyze your application's execution, let's consider some tips for improving the performance of that application.

Avoid Unnecessary Code Execution

This is "mom and apple pie" advice in the world of tuning, and may seem rather obvious. Surely, if the code is not necessary I would not include it in my program. Surely. And under the pressure of the moment, I would never take shortcuts or do bad things because I always have plenty of time to pay the necessary attention to write optimized code. Right.

The reality is that we usually rush headlong into our coding tasks, feeling just a bit panicky and overwhelmed, annoyed that management won't buy us good tools and in a frenzy to get the job done and done well. And that is why, contrary to the laws of logic, it is all too easy to end up with code that really does not need to be executed in our programs. Removing such code will usually improve performance, sometimes in a dramatic fashion.

The search for unnecessary code

In an application with thousands of lines of source, how should you look for potential problems? Here are my recommendations:

Check your loops
: Code within a loop (FOR, WHILE, and simple) usually executes more than once. Therefore, any inefficiency in a loop's scope can have a multiplying effect.

Check your SQL statements
: First of all, you should of course make sure that your SQL statements have been optimized. That topic is outside the scope of this chapter; there are many fine tools and books that will help you tune your SQL. There are situations, however, when pure SQL results in excessive execution—and when the judicious use of PL/SQL can improve that statement's performance.

Review heavily patched sections of code
: In any complex program that has a lifespan of more than six months, you will usually find a section that has been changed again and again and again. It is very easy to allow inefficiencies to slip in with such incremental changes.

Don't take the declaration section for granted

Sure, that's the place where you declare all variables, give them their initial values, and so on. It is quite possible, however, that some actions taken in that section (the declarations themselves or the defaulting code) are not always needed and should not always be run on startup of the block.

Let's take a closer look at a number of these topics.

Check your loops

Code within a FOR, WHILE, or simple loop executes more than once (usually), so any inefficiency in a loop's scope therefore tends to have a multiplying effect. In one tuning exercise for a client, I discovered a 30-line function that ran in less than half a second, but was executed so frequently that its total elapsed time for a run was five hours. Focused tuning on that one program reduced its total execution time to less than twenty minutes. Always go to your loops first and make sure you are not introducing such a problem.

Here is an obvious example. My procedure accepts a single name argument, then processes each record fetched from a packaged cursor:

```
PROCEDURE process_data (nm_in IN VARCHAR2) IS
BEGIN
   FOR rec IN my_package.my_cursor
   LOOP
      process_record (
         UPPER (nm_in),
         rec.total_production);
   END LOOP;
END;
```

The problem with this code is that I apply the UPPER function to the nm_in argument for every iteration of the loop. That is unnecessary because the value of nm_in never changes. I can easily fix this by declaring a local variable to store the uppercased version of the name:

```
PROCEDURE process_data (nm_in IN VARCHAR2)
IS
   v_nm some_table.some_column%TYPE := UPPER (nm_in);
BEGIN
   FOR rec IN my_package.my_cursor
   LOOP
      process_record (v_nm, rec.total_production);
   END LOOP;
END;
```

Of course, it is not always so easy to spot redundant code execution. In this example, one would assume that I uppercased the name either because I knew for certain that process_record would not work properly with a lower- or mixed-case string, or because I was not really sure how process_record works and therefore "took out insurance" to head off any possible problems.

If I have found the process_data procedure to be a bottleneck, it is very important that I understand how all of the code on which it depends works. An incorrect assumption can intersect in very nasty ways with the algorithms of underlying programs. It may well be the case, for example, that process_record always performs an uppercase conversion on its first parameter. That would make my UPPER unnecessary.

Here is another program with lots of processing inside the loop. Do you see any unnecessary execution?

```
 1  CREATE OR REPLACE PROCEDURE process_data (tab_in IN VARCHAR2)
 2  IS
 3     cursor_id   PLS_INTEGER;
 4     exec_stat   PLS_INTEGER;
 5  BEGIN
 6     FOR rec IN (SELECT ... FROM ...)
 7     LOOP
 8        cursor_id := DBMS_SQL.open_cursor;
 9
10        DBMS_SQL.parse (cursor_id,
11           'SELECT ...
12              FROM employee E, ' || tab_in ||
13            'WHERE D.department_id = ' || rec.id ||
14              'AND ...',
15          DBMS_SQL.native
16        );
17        exec_stat := DBMS_SQL.execute (cursor_id);
18        DBMS_SQL.close_cursor (cursor_id);
19     END LOOP;
20  END;
```

The problem is more subtle in this case. You need to understand the workings of DBMS_SQL (the dynamic SQL built-in package described in Chapter 15) to realize that:

- You can reuse cursors allocated by the DBMS_SQL.OPEN_CURSOR function. Consequently, you do not need to open and close a cursor with each iteration of the loop.
- More importantly, whenever you're working with dynamic SQL, you must closely analyze the dynamic SQL string. In this case, when I look more closely at lines 11 through 14, I realize that the only thing changing with each loop iteration is the value of the department ID. Currently, this is being concatenated into the string, which means that this query will be reparsed for every different value of the ID. A much more efficient approach is to use binding, as I show in the following example.

Here is a process_data replacement that executes only what is necessary within the loop:

```
CREATE OR REPLACE PROCEDURE process_data (tab_in IN VARCHAR2)
IS
   cursor_id   PLS_INTEGER;
```

```
   exec_stat   PLS_INTEGER;
BEGIN
   cursor_id := DBMS_SQL.open_cursor;

   DBMS_SQL.parse (
      cursor_id,
         'SELECT ... FROM employee E, '
      || tab_in
      || 'WHERE D.department_id = :my_ID AND ...',
      DBMS_SQL.native
   );

   FOR rec IN (SELECT ... FROM ...)
   LOOP
      DBMS_SQL.bind_variable (cursor_id, 'my_id', rec.id);
      exec_stat := DBMS_SQL.EXECUTE (cursor_id);
   END LOOP;

   DBMS_SQL.close_cursor (cursor_id);
END;
```

Defer execution until needed

Just because you have a declaration section positioned "before" your execution section does not mean that you should declare all your program's variables there. It is quite possible that some actions taken in that section (the declarations themselves or the defaulting code) are not always needed and should not always be run on startup of the block.

Consider the following block of code:

```
PROCEDURE always_do_everything (criteria_in IN BOOLEAN)
IS
   big_string VARCHAR2(32767) := ten_minute_lookup (...);
   big_list
      list_types.big_strings_tt := two_minute_number_cruncher (...);
BEGIN
   IF NOT criteria_in
   THEN
      use_big_string (big_string);
      process_big_list (big_list);
   ELSE
      /* Nothing big going on here */
      ...
   END IF;
END;
```

In this code, I declare a big string and call a function that takes ten minutes of elapsed time and lots of CPU time to assign the default value to that string. I also declare and populate a collection (via a package-declared table TYPE), again relying on a CPU-intensive function to populate that list. I take both of these steps because I know that I need to use the big_string and big_list data structures in my programs.

Then I write my execution section, run some initial tests, and everything seems OK—except that it runs too slowly. I decide to walk through my code to get a better understanding of its flow. I discover something very interesting: my program always declares and populates the big_string and big_list structures, but it doesn't use them unless criteria_in is FALSE, which is usually not the case!

Once I have this more thorough understanding of my program's logical flow, I can take advantage of nested blocks (an anonymous block defined within another block of code) to defer the penalty of initializing my data structures until I am sure I need them. Here is a reworking of my inefficient program:

```
PROCEDURE only_as_needed (criteria_in IN BOOLEAN)
IS
   PROCEDURE heavy_duty_processing
   IS
      big_string   VARCHAR2 (32767)
                          := ten_minute_lookup (...);
      big_list     list_types.big_strings_tt
                 := two_minute_number_cruncher (...);
   BEGIN
      use_big_string (big_string);
      process_big_list (big_list);
   END;
BEGIN
   IF NOT criteria_in
   THEN
      heavy_duty_processing;
   ELSE
      /* Nothing big going on here */
      ...
   END IF;
END;
```

One other advantage of this approach is that when the nested block terminates, the memory associated with its data structures is released. This behavior would come in handy in the above example if I needed to perform more operations in my program after I am done with my "big" variables. With the former approach, memory would not have been released until the entire program was done.

Be a Good Listener

Are you a good listener? When people speak, do you expend more effort figuring out how you will respond than attempting to truly understand what they mean? Being a good listener is, I believe, a sign of respect for others and a skill we should all cultivate. (I know that I need to make more of an effort in this area myself.)

Being a good listener is also a critical skill when a programmer uncovers requirements from users and translates them into code. All too often, we hear what our users say but we do not really listen. The consequence is that we often end up writing code that does not meet their requirements or does so in an inefficient manner. Consider the following example:

```
CREATE OR REPLACE PROCEDURE remove_dept (
   deptno_in IN emp.deptno%TYPE,
   new_deptno_in IN emp.deptno%TYPE)
IS
   emp_count NUMBER;
BEGIN
   SELECT COUNT(*) INTO emp_count
     FROM emp WHERE deptno = deptno_in;

   IF emp_count > 0
   THEN
      UPDATE emp
         SET deptno = new_deptno_in
       WHERE deptno = deptno_in;
   END IF;

   DELETE FROM dept WHERE deptno = deptno_in;
END drop_dept;
```

This procedure drops a department from the department table, but first reassigns any employees in that department to another. The logic of the program is as follows: If I have any employees in that department, perform the update effecting the transfer. Then delete that row from the department table.

Can you see what is wrong here? Actually, this program is objectionable at two different levels. Most fundamentally, a good part of the code is unnecessary. If an UPDATE statement does not identify any rows to change, it does not raise an error; it simply doesn't do anything. So the remove_dept procedure could be reduced to nothing more than:

```
CREATE OR REPLACE PROCEDURE remove_dept (
   deptno_in IN emp.deptno%TYPE,
   new_deptno_in IN emp.deptno%TYPE)
IS
   emp_count NUMBER;
BEGIN
   UPDATE emp
      SET deptno = new_deptno_in
    WHERE deptno = deptno_in;

   DELETE FROM dept WHERE deptno = deptno_in;
END drop_dept;
```

Suppose, however, that it really is necessary to perform the check for existing employees. Let's take a closer look at what really is going on here. The question I need to answer is "Is there at least one employee?", yet if you look closely at my code, the question I really answer is "How many employees do I have?" I can transform the answer to that question into the answer to my first question with a Boolean expression (emp_count > 0), but in the process I may have gone overboard in my processing.

There are, in fact, a number of ways to answer the question "Do I have at least one of X?" The path you take may have a serious impact on performance. For a comparison of these different approaches, try out the *atleastone.sql* script available from the O'Reilly site.

The beginning of the *atleastone.sql* script creates a rather large copy of the employee table; this code is commented out to avoid the overhead of this step when the table is already in place. You will want to uncomment this section the first time you try the script.

Here's my conclusion from running this script: using a straightforward explicit cursor to fetch a single time and determine that there is at least one item is a very efficient (though not quite the most efficient) and very readable approach. Most importantly, it is also responsive to the question being asked—that is, the user requirements.

Use Package Data to Minimize SQL Access

When you declare a variable in a package body or a specification, its scope is not restricted to any particular procedure or function. As a result, the scope of package-level data is the entire Oracle session, and the value of that data persists for the entire session. Take advantage of this fact to minimize the frequency with which you have to go to the System Global Area (SGA) to access data. Performing lookups against structures located in your own Program Global Area (PGA) is much faster than going through the SGA—even if the data you want is resident in shared memory.

This tip is most handy when you find that your application needs to perform multiple lookups that do not change during your session. One very obvious example is the value returned by the USER function. It never changes during your session because it returns the name of the currently connected session. So why would you ever want to call USER more than once?

You might be thinking that it can't be *that* slow to run that built-in function. Well, no, it isn't, but it does execute a "SELECT FROM dual", and if you happen to have an application that runs USER many, many times, it can make a difference. I ran into just that situation when I was building a code generator (called PL/Generator) several years ago. After doing some performance analysis, I discovered that I was executing the USER function 15,000 times in the process of generating a large, complex package. That statistic almost certainly indicated a problem in my code base, but I didn't have time to sweep through my code and re-architect. So I took a different approach. I created the following package:

```
CREATE OR REPLACE PACKAGE thisuser
IS
```

```
    name CONSTANT VARCHAR2(30) := USER;
END;
```

and then I very carefully performed a global search and replace operation (replace USER with thisuser.name). Recompile, execute...and, lo and behold, I shaved a few seconds off a 45-second generation session. That's not too bad. By using this packaged variable, I was able to call USER just once, and after that I simply evaluate the thisuser.name constant.

And that's the basic idea behind caching data in session-level data structures. Of course, you might have much more complex requirements—you might want to cache a bunch of related data, say in a record structure, or you might even want to keep track of an entire list of already queried data.

Rather than present each of these scenarios in detail, I offer the following scripts (available from the O'Reilly site) that you can download and try yourself. Once you are convinced of the value of this technique, you can adapt my code to fit your requirements.

Caching a single value
: Avoid repetitive queries for values like USER, SYSDATE (which, in Oracle9*i*, is finally no longer obtained with a "SELECT FROM dual") and even application-specific static values.

    thisuser.pkg
    : Creates a package that caches the USER value, both in a named constant and via a function (which is callable from client-side PL/SQL).

    thisuser.tst
    : A test script that demonstrates the improved performance of the cached approach.

Caching a single record of data
: In the following script, I extract data from a user configuration table for the current user and cache that information in a record defined at the package level.

    init.pkg
    : Creates the user configuration table and package, populates the table with test data.

    init.tst
    : An associated test script.

Caching multiple rows of data
: A more interesting and complex example, the following script demonstrates the use of a collection to cache multiple rows of data to avoid querying any single row more than once in a session. This technique works only when the data being queried is static for your entire session; this is probably most applicable to small code-description lookup tables.

emplu.pkg
: Creates two packages, one that retrieves data with a standard query against the database, and another that accesses the data via a collection-based cache.

emplu.tst
: A test script that demonstrates the improved performance of the cached approach.

You can find more information about data caching in package-level data in Chapter 17.

Use BULK COLLECT and FORALL

New to Oracle*8i*—and improved in Oracle*9i*—are the BULK COLLECT and FORALL statements. Both share a common potential to dramatically reduce (by an order of magnitude or more) the time it takes to execute SQL operations that affect multiple rows of data. If you are currently executing SQL statements that operate on more than ten rows at a time, you should test the impact of FORALL and BULK COLLECT.

FORALL looks like a FOR statement, but it is not any kind of loop. Instead, it collects together a number of individual DML operations and sends them over to the SQL engine in a single pass for processing. Here is an example:

```
CREATE OR REPLACE PROCEDURE update_tragedies (
   warcrim_ids IN name_varray,
   num_victims IN number_varray
   )
IS
BEGIN
   FORALL indx IN warcrim_ids.FIRST .. warcrim_ids.LAST
      UPDATE war_criminal
         SET victim_count = num_victims (indx)
       WHERE war_criminal_id = warcrim_ids (indx);
END;
```

BULK COLLECT can be used inside both implicit and explicit fetch operations to retrieve more than one row in a single pass to the database. Here is an example:

```
DECLARE
   names name_varray;
   mileages number_varray;
BEGIN
   SELECT name, mileage
     BULK COLLECT INTO names, mileages
     FROM transportation
       WHERE TYPE = 'AUTOMOBILE'
         AND mileage < 20;
```

```
    -- Now work with data in the collections
    ...
 END;
```

And, finally, here is an example of combing FORALL and BULK COLLECT in a single statement (with the latter used in the RETURNING clause):

```
CREATE OR REPLACE FUNCTION remove_emps_by_dept (deptlist dlist_t)
   RETURN enolist_t
IS
   enolist enolist_t;
BEGIN
   FORALL aDept IN deptlist.FIRST..deptlist.LAST
      DELETE FROM emp WHERE deptno IN deptlist(aDept)
         RETURNING empno BULK COLLECT INTO enolist;
   RETURN enolist;
END;
```

As you can see, you need to be comfortable working with collections in order to take advantage of FORALL and BULK COLLECTION; Chapter 11 will give you all the information you need about these array-like data structures. See also Chapter 14 for more information on BULK COLLECT, and Chapter 13 for additional information on FORALL.

PART VI

Advanced PL/SQL Topics

A language as mature and rich as PL/SQL is packed full of features that you may not use on a day-to-day basis, but that may make the crucial difference between success and failure. This part of the book contains an exploration into the PL/SQL runtime architecture (Chapter 20), including PL/SQL's use of memory and differences between server-side and client-side PL/SQL. Chapter 21 offers an in-depth guide to using the object-oriented features of Oracle (object types and object views). Chapters 22 and 23 show you how to invoke Java and C code from your PL/SQL applications.

Chapter 20, *PL/SQL's Runtime Architecture*

Chapter 21, *Object-Oriented Aspects of PL/SQL*

Chapter 22, *Calling Java from PL/SQL*

Chapter 23, *External Procedures*

In this chapter:

- Looking Under the Hood
- Dependency Management
- PL/SQL's Use of Memory in the Oracle Server
- Processing Server-Side PL/SQL
- PL/SQL Code on the Client
- Execution Authority Models
- Hardware for PL/SQL: Bigger = Better?
- What You Need to Know

CHAPTER 20

PL/SQL's Runtime Architecture

As we discussed in Chapter 2, there are many different programmatic environments from which you can call a PL/SQL program, but there are only two places that you can find a PL/SQL runtime engine:

- Inside the Oracle database server
- On a client machine running Oracle's Developer tools such as Oracle Forms Builder or Oracle Reports Builder

An application developer has a number of packaging and design decisions to make, such as:

- Should I put code on the server, on the client, or both?
- What's better: an anonymous block, a top-level procedure, or a package?
- Should server-side code use conventional compilation or native compilation?
- Which client-side programs would be better stored in PL/SQL libraries rather than inside an Oracle Forms program?

You must also decide whether a program should run with the privileges of its owner (the definer rights model) or of the user who is running it (the invoker rights model).

Even to an experienced programmer, the "correct" answers to these questions are not always obvious. However, understanding something about the inner workings of the PL/SQL environment will help you make informed decisions. This chapter takes a closer look at PL/SQL's internal runtime architecture. Our goal is to take you beyond mere packaging decisions, and assist you in improving the design and performance of your applications in many ways.

While the primary emphasis of this chapter is on those aspects of PL/SQL that are of interest to the application developer, there are also many aspects of the runtime environment that are generally the purview of the database administrator. For example, the way the server assigns computer memory to the running program depends on whether you're running Oracle in shared or dedicated server mode. Because these differences can have a major impact on application tuning and performance, this chapter also highlights those areas that are of critical importance.

Looking Under the Hood

You may have heard that PL/SQL is an "interpreted" language, yet it's quite common for books like this one to refer to PL/SQL's "compiler." So is PL/SQL interpreted or compiled? It's not too far off to say that it is halfway between the two. You do send your source code through a compiler, and the compiler produces machine-dependent bytecode. At runtime, the PL/SQL virtual machine inside the Oracle server *interprets* the bytecode. And, just to make things even more interesting, you can also have Oracle9*i* translate your PL/SQL into C, compile it into a shared library using the compiler native to the machine, and load this compiled version dynamically at runtime.

PL/SQL Concepts

Let's begin our journey under the hood with some important terms and concepts relevant to the way that Oracle processes PL/SQL source code:

PL/SQL compiler
: The Oracle component that parses your PL/SQL source code, checks the syntax, resolves names, checks semantics (for example, verifies that calls to other stored programs match its "signature"), and generates two binary forms of compiled code.

DIANA
: An intermediate tree-structured form of PL/SQL and its dependencies that the compiler generates for syntax and semantic analyses. This is the first of the major outputs from the compiler. DIANA includes a representation of the call specification of your stored objects—that is, data from the program header such as parameter names, sequence, position, and datatype. Even tables, views, and sequences can have DIANA. The literal expansion of this acronym is Distributed Intermediate Annotated Notation for Ada, although Oracle's form is a variant of Ada's.

Machine-dependent pseudocode (bytecode)
: The executable form of compiled PL/SQL; the second major output generated by Oracle's PL/SQL compiler, known in some Oracle documentation by the term *mcode* and occasionally as *P-code*. This is the form required by the PL/SQL runtime engine. It may be helpful to know that bytecode is roughly equivalent to a *.o* object file.

You may encounter (in the database build script *sql.bsq*, for example) references to a third form of compiled PL/SQL known as *portable pcode*, but Oracle no longer produces this form. It turns out that the storage space for portable pcode does get used, though—for the symbolic information that the PL/SQL compiler generates when you compile a program with the DEBUG option.

As a bit of an aside, you probably know that you don't really run the PL/SQL compiler the way you would run a C or even a Java compiler. Instead, Oracle calls the compiler on your behalf whenever necessary. In fact, beginning PL/SQL programmers may not even realize the compiler exists! Any time you create a stored PL/SQL program using a CREATE PROCEDURE (or whatever) statement, Oracle runs the compiler on your behalf. Later we'll take a look at the way that Oracle automatically recompiles stored code after an object it depends upon changes.

Despite the way that Oracle shields you from the compiler, a good PL/SQL programmer will want to have a solid understanding of what goes on behind the scenes. In addition, the concept of executing PL/SQL once it's compiled introduces additional important elements:

PL/SQL runtime engine (PL/SQL virtual machine)
: The Oracle component that executes a PL/SQL program's bytecode, making calls as necessary to the server's SQL engine and returning results to the calling environment. In client-side tools such as Oracle Forms, the runtime engine typically opens a session to a remote database, communicating with the SQL engine over a networking protocol.

(Oracle) session
: For server-side PL/SQL, the process and memory space associated with an authenticated user through a network or interprocess connection. Each session has its own memory area where it can hold an executing program's data. While most people think of sessions as beginning with logon and ending with logoff, there are also *recursive* sessions—which have no authentication—that Oracle uses as a temporary means of changing a user's identity. For example, Oracle always executes program units running with definer rights in recursive sessions.

To put these ideas into context, let's take a look at several variations on running a trivial program from a very common front end, SQL*Plus. This is a good representative of a session-oriented tool that gives you direct access to the PL/SQL environment inside the Oracle database server. (We introduced SQL*Plus and showed how to use it with PL/SQL back in Chapter 2.) Of course, in your shop, you may also be calling the server from other tools such as Oracle's other client-side tools or even a procedural language such as Perl, C, or Java. But don't worry; processing on the server side is relatively independent of the client environment.

PL/SQL execution launched directly from SQL*Plus always involves a top-level anonymous block. While you may know that the SQL*Plus EXECUTE command converts the call into an anonymous block, did you know that SQL's CALL statement uses a (simplified) kind of anonymous block? Actually, until Oracle9*i*'s direct invocation of PL/SQL from SQL, *all* PL/SQL invocations from SQL used anonymous blocks.

So let's begin with a look at the simplest possible anonymous block:

```
BEGIN
   NULL;
END;
```

...and find out just what happens when you send this block to the Oracle server (Figure 20-1).

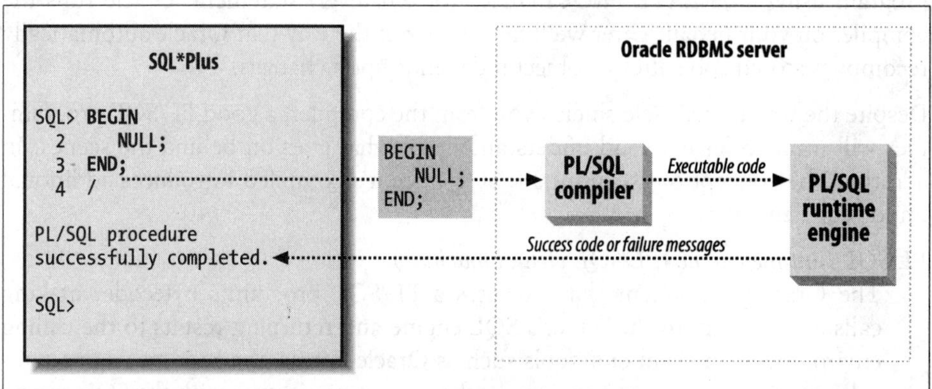

Figure 20-1. Execution of a do-nothing anonymous block

Let's step through the operations shown in this figure.

1. Starting on the left side of Figure 20-1, the user composes the block one line at a time and then gives SQL*Plus the "go-ahead" command (a slash). As the figure shows, SQL*Plus sends the entire code block, exclusive of the slash, to the server. This transmission occurs over whatever connection the session has established (for example, Oracle Net or interprocess communication).
2. Next, the PL/SQL compiler attempts to compile this anonymous block, generating internal data structures such as DIANA to help it analyze the code and generate bytecode.* A first phase is to check the syntax to ensure that the program adheres to the grammar of the language. In this simple case, there are no identifiers to figure out, only language keywords. If compilation succeeds, Oracle puts the block's bytecode into a shared memory area; if it fails, the compiler will return error messages to the SQL*Plus session.
3. Finally, the PL/SQL runtime engine interprets the bytecode and ultimately returns a success or failure code to the SQL*Plus session.

* Actually, if some session previously needed Oracle to compile the block, there is a good chance that the compile phase won't need to be repeated. This is because the server caches in memory and tries to share the output of relatively expensive operations like compilation.

Let's add an embedded SQL query statement into the anonymous block and see how that changes the picture. Figure 20-2 introduces some of the SQL-related elements of the Oracle server.

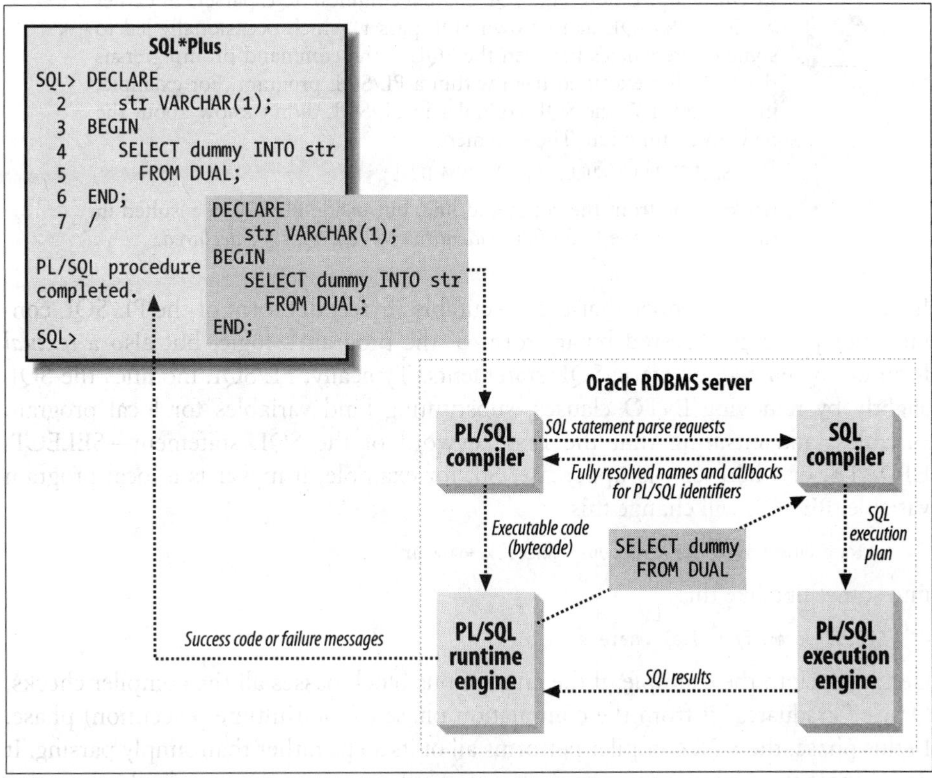

Figure 20-2. Execution of an anonymous block that contains SQL

This example fetches a column value from a well-known built-in table named DUAL.* The simple change introduces a surprisingly large number of new concepts.

After checking that the PL/SQL portions of the code adhere to the language's syntax, the PL/SQL compiler hands off the SQL statement to the SQL parser (parsing is the first of several compiler phases). The SQL parser first checks the SQL statement's syntax, and then it performs *name resolution*. This phase determines what each particular (non-keyword) identifier represents. In this example, the PL/SQL compiler has sent the SQL statement over to the SQL compiler with the identifiers DUAL, dummy, and str. The SQL parser will figure out that DUAL is a table and dummy is a column in that table, but it will call back to PL/SQL to resolve str. The

* According to Steve Adams' web site, the name DUAL is from its dual singularity: one row, one column.

SQL parser also checks permissions to make sure that the originating session has the authority to perform the requested SQL operation.

In Oracle9*i*, PL/SQL and SQL share a common SQL parser. In earlier versions, PL/SQL had its own SQL parser, which occasionally led to some discrepancies between the SQL at the command prompt versus the SQL that executed from within a PL/SQL program. For example, in Oracle 8.1.7, the SQL compiler in PL/SQL didn't know about the new NVL2 function. The statement:

```
SELECT NVL2(NULL, 1, 2) FROM DUAL;
```

worked fine from the command line, but inside PL/SQL it resulted in the error message *PLS-00201: identifier 'NVL2' must be declared.*

It's important to remember that the executable (bytecode) form of the PL/SQL contains not just a predigested binary form of the program's logic, but also a *textual* form of any embedded static SQL statements. Typically, PL/SQL modifies the SQL slightly by removing INTO clauses, substituting bind variables for local program variables, and ensuring that the first keyword of the SQL statement—SELECT, UPDATE, or whatever—is uppercase. So, for example, if myvar is a local program variable, PL/SQL will change this:

```
select dummy into str from dual where x = myvar
```

into something like this:

```
SELECT dummy from dual where x = :b1
```

Getting back to the example, if the anonymous block passes all the compiler checks, Oracle "graduates" it from the compilation phase to the runtime (execution) phase. In this phase, the SQL compiler performs all of its steps rather than simply parsing. It does repeat the syntax, name resolution, semantic, and permission checks, but goes on to compute what it thinks will be an efficient execution plan—in our example, one that's not too complicated. The SQL compiler hands the plan off to the SQL execution engine, which fetches the row and passes the results back to PL/SQL.

What if an anonymous block invokes a stored program? Figure 20-3 illustrates this case. To keep the picture as simple as possible, we'll go back to a no-SQL example.

Here, the compiler needs to resolve the external reference foo to determine whether it refers to a program that the user has privilege to execute. It will also need foo's DIANA to determine whether the anonymous block is, in fact, making a legal call to the stored program. Notice one of the benefits of stored code: having the DIANA and bytecode already stored in the data dictionary means that Oracle won't have to waste any time recompiling it. Even better, once the code is read from disk, Oracle will store that code in a memory area called the *library cache*, which will reduce or eliminate the need for any disk I/O to reread the code.

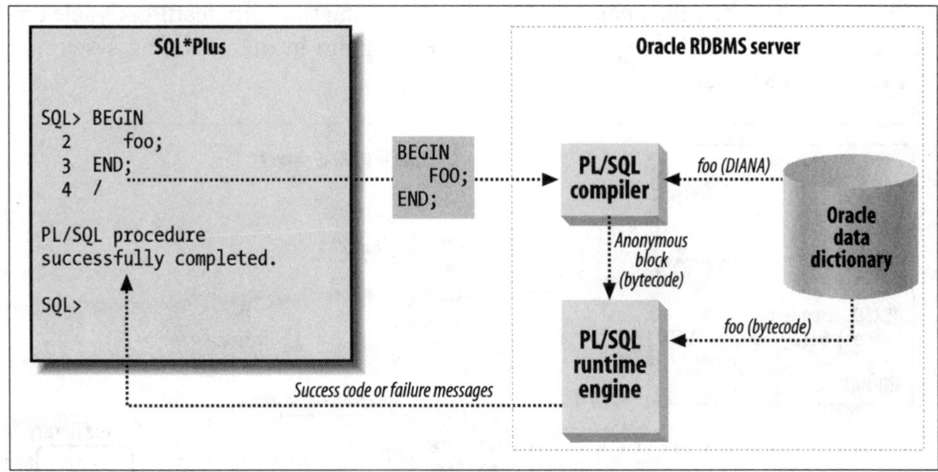

Figure 20-3. Execution of a program that calls a stored procedure

Further, after the initial compilation (and as long as there have been no changes in dependencies that would force an automatic recompilation), Oracle requires only bytecode in order to execute a program. In other words, when foo calls bar, Oracle can omit the reading of the DIANA for bar, thereby saving the expense of some I/O and library cache memory.

Suppose that the stored procedure *does* include embedded SQL—say, a nice long SELECT statement. Because Oracle compiles PL/SQL before it's stored in the data dictionary, resulting in speedier execution, you might be tempted to believe that the embedded SQL will also get this kind of performance boost. But in the same way that Oracle processes SQL in anonymous blocks, so it treats SQL in stored PL/SQL: saving it in textual form in PL/SQL's bytecode and compiling at runtime. There is no "precompiling" boost.

Nevertheless, PL/SQL performs several tricks at runtime to avoid "soft parses" of the query string. (A *soft parse* is how Oracle matches the query string to an in-memory compiled form of the SQL statement.) In contrast, if you run a SQL statement from a tool like SQL*Plus, there is no way to avoid soft parses. So you may, after all, see somewhat improved SQL parsing performance merely by wrapping up your SQL statements inside PL/SQL. It's true that some other programming environments may also avoid soft parses, but even something like the low-level C interface known as the Oracle Call Interface (OCI) will have communications overhead (network or IPC), which stored PL/SQL avoids.

Finally, let's take a look at native compilation—which may more properly be called *native execution*. This Oracle9*i* feature provides the option to convert server-side PL/SQL into C, and compile and link it into a shared object file. This form generally executes faster than conventionally compiled PL/SQL, unless the program spends a relatively large amount of time processing SQL statements.

If I have a procedure called bar that I've compiled using this nifty feature, Oracle creates and retrieves the corresponding compiled program in the operating system, as illustrated in Figure 20-4.

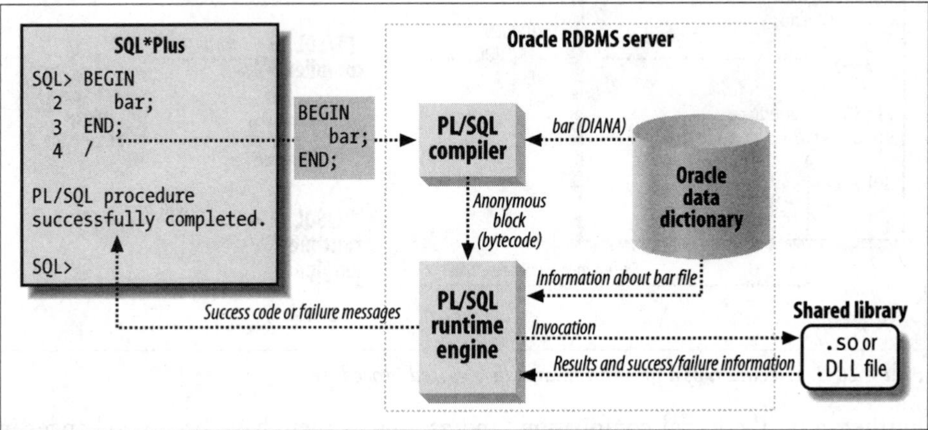

Figure 20-4. Execution of an anonymous block that calls a natively compiled program

In this case, the compiler did produce the usual DIANA during compilation, but there is no bytecode as such. Instead, the data dictionary and library cache structures that would otherwise store the bytecode contain the name and location of the object file. The called program, which lives in a shared library file, has no bytecode to interpret; Oracle makes operating system–level calls to load the shared library dynamically and run it natively.

There are other ways that you can build stored code and call it from PL/SQL:

Java stored procedures
: The default Oracle server installation includes not just a PL/SQL virtual machine but also a Java virtual machine. You can write a PL/SQL call spec whose logic is implemented as a static Java class. For details and examples, see Chapter 22.

External procedures
: You can also implement the executable portion of a PL/SQL subprogram in custom C code, and at runtime Oracle will run your code in a separate process and memory space from the main Oracle server. Chapter 23 discusses external procedures.

You can learn more about the runtime architecture of these two approaches in their respective chapters.

Physical Storage of Server-Side PL/SQL

Now that you've been introduced to the role that different components play in the compilation and execution of PL/SQL, let's take this abstract information and find out where the different forms of the language live on the disk. Table 20-1 lists the major hiding places in the Oracle database server.

Table 20-1. Locations of server-side PL/SQL code and metadata

Underlying location (all tables owned by SYS)	Name of view typically used by application developers	Applies to which PL/SQL objects	Most useful contents
OBJ$	USER_OBJECTS	All except anonymous blocks	Name, object type, last DDL time, compilation status (VALID or INVALID)
SOURCE$	USER_SOURCE	All except triggers and anonymous blocks	Source code
TRIGGER$	USER_TRIGGERS	Triggers	Source code, description of triggering event
ERROR$	USER_ERRORS	All except anonymous blocks	Most recent outstanding compilation error for any stored PL/SQL (including triggers)
DEPENDENCY$	USER_DEPENDENCIES	All except anonymous blocks	Object dependency hierarchy
SETTINGS$	USER_STORED_SETTINGS	All except anonymous blocks	PL/SQL compiler flags
IDL_UB1$ IDL_CHAR$ IDL_UB2$ IDL_SB4$	USER_OBJECT_SIZE	All except anonymous blocks	Internal storage of DIANA, bytecode, and debug data; used by the compiler and runtime engine
Directory in operating system, designated by PLSQL_NATIVE_LIBRARY_DIR database parameter	N/A	All that have been natively compiled	Shared object files natively compiled from PL/SQL via C

You probably haven't been lying awake at night wondering about these tables, so I'll mention a few reasons you might find them useful, along with the data dictionary views you can query for information:

- To find out which objects are in an INVALID state (USER_OBJECTS)
- To discover which programs have been compiled using native compilation (USER_STORED_SETTINGS)
- To find out what local objects will be invalidated by a change in a particular PL/SQL program (USER_DEPENDENCIES)
- To recover source code of programs whose original creation script has been lost (USER_SOURCE, USER_TRIGGERS)
- To get an idea of the relative sizes of stored programs (USER_OBJECT_SIZE)

Regarding that last item, if you look at the data dictionary view USER_OBJECT_SIZE, you can find the size of each stored portion of your programs. For each object, this view will tell you the following (these are column names):

SOURCE_SIZE
: Number of bytes on disk that the source code occupies.

PARSED_SIZE
: Number of bytes on disk that the DIANA occupies.

CODE_SIZE
: Sum of bytes on disk occupied by bytecode and debug data. For PL/SQL objects, the latter appears only if the program was compiled with the DEBUG option.

ERROR_SIZE
: Number of bytes on disk that the error text occupies; zero if no errors.

Don't get too excited—this information is less useful than it might seem. For example, when Oracle puts the DIANA in data dictionary tables, it's not stored in exactly the same form as when it's live in memory. On disk, it is "linearized" and compressed; in memory, it is expanded into its customary tree structure. Sooner or later, you are going to want to understand runtime memory requirements; see the later section "PL/SQL's Use of Memory in the Oracle Server" for more information about this important topic.

However, exploring the information in the USER_OBJECT_SIZE view does confirm one thing: Oracle discards DIANA for package bodies. The value of the PARSED_SIZE column for package bodies is always zero.

Because Oracle doesn't store DIANA for package bodies, putting PL/SQL programs into packages—rather than top-level functions, procedures, or types—can reduce the overall load on the server.

Does Oracle ever really need DIANA for a package body? Yes, but only during compilation, because the compiler uses DIANA to generate bytecode and to match the signatures in the package body with those of the package specification. Because no stored object will ever depend on the package body, Oracle discards its DIANA. If Oracle needs to recompile the body later (for example, if there has been a change in some object that it depends upon), the compiler will re-create the DIANA for the body, redo type checks, regenerate the bytecode, and throw that DIANA away again. Even if Oracle had retained the old DIANA, it would not have helped the recompilation in any way.

I am not, by the way, making a blind recommendation to put *everything* into packages no matter what. Objectives such as ease of development might outweigh the need to squeeze every drop of performance out of a given database machine. A good case in point is Oracle's PL/SQL Server Pages (PSP) feature, which generates top-level PL/SQL procedures from tagged HTML files.* As a general guideline, though, the larger the amount of code, the more significant the gain from using packages.

DIANAs Who Grew Too Much

Sometimes, large PL/SQL programs may encounter the server error *PLS-00123: Program too large*, or on the client side, *CDI-11005: (SQL execution error) line %1: End of line in string literal*. This means that the compiler, while attempting to create the DIANA parse tree, bumped into the maximum allowed number of "nodes" in the tree. The normal workaround for this error is to split the program up into several smaller programs. Sometimes, however, you just don't want to do that.

It's difficult to predict how many nodes a program will need because nodes don't directly correspond to anything easily measurable, such as tokens or lines of code. However, Table 20-2 shows the upper limits for different server versions and different types of PL/SQL programs. While the rightmost column purports to give an estimate of source code size, don't take it too literally. It's based on "typical" code that averages four bytes of source per DIANA node, but your code might not be typical.

Table 20-2. Some upper limits on PL/SQL program size

PL/SQL program types	Server version	Maximum size of DIANA parse tree (nodes)	Oracle's estimate of maximum size of source code (bytes)
Package and type bodies, standalone functions and procedures	7.3	2^{14} (16,384)	64K
	8.0.x and below	2^{15} (32,768)	128K
	8.1.5 and above	2^{26} (67,108,864)	256M
Signature (header) of standalone functions and procedures	7.3	2^{14}	64K
	8.0.x and above	2^{15}	128K
Package and type specifications, anonymous blocks	7.3	Theoretical limit: 2^{14}	64K in theory
	8.1.6 and below	2^{15} in theory, between 2^{13} and 2^{14} in practice	128K in theory, 32K to 64K in practice
	8.1.7 and above	2^{15}	128K

You can see from the table that Oracle has been working over the years to increase the limits. With the newer releases, it is fairly rare to run out of DIANA nodes.

As an aside, there are other documented limits in the PL/SQL compiler, such as the maximum number of levels of block nesting (255) and the number of parameters you can pass to a procedure or function (65,536). Few of these are likely to cause a

* I suppose you could bundle those PSP-generated procedures into packages, but if you're developing on "Internet time," your schedule might not allow it!

problem, but you can find a complete list of them in an appendix of Oracle's official PL/SQL documentation, *PL/SQL User's Guide and Reference*.

Dependency Management

Another important phase of PL/SQL compilation and execution is the checking of program *dependencies*, defined as follows. A dependency (in PL/SQL) is a usage relationship between a program and some Oracle object outside the program. Server-based PL/SQL programs can have dependencies on tables, views, types, procedures, functions, sequences, or package specifications, but not on package bodies or type bodies. Client-based PL/SQL programs can have additional dependencies on items such as form fields that exist only in the client-side module.

Oracle's basic dependency objective for PL/SQL is, loosely speaking:

> Do not allow a program to run if any of the objects on which it depends have changed since it was compiled.

The good news is that most dependency management happens automatically, from the tracking of dependencies to the recompilation required to keep everything synchronized. You can't completely ignore this topic, though, and the following sections should help you understand how, when, and why you'll need to intervene.

Dependencies in Server-Side PL/SQL

If you're working with server-side PL/SQL programs, you can use the server's data dictionary to explore usage relationships in quite a bit of detail.

Here's a simple illustration of this rule in action, using the data dictionary to give us eyes into the database. Let's say that I have a package named bookworm on the server. In this package is a function that selects from the books table. If I create the table and then create the package, I expect to see the following:

```
SQL> SELECT object_name, object_type, status
  2    FROM USER_OBJECTS
  3   WHERE object_name = 'BOOKWORM';

OBJECT_NAME                    OBJECT_TYPE       STATUS
------------------------------ ----------------- -------
BOOKWORM                       PACKAGE           VALID
BOOKWORM                       PACKAGE BODY      VALID
```

That is, there are two objects with the name BOOKWORM; the first is the package spec and the second is the body. Right now, they're both VALID.

Behind the scenes, Oracle has used its DIANA to determine a list of other objects that BOOKWORM needs in order to compile successfully. I can explore this dependency graph using a somewhat expensive (that is, slow) query of the data dictionary view USER_DEPENDENCIES:

```
SQL> SELECT name, type, referenced_name, referenced_type
  2    FROM USER_DEPENDENCIES
  3   WHERE name = 'BOOKWORM';

NAME            TYPE            REFERENCED_NAME REFERENCED_TYPE
--------------- --------------- --------------- ---------------
BOOKWORM        PACKAGE         STANDARD        PACKAGE
BOOKWORM        PACKAGE BODY    STANDARD        PACKAGE
BOOKWORM        PACKAGE BODY    BOOKS           TABLE
BOOKWORM        PACKAGE BODY    BOOKWORM        PACKAGE
```

Figure 20-5 illustrates this information as a directed graph, where the arrows indicate a "depends-on" relationship.

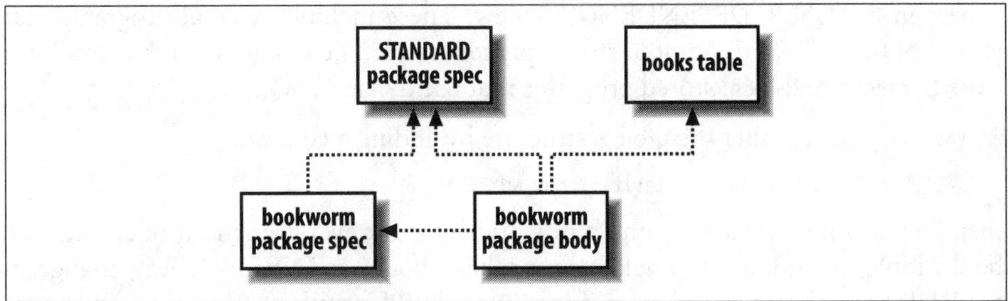

Figure 20-5. Dependency graph of the bookworm package

In other words, Figure 20-5 shows that:

- The bookworm package specification and body both depend on the built-in package named STANDARD (see the sidebar "Flying the STANDARD").
- The bookworm package body depends on its corresponding specification and on the books table.

For purposes of tracking dependencies, Oracle records the package specification and body as two different entities. Every package body will have a dependency on its corresponding specification, but the spec will never depend upon its body. Nothing depends upon the body. Hey, it might not even have a body.

If you've done much software maintenance in your life, you will know that performing impact analysis relies not so much "depends-on" information as it does on "referenced-by" information. Let's say that I'm contemplating a change in the structure of the books table. Naturally, I'd like to know everything that might be affected:

```
SQL> SELECT name, type
  2    FROM USER_DEPENDENCIES
  3   WHERE referenced_name = 'BOOKS'
  4     AND referenced_type = 'TABLE';
```

```
NAME                           TYPE
------------------------------ ------------
ADD_BOOK                       PROCEDURE
TEST_BOOK                      PACKAGE BODY
BOOK                           PACKAGE BODY
BOOKWORM                       PACKAGE BODY
FORMSTEST                      PACKAGE
```

Apparently, in addition to the bookworm package, there are some programs in my schema I haven't told you about, but fortunately Oracle never forgets. Nice! (By the way, you'll be even happier to hear that a query on the referenced_name column is *much* faster than the earlier query on the same column.)

As clever as Oracle is at keeping track of dependencies, it isn't clairvoyant: in the data dictionary, Oracle can only track dependencies of local stored objects written with static calls. There are plenty of ways that you can create programs that do not appear in the USER_DEPENDENCIES view. These include external programs that embed SQL or PL/SQL; remote stored procedures or client-side tools that call local stored objects; and local stored programs that use dynamic SQL.

As I was saying, if I alter the table's structure by adding a column:

```
ALTER TABLE books ADD popularity_index NUMBER;
```

then Oracle will immediately and automatically mark everything that references the books table, including the bookworm package body, as INVALID. Any change in the DDL time of an object—even if you just rebuild it with no changes—will cause Oracle to invalidate any programs that reference that object (see the later sidebar "A Little Validation, Please?"). Actually, Oracle's automatic invalidation is even more sophisticated than that; if you own a program that performs a particular DML statement on a table in another schema, and your privilege to perform that operation gets revoked, this action will also invalidate your program.

After the change, this is what I have:

```
SQL> SELECT object_name, object_type, status
  2    FROM USER_OBJECTS
  3   WHERE status = 'INVALID';

OBJECT_NAME                    OBJECT_TYPE        STATUS
------------------------------ ------------------ -------
ADD_BOOK                       PROCEDURE          INVALID
BOOK                           PACKAGE BODY       INVALID
BOOKWORM                       PACKAGE BODY       INVALID
FORMSTEST                      PACKAGE            INVALID
FORMSTEST                      PACKAGE BODY       INVALID
TEST_BOOK                      PACKAGE BODY       INVALID
```

By the way, this again illustrates a benefit of the two-part package arrangement: as the query shows, the package bodies appear in this list of invalids, but the specs do not. This is a wonderful thing; if the specs had become invalid too, everything dependent on those would also be marked invalid, and so on.

Using packages in your design can break the cycle of dependencies and recompilations.

Flying the STANDARD

All but the most pathologically ill Oracle installations will have a built-in package named STANDARD available in the database. This package contains many of the core features of the PL/SQL language, including:

- Functions such as INSTR and LOWER
- Comparison operators such as NOT, =, and >
- Predefined exceptions such as DUP_VAL_ON_INDEX and VALUE_ERROR
- Subtypes such as STRING and INTEGER

You can view the source code for this package by looking at the file *standard.sql*, which you would normally find in the *$ORACLE_HOME/rdbms/admin* subdirectory.

STANDARD's specification is the "root" of the PL/SQL dependency graph; that is, it depends upon no other PL/SQL programs, but most PL/SQL programs depend upon it. If you were to recompile the STANDARD specification, Oracle would invalidate virtually all the PL/SQL in the database.

The Oracle client-side PL/SQL environment also includes a version of STANDARD, which contains the same essential ingredients as the server version. (There is also a package of extensions to STANDARD that include tool-specific programs such as CALL_FORM.)

One final note: another way to look at programmatic dependencies is to use Oracle's DEPTREE_FILL procedure in combination with the DEPTREE or IDEPTREE views. As a quick example, if I run the procedure using:

```
SQL> EXEC DEPTREE_FILL('TABLE', 'SCOTT', 'BOOKS')
```

I can then get a nice listing by selecting from the IDEPTREE view:

```
SQL> SELECT * FROM IDEPTREE;

DEPENDENCIES
-------------------------------------------
TABLE SCOTT.BOOKS
   PROCEDURE SCOTT.ADD_BOOK
   PACKAGE BODY SCOTT.BOOK
   PACKAGE BODY SCOTT.TEST_BOOK
   PACKAGE BODY SCOTT.BOOKWORM
   PACKAGE SCOTT.FORMSTEST
      PACKAGE BODY SCOTT.FORMSTEST
```

This listing shows the result of a recursive "referenced-by" query. If you want to run this built-in yourself, execute the *utldtree.sql* script (from the *rdbms/admin* subdirectory) to build the utility procedure and views in your own schema. Or, if you prefer, you can emulate it with a query such as:

```
SELECT RPAD (' ', 3*(LEVEL-1)) || name || ' (' || type || ') '
  FROM user_dependencies
     CONNECT BY PRIOR RTRIM(name || type) =
            RTRIM(referenced_name || referenced_type)
       START WITH referenced_name = 'name' AND referenced_type = 'type';
```

Now that we have seen how the server keeps track of relationships among objects, let's explore one way that Oracle takes advantage of such information.

Healing Invalids

In addition to becoming invalid when a referenced object changes, a new program may be in an invalid state due to a failed compilation. In any event, no PL/SQL program marked as invalid will run until a successful recompilation restores its validity. Fortunately, there are at least three ways that can happen:

By hand
: Using an explicit ALTER command to recompile the package

By script
: Using a program that looks for invalid packages and issues the ALTER commands for you

Automatically
: Relying on Oracle's built-in recompilation rules

Recompiling by hand

The "by hand" method is simple, but it can be tedious. In the case presented earlier, I know by looking in the data dictionary that I need to recompile three stored programs, so I can just do this:

```
ALTER PACKAGE bookworm COMPILE BODY;
ALTER PACKAGE book COMPILE BODY;
ALTER PROCEDURE add_book COMPILE;
```

However, merely recompiling may be insufficient to recover from changes in the signature of a called program. You may have to edit the caller first!

Recompiling by script

Various scripts exist that can help you reduce the tedium of these recompilations. Oracle's own is called *utlrp.sql*, distributed in the usual *rdbms/admin* subdirectory—it works fine, but it does require DBA privileges. Generally, these kinds of scripts are not clever enough to recompile things in reverse dependency order. They simply iterate over the list of invalid programs, compiling each one; then they reread the list of invalid programs and repeat the process either until everything is valid or until recompiling has healed as many as it's going to heal. The scripts do tend to compile all the package headers before the bodies, though, which makes sense.

Solomon Yakobson has produced a recompile utility that *does* do things in the right order using CONNECT BY START WITH. This script is available from the Quest Pipelines PL/SQL Archive at:

http://www.quest-pipelines.com/Pipelines/PLSQL/archives.htm

under the header "A More Sophisticated Recompile Utility." It is also available in the *recompile.sql* file on the O'Reilly site.

If you have a large number of recompilations to perform and you have sufficient machine resources—CPUs, memory, disk—you should consider using Oracle's UTL_RECOMP package (found in *utlrcmp.sql*). This package allows you to recompile invalid objects in parallel, which it accomplishes by submitting multiple recompilation requests into Oracle's job queue. However, even Oracle warns that this package may not yield dramatic results because of write contention on system tables.

A Little Validation, Please?

When a database object's DDL time changes, Oracle's usual *modus operandi* is to immediately invalidate all of its dependents on the local database. From 8.1.7.3 onwards, there is a way to tell Oracle that you want to do a *conditional* invalidation of PL/SQL—that is, to invalidate dependents only if the object's source code has actually changed.

Be warned, though, that this is one of Oracle's undocumented and unsupported features—not for use by customers unless so advised by Oracle Support. You could be completely out of luck if it breaks something. The way to turn on the feature for the current session is:

```
SQL> ALTER SESSION SET EVENTS
  2  '10520 TRACE NAME CONTEXT FOREVER, LEVEL 10';

Session altered.
```

Now install your new code, and run a recompilation script such as *$ORACLE_HOME/rdbms/admin/utlrp.sql*.

Then, turn off the feature:

```
SQL> ALTER SESSION SET EVENTS
  2  '10520 TRACE NAME CONTEXT OFF';

Session altered.
```

This feature was designed as part of Oracle's ongoing initiative to speed up the process of applying database patch sets and upgrades. If you insist on using this feature for anything else, immediately afterwards you should shuffle the papers around on your desk, put on your best innocent look, and pretend that nothing happened.

Automatic recompilation

The third method, automatic recompilation, is even simpler, but it isn't without drawbacks. If you merely execute one of the programs implemented in the bookworm package body, Oracle will recompile it just prior to execution.

Production environments are likely to have strict policies on when you can and cannot recompile programs. That's because installing a new version of a PL/SQL program can force a lot of recompilation and can have disastrous side effects on programs currently running. You will probably want to run a script similar to *utlrp.sql* to find and recompile all invalid objects. Your DBA should help you schedule an upgrade procedure, which should include running the recompilation script.

Aside from a potentially unscheduled drain on performance, the biggest drawback to Oracle's automatic recompilation feature is that it can interfere with packages that are currently running. The telltale sign of this will be a series of messages:

```
ORA-04068: existing state of packages has been discarded
ORA-04061: existing state of package "SCOTT.P1" has been invalidated
ORA-04065: not executed, altered or dropped package "SCOTT.P1"
ORA-06508: PL/SQL: could not find program unit being called
```

This happens because automatically recompiling a package that is currently running invalidates the package. Not only that, Oracle shares the program's bytecode among different sessions, so this invalidation affects not just the session that triggered the recompilation, but *every* Oracle session that is running the package! Consequences of this devastation include the following:

- Executions terminate with an ORA-04068 error (unless programs have been written with some sophisticated exception handlers).
- All public and private package variables assume their default values; if you haven't supplied an explicit default value, it will revert to NULL. This effect applies to any package that the session has instantiated, not just the one that's getting recompiled. So, if you were in the middle of any computations that assign values to package variables, you will lose the contents of those variables.
- DBMS_OUTPUT stops working. Well, not really, but if you had previously enabled it, Oracle will disable it. This occurs because its on/off switch is really a package variable, and resetting the package reverts it to the default, which is off.
- Because all the packages executing in the current session have been reset, merely repeating the call should succeed; that is, the second call should not fail with the ORA-04068 error.

I have written a number of scripts attempting to demonstrate this behavior in various scenarios, and have wound up with some strangely inconsistent results—for example, a script that produces the error twice out of ten runs. I also have evidence, though, that recompiling the affected package with explicit ALTER...COMPILE statements reduces the ripple effect; instead of destroying the state of all packages for the current session, it seems to limit the "reset" to the package you're recompiling.

The bottom line on automatic recompilation bears repeating. In live production environments, do not do anything that will invalidate or recompile (automatically or otherwise) any stored objects for which sessions might have instantiations that will be referred to again. Also, use a recompilation script. Fortunately, development environments don't need to worry about ripple effects too much, and automatic recompilation outside of production is a huge plus.

Dependencies in Client-Side PL/SQL

If you're building applications using Oracle Forms and friends, a client-side PL/SQL program may have dependencies on any of the following:

- Other client-side PL/SQL programs
- Server-side objects such as tables, views, or PL/SQL programs
- Module-level items such as on-screen fields in Oracle Forms
- So-called "system variables" maintained by the development environment

You can attempt to explore these relationships by expanding the "References" items that appear under the program's name, as shown in Figure 20-6.

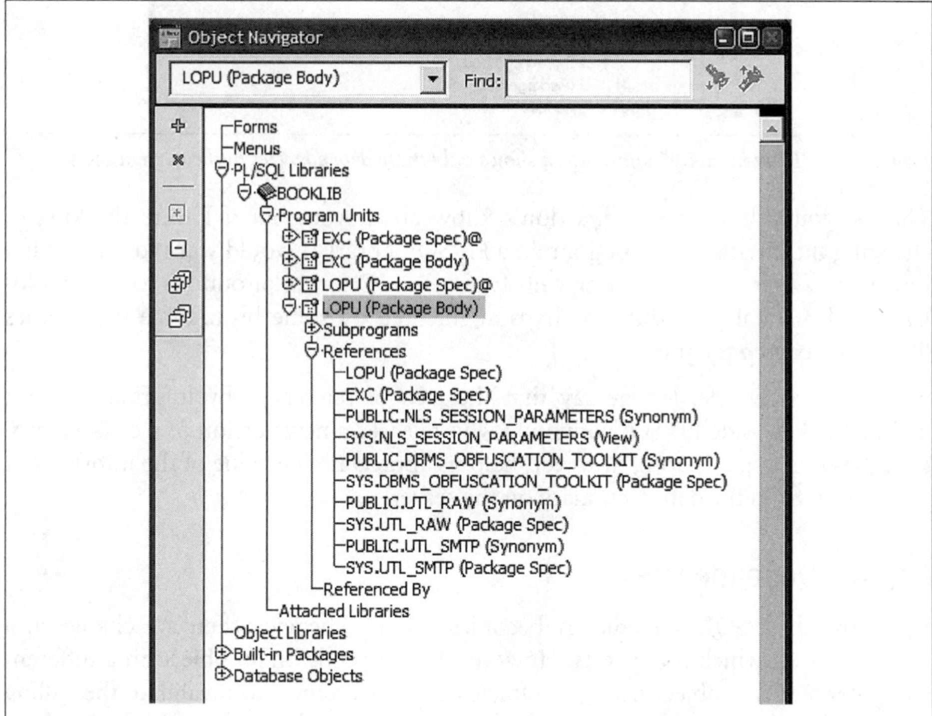

Figure 20-6. Viewing "References" information for a package body in a client-side PL/SQL library

Although the navigator successfully illustrates the external references for each client-side program unit, it does not show dependencies in client-side triggers. Moreover, the reverse dependency list—the "Referenced by" information—lists only referencing programs that happen to be *inside* the current module.

So, for example, let's say that you've created a client-side PL/SQL library that five different developers have been using in dozens of Oracle Forms modules. If you open up the library in the development environment and click on "Referenced by," you will see something like Figure 20-7.

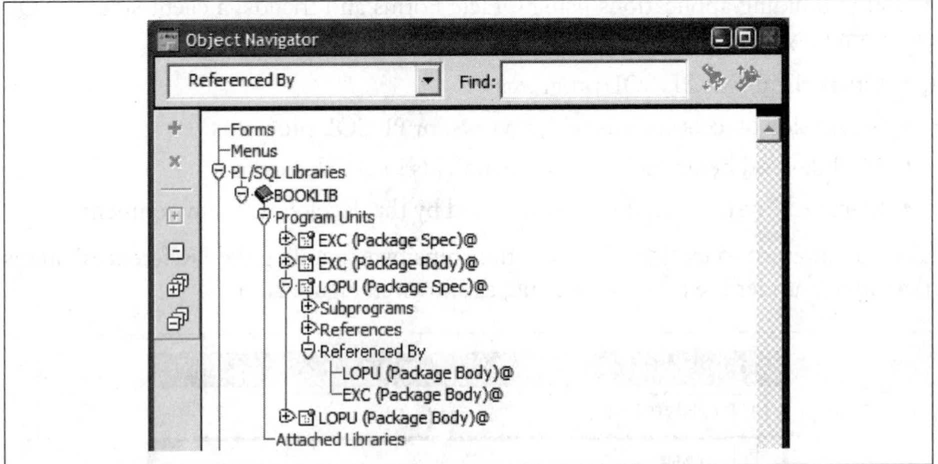

Figure 20-7. "Referenced By" information shows only those dependencies in the current module

That is, you will see nothing. I don't know about you, but if I were thinking of changing the interface of a program in a PL/SQL library, I would want to know what it will break before I start getting calls from users. One workaround is to use an old-fashioned manual procedure, perhaps augmented by some brute-force file utilities like the Unix *grep* program.

In fairness to Oracle, let me say that the lack of referenced-by information isn't unique to client-side PL/SQL; anybody who releases a new version of a callable program has this issue. It does, however, help us appreciate the value of the information you can get from the data dictionary on the server!

Remote Dependencies

Server-based PL/SQL immediately becomes invalid whenever there's a change in a local object on which it depends. However, if it depends on an object on a different computer and that object changes, Oracle does not attempt to invalidate the calling PL/SQL program in real time. Instead, Oracle defers the checking until runtime. This deferred checking applies to two situations:

- A client-side PL/SQL program, such as a procedure in an Oracle Forms module, calls out to a stored program on *any* database server.
- A server-side program makes a remote procedure call (RPC) over a database link. For example:

```
PROCEDURE synch_em_up (tax_site_in IN VARCHAR2, since_in IN DATE)
IS
BEGIN
   IF tax_site_in = 'LONDON'
   THEN
      recompute_prices@findat.ldn.world(cutoff_time => since_in);
   END IF;
```

In these situations, if the runtime engine decides that it won't execute the remote program, you'll see an ORA-04062 error with accompanying text such as *timestamp* (or *signature*) *of package "SCOTT.recompute_prices" has been changed.* To understand how the runtime engine makes this decision, you need to know that the PL/SQL compiler always stores two kinds of information about each referenced remote procedure: its *timestamp* and its *signature*.

Timestamp
: The most recent date and time (down to the second) when an object's specification was reconstructed, as given by the TIMESTAMP column in the USER_OBJECTS view. For PL/SQL programs, this is not necessarily the same as the most recent compilation time because it's possible to recompile an object without reconstructing its specification. (Note that this column is of the DATE datatype, not the newer datatype that also happens to have the name TIMESTAMP.)

Signature
: A footprint of the actual shape of the object's specification. Signature information includes the object's name and the ordering, datatype family, and mode of each parameter.

So when I compiled synch_em_up, Oracle retrieved both the timestamp and the signature of the remote procedure called recomputed_prices and stored a representation of them with the bytecode of synch_em_up.

How do you suppose Oracle uses this information at runtime? The model is simple: it uses either the timestamp or the signature, depending on the current value of the parameter REMOTE_DEPENDENCIES_MODE. If that timestamp or signature information, which is stored in the local program's bytecode, doesn't match the actual value of the remote procedure at runtime, you get the ORA-04062 error.

Oracle's default remote dependency mode is the timestamp method, but this setting can sometimes cause unnecessary recompilations. The DBA can change the system-wide setting via the initialization file or an ALTER SYSTEM command; an application developer can set it for the current session using the following command:

```
ALTER SESSION SET REMOTE_DEPENDENCIES_MODE = SIGNATURE;
```

or, inside PL/SQL:

```
EXECUTE IMMEDIATE 'ALTER SESSION SET REMOTE_DEPENDENCIES_MODE = SIGNATURE';
```

Thereafter, for the remainder of that session, every PL/SQL program run will use the signature method. As a matter of fact, Oracle's client-side tools always execute this ALTER SESSION...SIGNATURE statement as the first thing they do after connecting to the database, overriding whatever is in the Oracle initialization file (*INIT.ORA*).

Oracle recommends using signature mode on client tools like Oracle Forms, and timestamp mode on server-to-server procedure calls. Be aware that signature mode can cause false negatives—situations where the runtime engine thinks that the signature hasn't changed, but it really has—in which case Oracle does not force an invalidation of a program that calls it remotely. You can wind up with silent computational errors that are difficult to detect and even more difficult to debug. Here are several risky scenarios:

- Changing only the default value of one of the called program's formal parameters. The caller will continue to use the old default value.
- Adding an overloaded program to an existing package. The caller will not bind to the new version of the overloaded program even if it is supposed to.
- Changing just the name of a formal parameter. The caller may have problems if it uses named parameter notation.

In these cases, you will have to perform a manual recompilation of the caller. In contrast, the timestamp mode, while prone to false positives, is immune to false negatives. In other words, it won't miss any needed recompilations, but it may force recompilation that is not strictly required. This safety is no doubt why Oracle uses it as the default for server-to-server RPCs.

If you do use the signature method, Oracle recommends that you add any new functions or procedures at the *end* of package specifications, as doing so reduces false positives.

PL/SQL's Use of Memory in the Oracle Server

By economizing on its use of machine resources such as memory and CPU, Oracle can support tens of thousands of simultaneous users on a single database. Oracle's memory management techniques have become quite sophisticated over the years, and correspondingly difficult to understand. Although administrators of busy databases need a thorough knowledge of memory management, advanced PL/SQL programmers should also have a good understanding of this topic. Virtually all PL/SQL programmers will want to know how to avoid undermining Oracle's memory sharing algorithms.

Server Memory 101

Let's first look at some basics. An Oracle database *instance* consists of a shared memory area known as the System Global Area (SGA), plus a number of background processes.* Although a large part of the SGA typically consists of buffer pools that cache table data, another part that's of particular importance to PL/SQL performance is the *shared pool*. The shared pool performs two main caching functions:

- It holds metadata from the data dictionary
- It holds parsed representations of SQL statements and PL/SQL programs

The first time any user session runs a particular PL/SQL program, Oracle puts the executable portion of the program into the part of the shared pool called the *library cache*. When that session needs to execute the same PL/SQL program, Oracle will reuse the cached copy of it, saving a trip to the relatively slow disks. Oracle can even use this cached version when other sessions need to execute the same program. You may be surprised to learn that Oracle will share bytecode across sessions only under certain conditions. Before discussing the conditions for sharing PL/SQL bytecode, though, I'd like to mention other processes and memory areas important to application developers, including the often-confused PGA, CGA, and UGA.

When a client program such as SQL*Plus initiates a session with the database, Oracle assigns a "shadow" process on the database server machine to service that session. Program Global Area (PGA) is the name for the memory area associated with this process. Programmers have little or no control over the portion of the PGA that holds session information about the process state and the operating system resources that it uses; the variable portion of the PGA contains application data such as the CGA and, in dedicated server mode, the UGA.

Any time a session executes a SQL statement or PL/SQL block, Oracle temporarily allocates memory to execute the statement. This workspace is known as the Call Global Area (CGA), and Oracle always allocates CGA from PGA memory. CGA is used only for the duration of these server calls—that is, at the time the statement or block is actually executing. Oracle frees CGA memory as soon as the call completes.

Another important area in memory is known as the User Global Area (UGA). The UGA holds things like session state data and the private SQL and PL/SQL areas. So, for example, PL/SQL package variables and constants reside in the UGA. One important thing about UGA memory is that unlike the CGA, it persists across calls, and normally won't shrink or free until the session ends.

* The background processes do things like manage disk I/O, recover from failed processes and transactions, and monitor database processes.

One potentially confusing aspect of UGA memory is that it can live either in the PGA or in the SGA, depending on whether the session has connected to Oracle in a *dedicated* server configuration or in a *shared* server configuration.

Dedicated server
: Oracle spawns a dedicated process for the session, and puts the UGA and CGA into the PGA memory that this process allocates from the operating system where the server is running. This configuration is appropriate for heavy loads such as intensive OLTP or batch processing, long-running queries, and database backups.

Shared server (formerly known as "multithreaded server" or MTS)
: Oracle assigns multiple sessions to a shared back-end process, putting the UGA into memory allocated from the SGA. In this configuration, the shadow process and fixed portions of the PGA will be shared among multiple client processes rather than be dedicated to each. This introduces some overhead, though, and you probably won't get a real payback from using it unless you have many concurrent sessions (hundreds or more) with a lot of idle or "think" time.

The total size of the PGA can vary quite a bit based on what kind of operations your application requires the server to perform. For example, a SQL DML statement that requires a large sort can consume a lot of CGA memory; a PL/SQL package that populates a large PL/SQL collection in a package-level variable requires large amounts of UGA memory.

Figure 20-8 shows a simplified representation of these two different arrangements.*

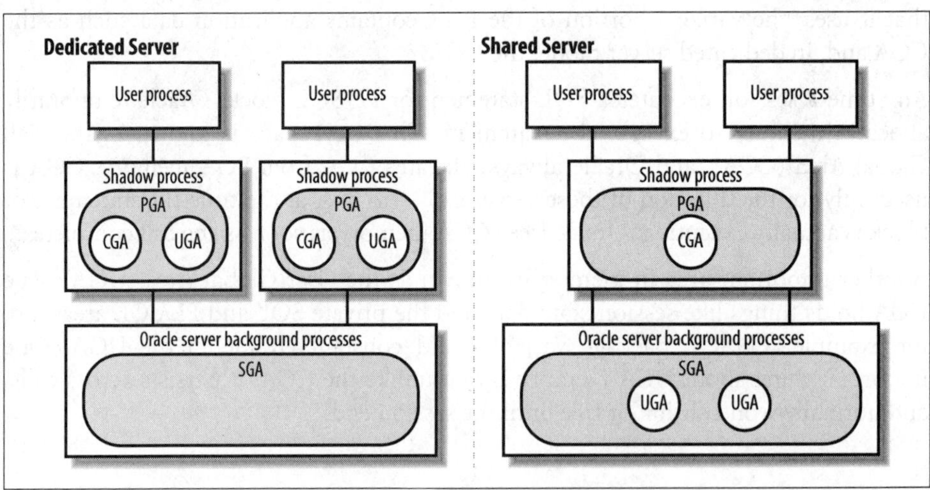

Figure 20-8. Oracle memory and process architecture in dedicated vs. shared server configurations

* The figure doesn't show the shared server's dispatchers and request/response queues, which are somewhat ancillary to this discussion.

If your application uses shared server, you need to realize that user processes can contend for time and memory in the shadow process. If your user processes invoke long-running PL/SQL blocks or SQL statements, the DBA may need to either configure the server with a greater number of shared shadow processes, or assign to those sessions a dedicated server.

After that whirlwind tour of the server memory, let's consider what memory looks like to an individual running program.

Cursors and Memory

At this point in your PL/SQL programming career, you no doubt have had some exposure to *cursors*. You may have written hundreds of programs that declare, open, fetch from, and close cursors. Perhaps you've even programmed with cursors at a relatively low level using the DBMS_SQL built-in package. It's impossible to execute SQL or PL/SQL without cursors, and statements often invisibly open recursive or child cursors to perform additional processing. And because every cursor, whether implicit or explicit, requires an allocation of memory on the database server, tuning Oracle often involves reducing the number of cursors required by an application.

Oracle assigns cursors to anonymous PL/SQL blocks in much the same way that it assigns cursors to SQL statements. For example, on the first parse call from a session, Oracle opens an area in PGA memory (the "private SQL area") where it will put things like bind data and other information specific to the run.

It turns out that some of the server-side data structures associated with cursors reside in the UGA, and some in the CGA. For example, because SELECT statements identify rows that need to be available during multiple fetches, Oracle allocates a work area for the cursor from UGA memory; because DML statements complete in a single call, Oracle allocates their work area from CGA memory. Similarly, when executing PL/SQL, Oracle allocates UGA memory to store state information, and uses CGA for other processing.

When executing a SQL statement or a PL/SQL block, the server first looks in the library cache to see if it can find a reusable parsed representation of it. If it does find such a shared PL/SQL area, the runtime engine establishes an association between the private SQL area and the shared SQL area. If no reusable shared area exists, Oracle will "hard parse" the statement or the block. (As an aside, note that Oracle also prepares and caches a simple execution plan for anonymous PL/SQL blocks, which consists of calling the PL/SQL engine to interpret the bytecode.)

Oracle interprets the simplest of PL/SQL blocks—those that call no subprograms and include no embedded SQL statements—using only the memory allocated for its primary cursor. If your PL/SQL program includes SQL or PL/SQL calls, though, Oracle requires additional private SQL areas in the PGA. Called statements execute in these recursive cursors that PL/SQL manages on behalf of your application. Oracle frees the private SQL areas used by the child cursors only after the private SQL area for the parent cursor is freed.

This brings us to another important fact about cursors: there are two ways a cursor can be closed. A *soft-closed* cursor is one that you can no longer use in your application without reopening it. This is what you get when you close a cursor using a statement such as this one:

```
CLOSE cursorname;
```

or even when an implicit cursor closes automatically. However, PL/SQL does not immediately free the session memory associated with this cursor. It assumes that you may actually open it again. You will see, if you look in the V$OPEN_CURSOR view, that the CLOSE alone does not reduce the count of this session's open cursors.

It turns out that PL/SQL maintains its own "session cursor cache;" that is, it decides when to close a cursor for good. This cache can hold a maximum number of cursors, as specified by the OPEN_CURSORS database initialization parameter. A least-recently-used (LRU) algorithm determines which of the soft-closed cursors need to be *hard-closed* and hence deallocated. With good programming practices such as closing your cursors immediately after you are through fetching with them, PL/SQL's approach usually results in a net performance gain.

You should always explicitly close cursors that you open explicitly. If you fail to close the cursors that you open, you may subvert PL/SQL's cursor management algorithm.

There are a few ways that Oracle allows PL/SQL programmers to intervene in the default behavior. One way you can close all of your session cursors, of course, is to terminate the session! Less drastic ways include:

- Reset the package state, as discussed at the end of the later section "Large collections in PL/SQL."
- Use DBMS_SQL to gain explicit control over low-level cursor behavior. On the whole, though, memory gains provided by this approach may not offset the corresponding performance costs and programming challenges.

Tips on Reducing Memory Use

Armed with a bit of theory, let's review some practical tips you can use in your day-to-day programming.

Statement sharing

Oracle can share the source and compiled versions of SQL statements and anonymous blocks even if they are submitted from different sessions by different users. For that to happen, though, certain conditions must be true. There are five major guidelines for getting Oracle to share SQL statements; the first three also apply to anonymous PL/SQL blocks.

1. The letter case and spacing conventions of the source code must match exactly.
2. External references must resolve to the same underlying object in order for the program to be shared.
3. Data values must be supplied via bind variables rather than literal strings (or the CURSOR_SHARING system setting must have an appropriate value).

Oracle caches SQL statements separately from any PL/SQL programs that contain them, and the sharing rules are slightly different. For SQL statements, the two additional rules are:

4. All database parameters influencing the SQL optimizer must match. For example, the invoking sessions must be using the same "optimizer goal" (ALL_ROWS versus FIRST_ROWS).
5. The invoking sessions must be using the same language (National Language Support, or NLS) environment.

Although I'm not going to talk more about these last two rules, I would like to explore the impact of the first three rules on your PL/SQL programs.

Rule #1, matching letter case and spacing, is a well-known condition to sharing statements. Despite the fact that PL/SQL is normally a case-independent language, the block:

```
BEGIN NULL; END;
```

does not match:

```
begin null; end;
```

nor does it match:

```
BEGIN NULL;   END;
```

This is a painful fact of life, and it also applies to SQL statements. However, if all your anonymous blocks are short and all your "real programs" are in stored code such as packages, there is much less chance of inadvertently disabling code sharing. The tip here is:

> Centralize your SQL and PL/SQL code in stored programs. Anonymous blocks should be as short as possible, generally consisting of a single call to a stored program.

In addition, an extension of this tip applies to SQL:

> To maximize the sharing of SQL statements, put SQL into programs. Then call these programs rather than write the SQL you need in each block.

I've always felt that trying to force statement sharing by adopting strict formatting conventions for SQL statements was just too impractical; it's much easier to put the SQL into a callable program.

Moving on, Rule #2 says that external references (to tables, procedures, etc.) must resolve to the same underlying object. Say that Scott and I are connected to Oracle, and we both run a block that goes like this:

```
BEGIN
   foo;
END;
```

Oracle's decision about whether to share the cached form of this anonymous block boils down to whether the name "foo" refers to the same underlying stored procedure. If Scott has a synonym foo that points to my copy of foo, then Oracle will share this anonymous block; if Scott and I own independent copies of foo, Oracle will not share this anonymous block. So even if the two copies of foo are line-by-line identical, Oracle caches these as different objects. Oracle also caches identical triggers on different tables as different objects. That leads to the following tip:

> Avoid proliferating copies of tables and programs in different accounts unless you have a very good reason.

Furthermore:

> To help Oracle economize memory, pull out code that is common to multiple programs (especially triggers) and incorporate it by call rather than by duplicating the code. Then, set up your system so that one database user owns the PL/SQL programs, and grant EXECUTE privilege to any other user who needs it. (The later section "Execution Authority Models" covers the overall topic of execution privileges more thoroughly.)

There is an important exception to this tip, and it applies if you are running in a high concurrency environment—that is, many users simultaneously executing the same PL/SQL program. Whenever these common bits of code are called, a "library cache latch" is needed to establish and then release a pin on the object. In high concurrency environments, this can lead to latch contention. In such cases, duplicating the code wherever it is needed is actually preferred, as doing so will avoid latching and improve performance.

Rule #3—the one about bind variables—is important enough to have an entire section devoted to it.

Bind variables

In PL/SQL, any variable you use in a statically parsed SQL statement automatically becomes a bind variable. If you follow the good programming practice of putting literal values in parameters and constants, and if you refer to these variables rather than the literal values in your SQL statements, you will generally be in good shape. Here's a simple example:

```
FUNCTION maxcats (threshhold_in IN NUMBER DEFAULT 100)
   RETURN NUMBER
IS
   CURSOR qcur IS
```

```
        SELECT category, COUNT(*)
          FROM booklist
         GROUP BY category
        HAVING COUNT(*) > threshhold_in;
    etc...
```

PL/SQL translates the threshhold_in parameter into a bind variable in the query.

A lesser-known fact is that you can also use bind variables in anonymous blocks in SQL*Plus. For example:

```
SQL> VARIABLE howmany NUMBER
SQL> EXEC :howmany := maxcats
```

Note that you cannot, however, assign a value to a SQL*Plus bind variable unless you do so in an anonymous block.

One problem with bind variables comes up when you use dynamic SQL to construct a SQL statement at runtime. Sloppy programming results in statements getting built with literal values. For example:

```
CREATE OR REPLACE FUNCTION count_recent_records (tablename_in IN VARCHAR2,
   since_in IN DATE)
RETURN PLS_INTEGER
AS
   count_l PLS_INTEGER;
BEGIN
   EXECUTE IMMEDIATE 'SELECT COUNT(*) FROM ' || tablename_in
      || ' WHERE lastupdate > TO_DATE('''
      || TO_CHAR(since_in, 'YYYYMMDD')
      || ''', ''YYYYMMDD'')'
      INTO count_l;
   RETURN count_l;
END;
```

This causes the dynamic construction of statements such as:

```
SELECT COUNT(*) FROM tabname WHERE lastupdate > TO_DATE('20020315', 'YYYYMMDD')
```

Repeated invocation with different since_in arguments can result in a lot of unsharable statements. For example:

```
SELECT COUNT(*) FROM tabname WHERE lastupdate > TO_DATE('20020105', 'YYYYMMDD')
SELECT COUNT(*) FROM tabname WHERE lastupdate > TO_DATE('20010704', 'YYYYMMDD')
SELECT COUNT(*) FROM tabname WHERE lastupdate > TO_DATE('20030101', 'YYYYMMDD')
```

A "bind variable" version of this would be:

```
CREATE OR REPLACE FUNCTION count_recent_records (tablename_in IN VARCHAR2,
   since_in IN DATE)
RETURN PLS_INTEGER
AS
   count_l PLS_INTEGER;
BEGIN
   EXECUTE IMMEDIATE 'SELECT COUNT(*) FROM ' || tablename_in
      || ' WHERE lastupdate > :thedate'
      INTO count_l
```

```
        USING since_in;
    RETURN count_1;
END;
```

which results in statements that look like this to the SQL compiler:

```
SELECT COUNT(*) FROM tabname WHERE lastupdate > :thedate
```

Not only is the second version prettier and easier to follow, but it should also perform better over repeated invocations with the same tablename_in but with different since_in arguments.

However, there is a way to relax the optimizer's rules on literal strings as of Oracle 8.1.6, which introduced a parameter called CURSOR_SHARING. You can turn on this feature using the command:

```
ALTER SESSION SET CURSOR_SHARING = FORCE; /* available in 8.1.6 or later */
```

or:

```
ALTER SESSION SET CURSOR_SHARING = SIMILAR; /* in 9.0 or later */
```

For the remainder of your session, Oracle will invisibly rewrite the literal queries from the first function into a single statement like this:

```
SELECT COUNT(*) FROM tabname WHERE lastupdate > TO_DATE(:"SYS_B_0", :"SYS_B_1")
```

This provides the same results to the application, but in a way that eases the burden on the library cache.

To turn off cursor sharing, specify:

```
ALTER SESSION SET CURSOR_SHARING = EXACT;
```

If you are using Oracle8*i*, you cannot set cursor sharing to SIMILAR; you must use either EXACT or FORCE. With FORCE, Oracle always rewrites the SQL with literals to use a bind variable, but this may decrease performance in some cases. With SIMILAR, Oracle will rewrite the literal to use bind variables only if the optimizer would not consider the literal during optimization.

Use bind variables and an appropriate setting of CURSOR_SHARING to help Oracle share SQL statements. Remember that the datatype and maximum length of the bind variables must match.

Packaging to improve memory use

When retrieving the bytecode (or, for that matter, the DIANA) of a stored PL/SQL program, Oracle reads the entire program. This rule applies not only to procedures and functions, but also to packages. In other words, you can't get Oracle to retrieve only a part of a package; the first time any session uses some element of a package, even just a single package variable, Oracle loads the compiled code for the entire package into the library cache. So a logical grouping of package elements is not just a good design idea, but it will also help your system's performance.

Because Oracle reads an entire package into memory at once, design each package with functionally related components that are likely to be invoked together.

Large collections in PL/SQL

Sharing is a wonderful thing, but of course not everything can be shared at runtime. Even when two or more users are executing the same program owned by the same Oracle schema, each session has its own private memory area, which holds run-specific data such as the value of local or package variables, constants, and cursors. It wouldn't make much sense to try to share values that are specific to a given session.

In my experience, the most common PL/SQL memory problems occur when manipulating large collections, which are a great example of runtime data that is not shareable. (Chapter 11 describes collections in detail.) Imagine that I declare a PL/SQL associative array—formerly known as an index-by table—as follows:

```
DECLARE
   TYPE number_tab_t IS TABLE OF NUMBER INDEX BY BINARY_INTEGER;
   number_tab number_tab_t;
   empty_tab number_tab_t;
```

Now I create a bunch of elements in this table:

```
   FOR i IN 1..100000
   LOOP
      number_tab(i) := i;
   END LOOP;
```

Oracle has to put all of those elements somewhere. Following the rules discussed earlier, memory for this array will come from UGA in the case of package-level data, or CGA in the case of data in anonymous blocks or top-level procedures or functions.

You may wonder how you can get that memory back once a program is through with it. This is a case where the natural and easy thing to do will help quite a bit. That is, you can use one of these two forms:

```
number_tab.DELETE;
```

or:

```
number_tab := empty_tab;
```

Using either of these statements will cause Oracle to free the memory into its originating free list. That is, package-level memory frees into the UGA, and call-level memory frees into the PGA. The same thing happens when the collection passes out of scope; that is, if you declare and use the collection only in a standalone procedure, Oracle realizes after the procedure finishes executing that you don't need it any more. Either way, though, this memory is not available to other sessions, nor is it available to the current session for CGA memory requirements. So, if a subsequent DML operation requires a large sort, you could wind up with some huge memory requirements. When the session ends, Oracle will release this memory to its parent memory heap.

I should point out that it is no great hardship for a virtual memory operating system with plenty of paging/swap space if processes retain large amounts of inactive virtual memory in their address space. This inactive memory consumes only paging space, not real memory. There may be times, however, when you don't want to fill up paging space, and you would prefer that Oracle release the memory. For those times, Oracle supplies an on-demand "garbage collection" procedure. The syntax is simply:

```
DBMS_SESSION.FREE_UNUSED_USER_MEMORY;
```

This built-in procedure will find most of the memory that is no longer in use by any program variables, and release it back to the parent memory heap—the PGA in the case of dedicated server, or the SGA in the case of shared server.

There are two ways you can tell Oracle that you no longer need a particular collection in PL/SQL. One way is for the collection to go "out of scope." However, that won't work for package-level data, in which case you would use the built-in DELETE method just shown.

I have run quite a few test cases to determine the effect of running garbage collection in different scenarios: for example, associative arrays versus nested tables, shared versus dedicated server, anonymous blocks versus package data. The following conclusions and tips apply to using large collections.

- Merely assigning a NULL to a nested table or VARRAY will fail to mark its memory as unused. Instead, you can do one of three things: use the *collection*.DELETE method; assign a null but initialized collection to it; or wait for it to go out of scope.
- If you need to release memory to the parent heap, use DBMS_SESSION.FREE_UNUSED_USER_MEMORY when your program has populated one or more large PL/SQL tables, marked them as unused, and is unlikely to need further large memory allocations for similar operations.
- Shared server mode can be more prone than dedicated server mode to memory-shortage errors. This is because the UGA is drawn from the SGA, which is fixed in size. As discussed in the later section "A Trace of Memory," you may get an ORA-04031 error.
- If you must use shared server connections, you cannot release the memory occupied by PL/SQL tables unless the table is declared at the package level.

As a practical matter, for a collection of NUMBER elements, there seems to be no difference in storage required to store NULL elements versus, say, 38-digit number elements. However, Oracle does seem to allocate memory for VARCHAR2 elements dynamically if the elements are declared larger than VARCHAR(30).

When populating an associative array in dedicated server mode, a million-element associative array of NUMBERs occupies about 38 MB; even if the million elements are just Booleans, Oracle9*i* will require almost 15 MB of memory. Multiply that by 100 users and you're talking some big numbers, especially if you don't want the operating system to start paging this memory out to disk.

If you'd like to discover for yourself how much UGA and PGA your current session uses, you can run a query like the following:

```
SELECT n.name, ROUND(m.value/1024) kbytes
  FROM V$STATNAME n, V$MYSTAT m
 WHERE n.statistic# = m.statistic#
   AND n.name LIKE 'session%memory%'
```

(You'll need nondefault privileges to read the two V$ views in this query.)

Incidentally, if you don't want to terminate the session, the only supported way I have found to release freed PGA memory to its parent heap is to do a hard reset of package state as follows:

DBMS_SESSION.RESET_PACKAGE
: Frees all memory allocated to package state. This has the effect of resetting *all* package variables to their default values. For packages, this built-in goes beyond what FREE_UNUSED_USER_MEMORY does, because RESET_PACKAGE doesn't care whether the memory is in use or not.

DBMS_SESSION.MODIFY_PACKAGE_STATE (action_flags IN PLS_INTEGER)
: You can supply one of two constants as the action flag: DBMS_SESSION.FREE_ALL_RESOURCES or DBMS_SESSION.REINITIALIZE. The first has the same effect as using the RESET_PACKAGE procedure. Supplying the latter constant resets state variables to their defaults, but doesn't actually free and re-create the package from scratch; also, it only soft-closes open cursors, and does not flush the cursor cache. If these behaviors are acceptable in your application, use the second constant, as it will perform better than a complete reset.

Preservation of state

Oracle normally maintains the state of package-level constants, cursors, and variables in your UGA for as long as your session is running. Contrast this behavior with the variables instantiated in the declaration section of a standalone module. The scope of those variables is restricted to the module. When the module terminates, the memory and values associated with those variables are released. They are no more.

In addition to disconnecting, several other things can cause a package to obliterate its state:

- Someone recompiles the program, or Oracle invalidates it, as discussed earlier.
- The DBMS_SESSION.RESET_PACKAGE built-in procedure executes in your session.

- You include the SERIALLY_REUSABLE pragma (see Chapter 17) in your program, which causes Oracle to retain state only for the duration of the call, rather than for the entire session.
- You are using the web gateway in the default mode which by default does not maintain persistent database sessions for each client.

Subject to these limitations, package data structures can act as "globals" within the PL/SQL environment. That is, they provide a way for different PL/SQL programs running in the same session to exchange data.

From an application design perspective, there are two types of global data: *public* and *private*.

Public

A data structure declared in the specification of a package is a global public data structure. Any calling program or user with EXECUTE privilege has access to the data. Programs can assign even meaningless values to package variables not marked CONSTANT. Public global data is the proverbial "loose cannon" of programming: convenient to declare but tempting to overuse, leading to a greater risk of unstructured code that is susceptible to ugly side effects.

The specification of a module should give you all the information you need to call and use that module. If the program reads and/or writes global data structures, you cannot tell this from the module specification; you cannot be sure of what is happening in your application and which program changes what data. It is always preferable to pass data as parameters in and out of modules. That way, the reliance on those data structures is documented in the specification and can be accounted for by the developer. In my own code, I try to limit global public data to those values that can truly be made CONSTANT.

Private

Not so problematic are global but private data structures (also called *package-level data*) that you might declare in the body of the package. Because it does not appear in the specification, this data cannot be referenced from outside the package—only from within the package, by other package elements.

Global, but only within a single Oracle session

Packaged data items are global only within a single Oracle session or connection. Package data is not shared across sessions. If you need to share data between different Oracle sessions, there are other tools at your disposal, including the DBMS_PIPE package, Oracle Advanced Queuing, and the UTL_TCP package.

Client-side application developers in particular need to be careful about assuming that different modules maintain a single Oracle connection. There are times when a tool may establish a new connection to the database to perform an action. If this occurs, the data stored in a package in the first connection will not be available.

Consider the scenario in Figure 20-9. An Oracle Forms application has saved values to data structures in a server-side package. When the form calls a stored procedure, this stored procedure can access these same package-based variables and values as the form because they share a single Oracle connection. The form then uses the RUN_PRODUCT built-in to display a chart with Oracle Graphics. By default, this will spawn a second connection to the database (same username and password) to run the report. So even if this report accesses the same package and its data structures, the values in those data structures will not match those used by the form. It is a different Oracle session, which means there is a new instantiation of the data structures. (In addition, different sessions won't share transactions, nor will they share the same read-consistent view.)

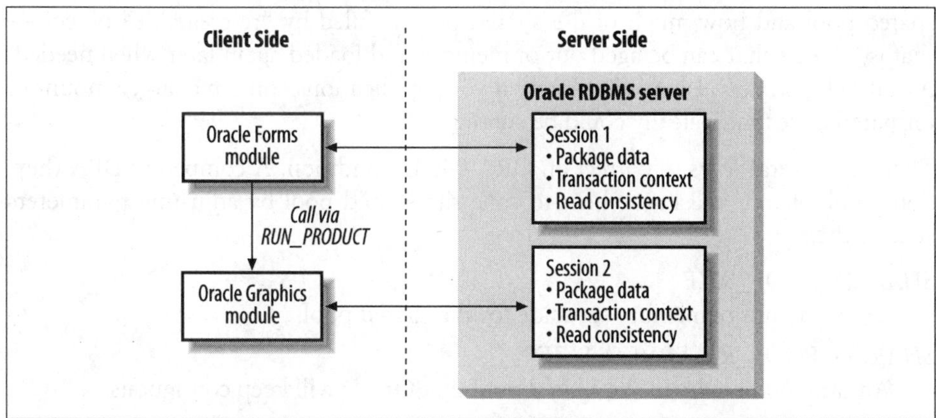

Figure 20-9. Two Oracle connections between Oracle Forms and Oracle Graphics

With client-side PL/SQL, there is a case where you have to take one extra step to share package state among different modules. See the later section "Client PL/SQL libraries at runtime" for this discussion.

A Trace of Memory

Let's say you're cruising along with your database running just fine, with lots of PL/SQL and SQL statements happily zipping by, and then it strikes: *ORA-04031: unable to allocate n bytes of shared memory*. I've seen this error only in shared server mode, which caps a shared server's UGA memory; in dedicated server mode, Oracle simply grabs more virtual memory from the operating system.

Even just to start a PL/SQL program, Oracle must load all of its bytecode into memory. To see how much space an object actually occupies in the shared pool, you can run the built-in procedure DBMS_SHARED_POOL.SIZES, which lists all objects over a given size. Here is an example:*

* If you're wondering why the columns of data do not line up properly with their headings, it's probably because of the severe limitations of DBMS_OUTPUT. If you don't like it, write your own (grab the query from V$SQLAREA after running the package).

```
SQL> SET SERVEROUTPUT ON SIZE 1000000
SQL> EXEC DBMS_SHARED_POOL.SIZES(minsize => 100)

SIZE(K) KEPT   NAME
------- ------ ---------------------------------------------------------------
371            SYS.STANDARD                  (PACKAGE)
166            SYS./5ee89977_NamespaceRDBMS  (JAVA CLASS)
101 YES        SYS.java/math/BigInteger      (JAVA CLASS)

PL/SQL procedure successfully completed.
```

This output shows that the package STANDARD occupies 371K of shared memory.* This is necessary, but not sufficient, information; you must also know the size of the shared pool and how much of the shared pool is filled by "re-creatable" objects—that is, objects that can be aged out of memory and loaded again later when needed. As a developer, you also need to know if your applications contain a large amount of unshared code that logically could be shared.

There are several ways to correct an ORA-04031 condition. A competent DBA (hey, don't look at me) will know how to tune the shared pool by adjusting parameters such as these:

SHARED_POOL_SIZE
: Total amount of memory set aside for the shared pool.

SHARED_POOL_RESERVED_SIZE
: Amount of memory in the shared pool that Oracle will keep contiguous.

LARGE_POOL_SIZE
: Optional region of memory, separate from the shared pool, that holds UGA for shared server connections. This prevents the UGA from competing for use of the shared pool.

SESSION_CACHED_CURSORS
: Number of entries in the session cursor cache.

CURSOR_SPACE_FOR_TIME
: If set to true, Oracle will deallocate a cursor from the library cache only if all applications have closed any cursors associated with it. This value is normally true.

If you're the application developer, though, you can do at least two things on your own:

- Modify code to ensure that the maximum number of SQL statements get shared.
- Petition the DBA to force certain PL/SQL programs and/or cursors to be kept in memory.

* There is a bug in most older versions of DBMS_SHARED_POOL.SIZES that results in the amount's being over-reported by about 2.3%. Oracle's package erroneously computes kilobytes by dividing bytes by 1000 instead of by 1024.

You can force the shared pool to hold a particular program in memory with the DBMS_SHARED_POOL.KEEP procedure.* For example, a DBA could run this:

```
BEGIN
   DBMS_SHARED_POOL.KEEP('SYS.STANDARD');
END;
```

This would force Oracle to keep the package SYS.STANDARD in memory.

Oracle provides a variety of dictionary views that may help you decide what to keep in memory. While most authors recommend pinning the STANDARD package in the shared pool, respected internals expert Steve Adams recommends keeping "everything that moves." This became less important from 8.1.6 onwards, when Oracle introduced a feature that eliminates latch contention when the shared pool gets fragmented. For more of Mr. Adams' sage counsel about Oracle internals, visit *http://www.ixora.com.au/*.

The KEEP tactic could be appropriate for large programs that go unused for a stretch of time because, on reload, they may force out many smaller objects. KEEP works for packages, procedures, functions, triggers, sequences, and, with a little extra effort on the part of the programmer, cursors.

Oracle follows a different memory-sharing tactic for PL/SQL programs that are compiled into C using the native execution feature. These get linked into shared-library files whose common code will load into memory only once, and they allocate memory from the operating system. Other programs called by the server, such as Java stored procedures and external (C) procedures, also use shared memory.

Another memory error you may encounter in shared server mode is *ORA-06500: PL/SQL: storage error*. Increasing the LARGE_POOL_SIZE will usually make this go away.

The Processing of Server-Side PL/SQL

To restate and amplify some of the main points covered so far, I'd like to enumerate the steps Oracle takes when you use a program such as SQL*Plus to submit PL/SQL to the server.

* In the fine print, Oracle says that it may obsolete the feature when it comes up with better memory management algorithms.

Compiling an Anonymous Block

Here are the major steps involved in compiling an anonymous block.

1. The PL/SQL compiler parses the code to check its syntax. If the code does not pass the syntax check, stop here and return a compile error to the calling environment.
2. The Oracle server determines whether valid parsed and executable versions of this block already exist in the library cache. It does this by computing the hash value of the text of the block, then by doing textual searches of potential matches using something like a *memcmp*, followed by a series of checks to make sure that the server environment hasn't changed. If it is OK to re-execute the block, skip to Step 1 of execution.
3. If the block is not already in the library cache, Oracle passes the block to the PL/SQL compiler.
4. The PL/SQL compiler resolves the names of PL/SQL identifiers, but sends any embedded SQL statements off to the SQL parser.
5. The SQL parser does its own syntax check, name resolution, and semantics checks, but calls back to PL/SQL to resolve any remaining identifiers (such as bind variables).
6. At the time of compilation, Oracle checks to make sure that the user who is compiling the code has privileges to (a) execute any referenced programs, and (b) perform the requested operations on SQL statements on any data structures, such as tables. This is true even when compiling invoker rights programs.
7. Automatic recompilation of invalid referenced objects (even remote procedures) occurs when the PL/SQL compiler encounters the reference to the objects (as described in the earlier section "Dependency Management").
8. The compiler reads the DIANA of any referenced objects (including remote procedures) in order to validate that the call matches their signature. If the DIANA for a referenced object is not already present in the data dictionary, then it is generated at this point and stored persistently.
9. If compilation succeeds, Oracle creates bytecode and loads it into library cache. The DIANA for the anonymous block is discarded.

Compiling a Stored Object

There are some variations on the compilation process for stored objects (package, package body, procedure, function, trigger, type, type body):

1. Before recompiling an existing program, Oracle determines whether it is already running and waits until the run completes before recompiling. Steve Adams points out that this is "a (S)hare mode KGL pin held during execution, and com-

pilation needs to take that pin in e(X)clusive mode." Watch out, because these pins can cause deadlocks or long-term waits.

2. If the object being compiled is a package with state information, Oracle will tear down this package state and possibly the state of other packages in session memory.
3. When you issue a DDL statement such as CREATE OR REPLACE PROCEDURE, Oracle saves the source code in the SOURCE$ table even if compilation ultimately fails. In addition, for each stored program, Oracle also stores the current compiler flags in the SETTINGS$ table.
4. Successful compilation causes DIANA to be stored in the database for everything except package bodies and type bodies (even for natively compiled programs).
5. Once the DIANA exists for a stored program, Oracle also saves information about the objects on which the program depends in the DEPENDENCY$ table.
6. If the program uses any remote procedures, at compilation time Oracle retrieves the timestamp and the DIANA-based "signature" of the remote object and saves it with the compiled code of the local program
7. If the session or database flags are set for native compilation, the PL/SQL compiler performs the usual syntax and semantic analysis. An internal translator then converts the PL/SQL into C and invokes the operating system's C compiler to generate a shared object file.
8. If compiling a stored object fails, Oracle makes an entry in the ERROR$ table, which users may see via the USER_ERRORS view. Successful compilation removes any previous error information from the ERROR$ table.
9. As with anonymous blocks, successful compilation loads all forms of compiled code into the library cache; with stored programs, Oracle also saves the DIANA, bytecode, and any debug data in the data dictionary.

Executing PL/SQL

Once the bytecode exists in the library cache, Oracle can execute it. Here are some of the steps involved in execution:

1. If the invoker of the program is not its owner, Oracle checks whether the invoker has been granted EXECUTE privilege on the program.
2. If the program is a stored program that has been marked AUTHID CURRENT_USER (invoker rights), the PL/SQL runtime engine re-resolves external references to SQL objects at runtime based on the identity of the invoker. External references to PL/SQL programs are not re-resolved unless they are embedded in an anonymous block.

3. Oracle opens a cursor and associates it with the program, even if it is an anonymous block.
4. If there are any remote procedures, the PL/SQL runtime engine compares the local copy of the timestamp or signature with its counterpart on the remote side. If they don't match, Oracle discards the current session state (ORA-04068) and gives an *ORA-04062: timestamp (or signature) of procedure* "procedure_name" *has been changed* error. A second invocation attempt will trigger an automatic recompilation of the local program; if it succeeds, it will execute.
5. The PL/SQL runtime engine makes any needed calls to Oracle's SQL processor, which opens and caches cursors as needed.
6. Normally, a PL/SQL program runs inside the transaction context established by the current session. If, however, the runtime engine calls a program marked as an autonomous transaction, the runtime engine suspends the current transaction and initiates a second transaction context for the called program. After the autonomous transaction commits or rolls back, the original transaction resumes. (See Chapter 13 for more details).
7. When a running PL/SQL program calls a second program and passes an IN OUT parameter to it, the runtime engine makes an internal copy of the argument before completing the call. If the called program ends with an unhandled exception, the runtime engine will revert the argument to its old value when control reverts to the caller. If you use the IN OUT NOCOPY compiler hint and Oracle accepts it, the runtime engine makes no copy and cannot reverse what may be partial or incorrect changes made by the called program. (See Chapter 16 for a discussion and examples).
8. For natively compiled PL/SQL, the runtime engine calls out to the appropriate shared library, which has already been linked with the Oracle executable. (See Chapter 19 for complete coverage.)
9. For external procedures, the Oracle Net listener spawns a session-specific process called *extproc* through which the PL/SQL runtime exchanges arguments and results with the shared library containing the external procedure. (See Chapters 22 and 23 for details).
10. When the program completes, Oracle passes the results back to the caller in the form of status information and/or return and OUT parameter values. If there were any unhandled exceptions, the runtime engine populates an error stack with information about the exception, which the calling environment normally interrogates and reports to the user.

PL/SQL Code on the Client

If you are using Oracle's application development tools, such as Forms or Reports, you can use PL/SQL as the language in which you create an application's graphical user interface and supporting logic. Technically, you don't even have to connect to a database to use this feature. Also, with a little effort, you can even hook up client-side PL/SQL to databases other than Oracle. The normal arrangement, though, looks like Figure 20-10.

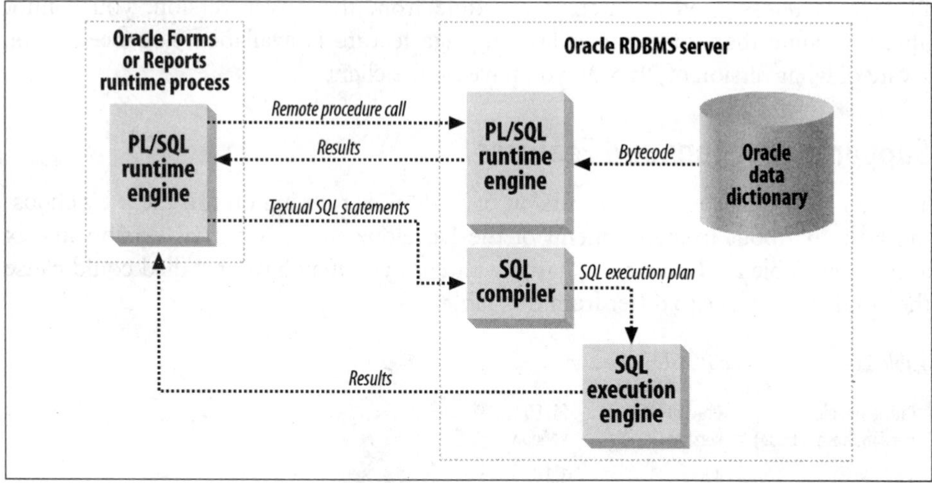

Figure 20-10. Oracle client-side runtime environment invoking a stored procedure

As illustrated, the client-side runtime environment—which may actually be running on a middle tier, such as an Oracle Forms "server"—communicates with both the server-side PL/SQL runtime and the server's SQL processing components. The remote procedure calls don't require the server to read the DIANA of any called programs in order to determine whether the referenced program has changed, as discussed earlier in the "Remote Dependencies" section of this chapter.

One of the great things that Oracle has done with the application development tools is to provide a wide range of extended functionality via built-in packages. So, on the client computer, for example, you can use PL/SQL to do things like:

- Define the behaviors of triggers that fire on events such as mouse clicks
- Provide data entry assistance to the user by encoding automatic lookups and data validation
- Specify what will happen when the user selects an item from a pull-down menu
- Store and retrieve data in local files using the TEXT_IO package
- Programmatically alter behavior and visual characteristics of user interface widgets

Up through Developer 6*i*, you could also use PL/SQL to interact with the client operating system. For example, on Microsoft Windows you could call DLLs directly, use OLE (Object Linking and Embedding) features, or make calls to the Windows API.

Oracle eliminated those Microsoft-specific features in Developer 9*i*, though. No comment.

Fortunately, making direct calls to server-side PL/SQL from the client PL/SQL environment is subject to only a few gotchas. For starters, because the client version of PL/SQL is released on a different schedule from the server version, you cannot always assume that some particular language feature is available. You need to be aware of what version of PL/SQL you have on the client.

Supported Versions and Features

You can always discover which version of PL/SQL is running on the client by choosing Help → About from the menu of the Developer tool. A partial version matrix appears in Table 20-3, but note that any patches you may have installed could cause the *n*th decimal place to differ from this table.

Table 20-3. Client-side PL/SQL versions

Oracle Developer version (base release)	Oracle Forms version	PL/SQL version
1.x	4.5	1.2
2.x	5.0	2.3
6.0	6.0.5	8.0.5
6*i*	6.0.8	8.0.6
9*i*	9.0.2	9.0.1

The next thing to realize is that just because the client has a particular PL/SQL release, that does not mean you have access to all of the corresponding *server* features you might expect from that version. With client PL/SQL 9.0.2, for example, you can do any of these things:

- Declare and use a local collection type inside a client program (and declare and use local variables of that type).
- Use a subtype, collection type, record type, or cursor variable type that has been declared in a package spec on the server.
- Declare a variable in a client program of a type that has been declared in a server-based package specification. This includes records and single-level collections.
- Declare and use variables as REFs to a user-defined object type.
- Base a block on a table with a collection-typed attribute.
- Base a block on an object table or on a table with an object column, as long as the object type does not include a collection-typed attribute.

But (and this is still on the client side, remember) you *cannot*:

- Create a standalone user-defined type (such as an object type or collection type).
- Declare a variable in a client program that is of a standalone user-defined type you have declared on the server.

There are two ways to work around this problem:

- Do not use any unsupported datatypes in the specifications of your server-side stored modules.
- Write a thin "translator" stored procedure to map server-side PL/SQL datatypes to the datatypes available on your client version of PL/SQL (where possible).

I strongly urge you to employ the second workaround. If you have built stored programs that make use of server-side PL/SQL datatypes in the parameter list, and if those datatypes are the most appropriate ones for the parameters, you shouldn't change that module's specification. You should always try to take advantage of the most advanced features of a language. Don't choose a lowest-common-denominator solution unless there are no other options.

In many situations, you won't have the opportunity to change the specification (parameter list) of a stored module. It might have been written by others, perhaps for another application, and cannot be modified without possibly affecting those other applications. In this case, the second workaround is annoying, but is thoroughly able to be implemented. If your pre-Oracle9*i* client-side code must call a procedure that accepts a TIMESTAMP parameter, for example, it may make sense to encapsulate it inside another stored procedure that instead accepts a DATE. In fact, you could just overload the procedure if it's in a package. Here is the specification:

```
PACKAGE logger
AS
   PROCEDURE note_the_time (event_time_in IN TIMESTAMP);
   PROCEDURE note_the_time (event_time_in IN DATE);
END;
```

The package body would include the following implementation of the DATE version:

```
PROCEDURE note_the_time (event_time_in IN DATE) IS
BEGIN
   note_the_time(TO_TIMESTAMP(event_time_in));
END;
```

Now logger.note_the_time can be called from a pre-9*i* client program because it accepts one of the supported datatypes.

When implementing overloading to support different datatypes, do *not* rely on implicit type conversions in the body of the procedure. I tried that:

```
PROCEDURE note_the_time (event_time_in IN DATE) IS
BEGIN
   note_the_time(event_time_in);  /* bad idea */
END;
```

Yup, that's an infinite recursive loop, and the means of escaping from it is not obvious (kill the shadow task using *orakill.exe* on Windows platforms, or *kill -9* on Unix). No doubt a real DBA would have long ago imposed CPU limits with Oracle's "profile" feature on a guy like me.

Note that if you are using Forms 9*i*, you won't have this particular problem with TIMESTAMP because it is a supported datatype. You will, however, run into another annoyance when you attempt to use server-side package variables, as the next section illustrates.

Limitations of Oracle's Remote Invocation Model

With the Oracle software available at the time of this writing, there is no direct way for any PL/SQL program to directly use any of the following package constructs on a remote server:

- Variables (including constants)
- Cursors
- Exceptions

This limitation applies not only to client PL/SQL calling the database server, but also to server-to-server RPCs.

The simple workaround for variables is to use "get-and-set" programs to encapsulate the data. In general, you should be doing that anyway, as it's an excellent programming practice.

The workaround for cursors is to encapsulate them with "open, fetch, and close" subprograms. For example, if you've declared a book_cur cursor in the specification of the book_maint package, you could put this corresponding package body on the server:

```
CREATE OR REPLACE PACKAGE BODY book_maint
AS
   prv_book_cur_status BOOLEAN;

   PROCEDURE open_book_cur IS
   BEGIN
      IF NOT book_maint.book_cur%ISOPEN
      THEN
         OPEN book_maint.book_cur;
```

```
      END IF;
   END;

   FUNCTION next_book_rec
     RETURN books%ROWTYPE
   IS
      l_book_rec books%ROWTYPE;
   BEGIN
      FETCH book_maint.book_cur INTO l_book_rec;
      prv_book_cur_status := book_main.book_cur%FOUND;
      RETURN l_book_rec;
   END;

   FUNCTION book_cur_is_found
     RETURN BOOLEAN
   IS
   BEGIN
      RETURN prv_book_cur_status;
   END;

   PROCEDURE close_book_cur IS
   BEGIN
      IF book_maint.book_cur%ISOPEN
      THEN
         CLOSE book_maint.book_cur;
      END IF;
   END;

END;
```

Unfortunately, this approach won't work around the problem of using remote exceptions; the exception "datatype" is treated differently from true datatypes. Instead, you can use the RAISE_APPLICATION_ERROR procedure with a user-defined exception number between –20000 and –20999. See Chapter 6 for a discussion of how to write a good package to help your application manage this type of exception.

Client-Side PL/SQL Libraries

Broadly speaking, PL/SQL lives in two major places on the client side:

- In a reusable PL/SQL "library"
- In the application module (form, report, etc.) itself

A library can contain any number of procedures, functions, and packages; it is a kind of "super-package" structure. The library construct is unique to Oracle's client-side tools, and using it properly bears some discussion. The first thing to realize is that, although PL/SQL code may reside in a lot of different places—as Table 20-4 shows—only libraries can contain PL/SQL that you can share among different client modules.

Table 20-4. Libraries and other file types on the client side that may contain PL/SQL

File extension	Expansion	Type of PL/SQL contained
.PLL	PL/SQL library	PL/SQL source, DIANA, and bytecode of procedures, functions, and packages
.PLX	PL/SQL library "executable"	Bytecode corresponding to the program units in the library
.PLD	PL/SQL library text	Optional readable text version of program units in the library
.FMB	Forms module binary	Any PL/SQL source code (and other source code) in an Oracle Forms module, but stored in a binary file along with DIANA and bytecode
.FMX	Forms module "executable"	Bytecode corresponding to any PL/SQL in the Oracle Forms module
.FMT	Forms module text	Optional text version of the Oracle Forms module; however, any PL/SQL appears only in hex
.RDF	Report definition file	Any PL/SQL that you've created in the Oracle Reports module, stored in a binary file along with DIANA and bytecode
.REP	Report runfile	Bytecode corresponding to any PL/SQL in the Oracle Reports module
.REX	Report text file	Optional text version of the Oracle Reports application, including readable PL/SQL source code
.MMB	Menu module binary	Any PL/SQL that you've created in the menu module, stored in a binary file along with DIANA and bytecode
.MMX	Menu module executable	Bytecode corresponding to any PL/SQL in the menu module
.MMT	Menu module text	Optional text version of menu module

Because PL/SQL libraries can dramatically improve the design and performance of your client-side applications, the next two sections present some of the concepts and non-obvious aspects of putting libraries to use.

Client PL/SQL libraries at design time

The usual convention of designing client PL/SQL is to put only module-specific code into the application module, and to put anything used by more than one module into a library.

When you put code into a library, you must "attach" the library to the module to be able to use its programs. This simple task is accomplished with the object navigator in the design-time tools. The PL/SQL library file and the application module file (for example, *.FMB*) do remain separate, though, and you must remember to copy them both when distributing your code.

One of the aspects of using libraries that confuses beginners is the prompt asking whether to remove path information from the library. Oracle wants to know which of two alternatives you intend to use at runtime:

- Retain full path information (such as *c:\apps\forms\libs*) because you will be deploying the library in exactly the same path in which you're developing it
- Remove path information and have the application tool search for the library according to certain system variables

The first option may be more expedient during development, but the second is more flexible and probably better in the long run, even though it requires the extra step of setting the path variables. The runtime search order is this:

1. First, check the tool-specific variable, such as FORMS90_PATH, REPORTS90_PATH, or GRAPHICS60_PATH.
2. Then, if the variable is not found, look in ORACLE_PATH.

On Windows environments, you can set these variables either via the control panel ("System Properties") or in the registry. Apparently, you cannot simply define them in a batch file.

To reveal a bit more of the story, the Oracle client tools I have tested seem to resolve external program references using the following search sequence:

1. Client-side built-in programs
2. "Program units" defined in the module itself (*.FMB*)
3. PLX versions of attached PL/SQL libraries on the path supplied by the environment variables discussed earlier
4. If no PLX version, the PLL versions of the attached PL/SQL libraries
5. Database server (using standard server name resolution)

When you are factoring programs into their best location during development, you will want to load both the PL/SQL library and an attaching application module (form, report, etc.) into the development environment at the same time. You will want to be conscious of saving a modified library before attempting to use any new features in the attaching module.

When modifying a library and an attaching module during the same editing session, you will need to do one or two things before the attaching module can see the changes. If you are using only the PLL version at runtime, you will need to save the PL/SQL library (File → Save). If you have also generated a PLX version of the library on the path, you will need to generate it (File → Administration → Compile File, or Program → Compile).

Client PL/SQL libraries at runtime

The runtime environment searches for PL/SQL libraries in the same way that the development environment does: if the library isn't called with explicit path information, the tool looks in the path given by the environment variables.

One of the selling points of PL/SQL libraries is the way that the client tools load them into memory. At startup, the runtime environment reads only a "directory" portion of the attached library into memory. Then, the first time that your module invokes a particular procedure, function, or package, the environment loads only that code into memory, in 4K chunks. Contrast this with what happens with PL/SQL code in an application module, where *all* of its local code gets loaded into memory at startup.

Because PL/SQL libraries load into memory as needed rather than all at once, putting large client programs into libraries instead of into individual application module files can help optimize memory use.

If you attach a PL/SQL library to multiple forms, you have the option of sharing library state—that is, using package variables as globals. The way to tell the runtime environment to do that is to specify a particular argument to CALL_FORM. For example:

```
CALL_FORM(formmodule_name => 'BOOKS', data_mode => SHARE_LIBRARY_DATA);
```

If you don't supply this value for the data_mode parameter, the default behavior is NO_SHARE_LIBRARY_DATA, which means that each running form separately instantiates any referenced program(s) in the library.

Deferring Item Name Resolution in Client PL/SQL

One of the quirks of attempting to put reusable code into PL/SQL libraries is the fact that you cannot refer directly to module-level objects in the library code, even though it is legal to do so in a module. The library code must compile successfully, independent from any particular application module. So, in an Oracle Forms module, I can include a statement such as this one:

```
IF :bookblock.summary IS NULL
THEN
   :bookblock.summary := 'TO BE SUPPLIED';
END IF;
```

where :bookblock.summary is the name of an on-screen field. However, if I try that in a program in a PL/SQL library, it won't compile because it knows nothing about that field. So I would like a way to *defer* resolution of the field reference until runtime.

Oracle solves this problem with two special built-ins: NAME_IN, which reads the value of an item whose name you supply as a string argument, and COPY, which assigns a value to the item. I could say this:

```
IF NAME_IN('bookblock.summary') IS NULL
THEN
   COPY('TO BE SUPPLIED', 'bookblock.summary');
END IF;
```

This solves the compile problem. As with any kind of dynamic coding technique, though, it creates a secondary problem: it defers the detection of errors until runtime. The compiler will not look inside those literal strings and try to determine whether they are real item names. As long as you test your code, however, I'd categorize this tradeoff as a minor irritant rather than a major obstacle.

Execution Authority Models

Back in the old days before Oracle8*i*, a stored program was always executed under the authority of its owner, or *definer*. This was not a big deal if your entire application—code and data—worked out of the same Oracle account. The centralized, stored code would not automatically apply the privileges of a user (also known as an *invoker*) to the code's objects. The user might not have had DELETE privileges on a table, but the stored code did, so delete away! Now, in some circumstances, that may have been just how you wanted it to work. In other situations, particularly when you were executing programs relying on the DBMS_SQL (dynamic SQL) package, awesome complications could ensue.

In Oracle 8.1, PL/SQL was enhanced so that at the time of compilation, the application programmer could decide whether a program (or all programs in a package) should run under the authority of the definer (the only choice in Oracle 8.0 and earlier) or of the invoker of that program.

The Definer Rights Model

You need to understand the nuances of both the definer rights model and the invoker rights model because many PL/SQL applications rely on a combination of the two.

Before a PL/SQL program can be executed from within a database instance, it must be compiled and stored in the database itself. Thus, a program unit is always stored within a specific schema or Oracle account, even though the program might refer to objects in other schema.

With the *definer rights model*, you should keep the following rules in mind:

- Any external reference in a program unit is resolved at compile time, using the directly granted privileges of the schema in which the program unit is compiled.
- Database roles are in effect when compiling anonymous blocks, but are ignored completely when compiling stored programs.
- Whenever you run a program compiled with the definer rights model (the default), its SQL executes under the authority of the schema that owns the program.
- Although direct grants are needed to compile a program, you can grant EXECUTE authority to give other schemas and roles the ability to run your program.

Figure 20-11 shows how you can use the definer rights model to control access to underlying data objects. All the order entry data is stored in the OEData schema. All the order entry code is defined in the OECode schema. OECode has been granted the direct privileges necessary to compile the Order_Mgt package, which allows you to both place and cancel orders.

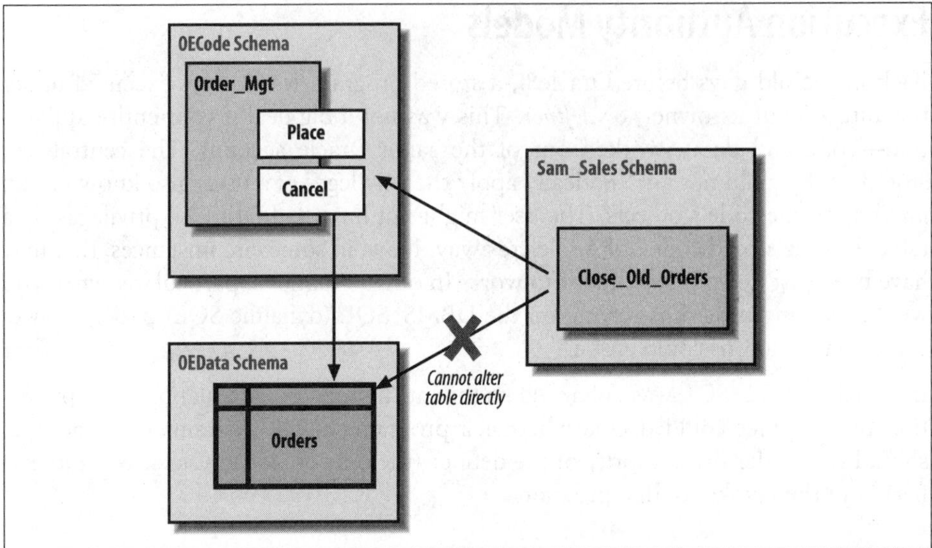

Figure 20-11. Controlling access to data with the definer rights model

To make sure that the orders table is updated properly, no direct access (either via roles or via privileges) is allowed to that table through any schema other than OECode. Suppose, for example, that the Sam_Sales schema needs to run through all the outstanding orders and close out old ones. Sam will not be able to issue a DELETE statement from the Close_Old_Orders procedure; instead, he will have to call Order_Mgt.cancel to get the job done.

Advantages of definer rights

Certain situations cry out for the definer rights model. That model has the following advantages:

- You are better able to control access to underlying data structures. You can guarantee that the only way the contents of a table can be changed is by going through a specific programmatic interface (usually a package).
- Application performance improves dramatically because the PL/SQL engine does not have to perform checks at runtime to determine if you have the appropriate privileges or—just as important—which object you should actually be manipulating (my accounts table may be quite different from yours!).
- You don't have to worry about manipulating the wrong table. With definer rights, your code will work with the same data structure you would be accessing directly in SQL in your SQL*Plus (or other execution) environment. It is simply more intuitive.

Disadvantages of definer rights

But there are problems with the definer rights model as well. These are explored in the next sections.

Where'd my table go? Let's see what all those definer rights rules can mean to a PL/SQL developer on a day-to-day basis. In many databases, developers write code against tables and views that are owned by other schemas, with public synonyms created for them to hide the schema. Privileges are then granted via database roles.

This very common setup can result in some frustrating experiences. Suppose that my organization relies on roles to grant access to objects. I am working with a table called accounts, and can execute this query without any problem in SQL*Plus:

```
SQL> SELECT account#, name FROM accounts;
```

Yet, when I try to use that same table (and the same query, even) inside a procedure, I get an error:

```
SQL> CREATE OR REPLACE PROCEDURE show_accounts
     IS
     BEGIN
        FOR rec IN (SELECT account#, name FROM accounts)
        LOOP
           DBMS_OUTPUT.PUT_LINE (rec.name);
        END LOOP;
     END;
     /

Warning: Procedure created with compilation errors.

SQL> sho err
Errors for PROCEDURE SHOW_ACCOUNTS:

LINE/COL ERROR
-------- ------------------------------------------------------
4/16     PL/SQL: SQL Statement ignored
4/43     PLS-00201: identifier 'ACCOUNTS' must be declared
```

This doesn't make any sense…or does it? The problem is that accounts is actually owned by another schema; I was unknowingly relying on a synonym and roles to get at the data. So if you are ever faced with this seemingly contradictory situation, don't bang your head against the wall in frustration. Instead, ask the owner of the object or the DBA to grant you the privileges you require to get the job done.

How do I maintain all that code? Suppose that my database instance is set up with a separate schema for each of the regional offices in my company. I build a large body of code that each office uses to analyze and maintain its data. Each schema has its own tables with the same structure but different data. (Yes, I know that this is rarely a good design, but please suspend your disbelief temporarily.)

Now, I would like to install this code so that I spend the absolute minimum amount of time and effort setting up and maintaining the application. The way to do that is to install the code in one schema and share that code among all the regional office schemas.

With the definer rights model, unfortunately, this goal and architecture are impossible to achieve. If I install the code in a central schema and grant EXECUTE authority to all regional schemas, then all those offices will be working with whatever set of tables is accessible to the central schema (perhaps one particular regional office or, more likely, a dummy set of tables). That's no good. I must instead install this body of code in each separate regional schema, as shown in Figure 20-12.

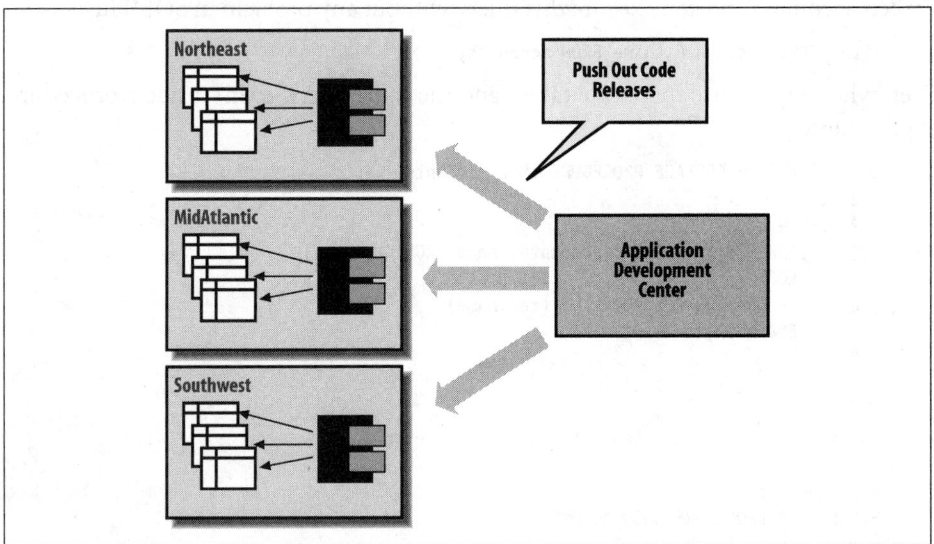

Figure 20-12. Repetitive installations of code needed with definer rights

The result is a maintenance and enhancement nightmare. Perhaps invoker rights will give us options for a better solution.

Dynamic SQL and definer rights. Another common source of confusion with definer rights occurs when using dynamic SQL (described in Chapter 15). Suppose that I create a generic "exec DDL" program as follows:

```
/* File on web: execddl.sp */
CREATE OR REPLACE PROCEDURE execDDL (ddl_string IN VARCHAR2)
   AUTHID CURRENT_USER IS
BEGIN
   EXECUTE IMMEDIATE ddl_string;
EXCEPTION
   WHEN OTHERS
   THEN
      DBMS_OUTPUT.PUT_LINE ('Dynamic SQL Failure: ' || SQLERRM);
```

```
        DBMS_OUTPUT.PUT_LINE (
           '  on statement: "' || ddl_string || '"');
        RAISE;
END;
```

Now, dynamic SQL can be tricky stuff (notice the exception handler that closes the cursor instead of leaving it hanging open—it's easy to forget housekeeping like this). So after testing it in my schema with outstanding results, I decide to share this neat utility with everyone else in my development organization. I compile it into the COMMON schema (where all reusable code is managed), grant EXECUTE to public, and create a public synonym. Then I send out an email announcing its availability.

A few weeks later, I start getting calls from my coworkers. "Hey, I asked it to create a table and it ran without any errors, but I don't have the table." "I asked it to drop my table, and the execddl procedure said that there is no such table. But I can do a DESCRIBE on it." You get the idea. I begin to have serious doubts about sharing my code with other people. Sheesh, if they can't use something as simple as the execddl procedure without screwing things up...but I decide to withhold judgment and do some research.

I log into the COMMON schema and find that, sure enough, all of the objects people were trying to create or drop or alter were sitting here in COMMON. And then it dawns on me: unless a user of execddl specifies his own schema when he asks to create a table, the results will be most unexpected.

In other words, this call to execddl:

```
SQL> EXEC execddl ('CREATE TABLE newone (rightnow DATE)')
```

would create the newone table in the COMMON schema. And this call to execddl:

```
SQL> EXEC execddl ('CREATE TABLE scott.newone (rightnow DATE)')
```

might solve the problem, but would fail with the following error:

```
ORA-01031: insufficient privileges
```

unless I grant CREATE ANY TABLE to the COMMON schema. Yikes . . . my attempt to share a useful piece of code got very complicated very fast! It sure would be nice to let people run the execddl procedure under their own authority and not that of COMMON, without having to install multiple copies of the code.

The Invoker Rights Model

To help developers get around the obstacles raised by the definer rights model, Oracle 8.1 and later offers an alternative: the *invoker rights model*. With this approach, all external references in the SQL statements in a PL/SQL program unit are resolved according to the directly granted privileges of the invoking schema, not those of the owning or defining schema.

Figure 20-13 demonstrates the fundamental difference between the definer and the invoker rights models. Recall that in Figure 20-12, it was necessary for me to push out copies of my application to each regional office so that the code would manipulate the correct tables. With invoker rights, this step is no longer necessary. Now I can compile the code into a single code repository. When a user from the Northeast region executes the centralized program (probably via a synonym), it will automatically work with tables in the Northeast schema.

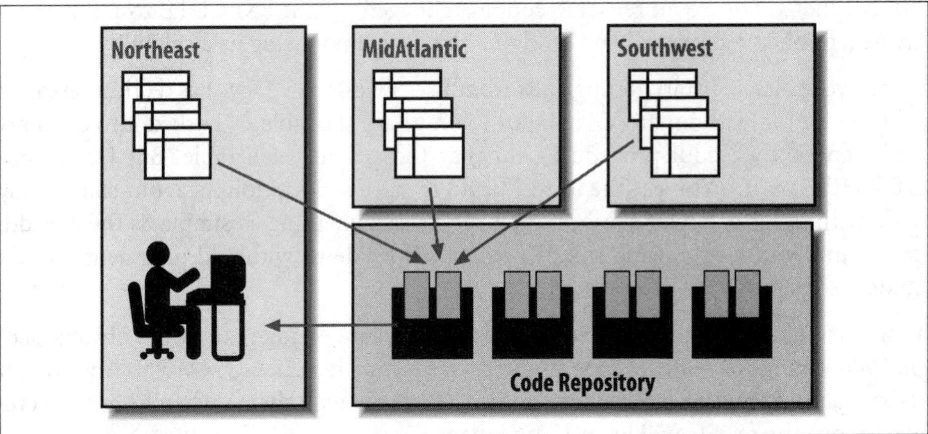

Figure 20-13. Use of invoker rights model

So that's the idea behind invoker rights. Let's see what is involved in terms of code, and then explore how best to exploit the feature.

Invoker rights syntax

The syntax to support this feature is simple enough. You add the following clause before your IS or AS keyword in the program header:

```
AUTHID CURRENT_USER
```

Here, for example, is that generic "exec DDL" engine again, this time defined as an invoker rights program:

```
/* File on web: execddl.sql */
CREATE OR REPLACE PROCEDURE execddl (ddl_in in VARCHAR2)
   AUTHID CURRENT_USER
IS
BEGIN
   EXECUTE IMMEDIATE ddl_in;
END;
```

The AUTHID CURRENT_USER clause before the IS keyword indicates that when execddl executes, it should run under the authority of the invoker or "current user," not the authority of the definer. And that's all you have to do. If you do not include the AUTHID clause, or if you include it and explicitly request definer rights as shown:

```
AUTHID DEFINER
```

then all references in your program will be resolved according to the directly granted privileges of the owning schema.

> **Invoker Rights for Dynamic SQL**
>
> I have written hundreds of programs using dynamic SQL, and prior to Oracle 8.1, I always had to worry about schema issues. Where is the program running? Who is running it? What will happen when someone runs it? These are scary questions to ask about your own code!
>
> You may be tempted to use the AUTHID CURRENT_USER clause with every stored program unit that uses any sort of dynamic SQL. Once you take this step, you reason, you can rest assured that no matter where the program is compiled and which schema runs the program, it will always act on the currently connected schema.
>
> The problem with this approach, though, is that the extra runtime checking Oracle must perform for invoker rights programs can be a real drag on performance. Use invoker rights sparingly.

Some rules and restrictions

There are a number of rules and restrictions to keep in mind when you are taking advantage of the invoker rights model:

- AUTHID DEFINER is the default option.
- The invoker rights model checks the directly granted privileges assigned to the invoker at the time of program execution to resolve any SQL-based references to database objects.
- With invoker rights, roles *are* in effect at runtime as long as the invoker rights program hasn't been called from a definer rights program.
- The AUTHID clause is allowed only in the header of a standalone subprogram (procedure or function), a package specification, or an object type specification. You cannot apply the AUTHID clause to individual programs or methods within a package or object type.
- Invoker rights resolution of external references will work for the following kinds of statements:
  - SELECT, INSERT, UPDATE, and DELETE data manipulation statements
  - LOCK TABLE transaction control statement
  - OPEN and OPEN FOR cursor control statements

— EXECUTE IMMEDIATE and OPEN FOR USING dynamic SQL statements
  — SQL statements parsed using DBMS_SQL.PARSE
- Definer rights will always be used to resolve all external references to PL/SQL programs and object type methods at compilation time.
- You can use invoker rights to change the resolution of static external data element references (tables and views).

You can also use invoker rights to resolve external references to PL/SQL programs. Here is one way to do it:

```
EXECUTE IMMEDIATE 'BEGIN someprogram; END;';
```

In this fragment, *someprogram* would get resolved at runtime according to the rights and namespace of the invoker. Alternatively, I could have used SQL's CALL statement instead of the anonymous block. (I can't just use a naked CALL statement because it is not directly supported within PL/SQL.)

Combining Rights Models

What do you think would happen when a definer rights program calls an invoker rights program? Or vice versa? The rules are simple:

- If a definer rights program calls an invoker rights program, the rights of the *calling* program's owner apply while the called program executes.
- If an invoker rights program calls a definer rights program, the rights of the *called* program's owner apply while the called program executes. When control returns to the caller, invoker rights resume.

To help keep all this straight in your head, just remember that definer rights are "stronger" than (take precedence over) invoker rights.

Here are some files on the O'Reilly web site that you can use to explore the nuances of the invoker rights model in more detail:

invdefinv.sql and invdefinv.tst
: Two scripts that demonstrate the impact of the precedence of definer rights over invoker rights.

invdef_overhead.tst
: Examines the overhead of reliance on invoker rights (hint: runtime resolution is slower than compile-time resolution).

invrole.sql
: Demonstrates how a change in roles can affect how object references are resolved at runtime.

irdynsql.sql
: Explores some of the complexities involved in using invoker and definer rights with dynamic SQL.

Hardware for PL/SQL: Bigger = Better?

Let's close out this chapter with a few observations about server hardware and its effect on PL/SQL performance. Typically, database server hardware is one of the following:

- A single-processor computer
- A symmetric multiprocessor (SMP) computer
- A "clustered" computer

Oracle, like any software that runs on SMP or clustered machines, won't *automatically* benefit from extra processors. Only when the software is carefully crafted to delegate computing tasks to different CPUs will those extra processors pay off. The smart programmers at Oracle have done a lot of work to enable the server to exploit multiprocessing hardware.

Not all Oracle editions have this capability, though. To take advantage of SMP hardware, you must be using either the Enterprise edition or the Personal edition of Oracle. The one exception to this rule has to do with bulk data loads; all editions of Oracle are capable of parallelizing loads on SMP machines. To take advantage of clustered computers, you must not only be running Oracle's Enterprise edition, you must also license an extra option called Real Application Clusters (RAC) in Oracle9*i*, or Oracle Parallel Server (OPS) prior to that.

But will the extra expense translate into better PL/SQL performance? Let's look at the three major processor families.

The Single-Processor Variation

If you're a lone developer running Oracle on a desktop machine, you're probably running Oracle on a single-processor computer. In this configuration, most computing tasks—including the execution of PL/SQL programs—are threaded through a single CPU. Modern operating systems schedule the CPU to rapidly cycle among multiple tasks so that they appear to be running concurrently.

In a single-processor arrangement, you may well be "compute-bound"—that is, you have unused memory capacity and disk throughput, but not enough CPU speed. In this case, the upgrade path on a single-processor machine might be to get a faster processor. However, given a well-tuned application running with sufficient memory and disk I/O bandwidth, fast single-processor machines can still provide Oracle database service for hundreds of simultaneous users, at least for some applications.

If you do upgrade the processor speed or power in a single-CPU machine, your PL/SQL will almost certainly experience a performance upgrade. Processing power doesn't automatically improve disk I/O, but a lot of PL/SQL's runtime performance depends on the raw speed of the CPU.

The Symmetric Multiprocessor (SMP) Variation

The next level of sophistication in server hardware is to have two or more CPUs inside a single computer, but with the CPUs sharing memory, disk, and other I/O pathways. In this arrangement, a single operating system manages all processors, which share access to disks, memory, and other input/output devices. It's called *symmetric* because any CPU can perform any task assigned by the operating system.*

As it turns out, though, some kinds of tasks are much more likely than others to benefit from parallel processing. If your PL/SQL program includes a SQL statement that sorts a million-row table, that is a good candidate, but one that retrieves one record via an indexed lookup is not. In general, good candidates are operations that are common in decision support systems (DSS) as opposed to those in online transaction processing (OLTP).

So, let's say that you've purchased an SMP machine that includes an SMP-aware operating system, licensed Oracle's Enterprise edition or Personal edition, and built a very large data warehouse. Now you write a PL/SQL program. Will this program enjoy all the benefits of symmetric multiprocessing? It depends. Your program must meet some very specific requirements:

- The program must be a function, not a procedure or an anonymous block.
- You must call the function from a SQL statement that the Oracle optimizer would otherwise want to execute in parallel.
- The function must not attempt to change data in the database via INSERT, UPDATE, or DELETE statements (and no, you can't get around this requirement by having it call another program to do so).
- The function must not read or modify any package data. This is because there is no way to share state information among the multiple instances of the program that are running in parallel.

The bottom line is that, yes, Oracle can distribute portions of a PL/SQL program to run on multiple processors, but only if it's a computational program that runs as a "helper" to a SQL statement. Chapter 16 contains more details about parallelizing stored funtions.

The Clustered Variation

Clustering is a way to join multiple computers, each with its own CPU and memory, so that they can divide and conquer large jobs. Prior to Oracle9*i*, the optional feature for this was named Oracle Parallel Server (OPS). As of Oracle9*i*, the new and

* Asymmetric computers, which assign different tasks such as disk I/O or network I/O to different processors, are virtually nonexistent these days.

improved technology is known as Real Application Clusters (RAC). With both technologies, Oracle runs separate instances on each machine in the cluster, and these instances communicate among themselves to respond to application requests while sharing a common database on disk.

One of Oracle's advertised improvements of RAC over OPS is the ease with which applications can take advantage of the extra hardware. Oracle marketing literature asserts that you can "scale up your applications without changing a line of code." However, the fine print says that you may first need to do two things:

- Design the database to take advantage of RAC
- Partition the application to distribute the workload

Then, as the database grows in size, you should be able to scale by adding another node to the cluster. If the number of users grows, though, you may need to repartition the application. To tell you the truth, I have not had a chance to test any of Oracle's claims in this area.

Another advertised benefit of running Oracle on clustered computers is increased availability—the database will keep running even if one of the computers in the cluster goes belly-up. With OPS or RAC, some of these benefits are available automatically, while deeper support (such as transparently preserving a user's session and even preserving incomplete transactions) requires configuring additional database features. Through Oracle8*i*, the relevant feature was called Oracle Parallel Fail Safe, but in Oracle9*i* it was replaced by Real Application Clusters Guard. These topics, while extremely important to some sites, are outside the scope of this book, so check Oracle's documentation for more information.

What You Need to Know

Do you really *need* to remember everything in this chapter? I certainly hope not, though your database administrator probably does. In addition to satisfying healthy curiosity, my goal in presenting this material was to help allay any misgivings programmers might have about what happens under the hood. Whether or not you've ever had such concerns, there are a number of important points to remember about PL/SQL's runtime architecture.

- To avoid compilation overhead, programs you plan to use more than a few times should be put in stored programs rather than stored in files as anonymous blocks.
- In addition to their unique ability to preserve state throughout a session, PL/SQL packages offer performance benefits. You should put most of your extensive application logic into package bodies.
- If you don't want to bother learning how to query Oracle's data dictionary, you should probably be using a front-end developer's tool of some kind.

- While Oracle's automatic dependency management approach relieves a huge burden on developers, upgrading applications on a live production database should be undertaken with great care.
- Oracle's sophisticated approaches aimed at minimizing the machine resources needed to run PL/SQL occasionally need a little help from developers and DBAs—for example, by explicitly freeing unused user memory or pinning objects in memory.
- When you OPEN an explicit cursor in a PL/SQL program, be sure to CLOSE it as soon as you are through fetching.
- Native compilation of PL/SQL may not offer any performance advantages for SQL-intensive applications, but it can significantly improve the performance of compute-intensive programs.
- Calling remote packages entails some special programming considerations if you want to take advantage of anything in the package other than procedures, functions, types, and subtypes.
- If you are using Oracle's client-side tools, putting reusable client-side code into PL/SQL libraries generally makes sense.
- Use definer rights to maximize performance and to help simplify the management and control of privileges on database tables. Use invoker rights to address particular problems (for example, programs that use dynamic SQL and that create or destroy database objects).
- Faster CPUs, more memory, and better disk I/O will improve PL/SQL performance, but taking advantage of parallel computing still requires conscious design effort.

In this chapter:

- Introduction to Oracle's Object Features
- An Extended Example
- Object Views
- Maintaining Object Types and Object Views
- Pontifications

CHAPTER 21

Object-Oriented Aspects of PL/SQL

PL/SQL has always been a language that supports traditional procedural programming styles such as structured design and functional decomposition. Using PL/SQL packages, it is also possible to take an object-based approach, applying principles such as abstraction and encapsulation to the business of manipulating relational tables. Later version of Oracle have introduced direct support for *object-oriented programming* (OOP), providing a rich and complex type system, complete with support for type hierarchies and "substitutability."

In the interest of summarizing this book-sized topic into a modest number of pages, this chapter presents a few choice code samples to demonstrate the most significant aspects of object programming with PL/SQL. These cover the following areas:

- Creating and using object types
- Inheritance and substitutability
- Type evolution
- Pointer (REF)-based retrieval
- Object views

Among the things you won't find in this chapter are:

- Comprehensive syntax diagrams for SQL statements dealing with object types
- Database administration topics such as importing and exporting object data
- Low-level considerations such as physical data storage on disk

I'd like to introduce the topic with a brief history.

Introduction to Oracle's Object Features

First released in 1997 as an add-on to Oracle8 (the so-called "object-relational database"), the "objects option" allowed developers to extend Oracle's built-in datatypes to include *abstract datatypes*. Oracle8's introduction of programmer-defined *collections* (described in Chapter 11) also proved useful, not only because application developers had been looking for ways to store and retrieve arrays in the database, but also because PL/SQL provided a new way of querying collections as if they were tables. While there were other interesting aspects of the Oracle8 object model such as pointer-based navigation, there was no notion of inheritance or dynamic polymorphism, making the object-relational features of Oracle8 an option that drew few converts from (or into) the camp of true OOP believers. The complexity of the object features, plus a perceived performance hit, also limited uptake in the relational camp.

Oracle8*i* introduced support for Java Stored Procedures, which not only provided the ability to program the server using a less proprietary language than PL/SQL, but also made it easier for the OOP community to consider using stored procedures. Oracle provided a way to translate object type definitions from the server into Java classes, making it possible to share objects across the Java/database boundary. Oracle released 8*i* during a peak of market interest in Java, so hardly anyone really noticed that Oracle's core object features were not much enhanced—except that Oracle quietly began bundling the object features with the core database server, meaning that using the features required no additional license fees. Around this time, I asked an Oracle representative about the future of object programming in PL/SQL, and the response was, "If you want real object-oriented programming in the database, use Java."

With Oracle9*i*, though, Oracle has significantly extended the depth of its native object support, becoming a more serious consideration for OO purists. Inheritance and polymorphism have become available in the database, and PL/SQL has gained new object features. Does it finally make sense to extend the object model of our system into the structure of the database itself? Should we repartition existing middleware or client applications to take advantage of "free stuff" in the database server? As Table 21-1 shows, Oracle has made great strides, and the move may be tempting. The table also shows that a few desirable features still aren't available.*

Table 21-1. Significant object programming features in the Oracle database

Feature	Oracle8	Oracle8*i*	Oracle9*i* Release 1	Oracle9*i* Release 2
Abstract datatypes as first-class database entity	✓	✓	✓	✓
Abstract datatypes as PL/SQL parameter	✓	✓	✓	✓
Collection-typed attributes	✓	✓	✓	✓
REF-typed attributes for intra-database object navigation	✓	✓	✓	✓
Implementing method logic in PL/SQL or C	✓	✓	✓	✓
Programmer-defined object comparison semantics	✓	✓	✓	✓
Views of relational data as object-typed data	✓	✓	✓	✓

* Perhaps I should say *arguably* desirable features. The missing features are unlikely to be showstoppers.

Table 21-1. Significant object programming features in the Oracle database (continued)

Feature	Oracle8	Oracle8*i*	Oracle9*i* Release 1	Oracle9*i* Release 2
Compile-time or static polymorphism (method overloading)	✓	✓	✓	✓
Ability to "evolve" type by modifying existing method logic (but not signature), or by adding methods	✓	✓	✓	✓
Implementing method logic in Java		✓	✓	✓
"Static" methods (executes without having object instance)		✓	✓	✓
Relational primary key can serve as persistent object identifier, allowing declarative integrity of REFs		✓	✓	✓
Inheritance of attributes and methods from a user-defined type			✓	✓
Dynamic method dispatch			✓	✓
Non-instantiable supertypes, similar to Java-style "abstract classes"			✓	✓
Ability to evolve type by removing methods (and adding to change signature)			✓	✓
Ability to evolve type by adding and removing attributes, automatically propagating changes to associated physical database structures			✓	✓
"Anonymous" types: ANYTYPE, ANYDATA, ANYDATASET			✓	✓
Downcast operator (TREAT) and type detection operator (IS OF) available in SQL			✓	✓
TREAT and IS OF available in PL/SQL				✓
User-defined constructor functions				✓
"Private" attributes, variables, constants, or methods				
Inheritance from multiple supertypes				
Sharing of object types or instances across distributed databases without resorting to object views				

Unless you're already a practicing object-oriented programmer, many of the terms in Table 21-1 probably don't mean much to you. However, the remainder of this chapter should shed some light on these terms and give some clues about the larger architectural decisions you may need to make.

An Extended Example

I'd like to point out that this example—indeed, most of this chapter—relies heavily on features introduced in Oracle9*i*. In a number of areas, this section focuses on features available only in Oracle9*i* Release 2. If you really want server-side object orientation, you probably won't want to use any version earlier than Oracle9*i* anyway, and you'll probably agree that ignoring the OO-challenged earlier versions is no great sacrifice.

A Tree of Types

In keeping with the sample general application area we explored in our introductory book, *Learning Oracle PL/SQL Programming* (O'Reilly), I'd like to build an Oracle system that will use an object-oriented approach to modeling a trivial library catalog. The catalog can hold books, serials (such as magazines, proceedings, or newspapers), and, eventually, other artifacts.

A graphic portrayal of the top-level types appears in Figure 21-1. Later on, we might want to add to the type hierarchy, as the dotted-line boxes imply.

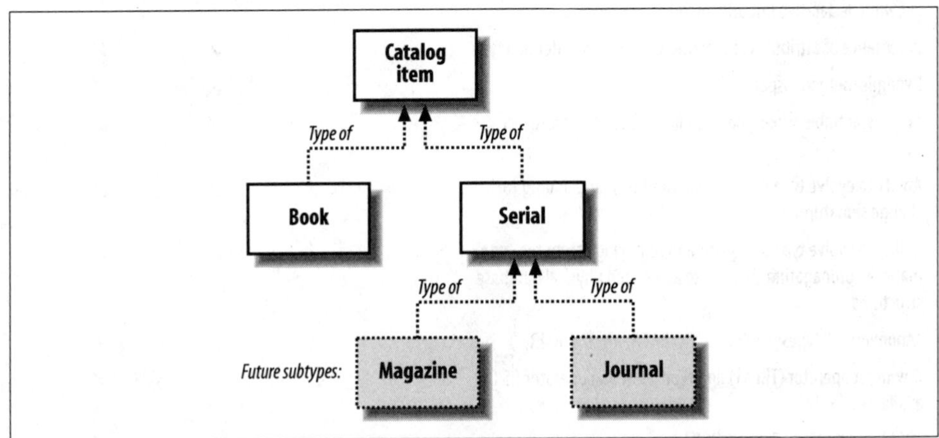

Figure 21-1. Type hierarchy for a trivial library catalog

Creating a base type

The "root" or top of the hierarchy represents the common characteristics of all the subtypes. For now, let's assume that the only things that books and serials have in common are a library-assigned identification number and some kind of filing title. We can create an object type for catalog items using the following SQL statement from SQL*Plus:

```
CREATE OR REPLACE TYPE catalog_item_t AS OBJECT (
   id INTEGER,
   title VARCHAR2(4000),

   NOT INSTANTIABLE MEMBER FUNCTION ck_digit_okay
      RETURN BOOLEAN,
   MEMBER FUNCTION print
      RETURN VARCHAR2
) NOT INSTANTIABLE NOT FINAL;
```

This statement creates an *object type*, which is similar to a Java or C++ *class*. In relational terms, an object type is akin to a record type bundled with related functions and procedures. These subprograms are known collectively as *methods*.

The NOT FINAL keyword at the end flags the datatype as being able to serve as the *base type* or supertype from which you can derive other types. I needed to include NOT FINAL because I want to create subtypes for books and serials; if this keyword is omitted, Oracle defaults to FINAL (no subtypes allowed).

Notice also that I've marked this type specification NOT INSTANTIABLE. Although PL/SQL will let me declare a variable of type catalog_item_t, I won't be able to give it a value—not directly, anyway. Similar to a Java *abstract class*, this kind of type exists only to serve as a base type from which to create subtypes—and objects of the subtype will, presumably, be instantiable.

For demonstration and debugging purposes, I've included a print method ("print" is *not* a reserved word, by the way) as a way to describe the object in a single string. When I create a subtype, it can (and probably should) "override" this method—in other words, the subtype will include a method with the same name, but will also print the subtype's attributes. Notice that instead of making print a procedure, which would have hardcoded a decision to use something like DBMS_OUTPUT.PUT_LINE, I made it a function whose output can be redirected later. This isn't particularly object-oriented, just good design.

I've also defined a ck_digit_okay method that will return TRUE or FALSE depending on whether the "check digit" is OK. The assumption here (which is a bad one, I admit) is that all subtypes of catalog_item_t will be known by some identifier other than their library-assigned id, and these other identifiers include some concept of a check digit.* I'm only going to be dealing with books and serials, normally identified with an ISBN or ISSN, so the check digit concept applies to all the subtypes.

Here are a few further comments before moving on to the next part of the example:

- The CREATE TYPE statement above creates only an object type specification. The corresponding body, which implements the methods, will be created separately using CREATE TYPE BODY.
- Object types live in the same namespace as tables and top-level PL/SQL programs. This is one of the reasons I use the "_t" naming convention with types.
- Object types are owned by the Oracle user (schema) that created them, and this user may grant EXECUTE privilege to other users.
- You can attempt to create synonyms on object types, but unless you're using Oracle9*i* Release 2, the synonyms won't work.
- As with conventional PL/SQL programs, you can create an object type using either definer rights (the default) or invoker rights (described in Chapter 20).

* A *check digit* is a number incorporated into an identifier that is mathematically derived from the identifier's other digits. Its accuracy yields a small amount of confidence that the overall identifier has been correctly transcribed. The ISBN (International Standard Book Number) and ISSN (International Standard Serial Number)—identifiers assigned by external authorities—both contain check digits.

- Unlike some languages' object models, Oracle's model does not define a master root-level class from which all programmer-defined classes derive. Instead, you can create any number of standalone root-level datatypes such as catalog_item_t.
- If you see the compiler error *PLS-00103: Encountered the symbol ";" when expecting one of the following...*, you have probably made the common mistake of terminating the methods with a semicolon. The correct token in the type specification is a comma.

Creating a subtype

I made catalog_item_t impossible to instantiate, so now would be a good time to show how to create a subtype for book objects. In the real world, a book is a type of catalog item; this is also true in my example, in which all instances of this book_t subtype will have four attributes:

id
: Inherited from the base catalog_item_t type

title
: Also inherited from the base type

isbn
: Corresponds to the book's assigned ISBN, if any

pages
: An integer giving the number of pages in the book

In code, I can make the equivalent statement as follows:

```
 1 CREATE OR REPLACE TYPE book_t UNDER catalog_item_t (
 2    isbn VARCHAR2(13),
 3    pages INTEGER,
 4
 5    CONSTRUCTOR FUNCTION book_t (id IN INTEGER DEFAULT NULL,
 6       title IN VARCHAR2 DEFAULT NULL,
 7       isbn IN VARCHAR2 DEFAULT NULL,
 8       pages IN INTEGER DEFAULT NULL)
 9       RETURN SELF AS RESULT,
10
11    OVERRIDING MEMBER FUNCTION ck_digit_okay
12       RETURN BOOLEAN,
13
14    OVERRIDING MEMBER FUNCTION print
15       RETURN VARCHAR2
16 );
```

The interesting portions of this code are as follows:

Line 1
: You can see that the syntax for indicating a subtype is the keyword UNDER in line 1, which makes a certain amount of intuitive sense. Oracle doesn't use the

phrase AS OBJECT here because it would be redundant; the only thing that can exist "under" another is an object type.

Lines 2–3
: I need to list only those attributes that are unique to the subtype; those in the parent type are implicitly included. Oracle orders the attributes with the base type first, then the subtype, in the same order as defined in the specification.

Lines 5–15
: Here are the method declarations. We'll look at these methods more closely in the next section.

Methods

I've used two kinds of methods in the previous type definition:

Constructor method
: A function that accepts values for each attribute and assembles them into a typed object. Declared in lines 5–9 of the example.

Member method
: A function or procedure that executes in the context of an object instance—that is, it has access to the current values of each of the attributes. Declared in lines 11–12, as well as in lines 14–15 of the example.

My example shows a user-defined constructor, a feature that was introduced in Oracle9*i* Release 2. Earlier versions provided only a system-defined constructor. Creating your own constructor for each type gives you precise control over what happens at instantiation. That control can be very useful for doing extra tasks like validation and introducing controlled side effects. In addition, you can use several overloaded versions of a user-defined constructor, allowing it to adapt to a variety of calling circumstances.

To see some types and methods in action, take a look at this anonymous block:

```
1  DECLARE
2     generic_item catalog_item_t;
3     abook book_t;
4  BEGIN
5     abook := NEW book_t(title => 'Out of the Silent Planet',
6        isbn => '0-6848-238-02');
7     generic_item := abook;
8     DBMS_OUTPUT.PUT_LINE('BOOK: ' || abook.print());
9     DBMS_OUTPUT.PUT_LINE('ITEM: ' || generic_item.print());
10 END;
```

Interestingly, the objects' print invocations (lines 8 and 9) return the following:

```
BOOK: id=; title=Out of the Silent Planet; isbn=0-6848-238-02; pages=
ITEM: id=; title=Out of the Silent Planet; isbn=0-6848-238-02; pages=
```

Lines 5–6

The constructor assembles a new object and puts it into a book. My example takes advantage of PL/SQL's named notation. It supplied values for only two of the four attributes, but the constructor creates the object anyway, which is what I asked it to do.

The syntax to use any constructor follows the pattern:

```
[ NEW ] typename ( arg1, arg2, ... );
```

The NEW keyword, introduced in Oracle9*i* Release 2, is optional, but is nevertheless useful as a visual cue that the statement will create a new object.

Line 7

Something very cool happens here: even though a catalog item is not instantiable, I can assign to it an instance of a subtype, and it will even hold all the attributes that are unique to the subtype. This demonstrates one nifty aspect of "substitutability" that Oracle supports in PL/SQL, which is that by default, an object variable may hold an instance of any of its subtypes.

In English, it certainly makes sense to regard a book as a catalog item. In computerese, it's a case of "widening" or "upcasting" the generic item by adding attributes from a more specific subtype. The converse operation, narrowing, is trickier but nevertheless possible, as you'll see later.

Lines 8–9

Notice that the calls to print() use the graceful object-style invocation:

```
object.methodname( arg1, arg2, ...)
```

because it is a member method executing on an already declared and instantiated object. Which version of the print method executes for objects of different types? The one in the *most specific subtype* associated with the currently instantiated object. The selection of the method gets deferred until runtime, in a feature known as *dynamic method dispatch*. This can be very handy, although it may incur a performance cost.

Let's turn now to the body of the book_t method, so we can better understand the result we've just seen. The implementation holds two important new concepts, which I'll describe afterwards.

```
CREATE OR REPLACE TYPE BODY book_t
AS
   CONSTRUCTOR FUNCTION book_t (id IN INTEGER,
      title IN VARCHAR2,
      isbn IN VARCHAR2,
      pages IN INTEGER)
      RETURN SELF AS RESULT
   IS
   BEGIN
      SELF.id := id;
      SELF.title := title;
      SELF.isbn := isbn;
```

```
      SELF.pages := pages;
      IF isbn IS NULL OR SELF.ck_digit_okay
      THEN
         RETURN;
      ELSE
         RAISE_APPLICATION_ERROR(-20000, 'ISBN ' || isbn
            || ' has bad check digit');
      END IF;
   END;

   OVERRIDING MEMBER FUNCTION ck_digit_okay
      RETURN BOOLEAN
   IS
      subtotal PLS_INTEGER := 0;
      isbn_digits VARCHAR2(10);
   BEGIN
      /* remove dashes and spaces */
      isbn_digits := REPLACE(REPLACE(SELF.isbn, '-'), ' ');
      IF LENGTH(isbn_digits) != 10
      THEN
         RETURN FALSE;
      END IF;

      FOR nth_digit IN 1..9
      LOOP
         subtotal := subtotal +
            (11 - nth_digit) * TO_NUMBER(SUBSTR(isbn_digits, nth_digit, 1));
      END LOOP;

      /* check digit can be 'X' which has value of 10 */
      IF UPPER(SUBSTR(isbn_digits, 10, 1)) = 'X'
      THEN
         subtotal := subtotal + 10;
      ELSE
         subtotal := subtotal + TO_NUMBER(SUBSTR(isbn_digits, 10, 1));
      END IF;

      RETURN MOD(subtotal, 11) = 0;

   EXCEPTION
      WHEN OTHERS
      THEN
         RETURN FALSE;
   END;

   OVERRIDING MEMBER FUNCTION print
      RETURN VARCHAR2
   IS
   BEGIN
      RETURN 'id=' || id || '; title=' || title
         || '; isbn=' || isbn || '; pages=' || pages;
   END;
END;
```

Lines 3–21

A user-defined constructor has several rules to follow:

1. It must be declared with keywords CONSTRUCTOR FUNCTION (line 3)
2. The return clause must be RETURN SELF AS RESULT (line 7)
3. It assigns values to any of the current object's attributes (lines 10–13)
4. It ends with a bare RETURN statement or an exception (line 16; lines 18–19)

A constructor would typically assign values to as many of the attributes as it knows about. As you can see from line 14, my constructor tests the check digit before completing the construction. Notice, by the way, that the ck_digit_okay function reads the current object's isbn attribute (line 30) even before the object has passed validation.

Lines 16–17 are merely a placeholder; you should definitely take a more comprehensive approach to application-specific exceptions, as discussed in the last section of Chapter 6.

Next I'd like to discuss the use of the SELF keywords that appears throughout the type body, which, for you Java programmers, is akin to Java's `this` keyword. Translation for non-Java programmers: SELF is merely a way to refer to the invoking (current) object when writing implementations of member methods. You can use SELF by itself when referring to the entire object, or you can use dot notation to refer to an attribute or a method.

```
IF SELF.id ...

IF SELF.ck_digit_okay() ...
```

The SELF keyword is not always required inside a member method, as you can see in lines 62–63, because the current object's attribute identifiers are always in scope. Using SELF can provide attribute visibility (as in lines 10–13, where the PL/SQL compiler interprets those unqualified identifiers as the formal parameters) and help to make your code *SELF*-documenting. (Ugh, sorry about that.)

There are a few more rules I'd like to mention about this keyword:

- SELF isn't available inside static method bodies because static methods have no "current object." (I'll define static methods later in this section.)
- By default, SELF is an IN variable in functions and an IN OUT variable in procedures and constructor functions.
- You can change the default mode by including SELF as the first formal parameter.

Lines 23–56

Computing the check digit is kind of fun, but my algorithm doesn't really exploit any new object-oriented features. I will digress to mention that the exception handler is quite important here; it responds to a multitude of problems such as the TO_NUMBER function encountering a character instead of a digit.

Next, on to creating a subtype for serials:

```
CREATE OR REPLACE TYPE serial_t UNDER catalog_item_t (
   issn VARCHAR2(10),
   open_or_closed VARCHAR2(1),

   CONSTRUCTOR FUNCTION serial_t (id IN INTEGER DEFAULT NULL,
      title IN VARCHAR2 DEFAULT NULL,
      issn IN VARCHAR2 DEFAULT NULL,
      open_or_closed IN VARCHAR2 DEFAULT NULL)
      RETURN SELF AS RESULT,

   OVERRIDING MEMBER FUNCTION ck_digit_okay
      RETURN BOOLEAN,

   OVERRIDING MEMBER FUNCTION print
      RETURN VARCHAR2
) NOT FINAL;
```

Again, no new features appear in this type, but it does give another example of subtyping. A serial item in this model will have its own constructor, its own version of validating the check digit, and its own way to print itself.*

In addition to constructor and member methods, Oracle supports two other categories of methods:

Static method
: A function or procedure invoked independently of any instantiated objects. Static methods behave a lot like conventional PL/SQL procedures or functions. See the sidebar "Static Method as Pseudo-Constructor" for an example.

Comparison method
: That is, a *map* or *order* method. These are special member methods that let you program what Oracle should do when it needs to compare two objects of this datatype—for example, in an equality test in PL/SQL or when sorting objects in SQL.

One final point before moving on. Objects follow PL/SQL's general convention that uninitialized variables are null;† the precise term is *atomically null*. As with collections, when an object is null, you cannot simply assign values to its attributes. Take a look at this short example:

```
DECLARE
   mybook book_t;       -- declared, but not initialized
BEGIN
   IF mybook IS NULL  -- this will be TRUE; it is atomically null
```

* In case you're curious, the open_or_closed attribute will be either (O)pen, meaning that the library can continue to modify the catalog entry (perhaps they do not own all the issues), or (C)losed, meaning that the catalog entry is complete.

† Associative arrays are a significant exception; they are non-null but empty when first declared.

```
      THEN
         mybook.title := 'Learning Oracle PL/SQL'; -- this line raises...
      END IF;
   EXCEPTION
      WHEN ACCESS_INTO_NULL                       -- ...this predefined exception
      THEN
         ...
   END;
```

Before assigning values to the attributes, you *must* initialize (instantiate) the entire object in one of three ways: by using a constructor method; via direct assignment from another object; or via a fetch from the database, as the next section discusses.

> **Static Method as Pseudo-Constructor**
>
> In Oracle8*i* through Oracle9*i* Release 1, the closest thing you could get to a user-defined constructor was a static method that returned an object created by the system-defined constructor. For example:
>
> ```
> STATIC FUNCTION make (id IN INTEGER, title IN VARCHAR2, isbn IN VARCHAR2,
>    pages IN INTEGER)
>    RETURN book_t
> IS
> BEGIN
>    IF <various attribute validation tests pass...>
>    THEN
>       RETURN book_t(id, title, isbn, pages);
>    ELSE
>       RAISE <some appropriate exception>;
>    END IF;
> END;
> ```
>
> The highlighted code shows where I am using the system-generated constructor, a function Oracle makes available as soon as you create an instantiable type. The constructor always has the same name as the object type, and requires a value for each attribute, in the default order in which attributes are declared in the object type definition. Calling the make function looks like a typical PL/SQL function call:
>
> ```
> DECLARE
>    a_book book_t := book_t.make(id => 111);
> ```
>
> Of course, static methods are good for other uses, too.

Storing, Retrieving, and Using Persistent Objects

Thus far, I've only been discussing the definition of the datatypes and the instantiation of objects in the memory of running programs. Fortunately, that's not even half the story! Oracle wouldn't be Oracle if there were no way to store an object in the database.

Method Chaining

An object whose type definition looks like this:

```
CREATE OR REPLACE TYPE chaindemo_t AS OBJECT (
   x NUMBER, y VARCHAR2(10), z DATE,
   MEMBER FUNCTION setx (x IN NUMBER) RETURN chaindemo_t,
   MEMBER FUNCTION sety (y IN VARCHAR2) RETURN chaindemo_t,
   MEMBER FUNCTION setz (z IN DATE) RETURN chaindemo_t);
```

provides the ability to "chain" its methods together. For example:

```
DECLARE
   c chaindemo_t := chaindemo_t(NULL, NULL, NULL);
BEGIN
   c := c.setx(1).sety('foo').setz(sysdate);  -- chained invocation
```

The executable statement above really just acts as the equivalent of:

```
c := c.setx(1);
c := c.sety('foo');
c := c.setz(sysdate);
```

Each function returns a typed object as the input to the next function in the chain. The implementation of one of the methods appears in the following code (the others are similar):

```
MEMBER FUNCTION setx (x IN NUMBER) RETURN chaindemo_t IS
   l_self chaindemo_t := SELF;
BEGIN
   l_self.x := x;
   RETURN l_self;
END;
```

Here are some rules about chaining:

- You cannot use a function's return value as an IN OUT parameter to the next function in the chain. Functions return read-only values.
- Methods are invoked in order from left to right.
- The return value of a chained method must be of the object type expected by the method to its right.
- A chained call can include at most a single procedure.
- If your chained call includes a procedure, it must be the rightmost method in the chain.

There are at least two main ways that I could physically store the library catalog as modeled thus far: either as one big table of catalog objects or as a series of smaller tables, one for each subtype. I'll show the former arrangement, which could begin as follows:

```
CREATE TABLE catalog_items OF catalog_item_t
   (CONSTRAINT catalog_items_pk PRIMARY KEY (id));
```

This statement tells Oracle to build an object table called catalog_items, each row of which will be an object of type catalog_item_t. An object table generally has one column per attribute. Remember, though, that catalog_item_t isn't instantiable, and each row in the table will actually be of a subtype such as a book or serial item. So, somewhere in this table, Oracle will have to come up with a place to store attribute values of each possible subtype. It does this by adding hidden columns to the table, one column per unique subtype attribute. From an object programming point of view, that's pretty cool, because it helps preserve the abstraction of the catalog item, yet provides a way to expose the additional subtype information when needed.

Moving right along, the CONSTRAINT clause designates the id column as the primary key. Yes, object tables can have primary keys too. And, by default, Oracle will also create a system-generated object identifier (OID), as described next.

Object identity

In the same way that relational databases include unique identifiers for every row in every table, object-oriented programming systems maintain the unique identity of each object. Generally, OOP systems assign invisible arbitrary numbers to serve as object handles. For any object table, Oracle can base its object identifier on one of two things:

The primary key value
: To use this feature, use the clause OBJECT IDENTIFIER IS PRIMARY KEY at the end of the CREATE TABLE statement.

A system-generated value
: In this case, Oracle adds another hidden column named SYS_NC_OID$ to the table and populates it with a unique 16-byte RAW value. This is the default behavior.

Not all objects have an object identifier. In particular, objects stored in PL/SQL variables lack a referenceable OID, as do column objects. Oracle takes the view that a column object is dependent on the row's primary key, and should not be independently identified.*

Which kind of OID should you use? While primary-key based OIDs typically use less storage than system-generated OIDs, the latter offer unique benefits, as I'll show later. For a more complete discussion of the pros and cons of these two approaches, check out Oracle's document *Application Developer's Guide—Object-Relational Features*. For now, you should know that a system-generated OID is:

* A contrary view is held by relational industry experts who assert that OIDs should not be used for row identification, and that *only* column objects should have OIDs. See Hugh Darwen and C. J. Date, "The Third Manifesto," *SIGMOD Record*, Volume 24 Number 1, March 1995.

Opaque

Although your programs can use the OID indirectly, you don't typically see its value.

Potentially globally unique across databases

The OID space makes provisions for up to 2^{128} objects (definitely "many" by the reckoning of the Hottentots).* In theory, these OIDs could allow object navigation across distributed databases without embedding explicit database links.

Immutable

Immutable in this context means incapable of update. Even after export and import, the OID remains the same, unlike a ROWID. To "change" an OID, you would have to delete and re-create the object.

The VALUE function

Data manipulation on object tables introduces a few twists into the SQL syntax. For example, I can create an object with my constructor and use it in a somewhat normal INSERT statement:†

```
INSERT INTO catalog_items
   VALUES (NEW book_t(10003, 'Perelandra', '0-684-82382-9', 222));
INSERT INTO catalog_items
   VALUES (NEW serial_t(10004, 'Time', '0040-781X', 'O'));
```

> **Emulating Global Constants with Object Methods**
>
> Students of the design approaches advocated elsewhere in this book series will immediately object to the hardcoding of magic values such as 'O' for Open. I could substitute a package constant there, or I could create a static method called something like open_c, which would return the chosen value. I would want to use a static method for this purpose because Oracle object types do not support global constants, global variables, or global anything, the way that packages do. In this case, my INSERT would look like this:
>
> ```
> INSERT INTO catalog_items
>    VALUES (NEW serial_t(10002, 'Time', '0040-781X', serial_t.open_c));
> ```
>
> The body of the corresponding static method is just a `RETURN 'O'` statement, but this coding practice has advantages such as ensuring consistency and accommodating requirements changes in the future.

* The Hottentots had a four-valued counting system: 1, 2, 3, and "many."

† I would prefer to use named notation in these static function calls, but Oracle does not support named notation when calling any kind of PL/SQL function from SQL (at least as of Oracle9*i* Release 2).

To retrieve an object from the database, Oracle provides the VALUE function in SQL. VALUE accepts a single argument, which must be a table alias in the current FROM clause, and returns an object of the type on which the table is defined. It looks like this in a SELECT statement:

```
SELECT VALUE(c)
  FROM catalog_items c;
```

I like short abbreviations as table aliases, which explains the c. The VALUE function returns an opaque series of bits to the calling program rather than a record of column values. SQL*Plus, however, has built-in features to display objects, returning the following result from that query:

```
VALUE(C)(ID, TITLE)
-------------------------------------------------
BOOK_T(10003, 'Perelandra', '0-684-82382-9', 222)
SERIAL_T(10004, 'Time', '0040-781X', 'O')
```

PL/SQL also has features to deal with fetching objects. Start with a properly typed local variable:

```
DECLARE
   catalog_item catalog_item_t;
   CURSOR ccur IS
      SELECT VALUE(c)
        FROM catalog_items c;
BEGIN
   OPEN ccur;
   FETCH ccur INTO catalog_item;
   DBMS_OUTPUT.PUT_LINE('I fetched item #' || catalog_item.id);
   CLOSE ccur;
END;
```

The argument to PUT_LINE uses *variable.attribute* notation to yield the attribute value, resulting in the output:

```
I fetched item #10003
```

The fetch assigns the object to the local variable catalog_item, which is of the base type; this makes sense because I don't know in advance which subtype I'll be retrieving. My fetch simply assigns the object—defined on some subtype I don't know in advance—into the variable. This is not only elegant, but also quite useful!

The example also illustrates (by printing catalog_item.id) that I have immediate access to the base type's attributes.

In case you're wondering, normal cursor attribute tricks work too; the previous anonymous block is equivalent to:

```
DECLARE
   CURSOR ccur IS
      SELECT VALUE(c) obj
        FROM catalog_items c;
   arec ccur%ROWTYPE;
```

```
BEGIN
   OPEN ccur;
   FETCH ccur INTO arec;
   DBMS_OUTPUT.PUT_LINE('I fetched item #' || arec.obj.id);
   CLOSE ccur;
END;
```

If I just wanted to print out all of the object's attributes, I could, of course, use the print method I've already defined. It's legal to use this because it has been defined at the root type level and implemented in the subtypes; at runtime, Oracle will find the appropriate overriding implementations in each subtype. Ah, the beauty of dynamic method dispatch.

As a matter of fact, the VALUE function supports dot notation, which provides access to attributes and methods—but only those specified on the base type. For example, the following:

```
SELECT VALUE(c).id, VALUE(c).print( )
  FROM catalog_items c;
```

yields:

```
VALUE(C).ID VALUE(C).PRINT( )
----------- ---------------------------------------------------------
      10003 id=10003; title=Perelandra; isbn=0-684-82382-9; pages=222
      10004 id=10004; title=Time; issn=0040-781X; open_or_closed=Open
```

If I happen to be working in a client environment that doesn't understand Oracle objects, I might want to take advantage of such features.

But what if I want to read only the attribute(s) unique to a particular subtype? I might first try something like this:

```
SELECT VALUE(c).issn   /* Error. Direct access to subtype attribute won't work. */
  FROM catalog_items c;
```

This gives me *ORA-00904: invalid column name*. Oracle is telling me that an object of the parent type provides no direct access to subtype attributes. I might try declaring book of book_t and assigning the subtyped object to it, hoping that it will expose the "hidden" attributes:

```
book := catalog_item;  /* Error. Direct assignment to subtype won't work either. */
```

This time I get *PLS-00382: expression is of wrong type*. What's going on? The non-intuitive answer to that mystery appears in the next section.

Before we move on, here are a few final notes about performing DML on object relational tables:

- For object tables built on object types that lack subtypes, it is possible to select, insert, update, and delete all column values using conventional SQL statements. In this way, some object-oriented and relational programs can share the same underlying data.

- You cannot perform conventional relational DML on hidden columns that exist as a result of subtype-dependent attributes. You must use an "object DML" approach.
- To update an entire persistent object from a PL/SQL program, you can use an object DML statement such as:

  ```
  UPDATE catalog_items c SET c = object_variable WHERE ...
  ```

  That will update all the attributes (columns), including those unique to a subtype.
- The only good way I have found to update a specific column that is unique to a subtype is to update the entire object. For example, to change the page count to 1000 for the book with id 10007, specify:

  ```
  UPDATE catalog_items c
     SET c = NEW book_t(c.id, c.title, c.publication_date, c.subject_refs,
                       (SELECT TREAT(VALUE(y) AS book_t).isbn
                          FROM catalog_items y
                         WHERE id = 10007),
                   1000)
    WHERE id = 10007;
  ```

The TREAT function

If I'm dealing with a PL/SQL variable typed as a supertype and it's populated with some subtype value, how can I gain access to the subtype-specific attributes and methods? In my case, I want to treat a generic catalog item as the more narrowly defined book. This operation is called *narrowing* or *downcasting*, and is something the compiler can't, or won't, accept. What I need to use is the special Oracle function called TREAT:

```
DECLARE
   book book_t;
   catalog_item catalog_item_t := NEW book_t();
BEGIN
   book := TREAT (catalog_item AS book_t);    /* Requires 9i R2 */
END;
/
```

or, in SQL (Oracle9*i* Release 1 PL/SQL doesn't directly support TREAT):

```
DECLARE
   book book_t;
   catalog_item catalog_item_t := book_t(NULL, NULL, NULL, NULL);
BEGIN
   SELECT TREAT (catalog_item AS book_t)
     INTO book
     FROM DUAL;
END;
```

The general syntax of TREAT is:

```
TREAT (object_instance AS subtype) [ . { attribute | method( args...) } ]
```

where *object_instance* is a value of a particular supertype in an object hierarchy, and *subtype* is the name of a subtype in the same hierarchy. It won't compile if you attempt to treat one type as another from a different type hierarchy. One nifty feature of TREAT is that if you have supplied an object from the correct type hierarchy, it will return either the downcasted object or NULL—but not an error.

As with VALUE, you can use dot notation with TREAT to specify an attribute or method of the TREATed object. For example:

```
DBMS_OUTPUT.PUT_LINE(TREAT (VALUE(c) AS serial_t).issn);
```

If I want to iterate over all the objects in the table in a type-aware fashion, I can do something like this:

```
DECLARE
   CURSOR ccur IS
      SELECT VALUE(c) item FROM catalog_items c;
   arec ccur%ROWTYPE;
BEGIN
   FOR arec IN ccur
   LOOP
      CASE
         WHEN arec.item IS OF (book_t)
         THEN
            DBMS_OUTPUT.PUT_LINE('Found a book with ISBN '
               || TREAT(arec.item AS book_t).isbn);
         WHEN arec.item IS OF (serial_t)
         THEN
            DBMS_OUTPUT.PUT_LINE('Found a serial with ISSN '
               || TREAT(arec.item AS serial_t).issn);
         ELSE
            DBMS_OUTPUT.PUT_LINE('Found unknown catalog item');
      END CASE;
   END LOOP;
END;
```

This block introduces the IS OF predicate to test an object's type. Although the syntax is somewhat brazen:

```
object IS OF ( [ ONLY ] typename )
```

the IS OF operator is much more limited than one would hope: it works only on object types, not on any of Oracle's core datatypes like NUMBER or DATE. Also, it will return an error if the *object* is not in the same type hierarchy as *typename*.

Notice the ONLY keyword. The default behavior—without ONLY—is to return TRUE if the object is of the given type or any of its subtypes. If you use ONLY, the expression won't check the subtypes, and returns TRUE only if the type is an exact match.

The IS OF predicate, like TREAT itself, became available in Oracle9*i* SQL, although direct support for it in PL/SQL didn't appear until Oracle9*i* Release 2. As a Release 1 workaround, I could define one or more additional methods in the type tree, taking advantage of dynamic method dispatch to perform the desired operation at the correct level in the hierarchy. The "correct" solution to the narrowing problem depends not just on the version number, though, but also on what my application is supposed to accomplish.

For the moment, I'd like to move on to another interesting area: exploring the features Oracle offers when (not if!) you have to deal with changes in application design.

Evolution and Creation

I have little but good news here: Oracle9*i* is light years beyond Oracle8*i* in the area known as *type evolution*. That is, Oracle now lets you make a variety of changes to object types, even if you have created tables full of objects that depend on the type. Yippee!

Earlier in this chapter, I did a quick-and-dirty job of defining catalog_item_t. As almost any friendly librarian would point out, it might also be nice to carry publication date information* about all the holdings in the library. So I just hack out the following (no doubt while my DBA cringes):

```
ALTER TYPE catalog_item_t
   ADD ATTRIBUTE publication_date VARCHAR2(400)
   CASCADE INCLUDING TABLE DATA;
```

Et voilà! Oracle propagates this change to perform the needed physical alterations in the corresponding table(s). It appends the attribute to the bottom of the supertype's attributes, and adds a column after the last column of the supertype in the corresponding object table. A DESCRIBE of the type now looks like this:

```
SQL> DESC catalog_item_t
 catalog_item_t is NOT FINAL
 catalog_item_t is NOT INSTANTIABLE
 Name                                      Null?    Type
 ----------------------------------------- -------- ----------------------------
 ID                                                 NUMBER(38)
 TITLE                                              VARCHAR2(4000)
 PUBLICATION_DATE                                   VARCHAR2(400)

METHOD
------
 MEMBER FUNCTION CK_DIGIT_OKAY RETURNS BOOLEAN
 CK_DIGIT_OKAY IS NOT INSTANTIABLE

METHOD
------
 MEMBER FUNCTION PRINT RETURNS VARCHAR2
```

* I can't make this attribute an Oracle DATE type, though, because sometimes it's just a year, sometimes a month or a quarter, and occasionally something completely offbeat. I might get really clever and make this a nifty object type...well, maybe in the movie version.

And a DESCRIBE of the table now looks like this:

```
SQL> DESC catalog_items
 Name                                      Null?    Type
 ----------------------------------------- -------- ----------------------------
 ID                                        NOT NULL NUMBER(38)
 TITLE                                              VARCHAR2(4000)
 PUBLICATION_DATE                                   VARCHAR2(400)
```

In fact, the ALTER TYPE statement fixes *nearly* everything—though alas, it isn't smart enough to rewrite my methods. My constructors are a particular issue because I need to alter their signature. Hey, no problem! I can change a method signature by dropping and then re-creating the method.

When evolving object types, you may encounter the message *ORA-22337: the type of accessed object has been evolved.* This condition may prevent you from doing a DESCRIBE on the type. You might think that recompiling it will fix the problem, but it won't. Moreover, if you have hard dependencies on the type, Oracle won't let you recompile the object type specification. To get rid of this error, disconnect and then reconnect your Oracle session. This clears various buffers and enables DESCRIBE to see the new version.

To drop the method from the book type specification, specify:

```
ALTER TYPE book_t
   DROP CONSTRUCTOR FUNCTION book_t (id INTEGER DEFAULT NULL,
      title VARCHAR2 DEFAULT NULL,
      isbn VARCHAR2 DEFAULT NULL,
      pages INTEGER DEFAULT NULL)
      RETURN SELF AS RESULT
   CASCADE;
```

Notice that I supply the full function specification. That will guarantee that I'm dropping the correct method, as multiple overloaded versions of it might exist. (Strictly speaking, though, the DEFAULTs are not required, but I left them in because I'm usually just cutting and pasting this stuff.)

The corresponding add-method operation is easy:

```
ALTER TYPE book_t
   ADD CONSTRUCTOR FUNCTION book_t (id INTEGER DEFAULT NULL,
      title VARCHAR2 DEFAULT NULL,
      publication_date VARCHAR2 DEFAULT NULL,
      isbn VARCHAR2 DEFAULT NULL,
      pages INTEGER DEFAULT NULL)
      RETURN SELF AS RESULT
   CASCADE;
```

Easy for me, anyway; Oracle is doing a lot more stuff behind the scenes than I will probably ever know.

The next steps (not illustrated in this chapter) would be to alter the serial_t type in a similar fashion and then rebuild the two corresponding object type bodies with the CREATE OR REPLACE TYPE BODY statement. I would also want to inspect all the methods to see whether any changes would make sense elsewhere (for example, it would be a good idea to include the publication date in the print method).

By the way, you can drop a type using the statement:

```
DROP TYPE typename [ FORCE ];
```

Use the FORCE option with care because it cannot be undone. Any object types or object tables that depend on a force-dropped type will be rendered permanently useless. If there are any columns defined on a force-dropped type, Oracle marks them as UNUSED and makes them inaccessible. If your type is a subtype and you have used the supertype in any table definitions, you might benefit from this form of the statement:

```
DROP TYPE subtypename VALIDATE;
```

VALIDATE causes Oracle to look through the table and drop the type as long as there are no instances of the subtype, avoiding the disastrous consequences of the FORCE option.

Now let's visit the strange and fascinating world of *object referencing*.

Back to Pointers?

The object-relational features in Oracle include the ability to store an *object reference* or *REF value*. A REF is a *logical pointer* to a particular row in an object table. Oracle stores inside each reference the following information:

- The target row's primary key or system-generated object identifier
- A unique identifier to designate the table
- At the programmer's option, a hint on the row's physical whereabouts on disk, in the form of its ROWID

The literal contents of a REF are not terribly useful unless you happen to like looking at long hex strings:

```
SQL> SELECT REF(c) FROM catalog_items c WHERE ROWNUM = 1;

REF(C)
--------------------------------------------------------------------------------
00002802099FC431FBE5F20599E0340003BA0F1F139FC431FBE5F10599E0340003BA0F1F130240000C0000
```

However, your queries and programs can use a REF to retrieve a row object without having to name the table where the object resides. Huh? Queries without table names? A pointer in a relational database? Let's take a look at how this feature might work in our library catalog.

Using REFs

Libraries classify their holdings within a strictly controlled set of subjects. For example, the Library of Congress might classify the book you're reading now in the following three subjects:

- Oracle (Computer file)
- PL/SQL (Computer program language)
- Relational databases

The Library of Congress uses a hierarchical subject tree: "Computer file" is the broader subject or parent of "Oracle," and "Computer program language" is the broader subject for "PL/SQL."

When classifying things, any number of subjects may apply to a particular catalog item in a many-to-many (M:M) relationship between subjects and holdings. In my simple library catalog, I will make one long list (table) of all available subjects. While a relational approach to the problem would then establish an "intersection entity" to resolve the M:M relationship, I have other options in object-relational land.

I will start with an object type for each subject:

```
CREATE TYPE subject_t AS OBJECT (
   name VARCHAR2(2000),
   broader_term_ref REF subject_t
);
```

Each subject has a name and a broader term. However, I'm not going to store the term itself as a second attribute, but instead a reference to it. The third line of this type definition shows that I've typed the broader_term_ref attribute as a REF to a same-typed object. It's kind of like Oracle's old EMP table, with a MGR column whose value identifies the manager's record in the same table.

I now create a table of subjects:

```
CREATE TABLE subjects OF subject_t
   (CONSTRAINT subject_pk PRIMARY KEY (name),
   CONSTRAINT subject_self_ref FOREIGN KEY (broader_term_ref)
      REFERENCES subjects);
```

The foreign key begs a bit of explanation. Even though it references a table with a relational primary key, because the foreign key datatype is a REF, Oracle knows to use the table's object identifier instead. This support for the REF-based foreign key constraint is a good example of Oracle's bridge between the object and relational worlds.

Here are a few unsurprising inserts into this table (just using the default constructor):

```
INSERT INTO subjects VALUES (subject_t('Computer file', NULL));
INSERT INTO subjects VALUES (subject_t('Computer program language', NULL));
INSERT INTO subjects VALUES (subject_t('Relational databases', NULL));
INSERT INTO subjects VALUES (subject_t('Oracle',
   (SELECT REF(s) FROM subjects s WHERE name = 'Computer file')));
```

```
INSERT INTO subjects VALUES (subject_t('PL/SQL',
   (SELECT REF(s) FROM subjects s WHERE name = 'Computer program language')));
```

For what it's worth, you can list the contents of the subjects table, as shown here:

```
SQL> SELECT VALUE(s) FROM subjects s;

VALUE(S)(NAME, BROADER_TERM_REF)
-------------------------------------------------------------------------------
SUBJECT_T('Computer file', NULL)
SUBJECT_T('Computer program language', NULL)
SUBJECT_T('Oracle', 00002202089FC431FBE6FB0599E0340003BA0F1F139FC431FBE6690599E03
40003BA0F1F13)

SUBJECT_T('PL/SQL', 00002202089FC431FBE6FC0599E0340003BA0F1F139FC431FBE6690599E03
40003BA0F1F13)

SUBJECT_T('Relational databases', NULL)
```

Even if that's interesting, it's not terribly useful. However, what's both interesting and useful is that I can easily have Oracle automatically "resolve" or follow those pointers. For example, I can use the DEREF function to navigate those ugly REFs back to their target row in the table:

```
SELECT s.name, DEREF(s.broader_term_ref).name bt
  FROM subjects s;
```

Dereferencing is like an automatic join, although it's more of an outer join than an equi-join. In other words, if the reference is null or invalid, the driving row will still appear, but the target object (and column) will be null.

Oracle introduced a dereferencing shortcut that is really quite elegant. You only need to use dot notation to indicate what attribute you wish to retrieve from the target object:

```
SELECT s.name, s.broader_term_ref.name bt FROM subjects s;
```

Both queries produce the following output:

```
NAME                           BT
------------------------------ ------------------------------
Computer file
Computer program language
Oracle                         Computer file
PL/SQL                         Computer program language
Relational databases
```

As a point of syntax, notice that both forms require a table alias, as in the following:

```
SELECT table_alias.ref_column_name
   FROM tablename table_alias
```

You can also use REF-based navigation in the WHERE clause. To show all the subjects whose broader term is "Computer program language," specify:

```
SELECT VALUE(s).name FROM subjects s
 WHERE s.broader_term_ref.name = 'Computer program language';
```

Although my example table uses a reference to itself, in reality a reference can point to an object in any object table in the same database. To see this in action, let's return to the definition of the base type catalog_item_t. I can now add an attribute that will hold a collection of REFs, so that each cataloged item can be associated with any number of subjects. First, I'll create a collection of subject references:

```
CREATE TYPE subject_refs_t AS TABLE OF REF subject_t;
```

And now I'll allow every item in the catalog to be associated with any number of subjects:

```
ALTER TYPE catalog_item_t
   ADD ATTRIBUTE subject_refs subject_refs_t
   CASCADE INCLUDING TABLE DATA;
```

Now (skipping gleefully over the boring parts about modifying any affected methods in the dependent types), I might insert a catalog record using the following exotic SQL statement:

```
INSERT INTO catalog_items
VALUES (NEW book_t(10007,
   'Oracle PL/SQL Programming',
   'Sept 1997',
    CAST(MULTISET(SELECT REF(s)
                    FROM subjects s
                   WHERE name IN ('Oracle', 'PL/SQL', 'Relational databases'))
      AS subject_refs_t),
   '1-56592-335-9',
   987));
```

The CAST/MULTISET clause performs an on-the-fly conversion of the subject REFs into a collection, as explained in the "Collection Pseudo-Functions" section of Chapter 11.

Here is a slightly more understandable PL/SQL equivalent:

```
DECLARE
   subrefs subject_refs_t;
BEGIN
   SELECT REF(s)
     BULK COLLECT INTO subrefs
     FROM subjects s
    WHERE name IN ('Oracle', 'PL/SQL', 'Relational databases');

   INSERT INTO catalog_items VALUES (NEW book_t(10007,
      'Oracle PL/SQL Programming', 'Sept 1997', subrefs, '1-56592-335-9', 987));
END;
```

In English, that code says "grab the REFs to three particular subjects, and store them with this particular book."

REF-based navigation is so cool that I'll show another example using some more of that long-haired SQL:

```
SELECT VALUE(s).name
  || ' (' || VALUE(s).broader_term_ref.name || ')' plsql_subjects
```

```
    FROM TABLE(SELECT subject_refs
                 FROM catalog_items
                WHERE id=10007) s;
```

This example retrieves values from the subjects table, including the name of each broader subject term, without ever mentioning the subjects table by name. (The TABLE function converts a collection into a virtual table.) Here are the results:

```
PLSQL_SUBJECTS
------------------------------------
Relational databases ()
PL/SQL (Computer program language)
Oracle (Computer file)
```

Other than automatic navigation from SQL, what *else* does all this effort offer the PL/SQL programmer? Er, well, not a whole lot. References have a slight edge, at least as theory goes, in that they are *strongly typed*—that is, a REF-typed column can point only to an object that is defined on the same object type as the REF. Contrast this behavior with foreign keys, which can point to any old thing as long as the target is constrained to be a primary key or has a unique index on it.

The REFTOHEX function

Earlier, I used the following query to show you the underlying hex value of a REF:

```
SELECT REF(c) FROM catalog_items c WHERE ROWNUM = 1;
```

The results of this query were displayed in hexadecimal because SQL*Plus knows how to convert the binary data of a REF to a printed hexadecimal form. You can explicitly specify that same conversion using the built-in REFTOHEX function, as follows:

```
SELECT REFTOHEX(REF(c)) FROM catalog_items c WHERE ROWNUM = 1;
```

If you're executing a query from SQL*Plus, using REFTOHEX is just so much extra typing. However, if you are executing a query from within PL/SQL and you want to return the hexadecimal value of a REF, you can use REFTOHEX in your SQL query to make your intentions, and the resulting conversion, explicit.

It would be ideal if REFTOHEX could also be invoked directly from PL/SQL. For example, the following code retrieves a REF from the database (itemref) and attempts to use REFTOHEX to convert that REF into its hexadecimal representation:

```
DECLARE
   itemref REF catalog_item_t;
   itemref_as_hex VARCHAR2(100);
BEGIN
   -- Retrieve a REF value from the database
   SELECT REF(c) INTO itemref
     FROM catalog_items c WHERE ROWNUM = 1;

   -- Use REFTOHEX to get the hexadecimal representation of the REF value
```

```
        itemref_as_hex := REFTOHEX(itemref);

        --Display the length of the result, and the result itself.
        DBMS_OUTPUT.PUT_LINE(LENGTH(itemref_as_hex));
        DBMS_OUTPUT.PUT_LINE(itemref_as_hex);

    END;
```

Unfortunately, this piece of code doesn't work. Try it, and you'll get the following results:

```
    ERROR at line 10:
    ORA-06550: line 10, column 22:
    PLS-00201: identifier 'REFTOHEX' must be declared
    ORA-06550: line 10, column 4:
    PL/SQL: Statement ignored
```

This message footprint indicates that PL/SQL can't always perform the same functions as SQL. Even though Oracle9*i* advertises a single parser shared by PL/SQL and SQL, support for REFTOHEX obviously requires something deeper than parsing. I doubt that there is any need to retrieve additional data from the database to convert from a REF to a hexadecimal value, so I would expect support for this particular function from PL/SQL. It would be great if application developers didn't face surprises like this one, but Oracle has added support in PL/SQL for a number of other built-in functions (like NVL2 and TREAT), so at least the trend is in the right direction.

The UTL_REF package

The UTL_REF built-in package performs the dereferencing operation without an explicit SQL call, allowing your application to perform a programmatic lock, select, update, or delete of an object given only its REF. As a short example, I can add a method such as the following to the subject_t type:

```
MEMBER FUNCTION print_bt (str IN VARCHAR2)
   RETURN VARCHAR2
IS
   bt subject_t;
BEGIN
   IF SELF.broader_term_ref IS NULL
   THEN
      RETURN str;
   ELSE
      UTL_REF.SELECT_OBJECT(SELF.broader_term_ref, bt);
      RETURN bt.print_bt(NVL(str,SELF.name)) || ' (' || bt.name || ')';
   END IF;
END;
```

This recursive procedure walks the hierarchy from the current subject to the "topmost" broader subject.

> **In C, Better Support for REFs**
>
> While PL/SQL offers few overwhelming reasons to program with object references, you would find more benefits to this programming style with the Oracle Call Interface (OCI), Oracle's C/C++ language interface, or even with Pro*C. In addition to the ability to navigate REFs, similar to what you find in PL/SQL, OCI provides *complex object retrieval* (COR). With COR, you can retrieve an object and all its REFerenced neighbors in a single call. Both OCI and Pro*C support a client-side object cache, allowing an application to load objects into client memory and to manipulate (select, insert, update, delete) them as if they were in the database. Then, in a single call, the application can flush all the changes back to the server. In addition to improving the programmer's functional repertoire, these features reduce the number of network round trips, improving overall performance.

When using the procedures in UTL_REF, the REF argument you supply must be typed to match your object argument. The complete list of subprograms in UTL_REF follows:

`UTL_REF.SELECT_OBJECT (`*`obj_ref`*` IN, `*`object_variable`*` OUT);`
: Finds the object to which *obj_ref* points and retrieves a copy in *object_variable*.

`UTL_REF.SELECT_OBJECT_WITH_CR (`*`obj_ref`*` IN, `*`object_variable`*` OUT);`
: Like SELECT_OBJECT, but makes a copy ("snapshot") of the object. This version exists to avoid a mutating table error (ORA-4091), which can occur if you are updating an object table and setting the value to a function, but the function uses UTL_REF to dereference an object from the same table you're updating.

`UTL_REF.LOCK_OBJECT (`*`obj_ref`*` IN);`
: Locks the object to which *obj_ref* points but does not fetch it yet.

`UTL_REF.LOCK_OBJECT (`*`obj_ref`*` IN, `*`object_variable`*` OUT);`
: Locks the object to which *obj_ref* points and retrieves a copy in *object_variable*.

`UTL_REF.UPDATE_OBJECT (`*`obj_ref`*` IN, `*`object_variable`*` IN);`
: Replaces the object to which *obj_ref* points with the value supplied in *object_variable*. This operation updates all of the columns in the corresponding object table.

`UTL_REF.DELETE_OBJECT (`*`obj_ref`*` IN);`
: Deletes the object to which *obj_ref* points.

REFs and type hierarchies

All of the above subprograms are procedures, not functions,* and the parameters have the characteristic of being semi-weakly typed. In other words, Oracle doesn't

* I'm somewhat mystified by this; it would be a lot handier if at least SELECT_OBJECT were a function.

need to know at compile time what the precise datatypes are, as long as the REF matches the object variable.

I'd like to mention a few more technical points about REFs when dealing with type hierarchies. Assume the following program declarations:

```
DECLARE
   book book_t;
   item catalog_item_t;
   itemref REF catalog_item_t;
   bookref REF book_t;
```

As you have seen, assigning a REF to an "exactly-typed" variable works fine:

```
SELECT REF(c) INTO itemref
  FROM catalog_items c WHERE id = 10007;
```

Similarly, you can dereference an object into the exact type, using:

```
UTL_REF.select_object(itemref, item);
```

or:

```
SELECT DEREF(itemref) INTO item FROM DUAL;
```

However, you cannot directly narrow a REF:

```
SELECT REF(c)
  INTO bookref      /* Error */
  FROM catalog_items c WHERE id = 10007;
```

One way to narrow a REF would be to use TREAT, which understands how to narrow references:

```
SELECT TREAT(REF(c) AS REF book_t)
  INTO bookref
  FROM catalog_items c WHERE id = 10007;
```

You can always widen or upcast while dereferencing, whether you are using:

```
UTL_REF.select_object(TREAT(bookref AS ref catalog_item_t), item);
```

(notice the explicit upcast) or:

```
SELECT DEREF(bookref) INTO item FROM DUAL;
```

And, although you cannot narrow or downcast while dereferencing with DEREF, as shown here:

```
SELECT DEREF(itemref)
  INTO book   /* Error */
  FROM DUAL;
```

TREAT can again come to the rescue:

```
SELECT DEREF(TREAT(itemref AS REF book_t))
  INTO book
  FROM catalog_items c WHERE id = 10007;
```

Or, amazingly enough, you can also perform an implicit downcast with UTL_REF:

```
UTL_REF.select_object(itemref, book);
```

Got all that?

Dangling REFs

Here are a few final comments about object references:

- A REF may point to nothing, in which case it's known as a *dangling REF*. This can happen when you store a reference to an object and then delete the object. Oracle permits such nonsense if you fail to define a foreign key constraint that would prevent it.
- To locate references that point to nothing, use the IS DANGLING operator:

  ```
  SELECT VALUE(s) FROM subjects s
  WHERE broader_term_ref IS DANGLING;
  ```

Now let's move on and take a look at some Oracle features for dealing with data whose type is either unknown or varying.

Generic Generics: The ANY Datatypes

As discussed in Chapter 12, Oracle provides several built-in datatypes that can extend the type model into the world of generics. With the built-in type called ANYDATA, a PL/SQL program can, for instance, store, retrieve, and operate on a data item declared on any SQL type in the database—without having to create dozens of overloaded versions. Sounds pretty good, right?

Before I demonstrate, here's a review of the built-in packages and types in this family:

ANYDATA type
: Encapsulation of any SQL-datatyped item in a self-descriptive data structure.

ANYTYPE type
: When used with ANYDATA, reads the description of the data structure. Can be used separately to create transient object types.

DBMS_TYPES package
: A package consisting only of constants that help interpret which datatype is being used in the ANYDATA object.

ANYDATASET type
: Similar to an ANYDATA, but the contents are one or more instances of a datatype.

Processing an ANYDATA value

I'll now show you what all this means, first with a program intended to return a string version of any variable's contents. For now, this program deals only with numbers, strings, dates, objects, and REFs, but you could extend it to almost any other datatype.

```
/* File on web: printany.fun */
CREATE OR REPLACE FUNCTION printany (adata IN ANYDATA)
   RETURN VARCHAR2
AS
   aType ANYTYPE;
   retval VARCHAR2(32767);
   result_code PLS_INTEGER;
BEGIN
   CASE adata.GetType(aType)
   WHEN DBMS_TYPES.TYPECODE_NUMBER THEN
      RETURN 'NUMBER: ' || TO_CHAR(adata.AccessNumber);
   WHEN DBMS_TYPES.TYPECODE_VARCHAR2 THEN
      RETURN 'VARCHAR2: ' || adata.AccessVarchar2;
   WHEN DBMS_TYPES.TYPECODE_CHAR THEN
      RETURN 'CHAR: ' || RTRIM(adata.AccessChar);
   WHEN DBMS_TYPES.TYPECODE_DATE THEN
      RETURN 'DATE: ' || TO_CHAR(adata.AccessDate, 'YYYY-MM-DD hh24:mi:ss');
   WHEN DBMS_TYPES.TYPECODE_OBJECT THEN
      EXECUTE IMMEDIATE 'DECLARE ' ||
                        '   myobj ' || adata.GetTypeName || '; ' ||
                        '   myad anydata := :ad; ' ||
                        'BEGIN ' ||
                        '   :res := myad.GetObject(myobj); ' ||
                        '   :ret := myobj.print( ); ' ||
                        'END;'
                        USING IN adata, OUT result_code, OUT retval;
      retval := adata.GetTypeName || ': ' || retval;
   WHEN DBMS_TYPES.TYPECODE_REF THEN
      EXECUTE IMMEDIATE 'DECLARE ' ||
                        '   myref ' || adata.GetTypeName || '; ' ||
                        '   myobj ' || SUBSTR(adata.GetTypeName,
                                   INSTR(adata.GetTypeName, ' ')) || '; ' ||
                        '   myad anydata := :ad; ' ||
                        'BEGIN ' ||
                        '   :res := myad.GetREF(myref); ' ||
                        '   UTL_REF.SELECT_OBJECT(myref, myobj);' ||
                        '   :ret := myobj.print( ); ' ||
                        'END;'
                        USING IN adata, OUT result_code, OUT retval;
      retval := adata.GetTypeName || ': ' || retval;
   ELSE
      retval := '<data of type ' || adata.GetTypeName ||'>';
   END CASE;

   RETURN retval;

EXCEPTION
   WHEN OTHERS
   THEN
      IF INSTR(SQLERRM, 'component ''PRINT'' must be declared') > 0
      THEN
```

```
51           RETURN adata.GetTypeName || ': <no print() function>';
52        ELSE
53           RETURN 'Error: ' || SQLERRM;
54        END IF;
55  END;
```

Here are just a few highlights.

Line 1

This function receives a single argument of type ANYDATA. In order to call the function, you must convert your variable to an ANYDATA; for example:

```
DBMS_OUTPUT.PUT_LINE(printany(ANYDATA.ConvertNumber(3.14159)));
```

Explicit conversions are sort of the dark side of ANYDATA.

Line 5

In cases where I need a temporary variable to hold the result, I assume that 32K will be big enough. Remember that PL/SQL dynamically allocates memory for large VARCHAR2s, so it won't be a memory pig unless required.

Line 6

The value of result_code (see lines 25 and 38) is irrelevant for the operations in this example, but is required by the ANYDATA API.

Line 8

The ANYDATA type includes a method called GetType that returns a code corresponding to the datatype. Here is its specification:

```
MEMBER FUNCTION ANYDATA.GetType (OUT NOCOPY ANYTYPE) RETURN typecode_integer;
```

To use this method, though, you have to declare an ANYTYPE variable into which Oracle will store detailed information about the type that you've encapsulated.

Lines 9, 11, 13, 15, 17, 27

These expressions rely on the constants that Oracle provides in the built-in package DBMS_TYPES.

Lines 10, 12, 14, 16

These statements use the ANYDATA.Convert*NNN* member functions introduced in Oracle9*i* Release 2. In Release 1, you can use the Get*NNN* member procedures for a similar result, although they require the use of a temporary local variable.

Lines 18–25

To get an object to print itself without doing a lot of data dictionary contortions, this little dynamic anonymous block will construct an object of the correct type and invoke its print() member method.

Lines 28–38

The point of this is to dereference the pointer and return the referenced object's content. Well, it will work if there's a print().

Lines 49–51

In the event that I'm trying to print an object with no print member method, the compiler will return an error at runtime that I can detect in this fashion. In this case the code will just punt and return a generic message.

Let's take a look at some simple invocations and what this returns:

```
DECLARE
   achar CHAR(20) := 'fixed-length string';
   abook book_t := NEW book_t(id => 12345, title => 'my book', pages => 100);
   sref REF serial_t;
   asub subject_t := subject_t('The World', NULL);
BEGIN
   DBMS_OUTPUT.PUT_LINE(printany(ANYDATA.ConvertNumber(3.141592654)));
   DBMS_OUTPUT.PUT_LINE(printany(ANYDATA.ConvertChar(achar)));
   DBMS_OUTPUT.PUT_LINE(printany(ANYDATA.ConvertObject(abook)));
   DBMS_OUTPUT.PUT_LINE(printany(ANYDATA.ConvertObject(asub)));
   SELECT TREAT(REF(c) AS REF serial_t) INTO sref
     FROM catalog_items c WHERE title = 'Time';
   DBMS_OUTPUT.PUT_LINE(printany(ANYDATA.ConvertRef(sref)));
END;
```

This yields:

```
NUMBER: 3.141592654
CHAR: fixed-length string
SCOTT.BOOK_T: id=12345; title=my book; publication_date=; isbn=; pages=100
SCOTT.SUBJECT_T: <no print() function>
REF SCOTT.SERIAL_T: id=10004; title=Time; publication_date=; issn=0040-781X;
open_or_closed=Open
```

As you can see, using ANYDATA is not as convenient as true inheritance hierarchies because ANYDATA requires explicit conversions. On the other hand, it does make possible the creation of a table column or object attribute that will hold any type of data.*

Creating a transient type

Although PL/SQL still does not support defining new object types inside a program's declaration section, it is possible to use these ANY built-ins to create this kind of "transient" type—that is, one that exists only at runtime. Wrapped up as an ANYTYPE, you can even pass such a type as a parameter and create an instance of it as an ANYDATA. Here is an example:

```
CREATE OR REPLACE FUNCTION create_a_type
   RETURN ANYTYPE
AS
   myany ANYDATA;
```

* As of this writing, it is impossible to store in a table an ANYDATA encapsulating an object that has evolved or that is part of a type hierarchy.

```
    mytype ANYTYPE;
BEGIN
    /* Create (anonymous) transient type with two attributes: number, date */
    ANYTYPE.BeginCreate(typecode => DBMS_TYPES.TYPECODE_OBJECT, atype => mytype);
    mytype.AddAttr(typecode => DBMS_TYPES.TYPECODE_NUMBER, aname => 'just_a_number',
       prec => 38, scale => 0, len => NULL, csid => NULL, csfrm => NULL);
    mytype.AddAttr(typecode => DBMS_TYPES.TYPECODE_DATE, aname => 'just_a_date',
       prec => 5, scale => 5, len => NULL, csid => NULL, csfrm => NULL);
    mytype.EndCreate;
    RETURN mytype;
END;
```

As you can see, there are three main steps:

1. Begin the creation by calling the static procedure BeginCreate. This returns an initialized ANYTYPE.
2. One at a time, add the desired attributes using the AddAttr member procedure.
3. Call the member procedure EndCreate.

Similarly, when you wish to use the type, you will need to assign attribute values in a piecewise manner:

```
DECLARE
    ltype ANYTYPE := create_a_type;
    l_any ANYDATA;
BEGIN
    ANYDATA.BeginCreate(dtype => ltype, adata => l_any);
    l_any.SetNumber(num => 12345);
    l_any.SetDate(dat => SYSDATE);
    l_any.EndCreate;
END;
```

If you don't know the structure of the datatype in advance, it is possible to discover it using ANYTYPE methods (such as GetAttrElemInfo) in combination with a piecewise application of the ANYDATA.Get methods. (See the *anyObject.sql* script on the O'Reilly site for an example.)

I Can Do It Myself

In object-oriented design, there is a school of thought that wants each object type to have the intelligence necessary to be self-sufficient. If the object needs to be stored persistently in a database, it would know how to save itself; similarly, it would include methods for update, delete, and retrieval. If I subscribed to this philosophy, here is one of the methods I would want to add to my type:

```
ALTER TYPE catalog_item_t
   ADD MEMBER PROCEDURE remove
   CASCADE;

CREATE OR REPLACE TYPE BODY catalog_item_t
AS
   ...
```

```
    MEMBER PROCEDURE remove
    IS
    BEGIN
       DELETE catalog_items
        WHERE id = SELF.id;
       SELF := NULL;
    END;
END;
```

(Oracle does not offer a destructor method, by the way.) By defining this method at the supertype level, all my subtypes are taken care of too. This design assumes that corresponding objects will live in a single table; some applications might need some additional logic to locate the object. (Also, a real version of this method might include logic to perform ancillary functions like removing dependent objects and/or archiving the data before removing the object permanently.)

Assuming that my applications would always modify a transient object in memory before writing it to disk, I could combine insert and update into a single method I'll call "save":

```
ALTER TYPE catalog_item_t
   ADD MEMBER PROCEDURE save,
   CASCADE;

CREATE OR REPLACE TYPE BODY catalog_item_t
AS
   ...
   MEMBER PROCEDURE save
   IS
   BEGIN
      UPDATE catalog_items c
         SET c = SELF
       WHERE id = SELF.id;
      IF SQL%ROWCOUNT = 0
      THEN
         INSERT INTO catalog_items VALUES (SELF);
      END IF;
   END;
```

You may correctly point out that this will replace all of the column values in the table even if they are unchanged, which could cause triggers to fire that shouldn't, and results in needless I/O. Alas, this is one of the unfortunate by-products of an object approach. It is true that with careful programming, you could avoid modifying columns from the supertype that haven't changed, but columns from any subtype are not individually accessible from any variation on the UPDATE statement that Oracle currently offers.

Retrieval is the most difficult operation to encapsulate, because of the many WHERE-clause permutations and the multi-set nature of the result. The specification of the query criteria can be a real rat's nest, as anyone who has ever built a custom query screen will attest. Considering only the result side, the options for what to return include:

- A collection of objects
- A collection of REFs
- A pipelined result set
- A cursor variable (strongly or weakly typed)

The requirements of the application and its programming environment will have the largest influence on how to choose from these options. Here's an example that uses the fourth approach, a cursor variable:

```
ALTER TYPE catalog_item_t
   ADD MEMBER FUNCTION retrieve_matching
      RETURN SYS_REFCURSOR
   CASCADE;
```

I use the built-in SYS_REFCURSOR type, which is a weak cursor type that Oracle provides just for convenience. The idea of this function is that the calling application will instantiate some object as a "sample record," invoke the retrieve_matching function on that object, and then use the returned cursor variable as the handle to the result set. Jumping ahead to how you might execute a query, let's look at this example:

```
DECLARE
   catalog_item catalog_item_t;
   l_refcur SYS_REFCURSOR;
   l_sample_object book_t := NEW book_t(title => 'Oracle%');
 BEGIN
   l_refcur := l_sample_object.retrieve_matching( );
   LOOP
      FETCH l_refcur INTO catalog_item;
      EXIT WHEN l_refcur%NOTFOUND;
      DBMS_OUTPUT.PUT_LINE(catalog_item.print);
   END LOOP;
   CLOSE l_refcur;
END;
```

One of the issues with this specification, though, is whether the query should retrieve all matching catalog items, or only those matching the datatype of the sample object. If the answer is "all," the corresponding implementation could look like this:

```
CREATE OR REPLACE TYPE BODY catalog_item_t
AS
   ...
   MEMBER FUNCTION retrieve_matching
      RETURN SYS_REFCURSOR
   IS
      l_refcur SYS_REFCURSOR;
   BEGIN
      IF SELF IS OF (book_t)
      THEN
```

```
         OPEN l_refcur FOR
            SELECT VALUE(c)
              FROM catalog_items c
             WHERE (SELF.id IS NULL OR id = SELF.id)
               AND (SELF.title IS NULL OR title LIKE SELF.title || '%')
               AND (SELF.publication_date IS NULL
                    OR publication_date = SELF.publication_date)
               AND (TREAT(SELF AS book_t).isbn IS NULL
                    OR TREAT(VALUE(c) AS book_t).isbn =
                          TREAT(SELF AS book_t).isbn)
               AND (TREAT(SELF AS book_t).pages IS NULL
                    OR TREAT(VALUE(c) AS book_t).pages =
                          TREAT(SELF AS book_t).pages);
      ELSIF SELF IS OF (serial_t)
      THEN
         OPEN l_refcur FOR
            SELECT VALUE(c)
              FROM catalog_items c
             WHERE (SELF.id IS NULL OR id = SELF.id)
               AND (SELF.title IS NULL OR title LIKE SELF.title || '%')
               AND (SELF.publication_date IS NULL
                    OR publication_date = SELF.publication_date)
               AND (TREAT(SELF AS serial_t).issn IS NULL
                    OR TREAT(VALUE(c) AS serial_t).issn =
                          TREAT(SELF AS serial_t).issn)
               AND (TREAT(SELF AS serial_t).open_or_closed IS NULL
                    OR TREAT(VALUE(c) AS serial_t).open_or_closed =
                          TREAT(SELF AS serial_t).open_or_closed);
      END IF;
      RETURN l_refcur;
   END;
END;
```

I'm not completely satisfied with this approach, because it requires modifying this method in the supertype every time I add a subtype to the inheritance tree. I could override retrieve_matching methods in the subtypes, but when I later want a result set that includes both books and serials, there is no way to invoke the method in the supertype. In that case, I would wind up with the non-intuitive situation of a book query retrieving serials, or vice versa.

Although I could change the supertype to be instantiable, perhaps a better approach would be to change the retrieve_matching function into a static method. I leave this change as an exercise for the reader.

Comparing Objects

So far, my examples have used object tables—tables in which each row constitutes an object built with the CREATE TABLE...OF type statement. As I've illustrated, such an arrangement enjoys some special features, such as REF-based navigation and the treatment of entire objects (rather than individual column values) as the unit of I/O.

You can also use an object type as the datatype for individual columns in a table. For example, imagine that I want to create an historical record of changes in the catalog_items table, capturing all inserts, updates, and deletes.*

```
CREATE TABLE catalog_history AS (
   id INTEGER NOT NULL PRIMARY KEY,
   action CHAR(1) NOT NULL,
   action_time TIMESTAMP NOT NULL DEFAULT TIMESTAMP,
   old_item catalog_item_t,
   new_item catalog_item_t
);
```

As soon as you start populating a table with column objects, though, you raise some questions about how Oracle should behave when you ask it to do things like sort or index on one of those catalog_item_t columns. Well, there are four different ways you can compare objects, though some are more useful than others:

Attribute-level comparison
: Include the relevant attribute(s) when sorting, creating indexes, or comparing.

Default SQL
: Oracle's SQL knows how to do a simple equality test. In this case, two objects are considered equal if they are defined on exactly the same type and every corresponding attribute is equal. This will work if the objects have only scalar attributes (no collections or LOBs) and if you haven't already defined a MAP or ORDER member method on the object type.

MAP member method
: You can create a special function method that returns a "mapping" of the object value onto a datatype that Oracle already knows how to compare, such as a number or a date. This will work only if no ORDER method exists.

ORDER member method
: This is another special function that compares two objects and returns a flag value that indicates their relative ordering. This will work only if no MAP method exists.

Default SQL comparison is not terribly useful, so I won't say any more about it. The following sections describe the other, more useful ways to compare objects.

Attribute-level comparison

Attribute-level comparison may not be precisely what you want, but it is fairly easy in PL/SQL, or even in SQL if you remember to use a table alias in the SQL statement. Oracle lets you expose attributes via dot notation:

* It might seem reasonable to expect DML triggers on the catalog_items table to populate this history table automatically. Unfortunately, inside a trigger there is no access to attributes specific to lower-level subtypes. With a trigger, you can only capture the history of the common (supertype) attributes.

```
SELECT * FROM catalog_history c
 WHERE c.old_item.id > 10000
 ORDER BY NVL(TREAT(c.old_item as book_t).isbn, TREAT(c.old_item AS serial_t).issn)
```

Attribute-level index creation is equally easy:

```
CREATE INDEX catalog_history_old_id_idx ON catalog_history c (c.old_item.id);
```

The MAP method

Both the MAP and the ORDER methods make it possible to perform statements such as the following:

```
SELECT * FROM catalog_history
 ORDER BY old_item;

IF old_item > new_item
THEN ...
```

First let's look at MAP. I can add a trivial MAP method to catalog_item_t as follows.

```
ALTER TYPE catalog_item_t
   ADD MAP MEMBER FUNCTION mapit RETURN NUMBER
   CASCADE;

CREATE OR REPLACE TYPE BODY catalog_item_t
AS ...
   MAP MEMBER FUNCTION mapit RETURN NUMBER
   IS
   BEGIN
      RETURN id;
   END;
   ...
END;
```

Assuming, of course, that ordering by id makes sense, now I can order and compare catalog items to my heart's content, and Oracle will call this method automatically whenever necessary. The function needn't be so simple; for example, it could return a scalar value computed from all the object attributes, melded together in some way that actually might be of some value to librarians.

Creating a MAP method like this has a side effect, though: the equality comparison gets defined in a way you might not like. "Equality" now becomes a matter of the mapped value's being equal for the objects you're comparing. If you want an easy way to compare two objects for attribute-by-attribute equality, you will want to either create your own (non-MAP) method and invoke it by name when needed, or use an ORDER method.

The ORDER method

The alternative to MAP is an ORDER member function, which compares two methods: SELF, and another object of the same type that you supply as an argument. You want to program the function to return an integer that is positive, zero, or negative, indicating the ordering relationship of the second object to SELF. Table 21-2 illustrates the behavior you need to incorporate.

Table 21-2. Desired behavior of ORDER member functions

For these desired semantics...	Your ORDER member function must return
SELF < *argumentObject*	Any negative number (typically –1)
SELF = *argumentObject*	0
SELF > *argumentObject*	Any positive number (typically +1)
Undefined comparison	NULL

Let's take a look at a nontrivial example of an ORDER method.

```
ALTER TYPE catalog_item_t
   DROP MAP MEMBER FUNCTION mapit RETURN NUMBER
   CASCADE;

ALTER TYPE catalog_item_t
   ADD ORDER MEMBER FUNCTION orderit (obj2 IN catalog_item_t)
      RETURN INTEGER
   CASCADE;

CREATE OR REPLACE TYPE BODY catalog_item_t
AS ...
   ORDER MEMBER FUNCTION orderit (obj2 IN catalog_item_t)
      RETURN INTEGER
   IS
      self_gt_o2 CONSTANT PLS_INTEGER := 1;
      eq CONSTANT PLS_INTEGER := 0;
      o2_gt_self CONSTANT PLS_INTEGER := -1;
      l_matching_count NUMBER;
   BEGIN
      CASE
         WHEN obj2 IS OF (book_t) AND SELF IS OF (serial_t) THEN
            RETURN o2_gt_self;
         WHEN obj2 IS OF (serial_t) AND SELF IS OF (book_t) THEN
            RETURN self_gt_o2;
         ELSE
            IF obj2.title = SELF.title
               AND obj2.publication_date = SELF.publication_date
            THEN
               IF obj2.subject_refs IS NOT NULL
                  AND SELF.subject_refs IS NOT NULL
                  AND obj2.subject_refs.COUNT = SELF.subject_refs.COUNT
               THEN
                  SELECT COUNT(*) INTO l_matching_count FROM
                     (SELECT *
                        FROM TABLE(SELECT CAST(SELF.subject_refs AS subject_refs_t)
                                     FROM dual)
                     INTERSECT
                     SELECT *
                        FROM TABLE(SELECT CAST(obj2.subject_refs AS subject_refs_t)
```

```
40                                     FROM dual));
41                   IF l_matching_count = SELF.subject_refs.COUNT
42                   THEN
43                      RETURN eq;
44                   END IF;
45                END IF;
46             END IF;
47             RETURN NULL;
48       END CASE;
49    END;
50    ...
51 END;
```

Here are the important things to note:

Lines 21–24
: This means that "books sort higher than serials."

Lines 26–46
: This is an equality test that uses a very cool feature. Because Oracle doesn't know how to compare collections, this code uses Oracle's ability to select from a collection as if it were a table. By checking to make sure that the relational intersection of these two collections has the expected number of elements, I can determine whether every element in the first collection has an equal counterpart in the second (which is my definition of "equality").

Overall, however, my ORDER method is still inadequate because it fails to treat the subtype-specific attributes, but anything longer would just be too unwieldy for this book.

Additional comparison recommendations

To close out this discussion, here are a few additional rules and recommendations for comparison methods:

- MAP and ORDER cannot coexist in the same object type; use one or the other.
- Oracle recommends MAP when you have a large number of objects to sort or compare, as in a SQL statement. This is because of an internal optimization that reduces the number of function calls. With ORDER, the function must run once for every comparison.
- Oracle ignores the method names; you can call them anything you want.
- Subtypes can include MAP methods, but only if the supertype also has one.
- Subtypes cannot have ORDER methods; you'll have to put all the comparison "smarts" into the supertype.

Object Views

Although Oracle's object extensions offer PL/SQL programmers rich possibilities for the design of new systems, it's unlikely that you will want to completely reengineer your existing systems to use objects. In part to allow established applications to take advantage of the new object features over time, Oracle provides *object views*. This feature offers several unique advantages:

"Object-ification" of remote data
: It's not yet possible in Oracle9*i* to use the object tables and physical REFs across a distributed database, but you can create object views and virtual REFs that cast remote relational data as objects.

Virtual denormalization
: In a relational database or even an object-relational database, you will usually find relationships modeled in only one direction. For example, a book has some number of subjects. With an object view, it's easy to associate a column that provides the inverse mapping; for example, a subject object could include a collection of REFs that point to all of the books in that subject.

Efficiency of object access
: In Oracle Call Interface (OCI) applications, object programming constructs provide for the convenient retrieval, caching, and updating of object data. By reducing trips between application and database server, these programming facilities may provide performance improvements, with the added benefit that application code can be more succinct.

Greater flexibility to change the object model
: Although Oracle9*i* has tremendous abilities in the area of type evolution, adding and removing object attributes still cause table bits to move around on the disk, which administrators may be loath to do. Recompiling object views suffers no such consequences.

On the other hand, there are some disadvantages to using object views:

View performance
: Object views are still views, and some Oracle shops are generally leery of the performance of any view.

No virtual REFs
: You cannot store virtual REFs in the database; instead, they get constructed on the fly. This may present some challenges if you someday want to convert those object views into object tables.

Other features of Oracle can improve the expressiveness of any types of views, not just object views. Two such features that are not strictly limited to object views are collections and INSTEAD OF triggers:

Collections
: Consider two relational tables with a simple master-detail relationship. You can create a view portraying the detail records as a single nonscalar attribute (collection) of the master.

INSTEAD OF triggers
: In addition, by using INSTEAD OF triggers, you can tell Oracle exactly how to perform inserts, updates, and deletes on the view.

From an object perspective, there is one slight disadvantage of object views when compared to comprehensive reengineering: object views cannot retrofit any benefits of encapsulation. Insofar as any applications apply INSERT, UPDATE, and DELETE statements directly to the underlying relational data, they may subvert the benefits of encapsulation normally provided by an object approach. Object-oriented designs typically prevent free-form access directly to data. However, because Oracle supports neither private attributes nor private methods, the incremental sacrifice here is small.

If you do choose to layer object views on top of an existing system, it may be possible for new applications to enjoy incremental benefit, and your legacy systems are no worse off than they were before. Figure 21-2 illustrates this use of object views.

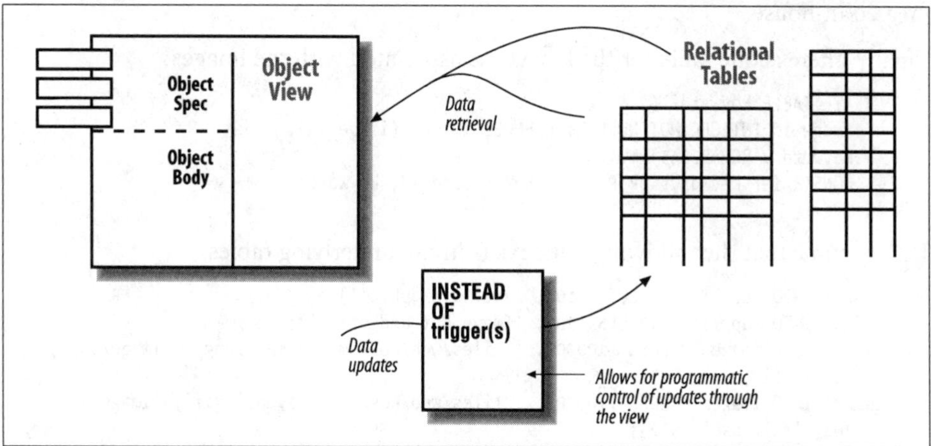

Figure 21-2. Object views allow you to bind an object type definition to (existing) relational tables

The following sections discuss aspects of using object views (including differences between object tables and object views) that PL/SQL programmers should find particularly useful and interesting.

The Existing Relational System

For this chapter's second major example, let's look at how object views might be used in a database application that supports a graphic design firm. Their relational application includes information about images (GIF, JPEG, etc.) that appear on web sites they design. These images are stored in files, but data about them is stored in relational tables. To help the graphic artists locate the right image, each image has one or more associated keywords stored in a straightforward master-detail relationship.

The legacy system has a table of suppliers:

```
CREATE TABLE suppliers (
   id INTEGER NOT NULL PRIMARY KEY,
   name VARCHAR2(400) NOT NULL
);
```

Here is the table for image metadata:

```
CREATE TABLE images (
   image_id INTEGER NOT NULL PRIMARY KEY,
   file_name VARCHAR2(512) NOT NULL,
   file_type VARCHAR2(12) NOT NULL,
   supplier_id INTEGER REFERENCES suppliers (id),
   supplier_rights_descriptor VARCHAR2(256),
   bytes INTEGER
);
```

Not all images originate from suppliers; if the supplier id is null, then the image was created in-house.

Finally, there is one table for the keywords associated with the images:

```
CREATE TABLE keywords (
   image_id INTEGER NOT NULL REFERENCES images (image_id),
   keyword VARCHAR2(45) NOT NULL,
   CONSTRAINT keywords_pk PRIMARY KEY (image_id, keyword)
);
```

Let's assume that the following data exists in the underlying tables:

```
INSERT INTO suppliers VALUES (101, 'Joe''s Graphics');
INSERT INTO suppliers VALUES (102, 'Image Bar and Grill');
INSERT INTO images VALUES (100001, '/files/web/60s/smiley_face.png', 'image/png',
   101, 'fair use', 813);
INSERT INTO images VALUES (100002, '/files/web/60s/peace_symbol.gif', 'image/gif',
   101, 'fair use', 972);
INSERT INTO images VALUES (100003, '/files/web/00s/towers.jpg', 'image/jpeg', NULL,
   NULL, 2104);
INSERT INTO KEYWORDS VALUES (100001, 'SIXTIES');
INSERT INTO KEYWORDS VALUES (100001, 'HAPPY FACE');
INSERT INTO KEYWORDS VALUES (100002, 'SIXTIES');
INSERT INTO KEYWORDS VALUES (100002, 'PEACE SYMBOL');
INSERT INTO KEYWORDS VALUES (100002, 'JERRY RUBIN');
```

In the next few sections, you'll see several object views defined on this data:

- The first view will be defined on an image type that includes the keywords as a collection attribute.

- The second view will be a "subview"—that is, defined on a subtype in an object type hierarchy. It will include characteristics for images that originate from suppliers.
- The final view will include keywords and their inverse references back to the relevant images.

Object View with a Collection Attribute

Before creating an underlying type for the first view, we need a collection type to hold the keywords. Use of a nested table makes sense here, because keyword ordering is unimportant and because there is no logical maximum number of keywords.*

```
CREATE TYPE keyword_tab_t AS TABLE OF VARCHAR2(45);
```

At this point, it's a simple matter to define the image object type:

```
CREATE TYPE image_t AS OBJECT (
    image_id INTEGER,
    image_file BFILE,
    file_type VARCHAR2(12),
    bytes INTEGER,
    keywords keyword_tab_t
);
```

Assuming that the image files and the database server are on the same machine, I can use an Oracle BFILE datatype rather than the filename. I'll need to create a "directory," that is, an alias by which Oracle will know the directory that contains the images. In this case, I use the root directory (on the target Unix system, this is represented by a single forward slash), because I happen to know that the file_name column includes full pathnames.

```
CREATE DIRECTORY rootdir AS  '/';
```

So far, I have not defined a connection between the relational tables and the object type. They are independent organisms. It is in building the object view that we overlay the object definition onto the tables, as the next statement illustrates:

```
CREATE VIEW images_v
   OF image_t
   WITH OBJECT IDENTIFIER (image_id)
AS
   SELECT i.image_id, BFILENAME('ROOTDIR', i.file_name),
      i.file_type, i.bytes,
      CAST (MULTISET (SELECT keyword
                        FROM keywords k
                       WHERE k.image_id = i.image_id)
        AS keyword_tab_t)
     FROM images i;
```

* If ordering were important or if there were a (small) logical maximum number of keywords per image, a VARRAY collection would be a better choice.

There are two components of this statement that are unique to object views:

OF image_t
: This means that the view will return objects of type image_t.

WITH OBJECT IDENTIFIER (image_id)
: To behave like a "real" object instance, data returned by the view will need some kind of object identifier. By designating the primary key as the basis of a virtual OID, we can enjoy the benefits of REF-based navigation to objects in the view.

In addition, the select list of an object view must correspond in number and datatype with the attributes in the associated object type.

OK, now that we've created an object view, what can we do with it? Most significantly, we can retrieve data from it just as if it were an object table.

Now, from SQL*Plus, a query like the following:

```
SQL> SELECT image_id, keywords FROM images_v;
```

yields:

```
 IMAGE_ID KEYWORDS
---------- -------------------------------------------------------
    100003 KEYWORD_TAB_T( )
    100001 KEYWORD_TAB_T('HAPPY FACE', 'SIXTIES')
    100002 KEYWORD_TAB_T('JERRY RUBIN', 'PEACE SYMBOL', 'SIXTIES')
```

In the interest of deepening the object appearance, I could also add methods to the type definition. Here, for example, is a print( ) method:

```
ALTER TYPE image_t
   ADD MEMBER FUNCTION print RETURN VARCHAR2
   CASCADE;

CREATE OR REPLACE TYPE BODY image_t
AS
   MEMBER FUNCTION print
      RETURN VARCHAR2
   IS
      filename images.file_name%TYPE;
      dirname VARCHAR2(30);
      keyword_list VARCHAR2(32767);
   BEGIN
      DBMS_LOB.FILEGETNAME(SELF.image_file, dirname, filename);
      IF SELF.keywords IS NOT NULL
      THEN
         FOR key_elt IN 1..SELF.keywords.COUNT
         LOOP
            keyword_list := keyword_list || ', ' || SELF.keywords(key_elt);
         END LOOP;
      END IF;
      RETURN 'Id=' || SELF.image_id || '; File=' || filename
         || '; keywords=' || SUBSTR(keyword_list, 3);
   END;
END;
```

> **Is It Null, or Is It Not?**
>
> A null collection is not the same thing as an initialized collection with zero elements. Image 100003 has no keywords, but the object view is mistakenly returning an empty but initialized collection. To get a true NULL instead, I can use a DECODE to test the number of keywords:
>
> ```
> CREATE OR REPLACE VIEW images_v
>    OF image_t
>    WITH OBJECT IDENTIFIER (image_id)
> AS
>    SELECT i.image_id, BFILENAME('ROOTDIR', i.file_name),
>           i.file_type, i.bytes,
>           DECODE((SELECT COUNT(*)
>                     FROM keywords k2
>                    WHERE k2.image_id = i.image_id),
>                  0, NULL,
>                  CAST (MULTISET (SELECT keyword
>                                    FROM keywords k
>                                   WHERE k.image_id = i.image_id)
>                    AS keyword_tab_t))
>      FROM images i;
> ```
>
> In other words, if there are no keywords, return NULL; otherwise, return the CAST/MULTISET expression. From this view, "SELECT ... WHERE image_id=100003" properly yields the following:
>
> ```
>   IMAGE_ID KEYWORDS
> ---------- -------------------------------------------------------
>     100003
> ```
>
> But you might conclude that this amount of conceptual purity is not worth the extra I/O (or having to look at the convoluted SELECT statement).

This example illustrates a way to "flatten" the keyword list by iterating over the virtual collection of keywords.

Other things you can do with object views include the following:

Use virtual REFs
: These are pointers to virtual objects. They are discussed in detail in the later section "Differences Between Object Views and Object Tables."

Write INSTEAD OF triggers
: These will allow direct manipulation of the view's contents. You can read more about this topic in the later section, "Discussion: INSTEAD OF Triggers."

Object Subview

In the case where I want to treat certain images differently from others, I might want to create a subtype. In my example, I'm going to create a subtype for those images that originate from suppliers. I'd like the subtype to include a REF to a supplier object, which is defined by:

```
CREATE TYPE supplier_t AS OBJECT (
   id INTEGER,
   name VARCHAR2(400)
);
```

and by a simple object view:

```
CREATE VIEW suppliers_v
   OF supplier_t
   WITH OBJECT IDENTIFIER (id)
AS
   SELECT id, name
     FROM suppliers;
```

I will need to alter or re-create the base type to be NOT FINAL:

```
ALTER TYPE image_t NOT FINAL CASCADE;
```

so that I can create the subtype under it:

```
CREATE TYPE supplied_images_t UNDER image_t (
   supplier_ref REF supplier_t,
   supplier_rights_descriptor VARCHAR2(256)
);
```

After all this preparation, I make the subview of this subtype and declare it to be UNDER the images_v view using the following syntax:

```
CREATE VIEW supplied_images_v
   OF supplied_images_t
   UNDER images_v
AS
   SELECT i.image_id, BFILENAME('ROOTDIR', i.file_name),
          i.file_type, i.bytes,
          CAST (MULTISET (SELECT keyword
                            FROM keywords k
                           WHERE k.image_id = i.image_id)
            AS keyword_tab_t),
          MAKE_REF(suppliers_v, supplier_id),
          supplier_rights_descriptor
     FROM images i
    WHERE supplier_id IS NOT NULL;
```

Oracle won't let a subview query through the superview, so this view queries the base table, adding the WHERE clause to restrict the records retrieved. Also notice that subviews don't use the WITH OBJECT IDENTIFIER clause because they inherit the same OID as their superview.

I have introduced the MAKE_REF function in this query, which Oracle provides as a way to compute a REF to a virtual object. Here, the virtual object is the supplier, as conveyed through suppliers_v. The specification of MAKE_REF is:

```
FUNCTION MAKE_REF (view, value_list) RETURN ref;
```

where:

view
    Is the object view to which you want *ref* to point.

value_list
    Is a comma-separated list of column values whose datatypes must match one for one with the OID attributes of *view*.

You should realize that MAKE_REF does not actually select through the view; it merely applies an internal Oracle algorithm to derive a REF. And, as with "real" REFs, virtual REFs may not point to actual objects.

Now I come to a surprising result. Although it seems that I have not changed the superview, images from suppliers now appear twice in the superview—that is, as duplicates:

```
SQL> SELECT COUNT(*), image_id FROM images_v GROUP BY image_id;

  COUNT(*)   IMAGE_ID
---------- ----------
         2     100001
         2     100002
         1     100003
```

Oracle is returning a logical UNION ALL of the query in the superview and that in the subview. This does sort of make sense; an image from a supplier is still an image. To eliminate the duplicates, add a WHERE clause on the parent that excludes records returned in the subview:

```
CREATE OR REPLACE VIEW images_v AS
   ...
   WHERE supplier_id IS NULL;
```

Object View with Inverse Relationship

To demonstrate virtual denormalization, I can create a keyword type for a view that links keywords back to the images they describe:

```
CREATE TYPE image_refs_t AS TABLE OF REF image_t;

CREATE TYPE keyword_t AS OBJECT (
   keyword VARCHAR2(45),
   image_refs image_refs_t);
```

And here is a keywords view definition:

```
CREATE OR REPLACE VIEW keywords_v
   OF keyword_t
   WITH OBJECT IDENTIFIER (keyword)
AS
   SELECT keyword, CAST(MULTISET(SELECT MAKE_REF(images_v, image_id)
                                   FROM keywords
```

```
                        WHERE keyword = main.keyword)
                AS image_refs_t)
    FROM (SELECT DISTINCT keyword FROM keywords) main;
```

Now, I don't promise that queries on this view will run *fast*—the query is compensating for the fact that the database lacks a reference table of keywords by doing a SELECT DISTINCT operation. Even if I weren't using any object features, that would be an expensive query.

You may correctly point out that using MAKE_REF is not mandatory here; I could have retrieved a REF by making the inner query on images_v rather than on the keywords table. In general, MAKE_REF should be faster than a lookup through an object view; on occasion, you may not have the luxury of being able to perform that lookup.

Anyway, at this point I can run such pithy queries as this one:

```
SQL> SELECT DEREF(VALUE(i)).print()
  2    FROM keywords_v v, TABLE(v.image_refs) i
  3   WHERE keyword = 'SIXTIES';

DEREF(VALUE(I)).PRINT()
------------------------------------------------------------------------------------
Id=100001; File=/files/web/60s/smiley_face.gif; keywords=HAPPY FACE, SIXTIES
Id=100002; File=/files/web/60s/peace_symbol.gif; keywords=JERRY RUBIN, PEACE SYMBOL,
SIXTIES
```

That is, I can show a list of all the images tagged with the keyword SIXTIES, along with their other keywords and attributes. I admit that I'm not sure how groovy that really is!

INSTEAD OF Triggers

Because Chapter 18 covered the syntax and use of INSTEAD OF triggers, I'm not going to discuss their mechanics here. Instead, I will explore whether they are a good fit for the problem of updating object views. If your goal is to migrate toward an object approach, you may ask whether INSTEAD OF triggers are just a relational throwback that facilitates a free-for-all in which any application can perform DML.

Well, they are and they aren't.

Let's examine the arguments for both sides, and come up with some considerations so you can decide what's best for your application.

The case against

On the one hand, you could use PL/SQL programs such as packages and object methods to provide a more comprehensive technique than triggers for encapsulating DML. It is nearly trivial to take the logic from our INSTEAD OF trigger and put it into an alternate PL/SQL construct that has more universal application. In other words, if you've already standardized on some combination of packages and methods as the means of performing DML, you could keep your environment consistent without using view triggers. You might conclude that view triggers are just added complexity in an increasingly confusing equation.

Moreover, even Oracle cautions against the "excessive use" of triggers, as they can cause "complex interdependencies." Imagine if your INSTEAD OF triggers performed DML on tables that had other triggers, which performed DML on still other tables with triggers...it's easy to see how this could get impossible to debug.

The case for

On the other hand, you can put much of the necessary logic that you would normally put into a package or method body into an INSTEAD OF trigger instead. Doing this in combination with a proper set of privilege restrictions could protect your data just as well as, or even better than, methods or packages.

If you happen to use a client tool such as Oracle Forms, INSTEAD OF triggers allow you to use much more of the product's default functionality when you create a Forms "block" against a view rather than a table.

Finally, if you use OCI, INSTEAD OF triggers are *required* if the object view is not inherently modifiable and you want to be able to easily "flush" cached object view data back to the server.

The bigger question

The bigger question is this: what's the best place for the SQL statements that insert, update, and delete data, especially when using object views? Assuming that you want to localize these operations on the server side, you have at least three choices: PL/SQL packages, object methods, and INSTEAD OF triggers.

Table 21-3 summarizes some of the major considerations of the three techniques. Note that this table is not meant to compare these approaches for general-purpose use, but only as they apply to localizing DML on object views.

Table 21-3. Assessment of techniques for encapsulating DML on object views

Consideration	PL/SQL package	Object method	INSTEAD OF trigger
Consistency with object-oriented approach	Potentially very good	Excellent	Potentially very good
Ability to modify when underlying schema changes	Excellent; can be easily altered and recompiled independently	Excellent, as of Oracle9*i*	Excellent
Risk of unexpected interactions	Low	Low	High; triggers may have unpredictable interactions with each other

Table 21-3. Assessment of techniques for encapsulating DML on object views (continued)

Consideration	PL/SQL package	Object method	INSTEAD OF trigger
Ease of use with client tool default functionality (specifically Oracle Developer)	Acceptable; programmer must add code for all client-side transactional triggers	Acceptable; programmer must add code for all client-side transactional triggers	Excellent for top-level types (however, there is no INSTEAD OF LOCK server-side trigger)
Can be turned on and off at will	No	No	Yes (by disabling and enabling the trigger)

As you can see, there is no clear "winner." Each technique has benefits that may be of more or less importance to your application.

One important point about using INSTEAD OF triggers in view hierarchies is that you will need a separate trigger for each level of the hierarchy. When you perform DML through a subview, the subview's trigger will fire; when you perform DML through the superview, the superview's trigger will fire.

And of course, you may decide that INSTEAD OF triggers make sense in combination with PL/SQL packages and/or object methods to provide layers of encapsulation. For example:

```
CREATE OR REPLACE TRIGGER images_v_insert
INSTEAD OF INSERT ON images_v
FOR EACH ROW
BEGIN
   /* Call a packaged procedure to perform the insert. */
   manage_image.create_one(:NEW.image_id, :NEW.file_type,
      :NEW.file_name, :NEW.bytes, :NEW.keywords);
END;
```

In an ideal world, developers would select an overall architecture and design approach before hurling every Oracle feature at their application. Use a feature only if it make sense for your design. I agree with Oracle's advice that if you do use triggers, you should use them in moderation.

Differences Between Object Views and Object Tables

In addition to the obvious difference between an object view and an object table, PL/SQL programmers should be aware of the more subtle differences. Areas of difference include the following:

- OID uniqueness
- "Storeability" of physical versus virtual REFs
- REFs to non-unique OIDs

Lets look at each difference in turn.

OID uniqueness

An object table will always have a unique object identifier, either system-generated or derived from the primary key. It is technically possible—though poor practice—to create an object table with duplicate rows, but the instances will still be unique in their object identifier. This can happen in two different ways.

Duplicate OIDs in a single view
: An object view can easily contain multiple object instances (rows) for a given OID. We've already seen a case where the superview can accidentally contain duplicates.

Duplicate OIDs across multiple views
: If your object view is defined on an underlying object table or view *and* if you use the DEFAULT keyword to specify the OID, the view contains OIDs that match the OIDs of the underlying structure.

It seems more likely that this second possibility of duplication would be legitimate in your application, because separate views are just separate stored queries.

"Storeability" of physical versus virtual REFs

If you've built an application with physical object tables, you can store REFs to those objects persistently in other tables. A REF is a binary value that Oracle can use as a pointer to an object.

However, Oracle returns an error if you attempt to store a virtual REF—that is, a REF to a row of an object view—in an actual table. Because the reference depends on some column value(s), you will need to save the underlying column value(s) instead of the virtual reference. From one perspective, this is an irritant rather than a major obstacle. Still, it's a bit unpleasant that we cannot intermingle object tables with object views, nor can we perform a simple transformation from an object view into an object table. I would like to be able to create an object table:

```
CREATE TABLE images2 OF image_t
   NESTED TABLE keywords STORE AS keyword_tab;
```

and then populate it from the view:

```
INSERT INTO images2       /* invalid because images_v includes a REF */
 SELECT VALUE(i) FROM images_v i;
```

But alas, Oracle tells me *ORA-22979: cannot INSERT object view REF or user-defined REF*. Life goes on, however.

REFs to non-unique OIDs

I don't believe that it is possible to have a REF to a non-unique OID when dealing with object tables. You may want to consider what will happen if you create a REF to an object in an object view, but the view has multiple object instances for the OID in question. Granted, this is a pretty weird case; you shouldn't be creating object views with ambiguous OIDs.

In my testing, DEREFing this type of virtual REF did indeed return an object—apparently, the first one Oracle found that matched. In previous versions of Oracle, this operation returns a NULL. I don't think I would count on either behavior in an application.

Maintaining Object Types and Object Views

If you work much with object types, you will learn a number of ways to get information about the types and views that you have created. Once you reach the limits of the SQL*Plus DESCRIBE command, this could involve direct queries from the Oracle data dictionary.

The dictionary term for user-defined types (objects and collections) is simply TYPE. Object type definitions and object type bodies are both found in the USER_SOURCE view (or DBA_SOURCE, or ALL_SOURCE), just as package specifications and bodies are. Table 21-4 lists a number of helpful queries you can use.

Table 21-4. Data dictionary entries for object types

To answer the question...	Use a query such as

What object and collection types have I created?	`SELECT * FROM user_types;`
	`SELECT * FROM user_objects`
	`   WHERE object_type = 'TYPE';`

What do my object type hierarchies look like?	`SELECT RPAD(' ', 3*(LEVEL-1)) || type_name`
	`  FROM user_types`
	` WHERE typecode = 'OBJECT'`
	`  CONNECT BY PRIOR type_name = supertype_name;`

What are the attributes of type foo?	`SELECT * FROM user_type_attrs` ` WHERE type_name = 'FOO';`
What are the methods of type foo?	`SELECT * FROM user_type_methods` ` WHERE type_name = 'FOO';`
What are the parameters of foo's methods?	`SELECT * FROM user_method_params` ` WHERE type_name = 'FOO';`
What datatype is returned by foo's method called bar?	`SELECT * FROM user_method_results` ` WHERE type_name = 'FOO' AND method_name = 'BAR';`

What is the source code for foo, including all ALTER statements?	`SELECT text FROM user_source`
	` WHERE name = 'FOO'`
	`   AND type = 'TYPE' /* or 'TYPE BODY' */`
	` ORDER BY line;`

What are the object tables that implement foo?	`SELECT table_name FROM user_object_tables` ` WHERE table_type = 'FOO';`

What are all the columns in an object table foo_tab, including the hidden ones?	`SELECT column_name, data_type, hidden_column,`
	`   virtual_column`
	`  FROM user_tab_cols`
	` WHERE table_name = 'FOO_TAB';`

Table 21-4. Data dictionary entries for object types (continued)

To answer the question...	Use a query such as
What columns implement foo?	`SELECT table_name, column_name FROM user_tab_columns WHERE data_type = 'FOO';`
What database objects depend on foo?	`SELECT name, type FROM user_dependencies WHERE referenced_name = 'FOO';`
What object views have I created, using what OIDs?	`SELECT view_name, view_type, oid_text FROM user_views WHERE type_text IS NOT NULL;`
What does my view hierarchy look like? (Requires a temporary table because you can't use a subquery with CONNECT BY)	`CREATE TABLE uvtemp AS SELECT v.view_name, v.view_type, v.superview_name, v1.view_type superview_type FROM user_views v, user_views v1 WHERE v.superview_name = v1.view_name (+); SELECT RPAD(' ', 3*(LEVEL-1)) || view_name || ' (' || view_type || ') ' FROM uvtemp CONNECT BY PRIOR view_type = superview_type; DROP TABLE uvtemp;`
What is the query on which I defined the foo_v view?	`SET LONG 1000 -- or greater SELECT text FROM user_views WHERE view_name = 'FOO_V';`
What columns are in view foo_v?	`SELECT column_name, data_type_mod, data_type FROM user_tab_columns WHERE table_name = 'FOO_V';`

One potentially confusing thing Oracle has done in the data dictionary is to make object tables invisible from the USER_TABLES view. Instead, a list of object tables appears in USER_OBJECT_TABLES (as well as in USER_ALL_TABLES).

Privileges

There are a handful of system-level privileges associated with object types, summarized here:

CREATE [ANY] TYPE
: Create, alter, and drop object types and type bodies. ANY means in any schema.

CREATE [ANY] VIEW
: Create and drop views, including object views. ANY means in any schema.

ALTER ANY TYPE
: Use ALTER TYPE facilities on types in any schema.

EXECUTE ANY TYPE
: Use an object type from any schema for purposes including instantiating, executing methods, referencing, and dereferencing.

UNDER ANY TYPE
: Create a subtype in one schema under a type in any other schema.

UNDER ANY VIEW
: Create a subview in one schema under a view in any other schema.

There are three kinds of object-level privileges on object types: EXECUTE, UNDER, and DEBUG. It is also important to understand how the conventional DML privileges apply to object tables and views.

The EXECUTE privilege

If you want your associate Joe to use one of your types in his own PL/SQL programs or tables, you can grant the EXECUTE privilege to him:

```
GRANT EXECUTE on catalog_item_t TO joe;
```

If Joe has the privilege needed to create synonyms and is running Oracle9*i* Release 2 or later, he will be able to create a synonym:

```
CREATE SYNONYM catalog_item_t FOR scott.catalog_item_t;
```

and use it as follows:

```
CREATE TABLE catalog_items OF catalog_item_t;
```

and/or:

```
DECLARE
   an_item catalog_item_t;
```

Joe can also use a qualified reference to the type scott.catalog_item_t.

If you refer to an object type in a stored program and grant EXECUTE privilege on that program to a user or role, having EXECUTE on the type is not required, even if the program is defined using invoker rights (described in Chapter 20). Similarly, if a user has a DML privilege on a view that has an INSTEAD OF trigger for that DML operation, that user doesn't need explicit EXECUTE privileges if the trigger refers to the object type because triggers run under the definer rights model. However, the EXECUTE privilege is required by users who need to run anonymous blocks that use the object type.

The UNDER privilege

The UNDER privilege gives the grantee the right to create a subtype. You can grant it as follows:

```
GRANT UNDER ON image_t TO scott;
```

For a schema to be able to create a subtype, the supertype must be defined using invoker rights (AUTHID CURRENT_USER).

This privilege can also grant the recipient the right to create a subview:

```
GRANT UNDER ON images_v TO scott;
```

An apparent bug prevented this from working on the Oracle version where I tested it, however.

The DEBUG privilege

If one of your associates is using a PL/SQL debugger to analyze code that uses a type you have created, you may wish to grant him the DEBUG privilege:

```
GRANT DEBUG ON image_t TO joe;
```

Doing so will enable the grantee to look "under the covers" to examine the variables used in the type and to set breakpoints inside methods.

The DEBUG privilege also applies to object views, providing a way to debug the PL/SQL source code of INSTEAD OF triggers.

The DML privileges

For object tables, the traditional SELECT, INSERT, UDPATE, and DELETE privileges still have some meaning. A user with only SELECT privilege on the object table may retrieve any relational columns in the base type on which the table is defined, but cannot retrieve the object-as-object. That is, VALUE, TREAT, REF, and DEREF are not available. Similarly, the other DML privileges, INSERT, UPDATE, and DELETE, also apply only to the relational interpretation of the table.

In the same fashion, the grantee will not have permission to use the constructor or other object methods unless the object type owner has granted the user EXECUTE privilege on the object type. Any columns defined on subtypes will be invisible.

Pontifications

I have to confess that I started programming before object approaches made any kind of inroads into business application development. I think I'm still waiting for that to happen.

Over the years, I've seen no compelling evidence that any particular programming style has a monopoly on the fundamental things we care about—fidelity to requirements, performance efficiency, developer effectiveness, and system reliability. I have seen a lot of fads, bandwagons, hand-waving, and unsupported assumptions (OK, I'm probably not entirely innocent myself), and object-oriented programming seems to attract quite a lot of it. That isn't to say that OOP fails to help you solve problems; it's just that OOP is not the magic bullet that many would have you believe.

Take, for example, the principle of object-based decomposition, particularly as it tends to generate inheritance hierarchies. By accurately modeling objects as they exist in the real world, software artifacts should be easier to comprehend, faster to assemble, and more amenable to large-scale system development. Sounds fabulous, doesn't it? Well, there are a lot of different ways to decompose something drawn from the real world.* It is a rare taxonomy that can exist in a simple hierarchy. My

* See "Object Oriented Programming Oversold!" by B. Jacobs, *http://www.geocities.com/tablizer/oopbad.htm*.

library catalog hierarchy could have been decomposed according to, say, media (print versus audio tape versus digital format...). And, although Oracle provides wonderful tools for type evolution, it may still be so painful to make sweeping changes in a type hierarchy that it will never happen. This isn't really the tool's fault; reality has a way of circumventing even the best-laid plans.

Nor is it even clear that co-locating the programming logic (methods) with the data (attributes) in an abstract datatype yields any measurable benefits. It looks reasonable and makes for some great sound bites, but how exactly will coupling data and behavior be better than keeping data structures (logical and physical table design) separate from processes (procedures, functions, packages)? Many development methods acknowledge that an organization's business data structures have a much slower rate of change than do the algorithms that manipulate them. It is a design truism (even for OOP) that the more volatile elements of a system should be kept separate from the more stable elements.

There is considerable inconsistency on this last point. Rich and famous object evangelists, while emphasizing the value of bundling data with behaviors, simultaneously promote a "model-view-controller" approach that "separates business logic from data." Are these emperors wearing clothes, or not?

Many OOP proponents have argued for years that its greatest benefit is the reuse of software. It has been said so many times that it must be true! Unfortunately, few observers have hard evidence for this,* in part because there is no consensus on what constitutes "reuse." Even object apologists began promoting higher-level "components" (whatever those may be) as a preferred unit of reuse precisely because objects proved very difficult to fit into situations beyond those for which they were designed. My sense is that OOP results in no more code reuse than well-designed subroutines.

It is certainly possible to use object-oriented approaches with PL/SQL and achieve reuse of software. Fellow author Don Bales, an accomplished object-oriented programmer, has been using PL/SQL packages as "types" for about a decade, and he says that he has been able to take entire packages (and any accompanying tables) and drop them into new software development projects without modification. He believes that the missing ingredient in most object approaches is an accurate model of the person who is actually executing the software—the user—whom Don models as an object with behaviors implemented in the actual program that is run.

Regardless of development method, some of the critical ingredients of software success are having prior expertise with similar problems, being able to employ seasoned project leaders, and incorporating a conscious software design phase. Introducing

* See "So Much OO, So Little Reuse," by Lawrence Finch, *Dr. Dobb's Journal*, May 7, 1998.

object methods or any other approach is likely to produce more positive results than an unplanned, organically grown system.

A few final thoughts on when to best use Oracle's object features:

- If you use the Oracle Call Interface (OCI), it's possible that the client-side cache and complex object retrieval would tip the scales in favor of heavy use of Oracle's object features. I'm not an OCI programmer, though, so I can't speak from experience in this regard.
- If your organization already uses object programming across the board, Oracle's object features will probably make it easier and more graceful to introduce database technology into your systems.
- Don't throw the collections baby out with the objects bathwater. Remember that you don't need to use object types or object views to take advantage of collections.
- If you've never used OOP before, these object features may seem quite complicated. I would encourage quite a bit of playing around before committing to an object approach. In particular, try out object views in conjunction with an existing system.
- I would caution against rejecting object types and object views on a vague performance argument. Oracle has made continuous progress in reducing overhead. If you perform some actual measurements, you might find OOP within acceptable bounds for your application.
- It turns out that Oracle delivers some of its built-in functionality (in features such as Oracle9*i* Advanced Queuing and Oracle Spatial) using object types. Using these features will require you to understand something about the object features even if you don't want to create your own custom types.

CHAPTER 22

Calling Java from PL/SQL

In this chapter:

In this chapter, I explore an exciting feature introduced in Oracle8*i* that allows a developer to call Java stored procedures (JSPs) from within PL/SQL. Java is a very powerful language, more robust in many ways than PL/SQL. Java also offers hundreds of classes that provide clean, easy-to-use Application Programming Interfaces (APIs) to a wide variety of functionality.

Oracle and Java

Beginning with the Oracle8*i* release, Oracle includes a product called JServer, which consists of the following elements:

- Oracle's Java Virtual Machine (JVM), called Aurora; the supporting runtime environment; and Java class libraries
- Tight integration with PL/SQL and Oracle RDBMS functionality
- An Object Request Broker (the Aurora/ORB) and Enterprise JavaBeans (EJB)
- The JServer Accelerator (native compiler)

The Aurora JVM executes Java methods (also known as *Java stored procedures*, or JSPs) and classes if they were stored in the database itself.

Java in the Oracle database is a big topic; Java programming all by itself is an even bigger topic. Complete treatment of either is outside the scope of this book. My objectives for this chapter are limited to the following:

- Providing the information you need to load Java classes into the Oracle database, manage those new database objects, and publish them for use inside PL/SQL
- Offering a basic tutorial in building Java classes that will provide enough guidance to let you construct simple classes to access underlying Java functionality

To access Java class methods from within Oracle, you must take the following steps:

1. Create the Java code elements. You can do this in Oracle's JDeveloper or in any other Java Integrated Development Environment. (In a pinch, *notepad.exe* will also do the trick!)
2. Load the Java classes into Oracle using the *loadjava* command-line utility or the CREATE JAVA statement.
3. Publish the Java class methods inside PL/SQL by writing wrapper programs in PL/SQL around the Java code.
4. Grant privileges as required on the PL/SQL wrapper programs and the Java class referenced by the PL/SQL wrapper.
5. Call the PL/SQL programs from any one of a number of environments, as illustrated in Figure 22-1.

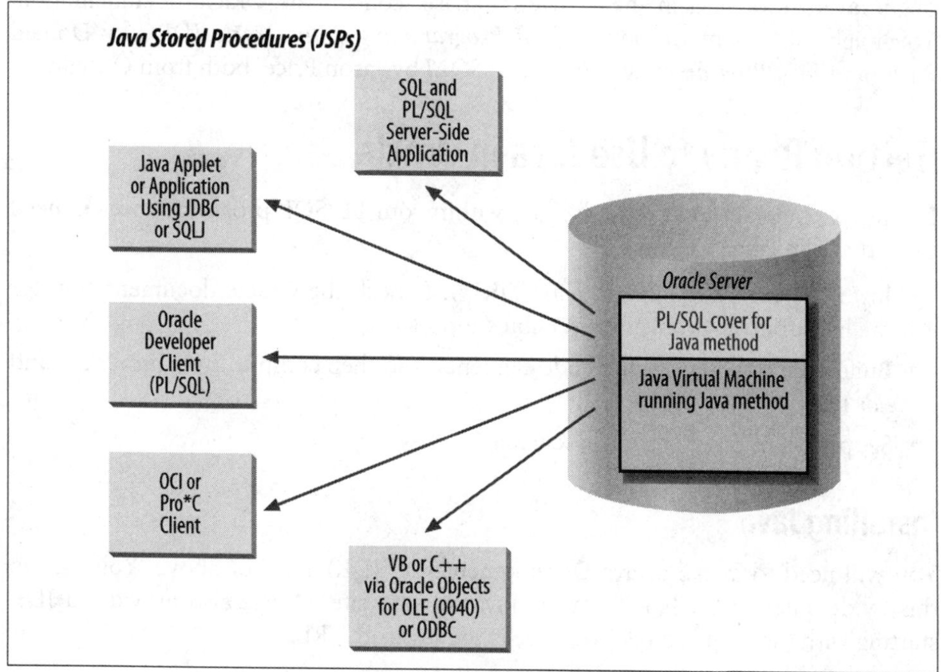

Figure 22-1. Accessing JSPs from within the Oracle database

Oracle offers a variety of components and commands to work with Java. Table 22-1 summarizes these different elements.

Table 22-1. Oracle components and commands for Java

Component	Description
Aurora JVM	The Java Virtual Machine (JVM) that Oracle implemented in its database server
loadjava	An operating system command-line utility that loads your Java code elements (classes, *.jar* files, etc.) into the Oracle database
dropjava	An operating system command-line utility that drops your Java code elements (classes, *.jar* files, etc.) from the Oracle database
CREATE JAVA DROP JAVA ALTER JAVA	New DDL statements that perform some of the same tasks as *loadjava* and *dropjava*
DBMS_JAVA	A built-in package that offers a number of utilities to set options and other aspects of the JVM
JPublisher	A utility used to build Java classes around object types and REFs defined in the Oracle database

The remainder of this chapter explains these steps and components. For more thorough coverage of Java in the Oracle database, consult the Oracle documentation. You might also want to look at *Java Programming with Oracle JDBC* by Donald Bales, and *Java Programming with Oracle SQLJ* by Jason Price, both from O'Reilly.

Getting Ready to Use Java in Oracle

Before you can call Java methods from within your PL/SQL programs you will need to do the following:

- Install a Java Development Kit (JDK™). (Check the Oracle documentation for the latest information about version support.)
- Build your Java classes and code elements, and then compile them into *.class* and *.jar* files.
- Set privileges on your Oracle schema.

Installing Java

You will need to install a Java Development Kit (JDK) 1.1.5 or above. You can do this by downloading a JDK from the Javasoft web site; Oracle also provides a JDK starting with the Oracle8*i* release. Here is the Javasoft URL:

http://www.javasoft.com/products/index.html

Make sure to set the environmental variable CLASSPATH so that the Java compiler (*javac*) can locate any references to your classes—and to the Oracle classes. Visit the following URL to get more information about CLASSPATH and general documentation on the Java language:

http://java.sun.com

Building and Compiling Your Java Code

Many PL/SQL developers (myself included) have never worked with an object-oriented language of any kind, so getting up to speed on Java can be a bit of a challenge. In the short time in which I have studied and used Java, I have come to these conclusions:

- It doesn't take long to get a handle on the syntax needed to build simple classes in Java.
- It's not at all difficult to start leveraging Java inside PL/SQL.
- Writing real object-oriented applications using Java requires significant rethinking for PL/SQL developers.

It would be impossible to offer a comprehensive primer on Java in this chapter. There are many (many, many, many) books available on various aspects of Java, and a number of them are excellent. I recommend that you check out the following:

- *The Java Programming Language,* by Ken Arnold, James Gosling, and David Holmes (Addison Wesley). James Gosling is the creator of Java, so you'd expect the book to be helpful. It is. Written in clear, simple terms, it gives you a strong grounding in the language.
- *Java in a Nutshell,* by David Flanagan (O'Reilly). This very popular and often-updated book contains a short, but excellent primer to the language, followed by a quick reference to all of the major language elements, arranged in an easy-to-use and heavily cross-referenced fashion.
- *Thinking in Java*, by Bruce Eckel (Prentice Hall). A very readable and creative approach to explaining object-oriented concepts. It is also available in a free, downloadable format at *http://www.mindview.net/Books/TIJ/*. If you like the feel of *Oracle PL/SQL Programming*, you will definitely enjoy *Thinking in Java*.

Later in this chapter, when I demonstrate how to call Java methods from within PL/SQL, I will also take you step by step through the creation of relatively simple classes. You will find that, in many cases, this discussion will be all you need to get the job done.

Setting Privileges for Java Development and Execution

Java security is handled differently in Oracle8*i* and Oracle9*i*, so we will look at each release individually in the following sections.

Oracle8i Java security

The Oracle8*i* database offers two roles that can grant privileges to allow access to different kinds of operations:

JAVAUSERPRIV
: Grants authority on relatively few Java permissions, including examining properties

JAVASYSPRIV
: Grants authority on major permissions, including updating JVM-protected packages

You grant these roles as you would any other database role. For example, if I want to allow Scott to perform any kind of Java-related operation, I would issue this command from a SYSDBA account:

```
GRANT JAVASYSPRIV TO SCOTT;
```

If I want to place some restrictions on what he can do with Java, I might execute this grant instead:

```
GRANT JAVAUSERPRIV TO SCOTT;
```

For example, to create a file through Java, I need the JAVASYSPRIV role; to read or write a file, I only need the JAVAUSERPRIV role. See the Oracle documentation for more details, including a table listing the different check methods of Java and which role is required to run those methods.

When the Aurora JVM is initialized, it installs an instance of java.lang.SecurityManager, the Java Security Manager. Each Oracle user has a *dynamic ID*, which will correspond to the session owner when you access the Java methods from within PL/SQL.

If a user lacking sufficient privileges tries to execute an illegal operation, the JVM will throw the java.lang.SecurityException. Here is what you would see in SQL*Plus:

```
ORA-29532: Java call terminated by uncaught Java exception:
           java.lang.SecurityException
```

When you run Java methods inside the database, different security issues can arise, particularly when interacting with the server-side filesystem or other operating system resources. Oracle follows the following two rules when checking I/O operations:

- If the dynamic ID has been granted JAVASYSPRIV, then Security Manager allows the operation to proceed.
- If the dynamic ID has been granted JAVAUSERPRIV, then Security Manager follows the same rules that apply to the PL/SQL UTL_FILE package to determine if the operation is valid. In other words, the file must be in a directory (or subdirectory) specified by the UTL_FILE_DIR parameter in the database initialization file.

Oracle9i Java security

Oracle9*i* JVM security is based on and supports Java 2 security, in which permissions are granted on a class-by-class basis. This is a much more sophisticated and fine-grained approach to security. A detailed treatment of this topic is outside the scope of this book; please see the Oracle documentation for details. I will, however, offer some examples in this section to give you a sense of the kind of security-related code you could write in Oracle9*i*.

Generally, you will use the DBMS_JAVA.GRANT_PERMISSION procedure to grant the appropriate permissions. Here is an example of calling that program to give the BATCH schema permission to read and write the *lastorder.log* file:

```
CALL DBMS_JAVA.GRANT_PERMISSION(
    'BATCH',
    'java.io.FilePermission', '/apps/OE/lastorder.log',
    'read,write');
```

And here is a sequence of commands that first grants permission to access files in a directory, and then *restricts* permission to perform operations on a particular file:

```
CONNECT OE_admin/OE_admin

REM Grant permission to all users (PUBLIC) to be able to read and write
REM all files in /tmp.
CALL DBMS_JAVA.GRANT_PERMISSION('PUBLIC',
     'java.io.FilePermission',
     '/tmp/*',
     'read,write');

REM Limit permission to all users (PUBLIC) from reading or writing the
REM password file in /tmp.
CALL DBMS_JAVA.GRANT_PERMISSION('PUBLIC',
     'java.io.FilePermission',
     '/tmp/password',
     'read,write');

REM By providing a more specific rule that overrides the limitation,
REM OE_admin can read and write /tmp/password.
CALL DBMS_JAVA.GRANT_PERMISSION('OE_admin',
     'java.io.FilePermission',
     '/tmp/password',
     'read,write');
COMMIT;
```

A Simple Demonstration

Before diving into the details, let's walk through all the steps needed to access Java from within PL/SQL. In the process, I'll introduce the various pieces of technology you need to get the job done.

Say that I need to be able to delete a file from within PL/SQL. Prior to Oracle 8.1, I had the following options:

- In Oracle 7.3 (and above), I could send a message to a database pipe, and then have a C listener program grab the message ("Delete file X") and do all the work.

- In Oracle 8.0, I could set up a library that pointed to a C DLL or shared library, and then from within PL/SQL call a program in that library to delete the file.

The pipe technique is handy, but it is a clumsy workaround. The external procedure implementation in Oracle 8.0 is a better solution, but it is also less than straightforward, especially if you don't know the C language. So the Java solution looks as if it might be the best one all around. Although some basic knowledge of Java is required, one does not need the same level of skill that would be required to write the equivalent code in C. Java comes with prebuilt (*foundation*) classes that offer clean, easy-to-use APIs to a wide array of functionality, including file I/O.

Here are the steps that I will perform in this demonstration:

1. Identify the Java functionality I need to access.
2. Build a class of my own to make the underlying Java feature callable through PL/SQL.
3. Compile the class and load it into the database.
4. Build a PL/SQL program to call the class method I created.
5. Delete files from within PL/SQL.

Oracle9*i* Release 2 offers an enhanced version of the UTL_FILE built-in package that allows you to delete a file by calling the UTL_FILE.FREMOVE program.

Finding the Java Functionality

My O'Reilly & Associates editor, Deborah Russell, was kind enough to send me a whole bunch of their Java books, so I grabbed the big, fat *Java Fundamental Classes Reference*, by Mark Grand and Jonathan Knudsen, and looked up "File" in the index (sure, I could use HTML documentation, but I *like* books). The entry for "File class" caught my eye and I hurried to page 161.

There I found information about the class named java.io.File, namely, that it "provides a set of methods to obtain information about files and directories." And it doesn't just let you obtain information—it also contains methods (procedures and functions) to delete and rename files, make directories, and so on. I had come to the right place!

Here is a portion of the API offered by the File class:

```
public class java.io.File {
   public boolean delete( );
   public boolean mkdir ( );
}
```

In other words, I will call a Boolean function in Java to delete a file. If the file is deleted, the function returns TRUE; otherwise, it returns FALSE.

Building a Custom Java Class

Now, you might be asking yourself why I had to build my own Java class on top of the File class. Why can't I just call that function directly inside my PL/SQL wrapper? There are two reasons:

- A Java class method is, in almost every case (except for static methods), executed for a specific object instantiated from the class. From within PL/SQL, I cannot instantiate a Java object and then call the method against that object.
- Even though Java and PL/SQL both have Boolean datatypes (Java even offers a Boolean primitive and a Boolean class), they do not map to each other. I cannot pass a Boolean from Java directly to a PL/SQL Boolean.

As a direct consequence, I need to build my own class that will:

- Instantiate an object from the File class
- Execute the delete method against that object
- Return a value that PL/SQL interprets properly

Here is the very simple class I wrote to take advantage of the File.delete method:

```
/* File on web: JDelete.java */
import java.io.File;

public class JDelete {

   public static int delete (String fileName) {
      File myFile = new File (fileName);
      boolean retval = myFile.delete( );
      if (retval) return 1; else return 0;
      }
}
```

Figure 22-2 explains each of the steps in this code, but the main effect is clear: the JDelete.delete method simply instantiates a dummy File object for the specified filename so that I can call the delete method for that file. By declaring my method to be static, I make that method available without the need to instantiate an object (which is necessary to be able to call this method from PL/SQL). Static methods are associated with the *class*, not with the objects declared from that class.

This class highlights a number of differences between Java and PL/SQL that you should keep in mind:

- There are no BEGIN and END statements in Java for blocks, loops, or conditional statements. Instead, you use an open-brace ({) to start a block of related code, and a close-brace (}) to close the block.
- Java is case-sensitive; "if" is definitely not the same thing as "IF".
- The assignment operator is a plain equals sign (=) rather than the complex symbol used in PL/SQL (:=).

- When you call a method that does not have any arguments (such as the delete method of the File class), you still must provide open and close parentheses. Otherwise, the Java compiler will try to interpret the method as a class member or data structure.

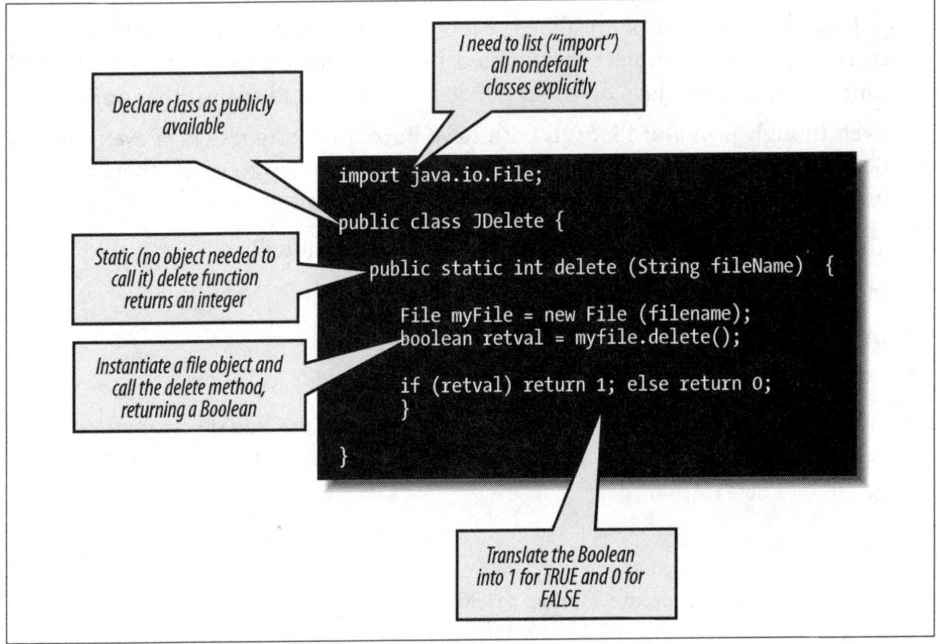

Figure 22-2. A simple Java class used to delete a file

Hey, that was easy! Of course, you didn't watch me fumble around with Java for a day, getting over the nuisance of minor syntax errors, the agony of a case-sensitive language, and the confusion setting the CLASSPATH. I'll leave all that to your imagination—and your own day of fumbling!

Compiling and Loading into Oracle

Now that my class is written, I need to compile. To do this I open an MS-DOS session on a Windows platform, change to the *d:\Java* directory (or wherever the Sun JDK is installed on your machine), and compile the class:

```
D:\Java> javac JDelete.java
```

Now that it's compiled, I realize that it would make an awful lot of sense to test the function before I stick it inside Oracle and try it from PL/SQL. You are always better off building and testing *incrementally*. Java gives us an easy way to do this: the main method. If you provide a void method (procedure) called main in your class—and give it the right parameter list—you can then call the class, and this code will execute.

The main method is one example of how Java treats certain elements in a special way if they have the right signature. Another example is the toString method. If you add a method with this name to your class, it will automatically be called to display your custom description of the object. This is especially useful when your object consists of many elements that make sense only when presented a certain way, or that otherwise require formatting to be readable.

So let's add a simple main method (shown in bold) to JDelete:

```
public class JDelete {
   public static int delete ...

   public static void main (String args[]) {
      System.out.println (
         delete (args[0])
         );
   }
}
```

In other words, you call delete for the first value passed to the class and then display the value being returned. Now I will recompile the class and run it (this example is taken from a DOS window):

```
D:\Java>javac JDelete.java

D:\Java>java JDelete c:\temp\te_employee.pks
1

D:\Java>java JDelete c:\temp\te_employee.pks
0
```

Notice that the first time I run the main method it displays 1 (TRUE), indicating that the file was deleted. So it will come as no surprise that when I run the same command again, main displays 0. It couldn't delete a file that had already been deleted.

That didn't take too much work or know-how, did it?

In another demonstration of the superiority of Java over PL/SQL, please note that while you have to type 20 characters in PL/SQL to display output (DBMS_OUTPUT.PUT_LINE), you needn't type any more than 18 characters in Java (System.out.println). Give us a break, you language designers! Though Alex Romankeuich, one of our technical reviewers, notes that if you declare "private static final PrintStream o = System.out;" at the beginning of the class, you can then display output in the class with the command "o.println"—only 9 characters in all!

Now that my class compiles and I have verified that the delete method works, I will load it into the SCOTT schema of the Oracle database using the *loadjava* command:

```
D:\Java>loadjava -user scott/tiger -oci8 -resolve JDelete.class
```

I can even verify that the class is loaded by querying the contents of the USER_OBJECTS data dictionary via a utility I'll introduce later in this chapter:

```
SQL> exec myjava.showobjects
Object Name Object Type  Status  Timestamp
---------------------------------------------
Hello        JAVA CLASS   VALID   1999-05-19:16:42
JDelete      JAVA CLASS   VALID   1999-06-07:13:20
JFile2       JAVA CLASS   VALID   1999-05-26:17:07
JFile3       JAVA CLASS   VALID   1999-05-27:12:53
```

That takes care of all the Java-specific steps, which means that it's time to return to the cozy world of PL/SQL.

Building a PL/SQL Wrapper

I will now make it easy for anyone connecting to my instance to delete files from within PL/SQL. To accomplish this goal, I will create a PL/SQL wrapper that looks like a PL/SQL function on the outside, but is really nothing more than a pass-through to the underlying Java code.

```
/* File on web: fdelete.sf */
CREATE OR REPLACE FUNCTION fDelete (
   file IN VARCHAR2)
   RETURN NUMBER
AS LANGUAGE JAVA
   NAME 'JDelete.delete (
            java.lang.String)
            return int';
```

The implementation of the fdelete function consists of a string describing the Java method invocation. The parameter list must reflect the parameters of the method, but in place of each parameter I specify the fully qualified datatype name. In this case, that means that I cannot simply say "String", but instead must add the full name of the package containing the String class. The RETURN clause simply lists int for integer. The int is a primitive datatype, not a class, so that is the complete specification.

Deleting Files from PL/SQL

So I compile the function and then perform my magical, previously difficult (if not impossible) feat:

```
SQL> @fdelete.sf

Function created.

Input truncated to 12 characters

SQL> exec DBMS_OUTPUT.PUT_LINE (
      fdelete('c:\temp\te_employee.pkb'))
1
```

```
SQL> exec DBMS_OUTPUT.PUT_LINE (
       fdelete('c:\temp\te_employee.pkb'))
0
```

I can also build utilities on top of this function. How about a procedure that deletes all of the files found in the rows of a nested table? Even better, how about a procedure that accepts a directory name and filter ("all files like *.tmp*", for example) and deletes all files found in that directory that pass the filter?

In reality, of course, what I should do is build a package and then put all this great new stuff in there. And that is just what I will do later in this chapter. First, however, let's take a closer look at each of the steps I just performed.

Using loadjava

The *loadjava* utility is an operating system command-line utility that uploads Java files into the database. The first time you run *loadjava* in a schema, it creates a number of elements for its own use:

CREATE$JAVA$LOB$TABLE
: A table created in each schema, containing Java code elements. Each new class you load using *loadjava* will generate one row in this table.

JAVA$CLASS$MD5$TABLE
: A *hash table*, also referred to as the *digest table*, used to track the loading of Java elements into a given schema.

LOADLOBS
: A package that is installed in each schema, used to load Java code elements as large objects (LOBs) into the database.

Using LOADLOBS, *loadjava* moves Java files into a BLOB column in the database table CREATE$JAVA$LOB$TABLE. It also checks the JAVA$CLASS$MD5$TABLE. MD5 hash value to see if the loaded classes have been loaded previously and whether they have been changed (thereby minimizing the need to reload).* This is done to avoid unnecessary invalidation of dependent classes. It then calls the new DDL command CREATE JAVA to load the Java classes from the BLOB column of CREATE$JAVA$LOB$TABLE into the RDBMS as schema objects. This loading occurs only if:

- The class is being loaded for the first time
- The class has been changed
- The -force option is supplied

* MD5 is RSA Data Security's MD5 message digest algorithm; more information can be found at *http://www.columbia.edu/~ariel/ssleay/rfc1321.html*.

Figure 22-3 illustrates the loading of Java objects into the Oracle database.

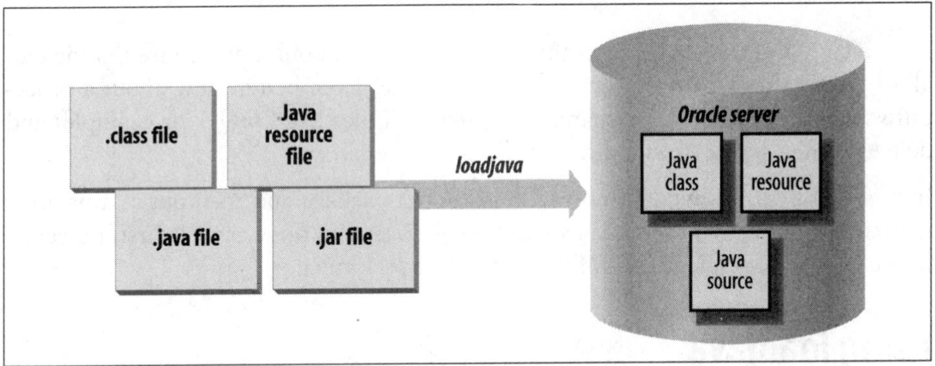

Figure 22-3. Loading Java elements into Oracle

Here is the syntax:

```
loadjava {-user | -u} username/password[@database]
  [-option_name [-option_name] ...] filename [filename ]...
```

where *option_name* can be one or more of many options, some of which are listed below:

```
  | debug
  | {definer | d}
  | {encoding | e} encoding_scheme_name
  | {force | f}
  | {grant | g} {username | role_name}[,{username | role_name}]...
  | {oci8 | o}
  | {resolve | r}
  | {resolver | R} "resolver_spec"
  | {schema | S} schema_name
  | {synonym | s}
  | {thin | t}
  | {verbose | v}
  | {nousage}
  | {noverify}}
```

On the command line, you can enter the names of Java source, class, and resource files, SQLJ input files (*.sqlj* files), and uncompressed *.jar* files and *.zip* archives, in any order.

The following command, for example, loads the JFile class into the SCOTT schema:

```
loadjava -user scott/tiger -oci8 -resolve JFile.class
```

You can run this command from within a DOS window on Windows platforms or from the command line in a Unix session. You can also execute it from within SQL*Plus as shown:

```
host loadjava -user scott/tiger -oci8 -resolve JFile.class
```

To make it easier to load Java resources into Oracle, I created a file named *lj.bat* for Windows as follows:

```
javac %1.java
loadjava -user %2 -oci8 -resolve %1.java
```

Now I can compile and load a Java class in one step:

```
D:\Java> lj scott/tiger JFile
```

Here are some things to keep in mind about *loadjava*. To display a help screen, use this syntax:

```
loadjava {-help | -h}
```

In a list of options or files, names must be separated only by spaces:

```
-force, -resolve, -thin  // No
-force -resolve -thin    // Yes
```

In a list of users or roles, however, names must be separated only by commas:

```
SCOTT, PAYROLL, BLAKE  // No
SCOTT,PAYROLL,BLAKE    // Yes
```

Table 22-2 summarizes the common *loadjava* command-line options.

Table 22-2. Common loadjava options

Option	Description
-debug	Generates debug information. This option is equivalent to javac -g.
-definer	Specifies that the methods of uploaded classes will execute with the privileges of their definer, not their invoker. (By default, methods execute with the privileges of their invoker.) Different definers can have different privileges, and an application can have many classes, so make sure the methods of a given class execute only with the privileges they need.
-encoding	Sets (or resets) the -encoding option in the database table JAVA$OPTIONS to the specified value, which must be the name of a standard JDK encoding scheme (the default is "latin1"). The compiler uses this value, so the encoding of uploaded source files must match the specified encoding. Refer to the section "GET_, SET_, and RESET_COMPILER_OPTION: Getting and Setting Compiler Options" for information on how this object is created and used.
-force	Forces the loading of Java class files, whether or not they have been loaded before. By default, previously loaded class files are rejected. You cannot force the loading of a class file if you previously loaded the source file. You must drop the source schema object first.
-grant	Grants the EXECUTE privilege on uploaded classes to the listed users or roles. (To call the methods of a class directly, users must have the EXECUTE privilege.) This option is cumulative. Users and roles are added to the list of those having the EXECUTE privilege. To revoke the privilege, either drop and reload the schema object without specifying -grant, or use the SQL REVOKE statement. To grant the privilege on an object in another user's schema, you must have the CREATE PROCEDURE WITH GRANT privilege.
-oci8	Directs *loadjava* to communicate with the database using the OCI JDBC driver. This option (the default) and -thin are mutually exclusive. When calling *loadjava* from a client-side computer that does not have Oracle installed on it, use the -thin option.

Table 22-2. Common loadjava options (continued)

Option	Description
-resolve	After all class files on the command line are loaded and compiled (if necessary), resolves all external references in those classes. If this option is not specified, files are loaded but not compiled or resolved until runtime. Specify this option to compile (if necessary) and resolve a class that was loaded previously. You need not specify the -force option because resolution is done independently, after loading.
-resolver	Binds newly created class schema objects to a user-defined resolver spec. Because it contains spaces, the resolver spec must be enclosed in double quotes. This option and -oracleresolver (the default) are mutually exclusive.
-schema	Assigns newly created Java schema objects to the specified schema. If this option is not specified, then the logon schema is used. You must have the CREATE ANY PROCEDURE privilege to load into another user's schema.
-synonym	Creates a public synonym for uploaded classes, making them accessible outside the schema into which they are loaded. To specify this option, you must have the CREATE PUBLIC SYNONYM privilege. If you specify this option for source files, it also applies to classes compiled from those source files.
-thin	Directs *loadjava* to communicate with the database using the thin JDBC driver. This option and -oci8 (the default) are mutually exclusive. When calling *loadjava* from a client-side computer that does not have Oracle installed on it, use the -thin option.
-verbose	Enables the verbose mode, in which progress messages are displayed.

As you can probably imagine, there are various nuances of using *loadjava*, such as whether to load individual classes or compressed groups of elements in a *.zip* or *.jar* file. The Oracle documentation contains more information about the *loadjava* command.

Using dropjava

The *dropjava* utility reverses the action of *loadjava*. It converts filenames into the names of schema objects, drops the schema objects, and finally deletes their digest table rows. Dropping a class invalidates classes that depend on it directly or indirectly. Dropping a source also drops classes derived from it.

Here is the syntax:

```
dropjava {-user | -u} username/password[@database]
  [-option_name [-option_name] ...] filename [filename] ...
```

where *option_name* can be one or more of many options, some of which are listed below:

```
{  {oci8 | o}
 | {schema | s} schema_name
 | {thin | t}
 | {verbose | v}
 | {help}
 | {encoding}
 | {synonym}}
```

On the command line, you can enter the names of Java source, class, and resource files, SQLJ input files, and uncompressed *.jar* files and *.zip* archives, in any order. Table 22-3 summarizes the common *dropjava* command-line options.

Table 22-3. Common dropjava options

Option	Description
-oci8	Directs *dropjava* to communicate with the database using the OCI JDBC driver. This option (the default) and -thin are mutually exclusive.
-schema	Drops Java schema objects from the specified schema. If this option is not specified, then the logon schema is used. You must have the DROP ANY PROCEDURE privilege to drop objects from another user's schema.
-thin	Directs *dropjava* to communicate with the database using the thin JDBC driver. This option and -oci8 (the default) are mutually exclusive.
-verbose	Enables the verbose mode, in which progress messages are displayed.

Managing Java in the Database

This section explores in more detail issues related to the way Java elements are stored in the database and how you can manage those elements.

The Java Namespace in Oracle

Oracle stores each Java class in the database as a schema object. The name of that object is derived from (but is not the same as) the fully qualified name of the class; this name includes the names of any containing packages. The full name of the class OracleSimpleChecker, for example, is as follows:

```
oracle.sqlj.checker.OracleSimpleChecker
```

In the database, however, the full name of the Java schema object would be:

```
oracle/sqlj/checker/OracleSimpleChecker
```

In other words, once stored in the Oracle RDBMS, slashes replace dots.

An object name in Oracle, whether the name of a database table or a Java class, cannot be longer than 30 characters. Java does not have this restriction; you can have much longer names. Oracle will allow you to load a Java class into Oracle with a name of up to 4000 characters. If the Java element name has more than 30 characters, Oracle will automatically generate a valid alias (less than 31 characters) for that element.

But don't worry! You never have to reference that alias. You can instead continue to use the real name for your Java element in your code. Oracle will map that long name automatically to its alias (the schema name) when necessary.

Examining Loaded Java Elements

Once you have loaded Java source, class, and resource elements into the database, information about those elements is available in several different data dictionary views, as shown in Table 22-4.

Table 22-4. Class information in data dictionary views

View	Description
USER_OBJECTS ALL_OBJECTS DBA_OBJECTS	Contains header information about your objects of JAVA SOURCE, JAVA CLASS, and JAVA RESOURCE types
USER_ERRORS ALL_ERRORS DBA_ERRORS	Contains any compilation errors encountered for your objects
USER_SOURCE	Contains the source code for your Java source if and only if you used the CREATE JAVA SOURCE command to create the Java schema object

You can write queries against these views, or you can build programs to access the information in a variety of useful ways. For example, here is a query that shows all of the Java-related objects in my schema:

```
/ *Files on web: showjava.sql and myJava.pkg */
COLUMN object_name FORMAT A30
SELECT object_name, object_type, status, timestamp
  FROM user_objects
 WHERE (object_name NOT LIKE 'SYS_%'
        AND object_name NOT LIKE 'CREATE$%'
        AND object_name NOT LIKE 'JAVA$%'
        AND object_name NOT LIKE 'LOADLOB%')
   AND object_type LIKE 'JAVA %'
 ORDER BY object_type, object_name;
```

The WHERE clause filters out those objects created by Oracle for managing Java objects. Here is some sample output:

```
SQL> exec myJava.showObjects
OBJECT_NAME           OBJECT_TYPE  STATUS  TIMESTAMP
--------------------- ------------ ------- -------------------
Hello                 JAVA CLASS   VALID   1999-05-19:16:42:27
JFile2                JAVA CLASS   VALID   1999-05-26:17:07:11
JFile3                JAVA CLASS   VALID   1999-05-27:12:53:46
plsolutions/java/putLn JAVA SOURCE VALID   1999-05-19:16:30:29
```

The *myjava.pkg* file on the O'Reilly site contains a packaged version of this query, allowing you to view your Java objects with this procedure call:

```
SQL> exec myJava.showobjects
```

The following lets you see a list of all the Java elements whose names start with OE:

```
SQL> exec myJava.showobjects ('OE%')
```

The USER_OBJECTS view's object_name column contains the full names of Java schema objects, unless the name is longer than 30 characters or contains an untranslatable character from the Unicode character set. In both cases, the short name is displayed in the object_name column. To convert short names to full names, you can use the LONGNAME function in the utility package DBMS_JAVA, which is explored in the next section.

Using DBMS_JAVA

The Oracle built-in package DBMS_JAVA gives you access to and the ability to modify various characteristics of the Aurora Java Virtual Machine.

The DBMS_JAVA package contains a large number of programs, many of which are intended for Oracle internal use only. Nevertheless, we can take advantage of a number of very useful programs; most can also be called within SQL statements. Table 22-5 summarizes some of the DBMS_JAVA programs. As noted earlier in the chapter, DBMS_JAVA also offers programs to manage security and permissions.

Table 22-5. Common DBMS_JAVA programs

Program	Description
LONGNAME function	Obtains the full (long) Java name for a given Oracle short name
GET_COMPILER_OPTION function	Looks up an option in the Java options table
SET_COMPILER_OPTION procedure	Sets a value in the Java options table and creates the table, if one does not exist
RESET_COMPILER_OPTION procedure	Resets a compiler option in the Java options table
SET_OUTPUT procedure	Redirects Java output to the DBMS_OUTPUT text buffer
EXPORT_SOURCE procedure	Exports a Java source schema object into an Oracle large object (LOB)
EXPORT_RESOURCE procedure	Exports a Java resource schema object into an Oracle large object
EXPORT_CLASS procedure	Exports a Java class schema object into an Oracle large object

These programs are explored in detail in the following sections.

LONGNAME: Converting Java Long Names

Java class and method names can easily exceed the maximum SQL identifier length of 30 characters. In such cases, Oracle creates a unique "short name" for the Java code element and uses that name for SQL- and PL/SQL-related access.

Use the following function to obtain the full (long) name for a given short name:

```
FUNCTION DBMS_JAVA.LONGNAME (shortname VARCHAR2) RETURN VARCHAR2
```

The following query displays the long names for all Java classes defined in the currently connected schema for which the long names and short names do not match:

```
/* File on web: longname.sql */
SELECT object_name shortname,
```

```
        DBMS_JAVA.LONGNAME (object_name) longname
   FROM USER_OBJECTS
   WHERE object_type = 'JAVA CLASS'
     AND object_name != DBMS_JAVA.LONGNAME (object_name);
```

This query is also available inside the myJava package (found in the *myJava.pkg* file); its use is shown here. Suppose that I define a class with this name:

```
public class DropAnyObjectIdentifiedByTypeAndName {
```

That is too long for Oracle, and we can verify that Oracle creates its own short name as follows:

```
SQL> exec myJava.showlongnames
Short Name | Long Name
----------------------------------------------------
Short: /247421b0_DropAnyObjectIdentif
Long:  DropAnyObjectIdentifiedByTypeAndName
```

GET_, SET_, and RESET_COMPILER_OPTION: Getting and Setting Compiler Options

You can also set compiler option values in the database table JAVA$OPTIONS (called the *options table* from here on). Then, you can selectively override those settings using *loadjava* command-line options. A row in the options table contains the names of source schema objects to which an option setting applies. You can use multiple rows to set the options differently for different source schema objects.

The compiler looks up options in the options table unless they are specified on the *loadjava* command line. If there is no options-table entry or command-line value for an option, the compiler uses the following default values (you can find more information about nondefault values in Oracle's *SQLJ Developer's Guide and Reference* documentation):

```
encoding = latin1
online = true       // applies only to SQLJ source files
```

You can get and set options-table entries using the following DBMS_JAVA functions and procedures:

```
FUNCTION DBMS_JAVA.GET_COMPILER_OPTION (
   what VARCHAR2, optionName VARCHAR2)

PROCEDURE DBMS_JAVA.SET_COMPILER_OPTION (
   what VARCHAR2, optionName VARCHAR2, value VARCHAR2)

PROCEDURE DBMS_JAVA.RESET_COMPILER_OPTION (
   what VARCHAR2, optionName VARCHAR2)
```

The parameter *what* is the name of a Java package, the full name of a class, or the empty string. After searching the options table, the compiler selects the row in which *what* most closely matches the full name of the schema object. If *what* is the empty string, it matches the name of any schema object.

optionName is the name of the option being set. Initially, a schema does not have an options table. To create one, use the procedure DBMS_JAVA.SET_COMPILER_OPTION to set a *value*. The procedure creates the table if it does not exist. Enclose parameters in single quotes, as shown in the following example:

```
SQL> DBMS_JAVA.SET_COMPILER_OPTION ('X.sqlj', 'online', 'false');
```

SET_OUTPUT: Enabling Output from Java

The System.out and System.err classes send their output to the current trace files (when executed within the Oracle database). This is not a very convenient repository if you simply want to test your code to see if it is working properly. DBMS_JAVA supplies a procedure you can call to redirect output to the DBMS_OUTPUT text buffer so that it can be flushed to your SQL*Plus screen automatically. The syntax of this procedure is:

```
PROCEDURE DBMS_JAVA.SET_OUTPUT (buffersize NUMBER);
```

Here is an example of how you would use this program:

```
//* File on web: ssoo.sql */
SET SERVEROUTPUT ON SIZE 1000000
CALL DBMS_JAVA.SET_OUTPUT (1000000);
```

Documentation on the interaction between these two commands is skimpy; my testing has uncovered the following rules:

- The minimum (and default) buffer size is a measly 2000 bytes; the maximum size is 1,000,000 bytes. You can pass a number outside of that range without causing an error; unless the number is *really* big, it will simply be ignored.
- The buffer size specified by SET SERVEROUTPUT supersedes that of DBMS_JAVA.SET_OUTPUT. In other words, if you provide a smaller value for the DBMS_JAVA call, it will be ignored, and the larger size will be used.
- If your output in Java exceeds the buffer size, you will *not* receive the error you get with DBMS_OUTPUT, namely:

  ```
  ORA-10027: buffer overflow, limit of nnn bytes
  ```

  The output will instead be truncated to the buffer size specified, and execution of your code will continue.

As is the case with DBMS_OUTPUT, you will not see any output from your Java calls until the stored procedure through which they are called finishes executing.

EXPORT_SOURCE, EXPORT_RESOURCE, and EXPORT_CLASS: Exporting Schema Objects

Oracle's DBMS_JAVA package offers the following set of procedures to export source, resources, and classes:

```
PROCEDURE DBMS_JAVA.EXPORT_SOURCE (
   name VARCHAR2,
   [ blob BLOB | clob CLOB ]
   );

PROCEDURE DBMS_JAVA.EXPORT_SOURCE (
   name VARCHAR2,
   schema VARCHAR2,
   [ blob BLOB | clob CLOB ]
   );

PROCEDURE DBMS_JAVA.EXPORT_RESOURCE (
   name VARCHAR2,
   [ blob BLOB | clob CLOB ]
   );

PROCEDURE DBMS_JAVA.EXPORT_RESOURCE (
   name VARCHAR2,
   schema VARCHAR2,
   [ blob BLOB | clob CLOB ]
   );

PROCEDURE DBMS_JAVA.EXPORT_CLASS (
   name VARCHAR2,
   blob BLOB
   );

PROCEDURE DBMS_JAVA.EXPORT_CLASS (
   name VARCHAR2,
   schema VARCHAR2,
   blob BLOB
   );
```

In all cases, *name* is the name of the Java schema object to be exported, *schema* is the name of the schema owning the object (if not supplied, then the current schema is used), and *blob* | *clob* is the large object that receives the specified Java schema object.

You cannot export a class into a CLOB, only into a BLOB. In addition, the internal representation of the source uses the UTF8 format, so that format is used to store the source in the BLOB as well.

The following prototype procedure offers an idea of how you might use the export programs to obtain source code of your Java schema objects, when appropriate:

```
/* File on web: showjava.sp */
CREATE OR REPLACE PROCEDURE show_java_source (
```

```
   NAME     IN   VARCHAR2,  SCHEMA   IN   VARCHAR2 := NULL
)
-- Overview: Shows Java source (prototype). Author: Vadim Loevski
IS
   b                      CLOB;
   v                      VARCHAR2 (2000);
   i                      INTEGER;
   object_not_available   EXCEPTION;
   PRAGMA EXCEPTION_INIT (object_not_available, -29532);

BEGIN
   /* Move the Java source code to a CLOB. */
   DBMS_LOB.createtemporary (b, FALSE );

   dbms_java.export_source (name,  NVL (SCHEMA, USER), b);

   /* Read the CLOB to a VARCHAR2 variable and display it. */
   i := 1000;
   DBMS_LOB.READ  (b, i, 1, v);
   DBMS_OUTPUT.PUT_LINE  (v);
EXCEPTION
   -- If the named object does not exist, an exception is raised.
   WHEN object_not_available
   THEN
      IF (SQLERRM) LIKE '%no such%object'
      THEN
         DBMS_OUTPUT.put_line ('Java object cannot be found.' );
      END IF;
END;/
```

If I then create a Java source object using the CREATE JAVA statement as follows:

```
CREATE OR REPLACE JAVA SOURCE NAMED "Hello"
AS
   public class Hello {
      public static String hello( ) {
         return "Hello Oracle World";}
      };
/
```

I can view the source code as shown here (assuming that DBMS_OUTPUT has been enabled):

```
SQL> exec show_java_source ('Hello')
public class Hello {
      public static String hello( ) {
         return "Hello
 Oracle World";
         }
      };
```

Publishing and Using Java in PL/SQL

Once you have written your Java classes and loaded them into the Oracle RDBMS, you can call their methods from within PL/SQL (and SQL)—but only after you "publish" those methods via a PL/SQL wrapper.

Call Specs

You need to build wrappers in PL/SQL only for those Java methods you want to make available through a PL/SQL interface. Java methods can access other Java methods in the Java Virtual Machine directly, without any need for a wrapper. To publish a Java method, you write a *call spec*—a PL/SQL program header (function or procedure) whose body is actually a call to a Java method via the LANGUAGE JAVA clause. This clause contains the following information about the Java method: its full name, its parameter types, and its return type. You can define these call specs as standalone functions or procedures, as programs within a package, or as methods in an object type:

```
CREATE [OR REPLACE] --Only if a standalone program
<Standard PL/SQL procedure/function header>
{IS | AS} LANGUAGE JAVA
NAME 'method_fullname (java_type_fullname[, java_type_fullname]...)
  [return java_type_fullname]';
```

where *java_type_fullname* is the full name of the Java type, such as java.lang.String.

The NAME clause string uniquely identifies the Java method being wrapped. The fully qualified Java names and the call spec parameters, which are mapped by position only, must correspond, one to one, with the parameters in the program. If the Java method takes no arguments, code an empty parameter list for it, but not for the function or procedure.

Here are a few examples:

- A standalone function calling a method:

```
CREATE OR REPLACE FUNCTION fDelete (
   file IN VARCHAR2)
   RETURN NUMBER
AS LANGUAGE JAVA
   NAME 'JDelete.delete (
           java.lang.String)
           return int';
```

- A packaged procedure with the LANGUAGE clause in the specification that passes an object type as a parameter:

```
CREATE OR REPLACE PACKAGE nat_health_care
IS
   PROCEDURE consolidate_insurer (ins Insurer)
      AS LANGUAGE JAVA
      NAME 'NHC_consolidation.process(oracle.sql.STRUCT)';
END nat_health_care;
```

- An object type method with the LANGUAGE clause in the specification:

```
CREATE TYPE pet_ AS OBJECT (
  name VARCHAR2(100),
  date_of_birth DATE,
  MEMBER FUNCTION age (
    name_in IN VARCHAR2) RETURN DATE
    AS LANGUAGE JAVA
    NAME 'petInfo.age (java.lang.String)
          return java.sql.Timestamp'
```

- A standalone procedure with an OUT parameter:

```
CREATE OR REPLACE PROCEDURE read_out_file (
   file_name  IN      VARCHAR2,
   file_line  OUT     VARCHAR2
)
AS
LANGUAGE JAVA
   NAME 'utils.ReadFile.read(java.lang.String
                            ,java.lang.String[])';
```

Some Rules for Java Wrappers

Note the following rules for Java wrappers:

- A PL/SQL call spec and the Java method it publishes must reside in the same schema.
- A call spec exposes a Java method's top-level entry point to Oracle. As a result, you can publish only public static methods, unless you are defining a member method of a SQL object type. In this case, you can publish instance methods as member methods of that type.
- You cannot provide default values in the parameter list of the PL/SQL program that will serve as a wrapper for a Java method invocation.
- A method in object-oriented languages cannot assign values to objects passed as arguments; the point of the method is to apply to the object to which it is attached. When you want to call a method from SQL or PL/SQL and change the value of an argument, you must declare it as an OUT or IN OUT parameter in the call spec. The corresponding Java parameter must then be a one-element array.

You can replace the element value with another Java object of the appropriate type, or (for IN OUT parameters only) modify the value if the Java type permits. Either way, the new value propagates back to the caller. For example, you might map a call spec OUT parameter of type NUMBER to a Java parameter declared as float[] p, and then assign a new value to p[0].

A function that declares OUT or IN OUT parameters cannot be called from SQL DML statements.

Mapping Datatypes

Earlier in this chapter, we saw a very simple example of a PL/SQL wrapper—a delete function that passed a VARCHAR2 value to a java.lang.String parameter. The Java method returned an int, which was then passed back through the RETURN NUMBER clause of the PL/SQL function. These are straightforward examples of datatype *mapping*, that is, setting up a correspondence between a PL/SQL datatype and a Java datatype.

When you build a PL/SQL call spec, the PL/SQL and Java parameters, as well as the function result, are related by position and must have compatible datatypes. Table 22-6 lists all the datatype mappings currently allowed between PL/SQL and Java. If you rely on a supported datatype mapping, Oracle will convert from one to the other automatically.

Table 22-6. Legal datatype mappings

SQL type	Java class
CHAR, NCHAR, LONG, VARCHAR2, NVARCHAR2	oracle.sql.CHAR java.lang.String java.sql.Date java.sql.Time java.sql.Timestamp java.lang.Byte java.lang.Short java.lang.Integer java.lang.Long java.lang.Float java.lang.Double java.math.BigDecimal byte, short, int, long, float, double
DATE	oracle.sql.DATE java.sql.Date java.sql.Time java.sql.Timestamp java.lang.String
NUMBER	oracle.sql.NUMBER java.lang.Byte java.lang.Short java.lang.Integer java.lang.Long java.lang.Float java.lang.Double java.math.BigDecimal byte, short, int, long, float, double
RAW, LONG RAW	oracle.sql.RAW byte[]
ROWID	oracle.sql.CHAR oracle.sql.ROWID java.lang.String
BFILE	oracle.sql.BFILE

Table 22-6. Legal datatype mappings (continued)

SQL type	Java class
BLOB	oracle.sql.BLOB oracle.jdbc2.Blob
CLOB, NCLOB	oracle.sql.CLOB oracle.jdbc2.Clob
OBJECT	oracle.sql.STRUCT oracle.SqljData oracle.jdbc2.Struct
REF	oracle.sql.REF oracle.jdbc2.Ref
TABLE, VARRAY	oracle.sql.ARRAY oracle.jdbc2.Array
Any of the above SQL types	oracle.sql.CustomDatum oracle.sql.Datum

As you can see, Oracle supports only automatic conversion for SQL datatypes. PL/SQL-specific datatypes, including BINARY_INTEGER, PLS_INTEGER, BOOLEAN, and associative table types, are not supported. In those cases, you will have to perform manual conversion steps to transfer data between these two execution environments. See the references in the "Other Examples" section for examples of non-default mappings; see the Oracle documentation for even more detailed examples involving the use of JDBC.

Calling a Java Method in SQL

You can call PL/SQL functions of your own creation from within SQL DML statements. You can also call Java methods wrapped in PL/SQL from within SQL. However, these methods must conform to the following purity rules:

- If you call a method from a SELECT statement or a parallelized INSERT, UPDATE, or DELETE statement, the method is not allowed to modify any database tables.
- If you call a method from an INSERT, UPDATE, or DELETE statement, the method cannot query or modify any database tables modified by that statement.
- If you call a method from a SELECT, INSERT, UPDATE, or DELETE statement, the method cannot execute SQL transaction control statements (such as COMMIT), session control statements (such as SET ROLE), or system control statements (such as ALTER SYSTEM). The method also cannot execute DDL statements, because they automatically perform a commit in your session. Note that these restrictions are waived if the method is executed from within an autonomous transaction PL/SQL block.

The objective of these restrictions is to control side effects that might disrupt your SQL statements. If you try to execute a SQL statement that calls a method violating any of these rules, you will receive a runtime error when the SQL statement is parsed.

It is also possible to call Java from PL/SQL via the SQL layer using the CALL command syntax and native dynamic SQL, as shown in the following code (the implementation of dropany is shown in the next section):

```
DECLARE
   Tp varchar2(30):='TABLE';
   Nm varchar2(30):='mytable';
BEGIN
   EXECUTE IMMEDIATE 'CALL dropany(:tp,:nm)' USING tp, nm;
END;
```

Exception Handling with Java

On the one hand, the Java exception-handling architecture is very similar to that of PL/SQL. In Java-speak, you throw an exception and then catch it. In PL/SQL-speak, you raise an exception and then handle it.

On the other hand, exception handling in Java is much more robust. Java offers a foundation class called Exception. All exceptions are objects based on that class, or on classes derived from (extending) that class. You can pass exceptions as parameters and manipulate them pretty much as you would objects of any other class.

When a Java stored method executes a SQL statement and an exception is thrown, that exception is an object from a subclass of java.sql.SQLException. That subclass contains two methods that return the Oracle error code and error message: getErrorCode( ) and getMessage( ).

If a Java stored procedure called from SQL or PL/SQL throws an exception that is *not* caught by the JVM, the caller gets an exception thrown from a Java error message. This is how all uncaught exceptions (including non-SQL exceptions) are reported. Let's take a look at the different ways of handling errors and the resulting output.

Suppose that I create a class that relies on JDBC to drop objects in the database (this is drawn from an example in Oracle documentation):

```
/* File on web: dropany.java */
import java.sql.*;
import java.io.*;
import oracle.jdbc.driver.*;

public class DropAny {
  public static void object (String object_type, String object_name)
  throws SQLException {
    // Connect to Oracle using JDBC driver
    Connection conn = new OracleDriver( ).defaultConnection( );
    // Build SQL statement
    String sql = "DROP " + object_type + " " + object_name;
```

```
        try {
            Statement stmt = conn.createStatement( );
            stmt.executeUpdate(sql);
            stmt.close( );
        } catch (SQLException e) {System.err.println(e.getMessage( ));}
    }
}
```

Of course, it doesn't really make any sense to rely on JDBC to perform a drop object action, as this can be done much more easily in native PL/SQL. On the other hand, building it in Java makes the functionality available to other Java programs.

This version traps and displays any SQLException with this line:

```
} catch (SQLException e) {System.err.println(e.getMessage( ));}
```

I load the class into the database using *loadjava*, and then wrap this class inside a PL/SQL procedure as follows:

```
CREATE OR REPLACE PROCEDURE dropany (
   tp IN VARCHAR2,
   nm IN VARCHAR2
   )
AS LANGUAGE JAVA
   NAME 'DropAny.object (
            java.lang.String,
            java.lang.String)';
```

When I attempt to drop a nonexistent object, I will see one of two outcomes:

```
SQL> CONNECT scott/tiger
Connected.

SQL> SET SERVEROUTPUT ON
SQL> BEGIN dropany ('TABLE', 'blip'); END;
/
PL/SQL procedure successfully completed.

SQL> CALL DBMS_JAVA.SET_OUTPUT (1000000);

Call completed.

SQL> BEGIN dropany ('TABLE', 'blip'); END;
/

ORA-00942: table or view does not exist
```

What you are seeing in these examples is a reminder that output from System.err.println will *not* appear on your screen until you explicitly enable it with a call to DBMS_JAVA.SET_OUTPUT. In either case, however, no exception was raised back to the calling block because it was caught inside Java. After the second call to dropany, you can see that the error message supplied through the getMessage() method is taken directly from Oracle.

If I comment out the try and catch lines in the DropAny.obj method, I will get very different behavior, as shown:

```
SQL> BEGIN
       dropany ('TABLE', 'blip');
     EXCEPTION
        WHEN OTHERS
        THEN
           DBMS_OUTPUT.PUT_LINE (SQLCODE);
           DBMS_OUTPUT.PUT_LINE (SQLERRM);
     END;

java.sql.SQLException: ORA-00942: table or view does not exist
  at oracle.jdbc.kprb.KprbDBAccess.check_error(KprbDBAccess.java)
  at oracle.jdbc.kprb.KprbDBAccess.parseExecuteFetch(KprbDBAccess.java)
  at oracle.jdbc.driver.OracleStatement.doExecuteOther(OracleStatement.java)
  at oracle.jdbc.driver.OracleStatement.doExecuteWithBatch(OracleStatement.java)
  at oracle.jdbc.driver.OracleStatement.doExecute(OracleStatement.java)
  at oracle.jdbc.driver.OracleStatement.doExecuteWithTimeout(OracleStatement.java)
  at oracle.jdbc.driver.OracleStatement.executeUpdate(OracleStatement.java)
  at DropAny.object(DropAny.java:14)

-29532
ORA-29532: Java call terminated by uncaught Java exception: java.sql.SQLException:
ORA-00942: table or view does not exist
```

This takes a little explaining. Everything between:

```
java.sql.SQLException: ORA-00942: table or view does not exist
```

and:

```
-29532
```

represents an error stack dump generated by Java and sent to standard output, regardless of how you handle the error in PL/SQL. In other words, even if my exception section looked like this:

```
EXCEPTION WHEN OTHERS THEN NULL;
```

I would still get all that output on the screen, and then processing in the outer block (if any) would continue. The last three lines of output displayed are generated by the calls to DBMS_OUTPUT.PUT_LINE. Notice that the Oracle error is not ORA-00942, but instead is ORA-29532, a generic Java error. This is a problem. If you trap the error, how can you discover what the real error is? Looks like it's time for Write-A-Utility Man!

It appears to me that the error returned by SQLERRM is of this form:

```
ORA-29532: Java call ...: java.sql.SQLException: ORA-NNNNN ...
```

So I can scan for the presence of java.sql.SQLException and then SUBSTR from there. The O'Reilly site contains a program in the *getErrorInfo.sp* file that returns the error code and message for the current error, building in the smarts to compensate for the Java error message format.

The main focus in the following sections is an expansion of the JDelete class into the JFile class, which will provide significant new file-related features in PL/SQL. Following that, we'll explore how to write Java classes and PL/SQL programs around them to manipulate Oracle objects.

Extending File I/O Capabilities

Oracle's UTL_FILE package is notable more for what it is missing than for what it contains. With UTL_FILE, you can read and write the contents of files sequentially. That's it. You can't delete files, change privileges, copy a file, obtain the contents of a directory, set a path, etc., etc. Java to the rescue! Java offers lots of different classes to manipulate files. You've already met the File class and seen how easy it is to add the "delete a file" capability to PL/SQL.

I will now take my lessons learned from JDelete and the rest of this chapter and create a new class called JFile, which will allow PL/SQL developers to answer the questions and take the actions listed here:

- Can I read from a file? Write to a file? Does a file exist? Is the named item a file or a directory?
- What is the number of bytes in a file? What is the parent directory of a file?
- What are the names of all the files in a directory that match a specified filter?
- How can I make a directory? Rename a file? Change the extension of a file?

I won't explain all the methods in the JFile class and its corresponding package; there is a *lot* of repetition, and most of the Java methods look just like the delete() function I built at the beginning of the chapter. I will instead focus on the unique issues addressed in different areas of the class and package. You can find the full definition of the code in the following files on the O'Reilly site:

JFile.java
: A Java class that draws together various pieces of information about operating system files and offers it through an API accessible from PL/SQL.

xfile.pkg
: The PL/SQL package that wraps the JFile class. Stands for "eXtra stuff for FILEs."

Oracle9*i* Release 2 offers an enhanced version of the UTL_FILE package that, among other things, allows you to delete a file using the UTL_FILE.FREMOVE procedure. It also supports file copying (FCOPY) and file renaming (FRENAME).

Polishing up the delete method

Before moving on to new and exciting stuff, we should make sure that what we've done so far is optimal. The way I defined the JDelete.delete() method and the delete_file function is far from ideal. Here's the code I showed you earlier:

```
public static int delete (String fileName) {
   File myFile = new File (fileName);
   boolean retval = myFile.delete( );
   if (retval) return 1; else return 0;
   }

CREATE OR REPLACE FUNCTION fDelete (
   file IN VARCHAR2) RETURN NUMBER
AS LANGUAGE JAVA
   NAME 'JDelete.delete (java.lang.String)
         return int';
```

So what's the problem? The problem is that I have been forced to use clumsy, numeric representations for TRUE/FALSE values. As a result, I must write code like this:

```
IF fdelete ('c:\temp\temp.sql') = 1 THEN ...
```

and that is very ugly, hardcoded software. Not only that, but the person writing the PL/SQL code would be required to know about the values for TRUE and FALSE embedded within a Java class.

I would much rather define a delete_file function with this header:

```
FUNCTION fDelete (
   file IN VARCHAR2) RETURN BOOLEAN;
```

So let's see what it would take to present that clean, easy-to-use API to users of the xfile package.

First, I will rename the JDelete class to JFile to reflect its growing scope. Then, I will add methods that encapsulate the TRUE/FALSE values its other methods will return—and call those inside the delete() method. Here is the result:

```
/* File on web: JFile.java */
import java.io.File;

public class JFile {

   public static int tVal ( ) { return 1; };
   public static int fVal ( ) { return 0; };

   public static int delete (String fileName) {
      File myFile = new File (fileName);
      boolean retval = myFile.delete( );
      if (retval) return tVal( );
         else return fVal( );
      }
}
```

That takes care of the Java side of things; now it's time to shift attention to my PL/SQL package. Here's the first pass at the specification of xfile:

```
/* File on web: xfile.pkg */
CREATE OR REPLACE PACKAGE xfile
IS
   FUNCTION delete (file IN VARCHAR2)
      RETURN BOOLEAN;
END xfile;
```

So now we have the Boolean function specified. But how do we implement it? I have two design objectives:

1. Hide the fact that I am relying on numeric values to pass back TRUE or FALSE.
2. Avoid hardcoding the 1 and 0 values in the package.

To achieve these objectives, I will define two global variables in my package to hold the numeric values:

```
/* File on web: xfile.pkg */
CREATE OR REPLACE PACKAGE BODY xfile
IS
   g_true INTEGER;
   g_false INTEGER;
```

And way down at the end of the package body, I will create an initialization section that calls these programs to initialize my globals. By taking this step in the initialization section, I avoid unnecessary calls (and overhead) to Java methods:

```
BEGIN
   g_true := tval;
   g_false := fval;
END xfile;
```

Back up in the declaration section of the package body, I will define two private functions whose only purpose is to give me access in my PL/SQL code to the JFile methods that have encapsulated the 1 and 0:

```
FUNCTION tval RETURN NUMBER
AS LANGUAGE JAVA
   NAME 'JFile.tVal () return int';

FUNCTION fval RETURN NUMBER
AS LANGUAGE JAVA
   NAME 'JFile.fVal () return int';
```

I have now succeeded in softcoding the TRUE/FALSE values in the JFile package. To enable the use of a true Boolean function in the package specification, I create a private "internal delete" function that is a wrapper for the JFile.delete() method. It returns a number:

```
FUNCTION Idelete (file IN VARCHAR2) RETURN NUMBER
AS LANGUAGE JAVA
   NAME 'JFile.delete (java.lang.String) return int';
```

Finally, my public delete function can now call Idelete and convert the integer value to a Boolean by checking against the global variable:

```
FUNCTION delete (file IN VARCHAR2) RETURN BOOLEAN
AS
BEGIN
   RETURN Idelete (file) = g_true;
EXCEPTION
   WHEN OTHERS
   THEN
      RETURN FALSE;
END;
```

And that is how you convert a Java Boolean to a PL/SQL Boolean. You will see this method employed again and again in the xfile package body.

Obtaining directory contents

One of my favorite features of JFile is its ability to return a list of files found in a directory. It accomplishes this feat by calling the File.list() method; if the string you used to construct a new File object is the name of a directory, it returns a String array of filenames found in that directory. Let's see how I can make this information available in PL/SQL.

I create a String method called dirContents, as follows:

```
/* File on web: JFile.java */
public static String dirContents (String dir) {
   File myDir = new File (dir);
   String[] filesList = myDir.list( );
   String contents = new String( );
   for (int i = 0; i < filesList.length; i++)
      contents = contents + listDelimiter + filesList[i];
   return contents;
   }
```

This method instantiates a File object called myDir and then assigns the myDir.list() to a String array called filesList. I then use a Java "for" loop to concatenate all of the files into a single String, separated by the listDelimiter, and return that String.

Over on the PL/SQL side of the world, I will create a wrapper that calls this method:

```
FUNCTION dirContents (dir IN VARCHAR2)
   RETURN VARCHAR2
   AS LANGUAGE JAVA
      NAME 'JFile.dirContents (java.lang.String)
               return java.lang.String';
```

But what am I to do with this string? Let's build some additional code elements on top of my wrapper functions to make the information more developer-friendly. First, I'd like to let users of xfile manipulate files either as string lists or as nested tables (this is more structured data, and easier to scan and manipulate). So I will define a nested table type as follows:

```
CREATE TYPE file_list_t IS TABLE OF VARCHAR2(2000);
```

Then I define a procedure to return the files in a directory in a nested table of this type. Note the call to the dirContents wrapper function and the reference to g_listdelim, which contains the delimiter passed back from JFile (just like the numeric values for TRUE and FALSE):

```
PROCEDURE getDirContents (
   dir IN VARCHAR2,
   files IN OUT file_list_t)
IS
   file_list VARCHAR2(32767);
   next_delim PLS_INTEGER;
   start_pos PLS_INTEGER := 1;
BEGIN
   files.DELETE;
   file_list := dirContents (dir);
   LOOP
      next_delim :=
         INSTR (file_list, g_listdelim, start_pos);
      EXIT WHEN next_delim = 0;
      files.EXTEND;
      files(files.LAST) :=
         SUBSTR (file_list,
            start_pos,
            next_delim - start_pos);
      start_pos := next_delim + 1;
   END LOOP;
END;
```

From there, it's all just fun and games with PL/SQL. You will find in the xfile package the following programs built on top of getDirContents:

getDirContents, the filter version
: Allows the user to pass a filter, such as *.tmp or %.tmp, and retrieve only files that match the filter. The character _ will be treated as a single-character wildcard, following the SQL standard.

showDirContents
: Displays all of the files found in the specified directory that match your filter.

chgext
: Changes the extension of the specified files.

In the xfile package, you will also find all of the entry points of the UTL_FILE package, such as FOPEN and PUT_LINE. I add those so that you can avoid the use of UTL_FILE for anything but declarations of file handles as UTL_FILE.FILE_TYPE and references to the exceptions declared in UTL_FILE.

Other Examples

You will find on the O'Reilly site three more interesting examples of using Java to extend the capabilities of PL/SQL or perform more complex datatype mapping.

utlzip.sql

Courtesy of reviewer Vadim Loevski, this Java class and corresponding package make zip/compression functionality available in PL/SQL. They also use the CREATE OR REPLACE JAVA statement to load a class directly into the database without relying on the *loadjava* command. Here is the header of the Java class creation statement:

```
CREATE OR REPLACE AND RESOLVE JAVA SOURCE NAMED "UTLZip" AS
import java.util.zip.*;
import java.io.*;
public class utlzip
{ public static void compressfile(string infilename, string outfilename)
...
}
/
```

And here is the "cover" for the Java method:

```
CREATE OR REPLACE PACKAGE utlzip
IS
   PROCEDURE compressfile (p_in_file IN VARCHAR2, p_out_file IN VARCHAR2)
   AS
   LANGUAGE JAVA
      NAME 'UTLZip.compressFile(java.lang.String,
                java.lang.String)';
END;
```

DeleteFile.java and deletefile.sql

Courtesy of reviewer Alex Romankeuich, this Java class and corresponding PL/SQL code demonstrate how to pass a collection (nested table or VARRAY) into an array in Java. The specific functionality implements the deletion of all files in the specified directory that have been modified since a certain date. To create the PL/SQL side of the equation, I first create a nested table of objects, and then pass that collection to Java through the use of the oracle.sql.ARRAY class:

```
CREATE TYPE file_details AS OBJECT (
   dirname       VARCHAR2 (30),
   deletedate    DATE)

CREATE TYPE file_table AS TABLE OF file_details;

CREATE OR REPLACE PACKAGE delete_files
IS
   FUNCTION fdelete (tbl IN file_table) RETURN NUMBER
   AS
   LANGUAGE JAVA
      NAME 'DeleteFile.delete(oracle.sql.ARRAY) return int';
END delete_files;
```

And here are the initial lines of the Java method. Note that Alex extracts the result set from the array structure and then iterates through that result set. See the *DeleteFile.java* script for the full implementation and extensive comments.

```
public class DeleteFile {
  public static int delete(oracle.sql.ARRAY tbl) throws SQLException {
    try {
      // Retrieve the contents of the table/varray as a result set
      ResultSet rs = tbl.getResultSet( );

      for (int ndx = 0; ndx < tbl.length( ); ndx++) {
        rs.next( );

        // Retrieve the array index and array element.
        int aryndx = (int)rs.getInt(1);
        STRUCT obj = (STRUCT)rs.getObject(2);
```

utlcmd.sql

Courtesy of reviewer Vadim Loevski, this Java class and corresponding package make it very easy to execute any operating system command from within PL/SQL.

CHAPTER 23
External Procedures

In this chapter:

Back in the Oracle7 days, it was common to hear the question "Can I call *whatever* from within Oracle?" Typically, *whatever* had something to do with sending email, running operating system commands, or using some non-PL/SQL language feature. Although email has pretty much been a non-issue since Oracle began shipping the built-in UTL_SMTP package, there are by now quite a handful of alternatives to calling "whatever." Here are the most common approaches:

- Write the program as a Java stored procedure and call the Java from PL/SQL
- Use a database table or queue as a place to store the requests, and create a separate process to read and respond to those requests
- Use a database pipe and write a daemon that responds to requests on the pipe
- Write the program in C and call it as an external procedure

Let's look at each of these approaches in turn. Java may work well, *if* it's fast enough for your application. Queueing is a very interesting technology, but even if you are simply using plain tables, this approach requires two Oracle sessions: one to write to the queue and one to read from it. Moreover, two sessions means two different transaction spaces, and that might be a problem for your application. Database pipe-based approaches also have the two-session problem, not to mention the challenge of packing and unpacking the contents of the pipe. In addition, handling many simultaneous requests using any of these approaches might require you to create your own listener and process-dispatching system.

Those are all reasons to consider the fourth option. *External procedures* allow PL/SQL to do almost anything that any other language can do, and can remedy the shortcomings of the other approaches just mentioned. PL/SQL programmers typically have many questions about using external procedures. How do external procedures work? Are they secure? How can I build my own? What are their advantages and disadvantages? This chapter addresses these questions and provides examples of commonly used features of external procedures.

Introduction to External Procedures

To call an external program from inside Oracle, the program must run as a shared library. You probably know this type of program as a DLL (dynamically linked library) on Microsoft operating systems; on Unix, you'll usually see shared libraries with a *.so* (shared object) file extension. In theory, you can write the external routine in any language you wish, but your compiler and linker will need to generate the appropriate shared library format that is callable from C. You "publish" the external program by writing a special PL/SQL wrapper, known as a *call specification*. If the external function returns a value, it maps to a PL/SQL function; if the external function returns nothing, it maps to a PL/SQL procedure.

Example: Invoking an Operating System Command

Our first example allows a PL/SQL program to execute any system-level command. Huh? I hope your mental "OracleHomeLand" security buzzer is going off right about now—that sounds like a really dangerous thing to do, doesn't it? Despite several security hoops you have to jump through to make it work, your database administrator will probably still want to intervene to really tighten up the ship. For now, try to suspend your disbelief, and start paddling.

This example uses a very simple C function, extprocsh( ), which accepts a string and asks the system function to execute it as a command:

```
int extprocsh(char *cmd)
{
   return system(cmd);
}
```

The function returns the result code as provided by system, a function normally found in the C runtime library (*libc*) on Unix, or in *msvcrt.dll* on Microsoft platforms.

After saving the function in a file named *extprocsh.c*, I can use the GNU C compiler to generate a shared library:

```
gcc -c extprocsh.c
gcc -shared -o extprocsh.so  extprocsh.o   -- Naming convention for most Unixes
gcc -shared -o extprocsh.dll  extprocsh.o  -- Microsoft Windows naming convention
```

These commands generate an object file, *extprocsh.o*, and a shared library file, *extprocsh.so* or *extprocsh.dll*. Now I need to put the library file somewhere that Oracle can find it.* Assuming that an ORACLE_HOME environment variable is set, I simply copy the file from wherever I compiled it:

```
cp extprocsh.so $ORACLE_HOME/lib/             -- Unix
copy extprocsh.dll %ORACLE_HOME%\bin\         -- Microsoft
```

* A security enhancement of Oracle Net in Oracle9*i* Release 2 restricts (by default) the allowed directory to those indicated. Unfortunately, putting custom files in the Oracle distribution directories in this way is a bad idea from an administrator's point of view.

I also need to define a "library" inside Oracle to point to the DLL. If the DBA has granted me the CREATE LIBRARY privilege, I can execute SQL commands such as those shown here:

```
CREATE OR REPLACE LIBRARY extprocshell_lib
   AS '/u01/app/oracle/9.2/lib/extprocsh.so';   -- Unix

CREATE OR REPLACE LIBRARY extprocshell_lib
   AS 'c:\oracle\ora92\bin\extprocsh.dll';      -- Microsoft
```

Now I have a library named *extprocshell_lib*. The term *library* is something of a misnomer because it's really a thin, sort of "see-through" object. It merely provides an alias for the operating system path that can live in the Oracle namespace.

I am now ready to create a PL/SQL call specification, as shown here:

```
CREATE OR REPLACE FUNCTION shell(cmd IN VARCHAR2)
   RETURN PLS_INTEGER
AS
   LANGUAGE C
   LIBRARY extprocshell_lib
   NAME "extprocsh"
   PARAMETERS (cmd STRING, RETURN INT);
```

This call spec maps the C parameters to PL/SQL parameters, making shell() callable from anywhere that you can invoke a PL/SQL function (SQL*Plus, Perl, Pro*C, etc.). From an application programming perspective, calling an external procedure is indistinguishable from calling a conventional procedure.

Assuming that the DBA has set up the system environment to support external procedures (see the "Specifying the Listener Configuration" section later in this chapter), it's easy to invoke the program. You can specify:

```
DECLARE
   result PLS_INTEGER;
BEGIN
   result := shell('operating system command'));
END;
```

Or perhaps:

```
SQL> VAR res NUMBER
SQL> CALL shell('operating system command') INTO :res;
```

Keep in mind that if the operating system command would normally display output to stdout or stderr, you can instead (if privileges permit) redirect that output to a file. Here is a trivial example of saving a file containing a directory listing:

```
result := shell('ls / > /tmp/extproc.out'));                    -- Unix
result := shell('cmd /c "dir c:\ > c:\temp\extproc.out"'));     -- Microsoft
```

These operating system commands will execute with the same privileges as the Oracle Net listener that spawns the *extproc* process. Hmmm, I bet your DBA or security guy will want to change *that*. Read on if you want to help.

Architecture of External Procedures

What happens under the covers when you invoke an external procedure? Let's first consider a case such as the example illustrated in the previous section, which uses the default external procedure "agent."

When the PL/SQL runtime engine learns from the compiled code that the program has been implemented externally, it looks for a TNS service named EXTPROC_CONNECTION_DATA, which must be known to the server via some Oracle Net naming method such as the *tnsnames.ora* file. As shown in Figure 23-1, the Oracle Net listener responds to the request by spawning a session-specific process called *extproc*, to which it passes the path to the DLL file along with the function name and any arguments. It is *extproc* that dynamically loads your shared library, sends needed arguments, receives its output, and transmits these results back to the caller. In this arrangement, only one *extproc* process runs for a given Oracle session; it launches with the first external procedure call and terminates when the session disconnects. For each distinct external procedure you call, this *extproc* process loads the associated shared library (if it hasn't already been loaded).

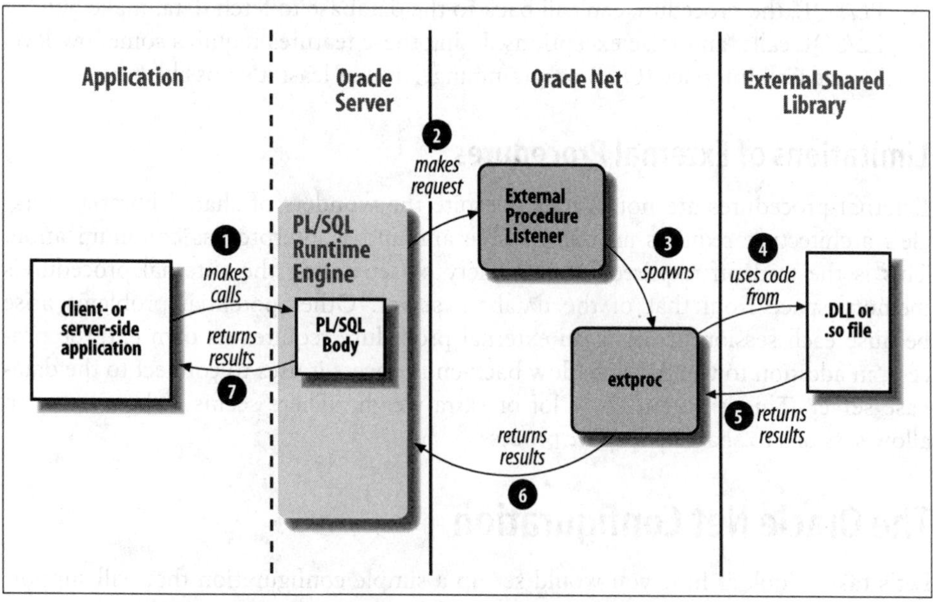

Figure 23-1. Invoking an external procedure that uses the default agent

Oracle has provided a number of features to help make external procedures usable and efficient:

Shared DLL
: The external C program must be in a shared dynamically linked library rather than in a statically linked module. Although deferring linking until runtime

incurs some overhead, there should be memory savings when more than one session uses a shared library; the operating system allows some of the memory pages of the library to be shared by more than one process. Another benefit of using dynamically linked modules is that they can be created and updated more easily than statically linked programs. In addition, there can be many subprograms in a shared library (hence the term "library"). This mitigates the performance overhead by allowing you to load fewer files dynamically.

Separate memory space
: Oracle external procedures run in a separate memory space from the main database kernel processes. If the external procedure crashes, it won't step on kernel memory; the *extproc* process simply returns an error to the PL/SQL engine, which in turn reports it to the application. Writing an external procedure to crash the Oracle server is possible, but it's no easier than doing so from a non-external procedure program.

Full transaction support
: External procedures provide full transaction support; that is, they can participate fully in the current transaction. By accepting "context" information from PL/SQL, the procedure can call back to the database to fetch data, make SQL or PL/SQL calls, and raise exceptions. Using these features requires some low-level Oracle Call Interface (OCI) programming...but at least it's possible!

Limitations of External Procedures

External procedures are not perfect. Despite the wonders of shared libraries, Oracle's architecture requires an unavoidable amount of interprocess communication. This is the tradeoff required for the safety of separating the external procedure's memory space from that of the database server. Other potential problems arise because each session invoking an external procedure requires its own extproc process, in addition to whatever shadow back-end process it uses to connect to the database server. This is potentially a lot of extra weight. There seems to be no way to allow sessions to share an *extproc* process.

The Oracle Net Configuration

Let's take a look at how you would set up a simple configuration that will support external procedures while closing up some of the glaring security gaps.

Specifying the Listener Configuration

It is the Oracle Net communications layer that provides the conduit between PL/SQL and the shared libraries. Although default installations of Oracle8*i* and later generally provide some support for external procedures, you probably don't want to use the out-of-the-box configuration until Oracle has made some significant security enhancements.

At the time of this writing, Oracle is still suffering a bit of a black eye from a security vulnerability arising from the external procedures feature. Specifically, a remote attacker could connect via the Oracle Net TCP/IP port (usually 1521) and run extproc with no authentication. So one of the things you could do to enhance your security would be:

Keep Oracle listeners behind a firewall; never expose a listener port to the Internet or any other untrusted network.

Getting the listener set up properly involves modifying the *tnsnames.ora* and the *listener.ora* files (either by hand or by using the Oracle Net Manager front end). Here, for example, is a simple *listener.ora* file that sets up an external procedure listener that is separate from the database listener:

```
LISTENER =
   (ADDRESS = (PROTOCOL = TCP)(HOST = hostname)(PORT = 1521))

EXTPROC_LISTENER =
   (ADDRESS = (PROTOCOL = IPC)(KEY = extprocKey))

SID_LIST_LISTENER =
   (SID_DESC =
      (GLOBAL_DBNAME = global_name)
      (ORACLE_HOME = oracle_home_directory)
      (SID_NAME = SID)
   )

SID_LIST_EXTPROC_LISTENER =
   (SID_DESC =
      (SID_NAME = extprocSID)
      (ORACLE_HOME = oracle_home_directory)
      (ENVS="EXTPROC_DLLS=ONLY:shared_object_file_list")
      (PROGRAM = extproc)
   )
```

where:

extprocKey
: A short identifier used by Oracle Net to distinguish this listener from other potential IPC listeners. Its actual name is arbitrary, because your programs will never see it. Oracle uses EXTPROC0 as the default name for the first Oracle Net installation on a given machine. This identifier must be the same in the address list of *listener.ora* and in the *tnsnames.ora* file.

hostname
: The name or IP address of this machine. This parameter does not apply to external procedures that listen only via interprocess communication (IPC).

oracle_home_directory
The full pathname to your ORACLE_HOME directory, such as */u01/app/oracle/product/9.2* on Unix or *C:\ORACLE\ora92* on Microsoft Windows. Notice that there are no quotation marks around the directory name, and no trailing slash.

extprocSID
An arbitrary unique identifier for the external procedure listener. In the default installation, Oracle uses the value PLSExtProc.

ENVS="EXTPROC_DLLS=ONLY:shared_object_file_list"
(Oracle9*i* Release 2) The ENVS clause sets up environment variables for the listener. This example sets the EXTPROC_DLLS environment variable to the setting that provides maximum security—as specified by the keyword ONLY—to allow execution of only those shared libraries given by the colon-delimited list.

Here is an example from my Solaris machine of what this might look like:

```
(ENVS="EXTPROC_DLLS=ONLY:/u01/app/oracle/admin/local/lib/extprocsh.so:/u01/app/
oracle/admin/local/lib/RawdataToPrinter.so")
```

And here is the entry on my laptop machine, which runs Windows XP:

```
(ENVS="EXTPROC_DLLS=ONLY:c:\oracle\admin\local\lib\extprocsh.dll:c:\oracle\admin\
local\lib\RawDataToPrinter.dll")
```

Strangely, the colon not only functions as the path delimiter, but also sets apart the normal DOS drive letter. Also note that although I've shown only two library files, you can include as many as you like.

If you're running Oracle9*i* Release 2 and you omit this value, Oracle only allows you to run those shared library files in one particular Oracle subdirectory: *bin* under Windows, and *lib* under Unix. There are additional ways that you can set this value; you can omit the ONLY keyword but still use delimited library files. In this case, both the default directories and the library files are available.

Or, you can throw caution to the wind and use the ANY keyword, which lets you use any shared library that is visible to the operating system user running the external procedure listener.

global_name
Fully qualified database name. This entry does not apply to external procedures.

Security Characteristics of the Configuration

The configuration we've established here accomplishes two important security objectives:

- It allows the system administrator to run the external procedure listener as a user account with limited privileges. By default, the listener would run as the account that runs the Oracle server.
- It limits the external procedure listener to accept only IPC connections from the local machine, as opposed to TCP/IP connections from anywhere.

But we're not quite done. The *tnsnames.ora* file for the database in which the callout originates will need an entry like the following:

```
EXTPROC_CONNECTION_DATA =
   (DESCRIPTION =
      (ADDRESS = (PROTOCOL = IPC)(KEY = extprocKey))
      (CONNECT_DATA = (SID = extprocSID) (PRESENTATION = RO))
   )
```

You'll recognize most of these settings from the earlier listener configuration. Note that the values you used in the listener for *extprocKey* and *extprocSID* must match their respective values here. The optional PRESENTATION setting is intended to improve performance a bit; it tells the server, which might be listening for different protocols, to assume that the client wants to communicate using the protocol known as "RemoteOps" (hence the RO).

You'll want to be careful about what privileges the supplemental listener account has, especially regarding its rights to modify files owned by the operating system or by the *oracle* account. Also, by setting the TNS_ADMIN environment variable on Unix (or in the registry of a Microsoft operating system), you can relocate the external procedure listener's *listener.ora* and *sqlnet.ora* files to a separate directory. This may be another aspect of an overall approach to security.

Setting up these configuration files and creating supplemental OS-level user accounts may seem rather distant from day-to-day PL/SQL programming, but these days, security is everybody's business!

Oracle professionals should keep up with Oracle's security alerts page at *http://otn.oracle.com/deploy/security/alerts.htm*. The external procedures problem I mentioned back in the "Specifying the Listener Configuration" section appears as alert number 29, but every Oracle shop should review the entire list of issues to discover what workarounds or patches to employ.

Creating an Oracle Library

The SQL statement CREATE LIBRARY defines an alias in the Oracle data dictionary for the external shared library file, allowing the PL/SQL runtime engine to find the library when it is called. The only users who can create libraries are administrators and those to whom they have granted the CREATE LIBRARY or CREATE ANY LIBRARY privilege.

The general syntax for the CREATE LIBRARY command is:

```
CREATE [ OR REPLACE ] LIBRARY library_name
AS
   'path_to_file' [ AGENT 'agent_db_link' ] ;
```

where:

library_name

A legal PL/SQL identifier. This name will be used in subsequent bodies of external procedures that need to call the shared object (or DLL) file. The library name cannot be the same as a table, top-level PL/SQL object, or anything else in the main namespace.

path_to_file

The fully qualified pathname to the shared object (or DLL) file, enclosed in single quotes.

In Oracle9*i*, it became possible to use environment variables in *path_to_file*. In particular, if the operating system–level account sets the variable before starting the listener, you can put this variable in the CREATE LIBRARY statement; for example:

```
CREATE LIBRARY extprocshell_lib AS '${ORACLE_HOME}/lib/extprocsh.so'; -- Unix
CREATE LIBRARY extprocshell_lib AS '%ORACLE_HOME%\bin\extprocsh.dll'; -- MS
```

This may be a good thing to do for the sake of script portability, although it is unclear to me whether using an environment variable in this fashion is good from a security standpoint.

Another way to make variables available to libraries is to add the variable to the ENVS setting of the external procedure listener. To make a MYLIBS variable available on Unix, you could use:

```
(ENVS="EXTPROC_DLLS=ANY,MYLIBS=/usr/local/extproclib")
```

Note that a comma separates the DLL path and the environment variable setting. You would therefore create a library using a statement such as:

```
CREATE LIBRARY extprocshell_lib AS '${MYLIBS}/extprocsh.so';  -- Unix
```

I have confirmed that putting the variable in ENVS and referring to it in the library path does in fact work on Unix systems, but my attempts to use the equivalent on Microsoft Windows XP did not succeed.

One final comment: another variable on Unix systems that you may want to set is LD_LIBRARY_PATH or its equivalent, in order to supply the external procedure a non-default search path for shared libraries it needs to open.

AGENT 'agent_db_link'

Optional database link (Oracle9*i* and later) to which the library owner has access; the link must be associated with a service name for an external procedure. Using the AGENT clause allows the external procedure to run on a different database server, although it must still be on the same machine.

Here are some things to keep in mind when issuing a CREATE LIBRARY statement:

- The statement must be executed by the DBA or by a user who has been granted CREATE LIBRARY or CREATE ANY LIBRARY privileges.

- As with most other database objects, libraries are owned by a specific Oracle user (schema). The owner automatically has execution privileges, and can grant and revoke the EXECUTE privilege on the library to other users.
- Other users who have received EXECUTE privilege on a library can refer to it in their own call specs using *owner.library* syntax, or they can create and use synonyms for the library if desired.
- Oracle doesn't check whether the named shared library file exists when you execute the CREATE LIBRARY statement. Nor will it check when you later create an external procedure declaration for a function in that library. If you have an error in the path, you won't know it until the first time you try to execute the function.

You need to create only a single Oracle library in this fashion for each shared library file you use. There can be any number of callable C functions in the library file, and any number of call specifications that refer to the library.

Let's take a closer look at how to write a PL/SQL subprogram that maps the desired routine from the shared library into a PL/SQL-callable form.

Writing the Call Specification

An external procedure can serve as the implementation of a program unit other than an anonymous block. In other words, a call specification can appear in a top-level procedure or function, a packaged procedure or function, or an object method. What's more, you can define the call spec in either the specification or the body of packaged program units (or in either the spec or body of object types). Here are some schematic examples:

```
CREATE FUNCTION name (args) RETURN datatype
AS callspec;
```

You should recognize the form shown here as that of the shell( ) function shown earlier in the chapter. You can also create a procedure:

```
CREATE PROCEDURE name
AS callspec;
```

In this case, the corresponding C function would be typed void.

The next form shows a packaged function that does not need a package body:

```
CREATE PACKAGE pkgname
AS
   FUNCTION name RETURN datatype
   AS callspec;
END;
```

However, when the time comes to modify the package, you would have to recompile the specification. Depending on the change you need to make, you may considerably reduce the recompilation ripple effect by moving the call spec into the package body:

```
CREATE PACKAGE pkgname
AS
   PROCEDURE name;
END;

CREATE PACKAGE BODY pkgname
AS
   PROCEDURE name
   IS callspec;
END;
```

Unpublished or private program units inside packages can also be implemented as external procedures. Using a call spec in an object type method is quite similar to using it in a package; that is, you can put the call spec in the object type specification or in the corresponding type body.

The Call Spec: Overall Syntax

The AS LANGUAGE clause* distinguishes the call spec. Syntactically, it looks like this:

```
AS LANGUAGE C
   LIBRARY library_name
   [ NAME external_function_name ]
   [ WITH CONTEXT ]
   [ AGENT IN (formal_parameter_name) ]
   [ PARAMETERS (external_parameter_map) ] ;
```

where:

AS LANGUAGE C
: Another option here is AS LANGUAGE JAVA, as covered in Chapter 22.

library_name
: Name of the library, as defined in a CREATE LIBRARY statement, which you have privilege to execute, either by owning it or by receiving the privilege.

external_function_name
: Name of the function as defined in the C language library. If the name is lowercase or mixed case, you must put double quotes around it. You can omit this parameter, in which case the name of the external routine must match your PL/SQL module's name (defaults to uppercase).

* Oracle 8.0 did not have this clause, offering instead a now-deprecated form, AS EXTERNAL.

WITH CONTEXT

The presence of this clause indicates that you want PL/SQL to pass a "context pointer" to the called program. The called program must be expecting the pointer as a parameter of type *OCIExtProcContext* * (defined in the C header file *ociextp.h*).

This "context" that we are passing via a pointer is a data structure that contains a variety of Oracle-specific information. The called procedure doesn't need to manipulate the data structure's content directly; instead, the structure simply facilitates other OCI calls that perform various Oracle-specific tasks. These tasks include raising predefined or user-defined exceptions, allocating session-only memory (which gets released as soon as control returns to PL/SQL), and obtaining information about the Oracle user's environment.

AGENT IN (formal_parameter_name)

This clause is a way of designating a different agent process, similar to the AGENT clause on the library, but deferring the selection of the agent until runtime. The idea is that you pass in the value of the agent as a formal PL/SQL parameter to the call spec; it will supersede the name of the agent given in the library, if any.

PARAMETERS (external_parameter_map)

This section gives the position and datatypes of parameters exchanged between PL/SQL and C. The *external_parameter_map* is a comma-delimited list of elements that match positionally with the parameters in the C function or that supply additional properties.

Getting the mapping right is potentially the most complex task you face, so the next section spends a bit of time examining the wilderness of details.

Parameter Mapping: The Example Revisited

Consider for a moment the problems of exchanging data between PL/SQL and C. PL/SQL has its own set of datatypes that are only somewhat similar to those you find in C. PL/SQL variables can be NULL and subject to three-valued truth table logic; C variables have no equivalent concept. Your C library might not know which national language character set you're using to express alphanumeric values. And should your C functions expect a given argument by value or by reference (pointer)?

I'd like to start with an example that builds on the shell program illustrated earlier in the chapter. When we last saw the shell() function, it had no protection from being called with a NULL argument instead of a real command. It turns out that calling shell(NULL) results in the runtime error *ORA-01405: fetched column value is NULL*. That may be a perfectly acceptable behavior in some applications, but what if I prefer that the external procedure simply respond to a null input with a null output?

Properly detecting an Oracle NULL in C requires PL/SQL to transmit an additional parameter known as an *indicator variable*. Likewise, for the C program to return an

Oracle NULL, it must return a separate indicator parameter back to PL/SQL. While Oracle sets and interprets this value automatically on the PL/SQL side, the C application will need to get and set this value explicitly.

It's probably simplest to illustrate this situation by looking at how the PL/SQL call spec will change:

```
CREATE OR REPLACE FUNCTION shell(cmd IN VARCHAR2)
    RETURN PLS_INTEGER
AS
    LANGUAGE C
    LIBRARY extprocshell_lib
    NAME "extprocsh"
    PARAMETERS (cmd STRING, cmd INDICATOR, RETURN INDICATOR, RETURN INT);
```

Although the PL/SQL function's formal parameters can appear anywhere in the PARAMETERS mapping, the items in the mapping must correspond in position and in associated datatype with the parameters in the C function. Any RETURN mapping that you need to provide must be the last item on the list.

You can omit RETURN from the parameter map if you want Oracle to use the default mapping. This would actually be OK in our case, although the indicator still has to be there:

```
CREATE OR REPLACE FUNCTION shell(cmd IN VARCHAR2)
    RETURN PLS_INTEGER
AS
    LANGUAGE C
    LIBRARY extprocshell_lib
    NAME "extprocsh"
    PARAMETERS (cmd STRING, cmd INDICATOR, RETURN INDICATOR);
```

The really good news is that even though we've made a number of changes to the call spec compared with the version earlier in the chapter, a program that invokes the shell( ) function sees no change in the number or datatype of its parameters.

Let's turn now to the new version of the C program, which adds two parameters, one for each indicator:

```
#include <ociextp.h>

int extprocsh(char *cmd, short cmdInd, short *retInd)
{
    if (cmdInd == OCI_IND_NOTNULL)
    {
        *retInd = (short)OCI_IND_NOTNULL;
        return system(cmd);
    } else
    {
        *retInd = (short)OCI_IND_NULL;
        return 0;
    }
}
```

Here are the important lines to note:

Line 1
: This include file appears in the *%ORACLE_HOME%\oci\include* subdirectory on Microsoft platforms; on Unix-like machines, I've spotted this file in *$ORACLE_HOME/rdbms/demo*, although it may be somewhere else on your system.

Line 3
: Notice that the command indicator is short, but the return indicator is short *. That follows the argument-passing convention of using call-by-value for input parameters sent from PL/SQL to C, but call-by-reference for output or return parameters sent from C to PL/SQL.

Lines 5, 7
: The indicator variable is either OCI_IND_NULL or OCI_IND_NOTNULL; these are special #define values from Oracle's include file. Here, explicit assignments in the code set the return indicator to be one or the other.

Lines 11–12
: The return indicator takes precedence over the return of 0; the latter is simply ignored.

Here are some simple commands that will compile and link the above program, first using Unix (still with GNU C):

```
gcc -c -I${ORACLE_HOME}/rdbms/demo -I$ORACLE_HOME/rdbms/public extprocsh.c
gcc -shared -o extprocsh.so extprocsh.o
```

And here are the equivalent commands using the Cygwin port of *gcc* on a Microsoft operating system:

```
gcc -I/cygdrive/c/oracle/ora92/oci/include/ -c extprocsh.c
gcc -shared -o extprocsh.dll extprocsh.o
```

And now, steel yourself to face the intimidating details of parameter mapping.

Parameter Mapping: The Full Story

As shown in the previous section, when moving data between PL/SQL and C, each PL/SQL datatype maps to an external datatype, identified by a PL/SQL keyword, which in turn maps to an allowed set of C types:

PL/SQL types ↔ External datatypes ↔ C types

You identify an external datatype in the PARAMETERS clause with a keyword known to PL/SQL. In some cases, the external datatypes have the same name as the C type, but in others they don't. For example, if you pass a PL/SQL variable of type PLS_INTEGER, the corresponding default external type is INT, which maps to an int in C. But Oracle's VARCHAR2 type uses the STRING external datatype, which normally maps to a char * in C.

Table 23-1 lists all the possible datatype conversions supported by Oracle's PL/SQL-to-C interface. Note that the allowable conversions depend on both the datatype and the mode of the PL/SQL formal parameter, as the previous example illustrated. The defaults, if ambiguous, are shown in bold in the table.

Table 23-1. Legal mappings of PL/SQL and C datatypes

Datatype of PL/SQL parameter	PL/SQL keyword identifying external type	C datatypes for PL/SQL parameters that are... IN or function return values	IN OUT, OUT, or any parameter designated as being passed BY REFERENCE
Long integer family: BINARY_INTEGER, BOOLEAN, PLS_INTEGER	**INT**, UNSIGNED INT, CHAR, UNSIGNED CHAR, SHORT, UNSIGNED SHORT, LONG, UNSIGNED LONG, SB1, UB1, SB2, UB2, SB4, UB4, SIZE_T	int, unsigned int, char, unsigned char, short, unsigned short, long, unsigned long, sb1, ub1, sb2, ub2, sb4, ub4, size_t	Same list of types as at left, but use a pointer (for example, the default is int * rather than int)
Short integer family: NATURAL, NATURALN, POSITIVE, POSITIVEN, SIGNTYPE	Same as above, except default is UNSIGNED INT	Same as above, except default is unsigned int	Same as above, except default is unsigned int *
Character family: VARCHAR2, CHAR, NCHAR, LONG, NVARCHAR2, VARCHAR, CHARACTER, ROWID	**STRING**, OCISTRING	**char ***, OCIString *	**char ***, OCIString *
NUMBER	OCINUMBER	OCINumber *	OCINumber *
DOUBLE PRECISION	DOUBLE	double	double *
FLOAT, REAL	FLOAT	float	float *
RAW, LONG RAW	**RAW**, OCIRAW	**unsigned char ***, OCIRaw *	**unsigned char ***, OCIRaw *
DATE	OCIDATE	OCIDate *	OCIDate *
Timestamp family: TIMESTAMP, TIMESTAMP WITH TIME ZONE, TIMESTAMP WITH LOCAL TIME ZONE	OCIDATETIME	OCIDateTime *	OCIDateTime *
INTERVAL DAY TO SECOND, INTERVAL YEAR TO MONTH	OCIINTERVAL	OCIInterval *	OCIInterval *
BFILE, BLOB, CLOB	OCILOBLOCATOR	OCILOBLOCATOR *	OCILOBLOCATOR **
Descriptor of user-defined type (collection or object)	TDO	OCIType *	OCIType *
Value of user-defined collection	OCICOLL	OCIColl **, OCIArray **, OCITable **	OCIColl **, OCIArray **, OCITable **
Value of user-defined object	DVOID	dvoid *	dvoid * for final types; dvoid ** for nonfinal types

In some simple cases where you are passing only numeric arguments and where the defaults are acceptable, you can actually omit the PARAMETERS clause entirely. However, you must use it when you want to pass indicators or other data properties.

Each piece of supplemental information we want to exchange will be passed as a separate parameter, and will appear both in the PARAMETERS clause and in the C language function specification.

More Syntax: The PARAMETERS Clause

The PARAMETERS clause provides a comma-delimited list that may contain five different kinds of elements:

- The name of the parameter followed by the external datatype identifier
- The keyword RETURN and its associated external datatype identifier
- A "property" of the PL/SQL parameter or return value, such as a nullness indicator or an integer corresponding to its length
- The keyword CONTEXT, which is a placeholder for the context pointer
- The keyword SELF, in the case of an external procedure for an object type member method

Elements (other than CONTEXT) follow the syntax pattern:

```
{ pname | RETURN | SELF } [ property ] [ BY REFERENCE ] [ external_datatype ]
```

If your call spec includes WITH CONTEXT, the corresponding element in the parameter list is simply:

```
CONTEXT
```

By convention, if you have specified WITH CONTEXT, you should make CONTEXT the first argument because that is its default location if the rest of the parameter mappings are defaulted.

Parameter entries have the following meanings:

pname | RETURN | SELF
: The name of the parameter as specified in the formal parameter list of the PL/SQL module, or the keyword RETURN, or the keyword SELF (in the case of a member method in an object type). PL/SQL parameter names are not necessarily the names of formal parameters in the C language routine. However, parameters in the PL/SQL parameter list must match one for one, in order, those in the C language specification.

property
: One of the following: INDICATOR, INDICATOR STRUCT, LENGTH, MAXLEN, TDO, CHARSETID, or CHARSETFORM. These are described in the next section.

BY REFERENCE
: Pass the parameter by reference. In other words, the module in the shared library is expecting a pointer to the parameter rather than its value. BY REFERENCE only has meaning for scalar IN parameters that are not strings, such as BINARY_INTEGER, PLS_INTEGER, FLOAT, DOUBLE PRECISION, and REAL. All others (IN OUT and OUT parameters, as well as IN parameters of type STRING) are *always* passed by reference, and the corresponding C prototype must specify a pointer.

external_datatype
: The external datatype keyword from the second column of Table 23-1. If this is omitted, the external datatype will default as indicated in the table.

PARAMETERS Properties

This section describes each possible property you can specify in a PARAMETERS clause.

The INDICATOR property

The INDICATOR property is a flag to denote whether the parameter is null, and has the following characteristics:

Allowed external types
: short (the default), int, long

Allowed PL/SQL types
: All scalars can use an INDICATOR; to pass indicator variables for composite types such as user-defined objects and collections, use the INDICATOR STRUCT property.

Allowed PL/SQL modes
: IN, IN OUT, OUT, RETURN

Call mode
: By value for IN parameters (unless BY REFERENCE specified), and by reference for IN OUT, OUT, and RETURN variables

You can apply this property to any parameter, in any mode, including RETURNs. If you omit an indicator, PL/SQL is supposed to think that your external routine will always be non-null (but it's not that simple; see the sidebar "Indicating Without Indicators?").

When you send an IN variable and its associated indicator to the external procedure, Oracle sets the indicator's value automatically. However, if your C module is returning a value in a RETURN or OUT parameter and an indicator, your C code must set the indicator value.

For an IN parameter, the indicator parameter in your C function might be:

```
short pIndicatorFoo
```

Or for an IN OUT parameter, the indicator might be:

```
short *pIndicatorFoo
```

In the body of your C function, you should use the #define constants OCI_IND_NOTNULL and OCI_IND_NULL, which will be available in your program if you #include *oci.h*. Oracle defines these as:

```
typedef sb2 OCIInd;
#define OCI_IND_NOTNULL (OCIInd)0            /* not NULL */
#define OCI_IND_NULL (OCIInd)(-1)            /* NULL */
```

Indicating Without Indicators?

What happens if you don't specify an indicator variable for a string and then return an empty C string? We wrote a short test program to find out:

```
void mynull(char *outbuff)
{
   outbuff[0] = '\0';
}
```

The call spec could look like this:

```
CREATE OR REPLACE PROCEDURE mynull(res OUT VARCHAR2)
AS
   LANGUAGE C
   LIBRARY mynulllib
   NAME "mynull";
/
```

When invoked as an external procedure, PL/SQL does actually interpret this parameter value as a NULL. The reason appears to be that the STRING external type is special; you can also indicate a NULL value to Oracle by passing a string of length 2 where the first byte is \0. (This works only if you omit a LENGTH parameter.)

But you probably shouldn't take this lazy way out; use an indicator instead!

The LENGTH property

The LENGTH property is an integer indicating the number of characters in a character parameter, and has the following characteristics:

Allowed external types
: int (the default), short, unsigned short, unsigned int, long, unsigned long

Allowed PL/SQL types
: VARCHAR2, CHAR, RAW, LONG RAW

Allowed PL/SQL modes
: IN, IN OUT, OUT, RETURN

Call mode
: By value for IN parameters (unless BY REFERENCE specified), and by reference for IN OUT, OUT, and RETURN variables

The LENGTH property is mandatory for RAW and LONGRAW, and is available as a convenience to your C program for the other datatypes in the character family. When passing a RAW from PL/SQL to C, Oracle will set the LENGTH property; however, your C program must set LENGTH if you need to pass the RAW data back.

For an IN parameter, the indicator parameter in your C function might be:

```
int pLenFoo
```

Or for an OUT or IN OUT parameter, it might be:

```
int *pLenFoo
```

The MAXLEN property

The MAXLEN property is an integer indicating the maximum number of characters in a string parameter, and has the following characteristics:

Allowed external types
: int (the default), short, unsigned short, unsigned int, long, unsigned long

Allowed PL/SQL types
: VARCHAR2, CHAR, RAW, LONG RAW

Allowed PL/SQL modes
: IN OUT, OUT, RETURN

Call mode
: By reference

MAXLEN is applied to IN OUT or OUT parameters and to no other mode. If you attempt to use it for an IN, you'll get the compile-time error *PLS-00250: Incorrect Usage of MAXLEN in parameters clause*.

Unlike the LENGTH parameter, the MAXLEN data is always passed by reference.

An example of the C formal parameter is:

```
int *pMaxLenFoo
```

The CHARSETID and CHARSETFORM properties

The CHARSETID and CHARSETFORM properties are flags denoting information about the character set, and have the following characteristics:

Allowed external types
: unsigned int (the default), unsigned short, unsigned long

Allowed PL/SQL types
: VARCHAR2, CHAR, CLOB

Allowed PL/SQL modes
: IN, IN OUT, OUT, RETURN

Call mode
: By reference

If you are passing data to the external procedure that is expressed in a nondefault character set, these properties will let you communicate the character set's ID and form to the called C program. The values are read-only and should not be modified by the called program. Here is an example of a PARAMETERS clause that includes character set information:

```
PARAMETERS (CONTEXT, cmd STRING, cmd INDICATOR, cmd CHARSETID,
            cmd CHARSETFORM);
```

Oracle sets these additional values automatically, based on the character set in which you have expressed the cmd argument. For more information about accommodating national language support in a C program, refer to Oracle's OCI documentation.

Raising an Exception from the Called C Program

If you think about it for a moment, the shell() program shown earlier in the chapter is arguably too "C-like" for PL/SQL: it is a function whose return value contains the status code, and the caller must check the return value to see if it succeeded. Wouldn't it make more sense—in PL/SQL, that is—for the program to be a procedure that simply raises an exception when there's a problem? Let's take a brief look at how to perform the OCI equivalent of RAISE_APPLICATION_ERROR.

In addition to the easy change from a function to a procedure, there are several other things I need to do:

- Pass in the context area
- Decide on an error message and an error number in the 20001–20999 range
- Add a call to the OCI service routine that raises an exception

The changes to the call spec are trivial:

```
/* File on web: extprocsh.sql */
CREATE OR REPLACE PROCEDURE shell(cmd IN VARCHAR2)
AS
   LANGUAGE C
   LIBRARY extprocshell_lib
   NAME "extprocsh"
   WITH CONTEXT
   PARAMETERS (CONTEXT, cmd STRING, cmd INDICATOR);
/
```

(I also removed the return parameter and its indicator because I don't need them any more.) The following code shows how to receive and use the context pointer in the call needed to raise the exception.

```
   /* File on web: extprocsh.c */
 1 #include <ociextp.h>
 2 #include <errno.h>
 3
 4 void extprocsh(OCIExtProcContext *ctx, char *cmd, short cmdInd)
 5 {
 6    int excNum = 20001;
 7    char excMsg[512];
 8    size_t excMsgLen;
 9
10    if (cmdInd == OCI_IND_NULL)
11       return;
12
13    if (system(cmd) != 0)
14    {
15       sprintf(excMsg, "Error %i during system call: %.*s", errno, 475,
16             strerror(errno));
17       excMsgLen = (size_t)strlen(excMsg);
18
19       if (OCIExtProcRaiseExcpWithMsg(ctx, excNum, (text *)excMsg, excMsgLen)
20             != OCIEXTPROC_SUCCESS)
21          return;
22    }
23
24 }
```

Note the following lines:

Line 4
: The first of the formal parameters is the context pointer.

Line 6
: You can use whatever number in Oracle's user-defined error number range you want; in general, I advise against hardcoding these values, but, er, this is a "do as I say, not as I do" example.

Line 7
: The maximum size for a user-defined error message is 512 bytes.

Line 8
: A variable to hold the length of the error message text, which will be needed in the OCI call that raises the exception.

Lines 10-11
: Here, I am translating the NULL argument semantics of the earlier function into a procedure: when called with NULL, nothing happens.

Line 13

A zero return code from system() means that everything executed perfectly; a nonzero code corresponds to either an error or a warning. A more sophisticated program might check for (and ignore) various warnings, based on the value that system() returns.

Lines 15, 16

These lines prepare the variables containing the error message and its length.

Lines 19-20

This OCI function, which actually raises the user-defined exception, is where the context pointer actually gets used.

Now, how do we compile this baby? First, Unix:

```
/* File on web: build_extprocsh.sh */
gcc -c -I$ORACLE_HOME/rdbms/public -I$ORACLE_HOME/rdbms/demo exp.c
gcc -shared -o exp.so exp.o
```

On Microsoft, I found that I needed an explicit *.def* file to identify the entry point.

```
/* File on web: build_extprocsh.bat */
echo LIBRARY extprocsh.dll > extprocsh.def
echo EXPORTS >> extprocsh.def
echo extprocsh >> extprocsh.def

gcc -c -I%ORACLE_HOME%\oci\include extprocsh.c
gcc -shared -o extprocsh.dll extprocsh.def extprocsh.o %ORACLE_HOME%\oci\lib\msvc\oci.lib
```

Let's run a simple test:

```
SQL> CALL shell('garbage');
CALL shell('garbage')
     *
ERROR at line 1:
ORA-20001: Error 2 during system call: No such file or directory
```

It's working! The "no such file or directory" message comes from the standard C error function strerror(). This is a Unix example; I discovered that the strerror function doesn't seem to be set meaningfully using GNU C on Microsoft, where the error message always comes out as *ORA-20001: Error error 0 during system call*. Oh well.

A number of other OCI routines are unique to writing external procedures. Here is the complete list:

OCIExtProcAllocCallMemory

Allocates memory that Oracle will automatically free when control returns to PL/SQL.

OCIExtProcRaiseExcp

Raises a predefined exception by its Oracle error number.

OCIExtProcRaiseExcpWithMsg
: Raises a user-defined exception, including a custom error message (illustrated in the previous example).

OCIExtProcGetEnv
: Allows an external procedure to perform OCI callbacks to the database to execute SQL or PL/SQL.

All of these require the context pointer. Refer to Oracle's *Application Developer's Guide—Fundamentals* for detailed documentation and examples of using these routines.

Nondefault Agents

As of Oracle9*i*, it became possible to run external procedure agents via database links that connect to other database servers. This functionality enables you to spread the load of running expensive external programs onto other database instances.

Even without other servers, running an external procedure through a nondefault agent launches a separate process. This can be handy if you have a recalcitrant external program. Launching it via a nondefault agent means that even if its extproc process crashes, it won't have any effect on other external procedures running in the session.

As a simple example of a nondefault agent, here is a configuration that allows an agent to run on the same database but in a separate extproc task. The *tnsnames.ora* file needs an additional entry such as:

```
agent1 =
  (DESCRIPTION =
    (ADDRESS = (PROTOCOL = IPC)(KEY=extprocKey))
    (CONNECT_DATA = (SID = PLSExtProc))
  )
```

Here, *extprocKey* can just be the same key as in your EXTPROC_CONNECTION_DATA entry.

Because agents are created with a database link, we'll need to create one of those:

```
SQL> CREATE DATABASE LINK agent1link
  2  CONNECT TO username IDENTIFIED BY password
  3  USING 'agent1';
```

Now, finally, the agent can appear in a CREATE LIBRARY statement such as:

```
CREATE OR REPLACE LIBRARY extprocshell_lib_with_agent
   AS 'c:\oracle\admin\local\lib\extprocsh.dll'
   AGENT 'agent1';
```

Any call spec that was written to use this library will authenticate and connect through this agent1 link, launching an extproc task separate from the default extproc task. As with the default arrangement, if more than one user invokes the external procedure, Oracle will still spawn one task per user; there is no way to get "pooling" of *extproc* processes.

Oracle also supports a more flexible arrangement that allows you to pass in the name of the agent as a parameter to the external procedure. To take advantage of this feature, use the AGENT IN clause in the call spec. For example (changes are printed in bold):

```
CREATE OR REPLACE PROCEDURE shell2 (name_of_agent IN VARCHAR2, cmd VARCHAR2)
AS
   LANGUAGE C
   LIBRARY extprocshell_lib
   NAME "extprocsh2"
   AGENT IN (name_of_agent)
   WITH CONTEXT
   PARAMETERS (CONTEXT, name_of_agent STRING, cmd STRING, cmd INDICATOR);
```

Notice that I had to include the name of the agent in the list of parameters. Oracle enforces a rule that every formal parameter must have a corresponding entry in the PARAMETERS clause. So I have to modify my external C library. In my case, I merely added a second entry point, extprocsh2( ), to the library with the following trivial function:

```
void extprocsh2(OCIExtProcContext *ctx, char *agent, char *cmd, short cmdInd)
{
   extprocsh(ctx, cmd, cmdInd);
}
```

My code just ignores the agent string. Now, though, I can invoke my shell2 procedure as in the following:

```
CALL shell2('agent1', 'whatever');
INSERT p. 949
```

If you want your stored program to somehow invoke an external procedure on a remote machine, you have at least three potential options. First, you could implement an external procedure on the local machine which is just a "pass-through" program, making a C-based remote procedure call on behalf of PL/SQL. Second, you could implement a stored PL/SQL program on the remote machine as an external procedure, and call it from the local machine via a database link. The third option—connecting directly to a remote agent from the local stored PL/SQL—does not seem to be officially supported by Oracle. While it is possible to set up an external procedure listener to accept connections over the network (TCP as opposed to IPC), all of my attempts to connect to a remote agent have failed. If I ever do get it working, though, I'll post a how-to on the O'Reilly web site.

A Debugging Odyssey

To help debug external procedures, Oracle supplies a script, *dbgextp.sql*, which you should be able to find it in the *plsql/demo* directory. The script builds a package named DEBUG_EXTPROC and an associated library named *debug_extproc_library*. Using this package, I was able to demonstrate that the GNU debugger (*gdb* 4.18) can attach to a running process and debug external procedures. Here's how I got this to work, first on Solaris, then on Windows XP.

As preliminary steps, I compiled the shared library file with the compiler option (-g) needed to include symbolic information for the debugger. I also ran the *dbgextp.sql* script. In a fresh SQL*Plus session, I then ran:

```
SQL> EXEC DEBUG_EXTPROC.startup_extproc_agent
```

This caused an *extproc* process to launch, whose process id (PID) I discovered using *ps -ef*. At this point I started the debugger and tried to attach to the running process.

```
gdb $ORACLE_HOME/bin/extproc pid
```

However, I got a "permission denied" error. Because I already had permission to read and execute the *extproc* program file, I wound up logging in as the *oracle* account to get past the error. (There is probably a better way.) I then set a breakpoint on the "pextproc" symbol per the instructions in the *dbgextp.sql* file.

Next, in my SQL*Plus session, I invoked the procedure using:

```
SQL> CALL shell(NULL);
```

When the external procedure was called, *extproc* hit the breakpoint. After executing a *gdb* "share" command so the debugger would read the symbols in my just-loaded external shared library, I was able to set a breakpoint on the extprocsh() external procedure. It worked pretty well after that.

While debugging on Microsoft platforms is also possible, I wouldn't exactly call what I did "graceful." These are the major changes in the debugging procedure:

1. I modified the external procedure listener service in the Windows control panel to execute under the authority of my own user account rather than under that of "Local System."
2. Because the debugger couldn't find pextproc and because the *gdb* "share" command doesn't seem to apply to MS Windows, I had to add the line of code "DebugBreak();" at the desired breakpoint in the C program and recompile. I also needed to "#include <windows.h>".
3. Instead of *ps -ef*, I used Microsoft's *tasklist.exe* program to obtain the extproc PID.

My Unix tests were on Solaris 2.6; my Microsoft tests were on Windows XP using the Cygwin *gdb* 5.0, which has both a console version and a GUI version.

Maintaining External Procedures

Here are some assorted bits of information that will assist you in creating, debugging, and managing external procedures.

Dropping Libraries

The syntax for dropping a library is simply:

```
DROP LIBRARY library_name;
```

The Oracle user who executes this command must have the DROP LIBRARY or DROP ANY LIBRARY privilege.

Oracle does not check dependency information before dropping the library. This fact is useful if you need to change the name or location of the shared object file to which the library points. You can just drop it and rebuild it, and any dependent routines will continue to function. (More useful, perhaps, would be a requirement that you use a DROP LIBRARY FORCE command, but such an option does not exist.)

Before you drop the library permanently, you may wish to look in the DBA_DEPENDENCIES view to see if any PL/SQL module relies on the library.

Data Dictionary

There are a few entries in the data dictionary that help manage external procedures. Table 23-2 shows the USER_ version of the dictionary tables, but note that there are corresponding entries for DBA_ and ALL_.

Table 23-2. Data dictionary views for external procedures

To answer the question...	Use this view	Example
What libraries have I created?	USER_LIBRARIES	`SELECT * FROM user_libraries;`
What stored PL/SQL programs use the foo library in a call spec?	USER_DEPENDENCIES	`SELECT * FROM user_dependencies WHERE referenced_name = 'FOO';`

Rules and Warnings

As with almost all things PL/SQL, external procedures come with an obligatory list of cautions:

- While the mode of each formal parameter (IN, IN OUT, OUT) may have certain restrictions in PL/SQL, C does not honor these modes. Differences between the PL/SQL parameter mode and the usage in the C module cannot be detected at compile time, and could also go undetected at runtime. The rules are what you would expect: don't assign values to IN parameters; don't read OUT parameters; always assign values to IN OUT and OUT parameters; always return a value of the appropriate datatype.

- Modifiable INDICATORs and LENGTHs are always passed by reference for IN OUT, OUT, and RETURN. Unmodifiable INDICATORs and LENGTHs are always passed by value unless you specify BY REFERENCE. However, even if you pass INDICATORs or LENGTHs for PL/SQL variables by reference, they are still read-only parameters.
- Although you can pass up to 128 parameters between PL/SQL and C, if any of them are float or double, your actual maximum will be lower. How much lower depends on the operating system.
- Because *extproc* might be a multithreaded process in future releases, and because the operating system won't ask permission before unloading shared libraries from memory, your external code should avoid the use of any internal or external "static" variables.
- Your external procedure may not perform DDL commands, begin or end a session, or control a transaction using COMMIT or ROLLBACK. (See Oracle's *PL/SQL User's Guide and Reference* for a complete list of unsupported OCI routines.)

Index

Symbols

We'd like to hear your suggestions for improving our indexes. Send email to *index@oreilly.com*.

Numbers

A

B

C

D

F

G

H

I

L

M

N

O

Q

R

T

U

V

W

X

Y

Z

About the Authors

Steven Feuerstein is considered one of the world's leading experts on the Oracle PL/SQL language. He is the author or coauthor of *Oracle PL/SQL Programming, Oracle PL/SQL Best Practices, Oracle PL/SQL Programming: Guide to Oracle8i Features, Oracle PL/SQL Developer's Workbook, Oracle Built-in Packages, Advanced Oracle PL/SQL Programming with Packages*, and several pocket reference books (all from O'Reilly & Associates). Steven is a Senior Technology Advisor with Quest Software, has been developing software since 1980, and worked for Oracle Corporation from 1987 to 1992.

In matters pertaining to humanity rather than programming, Steven is a past president of the Board of Directors of the Crossroads Fund, which makes grants to Chicagoland organizations working for social, racial, environmental, and economic justice (*http://www.CrossroadsFund.org*). He is a founder of Not In My Name, a gathering of Jews who seek a lasting and just peace between Israelis and Palestinians (*http://www.nimn.org*) and the Refuser Solidarity Network, which educates the public about the Israeli refuser movement (*http://www.refusersolidarity.net*). He also maintains his own web site with information about these and many other topics at *http://www.stevenfeuerstein.com*. You can reach Steven via email at *steven@stevenfeuerstein.com*.

Bill Pribyl, author, teacher, and software consultant, is the primary author of *Learning Oracle PL/SQL* and the coauthor of *Oracle PL/SQL Programming* and its companion pocket reference, all published by O'Reilly & Associates. An Oracle user since 1986, Bill has consulted on many aspects of using Oracle products. He recently spearheaded PLNet.org, a web-based repository where developers can share open source PL/SQL. At home with his family in Houston, Bill spends much of his free time as a "soccer dad," but also teaches religion to first-graders and volunteers with a Christian organization teaching computer skills to underemployed clients. Visit Bill's firm at *http://www.datacraft.com*.

Colophon

Our look is the result of reader comments, our own experimentation, and feedback from distribution channels. Distinctive covers complement our distinctive approach to technical topics, breathing personality and life into potentially dry subjects.

Ants are featured on the cover of *Oracle PL/SQL Programming*, Third Edition. At least 8,000 different species of ants can be found everywhere on Earth except the North and South Poles. Ants preserved in amber suggest that these insects existed 50 million years before humans.

Humans have long been fascinated by ants, because these tiny insects are accomplished builders, nurses, miners, and even farmers. Fables such as "The Ant and the Grasshopper" extol the virtues of hardworking, forward-looking ants. (Hail ants!) It is true that individual ants are able to perform amazing feats: an ant can carry up to 50 times its body weight, can travel the human equivalent of 40 miles a day, and can climb vertical heights the equivalent of Mount Everest. However, the greatest accomplishments of ants are those performed together for the good of their community.

Queen ants establish new communities, or nests, after their mating flight. On this flight the queen mates with several males. After mating, the males fall to Earth and die. The queen then finds an uninhabited nest, settles into it, and pulls her wings off. She will never fly again, and after removing her wings she is able to absorb the wing muscles as nutrients for her eggs. She will continue to lay eggs, thousands of them, for years.

During the three-stage development process, which takes about two months, the eggs, larvae, and pupae are cared for by the nurse ants, who feed, clean, and carefully move the young to warmer or cooler places in the nest, depending on the temperature. These nurse ants are, in turn, cared for by other worker ants, who feed the nurses with regurgitated food. The workers and the nurses will fight together to defend the young against enemies if the nest is invaded, either by another group of ants or by a larger animal.

Emily Quill was the production editor and copyeditor for *Oracle PL/SQL Programming,* Third Edition. Mary Anne Mayo, Sheryl Avruch, Matt Hutchinson, and Jane Ellin provided quality control. Phil Dangler, Derek DiMatteo, and Kimo Carter provided production assistance. Ellen Troutman wrote the index.

Edie Freedman designed the cover of this book. The cover image is a 19th-century engraving from the Dover Pictorial Archive. Emma Colby produced the cover layout with QuarkXPress 4.1 using Adobe's ITC Garamond font.

David Futato designed the interior layout. This book was converted to FrameMaker 5.5.6 with a format conversion tool created by Erik Ray, Jason McIntosh, Neil Walls, and Mike Sierra that uses Perl and XML technologies. The text font is Linotype Birka; the heading font is Adobe Myriad Condensed; and the code font is LucasFont's TheSans Mono Condensed. The illustrations that appear in the book were produced by Robert Romano and Jessamyn Read using Macromedia FreeHand 9 and Adobe Photoshop 6. The tip and warning icons were drawn by Christopher Bing. This colophon was written by Clairemarie Fisher O'Leary.

Other Titles Available from O'Reilly

Oracle PL/SQL

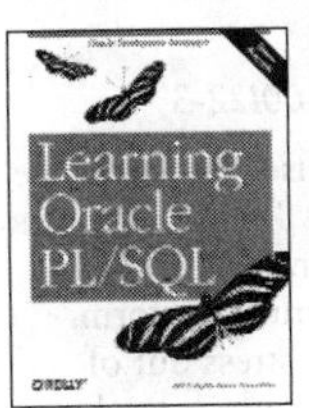

Learning Oracle PL/SQL

Bill Pribyl & Steven Feuerstein
1st Edition November 2001
424 pages, ISBN 0-596-00180-0

Among our best-selling books on PL/SQL, *Learning Oracle PL/SQL* is the first one a newcomer to the language will want to read. Beginning with a discussion of what PL/SQL is and what it's good for, this book then presents language features, one at a time, in an engaging and readable way. A consistent and understandable example application—the development of a library's electronic catalog system—runs through the chapters.

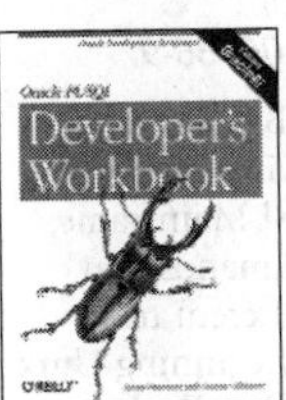

Oracle PL/SQL Developer's Workbook

By Steven Feuerstein with Andrew Odewahn
1st Edition May 2000
592 pages, ISBN 1-56592-674-9

A companion to Feuerstein's other best-selling Oracle PL/SQL books, this workbook contains a carefully constructed set of problems and solutions that will test your language skills and help you become a better developer. Exercises are provided at three levels: beginner, intermediate, and expert. It covers the full set of language features: variables, loops, exception handling, data structures, object technology, cursors, built-in functions and packages, PL/SQL tuning, and the new Oracle8i features (including Java and the Web).

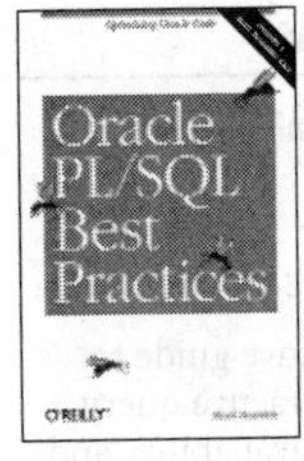

Oracle PL/SQL Best Practices

By Steven Feuerstein
1st Edition April 2001
202 pages, ISBN 0-596-00121-5

Oracle PL/SQL Best Practices is a concise, easy-to-use summary of best practices in the program development process. It covers coding style, writing SQL in PL/SQL, data structures, control structures, exception handling, program and package construction, and built-in packages. Complementary code examples are available on the O'Reilly web site. Includes a pull-out quick-reference card.

Oracle Essentials: Oracle9*i*, Oracle8*i* & Oracle8

By Rick Greenwald, Robert Stackowiak & Jonathan Stern
2nd Edition June 2001
381 pages, ISBN 0-596-00179-7

Updated for Oracle's latest release, Oracle9*i*, *Oracle Essentials* is a concise and readable technical introduction to Oracle features and technologies, including the Oracle architecture, data structures, configuration, networking, tuning, and data warehousing. It introduces such major Oracle9*i* features as Real Application clusters, flashback queries, clickstream intelligence, Oracle Database and Web Cache, XML integration, the Oracle9*i* Application Server, Oracle9*i* Portal, and much more.

The Oracle PL/SQL CD Bookshelf

By O'Reilly & Associates, Inc.
1st Edition July 2000
(Includes CD-ROM)
285 pages, ISBN 1-56592-849-0

The *Oracle PL/SQL CD Bookshelf* contains the complete text of seven books on CD-ROM: *Oracle PL/SQL Programming*; *Advanced PL/SQL Programming*; *Oracle Web Applications*; *Oracle Built-in Packages*; *Oracle PL/SQL Pocket Reference*; *Oracle Built-ins Pocket Reference*; and both electronic and print versions of *Oracle PL/SQL Programming: A Guide to Oracle 8i Features*.

Oracle SQL and SQL Plus

Oracle SQL: The Essential Reference

By David Kreines
1st Edition October 2000
415 pages, ISBN 1-56592-697-8

Everything Oracle developers and DBAs need to know about standard SQL (Structured Query Language) and Oracle's extensions to it is in this single, concise reference volume. Quick-reference chapters investigate basic SQL elements, Data Definition Language (DDL) and Data Manipulation Language (DML), SQL functions, PL/SQL, SQL*Plus, and Oracle SQL optimization and tuning. The book covers Oracle8*i*, release 8.1.6.

Mastering Oracle SQL

By Sanjay Mishra & Alan Beaulieu
1st Edition April 2001
336 pages, ISBN 0-596-00129-0

Mastering Oracle SQL goes far beyond other books, delivering the full power of SQL to write queries in an Oracle environment. It covers Oracle's vast library of built-in functions, the full range of Oracle SQL query-writing features, the newly supported SQL92 join syntax, Oracle's new analytic SQL features, hierarchical and time-based queries, implementing conditional logic in queries with DECODE and CASE, and much more. Not just a manual, this book is about creative techniques for writing effective and accurate queries.

Oracle SQL*Plus: The Definitive Guide

By Jonathan Gennick
1st Edition March 1999
526 pages, ISBN 1-56592-578-5

This book is the definitive guide to SQL*Plus, Oracle's interactive query tool. Despite the wide availability and usage of SQL*Plus, few developers and DBAs know how powerful it really is. This book introduces SQL*Plus, provides a syntax quick reference, and describes how to write and execute script files, generate ad hoc reports, extract data from the database, query the data dictionary tables, use the SQL*Plus administrative features (new in Oracle8*i*), and much more.

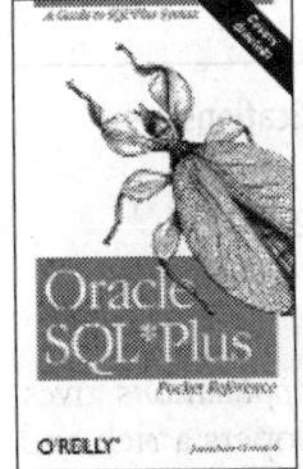

Oracle SQL*Plus Pocket Reference

By Jonathan Gennick
1st Edition April 2000
94 pages, ISBN 1-56592-941-1

This quick reference is an excellent, portable resource for every Oracle administrator and developer. It summarizes the syntax of SQL*Plus, Oracle's ubiquitous interactive query tool, including new Oracle8*i* release 8.1.6 features. It also summarizes how to interact with SQL*Plus and presents the basics of selecting data, formatting reports, and tuning SQL.

Oracle SQL Tuning Pocket Reference

By Mark Gurry
1st Edition January 2002
108 pages, ISBN 0-596-00268-8

One of the most important challenges faced by Oracle database administrators and Oracle developers is the need to tune SQL statements so that they execute efficiently. In this book, Mark Gurry shares his in-depth knowledge of Oracle's SQL statement optimizers. Mark provides solutions to many common problems that occur with both the rule-based and cost-based optimizers. Mark provides a number of handy SQL tuning tips, discusses the use of the DBMS_STATS package to manage database statistics, and shows you how to use outlines to specify execution plans for SQL statements in third-party applications that you can't otherwise modify.

Oracle

Building Oracle XML Applications

By Steve Muench
1st Edition September 2000
810 pages, Includes CD-ROM
ISBN 1-56592-691-9

Building Oracle XML Applications gives Java and PL/SQL developers a rich and detailed look at the many tools Oracle provides to support XML development. It shows how to combine the power of XML and XSLT with the speed, functionality, and reliability of the Oracle database. The author delivers nearly 800 pages of entertaining text, helpful and timesaving hints, and extensive examples that developers can put to use immediately to build custom XML applications. The accompanying CD-ROM contains JDeveloper 3.1, an integrated development environment for Java developers.

Java Programming with Oracle JDBC

By Donald K. Bales
1st Edition December 2001
496 pages, ISBN 0-596-00088-X

Learn how to leverage JDBC, a key Java technology used to access relational data from Java programs, in an Oracle environment. Author Don Bales begins by teaching you the mysteries of establishing database connections, and how to issue SQL queries and get results back. You'll move on to advanced topics such as streaming large objects, calling PL/SQL procedures, and working with Oracle9*i*'s object-oriented features, then finish with a look at transactions, concurrency management, and performance.

Perl for Oracle DBAs

By Andy Duncan & Jared Still
1st Edition August 2002 (est.)
624 pages (est.), ISBN 0-596-00210-6

Perl is a very helpful tool for Oracle database administrators, but too few DBAs realize how powerful Perl can be. *Perl for Oracle DBAs* describes what DBAs need to know about Perl and explains how they can use this popular open source language to manage, monitor, and tune their Oracle databases. The book also describes the Oracle/Perl software modules that tie these two environments together—for example, Oracle Call Interface (OCI), Perl DataBase Interface (DBI), DBD-Oracle, and mod_perl, etc. The book comes with a toolkit containing more than 100 ready-to-use programs that DBAs can put to immediate use in their Linux or Windows systems.

TOAD Pocket Reference for Oracle

By Jim McDaniel & Patrick McGrath
1st Edition August 2002 (est.)
128 pages (est.), ISBN 0-596-00337-4

This handy little book provides database developers and administrators with quick access to TOAD feature summaries, hot keys, productivity tips and tricks, and much more. A perfect pocket-sized guide that's easy to take anywhere, *TOAD Pocket Reference for Oracle* focuses on the major TOAD components, including the SQL Editor, Data Grid, Schema Browser, SQL Tuning module, and DBA tools (for database administration, user administration, and database performance).

How to stay in touch with O'Reilly

1. Visit our award-winning web site

http://www.oreilly.com/

★ "Top 100 Sites on the Web"—PC Magazine
★ CIO Magazine's Web Business 50 Awards

Our web site contains a library of comprehensive product information (including book excerpts and tables of contents), downloadable software, background articles, interviews with technology leaders, links to relevant sites, book cover art, and more. File us in your bookmarks or favorites!

2. Join our email mailing lists

Sign up to get email announcements of new books and conferences, special offers, and O'Reilly Network technology newsletters at:

http://www.elists.oreilly.com

It's easy to customize your free elists subscription so you'll get exactly the O'Reilly news you want.

3. Get examples from our books

To find example files for a book, go to:

http://www.oreilly.com/catalog

select the book, and follow the "Examples" link.

4. Work with us

Check out our web site for current employment opportunities:

http://jobs.oreilly.com/

5. Register your book

Register your book at:

http://register.oreilly.com

6. Contact us

O'Reilly & Associates, Inc.
1005 Gravenstein Hwy North
Sebastopol, CA 95472 USA
TEL: 707-827-7000 or 800-998-9938
(6am to 5pm PST)
FAX: 707-829-0104

order@oreilly.com
For answers to problems regarding your order or our products. To place a book order online visit:

http://www.oreilly.com/order_new/

catalog@oreilly.com
To request a copy of our latest catalog.

booktech@oreilly.com
For book content technical questions or corrections.

corporate@oreilly.com
For educational, library, and corporate sales.

proposals@oreilly.com
To submit new book proposals to our editors and product managers.

international@oreilly.com
For information about our international distributors or translation queries. For a list of our distributors outside of North America check out:

http://international.oreilly.com/distributors.html